1–2
THESSALONIANS

Baker Exegetical Commentary on the New Testament

ROBERT W. YARBROUGH
AND ROBERT H. STEIN, EDITORS

Volumes now available

Matthew *David L. Turner*

Mark *Robert H. Stein*

Luke *Darrell L. Bock*

John *Andreas J. Köstenberger*

Acts *Darrell L. Bock*

Romans *Thomas R. Schreiner*

1 Corinthians *David E. Garland*

Galatians *Douglas J. Moo*

Ephesians *Frank Thielman*

Philippians *Moisés Silva*

1–2 Thessalonians *Jeffrey A. D. Weima*

James *Dan G. McCartney*

1 Peter *Karen H. Jobes*

1–3 John *Robert W. Yarbrough*

Jude and 2 Peter *Gene L. Green*

Revelation *Grant R. Osborne*

Jeffrey A. D. Weima (PhD, Wycliffe College, University of Toronto) is professor of New Testament at Calvin Theological Seminary, where he has taught for more than twenty years. Among his published writings are *Neglected Endings: The Significance of the Pauline Letter Closings*, an annotated bibliography of works on 1 and 2 Thessalonians, and 1 and 2 Thessalonians in the *Zondervan Illustrated Bible Backgrounds Commentary*.

1-2
THESSALONIANS

JEFFREY A. D. WEIMA

Baker Exegetical Commentary on the New Testament

Baker Academic
a division of Baker Publishing Group
Grand Rapids, Michigan

© 2014 by Jeffrey A. D. Weima

Published by Baker Academic
a division of Baker Publishing Group
P.O. Box 6287, Grand Rapids, MI 49516-6287
www.bakeracademic.com

Printed in the United States of America

Library of Congress Cataloging-in-Publication Data
Weima, Jeffrey A. D.
    1–2 Thessalonians / Jeffrey A. D. Weima.
        pages   cm.   — (Baker exegetical commentary on the New Testament)
    Includes bibliographical references and index.
    ISBN 978-0-8010-2685-0 (cloth)
    1. Bible. Thessalonians—Commentaries. I. Title. II. Title: First–Second Thessalonians.
BS2725.53.W45 2014
227'.8107—dc23   2014016697

Unless otherwise indicated, all Scripture quotations are the author's own translation.

14   15   16   17   18   19   20   7   6   5   4   3   2   1

For my wife Bernice:
"How can I thank God enough for you?"
Τίνα εὐχαριστίαν δύναμαι τῷ θεῷ ἀνταποδοῦναι περὶ σοῦ;
(1 Thess. 3:9)

For my children Rebekah, Allison, Naomi, and Samuel:
For my sons-in-law Luke and Jeffrey:
For my grandsons Leo and Graham:
"I pray always about you that our God may make you worthy
of his calling."
Προσεύχομαι πάντοτε περὶ ὑμῶν, ἵνα ὑμᾶς ἀξιώσῃ τῆς κλήσεως ὁ θεὸς ἡμῶν.
(2 Thess. 1:11)

For my son David:
"I do not grieve like the rest who do not have hope."
Οὐ λυποῦμαι καθὼς καὶ οἱ λοιποὶ οἱ μὴ ἔχοντες ἐλπίδα.
(1 Thess. 4:13)

Contents

Series Preface

The chief concern of the Baker Exegetical Commentary on the New Testament (BECNT) is to provide, within the framework of informed evangelical thought, commentaries that blend scholarly depth with readability, exegetical detail with sensitivity to the whole, and attention to critical problems with theological awareness. We hope thereby to attract the interest of a fairly wide audience, from the scholar who is looking for a thoughtful and independent examination of the text to the motivated lay Christian who craves a solid but accessible exposition.

Nevertheless, a major purpose is to address the needs of pastors and others involved in the preaching and exposition of the Scriptures as the uniquely inspired Word of God. This consideration affects directly the parameters of the series. For example, serious biblical expositors cannot afford to depend on a superficial treatment that avoids the difficult questions, but neither are they interested in encyclopedic commentaries that seek to cover every conceivable issue that may arise. Our aim, therefore, is to focus on those problems that have a direct bearing on the meaning of the text (although selected technical details are treated in the additional notes).

Similarly, a special effort is made to avoid treating exegetical questions for their own sake, that is, in relative isolation from the thrust of the argument as a whole. This effort may involve (at the discretion of the individual contributors) abandoning the verse-by-verse approach in favor of an exposition that focuses on the paragraph as the main unit of thought. In all cases, however, the commentaries will stress the development of the argument and explicitly relate each passage to what precedes and follows it so as to identify its function in context as clearly as possible.

We believe, moreover, that a responsible exegetical commentary must take fully into account the latest scholarly research, regardless of its source. The attempt to do this in the context of a conservative theological tradition presents certain challenges, and in the past the results have not always been commendable. In some cases, evangelicals appear to make use of critical scholarship not for the purpose of genuine interaction but only to dismiss it. In other cases, the interaction glides over into assimilation, theological distinctives are ignored or suppressed, and the end product cannot be differentiated from works that arise from a fundamentally different starting point.

The contributors to this series attempt to avoid these pitfalls. On the one hand, they do not consider traditional opinions to be sacrosanct, and they are certainly committed to doing justice to the biblical text whether or not it supports such opinions. On the other hand, they will not quickly abandon a long-standing view, if there is persuasive evidence in its favor, for the sake of fashionable theories. What is more important, the contributors share a belief in the trustworthiness and essential unity of Scripture. They also consider that the historic formulations of Christian doctrine, such as the ecumenical creeds and many of the documents originating in the sixteenth-century Reformation, arose from a legitimate reading of Scripture, thus providing a proper framework for its further interpretation. No doubt the use of such a starting point sometimes results in the imposition of a foreign construct on the text, but we deny that it must necessarily do so or that the writers who claim to approach the text without prejudices are invulnerable to the same danger.

Accordingly, we do not consider theological assumptions—from which, in any case, no commentator is free—to be obstacles to biblical interpretation. On the contrary, an exegete who hopes to understand the apostle Paul in a theological vacuum might just as easily try to interpret Aristotle without regard for the philosophical framework of his whole work or without having recourse to those subsequent philosophical categories that make possible a meaningful contextualization of his thought. It must be emphasized, however, that the contributors to the present series come from a variety of theological traditions and that they do not all have identical views with regard to the proper implementation of these general principles. In the end, all that really matters is whether the series succeeds in representing the original text accurately, clearly, and meaningfully to the contemporary reader.

Shading has been used to assist the reader in locating salient sections of the treatment of each passage: introductory comments and concluding summaries. Textual variants in the Greek text are signaled in the author's translation by means of half-brackets around the relevant word or phrase (e.g., ⌜Gerasenes⌝), thereby alerting the reader to turn to the additional notes at the end of each exegetical unit for a discussion of the textual problem. The documentation uses the author-date method, in which the basic reference consists of the author's surname + year + page number(s): Fitzmyer 1992: 58. The only exceptions to this system are well-known reference works (e.g., BDAG, LSJ, *TDNT*). Full publication data and a complete set of indexes can be found at the end of the volume.

Robert Yarbrough
Robert H. Stein

Author's Preface

The completion of this major commentary on 1–2 Thessalonians is accompanied by a combination of competing emotions. The joy of finishing the volume is balanced somewhat by the sober realization that I began this project almost twenty years ago. I started off with a sense of idealism typical of someone fresh out of graduate school and one who had the vain ambition to write the definitive commentary on 1–2 Thessalonians. So instead of beginning the commentary proper, I first undertook exhaustive research of everything that had ever been printed on these two letters. This led to the publication of *An Annotated Bibliography of 1 & 2 Thessalonians* (Leiden: Brill, 1998) with Stanley E. Porter. After completing this extensive research, I then began to write the commentary—only to let my progress be interrupted frequently by the publishing of several journal articles and book chapters on various issues related to the Thessalonian correspondence. I also benefited greatly during this time from the feedback of students in my elective course on 1–2 Thessalonians taught annually at Calvin Theological Seminary. My understanding of these letters was further enhanced by participating in and later cochairing the five-year seminar titled "The Thessalonian Correspondence" held during the annual meetings of the Studiorum Novi Testamenti Societas (SNTS). The Baker commentary was also briefly put on hold for the writing of a much shorter and more user-friendly commentary on the same letters published by Zondervan in their *Illustrated Bible Background Commentary* (2002).

The unintended consequence of all these delays has been the opportunity to gain a more mature understanding of 1–2 Thessalonians. There have been many occasions when ideas and truths in Paul's correspondence to the Thessalonians that I had underplayed or missed completely during my initial interpretation of the letters suddenly became visible and compelling after the benefit of simply interacting with the text for a longer period of time. The passing years were also effective in shattering the naive idealism and vain ambition with which I began the project. I am now painfully aware of the shortcomings of what I have written and the issues in the text that I have not explained as convincingly as one would like. Nevertheless, I am very thankful to God both for the opportunity to write a commentary on a small portion of his Word and also for the diverse ways that he has been at work in my life and academic career such that this writing project has finally reached its conclusion. Additionally, I pray that God will use this commentary to give its readers a clearer understanding of what God was saying through the apostle Paul to the Christ-followers who lived in Thessalonica in the first century AD and how these ancient letters continue to communicate God's will for Christ-followers today.

I would like to acknowledge the help of others in the completion of this commentary. James (Jim) Kinney, editorial director of Baker Academic and Brazos Press, dealt graciously with my delays and was encouraging in moving the project along. Robert (Bob) Yarbrough, series editor, not only offered helpful revisions but also endorsed the volume despite its excessive length. Wells Turner did an excellent job of editing the commentary, thereby saving me from many errors and enhancing its overall quality. I am also thankful to Calvin Theological Seminary, both its administrators and its board of trustees, for granting a couple of sabbaticals and even a publication leave, all of which were very helpful in the research and writing of the commentary. Finally and most important, I want to thank my wife, Bernice: Thank you, dear, for your unflagging encouragement, self-sacrificial support, and continued love!

Abbreviations

Bibliographic and General

§/§§	section/sections
//	textual parallels
ABD	*The Anchor Bible Dictionary*, edited by D. N. Freedman et al., 6 vols. (New York: Doubleday, 1992)
AD	*anno Domini*, in the year of the Lord
ANRW	*Aufstieg und Niedergang der römischen Welt*, edited by H. Temporini and W. Haase, Part 2: *Principat* (Berlin: de Gruyter, 1972–)
Anth. Pal.	*Epigrammatum anthologia Palatina*, edited by F. Dübner, P. Waltz, et al. (Paris: Firmin-Didot; et al., 1864–)
ASV	American Standard Version
BAGD	*Greek-English Lexicon of the New Testament and Other Early Christian Literature*, by W. Bauer, W. F. Arndt, F. W. Gingrich, and F. W. Danker, 2nd ed. (Chicago: University of Chicago Press, 1979)
BC	before Christ
BDAG	*A Greek-English Lexicon of the New Testament and Other Early Christian Literature*, by W. Bauer, F. W. Danker, W. F. Arndt, and F. W. Gingrich, 3rd ed. (Chicago: University of Chicago Press, 2000)
BDF	*A Greek Grammar of the New Testament and Other Early Christian Literature*, by F. Blass and A. Debrunner, translated and revised by R. W. Funk (Chicago: University of Chicago Press, 1961)
ca.	*circa*, around
CEV	Contemporary English Version
cf.	*confer*, compare
chap(s).	chapter(s)
DPL	*Dictionary of Paul and His Letters*, edited by G. F. Hawthorne and R. P. Martin (Downers Grove, IL: InterVarsity, 1993)
ed.	edition
e.g.	*exempli gratia*, for example
Eng.	English Bible versification when this differs from the MT or LXX
esp.	especially
ESV	English Standard Version
ET	English translation
et al.	*et alii*, and others
frg(s).	fragment(s)
GNT	Good News Translation / Today's English Version
Grimm-Thayer	*A Greek-English Lexicon of the New Testament: Being Grimm's Wilke's "Clavis Novi Testamenti,"* translated, revised, and enlarged by J. H. Thayer (New York: American Book, 1889; plus reprints)
HCSB	Holman Christian Standard Bible
ISBE	*International Standard Bible Encyclopedia*, edited by G. W. Bromiley, fully revised, 4 vols. (Grand Rapids: Eerdmans, 1979–88)
ISV	International Standard Version
JB	Jerusalem Bible
KJV	King James Version

Knox Version	*The Holy Bible: A Translation from the Latin Vulgate in the Light of the Hebrew and Greek Originals*, trans. R. Knox (1946–50)
lit.	literally
LSJ	*A Greek-English Lexicon*, by H. G. Liddell, R. Scott, and H. S. Jones, 9th ed. with rev. supplement (Oxford: Clarendon, 1996)
LXX	Septuagint
𝔐	majority text
mg.	marginal reading
MHT	*A Grammar of New Testament Greek*, by J. H. Moulton, W. F. Howard, and N. Turner, 4 vols. (Edinburgh: T&T Clark, 1908, 1928, 1963, 1976)
MM	*The Vocabulary of the Greek Testament: Illustrated from the Papyri and Other Non-literary Sources*, by J. H. Moulton and G. Milligan (reprinted Grand Rapids: Eerdmans, 1976)
MS(S)	manuscript(s)
MT	Masoretic Text (Hebrew Bible)
n(n)	note(s)
NA²⁷	*Novum Testamentum Graece*, edited by Eberhard Nestle, Erwin Nestle, B. Aland, K. Aland, J. Karavidopoulos, C. M. Martini, and B. M. Metzger, 27th ed. (Stuttgart: Deutsche Bibelgesellschaft, 1993)
NA²⁸	*Novum Testamentum Graece*, edited by Eberhard Nestle, Erwin Nestle, B. Aland, K. Aland, J. Karavidopoulos, C. M. Martini, and B. M. Metzger, 28th ed. (Stuttgart: Deutsche Bibelgesellschaft, 2012)
NAB	New American Bible (1986, unless otherwise indicated)
NASB	New American Standard Bible
NCV	New Century Version
NEB	New English Bible
NET	New English Translation
NewDocs	*New Documents Illustrating Early Christianity*, edited by G. H. R. Horsley and S. R. Llewelyn (North Ryde, NSW: Ancient History Documentary Research Centre, Macquarie University, 1976–)
NIDNTT	*New International Dictionary of New Testament Theology*, edited by C. Brown, 4 vols. (Grand Rapids: Zondervan, 1975–85)
NIV	New International Version (2011, unless otherwise indicated)
NJB	New Jerusalem Bible
NKJV	New King James Version
NLT	New Living Translation
no(s).	number(s)
NRSV	New Revised Standard Version
NT	New Testament
OT	Old Testament
𝔓	papyrus
par.	parallel
PG	Patrologia graeca, edited by J.-P. Migne, 162 vols. (Paris, 1857–86)
Phillips	*The New Testament in Modern English*, by J. B. Phillips (New York: Macmillan, 1958)
REB	Revised English Bible
rev.	revised
RSV	Revised Standard Version
RV	Revised Version
Str-B	*Kommentar zum Neuen Testament aus Talmud und Midrasch*, by H. L. Strack and P. Billerbeck, 6 vols. (Munich: Kessinger, 1922–61)
TDNT	*Theological Dictionary of the New Testament*, edited by G. Kittel and G. Friedrich, translated and edited by G. W. Bromiley, 10 vols. (Grand Rapids: Eerdmans, 1964–76)

TLG	Thesaurus Linguae Graecae: A Digital Library of Greek Literature (Irvine: University of California, 2001–; http://www.tlg.uci.edu/)
TNIV	Today's New International Version
UBS⁴	*The Greek New Testament*, edited by B. Aland et al., 4th rev. ed. (Stuttgart: Deutsche Bibelgesellschaft/United Bible Societies, 1994)
v./vv.	verse/verses
v.l.	*varia lectio*, variant reading
W-H	*The New Testament in the Original Greek*, the text revised by B. F. Westcott and F. J. A. Hort (Cambridge et al.: Macmillan, 1881; 2nd ed., 1896)
x	number of times a form occurs

Hebrew Bible

Gen.	Genesis	Neh.	Nehemiah	Hosea	Hosea
Exod.	Exodus	Esther	Esther	Joel	Joel
Lev.	Leviticus	Job	Job	Amos	Amos
Num.	Numbers	Ps(s).	Psalm(s)	Obad.	Obadiah
Deut.	Deuteronomy	Prov.	Proverbs	Jon.	Jonah
Josh.	Joshua	Eccles.	Ecclesiastes	Mic.	Micah
Judg.	Judges	Song	Song of Songs	Nah.	Nahum
Ruth	Ruth	Isa.	Isaiah	Hab.	Habakkuk
1–2 Sam.	1–2 Samuel	Jer.	Jeremiah	Zeph.	Zephaniah
1–2 Kings	1–2 Kings	Lam.	Lamentations	Hag.	Haggai
1–2 Chron.	1–2 Chronicles	Ezek.	Ezekiel	Zech.	Zechariah
Ezra	Ezra	Dan.	Daniel	Mal.	Malachi

Greek Testament

Matt.	Matthew	Gal.	Galatians	Philem.	Philemon
Mark	Mark	Eph.	Ephesians	Heb.	Hebrews
Luke	Luke	Phil.	Philippians	James	James
John	John	Col.	Colossians	1–2 Pet.	1–2 Peter
Acts	Acts	1–2 Thess.	1–2 Thessalonians	1–3 John	1–3 John
Rom.	Romans	1–2 Tim.	1–2 Timothy	Jude	Jude
1–2 Cor.	1–2 Corinthians	Titus	Titus	Rev.	Revelation

Other Jewish and Christian Writings

'Abot R. Nat.	'Abot of Rabbi Nathan
Add. Esth.	Additions to Esther
An.	Tertullian, *De anima* (*The Soul*)
Antichr.	Hippolytus, *On the Antichrist*
1 Apol.	Justin Martyr, *First Apology*
2 Apol.	Justin Martyr, *Second Apology*
Ap. Const.	Apostolic Constitutions
Apoc. Ab.	Apocalypse of Abraham
Apoc. Mos.	Apocalypse of Moses
Apoc. Zeph.	Apocalypse of Zephaniah
Ascen. Isa.	Ascension of Isaiah
Ascens.	John Chrysostom, *On the Ascension of Our Lord Jesus Christ*
As. Mos.	Assumption of Moses
Autol.	Theophilus of Antioch, *To Autolycus*
Bar.	Baruch
2 Bar.	2 Baruch (Syriac Apocalypse)
3 Bar.	3 Baruch (Greek Apocalypse)
4 Bar.	4 Baruch (Paraleipomena Jeremiou, Things Omitted from Jeremiah)
Barn.	Epistle of Barnabas

Cat. Lect.	Cyril of Jerusalem, *Catechetical Lectures*	Midr. Ps.	Midrash on Psalms
Cels.	Origen, *Against Celsus*	Midr. Tanḥ.	Midrash Tanḥuma
City	Augustine, *The City of God*	*Or.*	Tertullian, *De oratione* (*Prayer*)
1–2 Clem.	1–2 Clement	*Or.*	Tatian, *Oration to the Greeks*
Comm. Dan.	Hippolytus of Rome, *Commentary on Daniel*	*Paed.*	Clement of Alexandria, *Paedagogus* (*Christ the Educator*)
Dial.	Justin Martyr, *Dialogue with Trypho*	Pesiq. Rab.	Pesiqta Rabbati
Did.	Didache	*Phil.*	Polycarp, *To the Philippians*
1 En.	1 Enoch (Ethiopic Apocalypse)	Pr. Man.	Prayer of Manasseh
2 En.	2 Enoch (Slavonic Apocalypse)	Pss. Sol.	Psalms of Solomon
Ep.	Augustine, *Epistles/Letters*	*Quis div.*	Clement of Alexandria, *Quis dives salvetur* (*Salvation of the Rich*)
Ep. Apos.	Epistle of the Apostles	*Res.*	Tertullian, *The Resurrection of the Flesh*
Ep. Olymp.	John Chrysostom, *Epistles/Letters to Olympias*	*Rom.*	Ignatius, *To the Romans*
Eph.	Ignatius, *To the Ephesians*	Sib. Or.	Sibylline Oracles
1 Esd.	1 Esdras (in the Apocrypha)	*Sim.*	Shepherd of Hermas, *Similitudes*
2 Esd.	2 Esdras (4 Ezra)	Sir.	Sirach (Ecclesiasticus)
Gen. Rab.	Genesis Rabbah	*Smyrn.*	Ignatius, *To the Smyrnaeans*
Haer.	Irenaeus, *Against Heresies*	*Strom.*	Clement of Alexandria, *Stromata*
Hom. 1 Thess.	John Chrysostom, *Homilies on 1 Thessalonians*	T. Ab.	Testament of Abraham
		T. Asher	Testament of Asher
		T. Benj.	Testament of Benjamin
Hom. 2 Thess.	John Chrysostom, *Homilies on 2 Thessalonians*	T. Dan	Testament of Dan
		T. Gad	Testament of Gad
Inst.	Lactantius, *The Divine Institutes*	T. Isaac	Testament of Isaac
Jdt.	Judith	T. Job	Testament of Job
Jos. Asen.	Joseph and Aseneth	T. Jos.	Testament of Joseph
Jub.	Jubilees	T. Jud.	Testament of Judah
L.A.B.	Liber antiquitatum biblicarum (Pseudo-Philo)	T. Levi	Testament of Levi
		T. Naph.	Testament of Naphtali
Leg.	Athenagoras, *Legatio pro Christianis* (*A Plea for the Christians*)	T. Reu.	Testament of Reuben
		T. Sim.	Testament of Simeon
Lit. James	Divine Liturgy of James	Tob.	Tobit
1–4 Macc.	1–4 Maccabees	*Ux.*	Tertullian, *Ad uxorem* (*To His Wife*)
Magn.	Ignatius, *To the Magnesians*		
Marc.	Tertullian, *Against Marcion*	*Vis.*	Shepherd of Hermas, *Vision(s)*
Mart. Isa.	Martyrdom and Ascension of Isaiah 1–5	Wis.	Wisdom of Solomon
Mart. Pol.	Martyrdom of Polycarp		

Rabbinic Tractates

These abbreviations below are used for the names of the tractates in the Mishnah (when preceded by *m.*), Tosefta (*t.*), Babylonian Talmud (*b.*), and Palestinian/Jerusalem Talmud (*y.*).

ʾAbot	ʾAbot
B. Bat.	Baba Batra
Ḥag.	Ḥagigah
Pesaḥ.	Pesaḥim

Qumran / Dead Sea Scrolls and Related Texts

CD	*Damascus Document*, from the Cairo Genizah	1QH	*Thanksgiving Hymns* [former numbers bracketed]
Ḥev	text from Naḥal Ḥever	1QM	*War Scroll*
Mas	text from Masada	1QpHab	*Pesher Habakkuk*
papMur	papyrus from Murabbaʿat	1QS	*Rule of the Community*
1Q27	*1QMysteries*	4Q416	*4QSapiental Work A^b*

Papyri, Inscriptions, and Coins

BGU   *Aegyptische Urkunden aus den Königlichen* [later *Staatlichen*] *Museen zu Berlin: Griechische Urkunden* (Berlin, 1895–)

CIG   *Corpus inscriptionum graecarum*, edited by A. Boeckh et al., 4 vols. (Hildesheim: G. Olms Verlag, 1977)

CIJ   *Corpus inscriptionum judaicarum*, compiled by J.-B. Frey (Rome: Pontificio Institutu di Archeologia Christiana, 1936–); reprinted as *Corpus of Jewish Inscriptions: Jewish Inscriptions from the Third Century B.C. to the Seventh Century A.D.* (New York: Ktav, 1975)

CIL   *Corpus inscriptionum latinarum* (Berlin: Reimer, 1862–)

IG   *Inscriptiones graecae*, editio minor (Berlin: de Gruyter, 1924–)

ILS   *Inscriptiones latinae selectae*, edited by H. Dessau, 3 vols. (Berlin: Weidmann, 1882–1916; plus various reprints)

IT   *Inscriptiones graecae*, vol. 10: *Inscriptiones Thessalonicae et viciniae*, edited by C. Edson (Berlin: de Gruyter, 1972)

OGIS   *Orientis graeci inscriptiones selectae*, edited by W. Dittenberger, 2 vols. (Leipzig: S. Hirzel, 1903–5)

P.Cair. Zen.   *Zenon Papyri: Catalogue général des antiquités égyptiennes du Musée du Caire*, edited by C. C. Edgar (Cairo, 1925–40)

P.Col.   *Columbia Papyri* (New York et al., 1929–)

P.Eleph.   *Aegyptische Urkunden aus den Königlichen Museen in Berlin: Griechische Urkunden*, Sonderheft: *Elephantine-Papyri*, edited by O. Rubensohn (Berlin, 1907–)

P.Freib.   *Mitteilungen aus der Freiburger Papyrussammlung* (Heidelberg et al., 1914–)

P.Giess.   *Griechische Papyri im Museum des oberhessischen Geschichtsvereins zu Giessen*, edited by O. Eger, E. Kornemann, and P. M. Meyer (Leipzig-Berlin, 1910–12)

PGM   *Papyri graecae magicae: Die griechischen Zauberpapyri*, edited by K. Preisendanz (Berlin, 1928–)

P.Grenf. II   *New Classical Fragments and Other Greek and Latin Papyri*, edited by B. P. Grenfell and A. S. Hunt (Oxford, 1897)

P.Lond.   *Greek Papyri in the British Museum* (London, 1893–)

P.Lond. Lit.   *Catalogue of the Literary Papyri in the British Museum*, edited by H. J. M. Milne (London, 1927)

P.Oslo   *Papyri Osloenses* (Oslo, 1925–36)

P.Oxy.   *The Oxyrhynchus Papyri*, published by the Egypt Exploration Society in Graeco-Roman Memoirs (London, 1898–)

PSI   *Papiri greci e latini*, edited by G. Vitelli, M. Norsa, et al. (Florence: Pubblicazioni della Società Italiana, 1912–)

P.Tebt.   *The Tebtunis Papyri*, edited by B. P. Grenfell, A. S. Hunt, et al. (London et al., 1902–)

P.Wisc.   *The Wisconsin Papyri*, edited by P. J. Sijpesteijn (Leiden, 1967; Zutphen, 1977)

RIC   *The Roman Imperial Coinage*, by H. Mattingly, E. A. Sydenham, et al., multiple editions, 10 vols. (London: Spink, 1926–2007)

SB   *Sammelbuch griechischer Urkunden aus Ägypten*, edited by F. Preisigke et al., vols. 1– (Strassburg: Trübner; et al., 1915–)

SEG   *Supplementum epigraphicum graecum* (Leiden: Brill; et al., 1923–)

UPZ   *Urkunden der Ptolemäerzeit (ältere Funde)*, edited by U. Wilcken (Berlin, 1927–)

Josephus

Ag. Ap.   *Against Apion*
Ant.   *Jewish Antiquities*
J.W.   *Jewish War*

Philo

Abraham	*Life of Abraham*	Migration	*Migration of Abraham*
Alleg. Interp.	*Allegorical Interpretation*	Names	*Change of Names*
Dreams	*Dreams*	Rewards	*Rewards and Punishments*
Embassy	*Embassy to Gaius*	Sacrifices	*Sacrifices of Cain and Abel*
Flaccus	*Against Flaccus*	Spec. Laws	*Special Laws*
Flight	*Flight and Finding*	Virtues	*Virtues*
Good Person	*That Every Good Person Is Free*		

Classical Writers

Aem.	Plutarch, *Aemilius Paullus*	Demon.	Isocrates, *To Demonicus (Oration 1)*
Age	Cicero, *Old Age (De senectute)*	Dio Cassius	Dio Cassius, *Roman History*
Alex.	Dio Chrysostom, *To the People of Alexandria (Or. 32)*	Diodorus Siculus	Diodorus of Sicily, *Library of History*
Ant.	Plutarch, *Antony*	Disc.	Epictetus, *Discourses*
Apol.	Plato, *Apologia of Socrates*	Div.	Cicero, *Divination*
Ass	Lucian of Samosata, *The Ass*	Duties	Cicero, *On Duties (De officiis)*
Att.	Cicero, *Letters to Atticus*	El.	Sophocles, *Elektra*
Busybody	Plutarch, *On Being a Busybody (De curiositate)*	Ep.	Julian, *Epistles*
		Ep.	Seneca, *Moral Epistles*
Cael.	Cicero, *Pro Caelio*	Flatterer	Plutarch, *How to Tell a Flatterer from a Friend (Mor. 4)*
Cat. Maj.	Plutarch, *Cato Major (Cato the Elder)*	Font.	Cicero, *Pro Fonteio*
Catullus	Catullus, *Poetry of Catullus*	Frat. amor.	Plutarch, *De fraterno amore (Brotherly Love)*
Char.	Theophrastus, *Characters*		
Cho.	Aeschylus, *Choephori (Libation-Bearers)*	Geogr.	Strabo, *Geography*
		Hell.	Xenophon, *Hellenica*
Claud.	Suetonius, *The Life of Claudius*	Herodotus	Herodotus, *History of the Persian Wars*
Con. Apoll.	Plutarch, *A Letter of Condolence to Apollonius*		
		Hist.	various authors, *Histories*
Cyr.	Xenophon, *Cyropaedia*	Icar.	Lucian of Samosata, *Icaromenippus*
Demetr.	Plutarch, *Demetrius*	Id.	Theocritus, *Idylls*

Il.	Homer, *Iliad*	*Pis.*	Cicero, *Against Piso*
Inst.	Quintilian, *Institutes of Oratory*	*Pol.*	Aristotle, *Politics*
Laws	Ulpian, *Comparison of Mosaic and Roman Laws*	*Polyb.*	Seneca, *To Polybius on Consolation*
		Pontic Ep.	Ovid, *Pontic Epistles*
Lives	Diogenes Laertius, *Lives of Eminent Philosophers*	*Prot.*	Plato, *Protagoras*
		Rep.	Plato, *Republic*
Livy	Livy (Titus Livius), *History of Rome*	*Rhet.*	Aristotle, *Rhetoric*
Marc.	Seneca, *Consolation to Marcia*	*Rom. Ant.*	Dionysius of Halicarnassus, *Roman Antiquities*
Med.	Marcus Aurelius, *Meditations*		
Misc.	Aelian, *Miscellaneous Stories*	*Sat.*	various authors, *Satires*
Mor.	Plutarch, *Moralia*	*Siege*	Aeneas Tacitus, *How to Survive under Siege*
Nat.	Pliny the Elder, *Natural History*		
Nic. Eth.	Aristotle, *Nicomachean Ethics*	*Symp.*	Plato, *Symposium*
Or.	various authors, *Orations*	Thucydides	Thucydides, *History of the Peloponnesian War*
Per.	Plutarch, *Life of Pericles*		
Phileb.	Plato, *Philebus*	*Vit. Apoll.*	Philostratus, *Life of Apollonius of Tyana*
4 Philip.	Demosthenes, *4 Philippic*		

Transliteration

Hebrew

Hebrew		Hebrew		
א	ʾ	בָ	ā	qāmeṣ
ב	b	בַ	a	pataḥ
ג	g	הַ	a	furtive pataḥ
ד	d	בֶ	e	sĕgôl
ה	h	בֵ	ē	ṣērê
ו	w	בִ	i	short ḥîreq
ז	z	בִ	ī	long ḥîreq written defectively
ח	ḥ	בָ	o	qāmeṣ ḥāṭûp
ט	ṭ	בוֹ	ô	ḥôlem written fully
י	y	בֹ	ō	ḥôlem written defectively
כ/ך	k	בוּ	û	šûreq
ל	l	בֻ	u	short qibbûṣ
מ/ם	m	בֻ	ū	long qibbûṣ written defectively
נ/ן	n	בָה	â	final qāmeṣ hēʾ (בָה = āh)
ס	s	בֵי	ê	sĕgôl yôd (בֶי = êy)
ע	ʿ	בֵי	ê	ṣērê yôd (בֵי = êy)
פ/ף	p	בִי	î	ḥîreq yôd (בִי = îy)
צ/ץ	ṣ	בֲ	ă	ḥāṭēp pataḥ
ק	q	בֱ	ĕ	ḥāṭēp sĕgôl
ר	r	בֳ	ŏ	ḥāṭēp qāmeṣ
שׂ	ś	בְ	ĕ	vocal šĕwāʾ
שׁ	š			
ת	t			

Notes on the Transliteration of Hebrew

1. Accents are not shown in transliteration.
2. Silent šĕwāʾ is not indicated in transliteration.
3. The spirant forms ב ג ד כ פ ת are usually not specially indicated in transliteration.

4. *Dāgēš forte* is indicated by doubling the consonant. Euphonic *dāgēš* and *dāgēš lene* are not indicated in transliteration.
5. *Maqqēp* is represented by a hyphen.

Greek

α	*a*	ξ	*x*
β	*b*	ο	*o*
γ	*g/n*	π	*p*
δ	*d*	ρ	*r*
ε	*e*	σ/ς	*s*
ζ	*z*	τ	*t*
η	*ē*	υ	*y/u*
θ	*th*	φ	*ph*
ι	*i*	χ	*ch*
κ	*k*	ψ	*ps*
λ	*l*	ω	*ō*
μ	*m*	ʽ	*h*
ν	*n*		

Notes on the Transliteration of Greek

1. Accents, lenis (smooth breathing), and *iota* subscript are not shown in transliteration.
2. The transliteration of asper (rough breathing) precedes a vowel or diphthong (e.g., ἁ = *ha*; αἱ = *hai*) and follows ρ (i.e., ῥ = *rh*).
3. *Gamma* is transliterated *n* only when it precedes γ, κ, ξ, or χ.
4. *Upsilon* is transliterated *u* only when it is part of a diphthong (i.e., αυ, ευ, ου, υι).

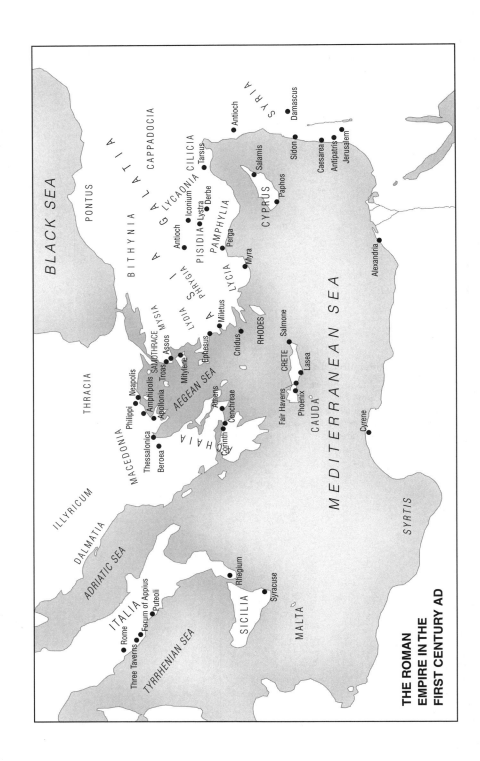

THE ROMAN
EMPIRE IN THE
FIRST CENTURY AD

Introduction to 1–2 Thessalonians

The City of Thessalonica

A Strategic Location

If the three most important factors affecting the value of real estate are "location, location, location," then Thessalonica was destined to be a prosperous and leading city. Two geographical factors resulted in Thessalonica becoming what its first-century BC native poet Antipater called "the mother of all Macedonia" (*Anth. Pal.* 4.428) and what a local inscription identified as "the metropolis ["mother city"], first of Macedonia" (*CIG* 1.1969). That these descriptions were not merely the exaggerated claim of overly proud native citizens is confirmed by Strabo, the historian and geographer (64 BC–ca. AD 24), who similarly referred to Thessalonica as the "metropolis of Macedonia" (*Geogr.* 7 frg. 21).

The first of these two geographical advantages involved the city's access to the sea: Thessalonica enjoyed a natural harbor that was perhaps the best in the entire Aegean Sea. This factor led to the creation of the city by Cassander, the king of Macedonia, in 316–315 BC. The capital city of his father-in-law, Philip II, the father of Alexander the Great, was located in nearby Pella: though situated inland, it had access to the Aegean Sea by means of the Loudias River. This river, however, suffered heavy silting, thereby forcing Cassander to establish a new port and town to serve as the center of his reign over the region of Macedonia. The king forcibly joined together the populations of twenty-six villages in the area and situated them on the existing town of Therme, naming the new city Thessalonica, after his wife[1] (Strabo, *Geogr.* 7 frgs. 21, 24; Dionysius of Halicarnassus, *Rom. Ant.* 1.49.4). This location on the most innermost part of the Thermaic Gulf was chosen because of the site's deep anchorage and excellent protection from dangerous southeast winds.[2] The advantages of this favorably situated harbor were noted by ancient authors (Herodotus 7.121; Livy 44.10), and the port of Thessalonica continues to be a busy and profitable one still today. Vacalopoulos (1972: 3) reports: "Thessaloniki is the

---

1. Cassander's wife was born on the day her father, Philip II, won an important battle in Thessaly, the region south of Macedonia, and was consequently named Thessalonike, which means "Thessalian Victory." She was the younger stepsister of Alexander the Great.

2. Although the Thermaic Gulf opens southeastward to the Aegean Sea, the inlet at Thessalonica opens almost at a right angle southwestward to the gulf, thereby giving the harbor shelter from the prevailing southeast winds.

only sea-board city of contemporary Greece that has never, from its foundation (316 BC) till today, lost its commercial importance."

The second of the geographical advantages benefiting Thessalonica involves the city's access to major land travel routes. The city was situated on or near[3] the Via Egnatia—the major east-west highway built by the Romans in the second century BC. This highway connected Thessalonica with the other major cities not only in Macedonia but also far beyond. Going west on this route some 260 miles from Thessalonica would bring one to the port of Dyrrachium on the Adriatic Sea, which could then be crossed by boat to the shore of Italy, where the Via Appia would lead directly into Rome. Going east on this route some 430 miles from Thessalonica would bring one to Byzantium, on the edge of the Black Sea, or even earlier to the Hellespont, which would allow access into Asia Minor. Thessalonica also was located on the intersection of the Via Egnatia with the major road north along the Axius River through the Balkans to the Danube region.

The benefits of Thessalonica's location with respect to both sea and land were key factors ensuring the prosperity and numerical growth of the city. As Green (2002: 6) observes: "The great success of Thessalonica was due in grand part to the union of land and sea, road and port, which facilitated commerce between Macedonia and the entire Roman Empire. No other place in all Macedonia offered the strategic advantages of Thessalonica." Additional geographical factors ensuring the success of the city were its favorable climate conditions, fertile plains nourished by abundant rivers, rich mineral deposits (gold, silver, iron, copper, lead), and vast forests to provide timber for building. Fearing a Macedonian revival (Livy 45.29), the Romans under General Aemilius Paullus imposed restrictions on the Thessalonians and others in Macedonia over the use of these natural resources after his victory at Pydna in 168 BC. This and the 300 million sesterces that this victory brought into the Roman treasury (Pliny the Elder [*Nat.* 33.17; Livy 45.40.1] gives the amount as 120 million sesterces) suggest the wealth that the region around Thessalonica could potentially produce. These geographical advantages were not lost on writers in the ancient world, as evidenced by the succinct comment of Miletius: "So long as nature does not change, Thessalonica will remain wealthy and fortunate" (cited by Lightfoot 1893: 255).

The city's prosperity not surprisingly attracted new inhabitants: in the years just before Paul's arrival, Thessalonica was "more populous than any of the rest" of the Macedonian cities (Strabo, *Geogr.* 7.7.4; see also Lucian, *Ass* 46.5, who, in the second century AD, refers to Thessalonica as "the largest city in Macedonia"). The exact size of the city's population is difficult to determine with certainty. If one uses the length of the city walls to determine the total living area and factors in the typical rates of population density for ancient cities, the population of Thessalonica can be calculated to have been from

3. There is evidence that the Via Egnatia did not pass directly through the city but rather was located nearby to the north: Vickers 1972: 157n4; Makaronas 1951: 387–88.

65,000 to 100,000 people (J. Hill 1990: 45–49; Riesner 1998: 314). This would rank Thessalonica among the top ten largest cities in the Roman Empire.[4]

A Favored Political Status

Thessalonica enjoyed a favored relationship with Rome—a relationship that it deliberately fostered in the hopes of political and financial gain. After the fall of Macedonia as an independent kingdom in the battle at Pydna in 168 BC, the victorious Romans followed the strategy of divide and conquer, splitting the region into four "districts" (μερίδες, *merides*; see Acts 16:12), with Thessalonica as the capital of the second district (Livy 44.32; 45.29.9; Diodorus Siculus 31.8.6–9; Strabo, *Geogr.* 7 frg. 47). The following years of Roman rule witnessed sporadic rebellions, finally suppressed in 146 BC, at which time the Romans expanded the boundaries of the region and reorganized Macedonia as a province, with Thessalonica alone elevated to the privileged status of capital city and as the home base of Rome's representative, the governor.

Rome's choice of Thessalonica as provincial capital was based not solely on the city's size and wealth but also on its loyalty to the Roman Empire rather than to local leaders heading up the rebellions. One inscription records how the Thessalonians honor Metellus, the Roman praetor who quelled the insurrection, identifying him as the city's "savior and benefactor" (*IT* 134). Several other inscriptions honor "Roman benefactors" (Ῥωμαῖοι εὐεργέται, *Rhōmaioi euergetai*), individuals who financed local cultural institutions (e.g., the gymnasium and its activities), helped protect the city from hostile neighbors and anti-Roman invaders, promoted the interests of Thessalonica in Rome, or provided aid in other ways. These honorific inscriptions reveal that a pro-Roman attitude existed in Thessalonica and that at least some of its leading citizens were willing not merely to endure but also eagerly to embrace Roman rule in order to enjoy more fully the benefits that this relationship brought (see esp. Hendrix 1984; also Green 2002: 16–17). This positive view of Rome was enhanced by Thessalonica's need for the empire's help in fending off the frequent raids by the barbarian tribes in northern Macedonia (Papagiannopoulos 1982: 36). Thus Cicero, the famous Roman statesman who spent six months in Thessalonica in exile in 58 BC, referred to Macedonia as "a loyal province, friend to the Roman people" (*Font.* 44).

The close relationship between Thessalonica and Rome can also be seen in the key role that the city played in the empire's civil wars, even though all too often this role involved initially backing the losing side. The city supported Pompey in his quest for power against Julius Caesar. Before his inglorious

---

4. Keener (2014: 2537): "Thessalonica was not one of the giant cities, such as Rome (with as many as a million inhabitants on a frequent estimate) and Alexandria (sometimes estimated at six hundred thousand), but with Smyrna it followed close after the second tier of cities (Carthage and Antioch, each with some half million, and Ephesus, with four hundred thousand, on the highest estimates), with more than two hundred thousand inhabitants on the highest estimates. More conservative estimates run from forty thousand to sixty-five thousand, but these figures remain substantial."

defeat at Pharsalus in 48 BC, Pompey prepared for battle by gathering in Thessalonica with the two consuls and over two hundred senators, turning the city into a kind of second Rome, where the "true" Senate was now held (Dio Cassius 41.18.4–6; 41.43.1–5). Some six years later Thessalonica was again at the center of the Roman internal wars, when the armies of Brutus and Cassius, the two leaders responsible for the assassination of Julius Caesar, faced off in battle on the plains of nearby Philippi against the armies of Marc Antony and Octavian (who later became Caesar Augustus), the two avengers of Caesar's murder. Thessalonica initially supported Brutus and Cassius but, between the two battles on the Philippian plains, switched their allegiance to Marc Antony and Octavian, causing Brutus to promise his soldiers the right to plunder Thessalonica following their anticipated victory (Appian, *Civil Wars* 4.118; Plutarch, *Brutus* 46.1). Fortunately for Thessalonica, that victory never came: both Brutus and Cassius went down to defeat at the hands of Marc Antony and, to a lesser extent, Octavian. A triumphal arch celebrating the two victors was built at the Vardar Gate, one of the major gates of the city wall, and commemorative medals were circulated with the inscription "for the freedom of the people of Thessaloniki" (Papagiannopoulos 1982: 39). A coin series was produced, presenting on one side a veiled female head with the inscription OMONIA (concord, harmony, like-mindedness) and on the other side a galloping free horse with the inscription ΘΕΣΣΑΛΟΝ[ΙΚΗΣ]/ΡΩΜ[ΗΣ] (Thessalonica/Rome), thereby celebrating how the victory of Antony and Octavian had restored concord between the two cities (Hendrix 1984: 162–65).

The city and the province came under the control of Marc Antony, who in 42 BC rewarded its citizens for their support by granting Thessalonica the status of a "free city" (*civitas libera*; Pliny the Elder, *Nat.* 4.17 [10]).[5] This favored classification meant that the inhabitants enjoyed a measure of autonomy over local affairs, the right to mint their own coins, freedom from military occupation within the city walls, and certain tax concessions. Hendrix (1984: 251) notes that this privileged status was "granted only to people and cities which had displayed remarkable loyalty to the interests of the Roman people." Nine years later the city found itself again backing the losing side in Rome's internal wars as Marc Antony fell at the hands of Octavian in the battle at Actium in 31 BC. Nevertheless, the city quickly either erased the name of Antony from inscriptions honoring the defeated general (a standard way of effecting *damnatio memoriae*—erasing the memory of someone formally esteemed who was now dishonored) or replaced his name with Octavian (*IT* 6, 83, 109), thereby ensuring good relations with Rome and maintaining their favored status as a free city.

During this time period the city's intimate relationship with Rome was fostered further with the establishment of a new cult of Roma and the Roman benefactors (Edson [1940: 133] dates its founding to 41 BC, while Hendrix

---

5. Evidence of Thessalonica's "freedom" is found in one inscription (*IT* 6) and in a series of coins issued by the city inscribed ΘΕΣΣΑΛΟΝΙΚΕΩΝ ΕΛΕΥΘΕΡΙΑΣ (Freedom of the Thessalonians).

[1987: 22] dates this new cult to 95 BC or earlier). Several inscriptions are addressed to "the gods and the Roman benefactors" (*IT* 4), "the priest of the gods . . . and of the priest of Roma and the Roman benefactors" (*IT* 133, 226), "of both Roma and the Roman benefactors" (*IT* 128), and "Roma and Romans" (*IT* 32). Once the cult to honor the goddess Roma and the Roman benefactors was established, it was natural to extend such honors to the most powerful and most important Roman benefactor, the emperor. A temple in honor of Caesar was built near the end of the first century BC, and a priesthood to service this temple was established: an important inscription refers to "the temple of Caesar" and to a person with the title "priest and *agōnothetēs* [games superintendent] of the Imperator Caesar Augustus son [of god]" as well as to the "priest of the gods . . . and priest of Roma and the Roman benefactors" (*IT* 31). This inscription, along with others (*IT* 32, 132, 133), also suggests the preeminence of officials connected with the imperial cult over other priesthoods.[6]

Further evidence of Thessalonica's aggressive pursuit of fostering good relations with Rome lies in a recent rediscovery of an archaic temple that the city had moved from its original location and reassembled in the most important location in town, where all the key sanctuaries were situated, including the Serapeion. The temple was first discovered in 1936 during the erection of a two-story building in the heart of the modern city, in Antigonidon Square. However, this finding soon disappeared due to the invasion and destruction of the Nazi occupation and the subsequent postwar urban development. The temple was rediscovered in 2000 when the two-story building located on top of it was demolished as part of a redevelopment project. It then became clear that this archaic temple dates back to the late sixth century BC but had been rebuilt as an Ionic-style temple on top of a Roman base. A statue of the goddess Roma and other imperial statues were also discovered here, but nothing dating to the pre-Roman period.[7] The presence of architectural marks to ensure the accurate reassembling of the temple confirmed that the temple had originally been built and located somewhere else in the late archaic period and then moved into the heart of Thessalonica during the Roman period. Its original location was likely Aineia (suburb of modern-day Michaniona), located about twelve miles south of Thessalonica, and the temple was dedicated to Aphrodite (Dionysius of Halicarnassus, *Rom. Ant.* 1.49.4). According to tradition, this goddess of love was the mother of Aeneas, who was the founder not only of Rome but also of the Julian line from whom Julius Caesar descended. It

---

6. "In every extant instance in which the 'priest and agonothete of the Imperator' is mentioned, he is listed first in what appears to be a strict observance of protocol. The Imperator's priest and agonothete assumes priority, the priest of 'the gods' is cited next, followed by the priest of Roma and Roman benefactors" (Hendrix 1984: 312).

7. Most of these recent findings are now exhibited in the lobby of the Archaeological Museum of Thessaloniki. Controversy continues over what to do with the temple base located in Antigonidon Square. For a website dedicated to saving the Aphrodite temple from development, see http://www.templeofvenus.gr/.

seems likely, then, that the Thessalonians, at great effort and expense, moved a temple that could be linked with Julius Caesar to a prime location in their city and turned it into a temple for imperial worship in order to demonstrate in a dramatic way their allegiance to Caesar's adoptive son, Octavian (later known as Augustus), even though they had supported Octavian's rival, Marc Antony, during Rome's civil war.

Coinage from the city reveals that Julius Caesar and Octavian received divine honors. In one series minted about 27 BC, the laureate head of Julius Caesar appears with the inscription "God." The reverse side of coins from this series has the image of Octavian, and though they do not have the similar inscription "God" or "son of god," his divinity is implied by his pairing with the divine Julius and by the title *Sebastos* or "Augustus" often found. A statue of Augustus discovered in Thessalonica depicts the emperor in a divine posture.[8] In contrast to the *Prima Porta* exemplar where Augustus is in full military garb, the Thessalonian statue of him omits these symbols of power and instead conveys the emperor as a man not of war but of peace.

The good relations that existed between Macedonia, including its leading city of Thessalonica, and Rome can also be seen in the so-called Augustan Settlement of 27 BC, when the emperor regulated the governance of the provinces, classifying them as either senatorial or imperial. Senatorial provinces were those considered to be peaceful and loyal to Rome and so were placed under the control of the Senate, governed by proconsuls (governors) who held office for only a one-year term. Imperial provinces were those typically located on the boundaries of the empire and whose commitment to Rome was considered weak or questionable. They were placed under the direct control of the emperor, who appointed procurators or prefects with military authority to hold office and govern these areas as long as the emperor desired. That Augustus designated Macedonia as a senatorial province (Dio Cassius 53.12.4) therefore is significant. It also suggests that the act of the subsequent emperor, Tiberius, in reclassifying Macedonia as an imperial province in AD 15 and placing this region under his direct control (Tacitus, *Hist.* 1.76.4), would have been viewed with alarm by those in Macedonia and Thessalonica who were concerned with maintaining good relations with Rome. Pro-Roman sensibilities in the region and capital city were encouraged, however, when Claudius in AD 44 annulled the decision of his predecessor and restored Macedonia's status as a senatorial province and Thessalonica as the dwelling place of the governor (Dio Cassius 60.24.1).

This historical survey makes clear that Thessalonica enjoyed a favored relationship with Rome and engaged in a variety of activities to strengthen that relationship, thereby securing political and financial benefits from the empire. As De Vos (1999: 125) states: "In light of this history, the city [Thessalonica] seems to have developed an attitude of strong dependence on Roman, and

8. Archaeological Museum, Thessaloniki, No. 1065, http://odysseus.culture.gr/h/4/eh430.jsp?obj_id=8164.

especially, Imperial, benefaction." What this historical survey also makes clear is how important Thessalonica's favored status would have been to both its city leaders and citizens, and how they would naturally be upset and deal aggressively with anyone or any group within the community whom they feared might jeopardize their favored status. Especially with the memory still fresh in their mind of the loss of their senatorial status under Tiberius and its recovery just six years earlier under Claudius, it is understandable why the crowd and city leaders "were disturbed" (Acts 17:8) on hearing about the anti-Roman charges brought against Paul and Silas as well as about those local citizens who had embraced their teachings (Riesner 1998: 357).

A Unique Governmental Structure

The special status that Thessalonica had as a free city meant, among other things, that it enjoyed a degree of autonomy over local affairs: instead of reorganizing their city governance according to Roman practices, they were permitted to keep their existing civic structure. This local governmental structure was composed of the following three main offices,[9] the first and last of which are explicitly mentioned in Acts 17:1–10, with its description of Paul's ministry in Thessalonica: (a) the citizen assembly; (b) the council; and (c) the politarchs or city officials.

a. *The citizen assembly.* The lowest level of city governance involved the *dēmos* (δῆμος, citizen assembly), whose existence is attested in local inscriptions (*IT* 6, 136). The *dēmos* pattern of government (from which we get the word "democracy") originated in Athens in the fifth century BC and subsequently spread from there throughout the Hellenistic cities. In a free city like Thessalonica, which was allowed to follow its traditional democratic traditions, the *dēmos* consisted of "a convocation of citizens called together for the purpose of transacting official business" (BDAG 223). This administrative body handled such city matters as financial affairs, festivals, issues connected to the various local cults, and certain judicial concerns (R. Evans 1968: 13). The mob in Thessalonica, enraged over the charges made against Paul and Silas, originally planned to bring the pair before this citizen assembly (Acts 17:5).

b. *The council.* The higher level of city governance involved the *boulē* (βουλή, council), whose existence is also attested in local inscriptions (*IT* 5, 6, 7, 14, 133, 137). The origin of this administrative body similarly goes back to the birth of democracy in Athens and was instituted in order to function as an

---

9. Additional city offices or administrators were commonly found in cities in that day. Inscriptions from Thessalonica refer to the "treasurer of the city" (ταμίας τῆς πόλεως: *IT* 31, 50, 133); the "treasurer of the Romans" (ταμίας Ῥωμαίων: *IT* 29, 135); the "marketplace ruler" (ἀγορανόμος: *IT* 7, 26), who regulated the commercial activity in the agora, or forum; the "gymnasiarch" (γυμνασίαρχος: *IT* 4, 133, 135, 201), who supervised the training and educational activities that took place in the gymnasium; the "agonothete" (ἀγωνοθέτης: *IT* 132, 226), who was in charge of the athletic and musical competitions; the "ephebarch" (ἐφήβαρχος: *IT* 133, 135; *IG* 10.1.4), who supervised the training of young men of citizen status; and the city "architect" (ἀρχιτέκτων: *IT* 31, 128, 133), who oversaw building projects (see also Green 2002: 22–24).

executive branch of the citizen assembly, making the governing process more efficient by filtering problems before they were brought to the lower body (Plutarch, *Solon* 19). This meant that the duties of the council overlapped with those of the citizen assembly, which is natural given that the former body was intended to be a preparatory institution for the latter. The close interaction of these two administrative bodies in Thessalonica can be seen in certain inscriptions where both the citizen assembly and the council are listed together as cosponsors of a proclamation (R. Evans 1968: 217n100; Green 2002: 22). Yet it was also natural for the council to exert undue influence in controlling not only what issues were brought before the citizen assembly but also what decisions about these issues ought to be adopted.

c. *The politarchs (city officials)*. Although the citizen assembly and council are administrative bodies typical of a classical Greek civic structure that can be found in virtually any Hellenistic city, the office of politarch (πολιτάρχης, *politarchēs*, city official) is distinctive and rare, thus justifying our heading of this larger introductory section as "A Unique Governmental Structure." It is often claimed that the term "politarch" does not occur in any extant Greek writing other than its twofold reference in Acts 17:6 and 17:8. Consequently, many biblical scholars prior to the late nineteenth century and some even in the early twentieth century questioned the historical accuracy of these two references in the Acts account. The claim about the term not occurring in any literary source other than Acts, however, is incorrect: the word does occur in the fourth-century BC Greek writer on the art of war, Aeneas Tacitus (*Siege* 26.12).[10] Furthermore, while literary evidence for the existence of this city office may be weak, with only one other occurrence apart from Acts, inscriptional evidence has become increasingly impressive, as more and more references to politarchs have been discovered. Although at the close of the nineteenth century, nineteen inscriptions attested to the office of politarch (Burton 1898), there are currently as many as seventy known nonliterary references to these unique city officials (Horsley 1994: 422; Riesner 1998: 355). Twenty-eight of these inscriptions (40 percent) are from Thessalonica, while the majority of the remaining attestations are from various communities in Macedonia (Amphipolis, Lete, Derriopus, Pella, Edessa). The few inscriptions with the term "politarch" coming from outside the borders of Macedonia were found in the nearby regions of Thrace and Thessaly, as well as in the farther province of Bithynia in Asia Minor.

Up to the 1970s the dominant view was that the office of politarch was introduced into Macedonia by the Romans, either after their key victory at Pydna in 168 BC or when they reorganized Macedonia as a province in 146 BC (see esp. Schuler 1960). But although the vast majority of inscriptions date from the Roman period, it has become clear in recent decades that the office of politarch existed already before the Roman takeover of Macedonia.

---

10. The form πολιτάρχος differs slightly in the suffix (-αρχος instead of -αρχης), which is merely a variation of dialect (Horsley 1982: 34).

In addition to the early citation from Aeneas Tacitus, there is, for example, one inscription from Amphipolis that dates between 179 and 171 BC (Helly 1977: 531–44; Koukouli-Chrysanthaki 1981).[11]

The inscriptions as a whole reveal several important facts about the office of politarch (see Burton 1898; Schuler 1960; Horsley 1982; 1994). In the province of Macedonia, this position was widespread, although not found in Roman colonies like Philippi (Acts, therefore, accurately employs a different title [στρατηγοί, *stratēgoi*] for the city leaders of Philippi: 16:20, 22, 35, 36, 38). The politarchs came from the wealthier families, and their number varied from city to city and from time to time. In Thessalonica at the end of the first century BC, there were five individuals who served as politarchs; that number varied from three to seven during the following two centuries. The politarchs, who could simultaneously hold other civic offices, functioned as the chief administrative and executive officers of their respective cities or communities. They served a one-year term, but the same person could hold office more than once. The politarchs had authority to convene meetings of the *boulē*, or council; introduce motions to that body; and confirm its decisions. For example, clay seals mentioning politarchs discovered at Pella suggest that a decree passed by the council would be ratified by the politarchs, who set their seal on the papyrus copy of the decision before it was stored in the city archives. They also had authority to deal with judicial matters, which is indicated by the action of the angry crowd in Thessalonica who failed to find Paul and Silas and instead grabbed their host Jason and some other Christians and brought them to the politarchs (Acts 17:6–9).

That the politarchs had ultimate local responsibility for maintaining peace and order (Gschnitzer 1973: 491) explains why these city officials in Thessalonica were "disturbed" (Acts 17:8) at the anti-Roman charges brought against Paul, Silas, Jason, and the other new believers. Although in theory the politarchs existed to serve and implement the will of the council and the citizen assembly, in reality they were all too aware that real power resided in Rome. Even in a large city like Thessalonica, the politarchs would have had a vested interest in any movement—even a relatively small one—within their city whose beliefs and actions might negatively attract the attention of Rome (see the appeal of the *grammateus* in Ephesus during the riot in that city: Acts 19:38–40) and perhaps ultimately lead to the loss not only of the city's advantageous "free status" but also of the privileged leadership position that they as city officials enjoyed.

A Religiously Pluralistic Environment

Athens was not the only place where Paul preached the gospel in a city that was "full of idols" (Acts 17:16). Thessalonica, as the "mother / mother city of

---

11. Additional key evidence for the pre-Roman existence of the office of politarch is provided by Gauthier and Hatzopoulos (1993) in their commentary on the gymnasiarchal law of "Béroia" (Berea).

all Macedonia" and one of the leading cities in the Roman Empire, also had a significant number of pagan cults and temples to diverse deities that competed for its citizens' attention and participation. Numismatic, inscriptional, and other archaeological evidence reveal that over twenty-five gods, heroes, and personifications of virtues were worshiped in Thessalonica (see the overview of Tzanavari 2003), thereby justifying the heading of this section "A Religiously Pluralistic Environment."[12] In these diverse sources, the specific gods mentioned most frequently include Dionysus, the gods of Egypt—especially Serapis and Isis but also Osiris, Harpocrates, and Anubis—and Cabirus, who served as the patron deity of Thessalonica. Also important in Thessalonica was the imperial cult—the worship of Roma as a personification of the Roman state and of individual emperors as gods. Other less commonly attested deities include Zeus Hypsistos (the "most high" Zeus), Hera, Athena, Apollo, Artemis, Aphrodite Epiteuxidia (the Aphrodite "giving success"), Demeter and her daughter (Persephone), Hermes Kerdoos (the "profitable" Hermes), Poseidon (connected with the important harbor at Thessalonica), Cybele (the Phrygian mother goddess), Asklepios (god of healing) and his daughter (Hygieia, Health), Nike (Victory), the Dioscuri, Heracles, Tyche (Fortune), and Nemesis (Retribution). Judaism and the likely presence of a local synagogue should also be added to this religious potpourri.

Since citizens were expected to participate in the local religious practices and festivals and sometimes were even given funds from civic leaders to ensure such participation, it is reasonable to assume that in their pre-Christian life the members of the Thessalonian church not only were very familiar with the various cults of their city but also had themselves actively participated in many of them. This assumption becomes a certainty in light of Paul's words to his Thessalonian readers concerning "how you turned to God from idols in order to serve a living and true God" (1 Thess. 1:9). A detailed study of that religiously pluralistic environment will yield a deeper understanding and appreciation of how traumatic an event it must have been for the predominantly Gentile congregation in Thessalonica, who had been immersed in the religious institutions of their city, to abruptly sever these ties and commit themselves solely to "God the Father and the Lord Jesus Christ" (1:1).

In sharp contrast to other leading cities of the ancient world connected with NT writings, such as Ephesus, Corinth, and Philippi—where the large amount of material brought to light over one hundred years of archaeological work has resulted in a clear picture of local worship practices—we know significantly less about religion in Thessalonica. Over sixty years ago Charles Edson (1948: 153) noted: "Yet few ancient cities of equal importance [to Thessalonica] have been the subject of so little investigation in modern times. Up to now, the inscriptions found in Salonica have all been chance discoveries." Sadly, the situation today is only slightly improved, as archaeological work

---

12. Thessalonica, of course, was not unique in this regard: all major cities in the ancient world had a religiously pluralistic environment.

in the modern city of Thessalonica, the second largest city in the country, has been limited to only the Roman forum and the third-century AD monuments connected with Galerius. Any conclusions we reach about religion in Thessalonica, therefore, must be of a provisional nature, contingent on what future discoveries may become available. Our survey will focus on those cults for which the evidence is most abundant and reliable.

a. *Dionysus cult*. Dionysus was worshiped in the surrounding Macedonian towns of Amphipolis, Vergina, Pella, Berea, and Dion (Tzanavari 2003: 210–12), and so also not surprisingly in Thessalonica. In fact, Dionysus ranks among the oldest of the deities worshiped in Thessalonica, dating to the very founding of the city. An altar found at the Golden (or Vardar) Gate, the western entrance to the city, honors a prominent city leader during the third century BC. This dedication was given by "the tribe Dionysus," one of the three tribes formed by the general Cassander at the time of the forced relocation and unification of the surrounding villages used to create the city of Thessalonica (Edson 1948: 160; R. Evans 1968: 71). That in this Hellenistic period Dionysus was one of the more popular gods worshiped in Thessalonica is indicated by the coinage, on which Dionysus appears beginning already in 187 BC (Gaebler 1935: nos. 1, 9, 15). Further evidence of devotion to Dionysus during this early period of the city's history exists in a brief inscription on a large base found not in its original location but as part of a Roman wall, near the Serapeion in the western part of the city. The inscription—"The city, to Dionysus, from the city leaders, Aristandros, son of Aristonos, Antmachos, son of Aristoxenos" (*IT* 28)—testifies to the presence of a state cult of the god.

Although during the Roman period the image of Dionysus disappears from the coinage of Thessalonica, this popular god does not vanish from the life of the city. In 1887 a large marble altar was found in the foundation of a home located near the Kassandreotic (Kalamari) Gate, on the east side of the city. The inscription on this altar reveals that it was erected in AD 132 in honor of someone who served not only as "priest of Dionysus" but also as *hydroscopus*—another official and likely higher post connected with the cult of Dionysus (*IT* 503). Further epigraphic evidence for the existence of a Dionysus cult in Thessalonica during the Roman period exists in two marble monuments located in or very near the Church of the Panagia Acheiropoietos (the mosque Eski Cuma under Turkish rule), in the eastern part of the city. The first monument is a funerary altar dated to AD 209, erected in honor of someone who had been priest of at least two *thiasoi*, religious associations of Dionysus (*IT* 506). The second monument contains a relief of a standing draped woman, and its two sides record a donation by a "priestess Evia of Prinophoros"—a priestess of Dionysus.[13] The rest of this inscription testifies to the existence of two *thiasoi*, religious associations dedicated to Dionysus (*IT* 260). Although it is impossible to determine with certainty, the evidence

---

13. The term *Prinophoros* (Πρινοφόρος), "Oak-Bearer," refers to Dionysus since cult epithets of this deity that have to do with plants are very common. See Edson 1948: 168; Tzanavari 2003: 213.

suggests that these two religious associations were not private groups but connected with the city cult of Dionysus (see argument forwarded by Edson 1948: 177–78; but Steimle [2008: 182–83] and Nigdelis [2010: 15n7] reject this view). Additionally, a gravestone discovered in 1904, during the demolition of the eastern city wall to the north of the Kassandreotic (Kalamari) Gate, dates to around AD 200 and commemorates a certain Makedon who was a member of "the *thiasos* of Asiani." Even though the god of the Asiani is not named, there is compelling evidence that the unspoken deity in view is Dionysus. Individuals who moved to Thessalonica from Asia apparently formed a religious association composed initially or primarily of members from their own province and devoted to one of the most popular gods of their homeland, Dionysus. Finally, Dionysus is among the deities on the pillars of the double portico of *Las Incantadas*, removed from the monument in 1864 and now in the Louvre,[14] and a second-century AD statuette of Dionysus crowned with an ivy wreath was found in the Roman forum (Tzanavari 2003: 213–14). Throughout both the Hellenistic and Roman periods, the popularity of the worship of Dionysus is evident in the plethora of personal names derived from the god: Dionysas, Dionysia, Dionysianos, Dionysis, Dionysodots, Bacchides, Bacchios, Bacchis, and Bachylos (Tzanavari 2003: 212).

Perhaps the most intriguing evidence for the worship of Dionysus in Thessalonica lies in a small herm—a statue in the form of a square stone pillar surmounted by a head—of Dionysus discovered in the crypt of the city's Serapeion. The presence of a herm of Dionysus in a building devoted to the Egyptian gods is surprising, but it can be explained by Dionysus's identification with the Egyptian god Osiris, an identification found already in the classical period with Herodotus ("Now Osiris in the tongue of Hellas is Dionysus" [2.144]). This linking of Dionysus with Osiris is likely due to the fact that, according to some traditions, both deities suffered dismemberment of their male sex organ, which makes the absence of the phallus in the herm of Dionysus significant. As Hendrix (1987: 9) observes: "The legendary reconstitution of the gods may have been ritually enacted by their devotees (note the suggestive absence of the herm's phallus), and would have affirmed the deities' powers of renewal and regeneration." There is no information about the worship practices and rites of the Dionysus cult at Thessalonica, though one can safely assume that features of Dionysus worship—processions in which imposing effigies of Dionysus along with his symbol, the phallus, were carried; ecstatic dances to the accompaniment of flutes and drums; excess of drinking wine and feasting at banquets; and so forth—were practiced there too.

14. The four portico two-sided Caryatids were part of a Corinthian colonnade located at the entrance to the ancient agora. Along with Dionysus, the other figures depicted in these second-century BC sculptures include the Maenad, Ariadne, Leda, Ganymede, one of the Dioscuri, the Aura, and Nike. Before their removal, these eight figures belonging to "Las Incantadas" were the symbol of Thessalonica, and only after their removal in 1864 did the White Tower rise to prominence as the city's symbol.

b. *Egyptian cult*. The gods of Egypt—especially Serapis and Isis but also Osiris, Harpocrates, and Anubis—received so much attention and devotion from the citizens of Thessalonica that outside Egypt in the Greek world, this city became the second most important center of the cult, after the island of Delos (Tzanavari 2003: 241). In 1939 the popularity of these Egyptian gods became clear with the discovery, in the western part of the city, of the so-called Serapis temple along with thirty-five inscriptions, and an additional thirty-four inscriptions dealing with Egyptian deities were subsequently found.[15] The building is technically neither a temple nor explicitly identified with Serapis, but a small assembly hall where Serapis, after whom the building is now conveniently named, and other Egyptian gods were worshiped (Fraikin 1974; Hendrix 1987: 6–9; Koester 2007: 46–49).

This Serapeion, as it is commonly called, consisted of a small entrance hall, which leads to a larger hall (36′ x 26′) with a far north wall containing a niche where a statue of one of the Egyptian gods would have been located. In front of the niche was a stone step or bench, which may have functioned as a sacred table for the cult's rituals. Situated directly below the entrance hall of the Serapeion was a modest-sized underground room or crypt (13′ x 5′). Access to this crypt was not possible from the main building above but rather by means of a long underground passageway (32′ x 3′), entered at the bottom of a flight of steps that started outside the assembly hall. The entrance to this passageway was discovered sealed at the top with marble slabs, thereby preserving it and the crypt in their original state, including various statues and inscriptions. One of these finds included the herm of Dionysus already discussed above, which stood in a niche in the crypt's east wall.

There is evidence that, like the cult of Dionysus, the worship of the Egyptian gods in Thessalonica took place throughout both Hellenistic and Roman periods. That the gods of Egypt migrated north to Macedonia very early is indicated by the presence of the Serapeion, whose original construction is dated to the late third century BC (Edson 1948: 181; Fraikin 1974: 4). Further evidence lies in a small stela found in the Serapeion that records a decree of the Macedonian king Philip V dated to 186 BC. In this recorded document the king forbids using funds from the temple for anything not connected with the Serapis cult and lays down specific penalties for the noncompliance with his command. Still additional support for Thessalonian participation in the Egyptian cult during the Hellenistic period exists in a votive relief to Osiris that was found in the Serapeion and dates to the late second century BC (*IT* 107).[16]

15. *IT* 3, 15, 16, 37, 51, 53, 59, 61, 73, 75–123, 221–22, 244, 254–59. The remains of the Serapis temple and its underground crypt are no longer visible today since they are covered by a street (junction of Vardari Square and Dioiketerion Street) and a private house. A model of the building was made and is now housed in the city's archaeological museum.

16. The inscription on this votive reveals that it was given by Demetrios in honor of his parents, who are depicted in the relief as standing on each side of an altar: the father Alexander is on the right, pouring out a libation; the mother, Nikaia, is on the left; and standing above them both in the middle is either the son and giver of the votive, Demetrios, or the god Osiris portrayed in a

The gods of Egypt continued to be venerated by the Thessalonians in the Roman period. An important inscription from the Serapeion dating to the first century AD testifies to the crucial role that this Thessalonian sanctuary played in the spread of the Egyptian cult to the city of Opus, located on the southern coast of mainland Greece (*IT* 255). This inscription records how the god Serapis appeared twice in a dream to Xenainetos, apparently a city official from Opus, while he was visiting Thessalonica and staying in the local Serapeion or one of the other sacred buildings connected with the Egyptian cult. It was common for a person to spend the night in the temple while waiting for the deity to convey a message, vision, or healing. The god informed Xenainetos that under his pillow he would find a letter that he should take back to his home city of Opus: it contained instructions to his political rival there to initiate the worship of both Serapis and Isis. This inscription suggests that the Egyptian cult in Thessalonica did not play merely a minor role in the religious milieu of that city but rather functioned as "a significant center for the propagation of the religion" (Hendrix 1987: 11). Other important finds from the Serapeion include larger than life-size heads of Isis and Serapis, a statuette of Harpocrates, a statue of Isis or a priestess of the goddess, and a cylindrical votive altar (see images in Tzanavari 2003: 245–48 [figs. 42–46]).

One of the reasons for the rising popularity of the Egyptian gods was the conviction that these deities were less distant and removed than the traditional Greco-Roman gods, and thus more attentive to the individual needs of their devotees. For example, one votive relief of stone discovered in the Serapeion and dating to the second or third century AD depicts two human ears and has a brief inscription: "According to a vow, Phouphikia to Isis for hearing" (*IT* 100). The ears represent those of Isis: this woman has made a vow to honor the Egyptian goddess for hearing her unstated request, which may have to do with healing. Another votive relief also discovered in the Serapeion and dating to the same time period involves the imprint of two feet with a brief inscription: "Venetia Prima. [Given] according to a command" (*IT* 120). The feet represent those of an unnamed god from the Egyptian cult who is claimed to have appeared to a female devotee named Venetia Prima and commanded her to offer this votive relief to commemorate the divine manifestation.

Several brief inscriptions that include the name of the devotee(s) and end simply with the word "thanksgiving" ([εὐ]χαριστήριον, [*eu*]*charistērion*) are dedicated to various Egyptian gods: "To Serapis, Isis, Anubis, and the gods of the same temple" (*IT* 78); "To Isis and Harpocrates" (*IT* 81); "To Serapis, Isis, Harpocrates, and the gods of the same temple and same altar" (*IT* 85); "To Eros, Isis, Serapis, and Harpocrates" (*IT* 87); "To Isis" (*IT* 96, 101). Instead of an expression of "thanksgiving," some inscriptions from the Serapeion consist

thoroughly hellenized style. On the arm of the father hangs a money purse, which may indicate that he was a patron of this Egyptian cult. Surprisingly, it is not the devotee, Demetrios, who is identified as the "initiate" but the god Osiris. This may indicate a belief that the god Osiris himself is the "initiate" in the cult who oversees the ongoing devotions of his human followers after they have died.

of a "vow" or "prayer" (εὐχή, *euchē*) whose contents are not spelled out and are also directed to the Egyptian gods: "To Sarapis, Isis, Anubus, and the gods of the same temple" (*IT* 80); "To the great gods" (*IT* 51). These inscriptions imply that devotees viewed their relationship with the various gods as one that could be summarized as quid pro quo: "Do this for me, and I'll do that for you." Although the dedications of thanksgivings no doubt were motivated by genuine gratitude for past blessings, they also were given with the implied expectation of receiving future answers from the gods to their subsequent requests (Green 2002: 33–34).

Thessalonian involvement with the Egyptian gods also is clear from the presence of three different religious associations dedicated to the financial support and activities of the cult (Tzanavari 2003: 249–50). We learn about one of these associations from a stela that contains a relief of Anubis found not in the Serapeion but outside the ancient city walls. This relief, located at the top of the narrow stela, consists of a pediment under which is the image of the dog-headed Anubis, who is robed and encircled by a wreath. The eighteen-line inscription under the relief dates to the first half of the second century AD (*IT* 58). The relief is dedicated to "Aulus Papius Chilon, who provided the meeting place [οἶκος, *oikos*]"—likely a small building where members of the voluntary association met for religious and social functions. Thirteen other members of this association who dedicated the stela to him identify themselves with two terms: "the bearers of sacred objects" (ἱεραφόροι, *hieraphoroi*) and "dining companions" (συνκλίται, *synklitai*). The first term reveals that the association's members perform a special role in the city cult of the Egyptian gods—a role that involves the bearing of sacred cult objects. The second term reveals that these individuals have formed themselves into a private club or association for the purposes of dining fellowship. Edson (1948: 188) summarizes the interpretation of this inscription as follows: "Outside the city walls of Thessalonica in the suburbs to the northwest Aulus Papius Chilon built an *oikos* for his fellow *hieraphoroi* where they could meet together at stated intervals presided over by their *archon*, perform rites to Anubis and dine together as friends united in their common interest and common duty as functionaries in the public cult of the Egyptian gods." That several of the listed names of the association members typically belong to slaves and freedpersons, whereas some of the offerings were quite lavish and expensive, has indicated to some that the Egyptian gods appealed to Thessalonians of varying social and economic backgrounds (Hendrix 1987: 15; Tzanavari 2003: 250; Koester 2007: 54).

c. *Cabirus cult*. The Cabirus cult is widely recognized as the most important center of worship in Thessalonica. Edson (1948: 188), for example, states, "From the Flavian period at the latest, Cabirus was the chief, the tutelary deity of Thessalonica." Robert Jewett (1986: 127) refers to "the ubiquity of evidence concerning the Cabiric cult in Thessalonica, indicating it was not only the most distinctive but also the most important factor in the religious environment."

But while compelling evidence exists as to the importance of the Cabirus cult among the various deities worshiped in Thessalonica, there is frustratingly little data to provide clarity about the myth connected with this god and the ritual practices and beliefs associated with his cult. For answers to these questions, some scholars have been tempted to look to information about the Cabiri (plural) worshiped in other places, such as Thebes, Delos, Imbros, Lemnos, and especially Samothrace (Witt 1977), which was apparently the center of this cult and the place from where it was introduced to Thessalonica (Edson 1948: 188–89). The problem with this, however, is that in sharp distinction from the two/twin Cabiri worshiped on the island of Samothrace, where they were also known as "the great gods," the Thessalonians venerated only a single Cabirus. Therefore information about the plural Cabiri worshiped in other places may be relevant in supplementing our understanding of the Cabirus cult in Thessalonica but must be used with great caution.

The date when the Cabirus cult was initiated in Thessalonica cannot be determined on the basis of the evidence currently available. Yet the Cabiri were known in Larisa, the capital of nearby Thessaly, by about 200 BC, and were also widespread in the northern Aegean: these facts suggest that it may well have been established in Thessalonica before the start of the common era (Hemberg 1950: 9). Early devotion to Cabirus in Thessalonica is further suggested by a series of coins the city issued in the late first century BC that contain the image of the Dioskouroi (or Dioskuri), twin gods often identified with the two Cabiri (Hendrix 1987: 24). Also highly suggestive are two inscriptions found in Samothrace: one lists pilgrims from Thessalonica who visited the Cabiri cult between 37 BC and AD 43; the other is a dedication to the Cabiri from a number of initiates from Thessalonica. These inscriptions cause Edson (1948: 190) to conclude that "by the reign of Augustus at the latest members of the city's upper classes were showing interest in the cult of the Samothracian gods," that is, the Cabiri.

The most compelling proof for the Thessalonian devotion to the singular Cabirus, however, lies in the numismatic evidence. Searchers have discovered some one hundred coins on which Cabirus is portrayed in the following conventional manner. He is clean-shaven and wearing the *chitōn*, or short tunic, and the *chlamys*, or billowing cloak—standard attire for youths and young men and thus a symbol of the god's eternal youthfulness. Resting on his shoulder and held in his left hand is a hammer or mallet, which resembles that carried by Hephaistos, Greek god of metalworks and patron of craftsmen, and thus serves as a symbol of the god's productivity. Held in his right hand is a *rhyton*, or drinking horn, which perhaps is influenced by another popular Thessalonian deity, Dionysus, and a likely symbol of the god's conviviality. On the imperial coinage minted in Thessalonica, that is, coinage whose obverse contains an image of the current emperor or other members of the imperial family, Cabirus appears on the reverse side far more frequently than any other god (Touratsoglou 1988: 24–81). Hendrix (1987: 25) thus speaks of the "ubiquitous presence" of Cabirus in the coinage of Roman Thessalonica and how this "indicates his importance as the city's chief deity." Witt (1977: 78) goes even further and states: "Thessalonike, on numismatic evidence, was addicted to the cult of what may perhaps be termed Kabeiric monotheism."

Inscriptional evidence for the Cabirus cult, in sharp contrast to the coinage, is surprisingly almost nonexistent: among the several hundred inscriptions discovered in Thessalonica, only one explicitly mentions the name of this enigmatic deity. Yet though it numbers as only one inscription, and though it dates rather late, to the first part of the third century AD, it nevertheless is important in confirming the evidence of the coins concerning Cabirus as the key god of Thessalonica. A marble altar found in 1927 refers to Cabirus as "the most holy and ancestral god" (*IT* 199). The adjective "ancestral" (πάτριος, *patrios*) conveys not only the importance of the Cabirus cult but also its longevity and the enduring status of Cabirus as a key god of the city.

Monumental evidence for the Cabirus cult exists in a marble pilaster capital discovered in the octagonal building that was part of Emperor Galerius's (AD 305–311) palace in Thessalonica. The relief in the capital portrays Cabirus in exactly the same way that the god is conventionally depicted on the coinage: a young, clean-shaven individual who wears a short tunic and holds a hammer in his left hand and a drinking horn in his right hand. Although the function of this octagonal building is not clear, there is good reason to believe that it served as a throne room for the emperor. The presence of a Cabirus relief in such a key location within the palace complex attests to the ongoing importance that this god still played in Thessalonica in the early fourth century AD. Further evidence of the enduring veneration of Cabirus may exist in the later Christian veneration of Saint Demetrius—a young man from a senatorial family in Thessalonica who was martyred about AD 306 during the persecutions under Diocletian or Galerius. There are compelling reasons to believe that the young god Cabirus, who was the patron deity of Thessalonica, influenced the iconography and hagiography of the young man Demetrius, who in later times became the patron saint of Thessalonica (so Edson 1948: 203; Hemberg 1950: 210; Witt 1977: 79; Koester 2007: 40).

In addition to the inscriptional and monumental evidence for the Cabirus cult at Thessalonica, there is also literary evidence, which must be used cautiously due to its late date and authorship by Christians concerned with repudiating pagan beliefs and practices. The fullest account of the myth connected with Cabirus is given by Clement of Alexandria in chapter 2 of his *Exhortation to the Greeks*, composed AD 180–190. Clement is actually describing the Corybantes, whom he says "are also called by the name Cabiri, and the ceremony itself they announce as the Cabiric mystery." His account describes three brothers, one of whom—Cabirus, though he is not named as such—is killed by the other two. To hide their murderous act and ward off any evil consequences, the two brothers wrapped the body of Cabirus in purple cloth, crowned his head, and carried the corpse on a brass shield to the base of Mount Olympus, where it was consecrated and buried. Clement also reports that the two brothers got possession of a box that contained the phallus of Dionysus, which they took to Tuscany, where they used the box and its contents for the purposes of worship. The same legend is recounted by Firmicus Maternus in his mid-fourth-century work, *The Error of the Pagan Religions*, but with an important additional comment that links this story with the Cabirus worshiped in Thessalonica: "This [the murdered brother] is the same person whom the Macedonians worship in their fatuous superstition. This is the Cabirus, the bloody one to whom the Thessalonians once offered prayers with bloody hands." Lactantius, another Christian apologist in the early fourth century, writes that Cabirus enjoyed the same position of preeminence among the Macedonians as Isis had among the Egyptians and Athena among the Athenians (*Inst.* 1.15.8).

These three pieces of literary evidence (Clement, Firmicus Maternus, Lactantius) certainly confirm the importance of the Cabirus cult in Thessalonica, but do they shed any light on the myth and cultic worship of this deity? On the one hand, it is intriguing to consider a possible connection between Cabirus, to "whom the Thessalonians once offered prayers with bloody hands," and the murder and dismemberment of Dionysus, especially in light of the herm of Dionysus with the removable phallus found in the crypt of the Serapeion. On the other hand, Firmicus's charge of blood sacrifice was a common one that Christian apologists raised against their pagan opponents and thus may not reflect a unique cultic practice of Cabirus in Thessalonica. Unfortunately, how the Thessalonian citizens venerated their city's patron deity cannot yet be known. Thus Hendrix (1987: 25–26) concludes his survey of this cult: "The Kabiros temple at Thessalonica has not been found, and until new material or literary evidence is discovered, the nature of the Thessalonian cult ritual and its 'legend' cannot be determined more precisely."

d. *Imperial cult*. The imperial cult—the worship of Roma as a personification of the Roman state and of individual emperors as gods—played an important role in the religiously pluralistic environment of Thessalonica. This is because the imperial cult here, as elsewhere in the ancient world, was not merely an expression of religious devotion but also one of political allegiance and economic dependence. As Mellor (1975: 16) summarizes: "For the Greeks such cults [worship accorded Roma and similar divinities] were political and diplomatic acts, sometimes sincere, sometimes not. . . . It [worship of Roma] was a cult based on political, rather than religious experience."

In our earlier discussion of Thessalonica's favored political status, we noticed how the city's veneration of Rome and its emperors was a natural outgrowth of the city's political and financial need to honor "Roman benefactors" (Ῥωμαῖοι εὐεργέται, *Rōmaioi euergetai*). These are individuals who financed local cultural institutions (e.g., the gymnasium and its activities), helped protect the city from hostile neighbors and anti-Roman invaders, promoted the interests of Thessalonica in Rome, or provided aid in other ways. The city's well-being and success "depended on its ability to attract and sustain influential Romans' commitments and favors" and an "institution developed by the Thessalonicans to attract and regularize such commitment as honors for their 'Roman benefactors'" (Hendrix 1984: 253). So great was Thessalonica's desire to honor those Roman individuals whose good works benefited the city that a new cult and priesthood was established in the first century BC to honor not just the human benefactors but also the goddess Roma and the unnamed "gods."

A temple in honor of Caesar was built near the end of the first century BC, and a priesthood to service this temple was established: an important inscription refers to "the temple of Caesar," the "priest and *agōnothetēs* [games superintendent] of Imperator Caesar Augustus son [of god]," and the "priest of the gods . . . and priest of Roma and the Roman benefactors" (*IT* 31). This inscription, along with others (*IT* 32, 132, 133), also suggests that officials connected with the imperial cult were preeminent over other priesthoods: "In every extant instance in which the 'priest and agonothete of the Imperator' is mentioned, he is listed first in what appears to be a strict observance of protocol. The Imperator's priest and agonothete assumes priority, the priest of 'the gods' is cited next, followed by the priest of Roma and Roman benefactors" (Hendrix 1984: 312). Coinage from the city reveals that Julius Caesar and his adoptive son, Octavian (Augustus), received divine honors. In one series minted about 27 BC, the laureate head Julius Caesar appears with the inscription "God." The reverse sides of coins from this series have the image of Octavian (Augustus), and though they do not have the similar inscription "God" or "son of god," his divinity is implied by his pairing with the divine Julius and by the oft-found title *Sebastos*, or "Augustus." It is also significant that in one standard series of coins the head of Zeus was replaced with that of Augustus (Hendrix 1984: 179, 188; Donfried 1997: 218; Green 2002: 40; S. Kim 2008: 5). A statue of Augustus, found in 1939 just north of the Serapeion, depicts the emperor in a divine posture: he is slightly larger than life-sized, semi-naked, and a voluminous robe wraps around his waist and over his left arm; his right arm is raised with closed fist and finger pointed upward as he strides forward.[17] It is "one of the best examples of the imperial propaganda statues—and is, indeed, one of the first of the series—that the Romans erected in various nerve-centres of their boundless empire" (Vokotopoulou 1996: 85). Another statue—this one headless but likely that of Claudius—was discovered close to that of Augustus; it also portrays this later emperor in a divine pose (Archaeological Museum, Thessaloniki, no. 2467).

Hendrix's thesis that the Thessalonians' practice of honoring the Roman emperors must be understood as an "innovative expansion of traditional honors to Romans and other foreign benefactors" (1984: 337) causes him to reject such labels as "imperial cult" and "emperor worship." As further support he appeals to the fact that neither Augustus nor any of his successors (with the exception of Nero) was designated as a god by the Thessalonians: "Be they magistrates, important Romans or emperors, it was the norm at Thessalonica

17. Archaeological Museum, Thessaloniki, no. 1065, http://odysseus.culture.gr/h/4/eh430.jsp?obj_id=8164.

to honor Romans as humans" (Hendrix 1986: 307). Several factors, however, suggest that the attention paid to the Roman emperors in Thessalonica went beyond benefaction to worship. The building of a temple dedicated to Caesar, the establishment of a priesthood to the goddess Roma, the divine titles found in the coinage, and the widespread bestowal of divine honors to the Roman emperors in other nearby places "all point to the presence of genuine religious sentiments" (Green 2002: 42). Furthermore, the distinction between honoring the emperors and worshiping them is not so great. As Ferguson (2009: 206) explains in his discussion of the imperial cult: "Sacrifices offered for or in honor of a person could easily become sacrifices to him."

e. *Judaism*. The clearest evidence that Judaism existed as one of the religious options in Roman Thessalonica lies in the Acts account of Paul's mission-founding activity in that city, which identifies not only the existence of a synagogue community but also one whose membership included both Jews and God-fearers, some of whom were women from leading families (Acts 17:1–9). Many scholars, of course, quickly dismiss this account on the grounds that Acts qualifies only as a "secondary source" and is historically unreliable. This objection, however, fails on two grounds. First, there exists a "primary source" that confirms the presence of Jews in Thessalonica who were involved in Paul's hasty departure from the city: the apostle himself in 1 Thess. 2:14–15 refers to "the Jews . . . who drove us out." Although there were other times and places where Paul faced opposition from Jews (Gal. 5:11; 2 Cor. 11:24–26; see also Acts 13:44–51; 14:2, 19; 17:5–9, 13–14; 18:12–18), this brief clause makes best sense in its context if Paul is referring to a situation that his readers knew all too well: the role that certain Jews in Thessalonica had in driving the missionaries out of town.[18] Second, Riesner (1998: 366–67) has shown that of the twenty-five individual pieces of information in the Lukan account of Paul's ministry in Thessalonica, nineteen are directly or indirectly confirmed by 1 Thessalonians, thereby demonstrating the historical reliability of that account.

Evidence outside the biblical record for the presence of a Jewish community in Thessalonica is admittedly sparse and at times inferential but by no means nonexistent (contra Koester 2007: 56, who asserts: "The archaeological record is silent about 'Judaism' in Thessalonike"). It is possible that Jews would have come to Thessalonica very early to pursue business opportunities in this rapidly growing harbor town. Vacalopoulos (1972: 9) writes in this regard: "Not only did foreign religions penetrate into Thessaloniki at a very early date but also various peoples resident in the East must have settled there on a temporary or even a permanent basis, attracted by the commerce of Thessaloniki which became more vigorous year by year—and the first of all surely were the Jews." This possibility gains support from Philo's recording of a letter from Herod Agrippa (AD 37–44) to the emperor Caligula, which observes that Jewish

18. Malherbe (2000: 175) observes: "It is only extreme skepticism about what Acts has to offer and the hypothesis that Paul did not write 2:13–16 that raise serious doubts that Paul here refers to his expulsion by Jews, probably engineered in the way Acts describes."

communities can be found among most of the provinces of Rome, including that of Macedonia (*Embassy* 281). Some scholars dismiss this testimony of Philo, claiming that it comes from "a completely apologetic document," which "suggests that his comments should be seen as over-generalization and treated cautiously" (De Vos 1999: 131–32; Ascough 2003: 192–93). But Jews lived throughout the Roman Empire, and it is entirely reasonable to expect them also to be living in Macedonia, just as Philo records, and in the largest city of that province, Thessalonica (so also Jewett 1986: 119–20). For example, a late second- or early third-century AD inscription from Stobi (*CIJ* 694), located some seventy-five miles northwest of Thessalonica, and a synagogue excavated there testify to the presence of a significant number of Jews (Hengel 1966; Schürer 1973–87: 3/1.67–68; Levine 2000: 270–73). This not only supports Philo's claim about the presence of Jews in Macedonia but, given Stobi's location relatively close to Thessalonica as an inland city of considerably less importance than that coastal capital, suggests that a Jewish community also existed in Thessalonica (J. Hill 1990: 53, 55–56).

The most important evidence for the presence of a significant number of Jews in Thessalonica lies in an inscription found on a sarcophagus that dates to the late second or early third century AD (*SEG* 44:556). The tomb belonged to a couple whose multiple names include a Jewish one for each: Marcus Aurelius Jacob, who was called Eutychios ("Lucky"), and his wife, Anna, who has the pet name Asyncrition ("Incomparable"). The inscription warns that any person who violates this tomb by placing within it another body will be punished with a fine of 75,000 denarii payable "to the synagogues" (ταῖς συναγωγαῖς, *tais synagogais*). The use of the plural "synagogues" is significant, for it "implies that in the third century there were several Jewish communities in Thessalonica" (Levinskaya 1996: 156).

Five other tomb inscriptions from Thessalonica are of possible relevance. One dating from the second century AD reads: "In memory of Abraham and his wife Theodote" (*CIJ* 693 = *IG* 10/2:633). This tomb contains no distinctively Jewish symbols other than the two names and hence may be a Jewish Christian epitaph. Another tomb has the symbol of the menorah and the phrase "The Lord is with us" (Κύριος μεθ' ἡμῶν, *Kyrios meth' hēmōn*; *CIJ* 693b)—a phrase that occurs elsewhere in Christian inscriptions. A third tomb has the inscription on its marble door: "Benjamin, the one also called Domitios" (Βενιαμῆς ὁ καὶ Δομείτιος, *Beniamēs ho kai Domeitios*; *CIJ* 693c). A fourth tomb, unfortunately now lost and dating to AD 155, was erected in honor of Phoebe (Φοίβη, *Phoibē*) by her mother, Paraskeue (Παρασκευή, *Paraskeuē*; *IG* 10/2:449). A fifth tomb, likewise lost and of uncertain date, may also be of Jewish origin (*IG* 10/2:632.1). Even if some or all of these sarcophagi belonged to Jewish Christians, they do testify to the presence of ethnic Jews in Thessalonica by the second and third centuries AD—ethnic Jews whose families in the city may possibly be traced back to earlier times.

Additional epigraphic evidence for the existence of a Jewish community in Thessalonica stems from a bilingual—Greek and Hebrew—inscription (*CIJ*

693a). It is often referred to as the "Samaritan inscription" because it contains the text of Numbers 6:22–27 taken from the Samaritan Pentateuch rather than the LXX. The text is variously dated as early as the fourth and as late as the sixth century AD and may refer to an actual synagogue building.

It is true that none of the epigraphic and archaeological evidence cited above dates back to the first century, other than the testimony of Paul's First Letter to the Thessalonians and Acts. But as Riesner (1998: 347) asserts: "By no means, however, does the lack hitherto of any evidence from outside the New Testament constitute a reason for doubting the existence of a synagogue during the period of Paul's arrival in Thessalonica." An argument from silence is never particularly persuasive, especially because the city of Thessalonica has never been subjected to any kind of systematic excavation.[19] The Jews who lived in Thessalonica and the larger region of Macedonia, for whom we do have evidence dating to the second and third centuries, did not suddenly appear out of nowhere but, in light of the testimony of both Paul and Acts, more plausibly are descendants of those Jews who lived in these places from the first century or even earlier.

f. *Summary*. The above survey has provided only a glimpse into the religiously pluralistic environment of Thessalonica. Hopefully, there will be future archaeological discoveries that provide a clearer picture of this city's religious life at the time of Paul. Nevertheless, enough can be known to make it obvious that the conversion of the Thessalonian Christians is described in Paul's First Letter to the Thessalonians in deceptively simple terms: "how you turned to God from idols" (1:9). For in a place where over twenty-five gods, heroes, or personifications of virtues were being worshiped, there was nothing simple about turning to God from idols. In fact, in a society where cultic activities were intimately connected with political, economic, and social interests, it is to be expected that there would be significant opposition to both Paul and his Thessalonian converts. The Christians' total renunciation of their former pagan religious practices evoked feelings of resentment and anger in their non-Christian family members and friends. The exclusivity of these

19. The danger of arguing from silence is well illustrated by Paul Perdrizet, a classical scholar from France, who in 1894 was examining the importance of the Egyptian gods in Macedonia during the Roman period. He observed that numismatic evidence in Macedonia demonstrating the popularity of Isis and Serapis was virtually nonexistent. Though a coin from nearby Stobi in northern Macedonia contained the image of Serapis, coins from Thessalonica did not honor these two key Egyptian gods, nor was there any evidence indicating that their cult was important enough for the state to honor them with a municipal priest. Such evidence led Perdrizet (1894: 419) to conclude: "It does not appear that the cult of the Alexandrian divinities was ever widespread in Macedonia" ("Il ne semble pas que le culte des divinités alexandrines ait jamais été fort répandu en Macédoine"; my translation). The great error of this conclusion, which seemed perfectly logical in that day, became clear shortly after the 1917 fire in Thessalonica, when a Serapis temple was discovered along with what ultimately numbered sixty-nine inscriptions to various Egyptian deities. As a result of this now-rich collection of inscriptional evidence, a conclusion completely opposite that forwarded by Perdrizet is reached today: the Egyptian gods were extremely popular in Thessalonica and elsewhere in Macedonia.

Christians—their seemingly arrogant refusal to participate in the worship of any god but their own—deeply wounded public sensibilities and even led to charges that they were "atheists" (Barclay 1993: 515). Citizens of Thessalonica worried whether the Greek gods, whose home on Mount Olympus they could see a mere fifty miles away to the southwest, might punish the whole city for the sacrilegious actions of a few by sending disease, famine, or other natural disasters. Turning to God from idols also meant a rejection of the imperial cult, thereby jeopardizing Thessalonica's favored political and economic status as a free city. The conversion of the Thessalonian Christians involved a truly radical break with the religious setting of Thessalonica—a break that naturally incurred the resentment and anger of their "fellow citizens" (1 Thess. 2:14). Such resentment and anger led not only to Paul preaching the gospel to the Thessalonians "in spite of strong opposition" (2:2), but also to the Thessalonian believers accepting that gospel "in spite of severe suffering" (1:6). Little wonder that the apostle worried about his "baby" converts in Thessalonica whom he had to leave far sooner than he wanted and who were left alone to face significant opposition to their fledgling faith.

The Church of Thessalonica

Sources

Our reconstruction of the historical events surrounding the founding and ongoing nurturing of the Thessalonian church by Paul makes use of two main sources: Paul's letters, particularly 1 and 2 Thessalonians, and the book of Acts, particularly the account of 17:1–9. Two objections are sometimes made against using the latter source for the establishment of the Thessalonian church as recorded in Acts. The first is a methodological objection by those who not only make a sharp distinction between a primary source (what Paul wrote himself: his letters) and a secondary source (what others wrote about Paul: Acts) but also assume that Acts is so theologically motivated that its recorded historical events cannot be trusted (the so-called Knox school: John Knox 1950; Donald Riddle 1940; John Hurd 1967; 1968; Robert Jewett 1979; Gerd Lüdemann 1984). While the distinction itself between primary and secondary sources is not problematic, the presupposition about the relative historical reliability of each type is. The absolute priority of statements by Paul himself over those of the writer of Acts is negated by the possibility that autobiographical accounts might have gaps or be biased, whereas a third-person account might actually be more objective (see Hemer 1989: 244; Riesner 1998: 29–30). I am not claiming that the apostle's own voice is not to be trusted; rather, I am highlighting the illogical nature or fallacy of assuming that Acts as a secondary source is necessarily unreliable.

A second objection stems from the seemingly stereotyped nature of the account in Acts 17:1–9, which has suggested to some that it does not reflect the actual historical situation. This suspicion is increased by a number of claimed conflicts between the Acts account and the Thessalonian Letters, such as these: Acts implies that Paul's ministry in Thessalonica lasted three Sabbaths, whereas his letters suggest a longer stay; Acts presents the church as consisting predominantly of Jewish Christians, whereas 1 Thess. 1:9 indicates a Gentile Christian audience. Thus Richard (1995: 5) states: "Careful analysis of the Lukan passage and of 1 Thessalonians shows on the one hand that the former is thoroughly Lukan in theme, pattern, and concern, and on the other that these features conflict with Paul's composition." Koester (1982: 108) boldly claims that "all the individual events of Paul's activity in this city [Thessalonica] are legendary."

It ought to be acknowledged, in response, that Luke selected, omitted, and arranged the events in his description of Paul's mission-founding visit to Thessalonica to better fit the larger interests and themes at work in his book as a whole.[20] Nevertheless, the account of Acts 17:1–9 agrees in a number of significant and even impressive ways with information derived from the Thessalonian Letters and other ancient sources about Thessalonica. To cite but one example to illustrate this important fact, Luke identifies the city leaders of Thessalonica twice with the distinctive term "politarchs" (Acts 17:6, 8)—a rare city office, whose existence, though questioned in the past, has now been verified by some seventy inscriptions discovered thus far (see the more extensive discussion of "politarch" above under "The City of Thessalonica"). Since Luke proves himself reliable in technical details like this, he is likely to be trustworthy in other details as well. Riesner (1998: 366–67) lists eighteen additional pieces of information derived from the brief account of Acts 17:1–9 that can be verified either directly or indirectly by 1 Thessalonians. As a result, the observation made some time ago by Bruce (1979: 339) remains just as compelling today: "The account of Paul's movements which can be gathered from 1 Thessalonians agrees so well with the fuller record of Acts xvi.6–xviii.5 that that record, though it is substantially later than 1 Thessalonians, may confidently be accepted as providing a historical framework within which the references in 1 Thessalonians can be read with greater understanding."[21]

Philippi to Thessalonica

Paul, still in the early phase of his second missionary journey, first arrived in Thessalonica after his ministry in Philippi, a place where both 1 Thessalonians and Acts agree he had suffered and been shamefully treated (1 Thess.

---

20. As Keener (2014: 2532–33) notes: "Luke's brevity in reporting about the church in Thessalonica is more likely due to his interest and his space and subject constraints than to a lack of available information; the testimony about the Thessalonian church was apparently widespread, even beyond Macedonia and Achaia (even if 1 Thess 1:7–9 is hyperbolic). Certainly, if Luke or his 'we' source was in Philippi at this time, he would have had access to some further information, and if his ideal target audience is partly in Achaia and Macedonia, they would have had some knowledge about this church. Luke apparently presupposed such knowledge, mentioning one 'Jason' (Acts 17:5) without explanation, as if this person was already familiar to the ideal audience that he takes for granted."

21. On the broad question of the historicity of Acts as a whole, see Keener's magisterial Acts commentary (2012: 166–220).

2:2; Acts 16:16–40). The apostle's traveling companions included Silas (Silvanus) and Timothy, which explains why both are included as cosenders of Paul's later letters to the Thessalonian church (1 Thess. 1:1; 2 Thess. 1:1). Luke explicitly refers to Silas's presence with Paul during the establishment of the new church in Thessalonica (Acts 17:4, 10). Timothy, by contrast, is not mentioned in the Acts account, likely because he was not targeted by the mob action against the Christian movement. Nevertheless, Timothy's presence during the mission-founding visit to Thessalonica is clearly implied in the Acts account from the surrounding context (16:1–3; 17:14–15). The band of three missionaries apparently left Luke behind in Philippi, since the first of the "we" sections in Acts stops here (16:10–18) and the second one begins again in the same city (20:5).

The most natural route from Philippi to Thessalonica in terms of both shortest distance and ease of travel would be to follow the Via Egnatia (Egnatian Way)—the major east-west highway constructed by the Romans in the second century BC. Following this important imperial road from Philippi to Thessalonica would take the traveler through two other key cities, exactly as the account of Acts indicates: "They passed through Amphipolis and Apollonia" (17:1a). The total distance of such a trip is 92 miles, made up of three stages of 30 miles (Amphipolis), 27 miles (Apollonia), and 35 miles (Thessalonica). Some have concluded that Paul and his companions thus took three days to complete their journey and that they must have had the use of mules or horses, since these distances are too far for a typical day of walking (Hemer 1989: 115; followed by Barrett 1998: 808; D. Peterson 2009: 477; Keener 2014: 2535). Although it is impossible to know for sure, the lists of trials that Paul has endured during his years of ministry such as being hungry, thirsty, in rags, and homeless (1 Cor. 4:11; 2 Cor. 11:27) suggest that he did not enjoy the luxury of traveling by animal instead of foot. If so, it would have taken him and his companions some five or six days to reach Thessalonica.

Converts from Judaism

Paul begins his ministry in Thessalonica by going first to the local synagogue. The observation in Acts that Thessalonica was a place "where there was a synagogue" (17:1b) implies that this was not the case in the preceding two cities just mentioned, Amphipolis and Apollonia, and that the apostle did not evangelize these communities because they lacked the presence of Jews. The existence of a synagogue in Thessalonica has been questioned by some scholars who see this simply as a Lukan invention. Yet, as noted above, the Jews who lived in Thessalonica and the larger region of Macedonia for whom we do have evidence dating to the second and third centuries (see the fuller discussion of this evidence above under "A Religiously Pluralistic Environment") did not suddenly appear out of nowhere but more plausibly are descendants of Jews who lived in these places from the first century or even earlier. Furthermore, Paul's reference to Thessalonian Jews "who drove us out"

(1 Thess. 2:14–15) presupposes not only the existence of a Jewish community but also Paul's missionary activity in their midst.

Paul went to the synagogue "as was his custom" (Acts 17:2). During his first missionary journey, the apostle often began his ministry in a given town in the synagogue (13:5, 14; 14:1) and he continues that pattern in Thessalonica (see also 17:10, 17; 18:4, 19; 19:8). This might appear to be at odds with Paul's own statements about his calling to evangelize the Gentiles (Gal. 1:16; 2:7–8; Rom. 1:5, 13–16; 15:9–12, 15–21). Such a calling, however, does not preclude a ministry also to Jews. Thus the apostle speaks clearly about becoming a Jew and living as one under the law in order to win over Jews (1 Cor. 9:20). Also, Paul's list of trials as a missionary includes receiving the Jewish punishment of forty lashes minus one (cf. Deut. 25:3) and having suffered in this way no fewer than five times (2 Cor. 11:24)—punishments that presuppose an active ministry among his fellow Jews.

Paul's ministry in the synagogue of Thessalonica took place "on three Sabbaths," a phrase that could be understood to describe the length of his entire stay in the city (Lake 1911: 64–66; Lüdemann 1984: 177). Yet the Acts account does not require this conclusion but instead allows for a post-synagogue ministry. A longer stay is even demanded by several considerations. First, the Thessalonian church was composed primarily of Gentiles who had "turned to God from idols" (1 Thess. 1:9) and some time would have been needed for these members to be evangelized. Second, Paul stayed in Thessalonica long enough for the Philippians to send him financial aid on more than one occasion (Phil. 4:15–16).[22] Third, the apostle lived among the Thessalonian believers for a period of time that allowed him to become established in his trade (1 Thess. 2:9) and thereby provide them with a model of self-sufficient work to imitate (2 Thess. 3:7–9). Fourth, Paul uses the imperfect tense several times to refer to his preaching ministry among the Thessalonians (1 Thess. 3:4; 2 Thess. 2:5; 3:10) in order to stress the repetitive nature of his speaking on specific subjects, which in turn is suggestive of a longer stay in their midst. Fifth, a three-week ministry does not likely provide sufficient time for Paul to appoint and train leaders in the church (1 Thess. 5:12–13), unless this happened under Timothy's subsequent ministry in their midst (1 Thess. 3:1–5). But while Paul clearly ministered in Thessalonica for more than three weeks, his stay was likely not much longer than that given that he was "driven out" of town earlier than he wished (1 Thess. 2:15), with the result that he was "orphaned" from his Thessalonian converts (2:17) and they were "lacking" instruction in certain areas of their newfound faith (3:10).

Paul is quickly given the opportunity to address the synagogue community. Not only was this the right of all male Jews over eighteen years old, but local Jews would also have been eager to hear from a fellow countryman who might

---

22. The phrase in Phil. 4:16 καὶ ἅπαξ καὶ δίς (*kai hapax kai dis*) indicates at least two times when the Philippian church sent financial aid to Paul while he was in Thessalonica but could also refer to still additional occasions ("several times": BDAG 252).

have news from Jerusalem and elsewhere. Furthermore, Paul had excellent credentials, having graduated from the "Harvard" school of Judaism: he had studied at the feet of the renowned Jewish teacher Gamaliel, "a teacher of the law, who was honored by all the people" (Acts 5:34; 22:3). But while access to the *bēma*, or speaker's platform, was easy for Paul, winning over his hearers was significantly more difficult in light of his message: "explaining and proving that it was necessary for the Christ to suffer and to rise from the dead, and saying, 'This Jesus, whom I proclaim to you, is the Christ'" (17:3). The idea of a suffering and dying (implied from the following words) Messiah was not a common expectation among first-century Jews, and there was no anticipation of a resurrection of an individual *within* history—Jews (other than the Sadducees) looked forward only to a universal resurrection at the *end* of history. Yet this was not Paul's first time to preach the difficult message of a messiah who suffered, was killed, and then raised to life again, and it would not be his last. The apostle had previously delivered just such a sermon to the Jews in Antioch of Pisidia during his first missionary journey (Acts 13:16–41). Many years later, Paul preached the same message to the Jewish king Agrippa II and his sister, Bernice, along with the Roman governor Festus, claiming: "I am saying nothing beyond what the prophets and Moses said would happen—that the Messiah would suffer and, as the first to rise from the dead, would bring the message of light to his own people and to the Gentiles" (Acts 26:22–23 NIV). In his message to the Jews in Thessalonica, Paul no doubt discussed OT texts such as Pss. 2:7; 16:10–11; 110:1; and Isa. 53 (see the texts cited by Paul in Antioch of Pisidia [Acts 13:16–41] as well as by Peter in Jerusalem [Acts 2:14–40]).

Despite the difficult content of his message, Paul's three-Sabbath preaching in the synagogue wins over a significant number of converts. The apostle's success, however, is due not so much to his rhetorical skill as to the working of the Holy Spirit. As Paul himself stresses in his opening thanksgiving, his gospel preaching in Thessalonica involved not just words but also the power of the Holy Spirit, who made that proclaimed word effective in the lives of the Thessalonian believers (see comment on 1 Thess. 1:5a). The account in Acts similarly emphasizes God's role in causing the Thessalonian converts to respond positively to Paul's preaching, placing in the passive voice the verbs "they were persuaded and were joined to" (Acts 17:4a, ἐπείσθησαν καὶ προσεκληρώθησαν, *epeisthēsan kai proseklērōthēsan*), a use of the "divine passive" (BDF §130.1; Porter 1992: 65; Wallace 1996: 437–38).

Acts breaks down these converts from Judaism into three groups, listing them from the more general to the specific. First, it states that "some of them were persuaded and were joined to Paul and Silas" (Acts 17:4a). Among this group was Jason (which is the Greek form of the Jewish "Joshua": see Josephus, *Ant.* 12.239), who was wealthy, as evident from his ability both to house the three missionaries (Keener [2014: 2549] notes the explicit reference to Jason's "house" in Acts 17:5) as well as to post bond for them when they later got into trouble. The Thessalonian church likely also gathered for worship at Jason's house, since this agrees with Paul's pattern elsewhere of finding a convert who is wealthy enough to own a home (most people in that day did not, since this was a privilege enjoyed by only the wealthy) and thereby provide the group of new Christians with a place to meet communally (cf. Lydia in Philippi [Acts 16:15, 40]; Gaius in Corinth [Rom. 16:23]; Philemon in Colossae [Philem. 2]; Nympha in Hierapolis [Col. 4:15]). This Jason was also with Paul (unless this is a different Jason) when he wrote to the Romans from either Corinth or its eastern port Cenchreae (Rom. 16:21; for a fuller discussion of Jason, see Morgan-Gillman 1990). Another Jewish convert from Thessalonica, though he might have become a believer at a later time, was Aristarchus,[23] who traveled with Paul on his third missionary journey to Ephesus (Acts 19:29) and Corinth (20:4), his prison journey to Rome (27:2), and who stayed with Paul during his Roman imprisonment (Col. 4:10; Philem. 24).

The second and larger group among the converts from Judaism involved "a great many of the devout Greeks" (Acts 17:4b). These "devout" ones (σεβόμενοι, *sebomenoi*), often translated as "God-fearers," refer to "former polytheists who accepted the ethical monotheism of Israel and attended the synagogue, but who did not oblige themselves to keep the whole Mosaic law; in particular, the males did not submit to circumcision" (BDAG 918). These members of the Thessalonian church, therefore, underwent a kind of double conversion: they first were converted from paganism to Judaism, attracted by its antiquity, morality, and other features; they now were being converted from Judaism to Christianity on the basis of Paul's explanation of the OT.

The third and most significant—not in size but in importance—group of converts from Judaism included "not a few of the leading [lit., "first"] women" (Acts 17:4c). It is possible to render this phrase as "not a few women/wives of leading [men]"—a meaning made certain by the Western text.[24] The difference is moot, however, for either sense shows Luke's audience that Christianity was appealing to all classes of society, including those who enjoyed power and prestige (Acts 13:7, 12, 50; 17:34; 19:47; 28:7).

Converts from Paganism

The account in Acts indicates that the Thessalonian church, though made up of some Jews, consisted of more members who were Greek. In a number of ways, Paul's two Letters to the Thessalonians also indicate that the apostle won

23. Aristarchus, along with Mark the cousin of Barnabas and Jesus who is called Justus, is explicitly identified by Paul as belonging to the "men of the circumcision" (Col. 4:10–11). Schnabel (2012: 705) observes: "There is the intriguing possibility that this Aristarchus might be identical with the 'Aristarchos son of Aristarchos' mentioned as a politarch in several inscriptions."

24. In Acts 17:4, Codex Bezae (D) changes γυναικῶν τε τῶν πρώτων to καὶ γυναῖκες τῶν πρώτων. The shift from the genitive γυναικῶν to the nominative γυναῖκες can now be read only as "wives of the leading men." Codex Bezae, along with other key MSS ($\mathfrak{P}^{74}$ A 33 *pc* lat bo), also adds the conjunction καί earlier in the sentence between "devout" and "Greeks," which creates four (rather than three) groups of converts: Jews, Greeks who are "devout" or "God-fearers," *pagan Greeks*, and wives of leading men.

converts from paganism and that these members, in fact, formed the majority of the Thessalonian church. The strongest evidence of this stems from Paul's statement that his readers "had turned to God from idols to serve a living and true God" (1 Thess. 1:9)—something that could never be said about Jews. In both letters further indications of the predominantly Gentile background of the congregation in Thessalonica include the absence of any explicit OT quotations as well as his exhortations against the common Gentile—since the Jewish Torah prohibited such conduct—problem of sexual immorality (1 Thess. 4:3–8). It appears, therefore, that after three weeks of preaching in the synagogue, Paul and his coworkers engaged in a post-synagogue ministry, a missionary pattern that was later followed also in Corinth (Acts 18:7), Ephesus (19:9), and likely elsewhere as well.

It is commonly held that Paul won converts from paganism by preaching in the marketplaces and on street corners, in company with other wandering philosophers, teachers, and miracle workers, who were all competing for the same audience. But while there is evidence that the apostle did evangelize at times in such public settings (Acts 17:17), such evidence is remarkably rare: Acts, despite its interest in portraying the public acceptance of Christianity, hardly ever records the apostle as ministering in public venues. A more likely setting for Paul's evangelistic ministry, both in Thessalonica and elsewhere, was in the semiprivate setting of a workshop (see Hock 1979; 1980: 26–49, 52–59; Malherbe 1987: 7–20). The apostle thus closely links his work and his preaching in 1 Thess. 2:9: "Working night and day, . . . we preached to you the gospel of God." Although the precise relationship between the actions of working and preaching is open to debate (see comments on 2:9 for a fuller discussion of this issue), a good case can be made that they happened contemporaneously: "*while* working night and day, . . . we preached to you the gospel of God." In other words, Paul presented the gospel to fellow workers and customers while laboring in the workshop. This scenario is supported by some ancient sources that depict the workshop as one of the conventional settings for intellectual discourse and instruction (Hock 1979: 444–45). A century after Paul, Celsus, an enemy of Christianity, complains how in Christian families the children are not being taught at home as they should be tutored, but are going "to the wool-dresser's shop, or to the cobblers or the washer-woman's shop" to be instructed in the faith there (Origen, *Cels.* 3.55). A modern analogy would be the barbershop in America in the 1950s and 1960s: people went to the barber not just to get a haircut but also to catch up on the latest news and engage in discussion and debate with others gathered there.

We can plausibly reconstruct, therefore, Paul's post-synagogue ministry in Thessalonica. The apostle was working in a local leather workshop, making or repairing tents, as well as producing a range of leather and woven goods (W. Michaelis, *TDNT* 7:393–94; P. W. Barnett, *DPL* 926). This shop might well be owned—following the analogy of the Jewish couple in Corinth, Aquila and Priscilla (Acts 18:1–3)—by his host, Jason, a wealthy Jew just converted to the Christian faith during Paul's three weeks of preaching in the synagogue.

The apostle's work not only allowed Paul to support himself, thereby freeing the church from the burden of providing for his daily needs (1 Thess. 2:9); it also provided a model of self-sufficient work for believers to follow (2 Thess. 3:7–9), especially a small and rebellious group within the congregation who were guilty of idleness. In addition, Paul's work allowed him the opportunity to evangelize. During the long hours at his workbench, "working night and day," he "preached the gospel of God" (1 Thess. 2:9) to fellow workers, customers, and others who heard about the Jewish leatherworker who had recently arrived in town with new and provocative ideas. Some who participated in these workshop discussions accepted Paul's words "not as the words of men but as what it truly is, the word of God" (2:13) and so "turned to God from idols to serve a living and true God" (1:9). These new believers would need further instruction about their newfound faith and so either returned to the workshop or met Paul and his fellow missionaries elsewhere for one-on-one discipleship (2:11: "we exhorted *each one of you*"—the Greek is emphatic). These converts from paganism soon constituted the majority of believers in the Thessalonian church.

Numbered among these earliest Gentile members of the congregation may have been Secundus (a name of Latin origin meaning "Second"). The date of his conversion, however, is unknown since we meet him only some seven years after the founding of the church, when he, along with the Jewish Christian Aristarchus, represented the Thessalonian congregation in the delivery of the collection to Jerusalem (Acts 20:4). The name Secundus ranks among the most frequently attested ones in inscriptions from Thessalonica; over 80 percent of these occurrences have the *cognomen* (surname or family name) of Roman citizens (see Riesner 1998: 351n79 for list of inscriptions), suggesting that the Secundus mentioned in Acts was also a Roman citizen. His role in representing the Thessalonian church in the collection clearly indicates his importance within the congregation and may also suggest that he was among those earliest Gentiles who became believers during Paul's mission-founding visit (Riesner 1998: 351). Another less probable member among the first Gentile converts at Thessalonica was Demas (likely a shortened form of Demetrios: BDAG 222; BDF §125.1), who was one of Paul's "fellow workers" (Philem. 24; Col. 4:14) but later deserted the apostle and went to Thessalonica (2 Tim. 4:10), suggesting that this city may have been his hometown.

Opposition to Paul's Ministry

Paul's success in winning some converts from Judaism and even more from paganism not surprisingly caused a negative reaction from both the Jewish and the larger pagan communities. The apostle testifies to the opposition that he, as well as his converts, faced during the founding of the Thessalonian church: Paul, along with Silas and Timothy, needed "courage in our God to declare to you the gospel of God in the face of great opposition" (1 Thess. 2:2), and the Christians in that city also "received the word in much affliction" (1:6), with the result that "you indeed suffered . . . from your own fellow citizens" (2:14).

Although there is uncertainty over the precise meaning of "fellow citizens" (συμφυλέται, *symphyletai*), there are good grounds for understanding this term not in an ethnic sense (i.e., it has in view only the Gentile citizens of the city) but a geographical sense of referring to all the inhabitants of Thessalonica: the vast majority of them would have been Gentiles, but some would have been Jews (see further the comments on these verses below). This sense agrees with Acts 17:5–9, which claims that local Jews and Greeks were both involved in the events that ultimately led to Paul's forced departure from Thessalonica.

Opposition to the fledgling Jesus movement during the first three-plus weeks of Paul's ministry was spontaneous and unorganized. This changed when the success of the apostle in securing converts from the synagogue caused the remaining Jews to pursue a planned course of action: "But the Jews were jealous, and taking some bad characters from the marketplace, they formed a mob and started a riot in the city" (Acts 17:5a). The loss of even a few syna-gogue members naturally would have aroused the jealousy and anger of Jewish leaders; how much more intense these hostile feelings must have been toward the apostle for stealing both a great number of God-fearers and several women from rich and powerful families![25] The Jewish leaders, therefore, came up with a strategy for removing Paul from their city. Jewish involvement in the apostle's exodus from Thessalonica cannot be dismissed as a Lukan creation, since Paul himself claims that it was "the Jews who . . . drove us out" (1 Thess. 2:14–15).

The plan involved hiring "some bad characters from the marketplace" (τῶν ἀγοραίων ἄνδρας τινὰς πονηρούς, *tōn agoraiōn andras tinas ponērous*)—a phrase that, with the addition of the adjective "bad," refers not in a neutral sense to common day laborers or marketplace traders but in a pejorative sense to louts, loafers, and lowlifes, those who hang around public spaces with nothing to do but get into trouble (Acts 17:5; Aristophanes, *Frogs* 1015 [1047]; Plato, *Prot.* 347C; Theophrastus, *Char.* 6.2; Herodotus 2.141; Xenophon, *Hell.* 6.2.23). These good-for-nothing men were nevertheless good at something: they were able to help the Jews form a crowd and get their Gentile fellow citizens to join them in a riot based on trumped-up charges against Paul and Silas. The historical plausibility of this scenario is supported by Plutarch, who describes a similar situation of "men who were of low birth and had lately been slaves but who were hanging around the marketplace [*agoraious*—the same term used in Luke's account] and able to gather a mob and force all issues by means of solicitations and shouting" (*Aem.* 38.4).

---

25. Schnabel (2012: 706) suggests that Jewish opposition to Paul's ministry stemmed not just from their negative self-interest over lost members but also from a more noble religious reason: "The motivation of the Jews who oppose the missionaries is described, as in Pisidian Antioch, with reference to 'jealousy,' a term that probably refers not only to their jealousy over the conversion of Jews and of a large number of Gentiles including God-fearers, but also to their 'zeal' for the traditional understanding of the Mosaic law." However, the use of the verb ζηλόω (*zēloō*), as well as its cognate ζῆλος (*zēlos*) elsewhere in Acts (5:17; 7:9; 13:45; 17:5) always has the sense of "to have intense negative feelings over another's achievements or success, *be filled w. jealousy, envy*" (BDAG 427.2).

The agitated mob "attacked the house of Jason," who was providing housing for the missionaries. The original plan was to bring the pair to the "citizens assembly" (δῆμος, *dēmos*), the lowest level of city governance, which handled such matters as financial affairs, festivals, issues connected to the various local cults, and certain judicial concerns (R. Evans 1968: 13). However, when they could not find Paul and Silas, the plan changed: they seized Jason and a few other converts and brought them instead to a higher power—the "city authorities" (politarchs). This distinctive and ancient office consisted of three to seven individuals serving multiple one-year terms and having ultimate local responsibility for maintaining peace and order (for a fuller introduction to the ancient and rare political office of politarchs, see the section "A Unique Governmental Structure" above).

The angry crowd lodged two charges against Paul and Silas, both of which were political and anti-Roman and thus very serious; such charges were cleverly intended to ensure the missionaries' arrest, severe punishment, and almost certain expulsion from the city. The first charge accused them of disturbing the peace: "These men who have caused trouble all over the world have now come here" (Acts 17:6). The gravity of this charge becomes clearer when one recognizes that the Romans actively and aggressively promoted themselves as providing "peace and security" (1 Thess. 5:3), and they did so through various public media. The minting of coins, the building of public monuments, the engraving of official proclamations, and the dissemination of literary works all served the common purpose of shaping public opinion and convincing the populace about the peace and security that Roman rule supplied (Weima 2012). The charge of disturbing the peace, therefore, accuses Paul and Silas of undermining the main benefit that Rome supposedly provided. Furthermore, that Thessalonica had a lengthy and close relationship with Rome (see the section "A Favored Political Status" above) would cause both the crowd and the city officials to be especially alarmed at such a charge (Acts 17:8).[26] It is ironic, of course, that Paul and Silas are accused of disturbing the peace by an angry mob that is guilty of the very thing with which they are charging the two missionaries.

The second charge has proved hard thus far to identify: "and they all are acting contrary to the decrees of Caesar, saying that there is another king—Jesus" (Acts 17:7).[27] Four possibilities have been proposed:

26. Most commentators fail to appreciate the gravity of the first charge, with some thereby asserting that the second charge is the more serious of the two (e.g., Witherington 1998: 507; Bock 2007: 552). Notice, however, the observation of Schnabel (2012: 707), who correctly states, "This charge is much more serious than translations such as 'these men who have upset the world' (NASB) or even 'these men who have turned the world upside down' (RSV, ESV, cf. NRSV) suggest."

27. Fitzmyer (1998: 596) claims that there are two charges here, bringing the total number of accusations against Paul and Silas to three: disturbing the peace, acting against the decrees of Caesar, and claiming that Jesus is another king. The grammar works against this possibility, however, since the supposed third charge involves not an independent clause but an adverbial participle that is dependent upon, and thus closely connected with, the second charge.

a. *Treason.* The traditional answer is that Paul and Silas's claims about the kingship of Jesus were interpreted as an attempt to overthrow the current emperor, Claudius, and that they were therefore accused of breaking the Roman law of treason (*maiestas*). The major weakness of this interpretation is that treason was forbidden by general public law, and so there was no need for a specific decree by Caesar to make it illegal (Sherwin-White 1963: 103; Judge 1971: 2).

b. *Jewish messianic agitation.* Another possibility is that the accusation refers to an imperial edict dealing with Jewish messianic agitation (Erhardt 1969: 96; Hemer 1989: 167; D. Peterson 2009: 482). Claudius issued a decree in AD 49, just a year or so prior to Paul's ministry in Thessalonica, in which Jews were banished from Rome because of their rioting over a certain Chrestus, that is, Christ (Suetonius, *Claud.* 25.4). A few years earlier, in AD 41, Claudius also wrote a letter to Alexandria (P.Lond. 1912) in which he banned the importation of Jewish agitators into the city. There may have existed, therefore, an official decree by the emperor against any kind of Jewish disturbance over the Messiah—a decree that Paul and Silas are accused of disobeying. This possibility is undermined, however, in that the actual charge against the missionaries does not include any claim that Jesus is "Christ" or "messiah." Additionally, the attack against Paul and Silas was instigated by local Jews, and it is unlikely that they would have brought a specific charge of messianic agitation, since such a charge might well cause a negative reaction against not merely the two missionaries but also their own Jewish community as a whole.

c. *Oath of loyalty to Caesar.* Yet a third possibility is that "the decrees of Caesar" have in view the oath of loyalty to Caesar that many Roman and non-Roman citizens made, even those living far from the imperial city (Jewett 1986: 125; Manus 1990: 34; De Vos 1999: 156–57; Witherington 2006: 7; Furnish 2007: 28; this view was first forwarded by Judge 1971: 5–6, who ultimately rejects it). One example of such an oath comes from Paphlagonia, a province located in north Anatolia, along the Black Sea, and dates to 3 BC: "I swear . . . that I will support Caesar Augustus, his children and descendants throughout my life in word, deed and thought, . . . that in whatsoever concerns them I will spare neither body nor soul nor life nor children, . . . that whenever I see or hear of anything being said, planned or done against them I will report it, . . . and whomsoever they regard as enemies I will attack and pursue with arms and the sword by land and by sea" (Judge 1971: 6). As attractive as this explanation is, it suffers from two weaknesses (Judge 1971: 6–7). First, the extant documents dealing with these loyalty oaths do not provide any grounds for describing such texts with the term used to accuse the apostles, namely, "decrees." Second, there is evidence that the violation of these loyalty oaths fell under the jurisdiction not of the local authorities (such as the politarchs in Thessalonica) but the emperor himself.

d. *Prediction of a change of ruler.* The most convincing explanation of "the decrees of Caesar" is that they refer to imperial edicts against predictions about the emperor, especially those dealing with his health, death, and successor (Judge 1971; followed by Bruce 1982: xxiv; Donfried 1985: 342–44; Hemer 1989: 167; Witherington 1998: 508; Riesner 1998: 356–57; Green 2002: 50). In AD 11 the seventy-four-year-old Augustus responded to widespread questions about his health and heir by passing an imperial edict that forbade astrologers, diviners, prophets, and all others from predicting anyone's death, especially that of the emperor (Dio Cassius 56.25.5–6). This prohibition was reaffirmed and extended by Tiberius in AD 16 (Dio Cassius 57.15.8, who refers to this decree as a "dogma" [δόγμα, *dogma*], the same term used in the second charge of Acts 17:7), and the ban continued to be in effect as late as the third century (Ulpian, *Laws* 15.2). A similar situation exists in our modern age, where the health of a given nation's leader is often kept secret to maintain political peace and guard against civil uprising. Paul's eschatological preaching in Thessalonica about a resurrected "Lord" who will soon reappear on earth as a universal king and judge could have been interpreted as a prediction about a change of ruler and thus a violation of "the decrees of Caesar."

The clarification of the second charge brought against Paul and Silas, their "saying that there is another king—Jesus" (Acts 17:7b), agrees with the apostle's claim in his letter that he preached during his mission-founding visit in Thessalonica about the "kingdom" (1 Thess. 2:12). As Donfried (1987: 188) observes:

> Paul's categorical statement in 1 Thess. 2:12 that he did speak to the Thessalonians about the kingdom during his presence in the city should help us understand the relative accuracy of the Acts 17 account, not only with regard to Paul's use of king/kingdom language but also with regard to the fact that this language may well have served as a catalyst for the animosity he and his co-workers aroused in Thessalonica.

The seriousness of the two charges brought against Paul and Silas, along with the presence of an angry mob, naturally caused both the citizens and the city officials—the politarchs—to become "disturbed" (Acts 17:8). It made no difference that the nascent Christian movement involved only a small percentage of the overall population of a large provincial capital city like Thessalonica. The anti-Roman nature of the two charges leveled against the church's founders would cause local citizens and authorities to fear that the presence of such a movement, however small, within their city might cost them their privileged status as a free city as well as their favorable (and thus profitable) relationship with Rome. This fear would have been exacerbated because in recent times they had lost some administrative privileges under Tiberius and did not get them back until six years earlier than Paul's visit, through the personal favor of Claudius himself (Riesner 1998: 357).

Consequently, the city officials took immediate yet moderate (given the seriousness of the charges) action: they did not cave in to the crowd's desire for punishment (L. Johnson 1992: 307) but instead settled for "taking bail from

Jason and the others" and then "released them" (Acts 17:9).[28] The expression "taking bail" (λαβόντες τὸ ἱκανόν, *labontes to hikanon*; Moule [1959: 192] identifies this phrase as a Latinism from *cum satis accepissent*) refers to the act of taking a security deposit or posting bond (BDAG 472.1), which in this context likely guaranteed that the infant church would maintain the peace and that the perceived troublemakers, Paul and Silas, would leave town and not return. This legal action, which is a well-attested practice (*OGIS* 484.50–51; 629.100–101; Sherwin-White 1963: 95–96), may well be lying behind Paul's veiled reference to how "Satan has hindered" his ongoing efforts to return to the believers in Thessalonica (1 Thess. 2:18; so Ramsay 1920: 230–31; Bruce 1982: 55; Williams 1992: 55; Schnabel 2012: 709n20). That Timothy was not implicated along with Paul and Silas would explain why he was later chosen to go back to Thessalonica and strengthen the believers there (1 Thess. 3:1–5).

Thessalonica to Berea

Just as Paul several years earlier had been sent by the believers from Jerusalem to his hometown of Tarsus so he would not be a catalyst for trouble upon the Judean believers (Acts 9:30), now also he, along with Silas (and Timothy, unless he joins them later), on the very night when the security deposit was paid ("immediately at night"), was sent by "the brothers" from Thessalonica to Berea in order to protect Jason and the other converts (17:10). In his First Letter to the Thessalonians, the apostle confirms that he did not want to leave the newly founded congregation but was forced for some reason to depart from Thessalonica (2:15, 17–20). Paul was certainly willing to appear before the city officials and face the charges brought against him, as his recent actions in Philippi clearly demonstrated (1 Thess. 2:2; Acts 16:19–39). Nevertheless, the apostle's sudden departure was later used against him: non-Christians in Thessalonica raised questions about his integrity, accusing him of being interested only in winning other people's money and praise, as well as fleeing town at the first sign of trouble (1 Thess. 2:1–16).

Berea is located about forty-five miles southwest of Thessalonica, a distance that would have taken Paul, Silas, and Timothy at least two days of walking. In contrast to the previous cities where the apostle recently traveled and ministered (Neapolis, Philippi, Amphipolis, Apollonia, Thessalonica), Berea was situated not on the Via Egnatia but just south of this major east-west highway. This suggests that Berea was not part of Paul's original itinerary but that he ended up there out of the need to avoid the political charges awaiting him in Thessalonica. Cicero reminds Piso, the Roman statesman, how in his attempt to avoid the complaints against him from angry citizens in Thessalonica, "you fled to Berea, a town *out of the way*" (*Pis.* 89). Yet Berea was an important city: it was a former capital

28. Keener 2014: 2558: "A fine constituted 'a relatively lenient penalty' in Roman justice and could be consistent with the view that the authorities treated the Christian gatherings merely as unauthorized associations with political interests. That is, it might be advisable to ban such meetings, but harsh punishments, such as executing leaders, would be unnecessary."

of one of the four districts of Macedonia before the Romans restructured the province in 148 BC, had a sizable population (Lucian [*Ass* 34] describes the city as "great and heavily populated"), and housed the provincial council (κοινόν, *koinon*) of Macedonia (Thessalonica, as a free city, did not belong to the council).

Berea also had a Jewish community among whom Paul, in keeping with his typical mission strategy, preached in its local synagogue (Acts 17:10). In contrast to the hostility of the Jews in Thessalonica, the apostle received a warmer welcome from his countrymen in Berea: "Now these Jews were more noble than those in Thessalonica, for they received the word with all eagerness, examining the scriptures daily to see if these things were so" (17:11). Whereas Paul only had weekly access to the Thessalonian Jews (three Sabbaths), he seems to have interacted each day with the Berean Jews, who tested the apostle's claims against the teaching of Scripture "daily." Paul's preaching passed the test, as "many of them believed" (17:12a). In addition to these Jewish converts, there were also "not a few Greek women and men of high standing" (17:12b). Although the term "devout" (σεβόμενοι, *sebomenoi*) is not used as earlier for Thessalonica (17:4), these Greek converts are "God-fearers"—pagans who were attracted to Judaism but were not full converts, since they did not submit to the whole Mosaic law, especially the law pertaining to circumcision. One of these Greek converts likely included Sopater, the son of Pyrrhus (probably identical with the Sosipater of Rom. 16:21; so Bruce 1982: xxv; Hemer 1989: 236), who seven years later represented the Berean church and their contribution to the relief fund by accompanying Paul on the return leg of his third missionary journey when he delivered this financial offering to the believers in Judea (Acts 20:4).

Berea to Athens

The success of Paul and his coworkers in Berea caused the Jews of Thessalonica to act yet again against the Christian missionaries. The depth of these Jews' jealousness or zealousness is indicated by their willingness to travel two days by foot to implement the same strategy that worked so well in their home city: "they stirred up and incited the crowds" (Acts 17:13b). The decision of the city authorities in Thessalonica would not be binding in Berea, and so there was a need for the Thessalonian Jews to again start a series of events that would hopefully lead to the expulsion of Paul from the city. Acts, with its abridged account of Paul's ministry in Berea, does not spell out what these events involved, but the reference to the "crowds" indicates that the Thessalonian Jews were able to arouse the anger of the larger pagan community against the apostle. Although there is no mention of the involvement of any city authorities in Berea, the analogous situation here to what occurred in Thessalonica, along with the strong attestation of the office of politarchs in Berea, suggests that these officials may have been drawn into the conflict to stop the disturbances in this city as well (Horsley 1994: 425).

The strategy of the Thessalonian Jews was once more successful, causing Paul yet again to be involuntarily sent out of town for the well-being of the new converts in Berea. This time, however, not only did Timothy escape any charges or official sanction, but so did Silas, which allowed these two coworkers of the apostle to remain behind and minister to the infant church of Berea. Paul alone is escorted by some of the Christians all the way to Athens, over two hundred miles to the south. The exact itinerary of this trip is not spelled out but almost certainly involved travel by sea. Not only does the statement that Paul was sent "as far as the sea" (Acts 17:14) imply a boat journey to Athens, but this conclusion is also supported by the difficulty of going south by land through the Olympic Mountains.[29] As Hemer (1989: 116) notes: "The implication of sea-travel is at once the most convenient way of reaching Athens with the favouring 'Etesian' winds of the summer sailing-season and also removed Paul to a different jurisdiction remote from nearer land-routes where opponents might be expecting him." The closest port to Berea was Pydna, but another possible departure point was Dion, which had a major port (the city was one of the first two Roman colonies established in Macedonia and possessed the privileged *ius Italicum* status) and was connected directly by road to Berea. Once Paul arrived in Athens, his escorts returned to Berea with a command from the apostle that Silas and Timothy should rejoin him "as soon as possible" (Acts 17:15). A command like this concerning the movement of his fellow workers is found frequently in Paul's Letters (1 Cor. 16:10–11; Phil. 2:19; Col. 4:10; 1 Tim. 1:3; 2 Tim. 4:21; Titus 3:12–13).

Athens to Corinth

Although Acts does not again refer to Silas and Timothy until they together are reunited with Paul when he later moves on to Corinth (Acts 18:5), there are clues from the apostle's words in 1 Thess. 3:1–5 that they returned to Paul earlier during his stay in Athens.[30] This understanding is supported by his command to come "as soon as possible" (Acts 17:15). It gains further strength from Paul's own words to the Thessalonians that he was willing to be left in Athens "alone" (1 Thess. 3:1), which implies that at one point, before sending Timothy back to Thessalonica, the apostle was not by himself in Athens but that his coworkers were with him once again. Their reunion with Paul was short: the apostle sent both back to Macedonia, though to different churches. Timothy was sent to Thessalonica in order to strengthen the faith of that young church in the midst of their afflictions (1 Thess. 3:1–5). The

29. Codex Bezae, with occasional support from other Western witnesses, envisions travel by land with an addition: "and he passed by Thessaly, for he was prevented from proclaiming the word to them." This addition was likely intended to explain why nothing is mentioned in Acts about Paul's journey from Berea to Athens (B. Metzger 1994: 403–4). The Byzantine MSS also suggest land travel to Athens by using ὡς (as) instead of ἕως (as far as, until), thus making Acts 17:14 read: "as [if it were] to the sea," i.e., those pursuing Paul were tricked into thinking that the apostle was escaping by sea when in reality he went by a land route (B. Metzger 1994: 404).

30. Many have found it difficult to reconcile the movements of Paul, Silas, and Timothy as recorded in Acts 17:1–15 and 18:5 with the apostle's words in 1 Thess. 3:1–5 (e.g., Best 1977: 131–32; Marxsen 1979: 13–14; Lüdemann 1984: 14). Yet if the "we" of 1 Thess. 3:1–5 is properly read as a literary plural (i.e., it refers to Paul alone), then it is possible to interpret this text in a way that essentially agrees with the testimony of Acts (Donfried 1991).

apostle worried about these young Christians from whom he was orphaned (2:17). He wanted to revisit them himself but was prevented from doing so (2:18), perhaps because of the bond that Jason and the other believers had to post guaranteeing that he would not return and further disturb the peace. This likely explains why Timothy was chosen for this mission over Silas: he, unlike Paul and Silas, was not caught up in the legal judgment of the city authorities in Thessalonica and thus was able to return for a second visit, whereas such a return by the other two missionaries would have proved too dangerous to either themselves or the local believers. The exact itinerary and purpose of Silas's trip to Macedonia is not clear, though a good possibility is that he revisited the Philippian church, where he received further gifts of financial support for Paul's ministry (Phil. 1:4; 4:16; 2 Cor. 11:8–9).

After a largely frustrating ministry in Athens, Paul arrived in Corinth "in weakness and in fear and in much trembling" (1 Cor. 2:3), no exaggeration in light of the opposition, punishments, and forced or hasty departures he endured in Philippi, Thessalonica, Berea, and Athens. The apostle began what would be a much longer stay in Corinth—eighteen months—than his previous stops. During this time both Silas and Timothy return to Paul from their trip to Macedonia (Acts 18:5), bringing with them financial support from the churches in that province (2 Cor. 11:8–9), which apparently allows the apostle to curtail his day job as a tentmaker and begin a full-time preaching ministry in Corinth. This return of Silas and Timothy corresponds to the return of Timothy that is reported by Paul in 1 Thess. 3:6: "But Timothy has now come to us from you and has brought good news about your faith and love and that you have a good remembrance of us always, longing to see us, just as we also long to see you." Paul's description of Timothy's report as "good news" (for the significance of Paul's verb choice here, see comments on 3:6) reveals the depth of the apostle's concern about the infant Thessalonian church he was forced to leave and also his relief at Timothy's positive account. The two specific things that Paul singles out in the report as giving him great comfort are "your faith and love," that is, the faith *in God and Christ* that the believers still had even in the face of great opposition (1 Thess. 1:6; 2:14–16; 3:1–5) and the love *that they had for Paul* despite the accusations made against his integrity by those outside the church (2:1–20).

As affirming and upbeat as Timothy's report was, however, it nevertheless also included several issues of concern in the church—issues that caused Paul to pray most earnestly and repeatedly that God would allow him to return to Thessalonica and "complete the things that are lacking in your faith" (1 Thess. 3:10). These issues of concern included the need for holiness in sexual conduct (4:1–8), brotherly and sisterly love within the community of faith (4:9–12), the fate of both deceased and living believers at the return of Christ (4:13–18; 5:1–11), the treatment of church leaders (5:12–13) and troubled congregational members (5:14–18), and the gift of prophecy (5:19–22). Since the apostle was not able to address these issues in person, he did it instead by sending a letter.

That letter is 1 Thessalonians, which Paul wrote in either late AD 50 or early 51 during his eighteen-month stay in Corinth.[31]

A short time later Paul received an alarming report that the Thessalonian church was badly shaken by a false claim, likely via a prophecy, that "the day of the Lord has come" (2 Thess. 2:2). He also learned that the problem of the "rebellious idlers"—a small group within the congregation who ever since the founding of the church had refused to work (1 Thess. 5:14; see also 4:11–12)—had become worse. The apostle wrote a second letter to the Thessalonian church to address these two issues (2 Thess. 2:1–17; 3:1–15) and also to commend them for their faith despite ongoing and even intensified persecution (1:3–12). It is impossible to determine with certainty the date of this letter and where it was written. Yet Silas and Timothy were still with Paul (1:1), and the major subjects addressed in the second letter are ones also taken up in the first letter—these facts strongly suggest that only a short time had passed between the two letters and that both were written from the same place.[32]

Later Visits to Thessalonica

Neither Paul's Letters nor Acts explicitly identify any later visits of Paul to Thessalonica. Nevertheless, it is clear that the apostle did have ongoing contact with these Macedonian Christians. About five years later on his third missionary journey, he probably revisited them on two occasions: he would have traveled through Thessalonica on the westward part of this journey through Macedonia, on his way to Corinth in Achaia/Greece (Acts 19:21; 20:1–2) and again on the eastward return leg of this same trip (20:3–6). Other contact between Paul and the Thessalonian church took place through their participation in the collection that Paul was gathering for the needy Christians

31. This date of 50–51 is determined by three pieces of information. First, Timothy's return from Thessalonica and report to Paul in 1 Thess. 3:6 is equated to the return of Timothy and Silas to Paul in Corinth recorded in Acts 18:5, which means that Paul must have written 1 Thessalonians during his eighteen-month stay in Corinth (Acts 18:11). Second, during Paul's eighteen-month stay in Corinth, he appeared before Gallio, the proconsul or governor of Achaia (Acts 18:12–17). Third, an inscription discovered in Delphi, which records a letter of the emperor Claudius (the so-called Delphic Inscription), dates the start of Gallio's one-year term as proconsul to either July 51 or 52. For objections to this traditional view of the dating of 1 Thessalonians as well as an evaluation of these objections, see Marshall 1983: 20–23; Jewett 1986: 49–60; Malherbe 2000: 71–74.

32. A small group of scholars have picked up a very old view (found already in Hugo Grotius's discussion of the antichrist in 1640) and have argued that the order of the two Thessalonian Letters should be reversed: West 1914: 66–74; J. Weiss 1937: 286–91; Bristol 1943–44; Manson 1953: 428–47; Gregson 1966; Buck and Taylor 1969: 140–45; R. Thurston 1973; Hurd 1984: 73–89; Wanamaker 1990: 37–45; Trudinger 1995: 31–35. There is, of course, no a priori reason against this possibility since the current sequence may well be due to length rather than date. Nevertheless, the vast majority of scholars have not found the arguments convincing, and the traditional ordering makes the best sense of several issues. For the counterarguments typically made to defend the traditional ordering of the letters, see Rongy 1909; Thompson 1944–45; Best 1977: 42–45; Bruce 1982: xli–xlii; Jewett 1986: 26–30; Morris 1991: 26–30; D. Martin 1995: 30–33; Malherbe 2000: 361–64; Green 2002: 64–69; Foster 2012: 161–62.

in Palestine (2 Cor. 8:1–5; 9:4; Rom. 15:26; see also Acts 20:4, which refers to Aristarchus and Secundus, both representatives from Thessalonica in the delivery of the collection). The Thessalonian church may also have continued to support Paul financially in his ministry (2 Cor. 11:9, though this may refer just to the Philippian church: Phil. 4:15–16).

The Authorship of 1 and 2 Thessalonians

1 Thessalonians

THE LETTER AS A WHOLE

First Thessalonians belongs to the category of letters that the academic community unanimously judges to be unquestionably Pauline. As Jewett (1986: 3) reports, "No one in the current scholarly debate doubts its authenticity."[33]

INTERNAL EVIDENCE

The internal evidence for the Pauline authorship of 1 Thessalonians lies in the two references to the apostle as the writer of the letter: one in the letter opening (1:1) and the other in the letter body (2:18). Although the inclusion of Silas and Timothy as cosenders (1:1) raises the question whether Paul is the only author lying behind the letter (on this issue, see comments on 1:1), there is no question that Paul is at least one of the authors. Further internal evidence for the Pauline authorship of 1 Thessalonians lies in the vocabulary, grammatical constructions, and literary style, all of which are typical of the apostle's writings.

EXTERNAL EVIDENCE

The external evidence confirms that 1 Thessalonians was accepted very early as a genuine letter of Paul. It is true that this evidence is not as widespread as for some of the other NT writings (perhaps because its contents were not as controversial as some of the other canonical documents that required comment by the church fathers), but it nevertheless agrees with the compelling internal evidence. There are a number of possible allusions to 1 Thessalonians in early Christian documents: compare (1) Did. (mid-to-late first century) 16.6 ("first the sign of the appearance in heaven, then the sign of the sound of the trumpet") with 1 Thess. 4:16; (2) Ignatius (early second century), *Rom.* 2.1

---

33. There has been no scholarly objection to the Pauline authorship of 1 Thessalonians since the nineteenth century except for the recent monograph of Crüsemann (2010). The first to question its authenticity was apparently Schrader (1836: 23ff.), whose position was picked up and developed by Baur (1845: 480–85; 1855: 141–68), who succeeded in convincing a few others (e.g., Holsten 1877). The objections raised, however, were quickly and easily refuted (see Grimm 1850; Lipsius 1854; Hilgenfeld 1862: 225–64; Lünemann 1885: 10–15; Soden 1885; Milligan 1908: lxxii–lxxvi; Frame 1912: 37–38; Rigaux 1956: 120–24) with the result that over a century of scholarship has now passed without any significant challenge to Paul's authorship of 1 Thessalonians. As Fee (2009: 4) pragmatically puts it: "Such denial [of the Pauline authorship of 1 Thessalonians] faces enormous historical difficulties—so much so that one wonders, 'Why bother?'"

("For I do not want you to be pleasing people but to please God") with 2:4; (3) Ignatius, *Eph.* 10.1 ("Pray without ceasing") with 5:17; (4) Shepherd of Hermas, *Vis.* 3.9.10 ("Therefore, discipline one another and be at peace with one another") with 5:13; and (5) Barn. (late first or early second century) 21.6 ("Be God-taught") with 4:9. Clearer and more important evidence is that 1 Thessalonians was included in Marcion's canon (ca. 140; so Tertullian, *Marc.* 5.15), the Muratorian Canon (ca. 170),[34] as well as in the Syriac, Vulgate, and Old Latin versions. Irenaeus (ca. 180) is the first writer to explicitly quote by name from 1 Thessalonians, citing 5:23 as the words of the "apostle" (*Haer.* 5.6.1). Milligan (1908: lxxiii) observes that there is no need to cite references to 1 Thessalonians from any later church fathers since "the very existence of 2 Thessalonians, whatever its exact date, implies the recognition of the Pauline authorship of the First Epistle at a very early period in the history of the Church—a recognition moreover which it continued uninterruptedly to enjoy until the middle of last century."

The internal and external evidence surveyed above led Kümmel (1977: 185) to conclude in the sixteenth edition of his influential *Introduction to the New Testament* that "there can be no justifiable doubt that all of 1 Thess is of Pauline origin."[35]

1 Thessalonians 2:13–16

Although over one hundred years of scholarship have passed without any significant challenge to the Pauline authorship of 1 Thessalonians as a whole, the same cannot be said about every passage within the letter. Scholars have singled out various sections of 1 Thessalonians as not coming from the hand of Paul,[36] but only one passage has attracted significant support as a later interpolation: 2:13–16.[37] Questions about the Pauline authorship of 2:13–16 had been raised already in the nineteenth century by Baur and others (see historical survey by Baarda 1985; Jewett 1986: 37), but the discussion was significantly advanced in the late twentieth century by Pearson (1971), who presented three major arguments—theological, historical, and form-critical— to substantiate the conclusion that 2:13–16 was a post-Pauline interpolation, inserted sometime after the fall of Jerusalem in AD 70. A fourth argument, based on linguistic observations, was added by D. Schmidt (1983); the result is that a number of contemporary scholars reject the Pauline authorship of

34. Although some have argued that this important fragment should be dated later, to the fourth century (Sundberg 1973; Hahneman 1992), support still remains for its traditional second-century date (Ferguson 1982; C. Hill 1995).

35. Challenges in the mid-and-late twentieth century to the integrity of 1 Thessalonians, however, forced Kümmel to nuance this conclusion in the seventeenth edition of his introduction (1973: 224–26).

36. For a survey of scholarship on this issue, see Clemen (1894) for the nineteenth-century situation and Collins (1984: 96–135) for the twentieth-century situation.

37. The only other passage to be seriously considered as a later interpolation is 1 Thess. 5:1–11. See the arguments forwarded by Friedrich (1973), which have not won scholarly support (Rigaux 1974–75; Plevnik 1979; Marshall 1983: 12–13; Wanamaker 1990: 33).

2:13–16 (e.g., Eckart 1961; Boers 1975–76; Koester 1979: esp. 38; Gager 1983: 255–56; Beck 1985: 42–44; Richard 1995: 17–18, 119–27). Nevertheless, a careful evaluation of each of these arguments reveals that they are not as compelling as their proponents claim (see esp. Wanamaker 1990: 29–33; Weatherly 1991; Schlueter 1994: 25–38; Still 1999: 24–45).

THEOLOGICAL ARGUMENT

It is claimed that 2:13–16 involves "some basic incompatibilities" with "Paul's thought as expressed elsewhere in his epistles" (Pearson 1971: 85). For example, there is an apparent theological contradiction with Rom. 9–11, where Paul not only speaks positively of the Jews and their role in salvation history but also holds out hope for their future salvation. Some have found Paul's negative judgment about the Jews in 1 Thess. 2:13–16 not merely contradictory but also anti-Semitic (e.g., Best 1977: 122: "It must be allowed that I Th. 2.16c shows Paul holding an unacceptable anti-Semitic position"). Another example involves a claimed contradiction between 2:15, which blames Jews for "killing the Lord Jesus," and 1 Cor. 2:8, which ascribes the crucifixion of Christ "to the rulers of this age."

Neither example, however, is as problematic as it is claimed to be. Paul's positive statements about the Jews in Rom. 9–11 must not overshadow the negative statements he makes in the same passage about his own people (9:3 implies that Jews are under a curse; 9:22, "vessels of wrath made for destruction"; 11:3, "they have killed your prophets"; 11:7–10; 11:28, "enemies of God"). It is also important to recognize that Paul's hope for the Jews' *future* is set against their *present* state of condemnation—a presupposition that underlies the whole discussion of Rom. 9–11. Furthermore, in 1 Thess. 2:14–16 Paul is speaking not about all Jews but about only a limited group of Jews, those responsible for the death of Jesus (Davies 1977–78: 8; Gilliard 1989). That Paul is thinking only about some Jews is also implied in the contrast of 2:14 between "fellow citizens" and "Jews": just as not all the "fellow citizens" are persecuting the Thessalonian believers, so also not all the Jews are responsible for killing Jesus. Actually, Paul's reference to the persecutors in 2:14 with the term τῶν Ἰουδαίων (*tōn Ioudaiōn*) likely does not have an ethnic sense but a geographical meaning: the churches of Judea are persecuted by the "Judeans," a variety of peoples in this region and not the Jews alone (Bruce 1982: 46; Weatherly 1991: 84–86). Finally, the prepositional phrase εἰς τέλος (*eis telos*) in 2:16 is best rendered as "until the end": God's wrath rests upon Israel only until the final days of judgment. This would leave open the possibility for the future salvation of Israel afterward, in agreement with Paul's words in Rom. 11:25–32 (Munck 1967: 64, 137; Donfried 1984: 252).

The second example of a claimed contradiction between 1 Thess. 2:15 and 1 Cor. 2:8 over who is responsible for Jesus's death is more imaginary than real. The expression "rulers of this age" may well refer broadly to political officials in Judea, among whom the Jewish leaders are just one subset of this larger group. Also, both of Paul's statements agree with all four Gospels and Acts, which identify Romans and Jews alike as having a hand in the killing of Jesus (e.g., Mark 10:33–34 par.; Luke 22:2–4; Acts 4:27–28; see Weatherly 1991: 83).

HISTORICAL ARGUMENT

Two references in 1 Thess. 2:13–16, it is claimed, refer to historical events that date after Paul's lifetime, thereby making it impossible for this passage to have come from the hand of the apostle. The first is the aorist verb ἔφθασεν (*ephthasen*) in 2:16c, which refers to a major event in the past: the destruction of Jerusalem in AD 70. As Pearson (1971: 82–83) explains it:

> The aorist ἔφθασεν must be taken as referring to an event that is now past, and the phrase εἰς τέλος underscores the finality of the "wrath" that has occurred. It need only be inquired further what event in the first century was of such magnitude as to lend itself to such apocalyptic theologizing. The interpretation suggested by Baur and others is still valid: I Thessalonians 2:16c refers to the destruction of Jerusalem in 70 A.D.

The second problematic reference is the comparison made in 2:14 between the suffering endured by the Thessalonian believers with the suffering endured by the Judean believers. The historical problem here, according to Pearson (1971: 87), is that "there was no significant persecution of Christians before the war," that is, prior to the first Jewish revolt of AD 66–70.

With regard to the first reference, Pearson is correct to assert that the verb *ephthasen* refers to a past event. Therefore we must reject proposals for reading this verb as a "prophetic" aorist, which has a future event in view (Dobschütz 1909: 115–16; Frame 1912: 114), or with a weaker sense of "has drawn near" or "is coming" (e.g., Clark 1940; Rigaux 1956: 452; Best 1977: 120; Marshall 1983: 80–81; Weatherly 1996: 91–92). Yet it does not logically follow that the only past event to which the text possibly refers is the destruction of Jerusalem. Jewett (1986: 37) rightly judges there to be "an unmistakable quality of retrospection in Pearson's argument. From the perspective of those who know about the Jewish-Roman war, it is surely the most appropriate choice. But to someone who lived before that catastrophe, several of the other events could easily have appeared to be a final form of divine wrath." Indeed, the apostle may be referring to any of several other significant calamities the Jewish people had to endure in the years immediately preceding Paul's writing of 1 Thessalonians (see comments on 2:16). Furthermore, instead of a specific event, Paul may have more generally viewed the Jews' rejection of either the gospel or Jesus as God's Messiah as wrathful (Gaventa 1998: 38; Holmes 1998: 86). The important point for the authorship of 2:13–16 is that the presence of the aorist verb *ephthasen* does not require a date after AD 70.

With regard to the second reference, Pearson is wrong to claim that there is no evidence for any kind of suffering endured by the Judean churches before AD 70. In 2:14 Paul's reference to the opposition experienced by Jewish Christians in Judea could refer to the early 30s AD—a period when he himself persecuted the believers in Jerusalem and the surrounding area (Gal. 1:13, 22–23; 1 Cor.

15:9; Phil. 3:6; see Acts 8:3; 9:21; 22:4; 26:9–11). The apostle may instead be thinking of the early 40s AD—a period when Herod Agrippa I (AD 41–44) killed James the brother of John and attempted to do the same to Peter (Acts 12:1–19). The best option is that Paul has in view the late 40s and very early 50s—a period that witnessed a rising Zealot movement in Palestine (Josephus, *Ant.* 20.105–6; see Jewett 1970–71, esp. 205–7; Reicke 1984). These Jewish nationalists were especially active during the governorship of Tiberius Julius Alexander (AD 46–48) and his successor, Ventidius Cumanus (48–52). They engaged in a militant program of purging Israel from all Gentile influence in the belief that such action would hasten, if not actually inaugurate, the messianic age. Such Zealot activity would have naturally included some degree of opposition to the Jewish Christian churches in Judea (see comments on 2:14 below). There is, therefore, corroborating evidence dating prior to the writing of 1 Thessalonians that supports Paul's claim in 2:14 that Judean Christians suffered at the hands of their fellow Jews.

FORM-CRITICAL ARGUMENT

The presence of a second thanksgiving in 2:13 is claimed to be an anomaly in Paul's Letters. It is further observed that if 2:13, along with 2:14–16, were deleted from the text, this would result in a smoother transition from 2:12 to the apostolic parousia that begins at 2:17 than if this questionable section were kept as part of the original letter. These literary considerations led Pearson (1971: 91) to state: "The conclusion, therefore, which form-critical analysis suggests is this: vv. 13–16 do not belong to Paul's original letter at all, but represent a later interpolation into the text" (so also Boers 1975–76: 151–52).

Several factors undermine the persuasiveness of these claims. First, the presence of a second thanksgiving is not unparalleled in Paul's Letters, since a similar phenomenon occurs in 2 Thess. 2:13–14. Although many scholars reject this parallel on the assumption that 2 Thessalonians does not come from the hand of the apostle, compelling reasons exist for maintaining the Pauline authorship of this letter (see discussion below).

Second, the claimed thanksgiving in 1 Thess. 2:13 differs formally in significant ways from the typical form of Paul's other thanksgivings,[38] thereby suggesting that the apostle did not intend this verse to be understood as a thanksgiving formula. If 2:13 should not be formally classified as a thanksgiving, then the claimed anomaly of a double thanksgiving disappears.

Third, even if 2:13 would be classified as a second thanksgiving, Paul does not have a rigid epistolary pattern that would preclude the possibility of his including a second thanksgiving. The apostle constantly adapts his epistolary conventions so that they better serve his persuasive purposes and better fit the specific historical context. Just as Paul strategically omits the thanksgiving in Galatians because of the particular problems faced in those churches, so he

---

38. On the form of a Pauline thanksgiving and the five distinct units that typically make up this epistolary convention, see the comments on 1:2–10 under "Literary Analysis."

can add a second thanksgiving in 1 Thessalonians if that matches the context of that congregation and the apostle's purpose in the letter (Still 1999: 29–30).

Fourth, the shift from defending the integrity of Paul's past "visit" (*eisodos*) or mission-founding activity in Thessalonica (in 2:1–12) to the Thessalonians' response to that past visit (in 2:13–16) is not a problem but an expected move for the careful reader of the letter. This shift follows exactly the same pattern foreshadowed twice in the thanksgiving section, where the apostle similarly begins with his conduct during the mission-founding visit to Thessalonica (1:5 and 1:9a) and then moves to the response of the Thessalonians to that visit (1:6–8 and 1:9b–10). In fact, at 2:13 the transition from Paul's past visit (2:1–12) to the Thessalonians' response to that visit (2:13–16) is signaled already in the immediately preceding clause of 2:12b, where the purpose of the apostle's fatherlike conduct is "in order that *you* may lead a life worthy of God."

Fifth, the opening words of 2:13 ("and because of this") almost certainly look *back* to the material of 2:1–12, thereby in an integral way connecting the content of the disputed verses of 2:13–16 with the preceding discussion (see further discussion in comments on these verses).

Sixth, if 2:13–16, with its shift away from Paul and his fellow workers to the Thessalonian believers (note the predominance of the second and third persons in these verses), is original to the letter, then the first-person pronoun "we" in 2:17—emphasized both by its mere presence (since the subject is already expressed in the main verb) and its location at the head of the sentence—fits well as a literary marker, setting the subsequent verses apart from the preceding material. Conversely, if 2:13–16 were removed from the letter, the emphatic "we" in 2:17 makes less sense (Weatherly 1991: 81).

Linguistic Argument

Daryl Schmidt (1983) supplemented the three arguments of Pearson with an additional one based on a number of claimed linguistic problems. For example, the opening of 2:13 has two unusual features: the conjunction "and" (καί, *kai*) that opens the verse occurs nowhere else in Thessalonians to join two "matrix sentences" (i.e., independent clauses) and no other undisputed letter of Paul uses the fuller expression "and because of this" (καὶ διὰ τοῦτο, *kai dia touto*). Another example involves "embedding," that is, the subordination of clauses: 2:14–16 has, according to Schmidt's calculation, seven levels of embedding compared to a maximum of five for any other section of 2:2–3:10. Yet another perceived problem is the non-Pauline way that the noun "Lord" is separated from "Jesus" by the participle "killing" in 2:15. These and a few other examples lead D. Schmidt (1983: 276) to conclude, "The linguistic evidence suggests that it [2:13–16] did not come from the same author as the rest of the letter but is rather built around a conflation of Pauline expressions."

A number of scholars have evaluated D. Schmidt's linguistic argument and not found his conclusion convincing (e.g., Jewett 1986: 40–41; Wanamaker 1990: 32–33; Weatherly 1991: 91–98; Schlueter 1994: 34–36; Still 1999: 32–35). A general weakness involves the diverse syntactical style of Paul exhibited in his various letters such that the linguistic variations in 1 Thess. 2:13–16 are not so unique as to demand non-Pauline authorship. Also, there is the possibility that Paul is borrowing from traditional material in 2:13–16 (Schippers 1966; Steck 1967: 274–77; Michel 1967; Hyldahl 1972–73: 238–54; Donfried 1984: 247–50; Malherbe 2000: 169, 174–75), which would explain some of the unique linguistic features of these verses. More specifically, the unusual features cited by D. Schmidt are not so persuasive when examined more closely. There are over thirty examples (see list in Weatherly 1991: 92) among the undisputed letters of Paul where the conjunction "and" introduces and joins matrix sentences, including 1 Thess. 1:6. The fuller expression "and because of this" does occur elsewhere in Paul's writings, in 2 Thess. 2:11. Daryl Schmidt dismisses this parallel text by assuming that 2 Thessalonians is pseudepigraphical, but this assumption is itself not free from criticism. The presence of seven levels of embedding in 2:13–16 becomes less significant once it is recognized that Phil. 1:12–15 has seven such levels, Phil. 1:27–30 has eight, and Rom. 4:16–17 has nine. Similarly, the separation of "Lord" and "Jesus" by a verbal form in 1 Thess. 2:15 can hardly be called "un-Pauline" when there are several instances where Paul separates a noun from an attributive adjective with an intervening verb (1 Cor. 7:7, 12; 10:4; 12:24; 2 Cor. 7:5; Phil. 2:20). Furthermore, this unusual word order likely stems from Paul's deliberate attempt to emphasize "the Lord" and thereby stress the heinous nature of the action: the Jesus whom the Jews killed was no mere human being but was, in fact, the Lord (Hendriksen 1955: 71; Best 1977: 115; Williams 1992: 47, 115).

Conclusion

Our survey of the four arguments sometimes used to prove that Paul did not write 1 Thess. 2:13–16 has shown them, both individually and collectively, to be unpersuasive. An additional flaw with the claim that this passage is a later interpolation is the universal textual support that it enjoys: unlike the so-called floating doxology of Rom. 16:25–27 or the command of 1 Cor. 14:34–35 for women to be silent—two passages that appear in different locations in different manuscripts—this disputed passage is found in every extant manuscript of 1 Thessalonians. There are compelling reasons, therefore, for including 2:13–16 as part of the original text of the letter.

2 Thessalonians

The majority opinion within biblical scholarship has always been that the author of 2 Thessalonians is Paul; that opinion, despite facing a strong challenge in recent decades, is still the widespread view held today[39] (for a historical

39. It is true that, after the Pastoral Letters (1 and 2 Timothy and Titus) and Ephesians, 2 Thessalonians is the most disputed Pauline letter in terms of its authorship and that it "is generally not included among the seven-letter Pauline canon-within-a-canon accepted by modern critical orthodoxy" (Carson and Moo 2005: 536). But when one surveys the whole field of NT scholarship, it is also true that, as Malherbe (2000: 364) states: "The majority of scholars still hold to the genuineness of 2 Thessalonians." Foster (2012: 153–54) similarly makes the case that

survey of this issue, see Frame 1912: 39–43; Rigaux 1956: 124–52; Trilling 1972: 11–45; Jewett 1986: 3–18; Wanamaker 1990: 17–28). No one in the early church doubted the authenticity of 2 Thessalonians. The external evidence that Paul penned this letter is actually both earlier and more extensive than that of 1 Thessalonians. Several early church fathers allude to 2 Thessalonians: Ignatius (ca. 35–108) in *Rom.* 10.3 possibly alludes to 2 Thess. 3:5; Polycarp (69–155) in *Phil.* 11.3–4 alludes to 1:4 and 3:15; and Justin (ca. 100–165) in *Dial.* 32.12 and 110.6 alludes to 2:3–4. Still others in the early church not only quote the letter but also explicitly attribute the citation to Paul or "the apostle": Irenaeus (130–202) in *Haer.* 3.7.2 cites 2:8; Clement of Alexandria (ca. 150–215) in *Strom.* 5.3 cites 3:1–2; and Tertullian (ca. 160–225) in *An.* 57 cites 2:4 and in *Marc.* 5.16 cites 1:6–9; 2:3–4, 9–12; 3:10. Second Thessalonians is also included as a Pauline letter in both Marcion's canon (ca. 140) and in the Muratorian Canon (ca. 170).

No one, therefore, questioned the Pauline authorship of 2 Thessalonians for almost two millennia until perceived internal difficulties became an issue. J. E. C. Schmidt in 1801 argued that the eschatology of 2 Thess. 2:1–12 contradicted that of 1 Thess. 4:13–5:11 and that consequently the former passage was an interpolation (by a Montanist pseudepigrapher) into an authentic letter of the apostle. In 1903 a more influential challenge to Pauline authorship was raised by Wrede, who stressed the literary dependence of 2 Thessalonians upon 1 Thessalonians, concluding that a pseudonymous author of the second letter was mimicking Paul's language and style in the first letter. Nevertheless, the number of scholars who found such arguments convincing was still relatively few. In 1972 the situation changed significantly, however, with the monograph of Trilling, who marshaled various arguments that cumulatively seem to prove that 2 Thessalonians is not a genuine letter of Paul.[40] The impact of Trilling's work is seen in the increasing number—though not the majority—of contemporary scholars who reject the Pauline authorship of 2 Thessalonians (J. A. Bailey 1978–79; Krodel 1978; Marxsen 1982; D. Schmidt 1983; Laub 1985; Hughes 1989: 75–95; D. Schmidt 1990; Laub 1990; Menken 1994; Richard 1995; Verhoef 1997; Gaventa 1998; Collins 1988; Holland 1990; B. Thurston 1995; Légasse 1999; Esler 2000; Furnish 2007; McKinnish Bridges 2008).

Four major arguments are typically used to reach the conclusion that 2 Thessalonians could not have come from the hand of Paul: (1) the colder,

---

"the supposed consensus [that 2 Thessalonians is non-Pauline] simply does not exist." At the end of his article, Foster also presents an appendix showing the results of his survey of those attending the British New Testament Conference in Nottingham in 2011. Of the 109 respondents (70 percent of those attending), 63 answered "yes" to the question whether Paul authored 2 Thessalonians, 13 answered "no," and 35 answered "uncertain."

40. Jewett (1986: 3): "A substantial shift in critical opinion among leading New Testament scholars has been visible since the publication of Wolfgang Trilling's monograph contesting its [2 Thessalonians] authenticity in 1972." This shift in scholarly opinion concerning the authenticity of 2 Thessalonians during the 1970s and 1980s (i.e., after the work of Trilling) is also noted by Marshall (1983: 29) and Goulder (1992: 96n2).

authoritarian tone of 2 Thessalonians; (2) the authenticating comment of 3:17; (3) the eschatological differences between the two Thessalonian Letters; and (4) the literary dependence of 2 Thessalonians on 1 Thessalonians.[41] An evaluation of these arguments, however, shows them to be less persuasive than is often asserted (see esp. Marshall 1983: 28–45; Wanamaker 1990: 17–28; Still 1999: 46–55; Malherbe 2000: 364–74; Foster 2012).

The Colder, Authoritarian Tone of 2 Thessalonians

Many commentators have drawn a sharp contrast between the claimed detached, formal tone of 2 Thessalonians and the warm, personal character of 1 Thessalonians. Illustrations of this difference in tone include the following: the obligation to give thanks ("We *ought* to give thanks," 2 Thess. 1:3; 2:13) instead of the expected statement of thanksgiving ("We give thanks," 1 Thess. 1:2; 2:13); the use of the strong verb "we command" to introduce the exhortations in 2 Thess. 3:6–15 instead of the softer, more user-friendly "we appeal" in 1 Thess. 4:1 and 5:14; the heavy-handed appeal to tradition in 2 Thess. 2:15 and 3:6 in contrast to the warm family metaphors of infants, nursing mother, and father in 1 Thess. 2:7a, 7b, 11. In light of such differences, J. A. Bailey (1978–79: 137) states: "II Thessalonians is entirely lacking in the personal warmth which is so distinctive an element of I Thessalonians." Even Jewett (1986: 17), who maintains the Pauline authorship of 2 Thessalonians, comments: "Yet the tone of 2 Thessalonians is substantially different from that of 1 Thessalonians, implying a more irritable relation between writer and audience." Several scholars claim that Paul would not have written two letters to the same church within a short period of time that differ so much in tone from each other.

There are two points to this argument, and both are vulnerable to strong criticism. The first point involves the claim that 2 Thessalonians exhibits a colder, authoritarian tone. This claim not only exaggerates the differences with the first letter but also fails to see the warm, affectionate tone actually found in the second letter. For example, the expression "We ought to give thanks" (1:3) actually involves a *more* affectionate tone: Paul is so impressed with the faith of the Thessalonians, which is not merely "increasing" but "increasing [so] *abundantly*" (note the prefix *hyper* added to the verb) in the midst of intensified persecution that the apostle feels obligated—not as a duty but as a joy—to give thanks to God for them. The parenthetical phrase "as it is fitting" (1:3) refers to the propriety of Paul in giving thanks to God for them, thereby adding emphasis to his overall commendation of the Thessalonian Christians. Their amazing faith additionally causes Paul, along with Silas and Timothy (note the emphatic "we ourselves"), to "boast of you in the churches of God"

---

41. The perennial way in which these four arguments have continued to play a key role in the ongoing debate over the authorship of 2 Thessalonians is seen in that Hollmann already in 1904 summarized the key reasons against the authenticity of this letter by citing exactly the same four arguments (1904: 38).

(1:4), again stressing the affectionate nature of the relationship between the apostle and his readers. Paul uses the vocative "brothers" to refer to the Thessalonian congregation at a higher rate per verse (7 occurrences in 47 verses) than in any other of his letters except for 1 Thessalonians (14 occurrences in 89 verses), so the rates virtually match. In light of these examples from 2 Thessalonians that reflect the warm relationship that existed between Paul and the church in Thessalonica (see also 2 Thess. 1:11–12; 2:13–14, 16–17; 3:3–5), the words of Marshall (1983: 34) spoken already thirty years ago ought finally to be accepted: "It is surely time that the myth of the cold tone of the letter was exploded."[42]

The second point involves an illogical conclusion based on the first (and as we have argued above, exaggerated) point: even if one grants that the tone of 2 Thessalonians is colder and more authoritarian than 1 Thessalonians, this difference can be plausibly explained other than by concluding that the second letter is pseudonymous. Paul was willing and ready to adapt his tone to fit better the specific historical context that he is addressing. Writing to the Corinthian church, the apostle wonders whether he needs to come to them either with a rod of discipline or a spirit of gentleness (1 Cor. 4:21). Writing to the Galatian churches, he exclaims: "How I wish I could be with you now and change my tone, because I am perplexed about you!" (Gal. 4:19–20). Writing to the Thessalonian church, where some members have foolishly believed a false prophecy about the day of the Lord (2 Thess. 2:1–17) and where the problem of the rebellious idlers has become worse instead of better (3:6–15), Paul fittingly writes in a firmer and more serious tone.[43]

THE AUTHENTICATING COMMENT OF 2 THESS. 3:17

A second argument frequently made to establish the non-Pauline authorship of 2 Thessalonians involves the authenticating comment of 3:17: "The greeting is in my own hand, that of Paul, which is a sign in every letter; this is the way I write." Elsewhere Paul also makes reference to writing "in my own hand" (1 Cor. 16:21; Gal. 6:11; Col. 4:18a; Philem. 19), which implies that to this point he was using a secretary (Rom. 16:22) but now takes up the pen himself to write personally to his readers. This is the only statement, however, that includes a note emphasizing that the closing autograph "is a sign in every letter; this is the way I write." Several scholars see in this emphatic authenticating comment evidence that Paul is not the author. Collins (1988: 223), for example, states: "The modern reader has the impression that

---

42. Malherbe (2000: 351) makes an important additional observation: "Furthermore, it cannot be stressed too strongly that the readers of 2 Thessalonians had also read 1 Thessalonians not too long before. . . . He [Paul] could assume that they had responded positively to his effort to cultivate a cordial relationship with them (see 1 Thess 3:6–9), and that there was no need to repeat his earlier effort to that end."

43. Menken (1994: 31), who argues that Paul did not write 2 Thessalonians, concedes: "The difference in tone *per se* is not a sufficient reason to deny Pauline authorship to 2 Thessalonians, but in combination with other factors, it has some weight."

the author of 2 Thessalonians, as Hamlet's queen, protests too much." Esler (2000: 1219) similarly states: "The self-conscious (and unique) way in which the author draws attention to the practice in 3:17 by saying that 'This is my mark' (*sēmeion*, sign) is itself suspicious" (see also, e.g., J. A. Bailey 1978–79: 138; Krodel 1978: 84–86; Trilling 1980: 158; Menken 1994: 35–36; Richard 1995: 394–95; Furnish 2007: 132–33). Some find additional evidence in the phrase "a letter as though from us" (2 Thess. 2:2), which is interpreted to refer to a forged Pauline letter, whose existence during the apostle's lifetime is considered to be improbable.

This second argument, however, suffers from several weaknesses. First, the claim that the author of 2 Thessalonians in 3:17 "protests too much" overstates the case, since there are other closing autographs where Paul similarly makes an emphatic statement (e.g., Gal. 6:11: "See with what large letters I write to you in my own hand!"). Second, the authenticating comment of 3:17 is exactly the kind of statement that Paul should make if he has suspected that a forged letter in his name (2 Thess. 2:2) was circulating in the Thessalonian congregation (as J. Hill [1990: 5] rhetorically asks: "How else would the real author have approached such a misunderstanding?"). Third, the author of 2 Thessalonians gives evidence of being familiar with no Pauline letter other than 1 Thessalonians, which strikingly does *not* contain a reference to Paul's closing autograph statement (Foster 2012: 165–67). Fourth and most important, there are compelling reasons to see 3:17 as stressing not the authenticity of the letter (as is commonly asserted) but the presence and authority of Paul (see comments on 3:17 for explanation and evidence supporting this interpretation). The apostle feels the need to emphasize his authority in light of the rebellious idlers, whom he anticipates will not all obey his command to be engaged in self-sufficient work (note the first-class condition in 3:14, which assumes the truth of the protasis: "But if anyone does not obey our command in this letter"). If this interpretation about the authoritative rather than authenticating function of 3:17 is correct, the key evidence in the second argument for postulating the non-Pauline authorship of 2 Thessalonians is no longer relevant.

The Eschatological Differences between the Two Letters

Several commentators have questioned the authenticity of 2 Thessalonians on the grounds that the eschatological events presented in 2 Thess. 2:1–12 differ from that found in 1 Thess. 4:13–5:11. The observation of J. A. Bailey (1978–79) is blunt, succinct, and typical of this third argument frequently made as to why Paul cannot be the author of 2 Thessalonians: "These two eschatologies [of 1 Thess. and 2 Thess.] are contradictory. Either the end will come suddenly and without warning like a thief in the night (I Thessalonians) or it will be preceded by a series of apocalyptic events which warn of its coming (II Thessalonians)" (so also, e.g., Krodel 1978: 74–77; Hughes 1989: 80–83; Koester 1990; Menken 1994: 28–30; Furnish 2007: 134).

This argument, however, misrepresents Paul's teaching in the first letter in a way that creates a contradiction with what the apostle writes in the second letter. For *unbelievers*, Jesus's return and the final judgment connected with the day of the Lord will indeed "come suddenly and without warning, like a thief in the night." For *believers*, however, the situation is completely different. The Christians in Thessalonica are not merely knowledgeable of the future events that will take place on the day of the Lord—these things are what they "know well" (1 Thess. 5:2). Furthermore, their status of being "sons of light and sons of the day" (5:5) means that they "are not in darkness with the result that the day [of the Lord] would surprise you like a thief" (5:4). Since the Thessalonian congregation already knows well what is going to happen, Paul exhorts them to live ready and steady lives (5:6–8)—lives that not only are ready for the imminent return of Jesus but lives that also are steady and not easily shaken or fearful about the day of the Lord. Paul comforts his readers, in the midst of their eschatological anxiety, by appealing to the electing work of God by which their salvation on the day of the Lord is guaranteed: "For God did not destine us for wrath but for the obtaining of salvation" (5:9).

Paul makes the same main points in the second letter (2 Thess. 2:1–17). Here too he reminds his readers that they already "know well" the future events surrounding the day of the Lord from his repeated instruction about these things to them (note the imperfect tense in the rhetorical question of 2:5, which expects an affirmative response: "You remember, don't you, that, when I was with you, I was *repeatedly* saying these things to you?"). As a result of his repeated instruction and their knowledge about end-time matters, Paul again calls them to live ready and steady lives, whereby they are "not easily shaken from your mind or alarmed" about a false claim that the day of the Lord has come (2:2). Here too he comforts his readers by appealing to the electing work of God, which ensures their salvation on the day of the Lord: "because God chose you as firstfruits for salvation" (2 Thess. 2:13).

A proper interpretation of 1 Thess. 4:13–5:11 and 2 Thess. 2:1–17, therefore, reveals that the two letters share a common basic eschatological perspective. What differences may exist are minor and stem not from a hand other than that of Paul but from the apostle's need to address the specific problem that has arisen since the writing of the first letter: someone has claimed, likely by means of a prophetic utterance claiming the authority of Paul, that the day of the Lord has come (see fuller discussion in the comments on 2 Thess. 2:2). Even Menken (1994: 29–30), who argues against Pauline authorship, concedes: "Paul is able to express his ideas in various ways, dependent upon the situation of audiences and of himself, and when it comes to a description of what will happen at God's final intervention in human history, it is only to be expected that a variety of ideas and images will be used. This means that, as far as eschatology is concerned, it is *possible* that Paul wrote 2 Thessalonians."

THE LITERARY DEPENDENCE OF 2 THESSALONIANS ON 1 THESSALONIANS

The most persuasive argument against the Pauline authorship of 2 Thessalonians, according to proponents of this position, is that the letter betrays a striking dependence on 1 Thessalonians with regard to its structure, vocabulary, and phrases while at the same time differing in its thought or theology. This argument was first forwarded by Wrede in 1903 and later supplemented in a forceful way by Trilling in 1972, whose work marked a decided shift in convincing many that 2 Thessalonians was not written by Paul but by a later forger. Furnish (2007: 132) is illustrative of the post-Trilling shift when he writes: "The most important literary argument is that this letter appears, in certain respects, to have been written in imitation of 1 Thessalonians. The structural similarities and numerous instances of correspondence in wording . . . are best explained if a later author has used the earlier Pauline letter as a model. This would also account for the fact that correspondence in wording is not always matched by correspondence in thought" (see also, e.g., Krodel 1978: 77–80; J. A. Bailey 1978–79: 132–36; Marxsen 1982: 18–28; Menken 1994: 36–40; Richard 1995: 20–29).

A detailed evaluation of the claims of Wrede and Trilling have already been made by others who ultimately reach the conclusion that, though there is clearly a close relationship between the two letters, the evidence does not require the literary dependency of 2 Thessalonians on 1 Thessalonians such that Paul cannot be its author (see esp. Frame 1912: 45–54; Marshall 1983: 28–45; Wanamaker 1990: 19–28). Therefore, there is no need nor is there sufficient space to rehearse here all the details of that evaluation. Nevertheless, three general comments are warranted.

First, there is a highly *subjective* aspect to the argument: whereas the close parallels between the two letters appear to some to be clear evidence of forgery (e.g., J. A. Bailey 1978–79: 136: "It is impossible to conceive of a man as creative as Paul drawing upon his own previous letter in such an unimaginative way"), the same parallels appear to others to be perfectly understandable and even expected when the same author writes two letters to the same church within a very short time and covers the same major topics.

Second, there is a *paradoxical* aspect to the argument: on the one hand, the author of 2 Thessalonians is faulted for being too much like Paul in the first letter in terms of structure, vocabulary, and phrases; on the other hand, the author of 2 Thessalonians is simultaneously faulted for being too different from Paul in the first letter in terms of theology. It is simpler and more convincing to conclude that the similarities of 2 Thessalonians with 1 Thessalonians, which are not as great as typically claimed (see the helpful chart and comments in Malherbe 2000: 356–58), stem from the letters being written by the same author, Paul—and that the differences in 2 Thessalonians, which are also not as great as typically claimed, are all due to the slightly changed and specific situation that has arisen in the Thessalonian church since the writing of 1 Thessalonians.

Third, there is an *illogical* aspect to the argument: the presence of close parallels in 2 Thessalonians only to 1 Thessalonians but to no other Pauline letter means it is highly unreasonable to believe that it was written by someone after Paul's lifetime who had access only to his first letter and none of his other later letters. As Fee (2009: 240) puts it: "What is perhaps the most significant feature of all regarding this letter is the fact that its author has a thorough-going acquaintance with, and use of, language and terms from the first letter, but knew next to nothing, if anything at all, of the Paul of the later letters. As many have pointed out before, this phenomenon in itself calls the theory of pseudepigraphy for 2 Thessalonians into an extremely high level of suspicion, while at the same time it makes it nearly impossible that someone with knowledge of the whole corpus wrote it at a later time" (so also Marshall 1983: 43).

Additional Considerations

Our survey and evaluation of the four arguments commonly used to establish the pseudepigraphic character of 2 Thessalonians has shown that none of them taken individually is convincing. It is telling that even proponents of the non-Pauline authorship of this letter concede the weakness of the arguments when viewed in isolation from each other. Menken (1994: 27–43) is more candid than most about this weakness: regarding the first argument, based on the colder, authoritarian tone of 2 Thessalonians, he states: "The difference of tone *per se* is not a sufficient reason to deny Pauline authorship to 2 Thessalonians" (31); for the third argument, on the eschatological differences between the two letters, he states: "I believe that this difference alone is not a sufficient argument" (29); for the fourth argument, on the literary dependence of 2 Thessalonians on 1 Thessalonians, he states: "There are of course several points of agreement which are not very impressive when taken in isolation" (38).

Yet despite these concessions, Menken and others who deny that Paul wrote 2 Thessalonians follow the lead emphasized already by Wrede and Trilling and stress the *cumulative force* of the four arguments. Krodel (1978: 77), for example, states: "If these items are viewed separately, in isolation from each other, one might be tempted to dismiss them. Viewed together they become a strong argument for assuming the pseudonymity of 2 Thessalonians." There is, however, a major flaw in such reasoning. As Jewett (1986: 14) rightly observes, "The degree of plausibility with which the general conclusion can be advanced decreases with each new piece of marginal evidence." Wanamaker (1990: 23) makes the same point more bluntly, stating that "a series of weak arguments based on marginal evidence does not add up to a strong case" (so also Marshall 1983: 34; Green 2002: 63; Fee 2009: 238).

The assertion that 2 Thessalonians stems from the hand of an author other than Paul also faces a number of additional problems. First, there is the difficulty in providing a convincing alternative explanation for the historical context (*Sitz im Leben*) from which the letter was written, especially given the highly specific subjects taken up in the document (increased persecution, eschatological confusion over a claim that the day of the Lord had come, church members who are rebelliously idle). Donfried (1993b: 132) reflects the skepticism of many: "It is difficult to imagine a setting where a letter specifically addressed to the Thessalonians by Paul would be relevant and convincing to a non-Thessalonian church some thirty or more years after the Apostle's death" (so also Still 1999: 58; Malherbe 2000: 373–74; Witherington 2006: 11).

Second, there is also a problem—an Achilles' heel (Marshall 1983: 44)—in dating the letter to a post-Pauline period and after the destruction of the temple in AD 70. The problem stems from the fact that 2 Thess. 2:4, "*the* temple of *the* God," almost certainly refers to the temple in Jerusalem (see comments on 2:4). If 2 Thessalonians were written after the temple's destruction in AD 70, it is hard to believe that the imitator or forger would have written about future events to take place that require the temple to still be standing (2 Thess. 2:3–4) rather than predict an upcoming scenario that would more closely agree with what actually happened to the temple at the hands of the Roman general Titus (so also Rigaux 1956: 145; Witherington 2006: 12–13).

Third, although the practice of writing in another person's name—pseudepigraphy—was relatively common in the ancient world, it is only rarely if ever found in the genre of letters. As Carson and Moo (2005: 541) note: "Pseudonymous writings were, of course, quite common, especially in the apocalyptic genre of the Jewish world. But the evidence for pseudonymous *epistles* is meager at best" (see also their longer discussion of pseudonymity on 337–44; also Witherington 2006: 11, 13). This is understandable given the ad hoc nature of letters, which typically address specific situations rather than general ones. Furthermore, it is clear that the earliest Christians did not view pseudepigraphy as an acceptable practice and were on their guard to ensure the authenticity of any document claiming apostolic authority (Wilder 2004: 246). These historical observations make it harder to believe that 2 Thessalonians is pseudonymous and, if it were so, was not recognized as a forgery but instead could be cited as Pauline by Polycarp (*Phil.* 11.3–4 cites 2 Thess. 1:4 and 3:15) already in the early part of the second century.

CONCLUSION

A judicious evaluation of all the various arguments used to establish the non-Pauline authorship of 2 Thessalonians reveals that they, both individually and also cumulatively, fail to make a convincing case that Paul did not write this letter as the document itself claims (2 Thess. 1:1; 3:17). In fact, our survey has demonstrated how subjective the arguments against Pauline authorship typically are: proponents far too often exaggerate both the similarities and differences between the two letters, as well as frequently distort the more natural meaning of certain key texts so that their theory of pseudonymity gains further support. One cannot escape the conclusion that for too many commentators of 2 Thessalonians, pseudonymity, like beauty, lies largely in the eye of the beholder.

The Structure of the Thessalonian Letters

When it comes to understanding the structure of Paul's Letters generally and thus also the Thessalonian Letters specifically, scholars typically follow one of three distinct approaches: thematic, rhetorical, or epistolary (see Jewett 1986: 68 and esp. the charts on 216–25). The thematic approach focuses solely on the content of the letter and seeks to determine the thematic shifts or developments in Paul's correspondence; the rhetorical and the epistolary approaches pay additional attention to the literary form in which that content is presented. Another way to express the differences between these three approaches is to say that the thematic approach seeks only to answer the "what" question, the religious content of the text; then the rhetorical and epistolary approaches seek also to answer the "how" question, the literary modes in which the content is embodied (Ryken 1993: 367).

It is not an exaggeration to claim that a paradigm shift has taken place in biblical studies over the past three or four decades: the old perspective, illustrated by the thematic approach, which views Scripture primarily as a historical or theological document, has been replaced by a new conviction that the Bible is literature and as such ought to be interpreted from a literary perspective. Literary criticism involves several different emphases (Weima 2001: 150–67), but a central tenet consists in a preoccupation with the form and structure of the text as an important supplementary aid to understand its meaning—a preoccupation shared by both the rhetorical and epistolary approaches. Among these two approaches, the rhetorical perspective has become quite popular as an interpretative method to understand Paul's Letters, including his two Thessalonian Letters (see, e.g., Jewett 1986: 71–76, 82–85; Holland 1988; Wanamaker 1990; Hughes 1990; Witherington 2006). If one defines *rhetoric* very broadly as the "art of persuasion," then it can be readily granted that Paul uses rhetoric in his letters. It is also clear that the apostle employs a variety of literary or so-called rhetorical devices that are universally practiced in the everyday use of language and that do not necessarily provide evidence for the training in and conscious use of ancient rhetorical rules. For example, one does not need formal training in rhetoric to make use of paraleipsis, a way of speaking that allows speakers or writers to address a subject that they outwardly claim does not need to be addressed (e.g., 1 Thess. 4:9: "You have no need to have anyone write to you about brotherly love"; 5:1: "You have no need to have anything written to you about the times and the seasons"). These concessions, however, do not outweigh the significant objections that have been raised against the widespread practice of taking the ancient Greco-Roman rules for speech and applying them in a direct and wholesale manner to the interpretation of Paul's Letters (Weima 1997b; also see Porter 1993; Stamps 1995; Classen 2000: 265–91; Porter and Dyer 2012).

This commentary takes seriously the fact that Paul wrote letters and that, consequently, the most important source for understanding the apostle's letters must naturally be the letter-writing practices of his day rather than the rules for oral discourse. An epistolary approach to 1 and 2 Thessalonians, however, must be part of a more broadly literary reading of the text, recognizing Paul's Letters as the result of conscious composition, careful patterning, and the strategic use of literary conventions prevalent in his day. Consequently, each passage in this commentary begins with a significant discussion of its formal features under the heading "Literary Analysis." This involves an analysis of the passage in terms of its literary character (e.g., the form and function of the Letter Opening, Thanksgiving, epistolary conventions [appeal formula, disclosure formula, vocative, etc.] or genre [autobiography, apostolic parousia, paraenesis] found in the Letter Body, and Letter Closing), its boundaries (where the literary unit begins and ends), and its internal structure (the logic of Paul's argument or treatment of a given subject). When Paul's two Letters to the Thessalonians are subjected to this kind of literary analysis, the persuasive skill of the apostle becomes clearly evident, especially his ability to adapt or expand epistolary conventions so that he more effectively communicates the message that he, under the inspiration of the Holy Spirit, was led to write.

The Structure of 1 Thessalonians

    I. Letter opening (1:1)
        A. Sender formula (1:1a)
        B. Recipient formula (1:1b)
        C. Greeting formula (1:1c)
    II. Thanksgiving (1:2–10)
        A. The statement of thanksgiving (1:2a)
        B. The manner of thanksgiving (1:2b)
        C. The immediate cause of thanksgiving (1:3)
        D. The ultimate cause of thanksgiving (1:4–5)
            1. God's election of the Thessalonians (1:4)
            2. The genuineness of the apostles' ministry to the Thessalonians (1:5)
        E. Additional causes of thanksgiving (1:6–10)
            1. The exemplary life of the Thessalonians (1:6–7)
            2. The evangelistic activity of the Thessalonians (1:8)
            3. The conversion of the Thessalonians (1:9–10)
   III. Defense of apostolic actions and absence (2:1–3:13)
        A. Defense of past actions in Thessalonica (2:1–16)
            1. Paul's integrity during his past visit (2:1–12)
                a. His bold preaching in the face of persecution (2:1–2)
                b. His God-examined speech (2:3–4)
                c. His "innocent as an infant" conduct (2:5–7b)
                d. His "loving as a nursing mother" conduct (2:7c–8)
                e. His self-sufficient labor (2:9)
                f. His "nurturing as a father" conduct (2:10–12)
            2. The Thessalonians' response to Paul's past visit (2:13–16)

a. Their acceptance of the word of Paul as the word of God (2:13)

b. Their imitation of the persecuted churches in Judea (2:14–16)

B. Defense of present absence from Thessalonica (2:17–3:10)

   1. Paul's concern over his absence from the Thessalonians (2:17–20)

   2. Paul's concern over the persecution endured by the Thessalonians (3:1–5)

   3. Both concerns answered: Timothy's "good news" about the Thessalonians (3:6–10)

C. Transitional prayers (3:11–13)

   1. Paul's prayer for himself (3:11)

   2. Paul's prayer for the Thessalonians (3:12–13)

IV. Exhortations to the Thessalonians (4:1–5:22)

A. Increasing in conduct that pleases God (4:1–12)

   1. Introduction (4:1–2)

   2. Holiness in sexual conduct (4:3–8)

     a. Statement of thesis (4:3a)

     b. Three exhortations (4:3b–6a)

       i. Separate yourselves from sexual immorality (4:3b)

       ii. Learn to control your sexual desires and conduct (4:4–5)

       iii. Do not harm others through your sexual conduct (4:6a)

     c. Three reasons (4:6b–8)

       i. The future judgment of the Lord Jesus (4:6b)

       ii. The past call of God (4:7)

       iii. The present gift of the Holy Spirit (4:8)

   3. Love for one another (4:9–12)

     a. General affirmation (4:9–10a)

       i. Opening assertion: No need to write to you about loving one another (4:9a)

       ii. Reason 1: You are taught by God to love one another (4:9b)

       iii. Reason 2: You already give evidence of loving one another (4:10a)

     b. Specific appeal (4:10b–12)

       i. Appeal 1: Increase in loving one another (4:10b)

       ii. Appeal 2: Live a quiet life (4:11a)

       iii. Appeal 3: Mind your own business (4:11b)

       iv. Appeal 4: Engage in self-sufficient work (4:11c)

       v. Purpose clause (4:12)

         (1) To win the respect of non-Christians (4:12a)

         (2) To be dependent on no one (4:12b)

B. Comfort concerning deceased Christians at Christ's return (4:13–18)

1. Opening assertion: Christians grieve with hope (4:13)
2. Reason 1: The confession of the church (4:14)
3. Reason 2: The "word of the Lord" (4:15–17)
4. Conclusion: Comfort one another (4:18)

C. Comfort concerning living Christians at Christ's return (5:1–11)
  1. Opening assertion: Christians need not fear the day of the Lord (5:1–3)
  2. Reason 1: You are "sons of light/day" (5:4–5)
  3. Result: Live ready and steady lives (5:6–8)
  4. Reason 2: God has destined us for salvation and life with Christ (5:9–10)
  5. Conclusion: Comfort one another (5:11)

D. Exhortations on congregational life and worship (5:12–22)
  1. Respecting congregational leaders (5:12–13)
  2. Ministering to troubled congregational members (5:14–15)
    a. Ministering to rebellious idlers (5:14a)
    b. Ministering to the fainthearted (5:14b)
    c. Ministering to the weak (5:14c)
    d. Ministering to all members (5:14d–15)
  3. Doing God's will in congregational worship (5:16–18)
  4. Testing prophecy (5:19–22)

V. Letter closing (5:23–28)
A. Peace benediction (5:23)
B. Word of encouragement (5:24)
C. Hortatory section (5:25)
D. Kiss greeting (5:26)
E. Hortatory section (autograph) (5:27)
F. Grace benediction (5:28)

The Structure of 2 Thessalonians

I. Letter opening (1:1–2)
A. Sender (1:1a)
B. Recipient (1:1b)
C. Greeting (1:2)

II. Thanksgiving (1:3–12)
A. Commendation for spiritual growth in the face of persecution (1:3–4)
B. Comfort concerning the just judgment of God (1:5–10)
  1. The just judgment of God: Its assertion (1:5)
  2. The just judgment of God: Its evidence stated briefly (1:6–7a)
    a. Negative judgment on the afflicters: Affliction (1:6)
    b. Positive judgment on the afflicted: Rest (1:7a)
  3. The just judgment of God: Its evidence restated more fully (1:7b–10)

a. Negative judgment on the afflicters: Eternal destruction (1:7b–9)

b. Positive judgment on the afflicted: Glorification (1:10)

C. Challenge: Prayer for God to work in the Thessalonians' lives (1:11–12)

III. Comfort concerning the day of the Lord (2:1–17)

A. Crisis: Fear over the claim that "the day of the Lord has come" (2:1–2)

1. The nature of the false claim (2:1)

2. The meaning of the false claim (2:2a)

3. The source of the false claim (2:2b)

4. The connection of the false claim to Paul (2:2c)

B. Correction: Events that must precede the day of the Lord (2:3–12)

1. Future: The apostasy and the man of lawlessness (2:3–5)

a. The apostasy (2:3a)

b. The man of lawlessness (2:3b–4)

c. A mild rebuke (2:5)

2. Present: The restraining thing/person and the mystery of lawlessness (2:6–7)

3. Future: The coming of the man of lawlessness and his deceived followers (2:8–10)

4. Present: The judgment of unbelievers (2:11–12)

C. Comfort: God ensures the salvation of the Thessalonians (2:13–14)

D. Command: Stand firm by holding fast to Paul's teachings (2:15)

E. Closing prayer that God will comfort the Thessalonians (2:16–17)

IV. Exhortations about the rebellious idlers (3:1–15)

A. General exhortations: The Lord's work in Paul's ministry and the Thessalonian church (3:1–5)

1. Command for intercessory prayer (3:1–2a)

2. Reason for the command (3:2b)

3. Word of encouragement (3:3)

4. Confidence formula (3:4)

5. Concluding prayer (3:5)

B. Specific exhortations: Discipline the rebellious idlers (3:6–15)

1. Opening command (3:6)

2. The example of Paul (3:7–9)

3. The teaching of Paul (3:10)

4. Applying Paul's example and teaching (3:11–12)

5. Closing commands (3:13–15)

V. Letter closing (3:16–18)

A. Peace benediction (3:16a)

B. Word of encouragement (3:16b)

C. Autograph greeting and explanatory comment (3:17)

D. Grace benediction (3:18)

1 Thessalonians

I. Letter Opening (1:1)

The letter opening (1:1) has not been formally altered in any noteworthy way vis-à-vis some of Paul's other letters—a likely reflection of the good relationship that exists between the apostle and the Thessalonian church as well as his overall pleasure at their spiritual condition. Yet even this relatively simple letter opening serves the important function of laying down at least three significant points that have bearing on the rest of the letter. First, the inclusion of Silvanus and Timothy as cosenders gives further weight or authority to Paul's letter, for it not only shows to the Thessalonians that the apostle is well informed by the recently returned Timothy (3:6) about the current situation in their congregation but also that there is agreement between Paul and these other leaders about the required response expected from the recipients in their present circumstances. Second, the identification of the recipients with the term "church" (ἐκκλησία, *ekklēsia*), a term used in the LXX to refer to Israel as God's covenant people, reflects Paul's understanding of the predominantly *Gentile* church of Thessalonica as the new people of God. This understanding manifests itself elsewhere in the letter as Paul similarly takes language formerly reserved for Israel and applies it to the Thessalonian congregation. Finally, the prepositional phrase "in God the Father and the Lord Jesus Christ" and the greeting "Grace to you and peace" both emphasize the primary and thus crucial role of the Divine—both God and Christ—in the origin, ongoing life, and salvation of the readers. The church in Thessalonica is not the result of the human work of "Paul and Silvanus and Timothy" or of the Thessalonian believers themselves; instead, it is the result of the divine initiative of "God the Father and the Lord Jesus Christ," who undeservedly grant "grace and peace" to the converts in Thessalonica.

Literary Analysis

The letter opening is the most formally consistent section of Paul's Letters, being made up of three epistolary conventions. First, there is the sender formula, which typically consists of three formal elements: (1) the name of Paul; (2) a title, most commonly "apostle" (1 Cor. 1:1; 2 Cor. 1:1; Gal. 1:1; Eph. 1:1; Col. 1:1; 1 Tim. 1:1; 2 Tim. 1:1; Titus 1:1) but sometimes also "servant" (Rom. 1:1; Phil. 1:1; Titus 1:1); and (3) a short descriptive phrase, indicating the source of his apostleship or servanthood: "of Christ Jesus" (missing only in 1 Thess. 1:1 and 2 Thess. 1:1). Atypical of letters of his day, Paul includes the name of cosenders at the end of this formula and identifies them as "brother(s)," in distinction from the more authoritative title of "apostle" used to identify himself. Second, there is the recipient formula, which consists of two formal elements: (1) the designation of the recipient, normally the noun "church" along with the name of the city or region where the church is located; and (2) a brief phrase that positively describes the readers' relationship to God and/or Christ, such as "in God (our) Father and the Lord Jesus Christ" (1 Thess. 1:1; 2 Thess. 1:1); "in Christ Jesus" (1 Cor. 1:2; Phil. 1:1). The third and final epistolary convention of the Pauline letter opening is the greeting formula, which includes three formal elements: (1) the greeting: "grace and peace"; (2) the recipient: "to you"; and (3) the divine source: "from God our Father and the Lord Jesus Christ." The typical or expected form of the Pauline letter opening, therefore, is as follows:

A. Sender formula (1:1a)
1. Name of sender
2. Title
3. Short descriptive phrase, indicating source of title
4. Cosender(s)
B. Recipient formula (1:1b)
1. Identification of recipient
2. Short phrase, positively describing the recipients' relationship to God
C. Greeting formula (1:1c)
1. Greeting
2. Recipient
3. Divine source

That these same three formulas (although in a much more simplified form) were typically included in the openings of secular letters of Paul's day (see letter openings in Exler 1923: 24–60; Roller 1933: 57–62; White 1986) shows that the apostle is obviously not the creator of this epistolary format but borrows from the letter-writing practices of his day. Nevertheless, Paul does not slavishly follow these practices but adapts them to suit his particular audience and specific needs, as seen in the way he "Christianizes" the greeting (see comments below). The apostle's skill as a letter writer also manifests itself in those letter openings where he adapts or significantly expands his expected epistolary conventions so that this opening unit functions not merely to establish or maintain contact with his readers but already anticipates key concerns or themes to be developed in the body of the letter. For instance, Paul significantly expands the sender formula in the letter opening of Romans in order to present himself to his unknown readers as the divinely appointed apostle to the Gentiles, who has a God-given responsibility to share with them his gospel (see Weima 1994b). Paul similarly embellishes the sender formula in the letter opening of Galatians so that it stresses the divine rather than human source of his apostleship ("Paul, an apostle not from men nor through any man but through Jesus Christ and from God the Father"), thereby issuing a preemptive strike for the defense of his authoritative status taken up in the lengthy autobiographical apology that opens the letter body (1:11–2:14). Compared to these expanded letter openings, however, the epistolary conventions that open Paul's First Letter to the Thessalonians are simple and unembellished. This is likely due to the good relationship that Paul enjoys with the Thessalonian congregation and the absence of any questions in this church about his apostolic status or authority.

Exegesis and Exposition

[1]Paul and Silvanus and Timothy. To the church of the Thessalonians in God the Father and the Lord Jesus Christ. Grace to you and peace ⌜ ⌝.

A. Sender Formula (1:1a)

The letter opens in typical fashion with the sender formula, including the mention of cosenders: "Paul and Silvanus and Timothy" (Παῦλος καὶ Σιλουανὸς καὶ Τιμόθεος, *Paulos kai Silouanos kai Timotheos*).

1:1a

The name "Paul" (the Greek *Paulos* is a transliteration of the Latin *Paulus* or its variant *Paullus*) is one of three names that the apostle, as a Roman citizen (Acts 16:37–38; 22:25–29; also implied from his appeal to appear before Caesar: 25:10–12, 21, 25; 26:32), likely had: the "given name" (*praenomen*), the name of the ultimate founder of the family (*nomen gentile*), and the family name (*cognomen*; Harrer 1940; Bruce 1977: 38). We do not know the apostle's first two names since in his letters he uses only the third, or family, name. When a slave or foreigner was granted citizenship, his first two names were that of the Roman who obtained the citizenship for him, but he retained his third name, or cognomen (Murphy-O'Connor 1996: 41). The name "Paul" is derived from his Hebrew name "Saul" (the Greek *Saulos* is a hellenized form of the Hebrew *Šā'ûl*), which the writer of Acts uses in the early part of his narrative dealing with the apostle's life (7:58; 8:1, 3; 9:1, 8, 11, 22, 24; 11:25, 30; 12:25; 13:1–2, 7, 9). "Paul" was a rather common cognomen and had either the affectionate meaning of "little" or the pejorative sense of "small" (Hemer 1985: 183).

Contrary to the epistolary practice of our day but entirely in keeping with that of the Greco-Roman world, Paul lists his name as the first element of the letter opening. The only exception to this practice was in letters of petition when one was addressing a person of higher rank. Paul, however, writes to his readers as neither an inferior nor even an equal but as one having authority over them, as indicated by his normal addition of the title "apostle" (1 Cor. 1:1; 2 Cor. 1:1; Gal. 1:1; Eph. 1:1; Col. 1:1; 1 Tim. 1:1; 2 Tim. 1:1; Titus 1:1). The absence of this title here in his letter to the Thessalonians is, therefore, striking. A likely explanation for this omission is that, in contrast to several other letters (esp. Romans, 1 and 2 Corinthians, Galatians), Paul's apostleship was not an issue with the Thessalonian congregation, and so in the letter opening he has no need to assert his authoritative status. Thus Paul mentions his apostleship only once in his two Letters to the Thessalonians (1 Thess. 2:7a), and this single instance serves not to stress his authority but to demonstrate the opposite point: that he did not, in a self-serving and heavy-handed manner, assert his right as an apostle to be supported financially by the Thessalonian congregation, but that he self-sacrificially worked with his hands to provide his own support rather than become a burden to them. Repeated challenges to his apostolic status in later years, however, caused Paul to become explicit in his letter openings not only about his own apostleship but also to distance his own authoritative status from that of various fellow workers included as cosenders (e.g., 1 Cor. 1:1, "Paul, an *apostle*, . . . and Sosthenes, the *brother*"; see also 2 Cor. 1:1; Col. 1:1).

Although not a common epistolary practice in the letters of that day, Paul includes here, as he typically does, the names of cosenders: Silvanus and Timothy. The mention of these two individuals raises two related questions: First, what role, if any, did the cosenders play in the writing of this letter? Second, if Paul emerges as the ultimate or real author of the letter, what is the significance of his including the names of Silvanus and Timothy as cosenders?

With regard to the first question, the widespread use of the first-person plural "we" in the rest of the letter has caused many to conclude that Silvanus and Timothy played an active role in the composition of the letter. The situation is likened to that of a group project in which all three individuals contribute to the subject matter, organizational structure, and perhaps even the vocabulary of the letter. Against this scenario, however, are three instances in the letter where the text shifts significantly to the first-person singular, suggesting that the first-person plurals in the letter ought to be read not *literally* but *literarily*. The first instance is 2:18, where Paul's desire to revisit the Thessalonians is originally expressed in the plural ("We wanted to come to you") but then clarified with a personal interjection in the singular ("In fact, I, Paul, wanted to do so more than once"). The second occurrence is the inclusio formed between 3:1–2 and 3:5: the plural expression "Because we could no longer contain it, . . . we sent Timothy . . . in order to comfort you concerning your faith" is replaced by the singular expression "Because I could no longer contain it, I sent [Timothy] in order to learn about your faith." The third occasion is 5:27, where the letter closes with a strong exhortation given in the singular: "I cause you to swear an oath in the name of the Lord that this letter be read to all the brothers." These three texts (see also 2 Thess. 2:5 and 3:17) suggest that, though the names of Silvanus and Timothy are included as cosenders, Paul is the real author of the letter, so that the plurals used throughout the correspondence ought to be taken literarily rather than literally.

This conclusion raises the second question: since Paul is the real author of the letter, why has he included Silvanus and Timothy as cosenders? That Paul's epistolary practices are never accidental but relate in some way to his persuasive strategy suggests that the mention of cosenders involves something more than mere courtesy (contra Williams 1992: 21). According to Doty (1973: 30), secular letters of that day often mentioned the name of the letter carrier to "guarantee that what he had to say in interpreting the letter was authorized by the writer"; thus Silvanus and Timothy may have been mentioned in the letter opening for this reason (see also Wanamaker 1990: 68). The mention or recommendation of a letter carrier, however, typically occurred not in the opening but in the closing section of the letter (C. Kim 1972), and this appears to be Paul's practice elsewhere (Rom. 16:1–2; Eph. 6:21–22; Col. 4:7–9). A more likely reason for including the names of Silvanus and Timothy is that both have played a key role in the Thessalonian congregation: Silvanus in the establishing of the church (Acts 17:1–10), and Timothy in the subsequent strengthening of the church (1 Thess. 3:1–5). The inclusion of these two men as cosenders, therefore, gives further weight or authority to Paul's letter; it not only shows the Thessalonians that the apostle is well informed about the current situation in their congregation but also that there is agreement between Paul and these other leaders about the response expected from the recipients in their present circumstances (Wanamaker 1990: 68).

Although the details of Paul's life are well known to most modern Christians, those of Silvanus and Timothy are not and thus require some general comment. The "Silvanus" mentioned in the letters of Paul and Peter is almost certainly the same person identified as "Silas" in Acts. The longer name was the one commonly known and used in Greek and Roman communities (2 Cor. 1:19; 1 Thess. 1:1; 2 Thess. 1:1; 1 Pet. 5:12), whereas the shorter name was employed in Jewish circles (Acts 15:22, 27, 32, 40; 16:19, 25, 29; 17:4, 10, 14, 15; 18:5). Silvanus (Silas) first appears on the biblical scene after the meeting of the Jerusalem Council, when he and Judas Barsabbas, both of them "leading men among the brothers" (Acts 15:22), are sent to the Antiochian church to convey in person the council's decision. After splitting with Barnabas following the first missionary journey, Paul chose Silvanus (Silas) to join him for the second missionary journey, during which time the two missionaries, along with Timothy, established the church in Thessalonica. Later in the second missionary journey, Silvanus (Silas) is sent from Athens to somewhere in Macedonia, perhaps Philippi, after which he rejoins Paul, who by this time is in Corinth (for a more detailed account of the movements of both Silvanus and Timothy during this time, see comments on 1 Thess. 3:1). Sometime after his ministry in Corinth, Silvanus (Silas) served as Peter's associate in Rome.

That the name of Silvanus is listed before that of Timothy as a cosender of 1 Thessalonians likely reflects the role that each one played in Paul's ministry. Silvanus took Barnabas's place as Paul's senior associate on his second missionary journey (Acts 15:36–41; note also how Acts 17:1–10 describes Silas's role in the mission-founding work at Thessalonica but says nothing about Timothy's involvement), and Timothy similarly replaced John Mark as Paul's junior associate (G. F. Hawthorne, *ISBE* 4:858).

Timothy, despite his junior associate status, enjoyed an especially close relationship with Paul, evident in the apostle's reference to him in the early days of his ministry as "my beloved and faithful child in the Lord" (1 Cor. 4:17) and similarly late in his ministry as "my true child in the faith" (1 Tim. 1:2). Paul, however, was not the only one who played a role in Timothy's conversion: he was also influenced by his grandmother Lois and mother, Eunice, a Christian Jew (2 Tim. 1:5; Acts 16:1). Timothy first joined Paul in his hometown of Lystra during the second missionary journey and from this time onward was heavily involved in the apostle's ministry, both in establishing new churches and also in returning to these churches as Paul's emissary. It is in both these capacities that the Thessalonians knew Timothy, since he was present during the mission-founding visit of Paul and Silas (Acts 17:1–10) and was soon thereafter sent back to this congregation to strengthen their faith in the face of opposition (1 Thess. 3:1–5). Timothy then rejoined Paul, who by this time was in Corinth, and brought to the apostle not only a good report about the Thessalonians' enduring faith despite persecution and their ongoing love for Paul (3:6) but also news about some areas where they were "lacking" in their faith (3:10). This information from Timothy motivated Paul to write 1 Thessalonians.

B. Recipient Formula (1:1b)

1:1b The second formal section of the Pauline letter opening, the recipient formula, occurs here in its typical or expected form, consisting of two formal elements: (1) the designation of the recipient with the noun "church," along with the name of the city or region where the church is located; and (2) a brief phrase that positively describes the readers' relationship to God and/or Christ: "To the church of the Thessalonians in God the Father and the Lord Jesus Christ" (τῇ ἐκκλησίᾳ Θεσσαλονικέων ἐν θεῷ πατρὶ καὶ κυρίῳ Ἰησοῦ Χριστῷ, *tē ekklēsia Thessalonikeōn en theō patri kai kyriō Iēsou Christō*).

To the modern hearer, the word "church" evokes images of ornate buildings or complex denominational structures—images that all too easily cause one to miss the significance of this term. For Paul's identification of the recipients of his letter with the designation "church" reveals an important theological truth about the way in which the apostle views his converts, particularly their continuity with ancient Israel as the people of God. Although the noun *ekklēsia* (church) in secular Greek refers to an officially summoned assembly of citizens (see Acts 19:32, 39, 41), in the LXX it (or its verbal cognate) describes the people of God, whether they are assembled for worship or not (see, e.g., Deut. 9:10; 18:6; 23:2–4; 31:30; Judg. 20:2; 1 Sam. 17:47; 1 Chron. 28:8; Neh. 13:1). In light of the Jewish heritage of Paul, as well as his references to the "church(es) of God," both later in this letter (1 Thess. 2:14) and elsewhere (e.g., 1 Cor. 1:2; 10:32; 11:16; 15:9; 2 Cor. 1:1; Gal. 1:13), "it seems unreasonable to doubt that in I Thess. 1,1 Paul is thinking of the Christians of Thessalonica as members of the 'Church of God,' and that he is fully aware of the biblical background and theological implications of his use of the term" (Deidun 1981: 11; also Malherbe 2000: 99). That the term *ekklēsia* reflects Paul's understanding of the predominantly *Gentile* church of Thessalonica as the new people of God is confirmed by his reference to them a mere three verses later as those who are "loved by God" and who know their "election" (1:4), terms similarly used in the OT to refer to Israel but now applied to NT believers (for more about these two expressions, see the comments on 1:4; on the phrase "God who indeed gives to you his Spirit, who is holy," see the comment on 4:8).

Paul distinguishes the Thessalonian church from all other *ekklēsiai* or assembled groups in Thessalonica—not only the Jewish synagogue but also other voluntary associations that might gather under the same designation—with the prepositional phrase "in God the Father and the Lord Jesus Christ" (*en theō patri kai kyriō Iēsou Christō*).[1] The wide range of meanings expressed by the jack-of-all-trades preposition *en* (for this preposition, BDAG 326–30 lists twelve different nuances) makes it difficult to determine its precise sense here. The two most commonly identified meanings are either a spatial/locative sense (i.e., the church of the Thessalonians lives in the presence of God and Christ) or an instrumental sense (i.e., the church of the Thessalonians is brought into being by God and Christ). As Holmes (1998: 37) admits, deciding between these two meanings is complicated by the fact that the phrase "in God (the Father)" is as rare in Paul (only six other occurrences, of which only one [2 Thess. 1:1] matches the usage here) as the phrase "in (the Lord Jesus) Christ" is common (some 170 occurrences), and it is not clear whether the atypical phrase ought to be understood in light of the typical or whether the reverse interpretive method should be followed. What ought not to be overlooked in this debate, however, is what both interpretations have in common: the primary and thus crucial role of the Divine, both God and Christ, in the origin and ongoing life of the Thessalonian congregation. Just as the following thanksgiving section (1:2–10) is directed not to the Thessalonian Christians but to God, who has elected them and is the ultimate cause of their "work of faith and labor of love and steadfastness of hope" (see comments on 1:3), so also the letter opening acknowledges that the church of the Thessalonians is the result not of the human work of "Paul and Silvanus and Timothy" but of the divine initiative of "God the Father and the Lord Jesus Christ."[2]

The occurrence of both divine persons ("God the Father and the Lord Jesus Christ") as the double object of the single preposition ("in") is significant. That the same pattern is found in Paul's other letter openings as well[3] is similarly important for understanding the apostle's Christology. The high frequency of this construction has wrongly caused many to dismiss the apostle's joining of God and Christ as merely a fixed or stereotyped expression. But as Fee notes (2007: 49n62): "It is easy to forget that here is a Jew who in his younger years would not have dared breathe the name of

1. That this prepositional phrase in 1:1 is not preceded by the article τῇ means that technically it could modify either (1) the preceding noun phrase "to the church of the Thessalonians," (2) the earlier three nominatives "Paul and Silvanus and Timothy," or even (3) the following greeting of "Grace to you and peace." The second and third possibilities, however, do not conform to Paul's epistolary practice elsewhere. Conversely, the apostle normally adds to his designation of the recipients some words that acknowledge their relationship to God and/or Christ. Finally, the simplest and thus preferred reading is to connect the prepositional phrase with the immediately preceding noun phrase "to the church of the Thessalonians."

2. So also Gaventa (1998: 12), who observes: "Far more important than resolving them [i.e., debates about the meaning of the prepositional phrase "in God the Father and the Lord Jesus Christ"] is lingering over the too obvious but often neglected point: God and Jesus Christ are the primary agents in the Thessalonian church. Whatever Paul, Silvanus, and Timothy began, whatever the Thessalonians themselves have accomplished, it is God who is to be thanked (1:2), God who directs and strengthens the church (3:11–13), God who is and will remain faithful (5:24)."

3. The only other occurrence of the double object of God and Christ with the single preposition ἐν is 2 Thess. 1:1. The same double object, however, occurs with the single preposition ἀπό in the opening greeting of all Paul's remaining letters and also in 2 Thessalonians.

YHWH but who now as a matter of course puts θεός and Jesus together as the compound object in a single prepositional phrase." Yet it is not just here and in other letter openings that Paul does this: throughout both of his Letters to the Thessalonians he frequently links God and Jesus in an intimate manner (see 1 Thess. 1:3; 3:11–13; 5:18; 2 Thess. 1:1, 2, 8, 12; 2:16–17; 3:5). That Paul does not feel the need to explain or justify this juxtaposition suggests that the apostle possesses a high Christology, which would have been an important part of his missionary preaching and which he can now safely assume to be accepted by his readers. The apostle's exalted view of Jesus Christ is reflected in the title "Lord," which was the regular word used in the Septuagint for Yahweh and also a common term used in Hellenistic sources for their pagan gods.[4]

C. Greeting Formula (1:1c)

1:1c The third and final element of the letter opening is the greeting, which here differs from the pattern followed in all his later letters in that it omits the divine source: "Grace to you and peace" (χάρις ὑμῖν καὶ εἰρήνη, *charis hymin kai eirēnē*).

The greeting "Grace and peace" sounds familiar to the ears of contemporary Christians because this is the greeting that opens virtually all the letters ascribed to Paul (a slightly expanded form "grace, mercy, and peace" is found in 1 Tim. 1:2 and 2 Tim. 1:2) and other NT writers (1 Pet. 1:2; 2 Pet. 1:2). This greeting would have sounded distinctive, however, to the predominantly Gentile congregation of Thessalonica since it differs from the common infinitive greeting that typically opened secular letters of their day: χαίρειν (*chairein*), which literally means "Rejoice!" but has the colloquial sense of "Greetings!" (so Acts 15:23; 23:26; James 1:1; 2 John 10, 11).[5]

The minority of Jewish members of the Thessalonian church would have similarly found Paul's greeting unique since the few surviving *primary* Semitic letters of that time period[6] have either the same form *chairein* in correspondence written in Greek (5/6 Ḥev 3, 6; Mas 1039–307/1) or the word שָׁלוֹם (*shālôm*, lit., "Peace!" but colloquially, "Greeting!") in correspondence written in Hebrew and Aramaic (5/6 Ḥev 1, 4, 10, 12; papMur 42, 43, 44, 46, 48; Mas 16–89). There are a few *secondary* Semitic letters—letters not discovered in their original manuscript form but as incorporated into existing documents—that have an apparent similarity with Paul's epistolary

---

4. Morris 1991: 36: "He [Paul] employs a term that conveys the idea that Jesus is divine, be the reader's background Jewish or pagan."

5. Although different opening greetings are occasionally used, these are quite rare and the most common form by far is χαίρειν (see the examples from various papyrus letters listed in Exler 1923: 24–40, 42–44, 50–56; Weima 1994a: 29–30, 36).

6. Compared to the thousands of examples of Hellenistic letters available, the number of Semitic letters that have been discovered is exceedingly small. Of these only a small percentage date within a century or two of the time of Paul (twenty-eight letters belonging to the Bar Kokhba revolt of AD 132–135), and many of these letters exist only in fragmentary form.

greeting: "Greetings . . . good peace" (*chairein . . . eirēnēn agathēn*: 2 Macc. 1:1); "Mercy and peace" (2 Bar. 78.3; Tob. 7:12 in Codex Sinaiticus). There are dangers, however, in using these secondary or incorporated Semitic letters. For example, the Hanukkah letters recorded in 2 Macc. 1:1–10 were originally written in Aramaic or Hebrew, but only a Greek version survives, so it is possible that the original epistolary greeting has been distorted or replaced in the translation process. Furthermore, the supposed parallel of 2 Macc. 1:1 is not exact, since the final words "true peace" are not part of the opening greeting (this phrase is separated from *chairein* by thirteen words) but constitute a different epistolary convention commonly found in the opening of letters, namely, the health wish.

Therefore neither Hellenistic nor Semitic letters provide an exact parallel to Paul's opening greeting "Grace to you and peace." This makes it difficult to explain the origin of the apostle's salutation. Here some see Paul's indebtedness to his Jewish background and claim he is borrowing or adapting the expression "mercy and peace" current in some Jewish writings (see Frame 1912: 72; Bruce 1982: 8; Richard 1995: 39; Malherbe 2000: 100). But in light of the problems with the claimed Jewish parallels cited above, it is more likely that the apostle takes the typically secular or Greek greeting *chairein* and "Christianizes" it into the similar-sounding *charis* (grace; so, e.g., Koskenniemi 1956: 162; Best 1977: 63; Marshall 1983: 49; Morris 1991: 37; Taatz 1991; Fee [2009: 17] calls this "a marvelous example of Paul's 'turning into gospel' everything he sets his hand to"). Thus Paul adds *charis* to the typically Jewish greeting "peace" so that the new combination of "Grace and peace" results in a salutation that is truly inclusive of his Gentile Christian and Jewish Christian audience. Here in the letter opening, Paul's skillful adaptation is similar to what he does in the letter closing, where he replaces the "farewell wish" that typically brings secular or Greek letters to a definitive close with a distinctively Christian formula, the "grace benediction" ("May the grace of our Lord Jesus Christ be with you"), which performs the same function.

The change from "Greetings" (*chairein*) to "Grace" (*charis*) may be slight in sound but is significant in sense. For, as with the prepositional phrase that precedes it ("in God the Father and the Lord Jesus Christ"), it evokes the crucial role of the Divine in the readers' salvation. Grace is the supreme gift of God's undeserved favor given to the Thessalonians by virtue of their relationship with Christ. Or, as Paul will put it later in the letter, it is God's work of electing them (1:4), of rescuing them from the coming wrath (1:10), of destining them for the obtaining of salvation through the Lord Jesus Christ (5:9). "Peace," or *shalom*, similarly evokes the work of God in the Thessalonians' lives. Peace involves not the Greek sense of the absence of conflict but the Jewish notion of wholeness—a restoration of the fellowship and harmony that before the fall characterized humankind's relationship with God, with each other, and with the creation (see Rom. 2:10; 8:6; 14:17; Eph. 6:15; W. Foerster, *TDNT* 2:402–8).

Additional Note

1:1. After the opening greeting "Grace and peace," several MSS, including some important ancient ones, add the prepositional phrase "from God our Father and the Lord Jesus Christ" (so ℵ A [D] I 𝔐 vg^{mss} sy^{h**} bo). Nevertheless, the short reading enjoys textual support from both Alexandrian and Western text types (B F G Ψ 0278 629 1739 1881 *pc* lat sy^p sa). Furthermore, there would be no compelling reason why copyists would delete the longer reading if it were original. Instead, the longer reading is almost certainly a later addition that attempts to make this brief greeting conform to the lengthier greeting found in Paul's other letters (so B. Metzger 1994: 561).

II. Thanksgiving (1:2–10)

Paul gives thanks to God in 1:2–10 for the vibrant faith and active Christian life of the Thessalonian believers. The thanksgiving section does not belong to the body of the letter but rather functions as an important introduction to the rest of the correspondence. Paul uses the thanksgiving section to accomplish three key goals: (1) to reestablish his relationship with his readers, (2) to implicitly exhort them to live up to the praise that he brings to God for them, and (3) to foreshadow the four major issues that he will address in the rest of the letter (the defense of Paul's integrity [2:1–20; 3:6–10]; the persecution endured by the Thessalonian believers [3:1–10]; proper moral conduct [4:1–12; 5:12–22]; and the second coming of Christ [4:13–18; 5:1–11]). It is clear from 1:2–10 that Paul enjoyed a warm relationship with the Thessalonian Christians and was truly thankful for their exemplary life, evangelistic activity, and conversion—events that ultimately originate from God's election of his converts in Thessalonica.

Literary Analysis

Character of the Passage

First Thessalonians 1:2–10 consists of a distinct epistolary unit within Paul's Letters, located between the letter opening and the letter body, in which the apostle gives thanks to God for the believers to whom he is writing. This unit is typically titled the "thanksgiving" section because of the opening verb "I/We give thanks" (εὐχαριστῶ/ οὖμεν, *eucharistō/oumen*) and the general content of this section. In order to understand better the meaning and significance of 1:2–10 and its function in the letter as a whole, it is helpful to survey the thanksgiving sections in all of Paul's Letters in terms of their source, form, and function.

Source. Is Paul's custom of including a thanksgiving section in his letters a standard practice of ancient letter writing or a new literary convention that he himself developed? Evidence for the former position can be found in those ancient letters that open with a brief thanksgiving or prayer to the gods, usually in connection with physical health and safety. For example, a third-century BC letter begins: "Toubias to Apollonios, greeting. If you are well and if all your affairs and everything else is proceeding according to your will, *many thanks to the gods*; we also are well, always remembering you, as I should" (P.Cair.Zen 59076). This custom of giving thanks to the gods in the opening of a letter continued till well past Paul's day, as evidenced by this second-century AD letter: "Apion to his father and lord, Epimachos, very many greetings. Before all else I pray that you are well and that you may prosper in continual health, together with my sister and her daughter and my brother. *I give thanks to the lord Sarapis* [the Egyptian deity Serapis] because, when I was endangered at sea, he rescued me immediately" (*BGU* 632). The similarities between Paul's thanksgivings and the letter openings of his day lead Schubert (1939: 184) to conclude that "Paul was not just a Jew who was 'exposed' to Hellenistic 'influences,' but that he was an indigenous Hellenist."

But while Paul's thanksgivings share with Hellenistic letters the voicing of thanks to the gods at the opening of the correspondence, they differ from common letters in at least three important ways. First, in terms of content, Paul's thanksgivings deal with the spiritual (rather than physical) well-being of his recipients. Second, in terms of form, Paul's thanksgivings are much longer and formally complex than anything found in ancient letters.[1] Third, in terms of frequency, virtually all of Paul's Letters include a thanksgiving section, but the vast majority of Greco-Roman letters do not.[2] These differences have thus led some scholars to see the Pauline thanksgiving as an epistolary form that is unique to the apostle's writings, perhaps reflecting a Jewish custom or influence in Paul's background. Rigaux (1968: 122), for example, states: "The Pauline use of the thanksgiving form in his letters does not seem to owe its origin to some external influence. According to a Jewish custom, Paul most likely simply used to begin his preaching with an expression of thanksgiving, a pattern which he later incorporated into his correspondence."

Which of the two positions about the origin of the Pauline thanksgivings is correct? The best answer is probably a synthesis of the two views: the *form* of the thanksgiving sections is largely Hellenistic, but its *content* is influenced mainly by Judaism. In other words, although to a large extent the Pauline thanksgiving owes its existence and structure to the standard epistolary form in Hellenistic letter writing, its contents are influenced by OT and Jewish thought (so Wiles 1974: 160; Fitzmyer 1968: 225; O'Brien 1977: 11; 1982: 8).

Form. The first significant formal analysis of the Pauline thanksgivings was undertaken some time ago by Schubert (1939). This comparative study led Schubert to propose that there are two basic types of thanksgiving, one being formally more complex than the other.[3] Schubert's identification of the formal elements of

---

1. White (1971: 30–31): "The Pauline thanksgiving differs, formally and functionally, from its common letter counterpart. Unlike the thanksgiving of the common letter tradition, thanks to the gods does not depend upon safety from great danger. Further, the addressees play a much more positive role; they are cited as the cause of thanksgiving." Berger (1974: 219) has found the differences so great that he states: "Thanksgivings in Hellenistic letters are relatively seldom [i.e., rare] and have no comparable contents" ("Danksagungen in hellenistischen Briefen sind vergleichsweise [!] selten und haben keinen vergleichbaren Inhalt").

2. Schubert (1939: 172–73) responds to this criticism by observing that the thanksgiving formula was used in common letters "only where genuine feeling (personal as well as religious) is involved. These facts fully explain the relative scarcity of the formula on the one hand and its unmistakable fixity on the other."

3. These two types may be best presented in the following schematic fashion:

Type 1a: Complex (Philippians; Colossians; 1 Thessalonians; Philemon)
   1. Principal Clause: εὐχαριστῶ/εὐχαριστοῦμεν τῷ θεῷ (I/We give thanks to God)
   2. Participial Clause(s): one, two, or three participles that modify the subject (Paul and his cowriters, if any) of the principal verb; typically, the first of the participial clauses indicates time, the second indicates cause, and the third also indicates cause; the final participle is invariably built on verbs of hearing, learning, or believing—i.e., ἀκούειν (*akouein*, to hear), μνημονεύειν (*mnēmoneuein*, to remember), εἰδέναι (*eidenai*, to know), and πείθεσθαι (*peithesthai*, to be persuaded)
   3. Purpose Clause: a closing clause (introduced by ἵνα, ὅπως, or εἰς τό with the infinitive) that expresses purpose

the Pauline thanksgiving has been followed by many biblical scholars, including O'Brien (1977) in his monograph-length study of this epistolary unit. Despite the importance of Schubert's groundbreaking work and its widespread acceptance, his formal analysis suffers from a couple of weaknesses. First, the two proposed formal types do not account for the structure of *all* the Pauline thanksgivings, thereby requiring Schubert to identify yet a third ("mixed") type (Romans). Second, and more significant, Schubert focused his attention only on the initial parts of the thanksgiving section, to a large extent ignoring the relatively consistent structure and function of the concluding parts.

An attempt to address both concerns has been undertaken by Jervis (1991: 86–109). By restating and realigning the formal elements of the thanksgiving section along more functional categories, Jervis proposes that there is only one type of Pauline thanksgiving, within which there may occur five distinct units:

1. Principal Verb: verb εὐχαριστῶ (I give thanks) and its personal object τῷ θεῷ (μου) (to [my] God)
2. Manner of Thanksgiving: adverbial and/or participial constructions that serve to indicate the manner in which Paul gives thanks; the pronominal object phrase περὶ (ὑπὲρ) ὑμῶν (*peri [hyper] hymōn*, concerning [on behalf of] you) typically occurs (except in Philemon)
3. Cause of Thanksgiving: causal constructions in the form of phrases using ἐπί (*epi*) or ὅτι and/or participial clauses (usually verbs of learning or hearing) that give the reason for Paul's thanksgiving
4. Explanation: this section, begun either with καθώς (*kathōs*, as), γάρ (*gar*, for), or ὥστε (*hōste*, so then), usually modifies the preceding causal unit and thus serves to elaborate on the cause for Paul's thanksgiving
5. Prayer Report: a report of what Paul prays for regarding his addressees, involving the verb προσεύχεσθαι (*proseuchesthai*, to pray) and a ἵνα, ὅπως, or εἴ πως construction, which gives the content of the prayer

Although not completely free of criticism, Jervis's proposal helpfully identifies the five formal features typically found in a Pauline thanksgiving.

Function. It is crucial to consider the function(s) that the thanksgiving plays in the persuasive strategy of Paul. The question naturally arises as to why the apostle does not move directly to the body of the letter but chooses instead to preface this material with an expression of thanks to God about his readers. What does Paul gain or accomplish by not immediately addressing the main concerns raised in the letter body but instead first articulating a word of thanks to God concerning his letter recipients?

The answer to this question lies in recognizing three important functions that the Pauline thanksgivings have in aiding the persuasive strategy of the apostle. First, this epistolary unit has a "pastoral" function: the thanksgiving reestablishes Paul's relationship with his readers by means of a positive expression of gratitude to God for specific good things that are happening within their congregation. The letter is typically the first communication that Paul has had with a given church

---

Type 1b: Simple (1 Corinthians; 2 Thessalonians)
1. Principal Clause: εὐχαριστῶ/εὐχαριστοῦμεν (I/we give thanks to God)
2. Causal Clause: introduced by ὅτι (*hoti*, because)
3. Consecutive Clause: introduced by ὥστε (*hōste*, so that)

after his original mission-founding ministry among them. It is important, therefore, for the apostle to reconnect with his readers if he wants them not only to accept his letter but also to obey his exhortations contained in it. The thanksgiving also reveals Paul's deep pastoral concern for his readers as evidenced by his comments in units 2 (the manner of thanksgiving) and 5 (the prayer report) that he regularly prays for them.

Second, the thanksgiving has an "exhortative" function: this epistolary unit is "implicitly or explicitly parenetic" (Schubert 1939: 26, 89; see also O'Brien 1977: 141–44, 165, 262–63). In other words, even though Paul is expressing his thankfulness to God, there is an implicit challenge for the letter recipients to live up to the praise that the apostle is giving them in his words of gratitude. For example, when the apostle gives thanks to God for the Thessalonians' "work of faith and labor of love and steadfastness of hope in our Lord Jesus Christ" (1 Thess. 1:3), there is implicit pressure for the readers to continue to exhibit in their lives such work, faith, and hope. In those thanksgivings where Paul includes a prayer report (2 Thess. 1:11–12; Phil. 1:9–11; Col. 1:9–14; also Rom. 1:10b), the challenge is no longer implicit but explicit: his readers know from the content of the apostle's prayer for them exactly what he expects from them. There is nothing subtle or hidden about Paul's desires for the Thessalonian church when he closes his thanksgiving in the second letter to this church with the prayer report: "To this end we also are praying always concerning you, that our God may make you worthy of the calling and may complete every desire of goodness and work of faith in power so that the name of the Lord Jesus may be glorified in you and you in him, according to the grace of our God and of our Lord Jesus Christ" (1:11–12).

Third, the thanksgiving has an "epistolary" or "foreshadowing" function. In modern movie jargon, it is a "preview of coming attractions" (Witherington 2006: 52). The thanksgiving anticipates not only the central themes and issues to be developed in the body of the letter but also the nature of the relationship that exists between Paul and the church as well as the overall tone of his correspondence to them.[4] As Schubert (1939: 77) observed already some time ago: "Each thanksgiving not only announces clearly the subject matter of the letter, but also foreshadows unmistakably its stylistic qualities, the degrees of intimacy and other important characteristics." In his treatment of the Pauline thanksgivings, O'Brien (1977: 263) also acknowledges this foreshadowing function as well as its other functions:

> Paul's introductory thanksgivings have a varied function: epistolary, didactic and paraenetic, and they provide evidence of his pastoral and/or apostolic concern for the addressees. In some cases one purpose may predominate while others recede into the background. But whatever the thrust of any passage, it is clear that Paul's introductory thanksgivings were not meaningless devices. Instead they were integral parts of their letters, setting the tone and themes of what was to follow.

Extent of the Passage

Determining the extent of the thanksgiving section in 1 Thessalonians is complicated because this letter presents not one but three expressions of thanks: (a) 1:2: "We

---

4. O'Brien (1977: 15): "We note in these periods an epistolary function, i.e., to introduce and indicate the main theme(s) of the letters."

give thanks to God always concerning you all" (Εὐχαριστοῦμεν τῷ θεῷ πάντοτε περὶ πάντων ὑμῶν, *Eucharistoumen tō theō pantote peri pantōn hymōn*); (b) 2:13: "And because of this we also give thanks to God constantly" (καὶ διὰ τοῦτο καὶ ἡμεῖς εὐχαριστοῦμεν τῷ θεῷ ἀδιαλείπτως, *kai dia touto kai hēmeis eucharistoumen tō theō adialeiptōs*); and (c) 3:9: "For what thanksgiving are we able to give to God concerning you?" (τίνα γὰρ εὐχαριστίαν δυνάμεθα τῷ θεῷ ἀνταποδοῦναι περὶ ὑμῶν, *tina gar eucharistian dynametha tō theō antapodounai peri hymōn*). According to Schubert (1939: 17–27), what appears to be three separate thanksgivings (1:2–5; 2:13; 3:9–13) is actually one long thanksgiving, with the two repetitions of the basic thanksgiving formula (2:13; 3:9) serving to unify the whole section of 1:2–3:13. Schubert also claims that, unlike Paul's other thanksgivings, which serve to *introduce* the body sections of their respective letters, the lengthy thanksgiving of 1:2–3:13 *is* the body of the letter: "Thus the conclusion is inevitable that the thanksgiving itself constitutes the main body of I Thessalonians. It contains all the primary information that Paul wished to convey; . . . the thanksgiving is the letter, i.e., the 'main body' of the letter" (Schubert 1939: 26). A significant number of scholars have found Schubert's argument convincing and so also view the thanksgiving in 1 Thessalonians as consisting of the lengthy section of 1:2–3:13.[5]

There are serious difficulties, however, with this conclusion. First, the length of the claimed thanksgiving section in 1 Thessalonians would be more than four times as long as any other recognized Pauline thanksgiving. Second, Schubert's position requires that the function of the thanksgiving in 1 Thessalonians (i.e., it serves as the body of the letter) differs greatly from all other Pauline thanksgivings (i.e., it serves as an introduction to the major issues and themes taken up in the body of the letter). Third, such a position works against the formal identification of some of the material found in chapters 1–3: a Pauline autobiographical section (2:1–12), an apostolic parousia (2:17–3:10), and two benedictions or "prayer-wishes" (3:11–13)—epistolary conventions that elsewhere in Paul's writings belong not to the thanksgiving but to the body of the letter. Fourth, the claimed thanksgivings of 2:13 and especially 3:9–10 differ formally in significant ways from the typical form of Paul's other thanksgivings, thereby suggesting that the apostle did not intend these two passages to be understood as thanksgiving formulas equivalent to the statement of thanksgiving found in 1:2–10.

In addition to these problems, there are compelling reasons for limiting the thanksgiving section to 1:2–10:

1. The contents of 1:2–10 (without the additional material of 2:1–3:10) introduce well the four major concerns taken up in the body of the letter, just as Paul's other thanksgivings do (see the third function of the thanksgiving section described above):

    a. The apologetic reference to Paul's original preaching ministry among the Thessalonians in 1:5a ("Our gospel was not among you in word alone but also in power—both in the Holy Spirit and much conviction") as well as

---

5. Best (1977: 65), for example, states: "The 'thanksgiving' in our letter appears to be much longer (1.2–3.13) than in Paul's other letters, though if Paul is evolving a new form and this is an early letter we need not expect consistency with the later letters." Similar conclusions are reached by Bjerkelund 1967: 125–38; Wiles 1974: 45–51, 175–76; O'Brien 1977: 141–66; Koester 1979: 36–37; Bruce 1982: 11; Lambrecht 1990; Malherbe 2000: 78–80, 130; Beale 2003: 44; Furnish 2007: 39.

the defense of the apostle's integrity in 1:5b ("as you know what kind of men we were among you because of you") foreshadow the lengthy defense of his integrity in 2:1–16. Also, the reference in 1:9a to Paul's original visit to Thessalonica by the striking term "visit" (εἴσοδον, *eisodon*)—a word not used by the apostle in any of his other letters—anticipates the opening verse of 2:1–16, where Paul claims that his "visit" (εἴσοδον, *eisodon*) among them was not "insincere" (2:1b; for this meaning of κενή, *kenē*, see the comment on this verse).

b. The theme of persecution found in 1:6b ("receiving the word in much affliction") is taken up briefly in 2:13–16 and at greater length in 3:1–5. There is also a significant lexical link between 1:6 ("and you became imitators, . . . receiving the word"; καὶ ὑμεῖς μιμηταὶ ἡμῶν ἐγενήθητε καὶ τοῦ κυρίου, δεξάμενοι τὸν λόγον, *kai hymeis mimētai . . . egenēthēte, . . . dexamenoi ton logon*) and 2:13–14 ("you received the word, . . . you became imitators"; ἐδέξασθε λόγον, . . . ὑμεῖς μιμηταὶ ἐγενήθητε, *edexasthe logon, . . . hymeis mimētai egenēthēte*).

c. The purpose of the Thessalonians' conversion, "to serve a living and true God" (1:9c), anticipates the exhortations to proper conduct in 4:1–12 and 5:12–22. The reference to the Thessalonians as "turning to God from idols" (1:9b) may foreshadow in a veiled way the specific subject of sexual immorality addressed in 4:3–8, since such behavior was commonly associated with the practices of some pagan cults (see comment on 4:3–8).

d. The eschatological subject of Christ's return, which is addressed indirectly in 1:3 ("the steadfastness of hope in our Lord Jesus Christ") and directly in 1:10a ("to wait for his Son from the heavens"), is covered at great length in 4:13–18 and 5:1–11. Two further clauses in 1:10b also look ahead in a more specific way to eschatological material treated in the body of the letter: First, the reference to Jesus's resurrection ("whom he *raised from the dead*") anticipates the appeal to Jesus's resurrection in 4:14 ("For since we believe that Jesus died and *rose again*, so through Jesus, God will bring with him those who have fallen asleep") as part of Paul's explanation regarding believers who die before Christ's return (4:13–18). Second, the reference to the final judgment ("Jesus, the one who rescues us from the coming *wrath*") foreshadows a similar reference to salvation from future wrath through Christ's work in 5:9 ("For God has destined us not for *wrath* but for the obtaining of salvation through our Lord Jesus Christ") as part of Paul's explanation regarding those who are alive at Christ's return (5:1–11). This reference to the final judgment in 1:10b also looks ahead to Paul's comments in 2:14–16, especially verse 16 ("God's *wrath* has come upon them at last").

In addition to these four major concerns, the thanksgiving of 1:2–10 anticipates other less weighty topics addressed later in the body of the letter:

e. The divine initiative in the conversion of the Thessalonians is presented in 1:4 ("your election/calling") as the ultimate cause for giving thanks. Although this theme is not developed in any substantive way in the letter, it does reappear throughout the correspondence, often in strategic locations (2:12; 3:3b; 4:7; 5:9, 24).

f. The theme of "joy" expressed in 1:6b ("with the joy that comes from the Holy Spirit") is picked up later, in 2:19–20 and 3:9.

g. In a general way the unparalleled vocative phrase "loved by God" (1:4) may look ahead to the ground of Paul's argumentation in 4:1–12. In 1:4 the apostle takes covenant language that was originally applied to Israel and reapplies it to the predominantly Gentile church in Thessalonica (see comment on 1:4). The appeals to holiness in 4:1–12 are similarly based on the new-covenant status that the Gentile believers in Thessalonica now enjoy (in addition to the comment on 4:1–12, see Weima 1996).

2. That some of the other thanksgiving sections end on an eschatological note (1 Cor. 1:7–8; Phil. 1:10; 2 Thess. 1:7–10) suggests that the thanksgiving of 1 Thessalonians closes at 1:10, with its reference to the return of Christ and the final judgment (on the eschatological climax as a transition from the thanksgiving to the letter body, see Sanders 1962: 348–62; Roberts 1986: 29–35; even Schubert [1939: 4–5] recognizes that an eschatological climax frequently marks the end of the thanksgiving). Furthermore, eschatological climaxes like that of 1:10 are used throughout 1 Thessalonians as a "sequence-terminating feature" (Johanson 1987: 86).

3. It is significant that 2:1 ("For you yourselves know . . .") opens with a disclosure formula—an epistolary convention that in Paul's Letters typically signals a transition to a new topic or unit of thought. In particular, the disclosure formula frequently marks, as it does here in 2:1, the beginning of the letter body (2 Cor. 1:8; Gal. 1:11; Phil. 1:12; see Rom. 1:13; Col. 2:1) and thus the end of the preceding thanksgiving section.

4. The vocative "brothers" (ἀδελφοί, *adelphoi*) in 2:1, especially when it is found in conjunction with a disclosure or an appeal formula, is frequently used in 1 Thessalonians, as in Paul's other letters, at the beginning of a new topic or section (e.g., 2:17; 4:1, 13; 5:1, 12).

5. The tone and subject matter of 1:2–10 (laudatory tone with a focus on the Thessalonian believers) differs significantly from that of 2:1–12 (defensive tone with focus on Paul and his coworkers), thereby suggesting a shift from one literary unit to another.

There is overwhelming evidence, therefore, that the thanksgiving section in 1 Thessalonians does not include the whole of 1:2–3:13 but is limited to 1:2–10 (so the majority of commentators, regardless of whether they adopt a thematic, epistolary, or rhetorical approach: see the charts in Jewett 1986: 216–21).

Structure of the Passage

A consideration of grammatical and epistolary features helps to identify the structure of 1:2–10. The thanksgiving section consists of four main clauses: verses 2–5, 6–7, 8, and 9–10 (contra Best 1977: 65, who states that 1:2–10 constitutes "one long untidily constructed sentence"; also Frame 1912: 85; Malherbe 2000: 105; McKinnish Bridges 2008: 21; Fee 2009: 19 sees "two very long and complex sentences: vv. 2–5 and 6–10"). The first main clause (vv. 2–5) is the thanksgiving proper and exhibits a pattern that is relatively consistent with that found in Paul's other thanksgiving sections (see the above discussion of "Form," under "Character of the Passage"):

Principal Verb of Thanksgiving:
"We give thanks to God always concerning you all" (1:2a)
Manner of Thanksgiving:
"by making mention of you in our prayers" (1:2b)
Cause of Thanksgiving:
"because we remember . . ." (1:3)
"because we know . . ." (1:4–5)

The final three main clauses (vv. 6–7, 8, 9–10) of the thanksgiving function as the "explanatory" unit and serve to elaborate on the cause for Paul's thanksgiving. The "and" (καί, *kai*) that opens the second clause (vv. 6–7) probably ought to be taken as a coordinating conjunction,[6] strengthening the link between this clause and the preceding verses. The presence of the explanatory conjunction "for" (γάρ, *gar*) at the beginning of both the third and fourth main clauses (vv. 8, 9–10) indicates that the ideas of these verses are closely connected to and thus further support the assertion of the second clause (vv. 6–7). The thanksgiving here in 1 Thessalonians lacks a concluding "prayer report," which is sometimes found at the close of this epistolary unit (see 2 Thess. 1:11–12; Phil. 1:9–11; Col. 1:9–14; also Rom. 1:10b).

A consideration of these grammatical and epistolary features, along with the content of the passage, leads to the following outline of 1:2–10:

A. The statement of thanksgiving (1:2a)
B. The manner of thanksgiving (1:2b)
C. The immediate cause of thanksgiving (1:3)
D. The ultimate cause of thanksgiving (1:4–5)
   1. God's election of the Thessalonians (1:4)
   2. The genuineness of the apostles' ministry to the Thessalonians (1:5)
E. Additional causes of thanksgiving (1:6–10)
   1. The exemplary life of the Thessalonians (1:6–7)
   2. The evangelistic activity of the Thessalonians (1:8)
   3. The conversion of the Thessalonians (1:9–10)

Exegesis and Exposition

[2]We give thanks to God always concerning you all, by making mention ⌜of you⌝ in our prayers, because we constantly [3]remember your work of faith and labor of love and steadfastness of hope in our Lord Jesus Christ before our God and Father, [4]because we know, brothers loved by God, your election, [5]namely, that ⌜our⌝ gospel was not among you in word alone but also in power—both in the Holy Spirit and ⌜ ⌝ much conviction, as you know what kind of men we were ⌜among⌝ you because of

6. Paul rarely begins sentences with καί (the technical term is *parataxis*: the use of καί in typical Semitic fashion instead of participles or subordinate clauses; see BDF §§458, 471), and when he does so, "in most cases it can be shown to be intentionally linking sentences that are coordinate in some way" (Fee 1994a: 45n30).

you; [6]and you on your part became imitators of us and of the Lord, receiving the word in much affliction with joy ⌐that comes from⌐ the Holy Spirit, [7]so that you became an ⌐example⌐ to all the believers in Macedonia and in Achaia. [8]For from you the word of the Lord has echoed forth not only in Macedonia and ⌐Achaia⌐, ⌐but⌐ in every place your faith toward God has gone forth, so that we have no need to say anything. [9]For they themselves report concerning ⌐us⌐ what kind of visit we had among you, and how you turned to God from idols in order to serve a living and true God [10]and to wait for his Son from the heavens, whom he raised from the dead, Jesus, the one who rescues us ⌐from⌐ the coming wrath.

A. The Statement of Thanksgiving (1:2a)

The opening words of the thanksgiving "We give thanks to God" (εὐχαριστοῦμεν τῷ θεῷ, *eucharistoumen tō theō*) introduce well the theme of the passage: thanksgiving to God for the vibrant faith and active Christian life of the Thessalonian believers. Despite the stereotyped nature of the thanksgiving formula, the rest of the passage and indeed the whole letter indicate that Paul is genuinely thankful to God for what has taken place in the Thessalonian church. The positive response of the Thessalonians to the gospel is a reality that motivates the apostle to speak first of all words of thanksgiving to God rather than words of congratulations to his audience or words of commendation to himself. Even though the Thessalonians are to be praised for their faith, love, and hope (1:3); their exemplary life amid persecution (1:6–7); their evangelistic activity (1:8); and their conversion (1:9–10); and even though Paul and his fellow missionaries are to be praised for the genuineness of their original ministry in Thessalonica (1:5), all of these good things that have happened in the Thessalonian church are ultimately due to God's work of election (1:4), and so God is the one to whom thanksgiving must be given.

1:2a

The thanksgiving to God by Paul is given "concerning you *all*" (περὶ πάντων ὑμῶν, *peri pantōn hymōn*).[7] Some have interpreted this prepositional phrase polemically, so that Paul here give thanks "not only for his faithful supporters, but for the idle, fainthearted, weak (5:14), and the ones who actually oppose him" (Wiles 1974: 180; see also Marshall 1983: 50; Weatherly 1996: 36; Fee 2009: 20). Although there is an obvious danger in reading too much into the occurrence of the adjective "all," it is important to note that only one other Pauline thanksgiving includes this word (Rom. 1:8; cf. 1 Cor. 1:4a; Phil. 1:3a; Col. 1:3; 2 Thess. 1:3a; Philem. 4a), so that its presence here cannot be easily dismissed as being merely "formulaic" (so Richard 1995: 46) or "simply part of the liturgical style of this section of the letter" (Malherbe 2000: 106).

---

7. In 1:2 the prepositional phrase "concerning you all" (περὶ πάντων ὑμῶν) can go either with the preceding main clause, "We give thanks to God," or the following participial clause, "by making mention." The pattern of Paul's other thanksgivings makes the former option more likely. This reading, however, results in there being no explicit direct object of the participial clause. Although the direct object "of you" is easily implied, a number of late MSS (see additional notes) have inserted the pronoun ὑμῶν ("by making mention *of you*").

Furthermore, the deliberate addition of "all" would certainly be in keeping with Paul's practice elsewhere of adapting the thanksgiving section so that it foreshadows issues addressed later in the body of the letter (see the "Literary Analysis" above for the general discussion of the three functions of the Pauline thanksgiving as well as the listing of the specific ways that 1 Thess. 1:2–10 foreshadows major concerns taken up in the rest of the letter). Finally, the intensity of Paul's deep love for the Thessalonian believers (see the next paragraph) and his care for them individually (2:11: "each one of you") provides further indirect evidence that the addition of "all" to the opening statement of thanksgiving may well be a deliberate attempt by the apostle to include all the believers in Thessalonica, including those who, later in the letter, will come under rebuke and may have been opposed to Paul and his appointed leaders in the church.

Whereas the adjective "all" does not normally occur in the opening statement of the Pauline thanksgiving, the adverb "always" (πάντοτε, *pantote*) is a regular feature of this epistolary section (2 Thess. 1:3; Rom. 1:10; 1 Cor. 1:4; Phil. 1:4; Philem. 4; Col. 1:3). This fact might naturally suggest that Paul's claim of "always" giving thanks to God for the Thessalonian believers, along with his following assertion (1:2–3) that he "constantly" (ἀδιαλείπτως, *adialeiptōs*) remembers them, is merely a rhetorical remark or epistolary nicety. But even though these claims are formulaic and somewhat hyperbolic, they may be more credible than first thought when one considers the intimate family language and imagery used in the letter to characterize the relationship between Paul and the Thessalonians (see Gaventa 1998: 24). In addition to addressing his readers as "brothers" (1:4; 2:1, 9, 14, 17; 3:7; 4:1, 10b, 13; 5:1, 4, 12, 14, 25), Paul says that his relationship to them was like "a nursing mother taking care of her own children" (2:7) and like "a father with his children" (2:11). The separation of Paul from the Thessalonians has resulted in his being "orphaned" from them (2:17). In light of the intimate parent-child relationship that existed between the apostle and his Thessalonian converts, it may well be true that Paul "always" gave thanks to God for them and "constantly" remembered them.

B. The Manner of Thanksgiving (1:2b)

1:2b

The main clause of 1:2a is followed by three dependent participial clauses:

> "making mention of you in our prayers" (1:2b)
> "remembering your work of faith and labor of love and steadfastness of hope . . ." (1:3)
> "knowing . . . your election" (1:4)

Although in terms of grammatical structure these three clauses are in a parallel relationship, in terms of meaning or function they are not. Whereas the first participial clause expresses the *manner* of giving thanks, the second and third clauses convey the *causes* or reasons for expressing gratitude to God (so, e.g., Ellicott 1880: 4; Hendriksen 1955: 46; Wanamaker 1990: 74; Richard 1995: 59; as well as the formal analysis of the Pauline thanksgivings by Jervis 1991: 91–92).

The manner, therefore, by which Paul and his fellow missionaries always give thanks to God for all the Thessalonian believers is "*by* making mention[8] of you in our prayers" (μνείαν ποιούμενοι ἐπὶ τῶν προσευχῶν ὑμῶν, *mneian poioumenoi epi tōn proseuchōn hymōn*). Here the reference to prayers, along with 3:10 ("praying night and day as earnestly as possible in order to see you face-to-face and complete the things that are lacking in your faith"), suggests a picture of Paul, Silvanus (Silas), and Timothy meeting daily for prayer and thanking God for the blessings evident in the lives of the converts in Thessalonica. The frequency of these prayers is indicated not only by the adverbs "always" and "constantly" (see comment on 1:2a) but also by the present tense (which highlights the ongoing or continuous nature of the action) of the participle "making mention" and the plural "prayers." Furthermore, as a Jew who came from the strict religious group of the Pharisees, Paul was certainly accustomed to the practice of regular prayer.

The content of these intercessory prayers—prayers by Paul not for himself but for his readers—clearly involves difficulties experienced by the church and areas where spiritual growth was needed (this conclusion is based by analogy on the "prayer reports" that conclude the thanksgiving section in Rom. 1:10; Phil. 1:9–11; Col. 1:9–14; and 2 Thess. 1:11–12). It is significant, however, that here, as elsewhere in his writings, Paul connects his intercessory prayers first of all with giving thanks to God rather than with petitioning God. Contrary to the practice of most contemporary believers, who think of prayer almost exclusively as a means to make known one's needs to God, Paul uses prayer primarily as a means to express his gratitude to God. Thus the Heidelberg Catechism (1563), a sixteenth-century Reformed confession, answers well the question about the need for Christians to pray by stating as the first reason: "Because prayer is the most important part of the thankfulness God requires of us" (Question and Answer 116).

The importance of prayer in Paul's ministry becomes readily apparent from a comparative analysis of the apostle's other thanksgiving sections. In virtually every occurrence of this epistolary unit, Paul makes mention of giving thanks to God for his readers by means of prayer (Rom. 1:9; Eph. 1:16; Phil. 1:4; Col. 1:3; 2 Tim. 1:3; Philem. 4) and/or includes a summary report of his actual prayers for them (Rom. 1:10; Phil. 1:9–11; Col. 1:9–14; 2 Thess. 1:11–12; the absence of such a reference in Galatians and 1 Corinthians almost certainly reflects the tensions experienced between Paul and those churches). That Paul

---

8. The phrase μνείαν ποιούμενοι, under the influence of the root meaning of the noun, could be translated in 1:2 as "making remembrance" (note also the occurrence of the same root in the participial clause in 1:3). Classical and nonclassical writers, however, use this phrase as a periphrasis of the simple verbal idea of "to make/do something for oneself," and this is probably the sense intended by Paul (so BDAG 841.7; see also Bruce 1982: 11–12; Richard 1995: 46).

valued intercessory prayer is also evident from his appeal at the end of the letter that the Thessalonians "pray also for us" (5:25).

C. The Immediate Cause of Thanksgiving (1:3)

1:3   The first reason *why* Paul and his fellow missionaries always give thanks to God is "because we constantly[9] remember your[10] work of faith and labor of love and steadfastness of hope in our Lord Jesus Christ before our God and Father" (μνημονεύοντες ὑμῶν τοῦ ἔργου τῆς πίστεως καὶ τοῦ κόπου τῆς ἀγάπης καὶ τῆς ὑπομονῆς τῆς ἐλπίδος τοῦ κυρίου ἡμῶν Ἰησοῦ Χριστοῦ ἔμπροσθεν τοῦ θεοῦ καὶ πατρὸς ἡμῶν, *mnēmoneuontes hymōn tou ergou tēs pisteōs kai tou kopou tēs agapēs kai tēs hypomonēs tēs elpidos tou kyriou hēmōn Iēsou Christou emprosthen tou theou kai patros hēmōn*).

This first or "immediate" reason for giving thanks in 1:3, which focuses on the activity of the Thessalonian believers, can be distinguished from the second or "ultimate" reason in 1:4, which focuses on the activity of God (so many commentators: Findlay 1891: 19; Frame 1912: 75; Hendriksen 1955: 46; Best 1977: 70; O'Brien 1977: 146; Richard 1995: 59; Holmes 1998: 44–45; Malherbe 2000: 109; Furnish 2007: 40, 42; Fee 2009: 27). Although this distinction between the two causes of thanksgiving is primarily a theological judgment by modern interpreters and not one explicitly made in the text, a similar pattern can be found in at least one other Pauline thanksgiving.[11] Additionally, the second cause of thanksgiving in 1:4 is distinguished from the first in 1:3 and emphasized somewhat by the addition of the striking vocative phrase "brothers loved by God" (see comment on 1:4).

The immediate cause of thanksgiving is for three things that the Thessalonians are doing: "your work of faith and labor of love and steadfastness of hope." Most commentators give attention to the *second* members of this triad—faith, love, and hope—rather than to the first: work, labor, and

9. At the end of 1:2, the adverb ἀδιαλείπτως (constantly) can be read with either the immediately preceding clause ("by constantly making mention") or this clause ("because we constantly remember"). Some have found the former option preferable because of the analogy with Rom. 1:9 and the pattern of the following clauses, where the participle is in the initial position (so, e.g., RSV, NEB, TNIV, GNT, NET, ESV, NLT, NJB, Milligan 1908: 6; Rigaux 1956: 361; Masson 1957: 18; Morris 1959: 50; Wanamaker 1990: 74; Richard 1995: 46; Fee 2009: 20–21). Most editors, translations, and commentators, however, choose the latter option on the grounds that adverbs are generally placed next to the verb that they modify (so, e.g., W-H, NA[28], UBS[4]; KJV, NIV, NRSV, NASB, JB, REB; Findlay 1891: 19; Dobschütz 1909: 64–65; Hendriksen 1955: 46; O'Brien 1977: 147; Bruce 1982: 11; Green 2002: 87; Beale 2003: 45). Happily, this issue, while difficult to settle with certitude, is not especially significant for the overall interpretation of the passage.

10. The personal possessive pronoun "your" (ὑμῶν) modifies all three of the following nouns (work, labor, steadfastness) and may well be in a position of emphasis.

11. The same pattern appears in the thanksgiving section in Philippians. O'Brien (1977: 150) states of 1 Thess. 1:4: "The relationship of this second causal participial clause to the immediate cause [1:3] is similar to that of the causal clause of Phil. 1:6, πεποιθὼς αὐτὸ τοῦτο, ὅτι . . . and the causal phrase ἐπὶ τῇ κοινωνίᾳ ὑμῶν . . . (Phil. 1:5). In both thanksgivings the ultimate basis (God's activity or prior action) appears at the end."

steadfastness. This is understandable given that these three virtues are found so often grouped together in the writings of Paul (1 Thess. 5:8; Rom. 5:1–5; 1 Cor. 13:13; Gal. 5:5–6; Eph. 4:2–5; Col. 1:4–5),[12] other NT writers (Heb. 6:10–12; 10:22–24; 1 Pet. 1:3–8, 21–22), and the early church (Barn. 1.4; 11.8; Polycarp, *Phil.* 3.2–3). Attention is also typically given to this triad because many believe it to be "a brief definition of true Christianity" (Calvin 1981: 239), "the quintessence of the God-given life in Christ" (Bornkamm 1971: 219), or "a shorthand summary of the essentials of Christianity" (Holmes 1998: 48).

The direct objects of the missionaries' act of remembering, however, are the *first* members of the triad, and so the emphasis is on the Thessalonians' "work, labor, and steadfastness" rather than their "faith, love, and hope." Nevertheless, the second members of the triad, as either subjective genitives or genitives of source,[13] are important in giving the origin or cause of the first members of the triad. The sense is captured well by the NIV, which renders these noun phrases as "your work produced by faith, your labor prompted by love, and your endurance inspired by hope." The seemingly formulaic character of the triad should not lead to the conclusion that Paul is merely mentioning three generic activities that could have been stated about any of his healthy congregations. Instead, the triad is connected specifically to the church of Thessalonica. The apostle has just received a largely positive report from the recently returned Timothy about the Thessalonian believers (3:6–10), and this good news causes Paul to give thanks to God for their "work of faith," "labor of love," and "steadfastness of hope."

The first noun phrase, "work of faith," is striking since it joins together rather intimately two nouns that are frequently found in Paul's Letters in an antithetical relationship with each other. But while the apostle often uses the plural "works" in a negative manner in opposition to faith, he does employ the singular "work" in a positive sense (Rom. 2:7; 13:3; 14:20; 1 Cor. 3:13–15; 15:58; 1 Thess. 5:13; 2 Thess. 1:11). Furthermore, although Paul was vehemently opposed to "legalism"—the belief that salvation comes through the works of the law, whether these works refer to acts of obedience to the law

12. Since this triad (faith, love, hope) first occurs in Paul's writings (as in 1:3), there is no need to suppose, as some have done, "that the triad in Paul is not his own creation, but something common and apostolic, perhaps a sort of compendium of the Christian life current in the early apostolic church" (Hunter 1961: 34–35; see the lengthy discussion of the possible source of this triad in Söding 1992: 38–64, and the more general analysis in W. Weiss 1993). Malherbe (2000: 103) rightly observes that Paul varies the order of the different elements in the triad, placing the one of greatest importance at the end, thus in the position of emphasis.

13. The genitives πίστεως (of faith), ἀγάπης (of love), and ἐλπίδος (of hope) are given various designations by commentators: e.g., "subjective" (MHT 3:67; Milligan 1908: 6; Dobschütz 1909: 65; Frame 1912: 76; Wiles 1974: 383; O'Brien 1977: 147; Best 1977: 67; Wanamaker 1990: 75; Malherbe 2000: 108; Witherington 2006: 58); "origin/source" (Lightfoot 1904: 10; Morris 1991: 51; Marshall 1983: 51); "descriptive" (Moore 1969: 25). As Hendriksen (1955: 47) points out, however, this variety in terminology "matters little," since the sense is basically the same: the first members of the triad (work, labor, steadfastness) are the result of the second members of the triad (faith, love, hope).

(traditional view) or to ethnic, Jewish, boundary markers (the so-called new perspective)—the apostle was by no means antinomian (against the law). As Morris (1991: 39) observes: "Paul is very emphatic that salvation is a matter of faith, not works, and he uses the very strongest of expressions to make clear that people are not saved by works of any kind. But when this truth is not in dispute he does not hesitate to speak of the good works that characterize the life of faith." Thus, in light of a proper understanding of Paul's statements of the law as a whole, the pairing of "work" and "faith" is readily understandable. The phrase "work of faith," then, refers to the Christian activity that results from faith—what Paul elsewhere refers to as "faith working itself out in acts of love" (Gal. 5:6).

Here Paul does not spell out what this "work" involves. The additional causes of thanksgiving in 1:6–10 might suggest that he is referring to the Thessalonians' evangelistic activities, especially preaching, through which they became examples to believers in Macedonia and Achaia (Hendriksen 1955: 48; Söding 1992: 71–72; Malherbe 2000: 108; Beale 2003: 46).[14] Another possibility is that the apostle has in view the outward and visible signs of a holy life, which testify to the Thessalonians' salvation in Christ and distinguish them from their unbelieving fellow citizens (Wanamaker 1990: 75).[15] The most likely option, however, is that Paul is thinking of the Thessalonians' loyalty to Christ (faith = "faithfulness": Best 1977: 68) amid persecution (1:6; Furnish 2007: 41: ". . . the congregation's continuing trust in God even in the face of hardships"). That the thanksgiving section looks ahead to the major themes taken up in the letter body strengthens the possibility that Paul's reference to "faith" here anticipates his multiple later references to the "faith" of the Thessalonian believers (1:8; 3:2, 5, 6, 7, 10; 5:8; 2 Thess. 1:3, 4, 11; 2:13; 3:2; see also the verbal form in 1 Thess. 1:7; 2:4, 10, 13; 4:14). The apostle's great concern about the faith of his Thessalonian readers reveals itself especially in his sending Timothy immediately back to the church "to strengthen you and comfort you concerning your faith" (3:2; see also 3:5, "to learn about your faith") in their trials and persecutions, in his great relief over the returning Timothy's "good news about your faith" (3:6; see also 3:7: "We were comforted . . . through this faith of yours"), and in his earnest and repeated prayers to come to them in person and "complete the things that are lacking in your faith" (3:10).

14. Malherbe (2000: 108) points out that elsewhere in Paul the noun "work" (ἔργον, *ergon*) refers to preaching (1 Cor. 3:13–15; Phil. 1:22; other NT examples: Acts 13:2; 14:26; 15:38).

15. Johanson (1987: 86) sees a link (what he calls a "general triadic conceptual recurrence") between the three noun phrases of 1:3 and the text of 1:9–10, in which "work of faith" is echoed by "how you turned to God from idols," "labor of love" is echoed by "to serve a living and true God," and "steadfastness of hope" is echoed by "to wait for his Son from heaven." If such a link between 1:3 and 1:9–10 were legitimate, the first noun phrase, "work of faith," would refer to the conversion of the Thessalonians, specifically to their abandonment of pagan gods. It is doubtful, however, that Paul intended 1:9–10 to echo the noun phrases of 1:3. Of the three links proposed by Johanson, only the third one seems justifiable, and even here there is only a very general connection to the theme of Christ's return.

The second noun phrase, "labor of love," can be easily misunderstood by English speakers since in that language this expression refers to doing various acts of service without hope for reward or praise. This phrase, however, means something different than doing things without the thought of personal gain. The parallel with the preceding noun phrase indicates that, as "work of faith" refers to the Christian activity that originates from faith, so "labor of love" refers to the deeds that stem from love. Although the point should not be pressed too much, the word "labor" (κόπος, *kopos*) is stronger than the preceding word "work" (ἔργον, *ergon*) and involves not just the notion of doing something but also includes an element of discomfort or hardship.

Here too Paul does not specify what activities of love he has in mind. One possibility is that Paul is referring to the evangelistic activities of the Thessalonian church, since "labor" is the term typically used by the apostle to describe the character of his own missionary activity (1 Thess. 2:9; 3:5; 2 Thess. 3:8; 1 Cor. 4:12; 2 Cor. 6:5; 11:23, 27; see further F. Hauck, *TDNT* 3:828–29; Malherbe 2000: 108). However, since the thanksgiving section looks ahead to the key themes of the letter body, a more likely interpretation is suggested: the apostle is thinking of the subject of love for others foreshadowed in the transitional prayer of 3:12–13 ("May the Lord cause you to increase and abound in love for one another") and taken up more fully in 4:9–12 so that the phrase "labor of love" refers rather generally to the love that the Thessalonians have demonstrated in their dealings with each other (Holmes 1998: 47; Fee 2009: 26). Paul ends the section of 4:9–12 by specifying how this mutual love ought to manifest itself: the believers in Thessalonica should not take advantage of the loving support of their fellow church members but instead work with their own hands (v. 11c) and so be dependent on no one (v. 12b). It may well be, therefore, that the phrase "labor of love" has in view the problem of the rebellious idlers who are addressed briefly in this letter (5:14 in addition to 4:11c, 12b) and extensively in the second correspondence (2 Thess. 3:6–15). The love for fellow members that characterized relationships within the Thessalonian church causes Paul to give thanks to God, even if some are wrongly taking advantage of such acts of charity.

The third noun phrase, "steadfastness of hope," stands in the final and thus climactic position in the triad (1 Cor. 13:13: "And now these three remain: faith, hope, and love. But the greatest of these is love"; see also the comment on 1 Thess. 5:8, where several factors reveal that the emphasis falls on the third and final element of "hope") and is the easiest of the three parallel phrases to understand. The word "steadfastness" (ὑπομονή, *hypomonē*) or its cognate is commonly used in both Thessalonian Letters and in the rest of the NT in connection with the difficulties and persecution faced by Christians (Rom. 5:3; 12:12; 2 Cor. 6:4; 2 Thess. 1:4; Luke 21:19; Heb. 10:32; 1 Pet. 2:20), especially in an eschatological context (Rom. 8:25; 2 Cor. 1:6; 2 Tim. 2:12; Mark 13:13), and both aspects are at work in 1:3. There is clear evidence in the Thessalonian Letters and elsewhere that the church in Thessalonica experienced significant opposition and affliction because of their newfound faith (1 Thess. 1:6b; 2:2b,

14–15; 3:1–5; 2 Thess. 1:4–7; see also 2 Cor. 8:1–2; Acts 17:5–7, 13). Paul and his fellow missionaries, therefore, give thanks to God for the Thessalonians' "steadfastness"—their endurance and ongoing faith even in the face of much affliction and opposition.

The "hope" from which this steadfastness originates is not a feeble wish or desperate desire that things will somehow turn out right in the end; rather, it is a confident belief "in our Lord Jesus Christ" (τοῦ κυρίου ἡμῶν ʼΙησοῦ Χριστοῦ, *tou kyriou hēmōn Iēsou Christou*).[16] Since Paul breaks the pattern of the two preceding noun pairs by adding this phrase here, it is possible to determine with a high degree of certainty what he specifically has in mind (contra Best 1977: 69, who states: "Paul may have some particular phase of the life of the Thessalonian church in mind when he made this reference, but if so it is lost to us"). In light of the eschatological concerns that permeate the letter, as well as the words of 1:10 ("to wait for his Son from the heavens, whom he raised from the dead, Jesus, the one who rescues us from the coming wrath") that conclude the thanksgiving section, it is clear that Paul is referring not merely to a *general* hope that the Thessalonians have in the person and work of Christ but to their very *specific* hope in Christ's imminent return from heaven to bring about their deliverance (Hendriksen 1955: 47; Wanamaker 1990: 76; Stott 1991: 30; Williams 1992: 27; Gaventa 1998: 26; Green 2002: 91; Furnish 2007: 42).

The first or immediate reason for giving thanks to God comes to a close with the prepositional phrase "before our God and Father" (ἔμπροσθεν τοῦ θεοῦ καὶ πατρὸς ἡμῶν, *emprosthen tou theou kai patros hēmōn*). There are three possibilities as to what this phrase modifies: (1) the participial "remembering" (so, e.g., RSV, NIV, NRSV, TNIV; Ellicott 1864: 6; Best 1977: 70; Marshall 1983: 52; Wanamaker 1990: 76; Richard 1995: 47; Malherbe 2000: 107; Green 2002: 88; Fee 2009: 22); (2) the three noun phrases "work of faith and labor of love and steadfastness of hope" (so Lenski 1937: 221; Rigaux 1956: 367–68; Bruce 1982: 12–13; D. Martin 1995: 56–57; Furnish 2007: 41); or (3) the third noun phrase, especially the word "hope" (Lightfoot 1904: 11–12; Milligan 1908: 7; Masson 1957: 19n1; Kelcy 1963: 55; Hendriksen 1955: 47n35; O'Brien 1977: 150; Morris 1991: 42n24; Williams 1992: 27; Witherington 2006: 59). Although many have found the first option to be most attractive, it is vulnerable to two objections. First, this reading would be tautological after the main clause, "We give thanks *to God*." Second, no good reason exists for this phrase to be standing so far removed from its referent. Although it is harder to decide between the second and third options, it is more natural to connect the

---

16. Although it is grammatically possible to take the phrase τοῦ κυρίου ἡμῶν ʼΙησοῦ Χριστοῦ (of our Lord Jesus Christ) with all three items in the triad (faith, love, and hope: so, e.g., Rigaux 1956: 367; Moore 1969: 25–26; Fee 2009: 22), it is more natural to see this phrase as working only with the noun that stands closest to it (so majority of commentators). Additionally, since the personal pronoun "your" is already doing triple duty by being linked with each item in the triad, it is less likely that the phrase "our Lord Jesus Christ" does so as well. Finally, it is best to take this phrase as an objective genitive after the verbal idea implicit in ἐλπίδος (hope): "hope *in* our Lord Jesus Christ."

phrase "before our God and Father" with the immediately preceding words, just as in 2:19 and 3:13. If so, the sense is not that the missionaries' act of remembering in prayer was done in the presence of God (first option) or that the Thessalonians' work, labor, and steadfastness were done in the presence of God (second option) but rather that the hope of the Thessalonians and of the missionaries (note the shift to the first person: "*our* Lord Jesus Christ, . . . *our* God and Father") in Christ's return was a hope they manifested together in the presence of the Father. The addition of this phrase has the rhetorical effect of adding more weight to Paul's praise of the Thessalonians, since God is brought in as a witness to the mutual hope that they have in Christ's return.

D. The Ultimate Cause of Thanksgiving (1:4–5)

1. God's Election of the Thessalonians (1:4)

The second or "ultimate" reason why Paul and his fellow missionaries always give thanks to God is "because we know, brothers loved by God, your election" (εἰδοτες, ἀδελφοὶ ἠγαπημένοι ὑπὸ τοῦ θεοῦ, τὴν ἐκλογὴν ὑμῶν, *eidotes, adelphoi ēgapēmenoi hypo tou theou, tēn eklogēn hymōn*).

1:4

The mention of "our God and Father" at the end of the previous verse serves as a natural transition from the focus in 1:3 on the Thessalonians' response to the call of God to the emphasis here in 1:4 on God's call itself. The former (the human response) may be logically the result of the latter (the divine initiative), but Paul has likely mentioned it first because it is the only one of the two actions that can be readily observed (Best 1977: 70). Paul's knowledge of their election, therefore, is based on the holy lives that the Thessalonians manifest through their "work of faith and labor of love and steadfastness of hope." Yet even these actions of work, labor, and steadfastness are ultimately not human accomplishments but activities that originate from faith, love, and hope—all of which are gifts from God. This is why Paul directs his thanksgiving not to the Thessalonian Christians but to God.

Before giving the ultimate cause of thanksgiving as "your election," Paul addresses the Thessalonians directly with the striking vocative phrase "brothers loved by God" (*adelphoi ēgapēmenoi hypo tou theou*). Already prior to the NT era, the word "brother" in the Greco-Roman world was used in a broader religious sense to refer to members of the same religious group (for texts, see ἀδελφός in H. F. von Soden, *TDNT* 1:144–46). The use of this word by Christians, however, was primarily influenced by Jewish practice (e.g., Exod. 2:11; Deut. 15:3, 12; Ps. 22:22 [21:23 LXX]; Jer. 22:18; Zech. 7:9; 1QS 6.10, 22; CD 6.20–21; Josephus, *J.W.* 2.122). This word fit especially well into the conviction of Christians that they were the adopted "children" of God (Rom. 8:14–23; Gal. 3:26; 4:4–7) and could call him their "father" (Rom. 8:15; Gal. 4:6) and his Son, Jesus Christ, their "brother" (Rom. 8:29). In this they were following the lead of Jesus himself, who said about the crowds following him: "Here are my mother and my brothers! Whoever does God's will is my brother and sister and mother" (Mark 3:34 NRSV; also Matt. 12:49–50; Luke

8:20). It is not surprising, therefore, that "brother" became a favorite term in Christianity (it occurs in Paul's Letters some 130 times and is found in every other NT writing except the very brief letters of 2 John and Jude) to describe not just male believers but all Christians.

In the two brief letters of Paul to the Thessalonians, the vocative plural "brothers" (ἀδελφοί) occurs twenty-one times[17]—the highest occurrence per number of verses by far of any of his extant letters. This testifies to the close and warm relationship that the apostle shares with his converts in Thessalonica (note also the other "familial" terms used in 1 Thess. 2: "infants" [2:7b]; "nursing mother" [2:7c]; "father" [2:11]; "orphans" [2:17]). Wanamaker (1990: 77) stresses the *sociological* function that this word has in contributing to a strong sense of kinship among the Thessalonian converts: "In this way they gained a new social identity as former kinship and social ties broke down under the demands of their new religious commitments." While this is an important point, it should not be overlooked that the vocative "brothers" in Paul's Letters (as in other biblical and nonbiblical letters of that day) also has an important *literary* function: as a transition marker indicating either a major or minor shift in the apostle's argument. The presence of the vocative "brothers" here in 1:4, therefore, is likely intended to distinguish and stress this second cause of thanksgiving from the first cause given in the previous verse.

The second cause of thanksgiving is further emphasized by the addition of the remarkable participial phrase "loved by God," which is not found elsewhere in Paul's writings (normally the adjective ἀγαπητός [*agapētos*, dear, beloved] is used: 1 Thess. 2:8; Rom. 1:7; 1 Cor. 15:58; etc.; yet see the verbal in 2 Thess. 2:13; Col. 3:12). As with the word "church" in the opening verse of the letter (see comment on 1:1), here too we have an instance of language that originally applied to Israel (Deut. 32:15; 33:12; Pss. 60:5; 108:6; Isa. 44:2; Jer. 11:15; 12:7; Sir. 45:1; Bar. 3:36; etc.) now being reapplied to the Christian church. Especially in this context where the emphasis is on God's election of the Thessalonian believers (see discussion below), there can be little doubt that Paul's application of terms originally reserved for Israel to the predominantly Gentile congregation of Thessalonica is not coincidental but stems from his conviction that the church—made up of both Jewish and Gentile Christians—now constitutes the renewed Israel of God (see Thielman 1994: 73–74; Weima 1996: esp. 101–3). As Marshall (1990: 262) observes: "It is clear [from the phrase "loved by God" in 1:4] that by this early stage in his thinking Paul has already developed the concept of the church as the Israel of God. The conviction that God's love is now extended to the church composed of Jews and Gentiles is already present, and it does not need to be defended in any way. The church has inherited the position of Israel."

After addressing the Thessalonians with the significant phrase "brothers loved by God," Paul gives the second reason for giving thanks to God: "because

---

17. The vocative "brothers" occurs fourteen times in the first letter and seven times in the second. The word appears an additional seven times in cases other than the vocative form of address.

we know . . . your election." Although this is the only occurrence of the noun "election" (ἐκλογή, *eklogē*) in 1 Thessalonians,[18] this subject nevertheless is important in the letter. This is evident not only by the prominent position that this theme has in the thanksgiving section (election is given as the ultimate cause of thanksgiving), but also by the language of God's "calling" and "appointing" found elsewhere in the letter (2:12; 3:3b; 4:7; 5:9, 24). Thus the understanding that the well-being of the readers rests ultimately not in their own hands but in the work of God—that notion stands as the backdrop to the whole letter.

By identifying the Thessalonians as God's elect, Paul once again (see comment on "church" in 1:1 and "loved by God" in this verse) applies in a striking manner language formerly reserved for Israel to the church. As Furnish (2007: 43) notes: "It is a radical departure from the Jewish view of divine election, according to which Israel alone constitutes God's people, when Paul identifies this *Gentile* congregation as beloved and chosen of God." Although the specific word "election" (ἐκλογή, *eklogē*) does not occur in the LXX, the concept runs throughout the OT: God chooses Abraham (Gen. 12:1–3; Neh. 9:7) as well as his offspring, the people of Israel, "out of all the nations" to be his "treasured possession, . . . a kingdom of priests and a holy nation" (Exod. 19:5–6; see also Deut. 4:37; 1 Kings 3:8; Isa. 41:8, 9; 43:10; 44:1, 2; 45:4; 49:7). In the NT this vocabulary is deliberately transferred to the Christian community (Rom. 8:33; 9:11; 11:5, 7, 23, 29; 16:13; 1 Cor. 1:27, 28; Eph. 1:4–6; 2 Thess. 2:13, 16; Col. 3:12; 2 Tim. 2:10, 19; Titus 1:1; 1 Pet. 1:10; 2:5, 9–10). That Paul uses the term "election" without explaining any of this implies that this subject must have been an integral part of his original preaching in Thessalonica; thus he could be confident that his readers would know well what he had in mind.

Many today find the teaching of election difficult to accept because it appears to exclude human freedom. Thus they refuse to see in this teaching the primary role of God in the work of salvation and understand election as being dependent on human choice (e.g., Williams [1992: 28] says of 1 Thess. 1:4: "If we choose to be in Christ, we have been chosen by God. . . . Our choice makes us his elect"). Yet when one considers what Paul says not only here but also elsewhere, it seems quite clear that the apostle believed election to be exclusively an act of God (see Rom. 8:33; 9:11; 11:5, 7, 28; 16:13; 1 Cor. 1:27, 28; Eph. 1:4–6; Col. 3:12–17; 2 Tim. 2:10, 19; Titus 1:1). Still others consider election to be not just difficult but, more than that, offensive; thus they misrepresent this teaching by depicting God as an arbitrary tyrant who saves or damns people without rhyme or reason. Yet here in 1:4, as in other occasions in Paul's Letters (2 Thess. 2:13; Eph. 1:4), election is intimately linked to God's love. The Thessalonians' election is not the result of God's capricious choice but of his great love.

18. The noun ἐκλογή occurs only five times in Paul's Letters (here in 1:4; Rom. 9:11; 11:5, 7, 28), and the verbal form ἐκλέγομαι is found only four times (1 Cor. 1:27–28 [3x] and Eph. 1:4).

In the debate to discover *what* Paul means by his use of the term "election," it is important not to lose sight of *how* he uses this teaching. The apostle's reference to election, while ostensibly a second cause for thanksgiving, functions both to comfort and to challenge the Thessalonian believers. First and foremost, it comforts the church because they know that, despite the heavy opposition and ostracism that they endure from their fellow citizens (2:14), their salvation and final destiny rests not in their own imperfect abilities and uncertain strength but in "the living and true God" (1:9), who has chosen them.[19] Yet the knowledge of their election also implicitly challenges them (recall the "exhortative" function of the thanksgiving section) to continue to live in a manner appropriate to their calling.[20]

2. The Genuineness of the Apostles' Ministry to the Thessalonians (1:5)

1:5   The reference to the Thessalonians' election becomes an occasion for Paul to introduce the topic of his and his coworkers' sincere motives and conduct during their original ministry in Thessalonica: "Our gospel was not among you in word alone but also in power—both in the Holy Spirit and much conviction, as you know what kind of men we were among you because of you."

A comparison of the thanksgiving section in 1 Thessalonians with the thanksgiving sections of Paul's other letters highlights the unique character of this verse. In all other thanksgivings Paul focuses primarily *on his readers* and his thanksgiving to God for *them*; here in 1:5 the apostle also focuses heavily on *himself* and the righteous character of *his* activity among them. One is struck, however, not just by the mere presence of this unparalleled statement in a thanksgiving section but also by the prominent location (prior to the additional causes of thanksgiving in 1:6–10), the length, and the apparent defensive tone of this verse. For in addition to using an antithetical construction (1:5a), Paul here deviates from his typical manner of referring to the gospel and employs the personal pronoun "our" (τὸ εὐαγγέλιον ἡμῶν, *to euangelion hēmōn*),[21] thereby stressing the crucial role that he and his fellow

19. Donfried (2002: 129–30) and Fee (2009: 31) rightly note that the reference to election in 1:4, along with the references to "brothers" and being "loved by God," are in direct response to the church's suffering at the hands of their fellow citizens.

20. Wanamaker (1990: 77–78) argues that the reference to "election" in 1:4 has an important sociological function. The term ἐκλογή, like the word ἀδελφοί, should be categorized as "the language of belonging"—language that helps to create among recent converts a sense of group identity and exclusiveness over against the various mystery religious and pagan cults. Wanamaker concludes: "Thus the belief of the Thessalonians in their election by God was of tremendous social significance, since on the one hand it gave them a new identity and sense of belonging to the saved community of God, while on the other it helped symbolically to annihilate the world of their previous social existence, an important and necessary step if they were to remain converted" (78).

21. The term εὐαγγέλιον occurs sixty times in the Pauline corpus, very often accompanied by the phrase "of God" or "of Christ." The personal pronoun "our" or "my" with "gospel" is found only six times (Rom. 2:16; 16:25; 2 Cor. 4:3; 1 Thess. 1:5; 2 Thess. 2:14; 2 Tim. 2:8). The

missionaries played in the Thessalonians' conversion and their experience of election. Paul also feels the need to use not one but three nouns ("power," "Holy Spirit," and "much conviction"; on the interrelationship of these three nouns, see exegesis below) to highlight the sincere nature of his preaching activity among them. But even this is not enough, apparently, to make his point. Thus he adds a comparative clause (1:5b) by which he appeals to the Thessalonians' firsthand knowledge of his and his coworkers' exemplary conduct among them. When these unique features of 1:5 are combined with the fact that the thanksgiving section typically functions to foreshadow the central concerns of the letter as a whole, it becomes clear that Paul in 1 Thessalonians is very much concerned with defending his character and already here in 1:5 anticipates the lengthy defense that he will present at the beginning of the letter body (2:1–16).[22]

The apologetic comment of 1:5 is connected to the preceding participial phrase of 1:4 by the conjunction ὅτι, which most commentators understand *causally* ("because . . .": e.g., Frame 1912: 78–79; O'Brien 1977: 151–52; Morris 1991: 45n27; Wanamaker 1990: 78; Williams 1992: 29; Richard 1995: 48; Holmes 1998: 49; Green 2002: 93–94). According to this view, 1:5 provides additional proof (the other proof being found in 1:3) of the Thessalonians' election. Two factors, however, indicate that the ὅτι here has an *epexegetical*, or *explanatory*, function ("namely, that . . ."; see BDAG 732.2, "marker of explanatory clauses"), giving "the historical occasion and manner of their election" (Best 1977: 73; so also, e.g., Lightfoot 1904: 12; Milligan 1908: 8; Rigaux 1956: 372–73; Johanson 1987: 83–84; Fee 1994a: 40n4; Malherbe 2000: 110; Fee 2009: 31n20). First, when ὅτι occurs, as it does here, after the verb "to know" (εἰδέναι, *eidenai*) and a direct object, it always appears to be epexegetical (see esp. 1 Thess. 2:1; also Rom. 13:11; 1 Cor. 16:15; 2 Cor. 12:3–4). Second, the references in the verse to "power," the "Holy Spirit," and "much conviction" function as proof not of the Thessalonians' election but of the sincere nature of the preaching of Paul and his fellow missionaries. Viewing the ὅτι clause as epexegetical does not, however, completely remove the awkwardness of the shift in this verse from the topic of thanksgiving for God's election of the Thessalonians (v. 4) to the topic of the genuineness of the apostles' ministry to the Thessalonians (v. 5)—a somewhat clumsy transition that is no doubt the result of Paul's deep concern in this letter to defend himself.

The first half of the verse (1:5a) defends the genuineness of the apostles' preaching through the use of an antithetical statement (not *x* but *y*):

---

use of "our" here in 1:5 emphasizes not the content of the gospel (i.e., a version of the gospel unique to Paul) but the preaching of the gospel by Paul and his coworkers (Wanamaker 1990: 78; Richard 1995: 48). As Malherbe (2000: 110) states: "Paul draws attention to his part (*hēmōn*) in the proclamation of the gospel."

22. Many recent commentators deny the apologetic function of 2:1–16 and thus fail to recognize the defensive function of 1:5, believing instead that in both places Paul is merely interested in presenting himself as an example to follow. For a fuller discussion of this issue, see Weima 1997a as well as the comments on 2:1–16 below.

Our gospel was *not* among you in word alone
but also in power—both in the Holy Spirit and much conviction.

While the sense of this statement as a whole is relatively clear, the inter-relationship and meaning of its constituent parts are not. At first blush, it would appear that Paul is contrasting "word" (λόγος, *logos*) with three things: "power" (δύναμις, *dynamis*), the "Holy Spirit" (πνεῦμα ἅγιος, *pneuma hagios*), and "much conviction" (πληροφορία πολλή, *plērophoria pollē*). This view sees the three nouns as a "triad" (Collins 1984: 192n95; Thomas 1978: 244) and thus in a parallel relationship with each other (so virtually all commentators).

A closer consideration of a textual matter in the verse, however, suggests another view. Although the first two nouns are each preceded by the preposition ἐv, the third noun is probably not,[23] thereby breaking the pattern of a parallel relationship between the three nouns. This in turn implies that the contrast is only between "word" and "power" (as is the case also in 1 Cor. 2:1–5 and 4:19–20) and that the subsequent two nouns ("Holy Spirit" and "much conviction") are intended to qualify "power" (Moffatt 1897: 24; Fee 1992: 170; Richard 1995: 48, 65; Fee 2009: 33–34). This sense is captured in the following translation and punctuation of 1:5a: "Our gospel was not among you in word alone but also in power—both in the Holy Spirit and much conviction."

In defending the sincere character of his preaching among them, Paul claims that his gospel was not "in word alone but also in power." The addition of the word "alone" (μόνον, *monon*) is important: it shows that the apostle was not denigrating the importance of presenting the gospel in word (i.e., preaching) but rather distinguishing his preaching, whose genuineness is attested by the accompaniment of "power," from the kind of insincere preaching that consists in word "alone." Paul thus anticipates the charges implied in 2:1–12 that he is no different than the wandering philosophers and teachers of his day, who among other things used a "word of flattery" (2:5) for personal gain and glory. The apostle dispels any such notion by asserting that the genuineness of his preaching was verified by the presence of "power."[24]

But what specifically does Paul have in mind in his reference to "power"? Many believe that the apostle is referring to miracles (so, e.g., W. Grundmann, *TDNT* 2:311; Giblin 1967: 45; Marshall 1983: 53–54; Wanamaker 1990: 79; D. Martin 1995: 58) and appeal for support to passages indicating that miracles regularly accompanied the ministry of not only Paul (2 Cor. 12:12; Rom. 15:18–19; see also Acts 14:3; 15:12) but other believers as well (Gal. 3:5; see

23. In 1:5 although some MSS have ἐv before πληροφορίᾳ, there is stronger MS support for its omission (see additional notes).

24. Although the historical context is somewhat different, note 1 Cor. 4:19–20, where Paul, in order to distinguish himself and his authoritative position from certain arrogant, or puffed-up, leaders in the Corinthian church who are opposed to his leadership, similarly makes use of the contrast between "word" and "power": "But I will come to you soon, if the Lord wills, and I will find out not the talk [λόγον] of these arrogant people but their power [δύναμιν]. For the kingdom of God does not consist in talk [ἐv λόγῳ] but in power [ἐv δυνάμει]."

Heb. 2:3–4). Others observe that the noun "power" refers to miracles only in the plural, in contrast to the singular used in 1:5 (note, however, that the singular is used in Rom. 15:18–19 to refer to miracles). Consequently, they see Paul here referring to the power from the Holy Spirit that causes the spoken word to penetrate the hearts and minds of its hearers (so, e.g., Ellicott 1864: 8; Hendriksen 1955: 51; Best 1977: 75; Fee 1994a: 44). Although this latter view probably comes closer to Paul's intent, the former is also part of the picture. Paul's point is that his gospel message was not only a "heard word" but also an "experienced power." In other words, the message of his gospel became an experienced reality in the hearts and lives of the Thessalonians through the power of the Holy Spirit. That same power of the Holy Spirit undoubtedly also manifested itself in miracles (see the texts listed above) and other ways (e.g., prophetic utterances; see 1 Thess. 5:19–20), and these "signs and wonders" would have further convinced the Thessalonians of the truth of Paul's proclamation.

The ambiguity of his reference to "power" leads Paul to qualify this word with the compound phrase "both with the Holy Spirit and much conviction." The first part of this phrase gives the divine *source* of the power: it is the "Holy Spirit"[25] who makes effective the preached word of the apostles in the lives of the Thessalonians. The second part of the phrase gives the *consequence* of this Spirit-given power: "much conviction."[26] But who experiences this conviction? One possibility is that the Thessalonian believers are in view. Bruce (1982: 14), for example, states: "The reference is to the Thessalonians' deep inward persuasion of the truth of the gospel, a token of the Holy Spirit's work in their hearts, more impressive and more lasting than the persuasion produced by spectacular or miraculous signs" (see also Findlay 1891: 53; Masson 1957: 20–21; Moore 1969: 27; Witherington 2006: 71n34). The difficulty with this view, however, is that Paul's focus throughout 1:5 is on himself and his fellow missionaries rather than on the Thessalonian believers. Thus the phrase "much conviction" is best seen as referring to the boldness and confidence with which the missionaries presented their message (so most commentators,

25. There is no need to conclude from the absence of the definite article before πνεύματι ἁγίῳ that Paul does not have the personal Holy Spirit in view but instead an impersonal divine spirit that inspires people (so MHT 3:175; see also Best 1977 : 75, who seems overly concerned against interpreting this verse in terms of a developed trinitarian doctrine, and Richard 1995: 69). The apostle frequently omits the definite article before πνεῦμα ἅγιος, especially in prepositional phrases where the context indicates that he is referring to the Holy Spirit (in addition to 1:6, see Rom. 5:5; 9:1; 14:17; 15:13, 16, 19; 1 Cor. 12:3; 2 Cor. 6:6; see also BDF §255). Therefore, with the references to the "Father" and the "Lord Jesus Christ" in 1:1, we have a reference to all three persons of the Trinity given within the opening five verses of the letter (see also 4:6b–8).

26. The noun πληροφορία occurs only once elsewhere in Paul's Letters (Col. 2:2; see Heb. 6:11; 10:22; 1 Clem. 42.3), although the verb πληροφορεῖν is somewhat more frequent (Rom. 4:21; 14:5; Col. 4:12; 2 Tim. 4:5, 17). The word means either (1) "fullness" or (2) "conviction, assurance." Despite Rigaux's (1956: 277–79) vigorous argument for the first meaning, this neither fits the context of 1:5 nor makes sense with the presence of the adjective "much" (as Best [1977: 75] explains, "fullness" is an absolute, so it is impossible to have more or less of it).

e.g., Lightfoot 1904: 13; Frame 1912: 81; Hendriksen 1955: 51; Holtz 1986: 47; Marshall 1983: 54; Malherbe 2000: 112)—a point that Paul emphasizes again in 2:2 ("We had courage in our God to speak to you the gospel of God in spite of great opposition"). This "conviction," so evident in Paul's preaching, along with the designation of the Holy Spirit as the source of the power to make the apostle's "word" or message effective in the lives of the hearers together provide a powerful defense of the sincere nature of his preaching.

The second half of the verse (1:5b) continues Paul's apologetic concern, this time by appealing to the firsthand knowledge that the Thessalonians have about the virtuous conduct of himself and his coworkers: "as you know what kind of men we were among you because of you." The expression "you know" (οἴδατε, *oidate*), a simplified form of the disclosure formula (Mullins 1964), is the first occurrence of a number of the letter's direct appeals to the Thessalonians' recollection to confirm the accuracy of what Paul is telling them (2:1, 2, 5, 10, 11; 3:3, 4; 4:2; 5:2; see also 4:6, 11). The use of repeated appeals to the readers' firsthand knowledge is an effective and persuasive strategy adopted by the apostle, since most people tend to trust their own experience. It is as if Paul is saying to his Thessalonian readers: "Don't listen to what your fellow citizens are saying about how we acted while we were with you. Listen instead to yourselves. You were there. You know from firsthand experience what kind of men we were among you." Paul's use of this kind of persuasive appeal here provides further evidence that 1:5 foreshadows the lengthy defense of 2:1–12, since it is in that section of the letter where Paul most frequently adopts the same strategy of appealing to the personal knowledge that the Thessalonians have of the "holy, righteous, and blameless" (2:10) conduct of himself and his fellow missionaries during their original ministry among them.[27] But however much Paul is interested in defending himself, his concern is ultimately not for himself but for his readers: it is "because of you" (δι' ὑμᾶς, *di' hymas*) that he demonstrated a blameless conduct. Paul was most concerned for the spiritual well-being of his readers and thus made sure that his behavior matched what he preached.

E. Additional Causes of Thanksgiving (1:6–10)

1. The Exemplary Life of the Thessalonians (1:6–7)

1:6 Paul leaves his apologetic concern behind for the moment (he will address it at length in 2:1–16) and returns to the overall theme of 1:2–10, namely, giving thanks to God for the vibrant faith and active Christian life of the Thessalonian believers: "and you on your part became imitators of us and of the Lord, receiving the word in much affliction with joy that comes from the Holy Spirit, so that you became an example to all the believers in Macedonia and in Achaia" (1:6–7).

27. So also Fee 2009: 36: "This [the appeal in v. 5b] is in clear anticipation of the defense of the apostles', especially Paul's, own character that will be picked up in 2:1–12."

There is a marked shift from 1:5, which concentrates on Paul's mission-founding visit to Thessalonica, to 1:6–7, which focuses on the response of the Thessalonians to that visit (a transition signaled by the double reference to the readers at the end of the previous verse ["among *you* because of *you*"] and the emphatic pronoun "you"[28] at the beginning of 1:6). This shift is the first of three similar movements in the opening chapters of the letter:

Paul's mission-founding visit	The response of the Thessalonians
1:5	1:6–8
1:9a	1:9b–10
2:1–12	2:13–16

The clear shift in content here in 1:6 has caused virtually all editors of the Greek text and modern translators to put a full stop at the end of 1:5, thereby beginning a new sentence with 1:6–7. The grammar, however, suggests that 1:6–7 still has a close connection with the preceding verses. As noted above (see "Structure of the Passage"), the "and" (καί, *kai*) that opens this clause probably ought to be taken as a coordinating conjunction (*parataxis*: see BDF §§458, 471) that functions to strengthen the link between 1:6–7 and the preceding verses.[29] Therefore, even though 1:6–7 (as well as the subsequent clauses of 1:8 and 1:9–10) give additional reasons for thanksgiving (hence the heading for 1:6–10), it must not be overlooked that this clause is closely connected to the ultimate cause of thanksgiving: God's election of the Thessalonians.

The first "additional cause of thanksgiving" to which Paul draws his readers' attention is that "you on your part became imitators of us and of the Lord" (ὑμεῖς μιμηταὶ ἡμῶν ἐγενήθητε καὶ τοῦ κυρίου, *hymeis mimētai hēmōn egenēthēte kai tou kyriou*). Although the *vocabulary* of imitation, either in its noun (μιμητής, *mimētēs*) or verbal (μιμέομαι, *mimeomai*) form, is not very frequent in Paul's Letters (1 Thess. 1:6; 2:14; 2 Thess. 3:7, 9; 1 Cor. 4:16; 11:1; Phil. 3:17; see Eph. 5:1), the *idea* of imitation is quite common. The apostle holds up not only himself (in addition to the aforementioned texts, see 1 Cor. 7:7–16; Gal. 4:12–20; Phil. 1:30; 4:9a) but also others (God: Eph. 5:1; Christ: 1 Thess. 1:6; 1 Cor. 11:1; Phil. 2:5–11; the churches of Judea: 1 Thess. 2:14; Timothy: Phil. 2:19–24; Epaphroditus: Phil. 2:25–30) as examples or models to

---

28. The pronoun ὑμεῖς is emphasized both by its placement (in 1:6 at the head of the sentence) and its presence (the pronoun is redundant, since the subject is already expressed in the main verb ἐγενήθητε).

29. Fee (1994a: 45–46; 2009: 37) observes that this link is obscured somewhat by the presence of the comparative clause in 1:5b ("as you know . . ."). He thus presents the following structure of 1:4–6 (abbreviated to show its essential parts):

Knowing your election,
> *that* our gospel came [ἐγενήθη] to you . . . with power,
>> (just as you know how we were toward you),
> *and* you became [ἐγενήθητε] imitators of us . . .

A number of earlier commentators have similarly noted with respect to the grammar of 1:6–7 that, though "the sentence is getting to be independent, ὅτι (v. 5) is still in control" (Frame 1912: 82; so also de Boer 1962: 114; Kelcy 1963: 60).

be emulated.[30] The theme of imitation, therefore, plays an important though sometimes misunderstood role in Paul's theology.

The misunderstanding of the imitation theme in Paul usually stems from reading too heavily the apostle's statements through the eyes of our contemporary cultural attitudes and concerns. For example, the individualism so characteristic of modern (mostly Western) civilization can easily lead to the notion that the imitation of another person involves the denial of one's true and unique identity and that such a person is really a "fake" or "phony." Or again, the contemporary concern with patriarchalism and hierarchical relationships can quickly create the conviction that any person urging others to imitate him is guilty of arrogance and an abuse of power. Castelli (1991), for example, identifies Paul's language of imitation as a "discourse of power" by which the apostle reinforces the hierarchical relationship between himself and his converts, suppresses any dissident voices, and perpetuates his position of power in the churches.

While Paul's use of the imitation theme may in an indirect way serve to reaffirm his position of authority,[31] a number of factors ought to be recognized before accusing the apostle of egoism and a manipulative use of power (see Gaventa 1998: 28–31; Clarke 1998: 329–59):

a. The notion of imitating some sort of moral exemplar was quite common in the ancient world since philosophers and teachers were expected to impart to their disciples not only their instruction (*logos*) but also their conduct and behavior (*ethos*) (e.g., Isocrates, *Demon.* 4.11; Seneca, *Ep.* 6.5–6; 7.6–9; 11.8–10; Quintilian, *Inst.* 2.28; Philostratus, *Vit. Apoll.* 1.19; 4 Macc. 9:23; 2 Macc. 6:27–28; see also Malherbe 1986: 164–65; Fiore 1986; M. Martin 1999: 41). Thus not only is Paul following a widespread practice of his day, but also his failure to make use of the imitation theme might have opened himself up to charges that he considered himself an unfitting or unworthy teacher for his followers to emulate.

b. Paul's call to imitate himself is rooted not in his own authority but in his imitation of Christ (1 Cor. 11:1: "Be imitators of me, as I am of Christ"; this is probably a fuller expression of what we find here in 1:6: "And you on your part became imitators of us and of the Lord," meaning "And you on your part became imitators of us [as we] also [are imitators] of the Lord"; so Richard 1995: 67). In this regard, Paul's

30. Getty (1990: 278): "The notion of imitation is missing only in Romans, a community to which Paul remained unknown. But in all the other authentic Pauline writings from 1 Thessalonians to Philippians and Philemon, and also the deutero-Pauline Pastorals and Captivity epistles, the notion of imitation of Paul, of 'example' and 'model' of Paul and Christ and of certain other members of the community, is present and developed."

31. Wanamaker (1990: 81) observes that, though Paul does not make mention of his apostleship in the letter opening of 1 Thessalonians, "the phrase 'you became imitators of us' asserts Paul's position as the superior in the relationship with his converts. It thereby legitimates his right to guide and instruct his readers in the ways of Christ."

status is no different than that of his readers: each one is called to be an imitator of Christ.

c. In almost any kind of learning situation of life (e.g., raising children, teaching a skilled trade), verbal instruction alone is usually insufficient to accomplish the goal, thereby requiring some kind of modeling of the desired behavior or skill. Similarly, Paul cannot simply share abstract concepts or even specific commands with his converts without also presenting himself as a concrete example to be imitated (although Paul sometimes uses others as a model, the example of himself and his coworkers is best known to his readers and thus more effective). Especially since at this time his churches had no normative book to follow with respect to ethical conduct, it was essential for Paul to use himself as a model for them to emulate. In light of these and other considerations, modern readers must guard against too quickly finding in the apostle's calls for others to imitate him an arrogant desire for self-aggrandizement.

What about Paul's use of the imitation theme in 1:6? First, it is noteworthy that here Paul uses the indicative (so also 2:14) rather than, as elsewhere, the imperative to speak of the Thessalonians' imitation of himself and of Christ. This confirms something implied by the rest of the thanksgiving section and the letter as a whole: the apostle is generally pleased with the conduct of the believers in Thessalonica. Thus instead of being exhorted to live a life consistent with their election by God, the exemplary life they already are exhibiting becomes an additional cause of Paul's thanksgiving to God. Yet the distinction between the indicative and imperative should not be overstated. For in light of the exhortative function of the thanksgiving section, Paul's praise of the Thessalonians' present conduct carries with it the implicit challenge that such behavior should continue in the future.

Second, the order "of us and of the Lord" is somewhat striking (it is even more noticeable in the Greek text where "imitators of us" occurs prior to the main verb, while "of the Lord" is located at the very end of the main clause). Some see in this word sequence simply the "logical" or "historical" order: the Thessalonians begin with their imitation of Paul, which then leads to their imitation of Christ (Hendriksen 1955: 52; Holtz 1986: 48–49; Morris 1991: 47). Others, on the basis of the order found in 2:5 and 2:10, argue that Paul typically puts the more powerful party second (Gaventa 1998: 28–29). It may well be the case, however, that the word order reflects Paul's apologetic concern of the previous verse, which foreshadows the larger defense of 2:1–12.[32] By

---

32. Reinhartz (1987: 402) argues that Paul's reference to imitation in 1 Thess. 1:6, as with all of his calls to imitation, "implies a perceived threat to his apostleship and the need to defend his authority." While Reinhartz is right in seeing in Paul's statement in 1:6 an apologetic concern, she is wrong about the direction of that concern. Here the apostle is concerned not with his *authority*—no one in the church is questioning his apostolic credentials—but with his *integrity*: some outside the church, "the fellow citizens" (2:14), were questioning Paul's motives, claiming he was interested only in obtaining financial gain or soliciting praise.

stating that the Thessalonians have become imitators "of us," Paul not only praises the Thessalonian believers but also affirms the conduct of himself and his coworkers among them as blameless and worthy of emulation.

Third, Paul speaks of imitation here not in general terms but very specifically as "receiving[33] the word in much affliction with joy that comes from the Holy Spirit" (δεξάμενοι τὸν λογον ἐν θλίψει πολλῇ μετὰ χαρᾶς πνεύματος ἁγίου, *dexamenoi ton logon en thlipsei pollē meta charas pneumatos hagiou*).[34] The focus cannot be merely on the Thessalonians' receiving the proclaimed word, since we know of no event in Christ's life when he received the word in a way that the Thessalonians could legitimately be said to have become imitators of him in this regard. This suggests that the emphasis is on their accepting the word "in much affliction." Here too, however, the parallel that Paul makes between himself and the Lord with the conduct of the Thessalonians is not exact. For even though both the apostle and Christ experienced much persecution in their lives, they did not endure this in a specific context of "receiving the word," as conversion. Thus it is possible that what Paul has in mind is that the Thessalonians imitate him and the Lord in the general sense that they demonstrate faithfulness in the midst of opposition (Gaventa 1998: 29). It seems more likely, though, that Paul is thinking specifically of the opposition that he endured during his original preaching ministry in Thessalonica (2:2: "We had courage in our God to declare to you the gospel of God in the face of great opposition")—an opposition that the Thessalonians also experienced after "receiving the word" such that they now could be said to have become imitators of him.

The exact nature of the trouble endured by the Thessalonian believers is not spelled out (the Thessalonians knew all too well what Paul was talking about) but only hinted at in the brief phrase "in much affliction" (*en thlipsei pollē*). Malherbe argues that this "affliction" does not refer to outward persecution against the Thessalonian believers because of their newfound faith but to inward anxieties typically experienced by converts to a new philosophical system or pagan religion with its differing worldview: "It is reasonable to understand *thlipsis* in 1:6 as the distress and anguish of heart experienced by persons who broke with their past as they received the gospel" (1987: 48; see

---

33. It is difficult to decide whether the aorist participle δεξάμενοι should be taken either temporally ("*when* you received . . .") or instrumentally ("*by* your receiving . . ."). With respect to the translation of the participle, the word "receiving" may be rather weak, especially in light of the contrast between δέχομαι and παραλαμβάνω in 2:13. A translation that better captures this distinction is "welcoming," i.e., a *willing* reception (see W. Grundmann, *TDNT* 2:50, who refers to the distinction between these two verbs made by Pseudo-Ammonius [ca. AD 100] in his lexicon of synonyms; followed by de Boer 1962: 114n67).

34. It is unlikely (contra Benson 1996) that Paul's statement here is a deliberate allusion to Jesus's words in his explanation of the parable of the sower (Luke 8:13): "And the ones on the rock are those who, when they hear [the word], receive the word with joy [μετὰ χαρᾶς δέχονται τὸν λόγον]." Benson argues that Paul in 1 Thess. 1:6 not only refers to the Lord as an example of holding on to the gospel with joy in the face of persecution ("You became imitators of us and of the Lord") but also to the teaching of the Lord, which tells believers to do this.

the larger discussion on 46–52; also Malherbe 2000: 127–29). But while the Thessalonian Christians did experience significant social dislocation (far more than is often recognized), it would be clearly wrong to limit the suffering to inward anxieties (see esp. Still 1999: 208–17).

The word *thlipsis* is also used in 3:3, where it obviously refers to external oppression. In fact, Paul's use of this word rarely if ever means "mental distress" (only perhaps in 2 Cor. 2:4 and Phil. 1:17) but "trouble that inflicts distress, *oppression, affliction, tribulation*" (BDAG 457.1; H. Schlier, *TDNT* 3:143–48). Furthermore, there are several indications both within the Thessalonian Letters and without that believers in Thessalonica have encountered open hostility and opposition for their faith (1 Thess. 2:2, 14–15; 3:1–5; 2 Thess. 1:4–7; see also 2 Cor. 8:1–2; Acts 17:5–7, 13). Also, it is hard to believe that Paul means that the Thessalonians have become imitators of himself and of the Lord in the sense that they have experienced the same internal anxiety over their conversion (Wanamaker 1990: 81). Paul nowhere speaks of any such anxiety with respect to his own conversion, and such an idea makes no sense with respect to Christ. Therefore, the "affliction" that Paul has in mind in 1:6 involves outward trials and not only the inward anxieties that quite naturally accompany such trials. Although the specific content of this external affliction is less clear, it probably did not involve physical death and martyrdom but more likely entailed severe social harassment and ostracism. This opposition involved "such difficulties as their alienation from unbelieving family members and friends; the curtailment of their opportunities to maintain, let alone to improve, their current economic and social status; the restriction of their access to the city's political and social institutions; and their constant subjection to harassment and public insults" (Furnish 2007: 46–47).

Paul gives thanks to God for the Thessalonians' ability not merely to endure such affliction but also to do so "with joy that comes from the Holy Spirit" (*meta charas pneumatos hagiou*).[35] Although the pairing of "joy" with "affliction" may appear at first hearing to be strange (not only to non-Christians but also to those contemporary believers who have bought into the health-and-wealth version of the gospel), their combination here is completely consistent with what Paul and other NT writers say elsewhere (Rom. 5:3–5; 2 Cor. 6:5, 10; 7:4; 8:2; Phil. 2:17; Col. 1:24; James 1:2; 1 Pet. 1:6; 4:13). The joy that the Thessalonian Christians experience does not stem from a naïveté or blindness to the seriousness of their current situation of affliction. Rather, their joy originates from the Holy Spirit,[36] who enables them to see beyond

---

35. Here πνεύματος ἁγίου is a genitive of source: a joy that "comes from" or is "given by" the Holy Spirit. On the absence of the definite article, see the footnote in my comments on 1:5.

36. This is the second reference to the Holy Spirit within two verses: 1:5 refers to the Spirit as the source of power in the gospel proclaimed by Paul and his associates, and 1:6 refers to the Spirit as the source of joy in the lives of the Thessalonians who received that gospel word. Thus the Spirit plays a crucial role in both parties involved in the Thessalonians' conversion: in the preachers and in the hearers. For further reflections on Paul's understanding of the Spirit as evidenced in these two verses, see the summary observations of Fee 1994a: 47–48.

their present suffering to their future deliverance. The Thessalonian converts are convinced that Christ will return from heaven to rescue them from the coming wrath of God (1:10), a wrath that will be fully experienced by their oppressors. It is because of this Spirit-given conviction that the Thessalonians are able to face even "much" affliction with an attitude of joy.

1:7 The Thessalonians' imitation of Paul and of the Lord has had a positive consequence or result (ὥστε [hōste, so that] introduces a result clause that is dependent on the preceding verse). The joyful lives that the Thessalonian Christians lead, even in the midst of severe affliction, serve as a powerful example to others: "so that you became an example[37] to all the believers in Macedonia and in Achaia" (ὥστε γενέσθαι ὑμᾶς τύπον πᾶσιν τοῖς πιστεύουσιν ἐν τῇ Μακεδονίᾳ καὶ τῇ Ἀχαΐᾳ, hōste genesthai hymas typon pasin tois pisteuousin en tē Makedonia kai tē Achaia).

The word "example" (typos) properly refers to a mold for producing a shape or to a wooden stamp for making an imprint in clay. Figuratively, the word was used to refer to a model or pattern for ethical conduct (L. Goppelt, TDNT 8:246–59; Spicq 1994: 3.384–87). The metaphor here in 1:7 is thus of the Thessalonians who are not just an example for others to follow but indeed a kind of "mold" from which the lives of other believers are cast. The Thessalonians' joyful reception of the gospel in spite of much affliction has had a formative influence on Christians located in their region since the imitators have now become the imitated. This is high praise indeed. For though Paul often uses the language or idea of imitation (see comment on 1:6), he nowhere else states that a particular church has served as an inspiring example for believers in other locations (D. Martin 1995: 62). Such praise not only encourages the Thessalonians to continue to persevere in the face of adversity but also reaffirms and strengthens the close relationship between the apostle and his church (recall the exhortative and pastoral functions of the Pauline thanksgiving section).

Those Christians who are modeling their lives after the example of the Thessalonians include "all the believers in Macedonia and in Achaia" (pasin tois pisteuousin en tē Makedonia kai en tē Achaia).[38] These two place names identify the two provinces comprising Greece. Before 27 BC and again from AD 15 to 44—less than a decade prior to the writing of 1 Thessalonians—both were administered under the control of the Romans as one province, and this close historical connection between the two provinces probably explains why Paul links their names together here (Marshall 1983: 55). At this time Macedonia had churches in Philippi, Berea, and possibly Amphipolis and

---

37. Here the singular "example" is used because Paul thinks of the church as a whole.

38. The repetition of the preposition and definite article before "Achaia" shows that Paul here is thinking of Macedonia and Achaia as two distinct provinces in contrast to the next verse (1:8), where the two (preposition and article) are correctly omitted by the better witnesses, thereby classifying Macedonia and Achaia together in opposition to the rest of the world. See further the additional notes for 1:8.

Apollonia (Acts 17:1), in addition to the congregation in Thessalonica. Achaia had churches in Athens, Corinth (from where Paul likely wrote this letter), and its eastern seaport, Cenchreae (Rom. 16:1), and other unnamed places in the region (2 Cor. 1:1, "all the saints in the whole of Achaia"). Wanamaker (1990: 82–83) interprets the unique standing that Paul ascribes to the Thessalonians among all these churches as evidence that the strong opposition to the Christians in Thessalonica was not the common experience of other believers in Macedonia and Achaia. But while the Thessalonian believers were subject to particularly heavy persecution for their faith, it would be wrong to conclude that believers in other surrounding cities were free of any such affliction (see Phil. 1:27–30; 3:1–11; Acts 16:19–40; 18:12–17).

Before concluding our study of the first additional cause of thanksgiving given in 1:6–7, let us recognize once more from these verses the important ways in which the thanksgiving section foreshadows the major concerns of the letter and so, in colloquial terms, is a "preview of coming attractions" (Witherington 2006: 52, who wrongly applies this description only to 1:2–3 instead of the larger unit of 1:2–10). As 1:5 anticipates the first major concern of the letter, the lengthy defense of Paul's original ministry in Thessalonica (2:1–16), so 1:6–7 looks ahead to the second major concern of the letter, the combined concern of explaining Paul's failure thus far to return to Thessalonica and of strengthening the believers there who are currently experiencing persecution for their faith (2:17–3:10). The phrase "receiving the word in much affliction" anticipates especially the discussion of persecution in 3:1–5 (see also 3:6, 7, 8b). The theme of joy ("with joy that comes from the Holy Spirit") is picked up again in 2:19–20 and 3:9. Finally, the theme of imitation ("and you on your part became imitators of us and of the Lord"), along with the phrase "receiving the word," looks ahead to the discussion of 2:13–16.

2. The Evangelistic Activity of the Thessalonians (1:8)

That the second "additional cause of thanksgiving" in 1:8 opens with the explanatory particle "for" (γάρ, gar) shows that this verse is intended to clarify *how* "you became an example to all the believers in Macedonia and Achaia" (1:7). Although Paul has already identified one way in which the Thessalonians have become an example to others (by their joyful reception of the gospel in spite of opposition: 1:6), he feels the need to explain this further: "For from you the word of the Lord has echoed forth not only in Macedonia and Achaia, but in every place your faith toward God has gone forth, so that we have no need to say anything."

1:8

The grammatical structure of 1:8 is awkward due to the introduction of both an additional subject ("your faith toward God") and verb ("has gone forth") after the antithetical statement ("not only in Macedonia and Achaia, but in every place"), thereby resulting in what Frame (1912: 85) calls "an innocent anacoluthon." In order to remove this awkwardness, some translators place a semicolon after "of the Lord" and thus divide the verse into two distinct parts, with the antithetical statement being usually joined to the second half ("For from you the word of the Lord has echoed forth; not only in Macedonia and Achaia, but in every place has your faith toward God gone forth"). As Best (1977: 80) observes, however, "This makes an awkward break and is clumsy since so much of the [second half of the] sentence precedes the subject and verb." Thus most commentators are inclined to let the text stand in its present form and attribute its clumsiness to Paul's "impetuous style" (Milligan 1908: 12), his "characteristic earnestness" (Lightfoot 1904: 15), or simply a lapse in his grammatical finesse. A more likely reason for the grammatical difficulty of this verse, however, is that Paul has combined into one sentence two related yet distinct evangelistic activities carried out by the Thessalonians: a proclaimed message ("the word of the Lord") and an exemplary conversion ("your faith toward God").[39]

The first of these two evangelistic activities is described with an infrequent noun phrase and a rare verbal form. The full phrase "the word of the Lord" (ὁ λόγος τοῦ κυρίου, *ho logos tou kyriou*) occurs only one other time in Paul's Letters (2 Thess. 3:1; see also 1 Thess. 4:15); usually the apostle has "the word of *God*" (Rom. 9:6; 1 Cor. 14:36; Eph. 6:17; Phil. 1:14; Col. 1:25; 1 Thess. 2:13; 1 Tim. 4:5; 2 Tim. 2:9; Titus 2:5) or uses "word" absolutely (e.g., 1 Thess. 1:5, 6). The full phrase does appear with great frequency in the OT (over 250 occurrences), and it is this likely source that sheds light on whether "of the Lord" ought to be understood objectively ("the word about the Lord") or subjectively ("the word that comes from the Lord"). The latter reading is preferred since Paul, in keeping with OT usage, emphasizes that the "word" or gospel message originates not from the Thessalonians but from "the Lord."[40] Paul differs from the OT use of this phrase, however, in that "the Lord" refers not to God (so wrongly Ellingworth and Nida 1975: 13; Williams 1992: 31; Richard 1995: 71–72) but to Jesus Christ, following the apostle's normal use of the term (so most commentators).

This word or gospel message from the Lord Jesus Christ "has echoed forth" (ἐξήχηται, *exēchētai*; our English word "echo" derives from this Greek root) from the Thessalonian believers. The verb *exēcheō* occurs only here in Paul's Letters (and in all of the NT), although the root is found in 1 Cor. 13:1. This rare word group is used by classical writers and the LXX to portray a wide

---

39. Richard (1995: 70–71) argues that the grammatical structure of 1:8 is understandable as a chiasm (the chiasm is more convincing when the various elements of the verse are listed not in terms of their content, as Richard does, but in terms of their grammatical category/form):

    A   Verb: "has echoed forth"
        B   Subject: "the word of the Lord"
            C   Antithetical statement: "not only in Macedonia and Achaia"
            C′ Antithetical statement: "but in every place"
        B′ Subject: "your faith toward God"
    A′ Verb: "has gone forth"

40. Note also the variation in Paul's use of prepositions: ἀφ' ὑμῶν (*from* you) but ἐξήχηται (echoed *forth*). Thus the Thessalonians were not the source from which the word sounded forth, but only the point from which it proceeded.

---

range of sounds (J. Schneider, *TDNT* 2:954–55). There is no justification, therefore, for specifying the noise as that of a trumpet (John Chrysostom, *Hom. 1 Thess.* 2; Bruce 1982: 17) or thunder (Lightfoot 1904: 15). Here the focus is not on the identity of the sound but on its expanding character: it is a sound that reverberates out in all directions (note Paul's use of the rarer compound form *exēcheō*: "to echo *forth*"). The ongoing or continuing nature of the sound is also emphasized by the use of the perfect tense. The image that Paul presents, therefore, is that of a sound—the gospel message—emanating from the Thessalonian Christians and continuing to echo on and on throughout the hills and valleys of Macedonia, Achaia, and beyond.

How did the believers at Thessalonica communicate the gospel to others? Some see in this verse evidence for "active evangelism," the kind of public preaching of the sort in which Paul himself engaged (Henneken 1969: 62–63; Marshall 1983: 56; Malherbe 2000: 117). Others envision a kind of "holy gossip," the excited transmission from mouth to mouth of the obvious impact that the gospel was having on the lives of fellow citizens in Thessalonica (Stott 1991: 38). Paul does not specify the precise way in which the gospel has echoed forth from the Thessalonian Christians, and so any conclusion on this matter must remain tentative. Nevertheless, the reference to "the word of the Lord" suggests that some form of verbal evangelism took place.[41]

While the first half of verse 8 focuses on the evangelistic endeavors that the Thessalonian believers accomplished through verbal means, the second half of this verse addresses their outreach activity carried out through nonverbal means: "Your faith toward God has gone forth." The formulation "your faith *toward God*" (πρὸς τὸν θεόν, *pros ton theon*) is unusual (one would expect "faith *in God*"), but it exactly parallels the description of the Thessalonians' conversion given in the immediately following verse: "how you turned toward God" (*pros ton theon*). It seems likely, then, that the reference to the Thessalonians' "faith toward God" already has in view their conversion. As Richard (1995: 73) states: "The focal point of verse 8b then is the community's conversion, a theme which Paul describes at great length in verses 9–10."

The evangelistic activity of the Thessalonians in both its verbal and nonverbal forms has occurred "not only in Macedonia and Achaia but in every place." In the preceding verse, Paul praised the Thessalonians for becoming an example to all the believers "in Macedonia and in Achaia" (1:7).[42] Now he

41. Ware (1992) draws attention to the striking fact that nowhere in his letters does Paul command his congregations to preach the gospel. The reason for this, Ware proposes, is that such a command would not be consistent with Paul's conviction that he, as a divinely appointed apostle, had been entrusted with the task of preaching the gospel. This does not mean, however, that the apostle did not expect his churches to be involved in evangelistic activities: "Yet Paul was confident that his congregations would continue his missionary activity, as the power of God at work in his preaching of the gospel continued to be active in those who had believed the message" (131).

42. There is a slight but significant difference between the phrase "in Macedonia and in Achaia" in verse 7 and the phrase "in Macedonia and Achaia" here in verse 8. See discussion of 1:8 in additional notes below.

expands the impact that the Thessalonian believers have had beyond that of ancient Greece to include "every place." On the one hand, this claim obviously involves the use of hyperbole to praise the Thessalonians for their positive response to the gospel, even in the face of much opposition.[43] On the other hand, the far-reaching impact of the Thessalonians' evangelistic work should not be overlooked. Thessalonica was, after all, one of the leading cities in the ancient world and enjoyed travel possibilities by both land and sea, which would allow news about the nascent Christian community to spread quickly to regions far and near. It is not hard to envision, for example, Paul in Corinth as meeting Aquila and Priscilla, recently expelled from their home city of Rome (Acts 18:2), and hearing from them a report about the Thessalonians that had reached the imperial city (Lightfoot 1904: 16; Morris 1991: 51).

The wide-ranging impact of the Thessalonians' evangelistic efforts is so impressive that Paul and his fellow missionaries now "have no need to say anything." Although the apostle does not specify to whom he is referring (the Thessalonian readers or Christians in other places?), the larger context (esp. the subject "they themselves" at the opening of verse 9, which cannot refer to the Thessalonian readers) clearly shows that he is thinking about those believers in Macedonia, Achaia, and elsewhere. The story about the Thessalonians has spread so far that Paul has no need to tell Christians elsewhere about them. That Paul later did boast about the Thessalonians to other Christians (2 Thess. 1:4: "We boast of you in the churches of God"; see also 2 Cor. 8:1–5, where the apostle speaks to the Corinthian Christians more generally about the "churches of Macedonia") should not lead to conjectures as to why Paul may have changed his mind, nor should it be seen as further evidence that 2 Thessalonians must have been written prior to this letter (so Wanamaker 1990: 84). Instead, the expression "We have no need" in 1:8 constitutes an example of paraleipsis, a literary device allowing writers to address a subject that they outwardly claim does not need to be addressed. In this specific context, Paul's use of paraleipsis functions to heighten his praise for the Thessalonian church and to prepare for the explanatory comments given in the following sentence (1:9–10).

3. The Conversion of the Thessalonians (1:9–10)

1:9 The third "additional cause of thanksgiving" in 1:9–10 also (see 1:8) opens with the explanatory particle "for" (γάρ, *gar*), thereby indicating that these verses are intended to spell out more fully the conversion of the Thessalonians alluded to in the preceding verse ("your faith toward God"). Paul and his fellow missionaries "have no need to say anything" about the Thessalonians' conversion "for they themselves report concerning us what kind of visit we had among you, and how you turned to God from idols in order to serve a living

---

43. Gaventa (1998: 18) gives a helpful contemporary analogy to Paul's use of hyperbole here. She suggests that it is somewhat like a person who estimates the size of a large crowd by claiming that "everyone and his grandmother was there."

and true God and to wait for his Son from the heavens, whom he raised from the dead, Jesus, the one who rescues us from the coming wrath."

The shift in focus at the beginning of 1:9 from the activities of the Thessalonian converts to that of Paul and his mission-founding visit ("report concerning *us* . . . what kind of visit *we* had") is, at first glance, unexpected. The apparent awkwardness of this shift led some scribes to "correct" the text to the smoother reading "concerning *you*" (see additional notes).[44] Such a switch is understandable, however, given the seriousness of Paul's apologetic concern in the letter. The apostle's desire to defend himself accounts for the repeated shift in focus from himself along with his coworkers and their mission-founding visit to Thessalonica, to discuss the Thessalonian believers' response to that visit—a pattern found not only here in 1:9–10 (v. 9a: Paul's mission-founding visit to Thessalonica; vv. 9b–10: the response of the Thessalonians), but also earlier in 1:5–8 (v. 5: Paul's mission-founding visit to Thessalonica; vv. 6–8: the response of the Thessalonians) and later in 2:1–16 (vv. 1–12: Paul's mission-founding visit to Thessalonica; vv. 13–16: the response of the Thessalonians).

In keeping with this pattern, the first part of the report (v. 9a) made by those "not only in Macedonia and Achaia but in every place" (v. 8; this is the antecedent of the personal pronoun "they themselves" in v. 9) concerns the conduct of Paul and his coworkers, specifically "what kind of visit we had among you" (v. 9a). The word εἴσοδον (*eisodon*, visit) occurs only twice in Paul's Letters, both of them in 1 Thessalonians (here and in 2:1). A number of leading translations wrongly render this word as "reception" or "welcome" (NIV: "what kind of reception you gave us"; NRSV: "what kind of welcome we had among you"; see also NAB, NASB) and so mislead the contemporary reader into believing that the emphasis here is on the Thessalonian believers and their warm reception of the missionaries and the gospel. The word, however, means "entrance" or "visit" (BAGD 233;[45] LSJ 496; W. Michaelis, *TDNT* 5:106: "εἴσοδος is a simple statement denoting entry") and clearly refers to the activities of Paul along with his fellow missionaries and not that of the Christians in Thessalonica. The correlative pronoun ὁποίαν (*hopoian*, of what sort) points to the nature of that original visit (note the similar use of οἷοι in 1:5), stressing either the effectiveness or, more likely, the sincerity of Paul's mission-founding visit (see the discussion of κενή in 2:1). The point the apostle makes is clear: there is a widespread report of the genuine character of his original visit to Thessalonica. In an age where traveling philosophers and orators frequently entered a city with extravagant pomp and self-serving motives of securing the praise and purse of its citizens (see Winter 1993), people throughout Macedonia, Achaia, and even beyond recognized that

44. There is no support for the conjectural emendation made some time ago by Harris (1898: 195) that the third-person form ἀπαγγέλλουσιν (*they* report) in 1:9 ought to be replaced by the second-person form ἀπαγγέλλετε (*you* report), as though Paul were referring to a letter sent to him from the Thessalonian church.

45. BDAG 294–95.3 gives a different sense for the meaning of εἴσοδος in 1:9 and 2:1 but still concedes that the term "can also mean *visit* . . . here."

Paul's mission-founding visit to Thessalonica exhibited none of these vain and dishonest practices. In this way, Paul not only further defends himself but also strengthens his relationship with his original readers by reminding them of the crucial role that he played in their conversion.

The second part of the report (vv. 9b–10), which is being heard everywhere, concerns the Thessalonians and their response to the mission-founding visit of Paul and his coworkers, namely, their conversion: "and how you turned to God from idols in order to serve a living and true God and to wait for his Son from the heavens, whom he raised from the dead, Jesus, the one who rescues us from the coming wrath." It is widely assumed that these words constitute pre-Pauline material that summarizes missionary preaching to the Gentiles, which the apostle has here quoted and adapted somewhat to describe his original ministry to the Thessalonians. A full discussion of this issue (including a detailed analysis of the terminology found in 1:9b–10) is found in excursus 1, at the end of this unit. Here it is enough to state our conclusion that these verses do not constitute pre-Pauline material but come from the hand of Paul. Furthermore, 1:9b–10, along with 1:9a, summarize not missionary preaching to the Gentiles but key issues that Paul is going to treat in the body of the letter.

The conversion of the Thessalonians is described in deceptively simple terms: "how you turned to God from idols" (πῶς ἐπεστρέψατε πρὸς τὸν θεὸν ἀπὸ τῶν εἰδώλων, *pōs epestrepsate pros ton theon apo tōn eidōlōn*).[46] Yet, in a society where cultic and social activities were intimately connected, there was nothing simple about turning to God from idols. Such a total renunciation of all pagan deities also meant a complete rejection of a variety of social events closely associated with the worship of these gods. Such action by Christians evoked feelings of resentment and anger in their non-Christian family members and friends. The exclusivity of these Christians—their seemingly arrogant refusal to participate in the worship of any god but their own—deeply wounded public sensibilities and even led to charges that they were "atheists" (Barclay 1993: 514–15). Citizens of Thessalonica worried whether the gods, whose home on Mount Olympus they could see a mere fifty miles away to the southwest, might punish the whole city for the sacrilegious actions of a few by sending disease, famine, or other natural disasters. Turning from idols also meant a rejection of the imperial cult, thereby potentially jeopardizing Thessalonica's favored status with Rome and the emperor. The conversion of the Thessalonian Christians involved a truly radical break with their previous

---

46. It is clear that the church consisted primarily of Gentiles, since the phrase "turned from idols" is not appropriate for Jews. Many commentators would add that the phrase "turned from idols" is also not appropriate for "God-fearers" and thus see here a conflict with the account in Acts 17, which depicts Paul's converts in Thessalonica as including many devout Gentiles who worshiped in the synagogue (see, e.g., Best 1977: 5–6). There is evidence, however, for the ongoing participation of God-fearers in the pagan cults (see Fredriksen 1991: esp. 541–43; also Levinskaya 1996: 78: "Some of the God-fearers were only one step from becoming converts, while others just added the Jewish God to their pantheon").

way of life—a break that naturally incurred the resentment and anger of their fellow citizens (2:14).

This radical break or conversion involved change not for change's sake but a transformation with two specific goals (the Greek text has two infinitive clauses expressing purpose): a present holiness ("in order to serve a living and true God") and a future hope ("and to wait for his Son from the heavens"). The first goal of conversion is that the Thessalonians will "serve" God. The verb δουλεύω (douleuō) means not merely "to serve" but "to serve as a slave." The ancient Greeks, much like our contemporary society, were generally adverse to using the "slave" (δοῦλος, doulos) word group to describe the idea of "service," especially service to the gods, since this was antithetical to their notion of individual freedom. In the OT (LXX), however, the verb douleuō functions as a common term for expressing total commitment to God (K. H. Rengstorf, TDNT 2:261–68). In keeping with this Semitic background, the first goal of conversion, therefore, is a wholehearted commitment to God, which involves not only a verbal acknowledgment of him but also an outward demonstration of that devotion. The Thessalonians' activity of turning from idols to God shows itself in concrete ways in their conduct as they "serve" God in an absolute manner and seek to do his will. In this way, the first goal of conversion foreshadows the concern for holiness and proper moral conduct found later in the letter body (4:1–12 and 5:12–22).

The God whom the Thessalonians serve with this total commitment is portrayed as "living" and "true."[47] These two adjectives are rarely employed by Paul as a description of God: the adjective "living" (ζῶντι, zōnti) is used alone on a few occasions (Rom. 9:26; 2 Cor. 3:3; 6:16; 1 Tim. 3:15; 4:10), and the adjective "true" (ἀληθινῷ, alēthinō) is found only here. In the OT, however, both are common descriptions of God ("living": Num. 14:21, 28; Deut. 32:40; Ps. 40:3 [41:2 Eng.]; Hosea 2:1 [1:10 Eng.]; etc.; "true": Exod. 34:6; 2 Chron. 15:3; Ps. 86:15; Isa. 65:16; etc.) and occur together in Jer. 10:10 ("But the LORD is the true God; he is the living God" [NRSV]; also in Jos. Asen. 11.10: "The God of the Hebrews is a true God and a living God"). This suggests that, like the verb "to serve" in the same clause, the meaning of the two adjectives originates from an OT background. Such a conclusion is strengthened by the fact that those few instances where Paul does describe God as "living" are often part of his citing or adapting an OT passage (e.g., Rom. 9:26, which cites Hosea 1:10; 2 Cor. 6:16, which comes immediately before a quote from Lev. 26:12). This OT background indicates, then, that the two adjectives "living" and "true" serve to highlight the contrast between the God of the Christian faith and the idols from which the Thessalonians have turned. They previously worshiped idols, dead "gods" from their local region, Rome, and Egypt, whose claims to power and influence are false, but now they serve the one and only God who is living and true.

---

47. In 1:9c the character of God is emphasized through the omission of the article before θεῷ. The presence of the article before θεόν in 1:9b stresses God's identity as the one to whom the Thessalonians have turned in contrast to the idols they had previously served.

1:10   The goal of the Thessalonians' conversion is not only that they live a life of holiness in the present but that they also have hope for the future: "and to wait for his Son from the heavens." Although an indirect reference to Christ's return was made earlier, in 1:3 ("the steadfastness of hope in our Lord Jesus Christ"), here we have the first explicit reference to the second coming, or parousia, of Christ. The conviction that Jesus would one day return was widespread in the early church and is one of the major themes of this letter. The second goal of conversion—the hope in the future coming of Christ—thus well anticipates the extended discussion of issues related to Christ's return taken up in 4:13–18 and 5:1–11.

Although the verb ἀναμένω (*anamenō*, to wait) occurs only here in Paul's Letters, the concept of eschatological waiting is found elsewhere (Rom. 8:23; 1 Cor. 1:7; Gal. 5:5; Phil. 3:20; the verb ἀπεκδέχομαι, *apekdechomai*, is normally used). The present tense highlights the ongoing nature of this waiting: the believers in Thessalonica are constantly awaiting the return of Christ. In the two goals of their conversion, therefore, the Thessalonian believers demonstrate a healthy balance between ethics and eschatology. Some contemporary Christians emphasize only serving God in the present and so fail to anticipate the glorious return of Christ in the future. Others stress the second coming and the new world order to such an extreme that they devote little thought or energy to serving God in this world. In contrast, the Thessalonians' passion for serving God and so living a holy life in the present is matched by their fervent hope in the future return of "his Son."

The description of the returning one as God's "Son" is a bit unexpected, since this title is not normally used by Paul when referring to the parousia (he typically uses the terms "Lord" or "Lord Jesus [Christ]": see 1 Thess. 1:3; 2:19; 3:13; 4:15; 5:2, 23; 2 Thess. 1:7; 2:1, 2, 8). Yet the apostle does frequently use the title "Son" in connection with other topics, especially to indicate the close relationship between Christ and God (for a discussion of the relevant texts, see Best 1977: 83; Marshall 1983: 59; Wanamaker 1990: 86–87; Fee 2007: 240–44, 293–303). There is no need, therefore, to postulate that the reference here to "Son" is due to the "fusion of the Son of Man and Son of God traditions, or that an original Son of Man title is replaced by Son (of God) to accommodate missionary preaching to Gentiles" (so Richard 1995: 56). Instead, in keeping with his practice elsewhere, Paul uses the title "Son" to emphasize the intimate association between the one whose coming they await and the God to whom they have turned and now serve. This sonship or close relationship with God means that Jesus will be able to return and rescue them from the coming wrath (see Rom. 5:9–10, where the idea of Christ's "sonship" and his ability to deliver believers from eschatological "wrath" are similarly linked).

The Son of God will return to earth "from the heavens" (ἐκ τῶν οὐρανῶν, *ek tōn ouranōn*). The use of the plural "heavens" might reflect the Jewish belief that the heavenly world consisted of a number of tiers. Pseudepigraphic and rabbinic writings refer to divisions of heaven that number five (3 Bar. 11.1), seven (T. Levi 3.1; 2 En. 8–22; Ascen. Isa. 9; *b. Ḥag.* 11b; Pesiq. Rab. 5; Midr.

Ps. 92; 'Abot R. Nat. 37), or even ten (2 En. 20.3). Paul seems to support a multileveled cosmology in his elliptical self-reference in 2 Cor. 12:2, where he says: "I know a man in Christ who fourteen years ago was caught up to the third heaven." Nevertheless, that the apostle frequently employs the singular "heaven" with no obvious difference of meaning suggests that one should not read too much into his use of the plural here (esp. note the use of the singular in 1 Thess. 4:16 and 2 Thess. 1:7, which both have almost the same context as here).

The second goal of the Thessalonians' conversion—their future hope—concludes with three additional descriptions of God's "Son," who will one day return from the heavens: (1) "whom he [God] raised from the dead"; (2) "Jesus"; and (3) "the one who rescues us from the coming wrath." The first phrase is virtually a formula (see Rom. 4:24; 10:9; Gal. 1:1; Acts 3:15; 4:10; 1 Pet. 1:21; etc.) for another central teaching of the early church: the resurrection of Christ. As elsewhere in Paul's writings and the rest of the NT, this activity of being raised is attributed not to Christ and his own power but to God. The mention of the resurrection here provides further support for the future hope of the Thessalonians. Not only is Christ identified intimately with God as "his Son"; he also has been "raised" by God and so is eminently qualified to return to earth and rescue his people from the coming wrath. The presence of this first additional phrase is at first glance surprising since it seems to interrupt the strong end-time theme found in the immediately surrounding clauses (v. 10a, "to wait for his Son from the heavens"; v. 10c, "who rescues us from the coming wrath"). However, rather than being a mere "afterthought" (Wanamaker 1990: 87) or "awkward addition" (Furnish 2007: 49), this addition skillfully anticipates Paul's eschatological discussion in 4:13–18, where the apostle grounds his words of comfort by first appealing to Jesus's resurrection (4:14: "For since we believe that Jesus died and rose again, so through Jesus, God will bring with him those who have fallen asleep"). This reveals the impressive writing skill of the apostle who foreshadows in 1:10b not only the subject of Jesus's return, which he will take up at great length in 4:13–18 (and 5:1–11), but also the first argument that he will use in that upcoming end-time discussion: an appeal to Jesus's resurrection.

The second addition is the identification of the returning Son of God as "Jesus." The mention of the personal name is not due to the desire of Paul to clarify the identity of God's Son, as if there may have been some doubt about whom the apostle had in view. Instead, the addition of the name "Jesus" serves to mark the transition away from the activity of God (his raising up of Christ) and back to the activity of his Son (his return from the heavens). Now there is no ambiguity in the immediately following phrase as to who will bring about eschatological deliverance. The name "Jesus," of course, means "Savior" (Matt. 1:21) and so is especially appropriate as a transition to the final clause, which refers to Christ's saving work. This second addition may well look ahead to the only other solo use of the personal name in the letter in 4:14 (contrast 1:1, 3; 2:14, 15, 19; 3:11, 13; 4:1, 2; 5:9, 18, 23, 28), where, as noted above, Paul appeals to the resurrection of Jesus in dealing with the issue of those who die before Christ's return (4:13–18).

The third addition further identifies the returning Son as "the one who rescues us from the coming wrath." The verb ῥύομαι (rhyomai, rescue), though not as frequent as σῴζω (sōzō, save), is by no means rare in Paul's writings (Rom. 7:24; 11:26; 15:31; 2 Cor. 1:10 [3x]; Col. 1:13; 2 Thess. 3:2; 2 Tim. 3:11; 4:17, 18) and typically conveys the idea of being rescued "out of" (ἐκ, ek) or "from" (ἀπό, apo) something negative or harmful. The danger from which Christ will rescue believers is "the coming wrath."[48] Paul's use of the noun "wrath" (ὀργή, orgē) elsewhere reveals that the source of this wrath is God, even though the designation "of God" is not present. This third additional phrase foreshadows a similar reference to salvation from future wrath through Christ's work in 5:9 ("For God has destined us not for wrath but for the obtaining of salvation through our Lord Jesus Christ"), where Paul comforts the Thessalonians about the fate of living Christians at Christ's return (5:1–11).

Today many stumble over the notion of an angry God, preferring instead to think of him as a kind of jolly, good-natured uncle who loves to give people a helping hand. Even more thoughtful Christians, however, struggle with the coexistence of love and wrath in the same God. It is not surprising, then, that some have embraced the view that wrath is an impersonal process of retribution operating in a moral universe and not the personal activity of God against sinful people (see Dodd 1932: 21–24). At odds with this conclusion, however, are the opening chapters of Romans, where Paul maintains that wrath is not merely something that can be attributed to the way the world is, but that it originates in God and is an activity of God (Dunn 1988: 55).

Furthermore, God's wrath must be seen in the light of his justice. God is indeed loving and kind, but his justice demands that sin, which is such an affront to his holiness and supreme majesty, be punished. It must also be remembered that the wrath of God is not like human anger, which so often is expressed in a vindictive and uncontrolled manner. God's wrath instead represents a necessary and just response to human sin. Although this wrath is a current reality for those who live in sin (Rom. 1:18, 24, 26, 28), it awaits its future completion (Rom. 5:9; 1 Thess. 1:10; Col. 3:6), just as salvation is present but will not be fully experienced until the last day (Rom. 5:21; 6:22).

Instead of fearing that future judgment, the believers in Thessalonica have a great hope, since Christ will return and "rescue" both them and the missionaries (note the switch to the first person) "from the coming wrath" (for a fuller survey of the notion of God's "wrath," see G. Stählin, TDNT 5:382–447;

---

48. In 1:10 the present tense of the participle ἐρχομένης (coming) does not indicate anything about the timing of this event, as though the outpouring of wrath is imminent (Milligan 1908: 15) or has begun but is not yet complete (Ellingworth and Nida 1975: 16). The present tense serves instead to make the coming of God's wrath more vivid and thus emphasizes this future event. A similar emphasis is achieved by the word order—placing the participle after the noun, with the repeated article ("the wrath—*the one that is coming*").

Morris 1960; Ridderbos 1975: 108–14; Travis 1986; G. L. Borchert, *DPL* 1993: 991–93).

Additional Notes

1:2. If, as seems likely, the prepositional phrase "concerning you all" ought to be taken with the preceding main clause "We give thanks to God," this results in there being no explicit direct object of the participial clause "making mention." Although the direct object "of you" is easily implied, a number of late MSS ($\aleph^2$ C D F G Y 𝔐 it sy; Ambst) have inserted the pronoun ὑμῶν to ensure this sense: "by making mention *of you.*"

1:5. Instead of ἡμῶν εὐαγγέλιον (*our* gospel), $\aleph^*$ has added τοῦ θεοῦ (our *God's* gospel), while $\aleph^c$ and C have the more typical Pauline expression τοῦ θεοῦ εὐαγγέλιον (God's gospel).

1:5. On external evidence alone, it is difficult to choose between the presence of the preposition ἐν before πληροφορίᾳ (so A C D F G Ψ 𝔐 r vg^{mss}) and its omission (so $\aleph$ B 33 lat), although the latter reading is slightly stronger. The internal evidence, however, clearly supports the omission of the preposition. It is easy to see why scribes would have added the preposition (to conform to the pattern of the two preceding nouns, which both are preceded by "in"), whereas no plausible reason can be given for its omission (so Rigaux 1956: 374; Koester 1985: 220; Fee 1992: 170; 2009: 28n5). The omission of the preposition has important consequences for how one ought to view the interrelationship of the three nouns ("power," "Holy Spirit," "much conviction") in this clause (see comment on 1:5).

1:5. There is strong textual support for both the presence of the preposition ἐν before ὑμῖν at the end of the verse (so B D F G Ψ 0278 𝔐 it sy^{(p)}) and its omission (so $\aleph$ A C P 048 33 81 104 326* 945 1739 1881 *pc* vg^{st}). Since the immediately preceding word ἐγενήθημεν ends with the letters -εν, this textual variant may have either been accidentally omitted through haplography (Best 1977: 76) or accidentally added through dittography (Fee 1994a: 41n7; Fee, however, later questions his previous decision: see 2009: 28n6). There is a slight difference in meaning between the two readings: the text without the preposition emphasizes Paul's relationship *toward* or *before* the Thessalonians (Frame 1912: 79), whereas the text without the preposition stresses the apostle's conduct *among* them (Fee 2009: 28n6). Since Paul is concerned in 2:1–16 to defend his conduct among the believers in Thessalonica, the larger clause of 1:5b should be seen as foreshadowing the apostle's upcoming defense—an interpretation that favors the presence of the preposition.

1:6. The important Vaticanus and a few much later Vulgate MSS add the conjunction καί, thereby changing the original "with the joy of the Holy Spirit" (i.e., a joy that comes from the Holy Spirit) to "with joy *and* the Holy Spirit." Not only does this altered reading lack strong textual support, but it also goes against Paul's understanding of joy/rejoicing as a gift that proceeds from the presence and working of the Holy Spirit (see comment on 1 Thess. 5:16; also see Gal. 5:22; Rom. 14:17).

1:7. The plural form τύπους (examples: so $\aleph$ A C F G Ψ 𝔐 sy^h) is likely an intentional correction so that the word agrees with the plural subject "you." The singular form τύπον (example: so B D^{(1)} 6 33 81 104 1739 1881 *pc* lat sy^p), however, is appropriate if Paul is referring in a collective manner to the Thessalonian church as a whole.

1:8. Despite the strong support for the addition of ἐν τῇ before Ἀχαΐα ($\aleph$ C D F G Ψ 𝔐 lat), it seems more likely that the preposition and the definite article have been added under the influence of the identical phrase in 1:7 than if these words had been omitted (a similar instance of the secondary addition of ἐν is found in Rom. 13:9; Col. 2:7). This preferred shorter reading (so B K 6 33 365 614 629 630 1505 1739 [1881] *al* r vg^{mss}), in which the single definite article does double duty for the nouns "Macedonia" and "Achaia," emphasizes the totality—all of Greece—in contrast to "in every place" elsewhere.

1:8. Instead of the simple ἀλλά (but), some MSS (א² D² 𝔐 m vg^cl; Ambst) have ἀλλὰ καί (but also)—clearly an elaboration by copyists in response to the preceding οὐ μόνον (not only).

1:9. The apparent awkwardness of the shift ("report concerning *us* . . . what kind of visit *we* had") led some scribes to "correct" the text to the smoother reading ὑμῶν (concerning *you*: B 81 323 614 629 630 945 *al* a d vg^mss sa^mss bo^ms). Yet ἡμῶν (concerning *us*) not only has stronger MS support but also is the more difficult (and thus preferred) reading (Best 1977: 81).

1:10. Wallace (1990) argues that the preposition ἐκ (א A B P 0278 33 81 1505 1739 1881 2464 *pc* latt) is an early corruption of ἀπό (C D E F G K L Ψ 𝔐) and that "there *might* be some support here for a pretribulational rapture" (478). Not only is the former reading (ἐκ) far superior on textual grounds, but Wallace's theological inference from the latter reading (ἀπό) must also be judged to be a good example of eisegesis.

Excursus 1
Is 1 Thessalonians 1:9b–10 Pre-Pauline?

The view that 1:9b–10 is pre-Pauline has become almost axiomatic in NT scholarship. Most consider these verses to be a summary of missionary preaching to the Gentiles (covering such topics as the rejection of idols, the existence of one God, Jesus and his resurrection, and the eschatological events of the parousia and final judgment), which Paul has borrowed and adapted somewhat to describe his original ministry activity in Thessalonica (so, e.g., Rigaux 1956: 389–97; Langevin 1965; Wilckens 1963: 80–91; Bussman 1971: 38–56; Best 1977: 85–87; Neyrey 1980: 220–21; Richard 1995: 53–58; et al.). This position is summarized well in the statement of Adolf von Harnack given some time ago: "Here [1:9b–10] we have the mission-preaching to pagans in a nutshell" (1924: 117; 1962: 1.89). Others agree that 1:9b–10 is pre-Pauline yet see this passage not as traditional missionary preaching but as fragments of either a creedal formula or, less likely, a baptismal hymn. Thus Collins (1984: 338–39), for example, states: "The pre-Pauline character of the creedal formula found 1 Thess 1,10 . . . is now almost universally recognized" (see also, e.g., Friedrich 1965; Kramer 1966; Wengst 1972; Havener 1981; for a brief survey of the scholarly debate over the nature of the pre-Pauline traditions underlying 1 Thess. 1:9b–10, see Collins 1984: 20–23).

Proponents of this pre-Pauline position typically appeal to the presence of several words that are not characteristic of the apostle: (1) Paul normally describes conversion not with the verb "to turn" (ἐπιστρέφω, *epistrephō*) but with other expressions such as "to believe" (Rom. 13:11; 1 Cor. 3:5; 15:2, 11; Gal. 2:16) or "to receive the word" (1 Thess. 1:6; 2:13); (2) Paul elsewhere writes only of serving "the Lord," meaning Christ Jesus (Rom. 12:11; 14:18; 16:18; Eph. 6:7; Col. 3:24), never "God"; (3) the adjective "true" (ἀληθινός, *alēthinos*), used here to describe God, does not occur anywhere else in Paul's Letters; (4) the verb "to wait" (ἀναμένω, *anamenō*) is a hapax legomenon (appears only once) in the NT, as Paul elsewhere uses compounds of δεχόμαι (*dechomai*) to express the idea of waiting, especially in connection with the return of Christ (Rom. 8:23; 1 Cor. 1:7; Gal. 5:5; Phil. 3:20); (5) Paul seldom uses the term "Son" (υἱός, *huios*) in references to the parousia, preferring instead the terms "Lord" or "Lord Jesus (Christ)" (e.g., 1 Thess. 1:3; 2:19; 3:13; 4:15; 5:2, 23; 2 Thess. 1:7; 2:1, 2, 8); (6) the phrase "from the heavens" (ἐκ τῶν οὐρανῶν, *ek tōn ouranōn*) differs from Paul's normal practice of using the singular form of the noun and omitting the article (Rom. 1:18; 1 Cor. 8:5;

15:47; 2 Cor. 5:2; Gal. 1:8; Col. 4:1; 1 Thess. 4:16; 2 Thess. 1:7); (7) the definite article in the phrase "from the dead" (ἐκ τῶν νεκρῶν, *ek tōn nekrōn*) usually is omitted in this formulaic expression (e.g., Rom. 4:24; 6:4, 9; 7:4; 8:11; 1 Cor. 15:12; Gal. 1:1; Phil. 3:11); and (8) the concept of eschatological deliverance is normally expressed in Paul not with the verb ῥύομαι (*rhyomai*, rescue) but σῴζω (*sōzō*, save). Further support for the pre-Pauline character of 1:9b–10 is often seen in the fact that these verses lack two distinctive features of Paul's teaching: the central role of the cross and God's justifying grace.

Despite the seemingly compelling nature of such arguments, a number of factors suggest that 1:9b–10 comes from the hand of Paul (see Wanamaker 1990: 84–88; Hooker 1996; Furnish 2007: 48–49). First, the evidence of the vocabulary is not as decisive as it initially appears:

1. The verb "to turn" is used twice elsewhere by Paul: 2 Cor. 3:16 speaks of turning to the Lord and Gal. 4:9 refers to turning away from God to other gods. Although the "turning" is in the reverse direction, the latter passage in an especially striking manner parallels the vocabulary of 1 Thess. 1:9b: "how you are turning/turned . . . in order to serve" (πῶς ἐπιστρέφετε/ἐπεστρέψατε . . . δουλεύειν). Since the Pauline character of the language of Gal. 4:9 is not questioned, it should also not be doubted in 1 Thess. 1:9b.

2. The claim that Paul normally uses the verb "to serve" only with Christ instead of God is misleading. Of the seventeen occurrences of this verb, only five have Christ as their object. The remaining instances contain a variety of objects, such as sin (Rom. 6:6), one's spirit (7:6), the law of God (7:25), the younger person (9:12), things that by nature are not gods (Gal. 4:8), the elemental spirits (4:9), other people (5:13), and Paul himself (Phil. 2:22). The apostle's language of serving "God" in 1 Thess. 1:9b, therefore, is not nearly the anomaly it is claimed to be.

3. Although the adjective "true" (ἀληθινός, *alēthinos*) used to describe God is found only here in Paul's Letters, the closely related form ἀληθής (*alēthēs*, true) does occur, one time similarly used to characterize God (Rom. 3:4). Furthermore, the adjective seems an obvious choice for the apostle in his contrast between God and idols, especially in view of the term's LXX background.

4. It is true that the verb "to wait" (ἀναμένω) is not typically Pauline. The significance of this is offset, however, by the fact that the word occurs nowhere else in the NT either. Thus there is no evidence either way as to its possible pre-Pauline character.

5. Paul does not normally use the title "Son" when discussing the parousia. The apostle does, however, frequently employ this term in other contexts, especially when he wants to stress the close relationship that Jesus shares with God the Father. Thus the presence of "Son" in 1 Thess. 1:10, though somewhat atypical of Paul's known practice, is not at all impossible. Moreover, the Pauline character of this verse is strengthened

by the parallel with Rom. 5:9–10, where the "Son" is similarly said to save believers from the future "wrath."

6. The use of the plural "heavens" with the definite article does not provide evidence of the pre-Pauline character of 1:9b–10. Paul uses the plural on a number of occasions (2 Cor. 5:1; Eph. 1:10; 3:15; 4:10; 6:9; Phil. 3:20; Col. 1:5, 16, 20; 1 Thess. 1:10), only one less time than the singular (Rom. 1:18; 10:6; 1 Cor. 8:5; 15:47; 2 Cor. 5:2; 12:2; Gal. 1:8; Col. 1:23; 4:1; 1 Thess. 4:16; 2 Thess. 1:7). Similarly, the definite article occurs only slightly less than its omission, and it is found in both the singular and plural form as well as both with and without a preposition. The evidence is inconclusive.

7. The definite article in the phrase "from the dead" is found two other times in Paul's Letters (Eph. 5:14; Col. 1:18), and so its presence in 1 Thess. 1:10 could well come from the hand of the apostle. Furthermore, there is also some textual support for the omission of the article here in 1:10. While the evidence for its omission is not strong (uncials A C K and a number of minuscules), it is nevertheless sufficient to cause the editors of NA[28] to place square brackets around the article, thereby indicating the questionable character of its presence.

8. The verb ῥύομαι (*rhyomai*, rescue), contrary to the claims of some (Best 1977: 85; Richard 1995: 57), does occur elsewhere in Paul's Letters in an eschatological context. The first instance is Rom. 7:24, where there is a rhetorical appeal for deliverance from "this body of death." The second instance is Rom. 11:26, which cites an OT passage to support the eschatological salvation of Israel through the coming of a savior out of Zion.

Although there are one or two unusual phrases in 1:9b–10, many other Pauline passages could provide an equal amount of unique vocabulary. For example, 1:9a makes use of the verb "report" (ἀπαγγέλλω, *apangellō*) and the noun "visit" (εἴσοδος, *eisodos*), each of which occurs elsewhere in Paul only once (1 Cor. 14:25 and 1 Thess. 2:1, respectively). Yet no one considers this sufficient evidence to conclude that the verse could not have been written by Paul. Furthermore, there are a number of words in 1:9b–10 that either are distinctly Pauline ("idol," "to rescue," "wrath") or are found commonly in his letters ("to raise"). Therefore, the first and primary reason for judging 1:9b–10 to be pre-Pauline, the presence of several words claimed to be atypical for the apostle, does not ultimately prove to be convincing.

The second reason for viewing 1:9b–10 as pre-Pauline is similarly unpersuasive. The omission of any reference to the cross and the redemptive significance of Christ's death in a description of his preaching ministry is notable for Paul. Yet it is equally strange to find such an omission in a pre-Pauline formulation of the gospel. If the apostle were borrowing from traditional missionary preaching to the Gentiles, would such material not have contained some reference to the death of Christ? Furthermore, what advocates of the pre-Pauline view do not seem to recognize is that the material in 1:9b–10 is not really a summary of missionary preaching at all. Instead of describing the *contents* of the gospel, these verses recount the *consequences* that the gospel has had in the lives of the Thessalonians.

The evidence indicates, therefore, that far too much has been made of the claimed anomalies in 1:9b–10 and that the data does not demand that this material be judged pre-Pauline. Instead, if these verses are viewed as coming from the hand of Paul, a compelling explanation exists for the presence of not just 1:9b–10 but 1:9a as well. These two verses summarize not traditional missionary preaching to Gentiles but what Paul is going to say in the body of the letter. The Pauline thanksgivings typically serve to introduce the major themes of the letter, and that same function is at work here in 1 Thessalonians. In 1:9a the reference to the original "visit" of Paul and his coworkers to Thessalonica foreshadows well the extended defense in 2:1–16 of that same "visit" as well as the subsequent explanation in 2:17–3:10 of why the apostle has not been able to return for a second visit (esp. note the repetition of the unusual term "visit" in 2:1). The reference to "turning to God from idols in order to serve a living and true God" has in view a radical change not just in the thinking and beliefs of the Thessalonian converts but also in their conduct and actions and thus anticipates the exhortations to proper conduct in 4:1–12 and 5:12–22. The notion of "waiting for his Son from the heavens" looks ahead in a general way to the lengthy eschatological discussion of 4:13–5:11, while the additional phrases of "whom he raised from the dead, Jesus, the one who rescues us from the coming wrath" foreshadows in a more specific way this same material. Therefore 1 Thess. 1:9b–10 ought to be viewed not as pre-Pauline but, along with the rest of the thanksgiving section, as originating from the hand of the apostle.

III. Defense of Apostolic Actions and Absence (2:1–3:13)

The body of the letter falls into two major sections: the first half (2:1–3:13) involves Paul's *defense* of the integrity of his motives and conduct, while the second half (4:1–5:22) involves Paul's *exhortations* to the Thessalonian church. The defense logically comes prior to the exhortations, since Paul first needs to reestablish his readers' trust and confidence so that they will accept the appeals and encouragements he gives them later in the letter. The apostle's extended defense consists of two parts that are also logically arranged in chronological order: Paul first defends the genuineness of his *past* actions during his mission-founding visit to Thessalonica (2:1–16) and then defends his *present* absence from the believers in this city (2:17–3:10). The first half of the letter body comes to a close with two transitional prayers (3:11–13): the first prayer (3:11) looks back to a major concern previously raised in the defensive half of the letter, while the second prayer (3:12–13) looks ahead to three key themes about to taken up in the exhortative half.

A. Defense of Past Actions in Thessalonica (2:1–16)

In 1 Thess. 2:1–16 Paul defends the integrity of his motives and conduct during his mission-founding visit to Thessalonica. Non-Christians in that city—the "fellow citizens" (2:14) of the believers—not only oppressed and harassed members of the church but also raised questions about the integrity of its founder, Paul. They claimed that the apostle was no different from the wandering philosophers or traveling teachers of that day who had a notorious reputation for being interested solely in winning human praise and financial gain. Although the Christians in Thessalonica had not bought into these charges, Paul—in the context of a young church separated from its leader and under heavy social pressure to resume their former pagan practices—felt the need to answer these accusations. He begins the body of the letter, therefore, with a lengthy autobiographical reminder of how both he and his readers conducted themselves during his past visit to them.

In 2:1–12 Paul first focuses on his own conduct and that of his co-missionaries during the original visit, highlighting in a variety of ways "how holy and righteous and blameless we were to you believers" (2:10). In 2:13–16 the apostle then shifts to the Thessalonians' response to that past visit. That this response of the Thessalonian Christians was positive—they not only accepted the word of Paul as the word of God (2:13) but also were willing to be persecuted for this word, thereby imitating the persecuted churches in Judea (2:14–16)—further confirms the genuine character of the apostle and his mission-founding work in their midst. The autobiographical material of 2:1–16, therefore, functions to defend the integrity of Paul's motives and conduct during his past visit and thereby to reestablish the confidence of his readers. This renewed trust in the apostle (and thus also in his gospel message) would not only encourage the Thessalonian believers to stand firm amid heavy social pressures (esp. 3:1–10) but also ensure that they obey the instructions that Paul will yet give them in the second half of this letter (4:1–5:22).

Literary Analysis

Character of the Passage

First Thessalonians 2:1–16 (esp. 2:1–12) belongs to the genre of autobiography or autobiographical report—a section of the letter in which Paul provides a self-description of his past activities.[1] Although these autobiographical sections do not possess any recognizable structure or other formal elements, they nevertheless can be identified and distinguished from their surrounding material by a common subject matter: Paul's life and the gospel that he preaches. Another common feature of these autobiographical sections is their location: most, like the one under consideration here, are located at the beginning of the letter body, immediately following the thanksgiving section (Rom. 1:11–16a; 2 Cor. 1:12–2:17, continued in 7:5–16 and 10:7–12:13; Gal. 1:11–2:21; Phil. 1:12–26; 3:2–14).

The function of these autobiographical reports has been traditionally understood to be that of not merely informing readers about Paul's life but also defending the apostle and reaffirming his authority over the letter recipients. This apologetic or defensive function explains why these autobiographical sections are typically located at the beginning of the letter body. If Paul wants to ensure that the contents of his letter will be accepted and obeyed, it is necessary for him to respond to any criticisms that may be directed against him and so win back the trust and confidence of his readers. As Boers (1975–76: 153) observes: "In most of Paul's letters, after the thanksgiving, characteristically follows as a discrete section the apostolic apology in which the apostle speaks of himself and the gospel he proclaims, evidently to establish or reaffirm himself and his proclamation with his readers."

The apologetic function of the autobiographical reports, however, is strongly rejected by Lyons (1985) in his extensive study of this epistolary section in two of Paul's Letters: Gal. 1:11–2:21 and 1 Thess. 2:1–16. Lyons argues that the apostle's self-descriptions are intended to provide his readers with a concrete illustration of someone who exemplifies the gospel. The autobiographical reports, therefore, have an implicit paraenetic, or exhortative, function:

> Succinctly and simply put, Paul's autobiographical remarks function not to distinguish him from his converts nor to defend his person or authority but to establish his ethos as an "incarnation" of the gospel of Jesus Christ. He highlights his "autobiography" in the interests of this gospel and his readers. He is concerned that, by imitating him, they too should incarnate the gospel. . . . His autobiographical remarks rarely supplement the major concern of a letter, but rather support it by means of a flesh-and-blood illustration. (1985: 226–27)

Although the majority of scholars have not found Lyons's argument to be convincing for the autobiographical statements in Gal. 1:11–2:21, there has been a rather wide acceptance of his analysis of Paul's self-description in 1 Thess. 2:1–16. This endorsement is largely due to a significant shift that had already taken place in scholarship over the perceived function of this specific passage. Thus I leave this general discussion of Paul's autobiographical statements and turn to the more narrow and controversial issue of the function of 1 Thess. 2:1–16.

Function of the Passage

Until relatively recent times there had been widespread agreement that Paul in 1 Thess. 2:1–16 was in some real sense defending himself. Some claimed that Paul was under attack from *inside* the church, from either Judaizers (Neil 1957: xv–xvi,

---

1. The fullest treatment of the autobiographical statements in Paul's Letters is that of Lyons 1985; see also Roetzel 1982: 34–35; Gaventa 1986; Aune 1987: 189–90.

33–47; Hendriksen 1955: 11), gnostics (Schmithals 1972: 128–218; Harnisch 1973), spiritual enthusiasts (Lütgert 1909; Jewett 1972), or millenarianists (Meeks 1983: 687–705; Jewett 1986: 102–4, 159–78). The majority, under the influence of Acts 17:1–9, saw the charges coming from *outside* the church, namely, from unbelieving Jews in Thessalonica (e.g., Milligan 1908: xxxi–xxxii; Lake 1911: 76; Frame 1912: 9–10, 90; Plummer 1918: xvii–xviii, 17–18; Morris 1959: 22; Unger 1962: 40–41; Holtz 1986: 65–66). But while scholars debated the exact identity of Paul's opponents in Thessalonica, they did agree that in 2:1–16 Paul was defending himself from actual accusations and that the function of this passage was apologetic. Thus in the early 1970s Schmithals (1972: 151) could say with justification: "On this point the exegetes from the time of the Fathers down to the last century have never been in doubt."

The situation dramatically changed, however, with the publication of Abraham Malherbe's 1970 article, "'Gentle as a Nurse': The Cynic Background to I Thess ii." Malherbe, developing to a greater degree the early claims of Dibelius (1937: 7–11) concerning the Cynic background of 1 Thess. 2, highlighted the striking parallels in language and thought between Paul in this passage and the orator-turned-Cynic philosopher Dio Chrysostom (AD 40–120) in his address *To the People of Alexandria* (dated AD 108–112). Here Dio identifies some problems with the actions and motives of certain Cynic philosophers and then contrasts these with the characteristics found in a true philosopher. Since Dio here was not responding to any specific accusations made against himself personally, Malherbe assumed that Paul in 1 Thess. 2:1–16 was also not defending himself against actual accusations. Instead, the antithetical statements of this passage should be viewed as traditional topos and vocabulary of the philosopher depicting himself. Malherbe concluded, therefore, that the function of 2:1–16 is not apologetic but paraenetic: Paul is presenting the behavior of himself and his fellow missionaries as a model for the Thessalonian believers to follow.

Malherbe's article, along with the later study of Pauline autobiography by Lyons (1985), caused a paradigmatic shift to take place in biblical scholarship concerning the function of 2:1–16. The widespread agreement among interpreters today is that the autobiographical statements of this passage have an exclusively exemplary or paraenetic function and that the traditional apologetic function is no longer a realistic option (so Stegemann 1985: 397–416; Wanamaker 1990: 91; A. Smith 1990: 78–79; Hughes 1990: 101; Schoon-Janssen 1991: 39–65; Richard 1995: 88–89; Walton 1995; Gaventa 1998: 5–6; Holmes 1998: 60; Malherbe 2000: 79–81, 134; McKinnish Bridges 2008: 43–44; Shogren 2012: 81–83).

Despite this new consensus, there are compelling grounds for viewing the primary function of 2:1–16 as defensive or apologetic (for a fuller justification of the traditional function of this passage, see Weima 1997a; Still 1999: 137–49; Weima 2000b: 114–23; Holtz 2000: 69–80; S. Kim 2005: 37–47; Fee 2009: 52–53):

1. There is the evidence of the thanksgiving section (1:2–10), particularly the lengthy reference to the mission-founding activity of Paul and his coworkers in 1:5. The significance of this verse becomes clear through a comparison of this thanksgiving section with the thanksgiving sections of Paul's other letters. Whereas in his other thanksgivings Paul focuses *on his readers* and his thanksgiving to God for *them*, here in 1:5 Paul focuses on *himself* and the righteous character of *his* activity among them. One is struck, however, not

just by the mere presence of this unparalleled statement in a thanksgiving section but also by the prominent location (prior to the additional causes of thanksgiving in 1:6–10), the length, and the apparent defensive tone of this verse. In light of the fact that the thanksgiving section typically functions to foreshadow the central issues of the letter as a whole, it appears that Paul in 1 Thessalonians is very much concerned about defending his character and already here in the thanksgiving anticipates the lengthy defense he will present in 2:1–16.

2. A defensive function for 2:1–16 is supported by the apostolic parousia—a section of the letter in which Paul seeks to make his parousia, or "presence," more powerfully felt among his readers—found in 2:17–3:10. Paul uses this epistolary convention in 1 Thessalonians to reassure the believers of his continued love and care for them. The need for Paul to reassure the Thessalonians of this fact was due to his sudden separation from them (2:17–20) and the subsequent persecution (3:1–5) that they had to endure—events that apparently left Paul feeling vulnerable to criticism for his failure thus far to return to them. There appears to exist, therefore, a parallel between the function of the apostolic parousia of 2:17–3:10 and the autobiographical section of 2:1–16. Just as 2:17–3:10 is a defense of Paul's *present* absence from the Thessalonians (*apologia pro absentia sua*), so 2:1–16 is a defense of Paul's *past* ministry among them (*apologia pro vita sua [et labore suo]*).[2]

3. A variety of unique features of the antithetical statements (not *x* but *y*) in 2:1–16 provide still further evidence that Paul is very much concerned with defending the integrity of his character and actions during his mission-founding work among them. One such unique feature is Paul's double appeal to God as a "witness" (2:5, 10). The apostle rarely invokes God as a witness in his letters (elsewhere only in Rom. 1:9; 2 Cor. 1:23; Phil. 1:8), and our passage is the only place where he does it twice. Another notable feature is Paul's twofold claim in 2:4 that God has "examined" him and his coworkers ("We have been examined by God to be entrusted with the gospel; . . . God, the one who examines our hearts"). Elsewhere Paul always uses the verb "examine" (δοκιμάζω, dokimazō) in the active voice, with one person or a group of persons as its subject; only here does he use it in the passive, where God is the one doing the examining. This striking twofold reference in 2:4 to God's activity of "examining" the missionaries adds significant weight to the legal-like language of 2:5 and 2:10, where the apostle appeals to God and the Thessalonians as witnesses and so further supports a polemical context.

4. Perhaps the most important feature about the antithetical statements in 2:1–16 is their frequency. Elsewhere in 1 Thessalonians, eight such statements can be found (1:5, 8; 2:17; 4:7, 8; 5:6, 9, 15). These antithetical statements, however, are scattered throughout the letter, whereas five occurrences can be found in just the first eight verses of 2:1–16 (vv. 1–2, 3–4, 4b, 5–7b, 8b; see also 2:13).

2. These Latin phrases for the function of 2:1–16 and 2:17–3:10 are found in a number of older commentators (e.g., Moffatt 1897: 4, 26, 29; Frame 1912: 14, 17, 140; Hendriksen 1955: 74; more recently Lambrecht 1990: 200). It is difficult to determine who first coined this phrase, though Thessalonian commentators may be borrowing from John Henry Newman's classic defense, *Apologia pro Vita Sua* (1864), which became a best seller and remained a well-known work in the late nineteenth and early twentieth centuries.

Furthermore, in contrast to the other antithetical statements in the letter, all of the five instances in 2:1–8 are autobiographical: they refer to Paul and his coworkers. Finally, some of these five autobiographical antithetical statements are clearly being emphasized with the repeated use of the negative: there is a threefold occurrence of the negative in the antithetical statement of 2:3–4 and a fivefold occurrence of the negative in the antithetical statement of 2:5–7b. Therefore, although the mere presence of antithetical statements does not necessarily prove the existence of a polemical context, the several unique features of the antithetical statements in 2:1–16 strongly suggest that here Paul is not merely presenting himself as a model to be imitated but rather is countering accusations of some kind. When it is further recognized that Paul explicitly identifies opponents who are persecuting the church (2:14, "your own fellow citizens"), this creates an even greater presumption that the antithetical statements of 2:1–16, even if they have a rhetorical flair, correspond to a historical reality.

5. The traditional defensive function of 2:1–16 gains still further support from Paul's repeated appeals to the Thessalonians' firsthand knowledge about him and, more specifically, about his conduct during his original ministry among them.[3] The disclosure formula in the simple form "you know" (οἴδατε, *oidate*) occurs nine times in the letter as a whole, with four of these occurrences in our relatively brief passage (2:1, 2, 5, 11; see also 1:5; 3:3, 4; 4:2; 5:2). Yet another appeal to the Thessalonian believers' personal knowledge about Paul is found in 2:9 with the use of the introductory expression "For you remember, brothers." Additionally, the second appeal to God as a witness in 2:10 ("You and God are witnesses") also includes the Thessalonians themselves (note the emphatic position of "you") as those who have observed with their own eyes the "holy, righteous, and blameless" conduct of the missionaries. Thus Paul makes no less than six explicit appeals in 2:1–16 to the firsthand knowledge that the readers have about him during his original ministry among them. Significantly, these repeated appeals are not, as elsewhere in the letter, directed to the teaching and commands that the apostle had previously shared with them (so 3:3, 4; 4:2; 5:2), but to the moral conduct and behavior of Paul during his original ministry among them.

The evidence surveyed above indicates that modern interpreters have too quickly abandoned the long-held view that Paul in 1 Thess. 2:1–16 is in some real sense defending himself.[4] Although not all the factors discussed above are equally significant, they have the cumulative effect of legitimizing the claim that

---

3. As Holtz (2000: 72) observes: "The intensity of the appeal to the church's own experience with their apostle is singular. It lends to this section a special urgency that goes beyond purely grateful recollections."

4. This conclusion is still valid regardless of whether Paul is responding to actual accusations raised against him or to potential charges that he feared might be made. For in either situation, the function of 2:1–16 remains the same: Paul in this passage is attempting to defend himself and so reestablish the trust and confidence of his readers. As Aristotle observed: "One way of removing prejudice is to make use of the arguments by which one may clear oneself from disagreeable suspicion; *for it makes no difference whether this suspicion has been openly expressed or not*" (*Rhet.* 3.15.1).

the primary function of this passage is defensive or apologetic.[5] Non-Christians in Thessalonica—the "fellow citizens" (2:14: συμφυλέται, symphyletai) of the believers in that city—not only oppressed and harassed the church but also raised questions about the integrity of its founder, Paul, and his coworkers. Although the Thessalonian believers had not bought into these charges, in the context of a young church separated from its leader and under heavy social pressure to resume their former pagan practices, Paul felt the need to answer these accusations. He effectively accomplished this goal by beginning the letter body with an autobiographical reminder of his original ministry among them: in a pointed fashion he defends the integrity of himself and his fellow missionaries, and so reestablishes the trust and confidence of his readers. This renewed trust in the apostle (and thus also in his message) would not only encourage the Thessalonian believers to stand firm amid heavy social pressures (esp. 3:1–10) but also ensure that they will obey the instructions he will yet give them in the second half of the letter (4:1–5:22).

Extent of the Passage

The beginning of the passage is clearly indicated by both subject matter and formal features. The content and tone in 2:1–16 shifts away from that of thanksgiving for the vibrant faith and active Christian life of the Thessalonians to that of defending the integrity of Paul and his coworkers during their mission-founding work in Thessalonica. Formally, the material of 2:1–16 is distinct from that of 1:2–10; thus 2:1–16 constitutes an autobiographical report, whereas 1:2–10 belongs to the genre of thanksgiving. That 2:1 marks a shift is further indicated by the presence of a disclosure formula ("For you yourselves know") and the vocative ("brothers")—epistolary conventions typically used to indicate transition. The disclosure formula, in particular, frequently marks the beginning of the body section in Paul's Letters (2 Cor. 1:8; Gal. 1:11; Phil. 1:12; see Rom. 1:13; Col. 2:1). Finally, the compelling thematic and literary evidence that 1:10 signals the end of the preceding thanksgiving section (e.g., the eschatological climax of 1:10) naturally implies that the immediately following material of 2:1 constitutes the beginning of the next major unit.[6]

But while the beginning of a new unit at 2:1 is clear, the ending of this passage is harder to determine with the same degree of certainty. The issue centers on whether 2:13–16 ought to be included as part of a larger unit consisting of 2:1–16, or whether 2:1–12 and 2:13–16 stand alone as separate and distinct units (this assumes the authenticity of 2:13–16 in contrast to the view that these verses are a non-Pauline interpolation; on this matter, see the commentary introduction). Although 2:13–16 is distinct in a number of ways from the material in 2:1–12, the two passages are closely linked as both deal with Paul's past "visit" (εἴσοδος, eisodos) or mission-founding activity in Thessalonica: 2:1–12 deals with the conduct of the apostle

---

5. Thus, if a paraenetic, or hortatory, function is present in 2:1–16, it must be secondary or subordinate to Paul's primary purpose of defending himself. Such a secondary paraenetic function is recognized by Marshall 1983: 61; Johanson 1987: 165; Gillman 1990: 68; Verhoef 1998: 93–94.
6. The particle "for" (γάρ, gar) in 2:1 does not negate this conclusion but rather serves to highlight the connection between 2:1–16 and the earlier reference to the missionaries' conduct in Thessalonica in the thanksgiving section—either to the defensive comments of 1:5 or, because of the use of the same rare word "visit" (εἴσοδον, eisodon) and prepositional phrase "to you" (πρὸς ὑμᾶς, pros hymas), more specifically to the words of 1:9 ("what kind of visit we had among you").

during that past visit, while 2:13–16 deals with the conduct of the Thessalonians during that past visit. This shift in focus from Paul and his mission-founding visit to Thessalonica to the response of the Thessalonians to that visit follows the same pattern witnessed already twice in the thanksgiving section in 1:5–8 (v. 5: Paul's visit; vv. 6–8: their response) and 1:9–10 (v. 9a: Paul's visit; vv. 9b–10: their response).

Various other factors provide further support that 2:13–16 ought to be read along with the preceding material of 2:1–12. First, 2:12 does not contain any eschatological climax—a "sequence-termination feature" (Johanson 1987: 87) commonly found in this letter (1:10 concludes 1:2–10; next 2:16 concludes 2:1–16; and 3:13 concludes 2:17–3:13; then 5:23 perhaps serves as an eschatological climax to the whole letter). Second, 2:13 lacks any of the transitional formulas used elsewhere in this letter to mark a shift to a new subject (see 2:1, 17; 3:11; 4:1, 9, 13; 4:18; 5:1, 12, 23). Instead, the "and" (καί, *kai*) that introduces 2:13–16 ought to be taken as a coordinating conjunction (see also 1:6; *parataxis*: BDF §458) and thus serves to strengthen the link between these verses and the preceding material of 2:1–12. Third, the phrase "because of this" (διὰ τοῦτο, *dia touto*), which also introduces 2:13–16, virtually always in Paul's Letters refers back to preceding material (anaphoric function) rather than to subsequent material (cataphoric function), consequently further supporting the connection between 2:13–16 and 2:1–12. Thus, despite the different focus found in 2:1–12 (Paul and his coworkers) and 2:13–16 (the Thessalonian believers), both sections belong together as a coherent section in which Paul deals with his past "visit" or ministry work in Thessalonica.

Structure of the Passage

There is an obvious thematic shift within 2:1–16 from a focus on the motives and conduct of Paul and his coworkers during their past visit (vv. 1–12) to the response of the Thessalonian Christians to that visit (vv. 13–16). Although there are no epistolary conventions at verse 13 to mark this transition, such a shift is foreshadowed by the similar movement found twice in the thanksgiving section: 1:5–8 (v. 5: Paul's visit; vv. 6–8: their response) and 1:9–10 (v. 9a: Paul's visit; vv. 9b–10: their response). Furthermore, the closing words of 2:12 move away from the mission-founding visit of Paul to the intended goal of that visit for the believers in Thessalonica ("in order that *you* may walk worthy of the God who calls *you* into his own kingdom and glory"). Thus it is clear that 2:1–16 falls into two parts: verses 1–12 and 13–16.

The first section, dealing with the missionaries' activity, consists of six main clauses: verses 1–2, 3–4, 5–7b, 7c–8, 9, 10–12. That the first four of these clauses all contain antithetical statements (not *x* but *y*) and the fifth one opens with the transitional vocative "brothers" may justify further subdividing this first section into two parts: verses 1–8 and 9–12 (so Johanson 1987: 87–88; Lee and Lee 1975: 31–32). Yet the content of Paul's argumentation here suggests that it is probably better not to distinguish verses 1–8 and 9–12 but in the whole of these verses to see a variety of evidences used to support (note how four of the six main clauses are introduced with the conjunction "for": vv. 1–2, 3–4, 5–7b, 9) the primary goal of defending the sincere motives and conduct of the apostle during his original visit to Thessalonica.

The second section, dealing with the Thessalonians' response to Paul's past visit, consists of two main clauses: verses 13 and 14–16. The first clause gives thanks for the Thessalonians' acceptance of the word of Paul as the word of God. The second clause continues to give thanks, this time for the Thessalonians' imitation of the persecuted churches in Judea, who likewise suffer for the sake of the gospel. The mention of "the Jews" in the last word of 2:14 becomes the occasion for a rather extended description (vv. 15–16) of the role that some members of the Jewish faith have played in hindering the spread of the gospel and the consequent judgment for such activity. These verses are often claimed to be not a key part of Paul's argument in verses 13–16 but functioning as a "vituperative digression" (Johanson 1987: 100; so also Wanamaker 1990: 108–9; Furnish 2007: 69) or "parenthetical editorial comment" (Holmes 1998: 85), prompted by the reference to "the Jews" at the end of verse 14. Yet the content of 2:14–16 does serve to prepare the readers for the upcoming two themes of (1) the defense of Paul's ongoing absence from the Thessalonian believers in 2:17–20 and that of (2) the persecution endured by the Thessalonian church in 3:1–5—two themes that are then skillfully combined in 3:6–10. Both themes are introduced already in 2:14–16: the Thessalonians have become imitators of the Judean churches in that they too are being persecuted by their own fellow citizens (v. 14); also the Jews in Thessalonica instigated the opposition against Paul (v. 15: "They [the Jews] drove us out"),[7] making it impossible for the apostle to return and visit his converts in Thessalonica.

Paul's defense of his past visit to Thessalonica in 2:1–16, therefore, possesses the following structure:

1. Paul's integrity during his past visit (2:1–12)
   a. His bold preaching in the face of persecution (2:1–2)
   b. His God-examined speech (2:3–4)
   c. His "innocent as an infant" conduct (2:5–7b)
   d. His "loving as a nursing mother" conduct (2:7c–8)
   e. His self-sufficient labor (2:9)
   f. His "nurturing as a father" conduct (2:10–12)
2. The Thessalonians' response to Paul's past visit (2:13–16)
   a. Their acceptance of the word of Paul as the word of God (2:13)
   b. Their imitation of the persecuted churches in Judea (2:14–16)

Exegesis and Exposition

[1]For you yourselves know, brothers, about our visit to you, namely, that it was not insincere, [2]but though we had suffered beforehand and had been shamefully mistreated in Philippi, as you know, we had courage in our God to speak to you the gospel of God in spite of great opposition. [3]For our appeal was not from deception, nor from an impure motive, nor made with deceit, [4]but as we have been examined by God to be entrusted with the gospel, so we speak, not as those who please people but those who please God, the one who examines our hearts. [5]For we never came with a word of flattery (as you know), nor with a motive of greed (God is our witness!)

---

7. This agrees with Acts 17:5: "But the Jews were jealous, and rounding up some bad characters from the marketplace, they formed a mob and started a riot in the city, and attacked the house of Jason, seeking to bring Paul and Silas out to the Citizens Assembly."

⁶nor were we demanding honor from people, neither from you nor from others ⁷(even though we could have insisted on our importance as apostles of Christ), but we became ⌜infants⌝ among you. As a nursing mother cherishes her own children, ⁸so we, ⌜because we cared so much⌝ for you, ⌜were pleased⌝ to share with you not only the gospel ⌜of God⌝ but also our own selves, because you ⌜became⌝ beloved to us. ⁹For you remember, brothers, our labor and toil; ⌜ ⌝ while working night and day in order not to burden any of you, we preached to you the gospel of God. ¹⁰You are witnesses, and God also, how holy and righteous and blameless we were to you believers, ¹¹just as you know how we dealt with each one of you like a father with his children, ¹²appealing and encouraging and imploring ⌜you⌝ in order that you may lead a life worthy of God, the one who ⌜is calling⌝ you into his own kingdom and glory.

¹³⌜And⌝ because of this, we indeed give thanks to God constantly, namely, that when you received the word of God that you heard from us, you accepted it not as the word of human beings but, as it truly is, the word of God, which is indeed at work in you believers. ¹⁴For you yourselves, brothers, became imitators of the churches of God in Christ Jesus that are in Judea, because you indeed suffered the same things from your own fellow citizens as they also did from the Jews—¹⁵those who killed both the Lord Jesus and ⌜the prophets⌝, and who drove us out, and who do not please God, and who are hostile to all people, ¹⁶by hindering us from speaking to the Gentiles in order that they may be saved, with the result that they have been constantly filling up the measure of their sins; but the wrath ⌜of God⌝ ⌜has come⌝ upon them until the end.

1. Paul's Integrity during His Past Visit (2:1–12)

The central topic or theme of 2:1–12 (and also of the larger section 2:1–16) is a defense of Paul's integrity during his past visit to Thessalonica. That this defense of his integrity was a major concern of Paul is clear because it is the first topic the apostle chooses to take up in the body of the letter. The importance of this subject is also evident from the twofold manner in which Paul has foreshadowed his defensive concern in the thanksgiving section: first, in the lengthy apology of 1:5 ("Our gospel was not among you in word alone but also in power—both in the Holy Spirit and much conviction, as you know what kind of men we were among you because of you"); and second, in the use of the rare (for Paul) term "visit" (εἴσοδον, *eisodon*) in 1:9a ("For they themselves report concerning us what kind of visit we had among you"), which occurs again here in 2:1 to open the first major section of the letter body. The link between the apologetic concern of 2:1–16 and the same issue foreshadowed in 1:5 and 1:9a is made explicit in the conjunction "for" that opens 2:1 (unfortunately omitted in several translations: NIV, NRSV, NJB, NEB, GNT).

The apologetic function of 2:1–12 leads to two distinct but related questions: First, from whom is Paul defending himself? Second, what is the character or content of the charges to which Paul responds? With respect to the first question, it is clear that Paul's opponents come from *outside* the church. The good report about the church from Timothy as referred to in 3:6, the exemplary character of the Thessalonian believers' lives (1:6–7), Paul's description of them as "our hope and joy and crown of boasting" at Christ's return (2:19–20), the positive status of the church implied in the repeated command to "increase even more" with respect to proper conduct (4:1b, 10b), the frequent use of the term "brothers," as well as the affectionate tone of the letter as a whole—all these make it impossible to believe that Paul was facing attack from believers inside the church.

When one considers the possible opponents outside the church, the best candidates are the "fellow citizens" (συμφυλέται, *symphyletai*) explicitly mentioned by Paul in 2:14. There is clear evidence both within the Thessalonian Letters and without that the predominantly Gentile church of Thessalonica experienced significant opposition and affliction because of their newfound faith (1 Thess. 1:6b; 2:2b, 14–15; 3:1–5; 2 Thess. 1:4–7; see also 2 Cor. 8:1–2; Acts 17:5–7, 13) and that the source of this abuse was their fellow citizens (2:14). As noted above (see introduction and comment on 1:6, 9), this persecution probably did not involve physical death and martyrdom but more likely entailed social harassment due to their refusal to participate in civic and cultic activities. Given, then, that a number of the citizens of Thessalonica were harassing and persecuting members of the local church, it is not at all surprising that these attacks were also aimed at the church's leader, Paul, whom some unbelievers in the city blamed as the source of the problem.

With respect to the second question, the nature and content of the charges against which Paul is defending himself in 2:1–12, one must proceed carefully to avoid the dangers that often accompany a mirror reading of the text, particularly the danger of overinterpreting the antithetical statements that occur in such a heavy concentration in this passage. This danger has appeared so great to some that they have written off mirror reading as an inappropriate procedure, concluding that the "methodological presuppositions on which it rests are arbitrary, inconsistently applied, and unworkable" (Lyons 1985: 96 [see also 105–12]). But while it is important to recognize the problems that often accompany a mirror reading of a particular text, it does not logically follow that *any* use of this method is automatically suspect and unjustified. In other words, one should not throw the methodological baby out with the exegetical bathwater. The issue, then, is not *whether* we should use the method of mirror reading, but *how* we should use it. That matter has been addressed in a number of studies that have established a set of criteria to ensure an appropriate use of mirror reading.[8] When these criteria are followed in a mirror reading of 2:1–12 and especially of the first four antithetical statements in 2:1–7b, the evidence leads clearly to the same conclusion: Paul is defending himself against attacks on his integrity and the genuineness of his motives.[9]

---

8. See esp. the seven criteria proposed by Barclay (1987: 84–85). For further comments about the appropriate use of mirror reading, see Sumney (1990: 95–113) and Silva (1996: 104–8).

9. In this discussion, we must be careful not to confuse the issue of apostolic *integrity* with that of apostolic *status*. The latter is a problem, for example, in Paul's Letter to the Galatians, where the opponents are "inside" the church and thus concerned with matters of authority

a. His Bold Preaching in the Face of Persecution (2:1–2)

2:1 The first antithetical (not *x* but *y*) statement of 2:1–2 introduces well the theme of Paul's defense of his integrity during his past visit to Thessalonica: "For you yourselves know, brothers, about our visit [εἴσοδον, *eisodon*] to you, namely, that it was *not* insincere, *but* though we had suffered beforehand and had been shamefully mistreated in Philippi, as you know, we had courage in our God to speak to you the gospel of God in spite of great opposition." The logic of Paul's argument in this first antithetical statement can be simplified as follows: "Our visit to you was not a scam or selfishly motivated but genuine and pure, as proved by our bold preaching even in the face of severe persecution."

The negative half of this antithetical statement suggests that some unbelievers in Thessalonica were claiming that the mission-founding visit of Paul and his coworkers was "insincere" (κενή, *kenē*). Uncertainty over the precise nuance of this word has led to three possible senses of Paul's thought in this verse.

1. The literal meaning of *kenē* as "empty" or "without content" has led a few commentators to understand the apostle as claiming that he did not come to the Thessalonians "empty-handed" but brought them something, either the gospel message (2:2, 8, 9, "the gospel of God") that he proclaimed or the miracles (1:5, "with power") that he performed. Hendriksen (1955: 60), for example, offers the following paraphrase of 2:1: "Far from aiming to take something away from you, we brought you something. When we came to you, our hands were not empty" (see also Frame 1912: 92; Richard 1995: 89–90). The biggest weakness of this view, however, is that it does not agree with Paul's metaphorical use of this word everywhere else in his letters (1 Cor. 15:10, 14 [2x], 58; 2 Cor. 6:1; Gal. 2:2; Eph. 5:6; Phil. 2:16 [2x]; Col. 2:8; 1 Thess. 3:5).

2. The figurative use of *kenē* has a variety of nuances (A. Oepke, *TDNT* 3:659–60), but most translations and commentators see Paul as emphasizing the *results* of his mission: his visit was not "in vain" (RSV/NRSV), "without results" (NIV), "ineffectual" (JB), or "without effect" (NAB). Although this agrees with the use of the same term later in the letter (3:5), it does not fit the immediate context of 2:2, which focuses on the *character* of Paul's original visit.

3. A few commentators view *kenē* as stressing the *character* of Paul's past ministry in Thessalonica and so translate the term as "empty of purpose, lacking earnestness, insincere" (so Lightfoot 1904: 18; Milligan 1908: 16; Marshall 1983: 62–63; Morris 1991: 58–59). That Paul is, in fact, here emphasizing the genuine character of his visit becomes clear from the second half of the antithetical statement in 2:2, where the apostle appeals to his boldness of preaching, despite the suffering he experienced both

---

and status. In this Letter to the Thessalonians, however, where the opponents are "outside" the church and thus understandably not concerned with such matters, their attack focuses instead on Paul's integrity.

in Philippi and Thessalonica.[10] Paul's bold proclamation of the gospel in the face of much opposition proves the genuine motives of his preaching, not the successful results of his preaching. This is confirmed by the larger context of 2:1–12, where the focus is similarly on the sincere character of Paul and his coworkers' visit rather than on the results of that visit. The sense of *kenē* as "insincere" is also anticipated by Paul's claim in 1:5 that his gospel was among the Thessalonians in "much conviction," meaning that the boldness and confidence with which the apostle preached testifies to the sincere nature of his ministry among them.[11]

It is true that the difference between the two metaphorical senses of *kenē* should not be overstated (Bruce [1982: 24] comments that "the character and result of the preaching cannot be separated"; also Green 2002: 115). Nevertheless, the first antithetical statement of 2:1–2 plays a key role in introducing the central theme for the larger passage of 2:1–16, and so this distinction between Paul's defending the genuine character of his visit in contrast to the successful results of that visit is important.

The positive half of the opening antithetical statement of 2:1–2 is intended to repudiate (note how the response is introduced with the strong adversative "but" [ἀλλά, *alla*]) the implicit charge of the negative half, that the mission-founding visit of Paul and his fellow missionaries in Thessalonica was "insincere." The apostle accomplishes this goal by reminding the Thessalonian believers of the adverse circumstances surrounding that original visit: "Though we had suffered beforehand and had been shamefully mistreated in Philippi, as you know, we had courage in our God to speak to you the gospel of God in spite of great opposition." In other words, that Paul and his fellow missionaries boldly proclaimed the word of God in spite of being physically harmed and shamefully treated in both Philippi and Thessalonica testifies to their sincerity. After all, what charlatan would continue to subject himself to such abuse!

2:2

Paul first reminds his readers of the suffering he and his coworkers endured in the nearby city of Philippi. The apostle does not spell out the exact details of that affliction, stating only in a rather general way that he both "had suffered beforehand" (προπαθόντες, *propathontes*) there as well as "had been shamefully treated" (ὑβρισθέντες, *hybristhentes*; this verb, which occurs only here in Paul's Letters, means "to treat in an insolent or spiteful manner" [BDAG 1022] and thus refers to a more intense suffering than the preceding verb does). There was no need, however, for Paul to be more specific; as the phrase "as you know" indicates, the Thessalonians clearly were familiar with the details of what had

10. Malherbe (2000: 136) rightly recognizes that the second half of the antithetical statement requires that *kenos* (as *kenē* in 2:1) "has to do, not with the result, but with the character of his ministry." But because Malherbe believes that in this section Paul is indebted to the philosophical tradition, he translates *kenē* as "powerless," a word that, when negated as it is here, highlights the boldness or frankness of the apostle's speech rather than its sincerity or genuineness.

11. The term κενή in 2:1 conveys an "emptiness of sincerity," which makes it the opposite of the "full conviction" expressed by the term πληροφορία in 1:5 (see Gribomont 1979: 313–38).

taken place in Philippi. During his original ministry in Thessalonica, Paul had apparently spoken of the suffering he previously endured in Philippi. Perhaps the apostle had raised this matter as part of his repeated instruction to them about the affliction that both he and they were sure to receive (3:4: "For when we were with you, we were telling you beforehand that we were to suffer affliction"). It is also possible that Christians in Philippi who traveled to Thessalonica at least more than one time to bring a financial gift to Paul (Phil. 4:16) either told or confirmed the details of the suffering endured by the apostle in their city. Acts 16:19–40 provides a much fuller picture of exactly what happened in Philippi: Paul and Silas were arrested, dragged into the marketplace before the rulers, charged with disturbing the peace and advocating unlawful customs, attacked by the crowd, stripped of their garments, beaten with rods, thrown into prison with their feet in the stocks, and denied the rights to which they were entitled as Roman citizens. Although many scholars reject the depiction of these events in Acts,[12] this account agrees rather well with Paul's claim here that he had not merely "suffered beforehand" in Philippi but that he also "had been shamefully treated" there (see also Phil. 1:29–30).

Second, Paul reminds his Thessalonian readers of the suffering he and his coworkers endured in their own city, stating that he had preached the gospel of God to them "in spite of great opposition" (ἐν πολλῷ ἀγῶνι, *en pollō agōni*). The word *agōn* literally refers to an athletic contest, but its metaphorical use here has prompted at least three other possible connotations: (1) the intense effort or exertion entailed in preaching the gospel, thus "with strenuous exertion" (so Dibelius 1913: 6; Richard 1995: 92–93); (2) the inner anxiety in the mind of Paul and others arising from the persecution encountered in Philippi, thus "in great anguish" (so Dobschütz 1909: 85; Frame 1912: 94; Rigaux 1956: 405; Malherbe 1987: 48; 2000: 137–38); or (3) the external conflict experienced by the missionaries from those opposed to their ministry, thus "in spite of great opposition" (so the majority of translations and commentators: e.g., Milligan 1908: 17; Best 1977: 91–92; Marshall 1983: 64; Wanamaker 1990: 93; Still 1999: 128–30; Fee 2009: 59). Overwhelming support for the third option exists in the clear evidence for opposition to the original preaching of the gospel in Thessalonica (1 Thess. 1:6; 2:14–15; see also Acts 17:5–7, 13) and the ongoing opposition currently experienced by the Thessalonian church (1 Thess. 3:1–5; 2 Thess. 1:4–7; 2 Cor. 8:1–12).

One justly expects that the suffering endured by Paul and his fellow missionaries in both Philippi and Thessalonica would quickly expose any false

12. The rejection of the account in Acts 16 by Richard (1995), for example, leads him in his translation and interpretation of the two participles in 1 Thess. 2:2, προπαθόντες and ὑβρισθέντες, to minimize the degree of suffering experienced by Paul. Although the majority of scholars take the first verb, προπάσχω (the prefix makes this form a hapax legomenon in the NT), in the passive sense of "to suffer," Richard opts for a rarer active sense of "to fight or struggle." Similarly, whereas most see in the second verb ὑβρίζω a reference to physical punishment received by Paul at the hands of officials (G. Bertram, *TDNT* 8:305), Richard restricts its meaning to verbal abuse and so translates it as "to insult or scoff" (see Richard 1995: 78, 91).

motives these preachers might have. But instead of responding to such adversity with a less offensive message, a more circumspect delivery, or simply a quick exit out of town, they proclaimed the gospel story with boldness: "We had courage in our God to speak to you the gospel of God." The verb παρρησιάζομαι (*parrēsiazomai*), along with the more common noun form παρρησία from which it is derived, originally had a political sense: the right of a citizen to make one's own thoughts known. Since this freedom to speak often involved challenging the opinions of others, even those of high rank, the term *parrēsia* frequently conveys the nuance of "courage, confidence, boldness, fearlessness" (BDAG 781–82; H. Schlier, *TDNT* 5:871–86; Spicq 1994: 56–62). The specific context of 2:2, the opposition faced by the missionaries in both Philippi and Thessalonica, clearly suggests, therefore, that Paul here is not merely highlighting their *freedom* of speech (so Richard 1995: 92) but rather their *boldness* of speech (as in the apostle's only other use of the verbal form in Eph. 6:20).[13]

As much as Paul here wants to draw attention to himself and especially the sincere nature of his original visit to Thessalonica, he does not want his readers to overlook God's role in the apostle's ministry among them. Indeed, this involvement of God is further evidence of the sincere nature of his visit. Thus Paul makes it clear that the boldness he and other missionaries exhibited was not of their own doing but something made possible only "in our God" (ἐν τῷ θεῷ ἡμῶν, *en tō theō hēmōn*). This phrase should not be interpreted by analogy with the common "in Christ" formula to refer to some kind of mystical union with God (thus Hendriksen 1955: 61), nor should it be seen as a reference to "frank speech" given in the presence of God (thus Richard 1995: 92). Rather, the preposition *en* frequently is used instrumentally, and so here Paul highlights God's role as the divine source of the missionaries' courage (so, e.g., Best 1977: 91; Bruce 1982: 25; Wanamaker 1990: 92). A second explicit reference to God is found in the phrase "the gospel of God" (τὸ εὐαγγέλιον τοῦ θεοῦ, *to euangelion tou theou*), which, although somewhat redundant after the preceding reference to God, has the rhetorical effect of emphasizing God's role as the divine source of not just the boldness exhibited by the gospel messengers but also of the gospel message itself (the genitive *tou theou* is almost certainly subjective: God's gospel).

b. His God-Examined Speech (2:3–4)

The second antithetical statement of 2:3–4 continues (the conjunction "for" [γάρ, *gar*] links these verses with the preceding material of 2:1–2) Paul's defense by appealing to the apostle's God-examined speech: **2:3**

> For our appeal was
> *not* from deception,
> *nor* from an impure motive,

13. The bold character of Paul's preaching is something that the apostle has already highlighted for his readers in 1:5 ("in much conviction").

> *nor* made with deceit,
> *but* as we have been examined by God to be entrusted with the
> gospel,
> > so we speak,
> > *not* as those who please people
> > *but* those who please God, the one who examines our
> > hearts.

The noun παράκλησις (*paraklēsis*) is a characteristically Pauline word (twenty of its twenty-nine occurrences in the NT are in Paul's Letters) that has a variety of meanings, ranging from "encouragement, exhortation," to "appeal, request," and to "comfort, consolation" (BDAG 766). A few commentators have argued here for the third option, claiming either that Paul is employing OT language (Isa. 49:10) to present himself as a messianic prophet with a message of consolation (Denis 1957), or that Paul is comforting believers who are discouraged over the apparent failure of the parousia to occur (Kemmler 1975: 175–77). The context, however, involves the initial communication of the gospel to the Thessalonians (note the twofold occurrence of the verb "to speak" in 2:2 and 2:4, which emphasizes the activity of preaching rather than its content); hence it is best to see the noun *paraklēsis* as referring to Paul's missionary preaching (O. Schmitz, *TDNT* 5:795). This preaching was no neutral presentation of the facts about Jesus but an urgent "appeal" to turn from idols to the living God and accept his Son as deliverer from the coming wrath (Best 1977: 92–93; Marshall 1983: 64).

But while some in Thessalonica accepted the gospel message, others raised questions about the gospel messenger. Paul's threefold denial that his appeal to them was "not from deception, nor from an impure motive, nor made with deceit" strengthens the impression made in the first antithetical statement of 2:1–2 that the attack against the apostle focused on his integrity.[14]

The first denial of Paul that his appeal or preaching to them was "not from deception" (οὐκ ἐκ πλάνης, *ouk ek planēs*) has two possible connotations. A first option is that *planē* refers to an *intellectual* defect (error): Paul's preaching did not contain any misunderstandings about God and his will.[15] A second possibility is that the word refers to a *moral* defect (deception, deceit, fraud): Paul's preaching was not intended to deceive the Thessalonians for his own personal gain.[16] Although it is impossible to determine with certainty which

14. Horbury (1982) uses this threefold denial to argue that Paul was defending himself from unbelieving Jews who accused him of false prophecy. Although Horbury presents a number of interesting parallels to 2:3, his whole argument rests on verbal matches with only this one verse and so involves the kind of mirror reading that ought to be rejected.

15. Mearns (1980–81: 145), for example, sees in this first denial evidence that Paul had been charged with "error" because he had changed his teaching from a realized eschatology to a futuristic eschatology.

16. Schmithals (1972: 145), for example, connects this first denial of "deception" to the charge that Paul had stolen some of the funds collected for the believers in Palestine (see also the

meaning is intended here, the latter view gains support from the parallelism with "deceit" (δόλος, *dolos*) in the same verse (see discussion below);[17] the positive half of this antithetical statement (2:4), which emphasizes the character of Paul; and the larger context of 2:1–12, especially the other antithetical statements in the passage.

The second denial of Paul that his appeal to them was "not from an impure motive" (οὐδὲ ἐξ ἀκαθαρσίας, *oude ex akatharsias*) is similarly open to differing interpretations. Since the word *akatharsia* is sometimes connected with sexual immorality (Rom. 1:24; 1 Thess. 4:7; see also 2 Cor. 12:21; Gal. 5:19; Col. 3:5), several commentators conclude that their opponents had linked Paul and his companions with the sexual activity that was so often a part of the mystery religions and civic cults (so Lightfoot 1904: 20–21; Milligan 1908: 19; Frame 1912: 95–96; Rigaux 1956: 407; Bruce 1982: 26; Morris 1991: 61–62; Beale 2003: 66). There is nothing in this letter or elsewhere, however, to suggest that Paul was ever accused of sexual misconduct. Also, the word *akatharsia* is understood to have a more general sense in Rom. 6:19 as well as perhaps in Eph. 4:19 and 5:3 (see also Matt. 23:27). Furthermore, given the very tolerant attitude toward sexual conduct in the Greco-Roman world, it is difficult to imagine the unbelieving "fellow citizens" (2:14) of Thessalonica even raising such a concern. These considerations, along with the observation that the surrounding nouns have ethical connotations, suggest that the word *akatharsia* should be understood in a more general sense of "impurity" or "impure motive" (so BDAG 34; F. Hauck, *TDNT* 3:428; Schmithals 1972: 145; Best 1977: 93–94; Marshall 1983: 65; Richard 1995: 94; Malherbe 2000: 140; Green 2002: 119; Fee 2009: 60). Such a meaning is also attested in Hellenistic Greek (Demosthenes, *Or.* 21.119; *BGU* 393.16; Dio Chrysostom, *Alex.* 11–12).

The third denial of Paul that his appeal to them was "not made with[18] deceit" (οὐδὲ ἐν δόλῳ, *oude en dolō*) is the least ambiguous of the apostle's disavowals. The word *dolos* originally referred to catching fish by using bait (Morris 1991: 62), and from this developed the metaphorical meaning of "deceit, cunning, treachery" (BDAG 256). Paul claims that he did not reel in any suckers who foolishly swallowed the bait of his deceitful message hook, line, and sinker. The Thessalonians, therefore, ought to see a big difference between the original visit of the apostle and the visits of wandering preachers and sophists, who

---

denial of 2:5 "not with a motive of greed"), a charge also reflected in 2 Cor. 12:16. This claim of Schmithals, along with that of Mearns in the previous footnote, are further examples of an inappropriate use of mirror reading.

17. Some, however, use this parallel to reach the opposite conclusion: in 2:3, if πλάνη is interpreted as "deception," it becomes difficult to distinguish this word from δόλος (so, e.g., Best 1977: 93; D. Martin 1995: 72).

18. Here in 2:3 is a slight shift from the first two denials, making use of the preposition ἐκ, to this third denial, making use of the preposition ἐν. Although not too much should be read into this switch, it appears that the first two prepositions express the idea of origin or source, while the third signifies instrumentality or means.

would resort to various methods of deception in order to gain followers (on the typical conduct of traveling orators, see Winter 1993: esp. 60–64).

2:4 In the positive half of the second antithetical statement of 2:3–4, Paul answers (note again how the rebuttal is introduced with the strong adversative "but") the implicit charge of the negative half concerning the integrity of his preaching. The structure of this response takes the form of a correlative clause (as *x*, so *y*) whose second member contains within it yet another antithetical statement:

> *As* we have been examined by God to be entrusted with the gospel,
> *so* we speak,
> > *not* as those who please people
> > *but* those who please God, the one who examines our hearts.

The structure of this clause shows that Paul's concern lies with the character of his speech ("so we speak"), a fact suggested already by his previous reference to "our appeal." What is also immediately noticeable is the double claim by Paul that God has "examined" him and his coworkers ("examined [δεδοκιμάσμεθα, *dedokimasmetha*] by God, . . . God, the one who examines [δοκιμάζοντι, *dokimazonti*] our hearts"). Although the verb *dokimazō* is a relatively common Pauline word, occurring some seventeen times in his letters (Rom. 1:28; 2:18; 12:2; 14:22; 1 Cor. 3:13; 11:28; 16:3; 2 Cor. 8:8, 22; 13:5; Gal. 6:4; Eph. 5:10; Phil. 1:10; 1 Thess. 2:4 [2x]; 5:21; 1 Tim. 3:10), only here is it found twice in the same context. It is also striking that, whereas elsewhere Paul typically uses the verb *dokimazō* in the active voice with one person or a group of persons as the subject, only here does he use it in the passive voice with God as the one who does the examining (the passive occurs elsewhere only in 1 Tim. 3:10, but there God is not the agent).[19] Paul's strategy in the second antithetical statement of 2:3–4, therefore, is to defend the integrity of his preaching by appealing to his "God-examined speech."

Paul begins this part of his defense by claiming that he and his coworkers "have been examined by God to be entrusted with the gospel" (δεδοκιμάσμεθα ὑπὸ τοῦ θεοῦ πιστευθῆναι τὸ εὐαγγέλιον, *dedokimasmetha hypo tou theou pisteuthēnai to euangelion*). The perfect tense of *dedokimasmetha* emphasizes that God's examination of the missionaries took place not only during their past ministry in Thessalonica but also continues right up to their present activities. This divine investigation of Paul has a specific purpose or goal: that the apostle "be entrusted with the gospel" (the verb πιστεύω, *pisteuō*, most commonly meaning "to believe," can also have the sense "to entrust [something to someone]": BDAG 818). In this polemical context, Paul's point is that God does not entrust his gospel message to just anyone but only to those whom

---

19. This fact leads Collins (1993: 22), who denies that Paul is defending himself in 2:1–16, to conclude: "Paul's phraseology is so unusual that it suggests that he has something in mind that does not usually occupy the focus of his thought." A probable candidate for the thought that was occupying Paul's attention is a charge directed against him and his coworkers.

he has examined and found worthy. The Thessalonians, therefore, ought to be reassured that Paul's speech to them, both in his initial preaching to them and now in this letter (note the present tense of "we speak" [λαλοῦμεν, *laloumen*]), is not tainted by the kind of false motives mentioned in 2:3 but rather is God-examined and thus sincere.

The pure and genuine character of Paul's speech is further emphasized by a third antithetical formulation. Paul and his coworkers speak "not[20] as those who please people, but those who please God, the one who examines our hearts" (οὐχ ὡς ἀνθρώποις ἀρέσκοντες, ἀλλὰ θεῷ τῷ δοκιμάζοντι τὰς καρδίας ἡμῶν, *ouch hōs anthrōpois areskontes, alla theō tō dokimazonti tas kardias hēmōn*). In the negative half of this antithetical statement, the apostle repudiates the implicit claim that he was a *people pleaser*—someone who will say anything to win the favor of others (see also Gal. 1:10; Col. 3:22). There is a sense, of course, in which Paul was very sensitive to the specific needs and situation of his audience. Thus the apostle states his willingness to "become all things to all people" for the sake of the gospel (1 Cor. 9:22). This concern for others, however, was motivated only out of a genuine desire that unbelievers would be saved, and it in no way came at the expense of compromising the truth of the gospel. The reference here to speaking "not as those who please people," therefore, has in view the kind of speech that originates from deceit, impure motive, or trickery (2:3) and that in a self-serving manner is interested only in winning the favor of others.

The positive half of this third antithetical statement contrasts such false motives: instead of being a *people pleaser* ("We speak not as those who please people") Paul claims to be a *God pleaser* ("but those who please God"). The idea of "pleasing God" as the ultimate goal of human conduct stems from the OT (see, e.g., Num. 23:27; 1 Kings 14:13; Job 6:9; 34:9; Pss. 19:14; 69:31; 104:34; Prov. 15:26; 16:7; Mal. 3:4) and is one of Paul's favorite expressions for right behavior (Rom. 8:8; 1 Cor. 7:32–34; Gal. 1:10; 1 Thess. 2:4, 15; 4:1; see also Eph. 6:6; 2 Cor. 5:9; Col. 1:10; 3:22). Later in this passage the apostle identifies certain Jews who hindered his ministry as those "who do not please God" (2:15), a charge that in his mind is so serious that it comes immediately after his description of them as "those who killed both the Lord Jesus and the prophets." The importance that Paul places on pleasing God is also seen later in the letter as he reminds the Thessalonian believers that he has taught

---

20. In 2:4, instead of the expected negative form μὴ with the participle ἀρέσκοντες (as in 2:15), we find here the negative form οὐ. Since οὐ is normally used with the indicative mood to negate statements of fact or reality, some commentators conclude that the use of this negative form in 2:4 shows that Paul is emphasizing the actuality of what he is saying. Best (1977: 97), for example, states: "The unusual negative οὐ which Paul uses here with the participle 'pleasing' means that he affirms not just his intention ('seeking to please') but the actual fact that it is being accomplished" (see also Milligan 1908: 19; Morris 1991: 63n22; on this grammatical construction more generally, see MHT 1:231–32). There is a real danger here, however, of reading too much into this construction, since there are other possible reasons for the few examples of οὐ with the participle in Paul (see BDF §430.3).

them "how you must . . . please God" (4:1)—a key verse that introduces the exhortation found in the second half of this correspondence (4:1–5:22).

Paul strategically describes the God whom he seeks to please as "the one who examines our hearts." The notion of God as the searcher and tester of human hearts occurs frequently in the OT (1 Chron. 28:9; 29:17; Pss. 7:9; 17:3; 139:23 [138:23 LXX]; Prov. 17:3; Jer. 11:20; 12:3; 17:10). Paul uses this common OT concept to show that the God who has examined him and found him worthy to be entrusted with the gospel (2:4a) also continues to examine him (the present tense of *dokimazonti* highlights the ongoing or continuous nature of this inspection) and so ensures that the apostle's motives are pure. As Bruce (1982: 27) states: "The writers are in effect invoking God as a witness to the integrity of their motives."

c. His "Innocent as an Infant" Conduct (2:5–7b)

2:5 The third main clause in 2:1–12 consists of another antithetical statement whose punctuation and text are unfortunately misrepresented by virtually all translations. Modern versions wrongly end the positive half of this antithetical clause too early after the phrase "apostles of Christ" in 2:7a and so begin a new clause already at 2:7b ("But we became . . ."). In addition to this punctuation error, most translations also wrongly adopt the reading "gentle" (ἤπιοι, *ēpioi*) in 2:7b instead of the more strongly attested reading "infants" (νήπιοι, *nēpioi*). Although this punctuation and textual issue is complex and the conclusion reached by most translators and commentators differs from my own, there is nevertheless compelling evidence that the antithetical statement concludes at 2:7b after the reading "but we became infants among you" (for a full justification of the proper textual reading and punctuation of this verse, see excursus 2, at the end of this unit; also Weima 2000a).

Denial 1:	[5]For we never came with a word of flattery,
Parenthetical Response:	—as you know—
Denial 2:	nor with a motive of greed,
Parenthetical Response:	—God is our witness!—
Denial 3:	[6]nor were we demanding honor from people,
	neither from you
	nor from others,
Parenthetical Response:	[7a]—even though we could have insisted on our importance as apostles of Christ—
Affirmation:	[7b]but we became infants among you.

The antithetical statement of 2:5–7b exhibits a greater degree of symmetry than is commonly recognized (see preceding table). This contrasting clause consists of a lengthy negative half that contains three[21] denials (balancing

---

21. That the negative conjunction οὔτε occurs five times in 2:5–7b might lead to the conclusion that there are five denials in this antithetical statement. The final three of these five negatives, however, all deal with the one denial of Paul in 2:6 that he did not seek honor from people. Thus

somewhat the three denials in the preceding antithetical statement of 2:3–4), each of which is followed by a brief aside or parenthetical comment that in some sense repudiates the implied charge lying behind each denial, and a positive half that contains a relatively brief affirmation.

The conjunction "for" (γάρ, *gar*) that opens this third main clause resumes the "for" of the second main clause (see 2:3) and introduces a further third argument in Paul's defense of his past visit to Thessalonica. Whereas the preceding main clause of 2:3–4 affirms the integrity of Paul's motives in his evangelistic activities in general, the third main clause of 2:5–7b shifts the focus more specifically to his conduct among the Thessalonians. This shift is evident both in the past tense of "we came" (ἐγενήθημεν, *egenēthēmen*)[22] and the appeal to the firsthand knowledge that the readers have ("as you know").

Denial 1. The first of the three denials that Paul makes is that he and his coworkers never came "with a word of flattery" (ἐν λόγῳ κολακείας, *en logō kolakeias*). Although the term *kolakeia* occurs only here in the NT, the meaning of this noun can be easily discerned from its use in the ancient world (see Spicq 1994: 2.319–21). Theophrastus, after defining flattery as "a shameful business, but profitable for the flatterer" (*Char.* 2.1), concludes his discussion by stating, "You will see the flatterer say and do all the things that he hopes will ingratiate him" (2.13). Aristotle claims that the person "whose goal is to make people happy in order to profit in money or in goods which can be bought with money is the flatterer" (*Nic. Eth.* 4.6.9). The term *kolakeia* frequently appears in catalogs of vices, such as in Philo who lists "flattery" alongside "trickery," "deceitfulness," and "false speaking" (*Sacrifices* 22). Plutarch condemns the use of flattery and contrasts it with *parrēsia*, "boldness of speech" (*Mor.* 48E–74E). Dio Chrysostom describes certain Cynics who deceive others through flattery rather than speaking with the boldness and frankness of the true philosopher (*Alex.* 9–12, 26).

These uses of *kolakeia* help determine in what sense Paul did not come to the Thessalonian Christians "with a word of flattery." The apostle denies that his original preaching to them (the noun *logos* in the phrase *en logō kolakeias* has in view Paul's mission-founding preaching: see 1:5) involved deceptive language, empty praise, or false promises to trick the hearers into accepting the gospel. The context of this first denial—where Paul has just claimed that he speaks "not as one who pleases people" (2:4) and where he will soon assert that he is "not demanding honor from people" (2:6)—suggests that the apostle wants to distance himself from street-corner philosophers and wandering rhetoricians who typically used flattering speech to ingratiate themselves with the crowds.

Since the first denial deals with outward behavior, in the first brief aside Paul can appeal yet again (see 2:1, 2) to the personal knowledge that the readers

---

it is preferable to speak of three denials and to view the fourth and fifth negatives as clarifying the third denial: "nor were we seeking glory from people, *neither* from you *nor* from others."

22. The verb ἐγενήθημεν in 2:7 literally means "we were/became," but is used here, as in 1:5, to refer to the mission-founding visit of the missionaries and so can be rendered as "we came."

have: "as you know." The Thessalonian Christians have seen how the apostle was different from other traveling speakers of his day who employed flattery to win followers and financial profits. They know from firsthand experience how Paul boldly preached to them the gospel, despite the persecution he experienced not only in Philippi but also in their city (2:1–2; also 1:5, "in much conviction").

Denial 2. The second of the three denials involves the inward motive lying behind Paul's past visit to Thessalonica as the apostle asserts that he also did not come "with a motive of greed" (ἐν προφάσει πλεονεξίας, *en prophasei pleonexias*). Although the noun *prophasis* sometimes occurs with a neutral sense of "actual motive," it most commonly has a negative or pejorative connotation of "pretext, a motive set forth deceitfully" (Spicq 1994: 3:204–6; see also BDAG 889). This, in fact, is how it is used in virtually all its other occurrences in the NT (Phil. 1:18; Matt. 23:14; Mark 12:40; Luke 20:47; Acts 27:30; the one exception is John 15:22, where it has the sense of "excuse"). Translations have attempted to capture this negative sense by rendering *prophasis* as "mask" (NIV), "cloak" (KJV, RSV, NKJV, REB), "cover" (JB), or "pretext" (NASB, NAB, NRSV). However, since the accompanying genitive ("of greed") already makes clear the pejorative use of the term, it is enough to translate the phrase simply as "with a motive of greed" (so Wanamaker 1990: 97; Richard 1995: 98).

It is hardly surprising that Paul mentions "greed" here, since the motive of avarice was frequently connected with "flattery" (see the ancient sources cited above). The noun *pleonexia* need not be limited to the desire for money. It is derived from the words "more" (*pleon*) and "to have" (*echō*), and so it can refer more broadly to the selfish desire to obtain anything that one does not already have. Thus, for example, *pleonexia* (or its cognate verb) can be associated with sexual immorality (1 Thess. 4:6; Eph. 4:19; 5:3; see also Rom. 1:29). The context of 1 Thess. 2:5, however, makes it almost certain that Paul is thinking specifically of financial greed, since wandering preachers of that day were typically accused of being interested solely in monetary gain. The very real possibility of such a charge being brought against Paul is evident in that later in the apostle's life he refutes the charge of *pleonexia* against himself in connection with the relief offering he is collecting for the needy Christians in Judea (2 Cor. 9:5; 12:17–18; see also Paul's defensive comments in his farewell speech to the Ephesian elders [Acts 20:33–35], where the apostle denies that he "coveted anyone's silver or gold or clothing").

Since the second denial deals with an inward motive that is impossible for the Thessalonian Christians to discern, Paul appeals in the second brief aside to the only one who can know and judge the integrity of his motive: "God is [our] witness!" (θεὸς μάρτυς, *theos martys*). The practice of appealing to God as a witness can be found in the OT (Job 16:19; Ps. 89:37; Wis. 1:6), although it is a common enough occurrence in Hellenistic writings as well. Paul, however, rarely invokes God as a witness in his letters, doing so elsewhere only three times (Rom. 1:9; 2 Cor. 1:23; Phil. 1:8).[23] That he makes an unparalleled second appeal to God as a witness a few verses later (2:10), along with the preceding double claim in 2:4 that God has "examined" him, is striking and supports the claim the Paul truly is defending himself in this passage. As Morris (1991: 65) declares: "There can be no mistaking the intense seriousness with which he writes, nor the depth of his conviction that the methods and motives of the preachers would bear the closest scrutiny."

Denial 3. The third of the three denials repudiates any notion that Paul's past ministry in Thessalonica was motivated by the selfish desire to gain human praise: "nor were we demanding honor from people, either from[24] you or from others" (οὔτε ζητοῦντες ἐξ ἀνθρώπων δόξαν, οὔτε ἀφ' ὑμῶν οὔτε ἀπ' ἄλλων, *oute zētountes ex anthrōpōn doxan, oute aph' hymōn oute ap' allōn*). Here the word *doxa*, used more often by Paul than any other biblical writer, does not have its usual NT meaning of "glory" in a religious sense (see, e.g., 2:12), but the common secular meaning of "fame, recognition, renown, honor, prestige" (BDAG 257; see, e.g., 2:20). The denial of demanding honor follows naturally after the denial of acting out of greed, since it is another insincere motive commonly ascribed to traveling speakers. The link between financial gain and human praise can be seen in Dio Chrysostom, who identifies false philosophers as those who deliver orations for "their own profit and glory (*doxa*)" (*Alex.* 10–11). Yet in Paul's world where public speaking was a major competitive sport, where successful rhetoricians and sophists were treated like superstar athletes or Hollywood celebrities, glory (*doxa*) alone was a powerful enough temptation even apart from financial gain. Plutarch, for example, speaks of those who were motivated not merely by money but also by public "glory [*doxa*]" (*Mor.* 131A). Epictetus cynically describes an orator who demanded from his audience "Praise me!" In response to the crowd's question, "What do you mean by praise?" he answered: "Cry 'Bravo!' 'Marvelous!'" (*Disc.* 3.23.23). Dio Chrysostom refers with contempt to the glory-seeking antics of sophists, calling them "gorgeous peacocks lifted up high on the wings of glory [*doxa*] and their disciples" (*Or.* 12.5; the last two quotes are cited by Winter 1993: 61–62).

The participle *zētountes* normally conveys the sense of "seeking" or "desiring," and this may well be the way it should be translated here. Sometimes, however, this verb has the stronger connotation of "demanding" or "requiring" something (BDAG 428), and such a rendering provides a better contrast with the third aside, which immediately follows in 2:7a (so Wanamaker 1990: 98; see also Frame 1912: 98–99; Green 2002: 123). The thought of the third denial, therefore, is that Paul and his fellow missionaries did not demand honor from

23. Note also two occurrences where Paul, without using the term "witness," claims in the presence of God that he is not lying: Gal. 1:20; 2 Cor. 11:31.

24. Contrary to the claims of some older commentators (e.g., Lightfoot 1904: 23; Milligan 1908: 20), there is no significance in the shift from ἐκ to ἀπό in 2:6: the two prepositions were often used interchangeably (MHT 3:259).

either the Thessalonian Christians ("neither from you") or believers in other places ("nor from others"),[25] even though they could have insisted on such honor as apostles of Christ.

Paul is not saying that they had not received honor from anyone or that they had no right to receive it, but only that they had not selfishly demanded such human praise. Also, though Paul does not require honor from "people" (anthrōpōn), perhaps the unspoken contrast is that honor is to be sought from God, just as in 2:4 Paul claims to speak not as one who "pleases people but God" (so Rigaux 1956: 415–16; Best 1977: 99; Marshall 1983: 67). There is no tension, therefore, between Paul's assertion here about not demanding honor and his later claim that the Thessalonian believers will be his "glory" (doxa) before the Lord Jesus Christ at his return (2:20).

2:7a   For yet a third time Paul follows his denial with an aside or parenthetical comment that functions to repudiate the implied charge lying behind the denial: "even though we could have insisted on our importance as apostles of Christ." The key word in this phrase is the noun βάρος (baros), which literally means "weight, burden." Here, however, the noun has an obviously figurative sense, and this has resulted in two possible meanings. The first is "financial burden," namely, the responsibility that the church has to financially support the apostles in their work. According to this interpretation, Paul is appealing to the fact that he did not require the Thessalonian congregation to back him financially, even though as an apostle of Christ he had a right to such monetary support. That baros and its cognates occur frequently in the Greek papyri with respect to financial charges (Strelan 1975), as well as Paul's use of the cognate verb in 2:9 to refer to monetary support and his denial in 2:5 that he came "with a motive of greed," have led a few scholars to adopt this first interpretation (Bruce 1982: 30–31; Morris 1991: 66–67; Shogren 2012: 98).

The majority of commentators, however, embrace the second figurative meaning of baros as "weight of authority or dignity," namely, the responsibility that the church has to respect and honor the apostles in their work (BDAG 167.2: "influence that someone enjoys or claims, claim of importance"). This meaning also occurs quite frequently in the Greek papyri[26] and resembles our contemporary colloquialism that designates someone important as "a

---

25. A number of commentators claim that it is impossible to know whether in the phrase "nor from others," Paul refers to Christians in other places or the general populace in Thessalonica (e.g., Best 1977: 99; Morris 1991: 66; Richard 1995: 99). The third aside of 2:7a that accompanies this denial, however, appeals to Paul and his coworkers' status as "apostles of Christ" and so would appear to have Christians in view, not unbelievers (contra Green 2002: 124: "the reference is not to Christians in other cities").

26. For example, Diodorus Siculus (4.61.9) records: "From that time onward the Athenians were filled with pride by reason of the weight [i.e., importance] of their state." Plutarch (Per. 37.1) writes: "The city [Athens] made trial of its other generals and counselors for the conduct of the war, but since no one appeared to have weight that was adequate or authority that was competent for such leadership, it yearned for Pericles, and summoned him back to the bema and the war-office." See also Polybius, Hist. 4.32.7.

heavyweight," "a heavy hitter," or "throwing his weight around." The strength of the second interpretation lies in the structure of the larger clause of 2:5–7b, which requires that this third parenthetical clause correspond with the preceding denial that Paul was "not demanding honor from people, neither from you nor from others." The proper ground of this denial is not that Paul did not demand financial support but that he did not selfishly insist that honor (*doxa*) be given to him by the congregation. That *doxa* in the Septuagint translates the Hebrew root *kbd*, meaning "be weighty," strengthens the link between the denial that Paul sought "honor" (*doxa*) from people and the parenthetical comment that he could have made use of his position of "weight" (*baros*), and so further supports the claim that *baros* here refers to the weight of authority or influence. Although Paul does bring up the issue of finances in 2:9, he seemingly presents this matter as a new subject rather than as a continuation of an earlier statement (Wanamaker 1990: 99).[27]

The phrase "apostles of Christ" (Χριστοῦ ἀπόστολοι, *christou apostoloi*)[28] is striking, not only because it is the first occurrence of the term "apostle" in the letter, but especially because it occurs in the plural form, thereby implying that Silvanus and Timothy share apostolic status with Paul. This is potentially problematic since Paul elsewhere grounds his apostleship in his divine commission at an encounter with the resurrected Jesus (1 Cor. 9:1; 15:8; Gal. 1:15–17), and Silvanus and Timothy had witnessed, as far as is known, no such resurrection appearance. It also seems to conflict with Paul's practice in several letter openings of not identifying Timothy as an apostle (2 Cor. 1:1, "Paul, an *apostle* . . . and Timothy, the *brother*"; see also Phil. 1:1; Col. 1:1; Philem. 1). In response to this apparent problem of Paul's use of the plural "apostles," at least four different solutions have been proposed:

1. The first proposal is that Paul is employing a "literary plural," where a writer or speaker uses the "we" form to make statements that in actuality apply only to himself. Although Paul does make use of the literary plural elsewhere in 1 Thessalonians and is clearly the primary voice in this letter, there is nothing in the phrase "apostles of Christ" or in the immediate context to justify limiting the referent to himself alone.

2. The second possibility is that the plural "apostles" includes both Paul and Silvanus but not Timothy, on the grounds that Silvanus was from Jerusalem (Acts 15:22), where he may well have been commissioned as an apostle by the risen Christ (just as another apostle from Jerusalem,

27. A number of commentators suggest that in 2:6 Paul may be playing on both figurative meanings of *baros* (Lightfoot 1904: 24; Milligan 1908: 20–21; Morris 1991: 66–67). To this claim, Marshall (1983: 68–69) responds: "While the Greek phrase used cannot mean 'to wield authority' and 'to be a material burden' simultaneously, the latter *thought* could already be in Paul's mind, and, having dealt with the primary contrast in vv. 7f., he takes up the secondary point in v. 9."

28. Milligan (1908: 20) draws attention to the word order in 2:7 where the possessive genitive "of Christ" is "placed emphatically first to show whose Apostles they were, and why therefore they were entitled to claim honour."

Barnabas, had apparently seen the risen Jesus: see 1 Cor. 9:1, 5–6), while Timothy was either a convert from paganism or a noncircumcised half-Jew who had no such divine encounter and appointment (so Schmithals 1971: 23, 65–67; Marshall 1983: 69–70; Wanamaker 1990: 99–100; Holmes 1998: 63n11). This proposal, however, suffers from the fact that there is no explicit evidence that Silvanus ever did meet the resurrected Christ, nor is there anything in Paul's discussion here of his past ministry in Thessalonica (2:1–16) to suggest that Timothy was not in view.

3. The third option is that Paul uses the term "apostles" in the more general sense of "messenger" or "agent"—a sense that can be legitimately applied to Silvanus and Timothy (Williams 1992: 40). Such a general and nontechnical sense of the term "apostle" does appear in Paul's Letters at least twice: the two brothers who are coming to Corinth to hasten that church's completion of the collection are said to be "messengers [*apostoloi*] of the [Macedonian] churches" (2 Cor. 8:23); and Epaphroditus is identified as the Philippian church's "messenger [*apostolos*] and minister to [Paul's] need" (Phil. 2:25). It is highly doubtful, however, whether the use of "apostles" in 1 Thess. 2:7a can be added to this list, since the term here clearly expresses the notion of authority (note the accompanying genitive "of Christ")—a notion associated with the much more common technical sense of "apostle."

4. The fourth and strongest proposal views the plural "apostles" as referring to all three of the missionaries involved in the founding of the Thessalonian church but recognizes Paul's evolutionary use of this term in response to repeated challenges to his apostolic status (Richard 1995: 110–11). There is nothing in the two Letters to the Thessalonians to suggest that Paul's apostleship was being questioned in any way. Consequently, as Paul feels free in the letter opening to bracket Silvanus and Timothy with himself on equal terms as cosenders (1:1), here too he has no hesitation to include them with him as "apostles of Christ." But as P. W. Barnett (*DPL* 49) notes: "From that time, doubtless due to mounting criticism, Paul became explicit about his status as an apostle (Gal 1:1; 1 Cor 1:1; 2 Cor 1:1; Rom 1:1), and was careful to distance himself as an apostle from various co-workers (1 Cor 1:1; 2 Cor 1:1; Col. 1:1; cf. Phil 1:1)."

2:7b   *Affirmation.* After the lengthy negative half of the antithetical statement with its three denials and three parenthetical responses, Paul finally completes his thought with the corresponding positive half that, though brief, is remarkable for the metaphor it contains: "but we became infants[29] among you" (ἀλλὰ ἐγενήθημεν νήπιοι ἐν μέσῳ ὑμῶν, *alla egenēthēmen nēpioi en mesō hymōn*).

29. For a justification of the reading "infants" (νήπιοι) instead of the reading "gentle" (ἤπιοι), as found in virtually all translations (notable exceptions include the TNIV, NIV, NET), see excursus 2, at the end of this unit; also Weima 2000a.

This is the first of three striking uses of familial imagery found in this passage: "infants" (2:7b), "nursing mother" (2:7c), and "father" (2:11). In light of the overall structure found in the lengthy antithetical clause of 2:5–7b, it is clear that this first metaphor of infants serves to contrast (note again the strong adversative "but": see also 2:2 and 2:4) not just the immediately preceding phrase in verse 7a but also the whole clause of verses 5–7a, particularly the three denials that Paul "came with a word of flattery," "with a motive of greed," and "demanding honor." In contrast to these impure motives—motives typically associated with the wandering philosopher-teachers of that day—Paul asserts that he and his fellow missionaries during their past ministry in Thessalonica "became infants among you." In this context, the infant metaphor functions to highlight the *innocence* of the apostle and his coworkers. Babies are not capable of using deceptive speech, having ulterior motives, and being concerned with receiving honor; in all these things they are innocent. Philo similarly speaks about the innocence of infants, claiming that "it is impossible for the greatest liar to invent a charge against them, as they are wholly innocent" (*Spec. Laws* 3.119).

Some have questioned the appropriateness of this infant metaphor, claiming that Paul's use of *nēpios* elsewhere is "almost always pejorative" and using this assertion as further support for the alternate reading of "gentle" (Wanamaker 1990: 100; Delobel 1995: 128–29).[30] But while the word *nēpios* is used to describe the immaturity of new believers (1 Cor. 3:1), a survey of Paul's other uses of this term (Rom. 2:20; 1 Cor. 13:11 [5x]; Gal. 4:1, 3; Eph. 4:14) reveals that it does not always have a negative connotation. Paul certainly does use the cognate verb in a positive manner in 1 Cor. 14:20 ("Be infants with respect to evil"). Thus Paul appears to use the infant metaphor in a somewhat "fluid" fashion (Fee 1992: 177) such that even within the same letter it can have a pejorative sense (1 Cor. 3:1), a neutral sense (1 Cor. 13:11 [5x]), and a positive sense (1 Cor. 14:20). Elsewhere in the Scriptures—both in the Septuagint (e.g., Pss. 18:8; 118:130 [19:7; 119:130 Eng.]; Wis. 10:21) and in the Gospels (Matt. 11:25; 21:16; Luke 10:21)—*nēpios* refers to those whose motives are pure and without guile (Gaventa 1991: 196). And an examination of the term outside of the Scriptures in the literature from the first centuries BC and AD similarly reveals how "infant" was used in a positive sense.[31]

Paul's affirmative use of the infant metaphor, therefore, should in no way be viewed as problematic for a writer of that day. Quite the contrary, this bold image of becoming infants serves as a fitting contrast to the impure motives of coming "with a word of flattery," "a motive of greed," and "demanding

30. For a more detailed response to the claim that νήπιοι was always used pejoratively by Paul such that a positive use of this term is impossible in 1 Thess. 2:7, see excursus 2.

31. The statistical analysis by Sailors (2000) reveals the following results: The term is used the vast majority of time (75 percent) as a neutral, purely descriptive term meaning "infant." The negative sense of "childish" or "foolish" occurs 18.68 percent of the time, whereas the positive sense occurs 6.23 percent of the time. Sailor reports that the percentage of positive uses of *nēpios* is dramatically higher among Christian authors.

honor." In this way, the metaphor provides a powerful defense for the integrity of Paul and his fellow missionaries during their past visit to Thessalonica.[32]

d. His "Loving as a Nursing Mother" Conduct (2:7c–8)

2:7c   The fourth main clause of 2:7c–8 contains a second remarkable family metaphor as Paul likens himself to a nursing mother. This clause takes the form of another correlative clause (see 2:4), whose second member consists of an assertion that is bracketed by two causal clauses and contains an antithetical statement (the fifth so far in this passage):

> *As* a nursing mother cherishes her own children,
> *so* we,
>> *because* we cared so much for you,
>> were pleased to share with you
>>> *not* only the gospel of God
>>> *but* also our own selves,
>> *because* you became beloved to us.

Whereas the first metaphor of infants highlights the *innocence* of Paul's conduct and motives during his past visit to Thessalonica, the second metaphor of a nursing mother focuses on the *love* that Paul had for Thessalonian believers during his past visit. That love is indeed the key aspect emphasized in this clause can be seen in (1) the use of the metaphor (Frame 1912: 100–101: "The point of the new metaphor is love, the love of a mother-nurse for her own children"); (2) the emotional warmth expressed in the rare participle "caring so much"; (3) the desire of Paul and his fellow missionaries to share with the believers in Thessalonica not just the gospel but also "our own selves"; and (4) the concluding causal clause, which explicitly states that these Christians "became beloved [*agapētoi*] to us." Thus Wanamaker (1990: 102) is not guilty of hyperbole in stating: "Certainly no other passage in the whole of the Pauline corpus employs such deeply affective language in describing Paul's relation with his converts."

The word used for "mother" is not the common word μήτηρ (*mētēr*) but τροφός (*trophos*), which properly refers to a "nurse," someone hired to care for children. Since this noun derives from the verb τρέφω (*trephō*), meaning "to feed, nourish, provide with food," it often has the more specified meaning of "wet nurse," someone who suckles children. The use of such wet nurses, or lactating nurses, was widespread in the Greco-Roman world among both the higher and the lower classes (K. Bradley 1986). Writers of that day typically

---

32. Fee (2009: 71): "Paul here is making his case by using the strongest kind of metaphor to declare his and his companions' 'innocence' of the kinds of deceptions of which they apparently have been accused. When it comes to our relationship with you, Paul expostulates, even though our position as apostles gave us the right to do so, we refused to throw our weight around. Rather, in terms of attitude, we were as innocent as infants."

portrayed the wet nurse as an important and beloved figure (Dio Chrysostom, *Or.* 4.73–139; 33.10; Plutarch, *Flatterer* 69B–C; see Malherbe 1970), and there are a number of ancient inscriptions in which adults honor those who nursed them (Gaventa 1991: 201; 1998: 27).

But while Paul's analogy to a *trophos* may be restricted to that of a "wet nurse," there are at least three reasons to extend the metaphor to that of a "mother," or better yet, "nursing mother." First and foremost, the reflexive pronoun in the phrase "her *own* children" (τὰ ἑαυτῆς τέκνα, *ta heautēs tekna*), emphasized by way of word order, indicates that the woman in the metaphor is the natural mother of the children.[33] Second, the use of *trophos* to refer to a mother has classical justification (BDAG 1017; see also the sources listed in Lightfoot 1904: 25). Third, the surrounding family metaphors of "infants" (2:7b) and "father" (2:11) suggest that here Paul has in view another member of the family, the mother, rather than the hired wet nurse.

Why, then, did the apostle use *trophos* instead of the more common word for "mother," *mētēr*? Malherbe (1970: 211–14; 2000: 146, 160) suggests that Paul is influenced by the philosophers of his day, who commonly used the metaphor of a nurse to depict the way such teachers should gently care for those whom they taught and nourished in the truth. Donfried (1985: 338, 340) suggests that the metaphor of a nurse may stem from various figures connected with the mystery religions practiced at Thessalonica: the divine women who play a central role in the Dionysiac mysteries are referred to as "nurses"; Tethys, wife of the river god, Okeanos (Oceanus), is described as the "kindly nurse and provider of all things." A simpler and more likely reason for Paul's choice of *trophos* over *mētēr* is that this metaphor underscores the apostle's love for his readers. A nurse competently cares for the children in her charge, but she "cherishes" (the rare verb θάλπω, *thalpō*, literally means "keep warm," but figuratively it has the sense of "cherish, comfort": see also Eph. 5:29) her own children even more (so, e.g., Marshall 1983: 71; Wanamaker 1990: 101; Holmes 1998: 64; Green 2002: 128).

After presenting the moving image of a nursing mother in the first half of the correlative clause ("As . . ."), Paul introduces the second half with the expected adverb "thus" (οὕτως, *houtōs*). But before giving the main assertion of this clause, he includes a causal participial clause that further conveys his great love for the Thessalonian believers: "because we cared so much for you" (ὁμειρόμενοι ὑμῶν, *homeiromenoi hymōn*). The etymology, meaning, and proper breathing of the participle *homeiromenoi* are all uncertain,[34] since this word is attested only four times in all Greek literature. The three remaining occurrences—in

2:8

33. Although the reflexive pronoun in late Greek was losing its emphatic force such that ἑαυτῆς (her own) sometimes was equivalent to αὐτῆς (her: see BDF §283), there is little justification in 2:7 for translating the phrase τὰ ἑαυτῆς τέκνα as "the children entrusted to her personal care" rather than "her own children."

34. Two suggestions have been forwarded concerning the derivation of ὁμείρομαι in 2:8. The first claims that the form comes from ὁμοῦ and εἴρειν and thus means "to be attached to." The second argues that the form derives from the verb μείρεσθαι (to divide, separate) with a prothetic

Job 3:21 LXX, Symmachus's translation of Ps. 63:1 (62:2 LXX), and a fourth-century AD tombstone inscription (*CIG* 3.4000.7) describing a couple's sad yearning for their deceased child—suggest that the term means "to have a strong yearning, *long for someone*" (BDAG 705), "have affection for someone" (LSJ 1221), "a warm inward attachment" (H. W. Heidland, *TDNT* 5:176). This sense is supported by early interpreters such as Hesychius of Alexandria (fifth century AD), who equates the term with ἐπιθυμέω (*epithymeō*, desire, long for), and the Vulgate, with *desidero*. It receives additional support from the tendency of some later copyists to replace this enigmatic verb with the more common ἱμείρομαι (*himeiromai*), meaning "long for," both here in 1 Thess. 2:8 and in Job 3:21 LXX. The participle *homeiromenoi*, therefore, reinforces the meaning of the nursing-mother metaphor as it expresses in a powerful way the deep and continuing (note the present tense) love that Paul has for his readers.

The apostle further emphasizes his love for the Thessalonian believers by asserting that "we were pleased to share with you not only the gospel of God but also our own selves" (εὐδοκοῦμεν μεταδοῦναι ὑμῖν οὐ μόνον τὸ εὐαγγέλιον τοῦ θεοῦ ἀλλὰ καὶ τὰς ἑαυτῶν ψυχάς, *eudokoumen metadounai hymin ou monon to euangelion tou theou alla kai tas heautōn psychas*). Although it is difficult to determine whether the verb *eudokoumen* (see also 3:1) expresses the notion of either resolve (NRSV: "we are determined") or joy (NIV: "we were delighted"), the strong, affectionate tone of the passage supports the latter option. Also somewhat ambiguous is the tense of the verb, whose form here can be either present or imperfect (the temporal augment of ευ- verbs is frequently missing in the NT period: see BDF §67.1). Here too the latter option is preferred, since the verse, along with the whole of 2:1–16, describes Paul's past visit to Thessalonica (note how some scribes replaced the ambiguous form with the aorist tense: 33 81 *pc* f vg). The imperfect tense, therefore, like the preceding present participle, stresses the ongoing nature of Paul's love for the Thessalonian Christians.

This love manifested itself in the apostle's joyful willingness to share with them "not only the gospel of God but also our own selves." In this context, the word *psychē* does not refer to physical "life," as if Paul were speaking of his willingness to lay down his life for the Thessalonian believers as proof of his love for them (so Lightfoot 1904: 26). The term rather describes the inner, emotional life of Paul, his "very self." The apostle, therefore, did not preach "the gospel of God" (see 2:2, 4) during his mission-founding visit in a cold and aloof manner but instead involved himself in a very personal and self-denying way in the lives of the Thessalonians. As Marshall (1983: 71) puts it: "The language is that of love in which a lover wants to share his life with the beloved in an act of self-giving and union."

That love was the motivation for Paul's sharing of the gospel and his personal involvement with the Thessalonian Christians is made clear in the concluding,

---

omicron and should be taken here in the passive sense, "having been separated" (Baumert 1987). For objections to each of these two possibilities, see Lightfoot 1904: 25–26.

causal clause: "because you became beloved to us" (διότι ἀγαπητοὶ ἡμῖν ἐγενήθητε, *dioti agapētoi hēmin egenēthēte*). The readers are thus "beloved" not only to God (1:4) but also to Paul and his fellow missionaries. Although this closing clause presents no new claims or ideas but repeats the message expressed in the rest of 2:7c–8, it has the rhetorical effect of further emphasizing the love that Paul has for his converts in Thessalonica. Within the larger context of 2:1–16, this "loving as a nursing mother" conduct of the apostle also provides additional support for the integrity of Paul during his past visit to Thessalonica.

e. His Self-Sufficient Labor (2:9)

With the fifth main clause, in 2:9, Paul continues his defense with an appeal to his self-sufficient labor: "For you remember, brothers, our labor and toil; while working night and day in order not to burden any of you, we preached to you the gospel of God." The opening conjunction "for" (γάρ, *gar*) suggests that this verse intends to explain the previous material, either the earlier denial that Paul had come "with a motive of greed" (2:5) or, more likely, the immediately preceding assertion about his loving-as-a-nursing-mother conduct (2:7c–8). Paul's love for the Thessalonian Christians, and especially his willingness to share with them not only the gospel but also his very self, is evident in the apostle's practice of working hard and providing for himself rather than making financial demands on his converts.

2:9

The verb "you remember" (μνημονεύετε, *mnēmoneuete*) involves an appeal to the firsthand knowledge that the Thessalonians have about Paul's conduct during his mission-founding visit. In the passage this constitutes the fourth of six explicit appeals to the personal knowledge that his readers have (see also 2:1, 2, 5, 10, 11). Here Paul calls them to remember "our labor and toil" (τὸν κόπον ἡμῶν καὶ τὸν μόχθον, *ton kopon hēmōn kai ton mochthon*). The two nouns, *kopos* and *mochthos*, are commonly used to refer to work generally, though sometimes the first term stresses the fatigue associated with labor, while the second term conveys the painfulness of work (LSJ 978, 1149). Since both nouns occur as a word pair two more times in Paul's Letters (2 Cor. 11:27; 2 Thess. 3:8), there is little justification for distinguishing here between "labor" and "toil." Instead, these terms constitute a fixed unit that the apostle uses to describe in a more emphatic way the difficult work that he and his companions undertook during their original stay in Thessalonica.

In the first half of the verse, the general appeal to "remember our labor and toil" is followed in the second half with a more specific description about the time and purpose of that work as well as its connection to preaching.[35] With respect to time, Paul claims that he and his fellow missionaries were "working night and day" (νυκτὸς καὶ ἡμέρας ἐργαζόμενοι, *nyktos kai hēmeras ergazomenoi*). The two nouns "night and day" occur as a word pair quite frequently in Paul's Letters (1 Thess. 3:10; 2 Thess. 3:8; 1 Tim. 5:5; 2 Tim. 1:3)

---

35. To reflect better the fact that the second half of 2:9 functions to explain the first half, several MSS have added an explanatory "for" (γάρ): D¹ 𝔐 sy^hmg.

and other documents of his day. The sequence of the terms in Greek writings is almost always the same (this is true also for Hebrew and Latin: see texts cited by Rigaux 1956: 423–24), so that no conclusions should be derived from the word order (i.e., that Paul worked by night and preached by day, or that the apostle rose up in the dark to work before the sun came up and continued his labor throughout the day: so wrongly Green 2002: 131). That the two nouns occur in the genitive means that Paul and his coworkers labored *both* during the night and during the day (the genitive expresses "time within which": BDF §186.2), not that the apostle claims in a hyperbolic manner that they worked for the whole day and whole night (the accusative would be used to express "extent of time": BDF §161.2).

Although Paul does not say here or elsewhere what kind of work he did, there are some clues as to his profession. In 1 Cor. 4:12 we learn that he and his colleagues worked "with our own hands" (which agrees with Paul's words to the Ephesian elders in Acts 20:34: "You yourselves know that these hands of mine have supplied my own needs and the needs of my companions"), something that he exhorted the Thessalonians to do both during his mission-founding visit and again in his first letter (1 Thess. 4:11). Acts 18:3 identifies Paul, along with the couple Aquila and Priscilla, as "tentmakers" (σκηνοποιοί, *skēnopoioi*). Since tents of antiquity were usually made of leather, it may be better to describe Paul as a "leatherworker," one who not only made and repaired tents but also a range of leather and woven goods (W. Michaelis, *TDNT* 7:393–94; P. W. Barnett, *DPL* 926). Paul probably learned this trade as part of his rabbinic training, since Jewish teachers were expected to support themselves by some form of labor (*m. 'Abot* 2.2; 4.7). Some have questioned this, however, finding fault with the late date of the Jewish sources that speak of the need for rabbis to learn a trade. They claim that Paul's decision to work parallels instead the practice of certain Hellenistic philosophers, who thought that it was good for others to see them living in the midst of society, where they could put their teachings into practice (so esp. Hock 1978; 1979; 1980: 22–49; see also Wanamaker 1990: 104; Holmes 1998: 66; Malherbe 2000: 160–61).

Paul's stated purpose for working is "in order not to burden any of you" (πρὸς τὸ μὴ ἐπιβαρῆσαί τινα ὑμῶν, *pros to mē epibarēsai tina hymōn*).[36] The rare verb *epibarēsai* (elsewhere in the NT only in 2 Cor. 2:5; 2 Thess. 3:8), which means "weigh down, burden" (see the cognate noun in 2:7a), clearly denotes material support such as financial remuneration, free food, and lodging. Although Paul vigorously defended his right as an apostle to receive financial support (1 Cor. 9:3–7), he chose not to make use of this right during his initial ministry in a particular city. During his mission-founding visit to Thessalonica,

---

36. In his later letter to the Thessalonians, Paul not only restates this purpose (in 2:9b) in word-for-word identical language ("in order not to burden any of you": 2 Thess. 3:8) but also adds a second purpose for his self-sufficient work: "in order that we might give ourselves to you as an example so that you might imitate us" (2 Thess. 3:10). This second purpose will become an effective argument that Paul can use to rebuke the rebelliously idle conduct of some within the Thessalonian congregation.

therefore, he worked hard ("Remember our labor and toil") and long ("working night and day") so that the new Christians in that city did not need to support him financially. The concern behind this practice of self-sufficient work was that he not "put an obstacle in the way of the gospel of Christ" (1 Cor. 9:12). The obstacle is that his hearers may view him as just another itinerant lecturer whose coming was rooted in a "motive for greed" (2:5). Once a church had been established, however, and Paul left that congregation, he expected them to contribute to the cause of the gospel (J. M. Everts, *DPL* 297). This explains why Paul accepts monetary support from the Philippian church (Phil. 4:15–16) at the very time when he is in Thessalonica and working so as to not become a financial burden to the converts in that city.

Paul links his self-sufficient work with his activity of preaching by stating in the final phrase of the verse, "We preached to you the gospel of God" (ἐκηρύξαμεν εἰς ὑμᾶς τὸ εὐαγγέλιον τοῦ θεοῦ, *ekēryxamen eis hymas to euangelion tou theou*). This raises the issue of the precise relationship between Paul's "working night and day" and his preaching the gospel. Under the assumption that a participle in the present tense describes an action taking place simultaneously with the main verb, some have concluded that Paul's working and preaching occurred at the same time (so, e.g., Wanamaker 1990: 104; Malherbe 2000: 149). In other words, the setting in which the apostle evangelized and discipled others was not solely, as is commonly assumed, the public marketplace but also the semiprivate workshop. Indeed, some ancient sources depict the workshop as one of the conventional settings for intellectual discourse and instruction. During the long hours at his workbench, while cutting and sewing leather to make tents and other related goods, Paul was not only supporting himself but also sharing the gospel with fellow workers and customers (Hock 1979; 1980: 26–49, 52–59; Malherbe 1987: 7–20).

Although the general thesis that Paul used the workshop as the setting for his evangelistic ministry is probably correct, the specific appeal to the present tense of the participle "working" (*ergazomenoi*) as support for this thesis needs to be nuanced. Recent studies in Greek grammar have demonstrated that participles do not express time but verbal aspect (see Porter 1989; Fanning 1990; see also the earlier work of van Elderen 1961). The present tense of "working," therefore, emphasizes the ongoing or continuous nature of the action rather than its time. Paul's action of working may be taking place simultaneously with his preaching activity, but this must be determined on grounds other than the tense of the participle.

f. His "Nurturing as a Father" Conduct (2:10–12)

The sixth main clause, in 2:10–12, though long and missing at one point a required verb, has a structure that is relatively clear. The first and longest part of the clause (vv. 10–12a) consists of two more appeals to the firsthand knowledge of the Thessalonians ("You are witnesses, and God also"; "just as you know"), each of which is followed in parallel fashion by the relative adverb

2:10

"how" (ὡς, *hōs*) which introduces an indirect statement giving the content of that knowledge.[37] The second and shorter part of the clause (v. 12b) consists of a purpose statement that marks a major transition away from the focus on Paul and his integrity during his mission-founding visit (2:1–12) to the Thessalonians and their response to Paul's past visit (2:13–16). Thus the text can be outlined as follows:

> [10]You are witnesses, and God also,
>   how holy and righteous and blameless we were to you believers,
> [11]just as you know
>   how we dealt with each one of you like a father with his children,
>   [12]appealing and encouraging and imploring you
>   in order that you may lead a life worthy of God,
>   the one who is calling you into his own kingdom and glory.

In this clause, the first of the two appeals to the personal knowledge that the Thessalonians have about Paul comes in the form of a simple declarative statement: "You are witnesses, and God also" (ὑμεῖς μάρτυρες καὶ ὁ θεός, *hymeis martyres kai ho theos*). This constitutes not only the fifth time in the passage that Paul reminds his hearers of what they already know from firsthand experience (see 2:1, 2, 5, 9, 11) but also the second time that he invokes God as a witness (see 2:5). As noted above, the apostle rarely summons God as a witness, and this is the only place where he does so twice. The significance of this is not missed by Marshall (1983: 73): "The solemnity of the tone suggests strongly that Paul was dealing with real accusations that were being used by the opponents of the church to denigrate the missionaries and their message and so to turn the converts against them."[38]

What the Thessalonian Christians and God have witnessed with respect to Paul's conduct is "how holy and righteous and blameless we were to you believers" (ὡς ὁσίως καὶ δικαίως καὶ ἀμέμπτως ὑμῖν τοῖς πιστεύουσιν ἐγενήθημεν, *hōs hosiōs kai dikaiōs kai amemptōs hymin tois pisteuousin egenēthēmen*). The grammar is somewhat unexpected since the verb "we were" more properly takes adjectives as its predicate instead of the adverbial forms found in the clause. Perhaps the adverbs emphasize more the conduct of Paul and his coworkers than their character (so, e.g., Wanamaker 1990: 104; Richard 1995: 85). It is questionable, however, whether the apostle would distinguish so carefully between conduct and character. Furthermore, adverbs were sometimes used in Classical Greek as adjectives (BDF §434).

These three adverbs are rare elsewhere in Paul's Letters (*hosiōs* occurs only here; *dikaiōs* elsewhere only in 1 Cor. 15:34 and Titus 2:12; *amemptōs* elsewhere

---

37. BDAG (1105.5) lists the use of ὡς in 1 Thess. 2:10 and 11 as "after verbs of knowing, saying (even introducing direct discourse), hearing, etc. = ὅτι *that*" (see also BDF §396).

38. This conclusion is more compelling than the claim of several recent commentators that Paul is not defending himself but instead "engaging in implicit parenesis about how the Thessalonians should act based on his example" (Wanamaker 1990: 104).

only in 1 Thess. 5:23 [but see 1 Thess. 3:13 v.l.]), though the corresponding adjectives are more common. On the basis of their meaning in Classical Greek, the first two adverbs are claimed to refer to conduct related to God and humans respectively (F. Hauck, *TDNT* 5:490; Lightfoot 1904: 27–28; Wanamaker 1990: 105; D. Martin 1995: 83; Richard 1995: 85, 104; Fee 2009: 79–80), while the third adverb serves as a summary for conduct directed to both God and humans (Richard 1995: 85, 104–5). These distinctions, however, are not always operative in Classical Greek (Milligan 1908: 24), and it is difficult to substantiate this in the NT (Morris 1991: 75). It is also unlikely that Paul as a Jew would distinguish so sharply between one's obligation to God and one's obligation to others (Best 1977: 105; Bruce 1982: 35–36). The significance of the three adverbs, therefore, lies not in their distinctive meanings (they ought to be viewed as virtually synonymous) but in their number. The piling up of three adverbs, all placed emphatically in the first part of the clause, serves to emphasize the irreproachable character of Paul's conduct "to you believers."[39]

2:11 Paralleling the pattern found in the preceding verse, there is a second appeal to the personal knowledge that the Thessalonians have followed by the relative adverb "how" (ὡς, *hōs*), which introduces an indirect statement giving the content of that knowledge: "just as you know how we dealt with each one of you like a father with his children" (καθάπερ οἴδατε ὡς ἕνα ἕκαστον ὑμῶν ὡς πατὴρ τέκνα ἑαυτοῦ, *kathaper oidate hōs hena hekaston hymōn hōs patēr tekna heautou*). The indirect-statement clause lacks a main verb in the Greek text, and it is not clear what should be supplied in the translation. Some have suggested that the verb "we were" (*egenēthēmen*) from the preceding clause (2:10) does double duty, functioning either alone in a predicate construction or with the following three participles (2:12) in a periphrastic construction.[40] Both options, however, appear to be grammatically impossible because of the accusative "each one of you," which cannot serve as the object of "we were" (a predicate *nominative* would be required) or of a possible periphrastic construction (the participles already have a direct object given: "you"). The best option is to treat this as an anacoluthon in which the verb must be supplied from the context (so Lightfoot 1904: 28–29; Wanamaker 1990: 105–6; Richard 1995: 105). The metaphor of a father suggests that a child-rearing verb like "raised," "trained," or "brought up" would be especially appropriate, as would the more neutral "dealt with" (ASV, NIV, NRSV) or "treated" (NCV, NLT).[41]

---

39. In 2:10, the precise force of the dative phrase ὑμῖν τοῖς πιστεύουσιν has been disputed. The proposals include a locative dative ("among you who believe"), a dative of advantage ("to the benefit of you who believe"), or a dative of indirect object ("to you who believe"). The last option seems preferable with the main verb ἐγενήθημεν. The force of the phrase, then, is that the Thessalonians did not merely observe the holy, righteous, and blameless conduct of Paul and his coworkers toward others, but this was how the missionaries had also acted toward them personally.

40. Some translations, for example, render the three participles in 2:12 as three main verbs: "We exhorted each one of you and encouraged you and charged you" (KJV, RSV, NCV, NLT, ESV).

41. Richard (1995: 86, 105) argues that the supplied verb in 2:11 should be in the present tense, since Paul is not referring simply to past conduct but also to a general principle concerning

The phrase "each one of you" (*hena hekaston hymōn*) is noteworthy, for it is stronger than the simple and commonly used *hekaston* (among its forty-two occurrences in Paul's Letters, the numeral "one" is added seven times) and thus puts an emphasis on the individual. This supports Paul's overall apologetic concern because it reminds the readers of the fatherly manner in which the apostle dealt with them all individually—further evidence of his "holy and righteous and blameless" conduct. This phrase may also lend further support to the claim that Paul's evangelistic activity took place not only in the public setting of the street corner but also in the semiprivate setting of the workshop, where such individual training would be possible.

For the third time in this passage, Paul makes use of a familial metaphor: "like a father with his own children." Whereas the first metaphor of infants (2:7b) highlights the *innocence* of Paul during his mission-founding visit and the second metaphor of a nursing mother (2:7c) stresses the *love* that motivated the apostle during that same visit, this third metaphor of a father conveys the *nurturing* role that Paul had during his stay. The apostle makes use of the father metaphor in his later letters as well (1 Cor. 4:14–15; Phil. 2:22; Philem. 10); there, as here, the focus is on the nurturing or instructional role that Paul plays in the lives of his converts. As John Chrysostom, Pelagius, and others in the early church recognized, Paul compares himself to a nurse or mother when he wants to highlight the love and affection he has for his readers, but he likens himself to a father when he wants to focus on his role in teaching and training converts. In the ancient world this nurturing aspect of the metaphor is supported by the role of the father, who was normally responsible for the education and training of his children. That Paul was highlighting his nurturing conduct is confirmed by the following three participles (2:12), which speak of the apostle's work of "appealing and encouraging and imploring" the Thessalonians to lead lives worthy of God.[42]

In the patriarchal society of the ancient world, the image of a father depicted him as possessing ultimate authority over all members of the household, including, of course, the children. Both Greco-Roman and Jewish sources emphasize the hierarchical relationship of father to their children, often with language that jars the egalitarian spirit of our modern age (for sources, see Osiek and Balch 1997: 54–64; Burke 2000; Weima 2002: 225; Burke 2003: 36–96, 131–50). Aristotle states, for example, "The father is a kind of god

---

his current practice of pastoral care. In a somewhat similar vein, Holmes (1998: 67) claims that "the absence of a verb gives the statement something of a timeless cast: Paul is indicating not only how he related to the Thessalonians in the past (during the original missionary visit) but also how he continues to relate to them." The larger context of 2:1–16, however, and especially the preceding parallel clause of 2:10, with the aorist form ἐγενήθημεν, make it clear that Paul's primary focus here is on his past conduct to the Thessalonians.

42. Fee (2009: 81): "The essential difference between the two metaphors [of "mother" and "father"] is in this case to be found in the three participles, which together describe what the ancients, both Greek and Roman, would have recognized as a father's duty, especially in the matter of the moral training of his children."

to his children, a full head and shoulders above them, and rightly so, for the father is a king" (*Pol.* 1.12.3; see also *Nic. Eth.* 8.11.2). Plutarch similarly locates parents on a hierarchical scale in which they are second in rank only to the gods: "Both Nature and the Law, which uphold Nature, have assigned to parents, after the gods, first and greatest honor" (*Frat. amor.* 7/479F). Jewish writers were influenced by the fifth commandment, to honor one's parents—a commandment that establishes the authority of the parents and especially that of the "father [who is] head of the house" (Philo, *Names* 217). In light of the overwhelming testimony of the Greco-Roman and Jewish sources that depict the father as an authoritative figure, it might be easy to create a stereotyped image of the father as a cold, omnipotent ruler of his household. This image, however, must be balanced by the many texts that clearly reveal the great affection that fathers had for their children (Burke 2000: 65–69; 2003: 36–96, 131–50). A father may have been a powerful figure in the ancient world, but the term "father" also served to evoke the emotion of devotion and love. It is this latter picture of affection that Paul is highlighting for his Thessalonian readers. As Furnish (2007: 61–62) observes: "In this context it [the father metaphor] is used more particularly to accent the seriousness with which he [Paul] has taken his responsibility to provide instruction and guidance (v. 12). He is emphasizing his pastoral *devotion to* his Thessalonian 'children,' not primarily his *authority over* them" (emphasis his).

Paul's role as a devoted and nurturing father is spelled out in three participles **2:12** that modify the omitted main verb:[43] "appealing and encouraging and imploring you" (παρακαλοῦντες ὑμᾶς καὶ παραμυθούμενοι καὶ μαρτυρόμενοι, *parakalountes hymas kai paramythoumenoi kai martyromenoi*). The first verb, *parakaleō*, is, by far, the most common of the three forms, occurring some fifty-four times in Paul's Letters as a whole and eight times in this letter (2:12; 3:2, 7; 4:1, 10, 18; 5:11, 14). Although the verb possesses a wide range of meanings (BDAG 764–65 lists five different senses), these possibilities can be grouped into two primary nuances: either command (appeal, exhort, request, implore) or comfort (encourage, comfort, cheer up, console). The second verb, *paramytheomai*, is much less frequent in Paul, appearing only here and later in the letter in 5:14 (see also John 11:19, 31). Outside of Scripture this term "almost always has affective connotations, with the highly nuanced meanings of 'advise, encourage, console, comfort, speak calming words to, appease, soothe'" (Spicq 1994: 3.30–35; see also G. Stählin, *TDNT* 5:816–23). The third verb, *martyromai*, is also infrequent in Paul, occurring elsewhere only in Gal. 5:3 and Eph. 4:17 (although the closely related form διαμαρτύρομαι [*diamartyromai*] is used in 1 Thess. 4:6; 1 Tim. 5:21; 2 Tim. 2:14; 4:1). Although no longer possessing its original sense of invoking witnesses (testify, bear witness), this verb still has a more authoritative nuance than the two preceding verbs: "insist, implore" (BDAG 619).

---

43. All three participles in 2:12 function adverbially to give the manner in which Paul "dealt with each one of you as a father with his children."

It is very difficult to determine the specific nuance Paul intends in these three participles, particularly the first two. The notion of comfort would fit the church's problem of suffering ridicule and ostracism for their newfound faith. The notion of command, however, agrees better with the metaphor of a father and his expected role as the authoritative figure in the household, who appeals, encourages, and even implores his children to pursue proper learning and conduct. But rather than concentrate on the distinctive meanings of the three participles, it is probably better to focus on their number. The piling up of three participles, like the use of three adverbs in the preceding verse, is somewhat of a literary device by which Paul emphasizes the fatherly role that he played during his past visit to Thessalonica.

This fatherly role that Paul played had a very specific purpose:[44] "in order that you may lead a life worthy of God" (εἰς τὸ περιπατεῖν ὑμᾶς ἀξίως τοῦ θεοῦ, *eis to peripatein hymas axiōs tou theou*). The verb *peripateō* literally means "to walk" but has the metaphorical sense of "living one's life." It is not only one of Paul's favorite words to describe the Christian life (it occurs some thirty-two times in his letters); it is also one of his more strategic terms as it is used to introduce themes that the apostle considered to be fundamental (Holloway 1992). This metaphorical use of "walking" to describe moral conduct and an ethical way of life has its roots in Paul's Jewish background (roughly 200 of the 1,547 occurrences of הלך [*hlk*] are metaphorical or figurative). The metaphor also occurs in nonbiblical Greek (but with much less frequency and normally with the verb πορεύομαι, *poreuomai*, go, conduct one's life) and thus would have been readily understood by his readers (H. Seesemann, *TDNT* 5:940–45; Holloway 1992: 1–27).

Since "walking" is a neutral concept that can denote either positive or negative conduct (for the latter, see 2 Cor. 4:2 and 10:2), more precision is almost always given to the term by the addition of a prepositional phrase, a dative of the attendant circumstance, or as here, an adverb: "to walk *worthily*" (see also Eph. 4:1; Col. 1:10).[45] The use of "worthily" (*axiōs*) as a qualifier suggests a life that is equivalent to or in agreement to some standard (W. Foerster, *TDNT* 1:379–80). This standard is itself further explained as "of God" (*tou theou*). The resultant phrase "worthily of God" is one that occurs in Hellenistic religion to describe the conduct of priests and other followers who were required to live in a way that corresponded to the character and demands of

44. The use of an articular infinitive with the preposition εἰς is an almost exclusively Pauline construction in the NT that normally expresses purpose or result (BDF §402.2). A few have questioned whether this function of the articular infinitive is present here in 2:12 (MHT 1:219: "Purpose is so remote here as to be practically evanescent") and argued that this construction instead gives the content of the preceding three participles (Milligan 1908: 26). It seems best, however, to view this construction as having its normal meaning of purpose or result (so the majority of commentators; note the mediating position of Marshall [1983: 74], who states: "Now comes the purpose of the ethical appeal, which is at the same time a statement of its content").

45. There is little support for the claim that the use of ἀξίως in 2:12 suggests that Paul is dependent on an early Christian baptismal tradition (Haufe 1985: 469; Donfried 1987: 182).

the particular god that they worshiped (see the inscriptions from Pergamum and Magnesia cited by Milligan 1908: 26 and Frame 1912: 105). By analogy, therefore, the Christians in Thessalonica must conduct themselves in a manner that corresponds to the character and demands of their God.

Instead of presenting a list of specific commandments that must be obeyed, Paul sets before his readers the goal of living in a way that is consistent with the nature of their God. What is this nature of God to which the conduct of the Thessalonian Christians must conform? Some commentators identify God's holiness, citing the words of Lev. 11:45 ("You shall be holy, for I am holy"), as well as the emphasis on "holiness" later in the letter, in 1 Thess. 4:3–8 (Marshall 1983: 74–75; Richard 1995: 108). Others refer more generally to "God's loving-kindness" (Morris 1991: 77) or his attributes of "love, patience, justice, and so forth" (Wanamaker 1990: 107).

Paul, however, focuses on a different aspect of God's character: "the one who is calling you into his own kingdom and glory" (τοῦ καλοῦντος ὑμᾶς εἰς τὴν ἑαυτοῦ βασιλείαν καὶ δόξαν, *tou kalountos hymas eis tēn heatou basileian kai doxan*). This phrase makes it clear that, though the Thessalonian Christians must live in a way that is worthy of God, such conduct in no way earns their salvation but rather is a response to the free and unmerited "call" of God. Paul has raised the theme of the Thessalonians' election already at the very beginning of the letter (1:4) and will do so four more times later in the correspondence (3:3b; 4:7; 5:9, 24). Elsewhere the apostle typically uses the aorist tense to refer to God's initial call at the time of conversion (4:7; 2 Thess. 2:14; Gal. 1:6; 1 Cor. 1:9). The use of the present tense here in 2:12 (see also 5:24; Gal. 5:8) by contrast highlights the ongoing and effective nature of the call (for the apostle, God's call is always effective: 1 Thess. 5:23–24; Rom. 8:30; 1 Cor. 1:9). To a church experiencing opposition because of their newfound faith, it is especially encouraging to know that God has not called them once in the past and subsequently abandoned them to their own resources, but rather continues to call them and so will ensure that they "be kept sound and blameless at the coming of our Lord Jesus Christ" (5:23). It is also, however, challenging to know that this ongoing call of God must be responded to with the ongoing need "to lead a life worthy of God."

The goal of God's call is entry "into his own kingdom and glory." The term *basileia*, traditionally rendered "kingdom" or more dynamically "reign," occurs rather infrequently in Paul's Letters (fourteen occurrences) in sharp contrast to the Gospels, where the theme of the kingdom plays an especially prominent part in the teaching of Jesus. Yet the apostle shares with the Gospels the view that the kingdom is both a present and future reality. On the one hand, the kingdom has been inaugurated through the coming and ministry of Jesus Christ and so is something present and experienced now (Rom. 14:17; 1 Cor. 4:20). On the other hand, the kingdom as a time when God will vindicate his people and as a place where God will fully establish his rule over all creation—all this has not yet happened and so is something future and experienced at Christ's glorious return (2 Thess. 1:5; 1 Cor. 6:9, 10; 15:24, 50; Gal. 5:21). That the reference to "kingdom" here belongs to this second and more frequent use of the term is clear not only from the context but also from the presence of the accompanying term "glory" (on this, see below).

Paul's claim that his original preaching in Thessalonica involved speaking about the "kingdom" provides an important and largely overlooked agreement with the description in Acts 17 of the apostle's ministry in that city. The charge brought against Paul and his converts is that "these men who have turned the world upside down have come here also, and Jason has received them, and they are all acting against the decrees of Caesar, *saying that there is another king*, Jesus" (Acts 17:6–7). As Donfried (1987: 188) correctly states: "Paul's categorical statement in 1 Thess 2:12 that he did speak to the Thessalonians about the kingdom during his presence in the city should help us to understand the relative accuracy of the Acts 17 account, not only with regard to Paul's use of king/kingdom language but also with regard to the fact that this language may well have served as the catalyst for the animosity he and his co-workers aroused in Thessalonica."

The term "glory" is closely aligned with "kingdom" by virtue of the single definite article and the one reflexive pronoun "his own" used for both nouns (see BDF §276). Although earlier in the passage (2:6) *doxa* has the common secular meaning of "fame, renown, honor," here it has the religious and more typical Pauline sense of "glory." There is a rich OT and Jewish background to the apostle's use of this term that cannot be fully explored here (see G. Kittel, *TDNT* 2:233–55; Spicq 1994: 1.353–61; R. B. Gaffin Jr., *DPL* 348–50). Basically, the noun describes the visible radiance of God's being or character that is revealed in heaven and given by him to his human creatures (Rom. 5:2; 8:18; Col. 1:27). Although humanity lost its original share in God's glory (Rom. 3:23), believers will recover this divine glory in the future resurrection (1 Cor. 15:42–44; Phil. 3:20–21), an eschatological event for which they are already being prepared (2 Cor. 3:18). It is this glorious future that Paul holds out as an incentive for the Thessalonian Christians to live in the present. To "walk worthily of God" means to act, speak, and think in a way that reflects the ultimate goal of believers: to live under the reign of God and to share in his divine glory.

2. The Thessalonians' Response to Paul's Past Visit (2:13–16)

After defending (in 2:1–12) the integrity of his past "visit" (*eisodos*) or mission-founding activity in Thessalonica, Paul in 2:13–16 shifts to the Thessalonians' response to that past visit. This shift, far from being problematic,[46] is an expected one for the careful reader of the letter, since it follows exactly

---

46. The judgment that this shift at 2:13 is awkward and abrupt, along with the harsh condemnation of the Jews found in 2:15–16 as well as other distinctive features in this passage, has caused some to claim that 2:13–16 is not from the hand of Paul but is rather a later interpolation into the letter. For a discussion of this complex issue and a defense of the genuineness of this passage, see the introduction to the commentary.

the same pattern foreshadowed twice in the thanksgiving section, where the apostle similarly begins with his conduct during the mission-founding visit to Thessalonica (1:5 and 1:9a) and then moves to the response of the Thessalonians to that visit (1:6–8 and 1:9b–10).[47] That this response of the Thessalonian Christians was positive—they not only accepted the word of Paul as the word of God (2:13) but also were willing to be persecuted for this word, thereby imitating the persecuted churches in Judea (2:14–16)—further confirms the genuine character of the apostle and his mission-founding work in their midst and so provides a further defense of his integrity. In this way, 2:13–16 supports the defensive or apologetic function that is operative not only in the preceding section (2:1–12) but also in the whole first half of the letter body (2:1–3:10). As Marshall (1983: 9) notes: "These verses [2:13–16] round off the 'apology' by claiming that the Thessalonians themselves accepted Paul's message as God's Word and thereby rejected any insinuations that might be made against him."

The material of 2:13–16, however, not only looks back to Paul's defense at work in the preceding section of 2:1–12 but also looks ahead to the following section of 2:17–3:10. It has already been noted above that verses 14–16 prepare the reader for the upcoming two themes of (1) the defense of Paul's present absence from the Thessalonian believers in 2:17–20 and (2) the persecution endured by the Thessalonian church in 3:1–5—two themes that then are skillfully combined in 3:6–10. Both themes are introduced in 2:14–16: the Thessalonians have become imitators of the Judean churches in that they too are being persecuted by their own fellow citizens (2:14), thereby anticipating the theme of persecution addressed in 3:1–5; also, the Jews in Thessalonica instigated the opposition against Paul (2:15: "They [the Jews] drove us out"), which has made it impossible for the apostle to return and visit his converts in Thessalonica, thereby anticipating Paul's defense of his present absence in 2:17–20.

a. Their Acceptance of the Word of Paul as the Word of God (2:13)

The first way in which the Thessalonians positively responded to Paul's original ministry in their city was to accept the word spoken by the apostle as the authoritative word of God: "And because of this, we indeed give thanks to God constantly, namely, that when you received the word of God that you heard from us, you accepted it not as the word of human beings but, as it truly is, the word of God, which is indeed at work in you believers."

2:13

The opening words of this verse ("And because of this, we indeed") may appear innocuous and simple to understand, but they are actually quite complicated since they are open to differing interpretations. The first occurrence of

---

47. The transition at 2:13 from Paul's past visit (2:1–12) to the Thessalonians' response to that visit (2:13–16) is signaled already in the immediately preceding clause of 2:12b, where the purpose of the apostle's fatherlike conduct is "in order that *you* may lead a life worthy of God."

kai (and), omitted in some translations (KJV, JB, NASB, NRSV), is important: it functions as a coordinating conjunction (see also 1:6; 1:9b) that strengthens the link between 2:13–16 and the preceding material of 2:1–12. Paul elsewhere uses this conjunction "to indicate a division of medium importance, to introduce a new development, but one which is nevertheless related to what has gone before. He is saying, in effect, 'Don't forget what I have just told you, but bear it in mind while I tell you something more'" (Ellingworth and Nida 1975: 37). Although *kai* occurs often enough before the phrase διὰ τοῦτο (*dia touto*, because of this) in other writers (e.g., Matt. 14:2; Mark 6:14; John 5:16; Heb. 9:15; Barn. 8.7; Ignatius, *Magn.* 9.2; Hermas, *Sim.* 7.2; 9.19), in Paul it is found only here and in 2 Thess. 2:11, which may explain why a number of late manuscripts omit the word.

The phrase "because of this" (*dia touto*) can refer either (1) back to preceding material (anaphoric function) or (2) forward to subsequent material (cataphoric function). If taken as backward looking, it might refer to (a) the immediately preceding claim in 2:12b concerning God's call of the Thessalonians (so Malherbe 2000: 165); (b) the key principle asserted in 2:1–4, that "the gospel is not human, as the Jews alleged, but divine" (so Frame 1912: 106); (c) the general subject matter in 2:1–12 concerning Paul's past ministry among them (Lightfoot 1904: 30); or (d) the earlier reasons for thanksgiving listed in 1:2–10 (so Rigaux 1956: 437). In view of the ambiguity suggested by these differing interpretations, several scholars (e.g., Best 1977: 109–10; Wanamaker 1990: 110; Richard 1995: 112; Green 2002: 139) prefer to take the phrase "because of this" as looking ahead to a new and additional cause of thanksgiving given in the following ὅτι (*hoti*, that) clause (hence the JB translation: "Another reason why we constantly thank God for you is that . . .").

Although the latter option is the simpler interpretation, it founders on the fact that the other instances of *dia touto* in Paul refer fairly clearly back to preceding material.[48] This, along with the opening conjunction "and," which also highlights the link with the preceding material, suggests that *dia touto* here also most likely looks backward. While it is not possible to identify the antecedent with certainty, the following ὅτι clause, dealing with the way in which the Thessalonians received and accepted the preached word of the apostles, recalls Paul's concern throughout 2:1–12 with defending his role in the proclamation of the gospel message during his mission-founding visit. The contrast between the "word of humans" and "the word of God" (2:13) especially echoes the antithetical statement of 2:4, where Paul claims to speak not as one who pleases "humans . . . but God." It therefore appears that the phrase *dia touto* looks back in a general way to Paul's preaching the word of God to the Thessalonians during his original ministry among them and

---

48. There are some twenty-two occurrences of διὰ τοῦτο in Paul's Letters: Rom. 1:26; 4:16; 5:12; 13:6; 15:9; 1 Cor. 4:17; 11:10, 30; 2 Cor. 4:1; 7:13; 13:10; Eph. 1:15; 5:17; 6:13; Col. 1:9; 1 Thess. 2:13; 3:5, 7; 2 Thess. 2:11; 1 Tim. 1:16; 2 Tim. 2:10; Philem. 15.

the Thessalonians' reception of that word—a point that is clarified by the following ὅτι clause.

The second occurrence of the conjunction *kai* in 2:13 is also open to multiple interpretations. First, it could function with the personal pronoun "we," as the word order might suggest, thereby implying a contrast between the missionaries who are sending this letter ("we also") and some other group of people. Such a contrast opens the door to a number of possibilities. (a) Harris (1898: 193) claims that the Thessalonians had written a letter to Paul (see the epistolary formula περὶ δέ in 4:9, 13; 5:1) in which they gave thanks to God and that the apostle here in similar fashion states that "we also" (i.e., in addition to the Thessalonian believers) give thanks to God (so also Lake 1911: 87; Frame 1912: 107). This view, however, depends on the larger and questionable issue of whether the Thessalonians did actually write to Paul. (b) Marxsen (1979: 47) claims that the contrast is between Paul and those in Macedonia and Achaia who had informed the apostle about the conversion of the Thessalonians (1:8), so that the "we also" refers to the activity of Paul and his fellow missionaries joining these distant believers in giving thanks. This view, however, suffers from the fact that there has been no earlier mention of a thanksgiving that these Macedonians and Achaians have made. (c) Still other commentators see a contrast between the letter writers and the Thessalonian readers, in which the conjunction has a weakened sense, emphasizing the "we" that can be rendered as "we for our part" (so Lightfoot 1904: 30; Rigaux 1956: 437–38; Best 1977: 110).

Second, it is more likely, however, that the second conjunction *kai* modifies the verb "we give thanks." For the expression *dia touto kai* "is so fixed a phrase that *kai* can even be separated from the verb which it emphasizes" (BDF §422.12), and this displacement of *kai* is characteristic of Paul (Moule 1959: 167). This interpretation in turn leads to two possibilities. (a) A few commentators translate *kai* as "also" so that the conjunction indicates a reiteration of the earlier thanksgiving in 1:2–10 (e.g., Dobschütz 1909: 103; Dibelius 1937: 11; O'Brien 1977: 154). (b) A better alternative, however, sees the conjunction as emphasizing the activity of giving thanks and so renders *kai* as "indeed" or "in fact." This latter view is supported by the similar construction in 3:5, where *dia touto kagō epempsa* . . . does not mean "because of this I *also* sent . . ." but "because of this I *indeed* sent . . ." (see also Rom. 3:7; Phil. 4:15; Moule 1959: 167). The second occurrence of *kai* in 2:13, therefore, stresses Paul's activity of giving thanks to God for the positive way that the Thessalonian Christians responded to his original ministry in their midst.

The opening statement of thanksgiving is followed by a ὅτι (*hoti*) clause that many take as causal so that Paul is seen here as offering an additional reason or ground for his thanksgiving (e.g., Wanamaker 1990: 110; Holmes 1998: 81; Malherbe 2000: 166). However, the conclusions we have reached above concerning the meaning of the opening words of 2:13 (the first *kai* functions as a coordinating conjunction that strengthens the link between 2:13–16 and the preceding material in 2:1–12; the phrase *dia touto* functions anaphorically—it looks back to preceding material; and the second *kai* serves to emphasize the main verb) demand that the *hoti* function epexegetically: it explains the phrase *dia touto* that looks back in a general way to Paul's concern throughout 2:1–12 with his mediation of the word of God during his mission-founding visit to Thessalonica. As the apostle follows his statement of thanksgiving in 1:2–4 with an epexegetical *hoti* clause in 1:5, here too he adopts the same pattern. That Paul in this explanatory clause is very concerned with his role in communicating the word of God to the Thessalonians is evident in that the noun "word" occurs three times and also serves as the subject of the closing relative clause.

The positive response of the Thessalonians to Paul's preaching is expressed by two verbs that are virtually synonymous: παραλαβόντες . . . ἐδέξασθε (*paralabontes . . . edexasthe*, receiving . . . you accepted). The first verb, *paralambanō*, especially when used in combination with (παρα)δέχομαι (*paradechomai*, accept), is a technical term in Paul's Letters for the passing on and accepting of traditional material. Although this technical usage has strong parallels in the rabbinic tradition that was an essential part of Paul's pre-Christian training (see Davies 1948: 247–50; Gerhardsson 1961: 265, 290–96), it also has roots in Hellenism for the instruction passed down from a philosopher to his students and in the mystery religions for the secrets handed on to new initiates (see G. Delling, *TDNT* 4:11–12). The content of this traditional material that Paul has received and passes on to his readers includes such matters as the eucharistic sayings of Jesus (1 Cor. 11:23), a confession about Jesus's death and resurrection (1 Cor. 15:1, 3), ethical teachings about proper conduct in general (1 Thess. 4:1) and self-sufficient work in particular (2 Thess. 3:6), and the gospel message itself (Gal. 1:9, 12). The verb *paralambanō* here in 2:13, therefore, likely refers to the Thessalonians' reception of traditional material: the gospel that Paul and his fellow missionaries had passed on to them during their mission-founding visit.

The direct object of the first verb involves a rather awkward expression in Greek that literally means "the word, heard from us, of God" (λόγον ἀκοῆς παρ' ἡμῶν τοῦ θεοῦ, *logon akoēs par' hēmōn tou theou*). Nevertheless, this clause succeeds in driving home the point that the "word" or gospel that Paul had passed on to them was no mere human word but the divine word of God. The apostle stresses his part in communicating to the Thessalonians the gospel by identifying the word that they received as one "that you heard from us" (*akoēs par' hēmōn*). The placement of this phrase between the noun "word" and its genitive modifier "of God" gives it a certain emphasis. Here the noun *akoē* more likely has the active sense of "hearing" than the passive sense of that which is heard ("account, report, message": BDAG 36.4.b),[49] though the general sense is not greatly affected either way (Rigaux 1956: 439). The more important point is that this noun highlights Paul's role—an emphasis that no doubt stems from

---

49. Schippers (1966) argues that ἀκοή in 2:13 should be understood passively as "tradition" (rather than a reference to the preaching of the gospel) and that Paul in 2:14–16 is creatively handling a presynoptic tradition.

the apologetic concern of 2:1–12: this "heard" word that the Thessalonians received was communicated through human agents, the apostle and his fellow missionaries (*par' hēmōn*, from us). But while Paul and his companions were a key immediate source of this word, its ultimate source was God (*tou theou*, of God, is a subjective genitive [= a word originating from God] rather than objective [= a word about God]). The juxtaposition of the expressions "from us" and "of God" clearly implies that the word of Paul to the Thessalonians is actually the word of God—a point explicitly stated in the following clause.[50]

The second verb used to describe the positive response of the Thessalonians to Paul's preaching is *edexasthe* (you accepted; see 1:6). Although in lexical terms this verb is synonymous with the preceding verb *paralambontes* (e.g., the Vulgate and Syriac translators render the two Greek verbs with only one word), its use in the present context suggests that each word has a slightly different emphasis (Richard 1995: 112). The first verb, frequently used in the passing on of traditional material, highlights the hearing and reception of the authoritative word preached by Paul and the other missionaries; the second verb stresses the actual acceptance or internal appropriation of this message by the Thessalonian believers. Most commentators do see a distinction in this verse between the external reception of the gospel message and its subjective acceptance. Gaventa (1998: 34) cleverly captures this distinction by noting in colloquial terms that "the Thessalonians not only 'took' the gospel but also 'took to it.'"

The most important contrast in the verse, however, lies not between the two verbs of "receiving" and "accepting" but between the human and divine source of the word that the Thessalonian Christians embraced: "You accepted it not as the word of human beings but, as it truly is, the word of God" (οὐ λόγον ἀνθρώπων ἀλλὰ καθώς ἐστιν ἀληθῶς λόγον θεοῦ, *ou logon anthrōpōn alla kathōs estin alēthōs logon theou*). Here the implicit claim made in the preceding participial clause concerning the proclaimed word, which was both "from us" and "of God," is made explicit. There is no difference between Paul's word and God's word. The gospel that the apostle proclaimed during his original ministry in Thessalonica (note the fourfold occurrence of "the gospel [of God]" in 2:2, 4, 8, 9) was no mere human word but instead was the divine word of God. That the Thessalonian Christians responded positively to this gospel message by accepting Paul's word not as the "word of human beings" (i.e., a message whose human source renders it untrustworthy and nonobligatory) but as "the word of God" (i.e., a message whose divine source renders it true and authoritative)—this is the reason why the apostle now constantly gives thanks to God.

---

50. Wanamaker (1990: 111) claims that the insertion of the modifier "of God" in 2:13 is not only "redundant" but also worse: "it makes the phrase preempt the thought of the clause as a whole and detracts from the force of the contrast that Paul seeks to make in v. 13c between a message originating with human beings and the message of Paul, which stemmed from God." One can argue with greater plausibility, however, that the expression "from us of God" anticipates and strengthens the contrast of the following clause between the word of humans and the word of God.

Not only was this divine word accepted by the Thessalonians during Paul's past mission work among them; it also continues to be operative in their present lives: "which is indeed at work in you believers" (ὃς καὶ ἐνεργεῖται ἐν ὑμῖν τοῖς πιστεύουσιν, *hos kai energeitai en hymin tois pisteuousin*). Grammatically, the relative pronoun *hos* can refer to either "word" or "God." Although the fuller expression *hos kai* in 5:24 refers to God, the immediate context ought to be a more decisive factor. That "word" is especially emphasized in this verse (by means of its three occurrences and the affirmation "as it truly is") strongly suggests that here too Paul continues his focus on the word of God (for the alternative view that the relative pronoun refers instead to God, see Richard 1995: 113–15, followed by Beale 2003: 77). Furthermore, the apostle elsewhere consistently uses the active form of *energein* when God is the subject (1 Cor. 12:6; Gal. 2:8 [2x]; 3:5; Phil. 2:13 [2x]), and the middle/passive form, as we have here,[51] when other subjects are in view. The difference in meaning, however, is minimal since Paul has just clearly asserted that the "word" the apostle proclaimed and the Thessalonians "heard," "received," and "accepted" was "the word of God" and so ultimately originates from God.

Paul's point, therefore, is that the Thessalonians not only "accepted" (past tense) the word or gospel at their conversion, but that this divine message "indeed" (the conjunction *kai* functions adverbially) continues to be "at work" (present tense) in their lives. Much more than a fancy human message that caught their fleeting attention at one brief moment in time, the gospel instead is an ongoing source of divine power in the lives of the Thessalonian Christians. Although Paul does not spell out how the gospel is working in these believers, the reader cannot help but recall such things as their "work of faith, labor of love, and steadfastness of hope" (1:3); their exemplary life (1:6–7); their evangelistic activity (1:8); and how they "turned to God from idols to serve a living and true God" (1:9). But as powerful as the word of God is, it is effective only where a believing attitude exists and continues (Rom. 1:16; 1 Cor. 1:18). Thus, instead of ending the sentence with the simple locative phrase "in you" (*en hymin*), Paul adds the present-tense participle "the ones who believe" (*tois pisteuousin*). Consequently, these final words are no mere verbose addition to the verse but an important reminder about the key role that faith plays in making effective the power of the gospel.

b. Their Imitation of the Persecuted Churches in Judea (2:14–16)

2:14 The second way in which the Thessalonians positively responded to Paul's mission-founding visit was their willingness to suffer for the word of God: "For you yourselves, brothers, became imitators of the churches of God in

---

51. If, as the evidence strongly suggests, the relative pronoun *hos* in 2:13 refers to "word," the form *energeitai* can be either middle ("is at work") or passive ("is made operative [by God]"). If, however, *hos* refers to "God," then only the middle voice is possible. A further strike against this latter possibility, however, is the fact that elsewhere in the NT, the middle of the verb *energeō* occurs only with an impersonal subject (BDAG 335.1.b).

Christ Jesus which are in Judea, because you indeed suffered the same things from your own fellow citizens as they also did from the Jews."

The vocative "brothers" (*adelphoi*), an epistolary device typically marking a transition, suggests a break with the preceding material and so justifies the identification of 2:14–16 as introducing a second way in which the Thessalonians have positively responded to Paul's original ministry among them. Yet the shift here is minor since the explicative "for" (*gar*) links these verses with 2:13. The proof or evidence that the Thessalonian believers accepted the word of Paul as the word of God and that this word is presently at work in their lives is found in their imitation of the persecuted churches in Judea.

The idea that for their part the Thessalonians (note the emphatic "you" that begins the sentence and is repeated later in the verse) had become imitators was foreshadowed in the thanksgiving section (1:6), and the reader of this commentary is directed to the observations on that verse for a fuller explanation about the important, though often misunderstood, role that the theme of imitation has in Paul's theology. As in 1:6 ("And you on your part became imitators . . . , receiving the word in much affliction"), here too imitation is linked with the reception of the word and persecution. Also in common with this earlier passage is the use of the indicative rather than, as elsewhere, the imperative to speak of the Thessalonians' imitation. This is a further indication that Paul is generally pleased with the conduct of the Christians in Thessalonica.

There is, however, one significant difference between the theme of imitation in 1:6 and here in 2:14: earlier Paul gave thanks for the Thessalonians' imitation "of us and of the Lord," but here he points to their imitation "of the churches of God in Christ Jesus which are in Judea" (τῶν ἐκκλησιῶν τοῦ θεοῦ τῶν οὐσῶν ἐν τῇ Ἰουδαίᾳ ἐν Χριστῷ Ἰησοῦ, *tōn ekklēsiōn tou theou tōn ousōn en tē Ioudaia en Christō Iēsou*). These churches that the Thessalonians have imitated are identified by three phrases.

First, they are the churches "of God" (*tou theou*). This genitive phrase, frequently used by Paul both with the singular "church" (1 Cor. 1:2; 10:32; 11:22; 15:9; 2 Cor. 1:1; Gal. 1:13; 1 Tim. 3:5, 15) and with the plural "churches," as we have here (1 Cor. 11:16; 1 Thess. 2:14; 2 Thess. 1:4), likely conveys the notion that these churches belong to God.

Second, they are "the ones that are in Judea" (*tōn ousōn en tē Ioudaia*). In this letter Paul has already referred to Christians in such other places as Macedonia, Achaia, and "everywhere" (1:7–8), and now he adds to that list by mentioning the churches in "Judea." These churches are probably not limited to those situated in the geographic area of Judea proper but also include those in Samaria and Galilee—a region often referred to as Palestine (for this broader sense of "Judea," see Luke 1:5; Acts 10:37; 21:20 [Codex Bezae; also a few versions]; Strabo, *Geogr.* 16.479–80; Josephus, *Ant.* 1.160; Tacitus, *Hist.* 5.9; so W. Gutbrod, *TDNT* 3:382).

Third, these imitated Judean churches are further identified as being "in Christ Jesus" (*en Christō Iēsou*). Perhaps this common Pauline prepositional phrase was added to distinguish these Christian churches in Judea from Jewish synagogues, since the Greek word *ekklēsia* did not yet have a Christian meaning, somewhat akin to our English word "assembly" (so, e.g., Lightfoot 1904: 32; Frame 1912: 109; Marshall 1983: 78). Best (1977: 114), however, suggests that the presence of "in Christ Jesus" after the plural "churches" denotes the unity of the Judean Christian communities, both among themselves and especially between them and the Christians in Thessalonica (see also Bruce 1982: 45–46). But while this notion of unity is surely part of the "in Christ" language frequently used by Paul, this phrase is also part of the apostle's normal description of the church (see, e.g., 1 Cor. 1:2; Gal. 1:22; Phil. 1:1; 1 Thess. 1:1; 2 Thess. 1:1), and so one ought to guard against reading too much into its presence here.

The second half of the verse is introduced by a causal ὅτι (*hoti*), thereby indicating that the following clause explains how the Thessalonians became imitators of the Judean churches. This subsequent explanation is given in the form of a comparative clause whose two constituent parts closely balance each other (the parallels are more striking in the original Greek than in the English rendering):

because			
you indeed	suffered the same things	from your own fellow citizens
as they also	did	from the Jews.

It is clear from this comparative clause that the specific way in which the Thessalonians have imitated the Judean churches is through the suffering they have endured for their newfound faith. Paul foreshadowed this theme of persecution in 1:6 with the phrase "receiving the word in much affliction." As with this earlier reference, here too the apostle does not in any significant way reflect on the subject of persecution, since his overall concern in 2:1–16 lies elsewhere. A fuller treatment of this theme by the apostle will need to wait until later in the letter, in 3:1–5. At this point it is enough for Paul simply to affirm that the Thessalonian Christians imitated the Judean churches through their suffering, thereby providing a second way in which they responded positively to his past ministry in their midst.

The brevity of Paul's comparison between the persecution endured by the Thessalonian believers and that of the Judean churches results in at least four questions for which there are no easy answers. First, why did Paul pick the remote Judean churches rather than some closer church that he himself had founded (note, e.g., how Paul holds up before the Corinthian believers the example of the Macedonian churches in 2 Cor. 8–9)? Some possible answers (see de Boer 1962: 103–6; Best 1977: 113; Marshall 1983: 78) include the following: (1) the Judean churches enjoyed a position of prestige due to their locale as the origin of Christianity; (2) they were the first Christians to be persecuted; (3) they had suffered greatly for their faith and were well known in the early church for enduring persecution; (4) they suffered at the hands of the Jews in the same way that the suffering of the Thessalonian Christians originally stemmed from the Jews (2:15, "the ones who drove us out"; Acts 17:5); (5) Paul's theological orientation in which the gospel goes "first to the Jew, then to the Gentile" (Rom. 1:16) leads the apostle to compare the current suffering of the largely Gentile Thessalonian church with the past suffering of the largely Jewish churches of Judea (Fee 2009: 93); or most likely, given the following context, (6) Paul's mention of the Judean churches allows him in the next two verses to go on to show the Thessalonians that they stand in a long and distinguished line of those in Palestine who were persecuted for their faith: the OT prophets, the Lord Jesus, the earliest Christians, and even the apostle himself.

Second, what are the specific historical circumstances that Paul has in mind when he refers to suffering endured by the Judean churches? The apostle may be referring to the opposition these Jewish Christians experienced in the early 30s AD—a period when he himself persecuted the believers in Jerusalem and the surrounding area (Gal. 1:13, 22–23; 1 Cor. 15:9; Phil. 3:6; see Acts 8:3; 9:21; 22:4; 26:9–11). Against this possibility, however, is the fact that Paul gives no hint here in 1 Thess. 2:14 as to his own personal involvement in such persecution of the Judean churches as he does in Gal. 1:13, 22–23. The apostle may instead be thinking of the early 40s AD—a period when Herod Agrippa I (AD 41–44) killed James the brother of John and attempted to do the same to Peter (Acts 12:1–19). Yet this persecution seems directed at select leaders of the church rather than at its regular members. The best option is that Paul has in view the late 40s and very early 50s—a period that not only came immediately before the writing of 1 Thessalonians (and so would be fresh in Paul's mind) but also witnessed a rising Zealot movement in Palestine (Josephus, *Ant.* 20.105–6; see Jewett 1970–71, esp. 205–7; Reicke 1984). These Jewish nationalists were especially active during the governorship of Tiberius Julius Alexander (AD 46–48) and his successor, Ventidius Cumanus (AD 48–52). They engaged in a militant program of purging Israel from all Gentile influence in the belief that such action would hasten, if not actually inaugurate, the messianic age. Such Zealot activity would have naturally included some degree of opposition to the Jewish Christian churches in Judea. Hence there is good reason to believe that precisely this Zealot pressure resulted in the problematic circumcising campaign in the churches of both Antioch and Galatia (see esp. Gal. 6:12). Furthermore, this persecution of the Judean churches by their Zealot compatriots may also account for Paul's rather harsh and unexpected outburst in the immediately following verses (1 Thess. 2:15–16) against those Jews who not only were originally responsible for the death of Jesus but were still now hindering the apostle's work in spreading the gospel (Wanamaker 1990: 113).

The kind of persecution endured by the Thessalonian Christians, of course, need not be identical to that endured by the Judean churches. The comparison that Paul makes in 2:14 rests not so much on similar suffering as on similar opponents: both groups suffered at the hands of their "own fellow citizens" (τῶν ἰδίων συμφυλετῶν, *tōn idiōn symphyletōn*). Here we face a third difficult question: to whom exactly is Paul referring? At first blush *symphyletai* (a hapax legomenon in Paul and the rest of the NT) seems to have an *ethnic* sense as referring only to the Gentile citizens of Thessalonica (the strongest defense of this position is that of Still 1999: 218–24). This understanding naturally emerges from the contrast Paul makes between the "fellow citizens" and "the Jews" (Frame [1912: 100]: "συμφυλέται are Gentiles as Ἰουδαίων shows"). It seems to gain further support from 1:9, which implies that the majority of the church consisted of Gentile believers so that their "own fellow citizens" must also therefore be Gentiles (so e.g., Dobschütz 1909: 109–10; Malherbe 2000: 168). But *symphyletai* can also be taken in a *geographical* sense as referring to the inhabitants of Thessalonica, the vast majority of whom would have been Gentiles, but some of whom would have been Jews. As Lightfoot (1904: 32) declares: "Thus συμφυλετῶν would include such Jews as were free citizens of Thessalonica." This latter meaning agrees with Acts 17:5–9, which claims that the opposition to the Thessalonian church originated from certain Jews who used some bad characters from the marketplace to stir up a crowd of citizens against the newly founded church (Best 1977: 114; Marshall 1983: 78–79; Donfried 1984: 247–48). A geographical understanding of "fellow citizens" is further supported by its parallel to "the Jews," which, as we will see, also ought to be understood in a local sense.

Fourth, whom does Paul have in view when referring to "the Jews" (τῶν Ἰουδαίων, *tōn Ioudaiōn*)? As with its counterpart *symphyletai*, the term *Ioudaioi* can have either an *ethnic* or *geographical* sense. That the latter option is intended by the apostle can be seen from the preceding specification of the churches "which are in Judea" (Weatherly 1991: 85–86). Paul, therefore, does not have all Jews in view but only those in Judea—the "Judeans" (Bruce 1982: 46: "One could translate Ἰουδαῖοι here as 'Judeans'"). What's more, the apostle is not even referring to all Judeans but only a portion of this group: those who participated in some way in one of the specific activities mentioned in the following verses (2:15–16). Thus the comma that many English and Romance-language translations place after the word "Jews"—a punctuation mark that introduces a general (i.e., it describes all Jews) rather than restrictive clause (i.e., it describes a narrow group of Jews)—must be removed (Gilliard 1989; Amphoux 2003; contra Verhoef 1995). Finally, Paul cannot have all Jews in mind, simply because a substantial portion of those who professed Jesus as Messiah, including both the churches in Judea whom he has just mentioned as well as the apostle himself, were Jews. The strong accusations that Paul makes in the following two verses, therefore, should not be judged, as they often are, to be anti-Semitic or anti-Jewish. The apostle's anger is directed not against the Jewish people in toto but against the Judean persecutors in particular.

2:15 Up to this point Paul has highlighted the positive response of the Thessalonians to his past visit that is evident in both their acceptance of his word as the word of God (v. 13) and their willingness to suffer for that word as demonstrated in their imitation of the persecuted churches in Judea (v. 14). Thus a certain conclusion in his lengthy defense is reached by the end of verse 14. In that verse the mention of persecution endured by the Thessalonians, however, causes Paul to turn away from the apologetic concern that has preoccupied his attention thus far in the letter body (2:1–12) to the two interrelated concerns that he will take up in the next section of the letter body: to defend his inability to return to Thessalonica (2:17–20) and to strengthen the infant faith of the Thessalonians in the face of strong opposition (3:1–5). The reference to "the Jews" at the end of verse 14 becomes an occasion for Paul in the following verses to make use of what quite likely is presynoptic traditional material.[52] This traditional material functions first to explain why Paul has not been able to return for a second "visit" (εἴσοδος, eisodos) to Thessalonica: the Jews "who drove us out" (v. 15) instigated an opposition to Paul and the fledgling church that has made it impossible for the apostle to come back in person, thereby requiring him to reassure the Thessalonian Christians of his continued love and concern for them, despite his ongoing absence (2:17–20). This traditional material functions, second, to encourage the Thessalonian Christians to remain steadfast in their faith, despite facing opposition (3:1–5). It would be encouraging to these recent converts to learn that their experience of suffering opposition, though by no means a happy experience, was nevertheless not only expected (3:4: "For indeed when we were with you, we kept telling you beforehand: 'We are destined to suffer affliction'") but also one that they shared in common with the OT prophets, their Lord Jesus, other believers ("the churches of Judea"), and even their founding pastor, Paul.

Verse 15 consists of four clauses introduced by a single definite article (τῶν, tōn), whose antecedent is the final words of the preceding verse: "the Jews" (τῶν Ἰουδαίων, tōn Ioudaiōn). The subsequent clauses, therefore, are intended to say something more about those Jews who are persecuting the Judean churches. These four clauses in verse 15 possess a fixed pattern consisting of three elements: the conjunction "and" (καί, kai), a direct object in the emphatic position prior to the verb, and an attributive participle (the fourth clause instead has an adjective). The parallel relationship of these four clauses, though more obvious in the Greek text, can also be seen in the following translation:

> . . . the Jews
>> who killed both [kai] the Lord Jesus and [kai] the prophets,
>> and [kai] who drove us out,
>> and [kai] who do not please God,
>> and [kai] who are hostile to all people.

52. A variety of unique features in 2:15–16—the balanced parallelism of its clauses, its literary parallels with Gospel material (Matt. 23:29–38; 24:2; Luke 11:49–50), and the presence of several words that are not characteristically Pauline—have led many to conclude that Paul has incorporated traditional material that was circulating in the early church: see, e.g., Orchard 1938; Schippers 1966; Steck 1967: 274–77; Broer 1983: 71–72; Donfried 1984: 247–49; Weatherly 1994; Malherbe 2000: 169, 174–75.

The first clause deals with the role that some Jews played in the death of Jesus and the prophets: "who killed both the Lord Jesus and the prophets" (τῶν καὶ τὸν κύριον ἀποκτεινάντων Ἰησοῦν καὶ τοὺς προφήτας, *tōn kai ton kyrion apokteinantōn Iēsoun kai tous prophētas*). Elsewhere Paul speaks of Jesus as being crucified (1 Cor. 1:23; 2:2, 8; 2 Cor. 13:4; Gal. 3:1) rather than killed, with the former term suggesting Roman responsibility for Jesus's death, since the Jews were not directly involved in the actual act of crucifixion. In the only other place where Paul specifies the agents of Jesus's death, he names "the rulers of this age" (1 Cor. 2:8), that is, malevolent spiritual powers who use humans as their instruments. In this passage, however, the apostle highlights the Jews' role in killing Jesus. Even though such a charge is leveled by Paul nowhere else in his letters, it is found in an old kerygmatic tradition (Acts 2:23, 36; 3:13–15; see also 4:10; 5:30; 7:52; 10:39; 13:27–28) and in the Gospel of John (5:18; 7:1; 8:59; 11:45–53; 18:14, 31). Paul's use of the verb "killed" rather than the expected "crucified" is likely due to his employment of a tradition concerning the killing of the prophets (see texts cited below). The separation of the nouns "Lord" and "Jesus" by the verb is striking (the word order is "the Lord they killed Jesus") and so prompted various explanations. The apostle most likely intended this unusual word order to highlight "the Lord" (just as the direct objects in the other three clauses are similarly emphasized by virtue of their location prior to the verb), thereby stressing the heinous nature of their action: the Jesus whom the Judean Jews killed was no mere human but was actually the Lord (so, e.g., Hendriksen 1955: 71; Best 1977: 115; Williams 1992: 47, 115).

Paul attributes responsibility to the Jews for killing not only the Lord Jesus but also "the prophets." The nonchronological sequence of mentioning the Lord Jesus first and then the prophets (so also Justin, *Dial.* 16.4; contra Acts 7:52) has prompted two suggestions: (1) "the prophets" refer not to OT prophets but to NT believers such as Stephen and James, who were martyred (so Lake 1911: 87n2; Gilliard 1994; Fee 2009: 97–98); and (2) "the prophets" function as the direct object of the second clause rather than the first so that this part of the verse should be translated: "who killed the Lord Jesus and who drove out both the prophets and us" (so Neil 1950: 51; D. Martin 1995: 91).

Both suggestions, however, must be rejected on three grounds. First, there is no evidence in any of the relevant literature dating to the time of the writing of 1 Thessalonians (AD 51) that Stephen, James, or any other martyred believer was referred to as a "prophet." Furthermore, if the apostle was, in fact, referring to people like Stephen who was stoned for his faith, "it would be odd for Paul to be this vehement against other Jewish leaders who had a role in that [killing] and say or imply nothing about his own complicity in that crime" (Witherington 2006: 85–86n104).

Second, the unexpected ordering of mentioning the killing of the Lord Jesus prior to that of the prophets reflects Paul's desire to emphasize the first-referenced event. The apostle has done a similar thing twice thus far in the letter: in 1:6 he mentions the Thessalonians' imitation of himself and his coworkers before that of the Lord ("You became imitators of us and of the Lord"); in 2:10 he appeals to his Thessalonian readers as witnesses of his holy, righteous, and blameless conduct before invoking God also as a witness ("You are witnesses and God also").

Third, Paul here is drawing on a well-known tradition concerning the killing of the OT prophets. This tradition goes back to the OT (1 Kings 18:4; 19:9–18; 2 Chron. 24:19–21; 36:15–16; Neh. 9:27, 30; Jer. 2:30; 26:8, 20–23) and is found in contemporary Jewish literature as well (Mart. Isa. 5; Jub. 1.12; Pesiq. Rab. 27 [129a]). By NT times, therefore, the killing of the prophets had become a common way to refer to the persecution of the faithful remnant within Israel by the unrighteous. This tradition appears frequently in Jesus's teaching (Matt. 5:12; 23:29–37; Luke 4:24; 6:23; 11:47–51; 13:33–34) and is also found in the preaching of the early apostles (Acts 7:52). In Paul's other letters the tradition concerning the killing of the prophets surfaces in Rom. 11:3, where he cites 1 Kings 19:10. The apostle's use of this tradition here in 1 Thess. 2:15 highlights the similarity between the persecutions currently experienced by the Thessalonian church, the Judean churches, and himself—and the persecutions constantly endured by God's righteous prophets.

The second clause deals with the role Jews played in opposing the missionary activities of Paul and his colleagues: "and who drove us out" (καὶ ἡμᾶς ἐκδιωξάντων, *kai hēmas ekdiōxantōn*). In light of the fate experienced by the Lord Jesus and the OT prophets, it is hardly surprising that those who follow Christ, such as Paul and his fellow missionaries,[53] likewise experience persecution at the hands of certain Jews. The addition of this second clause allows the apostle to align himself closely with the tradition concerning the persecution and killing of the prophets. The compound verb *ekdiōkō* occurs only here in Paul (and in the NT): elsewhere the apostle uses the simple form of the verb some twenty-one times. The preposition *ek* in the compound form of the verb, therefore, is significant and may function adverbially to intensify its meaning: "to persecute severely" (BDAG 301). The more likely force of the prepositional prefix, however, is to specify the nature of the persecution: "to drive out" (LSJ 504). This latter sense is supported by 2:17, which refers to some kind of forced departure by Paul and his colleagues from the Thessalonian church. It also agrees with the account in Acts 17:5–10, where Paul and Silas had to flee Thessalonica because of opposition instigated by certain local Jews. That the apostle here has in mind a single or specific event such as this is also suggested by the aorist tense of the participle *ekdiōxantōn*.[54] There

---

53. Although the personal pronoun "us" (ἡμᾶς) in 2:15 could refer to Christians in general and the opposition that the Thessalonian believers and others elsewhere experienced at the hands of certain Jews, it more likely has in view Paul and his coworkers. This is supported by the fact that (1) the apostle here is probably referring to his own forced expulsion from Thessalonica, and (2) the meaning of "us" in the next verse ("by hindering us from speaking to the Gentiles") is clearly limited to Paul and his fellow missionaries.

54. Many commentators claim that the aorist tense of the participle must refer to a *past* event and thus wonder why Paul didn't use a present tense in 2:15 to indicate the continuing

were other times and places, of course, where Paul faced opposition from Jews (Gal. 5:11; 2 Cor. 11:24–26; see also Acts 13:44–51; 14:2, 19; 17:5–9, 13–14; 18:12–18), and he could have these situations in view instead.[55] Yet the clause makes the best sense in its context if Paul is referring to a situation that his readers know all too well: the role that certain Jews in Thessalonica had in driving the missionaries out of town.[56]

The third clause in a more general manner addresses the conduct of those Jews who have done the specific things mentioned in the preceding two clauses: "and who do not please God" (καὶ θεῷ μὴ ἀρεσκόντων, *kai theō mē areskontōn*). After speaking about the "killing" of the Lord Jesus and the prophets as well as the "driving out" of Paul and his coworkers, the charge of "not pleasing God" may appear somewhat insignificant by comparison. The seriousness of this third charge, however, becomes clear when one recognizes that the notion of pleasing God "is one of Paul's favorite expressions for true behaviour (Rom. 8.8; 1 Cor. 7.32–34; Gal. 1.10; 1 Th. 2.4, 15; 4.1; cf. 2 Cor. 5.9); he uses it even of Jesus himself (Rom. 15.3)" (Best 1977: 117). Later in this letter the importance that Paul placed on pleasing God is seen when the apostle reminds the Thessalonians that he had taught them "how it is necessary for you . . . to please God" (4:1)—a key verse that introduces the exhortations found in the second half of the letter body (4:1–5:22). And when Paul is accused by the Galatians of pleasing himself rather than God (Gal. 1:10), he reacts with a vehemence that reveals the seriousness with which he understood such a charge. The condemnation expressed in the third clause is further highlighted by the shift to the present tense, thereby indicating the ongoing or continuous nature of the displeasing conduct practiced by certain Jews.

The fourth clause involves another general yet strong denunciation: "and who are hostile to all people" (καὶ πᾶσιν ἀνθρώποις ἐναντίων, *kai pasin anthrōpois enantiōn*). Initially these harsh words sound like those made by many other ancient writers who reacted negatively to the strict separation that many Jews practiced between themselves and other ethnic groups. For example, the Roman

---

state of persecution endured by the church. Some then further postulate that an "attraction" of the tense has taken place: the tense of this participle has been attracted to the past tense of the preceding participle (see, e.g., Best 1977: 116; Richard 1995: 121). The Greek verbal system, however, expresses real or actual time only in the indicative mood, so the aorist participle here conveys only *Aktionsart* (kind of action), thus a simple or nonemphasized action. The present-tense participle, by contrast, highlights an ongoing action and thus suggests that Paul has in view a more generic, continuous opposition from the Jews, while the aorist participle supports a specific act of Jewish opposition such as is described in Acts 17:5.

55. Fee (2009: 98–99), for example, is concerned to show that Paul's condemnation in this passage does not refer to all Jews but in a restricted way only to the Judean Jews, so he translates the clause more generically as "who persecuted us" and argues that "the clause makes especially good sense as referring to the Judean Jews' treatment of Paul."

56. Many scholars, unduly influenced by their suspicion about the reliability of Acts, reject this interpretation. Yet Malherbe (2000: 175) correctly observes: "It is only extreme skepticism about what Acts has to offer and the hypothesis that Paul did not write 2:13–16 that raise serious doubt that Paul here refers to his expulsion by Jews, probably engineered in the way Acts describes."

historian Tacitus claimed that Jews felt "hostility and hatred toward all people" (*Hist.* 5.5.2). The Egyptian Apion charged the Jews with regularly swearing a divine oath "to bear no goodwill to any foreigner, and especially to none of the Greeks" (Josephus, *Ag. Ap.* 2.121). The Roman satirist Juvenal asserted that the Jews were an unfriendly race who denied even the most common act of hospitality to strangers (*Sat.* 14.103–4). Diodorus Siculus, a Greek historian, wrote that Jews "looked upon all people as their enemy" and that they "made their hatred of humankind into a tradition" (34.1.1–2). And Philostratus, a Greek sophist of the Roman imperial period, claimed that "the Jews have long been in revolt not only against the Romans but against humanity" (*Vit. Apoll.* 5.33). Yet there is an important difference between all these harsh statements about the Jews and that of the apostle: "Pagan criticism was social, Paul's is theological" (Malherbe 2000: 170). As the following verse makes clear, Paul is angry at those Jews who are hampering his mission to the Gentiles and thereby preventing the salvation of these people.

The fixed pattern found in each of the preceding four clauses—the conjunction "and," a direct object in the emphatic position prior to the verb, and an attributive participle—is broken at verse 16. The participle that introduces this verse, therefore, is not parallel with the preceding clauses (contra Best 1977: 117; Wanamaker 1990: 115) but subordinate to the fourth one, giving the means by which certain Jews are hostile toward all people: "by hindering us from speaking to the Gentiles" (κωλυόντων ἡμᾶς τοῖς ἔθνεσιν λαλῆσαι, *kōlyontōn hymas tois ethnesin lalēsai*).

2:16

The present tense of *kōlyontōn* (the verb occurs elsewhere in Paul only in Rom. 1:13; 1 Cor. 14:39; 1 Tim. 4:3) implies a repeated or persistent opposition by the Jews to Paul's missionary efforts (see Gal. 5:11; 2 Cor. 11:24–26; also Acts 13:44–51; 14:2, 19; 17:5–9, 13–14; 18:12–18). Thus, whereas the earlier clause "and who drove us out" has in view the Jewish opposition experienced specifically at Thessalonica, here a more general opposition from the Jews in other places and times is considered, thereby explaining and justifying the preceding charge that they are "hostile to all people." This Jewish opposition was directed not merely against Paul's "speaking" to the Gentiles but also against his preaching to them, since the verb *lalēsai* clearly refers to the apostle's missionary preaching (see 2:2, "to speak to you the gospel of God"; also 2:4). That Paul explicitly identifies the target audience of his preaching as "the Gentiles" is important, since the congregation of Thessalonica consisted predominantly of this people group. This suggests that the apostle's primary concern in the admittedly harsh description of certain Jews found here in verse 15 lies less with condemning his native people than with encouraging his Gentile readers in Thessalonica.

The purpose (the *hina* clause likely expresses purpose rather than result, though the two often cannot be easily distinguished) of Paul's preaching to the Gentiles was nothing less than their salvation: "in order that they may be saved" (ἵνα σωθῶσιν, *hina sōthōsin*). Although the verb "to save" is used only here in the letter, the cognate noun "salvation" does occur twice in 5:8–9. Furthermore, the concept of salvation is frequently implied in the many blessings received by those in Thessalonica who have responded positively to the gospel. Foremost among these blessings is their rescue from the coming wrath (1:10), their call into God's own kingdom and glory (2:12), and their being "kept blameless at the coming of our Lord Jesus Christ" (5:23).

The long and consistent history of Jewish opposition to the Lord Jesus, the OT prophets, and the Pauline mission (vv. 15–16a) has a logical outcome: "with the result that they have been constantly filling up the measure of their sins" (εἰς τὸ ἀναπληρῶσαι αὐτῶν τὰς ἁμαρτίας πάντοτε, eis to anaplērōsai autōn tas hamartias pantote). Here one is confronted with three difficult questions of grammar. First, is this clause dependent only on the immediately preceding participial clause in verse 16a ("by hindering us from speaking to the Gentiles in order that they may be saved") or the whole of verses 15–16a? Some have chosen the former option on the grounds that it is in keeping with Paul's focus on preaching throughout this passage (so Malherbe 2000: 170–71). Yet the adverb "always," along with the plural "sins," strongly suggests that Paul has in view more than just Jewish opposition to his own mission work but also earlier persecution of the OT prophets and involvement in the death of Jesus. Thus it is more probable that 2:16b depends on the whole of verses 15–16a (so Best 1977: 118; Wanamaker 1990: 116).

Second, how can one explain the puzzling combination of the aorist tense anaplērōsai and the adverb pantote, since the former term conveys the notion of a simple (punctiliar) action while the latter term suggests continuous action? Dobschütz (1909: 114) attempted to minimize the tension between these two forms by suggesting that the adverb was equivalent to πάντως or παντελῶς, with the sense of "completely, altogether, in every way." Yet there is no evidence that pantote ever has this meaning. Furthermore, in every other occurrence of this adverb in the letter (1:2; 3:6; 4:17; 5:15, 16), as in the apostle's other letters, it means "constantly, always." It seems best, therefore, to give the temporal force of the adverb priority over the tense of the infinitive (note the adverb's position of emphasis at the end of the clause rather than next to the verb) and understand Paul to have in view a lengthy series of events through which certain Jews have "constantly" been adding to the allotted measure of their nation's sins. The aorist tense of the infinitive may then be explained as viewing these events collectively (so Frame 1912: 113, who is followed by most commentators).

Third, does the preposition eis with the articular infinitive express purpose or result (see BDF §402.2)? That in Paul's Letters this grammatical construction "expresses hardly anything but purpose" (MHT 3:143) leads most commentators to adopt the former option. And since the notion of purpose cannot apply to the Jews themselves (because they would not have done these things with the conscious desire to fill up their own sins), some commentators attribute the intentionality to God and so claim further that this has the consequence of placing Jewish opposition within his divine plan (see, e.g., Milligan 1908:

31; Malherbe 2000: 171). But not only does this interpretation seem forced; it also does not work well with the adverb "constantly," since, as Best (1977: 118) explains, "It is easier to envisage a continuous result than a purpose continuously achieved." It is simpler and thus preferable to see *eis* plus the articular infinitive as expressing result (so NASB; Lightfoot 1904: 34; Williams 1992: 48; Richard 1995: 122). In other words, throughout history there have been some Jews—whether the Judeans of Paul's day who persecuted the churches or earlier Jews who opposed the OT prophets and were involved in the killing of the Lord Jesus—whose disobedience against God and his spokespersons have resulted in the constant filling up of their nation's sins.

The key concept at work here is that there exists a fixed amount of sins to be committed, after which punishment will be meted out. The verb *anaplērōsai* suggests the picture of a vessel or cup that is in a slow but constant process of being filled up; once it is completely full, judgment will take place. The identical verb is used in Gen. 15:16 LXX to describe the sins of the Amorites, which are said "to be not yet filled up." This theme of "filling up the measure of one's sins" occurs also in Dan. 8:23; 2 Macc. 6:14; and Wis. 19:4. In the NT the same verb "to fill up" (though in its unaugmented form) is found in Matt. 23:32, where Jesus uses it to describe the scribes and the Pharisees, who likewise are linked to the killing of the prophets (Matt. 23:31). The notion that humans have a fixed limit to their actions, both good and evil, is widely attested in later Jewish writings as well (2 Esd. [4 Ezra] 4:34–37; 7:74; 2 Bar. 21.8; 48.2–5; L.A.B. 26.1–3). Thus Paul's judgment against his own people seemingly borrows from a common theme and conventional language within Judaism, used by Jews to express their anger at the faithlessness of certain members of their own nation.

Paul's lengthy description of the Jews found in 2:15–16b comes to an abrupt close with a brief phrase that bristles with interpretative difficulties: "But the wrath [of God][57] has come upon them until the end" (ἔφθασεν δὲ ἐπ' αὐτοὺς ἡ ὀργὴ εἰς τέλος, *ephthasen de ep' autous hē orgē eis telos*).[58] The verb φθάνω (*phthanō*) occurs seven times in the NT, all except two (Matt. 12:28; Luke 11:20) occurring in Paul's Letters (Rom. 9:31; 2 Cor. 10:14; Phil. 3:16; 1 Thess. 2:16; 4:15). The classical meaning of this term as "come before, precede" occurs only once (1 Thess. 4:15). Here in 2:16 the verb has the weaker meaning,

---

57. See the additional notes, which justify adding the words "of God" to the translation of 2:16 even though they are not found in the original text.

58. Virtually the identical expression occurs in T. Levi 6.11: ἔφθασεν δὲ αὐτοὺς ἡ ὀργὴ τοῦ θεοῦ εἰς τέλος. The relationship of T. Levi 6.11 with 1 Thess. 2:16c is difficult to determine. Some evidence suggests that T. Levi 6.11 is a Christian interpolation derived from Paul, while other data indicates that it is original to the Testament of Levi and that these words may be a common expression within Judaism for declaring God's judgment—thus used independently by both Paul and the Testament of Levi (see the discussion in Frame 1912: 115–16). The issue, however, is ultimately not relevant for our understanding of 1 Thess. 2:16c. As Schlueter (1994: 23) observes: "Unfortunately, the *Testament of Levi* cannot illuminate the meaning of 1 Thess. 2:14–16 and to what event v. 16 referred. Today, as in the early twentieth century, the relationship of T. Levi 6.11 to 1 Thess. 2:16 is still unsettled and cannot resolve the meaning of the words in our passage."

commonly found in the Septuagint, as "having just arrived" or simply "arrive, reach" (BDAG 1053; G. Fitzer, *TDNT* 9:88–92). Paul therefore is clearly talking about the wrath of God arriving or coming "upon them," upon the Jews whom he has been describing in the past two verses. But what specific time frame ought one to associate with this wrath?

A few commentators, driven by the conviction that Paul must be referring to a *future* event, either a specific incident such as the destruction of Jerusalem or more generally the eschatological day of judgment, claim that *ephthasen* is a "prophetic" aorist (Dobschütz 1909: 115–16; Frame 1912: 114). The idea is that the wrath of God has already been decided but will be carried out in the future. The use of the prophetic aorist, however, is very infrequent in the NT (MHT 1:841–42; Fanning 1990: 269–74; Porter 1992: 37–38). Furthermore, there is no compelling reason to account for its use here rather than the future tense if that were actually the intention of Paul.

Other scholars, though rejecting the prophetic aorist, nevertheless argue that *ephthasen* does not have its full past-tense meaning of "has come" but the weaker sense of "has drawn near" (so, e.g., Clark 1940; Rigaux 1956: 452; Best 1977: 120; Marshall 1983: 80–81; Weatherly 1996: 91–92). In other words, God's wrath has not yet actually come upon the Jews but is very near to them, so close that it has virtually come. The reluctance of such commentators to adopt the full force of the past tense apparently stems from the belief that the two other occurrences of "wrath" in the letter have an eschatological sense (1:10; 5:9) and so must similarly refer to a future judgment in 2:16 as well. Further, because some see the difficult phrase *eis telos* functioning intensively to mean "fully" or "to the uttermost" (see discussion below), they fail to find any calamity befalling the Jews in the recent past that could justly be identified as the full and final wrath of God. Finally, an appeal is often made to Matt. 12:28 (and its parallel in Luke 11:20), where it is claimed that the aorist *ephthasen* is equivalent to the aorist ἤγγισεν (*ēngisen*, has drawn near) and thus describes the kingdom of God as drawing ever so near without its actual arrival.

This interpretation of *ephthasen*, however, violates the natural sense of the aorist as referring to a *past* event—one that has already taken place. Furthermore, it fails to view this specific claim that wrath "has come" upon the Jews in light of Paul's broader eschatological framework. The theological perspective evident throughout his letters includes *both* a future and present dimension (see especially Malherbe 2000: 177). Salvation is not merely a future event to be experienced when Christ comes again (1 Thess. 1:10; see Rom. 5:9–10) but also a present reality that believers already enjoy (1 Cor. 1:18; 15:2). Similarly, the wrath of God is not only a future judgment from which believers have been rescued and are predestined to escape (1 Thess. 1:10; 5:9; see Rom. 2:5, 8, 16; 3:5; 5:9; 9:22), but it has already been revealed and experienced in the present (Rom. 1:18–31). It is not contradictory, therefore, to see *both the future and present* aspects of God's wrath in 1 Thess. 2:16. Whereas verse 16b describes the continuous filling up of sins by certain Jews, after which they will experience a future judgment, verse 16c asserts that this punishment is not only future, since the Jews have already experienced God's wrath in their recent past. As Malherbe (2000: 177) states: "The Jews, who hindered Paul from preaching to Gentiles so that the latter could now lay hold of a salvation still to be fully realized in the future, have now proleptically experienced God's wrath that will also be fully realized in the future (1:10; 5:9)."

What historical event, then, is Paul referring to when he claims that "the wrath of God has come upon them"? Several possibilities have been forwarded (in addition to the various commentaries, see Bacon 1922; S. Johnson 1941: 173–76; Baarda 1984: 51–52): (1) The apostle views the crucifixion of Jesus as the event in which "the disobedience of God's people reached its climax," with the result that "God's wrath has already come upon the Jews to the uttermost in the event of the Cross" (Cranfield 1979: 218–19; also see Donfried 1984: 251). (2) Paul refers to the recent expulsion of Jews from Rome in AD 49 by Emperor Claudius (Acts 18:1–13; Suetonius, *Claud.* 25.4; so, e.g., Bammel 1959: 300–301). (3) Another possibility is the massacre of thousands of Jews in Jerusalem in AD 49, which may have been a reprisal against the violent activity of Jewish nationalists (Josephus, *Ant.* 20.102, 105–15, 118–210; *J.W.* 2.225–27; so Jewett 1970–71: 205n5; 1986: 37–38; Elias 1995: 95). Other recent disasters to befall the Jews include (4) a great famine in AD 47 (Acts 11:28; Josephus, *Ant.* 20.51, 101); (5) the violent quelling of a revolt led by Theudas in AD 44–46 (Acts 5:36; Josephus, *Ant.* 20.98); and (6) the sudden death of Herod Agrippa I in AD 44 (Acts 12:23). (7) The fall of Jerusalem and the destruction of the temple in AD 70 is frequently proposed by both those who view the verb *ephthasen* as a prophetic aorist (so, e.g., Eadie 1877: 90–91; Findlay 1891: 56–57; Lightfoot 1904: 35–36) and those who believe 2:13[14]–16 to be a later interpolation (so, e.g., Baur 1875: 87–88; Pearson 1971: 82–84). (8) Instead of a specific event, Paul more generally viewed the Jews' rejection of either the gospel or of Jesus as God's Messiah as wrathful (Gaventa 1998: 38; Holmes 1998: 86).

From these numerous options, many choose Claudius's expulsion of Jews from Rome, because this event happened very close to the writing of 1 Thessalonians and also because this event brought Aquila and Priscilla from Rome to Corinth—the likely place from where the letter was written. But while the Thessalonians undoubtedly knew what Paul was referring to, it is impossible for us to know with any degree of probability. The important fact, however, is that there were several large-scale disasters endured by the Jews about which an ancient writer like Paul could have legitimately said: "But the wrath of God has come upon them."

This difficult verse finally comes to a close with a brief prepositional phrase that has also occasioned much debate: "until the end" (*eis telos*). Though found a few times in the Gospels (Matt. 10:22; 24:13; Mark 13:13; Luke 18:5; John 13:1), the exact form of this prepositional phrase occurs nowhere else in Paul's Letters. The apostle does, however, use the similar forms εἰς τὸ τέλος (*eis to telos*) in 2 Cor. 3:13 and ἕως τέλους (*heōs telous*) in 1 Cor. 1:8 and 2 Cor. 1:13. One possibility is that the prepositional phrase functions *quantitatively*, describing the intensity of the wrath: "to the uttermost" (KJV), "in full" (BDF §207.3; G. Delling, *TDNT* 8:56), "fully" (NIV mg.; Williams 1992: 49), "completely" (NRSV mg.; Moule 1959: 70; Dobschütz 1909: 115n3; Holtz 1986: 110). The parallelism between verse 16b and verse 16c, however, demands that *eis telos*, like the temporal adverb *pantote* (constantly) with which it is balanced, functions *temporally*, describing the timing of the wrath.[59]

Yet this does not solve the issue since a temporal understanding of *eis telos* leads in turn to three possibilities: (1) "at last" (RSV, NRSV, NIV; Frame 1912: 114; Best 1977: 121); "finally" (GNT, NJB, Phillips; Milligan 1908: 32); (2) "forever" (RSV mg., NEB; G. Stählin, *TDNT* 5:434); or (3) "until the end" (Munck 1967: 63–64; Donfried 1984: 252; Wanamaker 1990: 117–18; Gaventa 1998: 37; Malherbe 2000: 171). A choice between these options is difficult, since Paul nowhere else uses *eis telos* and this prepositional phrase in the rest of Scripture conveys each of these three temporal meanings (Luke 18:5 supports "at last"; then Pss. 76:9; 78:5; 102:9 [77:8; 80:4; 103:9 Eng.]; support "finally"; and Matt. 10:22; 24:13; Mark 13:13; John 13:1 support "until the end"). The apostle's own statements about a future for Israel in Rom. 11:25–32, however, make the third option most attractive, since the first two "tend to absolutize the divine wrath coming upon unbelieving Jews into a final rejection" (Wanamaker 1990: 117). Paul therefore claims that the wrath of God has come upon his people "until the end," meaning until the day of Christ's return (*eis telos* thus functions similarly to *heōs telous* [until the end] in 1 Cor. 1:8 and 2 Cor. 1:13). The apostle does not here spell out what happens to rebellious Israel after this.

Additional Notes

2:7. See excursus 2, "Textual Reading of 1 Thessalonians 2:7," after this unit for an extended defense of the reading νήπιοι (infants) over ἤπιοι (gentle), as well as a justification for repunctuating the sentence such that the phrase "we became infants among you" concludes the third main clause of 2:1–12 rather than begins the fourth main clause (so virtually all Greek editions and translations).

2:8. Instead of ὁμειρόμενοι (this verb is also spelled with a smooth breathing), some minuscules (323 629 630 945 1881 2495 *al*) have the classical form ἱμειρόμενοι, which, despite having the same meaning, is not etymologically related.

2:8. Since Paul is referring to his past sharing of the gospel with the Thessalonians during his mission-founding activity, the form εὐδοκοῦμεν, which might appear to be a present tense, is best read as an imperfect, even though it does not have the augmented form ηὐδοκοῦμεν. The absence of the temporal augment in verbs with an initial diphthong occurs with some frequency in Koine Greek

---

59. The parallelism between these two clauses and how this literary feature requires a temporal meaning for εἰς τέλος was first stressed by Frame (1912: 114). This parallelism can be clearly seen in the following schematic presentation of the text:

| 2:16b | ἀναπληρῶσαι | αὐτῶν | τὰς ἁμαρτίας | πάντοτε |
| 2:16c | ἔφθασεν | ἐπ' αὐτοὺς | ἡ ὀργὴ | εἰς τέλος |

(BDF §67). Some ancient scribes corrected this ambiguous form in 2:8 by replacing it with the aorist εὐδοκήσαμεν: 33 81 *pc* f vg (the aorist form of this verb also appears in 3:1).

2:8. A few MSS (2 *pc*; Hier), perhaps under the influence of 3:2, identify the gospel as τοῦ Χριστοῦ (of Christ) instead of τοῦ θεοῦ (of God). The genitive phrase is missing in 255 and Or^{lat}.

2:8. Instead of the widely attested aorist form ἐγενήθητε (you became), one uncial (Ψ) and 𝔐 have the perfect γεγένησθε (you had become).

2:9. To reflect better that the second half of 2:9 functions to explain the first half, several MSS have added an explanatory "for" (γάρ): D¹ 𝔐 sy^{hmg}.

2:12. The direct object ὑμᾶς is missing in ℵ and one Vulgate MS.

2:12. The aorist tense καλέσαντος is found, apparently under the influence of Gal. 1:6, in two leading uncial texts (ℵ A), a few minuscules (104 326 606 1611 1831 1906 1912 2005), and a variety of versions (the weight of whose testimony is weakened by idiomatic considerations). As B. Metzger (1994: 562) states, "The present tense καλοῦντος, which is appropriate in the context, is strongly supported by B D F G H K L P and most minuscules."

2:13. A number of late MSS omit the first conjunction, καί (D F G H 33 𝔐 lat sy^p), because it (either καί alone or the fuller phrase καὶ διὰ τοῦτο) does not fit typical Pauline style. Nevertheless, the presence of the conjunction has strong textual support (ℵ A B P Ψ 6 81 1739 1881 *pc* (m) sy^h; Ambst), and copyists would have had no reason to add it at a later stage.

2:15. Some late MSS (D¹ K Y 𝔐 104 181 326 330 451 syr^{p,h} goth *al*; Marcion?) add ἰδίους (their own prophets), most likely in order to strengthen the interpretation that Paul was referring not to Christian prophets from the church age (e.g., Stephen, James the son of Zebedee) but Jewish prophets from the OT era. It is also possible that this variant reading is influenced by the word ἰδίων found in the preceding verse. In any case, "the shorter reading is decisively supported by the best representatives of several text-types (ℵ A B D* G I P 33 81 1739 it vg cop^{sa,bo,fay} arm eth)" (B. Metzger 1994: 562).

2:16. The words τοῦ θεοῦ are found in only a few late MSS (D F G 629 latt) and so clearly do not belong to the original text of this letter. Yet, because elsewhere "wrath" originates with God and is an activity of God (see Rom. 1:18; 5:9; 12:19; Eph. 5:6; Col. 3:6; also John 3:36; Rev. 14:19; 15:1, 7; 19:15), the clarifying addition of the words "of God" to the ET is warranted.

2:16. In place of the aorist ἔφθασεν, a few MSS have the perfect ἔφθακεν: B D* Ψ 104 *pc*.

Excursus 2
Textual Reading of 1 Thessalonians 2:7

The debate over the proper reading of 1 Thess. 2:7 ranks as one of the better-known issues in textual criticism: Did Paul write "We were *gentle* [ἤπιοι] among you" or "we were *infants* [νήπιοι] among you"?[1] In the nineteen centuries since this question first occupied the attention of the earliest church fathers, biblical scholarship has swung back and forth between the two possible readings.[2] Until recent times, the pendulum has clearly been swinging in support of the reading "gentle." Not only is this reading adopted in the vast majority of commentaries published during the second half of the twentieth century (Rigaux 1956; Best 1977; Marxsen 1979; Bruce 1982; Marshall 1983; Laub 1985; Holtz 1986; Wanamaker 1990; Morris 1991; Holmes 1998; Malherbe 2000), it is also found in virtually all the standard English translations dating to this period (so KJV, RV, RSV, NRSV, NEB, NIV [1984], NASB, NAB, NJB, REB, Phillips; notable exceptions include TNIV, NIV [2011], NET). Despite this almost universal acceptance of the reading ἤπιοι, a careful review of the manuscript evidence and a proper evaluation of the arguments pro and con reveal that νήπιοι is by far the superior reading.

External Evidence

What is immediately striking about the external evidence is how strongly it supports the reading "infants." In terms of date, the oldest Greek witnesses all have νήπιοι: 𝔓⁶⁵ dates to the third century; Sinaiticus (ℵ*) and Vaticanus (B) both belong to the fourth century; and Ephraemi Syri Rescriptus (C*), Claromontanus (D*), and Washingtonensis (I) are fifth century. The existence of the reading "infants" by an early date is further supported by the versions (Old Latin, one Sahidic manuscript, and the entirety of the Bohairic witnesses) and the church fathers (Clement, Origen, Ambst). By contrast, the oldest attested reading of ἤπιοι is in Alexandrinus (A), which dates to the fifth century—some two hundred years after the oldest witness to the reading νήπιοι. Furthermore, in terms of text type and geographic distribution, the reading "infants" occurs in the majority of Alexandrian and Western texts,

---

1. The following excursus is largely taken from my article: Weima 2000a.
2. See Crawford (1973) for an overview of how this textual variant has been handled in the patristic, medieval, Reformation, and modern periods.

and it is supported by the earliest evidence in both the West (Old Latin) and the East (Clement; 𝔓⁶⁵).

It is not surprising, therefore, that the major Greek editions of the NT, the Nestle-Aland and the Greek New Testament published by the United Bible Societies, have both shifted in recent decades toward a greater support of the reading "infants."[3] Even those who adopt the reading "gentle" readily admit that the external evidence supports the alternate reading "infants" and that it does so in a rather decisive manner.[4] The full force of the external evidence, therefore, should not be overlooked or minimized. As Gordon Fee (1992: 176) notes: "The evidence for ἤπιοι is so much weaker than for νήπιοι that under ordinary circumstances no one would accept the former reading as original."

Internal Evidence

Despite the force of the external evidence in support of "infants," most have nevertheless sided with the reading "gentle" on the basis of internal considerations. Four internal arguments of unequal importance are commonly used to defend the choice of "gentle" over "infants." An evaluation of each of these four arguments reveals that they do not provide, neither individually nor even collectively, the needed justification for rejecting the clear testimony of the external evidence.

Argument 1: Νήπιοι Is the Result of Dittography

One argument frequently cited in support of ἤπιοι is to claim that νήπιοι is the result of dittography, the common error of scribes who copied a letter, word, or phrase twice when the original manuscript had it only once (so, e.g., Bruce 1982: 31). This argument can be quickly dismissed since the reading ἤπιοι could instead be the result of haplography, the equally common error of scribes who copied a letter, word, or phrase once when the original manuscript had it twice. The significant point here is that dittography and haplography are both equally possible; there is no scribal tendency toward committing the one error more than the other. This means that it is illegitimate to appeal to either dittography or haplography in determining whether Paul wrote νήπιοι or ἤπιοι. The appeal to either one of these scribal errors is relevant only at a later stage in this debate, as providing one possible explanation of how the secondary reading came about. But the decision as to which of the two readings is secondary must be determined on other grounds.

3. The 26th edition of the Nestle-Aland text replaced ἤπιοι (in the 25th ed.) with νήπιοι, as now in NA²⁷ and NA²⁸. The 4th revised edition of the Greek New Testament (UBS⁴) has upgraded νήπιοι from a previous rating of C ("considerable degree of doubt") to a new rating of B ("the text is almost certain").

4. Bruce Metzger (1992: 231), for example, concedes: "The weight and diversity of external evidence are clearly in favour of νήπιοι, which is supported by the earliest form of the Alexandrian text (𝔓⁶⁵ [3rd century], ℵ*, and B), the Western text (D* and Old Latin), as well as a wide variety of Versions and Fathers." Other scholars make a similar concession: see Delobel 1995: 127; Wanamaker 1990: 100; Koester 1985: 225; Collins 1984: 7.

Argument 2: Νήπιοι Is a Common Term Replacing the Rare Ἤπιοι

A second argument claims that scribes replaced the rare term ἤπιοι with the more common word νήπιοι (so, e.g., Hendriksen 1955: 64n48; Rigaux 1956: 418; Marshall 1983: 70; Richard 1995: 82; D. Martin 1995: 78–79). But is it really the case that the one term is "rare" while the other is "common"? Paul uses νήπιοι only ten other times in his letters (Rom. 2:20; 1 Cor. 3:1; 13:11 [5x]; Gal. 4:1, 3; Eph. 4:14), and even this relatively small total figure may be somewhat misleading, since five of these occurrences are found in one verse. Thus it is more accurate to state that, in Paul's extant letters, neither word is very familiar. Nor is the word νήπιοι a common word in the rest of the NT: it occurs elsewhere only four times (Matt. 11:25; 21:16; Luke 10:21; Heb. 5:13). The word νήπιοι, therefore, does not occur with a sufficiently greater frequency than ἤπιοι (elsewhere in the NT, only 2 Tim. 2:24) that a scribe would feel compelled to replace "infants" for "gentle."

As a further weakness with this second argument, it fails to recognize that the supposedly rare ἤπιοι was a familiar-enough word to scribes from its use in nonbiblical writings.[5] Already some time ago, Malherbe (1970: 203–17) pointed out that being ἤπιος (gentle) was a well-known virtue in the ancient world. More recently, the assistance of computer searches has confirmed that the word ἤπιος was common in ancient writings.[6] There is ample evidence, therefore, that scribes would have been familiar enough with the word ἤπιος and that it is by no means a rare term compared with the word νήπιος (infant).

Argument 3: Νήπιοι Is Always Used Pejoratively by Paul

A third argument claims that the apostle always uses νήπιοι in a negative or pejorative manner and so would not have used this term to refer to himself in 1 Thess. 2:7 (so, e.g., Delobel 1995: 128–29). This argument, however, is misleading and prejudicial. For though Paul employs the metaphor of infants most often in a pejorative manner, it is not the case that he always uses it in a negative sense or always with the same degree of pejorativeness. This is best illustrated from its occurrences in 1 Corinthians—the letter where Paul most frequently makes use of the infant metaphor (see Fee 1992: 177). In 3:1 νήπιοι has a negative sense: the Corinthians are compared to infants who are not yet ready for solid food. In 13:11 the five references to infants are either neutral

---

5. Fee (1992: 177n36) notes that "ἤπιοι is a common enough word, even if found only once in the NT." Fowl (1990: 470) likewise observes that "if one looks in any standard lexicon, it will be clear that both words are well attested in Greek contemporary with the NT."

6. Sailors (2000) has used the Thesaurus Linguae Graecae (TLG) to show that ἤπιος occurs 42 times in the first centuries BC and AD compared to 274 occurrences of νήπιος in its nominal, adjectival, and verbal forms, for a ratio of about 1:7. Sailors further reports that the frequency of ἤπιος actually increases rather dramatically during this time period so that by the second century AD the ratio shrinks to 1:5. A search of the Duke Data Bank of Documentary Papyri (DDBDP) that I conducted yielded 65 matches with the adjective ἤπιος compared to 170 matches with the noun νήπιος, for a ratio of just under 1:3.

or just mildly negative as Paul uses this metaphor to describe the spiritual progression that naturally takes place as one moves from childhood to adulthood. In 14:20, however, the apostle uses the infant metaphor—expressed this time with the verbal form νηπιάζω—with a positive sense: he commands the Corinthians to "be infants with respect to evil." Paul's use of the infant metaphor is apparently fluid enough that it does not always require a pejorative sense but can be employed positively as well.

The possibility that Paul employs νήπιοι in 2:7 with a positive sense receives further support from the use of this term by other biblical and nonbiblical writers. In three of the remaining four occurrences of νήπιοι in the NT, this term refers to the righteous to whom God has revealed his wisdom (Matt. 11:25; Luke 10:21) and who bring to God perfect praise (Matt. 21:16). The Gospel writers here are following the positive sense that νήπιοι has in many Septuagint texts, especially the Psalms (18:8; 114:6; 118:130 [19:7; 116:6; 119:130 Eng.]; Wis. 10:21). In Hosea 11:1 LXX νήπιος expresses the childlike innocence of the nation Israel during its early days, before falling into sin and idolatry under the influence of the Canaanites (G. Bertram, *TDNT* 4:916).

Nonbiblical writers also occasionally used the term νήπιος in a positive manner. Dio Chrysostom, for example, uses the deep longing of infants to be reunited with their parents from whom they have been separated as a metaphor for humanity's desire to be with and converse with the gods (*Or.* 12.61). Several ancient writers describe the death of infants in wars and other hostilities in a way that emphasizes the innocence of these babies and the merciless character of those who kill such blameless creatures (see Diodorus Siculus 20.72.2; Philo, *Flaccus* 68; Josephus, *Ant.* 6.133, 136, 138, 260; 14.480; *J.W.* 1.352; 2.307, 496; 4.82). The notion of innocence connected with infants is found elsewhere in Philo, who speaks a number of times about "the soul of an infant child, which has no share in either virtue or vice" (*Alleg. Interp.* 2.53; see also 2.64; 3.210; *Good Person* 160). Even more explicit is Philo's claim that "it is impossible for the greatest liar to invent a charge against them [infants], as they are wholly innocent" (*Spec. Laws* 3.119). Sailors (2000: 86–87) has examined all the occurrences of νήπιος in its various forms in the literature from the first centuries BC and AD and claims that νήπιος has a neutral sense the vast majority of the time (75 percent), a negative sense as "childish, foolish" over 18 percent of the time, and a positive sense over 6 percent of the time.

It is now clear that the argument that Paul *always* uses the word νήπιοι in a pejorative manner and so would not have used this term to refer to himself is misleading and thus flawed. The apostle uses the infant metaphor in a rather fluid manner by which it sometimes has a neutral sense, most often has a negative sense, and in at least one situation other than 1 Thess. 2:7 has a clearly positive sense. Furthermore, the term νήπιοι was used with a positive sense by both biblical and nonbiblical writers. It thus remains entirely possible that Paul in 1 Thess. 2:7 employed the infant metaphor in a positive manner and that such a usage by no means ought to be judged non-Pauline.

Argument 4: Νήπιοι *Creates the Problem of a Mixed Metaphor*

A fourth argument claims that νήπιοι would create the problem of a mixed metaphor occurring within the same sentence: on the one hand, Paul states that he and his colleagues were like infants; on the other hand, he claims that they are like a nursing mother who cares for her own children. This resulting mixed metaphor has appeared to many to be so problematic that even the great textual critic, Bruce Metzger (1992: 231)—someone not at all prone to hyperbolic statements—asserts: "Paul's violent transition in the same sentence from a reference to himself as babe to the thought of his serving as a mother-nurse has seemed to most editors and commentators to be little short of absurdity."

The force of this argument, however, is mitigated by at least four factors. First, the reading νήπιοι and the resulting double metaphor of "infants" and "nursing mother" means that it is clearly the more difficult reading (*lectio difficilior*) and so, in keeping with a long-cherished rule of textual criticism, ought to be preferred. The counterresponse to this, of course, is that the reading "infants" is too difficult: it is not merely the *lectio difficilior* but the *lectio impossibilis* (so Delobel 1995: 131).

Yet the perceived difficulty of mixing the two metaphors of infants and a nursing mother is greatly alleviated by a second factor: the proper punctuation of 2:7 (see Dibelius 1937: 8; Stegemann 1985: 405–6; Baumert 1987: 561; Fee 1992: 177–78). The key issue is the correct location of a full stop in this verse. The standard Greek editions (which follow the reading νήπιοι) and major translations (which follow the reading ἤπιοι) all place a full stop after the phrase "apostles of Christ" in 2:7a so that a new sentence begins with the words "But we were gentle among you" in 2:7b:

UBS⁴/NA²⁸	NRSV
⁶οὔτε ζητοῦντες ἐξ ἀνθρώπων δόξαν, οὔτε ἀφ' ὑμῶν οὔτε ἀπ' ἄλλων,	⁶nor did we seek praise from mortals, whether from you or from others,
⁷ᵃδυνάμενοι ἐν βάρει εἶναι ὡς Χριστοῦ ἀπόστολοι.	⁷ᵃthough we might have made demands as apostles of Christ.
⁷ᵇἀλλὰ ἐγενήθημεν νήπιοι ἐν μέσῳ ὑμῶν,	⁷ᵇBut we were *gentle* among you,
⁷ᶜὡς ἐὰν τροφὸς θάλπῃ τὰ ἑαυτῆς τέκνα,	⁷ᶜlike a nurse tenderly caring for her own children.
⁸οὕτως ὁμειρόμενοι ὑμῶν εὐδοκοῦμεν μεταδοῦναι ὑμῖν . . .	⁸So deeply do we care for you that we are determined to share with you . . ."

This punctuation means that, if the reading νήπιοι is adopted, Paul would indeed have two mixed metaphors in one sentence ("But we were *infants* among you, like a *nurse* tenderly caring for her own children"), and the objection to "Paul's violent transition in the same sentence" would appear to be justified.

There are, however, serious problems with punctuating the verse in this manner. A number of grammatical considerations in 2:7–8, as well as a literary pattern in the larger structure of 2:1–8, demands that a full stop (period) be placed after the phrase "but we became infants among you" in 2:7b so that the infant metaphor *concludes* the clause of 2:5–7b. Then the nursing-mother metaphor *introduces* the clause of 2:7c–8.

That this is indeed the required punctuation becomes clear from the following grammatical considerations. First, when the conjunction ἀλλά (but) in Paul's writings introduces a clause following a negative (as is found here in 2:7b), this clause serves as the second and concluding part of an οὐ . . . ἀλλά (not *x* but *y*) contrast—a structure typically identified as an antithetical clause. In fact, this οὐ . . . ἀλλά contrast occurs no less than five times in the opening eight verses of 1 Thess. 2. The ἀλλά in 2:7b, therefore, cannot introduce a new sentence but rather concludes the preceding negative phrases in 2:5–7a.

Second, a similar situation occurs with the ὡς . . . οὕτως combination found in 2:7c–8—a structure typically identified as a correlative clause. The grammar dictates that ὡς introduces the correlative clause and οὕτως concludes it (note the similar structure in 2:4). Most translations violate this pattern by wrongly beginning a new clause in 2:8 and rendering the normally correlative οὕτως as an adverb denoting degree (e.g., NRSV: "so deeply"; NIV [1984]: "so much")—a usage that has no exact parallel in Paul's writings and conflicts with ordinary Greek usage (Fee 1992: 178). Therefore, on the basis of the ὡς . . . οὕτως combination, as well as the οὐ . . . ἀλλά contrast, it is clear that a full stop is required after the phrase "but we became infants among you" in 2:7b.

The significance of identifying the proper punctuation of this verse is that it greatly alleviates the perceived problem of the mixed metaphors. It is now clear that the metaphors of infants and nursing mother are not part of the same sentence—a fact that seriously undermines the legitimacy of even referring to them as "mixed" metaphors. They are rather two distinct metaphors, each with its own meaning and function in the larger argument of 2:1–12. A third important factor in this textual debate is that the phenomenon of mixed or rapidly changing metaphors is found elsewhere in Paul's Letters (Lightfoot: 1904: 24–25; Gaventa 1991: 197). The best example occurs in Gal. 4:19: in a relative clause containing a mere eight words, the apostle first depicts himself as a pregnant mother giving birth to his Galatian converts and then shifts rather abruptly to the image of the Galatian converts themselves as being pregnant, with Christ as a fetus in their wombs, and needing a further gestation period for that fetus to be fully formed. Another example is 2 Cor. 2:14, where Paul begins with the imagery of Titus and himself as captives being led in a military procession and then unexpectedly shifts to a different image in which the two of them are likened to the aroma of incense burned on an altar.

Yet one does not need to look outside 1 Thessalonians or even outside the second chapter of this letter for evidence of Paul's practice of rapidly shifting metaphors. Shortly after likening himself to a "nursing mother" (2:7c), the apostle compares himself to a "father" (2:11) and the Thessalonians to being his "children" (2:11). A few verses later Paul makes use of yet another family metaphor, describing his separation from the Thessalonian church as a state of being "orphaned" (2:17). Therefore, a sudden shift from the image of infants to that of a nursing mother is supported not only by Paul's practice in his other letters but also by the frequent movement from one family metaphor to another in 1 Thess. 2.

A fourth and final factor involves the presence of the orphan metaphor in 2:17. Many NT commentators claim that the verb ἀπορφανίζω was used to refer either to children who had been orphaned from their parents or, conversely, parents who had been orphaned from their children (see, e.g., Best 1977: 124; Ellingworth and Nida 1975: 47; Marshall 1983: 85; Holtz 1986: 115; Wanamaker 1990: 120; Holmes 1998: 94). Consequently, these scholars believe that it is ambiguous in 1 Thess. 2:17 whether the participle ἀπορφανισθέντες—a hapax legomenon in the NT—conveys the image of Paul and his coworkers as children who have been orphaned from the believers in Thessalonica, or conversely, it is the Thessalonian Christians who are children orphaned from Paul and his coworkers. Since the closest previous metaphor used by Paul to describe his relationship with the Thessalonians is that of the apostle as a "father" and the readers as his "children" (2:11), many choose the latter option.

This conclusion, however, is contradicted by the use of the verb ἀπορφανίζω in the extant Greek literature (Faulkenberry Miller 1999). This verb occurs infrequently, with only one attestation in Classical Greek, two in Philo, one in the NT (1 Thess. 2:17), and twenty-eight in the patristic literature. An analysis of these occurrences in their respective contexts gives a clear and consistent picture of how the verb ἀπορφανίζω was used: it never refers to parents who are orphaned from their children but consistently refers to children who are orphaned from their parents. There is, therefore, no ambiguity in the orphan metaphor of 2:17. By using the verbal form ἀπορφανισθέντες, Paul presents himself and his coworkers as children whose forced departure from Thessalonica has meant that they are orphaned from the believers in that city.

The use of the orphan metaphor in 2:17 provides indirect evidence in support of the reading νήπιοι in 2:7 in at least three ways. First, it shows that Paul made use of inverted metaphors in referring to himself: since the apostle switches from the metaphor of himself as a father in 2:11 to that of an orphaned child in 2:17, it is entirely feasible that earlier in the passage he switches from the metaphor of himself as an infant to that of a nursing mother. Second, the orphan metaphor indicates that Paul is confident enough of his relationship with the Thessalonians to portray himself in the nonauthoritative position of an orphaned child and hence suggests that he similarly would not be afraid to depict himself as a lowly infant. Finally, while the orphan metaphor can stand on its own, it is more readily understood as an extension of a preceding depiction of the apostle as a child, such as found in the infant metaphor of 2:7 (Lightfoot 1904: 36).

In light of the four factors highlighted above, it is difficult to agree with B. Metzger's claim (1992: 231) that the shift in 2:7 from infants to a nursing mother is a "violent transition" that is "little short of absurdity." Although the transition may be somewhat abrupt, the proper punctuation of the verse reveals that the two metaphors are part of separate sentences, each with their own distinct meaning and function in the larger argument of 2:1–12. Furthermore, a sudden shift from the image of infants to that of a nursing mother is entirely in keeping with Paul's practice elsewhere, especially with the frequent movement from one family metaphor to another in 1 Thess. 2. Finally, Paul's presentation of himself as an orphan in 2:17 serves in a variety of ways to support the apostle's use of the infant metaphor in 2:7.

Conclusion

The debate over the proper reading of 1 Thess. 2:7 is much less ambiguous than it is typically portrayed to be. The external evidence is decisively in favor of νήπιοι (infants), which even those opposed to this reading readily admit. An evaluation of the internal evidence and the four arguments commonly used to justify the choice of ἤπιοι (gentle) reveals that none of them provides the needed grounds for overriding the testimony of the external evidence. Furthermore, the superior reading "infants" involves a striking metaphor that functions effectively in the overall argument of 1 Thess. 2:5–7b. There are compelling reasons, therefore, for allowing Paul to make the claim of innocence that he made to the Thessalonians long ago: "But we became *infants* among you."

B. Defense of Present Absence from Thessalonica (2:17–3:10)

After defending the integrity of his motives and conduct during his *past* mission-founding visit to Thessalonica (2:1–16), Paul addresses two closely connected concerns stemming from his present absence from the believers in this city (2:17–3:10).[1] The apostle is concerned first that his inability to return to the Thessalonian church for a second visit might be used by opponents outside the church—the "fellow citizens" (2:14) who were oppressing the church and questioning the integrity of its founder—to raise further doubts about the genuineness of his care and concern for the new converts. Paul responds in 2:17–20 to this danger over his ongoing absence by employing the apostolic parousia—an epistolary device that makes his presence more powerfully experienced among the readers such that they are reassured of his love and care for them.

The apostle is concerned, second, about the persecution that threatens the faith of the Thessalonian church. The same evil, supernatural power who lies behind Paul's inability to return to Thessalonica (2:18: "But Satan blocked our way") is also at work in the afflictions experienced by the Thessalonian believers (3:5: "The Tempter had tempted you"), threatening to destroy the success of the apostle's missionary work. In 3:1–5 Paul responds to this danger by similarly making his presence more powerfully felt in the church, this time by referring to the sending of his emissary Timothy, whose mission is to strengthen the Thessalonian church in their faith.

These two concerns are skillfully combined and answered in 3:6–10, which deals with Timothy's return and report. The first concern of Paul, to reassure the Thessalonians of his genuine love for them despite his ongoing absence, is answered in Timothy's report about "your love and that you have a good remembrance of us always, longing to see us just as we also long to see you" (3:6b). The second concern of Paul about the faith of the persecuted believers in Thessalonica is answered in Timothy's report about "your faith" (3:6a), a faith that remains strong in the face of affliction and that in turn also provides comfort to the apostle in his own distress.

---

1. Fee (2009: 103): "Beginning with verse 17, the narrative of Paul's relationship with the Thessalonians takes a decided turn. To this point everything has been about that relationship in the *past*. . . . Now Paul begins to narrate how he and his companions have handled the *absence* since their hasty withdrawing from the city some months past" (emphasis added).

Literary Analysis

Character of the Passage

On the basis of both its form and content, 1 Thess. 2:17–3:10 ought to be identified as an "apostolic parousia," that is, a section of the letter where Paul is particularly concerned to make his "presence" (the Greek word παρουσία [*parousia*] has not only the sense of "coming, arrival" but also "presence") more powerfully experienced by the readers (on this epistolary convention, see Funk 1967; White 1972: 98–109; Boers 1975–76, esp. 146–49, 153; Aune 1987: 190–91; Jervis 1991: 110–31; P. Trebilco, *DPL* 446–56). The apostle, of course, is already present in some sense to the recipients through the letter, which is a substitute for his actual presence. Yet in his letters we often find a distinct section where Paul tries to make his presence more fully felt by the recipients. The most effective way he accomplishes this is by referring to a future visit that he himself plans to make to his readers.[2] When such a visit is not possible, however, Paul makes his presence more powerfully experienced through two alternate means: he refers either to the sending of one of his emissaries for a visit, or to the act of his writing this letter to the recipients.[3]

Form. The apostolic parousia as an epistolary convention was first identified and formally analyzed by Robert Funk (1967). Using Rom. 15:14–33 as his model, Funk proposed that the apostolic parousia consists of five major units.[4] Funk's conclusions were later modified by Ann Jervis (1991: 112–14), who uses the three means by which Paul emphasizes his presence to suggest that the apostolic parousia consists instead of three functional units: (1) the Letter Writing Unit, which includes the manner in which Paul is writing, the apostolic authority he has to write, and an appeal for the readers to obey his teaching; (2) the Sending of Emissary Unit, which includes a reference to Paul's dispatch of his emissary, the credentials of this representative of the apostle, and what Paul expects his envoy to do; and (3) the Apostolic Visit Unit, which includes Paul's stated intention or desire to visit, his submission to God's will regarding this visit, the reason(s) for his past inability to visit, and the reason for the projected visit.

The difficulty with both these formal analyses is that the parallels between the various apostolic parousias are not great enough to warrant the identification of specific units and subunits. It is better, therefore, to speak of the apostolic parousia as a distinct epistolary convention that exhibits a rather loose form or structure in which certain key words and expressions are frequently found. As Aune (1987:

---

2. This point is challenged by Mitchell (1992), who argues that sometimes it was more effective not for Paul himself to make a personal visit but for him to send one of his envoys instead.

3. Some have wrongly focused only on Paul's references to visits that he himself hoped to make and thus identify such passages as a "travelogue" (see, e.g., Doty 1973: 43; Mullins 1973: 350–58). Yet there is an important distinction between the terms "travelogue" and "apostolic parousia": in a limited sense the former term refers to future visits or travels of Paul, whereas the latter term refers more comprehensively to the presence of Paul, whether this is experienced by means of a future visit from the apostle, the arrival of his emissary, or the letter itself (see Funk 1967: 249).

4. The five units may be summarized as follows (Funk 1967: 252–53): (1) reference to Paul's letter-writing activity, including his disposition and purpose; (2) reference to Paul's relationship with his letter recipients; (3) reference to plans for paying a visit (desire to visit, delays in coming, sending of an emissary, announcement of visit); (4) invocation of divine approval and support for visit; and (5) benefits of the impending visit.

190) states: "The absence of a consistent structure [in the apostolic parousia] suggests that we are dealing with a *topos* or theme with a number of subordinate motifs."[5] This means that, in contrast to a comparative analysis of the more formally consistent sections of Paul's Letters (i.e., the opening, thanksgiving, and closing), less significance ought to be attached to any variations in form between the various apostolic parousias.

Function. Paul does not inform his readers about the future travel plans of himself and his emissaries merely to satisfy their curiosity or to provide details about himself and others for their general interest. Instead, the apostolic parousia is an effective literary device by which Paul can exert his authority over his readers. As Funk (1967: 249) observes: "All of these [i.e., references to either Paul's impending visit, the sending of his emissary, or his writing of the letter] are media by which Paul makes his apostolic authority effective in his churches. The underlying theme is therefore the apostolic parousia—the presence of apostolic authority and power." This authoritative function of the apostolic parousia should not be interpreted as a power-hungry ego trip by the apostle but instead as a useful literary means of placing his readers under his authority such that they will obey the contents of the letter. As White (*ANRW* 2:1745) asks and answers in a rhetorical fashion: "How does he [Paul] purpose to rectify, if inadequate, or to reinforce, if right-minded, his recipients' present status? By referring to one or another aspect of his apostolic authority and power."

Thus, for example, Paul employs the apostolic parousia near the end of his Letter to the Romans (15:14–33) to make his presence and authority experienced among the Roman believers—several house churches in the imperial city that he neither founded nor even visited—in such a powerful way that he ensures their acceptance of his apostolic authority over them and the gospel about which he has written quite boldly in the body of the letter (Weima 1994b: 354–58). Or again, the announcement of Paul's impending visit in Philem. 22 ("At the same time, prepare a guest room for me, for I am hoping through your prayers to be granted to you") functions as an indirect threat to Philemon himself: the apostle promises to come to Colossae to check personally whether his petition on behalf of the slave Onesimus has been obeyed (Weima 2010a: 56–57).

The function of the apostolic parousia in 1 Thess. 2:17–3:10, however, differs slightly from that found elsewhere in Paul's Letters. Here the apostle makes his parousia, or presence, more strongly experienced among the Thessalonian believers not so much to exert his authority as to reassure them of his continued love and care for them. As Jervis (1991: 116) concludes in her comparative analysis of this epistolary device: "Thus the dominant function of the apostolic parousia of 1 Thessalonians is to express Paul's love for his Thessalonian converts and to encourage them in their faith."

There was little need for the apostle to emphasize his authority over the Christians in Thessalonica since he enjoyed a good relationship with them in which his apostolic status and power were not in doubt (see the comment on the letter opening in 1:1 and the expression "apostles of Christ" in 2:7). There was a need, however, for Paul to emphasize his ongoing love and concern for the Thessalonian believers

---

5. Mitchell (1992: 641n3) similarly states: "I do not consider this [the apostolic parousia] to be a form. Paul talks about his own presence and that via envoys and letters in a variety of ways in a variety of places, which should not be homogenized."

since his sudden separation from them (2:17–20) and the subsequent persecution they had to endure (3:1–5) apparently left the apostle feeling vulnerable to criticism about his failure thus far to return. The apostolic parousia, therefore, functions as an effective literary device by which Paul emphasizes his presence among the Christians in Thessalonica in such a powerful way that they are reassured of his continued love for them, and any lingering uncertainty over his inability to return is removed. This reassurance of the apostle's love in turn encourages the Thessalonian believers to remain steadfast in their faith despite the persecution that they are currently experiencing.

Paul's emphasis on his apostolic presence in 2:17–3:10, however, also has a larger function in the letter as a whole. As with the apostolic apology in 2:1–16, so also the apostolic parousia here in 2:17–3:10 serves to reestablish the trust and confidence of Paul's readers such that they will submit to the exhortative material (paraenesis) that follows in the second half of the letter (4:1–5:22).[6]

Extent of the Passage

The beginning of the passage is clearly marked by both subject matter and formal features. There is a clear shift away from Paul's defense of his *past* visit (εἴσοδος, *eisodos*) to Thessalonica (2:1–16) to Paul's defense of his present absence and inability to return to the city for a second visit (2:17–3:10). This shift in subject matter is signaled formally in 2:17 by the use of both the contrastive particle "but" (δέ, *de*) and the personal pronoun "we" (ἡμεῖς, *hēmeis*) in the emphatic position at the head of the sentence, thereby setting the subsequent verses apart from the preceding material. The break at 2:17 is further indicated by the presence of the vocative "brothers" (ἀδελφοί, *adelphoi*), a transitional device widely used by Paul and other letter writers in the ancient world. Finally, the beginning of a new section at 2:17 is also inferred from the eschatological climax of 2:16c ("But the wrath of God has come upon them until the end"), a "sequence-terminating feature" (Johanson 1987: 86) that marks the end of the preceding passage.

But while there is no debate about the beginning of the passage, there is some question as to where it ends. Many commentators view the two prayers in 3:11–13 as belonging to the discussion that begins in 2:17 (so, e.g., Rigaux 1956; Best 1977; Ellingworth and Nida 1975; Bruce 1982; Marshall 1983; Holtz 1986; Morris 1991). This position is supported by a number of thematic and verbal links between 3:11–13 and the preceding material of 2:17–3:10. For example, the wish of the first prayer in 3:11, that God and the Lord Jesus "clear the way for us to come to you," looks back to the frequently stated (four times) desire of Paul to revisit the Thessalonians (2:17, "to see you face-to-face"; 2:18, "to come to you"; 3:6, "just as we also long to see you"; 3:10, "to see you face-to-face"). The wish of the second prayer in 3:11–12, that the Lord increase them in love "in order to strengthen your hearts" (εἰς τὸ στηρίξαι ὑμῶν τὰς καρδίας, *eis to stērixai hymōn tas kardias*), provides a verbal link with 3:2, where Paul's goal in sending Timothy to the Thessalonians is "in order to strengthen you" (εἰς τὸ στηρίξαι ὑμᾶς, *eis to stērixai hymas*). There is also a further connection in the second prayer between the reference to the return

---

6. This point is rightly recognized, although from a rhetorical rather than epistolary perspective, by Malherbe 1983: 241; Wanamaker 1990: 119–20; Holmes 1998: 94; Malherbe 2000: 181.

of Jesus in 3:13 ("before our God and Father at the coming of our Lord Jesus") and the same subject in 2:19 ("before our Lord Jesus at his coming").

Despite these important links, however, there are compelling reasons for distinguishing 2:17–3:10 from the following material of 3:11–13 (so, e.g., Lightfoot 1904; Milligan 1908; Frame 1912; Wanamaker 1990; Holmstrand 1997: 59; Malherbe 2000):

1. These two passages consist of texts that are formally distinct: 2:17–3:10 constitutes an apostolic parousia, while 3:11–13 contains two prayers or benedictions.
2. An important inclusio exists between Paul's opening statement in 2:17—that he was orphaned from the Thessalonian Christians "with respect to the face but not the heart" (προσώπῳ οὐ καρδίᾳ, prosōpō ou kardia) and that he therefore "most earnestly" (περισσοτέρως, perissoterōs) desired "to see you face-to-face" (τὸ πρόσωπον ὑμῶν ἰδεῖν, to prosōpon hymōn idein)—and his closing petition in 3:10 that he was "most earnestly" (ὑπερεκπερισσοῦ, hyperekperissou) begging "to see you face-to-face" (εἰς τὸ ἰδεῖν ὑμῶν τὸ πρόσωπον, eis to idein hymōn to prosōpon).
3. Another inclusio involving the theme of "joy" (χαρά, chara) is formed between 2:19–20 ("For who is . . . our joy? . . . For you are our joy") and 3:9 ("the joy with which we rejoice").
4. Then 3:10 closes with a reference to the word "faith" ("complete the things that are lacking in your faith"), a key term in both the sending of Timothy by Paul (3:2, "to strengthen you and comfort you concerning your faith"; 3:5, "to learn about your faith") and in Timothy's report (3:6, "good news about your faith"; 3:7, "We were comforted . . . through this faith of yours"), whereas this important word is lacking in the prayers of 3:11–13.
5. Though the two prayers of 3:11–13 contain key links with the preceding material of 2:17–3:10, they also foreshadow the major themes of the following material in 4:1–5:11 (see literary analysis of 3:11–13).

It is best, therefore, to treat 3:11–13 as an independent, transitional unit in the letter—one that not only echoes material in the first half of the letter but also anticipates the issues to be developed in the second half.

Structure of the Passage

On the basis of both its content and the presence of several transitional markers, 2:17–3:10 consists of three distinct units: 2:17–20; 3:1–5; and 3:6–10.

The first unit (2:17–20) deals with Paul's concern over his absence from the Thessalonians. As noted above, the beginning of this first unit is indicated not only by a shift in subject matter but also by the three formal markers found in 2:17: the adversative particle "but," the personal pronoun "you" at the head of the sentence, and the vocative "brothers." The ending of this unit is inferred from both the eschatological climax reached in the reference to Christ's return in 2:19b ("before our Lord Jesus at his coming") and the clear inclusio formed between 3:1–2 and 3:5 (see next paragraph).

The second unit (3:1–5) shifts the topic away from the absence of Paul to the persecution that the Thessalonians are enduring for their newfound faith. This shift is signaled in 3:1 with the inferential conjunction διό (dio, therefore). The boundaries of this second unit are even more clearly indicated in the inclusio formed between 3:1–2 and 3:5: the plural expression (of 3:1–2) "because we could no longer contain it, . . . we sent Timothy . . . in order to comfort you concerning your faith" (μηκέτι στέγοντες . . . ἐπέμψαμεν Τιμόθεον . . . εἰς τὸ . . . παρακαλέσαι ὑπὲρ τῆς πίστεως ὑμῶν, *mēketi stegontes . . . epempsamen Timotheon . . . eis to . . . parakalesai hyper tēs pisteōs hymōn*) is virtually repeated in singular form in the expression (of 3:5) "because I could no longer contain it, I sent [Timothy] in order to learn about your faith" (κἀγὼ μηκέτι στέγων ἔπεμψα εἰς τὸ γνῶναι τὴν πίστιν ὑμῶν, *kagō mēketi stegōn epempsa eis to gnōnai tēn pistin hymōn*).[7]

The third unit (3:6–10) picks up both of the concerns raised in the previous two units: the absence of Paul from the Thessalonians (2:17–20) and the persecution endured by the Thessalonians (3:1–5). The opening of this unit is not only inferred from the preceding inclusio (3:1–2 and 3:5) but also signaled by the adversative particle "but" (δέ, *de*) in 3:6 and the vocative "brothers" in 3:7 (the vocative is pushed back from its expected position at the beginning of this unit by the lengthy genitive-absolute construction that opens 3:6). The adverb "now" (ἄρτι, *arti*) in the emphatic position at the head of 3:6 serves to contrast Paul's *present* thankfulness in 3:6–10 with his *past* fear in 3:1–5. This shift from the past perspective of the second unit to the present time frame of the third unit is also signaled by another adverb meaning "now" (νῦν, *nun*) in 3:8.

The two distinct topics of Paul's absence from the Thessalonians in the first unit (2:17–20) and the persecution experienced by the Thessalonians in the second unit (3:1–5) become joined in the third unit (3:6–10). The first concern of Paul—to reassure the Thessalonian Christians of his continued love and concern for them, despite his failure thus far to return for a second visit (unit 1)—is answered in Timothy's report about "your love, and that you have a good remembrance of us always, longing to see us just as we also long to see you" (3:6b). The second concern of Paul—to encourage the Thessalonian Christians to remain steadfast in their faith, despite facing opposition (unit 2)—is answered in Timothy's report about "your faith" (3:6a) and the resulting comfort that the apostle has experienced "through this faith of yours" (3:7). These two concerns are also joined in the closing words of the third unit (3:10), where Paul prays that he might "see you face-to-face [first concern: Paul's absence] and complete the things that are lacking in your faith [second concern: persecution]."

The question naturally arises over why Paul in 2:17–3:10 chose to combine the differing concerns of absence and persecution rather than treat these two issues separately. The answer lies in that Paul's forced departure from Thessalonica and his inability to return were both the result of the same persecution that the believers in that city are currently experiencing. The apostle is also convinced that the same evil, supernatural power lies behind both his absence from the Thessalonian believers (2:18b: "But Satan blocked our way") and the suffering that they face for their faith (3:5b: "The Tempter had tempted you").

---

7. The NLT and ESV wrongly begin a new paragraph at 3:5. This paragraph division not only goes against the obvious inclusio that 3:5 forms with 3:1–2; it also suggests that 3:5 functions as an introduction to the following verses (6–10), which it clearly does not do, or at least does not do very well.

Therefore, despite the distinct issues that are addressed, 2:17–3:10 follows a logical line of argumentation that can be outlined as follows:

1. Paul's concern over his absence from the Thessalonians (2:17–20)
2. Paul's concern over the persecution endured by the Thessalonians (3:1–5)
3. Both concerns answered: Timothy's "good news" about the Thessalonians (3:6–10)

Exegesis and Exposition

[17]But we, brothers, having been orphaned from you for a short time, in person but not in heart, most earnestly made every effort to see you face-to-face with great desire. [18]It is for this reason that we wanted to come to you—in fact, I, Paul, wanted to do so more than once—but Satan blocked our way. [19]For who is our hope and joy and crown of ⌜boasting⌝—Is it not, in fact, you?—before our Lord Jesus at his coming? [20]For you are our pride and joy.

[3:1]Therefore, because we could no longer contain it, we thought it best to be left behind in Athens alone, [2]and we sent Timothy, our brother and ⌜coworker of God⌝ in the gospel of Christ, in order to strengthen you and comfort ⌜you⌝ ⌜concerning⌝ your faith, [3]so that ⌜no one may be shaken⌝ by these afflictions. For you yourselves know that we are destined for this. [4]For indeed when we were with you, we kept telling you beforehand: "We are destined to suffer affliction," as indeed it has happened and you know. [5]For this reason, because I could no longer contain it, I sent in order to learn about your faith, fearing that in some way the Tempter had tempted you and that our work might have been in vain.

[6]But Timothy has now come to us from you and has brought good news about your faith and love and that you have a good remembrance of us always, longing to see us just as we also long to see you—[7]for this reason, we were comforted, brothers, because of you in all our distress and affliction through this faith of yours. [8]For now we live, if you continue to ⌜stand firm⌝ in the Lord. [9]What thanksgiving, then, can we pay back to ⌜God⌝ concerning you because of all the joy with which we rejoice because of you before our ⌜God⌝, [10]pleading night and day as earnestly as possible in order to see you face-to-face and complete the things that are lacking in your faith?

1. Paul's Concern over His Absence from the Thessalonians (2:17–20)

The central topic or theme of 2:17–20 (and of 2:17–3:10 as a whole) is Paul's concern about his absence from the Thessalonian believers.[8] The apostle felt the need to defend not only his integrity during his past "visit" (2:1, εἴσοδος,

---

8. As demonstrated above (see "Structure of the Passage"), 2:17–3:10 also involves the closely connected theme of the persecution endured by the Thessalonians.

eisodos) to Thessalonica, but also his inability to return for a second visit.[9] The length of Paul's response to this problem, as well as the excessive nature of his highly affectionate comments in 2:17–20 (on this, see comments below), suggests the seriousness with which the apostle treats this concern. Yet here one must avoid the danger associated with mirror reading: inferring too much from the text. Nevertheless, when this passage is read in light of our earlier observations about the historical context of 2:1–16, there is sufficient evidence to understand the serious threat posed by Paul's inability to return to Thessalonica for a second visit.

One possibility is that Paul's absence might easily be used by opponents outside the church—the "fellow citizens" (2:14) who were oppressing the church and questioning the integrity of its founder—to raise further doubts about the genuineness of his motives and love for the Thessalonian believers (so, e.g., Frame 1912: 116–17; Hendriksen 1955: 74; Marshall 1983: 85; Morris 1991: 86; Beale 2003: 90). Another possibility is that Paul's absence might be wrongly interpreted by the recent (immature?) converts who understandably could feel that their "father" (2:11) had deserted them during their difficult days of persecution (see Calvin 1981: 261; Johanson 1987: 101). It is impossible to know with certainty whether Timothy reported either of these two scenarios to Paul as an actual problem or the apostle intuitively anticipated them as potential dangers. What is clear, however, is the very real threat posed by his continued inability to return in person to Thessalonica for a second visit. Paul responds to this serious concern over his absence, therefore, by employing the apostolic parousia—an epistolary device that makes his presence more powerfully experienced among the readers such that they are reassured of his love and joy over them.

The opening phrase "But we,[10] brothers" (ἡμεῖς δέ, ἀδελφοί, *hēmeis de, adelphoi*) signals a sharp break from the preceding comment about the Jews in 2:15–16. While Paul's words about some of his fellow Jews are striking for their harsh and vitriolic tone, his subsequent words in 2:17–20 are equally remarkable for their extremely touching and affectionate character. As Gaventa (1998: 40) observes: "Perhaps the most outstanding feature of this text is the way it interweaves a straightforward account of events with highly emotional interpretative remarks and asides." In this light, Paul's reference to the readers

2:17

---

9. A number of older commentators refer to 2:1–16 as Paul's *apologia pro vita sua* (apology for his life) in contrast to 2:17–3:10, which is Paul's *apologia pro absentia sua* (apology for his absence): so, e.g., Moffatt 1897: 4, 26, 28; Frame 1912: 14, 17, 140; Hendriksen 1955: 74; more recently Lambrecht 1990: 200.

10. In 2:17 it is difficult to determine whether ἡμεῖς δέ is meant to be (1) contrastive ("But we . . ."), distinguishing Paul and his fellow missionaries from either (a) the Thessalonian believers in 2:14 (so Moore 1969: 47) or (b) the Jews in 2:15–16 (so Frame 1912: 117; Morris 1991: 86); (2) resumptive ("Now we . . ."), continuing the description of either the missionaries' life with the Thessalonians in 2:1–12 or the "us" in 2:16 (Marshall 1983: 85); or (3) transitional, marking the introduction of a new idea or theme (Rigaux 1956: 457; Best 1977: 124; Marxsen 1979: 52).

as "brothers" ought to be viewed not merely as an epistolary convention to mark transition but also as an important expression of the deep affection that the apostle still has for his Thessalonian converts (for more on the use of the designation "brothers," see the comment on 1:4).

Paul further reassures the believers in Thessalonica of his deep love for them, despite his continued absence, by making use of another vivid family metaphor (see also 2:7b, "infants"; 2:7c, "nursing mother"; 2:11, "father"): "having been orphaned from[11] you" (ἀπορφανισθέντες ἀφ' ὑμῶν, *aporphanis-thentes aph' hymōn*). The emotional power contained in this metaphor is unfortunately weakened in many translations in one of two ways. Most problematic are those renderings that hide the metaphor of orphans completely by emphasizing instead the figurative sense of separation in the verb *aporphanizō*. For example, the RSV simply reads "We were bereft of you," and an older edition of the NIV (1984) has "We were torn away from you" (see also the KJV, NKJV, NASB, NAB, JB).[12] Some commentators similarly claim that the metaphor cannot be pressed since this verb came to have the more generalized sense of "deprived of" or "separated from" someone (so, e.g., Milligan 1908: 33; Richard 1995: 128–29). But as John Chrysostom (*Ep. Olymp.* 8.12.37–41) observed long ago: "He [Paul] did not say, 'separated from you,' nor 'torn from you,' nor 'left behind,' but 'orphaned from you.' He sought for a word that might sufficiently show the pain of his soul."

But even the translations and commentators who do rightly include the metaphor of orphans nevertheless minimize the force of Paul's language by failing to see that it is the apostle and his coworkers who are the children orphaned from the Christians in Thessalonica rather than the Thessalonian believers who are the children orphaned from Paul and his fellow missionaries. This error is rooted in the belief that the verb *aporphanizō* was used to refer either to children who had been orphaned from their parents, or conversely, parents who had been orphaned from their children (so, e.g., Best 1977: 124; Ellingworth and Nida 1975: 47; Marshall 1983: 85; Holtz 1986: 115; Wanamaker, 1990: 120; Holmes 1998: 94; Furnish 2007: 75). Since the closest previous metaphor used by Paul to describe his relationship with the Thessalonians is that of the apostle as "father" and the readers as his "children" (2:11; the notion of the Thessalonians as Paul's children is also implied in the nursing metaphor of 2:7c), many conclude that the orphan metaphor in 2:17 envisions Paul as the father who is separated from his Thessalonian children.[13]

11. In 2:17 the repetition of the preposition ἀφ' (from), redundant due to its presence already in the prefix of the participle, serves to stress the separation of Paul from his Thessalonian converts.

12. This problem has been corrected in recent revisions of these two popular translations. NRSV reads, "We were made orphans by being separated from you"; and NIV (2011): "We were orphaned by being separated from you."

13. Some appeal to the use of the adjective ὀρφανός, which, despite referring most often to children who have lost their parents, was sometimes used of parents bereft of children (see ὀρφανός in H. Seesemann, *TDNT* 5:487). Richard (1995: 129) also claims that this interpretation is a more logical reflection of the authority that Paul has over his converts in Thessalonica.

This conclusion is contradicted, however, by the use of the verb *aporphanizō* in the extant Greek literature (see Faulkenberry Miller 1999). This verb occurs infrequently, with only one attestation in Classical Greek, two in Philo, one in the NT (1 Thess. 2:17), and twenty-eight in the patristic literature. An analysis of these occurrences in their respective contexts gives a clear and consistent picture of how the verb *aporphanizō* was used: it never refers to parents who are orphaned from their children but always refers to children who are orphaned from their parents. There is, therefore, no ambiguity with the orphan metaphor in 2:17. By employing the verbal form *aporphanisthentes*, Paul presents himself and his coworkers as children whose forced[14] departure from Thessalonica has meant that they are orphaned from the believers in that city. Not only is this interpretation demanded by the use of the verb elsewhere in Greek literature, but it also is supported by the earlier metaphor of 2:7b, where Paul similarly depicts himself and his fellow missionaries as infants. Furthermore, this interpretation results in a more vivid metaphor: in a powerful fashion Paul evokes not only his forced absence from his Thessalonian converts, but also the deep sense of loss and grief that accompanies this absence. As Malherbe (2000: 187) observes: "The image of an orphan describes Paul in the most poignant way possible as in need. One could have expected Paul to say that his separation had made him bereft of his Thessalonian children or that the Thessalonians had been orphaned by his absence, but Paul wrenches the metaphor to extract the most emotion possible from it."

Two further phrases in the participial clause that opens 2:17 serve to minimize the problem of Paul's absence and add to his apostolic presence: "for a short time, in person but not in heart" (πρὸς καιρὸν ὥρας, προσώπῳ οὐ καρδίᾳ, *pros kairon hōras, prosōpō ou kardia*). The first phrase, *pros kairon hōras*, consists of a combination of *pros kairon* (1 Cor. 7:5; Luke 8:13) and *pros hōran* (2 Cor. 7:8; Gal. 2:5; Philem. 15; John 5:35), both of which mean a short or limited period of time. The combined phrase, therefore, intensifies this sense: "for a short time" (BDAG 497). Paul has apparently created this striking phrase (it occurs nowhere else in the LXX and NT) to stress that his absence is for a limited rather than indefinite or permanent time (so, e.g., Milligan 1908: 33; Bruce 1982: 54; Wanamaker 1990: 120). The natural implication for Paul's readers is that the apostle will soon be reunited with them.

The second phrase, *prosōpō ou kardia*, emphasizes that, though Paul may be absent from the Thessalonians "in person," he is present with them "in heart" (a similar, though slightly different, contrast is found in 1 Cor. 5:3; 2 Cor. 5:12; Col. 2:5). In other words, though the apostle could not have a face-to-face meeting with them (*prosōpō*, lit., "in face"), they were nevertheless very much in his thoughts (the "heart," for Paul the Jew, is the center

---

14. Best (1977: 124) comments: "No one is orphaned voluntarily; Paul was forcibly separated from the Thessalonians (Acts 17:10)." The orphan metaphor, therefore, along with the passive voice of the participle in 2:17 and Paul's previous statement concerning those "who drove us out" (2:15), support the account in Acts that the apostle did not leave Thessalonica voluntarily but was forced to flee the city.

of one's thinking and emotion). To use a comparable expression of our day, the believers were "out of sight but not out of mind."

The main clause of 2:17 continues the highly emotional, almost hyperbolic, language that Paul uses to express his love and longing for the Thessalonians: "We most earnestly made every effort to see you face-to-face with great desire" (περισσοτέρως ἐσπουδάσαμεν τὸ πρόσωπον ὑμῶν ἰδεῖν ἐν πολλῇ ἐπιθυμίᾳ, *perissoterōs espoudasamen to prosōpon hymōn idein en pollē epithymia*). The adverb *perissoterōs* has two possible senses: comparative (*more* earnestly) or superlative (*most* earnestly). More important than the difficult choice between these two options,[15] however, is the rhetorical effect that the addition of this adverb has in the sentence: it intensifies the expressed attempt of Paul to visit his converts once again.

The apostle's passionate feelings for the Thessalonians are further expressed in the verb σπουδάζω, which conveys the notion of being "especially conscientious in discharging an obligation" (BDAG 939). Paul did not merely harbor a private wish to return to Thessalonica but took concrete action to make this wish a reality: "We made every effort to see you face-to-face." As Wanamaker (1990: 121) observes: "σπουδάζειν indicates more than mere desire; it denotes actual effort on Paul's part to fulfill his desire."

After the comparative adverb "most earnestly" and the verbal choice of *espoudasamen*, the addition of the prepositional phrase "with great desire" (*en pollē epithymia*) might well appear to be redundant. Yet it is part of Paul's deliberate piling up of words to convey the intensity of his feelings toward the Thessalonian believers. The word *epithymia* in the writings of Paul and the rest of the NT almost always has the negative sense of "lust" and thus is regularly condemned. Here, however, the apostle uses the term in the positive sense of "desire" (see also Phil. 1:23; Luke 22:15) to express the "great" (note the addition of the adjective) longing that he has to see his readers again in person.

2:18 The close connection between this verse and the preceding one is indicated, first, by the conjunction διότι, which is an abbreviation of διὰ τοῦτο ὅτι (*dia touto hoti*, it is for this reason that) and functions as a "marker used to indicate why something just stated can reasonably be considered valid" (BDAG 251.3). The intimate link with the preceding verse is signaled, second, by the restatement of that verse's main clause: "We made every effort to see

---

15. Some commentators choose the former option (*more*), not only appealing to the obvious fact that this word is comparative in form but also claiming that this word always has a comparative meaning in Paul's Letters (so, e.g., Lightfoot 1904: 37; Milligan 1908: 34; Best 1977: 125; Marshall 1983: 85). Yet the comparative meaning raises a further issue on which there is no consensus: what is being compared here (see Frame 1912: 119 and those cited above for some possibilities)? Others choose the latter option (*most*) on the grounds that (1) the proposed possibilities for what is being compared are unconvincing, even nonsensical; (2) Paul uses this word in a superlative sense in three other places (2 Cor. 1:12; 2:4; 7:15); and (3) the comparative adjective and adverb in late Greek often replace the superlative (so, e.g., BDAG 806; Ellingworth and Nida 1975: 48; Wanamaker 1990: 121; Morris 1991: 87; Richard 1995: 129–30).

you face-to-face" is rephrased as "We wanted[16] to come to you" (ἠθελήσαμεν ἐλθεῖν πρὸς ὑμᾶς, *ēthelēsamen elthein pros hymas*). Although the main clause of 2:18 contributes virtually no new information but repeats Paul's previous assertion concerning his great desire to visit the Thessalonians, it fulfills the important rhetorical function of conveying yet again the magnitude of the apostle's feelings for his readers.

Paul continues to make his presence more powerfully felt among his readers, this time by means of a personal interjection: "In fact, I, Paul, wanted to do so more than once" (ἐγὼ μὲν Παῦλος καὶ ἅπαξ καὶ δίς, *egō men Paulos kai hapax kai dis*). The additions of the personal pronoun "I"[17] and the proper name "Paul"[18] both serve to emphasize that the apostle's stated wish to return to Thessalonica is no mere stereotyped formula, but rather a highly personalized expression of his own feelings. The emotionally charged state of Paul is also conveyed in the particle *men*. This particle is commonly used with a corresponding δέ to indicate contrast (on the one hand . . . on the other hand . . .). When it occurs alone, however, as it does here, it emphasizes the writer's emotional state (BDAG 630.2.a; see also Rom. 10:1). The intensity of Paul's emotion is still further heightened by the idiomatic expression "more than once" (*hapax kai dis*; elsewhere in the NT only in Phil. 4:16). Although this phrase literally means "once and twice," it does not signify that Paul tried to return to Thessalonica only two times. On the basis of its usage in the Septuagint (Deut. 9:13; 1 Sam. 17:39; Neh. 13:20; 1 Macc. 3:30), this saying denotes a plurality of occasions (two or more), with no attempt at exact specification (Morris 1956). The initial *kai* is not likely part of the idiomatic expression and is added for emphasis.

Paul not only reassures his readers of his repeated attempts to return to them but also provides them with a compelling reason why those efforts have thus far failed: "but[19] Satan blocked our way" (καὶ ἐνέκοψεν ἡμᾶς ὁ σατανᾶς, *kai*

16. A few commentators translate ἠθελήσαμεν in 2:18 with the slightly stronger rendering "we resolved" on the grounds that this verb has "the idea of active decision or purpose which as a rule distinguishes θέλω in the NT from the more passive βούλομαι 'desire,' 'wish'" (Milligan 1908: 34). It is questionable, however, whether such a distinction between these two common verbs exists in the NT generally and in Paul's Letters particularly. Some have even argued for the reverse interpretation (see the elaborate note under θέλω in the Grimm-Thayer lexicon). More convincing is the claim that the context, both the strong language of the previous verse as well as the subsequent personal interjection of Paul ("in fact, I, Paul, wanted to do so more than once"), shows that this verb "refers to more than a wish or desire here; it has the connotation of a wish made with resolve to fulfill it" (Wanamaker 1990: 121; see also Richard 1995: 130; Malherbe 2000: 183).

17. The singular "I, Paul" in 2:18, along with the singular in 3:5 and 5:27, reveals that Paul rather than all three missionaries is the real author of the letter; the plural "we" in the rest of the letter ought also to be interpreted as a literary plural, not as literal. See the comments on 3:1.

18. Other than in opening and closing formulas, Paul refers to himself by name elsewhere only in 2 Cor. 10:1; Gal. 5:2; Eph. 3:1; Col. 1:23; and Philem. 9 (the references to himself in 1 Cor. 1:12, 13 [2x]; 3:4, 5, 22 are due to what others have said about him). These five further references to the name of Paul in a letter body also serve to heighten the emotion (Malherbe 2000: 184).

19. The context strongly suggests that the conjunction καί in 2:18c has an adversative function and thus should be translated as "but" (BDAG 495.1.b.η).

enekopsen hēmas ho satanas). The verb ἐγκόπτω (*enkoptō*; elsewhere in NT only in Rom. 15:22; Gal. 5:7; Acts 24:4; 1 Pet. 3:7) derives its general sense of "hinder, thwart" (BDAG 274) from "the military practice of making slits in the road to hold up a pursuing enemy. Hence the basic meaning is 'to block the way'" (G. Stählin, *TDNT* 3:855). That Paul here does have this specific military practice in view appears to be confirmed by the later prayer of 3:11, which answers directly the problem of Satan's activity described here in 2:18: "May God himself . . . *clear the way* for us to come to you." The apostle, therefore, refers to the military tactic of cutting up a road so as to make it impassable as a powerful metaphor that excuses his failure to return to the Thessalonian believers.

Paul does not explain precisely how Satan has hindered his return, since he likely assumes either that the Thessalonians will readily understand what he is referring to or that Timothy (or whoever delivered this letter) will fill in the missing details. The apostle's silence on this matter, however, has not prevented scholars from offering their conjectures as to what happened. Some look for a cause in the Thessalonians' situation. For example, John Chrysostom (*Hom. 1 Thess.* 3) believed that it was ongoing Jewish opposition to Paul and the church in Thessalonica, even "a plot . . . being formed against him by the Jews" (note the description of Jewish opposition to Paul's missionary efforts in the immediately preceding verses, 2:15–16). Ramsay (1920: 230–31) suggested instead that the satanic hindrance was the legal ban and security deposit that the city leaders—the "politarchs"—required from Jason and the other Thessalonian Christians (Acts 17:9; so also Bruce 1982: 55; Hemer 1989: 186; Williams 1992: 55; Witherington 1998: 509; Riesner 1998: 359; Schnabel 2012: 709n20; Keener 2014: 2558). Others look for a cause in the circumstances of Paul. For example, Lightfoot (1904: 38) proposed that Paul was alluding to a "bodily ailment" (Gal. 4:13), likely the same debilitating illness that he later called his "thorn in the flesh, a messenger of Satan" (2 Cor. 12:7; so also Marshall 1983: 86; Wanamaker 1990: 122; Fee 2009: 107n18). But while some of these conjectures appear more plausible than others, they ultimately remain mere speculation because Paul fails even to hint at the specific nature of the problem. What is of more importance is the rhetorical effect that the reference to the satanic hindrance has: it allows Paul to avoid personal responsibility for his failure to revisit the Thessalonian believers and thus minimizes any criticism over his ongoing absence from them.

The name or title "Satan" is a transliteration of the Hebrew שָׂטָן (*śāṭān*), meaning "accuser" (it also has the nuance of "adversary" or "slanderer" in certain contexts: see "Satan" in V. P. Hamilton, *ABD* 5:985–86). This is the term that Paul most frequently uses, especially in his early letters, to refer to a personal, evil, spiritual being whose purposes are opposed to God and his people (Rom. 16:20; 1 Cor. 5:5; 7:5; 2 Cor. 2:11; 11:14; 12:7; 1 Thess. 2:18; 2 Thess. 2:9; 1 Tim. 1:20; 5:15). Some of the other terms that the apostle employs include "the devil" (Eph. 4:27; 6:11; 1 Tim. 3:6, 7; 2 Tim. 2:26), "Beliar" (2 Cor. 6:15), "the serpent" (2 Cor. 11:3), "the Tempter" (1 Thess. 3:5), and "the evil one" (2 Thess. 3:3; Eph. 6:16). Paul nowhere presents an extended and systematic discussion of Satan, but the picture that emerges from his letters as a whole largely agrees with the views commonly found in the Jewish literature of the Second Temple era (see σατανᾶς in W. Foerster, *TDNT* 7:151–63; see also "Satan, Devil" in D. G. Reid, *DPL* 862–67). In the OT the Hebrew noun *śāṭān* is used of a transcendent being in just three instances (Job 1–2; 1 Chron. 21:1; Zech. 3:1–2), where only a very vague picture of this supernatural figure emerges. These three texts apparently served as the basis for a later development in Jewish thought, where the origin, diverse names, activities, and final destiny of this evil, transcendent spiritual being were spelled out in great detail.

Paul, however, does not dwell on any of these matters. Instead, he theologically interprets the historical circumstances surrounding his inability to revisit the Thessalonians as the work of Satan. Paul's interpretation of these events should not be cynically dismissed as merely a ploy of the apostle to excuse his absence. For though Paul is surely trying to persuade his readers, he is also surely reflecting his genuine conviction that Satan is not only the enemy of God (Rom. 16:20) who tempts the followers of Christ (1 Thess. 3:5; 1 Cor. 7:5) and works against the well-being of the Christian community in a variety of deceptive ways (2 Cor. 2:11; 11:14), but one who also directly attacks the health and well-being of Paul as God's apostle (2 Cor. 12:7). Paul's worldview was one where he firmly believed that his struggle was "not against flesh and blood, but against the rulers, against the authorities, against the powers of this dark world, and against the spiritual forces of evil in the heavenly realms" (Eph. 6:12).

The two opening clauses of 2:17–20 that express Paul's repeated attempts to return to the Thessalonian believers (vv. 17–18) are balanced somewhat by two clauses that provide the reason *why* (note the conjunction "for" [γάρ, *gar*] that opens each clause) the apostle so often tried to revisit them (vv. 19–20). Both explanatory clauses continue Paul's pattern in 2:17–20 of piling up words and phrases that powerfully express his deep devotion to the Thessalonian believers. The highly affectionate character of the apostle's language led some of the church fathers to observe that Paul in verses 19–20 sounds like a mother lovingly addressing her children (see the references cited by Malherbe 2000: 184).

2:19

The first explanatory clause (v. 19) comes in the form of a rhetorical question that is affirmatively answered by means of an interjection that in turn involves yet another rhetorical question: "For who is[20] our hope and[21] joy and crown

---

20. In 2:19a it is not clear whether the implied verb "to be" has a present ("is") or future ("will be") meaning. Most commentators opt for the present tense on the grounds that the immediately following verse (20), which answers the rhetorical question of verse 19, uses the present tense. Some argue instead that the future tense fits more naturally the reference at the end of verse 19 to the return of Jesus as well as the eschatological sense of the three nouns "hope and joy and crown of boasting" (see esp. Richard 1995: 131–33, 137).

21. The two particles ἤ . . . ἤ in 2:19a have a conjunctive ("and . . . and") rather than disjunctive ("or . . . or") sense (so BDF §446). Paul is not selecting which of the three nouns ("hope,"

of boasting—Is it not, in fact, you?—before our Lord Jesus at his coming?" (τίς γὰρ ἡμῶν ἐλπὶς ἢ χαρὰ ἢ στέφανος καυχήσεως—ἢ οὐχὶ καὶ ὑμεῖς—ἔμπροσθεν τοῦ κυρίου ἡμῶν Ἰησοῦ ἐν τῇ αὐτοῦ παρουσίᾳ; *tis gar hēmōn elpis ē chara ē stephanos kauchēseōs—ē ouchi kai hymeis—emprosthen tou kyriou hēmōn Iēsou en tē autou parousia?*). Paul's repeated attempts to return to Thessalonica were motivated not out of any sense of obligation but out of the affectionate belief that these believers were his "hope and joy and crown of boasting."

The first item in this triad, "hope" (*elpis*), occurs thirty-six times in Paul's Letters (thirteen times in Romans alone) and thus plays a key role in the apostle's theology (see R. Bultmann, *TDNT* 2:530–33; J. M. Everts, *DPL* 415–17). Paul normally speaks of the believer's hope in God or Christ and in what the Deity will surely do. This notion of hope, for example, is found earlier in the letter where the reference to "your steadfastness of hope in our Lord Jesus Christ" (1:3) refers to the Thessalonians' hope in Christ's imminent return from heaven to bring about their deliverance (see comment on 1:3). Here the second reference to hope in the letter also has an eschatological focus involving the coming of Christ. Yet surprisingly Paul speaks not of a hope in Christ or God but in the Thessalonian believers who are "our hope." There is almost certainly a juridical context (see the closing words of the verse, "before our Lord Jesus at his coming," as well as the discussion of the terms "joy" and "crown of boasting" below) in which Paul views the converts in Thessalonica as evidence or proof of the faithful manner in which he has carried out his apostolic calling (Marshall 1983: 87; Richard 1995: 133). Just as Paul will later describe the difficult Corinthian church as "the seal of my apostleship" (1 Cor. 9:2) and his "letter of commendation" (2 Cor. 3:2), here the apostle somewhat similarly states his confident hope or certainty[22] that the Thessalonian congregation will be the proof he will present before the returning Jesus—proof that he has faithfully fulfilled his apostolic commission.

The second item in the triad, "joy" (*chara*), is also an important term in Paul's Letters, with twenty-one occurrences (see H. Conzelmann, *TDNT* 9:359–72; also "Joy" in W. G. Morrice, *DPL* 511–12). Its meaning here is clarified by a parallel expression in the Letter to the Philippians where the apostle similarly describes that church as "my joy and crown" (Phil. 4:1). The parallel, however, goes beyond vocabulary, as this expression also occurs in an eschatological context (see the immediately preceding verses of Phil. 3:20–21) in which Paul views the Philippian congregation as evidence in which he might "boast" before the returning Christ (Phil. 2:16, "so that in the day of Christ I may be proud [καύχημα, *kauchēma*] that I did not run in vain or labor in vain"). The notion of joy in 1 Thess. 2:19 is thus clear: with great joy Paul anticipates the day when the Thessalonian church, along with his converts

---

"joy," "crown of boasting") best describes what the Thessalonians mean to him but instead asserting that the believers are all three things. The conjunctive sense is also supported by the following verse, which answers the rhetorical question of verse 19: "For you are our pride *and* joy."

22. Fee (2009: 108): "Over against the watered-down sense that the word 'hope' has for most people in English, this word is Paul's primary way of speaking about the *certainty* of the future."

in Philippi and elsewhere, will be presented by him to the returning Lord as proof of his faithful missionary labors.

The third item in the triad, "crown of boasting" (*stephanos kaucheseōs*), is an expression found three times in the Septuagint (Ezek. 16:12; 23:42; Prov. 16:31). The word "crown," though with a different appellation ("crown of glory"), also occurs with a figurative meaning in the Septuagint (Jer. 13:18; Lam. 2:15) and the Jewish literature of the intertestamental period (T. Benj. 4.1; 2 Bar. 15.8; 1QS 4.7), and this appears to have influenced at least one NT writer (1 Pet. 5:4; "crown of life": James 1:12 and Rev. 2:10). Paul's use of the expression "crown of boasting," however, does not likely stem from these OT and Jewish texts (contra Lightfoot 1904: 38; Richard 1995: 133–34) but from the Hellenistic athletic contests where the victor received a wreath (so virtually all commentators). The apostle frequently employs the metaphor of the games to depict the Christian life in general and his apostolic ministry in particular (see Pfitzner 1962). The crown that Paul refers to is not a royal tiara or diadem (διάδημα, *diadēma*) but a wreath woven out of palm or other branches, flowers, or certain plant life (e.g., celery, parsley). Such crowns or wreaths would thus soon deteriorate—unlike the "imperishable" (1 Cor. 9:25) and "unfading" (1 Pet. 5:4) crown given to believers.

The metaphor that Paul uses, therefore, is powerful: just as a winning athlete boasts of his victory wreath, so the apostle will boast of the Thessalonian congregation, who are his victory wreath. As with the two preceding nouns, "hope" and "joy," here too "crown of boasting" has both an eschatological and legal sense: it is at the coming of Christ that the believers in Thessalonica will be the evidence or proof that Paul has faithfully fulfilled his apostolic calling (see Phil. 4:1, where, as noted above, these two senses similarly appear). The word "boasting" (καύχησις, *kauchēsis*) needs to be understood in light of the apostle's strong denunciation elsewhere of pride in human achievements before God (Rom. 3:27; 1 Cor. 1:29). Consequently, the *kauchēsis* of which Paul speaks here is not a false boasting or vain pride in his own accomplishments but a vindicating note of exultation for the work in Thessalonica that God brought about through him (1 Cor. 15:10).[23]

Paul's deep affection for the Thessalonians prevents him from finishing his rhetorical question as he interrupts the thought of 2:19 with a second rhetorical question, which answers the first: "Is it not, in fact, you?" By introducing this question with the negative οὐχί (*ouchi*, not?), Paul clearly signals that an affirmative answer is expected (BDAG 742; BDF §427)—a reply confirmed by the immediately following statement of verse 20 ("For you are our pride and joy"). Prior to the negative is the single Greek letter *eta* (ἡ), which virtually all editors and commentators give a grave accent (ἢ), thereby making it a

23. Notice how Paul in 2 Cor. 1:12 utters his "boast" (καύχησις) that he and his fellow missionaries have conducted themselves with "holiness and godly sincerity" but in the same breath asserts that their boasted conduct was due to "the grace of God." The apostle goes on in 1:14 to express his hope that the Corinthians "can be as proud [καύχημα] of us as we can be proud of you on the day of the Lord Jesus."

disjunctive particle (meaning "or"), whose function is to introduce a rhetorical question (see BDAG 432.1.d.α). The difficulty with this view is that it implies a contrast between the Thessalonians and some other unidentified group ("Or [if others are our hope and joy and crown of boasting] are you not also?"). An alternate reading that better fits this context, where Paul's attention is so sharply focused on the Thessalonians alone, is to give the letter a circumflex accent (ἤ), thereby making it an adverb ("truly, indeed") that serves to introduce a question which does not permit an alternative answer (see BDAG 433; so Bruce 1982: 53; Wanamaker 1990: 124; Malherbe 2000: 185). This position further suggests that the conjunction *kai*, which could function as an adverb ("Is it not *also* you?," i.e., you in addition to other Pauline churches), is best understood as providing emphasis ("Is it not, *in fact*, you?").

Now that his emotional interjection is finished, Paul is able to return to the first rhetorical question that opened verse 19. The apostle concludes that interrupted question with the prepositional phrase "before our Lord Jesus at his coming." This phrase makes clear the point observed above, noticing the eschatological and juridical context in which the triad "hope and joy and crown of boasting" ought to be understood. The Lord Jesus will return as a judge (see also 2 Cor. 5:10) before whom the Thessalonian church will appear as evidence or proof of the faithful way that Paul has fulfilled his apostolic calling.

Paul has already referred to the return of Christ two times in the letter thus far: implicitly in 1:3 ("hope in our Lord Jesus Christ") and explicitly in 1:10 ("to wait for his Son from the heavens"). His third reference here in 2:19 makes use of the key term *parousia*. This Greek word has two distinct senses (BDAG 780–81): (1) "the state of being present, *presence*"; and (2) "arrival as the first stage in presence, *coming*."[24] Thus, when Paul uses this term to describe the activities of himself or others, it sometimes conveys the notion of "presence" (1 Cor. 16:17; 2 Cor. 10:10; Phil. 2:12), while at other times the notion of "coming" (2 Cor. 7:6, 7; Phil. 1:26). When the apostle uses this term to refer to Jesus, however, it always refers to his "coming," yet in a very specific sense. In the Hellenistic world the word *parousia* was a technical term that referred either to the coming of a particular deity to help his worshipers or, more commonly, the coming of kings or high-ranking leaders (who were often considered to be divine) to a city for an official visit, where appropriate ceremonies were held and honors were bestowed. On such visits, a delegation of leading citizens would typically meet the coming dignitary outside the city and formally escort him for the remainder of his journey (see comment on the term ἀπάντησις in 4:17). The word *parousia*, therefore, with this technical meaning of a coming king, served as a key term used not only by Paul (1 Cor.

---

24. There remains, however, a close connection between these dual possibilities. As Marshall (1983: 88) observes: "The concept of 'arrival' can pass over easily into that of the 'presence' which is consequent upon a person's arrival, and here the thought may well be of the abiding presence of Jesus which follows on from his coming." Note also 4:17, where Paul concludes his description of the "coming" of Jesus with a statement about the eternal "presence" of the returning Lord with believers: "And so we will always be with the Lord."

15:23; 1 Thess. 2:19; 3:13; 4:15; 5:23; 2 Thess. 2:1, 8; see also the "coming" of the antichrist in 2 Thess. 2:9) but other biblical writers as well (Matt. 24:3, 27, 37, 39; James 5:7, 8; 2 Pet. 1:16; 3:4, 12; 1 John 2:28) to refer to the future coming of Jesus.

But while the term *parousia* is clearly Hellenistic, the roots of the idea quite likely go back to the OT, as concepts associated with the coming of Jesus are anticipated in the OT prophetic literature and Jewish apocalyptic writings (see Sabbe 1961; Kreitzer 1987; Glasson 1988; Ahn 1989). Some of these key OT ideas include the day of the Lord, when God will come to both judge the wicked and save the righteous (Isa. 2:10–12; 13:6, 9; Ezek. 7:19; 13:5; 30:3; Joel 1:15; 2:1, 11, 31; 3:14; Amos 5:18–20; Zeph. 1:7–8, 14, 18; 2:2–3; Zech. 14:1; Mal. 3:2; 4:5) and the "visit" of God in judgment (Jer. 5:9; Hosea 2:13; Zech. 10:3). Despite these OT roots, however, the predominately Gentile church of Thessalonica would naturally have understood the parousia in terms of the royal visits of the Roman emperors and officials. This Hellenistic understanding of the term *parousia* with its political overtones may well explain why the city authorities of Thessalonica accused Paul and his fellow missionaries of "saying that there is another king, Jesus" (Acts 17:7). This danger of too close an association with the Hellenistic notion of parousia may also explain why Paul used different terms in his later letters to refer to the coming of Jesus (Best 1977: 354; Furnish 2007: 76).

The rhetorical question of verse 19, already answered implicitly in the interjec- **2:20** tion of v. 19b ("Is it not, in fact, you?"), is now answered explicitly in a second explanatory clause (note the repeated γάρ, *gar*, for): "For you are our pride and joy" (ὑμεῖς γάρ ἐστε ἡ δόξα ἡμῶν καὶ ἡ χαρά, *hymeis gar este hē doxa hēmōn kai hē chara*). A positive response is immediately anticipated by the explanatory conjunction *gar*, which, when replying to a question as it does here, affirms what was asked by giving a reason for a tacit "yes" (BDF §452.2). This positive answer is then confirmed by the rest of the sentence, which affirms that "*you* [the personal pronoun is in the emphatic position] are our pride and joy." The double attributes of "pride" and "joy" are essentially parallel to the triad of the preceding verse ("hope and joy and crown of boasting") and therefore also ought to be understood in light of an eschatological and juridical context. The Thessalonian church will be evidence of the faithful fulfillment of Paul's apostolic calling at the return of Jesus because they are already now (note the present tense of *este*) the source of his pride and joy.

Here the word *doxa* has the common secular meaning of "fame, recognition, renown, honor, prestige" (so BDAG 257; see also 2:6) rather than the religious sense of "glory" (see 2:12). Since *doxa* is paralleled by the expression "crown of boasting," the word "pride" is an appropriate translation, especially since the fuller expression "our pride and joy" captures nicely in contemporary terms the deep affection that Paul has for his Thessalonian converts. The word "joy" (*chara*) is repeated from 2:19 (see comment on that verse) and will be used again in this passage to describe Paul's relationship with the believers in Thessalonica (3:9, "the joy with which we rejoice"). This second description of the Thessalonian believers as "joy" serves to convey even further the apostle's strong feelings for his readers.

2. Paul's Concern over the Persecution Endured by the Thessalonians (3:1–5)

The focus of Paul's attention shifts somewhat in 3:1–5. Although he continues to be concerned about his absence from Thessalonica, the apostle raises a new concern closely connected with his inability to return to them: the persecution that they must endure for their faith. This new topic of persecution is not unexpected for the careful reader of this letter. The issue of Christian suffering was foreshadowed in the thanksgiving section (1:6b, "receiving the word in much affliction") and has also been addressed as part of Paul's defense of his past ministry in Thessalonica (2:2b, 14–16). Now, as part of his defense for his present absence from Thessalonica, Paul again raises the issue of persecution and does so at a greater length than previously in the letter.

The reason for combining the differing topics of his absence (2:17–20) and of their persecution (3:1–5) lies in that Paul's forced departure from Thessalonica and his inability to return are both due to the same persecution that the believers in that city currently experience. Although Paul is not able to be with them in person, he continues to make his presence among them more powerfully felt (the apostolic parousia) by referring to the sending of his emissary, Timothy. Thus, despite his absence, the apostle manages to strengthen the faith of the Thessalonian church during this difficult time of affliction.

3:1 Paul's growing frustration over his continued inability to return in person to the Thessalonians finally caused him to act: "Therefore, because we could no longer contain it, we thought it best to be left behind in Athens alone" (διὸ μηκέτι στέγοντες εὐδοκήσαμεν καταλειφθῆναι ἐν Ἀθήναις μόνοι, *dio mēketi stegontes eudokēsamen kataleiphthēnai en Athēnais monoi*). The inferential conjunction *dio* (therefore) highlights the connection between what follows in 3:1–5 and the preceding discussion of 2:17–20. Thus, even though Paul does not state explicitly in the subsequent participial clause precisely what it is that he is no longer able to contain (there is no direct object), the conjunction *dio* makes it clear that the apostle has in view the preceding section (2:17–20), which expresses his deep affection for the Thessalonians.[25]

It was this great love and concern for the persecuted believers in Thessalonica that Paul "could no longer contain" (*mēketi stegontes*). The verb στέγω (*stegō*), used only four times in the NT (here in 3:1, 5; also in 1 Cor. 9:12; 13:7) and rarely in other Greek writings, originally denoted substances that do not allow

---

25. Some commentators make the connection with the preceding verses explicit in their translation by supplying a direct object to the participial clause. For example, Milligan (1908: 36) renders the opening of 3:1 as follows: "Unable to bear the thought of *this continued separation* any longer . . ." Similarly, Frame (1912: 124) translates: "Wherefore, since we intended no longer to endure *the separation* . . ."

themselves to be penetrated by air, light, fire, water, or anything else. The verb was especially used to describe watertight ships that kept water from seeping in and bowls that prevented their contents from leaking out. Thus, "at the core of its meaning στέγω denotes an activity or state which blocks entry from without or exit from within" (W. Kasch, *TDNT* 7:586).[26] Consequently, the image that Paul evokes with this verb is one where he is so full of love and concern for the Thessalonians that he is no longer able to prevent his strong emotions for them from leaking out (see Whitaker 1921).[27] The apostle's thought is similar to Philo's description of Moses, who was "unable to contain [μὴ στέγων, *mē stegōn*] a feeling of reciprocal love and affection for his people" (*Virtues* 69).

This irrepressible emotion caused Paul to act: "We thought it best to be left behind in Athens alone." The verb *eudokēsamen* expresses not joy (BDAG 404.2; see comment on 2:8), as if Paul were happy to remain alone in Athens, but resolve (BDAG 404.1): this was the best course of action to take. The passive voice of the complementary infinitive *kataleiphthēnai*, the prefixed preposition *kata-* (to be left *behind*), and the addition of the adjective *monoi* (alone)—all serve to stress the loneliness that resulted from this course of action and so echoes the earlier metaphor of his "being orphaned" (2:17). Paul does not spell out the circumstances surrounding his solitary stay in Athens. Presumably the Thessalonians know about these details from Timothy. Acts 17:16–34 describes how Paul's preaching in Athens yielded only few converts and how the philosophers in that city mocked his message about the resurrection of the dead. The apostle, however, says nothing about this matter to his Thessalonian readers. That he was willing to suffer the state of ministering alone in Athens testifies to his deep love and concern for the believers in Thessalonica.

There are two related issues in this verse that still need to be addressed: (1) clarifying the ambiguous use of the first-person plural, and (2) correlating the movements of Paul and his coworkers here with the account in Acts. The first issue deals with the difficulty in determining whether the "we" should be read as a literal plural or a literary plural. The reference to Silvanus (Silas) and Timothy as cosenders of the letter (1:1), the plural form of the adjective *monoi* in 3:1, and the apostle's general practice in his other letters of using the singular "I" have led several commentators to conclude that the "we" ought

---

26. This sense of στέγω in 3:1 is also found in the related noun στέγη (roof: Matt. 8:8; Mark 2:4; Luke 7:6) and the compound verb ἀποστεγάζω (to unroof: Mark 2:4).

27. Virtually all translations and commentators miss this image because they understand the verb to express the idea of bearing up against difficulties: "bear, stand, endure" (BDAG 942.2). Yet the core sense of preventing something from either coming in or out can also be found in Paul's two other uses of *stegō*. Thus 1 Cor. 9:12 should not be translated "we endure/bear all things," for the context makes it clear that Paul is referring not to sufferings but to the rights of an apostle to claim financial support (so W. Kasch, *TDNT* 7:586). Instead, here the image depicts Paul as containing or "keeping in" his rights as an apostle in order not to cause an offense or hindrance to the gospel. Similarly, 1 Cor. 13:7 should not be rendered as "Love endures/bears all things," for the image instead is one where love contains or "keeps in" anything negative about another person rather than allow such information to leak out and harm a relationship (so Whitaker 1921; Spicq 1994: 3.290; see BDAG 942.1: "to keep confidential, *cover, pass over in silence*").

to be understood literally: Paul was left behind in Athens with either other believers in that city or, more likely, Silas (NIV: "we thought it best to be left by *ourselves* in Athens"; so, e.g., Frame 1912: 125; Best 1977: 131; Bruce 1982: 60). Over against this conclusion, however, are several important factors: the plural of 3:1–2 is clarified by the emphatic use of the singular in 3:5, which forms an inclusio with the earlier verses; the adjective *monoi*, though plural in form, refers most naturally in meaning ("alone") to one person; the highly personal nature of Paul's language in 2:17–20 and the use of the emphatic singular in 2:18 also suggest that the plural ought not to be taken literally (see further the comment on 1:1). Most commentators, therefore, view the "we" in 3:1 as a literary or epistolary plural: Paul was left behind in Athens *by himself* (so, e.g., Wanamaker 1990: 126–27; Donfried 1991b; Morris 1991: 93; Malherbe 2000: 190; Donfried 2002: 209–12; Beale 2003: 95).

The second issue concerning the attempt to reconstruct the movements of Paul, Silas, and Timothy presupposes the historical reliability of Acts. It is true that this document omits certain details referred to in 1 Thess. 3:1–10. But rather than proof of Acts's untrustworthiness, this silence is more likely due either to Luke's lack of specific knowledge about the missionaries' travels or to his deliberate choice not to include such information. A comparison of the two sources suggests that the following sequence of events likely took place:

1. Paul arrives in Athens (2 Thess. 3:1; Acts 17:15–34), having left Silas and Timothy behind in Berea with instructions to join him "as soon as possible" (Acts 17:15b).
2. After his two coworkers return to him in Athens, Paul sends Timothy back to Thessalonica in order to encourage the believers, who were being persecuted for their newfound faith (1 Thess. 3:1–5). The apostle also sends Silas away with the result that he (Paul) was left behind in Athens by himself (3:1). The exact itinerary and purpose of Silas's trip is not clear. Although some have claimed that he was sent to the churches in Galatia to address the pressing problems faced there (Wainwright 1980), it is more likely that Silas also went to Macedonia and revisited the Philippian church, where he received further gifts of financial support for Paul's ministry (Phil. 1:5; 4:16).
3. After accomplishing his mission in Thessalonica, Timothy returns to Paul (1 Thess. 3:6), who by this time has left Athens to begin an eighteen-month ministry in Corinth (Acts 18:1–17). This return of Timothy probably corresponds to the return of both Timothy and Silas from Macedonia (Acts 18:5). Timothy gives an essentially good report about the Thessalonian church (1 Thess. 3:6–10) but also informs Paul of several concerns, thereby prompting the apostle to write 1 Thessalonians.

3:2   Paul continues to make his parousia or presence experienced more fully among the Thessalonian believers by reminding them of how he sent to them Timothy as his representative: "and we sent Timothy, our brother and coworker of

God in the gospel of Christ" (καὶ ἐπέμψαμεν Τιμόθεον, τὸν ἀδελφὸν ἡμῶν καὶ συνεργὸν τοῦ θεοῦ ἐν τῷ εὐαγγελίῳ τοῦ Χριστοῦ, *kai epempsamen Timotheon, ton adelphon hēmōn kai synergon tou theou en tō euangeliō tou Christou*). The apostle frequently sent (or attempted to send) to his various churches not only Timothy (1 Cor. 4:17; 16:10; Phil. 2:19, 23) but others as well (Epaphroditus: Phil. 2:25, 28; Apollos: 1 Cor. 16:12; Titus: 2 Cor. 8:6; 12:18; a companion of Titus: 2 Cor. 8:18; an unnamed "brother": 2 Cor. 8:22; 12:18; Tychicus: Col. 4:7–8; Eph. 6:21–22; Titus 3:12; 2 Tim. 4:12; Artemus: Titus 3:12), whenever he was unable to pay a personal visit himself. This suggests that Paul occupied a position of authority over his fellow missionaries. It is impossible to know with certainty why the apostle chose Timothy rather than Silas to return to Thessalonica. One plausible explanation is that Timothy was the only one of the three missionaries not specifically connected with the legal ban and security deposit that the city leaders—the politarchs—required from Jason and the other Thessalonian believers (note the absence of Timothy's name in Acts 17:1–10).[28]

Paul ascribes two titles to Timothy, and these designations are not as insignificant as they may initially appear. The first title of "our brother" is quite likely not merely an expression of endearment but also a technical term used by Paul to refer to someone engaged with him in the work of Christian ministry, as a "coworker" (Ellis 1978: 13–22). This more restricted sense of the common term *adelphos* is supported by a number of texts where "brother(s)" appears to be distinguished from the church membership as a whole (see, e.g., 1 Cor. 16:19–20; 2 Cor. 8:18, 23; 9:3, 5; Eph. 6:23–24; Phil. 1:14; 4:21–22; Col. 4:15). The second title of "coworker of God" is even more striking for the bold and lofty status that it ascribes to Timothy—a status so privileged that it not only caused many ancient copyists to alter the text (see additional notes) but also many contemporary translations to weaken Paul's claim ([italics added] NIV: "co-worker *in God's service*"; NRSV: "co-worker *for God*").

What did Paul hope to accomplish by using these two titles to describe Timothy? Since Timothy was personally well known to the Thessalonian church from both the missionaries' original ministry in the city as well as his return visit, there is obviously no need for Paul to describe his helper in ministry for the purpose of identifying for the readers who he is. Instead, both titles have the function of stressing the authoritative status of Timothy: he is no mere mailman or messenger boy but an authoritative coworker of both Paul and even God. By attributing considerable status to Timothy, Paul strengthens the defense of his present absence from the Thessalonians. Even though he has not been able to return to them personally, Paul nevertheless has been present with them through Timothy, who is no mere underling but an important, authoritative representative of the apostle.[29]

28. This explanation would be strengthened if this is the historical situation that Paul is alluding to in his previous reference to the hindering activity of Satan (see comment on 2:18).
29. Fee (2009: 115) argues that in 3:2 the unique title "coworker" has a different function: it is a "pro forma" commendation typical of letter carriers, since Timothy will be the bearer of the present letter. Such commendations of letter carriers, however, normally occur at the *end*

The purpose (εἰς τό + infinitive = purpose; BDF §402.2) for which Paul sent Timothy to the Thessalonian church was "in order to strengthen you and comfort you concerning your faith" (εἰς τὸ στηρίξαι ὑμᾶς καὶ παρακαλέσαι ὑπὲρ τῆς πίστεως ὑμῶν, *eis to stērixai hymas kai parakalesai hyper tēs pisteōs hymōn*). The two articular infinitives, *stērixai* and *parakalesai*, are closely linked by means of the one definite article, which does double duty for both. These same two verbs are elsewhere similarly joined in a word pair (2 Thess. 2:17; Acts 14:22; 15:32) or in close proximity to each other (Rom. 1:11–12); hence it would be wrong to distinguish too sharply between them.

The first infinitive, *stērixai*, literally means to "set up, establish" something such as a building, city, or even the world, but when used of things that are already in existence it has the more figurative sense of "confirm, establish, strengthen" (BDAG 945). Here the word serves to contrast the danger of being "shaken" (see comment on 3:3) in one's thinking or beliefs and thus expresses the goal that Timothy's past mission was to ensure that Thessalonian believers remained "firm" or "established" in their faith despite the persecutions that they continue to endure.

The second infinitive, *parakalesai*, involves a favorite Pauline term, occurring some fifty-four times in his letters as a whole and eight times in this letter (2:12; 3:2, 7; 4:1, 10, 18; 5:11, 14). Although this verb possesses a wide range of meanings (BDAG 764–65 lists five different senses), these possibilities can be grouped into two primary nuances: either the more authoritative sense of command ("appeal, exhort, request, implore") or the more pastoral sense of comfort ("encourage, comfort, cheer up, console"). That Paul has in mind the latter notion here in 3:2 seems evident from (1) the immediately following verse, which refers to the persecutions endured by the Thessalonian believers, thereby providing a historical context in which comfort is needed; and (2) the use of the same verb in 3:7 to convey the comfort that Paul and his fellow missionaries received from the report of Timothy.

This strengthening and comforting ministry of Timothy was specifically directed at the *faith* of the Thessalonian Christians: "concerning[30] your faith" (*hyper tēs pisteōs hymōn*). The word "faith" is a key term not only in this second unit of 3:1–5 but also in the concluding third unit of 3:6–10, occurring five times within ten verses. It appears here in verse 2 and again in verse 5 as part of the inclusio that clearly defines the boundaries of the second unit. It also appears three times in the third unit: in the opening report of Timothy, who "brought good news about your faith" (v. 6); in the comfort that Paul and his fellow missionaries derived "through this faith of yours" (v. 7); and in

---

of the letter as part of the closing (e.g., Rom. 16:1–2 [Phoebe]; Eph. 6:21–22 and Col. 4:7–9 [Tychicus]), not in the middle of the letter body, as would be the case here.

30. In 3:2c the preposition ὑπέρ functions as a marker of general content ("about, concerning") and is equivalent to περί, with which it is frequently interchanged in the MSS (see additional notes). It is too much to claim (see, e.g., Milligan 1908: 38; Best 1977: 134; Morris 1991: 95n6; Wanamaker 1990: 128) that the preposition here carries the additional connotation of "for the advantage of" such that Timothy's visit will result in an increase of the Thessalonians' faith.

the closing desire of Paul to see them face-to-face and "complete the things that are lacking in your faith" (v. 10). The apostle has earlier twice referred to the faith of the Thessalonians in the thanksgiving section, where he expresses gratitude to God for their "work of faith" (1:3) and how "in every place your faith toward God has gone forth" (1:8). These two earlier references suggest that "faith" here in 3:2 (and in the subsequent verses) refers not merely to the trustful response of the Thessalonian Christians to what God has done through Jesus Christ but to a whole range of Christian activities that result from their faith in God.

This new verse begins at an unfortunate spot, as the first part of 3:3 continues the clause begun in the preceding verse. The precise nature of its grammatical link to 3:2, however, remains unclear. The best explanation is to view the preposition εἰς before the two articular infinitives in 3:2 as serving double duty for the articular infinitive that opens 3:3, so that this third infinitive similarly expresses purpose or result:[31] "so that no one may be shaken by these afflictions" (τὸ μηδένα σαίνεσθαι ἐν ταῖς θλίψεσιν ταύταις, to mēdena sainesthai en tais thlipsesin tautais).

3:3a

There are two possible meanings for *sainesthai*, which occurs only here in the Bible. The verb originally referred to the wagging of a friendly dog's tail as it approaches someone, and this led to its figurative sense of "to flatter," whether in expression of genuine affection or as a deceptive means of winning over another person for one's own benefit or gain. Thus one possible sense of the verb is "to try to win favor by an ingratiating manner, *fawn upon, flatter*" (BDAG 910.1). According to this view, Paul sent Timothy to prevent the Thessalonian believers from being tricked or deceived by clever-speaking opponents of the Christian faith (so, e.g., Lightfoot 1904: 42; Frame 1912: 128; Heikel 1935: 316; Hendriksen 1955: 84; Morris 1991: 96; Baumert 1992; Richard 1995: 141–42).

The difficulty with this interpretation, however, is that the ancient translations (e.g., Latin *moveatur*) and the patristic commentators, apparently without exception, derived a different figurative sense in which the wagging action became an image of instability or wavering, and thus render *sainesthai* as "to be moved, shaken, unsettled" with respect to one's thinking or emotions (F. Lang, *TDNT* 7:54–55). Thus a second and more probable meaning of the verb is "to cause to be emotionally upset, *move, disturb, agitate*" (BDAG 910.2; so most modern translations and commentators). This latter sense

---

31. In 3:3a most exegetes see a statement of purpose or result, though their explanation for this interpretation differs from one to another. Some view τὸ μηδένα σαίνεσθαι as a substantive infinitive in which τὸ μή is the equivalent of a ἵνα μή clause (BDF §399.3; Malherbe 2000: 192). Others see the infinitive as being in apposition to the preceding infinitives (Milligan 1908: 38; also Findlay 1891). A few understand the preposition εἰς in the preceding verse as doing double duty (Lightfoot 1904: 41–42; Bruce 1982: 59). Less common are the claims that the infinitive serves as the direct object of the preceding infinitive παρακαλέσαι and thus as part of indirect discourse (i.e., "in order to appeal that no one be shaken"; Eadie 1877: 105; Ellicott 1880: 39) or that it comes after an unexpressed verb of hindering in keeping with Classical Greek (Frame 1912: 128).

not only better fits the context but also receives further support from two contemporary texts. In the first, Diogenes Laertius, after describing a crowd who hears about Pythagoras's journey to Hades, states: "The ones who were shaken [σαινόμενοι] by the things that were spoken wept" (*Lives* 8.41). The second text contains a discussion between Origen and Bishop Heraclides, whose orthodoxy had been questioned by some in the Christian community. At the end of this discussion, Origen states: "All the questions of faith which shook [ἔσηνεν] us have been examined" (Chadwick 1950).

The specific cause of Paul's concern that the Thessalonians might be shaken in their faith is finally stated: "by these afflictions" (*en tais thlipsesin tautais*). As with his earlier reference to "affliction" (1:6), here too Paul neither spells out the exact nature of this suffering nor whose suffering he has in view, since the Thessalonian believers already knew these things all too well. Some have used Paul's silence on these matters to argue that "afflictions" does not refer to the outward persecution of the Christians in Thessalonica because of their newfound faith but to inward anxieties typically experienced by converts to a new philosophical system or pagan religion with its differing worldview: "Paul refers to the alienation caused by the converts' adoption of a new value system which radically changed their social, cultic, and religious affiliations and loyalties" (Richard 1995: 149; so also Malherbe 1987: 46–52; 2000: 193). It would be wrong, however, to limit the *thlipsesin* referred to in 3:3 as inward anxieties (see Still 1999: 208–27). Among the twenty-four occurrences of the noun "affliction" in Paul's Letters, only two (2 Cor. 2:4; Phil. 1:17) possibly refer to the "inward experience of distress" (BDAG 457.2), and both texts might well speak of outward opposition instead of emotional distress. Furthermore, both within the Thessalonian Letters and without are several indications that the believers in Thessalonica encountered open hostility for their faith (1 Thess. 2:2, 14–15; 3:1–5; 2 Thess. 1:4–7; see also 2 Cor. 8:1–2; Acts 17:5–7, 13). Especially important is Paul's previous statement that the Thessalonians suffered at the hands of their fellow citizens (2:14). This external opposition likely involved severe social harassment and ostracism rather than physical death.

Who is experiencing this persecution? The antecedent of *tautais* is not clear, and this has allowed some to argue that the apostle is referring not to the afflictions endured by the Thessalonians but to his own suffering (Dobschütz 1909: 134–35; Holtz 1986: 127; Malherbe 2000: 193). According to this view, Paul worries that the Thessalonian Christians may be shaken in their faith once they discover that their spiritual father is being persecuted. This seems highly improbable, however, given the Thessalonians' knowledge that Paul has already suffered during his mission visit in their city and even before that in Philippi (2:2). Instead, the second-person personal pronouns in the preceding verse ("in order to strengthen *you* and comfort you concerning *your* faith") suggest that Paul is thinking primarily of the afflictions that the Thessalonians were enduring. This is supported by the corresponding part of the inclusio in verse 5, which also speaks of "*your* faith" and articulates Paul's fear that "the Tempter had tempted *you*." Yet the shift to the first-person plural in verses 3b–4 indicates that Paul's own suffering is not a distant thought (see also "our affliction" in 3:7).

Verses 3b–4 are no mere "digression" (Wanamaker 1990: 130; Green 2002: 164), "parenthesis" (D. Martin 1995: 103), or interruption (Fee 2009: 118) but provide an important reason *why* the Thessalonian believers do not need to be shaken by these afflictions. The double use of the conjunction "for" (γάρ, *gar*) to introduce each clause in this section and the repetition of the disclosure formula "you know" (οἴδατε, *oidate*) at its opening and close function to both delimit these verses and give emphasis to the importance of what is said (Johanson 1987: 104).

3:3b

The first explanatory clause reminds the readers that their afflictions, as difficult as they may be, are nevertheless a normal and expected part of God's will: "For you yourselves know that we are destined for this" (αὐτοὶ γὰρ οἴδατε ὅτι εἰς τοῦτο κείμεθα, *autoi gar oidate hoti eis touto keimetha*). As Paul has done throughout the letter so far (1:4, 5; 2:1, 2, 5, 11; see 2:9), here too he appeals to the knowledge that the Thessalonian believers themselves (*autoi oidate* is emphatic) already have. They know that their afflictions are hardly a rare or unanticipated product of fate but an expected feature of the life that has been "destined" (κεῖμαι with the preposition εἰς = "be appointed, set, destined" for something: BDAG 537) for them by God (the passive voice[32] implies an activity of God: the so-called divine passive). This belief that the Christian faith inevitably evokes opposition and suffering is a conviction common not only to Paul (e.g., Rom. 5:3; 8:17; 2 Cor. 4:7–12; 6:3–10; 11:23–33; Phil. 1:29; 2 Tim. 3:12) but also other NT writers (e.g., Matt. 5:11–12, 44; 10:17–23; 23:34; 24:9–10; Mark 8:34–35; John 16:33; Acts 9:16; 14:22; 1 Pet. 1:6; 3:13–17; Rev. 2:10). This widespread and consistent testimony of Scripture leads Best (1977: 135) to forward the maxim: "Normality is persecution." There is no justification here or anywhere else in Scripture for a health-and-wealth gospel in which believers are guaranteed a life free from difficulty and suffering.

The second explanatory clause does not introduce a new reason why the Thessalonians need not be shaken by their afflictions but clarifies the reason already forwarded in the first explanatory clause: "For indeed when we were with you, we kept telling you beforehand: 'We are destined to suffer affliction'" (καὶ γὰρ ὅτε πρὸς ὑμᾶς ἦμεν, προελέγομεν ὑμῖν ὅτι μέλλομεν θλίβεσθαι, *kai gar hote pros hymas ēmen, proelegomen hymin hoti mellomen thlibesthai*). The reason why the Thessalonian believers already know the truth of the first explanatory clause (v. 3b), that they are destined to suffer for their faith, is because this truth had often been taught (the imperfect tense of *proelegomen* stresses the repeated nature of this action) to them by Paul and his coworkers. That the apostle included this truth as part of his missionary preaching in

3:4

---

32. In 3:3b κεῖμαι serves as a quasi-passive of τίθημι (as also in Phil. 1:16; Luke 2:34) in place of the rarely used τέθειμαι.

Thessalonica and that he did so repeatedly reveals what a fundamental role suffering played in his life and thought.

Although virtually all translations and commentators view *hoti* as introducing indirect discourse, it could equally function to introduce direct speech. Tentative support for the latter option can be derived from (1) the use of the present rather than past tense for *mellomen* (Lightfoot 1904: 43; Johanson 1987: 105n505); (2) the parallel with 2 Thess. 3:10, where the virtually identical expression ("for indeed when we were with you": there is only a minor change in word order) does likely introduce a direct quote (Malherbe 2000: 194); and (3) the fact that direct speech would make more vivid and persuasive the use of the prophecy-fulfillment argument that Paul employs in this verse (see discussion below). Within this direct speech, the present tense of the infinitive *thlibesthai* after *mellomen* is significant, since this construction "denotes an action that necessarily follows a divine decree, *is destined*" (BDAG 628). Thus this direct statement does not merely express the future reality of Christian suffering ("We *are about to* suffer affliction"), but also implies that such suffering is part of God's divine plan ("We *are destined to* suffer affliction"), such that it reiterates well the truth highlighted in the preceding explanatory clause of 3:3b ("We are destined [*keimetha*] for this").

It is important for Paul to let his Thessalonian readers know that they are not suffering alone but that he and his fellow missionaries also must endure such affliction for their faith. The first-person plural in both *keimetha* and *mellomen* is almost certainly an inclusive "we" as the apostle expresses his solidarity with his suffering readers. The Thessalonians, therefore, share in the same persecution endured by not only the Christians in Judea (2:14) and the great heroes of the faith—the prophets as well as the Lord Jesus himself (2:15–16)—but also their spiritual father, Paul. This inclusive "we" serves as an important antidote to any accusation, actual or perceived, that the apostle's ongoing absence from Thessalonica stems from a selfish desire on his part to avoid the kind of suffering that his converts had to endure (Johanson 1987: 105).

The second explanatory clause of 3:4 closes with a simple declaration that at first glance may seem insignificant: "as indeed it has happened and you know" (καθὼς καὶ ἐγένετο καὶ οἴδατε, *kathōs kai egeneto kai oidate*). Yet this statement functions as part of the prophecy-fulfillment argument that Paul effectively employs. The truth of his words is evident in that his repeated prediction during his original ministry in Thessalonica—that both he and his converts would suffer affliction for their faith—has indeed become true (*kathōs kai egeneto*), as the readers themselves know from firsthand experience (*kai oidate*). Paul's persuasive strategy is similar to that of a concerned parent who tells the child after the fact: "I told you beforehand about this, and so you shouldn't be surprised that now it has come true!" In this way the prophecy-fulfillment argument serves the larger function of reestablishing the credibility of Paul and his message.

3:5

After the two explanatory clauses of verses 3b–4, which provide the reason why the Thessalonian believers should not be shaken by the afflictions that they are enduring, in verse 5 Paul returns to the thought of verses 1–2, which describes the sending of Timothy to strengthen the faith of these persecuted Christians. That Paul intends to create an inclusio between verses 1–2 and 5 is obvious because this latter verse repeats verbatim many of the key words belonging to the former verses, with the notable difference that the plural has now been replaced by the singular: "For this reason, because I could no longer contain it, I sent in order to learn about your faith" (διὰ τοῦτο κἀγὼ μηκέτι στέγων ἔπεμψα εἰς τὸ γνῶναι τὴν πίστιν ὑμῶν, *dia touto kagō mēketi stegōn epempsa eis to gnōnai tēn pistin hymōn*).

Since this verse repeats almost exactly the words of 3:1–2, it naturally adds very little in terms of new content or information. Yet this repetition has the rhetorical effect of emphasizing the depth of Paul's concern for the Thessalonian converts. Even though he has not been able to return and strengthen them personally in the afflictions that they are enduring, he is still very much concerned about them, as evident in his now twice-stated role of sending Timothy to them. The switch from the plural to the singular similarly stresses the concern that Paul personally has for his readers and thus provides a further defense for any lingering uncertainty over the reason for his ongoing absence from them.

The expression *dia touto* (for this reason) in Paul's Letters normally refers back to previous material (anaphoric function).[33] Here too it similarly refers to the immediately preceding material of 3:1–5, which details the afflictions endured by the Thessalonian believers as the reason why Timothy was sent. Yet the parallel between *dia touto* and the conjunction *dio* in 3:1 (which has in view preceding material: see comment on 3:1) suggests that *dia touto* also looks back even further, to the material of 2:17–20, which expresses Paul's deep affection for the Thessalonians despite his absence from them. Thus throughout this passage there continues to be an intimate link between Paul's twin concerns: his concern in 3:1–5 over the persecution endured by the Thessalonians (primary antecedent of *dia touto*) and his concern in 2:17–20 over his absence from these persecuted believers (secondary antecedent of *dia touto*).

The form *kagō* (a combination of the conjunction *kai* and the first-person personal pronoun *egō*) can be interpreted in two different ways. If the "we" used throughout this letter is a literal or real plural, then *kagō* ought to be translated as "I for my part" and functions as a way by which Paul distinguishes his role in the sending of Timothy from the two other cosenders of the letter, Silas and Timothy. The "we," however, is more likely a literary or epistolary plural (see comment on 3:1), and so *kagō* is better rendered

---

33. See comment on 2:13 and its accompanying footnote, which lists the twenty-two occurrences of διὰ τοῦτο in Paul's Letters. Note especially the occurrence of this expression a few verses later in 3:7, where it clearly looks back to the just-mentioned return and report of Timothy as the reason why Paul and his fellow missionaries "were comforted."

simply as "I" (BDAG 487.3.c), and the *kai* in this form serves to emphasize the personal pronoun. A similar shift from the plural to the singular in order to emphasize Paul's role occurs earlier in this passage in 2:18 and again at the end of the letter in 5:27.

The repeated presence of the participle *stegōn* (also 3:1) and the unique image or metaphor that this verb evokes (see comment on 3:1) allows Paul once again to express the idea that he was so full of love and concern for the Thessalonians that he was no longer able to prevent his strong emotions for them from leaking out. As a consequence of this irrepressible emotion, the apostle sent Timothy,[34] whose stated purpose for this trip shifts slightly from an equipping mission in 3:2 that benefits the Thessalonian believers ("in order to strengthen you and comfort you concerning your faith") to a fact-finding mission in verse 5 that benefits Paul ("in order to learn about your faith"). Although one ought not to read too much into this shift, it does have the consequence of conveying to the readers the degree of personal concern that Paul obviously has for them. That he is emotionally invested in their well-being can be seen in that he sent Timothy to find out about their "faith." As with its previous occurrence in verse 2, here too *pistin* refers to a broad range of Christian activities that result from the readers' faith in God. This term "faith," which plays a key role in the second unit of 3:1–5, occurs three more times in the third and concluding unit of 3:6–10.

The numerous parallels between verses 5 and 1–2 now come to an end as Paul's primary concern in the second unit (3:1–5) over the persecution endured by the Thessalonians reaches a certain climax in a closing expression of apprehension or fear (BDF §370): "fearing that in some way[35] the Tempter had tempted you and that our work might have been in vain" (μή πως ἐπείρασεν ὑμᾶς ὁ πειράζων καὶ εἰς κενὸν γένηται ὁ κόπος ἡμῶν, *mē pōs epeirasen hymas ho peirazein kai eis kenon genētai ho kopos hēmōn*).[36] The two verbal clauses within this expression of fear display an important shift in mood. The first

---

34. In 3:5b the absence of an explicit direct object after ἔπεμψα has led some to postulate that the apostle refers to sending someone in addition to Timothy: after the three missionaries first sent Timothy, Paul was still so anxious about the welfare of the Thessalonians that he also (κἀγώ = I also; 3:5a) dispatched a second envoy (so J. C. K. von Hofmann 1869, cited by Milligan 1908: 39). The close parallel between 3:5 and 3:1–2, however, clearly supports Timothy and no additional person as the implied object of Paul's activity of sending. This is confirmed by 3:6, which speaks only of Timothy's return.

35. In 3:5c the enclitic particle πῶς, a marker of undesignated means or manner, often occurs with μή after verbs of apprehension with the sense "that perhaps, lest somehow" (BDAG 901.2.b).

36. This last clause in 3:5 is not dependent on the preceding main verb ἔπεμψα (so Wanamaker 1990: 132) but the implied verb φοβέομαι (I am afraid). The grammatical construction of φοβέομαι followed by μή (not the common marker of negation ["no"] but a conjunction approaching the sense of ὅτι in introducing indirect discourse ["that"]: see BDAG 646.2) is common in Classical Greek. When this construction appears in Paul's Letters, it occurs a few times with the main verb of fear explicitly written (2 Cor. 11:3; 12:20; Gal. 4:11), but more often with the main verb of fear implied, as is the case here (see also, e.g., Gal. 2:2; 6:1). The expression of fear in Paul's Letters is also sometimes introduced with a warning verb such as βλέπετε ("Watch out lest . . ."; e.g., Col. 2:8) or ὁράτε ("Look out lest . . ."; e.g., 1 Thess. 5:15).

verb, *epeirasen*, occurs in the indicative (instead of the expected subjunctive) mood, reflecting Paul's certainty that the Tempter had indeed been at work in the Thessalonian church. By contrast, the second verb, *genētai*, occurs in the subjunctive mood, reflecting Paul's uncertainty about the outcome of that work of temptation.

The evil, spiritual being whom Paul identified earlier, in 2:18, as "Satan" is now named as "the Tempter" (*ho peirazōn*) in agreement with his malevolent work of tempting[37] the believers in Thessalonica. The apostle employs this title in no other place (elsewhere in Scripture only in Matt. 4:3), though he does refer to Satan's work of tempting believers to yield to their sexual desires (1 Cor. 7:5). As Paul interpreted the historical events that prevented him from returning to Thessalonica theologically as the work of Satan (1 Thess. 2:18), he similarly views the afflictions that the readers have endured at the hands of their fellow citizens as ultimately being the work of this same evil, supernatural figure. In this way, the believers in Thessalonica are encouraged to view their suffering as a small manifestation of the larger conflict that is taking place between the kingdom of God and the kingdom of evil. Paul's theological interpretation of their suffering also serves to strengthen the church's sense of self-identity: that the Tempter has targeted them means that they are indeed the people of God, in contrast to their neighbors, whose persecuting activity marks them as agents of Satan.

Paul shifts from the certainty (indicative mood) of Satan's temptations to the uncertainty (subjunctive mood) of how the Thessalonians will respond to those temptations, expressing his concern that his missionary labors among them, done at great personal cost (2:2), might have been "in vain." Whereas the apostle had earlier used the adjective *kenos* (empty) in a predicate construction with the metaphorical sense of being "empty of purpose, insincere" (2:1; see also 1 Cor. 15:14 [2x]; Eph. 5:6; Col. 2:8), here he employs it in a prepositional phrase (*eis kenon*)—a common construction in the LXX and Hellenistic texts but occurring only in Paul in the NT—with the alternative figurative meaning of being "empty of result, in vain" (see 2 Cor. 6:1; Gal. 2:2; Phil. 2:16 [2x]; also see 1 Cor. 15:10, 58).

Here Paul's language raises a difficult theological problem. It may appear that the apostle believed that the satanic temptations might actually result in the Thessalonians' loss of faith. But how would this relate to his language elsewhere in the letter concerning their "election" (1 Thess. 1:4; 5:9) and "call" (2:12; 4:7; 5:24) by God? This issue of perseverance and falling away is a complicated one, with no easy solution. Some argue that the warnings in Paul's Letters against apostasy are the means used by God to preserve his elect from succumbing to this danger and that the language of election and

---

37. The verb πειράζω occurs seven times in Paul's Letters, referring either to the attempt to discover the true nature or character of someone by testing (1 Cor. 10:9, 13; 2 Cor. 13:5; the compound form ἐκπειράζω also occurs in 1 Cor. 10:9) or, as here in 3:5, to entice someone to improper behavior (1 Cor. 7:5; Gal. 6:1; 1 Thess. 3:5 [2x]: see BDAG 792–93).

calling assures believers of their final salvation, even in the face of fearsome afflictions (Gundry Volf 1990). Others claim that Paul uses the language of election and calling to encourage persecuted believers but that this in no way guarantees their ultimate destiny (Marshall 1990: 259–76). Within this theological debate, however, one ought not to lose sight of the rhetorical effect of Paul's statement in 3:5b. The apostle's words create a sense of obligation for the Thessalonian believers: they must withstand these afflictions not only for their own sake but also for that of Paul so that his hard mission-founding work will not ultimately be "in vain."

3. Both Concerns Answered: Timothy's "Good News" about the Thessalonians (3:6–10)

The two concerns of 2:17–20 and 3:1–5 are skillfully combined and answered in 3:6–10, which deals with the return and report of Timothy. The first concern of Paul to reassure the Thessalonians of his ongoing *love* for them, despite his inability to visit them a second time in person, is answered in Timothy's report about "your love, and that you have a good remembrance of us always, longing to see us just as we also long to see you" (v. 6b). In other words, the Thessalonian church continues to have a loving relationship with the apostle, just as he does with them. The second concern of Paul, to strengthen the *faith* of the Thessalonians—a faith that is arousing strong opposition from their fellow citizens—is answered in Timothy's report about "your faith" (v. 6a). In other words, the Thessalonian church has not abandoned its faith but continues to give evidence of it not only to Timothy but also to believers in Macedonia, Achaia, and "in every place" (1:8). As a result, Paul was comforted in his own persecution "through this faith of yours" (3:7). But as comforting as the report of Timothy is to Paul, it apparently does not result in the complete removal of the apostle's original worries. For the final words of 3:6–10 combine these two concerns yet again, as Paul prays that he might "see you face-to-face [first concern of Paul's absence] and complete the things that are lacking in your faith [second concern of Thessalonians' persecution]."

3:6 The third unit of 3:6–10 opens with a lengthy, double genitive-absolute construction (BDF §423) that provides the reason for the comfort spoken of in the main verb of verse 7. The first genitive-absolute clause refers to the *return* of Timothy: "But Timothy has now come to us from you" (ἄρτι δὲ ἐλθόντες Τιμοθέου πρὸς ἡμᾶς ἀφ᾽ ὑμῶν, *arti de elthontes Timotheou pros hēmas aph᾽ hymōn*). The adversative particle "but" (*de*), along with the vocative "brothers" in the following verse,[38] serves to signal a transition in Paul's argument. That this transition involves a chronological shift from the apostle's *past* fear in 3:1–5 to his *present* thankfulness in 3:6–10 is indicated by the temporal

---

38. As noted above, the vocative is pushed back from its expected position at the beginning of the third unit in 3:6 to the following verse (7) by the lengthy genitive-absolute construction that opens this section.

adverb "now" (*arti*) located in the emphatic position at the head of the verse.[39] This return of Timothy probably corresponds to the return of both Timothy and Silas from Macedonia (Acts 18:5) to Paul, who has recently left Athens and is now ministering in Corinth. This likelihood in turn suggests that the plural "to us" (*pros hēmas*) does not refer to both Paul and Silas but either to Paul alone (a literary plural) or to the apostle along with the Christian community in Corinth. The fuller phrase "to us from you" (*pros hēmas aph' hymōn*) is excessive: Paul could have more briefly stated, "But Timothy has now returned." Actually, throughout this closing third unit, there is a plethora of personal pronouns: the first-person plural ("we, us, to us, our") occurs seven times, while the second-person plural ("you, to you, your") occurs ten times. This serves to highlight the depth of Paul's love and affection for his Thessalonian readers (see Best 1977: 139; Ellingworth and Nida 1975: 58; Furnish 2007: 79).

The second and longer genitive-absolute clause refers to the *report* of Timothy: "and has brought good news about your faith and love and that you have a good remembrance of us always, longing to see us just as we also long to see you" (καὶ εὐαγγελισαμένου ἡμῖν τὴν πίστιν καὶ τὴν ἀγάπην ὑμῶν καὶ ὅτι ἔχετε μνείαν ἡμῶν ἀγαθὴν πάντοτε, ἐπιποθοῦντες ἡμᾶς ἰδεῖν καθάπερ καὶ ἡμεῖς ὑμᾶς, *kai euangelisamenou hēmin tēn pistin kai tēn agapēn hymōn kai hoti echete mneian hēmōn agathēn pantote, epipothountes hēmas idein kathaper kai hēmeis hymas*). The choice of the verb *euangelizō* is striking, since in its twenty remaining occurrences in Paul, it is a technical term that always refers to the specific act of preaching the gospel (Rom. 1:15; 10:15; 15:20; 1 Cor. 1:17; 9:16 [2x], 18; 15:1, 2; 2 Cor. 10:16; 11:7; Gal. 1:8 [2x], 9, 11, 16, 23; 4:13; Eph. 2:17; 3:8). This has led some to believe that the apostle depicts the good report of Timothy as a kind of preaching of the gospel itself (so, e.g., Masson 1957: 41; Best 1977: 139–40; Marshall 1983: 94). The verb, however, occurs elsewhere in the NT with the more general meaning of bringing good news (Luke 1:19; 2:10; Rev. 14:6); thus, in light of the larger context of 3:6, most commentators view its occurrence here as the only nontechnical use in Paul. But even if *euangelizō* does have the more general sense of bringing good news, the choice of this verb over other more common verbs for speech (λέγω, λαλέω, ἀναγγέλλω) clearly emphasizes how thankful Paul was to receive the positive report of Timothy.

---

39. The adverb ἄρτι can refer either to the immediate present ("at once, immediately, just now") or more generally to the present ("now, at the present time": see BDAG 136). Most translations and commentators choose the former option and thus claim that Paul wrote to the Thessalonians immediately upon the return of Timothy (hence the translation: "But Timothy has *just now* come"). Elsewhere in Paul's Letters, however, this adverb is used only in the latter sense of referring in general to the present (1 Cor. 4:11, 13; 8:7; 13:12 [2x]; 15:6; 16:7; Gal. 1:9, 10; 4:20; 2 Thess. 2:7). That this latter sense is intended also here in 3:6a is further suggested by the presence of the general temporal adverb νῦν (now) a couple verses later, in 3:8. Therefore, although Paul no doubt wrote to the Thessalonians soon after the coming of Timothy, it does not appear that he is here emphasizing that he sent his letter immediately upon the return of his envoy.

The good news that Timothy brought about the Thessalonians concerned two matters: "your faith and love" (*tēn pistin kai tēn agapēn hymōn*).[40] These two terms occur elsewhere in Paul's Letters as a word pair (Eph. 1:15; Col. 1:4; Philem. 5), suggesting that it might well be wrong to distinguish too sharply between them (see Gal. 5:6, where the apostle speaks of "faith working through love"). Nevertheless, in this specific context of the dual concerns of Paul's absence (2:17–20) and of the Thessalonians' persecution (3:1–5), there is justification for distinguishing between these two terms. The first word, "faith," has in view the two earlier references to Paul's purpose in sending Timothy to visit the persecuted church: "to comfort you concerning your faith" (3:2), and "to learn about your faith" (3:5). Thus one aspect of the good news that Timothy "preached" or announced to Paul is that the Thessalonians' newfound faith has not been shaken by the afflictions that they endure from their fellow citizens.

Just as the first word, "faith," answers the earlier worry of 3:1–5, the second word, "love," has in view the previous concern of 2:17–20, that Paul's ongoing absence from Thessalonica might cause some in the church to question the genuineness of his feelings for them. The apostle does not provide any explicit object for the Thessalonians' love, leaving the door open for most commentators to conclude that the apostle is referring generally to the love that these believers have for either other Christians or all people (see 3:12; 4:9–10a; 5:15). In this context, however, the word "love" almost certainly refers specifically to the Thessalonians' continued affection for Paul, despite his inability to return to them thus far for a second visit.[41]

If the Thessalonians' fondness for the apostle is only hinted at in the single word "love," it is spelled out in the following *hoti* clause: "and that you have a good remembrance of us always." The addition of the adjective "good" (*agathēn*) gives the expression "you have a remembrance" (*echete mneian*) a greater warmth than Paul's similar statement in the opening thanksgiving that he "makes remembrance" (*mneian poioumenoi*) of them in his prayers (1:2). The adverb "always" (*pantote*)[42] stresses the ongoing nature of their affection and so also adds to the warmth of this expression. The intensity of the Thessalonians' feeling for Paul is even further stressed in the following participial phrase: "longing to see us" (*epipothountes hēmas idein*). It is not clear whether the prefix *epi* adds a degree of emphasis to the basic verb, since

40. On the claimed significance of no reference to "hope" (in 3:6) as the third member of the triad (1:3; 5:8), see comment on 3:10b.

41. Fee (2009: 123n64) states: "It is of some interest that so few see the word ["love"] as related to the immediate situation—as though Paul were suddenly 'spiritualizing' in some way. Since 'faith' in this phrase is not 'in general' but is especially case specific, why, one wonders, does 'love' suddenly lose that same specificity?"

42. Although Pauline usage allows for the possibility that the adverb "always" modifies the following participle ("always longing"), in this context (3:6b) it more likely goes with the preceding verb ("you have . . . always"), as often elsewhere (see Rom. 1:10; 1 Cor. 1:4; 15:58; Phil. 1:4; 4:4; 1 Thess. 1:2; Philem. 4).

Hellenistic writers display a common love for compound forms, and neither Paul nor any other NT author employs the simple form *potheō* (Spicq 1994: 2.58–60). What cannot be disputed, however, is that Paul uses the compound verb *epipotheō* to express no mere wish but an intense longing, whether to see loved ones (Rom. 1:11; Phil. 2:26; 2 Tim. 1:4; see *epipothia* in Rom. 15:23) or to put on the glorious resurrected body (2 Cor. 5:2). The use of this verb in 3:6, therefore, powerfully expresses the deep and ongoing (note the present tense) desire of the Thessalonians to see their spiritual father again. That this desire is a mutual one is made clear by the elliptical phrase "just as we also [long to see] you" (*kathaper kai hēmeis hymas*), a longing already expressed at the opening of this passage (2:17).

Some commentators fail to see any apologetic concern at work in this verse. Malherbe (2000: 201), for example, states: "The interpretation that sees in the phrase [of 3:6] Paul's relief that the Thessalonians still held him in high regard despite a charge by opponents that he had deserted the Thessalonians [Frame 1912: 132; Best 1977: 140] . . . is not on target." Yet the striking language employed by the apostle—particularly the excessive phrase "to us from you," and the choice of the verbs *euangelisamenou* and *epipothountes*—suggests that more is at work in this verse than mere conventional language of friendship between absent comrades. Even Wanamaker (1990: 134), who strongly rejects any defensive function at work in the earlier material of 2:1–16, states of 3:6: "This perhaps implies that he [Paul] was concerned about how the Thessalonians viewed him after his departure" and "This looks like an apology for his failure to return."

The lengthy genitive-absolute construction concerning Timothy's return and report finally comes to a close, and we reach the first and only main clause of the concluding unit of 3:6–10: "For this reason, we were comforted, brothers" (διὰ τοῦτο παρεκλήθημεν, ἀδελφοί, *dia touto pareklēthēmen, adelphoi*). Since the preceding participial clauses in verse 6 are causal, giving the reason for Paul's comfort, the presence of the causal phrase "for this reason" (*dia touto*) is redundant and interferes with the syntactical flow of the sentence. But even though the addition of this causal phrase results in an anacoluthon, it does draw the readers' attention to the antecedent of *touto*: Timothy's good report. Just as Timothy had been sent by Paul "to comfort" (*parakalesai*) the Thessalonian church concerning their faith (3:2), now conversely the apostle and those with him "were comforted" (*pareklēthēmen*) by Timothy's good report about the Thessalonians and their faith (see comment on 3:2 for the meaning of *parakaleō*). It is common for the apostle not only to comfort his converts but also to speak of how they in turn have comforted him (Rom. 1:12; 2 Cor. 7:4, 13; Philem. 7; see 2 Cor. 7:7). Paul continues to reveal his affection for the Thessalonians by identifying them once again (also 1:4; 2:1, 9, 14, 17) with the familial language of "brothers."

The main clause "we were comforted" is modified by three prepositional phrases: "because of you in all our distress and affliction through this faith

3:7

of yours" (ἐφ' ὑμῖν ἐπὶ πάσῃ τῇ ἀνάγκῃ καὶ θλίψει ἡμῶν διὰ τῆς ὑμῶν πίστεως, *eph' hymin epi pasē tē anankē kai thlipsei hēmōn dia tēs hymōn pisteōs*). The first prepositional phrase, *eph' hymin*, likely expresses cause ("because of you"), since *epi* after verbs of emotion "most frequently denotes the basis for a state of being, action, or result" (BDF §235.2; see also BDAG 365.6.c). This causal sense is rejected by some, however, on the grounds that this first prepositional phrase would be tautological with the third prepositional phrase, which also seemingly gives the cause for Paul's comfort. Consequently, they translate *eph' hymin* as "about you" or "with regard to you," thereby making the Thessalonians the object of Paul's comfort rather than its cause (so, e.g., NIV, NRSV, NASB, NAB, NKJV; Bruce 1982: 67; Richard 1995: 154). But if this indeed were Paul's intention, he could have easily expressed this idea by employing the preposition περί or ὑπέρ (as in 3:2). Also, the third prepositional phrase expresses the means through which (*dia* with the genitive) the Thessalonians comforted Paul and thus does not in a redundant manner repeat the first prepositional phrase (*epi* with the dative). Furthermore, the causal sense is rhetorically effective: by mentioning the Thessalonians first as the basis of his comfort, "Paul once more strengthens the personal bond with them" (Malherbe 2000: 202).

The second prepositional phrase, *epi pasē tē anankē kai thlipsei hēmōn*, is temporal ("in, at the time of, during": BDF §235.5; BDAG 367.18.b): Paul was comforted "in all our distress and affliction." The nouns *anankē* and *thlipsis* occur as a word pair elsewhere in 2 Cor. 6:4 and in the LXX (Job 15:24; Pss. 24:17; 118:143 [25:17; 119:143 Eng.]; Zeph. 1:15), suggesting that it would be wrong to distinguish these two terms. This is supported by the presence of only one definite article, which links *anankē* and *thlipsis* together as a collective whole.[43] Some claim, on the basis of *anankē* and *thlipsis* in 1 Cor. 7:26, 28 and the word pair in Zeph. 1:15, that these two terms have a special eschatological focus as denoting the persecutions and sufferings connected with the last days (so, e.g., Best 1977: 141; Wanamaker 1990: 135). But while Paul's worldview is one in which he counts all his missionary activities as taking place in the final days, there is nothing to suggest that in 3:7 he gives "all our distress and affliction" a special eschatological focus. Instead, the two terms are a general description of the hardships that Paul endures for his Christian faith.

Once again there is the question as to the specific nature of the "distress and affliction" experienced by Paul. Although some limit the apostle's suffering to internal emotional anguish (Malherbe 2000: 202: "Paul's feeling of desolation caused by his separation from the Thessalonians"), there are compelling reasons to believe that he has in mind the kind of external opposition encountered throughout his apostolic ministry (see the comment on *thlipsis* in 1:6 and 3:3a). More specifically, Paul is referring to the difficulties that he

---

43. Thus there is no justification for the claim of some older commentators that in 3:7 *anankē* refers to "physical privation" and *thlipsis* to "sufferings inflicted from without" (Lightfoot 1904: 45; see also Frame 1912: 133).

and his fellow missionaries have experienced since their forced departure from Thessalonica: not only the past problems in Berea (Acts 17:10–14) and the difficulty of ministering "alone" in the challenging environment of Athens (1 Thess. 3:1; Acts 17:15–34), but especially the current opposition he faces in Corinth (Acts 18:1–17). Paul himself later testifies to the Corinthians that such afflictions were a constant companion in his life (2 Cor. 4:8–12; 6:4–5; 11:23–28).

Paul's reference to his own suffering may appear somewhat out of place in a discussion where he is primarily concerned with the afflictions endured by the Thessalonians. Yet this reference confirms Paul's previous point that the Thessalonian church does not suffer alone; instead, he shares with them such affliction (recall the inclusive "we" of *keimetha* in 3:3b and *mellomen* in 3:4). In this way, the apostle strengthens the bond that exists between him and the church. This reference to his own suffering also serves to reestablish the credibility of Paul and his message, since the apostle's current affliction is another fulfillment of his repeated prophecy that believers are destined to suffer for their faith (3:4).

The third prepositional phrase, *dia tēs hymōn pisteōs*, provides the means by which the Thessalonians have comforted Paul during his time of affliction: "through this faith of yours." The word order in Greek reflects an emphasis that is lost in most translations. Whereas the possessive pronoun *hymōn* (of you, your) elsewhere in the letter always follows the noun "faith" (1:8; 3:2, 5, 6, 10), here it is in the attributive position, immediately before the noun, a position of emphasis (MHT 3:190): "through *your* faith" or, even better, "through this faith of yours." Similar to the first prepositional phrase ("because of you"), here too the Thessalonian believers are identified in the emphatic pronoun ("of yours") as the cause of Paul being comforted. Different from that earlier phrase, however, is the reference to the "faith" of the Thessalonians, which identifies the specific means by which this church comforted the apostle.

3:8   Paul further explains the comfort that the Thessalonian believers have been to him: "For now we live, if you continue to stand firm in the Lord" (ὅτι νῦν ζῶμεν ἐάν ὑμεῖς στήκετε ἐν κυρίῳ, *hoti nun zōmen ean hymeis stēkete en kyriō*). The conjunction *hoti* makes this verse subordinate to the preceding main clause "We were comforted," but the causal translation "because" does not fit the context, where Paul does not so much provide an additional reason why the Thessalonians have been a comfort to him as explain how they have comforted him (see also Wanamaker 1990: 136). The subordination with the causal *hoti* here is "so loose that the translation 'for' recommends itself" (BDAG 732.4.b; see also BDF §456.1).

The temporal adverb *nun* (now) reinforces the earlier temporal adverb *arti* (now) in 3:6, which marks the chronological shift from Paul's *past* fear in 3:1–5 to his *present* thankfulness in 3:6–10. Before the return and report of Timothy, the apostle's concern for his beloved converts in Thessalonica was so great that he was, in a certain sense, dying. But now the "good news" from the returning

Timothy means for Paul and those with him that "we live" (*zōmen*). This verb should be interpreted not theologically as a reference to eternal life (so some church fathers: see Rigaux 1956: 480) but metaphorically as the "removal of anxiety" (BDAG 425.1.γ). Some translations add the adverb "really" (e.g., NIV: "For now we really live") to highlight the fact that the issue is about quality of life: Paul is able to enjoy life fully once again because he now knows about the Thessalonians' continued love for him and their steadfast faith even amid persecution.

It is preferable, however, not to embellish Paul's words but leave them in their current form so that they are less a statement about quality of life than hyperbole (D. Martin 1995: 107). In ancient letters it was common to speak in hyperbolic language about separation from friends as well as the willingness of friends to live and die together. For example, one letter writer implores: "I beg you to send for me; else I die because I do not see you daily" (P.Giess. 17; see other parallels cited by Malherbe 2000: 202). A closer parallel to Paul's words in 3:7–8 is found in 2 Cor. 7:3–7, where in the context of speaking about the "affliction" (*thlipsis*: vv. 4–5) that he had to endure in Macedonia and the "comfort" (*parakaleō*: vv. 4, 6 [2x], 7 [2x]) that he received at the return and report of Titus, Paul says: "You are in our hearts, to die together and to live together" (v. 3 NRSV). The apostle's claim to the Thessalonians that "now we live," therefore, ought to be interpreted as a hyperbolic expression that powerfully conveys his deep love for the believers in that city.

Yet this strong statement of affection comes with a condition: "if you continue to stand firm in the Lord" (1 Thess. 3:8b). Instead of the expected subjunctive with the conditional conjunction *ean*, the indicative form *stēkete* is found. Although this construction appears with increasing frequency in the post-NT period, as εἰ and ἐάν are beginning to be confused (MHT 3:115–16), it occurs nowhere in Paul's Letters.[44] In the indicative form, some exegetes see Paul's confidence that the Thessalonians are actually fulfilling the condition and so translate this clause as "*since* you are standing firm in the Lord" or "if, *as indeed you do*, you stand firm in the Lord" (so, e.g., Milligan 1908: 41; Best 1977: 143; Ellingworth and Nida 1975: 61–62; Morris 1991: 103n26; Fee 2009: 125). The consistency of Paul's practice elsewhere, however, suggests that the use of *ean* with the indicative was not a careless slip on the apostle's part but a deliberate attempt to give the conditional clause a hypothetical and thus hortatory quality (so, e.g., Dobschütz 1909: 143; Rigaux 1956: 481; W. Grundmann, *TDNT* 7:636; Wanamaker 1990: 136). Although Timothy's report about the Thessalonians' ability to not be shaken by their afflictions was positive enough to warrant Paul's use of the indicative form *stēkete*, his concern for them remains great enough to substitute the conditional conjunction *ean* for the expected *ei*, thereby implicitly exhorting the church to

---

44. The apparent use of ἐάν with the imperfect of εἰμί in 1 Cor. 7:36 and 14:28 is "probably an illusion, since these forms are intended as [present] subjective" (MHT 3:116; so also BDF §372.1.a). The construction ἐὰν ἔχω in 1 Cor. 13:2 is better read as a subjunctive than an indicative.

continue to stand fast. This interpretation is supported by the final words of this passage (v. 10: "to complete the things that are lacking in your faith"), which also hint of Paul's ongoing concern for his readers.

The implicit appeal that "you (continue to)[45] stand firm" (*stēkete*) is chiefly a Pauline term in the NT (seven of its nine occurrences).[46] Whereas other biblical writers use this verb with its literal sense of being in a standing position (Mark 3:31; 11:25; see also John 1:26 v.l.; Rev. 12:4 v.l.), Paul always has the figurative meaning of being firmly committed in conviction or belief: "stand firm, be steadfast" (Rom. 14:4; 1 Cor. 16:13; Gal. 5:1; Phil. 1:27; 4:1; 1 Thess. 3:8; 2 Thess. 2:15). This verb clearly looks back to the apostle's earlier concern that the Thessalonians "not be shaken by these afflictions" (3:3a) and serves as a fitting antidote to that fear. Elsewhere Paul exhorts his readers to "stand firm in the faith" (1 Cor. 16:13), "stand firm in one spirit" (Phil. 1:27), or simply "stand firm" (Gal. 5:1; 2 Thess. 2:15). Here, as in Phil. 4:1, he directs the Thessalonian believers to "stand firm *in the Lord*" (*en kyriō*)—a phrase that, similar to the more common "in Christ," refers to the relationship believers have with the Lord Jesus Christ. The key to the Thessalonians' ability to stand firm in their faith even in the midst of affliction is to rely not on their own native gifts and strength but rather in the one whose power is so great that he is able to deliver them from the wrath to come (1:10).

The concluding unit of 3:6–10 ends with a lengthy and grammatically complicated sentence (vv. 9–10), which is composed of four parts: (1) an inferential clause in the form of a rhetorical question (v. 9a); (2) a relative clause (v. 9b); (3) a participial clause with only a loose relationship to the preceding relative clause (v. 10a); and (4) a double articular-infinitive clause (v. 10b).

3:9

The first part (v. 9a) expresses Paul's deep thanksgiving to God because of the joy that results from the good report about the Thessalonians: "What thanksgiving, then, can we pay back to God concerning you because of all the joy[?]" (τίνα γὰρ εὐχαριστίαν δυνάμεθα τῷ θεῷ ἀνταποδοῦναι περὶ ὑμῶν ἐπὶ πάσῃ τῇ χαρᾷ, *tina gar eucharistian dynametha tō theō antapodounai peri hymōn epi pasē tē chara*). The conjunction *gar* often occurs in questions with self-evident answers, where the English idiom best leaves it untranslated and adds "then" (BDAG 189.1.f; BDF §452.1). The rhetorical question asked here concerns the reciprocity (the double preposition *anti* + *apo* in the rare verb *antipodidōmi* [elsewhere in Paul only in 2 Thess. 1:6 and his OT quotes in Rom. 11:35; 12:19] emphasizes the notion of a complete return of that which is owed) of thanksgiving due to God, a sentiment similar to that of the psalmist: "What shall I pay back to the LORD for all his bounty to me?" (Ps. 116:12 [115:3 LXX]). That God and not the Thessalonian church is the recipient of

---

45. The addition of the words "continue to" in 3:8 reflects the reality that the Thessalonians thus far have been standing firm in their faith.

46. The verb στήκω is a new word that first appears in the NT as a late formation from ἕστηκα (the perfect of ἵστημι), due to the popular dislike in the postclassical period for verbs ending in -μι (BDAG 944; BDF §73; W. Grundmann, *TDNT* 7:636–38).

this thanksgiving is important and entirely in keeping with Paul's theology, where the praiseworthy conduct of his readers is always due to the prior work of God in their lives.

The subject matter of the thanksgiving owed to God is "concerning you" (*peri hymōn*), a general reference to the preceding good news about the Thessalonians' steadfast faith in the midst of affliction and their ongoing love for the apostle. The specific reason for this thanksgiving, however, is not the Thessalonians themselves but the joy that they have become to the apostle: "because of all the joy" (*epi pasē tē chara*). The causal force of this prepositional phrase is questioned by some (e.g., Best 1977: 144) who view it as a deliberate parallel and contrast to the prepositional phrase "in all our distress and affliction" (*epi pasē tē anankē kai thlipsei hēmōn*) in 3:7, which does not express cause but time. Yet exactly the same grammatical construction of a verb of thanksgiving followed by *peri* with the genitive and *epi* with the dative occurs in 1 Cor. 1:4, where it is clear that the first preposition provides the content of thanksgiving while the second gives the reason for thanksgiving (Richard 1995: 163). Further support lies in the causal constructions that occur both before (1 Thess. 3:7: *eph' hymin*) and after (v. 9b: *di' hymas*) this prepositional phrase. By specifying joy rather than the Thessalonians themselves as the cause of his thanksgiving, Paul recalls his similar identification of the believers in Thessalonica earlier in the passage (2:19–20: "For who is our . . . joy? . . . For you are our . . . joy").

The self-evident answer to the rhetorical question that opens verses 9–10, therefore, is that any thanksgiving Paul could offer to God for the joy that he [God] has caused the Thessalonians to be to the apostle would be woefully inadequate. Words cannot adequately express the deep thanksgiving that Paul feels toward God for the fact that the two concerns of 2:17–20 and 3:1–5 have been replaced with "all the joy" because the Thessalonians both continue their love for him despite his absence and remain steadfast in their faith despite enduring affliction.

The second part (v. 9b) of the lengthy construction of 3:9–10 consists of a relative clause that emphasizes further[47] the joy for which Paul is thankful: "with which we rejoice because of you before our God" (ᾗ χαίρομεν δι' ὑμᾶς ἔμπροσθεν τοῦ θεοῦ ἡμῶν, *hē chairomen di' hymas emprosthen tou theou hēmōn*). The relative pronoun *hē* is a cognate dative (BDF §198.6; MHT 2:419): a cognate word in the dative that functions to strengthen the verb, analogous to the use of the infinitive absolute in Hebrew (see Isa. 66:10 LXX; John 3:29).[48] Thus, although the fuller phrase "the joy with which we rejoice" is a tautology, it expresses in an emphatic way the intense joy that Paul has experienced "because of you" (*di' hymas*). This prepositional phrase identifies the Thessalonians

---

47. The note of joy that Paul expresses in 3:9 is already emphasized by the adjective πάσῃ: "*all* joy."

48. In 3:9, BDAG 1074.1 identifies the dative case ᾗ as due to attraction to its antecedent χαρᾷ, replacing the expected accusative form ἥν, which would function as a cognate accusative (see Matt. 2:10; also Isa. 35:2; Jon. 4:6).

yet again (see *eph' hymin* in v. 7) as the cause of the apostle's comfort and joy, and it also continues the excessive repetition of the personal pronoun "you" (ten occurrences) throughout the concluding third unit of 3:6–10. The expression "before our God" reflects Paul's conviction that he, along with the Thessalonians (note the personal pronoun "*our* God"), lives in the presence of God—not merely at the future return of Jesus (see 2:19 and 3:13, where *emprosthen* is used in an eschatological context) but also already now, through his present prayers[49] of thanksgiving and rejoicing. This consciousness of the divine presence explains why Paul does not direct his thanksgiving to the Thessalonians themselves but to God who is the ultimate reason for the good report about the church.

The third part (v. 10a) of the long rhetorical question makes explicit that Paul's thanksgiving and rejoicing was done in the context of prayer: "pleading night and day as earnestly as possible" (νυκτὸς καὶ ἡμέρας ὑπερεκπερισσοῦ δεόμενοι, *nyktos kai hēmeras hyperekperissou deomenoi*). The connection of the participle "pleading" with "we rejoice"[50] is not obvious. Some commentators say the grammatical link to that preceding verb is "loose" (Frame 1912: 135; Malherbe 2000: 204) and "not of an argumentative kind, but . . . simply due to the association of ideas" (Lightfoot 1904: 47). Most contemporary translations ignore the connection and make a full break here, ending the rhetorical question of verse 9 and beginning a new affirmative sentence (so, e.g., NIV, NRSV, JB, NAB, NLT). The pattern of Paul's opening thanksgivings, however, is to follow a verb of thanksgiving with a participle that expresses the manner of giving thanks, namely, by praying (1 Thess. 1:2b; Rom. 1:9–10; Eph. 1:16; Phil. 1:4; Col. 1:3; Philem. 4), and that is the likely function of the participle here ("we rejoice because of you before our God *by* pleading . . .").

Instead of the more common verb for prayer (προσεύχομαι, *proseuchomai*), the apostle uses the rarer (six times in Paul: Rom. 1:10; 2 Cor. 5:20; 8:4; 10:2; Gal. 4:12; 1 Thess. 3:10) and stronger verb *deomai*: "to ask for something pleadingly" (BDAG 218). Paul does not merely "pray" for the Thessalonians; he "pleads" to God on their behalf. The apostle adds greater emphasis to his pleading with the temporal expression "night and day" (*nyktos kai hēmeras*), an idiom that emphasizes the repeated prayers that he makes about them (for more on this word pair, see comment on 2:9). Still further emphasis is made with the hyperbolic adverb "as earnestly as possible" (*hyperekperissou*), an uncommon form (elsewhere only Eph. 3:20 and 1 Thess. 5:13; but see the related verbal form in Rom. 5:20 and 2 Cor. 7:4) whose double prefixes *hyper* and *ek* give the adjective *perissos* the superlative sense of the "highest form

3:10

---

49. That Paul is here alluding to the prayer as the means by which he brings his thanksgiving to God and rejoices over the Thessalonians is supported by the use of the phrase "before our God and Father" in the context of prayer in 1:3 as well as the reference to prayer in the next verse (3:10).

50. Although the participle *deomenoi* (3:10) could instead modify the earlier verbal phrase τίνα εὐχαριστίαν δυνάμεθα ἀνταποδοῦναι (in v. 9; so Ellicott 1880: 45; Lenski 1937: 293; Kelcy 1963: 128), it is more closely and easily linked with χαίρομεν (in v. 9; so most commentators).

of comparison imaginable" (BDAG 1033). Thus, while "night and day" refers to the frequency of Paul's prayers, the adverb addresses the intensity of those prayers.

The fourth and concluding part (1 Thess. 3:10b) of the lengthy rhetorical question of verses 9–10 consists of a double articular infinitive clause, which gives the twofold purpose[51] of Paul's prayers: "in order to see you face-to-face and complete the things that are lacking in your faith?" (εἰς τὸ ἰδεῖν ὑμῶν τὸ πρόσωπον καὶ καταρτίσαι τὰ ὑστερήματα τῆς πίστεως ὑμῶν, *eis to idein hymōn to prosōpon kai katartisai ta hysterēmata tēs pisteōs hymōn*). The two purposes are directly linked to the two concerns that have been at work throughout this passage. The first desire "to see you face-to-face" (*eis to idein hymōn to prosōpon*) looks back generally to the overall concern of 2:17–20 about Paul's ongoing absence from the Thessalonians and specifically to his opening claim that he was orphaned from them "in person [lit., "with respect to the face"] but not the heart" and that he desired "to see you face-to-face" (2:17), thereby forming an inclusio with those earlier words. Similarly, in 3:10 the second and closely connected[52] desire "to complete the things that are lacking in your faith" (*eis to . . . katartisai ta hysterēmata tēs pisteōs hymōn*) looks back generally to the overall concern of 3:1–5 about the persecution that threatens the faith of the Thessalonians and specifically to Paul's action of sending Timothy "in order to strengthen you and comfort you concerning your faith" (3:2) and "in order to learn about your faith" (3:5). But while both purposes clearly refer back to the two concerns at work earlier in the passage, the second purpose also looks ahead to the rest of the letter, which will presumably "complete the things that are lacking in your faith."

Two questions naturally emerge from this second stated purpose. First, what does Paul have in mind in his reference to "the things that are lacking"? Some exegetes find it significant that Timothy's report in 3:6 does not include any reference to "hope" as the third member of the triad faith, love, and hope (1:3; 5:8), suggesting that he reported positively about the Thessalonians' "faith and love" but negatively about their "hope." Consequently, it is then claimed that "the things that are lacking" refers to their lack of hope, particularly their eschatological hope in the return of Christ, thereby requiring Paul to take up this subject in the eschatological material of 4:13–5:11 (so, e.g., Dobschütz 1909: 140; Rigaux 1956: 478; Gaventa 1998: 45). However, there are several weaknesses with this interpretation: (1) It makes too much out of an

51. The context in 3:10 of "begging" or "asking" leads some commentators to view the infinitives as objective, giving the content of Paul's prayers (so, e.g., Milligan 1908: 42; Lenski 1937: 293; Robertson 1934: 1072). However, the construction εἰς τό + infinitive normally expresses purpose (BDF §402.2), "especially in Paul where it expresses hardly anything but purpose" (MHT 3:143), and this is its function elsewhere in 1 Thessalonians (2:12, 16; 3:2, 5, 13; 4:9). Nevertheless, the distinction between content and purpose should not be pressed, since there is obviously a close connection between the two in prayers.

52. The two articular infinitives of 3:10 are closely linked by means of the one definitive article τό, which does double duty for both.

argument from silence. (2) It is contradicted by Paul's opening thanksgiving for the Thessalonians' "hope in our Lord Jesus Christ"—not a general hope in the person and work of Christ, but a specific hope in his imminent return. (3) Paul takes up noneschatological subjects in the rest of the letter, including the matter of love (4:9–12), about which Timothy gave a positive report. And (4) the plural *hysterēmata* suggests that Paul has in view more things than a singular concern about the church's lack of hope. Therefore, the phrase "the things that are lacking" does not refer specifically to a lack of eschatological hope but more generally to a variety of concerns that Paul has about the Thessalonian congregation (holiness in sexual conduct, brotherly and sisterly love within the community of faith, the fate of both deceased and living believers at the return of Christ, the treatment of leaders and troubled congregational members, and the gift of prophecy), concerns he will take up in the second half of the letter (4:1–5:22).

Second, do Paul's words here imply that he finds fault with the Thessalonians? The noun *hysterēmata*, which occurs eight times in Paul (1 Cor. 16:17; 2 Cor. 8:14 [2x]; 9:12; 11:9; Phil. 2:30; Col. 1:24; 1 Thess. 3:10) has both the neutral meaning of "the lack of what is needed or desirable" and the negative connotation of "a defect that must be removed" (BDAG 1044). The positive nature of Timothy's report, along with Paul's praise in the opening thanksgiving, might be seen to support the former meaning. Indeed, most commentators downplay any notion that the faith of the Thessalonians was deficient or defective. The infinitive *katartisai*, however, normally refers to the restoring of something currently flawed to its proper condition (BDAG 526), and this is its primary meaning in Paul (1 Cor. 1:10; 2 Cor. 13:11; Gal. 6:1; 1 Thess. 3:10) and other NT writers (Matt. 4:21; Mark 1:19; Luke 6:40; Heb. 13:21; 1 Pet. 5:10). This suggests that the apostle is not merely referring in a neutral manner to what is needed or desirable for the faith of the Thessalonians but somewhat more seriously to what is lacking or deficient in that faith. As thankful as Paul is for the "good news" about the Thessalonians, he still remains concerned about them—a concern hinted at already in the earlier condition "if you continue to stand firm in the Lord" (3:8).

But do Paul's words go beyond concern to blame? In the second half of the letter, the apostle explicitly reminds the church that some of "the things that are lacking in your faith" (holiness in sexual conduct, brotherly and sisterly love within the community of faith, fate of living believers at the return of Christ) had already been taught and discussed during his mission-founding visit (4:1, "as you received from us"; 4:2, "for you know what commands we gave you"; 4:6, "as we indeed told you before and solemnly warned"; 4:11, "just as we commanded you"; 5:2, "for you yourselves accurately know"), implying a greater degree of culpability on their part. Paul introduces other topics (fate of deceased believers at the parousia), however, in such a way that clearly shows them to be new instruction that he had not previously shared with the church (4:13, "we do not want you not to know about . . ."), implying a lesser degree of culpability on their part. But while these matters are of concern to the apostle, he is nevertheless sufficiently pleased with the present conduct of his converts that he can exhort them "to do so more and more" (4:1, 10b). Therefore, although Paul's stated purpose "to complete the things that are lacking in your faith" refers to actual or genuine concerns that he takes up in the second half of the letter, these concerns are not so great as to imply blame on the Thessalonians' part or to negate the strong note of thanksgiving and praise found in the first half.

Additional Notes

2:19. One major uncial (Alexandrinus) has replaced καυχήσεως (boasting) with ἀγαλλιάσεως (exultation), perhaps to avoid any negative notion associated with Paul's pride or boasting in the Thessalonian Christians (see also Tertullian, *Res.* 24, who has *exultationis corona*).

3:2. There are five different readings for the second title used to describe Timothy in 3:2:

1. συνεργὸν τοῦ θεοῦ (coworker of God): D* 33 it[d, e, mon]* Ambst Pel Ps-Jerome
2. συνεργόν (coworker): B 1962 vg[mss]
3. διάκονον τοῦ θεοῦ (servant of God): ℵ A P Ψ 6 81 629* 1241 1739 1881 2464 *pc* lat sy[h] co[sa.bo.fay] goth eth
4. διάκονον καὶ συνεργὸν τοῦ θεοῦ (servant and coworker of God): F G
5. διάκονον τοῦ θεοῦ καὶ συνεργὸν ἡμῶν (servant of God and our coworker): D[2] K 88 104 614 𝔐 vg[mss]

Although there is strong external support for the third reading (adopted by Hendriksen 1955: 83n66; Morris 1991: 94), the first option is more probable for three reasons. First, it is the most difficult reading, since scribes would have hesitated to apply the bold and lofty title "coworker of God" to any person, least of all the young Timothy, who was merely Paul's helper. Second, it is a Pauline title, since the same designation is applied to Paul and Apollos in 1 Cor. 3:9. Third and most important, this is the reading that best explains the rise of the other four readings (see B. Metzger 1992: 240–42; also 1994: 563).

3:2. Some scribes (D[1] 𝔐 vg[ms] sy[p]) found it necessary to add the direct object ὑμᾶς after the second articular infinitive παρακαλέσαι. This is not necessary, however, since the ὑμᾶς located after the first articular infinitive στηρίξαι does double duty as the implied direct object of the second articular infinitive.

3:2. The preposition ὑπέρ functions as a marker of general content ("about, concerning") and is equivalent to περί (BDAG 1031.3), with which it is frequently interchanged in the MSS (so D[2] 𝔐).

3:3. The confusion over the precise meaning of σαίνεσθαι accounts not only for the origin of the alternate reading σιαίνεσθαι (to get disheartened, disgusted, unnerved) in MSS F and G (supported by Nestle 1906; Parry 1923–24) but also the numerous textual emendations that have been forwarded. Perdelwitz (1913) conjectured that τὸ μηδένα σαίνεσθαι ought to be read as τὸ μὴ δειλαίνεσθαι (not to be cowardly). A. Knox (1924) proposed the reading παθαίνεσθαι (to be filled with emotion), with the resulting translation "that no one break down in these persecutions." Hermann Venema conjectured a different word division, μηδὲν ἀσαίνεσθαι (a verb cited by the lexicographer Hesychius, meaning "to suffer violence or outrage"), while Theodore Beza and Richard Bentley, under the influence of 2 Thess. 2:2, postulated the reading σαλεύεσθαι (to be shaken): see Bruce 1982: 59. For a fuller discussion of these proposed textual emendations, see Rigaux 1956: 470–71.

3:8. The unexpected indicative form στήκετε was changed by some pedantic scribes to the subjunctive στήκητε (ℵ* D E *pc*)—the mood normally used with the conditional conjunction ἐάν.

3:9. Some MSS have substituted κυρίῳ (ℵ* D* G a b vg^mss bo^mss) for the better-attested θεῷ (ℵ² A B D² Ψ 𝔐 f m vg sy co; Ambst), no doubt under the influence of ἐν κυρίῳ, which concludes the previous verse (3:8). Yet as in 1:2; 2:13; and elsewhere in the apostle's letters (Rom. 1:8; 14:6 [2x]; 1 Cor. 1:4, 14; 14:18; 2 Cor. 9:11, 12; Eph. 5:20; Phil. 1:3; Col. 1:3, 12; 3:17; 2 Thess. 1:3; 2:13; Philem. 4), thanksgiving is always directed "to God" rather than "to the Lord," i.e., Jesus Christ. A similar substitution of κυρίου (ℵ* 181 a b m vg^mss) for θεοῦ takes place at the end of 3:9, likely due to the reading "before our Lord Jesus" in 2:19.

C. Transitional Prayers (3:11–13)

The two prayers of 3:11–13 not only summarize the two major concerns developed in the first half of the letter but also foreshadow three key themes that will be addressed in the second half. These two petitions, therefore, are *transitional* prayers in which Paul skillfully concludes the apologetic concerns at work in 2:1–3:10 and foreshadows the exhortative material of 4:1–5:22, where he will fulfill his just-stated desire to "complete the things that are lacking in your faith" (3:10).

Literary Analysis

Character of the Passage

Form. First Thessalonians 3:11–13 consists of two prayers that have been formally identified as "benedictions" (Champion 1934: 29–30; Jewett 1969: 18–34; Mullins 1977; Weima 1994a: 101–4) or "wish-prayers" (Wiles 1974: 45–71). Prayers or benedictions occur with some frequency in Paul's Letters, and commentators typically group these passages together into the same formal category. Yet three distinct types of prayers can be identified (Weima 1994a: 78–104): (1) the grace benediction; (2) the peace benediction; and (3) the "body" benediction. Whereas the first two types belong to the letter closing and possess a consistent form or structure, the third type is found in the letter body and exhibits greater formal variation. Nevertheless, these prayers or benedictions located in the letter body have a common structure consisting of five basic elements: (1) the introductory element, always the adversative particle δέ (*de*) in its expected postpositive position; (2) the divine source of the prayer, given in the nominative and usually elaborated on by means of a genitive phrase or participial clause; (3) the content of the prayer, normally expressed by the verb in the optative mood; (4) the object of the prayer, in every case except one involving some form of the personal pronoun "you"; and (5) the purpose of the prayer, expressed by either a ἵνα (*hina*) or εἰς (*eis*) clause. In 3:11–13, therefore, we encounter two of these body benedictions or prayers: the first in verse 11, the second in 12–13 (other instances of this third type of benediction or prayer include Rom. 15:5–6; 15:13; 2 Thess. 2:16–17; 3:5; see also Heb. 13:20–21).[1]

Function. These prayers possess a summarizing function: Paul adapts the conventional elements of the prayers such that they recapitulate and place the

---

1. These benedictions or prayers are formally distinct from: (1) the reference to prayer commonly found in the second part of the opening thanksgiving—the manner of giving thanks (Rom. 1:9; Eph. 1:16; Phil. 1:4; Col. 1:3; 1 Thess. 1:2; Philem. 4); and (2) the prayer reports that sometimes conclude the opening thanksgiving (Phil. 1:9–11; Col. 1:9–14; 2 Thess. 1:11–12; see Rom. 1:10) and the other prayer reports occasionally found in the body of the letter (1 Thess. 3:10; see Eph. 3:14–19).

spotlight on the letter's major concerns and themes (Jewett 1969: 24; Wiles 1974: 68; Weima 1994a). This summarizing function also manifests itself in the two prayers of 3:11–13. In verse 11 the wish of the first prayer that God and the Lord Jesus "clear the way for us to come to you" echoes the repeatedly stated (four times) desire of Paul in the preceding passage to revisit the Thessalonians (2:17, "to see you face-to-face"; 2:18, "to come to you"; 3:6, "just as we also long to see you"; 3:10, "to see you face-to-face"). In this first prayer the specific wish that God and Jesus *"clear the way* [lit., "road"] for us to come to you" also looks back to the military metaphor of 2:18b, where Paul excuses his failure to return thus far to Thessalonica by claiming that Satan "blocked our way"—a reference to the military practice of making cuts in the road to prevent an enemy army from advancing.

In 3:12–13 the second prayer also addresses the two main concerns of the preceding passage. The elliptical phrase "just as we also [abound and increase in love for] you" (v. 12b) echoes virtually verbatim the elliptical phrase "just as we also [long to see] you" in 3:6 and so recalls in a general way Paul's concern throughout 2:17–3:10 to reassure the Thessalonians of his continued love for them despite his absence. The wish of the second prayer, that the Lord increase them in love "in order to strengthen your hearts" (εἰς τὸ στηρίξαι ὑμῶν τὰς καρδίας, *eis to stēriksai hymōn tas kardias*), provides a verbal link with 3:2, where Paul's purpose in sending Timothy to the persecuted Thessalonian church is "in order to strengthen you" (εἰς τὸ στηρίξαι ὑμᾶς, *eis to stērixai hymas*). The two prayers, therefore, summarize well Paul's two primary concerns in the preceding passage: the absence of Paul from the Thessalonians (2:17–20) and the persecution endured by the Thessalonians (3:1–5).

The second prayer (3:12–13), however, does not only recap the major concerns of the preceding material: it also foreshadows three key themes that will be developed in the second half of the letter (see also Fee 2009: 129). First, the wish of the prayer that the Lord cause the Thessalonians to abound and increase "in love for one another and for all" anticipates the discussion of brotherly and sisterly love in 4:9–12 and the implications of loving one another in 5:12–22. Second, the purpose of the prayer, that the Thessalonians be "blameless in holiness," and also the final prepositional phrase "with all his holy ones"—both look ahead to the discussion of holiness in sexual conduct in 4:3–8, where the word "holiness/holy" in various forms plays a key role, occurring no less than four times (4:3, 4, 7, 8). Third, the closing temporal reference in the prayer to "the coming of our Lord Jesus" and the "all" in the final phrase, "with all his holy ones," have in view Paul's lengthy discussion of the return of Christ in 4:13–18 and 5:1–11.

The prayers of 3:11–13, therefore, are not merely *concluding* prayers (the title used by some commentators: e.g., Oepke 1963: 166, "der Schlußsegenswunsch"; Gaventa 1998: 45; Reinmuth 1998: 135: "Abschliessende Fürbitte"; Malherbe 2000: 211) but *transitional* prayers (so also Witherington 2006: 101, but from a rhetorical perspective). In fact, the emphasis in these prayers is less on the apologetic concerns found in the first half of the letter than on the exhortative concerns in the second half, where Paul will fulfill his just-stated desire to "complete the things that are lacking in your faith" (see Frame 1912: 136). The prayers or benedictions in Paul's Letters generally have not only a summarizing function but also a paraenetic, or exhortative, function: "By mentioning the needs of the readers in prayers which they themselves will read together during worship, the apostle is encouraging them before God to strive still harder" (Wiles 1974: 69) to do that which he prays for them. As the opening thanksgiving (1:2–10) implicitly exhorts the Thessalonians to live up to the praise that they receive from Paul, so the prayers of 3:11–13 implicitly challenge the believers in Thessalonica to make the divine petitions of the apostle a reality in their daily lives.

Extent of the Passage

Some scholars argue that a new section in the letter begins not in 3:11 but earlier, in 3:9, and defend this position on thematic grounds: Paul's two prayers in 3:11–13 ought to be linked with the report about his prayer in the preceding verses of 3:9–10 so that 3:9–13 is a unit (so, e.g., O'Brien 1977: 156–64; Richard 1995: 163–78; Holmes 1998: 113–22). There are compelling grammatical and literary grounds, however, for beginning a new section in 3:11. First, the contrastive particle δέ (*de*, but) distinguishes the following material from what comes before it. Second, this transition is further signaled by the change of subject: the "we" and "you" found throughout 2:17–3:10 are replaced in 3:11 by "our God and Father and our Lord Jesus," and this new subject is stressed by the intensive pronoun "himself" (αὐτός, *autos*). Third, the shift in the main verbs from the indicative to the optative mood indicates that the material of 3:11–13 belongs to the genre of prayer or benediction and thus is formally distinct from the apostolic parousia of 2:17–3:10. Finally, the inclusio and other literary evidence that supports the ending of the preceding passage in 3:10 (see "Extent of the Passage" for 2:17–3:10) implies that the following verse in 3:11 begins a new section in the letter.

Several features similarly mark the ending of this new section in 3:13. The two prayers reach an eschatological climax in the reference to "the coming of our Lord Jesus"—a "sequence-termination feature" (Johanson 1987: 87) commonly found in this letter (see also 1:10; 2:16; 5:23). The "Amen," which probably should be included in the text (see additional notes), clearly signals a conclusion. The prayers of 3:11–13 are formally distinct from the exhortative material of 4:1–5:22. The ending at 3:13 is confirmed by the clear new beginning in 4:1, signaled by several transitional devices such as the introductory phrase "Finally, then," the vocative "brothers," the appeal formula ("we ask and appeal"), and the disclosure formula ("For you know . . . ," in 4:2). There can be little doubt, therefore, that 3:11–13 constitutes a distinct unit within the letter.

Structure of the Passage

The unit 3:11–13 consists of two prayers: a petition in verse 11 that is relatively brief due to the absence of any purpose statement (see discussion above concerning the five basic elements that typically make up these "body" benedictions or prayers) and a longer and formally more complex petition in verses 12–13. Many contemporary translations divide the lengthy second prayer into two distinct parts, thereby wrongly suggesting to their readers that the apostle utters three prayers instead of two (so, e.g., NIV, NRSV, NJB). The two prayers are distinct not only in length and form but also in content: the first petition in verse 11 focuses on Paul and his particular situation; the second petition in verses 12–13 deals with the Thessalonians and their specific needs.

The structure of Paul's transitional prayers in 3:11–13, therefore, is simple and clear:

1. Paul's prayer for himself (3:11)
2. Paul's prayer for the Thessalonians (3:12–13)

Exegesis and Exposition

[11]But may our God and Father himself and our Lord Jesus clear the way for us to come to you. [12]But as for you, may the Lord cause you to abound and increase in love for one another and for all, just as we also abound and increase in love for you, [13]in order to strengthen your hearts as ⌜blameless⌝ in ⌜holiness⌝ before our God and Father at the coming of our Lord Jesus with all his holy ones. ⌜Amen⌝.

1. Paul's Prayer for Himself (3:11)

The first of Paul's two transitional prayers focuses on himself (although the prayer also has an obvious benefit for his readers) and looks back to the earlier concern in 2:17–3:10 over the apostle's absence from the Thessalonians: "But may our God and Father himself and our Lord Jesus clear the way for us to come to you" (αὐτὸς δὲ ὁ θεὸς καὶ πατὴρ ἡμῶν καὶ ὁ κύριος ἡμῶν Ἰησοῦς κατευθύναι τὴν ὁδὸν ἡμῶν πρὸς ὑμᾶς, *autos de ho theos kai patēr hēmōn kai ho kyrios hēmōn Iēsous kateuthynai tēn hodon hēmōn pros hymas*).

This prayer, like all the other prayers that occur in the letter body of Paul's Letters (1 Thess. 3:12–13; 2 Thess. 2:16–17; 3:5; Rom. 15:5–6, 13), is introduced with the particle *de*. Virtually all commentators fail to find any adversative force in this particle and so translate it as "now" rather than "but" (BDAG 213.2). Yet this particle does more commonly have an adversative sense, and this is how it functions in its previous uses in the letter (2:16, 17; 3:6), in the immediately following prayer (3:12), and in the rest of the letter (4:9, 10, 13; 5:1, 4, 8, 12, 14, 21, 23). Furthermore, Paul could have more closely linked the prayer with the immediately preceding material by shifting from *de* to the simple conjunction καί (*kai*, and), as he does in some closing prayers or benedictions for peace.[2] Finally, the presence of the intensive pronoun "himself" (*autos*) at the head of the prayer suggests that, though the contrastive force of *de* should not be overstated (it is much more moderate than ἀλλά), it does have a slight adversative sense: in contrast to the repeated and ineffectual attempts of Paul to overcome the blocking work of Satan (2:18b) and see the Thessalonians again "face-to-face" (2:17, 18a; 3:10), God himself and the Lord Jesus will

---

2. In instances where the peace benediction is the first element in the letter closing, it is always introduced with the particle δέ, whose adversative sense serves to mark the transition from the letter body to the letter closing (Rom. 15:33; 16:20a; 1 Thess. 5:23; 2 Thess. 3:16). In those instances, however, where other epistolary conventions such as final commands or autograph statements are the first element in the closing, the peace benediction is instead always introduced with the conjunction καί (2 Cor. 13:11b; Gal. 6:16; Phil. 4:9b). See Weima 1994a: 88–90.

clear the way for the apostle to revisit his converts in Thessalonica (so some older commentators: see those cited in Frame 1912: 137; also Moore 1969: 59).

The second part of the prayer, the divine source, is striking not only because of the addition of the intensive pronoun "himself" but even more for the use of two subjects ("our God and Father himself and our Lord Jesus") with a singular verb.[3] The similar use of a compound subject with a singular verb occurs elsewhere in the NT (e.g., 1 Cor. 15:50; Matt. 5:18; Mark 4:41; James 5:3). These examples, however, virtually always involve a conventional word pair ("flesh and blood," "heaven and earth," "wind and sea," "gold and silver") so that the parallel with two persons mentioned in the transitional prayer of 3:11 is not exact. The issue at stake is whether this grammatical construction indicates anything about Paul's view of the deity of Jesus. Some boldly assert that "this plural subject with a singular verb makes God our Father and the Lord Jesus one, which stresses the lordship and deity of Jesus Christ" (Hobbs 1971: 276). Others state with equal conviction that "this does not imply Paul held a Trinitarian or Binitarian theology" (Best 1977: 147; Furnish 2007: 83: "Nor is there any theological significance to his use of a singular verb following the compound subject").

Both extremes, however, go beyond the evidence. On the one hand, the grammar alone is not enough to establish the deity of Jesus. Indeed, the repetition of the definite article for both nouns suggests that Paul views God the Father and Jesus our Lord as two individual entities and so avoids the danger of a *complete merging* of the two figures to whom he prays. On the other hand, that these two individual figures are closely linked by a singular verb—a grammatical construction that Paul repeats (though in reverse order) in another prayer for the Thessalonians (2 Thess. 2:16–17)—suggests that Paul views Jesus as sharing the deity of God and so avoids the danger of a *complete separation* of these two figures to whom he prays (Hewett 1975–76: 54).

The intimate relationship between God and Jesus is never explained by Paul but simply assumed. The readers are identified in the letter opening, for example, as "the church of the Thessalonians in God the Father and the Lord Jesus Christ" (1:1). Paul gives thanks for their steadfast hope "in our Lord Jesus Christ before our God and Father" (1:3). The purpose of Paul's prayer for them is that they be blameless in holiness "before our God and Father at the coming of our Lord Jesus" (3:13). As Marshall (1983: 100) declares: "It would be more exact to say that Paul *assumes* the divinity of Jesus—to call him 'Son of God' in the way in which Paul uses the phrase cannot mean anything else." Similarly Fee (2009: 130–31), observing the "remarkable inclusion of the Son as the compound subject of the singular verb," states: "That he [Paul] does this in

---

3. Richard (1995: 168) proposes that 3:11 has been "clumsily modified by a later scribe" who took the original words in the genitive, which read "the God and Father of us *and of the Lord Jesus*" (see Rom. 15:6; 2 Cor. 1:3; 11:31) and changed them into the nominative, thereby resulting in a second subject of the prayer. There is, however, no MS evidence to support Richard's proposed original reading. This proposal further suffers from the fact that it adds yet another level of development to Richard's already-complicated partition theory concerning the composite character of 1 Thessalonians.

such a matter-of-fact way, and without explanation or argumentation, is at the same time sure evidence that he must have previously instructed them not only on the saving work of Christ, but also on *who* the divine Savior actually was."

The third part of the prayer, the content, is that God and Jesus "may clear the way for us to come to you." In the NT the optative mood often takes on a force similar to that of the imperative; thus it is legitimate to speak of an "imperatival optative," an optative that expresses a stronger sense than mere volition: "The speaker intends more than a wish ('may it be so-and-so'); he expresses this with a strong sense of fulfillment ('let it be so-and-so')" (van Elderen 1967: 48; BDF §384: "The optative proper used to denote an attainable wish"). The optative *kateuthynai*, therefore, conveys not merely Paul's faint hope but rather his confident prayer that God and Jesus will, in fact, make it possible for him to be reunited with the believers in Thessalonica.

The verb *kateuthynai* is not a common word in either Paul's Letters (elsewhere only 2 Thess. 3:5, also in a prayer) or other NT writings (only Luke 1:79). It does, however, occur with some frequency in the Septuagint, where it possesses a metaphorical or ethical sense: to make straight (i.e., to correct) a person's ways (Pss. 36:23; 39:3 [37:23; 40:2 Eng.]; Prov. 4:26) or to direct a person's heart to God (1 Chron. 29:18; 2 Chron. 12:14; 19:3; 20:33; Prov. 21:2; Sir. 49:3; 51:20). Although Paul employs *kateuthynai* with this metaphorical sense in 2 Thess. 3:5, here in 3:11 the verb has the literal meaning to "lead, direct" (BDAG 532). Yet Paul is not asking in a general way for divine guidance ("Direct our way") but specifically has in mind the removal of the satanic obstacles referred to in 2:18: Satan has "blocked our way," but now God and Jesus will "clear our way to you." Paul's first transitional prayer, therefore, looks back to the apostle's repeatedly stated desire to revisit the Thessalonians (2:17, 18a; 3:6, 10) and especially to the military metaphor of 2:18.

2. Paul's Prayer for the Thessalonians (3:12–13)

The second of Paul's two transitional prayers shifts the focus away from the apostle and onto the Thessalonians and their specific situation: "But as for you, may the Lord cause you to abound and increase in love for one another and for all, just as we also abound and increase in love for you" (ὑμᾶς δὲ ὁ κύριος πλεονάσαι καὶ περισσεύσαι τῇ ἀγάπῃ εἰς ἀλλήλους καὶ εἰς πάντας καθάπερ καὶ ἡμεῖς εἰς ὑμᾶς, *hymas de ho kyrios pleonasai kai perisseusai tē agapē eis allēlous kai eis pantas kathaper kai hēmeis eis hymas*).

3:12

The first part of the prayer, the introductory element, is the expected particle *de*, which here plainly has an adversative force: "but." That Paul intends to make a contrast with the first prayer is made clear by the presence of the personal pronoun "you" (*hymas*) in the emphatic position at the head of the second prayer. This relocation of the object of the prayer from its normal position as the fourth part is made even more dramatic because this results in the same pronoun occurring twice back-to-back: the "you" that introduces the second prayer comes immediately after the "you" that concludes the first prayer. All this serves to highlight Paul's shift from praying for himself in 3:11 to his prayer for the Thessalonians in 3:12–13, a shift nicely captured in the English phrase "But as for you . . ." (Frame 1912: 137) or "But as regards you . . ." (Richard 1995: 165).

The second part of the prayer, the divine source, is no longer both "our God and Father himself and our Lord Jesus" but only and more simply "the Lord" (*ho kyrios*). Since "Lord" in the surrounding verses of 3:11 and 3:13 refers to Jesus, that must also be its referent here. This is further supported by Pauline use in general, where the designation "Lord" almost always (except in some OT citations) refers to Jesus and not to God (L. W. Hurtado, *DPL* 560–69). Although the apostle directs his prayers most often to God, he also addresses them with some frequency to Jesus (2 Cor. 12:8; 2 Thess. 3:5, 16; 2 Tim. 1:16) or even to both (1 Thess. 3:11; 2 Thess. 2:16–17). The ease with which Paul can interchange God and Jesus as the divine source of his prayers supports our earlier observation about the first prayer: Paul assumes the divine status of Jesus.[4]

The third part of the prayer, the wish or content, is again expressed by verbs in the optative mood and thus expresses not merely a faint wish but a confident prayer that has a strong expectation of fulfillment (see comment on 3:11). The first verb, *pleonasai*, occurs elsewhere in Paul's Letters (Rom. 5:20 [2x]; 6:1; 2 Cor. 4:15; 8:15; Phil. 4:17; 2 Thess. 1:3) but only here as a transitive: "to cause increase" (BDAG 824). Similarly the second verb, *perisseusai*, more common in Paul, is typically used intransitively (Rom. 3:7; 5:15; 15:13; 1 Cor. 8:8; 14:12; 15:58; 2 Cor. 1:5 [2x]; 3:9; 4:15; 8:2, 7 [2x]; 9:8 [2x], 12; Eph. 1:8; Phil. 1:9, 26; 4:12 [2x], 18; Col. 2:7; 1 Thess. 4:1, 10) but here has the rarer transitive meaning: "to cause something to increase, abound" (so also 2 Cor. 4:15; 9:8a; Eph. 1:8; see BDAG 805.2). These two verbs are synonymous (Rom. 5:20; 2 Cor. 4:15) so that it would be wrong to distinguish between them, as some older commentators have tried to do (e.g., Ellicott 1880: 47; Lightfoot 1904: 48; Milligan 1908: 43). Instead, the combination of *pleonasai* and *perisseusai* serves to intensify the idea of abundance and increase. As Green (2002: 177) notes: "Taken together, the verbs show the superlative degree to which the apostles wanted the church's love to grow. The prayer is not simply that their love increase but that it abound beyond limits, being exceedingly great and overflowing."

The specific item for which Paul asks the Lord to bring about abundance and increase in the lives of the Thessalonians is "love for one another and for all" (*tē agapē eis allēlous kai eis pantas*). It is true that the apostle wishes that mutual love would abound in all his congregations, since this is the "glue" needed to

---

4. There is no apparent explanation as to why Paul chooses to direct this second prayer (3:12–13) to "the Lord" in contrast to the first prayer, which is addressed to both God and Jesus. Marshall's tentative suggestion that the shift to Jesus as the divine source of the prayer is appropriate "since the command to love one another is particularly linked with the teaching of Jesus" (1983: 100) is not convincing, since God the Father is equally identified in Paul's writings as a God of love, who expects his chosen people to also act in love.

bind together converts from differing social and economic strata within the community (Wanamaker 1990: 142–43). Yet this prayer for increased love is not a generic request but one that specifically arises out of the Thessalonian situation. Love is one of the "things that are lacking in your faith" that Paul seeks to "complete" (3:10) in the second half of the letter, specifically in his extended discussion of "brotherly and sisterly love" in 4:9–12 and also in his closing exhortations in 5:12–22, which spell out the implications of loving one another. Although the apostle commends the Thessalonians for the love that they already exhibit (4:9–10a), he nevertheless appeals to them "to increase" (same verb as in the prayer of 3:12) even more (4:10b). In this way, the second prayer for increased mutual love foreshadows one of the key themes to be addressed in the second half of the letter.

The love that the Thessalonians ought to demonstrate is not limited to the congregational members ("for one another") but must be extended to the non-Christian community as well ("and for all"). Since Paul does not emphasize this theme elsewhere in his letters (only Gal. 6:10: "Let us do good to all people, but especially to those who are of the household of faith"; perhaps also Rom. 12:9–14, 17–21), he may well be thinking of something specific in the Thessalonian situation. This possibility is strengthened by the fact that the conduct of believers toward non-Christians is addressed in both passages that this prayer for increased love foreshadows: in the latter part of 4:9–12 Paul exhorts the Thessalonians "to make it your ambition to live a quiet life and to mind your own affairs and to work with your own hands, just as we instructed you, so that you may command the respect of outsiders" (4:11–12); in the final exhortations of 5:12–22, the apostle warns the church: "See to it that no one pays back evil for evil to anyone, but at all times pursue what is good both *for one another and for all*" (5:15)—the italicized phrase being identical to that found in the prayer of 3:12. This call to extend love to the non-Christian community would be especially challenging for the Thessalonian believers, who continue to endure much affliction at the hands of their fellow citizens.

Paul asserts that he and his fellow missionaries have exemplified the kind of love that the Thessalonians ought to have in the elliptical phrase "just as we also [abound and increase in love] for you" (the omitted verbs are easily supplied from the context). To make the parallel with the preceding main clause more exact, we might well have expected the apostle to use the accusative "us" instead of the nominative "we" so that Paul prays that the Lord will also increase his love for the Thessalonians (Best 1977: 149). The present form of the elliptical phrase, however, allows the apostle to assert that he already does have abounding love for his readers, thereby echoing Paul's concern in 2:17–3:10 to reassure the Thessalonians of his continued love for them despite his absence. That Paul deliberately intends this elliptical phrase to look back to that previous concern is supported by the fact that he repeats virtually verbatim the elliptical phrase "just as we also [long to see] you" in 3:6. As Wiles (1974: 59) observes: "It is therefore no merely accidental aside when he now prays that their increase in love might be as his own love for them."

3:13   The fifth and final part of Paul's second prayer expresses the purpose of his petition: "in order to strengthen your hearts as blameless in holiness before our God and Father at the coming of our Lord Jesus with all his holy ones" (εἰς τὸ στηρίξαι ὑμῶν τὰς καρδίας ἀμέμπτους ἐν ἁγιωσύνῃ ἔμπροσθεν τοῦ θεοῦ καὶ πατρὸς ἡμῶν ἐν τῇ παρουσίᾳ τοῦ κυρίου ἡμῶν Ἰησοῦ μετὰ πάντων τῶν ἁγίων αὐτοῦ, *eis to stērixai hymōn tas kardias amemptous en hagiōsynē emprosthen tou theou kai patros hēmōn en tē parousia tou kyriou hēmōn Iēsou meta pantōn tōn hagiōn autou*). On the one hand, the purpose (εἰς τό + infinitive = purpose; BDF §404.2; so also 2:12, 16; 3:2, 5, 10) of the prayer looks back to another major concern in the preceding passage: the afflictions endured by the Thessalonian church. For the goal that the Lord "strengthen your hearts" (*eis to stērixai hymōn tas kardias*) recalls in an explicit way Paul's stated goal in sending Timothy to "strengthen you" (3:2, *eis to stērixai hymas*) as well as in a general way the apostle's desire that "no one may be shaken by these afflictions" (3:3a) but "continue to stand firm in the Lord" (3:8).[5] The combination of the verb "to strengthen" with the noun "heart," which is found in Paul only here and in 2 Thess. 2:17, occurs in the OT with a variety of meanings: the strengthening of the physical body, via nourishment (Judg. 19:5, 8; Ps. 103:15 [104:15 Eng.]); the strengthening of the mind, as insight (Sir. 6:37; 22:16); or the strengthening of the emotions, as courage (Ps. 111:8 [112:8 Eng.]; see also James 5:8). It is this last sense that Paul intends here; he prays that the Thessalonians will have courage to stand firm in their faith, even in the face of persecution.

On the other hand, the purpose of the prayer looks ahead to two more themes (in addition to the theme of mutual love) taken up in the second half of the letter. The theme of holiness, which will be treated in 4:3–8 (note the three occurrences of the noun "holiness" in 4:3, 4, 7, and also the description of God's Spirit in 4:8, which emphasizes his "holy" character), is foreshadowed in the somewhat awkward[6] phrase "blameless in holiness" (*amemptous en hagiōsynē*). The adjective "blameless" was used in the Greco-Roman world to describe people of exceptional merit or extraordinary civic consciousness (BDAG 52). Paul has already used this word in the adverbial form to defend "how holy and righteous and blameless" he acted among the Thessalonians during his mission-founding visit (2:10; see also Phil. 2:15; 3:6; 1 Thess. 5:23; Luke 1:6; Heb. 8:7). Now he prays that the believers in Thessalonica will be strengthened by the Lord in their current afflictions such that they may similarly live a "blameless" or exceptional life.

---

5. Wiles (1974: 61): "The language details of this final petition link closely with the wording and mood of the preceding passage."

6. In 3:13 the accusative "blameless" is a bit awkward grammatically, since the infinitive "to strengthen" already has a direct object ("your hearts"). Thus "blameless" might be a second direct object: a double accusative with "to strengthen" (Richard 1995: 166). However, since none of the remaining twelve occurrences of στηρίζω in the NT have the double accusative, "blameless" more likely is in apposition to the direct object: "to strengthen your hearts *as blameless*."

Paul specifies the particular area of life where the Thessalonians are to be blameless with the prepositional phrase "in holiness."[7] Whereas "blameless" is a common term within the Greco-Roman world, "holiness" is a word and concept that originates from the OT, where it is the defining characteristic and desired purpose for God's covenant people, Israel (see Weima 1996: esp. 101–2). When God constitutes the nation of Israel at Mount Sinai, he explicitly states: "You will be to me a kingdom of priests and a *holy* nation" (Exod. 19:6). This goal for Israel is repeated in the renewal of the Sinai covenant: "in order that you may be a *holy* people to the Lord your God" (Deut. 26:19). Similarly, the book of Leviticus repeatedly calls on Israel to imitate the holiness of their God: "You shall be *sanctified/made holy*, and you shall be *holy*, because I, the LORD your God, am *holy*" (11:44; see also 11:45; 19:2; 20:7; 22:32). That Paul considers holiness still to be a desired goal for God's covenant people, including the predominantly Gentile church in Thessalonica, is clear from both 4:3, where "your holiness" is explicitly identified as "the will of God," and the whole of 4:3–8, where the term "holiness" plays a key role in the apostle's discussion of sexual conduct. The phrase "blameless in holiness" in the prayer of 3:13, therefore, clearly looks ahead to the discussion of 4:3–8.

A third way in which the prayer foreshadows key themes to be developed in the second half of the letter is in its three concluding prepositional phrases: (1) "before our God and Father," (2) "at the coming of our Lord Jesus," and (3) "with all his holy ones." Since all three refer to the future return of Christ and the divine judgment that will take place at that time, they anticipate well the upcoming lengthy discussion of eschatological matters: the fate of deceased believers at the second coming of Christ (4:13–18) and the fate of living believers in the final judgment, to take place at Christ's return (5:1–11).

The first phrase, "before our God and Father" (*emprosthen tou theou kai patros hēmōn*), does not by itself necessarily have a future focus, but it could refer more broadly to God's ever-present presence in the lives of believers (so 1:3; 3:9). The two subsequent phrases, however, clearly indicate that Paul specifically has in view the future judgment, to take place at Christ's return—a time when "we all will stand before the judgment seat of God" (Rom. 14:10; see 2 Cor. 5:10). The identification of God as "our Father" has led some to see a deliberate attempt by the apostle to comfort the Thessalonians: they will appear before one who is not merely their judge but also their loving father (Rigaux 1956: 490; Richard 1995: 166). Others, however, observe that the epithet "our God and Father" repeats the divine address used in the preceding prayer of 3:11 (see also 2 Thess. 2:16) and that the description of God as "Father" occurs frequently in Paul's Letters in conventional formulas such as the opening greetings (e.g., Rom. 1:7; 1 Cor. 1:3; 2 Cor. 1:2; Gal. 1:1) or

---

7. In 3:13 Paul expresses the idea of "holiness" with the noun ἁγιωσύνη (Rom. 1:4; 2 Cor. 7:1; 1 Thess. 3:13), which is slightly more common than the rare ἁγιότης (Heb. 12:10; see 2 Cor. 1:12 v.l.), but less frequent than ἁγιασμός (Rom. 6:19, 22; 1 Cor. 1:30; 1 Thess. 4:3, 4, 7; 2 Thess. 2:13; 1 Tim. 2:15; Heb. 12:14; 1 Pet. 1:2).

liturgical material (e.g., Rom. 6:4; 8:15; 15:6; 1 Cor. 8:6; 2 Cor. 1:3 [2x]; Phil. 2:11; Eph. 4:6). Consequently, they claim that this fuller designation of God in 3:13 is formulaic and that the apostle is not deliberately highlighting the fatherly role of God in the future judgment (so, e.g., Best 1977: 151–52; Malherbe 2000: 213–14). But while it is wrong to read too much into the appellation "our Father," it is similarly mistaken to claim that it is merely formulaic and devoid of any significance. This would appear to be especially true in a letter where Paul makes great use of familial language and metaphors, and in a prayer where the apostle gives clear evidence that he has chosen his words with much care so as to connect the petition specifically to the situation of the Thessalonian church.

The second phrase, "at the coming of our Lord Jesus" (*en tē parousia tou kyriou hēmōn Iēsou*), makes clear the eschatological focus implied in the first phrase: the time when the Thessalonian Christians will appear in judgment before God so as to determine whether they are blameless in holiness is at the future return of Christ. Just as Paul earlier (in 1:10) links the second coming of Jesus ("to wait for his Son from the heavens") with the final judgment ("who rescues us from the coming wrath"), so also here these two eschatological events are joined together. For the second time in this letter, the apostle uses the term *parousia* to describe Christ's return, thereby evoking the image of a royal visit by a Roman emperor or official (see the fuller discussion of this key term in the comment on 2:19, as well as the comment on the technical term ἀπάντησις, *apantēsis* in 4:17).

The third phrase, "with all his holy ones" (*meta pantōn tōn hagiōn autou*), has generated much debate over whether it refers to angels or believers ("saints"). Most commentators (e.g., Dobschütz 1909: 152–53; Frame 1912: 139; Cerfaux 1925; Ross 1975; Wanamaker 1990: 145; Malherbe 2000: 214; Green 2002: 181; Witherington 2006: 104) believe that Paul is referring to angels for the following reasons (see esp. Richard 1995: 177–78; Fee 2009: 134–36). First, the term *hagioi* in the OT (e.g., Job 5:1; 15:15; Ps. 89:7–8; Dan. 7:17–18; 8:13; Zech. 14:5) and the intertestamental literature (e.g., 1 En. 1.9; Tob. 11:14; 12:15) sometimes refers to the presence of angels at the final judgment—a picture of the end times found elsewhere in Paul (2 Thess. 1:7). Second, there is good evidence that Paul in 3:13 is dependent on Zech. 14:5 LXX ("And the Lord my God will come, and all the holy ones with him"), a text that refers to angels. In fact, in Matt. 25:31, which borrows from this same OT text, the term "holy ones" is changed to "angels." Third, if *hagioi* in 1 Thess. 3:13 refers to angels, then this text will not disagree with 4:14–17, which describes deceased believers rising and joining their Lord in the air only after Christ has returned.

There remains compelling evidence, however, in support of the second option, that "holy ones" refers to believers or "saints" (so, e.g., Calvin 1981: 271–72; Findlay 1891: 77; Hendriksen 1955: 93; Ellingworth and Nida 1975: 71; Williams 1992: 67–68; Weatherly 1996: 122–23). First, the plural *hagioi* in every other occurrence in Paul refers clearly to Christians (Rom. 1:7; 8:27;

12:13; 15:25; 1 Cor. 1:2; 6:1–2; 2 Cor. 1:1; Eph. 2:19; 3:8; Phil. 1:1; 4:22; Col. 1:4, 26; 3:12; 1 Tim. 5:10) so that there would need to be weighty grounds to interpret this word differently in 1 Thess. 3:13. Second, the supposed Pauline parallel in 2 Thess. 1:7 (see the first reason cited above in support of angels) is not exact, since the key term "holy ones" does not occur here but instead the noun "angels." Indeed, just a few verses later, in 2 Thess. 1:10, which like 3:13 describes the coming judgment at Christ's return, Paul uses "holy ones" to refer to believers (it is parallel to "the ones who believe"). Third, the skillful way in which the second prayer of 3:12–13 anticipates the major themes to be developed in the second half of the letter suggests that this third phrase similarly looks ahead to key topics yet to be discussed. This is exactly what one finds. The reference to believers as "the holy ones" reinforces the goal of the prayer that the Thessalonians be "blameless in holiness" and foreshadows the discussion of the key word "holiness" in 4:3–8. Also, the statement that "all" of the holy ones will be with Jesus at his coming anticipates Paul's claim in 4:13–18 that *all* believers—not only the living Christians in Thessalonica but also "those who have fallen asleep," over whom the church is grieving—will be present and reunited at Christ's return.[8]

As for the claimed conflict with 4:14–17 (see the third reason cited above in support of angels), this is more imagined than real. For once all believers are reunited with one another and with Jesus in the air, they proceed (in keeping with the imagery evoked by the term ἀπάντησις, *apantēsis*, in 4:17) to escort the descending and reigning Christ to earth in a manner by which he does come "with all his holy ones" (3:13; see further Hendriksen 1955: 93–94). Additionally, one should not press the details too far since Paul's language about Christ's coming, though referring to an actual historical event yet to come, makes use of apocalyptic imagery and is thus by nature figurative (Weatherly 1996: 122).

Although the concluding "Amen" is omitted in virtually all the leading translations and ignored in most commentaries, it does have more textual support than is usually recognized (see additional notes). If included in the original text, the "Amen" forms a fitting conclusion not merely to the transitional prayers of 3:11–13 but also to the first half of the letter and so marks a clear shift to the exhortative concerns taken up in the second half.

Additional Notes

3:13. The adjective ἀμέμπτους (blameless) was changed in some MSS (B L 33 81 104 365 1241 *pc* latt) to the adverb ἀμέμπτως (blamelessly). There are two likely reasons for this change: first, it

8. The reference to "all" in the phrase "with all his holy ones" (3:13), along with the evidence that can be cited in support of interpreting "holy ones" as either angels or believers, has led several commentators to conclude that Paul here has *both* groups in view: Ellicott 1880: 49; Lightfoot 1904: 50; Milligan 1908: 45; Morris 1991: 111–12; Holmes 1998: 116n5; Nicholl 2004: 30.

removes the grammatical awkwardness of having two direct objects (see further the comment on 3:13); second, it conforms to Paul's use of the adverb form elsewhere in the letter (2:10; 5:23).

3:13. In place of ἁγιωσύνη (holiness), one major uncial (Alexandrinus, followed by a few minuscules) has δικαιοσύνη (righteousness), no doubt under the influence of Phil. 3:6, where the adjective "blameless" is similarly linked with the noun "righteousness" (see also 1 Thess. 2:10; Luke 1:6).

3:13. Although ἀμήν (Amen) is omitted in many MSS (ℵ¹ B D² F G Ψ 𝔐 it sy sa bo^mss), it is nevertheless found in many others, including a few important early witnesses: ℵ*,² A D* 81 629 *pc* a m vg bo. Although scribes may have deliberately added the ἀμήν as a natural conclusion to the prayers of 3:11–13, this possibility is weakened by the fact that these same copyists did not feel compelled to add ἀμήν to the other prayers of Paul (see Rom. 15:5–6; 15:13; 2 Thess. 2:16–17; 3:5). Instead, it seems more probable that some scribes deleted the ἀμήν because they believed this liturgical element to be inappropriate either for the genre of a letter generally or specifically for its location in the middle of a letter (similar to the deletion of ἀμήν in some MSS at the close of Rom. 15:33 and 16:24; see B. Metzger 1994: 563). Therefore, there appears to be slightly stronger evidence for the inclusion of ἀμήν than for its omission (note the decision of the UBS⁴ committee to include the word in the main text, albeit in square brackets).

IV. Exhortations to the Thessalonians (4:1–5:22)

A major shift in the body of the letter takes place at 4:1 as Paul has now completed the apologetic purpose that characterizes the first half (2:1–3:13) and moves on to the exhortative purpose at work throughout the second half (4:1–5:22). The apostle has effectively defended both his past actions during his mission-founding visit to Thessalonica (2:1–16) and his present absence from the believers in that city (2:17–3:10) so that his readers are reassured about the integrity of Paul's motives and conduct and are thus ready to accept the appeals and encouragements he is about to give in the rest of the letter. The apostle has been earnestly praying night and day that he will be able to return to the Thessalonian church and "complete the things that are lacking in [their] faith" (3:10). Since Paul is not able to do this in person, he will do it instead in this letter, addressing the different areas of concern that the just-returned Timothy has reported to him (3:6): the Thessalonian church needs to increase in conduct that pleases God (4:1–12), to be comforted both in their grief over the fate of their fellow believers who have died before Christ's return (4:13–18) and in their fear over the fate of living believers at Christ's return (5:1–11), and to be exhorted on various matters relating to congregational life and worship (5:12–22).

A. Increasing in Conduct That Pleases God (4:1–12)

Paul leaves behind the apologetic concerns that have preoccupied his attention in the first half of the letter body (2:1–3:10) and takes up the exhortative concerns that dominate the second half (4:1–5:22), where he fulfills his just-stated desire to "complete the things that are lacking in your faith" (3:10). The apostle begins the exhortative half by addressing the sexual conduct of the Thessalonians as well as their practice of mutual love within the church, two concerns foreshadowed already in the transitional prayer of 3:12–13 (the third concern anticipated in that prayer, dealing with Christ's return, will also be taken up later in the second half of the letter: 4:13–18; 5:1–11). These disparate subjects of sexual conduct (vv. 3–8) and mutual love within the church (vv. 9–12) are combined in 4:1–12 under the overall theme of *increasing in conduct that pleases God* (vv. 1–2).

The first specific way in which the Thessalonians can fulfill the general exhortation to increase in conduct that pleases God involves the need for holiness to characterize their sexual conduct (vv. 3–8). In this section Paul's exhortations stem from his conviction that the predominantly Gentile believers in Thessalonica, as part of the renewed Israel or the eschatological people of God, already possess the gift of holiness, which was one of the anticipated blessings of the "new" covenant in the messianic age (see comment on 4:8). Consequently, the distinguishing sign or boundary marker that separates the sexual attitudes and practices of the Thessalonian believers from that of their unbelieving fellow citizens is holiness.

The second specific way in which the Thessalonians can fulfill the general exhortation to increase in conduct that pleases God involves loving one another (4:9–12). After a general affirmation of the mutual love that already exists in the church (vv. 9–10a), Paul issues a specific appeal that in four concrete ways spells out how this love must yet be demonstrated within their fellowship (vv. 10b–12). The apostle is especially concerned with the rebellious refusal of some in the church to work but instead take advantage of the generosity of their fellow believers, thereby violating the principle of *philadelphia*, or mutual love.

Literary Analysis

Character of the Passage

The material of 4:1–12 and indeed of the whole second half of the letter body (4:1–5:22) can best be identified as "paraenesis" (on this formal category generally, see D. Bradley 1953; Doty 1973: 37–39; Roetzel 1982: 35–36; Aune 1987: 191, 194–97; Malherbe 1986: 124–29; Stowers 1986: 91–106; Popkes 1996; M. B. Thompson, *DPL* 922–23). This term (also spelled "parenesis") is a transliteration of the Greek noun παραίνεσις (*parainesis*), meaning "exhortation, advice, urging,"[1] and refers to traditional moral and religious exhortation dealing with practical issues of living. The ancient epistolary theorist, Libanius, lists the paraenetic letter as the first of his many types or "styles" of letters, defining such correspondence as "that in which we exhort someone by urging him to pursue something or to avoid something" (Malherbe 1988: 68–71).

In letters from the Greco-Roman world, paraenesis covers a wide range of moral matters, such as the handling of finances, labor, slavery, marriage, the upbringing of children, patriotism, and as in 4:1–12, sexual conduct and one's relationships with others, especially friends (the specific subject of "brotherly love" is widely discussed, though referring to the relationship between siblings). The key characteristics of paraenesis include the following (Aune 1987: 191; M. B. Thompson, *DPL* 922): (1) it involves traditional moral material, reflecting the conventional wisdom that is widely adopted in society; (2) it is general in nature and thus easily applied to many situations; (3) it is so familiar and widely held that it is frequently presented as a reminder to the audience of what they already know and believe; (4) it is commonly illustrated by individuals who serve as models of virtues to be imitated; and (5) it is typically given by those in authority or those who consider themselves to be morally superior to those whom they exhort.

Paraenesis in the NT Letters exhibits a variety of different forms. Although exhortations are found scattered throughout the letters, it is important to distinguish these intermittent commands from those places where they occur as a distinct literary type. Paul, for example, frequently gives lists of various vices that are to be avoided (Rom. 1:29–31; 13:13; 1 Cor. 5:10–11; 2 Cor. 6:9b–10; 12:20; Eph. 5:3–5; Col. 3:5, 8; 1 Tim. 1:9–10; 6:4–5; 2 Tim. 3:2–4), virtues that are to be adopted (2 Cor. 6:6–7; Gal. 5:22–23; Eph. 4:2–3), or mixed vice-and-virtue lists (Gal. 5:19–23; Eph. 4:31–32; Titus 1:7–10). Another distinct type of paraenesis is the "household codes" (often referred to by the German *Haustafeln*, meaning "house-tables"), which deal with the responsibilities of the various members of the household: wives and husbands, children and parents, slaves and masters (Col. 3:18–4:1; Eph. 5:21–6:9; 1 Tim. 2:1–15; 5:1–8; 6:1–2; Titus 2:1–10; 1 Pet. 2:11–3:7).

In a number of Paul's Letters, including 1 Thessalonians, it is possible to identify material as "concluding paraenesis": larger units of exhortation— prolonged exhortation of either mixed subject matter or centered on a particular topic—that occur at or toward the end of the letter body (Rom. 12:1–15:13; Gal. 5:1–6:10; 1 Thess. 4:1–5:22; Eph. 4:1–6:20; Col. 3:1–4:6). The reason for locating such larger units of paraenetic material at the close of the letter can be readily supplied. In writing to certain churches, Paul must first respond to any questions or criticisms about either his integrity (1 Thessalonians) or status as an apostle (Romans, Galatians) before he can confidently expect his readers to accept and obey the teaching and exhortations that he issues. A secondary reason lies in the general movement in some letters (Ephesians, Colossians) from "the indicative to the imperative"—from what God has done for the readers to what God has

---

1. Only the verbal form παραινέω (*paraineō*, to advise strongly, recommend, urge: BDAG 764) occurs in the NT (Acts 27:9, 22; see Luke 3:18 v.l.).

now called the readers to do. Several commentators view the closing paraenesis, including 1 Thess. 4:1–5:22, as a major unit within Paul's Letters, along with the opening, thanksgiving, body, and closing sections (so, e.g., Schubert 1939: 17–27; J. W. Bailey and Clarke 1955; Hurd 1972: 18; Doty 1973: 43; Roetzel 1982: 35–36; Hurd 1983: 13). However, a survey of all the Pauline Letters, as well as of other letters of that day, suggests that the closing paraenesis ought to be seen as one of the many different epistolary conventions that comprise the letter body.

The traditional nature of paraenesis and its easy application to a variety of situations (see the first two of the five key characteristics listed above) has caused some to argue that the exhortations of NT writers have little, if any, connection with the specific situation of their audience. The thesis of Martin Dibelius (1937: passim), for example, is that the hortatory sections of the NT are made up of rather stock ethical maxims or *topoi* (topics) drawn from the moralistic teachings of the Greco-Roman world and were used in only a general fashion, without any direct application to matters being discussed. Several commentators have followed this thesis in claiming that Paul's exhortations in 1 Thess. 4:1–12 are only of a general nature and do not reflect the actual problems in the Thessalonian church (so, e.g., Eckart 1961, esp. 35–36; Schmithals 1964; Laub 1973: 51–52; Koester 1979: 38–40; Schnelle 1990).

Most scholars today, however, recognize that Paul has used the source materials for his paraenesis with great care, modifying them so that they better relate to the specific historical situation that he is addressing. This also appears to be the case in 1 Thess. 4:1–12. The specificity of the exhortations of verses 3b–6a and 10b–12, coupled with their strategic location at the beginning of the paraenetic section of 4:1–5:22, the threatening tone of 4:6b–8, and the widespread nature of sexual immorality among Gentile Christians in the early church—all strongly suggest that Paul actually is addressing a real situation at work among the Thessalonian believers. Although the topics of holiness in sexual conduct and brotherly (and sisterly) love would no doubt be relevant for any of his churches, these two specific subjects were part of Timothy's report about the Thessalonians (3:6) and what Paul has in mind in his earlier reference to "the things that are lacking in your faith" (3:10).[2]

There is debate over the background or determining influences of Paul's paraenesis. Some believe that the apostle was impacted most by the Greco-Roman setting of his birthplace, Tarsus (Acts 22:3), and the Hellenistic culture that permeated the ancient world generally; they therefore stress the parallels between Paul's exhortations and those found in Cynic and Stoic thought (so esp. Malherbe 1989; 1992; also Hock 1980: 44–47). Others argue that the content of his paraenesis instead reflects his Jewish background and hence highlight the connections between his exhortations and those in OT thought and in the ethical traditions (halakah) that were part of his training as a Pharisee (Tomson 1990). With regard to the paraenetical material in 1 Thess. 4:1–12, a variety of factors indicate the apostle's indebtedness to the Jewish moral tradition (so, e.g., Hodgson 1982: 199–215; Collins 1983: 324–25; Carras 1990: 306–15; Rosner 1995: 352–54; Collins 1998: 406–10, 414): (1) Paul's use of key Hebrew verbs such as "to receive" (v. 1), a technical term in rabbinic writings for

---

2. On the basis of the περὶ δέ formula in 4:9, some claim that Paul is specifically responding in 4:9–12 (and probably also in 4:13–18 and 5:1–11) to a letter that the Thessalonians wrote to him (Milligan 1908: 126; Frame 1912: 140; Faw 1952; Malherbe 1990; 2000: 217, 243; Green 2002: 202). For an evaluation of this possibility, see comment on 4:9.

the transmission of traditional material, and "to walk" (vv. 1 [2x], 12), a common OT and rabbinic term denoting moral conduct; (2) the notion of "pleasing God" (v. 2) as the goal of human conduct, which stems from the OT (see, e.g., Num. 23:27; 1 Kings 14:13; Job 6:9; 34:9; Pss. 19:14; 69:31; 104:34; Prov. 15:26; 16:7; Mal. 3:4); (3) his allusions to OT texts in verses 8b and 9a (see comment on these verses below); (4) his emphasis on "holiness" in verses 3–8, a defining characteristic and desired purpose for Israel as God's covenant people (see comment on v. 3a); (5) the use of "brother" (4:1, 6, 10a, 10b) to refer to members of the church community, a use primarily influenced by Jewish practice (see comment on 1:4); and (6) the desire in 4:12 to make a good impression on those outside the community, an aspiration found throughout the OT (e.g., Exod. 32:12, 25; Num. 14:14–16; Deut. 9:25–29; 1 Kings 20:28) and developed in intertestamental Jewish writings (Unnik 1964).

Extent of the Passage

Several grammatical, literary, and thematic features clearly identify the beginning of a new section in 4:1. First, this section opens with the adverbial use of λοιπόν (*loipon*, finally) and the transitional particle οὖν (*oun*, therefore), a combination found only here in the NT. Although there is some confusion over the precise nuance of this word pair (see comment on 4:1), it clearly serves "as a transition to something new" (BDAG 603.3.b). Second, there is the presence of the vocative "brothers," which frequently occurs in the Letters of Paul and other NT writers at the opening of new epistolary units. Third, Paul begins this section with two other transitional devices common to letters of his day: the appeal formula in 4:1 ("we ask you and appeal in the Lord Jesus that . . .") and the disclosure formula in 4:2 ("For you know . . ."; see the similar use of this formula in 2:1 and 5:2). Fourth, the various features that plainly mark the ending of the preceding passage in 3:13 (see "Extent of the Passage" for 3:11–13) naturally lead the reader to expect a new section to begin in the immediately following material of 4:1. Finally, there is a rather obvious shift in both form and content from the largely apologetic material of 2:1–3:10, which focuses on the past and present relationship between Paul and the Thessalonian church, to the paraenetic, or exhortative, material of 4:1–5:22, which focuses on the Thessalonians alone and their required conduct in the future.

The presence of so many obvious transitional features suggests that 4:1 marks not merely the beginning of a new section but also a major shift in the letter. Paul leaves behind the apologetic concerns that have preoccupied his attention in the first half of the letter and moves to the exhortative concerns of the second half, where he fulfills his just-stated desire to "complete the things that are lacking in your faith" (3:10).

But while there is no question that a new section begins at 4:1, there is debate over where this passage ends. The presence of such transitional epistolary devices as the περὶ δέ (*peri de*, now concerning) formula in 4:9 (see also 5:1; 1 Cor. 7:1, 25; 8:1; 12:1; 16:1, 12) and the appeal formula in 4:10b (see also 4:1; 5:14; Rom. 12:1; 15:30; 16:17; 1 Cor. 1:10; 2 Cor. 10:1; Eph. 4:1; Phil. 4:2), as well as the shift in topic from that of holiness in sexual conduct in 4:3–8 to that of love for one another in 4:9–10a, then to other related problems in 4:10b–12—all this has led several commentators to believe the new passage ends at either 4:8 or 4:10a. Those who reach this conclusion typically view the opening verses of the new passage (4:1–2) as introducing not just the material of 4:3–12 but the entire second half of the letter (so, e.g., Moore 1969: 61; D. Martin 1995: 115; Holmes 1998: 123–24; Malherbe 2000: 217; Green 2002: 182).

There is compelling evidence, however, that supports the coherence of 4:1–12 and in turn suggests that the transitional formulas at 4:9 and 4:10b introduce minor subunits (rather than major new units) within this larger passage. Most important, three inclusios—the repetition of a key word or phrase—exist within the opening and closing verses of 4:1–12, serving to mark the boundaries of this literary unit: (1) the double reference in verse 1 to the crucial verb "to walk" as a metaphorical reference to moral conduct (περιπατεῖν/περιπατεῖτε, *peripatein/ peripateite*) is repeated in the closing words of verse 12 (περιπατῆτε, *peripatēte*); (2) the opening exhortation of verse 1, "Brothers, we ask you and appeal . . . that you increase more and more" (ἀδελφοί, ἐρωτῶμεν ὑμᾶς καὶ παρακαλοῦμεν, . . . ἵνα περισσεύητε μᾶλλον, *adelphoi, erōtōmen hymas kai parakaloumen, . . . hina perisseuēte mallon*), reappears virtually verbatim in the closing exhortation of verse 10: "But we appeal to you, brothers, to increase more and more" (παρακαλοῦμεν δὲ ὑμᾶς, ἀδελφοί, περισσεύειν μᾶλλον, *parakaloumen de hymas, adelphoi, perisseuein mallon*); and (3) the reminder that "you know what commands (παραγγελίας, *parangelias*)[3] we gave to you" in verse 2 is echoed in the closing aside in verse 11, "just as we commanded (παρηγγείλαμεν, *parēngeilamen*) you."

The coherence of 4:1–12 is further evident in that the exhortations given in this passage all constitute previously shared material. Four times Paul asserts that he is not presenting the Thessalonians with new exhortations but rather is repeating and clarifying matters already dealt with during his mission-founding visit: "as you received from us how you must walk and so please God" (v. 1); "for you know what commands we gave to you" (v. 2); "just as we indeed told you before and solemnly warned" (v. 6); "just as we commanded you" (v. 11). Not only do these expressions of reminder give 4:1–12 formal coherence, but they also serve to contrast this passage from the immediately following passage of 4:13–18, where Paul introduces his readers to a new subject not covered during his original ministry in their city (note the unique form of the disclosure formula in 4:13, "We do not want you not to know . . . ," a sharp contrast to the simple form "you know" commonly found throughout the letter).

The unity of 4:1–12 is finally also seen in its common subject matter. In this passage, although Paul treats the differing topics of holiness in sexual conduct (vv. 3–8) and issues connected with the practice of mutual love (vv. 9–12), these diverse subjects are nevertheless linked under the common theme introduced in verses 1–2: walking (i.e., living morally) in a way that pleases God. As Johanson (1987: 112) states: "This gives 4:1–12 an overall semantic coherence." The theme of the following passages in 4:13–18 and 5:1–11, by contrast, deals less with moral conduct that pleases God than with the comfort (note the concluding verses of 4:18 and 5:11: "Therefore comfort one another") that the Thessalonians have not only for their deceased fellow believers at Christ's return but also for themselves at that eschatological event.

To conclude: The strong literary and thematic evidence in support of the coherence of 4:1–12 indicates that the transitional formulas at 4:9 and 4:10b introduce minor

---

3. The plural "commands" in 4:2 is yet another clue that 4:1–2 introduce not merely the single subject of sexual conduct in 4:3–8 but also the subject of mutual love and its related exhortations taken up in 4:9–12 (Fee 2009: 138).

subunits (rather than major new units) within this larger passage. Although the topics of verses 3–8 and 9–12[4] are clearly distinct from each other, these two sections ought to be treated together since they are joined in the central theme of 4:1–12, to increase in conduct that pleases God (vv. 1–2).

Structure of the Passage

The passage consists of three sections: verses 1–2, 3–8, and 9–12. The first section of verses 1–2 introduces the overall theme of 4:1–12: increasing in conduct that pleases God. This opening unit is set apart from the rest of the passage by the very general nature of Paul's exhortation. In contrast to the later specific exhortations pertaining to holiness in sexual conduct and mutual love, these two opening verses include only general references to "how you must walk and so please God" and the "commands" that he has previously given them. The disclosure formula in verse 2 ("For you know . . .") provides further evidence that this verse belongs to the opening unit and not with the subsequent material, since this formula typically serves to introduce new material (see also 2:1; 5:2). The double reference to the lordship of Jesus as the authority by which Paul issues his exhortation (v. 1, "in the Lord Jesus"; v. 2, "through the Lord Jesus") also links these two opening verses.

The second section, 4:3–8, is defined not only by its common subject matter of sexual conduct[5] but also by the repetition of words derived from the root "holy" (ἁγι-, hagi-): the noun "holiness" (ἁγιασμός, hagiasmos) occurs three times (vv. 3, 4, 7), and the adjective "holy" (ἅγιον, hagion) is found in a unique description of God's Spirit, intended to emphasize his holy character (v. 8). This fourfold reiteration of the root word "holy" gives 4:3–8 lexical coherence. The ending of the second unit is indicated by the περὶ δέ (peri de, now about) formula in verse 9, marking the transition to the new unit dealing with love for one another, as well as the emphatic particle τοιγαροῦν (toigaroun, therefore) in verse 8, which anticipates a closing or concluding statement. The ending at verse 8 is also suggested by the natural climax that is reached in the three successive causal statements of verses 6b, 7, and 8, each one appealing to the activity of a different divine person: "the Lord" [i.e., Jesus] (v. 6b), "God" (v. 7), and "his Spirit, who is holy" (v. 8).

The third section, 4:9–12, clearly opens with the transitional peri de formula in verse 9 and the introduction of the new topic on "love for one another." The ending of this unit, however, is complicated by the presence of the appeal formula in verse 10b, which has suggested to some the presence of a fourth section dealing with yet another topic, that of idleness (so, e.g., Frame 1912: 159; Morris 1991: 130). Nevertheless, against this possibility is the fact that the first of the four infinitives linked to this appeal formula is "to increase more and more"—an exhortation that looks *back* to the preceding discussion of mutual love, just as the identical exhortation in verse 1c ("that you increase more and more") looks back to the preceding general exhortation in verse 1b ("how you must walk and so please God"). Consequently, verses 9–12 are linked by common subject matter: the topic of love for others found in the first half of this unit (vv. 9–10a: "love for one another" in

4. For the justification in treating 4:9–10a and 4:10b–12 together as one unit consisting of 4:9–12, despite the presence of the transitional appeal formula in 4:10b, see "Structure of the Passage."

5. Contrary to the claim of several commentators, Paul does not shift to the new topic of business practices in 4:6 (see comment on this verse below).

v. 9a; "to love one another" in v. 9b; "for indeed you are doing *this* [i.e., loving one another] to all the brothers" in v. 10a) is continued in the second half (vv. 10b–12): the first appeal "to increase more and more" looks backward, challenging the Thessalonians to abound in mutual love, while the three subsequent appeals spell out how this mutual love manifests itself in specific ways, such as leading a quiet life, minding one's own business, and being engaged in self-sufficient work. The coherence of verses 9–12 is further supported by the inclusio formed between the phrase "You have no need" in verse 9 with the similar phrase "You have need of no one/nothing" in verse 12.

The structure of 4:1–12, therefore, is as follows:[6]

1. Introduction (4:1–2)
2. Holiness in sexual conduct (4:3–8)
    a. Statement of thesis (4:3a)
    b. Three exhortations (4:3b–6a)
        i. Separate yourselves from sexual immorality (4:3b)
        ii. Learn to control your sexual desires and conduct (4:4–5)
        iii. Do not harm others through your sexual conduct (4:6a)
    c. Three reasons (4:6b–8)
        i. The future judgment of the Lord Jesus (4:6b)
        ii. The past call of God (4:7)
        iii. The present gift of the Holy Spirit (4:8)
3. Love for one another (4:9–12)
    a. General affirmation (4:9–10a)
        i. Opening assertion: No need to write to you about loving one another (4:9a)
        ii. Reason 1: You are taught by God to love one another (4:9b)
        iii. Reason 2: You already give evidence of loving one another (4:10a)
    b. Specific appeal (4:10b–12)
        i. Appeal 1: Increase in loving one another (4:10b)
        ii. Appeal 2: Live a quiet life (4:11a)
        iii. Appeal 3: Mind your own business (4:11b)
        iv. Appeal 4: Engage in self-sufficient work (4:11c)
        v. Purpose clause (4:12)
            (1) To win the respect of non-Christians (4:12a)
            (2) To be dependent on no one (4:12b)

Exegesis and Exposition

¹⌜And so⌝, brothers, we ask you and appeal in the Lord Jesus ⌜that⌝—just as you received from us how you must walk and so please God, ⌜just as you are indeed

6. The justification for the internal structure of sections 2 (4:3–8) and 3 (4:9–12) is given in the comments below.

walking⌐—that you increase more and more. ²For you know what commands we gave to you through the Lord Jesus.

³For this—namely, your holiness—is the will of God: that you separate yourselves from ⌐sexual immorality⌐; ⁴that each one of you know how to control his own vessel in holiness and honor, ⁵not in lustful passion, just as also the Gentiles who do not know God; ⁶that one not trespass or take advantage of his brother in this matter, because the Lord is an avenger concerning all these things, just as we indeed told you before and solemnly warned. ⁷For God did not call us for impurity but in holiness. ⁸Therefore the one who rejects these exhortations rejects not a human being but God, who ⌐indeed⌐ ⌐gives⌐ his Spirit, who is holy, into ⌐you⌐.

⁹Now about your love for one another, ⌐you have no need for us to write⌐ to you, for you yourselves are taught by God to love one another; ¹⁰ᵃfor indeed you are doing it to all the brothers ⌐in the whole of Macedonia⌐. ¹⁰ᵇBut we appeal to you, brothers, to increase more and more, ¹¹and to make it your ambition to live a quiet life, and to mind your own business, and to work with your ⌐hands⌐, just as we commanded you, ¹²in order that you may walk appropriately before outsiders and may have need of no one.

1. Introduction (4:1–2)

Paul presents the overall theme of 4:1–12 in an opening exhortation whose grammatical structure is more complex than most translations reveal.[7] The content of the exhortation is introduced by a ἵνα (*hina*, that) clause, which is immediately interrupted by two parenthetical καθώς (*kathōs*, just as) clauses of such length that a second *hina* was considered necessary:

4:1

> And so, brothers, we ask you and appeal in the Lord Jesus
> that—
>> just as you received from us how you must walk and so please God,
>> just as you are indeed walking—
> that you increase more and more.

The major shift in the letter that takes places here at 4:1 is marked first by the adverbial use of λοιπόν (*loipon*, finally) and the transitional particle οὖν (*oun*, therefore). The precise nuance of this word pair is difficult to determine, especially since this combination occurs nowhere else in the NT.[8] The renderings "as far as the rest is concerned, beyond that, in addition, finally" (BDAG 602.3.b; see also BDF §§160; 451.6) or "as for other matters" (NIV 2011) all suggest that Paul is introducing something new that has no link with

---

7. The NIV of 4:1, for example, (1) creates two independent clauses in English out of the single Greek sentence; (2) moves the opening main clause ("We ask you and urge you in the Lord Jesus") to the newly created second clause; (3) turns the first καθώς clause into an opening main clause; and (4) converts the passive "you received from us" into the active "we instructed you."

8. The particle οὖν is omitted in some MSS (see additional notes below).

the preceding material. The translation "finally," adopted in most versions (RSV, NRSV, NKJV, NASB, NLT, NJB, NAB, NIV [1984]), has an additional temporal sense, implying that Paul has finished most of the matters he wished to address and is now finally reaching the end of his letter (cf. 2 Cor. 13:11; Phil. 4:8; BDAG 603.3.b also cites 1 Thess. 4:1; 2 Thess. 3:1; UPZ 78.43; P.Oxy. 119.13; BGU 1079.6; 1 Clem. 64.1).

The adverbial use of *loipon*, however, sometimes has an inferential sense ("therefore, consequently, it follows that") that stresses the connection of the following statement with the immediately preceding material (1 Cor. 4:2; 7:29; 2 Tim. 4:8; BDAG 603.3.b also cites Epictetus, *Disc.* 1.24.1; 1.27.2; P.Oxy. 1480.13; T. Ab. A 7; T. Job 53.4; Ignatius, *Eph.* 11.1). This inferential sense is supported by the use of *oun* in Paul's other letters to introduce exhortation (paraenesis) as the natural result of teaching that he has just finished presenting (Rom. 12:1; Gal. 5:1; 6:10; Eph. 4:1; Col. 3:5). Since it is not obvious *how* the exhortation of 4:1 follows as an expected consequence from the preceding prayers of 3:11–13, most scholars who adopt the inferential sense of *loipon oun* claim that it has in view "the whole sweep of Paul's thought implicit in the preceding chapters" (Best 1977: 154; see also, e.g., Holtz 1986: 151; Morris 1991: 113–14; Rosner 1995: 358; Weatherly 1996: 127; Furnish 2007: 87). A better explanation, however, is that Paul's exhortation to increase in conduct that pleases God follows naturally from his just-stated desire to "complete the things that are lacking in your faith" (3:10) and his prayer that they might "abound and increase in love for one another and for all, . . . in order to strengthen your hearts as blameless in holiness" (3:12–13). The rendering of *loipon oun* as "and so" (Moule 1959: 161) more accurately expresses the somewhat veiled nature of the link to the preceding material than the stronger inferential translation "therefore." A fuller paraphrase of this unique word pair would be "And so, brothers, let me spell out what I was hinting at in my closing words of 3:10 and foreshadowed in my prayer of 3:12–13."[9]

The exhortation comes in the form of an epistolary convention widely used in the ancient world: the appeal formula (see esp. Mullins 1962; Bjerkelund 1967). This formula occurs in both private letters and official correspondence for requesting the readers to take some course of action. The appeal formula typically consists of four elements (Bjerkelund 1967: 43–50): (1) the verb of appeal, παρακαλέω (*parakaleō*, or its synonym ἐρωτάω, *erōtaō*), from which this epistolary convention derives its name, in the first person; (2) a reference to the recipients of the appeal; (3) a prepositional phrase indicating the source of authority by which the letter sender issues the appeal (this element normally occurs only in official correspondence and not in private letters); and (4) the content of the appeal, typically introduced by either a ἵνα (*hina*, that) or infinitive clause.

The parallels with Paul's appeal not only here in 4:1 but also elsewhere (Rom. 12:1–2; 15:30–32; 16:17; 1 Cor. 1:10; 4:16; 16:15–16; 2 Cor. 10:1–2; Phil. 4:2

---

9. See Malherbe (2000: 218), who translates λοιπὸν οὖν as "well then" and cites the paraphrase of Milligan (1908: 45): "And now, brethren, to apply more directly what we have been saying."

[2x]; 1 Thess. 4:10b–12; 5:12, 14; 2 Thess. 2:1–2; Philem. 9–10 [2x]) are obvious and reveal the apostle's frequent use of this formula. The presence of the third element—the prepositional phrase—in Paul's Letters suggests that his employment of the appeal formula conforms most closely to that of rulers and other officials writing to those under their authority. This is significant, since the appeal formula was typically used in official correspondence to express a friendlier, less heavy-handed tone. Paul deliberately uses the appeal formula in this nuanced manner: in situations where his authority is not questioned and he is confident that his exhortation will be obeyed, the apostle chooses not in a heavy-handed manner to "command" his readers but rather in a more user-friendly way to "appeal" to them. Paul's awareness of this softer sense expressed by the appeal formula is clear from its twofold occurrence in his Letter to Philemon, where the apostle emphasizes that he appeals to the slave owner (vv. 9–10) rather than commands him (v. 8).[10] In addition to giving his exhortations a warmer or friendlier tone, the appeal formula in Paul consistently appears at a turning point in the development of his thought and thus also functions as a transitional formula.

The appeal formula in 4:1 exhibits both the form and the function that this epistolary convention typically possesses, though there are some distinctive features. The first element, the verb of appeal, is expressed not by the expected single verb but by two: "we ask and appeal" (ἐρωτῶμεν καὶ παρακαλοῦμεν, *erōtōmen kai parakaloumen*). The first verb, *erōtōmen*, appears only four times in Paul's Letters, normally linked in close fashion to the second verb, *parakaloumen*, and as a synonym for this verb in an appeal formula (1 Thess. 4:1; 5:12; 2 Thess. 2:1; Phil. 4:3). The second verb, by contrast, appears with great frequency in the apostle's writings (54x) and possesses a wide range of meanings (BDAG 764–65 lists five different senses). Although the three occurrences of this verb earlier in the letter (2:12; 3:2, 7) express the nuance of comfort (so also later in 4:18; 5:11), when *parakaleō* occurs in the first person and as the first element in an appeal formula, it expresses the authoritative notion of exhortation.

The combined use of *erōtōmen* and *parakaloumen* as part of the same appeal formula occurs only here among Paul's many uses of this epistolary convention and thus is significant (the pair also occurs in the same order in P.Oxy. 294.28; 744.6; P.Freib. 39; and twice in P.Col. 8.8–9, 21). The presence of *erōtōmen*, especially in the first position prior to *parakaloumen*, reinforces the warmer or friendlier tone already expressed by the appeal formula: Paul

10. Note also the shift from 1 Thessalonians to 2 Thessalonians in Paul's treatment of the problem of idleness. In the first letter, Paul twice "appeals" to his readers "to work with your hands, . . . in order that you may have need of no one" (4:10b–12) and to "admonish the rebellious idlers" (5:14). In the second letter, however, the problem of idleness has worsened rather than improved, thereby causing Paul not only to treat the matter at much greater length (2 Thess. 3:6–15) but also to "command" his readers on this matter rather than appeal to them (2 Thess. 3:6). Note still further the absence of the appeal formula in Galatians, which is hardly accidental or surprising given the apostle's strained, if not broken, relationship with these churches.

is not commanding his readers in a domineering manner but asking and appealing to them. Nevertheless, the use of both verbs in the same formula adds a certain emphasis to the appeal that is being made.

The second element of the appeal formula is a reference to the recipients of the exhortation, and this is expressed rather simply in 4:1 by the second-person pronoun "you" (ὑμᾶς, hymas). As is often the case with this formula, however, Paul further specifies the recipients with the vocative "brothers" (ἀδελφοί, adelphoi). In addition to functioning as yet another transitional device marking the major shift that takes place here in 4:1, this seventh occurrence of "brothers" in the letter so far (1:4; 2:1, 9, 14, 17; 3:7; see 3:2) supplements the familial language and metaphors ("beloved" [1:4], "infants" [2:7b], "nursing mother" [2:7c], "father" [2:11], "orphaned" [2:17]) found elsewhere in 1 Thessalonians, intended to create community cohesion among the converts in Thessalonica who may have had little or no previous social interaction or commitment to each other and none to Paul (Meeks 1986: 129; Wanamaker 1990: 147–48; Malherbe 1995; see also comment on 1:4).

The third element frequently found in an appeal formula is a prepositional phrase indicating the source of authority by which the letter sender issues his appeal, and this corresponds to Paul's words "in the Lord Jesus" (ἐν κυρίῳ Ἰησοῦ, en kyriō Iēsou). Even though the appeal formula conveys a friendly and less heavy-handed tone, Paul still speaks authoritatively. As Wanamaker (1990: 148) states: "The prepositional phrase . . . serves to emphasize Paul's position as an authoritative representative of Jesus and to remind the Thessalonians that their lives were under Jesus' control."

Some commentators, however, fail to see any reference to authority in this phrase, claiming that the seemingly authoritative verb "we appeal" takes its meaning from the softer "we ask," and that the third element of the appeal formula elsewhere does not use the preposition en (as here) but διά (dia; see Rom. 12:1; 15:30; 1 Cor. 1:10; 2 Cor. 10:1). Consequently, they conclude that the phrase "in the Lord Jesus" qualifies not just the subject of the two verbs ("we") but also their object ("you"), thereby highlighting the communal perspective with which Paul issues his appeal (Dobschütz 1909: 156; Williams 1992: 70; Malherbe 2000: 219). Against this interpretation, however, is (1) the word order in Greek, where the prepositional phrase "in the Lord" is separated from the object "you" and more naturally connected with the immediately preceding verb "we appeal" and its subject; (2) the parallel prepositional phrase in verse 2 ("through the Lord Jesus"), which almost certainly also refers to the authority of the Lord Jesus (NIV, "by the authority of the Lord Jesus"); (3) the form of the appeal formula, which often uses a prepositional phrase at this point to convey the authority by which the appeal is given; and (4) the authoritative sense that the similar phrase "in the Lord" has in 5:12. Therefore, most scholars rightly see Paul as grounding the appeal in his position as an authoritative spokesperson of the Lord Jesus (e.g., Milligan 1908: 46; Frame 1912: 142; Marshall 1983: 104; Ellingworth and Nida 1975: 75; D. Martin 1995: 118; Collins 1998: 406; Witherington 2006: 111).

The fourth and final element involves the content of the appeal, and this is introduced here, as it is sometimes elsewhere (Rom. 15:30–31; 1 Cor. 1:10; see also Matt. 14:36; Mark 5:18; 6:56; 7:32; 8:22; Luke 8:32), with the conjunction ἵνα (*hina*, that).[11] But before this content clause is completed, it is interrupted by two *kathōs* clauses, each of which functions as a parenthesis within the opening exhortation.

The first *kathōs* clause reminds the Thessalonians of the paraenesis, or moral exhortation, that Paul passed on to them already during his mission-founding visit: "just as you received from us how you must walk and so please God" (καθὼς παρελάβετε παρ' ἡμῶν τὸ πῶς δεῖ ὑμᾶς περιπατεῖν καὶ ἀρέσκειν θεῷ, *kathōs parelabete par' hēmōn to pōs dei hymas peripatein kai areskein theō*). The verb "you received" (*parelabete*) is a technical term in Paul's Letters for the passing on and reception of traditional material (cf. 1 Cor. 11:23; 15:3). Although this technical usage has roots in Hellenism for the instruction passed on from a philosopher to his students (see G. Delling, *TDNT* 4:11–12), it has a stronger parallel in the rabbinic tradition, which was an essential part of Paul's pre-Christian training (see Davies 1948: 247–50; Gerhardsson 1961: 265, 290–96). This is the second time in the letter that Paul refers to traditional material that he has shared with the Thessalonians. The content of the traditional material referred to earlier (in 2:13) is the gospel message itself (see also Gal. 1:9, 12); here in 1 Thess. 4:1 it involves ethical teachings on "how[12] you must[13] walk and so please God."

The first infinitive, *peripatein* (see also 2:12), literally means "to walk" but has the metaphorical sense of "to conduct one's life" (BDAG 803.2). This is one of Paul's favorite terms (32 occurrences) to describe the Christian life, and he commonly uses it to introduce themes that he considers to be fundamental (Holloway 1992). Although this metaphorical use of "walking" to describe moral conduct clearly stems from Paul's Jewish background, it also occurs in nonbiblical Greek (but with much less frequency and normally with the synonymous verb πορεύομαι) and thus would have been readily understood by his readers (H. Seesemann, *TDNT* 5:940–45; Holloway 1992: 1–27).

The conjunction *kai* is consecutive (BDF §442.2) so that the following infinitive "to please" (*areskein*) does not list a second, parallel requirement for the Thessalonians but instead provides the purpose or result of the preceding infinitive: "to walk *and so please* God."[14] The notion of pleasing God as the

11. The conjunction ἵνα in 4:1b does not have its common function as a marker denoting purpose, aim, or goal but as a marker denoting the content of the preceding main verb (BDAG 476.2; Moule 1959: 145–46).

12. In 4:1b the neuter article τό functions to substantivize the indirect question introduced by πῶς (BDF §267.2); the resulting noun clause (τὸ πῶς δεῖ ὑμᾶς περιπατεῖν καὶ ἀρέσκειν θέω) serves as the direct object of παρελάβετε.

13. The NIV of 4:1b ("how to live") omits the verb δεῖ ("how you *must* walk") and so fails to capture the obligatory nature of this traditional, moral exhortation.

14. Bruce (1982: 79) somewhat similarly identifies the two infinitives as a hendiadys: "to walk and to please God" means "to walk *so as to please* God" (so also Gaventa 1998: 50; Shogren 2012: 156).

goal of human conduct stems from the OT (see, e.g., Num. 23:27; 1 Kings 14:13; Job 6:9; 34:9; Pss. 19:14; 69:31; 104:34; Prov. 15:26; 16:7; Mal. 3:4) and is one of Paul's favorite expressions for right behavior (Rom. 8:8; 1 Cor. 7:32–34; Gal. 1:10; 1 Thess. 2:4, 15; 4:1; see also Eph. 6:6; 2 Cor. 5:9; Col. 1:10; 3:22). Earlier in the letter the apostle defends his integrity by asserting that he speaks "not as those who please people but those who please God" (2:4). He also identifies certain Jews who hindered his ministry as those "who do not please God" (2:15), a charge that in Paul's mind is so serious that it comes immediately after his description of them as "those who killed both the Lord Jesus and the prophets." Now he reminds the Thessalonians that the traditional material—the moral teachings and exhortations—that he first passed on to them during his mission-founding visit has the ultimate goal of helping them lead lives that "please God."

This first *kathōs* clause reveals that moral exhortation was an essential part of Paul's missionary preaching in Thessalonica. For the apostle, paraenesis cannot be separated from kerygma: ethical instruction was intimately intertwined with theology at the very beginning of his ministry to the Thessalonians (Collins 1998: 404; Gaventa 1998: 50). The gospel message that caused them "to turn to God from idols" involved not merely an adjustment in their thinking or beliefs but a profound change in their lifestyle, as they sought "to serve a living and true God" (1:9). In addition to the gospel, therefore, Paul passed on to them teachings and exhortations whereby they could live a life that pleases God. Some commentators emphasize the sociological function that such paraenetical instruction has: "The patterns of conduct Paul enjoined on his converts were intended to separate them from the pagan social world out of which they had come and to facilitate harmony and a common identity among the members of the newly formed community" (Wanamaker 1990: 149; see also Meeks 1983: 97–103). It is true that Paul in 4:1–12 is concerned with strengthening the identity of the small and persecuted community of believers in Thessalonica and sharpening the boundaries that distinguish it from "the Gentiles who do not know God" (v. 5) and "outsiders" (v. 12). The apostle's motivation, however, is not solely sociological but also stems from his theological conviction that "pleasing God"—whether in sexual conduct that is holy (vv. 3–8) or in love for one another (vv. 9–12) or indeed in any activity of life—is the defining characteristic that distinguishes members of the covenant community from those who are of the world (see Weima 1996).

It was noted earlier that Paul gives a warmer tone to his opening exhortation by (1) appealing rather than commanding the Thessalonians and by (2) adding the softer "we ask" before the stronger "we appeal." The apostle now further softens the content of the appeal that he has strategically delayed and still not yet explicitly shared with his readers by the insertion of a second *kathōs* clause, which acknowledges that the Thessalonians are already living up to his previously shared call to "walk and so please God": "just as you are indeed walking" (καθὼς καὶ περιπατεῖτε, *kathōs kai peripateite*). This affirmation will be repeated two more times in Paul's later discussion of love for one another (4:10, "for you indeed are doing it") and eschatological matters (5:11, "just as indeed you are doing"). These statements of affirmation do not mean, however, that Paul has no concerns about the believers in Thessalonica or that in 4:1–12 he is not addressing concrete problems (see discussion in "Character of the Passage"). As pleased as the apostle is with the progress of his converts, he nevertheless remains concerned about the very real danger of their reverting to previous pagan practices (so, e.g., Frame 1912: 14–15, 145; Best 1977: 160; Wanamaker 1990: 158–59).

This concern of Paul, implicitly given in the two *kathōs* clauses, now finally manifests itself in an explicit way in the content of the appeal: "that[15] you increase more and more" (ἵνα περισσεύητε μᾶλλον, *hina perisseuēte mallon*). The absence of any direct object for the verb *perisseuēte* (see comment on 3:12) results in an appeal that at first glance may appear quite vague: what are the Thessalonian believers to increase more and more in doing? The answer lies in the two preceding *kathōs* clauses, which clarify the content of the appeal: they must increase in conduct (lit., "walking") that pleases God. But even with the clarifying comments of both *kathōs* clauses, the content of the appeal remains rather general: nothing specific is said about what such God-pleasing conduct involves. This general or generic nature of the appeal, however, is fitting for its function in introducing the overall theme of 4:1–12: *increasing in conduct that pleases God*. How this general appeal relates to the specific subjects of sexual conduct and love for one another will be spelled out in the rest of the passage.[16]

Before Paul takes up the first specific way that the Thessalonians can increase in conduct that pleases God, he reminds them again (see the first *kathōs* clause) that what he is about to say involves nothing new but was part of his mission-founding message to them: "For you know what commands we gave to you through the Lord Jesus" (οἴδατε γὰρ τίνας παραγγελίας ἐδώκαμεν ὑμῖν διὰ τοῦ κυρίου Ἰησοῦ, *oidate gar tinas parangelias edōkamen hymin dia tou kyriou Iēsou*). This statement adds nothing new in terms of specifying the content of

4:2

15. This second ἵνα is grammatically not necessary, since the first ἵνα earlier in 4:1 already serves to introduce the content of the appeal. Yet, due to the length of the two καθώς clauses that have interrupted the flow of the main clause after the first ἵνα, a second ἵνα was added to make clear the grammatical connection with the main verbs "we ask and appeal."

16. Fee (2009: 139) interprets the generic nature of 4:1 as a "considerable reluctance" by Paul to exhort the Thessalonian church in a more direct manner, since Timothy's report was that the majority of the congregation were living properly and that the exhortations in 4:1–12 are therefore "aimed at so few of them that he feels the need to ease his way into speaking to a decided minority." However, as we have argued above, the generic nature of Paul's wording in 4:1 (and also v. 2) stems not from reluctance but from a desire to introduce in a fitting manner the broad theme of pleasing God—a theme that will be spelled out via very specific exhortations in the following sections of 4:3–8 and 4:9–12. Furthermore, on the topic of sexual conduct (vv. 3–8), Paul issues not one but three exhortations (vv. 3b, 4–5, 6a) and also grounds them with three strong causal statements (note esp. v. 6b, "because the Lord is an avenger concerning all these things"; also vv. 7, 8); likewise he gives multiple reminders that sexual conduct and mutual love are subjects about which he has previously instructed them (vv. 1, 2, 6b, 11b)—all these facts suggest that Paul considers the problems in the Thessalonian church to be more serious and widespread than Fee recognizes.

the preceding appeal in verse 1 but refers in a similarly general way to undefined "commands." Yet the statement of verse 2 functions rhetorically in a variety of ways to lend a more emphatic and authoritative tone to the preceding appeal.

First, the opening "for" (*gar*), along with yet another use of the disclosure formula "you know" (see also 1:5; 2:1, 2, 5, 11; 3:3, 4; 5:2), looks back to and thus strengthens the point already made in the first *kathōs* clause: the appeal to conduct themselves in a God-pleasing manner is one that they "received" from Paul during his mission-founding visit and that they now still "know." Consequently, there is a greater degree of expectation on the apostle's part that they fulfill this appeal compared to other matters on which they have not yet been taught (e.g., the fate of deceased believers at Christ's return, taken up in 4:13–18). Second, the rare noun "commands" (*parangelias*; elsewhere in Paul's Letters only 1 Tim. 1:5, 18), like the common verb from which it is derived (1 Cor. 7:10; 11:17; 1 Thess. 4:11; 2 Thess. 3:4, 6, 10, 12; 1 Tim. 1:3; 4:11; 5:7; 6:13, 17), was originally used for military commands given to a soldier (see 1 Tim. 1:18; 2 Tim. 2:3) or strict orders issued by civil magistrates (see Acts 5:28; 16:24), and thus conveys the authoritative notion of "something that must be done, *order, command*" (BDAG 760).[17] Third, although there is uncertainty over the precise nuance of the words "through the Lord Jesus,"[18] this prepositional phrase at least means that the "commands" the Thessalonians originally "received" from Paul during his original visit to their city (v. 1), which they now still "know" (v. 2), are connected to "the Lord Jesus" in such a way that these commands are not optional requests but authoritative requirements (NIV: "by the authority of the Lord Jesus"). Therefore, although the appeal formula of verse 1 conveys a friendly and less heavy-handed tone than the verb "command," the presence of verse 2 adds emphasis to the preceding appeal and gives it a slightly more authoritative character.

2. Holiness in Sexual Conduct (4:3–8)

The first specific way in which the Thessalonians can fulfill the general exhortation to increase in conduct that pleases God involves the need for holiness

17. Despite the attempt to soften the authoritative sense of παραγγελίας into "instruction" or "advice" (4:2; see Malherbe 2000: 221), the use of the noun and the cognate verb elsewhere (see texts cited above) consistently describes authoritative demands. O. Schmitz (*TDNT* 5:764) summarizes his discussion of this noun by claiming, "In general his [Paul's] instructions . . . have the character of authoritative apostolic ordinances, behind which stands the full authorization of Christ Himself" (cited by Wanamaker 1990: 149). Spicq (1994: 3.10) similarly concludes: "Consequently, *parangelia* would normally be an injunction, command, order."

18. The issue is whether διά plus the genitive here expresses (1) agency: the commands are passed on by Paul from God through the Lord Jesus; (2) source: the commands are based on the actual teaching and words of the Lord Jesus; (3) mystical union with Christ: the commands are given "through the activity of Christ in whom we are" (Best 1977: 158); or (4) authority: the commands carry the authority of the Lord Jesus. Although their reasons differ, the majority of commentators adopt the fourth option (so, e.g., Hendriksen 1955: 99; Ellingworth and Nida 1975: 76; Collins 1984: 306; Wanamaker 1990: 149; Morris 1991: 117; Williams 1992: 71; D. Martin 1995: 118–19; Richard 1995: 181).

to characterize their sexual conduct. Paul foreshadowed his concern here with holiness in the transitional prayer of 3:12–13, where the goal of his petition is that the Thessalonians will be "blameless in *holiness*" at the coming of the Lord, when he arrives "with all his *holy* ones." By his earlier reference to the Thessalonians as "turning to God from idols" (1:9b), Paul in a veiled way may have also anticipated the topic of sexual immorality taken up here in 4:3–8, since such conduct was at times associated with the practices of pagan cults and mystery religions (see discussion below).

To understand better Paul's exhortations in 4:3–8, we need to give some attention to the historical and social context of this passage, especially the topic of sexual conduct and morality in the Greco-Roman world of the first century.[19] When examining the sexual attitudes and practices of the ancient world, one must guard against oversimplifying a complex topic that involves a host of larger issues. Nevertheless, it can be confidently stated that there existed in the Greco-Roman world of Paul's day a very tolerant attitude toward sexual conduct, particularly sexual activity outside of marriage.

In Greco-Roman society, marriages were usually family arrangements rather than love matches. Typically men in their middle twenties were paired with young women barely in their teens, whom they usually had never met. So it was expected that married men would have sexual relations with other women, such as prostitutes, female slaves, or mistresses from lower social classes. This explains why Demosthenes (384–322 BC), probably the greatest of the Greek orators and a respected citizen of Athens, could state matter-of-factly in his attempt to praise wives: "Mistresses we keep for our pleasure, concubines for our day-to-day physical well-being, and wives in order to bear us legitimate children and to serve as trustworthy guardians over our households" (*Or.* 59.122). That attitudes had not changed at all some three centuries later is evident from the words of the Stoic philosopher and moralist Cato (95–46 BC), who praised those men who satisfied their sexual desires with a prostitute rather than with another man's wife (reported by his contemporary Horace, *Sat.* 1.2.31–35). The permissive perspective toward sex outside of marriage is also reflected in the following comment of Cicero (106–43 BC), one of Rome's most famous politicians and orators:

> If anyone thinks that young men should be forbidden to have affairs even with prostitutes, he is very strict indeed . . . for his view is contradictory not only to the law of the present age but even with the habits of our ancestors and with what they used to consider allowable. For when was this not a common practice? When was it blamed? When was it forbidden? When, in fact, did that which was lawful become that which was not lawful? (*Cael.* 48; Gardner 1958, altered)

To give yet another example, Plutarch (ca. AD 46–120), the Platonist philosopher, advised prospective brides that it was better to close their eyes to the

---

19. The following discussion is developed from my earlier examination of this passage: Weima 1996: 104–6.

philandering activities of their husbands than to complain and so jeopardize good relations with them (*Mor.* 104B, 144F).

A very tolerant view toward adultery and other sexual practices can also be demonstrated from a variety of other sources. For example, funerary inscriptions evidence that concubinage was common. Prostitution was a business like any other, and profit from prostitutes working at brothels was an important source of revenue for many respectable citizens. In addition, innkeepers and owners of cookshops frequently kept slave girls for the sexual entertainment of their customers. Adulterous activity was so widespread that the emperor Augustus (63 BC–AD 14) established a new code of laws having to do with adultery and marriage—the Julian Laws (since he assumed the name Julius and the title Caesar, adding them to his own name)—in a failed attempt to reform sexual practices. Within such a social context, it is not at all surprising that the Jewish Christian leaders of the Jerusalem church felt the need to include in their letter to Gentile Christians in Syria and Cilicia—the so-called apostolic decree—a warning "to abstain from sexual immorality" (Acts 15:20, 29; 21:25).

Sexual activity was frequently connected with pagan religious practice. As a result, temples often had a reputation for immorality (see Ovid, *Art of Love* 1.77–78; Juvenal, *Sat.* 6.486–89, 526–41; 9.22–26; Josephus, *Ant.* 18.65–80). A link between temples and sexual activity is strongly suggested by the fact that every NT reference to "meat sacrificed to idols" (εἰδωλόθυτα, *eidōlothyta*)—meat often eaten in a dining room located in the temple of the god to whom the food was offered—is mentioned in the same breath as "sexual immorality" (πορνεία, *porneia*; see 1 Cor. 10:7–8; Acts 15:29; Rev. 2:14, 20; 9:20–22). Especially significant for the study of 1 Thess. 4:3–8 is the evidence that a number of religious cults in Thessalonica incorporated sexual activity as part of their worship practices (for the following discussion, see Edson 1948; Witt 1977; Donfried 1985; Jewett 1986: 126–33). In the time of Paul, the most popular such religion at Thessalonica was the Cabirus cult (see the fuller discussion of the Cabirus and other cults in the introduction to this commentary, under the heading "A Religiously Pluralistic Environment"). Although many of the ritual practices associated with this cult remain a mystery, the available sources suggest that they had a strong phallic and sexual character. Witt (1977: 72–73), for example, after referring to the "grotesquely phallic" scenes in Cabiric art, concludes that "the core of the mystery was a phallic ritual" and that "the stress during the initiation ceremony fell . . . on sex." Another popular cult in Thessalonica was that of Dionysus. A small herm of Dionysus, found in the crypt of the city's Serapeion, was designed in such a way as to allow for the reconstruction of his symbol, the phallus—a key ritual in celebrations by this god's followers. Donfried (1985: 337), after noting the sexual symbols and erotic activity associated with Dionysiac worship, states: "Already in an anticipatory way we might ask whether this emphasis on the phallus and sensuality offers a possible background for the exhortations in 1 Thess 4.3–8." The cults of Isis and Aphrodite have also been connected with sexual activity. Therefore, while sexual immorality may not necessarily have been an everyday occurrence in the pagan temples of the city, such activity at Thessalonica was by no means rare or unexpected.

In light of the general sexual laxity and promiscuity practiced throughout the ancient Greco-Roman world—as well as the sexual component in a number of the pagan religions of the day, particularly in the most popular cults of Thessalonica—we can better appreciate Paul's concern in 1 Thess. 4:3–8 that his Gentile converts not revert to their former pagan practices. In fact, there is evidence in the letter that the Thessalonian believers were not merely being tempted to revert to their previous lifestyle but were also strongly pressured by their "fellow citizens" (2:14) to do so. For as we have noted before, the many references in 1 Thessalonians to the suffering being experienced by the church (1:6b; 2:2, 14–15; 3:1–5; see also 2 Thess. 1:4–7; 2 Cor. 8:1–2; Acts 17:5–7, 13) are best understood as referring not primarily to physical persecution but to social harassment for the Christians' refusal to take part in their former cultic activities. Knowing full well from the report of Timothy (3:6) the temptations and pressures faced by his young converts, Paul exhorts the Thessalonian believers to let their sexual conduct be characterized by holiness.

The apostle's exhortations in 1 Thess. 4:3–8 regarding sexual conduct follow a clear tripartite structure. First, in verse 3a he opens with a thesis-like statement that God's will for the lives of his readers involves holiness. Second, in 4:3b–6a he issues three exhortations (expressed in three infinitival clauses that function epexegetically with the opening noun phrase "your sanctification"), which spell out in concrete terms how holiness ought to control their sexual behavior. The first exhortation (v. 3b) is a general appeal to abstain from sexual immorality, while the second (vv. 4–5) and third (v. 6a) exhortations involve specific appeals that have occasioned much debate as to their correct interpretation. Third, in 4:6b–8 Paul concludes by giving three reasons why the Thessalonians ought to be holy in their sexual conduct. Each reason is introduced by a different causal conjunction (διότι, γάρ, τοιγαροῦν) and describes an action associated with a particular person of the Trinity: the future judgment of the Lord Jesus (v. 6b), the past call of God (v. 7), and the present gift of the Holy Spirit (v. 8).

a. Statement of Thesis (4:3a)

Paul begins his treatment of proper sexual conduct by placing this specific topic within the broader theme of holiness as the will of God: "For this[20]— **4:3a**

---

20. It is impossible to determine with certainty whether the demonstrative pronoun "this" (*touto*) is the subject and the noun pair "will of God" (*thelēma tou theou*) is the predicate nominative (so most commentators) or whether the reverse is true (so Frame 1912: 146; Marshall 1983: 106). It is also unclear why the first word of the noun pair "will of God" lacks the definite article. Some have explained the anarthrous *thelēma* by saying that Paul is giving only one aspect of the will of God, which has a much broader and fuller content (so, e.g., Lightfoot 1904: 53; Frame 1912: 146; Best 1977: 159; Marshall 1983: 106; Morris 1991: 119; Green 2002: 189), while others have claimed that the article was omitted because the phrase "the will of God" was a well-known formula (Wanamaker 1990: 150, who cites BDF §252). Against both

namely, your holiness—is the will of God" (τοῦτο γάρ ἐστιν θέλημα τοῦ θεοῦ, ὁ ἁγιασμὸς ὑμῶν, *touto gar estin thelēma tou theou, ho hagiasmos hymōn*). The conjunction "for" (*gar*), omitted in some translations (NIV, NJB, NLT, NAB, REB), is important, for it connects the subsequent material of 4:3–8 with the preceding exhortation of verses 1–2, particularly the appeal of verse 1 to increase in conduct that pleases God. It functions as a marker not of cause or reason (as in v. 7) but of clarification (BDAG 189.2), a function captured in the paraphrase "Well, to be explicit . . ." (Frame 1912: 146, cited by Malherbe 2000: 224) or "In particular . . ." (Milligan 1908: 47).

The placement of the noun "holiness" (*hagiasmos*)[21] in apposition to the demonstrative pronoun "this" gives that abstract term content or meaning. The importance of the concept of holiness for Paul is indicated by his equating it with the will of God and by including it as part of the key statement that introduces his discussion of sexual conduct. It is further revealed in the two additional references to the noun "holiness" in this passage (vv. 4, 7) and in the closing description of God's Spirit, which emphasizes his "holy" character (v. 8). The importance of the holiness theme is also foreshadowed by Paul in the transitional prayer of 3:13, where he calls upon the Lord to strengthen the hearts of the Thessalonians such that they may be "blameless in *holiness*" when Jesus comes again "with all his *holy ones*." The apostle's emphasis on holiness manifests itself finally in his deliberate expansion of the closing peace benediction of 5:23, where, instead of the simple and expected formula "May the God of peace be with you" (see Rom. 15:33; 2 Cor. 13:11; Phil. 4:9b), Paul writes: "May the God of peace himself *make you holy* through and through; and may your whole spirit, soul, and body *be kept blameless* at the coming of our Lord Jesus Christ."

This persistent emphasis on holiness reveals an important truth about the theological perspective from which Paul views the Thessalonian believers and issues his exhortations to them (Weima 1996: esp. 101–3). Holiness was the defining characteristic and desired purpose for Israel, God's covenant people.

---

proposals, however, are the thirteen remaining occurrences of "the will of God" in the apostle's letters, which do not reveal any clear pattern or explanation why the definite article is included in some places (Rom. 1:10; 12:2; Eph. 6:6; see 5:17) but not in others (Rom. 15:32; 1 Cor. 1:1; 2 Cor. 1:1; 8:5; Eph. 1:1; Col. 1:1; 4:12; 1 Thess. 5:18; 2 Tim. 1:1). Happily, these unanswered questions do not greatly affect our understanding of this passage. A third proposal is that the article is frequently omitted "after verbs substantive [like "is"] or nuncupative [designative]" (Ellicott 1880: 51, who cites Greek grammarians).

21. Commentators typically identify the noun ἁγιασμός (Rom. 6:19, 22; 1 Cor. 1:30; 1 Thess. 4:3, 4, 7; 2 Thess. 2:13; 1 Tim. 2:15; also Heb. 12:14; 1 Pet. 1:2) with its -μος ending as a *nomen actionis* (action noun), which stresses the *action* or *process* of sanctification in contrast to the related noun ἁγιωσύνη (Rom. 1:4; 2 Cor. 7:1; 1 Thess. 3:13), which emphasizes the *state* of holiness as a result of the sanctifying process. Consequently, many emphasize this distinction in the shift from ἁγιωσύνη in the prayer of 3:13 to ἁγιασμός in 4:3, 4, 7 (so, e.g., Best 1977: 160; Williams 1992: 71; Malherbe 2000: 25). It is questionable, however, whether this distinction is justified. Note the comment in BDAG 10 about the use of ἁγιασμός "in a moral sense for a process, or, more often, its result (the state of being made holy)."

It was the attribute by which the people of God were to be distinguished from all other nations. This is explicitly stated by God when he constitutes the nation of Israel at Mount Sinai as his chosen covenant people: "And now if you indeed obey my voice and keep my covenant, you will be to me a *distinctive* people out of all the nations. For the whole earth is mine. You will be to me a kingdom of priests and a *holy* nation" (Exod. 19:5–6 LXX). This divine command for Israel to let holiness be the distinguishing feature of its existence is repeated in the renewal of the Sinai covenant: "And the Lord has chosen you today that you may be to him a *distinctive* people, as he promised, that you may keep his commandments, and that you may be above all the nations, as he has made you renowned and a boast and glorious, in order that you may be a *holy* people to the Lord your God, as he promised" (Deut. 26:18–19 LXX). Likewise, the book of Leviticus repeatedly calls on Israel to imitate the holiness of their God: "You shall be *sanctified/made holy*, and you shall be *holy*, because I, the Lord your God, am *holy*" (Lev. 11:44 LXX; see also 11:45; 19:2; 20:7, 26; 22:32).

The basic concept associated with this call to holiness is that of "separation"—that is, of the need for Israel to "come out" and be "distinct" from the surrounding peoples (Snaith 1944: 24–32). Thus holiness is the boundary marker that separates God's people from all other nations: "And do not follow the practices of the nations whom I am driving out before you. . . . I am the Lord your God who has *separated you from all the nations*. You shall therefore make a distinction between clean and unclean. . . . And you will be holy to me, because I, the Lord your God, am holy, the one who *separated you from all the nations* to be mine" (Lev. 20:23–26 LXX).

Any first-century Jew would have been familiar with all of this. Leviticus 17–26 (the so-called Holiness Code), where God's call to holiness is clearly set forth, was well known among Jews in both Palestine and the Diaspora (Hodgson 1982: 199–215). Certainly Paul was familiar with the material in Lev. 17–26. After all, he had been an active member of the Pharisees, a group within Judaism whose name, "the separated ones" (Greek *Pharisaioi* comes from the Aramaic and Hebrew verb *pāraš*, "separate, make distinct"), reflected their desire to distance themselves not just from Gentiles but also from other Jews who did not share their passion for following the Torah's call to holiness. It is not at all surprising, therefore, that Paul viewed holiness as God's desired purpose for and defining characteristic of Israel, his covenant people.

What is surprising and even astonishing, however, is that Paul applies this standard of holiness to predominantly Gentile believers in Jesus at Thessalonica. The holiness that previously has been the exclusive privilege and calling of Israel has now also become God's purpose for Gentiles at Thessalonica who have "turned to God from idols to serve a true and living God" (1:9). The holiness that has previously been the characteristic distinguishing Israel from the Gentile nations has now also become the boundary marker that separates the Thessalonian Gentile believers from "the Gentiles who do not know God" (4:5), those who are "outside" God's holy people (4:12).

Paul, it seems clear, views his Gentile converts at Thessalonica as the renewed Israel—as those who, together with Jewish Christians, are now full members of God's covenant people. And on the basis of their privileged new position, he exhorts them in 4:3–8 to exhibit the holiness that God's people have always been called to possess.

b. Three Exhortations (4:3b–6a)

i. Separate Yourselves from Sexual Immorality (4:3b)

4:3b The general thesis that holiness constitutes the will of God (v. 3a) is applied to the specific topic of sexual conduct by means of three infinitival clauses (vv. 3b, 4–5, 6a), all in apposition to and thus explaining (epexegetical function: BDF §394) the noun phrase "your holiness." The first of these three explanatory infinitives or exhortations[22] is rather brief and general: "that you separate yourselves from sexual immorality" (ἀπέχεσθαι ὑμᾶς ἀπὸ τῆς πορνείας, *apechesthai hymas apo tēs porneias*). The compound verb ἀπέχω (*apechō*) in the active voice expresses a variety of meanings. But when it occurs in the middle voice, as here (also 1 Thess. 5:22; 1 Tim. 4:3; Acts 5:39 v.l.; 15:20, 29; 1 Pet. 2:11), this verb means "to avoid contact with or use of something, *keep away, abstain, refrain from*" (BDAG 103.5). The translation "separate yourselves" is intended to highlight the play on words that Paul makes with the noun "holiness," which similarly emphasizes the idea of being separate, distinct, or set apart.

The thing from which the Thessalonians are to separate themselves is "sexual immorality" (*tēs porneias*). The range of meanings that *porneia* has within the NT (commercial or cultic prostitution; marriage within forbidden degrees of kinship; sexual immorality in general, including fornication; figurative term for idolatry; for texts supporting each of these possible meanings, see Jensen 1978: 180) has opened the door for a debate over its precise meaning here in 1 Thess. 4:3b. Some argue for the restricted sense of "fornication," sexual intercourse between a man and a woman not married to each other (so NRSV), implying that Paul did not have in view other forms of sexual activity (Malina 1972; see the critique of Malina by Jensen 1978). A few assert that Paul is narrowly referring to incest (see 1 Cor. 5:1) or marriage between close relatives prohibited in Lev. 18:6–23 (Matt. 5:32; 19:9; Acts 15:20, 29; 21:25), that of an uncle and niece being especially common due to a particular inheritance law (Baltensweiler 1963; 1967: 135–49).

Most scholars, however, understand *porneia* to refer in a general way to all kinds of sexual misconduct, including both premarital and extramarital sex as well as homosexual activity (Witherington 2006: 112, "an umbrella term for any and all sorts of sexual sin"; see also the brief but helpful survey of the term

---

22. In the larger context—with its references to how the Thessalonians "must" walk (v. 1), the "commands" that they were given through the authority of the Lord Jesus (v. 2), and "the will of God" (v. 3a)—the explanatory infinitives (vv. 3b, 4–5, 6a) have an implicit imperative force that justifies referring to them as exhortations.

porneia by Shogren 2012: 159–60). This broad understanding of the term best fits the context where a brief, general exhortation against sexual immorality (v. 3b) introduces two following exhortations (vv. 4–5, 6a) that give greater clarification on how the Thessalonians are to be holy in their sexual conduct. In the following verses, the references to "in lustful passion" (ἐν πάθει ἐπιθυμίας, *en pathei epithymias*) in verse 5 and "impurity" (ἀκαθαρσία, *akatharsia*) in verse 7 also "shows that Paul has in view general pagan immorality" (Malherbe 2000: 226). Some manuscript correctors and copyists tried to ensure a broad understanding of *porneia* by adding the adjective "all" (see additional notes).

The full force of Paul's first exhortation can be appreciated only in light of the prevailing sexual practices and attitudes of his day (see the lengthy discussion at the opening treatment of 4:3–8). For his challenge to the Thessalonians that they separate themselves from all kinds of sexual immorality would have surely sounded strange in a Greco-Roman world that tolerated and even encouraged, at least in the case of men, various forms of extramarital sexual activity. There were, to be sure, some voices within the Hellenistic world, especially among the Stoics, that similarly advised fidelity in marriage and a restriction on certain types of sexual activity (see the citations of certain Hellenistic moralists in Malherbe 1983: 250; O. Yarbrough 1986: 46–52, 80–81; Meeks 1986: 128–29; Malherbe 2000: 230). Nevertheless, such voices were a distinct minority: the widespread conduct and opinion on these matters was one of great tolerance. The converts in Thessalonica, however, were to follow a different standard of behavior, that of holiness. And this standard of holiness demands that they "separate themselves from sexual immorality," that they make holiness in sexual conduct a boundary marker that separates or distinguishes them from the pagan community to which they previously belonged.

ii. Learn to Control Your Sexual Desires and Conduct (4:4–5)

The second of the three explanatory infinitives or exhortations involves a certain knowledge or ability that the Thessalonians ought to have: "that each one of you know how to . . ." (εἰδέναι ἕκαστον ὑμῶν, *eidenai hekaston hymōn*). When the common verb οἶδα (*oida*, know) is followed by an infinitive without a connective particle, as happens here, it has the meaning "to know *how to*" do something (see BDAG 694.3). This means that κτᾶσθαι (*ktasthai*)—the second infinitive in verse 4 (but the third in the succession of five infinitives in 4:3b–6a)—is not parallel to but dependent on the preceding infinitive *eidenai* (so virtually all commentators).[23] Whereas the subject of the earlier explanatory infinitive *apechesthai* in verse 3 was the general "you" (*hymas*), here the subject

4:4

23. But in 4:4 see Frame (1912: 147–48), who (1) views κτᾶσθαι as independent and parallel to εἰδέναι; (2) places a comma after σκεῦος, so that it now functions as both the direct object of the first infinitive and the implied direct object of the second infinitive; and (3) interprets εἰδέναι in light of its use in 5:12, to mean "respect." This results in there being two exhortations in 4:4 rather than one: "that each of you respect his own wife; that each of you get his own wife in the spirit of consecration and honour" (see also Dobschütz 1909: 161–63).

of the second explanatory infinitive *eidenai* is "each one of you" (*hekaston hymōn*), a change that individualizes and so emphasizes this second exhortation (see also 2:11, "just as you know how we dealt with each one of you").

While the first part of 4:4 is clear and devoid of controversy, the second part of this verse has generated a great deal of debate.[24] The controversy centers on the intended meaning of two words: (1) the noun *skeuos* and (2) the infinitive *ktasthai*. The noun *skeuos* literally means "vessel," such as a household jar or dish, but obviously has here (as elsewhere in Paul: Rom. 9:21, 22, 23; 2 Cor. 4:7; 2 Tim. 2:20, 21) a figurative sense. Ever since the earliest days of the church, *skeuos* has been taken as a metaphorical reference to either (1a) one's *wife* or (1b) one's *body*. In more recent times, a narrower view of the second option has become increasingly accepted: *skeuos* refers euphemistically to a particular part of one's body, the *male sex organ*. There are similarly two options for interpreting the second key word, the infinitive *ktasthai*: either (2a) the ingressive sense of "to procure for oneself, acquire, get" (BDAG 572.1), or (2b) the durative sense of "to possess" (though normally only in the perfect tense; BDAG 572.3), which in this context has the extended meaning of either "to live with sexually" or "to control." The combination of these options has resulted in three interpretations of 4:4 that are worthy of consideration.

Interpretation 1: To acquire a wife. The first interpretation involves a combination of options 1a and 2a: "that each one of you know how *to acquire a wife for himself*" (so RSV, NRSV^mg, GNT, NAB, NIV^mg, NLT^mg; Theodore of Mopsuestia; Augustine; Aquinas; Alford 1865: 268–70; Linder 1867; Ellicott 1880: 53; Findlay 1891: 81; Wohlenberg 1909: 91–92; Oepke 1933; Hendriksen 1955: 102; Friedrich 1976: 237–38; Klassen 1978: 166–67; Marxsen 1979: 60–61; Collins 1983: 27–53; O. Yarbrough 1986: 69–73; Malherbe 2000: 227–28; Burke 2003: 185–93). In other words, the thrust of the exhortation is that the unmarried male believers in Thessalonica ought to take a wife in marriage rather than remain single. The key evidences cited in support of this interpretation include the following: (1) It preserves the usual ingressive sense of the verb *ktaomai* as "acquire." (2) This verb is used elsewhere with the noun γυνή (*gynē*, woman/wife) so that the fuller phrase "to acquire a woman/wife" is a well-known expression, corresponding to the Hebrew idiom *bāʿal ʾiššâ*, which is used in the OT of getting married and engaging in sexual relations. (3) There is a parallel with 1 Pet. 3:7, where the noun *skeuos* refers to a wife ("the weaker vessel"). (4) Another parallel occurs in the rabbinic writings of later Judaism, where the Hebrew כְּלִי (*kĕlî*), corresponding to the Greek *skeuos*, was used to refer in a figurative way to women. (5) It agrees with 1 Cor. 7:2–9, where Paul presents marriage as a safeguard against sexual immorality.

---

24. Almost certainly 4:4 is the most debated text in the whole letter: it has occasioned more than twenty academic journal articles or chapters in monographs, as well as one doctoral dissertation. For bibliography, see Weima and Porter 1998: 182–96. More recent publications on this passage include Collins 1998; R. Yarbrough 1999; J. Smith 2001a; 2001b; Caragounis 2002.

These points, however, are not as compelling as they may initially appear: (1) Although the ingressive sense of *ktaomai* is admittedly more common, examples of the durative sense can be cited in support of a similar meaning in 1 Thess. 4:4. (2) The phrase "to acquire a woman/wife," which never uses the noun *skeuos*, occurs only five times in the extant Greek literature, hardly making it a well-known expression. Furthermore, if Paul truly were exhorting the single males in Thessalonica "to acquire a wife," he could have employed the idiom γυναῖκα λαβεῖν (*gynaika labein*), frequently found in the Septuagint and NT. (3) The reference to "the weaker vessel" in 1 Pet. 3:7 implies that *both* the woman and the man are "vessels," not just the woman alone. As a result this text actually supports rendering *skeuos* more generally as "body" rather than restricting it to "wife." (4) The claimed parallel in the rabbinic writings suffers from the fact that these texts are written not in Greek but in Hebrew (making it doubtful that the Thessalonians would pick up on any connection with *kĕlî*) and date to a decidedly later period than the time of Paul. (5) The claimed parallel to 1 Cor. 7:2–9 is weakened by the larger context, in which believers are encouraged to remain single (7:7–8, 25–40)—in contrast to 1 Thess. 4:4, which, according to the first interpretation, exhorts single male believers to take a wife in marriage. Also, Paul's balanced directives in 1 Cor. 7:2–9 to both husband and wife concerning their sexual conduct conflicts with his alleged one-sided exhortation in 1 Thess. 4:4 that only males obtain a wife, here referred to in a rather disparaging manner as "vessel." Furthermore, 1 Cor. 7:2–9 instructs men who are already married to have sexual relations with their wives rather than fall prey to sexual immorality, whereas 1 Thess. 4:4 exhorts single men to obtain a wife.

There are also a number of additional points that make the first interpretation, "to acquire a wife for himself," untenable: (6) According to this interpretation, the infinitive *eidenai*, which refers to a certain knowledge or skill that the Thessalonians ought to have, makes little sense. For Paul doesn't merely exhort his readers "to acquire a wife" but rather "to *know how* to acquire a wife." (7) The use of the definite article before *skeuos* and the reflexive pronoun in the genitive case is problematic, since one does not normally acquire "*the* wife of *himself*" (genitive ἑαυτοῦ, *heautou*), but instead he acquires "*a* wife *for himself*" (dative ἑαυτῷ, *heautō*). (8) The negative assertion "not in passionate lust like the Gentiles who do not know God" is similarly difficult for this interpretation, for how can one "acquire a wife" not in passionate lust like the Gentiles? (9) That most marriages in the ancient world were arranged, especially for the lower class, among whom the majority in the Thessalonian church numbered, makes an exhortation "to take a wife for himself" not applicable to the social situation of most congregational members (note how the exhortation involves "each one of you").

Interpretation 2: To live with one's own wife. The second interpretation involves a combination of options 1a and 2b: "that each one of you know how to *live with his own wife* (so GNT, CEV, NIV^mg; C. Maurer, *TDNT* 7:366; Best 1977: 162; Thomas 1978: 271; Collins 1984: 314; Holtz 1986: 158; Witherington

1990: 141–42; 2006: 113–16; see also Vogel 1934). In other words, the thrust of the exhortation is that the married men in the Thessalonian church will have a proper sexual relationship with their wives—a sexual relationship in which they treat their spouses respectfully ("in holiness and honor") and not merely as a sex object or a means to satisfy their lustful desires ("not in passionate lust like the Gentiles who do not know God"). While agreeing that *skeuos* refers figuratively to one's wife, this second interpretation differs from the first in adopting a durative sense of the infinitive *ktaomai*: "to continue to have, possess, keep." And when this durative sense of *ktaomai* is combined with the noun *skeuos* in the larger context of a discussion about "sexual immorality" (*porneia*) and "passionate lust" (*en pathei epithymias*), advocates claim that it has the extended sense of "to live with sexually" and thus refers to sexual conduct within marriage.

The strength of this second interpretation over the first lies in its ability to account for the four additional problems cited above. According to this alternate view, the infinitive *eidenai* refers to the ability that one has in knowing how to have a proper sexual relationship with one's wife (point 6). The definite article before *skeuos* and the genitive reflexive pronoun fittingly refers to the proper sexual relationship that one ought to have with "*his own* wife" (point 7). The negative assertion "not in lustful passion like the Gentiles who do not know God" serves as a powerful contrast to the holy and honorable manner in which a Christian husband lives sexually with his own wife (point 8). The exhortation for a proper sexual relationship with one's spouse is applicable to far more members of the church than a command for single men to marry a wife (point 9). But despite all these advantages, the second interpretation still suffers from the significant problems connected with viewing *skeuos* as a reference to "wife" (points 1–5 above).

Interpretation 3: To control one's own body/sex organ. The third interpretation involves a combination of options 1b and 2b: either "that each one of you know how *to control his own body*" (so NIV, NRSV, NJB, NEB, REB, ESV, GNT^mg; Tertullian, *Res.* 16; John Chrysostom, *Hom. 1 Thess.* 5; Theodoret; Pelagius; Calvin; Beza; Grotius; Milligan 1908: 49; Ogara 1938: 65–72; Rigaux 1956: 505; Morris 1959: 121; Collins 1983; McGehee 1989; Richard 1995: 198; Green 2002: 191–94; Beale 2003: 116–19; Shogren 2012: 161–64) or more specifically "that each one of you know how *to control his own sex organ*" (so BDAG 928.3; NAB [1970: "guarding his member"]; Reese 1979: 44; Bruce 1982: 83; Whitton 1982; Marshall 1983: 108–9; Donfried 1985: 337, 342; Wanamaker 1990: 152; Fee 1994a: 51–52n59; Elgvin 1997; Légasse 1997: 105–15; R. Yarbrough 1999: 220–21; J. Smith 2001b: 90–105; Fee 2009: 149–50). Whether Paul is referring to the body in general or the male genital organ in particular, the intent of the exhortation is the same: all[25] Christians, whether single or married,

25. In 4:4 the masculine form of the pronouns ἕκαστον (each one) and ἑαυτοῦ (his own) and especially the likelihood that σκεῦος refers to the *male* sex organ suggest that Paul is addressing primarily the male members of the Thessalonian church and only indirectly the female

must control their sexual urges and activities, conducting themselves according to the standard of holiness ("in holiness and honor")—a moral standard that distinguishes believers in Thessalonica from their non-Christian fellow citizens ("not in passionate lust like the Gentiles who do not know God").

This third interpretation differs from the preceding two in taking the noun *skeuos* as a figurative reference to either one's body or genitalia. In support of this meaning, the following evidence can be cited: (1) In 1 Sam. 21:5 (21:6 MT) the Hebrew כְּלִי (*kĕlê*, vessels), rendered as *skeuos* in the LXX, functions twice as a euphemistic reference to the sexual organs of David's men, who have kept themselves from women (Whitton 1982). (2) Another important parallel is found in 4Q416 frg. 2 2.21, where the Hebrew כְּלִי once again serves as a euphemism for the male sex organ (Elgvin 1997; J. Smith 2001a). (3) The Greek noun *skeuos*, as well as the Latin equivalent *vas*, occurs frequently in the secular writings of Paul's day as a euphemism for genitalia. (4) This meaning fits the immediate context with its call to abstain from "sexual immorality" (1 Thess. 4:3) and its contrast between "in holiness and honor" (v. 4b) and "not in lustful passion" (v. 5a), similar to Paul's language of "honor" and "dishonor" when referring to the genitalia in 1 Cor. 12:23–24 (τιμή, *timē*, honor—the term is in both texts). (5) Such a euphemistic reference is supported by the strongly phallic character of the Cabirus and Dionysian cults, which were popular at Thessalonica. (6) There are numerous parallels from both biblical and secular writings where *skeuos* refers in a broader way to the "body." (7) Throughout his letters, Paul's concern (Rom. 1:24; 6:12; 1 Cor. 6:12–20; 7:34; 12:22–24; 1 Thess. 5:22–23) with how believers treat their body (σῶμα, *sōma*) strengthens the likelihood that *skeuos* in 1 Thess. 4:4 refers to the body or a specific part of the body, especially in light of the numerous verbal and conceptual similarities that exist between 1 Thess. 4:3–8 and these other passages (see J. Smith 2001b: 96–100).

In this third interpretation, the infinitive *ktasthai* typically is understood to have a durative sense: "to possess" one's body or sexual organ such that one acquires control over it. Yet this notion of acquiring control can also be derived from an ingressive sense of *ktasthai*. The use here in 4:4 of the present tense of this infinitive implies not a onetime occurrence but a continuous or repeated action. This is confirmed by the preceding infinitive, *eidenai*, which signifies a *process* of learning. In Phil. 4:12, for example, Paul employs this exact construction (the verb "to know" [*oida*] followed by an infinitive: "to

members. Some object to this conclusion, arguing (1) that the pronouns can be used inclusively (note how modern versions no longer render ἑαυτοῦ with the masculine "*his* own" but with the inclusive "*your* own": NIV, NRSV, NLT) and (2) that σκεῦος can refer to the sexual organs of both sexes. The first point may be granted, but the evidence for the second is very weak (J. Smith [2001b: 103n133] cites only the much later example of Augustine, who uses the Latin *vasa* to refer to both male and female genitalia). That Paul is primarily addressing males in the church and only indirectly female members is supported by Paul's seemingly noninclusive reference in 4:6 to a "brother" being wronged as well as by the patriarchal model of family and household structures of that day.

know how to . . .") to describe the repeated process by which he learned how to live with little and how to live in abundance (Caragounis 2002: 147). Thus one can understand *ktasthai* in 4:4 ingressively, as "to be in the process of gaining possession, i.e., control" (Williams 1992: 73). As Elgvin (1997: 613) explains: "Even if one grants the ingressive meaning in this case, one could still translate: '. . . that each one of you knows how to get in control of your sex organ [= passions].'"

The biggest objection typically raised against this third interpretation (in addition to the question over the durative force of the infinitive *ktasthai*) is that it fails to do justice to the reflexive pronoun "his own," which might be seen to emphasize one person's possession in contrast to that of someone else—an emphasis that fits well with the reading "wife" but not with one's own body or genitalia, which someone else cannot possess. Yet the reflexive pronoun was losing its emphatic function in Hellenistic Greek (BDF §283) and increasingly functioned in place of the simple personal pronoun, as is the case earlier in the letter, in 2:12. Furthermore, Paul elsewhere does use the reflexive pronoun to refer to a person's own body (Rom. 4:19; Eph. 5:28, 29).

Conclusion. Our survey of the three major interpretations that have been proposed for the exhortation of 1 Thess. 4:4 clearly demonstrates the complexity of this debate and that no interpretation is completely free of criticism. Nevertheless, the interpretation that has the strongest support and the fewest objections is the third: "that each one of you know how to control his own body/sex organ," that is, that the Thessalonians learn how to control their sexual urges and conduct. In light of the uncertainty of whether Paul is referring to the body in general or, as seems more likely, a specific part of the body (the genitalia), it is perhaps wisest to translate the noun *skeuos* with its literal meaning of "vessel." Such a translation not only retains the ambiguous character of Paul's language but also forces the modern reader to consider the different possibilities (body or sex organ) that the apostle evokes through his figurative use of this term.

The standard by which believers must learn to control their sexual desires and practices is spelled out both positively and negatively: "in[26] holiness and honor, not in lustful passion" (ἐν ἁγιασμῷ καὶ τιμῇ, μὴ ἐν πάθει ἐπιθυμίας, *en hagiasmō kai timē, mē en pathei epithymias*). The positive half of this antithetical statement involves two nouns, with the first term, "holiness," repeating and thus also recalling the opening thesis (4:3a) that God's will for the Thessalonians involves holiness. Paul again presents holiness—this time holiness in the specific matter of controlling one's sexual desire and conduct—as a key attribute that identifies the Thessalonians as belonging to the people of God and distinguishes them from "the Gentiles who do not know God" (v. 6; for more on the significance of the term "holiness," see comment on 4:3a).

26. The preposition ἐν functions adverbially (BDAG 330.11; Moule 1959: 78) with the infinitive κτᾶσθαι in 4:4 and thus provides the manner in which one "controls his own vessel."

The second term, "honor" (*timē*), typically refers to the respect or esteem that is given to a person or thing other than oneself: what God will give to believers at the final judgment (Rom. 2:7, 10), what believers now give to God (1 Tim. 1:17; 6:16), what believers ought to give to other people (Rom. 12:10; 13:7; 1 Tim. 5:17; 6:1), and what people give to parts of their body (1 Cor. 12:23–24). The term, therefore, is primarily "*other*-centered" (Holmes 1998: 126), so that "in honor" in 4:4 refers to controlling one's sexual desire and conduct in a way that treats others with respect. It is the opposite of acting "in lustful passion," that is, in a "*self*-centered" manner whereby a person is preoccupied with one's own sexual desire and conduct. Paul believes that the sexual activity of an individual impacts not just the self but also others, as he will spell out in the following infinitive clause (4:6a). The apostle, therefore, exhorts the Thessalonians to control their sexual desire and conduct in a way that gives "honor" or respect both to oneself and to others.

The negative half of the antithetical statement similarly involves two nouns, though this time joined not with a simple conjunction but with a genitive construction: literally, "in a passion of lust" (*en pathei epithymias*). The first term, *pathos*, refers to the "experience of strong desire, *passion*" (BDAG 748.2) and was used most often by ancient writers to describe passion of a sexual nature. This notion of erotic passion is found in Paul's two other uses of the term (Rom. 1:26; Col. 3:5) and clearly fits the discussion of sexual conduct found in the larger context of 1 Thess. 4:5 (contra Richard 1995: 190–92). The second term, *epithymia*, also refers to strong desire but is more ambiguous than the first term since it can be used positively to describe a desire for something good (like Paul's desire in 2:17 to revisit the Thessalonians; see also Phil. 1:23; Luke 22:15) or neutral (Mark 4:19; Rev. 18:14). Far more frequently (twenty-eight times), however, it refers to "a desire for someth[ing] forbidden or simply inordinate, *craving, lust*" (BDAG 372.2). The genitive is qualitative (BDF §165) so that the phrase *en pathei epithymias* should be rendered as "in lustful passion." The positive phrase "in holiness and honor" stresses the godlike and other-centered focus that distinctively marks believers in the control of their sexual desires and conduct; the negative phrase "not in lustful passion" refers to the unrestrained conduct of those who selfishly satisfy their own sexual needs, regardless of the harmful consequences for oneself or others.

4:5

Paul continues to contrast the sexual conduct of the Thessalonian believers with that of their unbelieving fellow citizens with a comparative clause (καθάπερ καί; see 3:6, 12) that not only explicitly identifies the latter group but also provides the theological reason for their acting in lustful passion: "just as also the Gentiles who do not know God" (καθάπερ καὶ τὰ ἔθνη τὰ μὴ εἰδότα τὸν θεόν, *kathaper kai ta ethnē ta mē eidota ton theon*). The apostle identifies unbelievers as "the Gentiles who do not know God"—an expression that he likely borrows from the OT (Job 18:21; Ps. 79:6 [78:6 LXX]; Jer. 10:25) and uses in his other letters as well (Gal. 4:8–9; 2 Thess. 1:8; see also 1 Cor. 1:21)—and so roots their immoral sexual conduct in their ignorance of God (so also Rom. 1:24–28, where humankind's failure to retain the knowledge of God leads to their sexual misbehavior; cf. Wis. 14:12, 22–26; Sib. Or. 3.29–45). The phrase "the Gentiles who do not know God" immediately places this verse in a covenant context, for "to know God" is a technical reference in the OT, especially in Jeremiah (see 31:34), to the covenant relationship (Deidun 1981: 19n61).

Paul's placing of the Thessalonian Christians, who were themselves Gentiles, in sharp antithesis to "the Gentiles who do not know God" is striking and, at first, incomprehensible: Why does Paul tell *Gentile* Christians in Thessalonica to stop acting in their sex life like Gentiles? The apostle's statement does make sense, however, if he no longer views these converts as Gentiles but with a new identity: they are now members of God's covenant people. The comparative clause of 1 Thess. 4:5, therefore, provides additional support to two principal claims made above (see comment on 4:3a). First, it shows that Paul perceives the Gentile believers at Thessalonica to be members of the renewed Israel, the covenant people of God. Second, it illustrates once again that Paul viewed holiness—here specifically holiness in sexual conduct—as a distinguishing sign or boundary marker of believers that sharply separates them from the world, from "those who do not know God."

iii. Do Not Harm Others through Your Sexual Conduct (4:6a)

4:6a

The last of the three exhortations consists of two articular infinitives that, like the preceding epexegetical infinitives *apexesthai* and *eidenai*, are in apposition to "your holiness" and thus explain more concretely how the overall theme of holiness applies to sexual conduct: "that one[27] not trespass or take advantage of his brother in this matter" (τὸ μὴ ὑπερβαίνειν καὶ πλεονεκτεῖν ἐν τῷ πράγματι τὸν ἀδελφὸν αὐτοῦ, *to mē hyperbainein kai pleonektein en tō pragmati ton adelphon autou*).

A number of commentators disagree with this translation, claiming that Paul is no longer talking about sexual conduct but has moved on to the new subject of business practices (so, e.g., early Latin commentators; Calvin 1981: 274–75; Dobschütz 1909: 167; Dibelius 1913: 22; Beauvery 1955; Merk 1968: 47–48; J. Schneider, *TDNT* 5:744; G. Delling, *TDNT* 6:271; Marxsen 1979: 62; Holtz 1986: 161–62; Richard 1995: 200–202). In support of this "business" or "commercial" interpretation, the following points are typically made: (1) The second infinitive *pleonektein* is used two times elsewhere in Paul's Letters to refer to the financial collection (2 Cor. 12:17, 18), where it has the commercial sense of "defraud." (2) The cognates of *pleonektein*—the noun *pleonexia* (greediness) and the verbal adjective *pleonektēs* (a greedy person)—are at times found alongside the noun *porneia* or its cognate (Rom. 1:29 [some MSS]; 1 Cor. 5:9–11; 6:9–10; Eph. 5:3, 5; Col. 3:5), suggesting that Paul typically

---

27. The subject of the two infinitives in the third exhortation (4:6a) is omitted and so must be supplied from the subject of the second exhortation (vv. 4–5): either "each one of you" (ἕκαστον ὑμῶν) or "a subject understood from ἕκαστον ὑμῶν such as τινα" (Lightfoot 1904: 56).

combines the differing subjects of sexual immorality and greed, and that this same pairing occurs here in 4:3–6. (3) The grammatical shift from the first two exhortations, which both employ anarthrous infinitives, to the third exhortation, where an articular infinitive is used, supports a topical shift from sexual immorality to a new subject. These three points, therefore, are thought to justify translating the third exhortation of 1 Thess. 4:6 as "that no man transgress and defraud his brother in business" (RSV[mg]).

There are, however, several reasons why this business or commercial interpretation ought to be rejected: (1) There is no transitional epistolary formula here to mark the beginning of a new topic, as can be consistently found in the surrounding context: 4:1 begins with an appeal formula ("We ask you and appeal that . . ."), 4:9 begins with a *peri de* formula ("Now about . . ."); and 4:13 begins with a disclosure formula ("We do not want you not to know . . ."). (2) That 4:3–6a constitutes a single sentence, with the first two infinitive clauses plainly dealing with sexual conduct, makes it unlikely that in the third infinitive clause Paul shifts to a new topic dealing with business practices. The grammatical shift from the anarthrous infinitives in the first two clauses (vv. 3b, 4–5) to the articular infinitive in the third (v. 6a) is better explained as a shift in focus from the consequences of sexual conduct on one's own life to that of *others*—a shift anticipated by the reference to controlling oneself "in honor." (3) The noun "holiness" (*hagiasmos*) in verse 7 and the adjective "holy" (*hagion*) in verse 8 combine with the two previous references to "holiness" (vv. 3, 4) to give 4:3–8 lexical coherence, thus reducing the possibility that Paul has introduced a new subject in verse 6. (4) The presence in verse 7 of the noun "impurity" (ἀκαθαρσία, *akatharsia*)—a term frequently found with *porneia* (2 Cor. 12:21; Gal. 5:19; Eph. 5:3; Col. 3:5; see 1 Thess. 4:3b) and used "especially of sexual sins" (BDAG 34.2; see also Rom. 1:24; Eph. 4:19)—suggests that Paul is still concerned with the subject of sexual conduct. It appears clear, therefore, that the rather ambiguous words in the third exhortation—the two infinitives and the prepositional phrase "in the/this matter"—ought to be interpreted as giving further instruction dealing with holiness in sexual conduct rather than with a new subject of proper business practices (so the great majority of scholars).

The first infinitive in 4:6, *hyperbainein*, which occurs only here in the NT, literally means "to go beyond a high point" and was used by other writers of that day in the moral sense of overstepping or breaking laws and commandments: "trespass, sin" (BDAG 1032). In this context, it refers to sexual activity in which one goes beyond the boundary of acting "in holiness and honor" and instead trespasses (sexually) on forbidden territory, where one ought not to be (Bruce 1982: 84). The second infinitive, *pleonektein*, appears only four other times in Paul's Letters: it refers to the apostle's denial that he has "taken advantage of" the Corinthians (2 Cor. 7:2; 12:17, 18) and to the prevention of Satan "taking advantage of" Paul and his fellow workers as a result of their having forgiven the Corinthians (2 Cor. 2:11). The verb conveys the notion of using trickery or deception to take advantage of another person for one's own selfish gain. Although Paul does not spell out the precise nature of this advantage or gain, the context clearly suggests that he has in mind some form of improper sexual activity. This seems confirmed by the fact that the most natural meaning of the prepositional phrase *en tō pragmati* is "in *this* matter," that is, the singular definite article refers back to the specific issue of sexual conduct dealt with in the two preceding exhortations (BDAG 859.3 identifies *pragma* here as probably a euphemism for an "illicit sexual affair"; note also our English word "affair," with a similar euphemistic meaning).[28]

The third exhortation of 1 Thess. 4:6a, therefore, warns against some form of improper sexual activity that results in one Christian taking advantage of "his brother." Although it is possible that Paul may be alluding to homosexual acts that directly involve the "brother" (Best 1977: 166), it is more likely that the apostle has in view the illicit sexual conduct of a male believer with either the wife, daughter, or another female member belonging to the extended household of his fellow Christian.[29] In our contemporary, gender-sensitive culture, some may very well take offense that Paul speaks against taking advantage of a "brother" but not a "sister." The apostle's language, however, reflects the patriarchal model of family and household structures of his day. Just as the second exhortation (vv. 4–5), with its likely euphemistic reference to the male sex organ, is primarily addressed to men and only indirectly to women (note also in these verses the masculine form of the pronouns "each one" and "his own"), so also here in the third exhortation (v. 6a) Paul's warning is directed primarily to the male members of the church community. To conclude that the apostle does not hold out the same standard for the women members of the church is as unjustified as it is to conclude that he cares only about sexual conduct that harms other Christians and remains unconcerned about harm done to non-Christians.

28. The possibility that πρᾶγμα in 4:6a refers to a "lawsuit" (1 Cor. 6:1) has been explored by Baltensweiler (1963), who proposes that the Thessalonians raised a question connected to a distinctive Greek custom—the right of a daughter who inherits her father's property when there are no surviving sons. In such situations the next of kin had the first claim to her hand. As a result male relatives frequently obtained divorces so that they might profit by entering into a new union with the daughter, and marriages between close relatives resulted, that of an uncle and a niece being especially common. Not only were such marriages perceived by some to constitute a situation of sexual immorality, but also the daughter's right to inheritance was often challenged in court, resulting in lawsuits. Paul's answer to the question raised by the Thessalonians about this widespread Greek custom is clear: such marriages and the resulting lawsuits are forbidden. Baltensweiler's proposal, albeit ingenious, suffers from a number of weaknesses, including that the evidence of the text does not support such a specific and complex historical situation (see further the six difficulties listed by Best 1977: 164). Consequently, despite being often presented as a possible historical context for the exhortations of 4:3b–6a, this theory has failed to win virtually any support (but see the explanatory notes in the Catholic Study Bible [Senior 1990: 327]).

29. Fee 2009: 150: "The best answer overall [to the question of the specific situation lying behind the exhortation of 4:6a] is that at least one case of sexual sin has been an adulterous situation with another man's wife, or perhaps with a household slave."

c. Three Reasons (4:6b–8)

The three exhortations to holiness in sexual conduct in 4:3b–6a are followed in verses 6b–8 by three reasons why the Thessalonian converts are to be holy in this area of their lives. Although not stressed in the text and thus not likely to be a conscious creation of Paul, it is nevertheless worth noting that each of the three reasons involves a different person of the Trinity and focuses on a different time period.

i. The Future Judgment of the Lord Jesus (4:6b)

The first reason concerns the future judgment of the Lord Jesus: "because the Lord is an avenger concerning all these things" (διότι ἔκδικος κύριος περὶ πάντων τούτων, *dioti ekdikos kyrios peri pantōn toutōn*). The causal conjunction *dioti* (omitted in NIV) connects this first reason not just to the immediately preceding command but also to all three of the earlier exhortations, as is clear from the plural "concerning all these things." The motivation for believers to separate themselves from sexual immorality (v. 3b), learn to control their sexual desires and conduct (vv. 4–5), and not harm another person through their own sexual misconduct (v. 6a) is that "an avenger is the Lord." The adjective *ekdikos* (elsewhere only Rom. 13:4), like its related verbal (Rom. 12:19; 2 Cor. 10:6) and noun forms (Rom. 12:19; 2 Cor. 7:11; 2 Thess. 1:8), refers to the infliction of an appropriate penalty for wrong done: "one who punishes, exacts vengeance" (see BDAG 301; G. Schrenk, *TDNT* 2:442–46). Its location in the emphatic position at the head of the causal clause adds even greater force to the threatening tone that the content of this term already conveys. The word "avenge" or "vengeance" in English unfortunately carries the negative connotation of acting out of personal vindictiveness or seeking revenge. The Greek term *ekdikos* and its related verbal and noun forms, however, have the positive sense of bringing about justice (the root *dik-*) by rightly punishing the wicked for their sins against God and others. In a world where evildoers all too often unjustly oppress others seemingly without penalty, it is comforting to hear about a future day when an avenger will come and take what is wrong and make it *dik-*, that is, "right."

There is some question as to who metes out this just punishment: God or Jesus? Note that (1) these words may be an allusion to Ps. 94:1 (93:1 LXX), (2) the theme of God as judge who exacts vengeance is widely found in both the OT (Exod. 7:4; 12:12; Deut. 32:35; Ps. 18:47; Jer. 11:20; Amos 3:2, 14; Mic. 5:15; Nah. 1:2) and the intertestamental literature (T. Reu. 6.6; T. Levi 18.1; T. Gad 6.7; T. Jos. 20.1; T. Benj. 10.8–10; Jos. Asen. 23.13), and (3) there are multiple references to "God" in the rest of 4:3–8 (vv. 3, 5, 7, 8). On this basis some deduce that Paul is referring to the judgment that God will distribute (so, e.g., Holtz 1986: 164; Morris 1991: 124; Richard 1995: 203–4; Malherbe 2000: 233). Against this conclusion, however, are at least three factors. First, the term *kyrios* has occurred numerous times in the letter thus far, always referring to Jesus (1:1, 3, 6, 8; 2:15, 19; 3:8, 11, 12, 13; 4:1, 2). Indeed, this is

4:6b

Paul's favorite designation for Jesus. Second, if *kyrios* does refer to God, it would make the explicit introduction of the subject "God" in the following verse unnecessary. Third, throughout both Thessalonian Letters, Paul makes several references to the future coming of Jesus, who will punish the wicked and serve as the agent of God's wrath (1 Thess. 1:10; 5:1–11; 2 Thess. 1:7–10; 2:8–10; see also Rom. 12:19; Col. 3:23–25).

This image of the Lord Jesus as the coming avenger is hardly a new one for the Thessalonian believers, as the following parenthetical καθώς clause makes clear: "just as we indeed told you before and solemnly warned" (καθὼς καὶ προείπαμεν ὑμῖν καὶ διεμαρτυράμεθα, *kathōs kai proeipamen hymin kai diemartyrametha*). The first verb, *proeipamen*, does not likely have the predictive sense of "foretell, tell/proclaim beforehand," as if Paul had prophesied the future coming of the Lord Jesus in judgment, but rather the temporal sense of "having said something before" (BDAG 868.2; see also 2 Cor. 13:2; Gal. 1:9; 5:21). The second verb *diemartyrametha* (1 Tim. 5:21; 2 Tim. 2:14; 4:1; Luke 16:28; Acts 8:25; 20:21) is a strong term meaning "to declare emphatically in the sense of a warning" (H. Strathmann, *TDNT* 4:512), "to make a solemn declaration about the truth of something" (BDAG 233.1).

Although these two verbs could form a hendiadys in which the second term is synonymous with and thus adds emphasis to the first (RSV: "as we solemnly forewarned you"; also NEB, NLT), the *kathōs kai . . . kai* construction more probably expresses two separate though closely connected ideas (so the identical construction in 3:4). This double reference to the past teaching and solemn warning suggests that the apostle's original exhortation against sexual immorality during his mission-founding visit to Thessalonica was an important and heavily stressed matter—the kind of exhortation that the readers should not easily forget or dismiss. That this constitutes the third reference in the passage thus far to previously shared material (also v. 1, "just as you received from us"; v. 2, "For you know what commands we gave to you") also adds a greater degree of culpability for the readers' failure to obey these exhortations.

ii. The Past Call of God (4:7)

4:7 The second reason why believers ought to be holy in their sexual conduct concerns the past call of God: "For God did not call us for impurity but in holiness" (οὐ γὰρ ἐκάλεσεν ἡμᾶς ὁ θεὸς ἐπὶ ἀκαθαρσίᾳ ἀλλ᾽ ἐν ἁγιασμῷ, *ou gar ekalesen hēmas ho theos epi akatharsia all' en hagiasmō*). The conjunction *gar* functions as a marker of cause and looks back not just to verse 6b but also the whole of 4:3b–6a, so that this verse parallels verse 6b and introduces yet another reason why the preceding exhortations must be obeyed: the past call of God. At the beginning of the letter, Paul already raised the theme of the Thessalonians' election as the ultimate cause for his thanksgiving to God (see comment on 1:4). He also used the present tense of *kaleō* in 2:12 (see also 5:24) to highlight the ongoing and effective nature of God's call, thereby encouraging the persecuted believers in Thessalonica with the knowledge that God did not call them once in the past and subsequently abandon them to their own resources, but rather continues to call them such that they will "be kept sound and blameless at the coming of our Lord Jesus Christ" (5:23). Here in verse 7 the apostle follows his more typical practice of using the aorist tense to refer to God's initial call at the time of conversion (so also 2 Thess. 2:14; Gal. 1:6; 1 Cor. 1:9). An important part of that past call of God, in which he caused the Thessalonian converts to "turn to God from idols in order to serve a living and true God" (1:9), is that their sexual conduct is characterized no longer by the attitude and practices of their pagan culture but now by God's will for their lives, namely, holiness.

Paul communicates this point by employing his favorite "not . . . but" (antithetical) construction: God called the Thessalonians, along with the apostle and his fellow missionaries (note the shift to the first-person plural, "us"), "not for impurity but in holiness." The negative half is expressed by the preposition *epi* with the dative, a combination that can express almost a dozen different nuances. Although some have argued for a causal sense (God did not call them *because of* their impurity: so Masson 1957: 49–50; Best 1977: 168; Marshall 1983: 113), most translations and commentators render the prepositional phrase (*epi* + dative) as expressing purpose or result: God did not call them *for the purpose of* impurity (so BDAG 366.16, "marker of object or purpose"; BDF §235.4; see also Gal. 5:13; Eph. 2:10; 2 Tim. 2:14). The noun *akatharsia* can refer to immoral conduct that is not of a sexual nature (see comment on 2:3), thus leading to the proposal that the term here refers to immoral business practices (see further comment on 4:6a). Yet that *akatharsia* is frequently found with *porneia* (2 Cor. 12:21; Gal. 5:19; Eph. 5:3; Col. 3:5) indicates that it most commonly refers to sexual immorality (BDAG 34.2; see also Rom. 1:24; Eph. 4:19). Especially in light of the earlier reference to *porneia* in the first exhortation of 1 Thess. 4:3b and the concern with sexual conduct in the second and third exhortations of 4:4–5 and 6a, this must be its meaning here: God did not call the Thessalonians for the purpose of their continuing to practice sexual immorality.

The positive half of the "not . . . but" (antithetical) construction is expressed not with the expected preposition *epi* but *en*—a different preposition that also can express a variety of nuances. The parallelism with the negative half has led some to see here also the idea of purpose or result: God called the Thessalonians *for the purpose of* their being holy (so, e.g., NIV, NAB, NLT, NJB, REB; Rigaux 1956: 512–13; Best 1977: 168; Holtz 1986: 165; Richard 1995: 189). But if this had been Paul's intention, he could have used *epi* once again, as in the negative half, or *eis* with the accusative, a relatively common means of expressing purpose or goal (see BDAG 288–90.1 and 4) that Paul frequently uses elsewhere with the verb *kaleō* (1 Cor. 1:9; Col. 3:15; 2 Thess. 2:14; 1 Tim. 6:12). The shift to *en*, therefore, appears to be significant. As N. Turner (MHT 3:263) noted already some time ago: "Paul carefully distinguishes ἐπί from ἐν in 1 Th 4⁷ and has a reason for the change from one preposition to the other."

Just what that reason is, however, remains difficult to determine with certainty. The preposition *en* commonly functions as a "marker of a state or condition" (BDAG 327.2), and this appears to be the sense expressed in the other instances where Paul combines *en* with the verb *kaleō* (1 Cor. 7:15, 18, 24; Gal. 1:6; Eph. 4:4; Col. 3:15). If Paul here in 1 Thess. 4:7 similarly is referring to the state or condition of the Thessalonians at their calling, his point is that holiness is not so much a future goal as a past and present reality—a state of holiness that started already at their conversion and continues in their current lives. As Moore (1969: 65) puts it: "The implication is that the process of sanctification has already begun and is to continue" (see also Best 1977: 168; Collins 1984: 320). What ought not to be overlooked in this debate over the proper meaning of the prepositional phrase "in holiness" is that this constitutes the third time in verses 3–8 that Paul employs the key term *hagiasmos*, thereby once again (see v. 4 "in holiness and honor") recalling the opening thesis (v. 3a) that God's will for the Thessalonians involves holiness.

iii. The Present Gift of the Holy Spirit (4:8)

4:8 The third reason why holiness ought to be a distinctive characteristic of one's sexual conduct concerns the present gift of the Holy Spirit: "Therefore the one who rejects these exhortations rejects not a human being but God, who indeed gives his Spirit, who is holy, into you" (τοιγαροῦν ὁ ἀθετῶν οὐκ ἄνθρωπον ἀθετεῖ ἀλλὰ τὸν θεὸν τὸν καὶ διδόντα τὸ πνεῦμα αὐτοῦ τὸ ἅγιον εἰς ὑμᾶς, *toigaroun ho athetōn ouk anthrōpon athetei alla ton theon ton kai didonta to pneuma autou to hagion eis hymas*). The rare particle *toigaroun* (elsewhere in the NT only in Heb. 12:1), due to its compound character (the enclitic particle τοί [*toi*], which stresses the reliability of the following statement + the conjunction γάρ [*gar*] + the inferential particle οὖν [*oun*]), is emphatic and thus brings the list of three reasons for holy conduct to a certain climax or conclusion. It introduces a strong inference from what has been previously stated, not merely the preceding reason of verse 7 but also everything asserted from verse 3 onward. If "your holiness" involves *God's* will for the Thessalonians (v. 3a) and if they have been called "in holiness" by *God* (v. 7), then it logically follows (*toigaroun* = therefore) that any rejection on their part of the exhortations in verses 3b–6a involves a rejection not just of the human who issued those exhortations but of God himself.

Paul frames this third reason, like the second reason of verse 7, in the form of another "not . . . but" construction. The subject of this antithetical clause is "the one who rejects" (the verb *atheteō* here expresses not merely the act of ignoring something or someone ["disregards": so RSV, NAB] but a strong rejection: BDAG 24). Although the substantive participle phrase *ho athetōn* lacks any expressed object, there is no need to treat it absolutely as meaning "the one who acts wickedly" (so Richard 1995: 190). The context makes it clear that the implied object involves the three exhortations concerning sexual conduct in verses 3b–6a: "the one who rejects *these exhortations*." The negative half of the "not . . . but" construction consists of the anarthrous *anthrōpon*, which almost certainly involves a veiled reference by Paul to himself as the one who gave these exhortations (contra Best 1977: 169).[30] The absence of the definite article stresses the quality of the noun, the humanness of the one (Paul) issuing the three commands (Wanamaker 1990: 158). This implies, in turn, that the positive half of the "not . . . but" contrast, with its mention of "God" including the definite article, stresses the divine character of the one and only true God from whom these exhortations ultimately originate (recall the similar human/divine contrast in 2:13). Here Paul's words echo, though not likely in a conscious manner, the words of Jesus in the Gospels (esp. Luke 10:16: "The one rejecting you rejects me"; also Matt. 10:40; Mark 9:37; John 12:44, 48; 13:20), which are themselves an echo of God's words in the OT (1 Sam. 8:7; also Exod. 16:8).

In the positive half of the antithetical statement, however, the emphasis is not merely on God as the divine figure whom the Thessalonians ultimately reject through any rejection of Paul's exhortations, but also on God as the giver of his Spirit, whose holy character empowers the Thessalonians to obey these exhortations to holiness. This is clear from the apostle's closing words, which stress that God is the one "who indeed [the conjunction *kai* is likely original (see additional notes) and functions adverbially with the following verbal form: see also 2:13; 5:24] gives his Spirit, who is holy [the word order emphasizes the holy character of God's Spirit] to you." This statement is of great significance for understanding the theological perspective from which Paul views his Thessalonian converts and issues to them the call to holiness. In a deliberate way, Paul here picks up the language of the OT prophets about the blessed presence of God's Spirit in the messianic age—language associated with the "new" or "everlasting" covenant—and applies it to the Thessalonian believers (see Deidun 1981: 19, 53–56; Thielman 1994: 76–77; Weima 1996: 110–12; 2007: 878–79). It ought to be recognized that Paul is not teaching this here; the logic of his argument "assumes far more than it actually says" (Fee 2009: 153). Yet the apostle's words about God, "who indeed gives his Spirit, who is holy, into you," provide an important window into Paul's theological framework or worldview.

Jews of the first century were painfully aware that their nation, both in its past and in its present, was not living according to the standard of holiness that God had called for when he first established his covenant with them. Yet most Jews also believed, on the basis of his promise given through the prophets,

---

30. Green (2002: 200) illustrates the danger of mirror reading by discovering in this veiled self-reference by Paul "someone or some people in the church who had questioned the apostle's authority and therefore his teaching. . . . Such people would have distinguished between the gospel proclamation, which they received as divine (2.13), and the moral teaching on sexuality, which they rejected as coming simply from a man." Paul's point in this antithetical statement is not to defend himself from those in the church who rejected his authority or teaching but to impress upon the Thessalonian readers the divine origin of the three exhortations in 4:3b–6a and the consequent obligation to obey them.

that God would not abandon his people, but would restore their holiness by pouring out his Spirit on them as part of the covenant blessings to be enjoyed in the messianic era. This eschatological hope for holiness, which is made possible through the presence of God's Spirit, is most clearly seen in Ezek. 36:25–27 LXX: "I will sprinkle clean water on you, and you will be purged from all your uncleanness and from all your idols, and I will cleanse you. And I will give you a new heart, and I will put a new spirit in you [*pneuma kainon dōsō en hymin*]; and I will take away the heart of stone out of your flesh, and I will give you a heart of flesh. And I will put my Spirit in you [*to pneuma mou dōsō en hymin*] and will cause you to walk in my commands and to keep my judgments and do them" (see also Ezek. 11:19).

The gift of God's Spirit as a key blessing of the eschatological age is also stressed in Ezek. 37:6 and 14 LXX, where it is twice stated: "I will put my Spirit into you [*dōsō pneuma mou eis hymas*]." And while other prophets like Jeremiah and Isaiah do not highlight the gift of God's Spirit quite as explicitly as Ezekiel does (but see Isa. 59:21), they do hold out the future hope of a "new" or "everlasting" covenant, in which God will live in and among his people in such an intimate way that they will be able to obey his commands and live holy lives (see, e.g., Jer. 31:31–34 [38:31–34 LXX]; 32:40; 50:5; Isa. 55:3; 59:21).

Paul takes this new-covenant language, which articulates the eschatological hope of the Jewish people, and applies it to Gentile Christians at Thessalonica. The parallels with Ezek. 36:25–27 are especially striking. For as Ezekiel prophesied (36:25: "You will be clean from all your uncleannesses, . . . and I will cleanse you"), God has cleansed the Thessalonian believers from their "uncleanness/impurity" (1 Thess. 4:7) so that their sexual conduct now is to be controlled by "holiness" (4:3, 4, 7). And as Ezekiel prophesied (26:25: "and from all your idols"), God has cleansed Paul's converts at Thessalonica from their idolatry, with the result that they have "turned to God from idols to serve a living and true God" (1:9). Likewise, as Ezekiel prophesied (26:27: "I will cause you to walk in my commands, and to keep my judgments and do them"), God has now enabled Gentile Christians at Thessalonica to "walk" (*peripatein*) according to his commands (4:1 [2x], 12). But most significantly, as Ezekiel prophesied (36:27: "I will put my Spirit in you"; also 37:6, 14), Paul can now say to Gentile believers at Thessalonica that God is the one "who indeed gives his Spirit, who is holy, into you" (4:8).

That Paul did quite consciously have in mind the eschatological age envisioned by Ezekiel can be seen in his description of God as giving his Spirit "into you" (*eis hymas*). For though this expression is somewhat awkward (the more natural and expected expression is the dative *en hymin*: "in you"), it echoes exactly the words of Ezekiel: "I will put my Spirit *into you*" (*eis hymas*; Ezek. 37:6, 14 LXX). As Fee (2009: 154) notes: "This unusual usage [*eis hymas* instead of the expected *en hymin*] is most likely an intentional echo on Paul's part of the Septuagint of Ezekiel 37:6 and 14. . . . This usage reflects a Pauline understanding of the gift of the Spirit as the fulfillment of Old Testament promises that God's own Spirit will come to indwell his people." But while the gift of God's Spirit was for Ezekiel and others in Judaism only a future hope ("I *will* give my Spirit"), for Paul it has become a present and ongoing reality, as indicated by the present tense of the participle *didonta* (see Deidun 1981: 56; Fee 1994a: 52–53; 2009: 154).[31]

It seems clear, therefore, that Paul views the conversion of Gentiles at Thessalonica as a fulfillment of the eschatological promises made to Israel. The Thessalonian believers are no longer simply "Gentiles who do not know God," but now are members of the renewed Israel, the covenant people of God. This privileged status meant that in their sexual conduct they are to observe the boundaries of holiness that the new covenant marks out for them. The key to living such lives of holiness is the present and ongoing presence of God's Spirit. So here, as elsewhere in Paul's Letters, the Holy Spirit is the power that enables believers to live holy lives.

3. Love for One Another (4:9–12)

The second specific way in which the Thessalonians can fulfill the general exhortation to increase in conduct that pleases God (vv. 1–2) involves loving one another. As with the preceding topic of holiness in sexual conduct, here too the subject of mutual love was foreshadowed in the transitional prayer of 3:12–13, where Paul asks that the Lord may cause the Thessalonians "to abound and increase in love for one another and for all." There is no obvious connection between the disparate topics of sexual conduct and of mutual love. Perhaps the third and final exhortation that the Thessalonians' sexual conduct ought not to wrong a "brother" (v. 6a) was linked in the apostle's mind with another way that some (Fee 2009: 157: "a small minority") in the church were also wronging a fellow Christian, namely, the problem of idleness as a violation of *philadelphia*—love for brother (and sister).

Paul's treatment of the new topic of loving one another falls into two distinct yet related sections. The first section (vv. 9–10a) involves a general affirmation of the mutual love that already exists within the Thessalonian congregation. This general affirmation consists of an opening assertion (v. 9a), which is grounded by two causal γάρ (*gar*, for) clauses (vv. 9b, 10a). The second section (vv. 10b–12) involves a lengthy appeal formula, which specifies how this mutual love ought to manifest itself. The content of this appeal consists of four exhortations given in the form of infinitives in indirect command. The first of these exhortations forms an important link with the preceding general affirmation of verses 9–10a, while the remaining three spell out in concrete ways how the Thessalonians ought to demonstrate love for one another. The lengthy

---

31. Contra Green (2002: 201n63), who states on 4:8: "The present participle [*didonta*] means simply that God is the source of the Spirit as the 'one who gives' and should not be pressed to mean that God constantly supplies them with the Holy Spirit" (so also Marshall 1983: 114; Wanamaker 1990: 158; Shogren 2012: 167n47). However, the verbal aspect of the rarer (compared to the aorist) present participle typically emphasizes the ongoing or continuous nature of the action. Furthermore, this ongoing or continuous nature is likely expressed by the present participle, which partly explains why some scribes changed the tense to the aorist (see additional notes).

appeal closes with a purpose (ἵνα, *hina*) clause that provides two reasons why the Thessalonians ought to demonstrate mutual love in these specific ways.

The fourth and final exhortation (that you "work with your own hands") seems to be most prominent in Paul's mind. The importance of this exhortation to the apostle is suggested first by his choice to follow it immediately with a parenthetical καθώς clause ("just as we commanded you"), which reminds the Thessalonians of the command against idleness that the apostle already gave during his mission-founding visit (so also 2 Thess. 3:6, 10). Second, Paul's preoccupation with the last exhortation against idleness is indicated in the purpose clause (v. 12), where the apostle chooses once again to take up this fourth concern rather than the preceding three, expressing his desire that the Thessalonian believers "be dependent on no one." Third, there is a discernible progression in the exhortations as each activity mentioned is more specific than the one before (so also perhaps the three exhortations of vv. 3b–6a) so that a certain climax is reached in the closing command "to work with your own hands" (Ellingworth and Nida 1975: 88; Malherbe 2000: 246). This progression is natural and expected in a discussion of any sensitive matter, where one tactfully begins by addressing the subject in a rather vague way and then becomes progressively more explicit as the discussion reaches its conclusion.

This observation that Paul is especially concerned with the problem of idleness in the specific appeal of 4:10b–12 impacts how one ought to read the general affirmation of verses 9–10a. It suggests that Paul's references to the proper exercise of mutual love in the opening verses of this section are intended to function as a corrective to the specific problem of idleness taken up in the closing verses. In other words, the refusal of some in the church to work but instead take advantage of the generosity of fellow believers is a clear violation of the call for Christians to love one another.[32]

a. General Affirmation (4:9–10a)

i. Opening Assertion: No Need to Write to You about Loving One Another (4:9a)

4:9a   Paul opens the new topic of love for one another with an assertion about the superfluous nature of his writing to the Thessalonians on this subject: "Now about your love for one another, you have no need for us to write to you" (περὶ δὲ τῆς φιλαδελφίας οὐ χρείαν ἔχετε γράφειν ὑμῖν, *peri de tēs philadelphias*

---

32. Fee (2009: 158) also rightly sees the connection between the general affirmation of 4:9–10a and the specific appeal of 4:10b–12: "To be sure, some scholars have found the paragraph [4:9–12] as a whole difficult to negotiate as dealing with a single issue, and have posited that Paul is here taking up two different issues. But the grammar and structure of the two sentences seem conclusively to disallow such an option. Thus Paul begins with a commendation of the majority (vv. 9–10a), in which the entire matter is put in the context of believers' having familial love for one another. This is followed by a sentence that begins with an exhortation to do so all the more (v. 10b), before he goes on to deal directly with those who are not working so as to provide for their sustenance (v. 11)."

ou chreian echete graphein hymin). The combination *peri de* is an epistolary formula commonly used in both secular (see White 1986 for examples from papyrus letters) and Pauline Letters (1 Cor. 7:1, 25; 8:1, 4; 12:1; 16:1, 12; 1 Thess. 4:9, 13; 5:1) as a shorthand way of introducing a new topic that is readily known by both author and reader. That this formula introduces Paul's response to a letter sent to him from the Corinthians (1 Cor. 7:1) has led some to conclude that the apostle here is similarly responding to a letter sent to him from the Thessalonians, who asked not only about the practice of mutual love (4:9) but also about the fate of deceased believers at Christ's return (4:13) and the fate of living believers at "the times and seasons" (5:1) connected with the final judgment (so Milligan 1908: 126; Frame 1912: 140, 157; Faw 1952; Masson 1957: 51–52; Malherbe 2000: 217, 243, 255; Green 2002: 202).[33] The use of this formula, however, need not necessarily imply the existence of a previous letter (Mitchell 1989). Since there is no explicit reference to a letter from the Thessalonians (as there is in 1 Cor. 7:1), it is better to conclude that *peri de* introduces a new subject that Paul raises in response to the oral report of Timothy (3:6).

The new subject that Paul raises concerns *philadelphia*, "love for one another." This term is somewhat rare in pre-Christian literature, where it always refers in an inclusive manner to the mutual love between not only blood brothers but also sisters (for texts, see BDAG 1055; Kloppenborg 1993: 272n31). In NT writings, *philadelphia* is used of extrafamilial relationships and refers in a figurative yet still inclusive manner to the mutual love that exists between fellow Christians, both male and female (Rom. 12:10; 1 Thess. 4:9; Heb. 13:1; 1 Pet. 1:22; 2 Pet. 1:7; see also the adjectival form in 1 Pet. 3:8). Paul's use of this term here matches well the intimate family language and metaphors employed throughout the letter: "infants" (2:7b), "nursing mother" (2:7c), "father" (2:11), "orphaned" (2:17), and "brothers" (1:4; 2:1, 9, 14, 17; 3:7; 4:1, 10, 13; 5:1, 4, 12, 14, 25, 26, 27). That *philadelphia*—mutual love among blood brothers and sisters—was one of the more powerful images of solidarity in Greek and Roman culture highlights the potential impact of its use by Paul to describe the relationship that exists among the Thessalonian believers. It implies that the believers in Thessalonica enjoy the kind of solidarity that their fellow citizens prized so highly yet, as the sources ruefully concede, found so difficult to achieve (Kloppenborg 1993: 273).

Paul's assertion that on this matter of *philadelphia* "you have no need for us to write to you" (on the textual problems here, see additional notes) ought not be taken literally, as if the apostle actually believed that there was no legitimate reason to take up this subject (so Milligan 1908: 52). Otherwise his statement might come across as somewhat of a rebuke, especially if the Thessalonians themselves had raised a question about the proper manifestation of

---

33. The first to propose that 1 Thessalonians was written in response to a letter from the Thessalonians, though for reasons other than the presence of the *peri de* formula (as in 4:9), was Harris 1898.

philadelphia. Rather, Paul's opening assertion is an example of paraleipsis, a rhetorical device that allows speakers or writers to address a subject that they outwardly claim does not need to be addressed (BDF §495; so also 1:8; 5:1; 2 Cor. 9:1; Philem. 19). It implies that the Thessalonians are already sufficiently demonstrating love for one another such that this matter does not need to be taken up. Thus, instead of a mild rebuke of the Thessalonians for asking a question that does not need to be addressed, this assertion actually involves a commendation of the Thessalonians (Malherbe 2000: 244; Witherington 2006: 119).

ii. Reason 1: You Are Taught by God to Love One Another (4:9b)

4:9b

The first reason (*gar* functions as a marker of cause or reason) for the superfluous nature of writing to the Thessalonians about loving one another concerns some form of divine instruction that they are receiving: "for you yourselves[34] are taught by God to love one another" (αὐτοὶ γὰρ ὑμεῖς θεοδίδακτοί ἐστε εἰς τὸ ἀγαπᾶν ἀλλήλους, *autoi gar hymeis theodidaktoi este eis to agapan allēlous*). The term *theodidaktoi*, a passive verbal adjective meaning "taught by God," is striking since there are no known occurrences of this term anywhere in Greek literature before its appearance in this verse, thereby suggesting that it is a new word created by Paul (so many commentators; see esp. Witmer 2006). The remarkable character of this term is also evident in that it occurs nowhere else in the NT, only rarely in later Christian literature, and never in non-Christian writings.[35]

But while virtually all scholars recognize the importance of this key term, they do not agree as to its intended meaning or use by Paul. Some of the different proposals that have been forwarded include the following:

1. Koester (1979: 39) suggests that Paul employed this term in order to create a sense of independence in the Thessalonians, whereby they will not be overly reliant on his instructions. In support, Koester cites Philo's repeated assertion that the truly wise man is someone who is a "self-learner" (αὐτομαθής, *automathēs*) and "self-taught" (αὐτοδίδακτος, *autodidaktos*) and "finds wisdom readily prepared, rained down from heaven above"

---

34. In 4:9 the addition of the third-person personal pronoun αὐτοί to the subject ὑμεῖς expresses emphasis: "you yourselves." Paul may be intending a contrast with the implied ἡμᾶς before γράφειν: "You have no need *for us* to write to you, for *you yourselves* are taught by God" (so Frame 1912: 158; Ellingworth and Nida 1975: 87). Another possibility is that Paul is emphasizing the knowledge that the Thessalonians already have about the practice of *philadelphia*, similar to his other emphatic statements in the letter (2:1; 3:3; 5:2) about what they already know (Malherbe 2000: 244).

35. Most of the few occurrences of θεοδίδακτος in later Christian literature involve references to 1 Thess. 4:9, as in Barn. 21.6; Athenagoras, *Leg.* 11, 32; Theophilus, *Autol.* 2.9; Tatian, *Or.* 29; Clement of Alexandria, *Paed.* 1.6.27; 1.20.98; 2.11.48; 2.18.84; 6.18.166; *Quis div.* 20.2. The term does appear in one non-Christian text: the commentary (*Prolegomenon sylloge*, p. 91, line 14) of John Doxapatres on Aphthonius's *Progymnasmata* (see BDAG 449). This usage, however, is very late, dating to the eleventh century AD.

(*Flight* 166). Yet this proposal founders on, among other things, Paul's repeated appeals in this section to his previous instructions (4:1, 2, 6, 11), which is hardly conducive to instilling in the Thessalonians a greater degree of self-reliance and independence from their apostle.

2. Malherbe (1983a: 253–54), quite opposite to the proposal of Koester, claims that Paul uses *theodidaktoi* in a deliberate attempt to highlight the Thessalonians' dependence on divine teaching in contrast to the Epicurean ideal of being "self-taught" and independently discovering the truth that exists within each person. Yet it is hard to discover anywhere in 1 Thess. 4:9–12 an anti-Epicurean polemic, a fact that leads even Malherbe to concede that his proposal may be considered by others too speculative (this concession, however, is dropped in Malherbe's later writings: 1987: 104–5; 2000: 244–45).

3. Roetzel (1986) argues that the Thessalonians had adopted a Hellenistic Jewish piety similar to that of Philo, in which it was held that those who possessed a wisdom learned not from any human teacher but given directly from God now enjoy the eschatological blessing of release from work (see *Flight* 166–73; *Migration* 29–30). Roetzel further claims that the term *theodidaktoi* involves Paul's "radically recasting" of the traditional meaning of the word *autodidaktos* (self-taught), widely known in Hellenistic Jewish circles, in order to emphasize the work and other social responsibilities of those who are "God-taught." The Thessalonian Letters, however, provide no evidence for the influence of Hellenistic Judaism among the members of this congregation. Furthermore, it is difficult to see how Paul's use of *theodidaktoi* corrects in any substantive way the proposed errant piety, since individuals could now claim divine authority for the wisdom that they possess and use this to justify their eschatological freedom from work.

4. Kloppenborg (1993) contends that Paul in verses 9–12 presupposes that the Thessalonian believers are familiar with the mythical traditions surrounding the Dioscuri—the twin pagan gods, Castor and Polydeuces—who were well known in the ancient world and especially in Thessalonica as paradigms of *philadelphia*, brotherly love. The apostle deliberately coined the new term "god-taught" and coupled it with the word *philadelphia* in order to evoke in his readers' minds the myths associated with these divine siblings and their mutual love for each other as a model for them to imitate. In this way, then, the Thessalonians are "god-taught," that is, they are taught by the example of these twin pagan gods how they should practice love for one another. As ingenious as this proposal may be, it is difficult, if not impossible, to believe that Paul would appeal to pagan deities as models to be imitated, especially in the very same letter where he gives thanks that his readers have "turned to God from idols in order to serve a living and true God" (1:9). Kloppenborg cannot so easily dismiss this criticism by claiming that "Paul's allusion to the

Dioscuri is a rhetorical strategy rather than a theological inconsistency" (289).[36]

5. The majority of commentators see in Paul's use of the term *theodidaktoi* an allusion to Isa. 54:13 LXX: "And I will cause all your sons to be *taught of God* [*didaktous theou*]." Within the context of Isaiah's description of the blessings to be enjoyed in the messianic age, these words refer to a future time when God will live so intimately in and among his people through his Spirit that they will no longer need to be taught by human intermediaries but will instead be "taught of God." This idea of divine instruction as an eschatological blessing enjoyed by God's covenant people is more widespread than scholars typically recognize (for the following, see Weima 2007: 879–80; also Witmer 2008: 153–64). Jeremiah similarly portrays the new covenant as a period when God's people will not need others to teach them the law but will know it innately, for God will write it on their hearts (Jer. 31:33–34 [38:31–34 LXX]). Isaiah, earlier in his prophecy, also envisions a future age when all the nations will stream to Mount Zion in order that "he [God] may teach us his ways and that we may walk in his paths" (Isa. 2:3 NRSV). The importance that Jews attached to this idea of divine instruction as an eschatological blessing is further evidenced in that Isaiah's vision of 2:2–4 is repeated in Mic. 4:1–3. This idea also manifests itself in Pss. Sol. 17.32, which speaks of the future king who will rule in the messianic age as one who is "taught by God" (*didaktos hypo theou*). That this eschatological blessing was still anticipated in NT times is clear from Jesus's citation of Isa. 54:13 to show that "all will be taught by God [*didaktous theou*]" in the messianic age (John 6:45). This expected eschatological blessing also likely lies behind the statement of 1 John 2:27 that, due to the enlightening grace of the Holy Spirit, "you have no need for anyone to teach you" (note also the earlier words of 1 John 2:20).

Paul's use of the term *theodidaktoi*, therefore, is significant (contra the statement of Best 1977: 173 that "perhaps nothing very deep is intended, only that the command to brotherly love is divine in origin"). The apostle's allusion in this term—either specifically to Isa. 54:13, with its juxtaposition of *didaktous* and *theou*, or more generally to the anticipation of divine instruction as an eschatological blessing (an anticipation expressed in several OT, intertestamental, and NT texts), so soon after his clear allusion in the previous verse (4:8b) to Ezekiel's description of the gift of God's Spirit in the messianic age[37]—suggests that here too Paul views the Thessalonians' prac-

---

36. Witmer (2006: 240–41) raises further weaknesses with Kloppenborg's proposal: Paul makes no mention of the Dioscuri anywhere in his extant letters; there are no Greek texts that refer to the Dioscuri as "teaching" brotherly love or "teaching" anything at all; and the foreshadowing prayer of 3:12–13 refers to "the Lord" as the one who will cause the Thessalonians to "abound and increase in love for one another and for all," not the Dioscuri.

37. Deidun (1981: 21) states: "By utilizing the parallel texts of Jeremiah and Ezekiel in I Thess. 4,8b–9, Paul wishes to recall to the Thessalonians their unique Covenant relationship with God."

tice of *philadelphia*, or mutual love, as an eschatological blessing of God's covenant people. Though this blessing of divine instruction was originally intended primarily for Israel (but see the reference to "all nations" in Isa. 2:2 and "many nations" in Mic. 4:2), Paul believes that it extends also to the predominantly Gentile believers at Thessalonica. This new-covenant language of being "God-taught," therefore, further supports my claim, already made above, that Paul's exhortations in 1 Thess. 4:1–12 are rooted in his conviction that the Gentile Christians at Thessalonica are included in the renewed Israel, the eschatological people of God who enjoy both the blessings and the challenges of that privileged relationship.

Paul does not specify how the Thessalonians are "taught by God." Nevertheless, the preceding reference to the gift of the Spirit (v. 8b) strongly suggests that the apostle has in mind the Holy Spirit's role in teaching and empowering believers to exhibit the kind of God-pleasing conduct that is characterized by *philadelphia* (so, e.g., Marshall 1983: 115; Williams 1992: 76; Richard 1995: 216). The Spirit's role in teaching the followers of Jesus is asserted in Paul's later letter to the Corinthians, where he claims to speak words of wisdom that are "taught by the Spirit" (1 Cor. 2:13, *en didaktois pneumatos*), another reference to divine instruction that may well reflect the influence of Isa. 54:13 on the apostle's thinking (Witmer 2008: 157). This, of course, is entirely in keeping with Paul's overall theology, in which the Spirit is "God's empowering presence" (Fee 1994a)—the person of God who indwells believers such that they are empowered to do his will.

Paul does specify, however, the purpose[38] of the divine teaching: "to love one another." This desire of the apostle that believers love one another appears in each of his other letters (see, e.g., Rom. 13:9–10; 1 Cor. 13; 2 Cor. 2:8; Gal. 5:13–14; Eph. 5:2; Phil. 2:2; Col. 3:14; 2 Thess. 1:3; 1 Tim. 6:11; 2 Tim. 2:22; Titus 2:2; Philem. 5), not a surprising fact in light of the central role that love for others has in both the teaching and example of Jesus (Mark 12:31 par.; John 13:34–35; 15:12, 17; see Lev. 19:18). The rest of this letter also illustrates Paul's desire that believers in Thessalonica exhibit love for each other (1:3; 3:6, 12; 5:8, 13), just as they themselves are loved by God (1:4) and Paul (2:8).

iii. Reason 2: You Already Give Evidence of Loving One Another (4:10a)

The second reason (*gar* parallels the use of the same conjunction in the preceding clause of v. 9b) why Paul does not need to write to the Thessalonians

4:10a

Deidun also observes that the combination of the two prophetic texts of Jer. 31:34 (38:34 LXX) and Ezek. 37:14 (cf. also 36:27) "is widely attested in Jewish tradition in contexts concerning messianic times, and with particular reference to the immediacy of God's teaching" (20).

38. Although the context in 4:9 might suggest that εἰς τὸ ἀγαπᾶν gives the *content* of what the Thessalonians have been taught by God, this grammatical construction normally expresses *purpose* (BDF §402.2). The distinction between content (*what* God taught them) and purpose (*why* God taught them), however, should not be stressed since the two are closely related.

about *philadelphia* is that they already give clear evidence of this mutual love: "for indeed you are doing it to all the brothers in the whole of Macedonia" (καὶ γὰρ ποιεῖτε αὐτὸ εἰς πάντας τοὺς ἀδελφοὺς ἐν ὅλῃ τῇ Μακεδονίᾳ, *kai gar poieite auto eis pantas tous adelphous en holē tē Makedonia*). This second reason advances Paul's argument by making two points (Frame 1912: 159): first, the Thessalonians not only have been taught by God to love another, but they also are indeed doing what they have been taught; second, they are doing it not only to believers in their own local congregation but also to all the believers in the whole of Macedonia.

On the first point, the statement "indeed you are doing it" affirms that the Thessalonians already are living up to the God-taught purpose of loving one another, similar to the statements of 4:1 ("just as you are indeed walking") and 5:11 ("just as you are indeed doing"). This affirmation does not mean, however, that Paul has no concerns about the Thessalonian church—something that becomes clear in the specific appeal of 4:10b–12.

On the second point, the statement "to all the brothers in the whole of Macedonia" refers to the Thessalonians' practice of extending mutual love to members beyond their home church, to those from other congregations in the area: Philippi, Berea, possibly Amphipolis and Apollonia (Acts 17:1), and other locales in Macedonia where the evangelistic activity of the Thessalonians has resulted in the formation of new churches (1:8). Paul's claim may at first appear to be hyperbole (so, e.g., Richard 1995: 217; Malherbe 2000: 245; Witherington 2006: 120). Yet his words should not be dismissed as mere rhetorical flourish, since the number of believers in the whole of Macedonia would not have been so great to make it impossible for the apostle's words to be understood in a more straightforward manner (note also the omission of a reference to the believers "in Achaia," as in 1:7, or even more broadly "in every place," as in 1:8).

Paul does not state *how* the Thessalonians have demonstrated this mutual love for all the Macedonian believers. He may be thinking of their provision of finances and personnel for the evangelistic activity that is taking place within both their own province and Achaia (1:7–8), similar to the support that the Philippians provided the apostle throughout various stages in his missionary activities (Phil. 1:5; 4:15–16), including his current stay in Corinth (2 Cor. 11:7–9; Acts 18:5). This possibility, however, suffers from the fact that the focus in 1 Thess. 4:9–10a is not on evangelism but on mutual love. Another option is that Paul has in mind the hospitality that the Thessalonians extended to fellow believers from their province, who, due to the importance of Thessalonica as the economic and political center of Macedonia, frequently traveled to this city and needed housing. Hospitality extended to traveling Christians was an important ministry in the early church (Rom. 16:1–2; 1 Pet. 4:9; 3 John 5–8, 10), even though it sometimes exposed congregations to the influence of false teachers (2 John 10–11; Jude 4–16; Rev. 2:2).

A third and more likely possibility, however, is that Paul alludes here to the economic aid that the Thessalonians were providing for needy Christians within their region. The apostle does speak elsewhere of the "extreme poverty" endured by the churches of Macedonia (2 Cor. 8:1–2). Also, Paul's claim that the Thessalonians had demonstrated love to "all" the brothers in the whole of Macedonia would be more appropriate as a reference to economic aid, which the majority of the Macedonian believers apparently needed, than a reference to the considerably fewer number of believers whose status and circumstances allowed them to travel to Thessalonica and need hospitality. Finally, the subsequent appeal that the Thessalonians "work with your hands" in order that they "may have need of no one" (vv. 11b–12) better fits a context in which some local believers are taking advantage of the Thessalonians' ongoing aid for the needy (food, money) than of the church's provision of temporary housing for travelers.

b. Specific Appeal (4:10b–12)

Paul's general affirmation of the love that the Thessalonians demonstrate toward fellow believers both within and beyond their own congregation (vv. 9–10a) gives way to an appeal formula (on the form and function of this epistolary convention, see comment on 4:1), which in concrete terms spells out how this mutual love ought to manifest itself. This specific appeal consists of four exhortations, all given in the form of infinitives in indirect command.[39] Although there is widespread agreement about the meaning of the first exhortation, there is much less unanimity about the final three, especially the historical situation to which they are referring and the specific problem that Paul tries to correct. The different explanations that have been forwarded will be presented below. For now we repeat our earlier observation that the fourth and final appeal that you "work with your hands" seems to be most prominent in Paul's mind; hence the problem of idleness provides the historical context (*Sitz im Leben*) in which the preceding exhortations, as well as the general affirmation of 4:9–10a, ought to be understood.

i. Appeal 1: Increase in Loving One Another (4:10b)

The first appeal establishes an important link between the specific appeal of 4:10b–12 and the preceding general affirmation of verses 9–10a: "But we appeal to you, brothers, to increase more and more" (παρακαλοῦμεν δὲ ὑμᾶς, ἀδελφοί, περισσεύειν μᾶλλον, *parakaloumen de hymas, adelphoi, perisseuein mallon*). As

4:10b

---

39. In 4:11 the second infinitive φιλοτιμεῖσθαι (to make it one's ambition) of the sentence (4:10b–12) takes an infinitive as its object (a complimentary infinitive). Thus the following grammatical constructions are possible: (1) only the first of the following infinitives, ἡσυχάζειν (to live a quiet life) is dependent on φιλοτιμεῖσθαι (so most commentators); (2) the first and second of the following infinitives are dependent on φιλοτιμεῖσθαι (so Richard 1995: 211; Holmes 1998: 136n2); or (3) all three of the following infinitives are dependent on φιλοτιμεῖσθαι (so Weatherly 1996: 145; Malherbe 2000: 246; Green 2002: 209). From a purely grammatical perspective, these options impact the number of indirect commands or appeals that Paul gives: four (option 1), three (option 2), or two (option 3). From a content perspective, however, four differing or distinct appeals remain, regardless of how one configures the grammatical construction.

with the similar expression in 4:1, here too the absence of any direct object for the verb *perisseuein* results in an appeal that at first glance appears ambiguous: What are the Thessalonians to increase more and more in doing? The context, however, provides the clear answer: just as the expression to "increase more and more" in 4:1 refers *back* to the preceding discussion of walking in a manner that pleases God, so also here it refers *back* to the preceding discussion of *philadelphia* and the practice of loving one another. The first appeal, therefore, involves an exhortation for the Thessalonians to increase even more in their practice of mutual love, the very thing that Paul prayed for them to do in 3:12 ("May the Lord cause you to abound and increase in love for one another and for all").

Although Paul has not yet explicitly raised the problem of idleness, there is good reason to believe that this problem is already in his mind with this first exhortation. This is suggested by the fact that the progressively specific appeals that climax in the call "to work with your hands" are intended to spell out how this love for others is to manifest itself in their relations with fellow believers. That Paul already has the problem of idleness in view with the first appeal is suggested further by his similar treatment of this same problem in the Second Letter to the Thessalonians. Just as the apostle in 2 Thess. 3:6–15 balances his negative rebuke of the idlers and his command that they work for their own bread with the positive exhortation that the church nevertheless "not be weary in doing good" for those who are genuinely in need (v. 13), so also here in 4:9–12 he balances his warning against idleness and the need for self-sufficient work (vv. 11b–12) with not only the positive affirmation of the church's demonstration of love for fellow believers (v. 10a), likely through the provision of aid to the needy, but also the positive exhortation that they "increase more and more" in such conduct.

ii. Appeal 2: Live a Quiet Life (4:11a)

4:11a The second appeal[40] specifies how the Thessalonians are to increase in mutual love toward fellow believers, though the exact meaning of this directive still remains rather ambiguous: "and to make it your ambition to live a quiet life" (καὶ φιλοτιμεῖσθαι ἡσυχάζειν, *kai philotimeisthai hēsychazein*). The verb *philotimeisthai*, which literally means "to love honor," was used by Hellenistic writers to refer to an intense desire or strong ambition for honor, sometimes with the negative connotation of a selfish desire to improve one's reputation, but more often with the positive sense of a laudatory desire to do something noble and good (LSJ 1941; for texts see Malherbe 2000: 246–47). The two other occurrences of this verb in Paul's Letters both express the strong desire

---

40. The NIV 1984 wrongly starts a new paragraph at 4:11, thereby suggesting that Paul has left behind the subject of mutual love and moved on to a new topic. Such a major break here, however, is grammatically impossible, since 4:11 opens with an infinitive that is dependent on the main verb "we appeal," found in the preceding 4:10b. Worse, beginning a new paragraph at 4:11 hides the important link that exists in Paul's argument between the general affirmation of 4:9–10a and the specific appeals of 4:10b–12. Thankfully, the NIV 2011 has corrected this problem and presents 4:9–12 as a single, unified paragraph.

of the apostle to do something that is described, as here in verse 11a, by a complimentary infinitive: "thus making it my ambition to preach the gospel" (Rom. 15:20); "Therefore, we make it our ambition . . . to be pleasing to him [the Lord]" (2 Cor. 5:9).

The strong desire or ambition that Paul exhorts the Thessalonians to have is "to live a quiet life." The verb *hēsychazein* in the Lukan writings means either to refrain from saying something, thus to "be quiet, remain silent" (Luke 14:4; Acts 11:18; 21:14; cf. 22:2); or to refrain from doing something, thus to "rest" (Luke 23:56). Here, however, in the only occurrence of the verb in Paul's Letters, *hēsychazein* clearly refers to something different than either saying nothing or doing nothing. Its meaning is clarified somewhat by the apostle's response to the problem of idle church members in his Second Letter to the Thessalonians (3:6–15).[41] After identifying those in the Thessalonian church who are "not busy" doing their own work but are instead "busybodies," Paul commands these idle members to earn their own living by "working with quietness" (3:12, *meta hēsychias ergazomenoi*). This suggests that the idleness of some at Thessalonica allowed them the time and opportunity to be involved in the kind of meddling and busybody activity that offends others. Philo (*Abraham* 20) contrasts the "quiet" life with the

> vulgar man, who spends his days meddling, running around in public, in theaters, tribunals, councils, and assemblies, meetings and consultations of all sorts; he prattles on without moderation, fruitless, to no end; he confuses and stirs up everything, mingling truth with falsehood, the spoken with the unspoken, the private with the public, the sacred with the profane, the serious with the ridiculous, not having learning to remain quiet [*hēsychian*], which is the ideal when the situation calls for it; and he pricks up his ears in an excess of bustling busyness.

41. Many scholars are reluctant to use 2 Thess. 3:6–15 to interpret 4:10b–12 (and 5:14) on the grounds that either (1) Paul did not write 2 Thessalonians, or (2) it is awkward to interpret the earlier letter (1 Thessalonians) in light of the later letter. In response to the first ground, we note that there is compelling evidence that 2 Thessalonians is an authentic letter of Paul (see the extended discussion of this issue in the commentary introduction). In response to the second ground, the striking parallels between the two letters in their respective treatment of the problem of idleness warrant interpreting the one letter in light of the other:

1 Thessalonians	2 Thessalonians
ἡσυχάζειν (4:11b)	μετὰ ἡσυχίας ἐργαζόμενοι (3:12)
ἐργάζεσθαι (4:11c)	same verb occurs five times (3:8, 10, 11 [2x], 12)
"as we commanded [παρηγγείλαμεν] you" (4:11c)	"we were commanding you" (same verb occurs three times: 3:6, 10, 12)
appeal to previously shared material (4:11c)	also 3:6, 10
"to mind your own business" (4:11b)	"being busybodies" (3:11)
ἀτάκτους (5:14)	root ἀτακτ- occurs three times (3:6, 7, 11)

These parallels lead Russell (1988: 114n10) to conclude that "2 Thess 3.6–13 is a commentary on 1 Thess 4.11–12 and 5.14."

This passage is frequently cited by commentators (e.g., Spicq 1994: 2.181; Holmes 1998: 137n4; Green 2002: 210).

Hence this second appeal, in verse 11a, challenges the Thessalonian believers to develop a strong desire to live the kind of quiet life that is free from any form of activity that disturbs others.

The brevity of this exhortation and the generic quality of its content make it difficult to reconstruct with confidence the specific historical situation that Paul is addressing. The two main options involve either an *inner-community context* (an in-house situation involving only church members) or a *public setting* (a situation involving contact between believers and nonbelievers). The first option is adopted, for example, by Frame (1912: 162), who argues that the situation "was not simply that some were idle and in their want had asked support from the church, but also that, being refused, they had attempted to interfere in the management of its affairs." Morris (1991: 132) similarly postulates "a tendency to interfere in the running of the church" (see also Hendriksen 1955: 105; Rigaux 1956: 521). Others stress the disorderly aspect of certain members, which included not merely their rejection of work but also their disregard of church order, thereby causing unrest within the church community: instead of being passive or "quiet," they were "busybodies," thrusting their unsolicited advice on other congregational members (Russell 1988: 108). What these proposals have in common is that the focus in the passage is on internal church relations and the practice of *philadelphia* as a means to maintain peace among fellow believers (see 5:12–13), a peace that presents a positive picture of the church to those outside its membership.

Most commentators, however, envision a public setting involving some kind of conflict between the Thessalonian believers and their fellow citizens. Support for a public setting lies in the fact that the verb *hēsychazein* and its cognate *hēsychia* were widely used by the Greco-Roman moralists to refer to withdrawal from active participation in political and social affairs (for texts, see Hock 1980: 46–47; Malherbe 2000: 247–49). Dobschütz (1909: 180–83), for example, proposed that some members of the Thessalonian church were proving troublesome in local politics by being preoccupied with preaching rather than carrying out their civic responsibilities. The common criticism of this "political" interpretation, however, is that the majority of believers were lower-class working people, who lacked the financial resources and status to hold public office and be involved in local politics.

More recently, variations of the political interpretation have been forwarded. For example, De Vos (1999: 160–70) argues that the Thessalonian believers were most likely citizens of the city and thus members of the *demos*, or citizen assembly, where they did play a political role. He further proposes that some of the church members retaliated against the repression they were experiencing for their newfound faith by "disrupting the *demos* meetings through their preaching and their protestation at the treatment they were receiving" (170). Thus he understands the exhortation "to live a quiet life" as Paul's instruction to his politically provocative and disruptive converts "to renounce their citizenship and become like metics [i.e., those who do not have rights as citizens]" (175).

Winter (1989: 313; 1994: 48–50) and Green (2002: 210–11) link the political interpretation with their conviction that the patron-client relationship lies behind the problem of idleness. A client who had citizenship would be obligated to support his patron's cause by speaking and casting the appropriate vote in the citizen assembly. Members of the Thessalonian church who had such a relationship with a powerful patron and who supported that person in the political assembly could easily arouse public opposition to Christians in general. Believers in these relationships might also be tempted to follow the "worldly" practice of turning to their powerful patrons to help solve the conflict that existed between church members and their fellow citizens (2:14). Accordingly, Paul's exhortation "to live a quiet life" urges believers to stay out of political affairs typically involved with the patron-client relationship. It is not certain, however, that the apostle has in view these patron-client relationships (see comment on 4:11c).

Others reject the connection to political office found in Dobschütz's proposal (above) but embrace his suggestion that believers gave up work in order to evangelize. Barclay (1993: 522–23), for example, claims that the Thessalonians were involved in the kind of aggressive evangelistic activity that included the public denigration of the so-called gods of nonbelievers, the prediction of their forthcoming doom, and perhaps even the vandalization of temples or shrines. Still (1999: 245–50) similarly finds in Paul's appeal to lead a quiet life a correction of the Thessalonians' active Christian proselytism (see also Furnish 2007: 98). That the church was involved in evangelism may be readily granted (1:8). Yet the depth of Paul's concern about their ability to not be shaken in their faith by their afflictions and his desire to send Timothy to them so as to strengthen their faith (3:1–5)—such concerns do not suggest a congregation that aggressively and defiantly preaches the gospel.

Although some of these diverse proposals for the historical context of 4:10b–12 are more compelling than others, they all run the danger of reading too much into the meager information that is available. Most commentators, therefore, settle for understanding Paul's exhortation "to live a quiet life" in a more general manner (so, e.g., Marshall 1983: 116; Wanamaker 1990: 163; D. Martin 1995: 137; Holmes 1998: 138). The apostle here and in the subsequent exhortation "to mind your own business" is calling the Thessalonians to maintain a low profile in the public arena, keep to themselves as much as possible, and practice *philadelphia* within the church, thereby minimizing the danger of arousing further opposition to the Christian movement.

iii. Appeal 3: Mind Your Own Business (4:11b)

The third appeal further spells out how the Thessalonians are to demonstrate mutual love, though again the precise historical context of this directive continues to remain vague: "and to mind your own business" (καὶ πράσσειν τὰ ἴδια, *kai prassein ta idia*). The expression *prassein ta idia* (lit., "to do one's own things") does not appear anywhere else in the NT or the LXX. The idea of sticking to one's own affairs rather than meddling into other people's business

4:11b

occurs frequently, however, in secular writings of this period, and at times it is linked with the notion of living a "quiet" life (for texts, see Malherbe 2000: 248–49). Plato, for example, describes the philosopher as one who "lives quietly [*hēsychian*] and minds his own business [*ta hautou prattein*]" (*Rep.* 6.496D). The two ideas are also juxtaposed in Dio Cassius (60.27), who similarly speaks of "living quietly [*hēsychian*] and minding one's own business [*ta heautou prattōn*]." Also of interest is Plato's comment that the saying "To mind one's own business [*ta hautou prattein*] and not to be a busybody is justice" (*Rep.* 4.441D–E) was well known and often repeated.

The cryptic nature of this third exhortation makes it possible to understand Paul's words here as fitting into any of the different historical situations proposed above. If the apostle is addressing internal church relations, this exhortation ought to be understood in light of 2 Thess. 3:11, which describes the conduct of certain congregational members who are "not busy" doing their work but are using their free time to become "busybodies" (see also 1 Pet. 4:15, which warns believers not to get into trouble as a meddler in other people's business). These believers are thus exhorted "to mind your own business." If, however, Paul is concerned about the interaction of the Thessalonian believers with their unbelieving fellow citizens, this third appeal calls on congregational members to minimize their activity in the public arena, regardless of whether that activity involves serving in public office, participating in the citizen assembly, carrying out one's responsibilities in a patron-client relationship, or preaching the gospel.

iv. Appeal 4: Engage in Self-Sufficient Work (4:11c)

4:11c

The fourth appeal is the clearest in showing how the Thessalonians are specifically to manifest *philadelphia*: "and to work with your hands" (καὶ ἐργάζεσθαι ταῖς χερσὶν ὑμῶν, *kai ergazesthai tais chersin hymōn*). Modern readers might well understand the expression "to work with your hands" as a metaphorical reference to the principle of working. Ancient readers, however, would have interpreted these words literally as referring to manual labor. This fourth appeal, therefore, implies that the great majority of the Thessalonian believers were manual workers, either artisans or unskilled laborers. Paul does not mean, of course, that those who could not work, whether through lack of opportunity or infirmity, should not turn to the church for support (cf. Eph. 4:28; 1 Tim. 5:3–8). Rather, he is addressing the specific problem at Thessalonica of those who were unwilling to work (2 Thess. 3:10b: "If anyone is *not willing* to work . . ."), content to live instead as parasites on the Christian community. Although the church must continue to practice *philadelphia* (4:9–10a) to all those in their fellowship who are genuinely in need, even increasing in such mutual love (4:10b), members who are capable of obtaining employment must not exploit the generosity of other believers but instead "work with your hands." Paul calls on his readers to be self-supporting and contributing members of the church, the very thing that he himself had done during his mission-founding work in their midst (2:9; 2 Thess. 3:7–9).

While the content of the fourth appeal is relatively clear, the reason for its presence is not. In other words, it is not obvious *why* some members of the Thessalonian church were idle and thus had to be exhorted to work. The traditional explanation is that their idleness was rooted in their eschatological excitement over the imminent return of Christ (so, e.g., Lightfoot 1904: 60–62; Milligan 1908: xlvi–xlvii, 53; Frame 1912: 160, 307; Rigaux 1956: 519; Best 1977: 175; Bruce 1982: 91; Jewett 1986: 172–75; Morris 1991: 9, 130; Gaventa 1998: 59). The belief that Christ would return soon led some in the church to abandon ordinary earthly pursuits, such as working for a living, reasoning to themselves: "Since the end is near, work is a waste of time."

Although nowhere in the two Thessalonian Letters does Paul explicitly make a direct connection between eschatological excitement and the problem of idleness, at least three factors can be cited to support such a link. First, the problem of idleness, which is raised twice in 1 Thessalonians (4:11c–12; 5:14), frames the extended discussion of matters concerning Christ's return (4:13–5:11)—thereby suggesting that the two topics are related. And this juxtaposition of topics occurs also in 2 Thessalonians, where the treatment of idleness (3:1–15) appears immediately after a lengthy discussion of the day of the Lord (2:1–17). Second, the frequent and lengthy references in both letters to the expected return of Christ—far more than in any of Paul's other letters—suggest that the Thessalonian church possessed a heightened expectancy regarding Christ's return. Third, the frequency with which eschatological excitement has led to idleness in a variety of religious groups over the centuries testifies to how easily this problem could have occurred at Thessalonica.[42]

Not all scholars, however, have found the "eschatological" argument convincing. They stress the already-noted fact that Paul never explicitly links the problem of idleness with a belief in the imminent return of Christ. They also point out that Paul needed to command the Thessalonian believers to work during his mission-founding visit (4:11; 2 Thess. 3:6, 10), which suggests that idleness was already a problem before their conversion. Thus, instead of an eschatological cause for the unwillingness of some in the Thessalonian church to work, these scholars argue for a sociological origin of the problem.

A few appeal to the general disdain toward physical labor that was prevalent in the Greco-Roman world (Bienert 1954: 270–72; Seventer 1961: 213; Marshall 1983: 116, 223). Cicero, for example, pejoratively refers to "the means of livelihood of all hired workmen whom we pay for mere manual labor, not for artistic skill" (*Duties* 1.150–51). This negative view toward work, however, was a viewpoint that only the wealthy upper class could afford to have. Laborers

---

42. Two recent examples can be briefly mentioned. The first is that of the Dami Mission Church in Korea, whose numerous members, in the belief that Christ was going to return on Reformation Day 1992, sold their homes, emptied their bank accounts, and quit their jobs. The second is the American Christian radio broadcaster Harold Camping's claim that Jesus would return on May 21, 2011, thereby causing a small group of followers to quit their jobs, give up planning for the financial future of themselves and their children (e.g., saving for college), and engage in a full-time preaching ministry.

and artisans, who probably made up the majority of the Thessalonian believers, would not have had the luxury of such an outlook.

Most in the sociological camp have tried to explain the problem of idleness
at Thessalonica in terms of the patron-client relationship that was popular in
that day (so, e.g., Russell 1988; Winter 1989; Aune 1989; Williams 1992: 150;
Green 2002: 208–13). In this relationship, members of the lower class would
attach themselves to benefactors from among the upper class, from whom
they would then receive sustenance and help in various matters in exchange for
the obligation to reciprocate with expressions of gratitude and support. It is
argued that Paul's converts included those of the urban poor who had formed
client relationships with wealthy members in the Thessalonian church, but who
exploited the generosity of their new Christian patrons. But while patron-client
relationships may well have existed in the congregation, this relationship in and
of itself may not be the specific cause of the idle behavior of some Christians in
the city. For the obligations that clients typically had to fulfill for their wealthy
patrons (e.g., greet them in the morning with the *salutation*, or "morning
salute"; appear with them in public; work in their public campaigns) involved
sufficient activity that clients would not likely be accused of idleness.

It appears, therefore, that there is insufficient evidence available to determine
with any high degree of certainty why some in the Thessalonian church were
guilty of idleness. Nevertheless, if one is forced to make a decision, the eschatological argument seems to provide a slightly more convincing explanation
than any of the sociological arguments for this state of affairs at Thessalonica.
That Paul warned against idleness from the very beginning of his ministry at
Thessalonica in no way negates this conclusion. For his ministry there, though
not lengthy, lasted long enough for the problem of eschatological enthusiasm
to manifest itself in the church.

The fourth appeal "to work with your hands" is emphasized somewhat
by a parenthetical καθώς clause, which reminds the Thessalonians that Paul
had given them the very same command already during his mission-founding
visit: "just as we commanded you" (καθὼς ὑμῖν παρηγγείλαμεν, *kathōs hymin
parēngeilamen*). Although the *kathōs* clause may refer to all four of the preceding appeals (so most commentators), two factors suggest that it perhaps should
be restricted only to the fourth and final one. First, the *kathōs* clause of 4:6c,
where Paul similarly reminds his readers that he had already taught them about
this subject during his mission-founding visit, refers only to the immediately
preceding reason concerning the future judgment of Jesus Christ (v. 6b), not
the subsequent reasons concerning the past call of God (v. 7) and the present
gift of the Holy Spirit (v. 8). While not decisive for understanding the *kathōs*
in verse 11, the parallel suggests that here too Paul has in view only the immediately preceding exhortation. Second, 2 Thess. 2:6, 10 show that Paul had
indeed previously commanded the Thessalonians on the requirement to work
with their hands, whereas there is no similar substantiation that the apostle
commanded the Thessalonians to increase more and more in the practice of
philadelphia, to make it their ambition to lead a quiet life, or to mind their

own business (so Frame 1912: 160, 162). But even if it is granted that the *kathōs* clause does refer to all four appeals, that it comes immediately after the fourth lends a certain emphasis to that appeal to self-sufficient work.

v. Purpose Clause (4:12)

The four exhortations contained in the appeal formula close with a purpose (ἵνα, *hina*) clause[43] that provides two reasons why the Thessalonians ought to demonstrate mutual love in these specific ways: "in order that you may walk appropriately before outsiders and may have need of no one" (ἵνα περιπατῆτε εὐσχημόνως πρὸς τοὺς ἔξω καὶ μηδενὸς χρείαν ἔχητε, *hina peripatēte euschēmonōs pros tous exō kai mēdenos chreian echēte*). Some commentators (Ellicott 1864: 60; Lünemann 1885: 526; Bornemann 1894: 182; Wanamaker 1990: 164; Holmes 1998: 138) try to link the first half of this purpose clause (to win the respect of non-Christians) to the second and third appeals ("Make it your ambition to live a quiet life, and to mind your own business"), and the second half of this purpose clause (to be self-sufficient) to the fourth appeal ("to work with your hands"). The possibility of these connections would be strengthened if in the second and third appeals Paul were clearly dealing with a public setting in which believers are called on to withdraw from active participation in political and social affairs. As we have seen, however, there is not enough evidence to conclude whether these preceding appeals refer to a public setting or an inner-community context. Although the reference to the Thessalonians as winning the respect of outsiders might appear to support the former option, this is not necessarily so, since internal conflict among fellow Christians also has a potentially powerful impact on how unbelievers view the church. An inner-community context indeed is supported by the first and fourth appeals, which urge them to increase in loving conduct toward fellow believers and work in a self-sufficient way whereby one is not dependent on the generosity of other Christians.

(1) To Win the Respect of Non-Christians (4:12a)

The first reason why the Thessalonians ought to follow the four specific appeals of verses 10b–11 is that this will ensure that they conduct themselves (lit., "walk"; for the metaphorical use of *peripatēte*, see comment on 2:12 and 4:1) in a manner that is appropriate or fitting (the adverb *euschēmonōs* occurs elsewhere only in Rom. 13:13 and 1 Cor. 14:40) in the eyes of their fellow unbelieving citizens. Paul elsewhere is similarly concerned about the public reputation of believers and expresses the desire that his converts present a positive image of the church to those who are not Christians (1 Cor. 10:32–33; Col. 4:5; 1 Tim. 3:7; Titus 3:1–2; see also 1 Pet. 2:12). The apostle's concern

4:12a

---

43. It is grammatically possible, though not likely from the context of 4:12, that this is a result clause (so Masson 1957: 52; Ellingworth and Nida 1975: 90; D. Martin 1995: 139). It is frequently difficult to distinguish between purpose and result. Much less probable is the claim that the ἵνα clause functions as the object of παρηγγείλαμεν (in v. 11), giving the content of what Paul has previously commanded the Thessalonians to do (so Dobschütz 1909: 181; Lenski 1937: 322).

in this regard may simply have the pragmatic goal of freeing the church from further persecution or enhancing their evangelistic efforts. Yet, in light of Paul's earlier emphasis on the need for holiness to characterize the sexual conduct of believers (1 Thess. 4:3–8), his concern here for appropriate conduct in the presence of unbelievers may instead stem from his theological conviction that the church, as the covenant people of God, must exhibit holiness as the attribute that distinguishes believers from the rest of the world (see comment on 4:3a). The apostle's final words in 4:1–12 should not be misunderstood as referring to personal autonomy: to "have need of no one" does not imply an insular or self-centered disregard for others, since this would violate the principle of loving others. Paul is instead highlighting the necessity of personal responsibility: *philadelphia* means that Christ-followers will not wrongly take advantage of the kindness of fellow believers but instead will live as best as possible in a self-sufficient manner.

The identification of non-Christians as "outsiders" (*tous exō* is found elsewhere only in 1 Cor. 5:12–13; Col. 4:5; Mark 4:11) is significant in this regard. For as in the preceding section (1 Thess. 4:3–8), where Paul views holiness in sexual conduct as a distinguishing sign of the Thessalonian church that separates it from "the Gentiles who do not know God" (v. 5), here in this current section (vv. 9–12) he similarly sees self-sufficient work as a boundary marker that sets the church apart from "outsiders." As full members of God's covenant people, Gentile believers at Thessalonica are and must continue to be a holy community whose conduct in all aspects of life distinguishes them from the surrounding world.

(2) To Be Dependent on No One (4:12b)

4:12b The second reason for following the four exhortations is grammatically ambiguous, as *mēdenos* can be either neuter ("in order that . . . you may have need of *nothing*") or masculine ("in order that . . . you may have need of *no one*"). Although the noun *chreia* ("need") more often takes the genitive of the thing (see texts cited in BDAG 1088), the context better fits the masculine form. Ultimately, however, there is little difference in meaning among these two possibilities. What is of more importance is that this second reason echoes and so adds emphasis to the fourth and final appeal: "to work with your hands." Paul's overall concern in 4:9–12 is that the proper practice of *philadelphia* means that believers will not be idle but will engage in self-sufficient work, thereby visibly demonstrating the distinctive character of the church and not exploiting the generosity of fellow believers.

Additional Notes

4:1. The omission of the particle οὖν in some MSS (B* 33 629 630 1175 1739 vg^mss sy^p bo) reflects the uncertainty of ancient scribes over both the meaning and single occurrence of the combination λοιπὸν οὖν in 4:1. The external evidence strongly supports the inclusion of the particle, as does the greater likelihood that it was deliberately deleted (so as to fit the use of λοιπόν by itself as elsewhere in the NT) than consciously added to the original text.

4:1. Although there is stronger external evidence for the omission of ἵνα (א A D² Ψ 𝔐 syʰ) than for its inclusion (B D* F G 33 2464 *pc* syᵖ co), it is far easier to explain its deliberate deletion than its addition. Scribes deleted the word in an attempt to remove the awkwardness that resulted from (1) having the first ἵνα separated from the rest of its clause (περισσεύητε μᾶλλον) by the two καθώς clauses, and (2) having a second ἵνα later in the verse that is grammatically not necessary. The internal evidence, therefore, clearly supports the presence of the first ἵνα.

4:1. The whole of the second parenthetical clause (καθὼς καὶ περιπατεῖτε) is missing in some MSS (D² K L Ψ 𝔐 177 206 257 623 917 1175 1518 1739 syᵖ). The external evidence for its inclusion, however, is very strong (א A B D* F G 33 104 181 218 330 1311 1611 1836 1906 1912 2005 2127 itᵈ·ᵍ vg syʰ copˢᵃ·ᵇᵒ goth arm eth) as is the internal evidence (B. Metzger 1994: 564: "ἵνα περισσεύητε presupposes the earlier mention of the Thessalonians having begun the Christian life, but such a beginning is not implied in the preceding text without καθὼς καὶ περιπατεῖτε"). The deletion of this clause, therefore, can be explained as either accidental (through confusion with the first καθώς clause) or intentional (it might have seemed to some copyists as either superfluous or cumbersome in an already lengthy, complex sentence).

4:3. A few correctors and copyists either replaced the definite article in the prepositional phrase ἀπὸ τῆς πορνείας with the adjective πάσης (all: א² Ψ 104 365 *pc*) or added πάσῃ before the article (F Gᶜ). The omission of this adjective is supported not only by the external evidence (א* A B D G* 0183 𝔐 lat syʰ co; Tert Cl) but also by the internal evidence: "all" was intentionally added by some scribes to ensure a broad meaning for the somewhat ambiguous noun πορνεία: "from *all* sexual immorality."

4:8. The external evidence for the omission of the conjunction καί (A B D¹ I 33 365 614 1739* 2464 *al* b syᵖ bo; Ambst Spec) as well as its inclusion (א D*·² F G Ψ 𝔐 lat syʰ samss; Clement) is rather evenly divided, thereby making it difficult to reach a definitive conclusion about this textual variant (the editors of NA²⁸ include it in the main text but enclose it within square brackets). The internal evidence, however, favors its inclusion, since it is more likely that scribes deleted the word as either confusing (does it mean "indeed" or "also"?) or unnecessary, and it is hard to find a compelling reason why scribes deliberately added it to the text.

4:8. The more strongly attested present tense διδόντα (א* B D F G I 365 2464 *pc*) was replaced with the aorist δόντα in some MSS (א² A Ψ 𝔐 sy co; Clement) in order to conform either to the preceding reference in v. 7 to the past call of God (so Frame 1912: 156) or to the pattern of Paul's usage elsewhere (Rom. 5:5; 2 Cor. 1:22; 5:5; see also Rom. 8:15; Gal. 3:2; 4:6; so Fee 1994a: 50n54; 2009: 142n20).

4:8. Instead of the second-person pronoun ὑμᾶς, some MSS have the first person ἡμᾶς: A 6 365 1739 1881 *pc* a f m t vgᶜˡ syʰ; Ambr Spec. This variation is almost certainly an intentional harmonization with the use of the first person ἡμᾶς in the preceding verse.

4:9. The omission of the implied subject ἡμᾶς of the infinitive γράφειν (for us to write/that we write) has resulted in an awkward construction that reads, lit.: "For you have no need to write to you." In order to create a smoother reading, many scribes changed the second person ἔχετε to the first person ἔχομεν: "*We* have no need to write to you" (א² D* F G Ψ 6 104 365 1739 1881 2464 2495ᶜ *pc* lat syʰ). This change to the first person was an attractive solution to a few other scribes who, in the attempt to correct even further this difficult reading, also changed the tense from the present to the aorist εἴχομεν: "We *had* no need to write to you" (B I t vgᵐˢˢ). The awkwardness of this construction was solved differently by a few other scribes, who, under the influence of 5:1, changed the infinitive γράφειν from the active to the passive γράφεσθαι: "You have no need *to be written* to you" (H 81 *pc*; Aug). Despite the awkwardness of this construction, however, the second person ἔχετε (1) has the strongest textual support (ℵ* A D¹ H 𝔐 sy^p co; Aug), (2) is the more difficult and thus preferred reading, and (3) best accounts for the rise of the alternate readings (see B. Metzger 1994: 564).

4:10. Some MSS (ℵ² B D¹ H Ψ 𝔐 vg^ms) repeat the definite article from τοὺς ἀδελφούς before the prepositional phrase ἐν ὅλῃ τῇ Μακεδονίᾳ: "the brothers, *the ones* in the whole of Macedonia." The external evidence for the omission of the repeated definite article is slightly stronger (ℵ* A D* F G 629 lat), especially since this reading goes against the tendency of D to embellish the text. The internal evidence is more difficult to determine: its omission could be a case of homoeoteleuton (same ending) with ἀδελφούς, while its addition could be a deliberate attempt to improve the style. The meaning of this verse is not significantly affected by either reading.

4:11. The adjective ἰδίαις is added before χερσὶν ὑμῶν (your *own* hands; see also 1 Cor. 4:12) in a couple of important early uncials (ℵ* A D¹) as well as the later Byzantine texts (𝔐), thus leading the editors of NA²⁸ to include it in the text (though within square brackets). There is also weighty support, however, for the omission of this adjective (ℵ² B D* F G Ψ 0278 6 104 365 1175 1505 1739 1881 *pc* sy^h). It is more likely that this is a later addition in keeping with the tendency of some scribes toward greater precision (see Eph. 4:28), probably under the influence of the same adjective in the preceding exhortation.

B. Comfort concerning Deceased Christians at Christ's Return (4:13–18)

In the second half of the letter body (4:1–5:22), Paul continues to fulfill his stated desire to "complete the things that are lacking in your faith" (3:10). Of the three topics foreshadowed in the transitional prayer of 3:12–13, two have already been taken up in 4:1–12: holiness in sexual conduct (vv. 3–8) and the practice of *philadelphia*, mutual love (vv. 9–12). Paul now turns to the third topic, the return of Christ. The first of the two following discussions that deal with the future coming of the Lord is 4:13–18, where the apostle speaks about the comfort the Thessalonians have concerning the fate of deceased believers at Christ's return.

The Christians in Thessalonica were grieving over fellow members of their church who died prior to Christ's return (v. 13), fearing that these deceased believers would not be able to participate equally with living believers in the glorious events connected with the coming of the Lord. First, Paul responds to their grief by appealing to a creedal statement—an authoritative confession of the church concerning the resurrection of Jesus, which in turn guarantees the resurrection of deceased believers such that they will be alive and with Jesus at his return (v. 14). Second, the apostle appeals to the "word of the Lord," an authoritative saying of Jesus guaranteeing that deceased believers will in no way be at a disadvantage at Christ's return compared to living believers but will participate equally with them in that eschatological event (vv. 15–17). After providing his Thessalonian readers with these two compelling reasons why they ought not to grieve over their deceased members with the kind of hopelessness that characterizes the non-Christians' experience of death, Paul concludes by exhorting the church to "comfort one another with these words" (v. 18).

Literary Analysis

Character of the Passage

At first glance the material of 4:13–18 appears to belong to a different classification from that of 4:1–12. The preceding passage contains several explicit exhortations about sexual conduct and the practice of *philadelphia* that justify identifying this material as paraenetic (exhortative). The present passage, however, primarily contains teaching about the return of Christ such that Paul's purpose seems to be didactic rather than paraenetic. Nevertheless, the intention of the apostle's instruction is not merely to inform but also to change the conduct of the Thessalonians, so that their grief over the uncertain fate of believers who have died before Christ's return would be replaced with the comfort that comes from knowing that these deceased Christians will share equally with living Christians in the blessedness of that future event. That the opening disclosure formula (v. 13a) is immediately followed by a purpose clause (v. 13b) suggests that the teaching of new information has a paraenetic purpose, something that is made explicit in the closing exhortation (Howard 1988: 166–70; Holmstrand 1997: 64–65). Consequently, as Malherbe (2000: 279, citing Radl 1981: 154–55) observes: "These verses . . . do not interrupt Paul's paraenesis, but are themselves hortatory."

Extent of the Passage

The beginning of a new section in 4:13 is suggested by the obvious shift in topic from conduct that pleases God (4:1–2) in the specific areas of sexual practice (4:3–8) and the demonstration of mutual love (4:9–12), to the fate of deceased believers at Christ's return. This shift in topic is confirmed by several epistolary and other more broadly literary features. First, this new section opens with a disclosure formula ("We do not want you not to know . . ."), a common transitional device in the letters of Paul and other writers of his day (Mullins 1964). But in contrast to the form of this formula ("You know that . . .") found elsewhere in the letter (2:1; 4:2; 5:2), Paul here employs a different version ("I do not want you not to know that . . .") to make it clear that he is about to present new information that he has not up to that time shared with the Thessalonians. In this way, a clear contrast is formed between 4:13–18 and the surrounding passages of 4:1–12 and 5:1–11, where the apostle stresses that the Thessalonians already know about these matters from his original preaching ministry in their midst (4:1, "just as you received from us how you must walk and so please God"; 4:2, "For you know what commands we gave to you"; 4:6, "just as we indeed told you before and solemnly warned"; 4:11, "just as we commanded you"; 5:2, "For you yourselves accurately know that . . ."). This likely explains why Paul does not open the new section of 4:13–18 with the "now about" (περὶ δέ, peri de) formula as he does in 4:9 and 5:1: a different form of the disclosure formula is needed to distinguish the new material of 4:13–18 from the previously shared material of 4:1–12 and 5:1–11.

Second, a break at 4:13 is indicated by the presence of the vocative "brothers," another common transitional device. Third, Paul once again (see 4:9; 5:1) uses the "now about" (peri de) formula, though its presence here is not so obvious. This is because the needed disclosure formula (see preceding paragraph) requires that the preposition peri be bumped from its normal position at the head of the sentence to the end, while the particle de retains its postpositive position. Finally, the various features that plainly mark the ending of the preceding passage in 4:12 (see "Extent of the Passage" for 4:1–12) naturally lead the reader to expect a new section to begin in the immediately following material of 4:13.

That Paul's discussion of eschatological matters continues through 5:11 might lead to the conclusion that this verse marks the end of the new passage begun in 4:13. There actually are striking similarities in both content and form between 4:13–18 and 5:1–11 (see Plevnik 1979; Collins 1984: 154–72; Johanson 1987: 118–19; Howard 1988; Luckensmeyer 2009: 181). Both passages deal generally with the return of Christ, though 4:13–18 focuses on the fate of the *deceased* believers at that eschatological event, while 5:1–11 deals with the fate of *living* believers on that day. In the first passage the references to "those who have fallen asleep" (4:13, 14,

15), "the dead in Christ" (4:16), and "we who are alive" (4:15, 17) are echoed in the second passage in the phrase "whether we wake or sleep we may live with him" (5:10). Both passages make ample use of apocalyptic motifs in contrast to the preceding (4:1–12) and following (5:12–22) passages, which do not. Both passages cite what is quite likely creedal material: "that Jesus died and rose" (4:14); "Jesus Christ, who died on behalf of us" (5:9–10). Both passages sharply contrast the condition of the Thessalonian believers with that of their fellow citizens, identifying them as "the rest" (οἱ λοιποί, *hoi loipoi*): those who grieve without hope (4:13) and who are spiritually asleep (5:6). Both passages make use of the emphatic future negation: "we . . . will certainly not precede" (4:15); "they will certainly not escape" (5:3). Both passages close by referring to the presence of believers with the returning Lord: "and so we will always be with the Lord" (4:17); "we will live together with him" (5:10). Both passages come to a definitive conclusion with the exhortation "comfort one another" (4:18; 5:11).

Nevertheless, despite these impressive links between 4:13–18 and 5:1–11, there are compelling grounds that these verses consist of two distinct passages, the first of which concludes at 4:18. This is indicated first in 4:18 by the particle ὥστε (*hōste*, therefore), introducing a concluding clause that, from a content perspective, appears to bring the preceding discussion to a close. The word "therefore" leads an audience to expect that the writer or speaker is wrapping up the discussion. This concluding function of *hōste* is confirmed by its use in Paul's other letters to mark the ending of a particular discussion (1 Cor. 7:38; 11:27, 33; 14:39; 15:58). Second, the fuller phrase in 4:18, "Therefore comfort one another" (ὥστε παρακαλεῖτε ἀλλήλους, *hōste parakaleite allēlous*), appears to function as a stereotyped expression that concludes the preceding material of 4:13–17, just as the virtually identical phrase in 5:11, "Therefore comfort one another" (διὸ παρακαλεῖτε ἀλλήλους, *dio parakaleite allēlous*), concludes the preceding material of 5:1–10. Third, this concluding exhortation to "comfort one another" forms a thematic inclusio[1] with the opening purpose statement of 4:13b that Thessalonians "not grieve" (so also Gillman 1985: 272; Plevnik 1997: 68; Luckensmeyer 2009: 179). Fourth, the closing prepositional phrase "with these words" (4:18) looks back to the preceding statements of 4:13–18. Fifth, that a new section begins in the immediately following verse of 5:1 is clear from the presence of two transitional markers: the "now about" (*peri de*) formula ("Now about times and dates") and the vocative "brothers." Sixth, the use of paraleipsis ("you have no need to have anything written to you"; for an explanation of this rhetorical device, see comment on 4:9a) in 5:1 and the particular form of the disclosure formula ("For you yourselves accurately know that . . .") in 5:2 indicate that Paul has left the new material introduced in 4:13–18 and returned to material that the Thessalonians already know from his mission-founding ministry in their midst.

Finally, the coherence of 4:13–18 is supported by the following lexical or conceptual recurrences (Johanson 1987: 119; Jurgensen 1994: 86): (1) "those who are/have fallen asleep" (κοιμωμένων [*koimōmenōn*] and κοιμηθέντας [*koimēthentas*;

---

1. An inclusio is typically formed by the repetition of the same key word, words, or phrase at the beginning and ending of a literary unit, thereby marking its boundaries. This inclusio, however, involves not a lexical link but one based on theme or content: the problem introduced at the beginning of the passage in 4:13 (the Thessalonians are ignorant and grieving) is solved by the end of the passage in verse 18 (the Thessalonians are now informed and comforted).

2x]: vv. 13, 14, 15) and its semantic equivalent "the dead in Christ" (οἱ νεκροὶ ἐν Χριστῷ, *hoi nekroi en Christō*: v. 16); (2) the double occurrence of the phrase "we who are alive, who are left" (ἡμεῖς οἱ ζῶντες οἱ περιλειπόμενοι, *hēmeis hoi zōntes hoi perileipomenoi*: vv. 15, 17); and (3) the conceptual parallels between "he will bring with him" (ἄξει σὺν αὐτῷ, *axei syn autō*: v. 14) and "we will be with the Lord" (σὺν κυρίῳ ἐσόμεθα, *syn kyriō esometha*: v. 17), and also between "Jesus . . . rose" (Ἰησοῦς . . . ἀνέστη, *Iēsous . . . anestē*: v. 14) and "the dead in Christ will rise" (οἱ νεκροὶ ἐν Χριστῷ ἀναστήσονται, *hoi nekroi en Christō anastēsontai*: v. 16). There can be little doubt, therefore, that 4:13–18 constitutes a distinct epistolary unit within 1 Thessalonians.

Structure of the Passage

Paul's discussion in 4:13–18 concerning the fate of deceased believers at Christ's return exhibits a clear structure or pattern. In verse 13 the apostle opens with an assertion that the Thessalonian Christians should not grieve for their deceased members with the kind of hopelessness that characterizes the way non-Christians experience death. This opening assertion is then followed with two causal clauses (vv. 14, 15), each introduced with γάρ (*gar*, for), and each providing one of the two reasons why the Thessalonians should not grieve as unbelievers do. The first reason (v. 14) involves a citation of confessional material about the resurrection of Jesus and so constitutes an authoritative word of the church—a confession that the Thessalonian church shares with other Christian congregations. Paul uses the church's confession concerning the resurrection of Jesus as a guarantee of the resurrection of deceased believers such that they will be alive and present at Christ's return. The second reason (v. 15) involves a "word of the Lord"—an authoritative saying of Jesus Christ guaranteeing that deceased believers will in no way be at a disadvantage at Christ's return as compared to living believers but will be equally present with them at that eschatological event. This "word of the Lord" is probably first summarized by Paul in his own words in verse 15b and then directly presented in verses 16–17a, with another Pauline summary in verse 17b. The particle ὥστε (*hōste*, therefore) in verse 18 leads readers to expect a concluding statement, here given in the form of an exhortation that the Thessalonians comfort one another with the preceding words of the passage.

Thus the structure of 4:13–18, "Comfort concerning Deceased Christians at Christ's Return," is as follows:

1. Opening assertion: Christians grieve with hope (4:13)
2. Reason 1: The confession of the church (4:14)
3. Reason 2: The "word of the Lord" (4:15–17)
4. Conclusion: Comfort one another (4:18)

Exegesis and Exposition

[13]⌐We⌐ do not want you not to know, brothers, about those who ⌐are asleep⌐ in order that you may not grieve like the rest who have no hope. [14]For since we believe that Jesus died and rose, so also, through Jesus, God will bring with him those who

have fallen asleep. ¹⁵For this we say to you by the word of the Lord, namely, we who are alive, who are left until the coming of the ⌜Lord⌝, will certainly not precede those who have fallen asleep, ¹⁶because the Lord himself will descend from heaven, with a commanding shout, with a voice of an archangel, and with a trumpet call of God, and the dead in Christ will rise ⌜first⌝; ¹⁷then we who are alive, ⌜who are left⌝, will be snatched up together with them by means of clouds for a ⌜reception⌝ of the Lord in the air; and so we will always be with the Lord. ¹⁸Therefore comfort one another with these ⌜words⌝.

1. Opening Assertion: Christians Grieve with Hope (4:13)

The first half of Paul's opening assertion in verse 13 introduces the topic that will occupy his attention in the subsequent verses: "We do not want you not to know, brothers, about those who are asleep" (οὐ θέλομεν δὲ ὑμᾶς ἀγνοεῖν, ἀδελφοί, περὶ τῶν κοιμωμένων, *ou thelomen de hymas agnoein, adelphoi, peri tōn koimōmenōn*).

4:13

The apostle clearly signals the beginning of a new topic and major section of the letter by effectively combining three transitional devices: the disclosure formula, the vocative, and the "now about" (*peri de*) formula. The first, the disclosure formula, occurs in the double negative form "we do not want you not to know" (so also Rom. 1:13; 11:25; 1 Cor. 10:1; 12:1; 2 Cor. 1:8). This serves as an emphatic equivalent of the positive form "I/We want you to know" (1 Cor. 11:3; Phil. 1:12; Col. 2:1) or "I make known to you" (1 Cor. 12:3; 15:1; 2 Cor. 8:1; Gal. 1:11). As in secular letters, where the disclosure formula frequently appears at the beginning of the correspondence and thus functions to introduce the main topic taken up in the letter body (see examples cited in Milligan 1908: 55; Koskenniemi 1956: 77–79; Mullins 1964; White 1986: 207), so also in Paul's Letters, but to an even greater degree this formula serves to introduce either the body of the letter or more often, as here, a new topic taken up within the document.

The form of the disclosure formula used in 4:13 suggests that the apostle is about to present something new and previously not taught to the Thessalonians (so, e.g., Best 1977: 184; Lüdemann 1984: 214–15; Morris 1991: 135; Plevnik 1997: 71; Nicholl 2004: 20–22; Fee 2009: 164). Some have objected to this conclusion (see, e.g., Dobschütz 1909: 186; Rigaux 1956: 239, 526–27; D. Martin 1995: 143; Luckensmeyer 2009: 212–13), claiming that this phrase should not "be read in a too literal sense" (Richard 1995: 233; see also Gaventa 1998: 62) and that Paul's varied use of the negative and positive forms of this formula "makes it impossible to draw rigid conclusions about their significance" (Malherbe 2000: 262). The larger context, however, clearly presents the topic of 4:13–18 as something unfamiliar to the Thessalonians, in contrast to the surrounding passages of 4:1–12 and 5:1–11, where Paul repeatedly draws their attention to the fact that these matters were part of his original preaching in Thessalonica (4:1, 2, 6, 11; 5:2) and thus are so well known to them that there is really "no need to write" about such things (4:9; 5:1). In fact, compared to the rest of the letter, where the apostle repeatedly refers to his readers' existing knowledge with expressions like "you know" (1:5; 2:1, 2, 5, 11; 3:3, 4; 4:2; 5:2) and "you remember" (2:9), such language is strikingly absent in 4:13–18. Although the apostle had taught the Thessalonians about the bodily resurrection of believers, he did not provide them with sufficient details about the specific matter of how the resurrection of these deceased believers coordinates with the event of Christ's return such that they need not grieve over "those who are asleep" (see further the discussion below concerning the specific reason for the grief of the Thessalonians).

The second transitional device in verse 13 is the vocative "brothers." Best (1977: 184) reasons that "since 'brothers' is always a part of the phrase [the disclosure formula: "we do not want you not to know"], it can have no special significance here." Nevertheless, this marks the ninth time in the letter thus far that Paul has addressed his readers as "brothers" (1:4; 2:1, 9, 14, 17; 3:7; 4:1, 10b; see also 5:1, 4, 12, 14, 25), indicating that it functions not merely as an epistolary convention marking transition but also as an important expression of the deep affection that the apostle still has for his Thessalonian converts—an affection also expressed in the other familial terms that he employs ("beloved," 1:4; "infants," 2:7b; "nursing mother," 2:7c; "father," 2:11; "orphaned," 2:17; for more on the designation "brothers," see the comment on 1:4).

The third transitional device is the "now about" (*peri de*) formula, commonly used in both secular (see White 1986 for examples from papyrus letters) and Pauline letters (1 Cor. 7:1, 25; 8:1, 4; 12:1; 16:1, 12; 1 Thess. 4:9, 13; 5:1) to introduce a new topic. Several commentators believe that the presence of the "now about" formula indicates that the Thessalonians had sent Paul a letter with a series of questions to which he responds in 4:9; 4:13; and 5:1 (so Milligan 1908: 126; Frame 1912: 140, 147, 164; Faw 1952; Masson 1957: 51–52; Malherbe 2000: 217, 243, 255; Green 2002: 202). Two factors, however, work against this conclusion. First, the "now about" formula occurs frequently in letters that do not involve a response to some earlier correspondence, and so its use does not necessarily imply the existence of a previous letter (Mitchell 1989). Second, unlike the Corinthians in 1 Cor. 7:1, there is no explicit reference to a letter sent to Paul from the Thessalonians. It appears more probable, therefore, that the "now about" formula introduces a new subject that Paul takes up in response to the oral report of Timothy (3:6).

The new topic that Paul takes up concerns "those who are asleep" (note the present tense of this participle in contrast to the aorist used in vv. 14, 15).[2] The verb *koimaō* literally means "sleep, fall asleep" (no Pauline examples of this literal meaning; Matt. 28:13; Luke 22:45; John 11:11, 12; Acts 12:6) but

---

2. There is likely little or no significance in the shift from the present participle to the aorist participle. Some suggest that the present tense "is a more expressive term, pointing forward to the future awakening and so implying the Resurrection more definitely" than the aorist (Lightfoot 1904: 63; Milligan 1908: 55). This conclusion probably derives too much from the tense. Furthermore, if this really were Paul's intention, why did he not use the present tense also in 4:14 and 15?

figuratively refers to the state of being dead—a usage also found in some NT writers (Matt. 27:52; Acts 7:60; 13:36; 2 Pet. 3:4) and consistently in Paul (1 Cor. 7:39; 11:30; 15:6, 18, 20, 51; 1 Thess. 4:13, 14, 15). Just as people today avoid the harshness of saying that someone has died by employing a variety of circumlocutions (e.g., "John has passed away"; "Joanne is no longer with us"), so the ancient world similarly used the verb "to sleep" as a euphemism for death. The description of death as sleep was widespread in the Greco-Roman world, appearing in Greek and Latin writings as early as the time of Homer (*Il.* 11.241; see also Sophocles, *El.* 509; Aelian, *Misc.* 2.35; Cicero, *Age* 81; Catullus 5.4–6) and also on many epitaphs (Lattimore 1942: 59, 164–65). The use of "sleep" as a euphemism for death also occurs in many OT (Gen. 47:30; Deut. 31:16; 2 Sam. 7:12; 1 Kings 2:10; 11:43; 22:50; Job 14:12; Ps. 13:3; Isa. 14:8; 43:17; Jer. 51:39; Dan. 12:2) and intertestamental writings (2 Macc. 12:45; As. Mos. 1.15; 10.14; 1 En. 92.3; 100.5; 2 Esd. [4 Ezra] 7:32; T. Jos. 20.4). Some of these writings not only refer to death as "sleeping" but also continue the metaphor by referring to the resurrection as an awakening from this sleep (Dan. 12:2; 2 Macc. 12:44–45; 1 En. 92.3; 2 Esd. [4 Ezra] 7:32).

In light of the widespread practice of euphemistically referring to death as "sleep," there is no justification for finding in 1 Thess. 4:13 any support for the notion of "soul sleep," that in the time immediately following death the soul of a person "sleeps," or exists in an unconscious state, unaware of its surroundings, until it is awakened at Christ's return, when the resurrection of the body takes place. This idea is further repudiated by NT passages that suggest the conscious and more blessed (compared to their previous fallen bodily condition) existence of believers during the intermediate state (Matt. 17:1–8 par.; Luke 23:43; 2 Cor. 5:8; Phil. 1:20–23; Rev. 6:9–11). The common practice of euphemistically referring to death as "sleep" also suggests that, though Paul makes use of this metaphor three times in this passage (vv. 13, 14, 15), it does not involve a "significant, if subtle, affirmation . . . that deceased Christians will rise" (Nicholl 2004: 23; also Fee 2009: 168). On this debatable point, it is significant that later in this passage Paul does not hesitate to identify deceased believers explicitly as "the dead" (v. 16).

The apostle nowhere indicates *how* these Thessalonian believers have died. Several commentators argue that some in the church had been martyred for their faith (e.g., Wohlenberg 1909: 101; Lake 1911: 88; Pobee 1985: 113–14; Donfried 1985: 349–51; 1993a: 21–23; Collins 1993: 112; Chapa 1994; Riesner 1998: 386–87; Still 1999: 215–17; Witherington 2006: 139). In support they appeal not only to the scattered references in 1 Thessalonians to the afflic-tion endured by the believers in Thessalonica (1:6; 2:2, 14–15; 3:1–5; see also 2 Thess. 1:4–7; 2 Cor. 8:1–2; Acts 17:5–7, 13) but especially to the parallel that Paul establishes between the persecution experienced by the Judean churches with that faced by the Thessalonian church (1 Thess. 2:14: "You suffered the same things"). The scattered references to affliction, however, more likely have in view severe social harassment and ostracism rather than physical death and martyrdom. As Bruce (1982: 98) notes: "The references in both 1 and

2 Thessalonians to the 'afflictions' endured by the Christians of Thessalonica scarcely give the impression that positive martyrdom was involved." Also, the parallel that Paul sets up in 2:14 rests not so much on similar suffering as on similar opponents: both groups suffered at the hands of their "own fellow citizens." Furthermore, if some Thessalonians had actually been martyred, Paul would surely have praised them for this act, just as he elsewhere (Rom. 16:4; Phil. 2:25–30) pays tribute to those who risk their lives for the Christian faith (Barclay 1993: 514).

Whereas the first half of verse 13 functions to introduce the topic of the new passage (i.e., the fate of deceased believers), the second half serves to present the assertion or thesis that Paul will establish in the subsequent verses: "in order that you may not grieve like the rest who have no hope" (ἵνα μὴ λυπῆσθε καθὼς καὶ οἱ λοιποὶ οἱ μὴ ἔχοντες ἐλπίδα, *hina mē lypēsthe kathōs kai hoi loipoi hoi mē echontes elpida*).

From this purpose clause, it is clear that the Christians in Thessalonica were "grieving" (the passive of *lypeō* means "be sad, be distressed, grieve": BDAG 604.2) over the death of their fellow believers. The use of the present tense highlights the ongoing nature of the action and so hints at the great depth of the Thessalonians' grief. What is not clear, however, is *why* the church was grieving to such a degree over their deceased members: what historical reconstruction of the situation in Thessalonica provides a plausible reason for their intense grief? This important question is not easily answered (Luckensmeyer 2009: 173 identifies it as the *crux interpretum* of this passage), and consequently a variety of hypotheses have been proposed (see the surveys provided by Marshall 1983: 120–22; Wanamaker 1990: 165–66; Richard 1995: 231–32; Malherbe 2000: 283–84; Green 2002: 213–15; see especially the helpful table in Luckensmeyer 2009: 192–211):

1. One hypothesis is that gnostic teachers had invaded the Thessalonian church, claiming among other things that the resurrection had already taken place (2 Tim. 2:18; see also 1 Cor. 15:12 and 2 Thess. 2:2). As a result, when some Christians died, the remaining members of the church grieved, thinking their fellow deceased believers were excluded from salvation (so Schmithals 1972: 160–64; Harnisch 1973: 16–51). It is questionable, however, whether gnosticism as a developed movement existed at this early date. And if it did, there is no compelling evidence for the presence of gnostic teachers in Thessalonica, a situation that would surely have provoked a much stronger reaction from Paul. Furthermore, it does not appear from the apostle's response that the problem at Thessalonica involved a denial of the resurrection doctrine.

2. A second proposal is that, due to Paul's belief in the imminent return of Christ, he did not teach the Thessalonians or other churches that he established early in his ministry anything about the resurrection of deceased believers. It was only with the passing of time and the passing away of Christians that the apostle's thinking developed from his early

position as reflected in 1 Thess. 4:13–18 to the full-fledged understanding of the resurrection found in 1 Cor. 15 (so, e.g., Marxsen 1969; Becker 1976: 46–54; Lüdemann 1984: 212–38, who uses the "early" character of Paul's parousia/resurrection teaching in 1 Thessalonians as evidence for dating this letter and the apostle's ministry in Thessalonica well before the traditional time of AD 51; see also Mearns 1980–81; Nicholl 2004: 35–38). Yet it strains credibility to believe that Paul had never previously encountered the death of Christians during the more than fifteen years that had passed from his conversion to the writing of 1 Thessalonians. Also, as 1 Cor. 15:3–8 ("I passed on to you . . .") suggests, the apostle typically included teaching on the resurrection of Jesus as part of his mission-founding message, and this teaching would have also included the resurrection of believers, given the intimate relationship in Paul's thinking between these two events (Rom. 8:11; 1 Cor. 6:14; 15:12–23; 2 Cor. 4:14; Col. 1:18). Furthermore, that the apostle can cite a "word of the Lord" about the resurrection of believers in verse 16b ("and the dead in Christ will rise") without any explanation about what this means indicates that the Thessalonian church is already familiar with this topic. Finally, the resurrection of the dead was affirmed not just by virtually all Jews but especially by the Pharisees, and so clearly was something that Paul had thought about and believed already before his conversion (see Acts 23:6). This would also be true for the few members of the Thessalonian church—Jews and God-fearers—who were converted from Paul's synagogue ministry in that city (Acts 17:1–4).

3. A third option grants that Paul had taught the Thessalonians about the resurrection of believers but that the church nevertheless became overwhelmed with grief when faced with the actual death of some of its members. Marshall (1983: 120–21), for example, observes that it is "one thing to have a theoretical belief in resurrection and quite another to maintain that belief in the actual presence of death and physical decay." Green (2002: 215) similarly suggests that "at the moment of confronting the reality of death, the Thessalonians did not allow their confession [in the resurrection of believers] to inform their reaction to this human tragedy" (see also Shogren 2012: 188). Paul's focus in 1 Thess. 4:15–17, however, lies not merely in reaffirming the resurrection of deceased believers but also in clarifying the connection between this event and the return of Christ (see further option 6 below).

4. A fourth proposal claims that the problem at Thessalonica is connected not with the resurrection of believers but with the return of Christ. Hyldahl (1980) argues that the death of some congregational members so devastated the remaining church members that they abandoned their former confidence in the second coming of Christ. The difficulty with this view, however, is that in 4:13–18 or anywhere else in the letter, Paul does not try to prove the parousia. What's more, the apostle opens the letter by thanking God for the Thessalonians' continued expectation in

the return of Christ (1:3, "your steadfastness of hope in our Lord Jesus Christ"; 1:10, "to wait for his Son from the heavens").

5. A fifth hypothesis involves the assumption of living believers in distinction from the resurrection of deceased believers. Plevnik (1984; 2000; see also 1997: 60–63), taking up the earlier work of Lohfink (1971: 32–78), argues that Paul had previously taught the Thessalonians that at Christ's parousia they would be assumed, that is, taken up to heaven. Since, according to OT and Jewish apocalyptic writings, only the living are assumed or transported to heaven, the Thessalonians feared that their deceased members would not be in a condition to be taken up at the return of Christ. Paul responds to their grief by affirming the resurrection of these deceased members (though this resurrection, according to Plevnik, involves not a new transformed body but simply a return to their previous earthly existence) such that they will be alive at Christ's return and able to be assumed to heaven along with those members who are currently living (see also Johanson 1987: 124–25; Wanamaker 1990: 166; Jurgensen 1994: 85n10). One wonders, however, to what degree the predominantly Gentile church at Thessalonica, among whom Paul had only a brief ministry, would be familiar with and influenced by Jewish apocalyptic writings involving the idea of an assumption. Also, the idea that Paul had taught the Thessalonians that they would be assumed or taken up to heaven is unlikely in light of the apostle's depiction of Christ's coming with the metaphor of a Hellenistic formal reception (see comment on the term ἀπάντησις, apantēsis in v. 17). This metaphor does not involve the movement of the church away from earth to heaven (the destination involved in assumption) but the reverse: the church meets the returning Christ in the air and escorts him the remainder of the way to his destination: earth.

6. A sixth and most likely explanation is that the Thessalonians' confusion over how precisely the one eschatological event involving the resurrection of deceased believers coordinated with the other future event involving Christ's return led to the fear that their fellow church members who had already died would be at some kind of disadvantage at the parousia compared to themselves, who were still alive (so, e.g., Luz 1968: 318–31; Siber 1971: 20–22; Merklein 1992: 407–8; Richard 1995: 232; Malherbe 2000: 284). That the relative status of deceased believers vis-à-vis living believers at Christ's return lies at the heart of the problem is indicated by a variety of factors:

a. Most important is verse 15b, where Paul summarizes the significance of the "word of the Lord" given in verses 16–17. The apostle uses the strongest form of negation possible (the "emphatic future negation": οὐ μή + aorist subjunctive; see BDF §365) to assert that those who are alive at the return of Christ "will certainly not precede" believers who have already died. Such an emphatic negative would be an appropriate corrective to the idea that living believers would actually precede deceased believers such that the latter group would be at a disadvantage compared to the former group.

b. Paul sequences the eschatological events such that deceased believers will rise "first" (v. 16), and only "then" (v. 17) will the next event involving living believers occur. The unusual placement of the adverb of time "first" as the very last element of the sentence (contrast Rom. 1:8; 3:2; 10:19; 15:24; 1 Cor. 11:18; 12:28; 15:46; 2 Cor. 8:5; 1 Tim. 2:1; 5:4), where it is immediately followed by the temporal adverb "then," gives an even stronger emphasis on the ordering of events that will occur (see also 1 Tim. 3:10).

c. The equality of deceased believers with those who are alive at Christ's return is emphasized in the first prepositional phrase of verse 17 ("we who are alive, who are left, . . . *together with them*") in two ways: first, the addition of *hama* to *syn autois* (not simply "with them" but "*together* with them"); and second, the placement of this prepositional phrase before the main verb.

d. The likelihood that the Thessalonians feared their fellow believers to be at some kind of disadvantage at the parousia is strengthened by the fact that several intertestamental writings reveal the similar conviction that at the inauguration of the messianic age, "those who are left are more blessed than those who had died" (2 Esd. [4 Ezra] 13:24; see also 6:25; 7:26–44; Pss. Sol. 17.44; 18.6).

This sixth explanation is frequently rejected on the grounds that, since the Thessalonians believe their deceased fellow members will ultimately be resurrected (albeit sometime later, after Christ's return), it is hard to understand why they grieved so deeply over these Christians who had died. But this objection underestimates the great anticipation and hope that the Thessalonians have about participating in the glory of the parousia event (1:3, 10; 2:19)—a time when their faith would be vindicated and they would enjoy eternal life with Christ (4:17; 5:10), while their fellow citizens who caused them so much affliction would be justly punished in the "coming wrath" (1:10; 5:9). And if the Thessalonians thought of Christ's coming in terms of a Hellenistic formal reception (ἀπάντησις, *apantēsis*), they would have especially looked forward to their privileged position of going out to meet Jesus as the visiting king and participating in the pomp and circumstance associated with his regal return (see further the comment on 4:17). In such a context it is not hard to comprehend the grief that these Thessalonian believers had, believing that their fellow church members who died before Christ's return would be at some kind of disadvantage compared to themselves, who expected to be still alive at this glorious event.

Everything that Paul has stated thus far in verse 13 functions to introduce the new topic of the passage: the Thessalonians' lack of knowledge about the fate of their deceased members and their subsequent grief over these fellow Christians who have died. The apostle closes this opening verse with a comparative καθώς clause ("like the rest who have no hope"), which presents the assertion or thesis that he will seek to prove in the following verses: in contrast to the hopelessness or despair that characterizes the way those outside the church face the death of others, *Christians grieve for deceased believers with hope.*

Several commentators disagree that this is the point being asserted by Paul, arguing instead that the apostle is making an absolute prohibition: Christians are not to grieve at all for deceased believers (see, e.g., Lightfoot 1904: 63; Milligan 1908: 56; Frame 1912: 167; Best 1977: 186; Malherbe 2000: 264).[3] The parallel with 4:5 is typically cited in support: just as *kathaper kai* in this earlier verse does not mean in the same manner or degree of lust as the Gentiles, so *kathōs kai* here does not mean that Christians are permitted to grieve but not in the same manner or degree as those outside the church. Though these commentators recognize that a total prohibition against grieving over the death of a loved one is rather extreme, it is explained that "here, as elsewhere, he [Paul] states his precept broadly, without caring to enter into the qualifications which will suggest themselves at once to thinking men" (Lightfoot 1904: 63; also cited by Milligan 1908: 56).

The majority of commentators, however, from the time of Augustine and Theodoret until modern times, recognize that the purpose of Paul's contrast between non-Christians and Christians cannot be to forbid the latter group from any expression of grief in the context of death.[4] This is obvious from the apostle's words to the Philippians that, if their messenger and his coworker, Epaphroditus, had died from his illness, Paul would have had "sorrow upon sorrow" (Phil. 2:27). It is also clear from Paul's general exhortation to the Romans to "weep with those who weep" (Rom. 12:15). It is further supported by the apostle's identification of death as "the last enemy" (1 Cor. 15:26), as well as by the example of Jesus, who wept over the death of his dear friend Lazarus (John 11:35). There is no justification here or anywhere else in Scripture for Christians to gloss over the pain of death and glibly utter pious phrases about the deceased "being in a better place." Tears and other expressions of grief by believers in these situations are not evidence of a weak faith but only of a great love (John 11:35–36: "Jesus wept [over the death of Lazarus]. So the Jews said, 'See how he loved him!'"). But while both non-Christians and Christians grieve at the death of loved ones, there is a critical difference: in contrast to the hopelessness that characterizes those outside the faith, believers grieve with hope.

3. A few Bible translations reflect this view: "to make sure that you do not grieve for them, as others do who have no hope" (NJB); "Then you won't grieve over them and be like people who don't have any hope" (CEV); "so that you will not be sad, as are those who have no hope" (GNT).

4. Those who argue that Paul is forbidding any form of grief usually feel compelled to make some kind of concession. Lightfoot (1904: 63), for example, states: "That St. Paul would not have forbidden the reasonable expression of sorrow at the loss of friends we cannot doubt." Malherbe (2000: 264) suggests that Paul is not prohibiting "any grief at all in any circumstance surrounding the death of Christians" but only "in reply to the specific question the Thessalonians had addressed to him."

It is true that some Greek philosophers maintained that the soul was immortal and continued to exist after death and also that some mystery religions (e.g., Eleusinian mysteries) promised their initiates an afterlife. Thus Best (1977: 185) is technically correct to state: "It is wrong to say that 'the rest of men' had no hope whatsoever." Nevertheless, these ideas were not well defined or widely adopted at a popular level so that Paul's assertion about the hopelessness of those outside the faith is accurate (MacMullen 1981: 53–57). For example, Seneca (ca. 4 BC–65 AD), the Roman philosopher and statesman, refers to the deification and immortality promised by the mystery religions as "human pipe dreams" (*NIDNTT* 2:239, cited by Green 2002: 218). The hopelessness that characterized the attitude of most with respect to death is succinctly captured by Theocritus, writer of Greek bucolic poetry during the third century BC, who states: "Hopes are for the living; without hope are the dead" (*Id.* 4.42). The Latin poet Catullus (ca. 84–54 BC) writes pessimistically about death: "The sun can set and rise again, but once our brief light sets, we must sleep a never-ending night" (5.4–6).

Grave inscriptions present a similar picture of despair in the face of death. One such dedication from a husband to his wife discovered in Thessalonica reads: "Because of her special disposition and good sense, her devoted husband Eutropos created this tomb for her and also for himself, in order that later he would have a place to rest together with his dear wife, when he looks upon the end of life that has been spun out for him by the indissoluble threads of the Fates" (*CIG* 2.1973). This inscription is one of many from Thessalonica that illustrate how little expectation for a life after death existed among the general population: being together with one's spouse in the grave is the final expectation. A popular tomb inscription found in both Greek and Latin throughout the ancient world also indicates that death was widely accepted as the complete end: "I was not and I was, I am not and I care not" (*CIL* 5.2283). This inscription was so popular that it was often simply abbreviated N F F N S N C (*non fui, fui, non sum, non curo*; Hopkins 1983: 230; Ferguson 1993: 232). Another grave inscription from Rome states pessimistically: "We are nothing. See, reader, how quickly we mortals return from nothing to nothing" (*CIL* 6.26003). Still another Latin grave inscription from Beneventum, Italy, reads: "If you want to know who I am, the answer is ash and burnt embers" (*CIL* 9.1837).

A second-century AD letter of consolation (*P.Oxy.* 115) provides an interesting contrast with Paul's words to the Thessalonians. This letter was written by a woman named Irene, who had recently lost either her husband or son, to a couple, Taonnophirs and Philo, whose son had just died. After stating that she and her family have fulfilled the customary duties in this situation (perhaps religious rites or prayers), Irene tries to comfort the grieving couple by stating: "But nevertheless, one is able to do nothing against such things [i.e., death]. Therefore comfort yourselves." In other words, these parents were helpless to do anything to prevent the death of their son, and so they should comfort themselves in their helplessness. Such logic and words stand in sharp contrast to Paul's closing exhortation in 1 Thess. 4:18: "Therefore comfort one another with these words."

There is ample proof, therefore, of the hopelessness that characterized the way the vast majority of people in the ancient world experienced death. But even without the kind of historical evidence provided in the statements cited above, Paul has a theological reason for asserting the lack of hope experienced by non-Christians: that they are "without God in the world" means that they are those "having no hope" (Eph. 2:12). By contrast, the Christians in Thessalonica do have hope, not only for themselves but also for their fellow believers who have fallen asleep. Paul spells out the two reasons for this Christian hope in the following verses.

2. Reason 1: The Confession of the Church (4:14)

4:14   The first reason (*gar* functions as a marker of cause or reason) why the Thessalonian Christians have hope as they grieve for deceased believers involves a confession or authoritative word of the church about the death and resurrection of Jesus Christ: "For since we believe that Jesus died and rose" (εἰ γὰρ πιστεύομεν ὅτι Ἰησοῦς ἀπέθανεν καὶ ἀνέστη, *ei gar pisteuomen hoti Iēsous apethanen kai anestē*). The pairing of the particle *ei* with the indicative in a conditional clause (a first-class condition) assumes the truth of the protasis (BDF §372.1). Paul, therefore, presents the first half of verse 14 not as a disputable point ("*If* we believe that . . .") but as an accepted fact ("*Since* we believe that . . ."). That the Thessalonians do indeed believe in the resurrection of Jesus is suggested not just by this grammatical construction but also by Paul's earlier thanksgiving that his readers are awaiting the return of God's Son from the heavens, "whom he [God] raised from the dead" (1:10). The message of Christ's death and resurrection was something that Paul passed on to all his converts "as of first importance" (1 Cor. 15:3); so clearly this message was an essential part of his mission-founding preaching in Thessalonica.

But Paul in verse 14 is not merely reminding the Thessalonians of his own preaching on the death and resurrection of Christ; instead, he is quite likely quoting for them a confession of the broader church about this belief. Several factors strongly suggest that the words "Jesus died and rose" is a creedal formula that the apostle here cites in part (so most commentators; see also Schlier 1963: 20; Vidal Garcia 1979; Havener 1981; Collins 1984: 158; Luckensmeyer 2009: 220–21):

1. The introductory phrase "we believe that" is used elsewhere to introduce a creedal formula (Rom. 10:9) and assumes that what follows is already well known to the Thessalonians.
2. The use of "Jesus" alone is rare for Paul, as he normally employs the fuller designations "Jesus Christ," "Christ Jesus," or "the (our) Lord Jesus Christ." The meager sixteen occurrences of "Jesus" alone—seven of which occur in a single text (2 Cor. 4:5–14)—among the hundreds of

Pauline references to Christ cause W. Foerster (*TDNT* 3:289) to state: "It is still astonishing that the simple Ἰησοῦς is so rare in the NT epistles."

3. Even more striking is the presence of the verb *anistēmi* (to rise), which Paul uses only here and in verse 16 (perhaps under the influence of v. 14) and in quotations from the OT (Rom. 15:12; 1 Cor. 10:7) and other sources (Eph. 5:14). Paul's preferred verb by far when referring to the resurrection is *egeirō* (thirty-seven times). The apostle's favored term is made even more unique when contrasted with other NT authors who do employ *anistēmi* to speak of the resurrection (Mark 8:31; 9:9, 10, 31; 10:34; 12:25; 16:9; Luke 18:33; 24:7, 46; John 6:39, 40, 44, 54; 11:23, 24, 25 [cognate noun]; 20:9; Acts 2:24, 32; 13:33 [noun], 34; 17:3, 31).

4. Elsewhere Paul always refers to God's activity in raising Jesus rather than, as here, of Jesus as rising (Rom. 4:24, 25; 6:4, 9; 7:4; 8:11, 34; 10:9; 1 Cor. 6:14; 15:4, 12, 13, 15, 16, 17, 20, 29, 32, 35, 42, 43, 44; 2 Cor. 1:9; 4:14; 5:15; Gal. 1:1; Eph. 1:20; Col. 2:12; 1 Thess. 1:10; 2 Tim. 2:8). The presence of a creedal formula would account for not only this change but also the break in the expected parallelism between the first half of the verse, where Jesus is the subject, and the second half, where God is the subject.

5. Finally, "the sheer economy of words ('Jesus died and rose') is consistent with the notion of traditional language that has been pared down to the essentials" (Gaventa 1998: 64).

Paul's citation of this creedal confession has the rhetorical effect of increasing the authority of his words: the death and resurrection of Jesus is not merely a private belief of Paul, nor even of just the Thessalonian congregation, but is something affirmed by the entire church.

Having established in the first half of verse 14 the unquestioned belief in the death and, more important for his purposes here, the resurrection of Jesus, Paul proceeds in the second half to draw out the implications of this belief as it relates to the deceased believers, about whom the Thessalonians are grieving: "so also, through Jesus, God will bring with him those who have fallen asleep" (οὕτως καὶ ὁ θεὸς τοὺς κοιμηθέντας διὰ τοῦ Ἰησοῦ ἄξει σὺν αὐτῷ, *houtōs kai ho theos tous koimēthentas dia tou Iēsou axei syn autō*).

Grammatically, the conditional clause in verse 14a ("Since we believe that . . .") is followed by a correlative clause in verse 14b ("so also . . ."). The logical link between the two parts of this verse is clear: the resurrection of Jesus functions as the guarantee of the resurrection of deceased believers such that they will be alive and with Jesus at his return. The crucial connection that exists in Pauline thought between the resurrection of Jesus and the resurrection of believers is indicated by the several passages where the apostle links these two events together (Rom. 8:11; 1 Cor. 6:14; 15:12–23; 2 Cor. 4:14; Col. 1:18). It is also seen in his use of the agricultural metaphor of Christ's resurrection as being the "firstfruits" of the believers' resurrection (1 Cor. 15:20, 23): just as the first ear of corn on the stalk or the first grape on the vine is a confirming sign of the rest of the harvest that will surely come, so also Christ's resurrection is a confirming sign of the resurrection of God's redeemed people, including the deceased believers in Thessalonica, that will surely happen. These two events are so intimately connected in Paul's mind that conversely a denial of believers' resurrection involves a denial of Christ's resurrection (1 Cor. 15:13, 16). Therefore, since the Thessalonian Christians believe the church's confession concerning the resurrection of Jesus, they can also believe that the deceased believers in their congregation will be resurrected at Christ's return and so be alive and able to participate equally with living believers in the glorious events connected with his coming.

But while this logical connection between the half verses 14a and 14b is clear, Paul's words are elliptical. The introductory phrase "we believe that" in the first half of the verse is not repeated in the second half but implied: "Since we believe that Jesus died and rose, so also *we believe that* . . ." Another matter not explicitly stated but implied is the resurrection of believers. After referring in verse 14a to the past resurrection of Jesus ("Jesus rose"), one expects Paul in verse 14b to refer to the future resurrection of believers, saying something like "the dead in Christ will rise," as he does later (v. 16b), or to refer to God's activity of bringing the dead back to life, as he does elsewhere (Rom. 8:11; 1 Cor. 6:14; 15:12–23; 2 Cor. 4:14). Instead, the apostle states: "Through Jesus, God will bring with him those who have fallen asleep." This statement presupposes the resurrection of believers, since obviously these dead Christians have to be restored to life before God can bring them with Jesus at his coming.[5]

Why, then, does Paul only implicitly refer to the resurrection of believers and instead choose to talk about their presence with Jesus at his return? The answer must be, as we have already observed above, that the problem at Thessalonica was not a denial of believers' resurrection but an uncertainty of how this event coordinated with the parousia of Christ. The Thessalonian church feared that their church members who died before Christ's return would be at some disadvantage compared to themselves who are still alive. Paul responds to this concern by stressing their presence at Christ's coming.

Although the overall meaning of verse 14 and its function within the larger unit of 4:13–18 is readily apparent, there is a lesser yet noteworthy problem faced in the second half of this verse, whose solution is not so obvious: does the prepositional phrase "through Jesus" (*dia tou Iēsou*) (1) modify the preceding substantival participle, "those who have fallen asleep" (*tous koimēthentas*), or (2) the following main verb, "he will bring" (*axei*)? In option 1, the resulting phrase "those who have fallen asleep through Jesus" has been interpreted in a variety of ways (see survey in Best 1977: 188–89; Nicholl 2004: 27–28). The most common view, however, is that "through Jesus" is equivalent to "in

---

5. Nicholl (2004: 31) correctly observes: "Paul has apparently omitted a step in his argumentation, and that step seems to be the resurrection of the saints and their ascending to meet Christ, which are needed to explain how the deceased Christians get from the grave to the company of the Lord at the parousia and why the death and resurrection of Jesus can serve as the grounds for confidence that the deceased will participate in the parousia."

Christ" (v. 16; see 1 Cor. 15:18), so that Paul is emphasizing the relationship these deceased believers have with Jesus even in death (NIV: "those who have fallen asleep *in him*"; REB: "those who died *as Christians*"; NKJV: "sleep *in Jesus*"). Yet the preposition *dia* with the genitive normally expresses agency so that its claimed use here to express the idea of a relationship with Jesus would be highly unusual. Furthermore, if this truly were Paul's intention, he could have easily expressed this with the prepositional phrase *en Christō*, a favorite expression of the apostle.

In option 2, the resulting phrase "he will bring through Jesus" refers to how God's future action of ensuring the presence of deceased believers at Christ's return happens through the agency of Jesus (NRSV: "even so, *through Jesus*, God will bring with him those who have died"). Although most commentators who adopt this position believe that Paul is making a general reference to the salvation of believers accomplished through the agency of Christ (so, e.g., Collins 1984: 159; D. Martin 1995: 146; Nicholl 2004: 28), it is more likely that the apostle is thinking specifically about the resurrection of Christ as the means by which believers are resurrected and able to be with Jesus at his return. The phrase "through Jesus," therefore, looks back to the first half of the verse (this accounts for the second occurrence of the rare simple "Jesus") and its reference to the resurrection of Christ as guaranteeing the future resurrection of believers. This understanding agrees with Paul's claim elsewhere that the resurrection of believers is made possible "through" (*dia*) the resurrection of Christ (1 Cor. 15:21).

Commentators spend so much energy debating the meaning of "through Jesus" that they often overlook the second and more important prepositional phrase that concludes the verse: "with him" (*syn autō*). Paul's argumentation in not only 4:13–18 but also 5:1–11 leads up to the climax of the believer's presence with Christ at his return: 4:17, "And so we will always be *with the Lord* [*syn kyriō*]"; 5:10, "in order that, whether we wake or sleep, we may live *with him* [*syn autō*]." The reason why the Thessalonian Christians can have hope as they grieve for the dead members of their church is that God "will bring" them, that is, he will resurrect these deceased believers and cause them to be present at Christ's return, such that they will be "with him." The implication is that these deceased believers will not be at some kind of disadvantage at the parousia of Christ but will be "with him" in such a way that they share equally with living believers in the glory associated with his return.

Paul does not spell out the location of where these believers are brought by God: heaven or earth? Some argue for a heavenly site, reasoning that Jesus's resurrection in verse 14a implies an upward movement from earth to heaven and that the subsequent verses refer to believers as being caught up into the clouds to meet the Lord in the air (Ellingworth 1974). Others also advocate a heavenly locale, based on the conviction that in this passage Paul is describing the assumption of believers, that is, their being taken up to the place of God in heaven at the parousia of the Lord (Plevnik 1984: 274–83; 2000: 83–95; Johanson 1987: 121–22; Wanamaker 1990: 169–70). But the language and imagery that Paul employs in this passage is not that of an assumption but of an official visit by a king or high-ranking official, in which the leading citizens go out to meet the person in order to escort him on the final stage of his journey into the city (see comment on *apantēsis* in 4:17). The picture, then, is one in which both resurrected (those who were dead at Christ's return) and transformed (those who were still alive at Christ's return) believers are gathered together to meet Jesus on the clouds in the air, where they proceed to escort him on the remainder of his journey to earth. This agrees with Paul's depiction elsewhere of the earth as a woman in labor, eagerly awaiting Christ's return, when it will be freed from the destructive power of sin and restored to its former perfection (Rom. 8:19–22). Other NT writers similarly anticipate a renewed earth as the ultimate destiny of God's people (2 Pet. 3:1–13; Rev. 21:1–2, 10). An earthly locale is also supported more generally by the inherent "goodness" of all that God created (Gen. 1) and the promise that the earth is not to be destroyed (God's promise to Noah in Gen. 8:21–22; 9:11) but also is part of God's redemptive activity (Rom. 8:19–22; 2 Pet. 3:10, which depicts the purification of the earth by fire rather than its destruction).

3. Reason 2: The "Word of the Lord" (4:15–17)

4:15   The second reason (*gar* parallels the use of the same conjunction in the preceding verse)[6] why the Thessalonian Christians have hope as they grieve for deceased believers involves a "word of the Lord," that is, an authoritative teaching of Jesus Christ: "For this we say to you by the word of the Lord" (τοῦτο γὰρ ὑμῖν λέγομεν ἐν λόγῳ κυρίου, *touto gar hymin legomen en logō kyriou*). The demonstrative pronoun "this" that opens the verse does not look back (anaphoric function) to the preceding argument of verse 14 (*pace* Richard 1995: 226, 240) but ahead (cataphoric function) to the subsequent material of 4:15–17 (so virtually all commentators). This immediately raises three questions: First, what in the following verses constitutes the "word of the Lord"? Second, what is the source of this "word of the Lord"? And third, *why* does Paul cite this "word of the Lord"?

Concerning the first question, there is increasing agreement among commentators that Paul does not immediately cite the "word of the Lord" in verse 15b but instead begins by giving in his own words a summary statement that applies this saying or teaching from Jesus to the specific Thessalonian situation ("We who are alive, who are left until the coming of the Lord, will certainly not precede those who have fallen asleep"). Then Paul proceeds in verses 16–17a to present the authoritative word of the Lord ("because the Lord himself will descend from heaven . . . for a reception of the Lord in the air"), to which he adds his own conclusion in verse 17b, which, like his summary statement in verse 15b, stresses again the significance of this Jesus logion for

---

6. Note, however, the claim of some commentators (Frame 1912: 171; Malherbe 2000: 267; Nicholl 2004: 35; Luckensmeyer 2009: 177; Shogren 2012: 183) that γάρ is explanatory and confirms the point of 4:14 rather than provides a new and second reason for the assertion of 4:13.

the particular problem faced in Thessalonica ("and so we will always be with the Lord").[7] This understanding of verses 15–17 is based primarily on their vocabulary and style: verses 15b and 17b are typically Pauline, whereas verses 16–17a contain several unique features. Additionally, many of these unique features have parallels with Jesus's sayings recorded in the Gospels, but no such parallels can be found in the surrounding verses of 15b and 17b (on this, see discussion below). The relatively few distinctively Pauline elements found in verses 16–17a are due to the apostle's redaction of "the word of the Lord," which he is loosely citing.

Concerning the second question, a number of explanations have been forwarded as to where Paul derives the "word of the Lord" (for a fuller survey and evaluation of the options, see Best 1977: 189–93; Marshall 1983: 125–27; Malherbe 2000: 267–70): (1) The apostle is quoting an *agraphon*, an otherwise unknown saying of Jesus not preserved in the Gospels (see John 20:30; Acts 20:35) but passed on to Paul orally (so, e.g., Frame 1912: 171; Jeremias 1964: 80–83; Morris 1991: 140–41; Holtz 1991: 389; Nicholl 2004: 38–41). (2) Paul cites a saying of Jesus found in the Gospels but doesn't quote it exactly, in keeping with his practice elsewhere of loosely referring to passages in the Synoptic tradition (1 Cor. 7:10, 25; 9:14; 11:23–25). The best candidate is Matt. 24:29–33, 40–41 (so Howard 1988; Wanamaker 1990: 171; Green 2002: 222; Witherington 2006: 135–36, with a helpful chart of parallels),[8] though a number of striking parallels with the parable of the wise and foolish virgins in Matt. 25:1–13 can also be discovered (Wenham 1985). (3) Paul is neither citing nor even paraphrasing a specific saying but more generally summarizing the teaching of Jesus about the end times (Rigaux 1956: 538–39). (4) Since the phrase "the word of the LORD" in the OT was commonly used to introduce prophecy (e.g., Isa. 1:10; Jer. 1:4; Ezek. 1:3; Hosea 1:1; Joel 1:1; Amos 5:1; Mic. 1:1), its presence here suggests that Paul presents himself as a prophet who is authorized to speak "a message from the Lord" (so, e.g., Lightfoot 1904: 65; Luz 1968: 327–28; Best 1977: 193; Bruce 1982: 98–99; Donfried 1993a: 39–40; Richard 1995: 226, 240; Malherbe 2000: 268–69; Shogren 2012: 184).

Although each of these proposals has its own strengths and weaknesses, two factors lend support to the second option. First, Paul elsewhere makes a special point of distinguishing his teaching from that of Jesus (1 Cor. 7:10–12), so that his reference here to the "word of the Lord" would similarly suggest that the apostle has in view a specific saying or teaching that comes from Jesus. Second, "the several and clear echoes of Jesus's sayings in the passage seem to suggest that Paul must be conscious of the material he is using as Jesus material and

---

7. Several scholars understand these verses differently, claiming that the "word of the Lord" is given first in 4:15b and that Paul then explains this "word" in 4:16–17 (so, e.g., Dobschütz 1909: 193–94; Holtz 1986: 184–85; Merklein 1992: 410–15; Donfried 1993a: 39–41). Yet 4:15b does not contain any terms that are similar to a saying of Jesus recorded in the Gospels, whereas parallels can be found to the words of 4:16–17.

8. Gundry (1987) argues that Paul is drawing on Jesus's saying in John 11:25–26, whose original form may have been: "The one who has died will rise, and the one who is alive will never die."

therefore that with 'the word of the Lord' here Paul is referring to the word(s) of the historical Jesus he is using rather than a prophetic oracle spoken in the name of the Lord" (S. Kim, *DPL* 476; see also S. Kim 2002). The apostle does not cite Jesus's words verbatim but recalls them in such a way that it more effectively applies to the specific situation he is addressing in Thessalonica.

The third question concerning Paul's purpose in citing the "word of the Lord" is more important than identifying either what in these verses constitutes the word of the Lord or its source, since one must not miss the rhetorical or persuasive force of Paul's appeal to the teaching of the historical Jesus. Just as the apostle's earlier citation of a creedal formulation adds authority to his first argument of verse 14, so his reference to the "word of the Lord" lends greater weight to his second argument of verses 15–17. Paul is sharing with the Thessalonians the authoritative word of Jesus, not merely his personal opinion. As Wanamaker (1990: 171) observes: "By placing his assurance that the living would not have precedence over the dead at the coming of the Lord under the rubric 'a word of the Lord,' Paul attributed the highest possible authority to his assertion in v. 15b." That the apostle in both arguments (vv. 14 and 15–17) appeals to such weighty authorities (a creedal formulation and an authoritative word of Jesus) suggests that Paul views the grieving of the Thessalonian believers (v. 13) as a significant problem that requires such strong responses on his part.

As noted above, Paul does not immediately proceed to cite the "word of the Lord" but instead first gives in his own words a summary statement that applies this authoritative saying of Jesus to the specific Thessalonian situation: "namely,[9] we who are alive, who are left until the coming of the Lord, will certainly not precede those who have fallen asleep" (ὅτι ἡμεῖς οἱ ζῶντες οἱ περιλειπόμενοι εἰς τὴν παρουσίαν τοῦ κυρίου οὐ μὴ φθάσωμεν τοὺς κοιμηθέντας, *hoti hēmeis hoi zōntes hoi perileipomenoi eis tēn parousian tou kyriou ou mē phthasōmen tous koimēthentas*). The use of the personal pronoun "we" is emphatic and highlights the contrast that Paul establishes between those who are still alive at Christ's return ("we who are alive, who are left") and those who have already died ("those who have fallen asleep"). Such a contrast involving these two groups supports my contention that the problem Paul is trying to address in this passage concerns the relative status of deceased believers at the parousia in relation to living believers.

This reconstruction of the problem being corrected in 4:13–18 receives further support from the apostle's emphatic assertion that believers who are alive at Christ's return "will certainly not precede" those believers who have died. The verb *phthanō* occurs seven times in the NT, all except two (Matt. 12:28; Luke 11:20) occurring in Paul's Letters (Rom. 9:31; 2 Cor. 10:14; Phil. 3:16; 1 Thess. 2:16; 4:15). The apostle has already used this verb earlier in the letter, also in an eschatological context where it has the meaning "have just

---

9. The ὅτι in 4:15 is epexegetical (BDF §394; BDAG 732.2), functioning to introduce a clause that will explain the preceding τοῦτο.

arrived" or simply "arrive, reach" in referring to the wrath of God (2:16). The second appearance of *phthanō* here in 4:15 is unique not only because this is its only occurrence in the NT without an accompanying prepositional phrase but also because this is the one instance where it has the classical meaning of "come before, precede" (BDAG 1053). That Paul here is stressing the temporal aspect of the verb is clear from the two adverbs found in the following verses, where the apostle states that the dead in Christ will rise "first," and "then" both living and deceased believers will be taken up to meet the Lord. Thus the statement that living believers "will certainly not precede" deceased believers appears to address a situation in which the Thessalonian church feared that those who were still alive at Christ's return might "precede" and so enjoy some kind of temporal advantage over the believers who had already died.

That this fear of the Thessalonians was not merely theoretical but a real concern is suggested by Paul's use of the emphatic future negation (οὐ μή + aorist subjunctive)—the strongest form of negation possible (see BDF §365). Although the double negative *ou mē* is quite rare and very emphatic in nonliterary papyri, it occurs some ninety-six times in the NT, causing some grammarians to conclude that it had lost its significance (note its omission in several translations: RSV, JB, REB, NLT). Yet 90 percent of these occurrences involve the special class of texts that consist of quotations from the LXX and sayings of Jesus so that "οὐ μή is quite as rare in the NT as it is in the papyri" (MHT 1:192; see the extended discussion on 187–92). Paul uses this construction only four times (excluding his citations from the LXX), and each occurrence possesses its typical strong emphasis (1 Cor. 8:13; Gal. 5:16; 1 Thess. 4:15; 5:3). In fact, the apostle's statement here in 4:15 "is so strong that it sounds like a denial of an opinion actually held by some people in Thessalonica" (Malherbe 2000: 272), just as its parallel in 5:3 (*ou mē ekphygōsin*, "they will certainly not escape") is aimed at those who actually believe and proclaim the Roman political mantra "peace and security." In contrast to those who fear that living believers will enjoy some kind of advantage over deceased believers at the return of Christ, the Thessalonians have "a word of the Lord," an authoritative teaching of Jesus Christ to the effect that "we who are alive, who are left until the coming of the Lord, will *certainly not* precede those who have fallen asleep." Both living (transformed) and deceased (resurrected) believers alike will share equally in the glory connected with the parousia. This constitutes the second reason why the Thessalonians are to have hope as they grieve over deceased members of their church.

Scholars have made much out of the addition of the personal pronoun "we" to the more generic phrase "those who are alive, who are left until the coming of the Lord," concluding that here the apostle expects to still be living at Christ's return (see also 1 Cor. 15:51–52). They then typically contrast this expectation with other texts where Paul either implies his death by including himself among those who will be resurrected (1 Cor. 6:14; 2 Cor. 4:14; 5:1) or seems to acknowledge that he will not live until the parousia of the Lord (2 Cor. 1:8–9; 5:8; Phil. 1:21–24; 2:17). Consequently, many conclude that the apostle's view on this matter changed over time (so, e.g., Beker 1980: 178; Bruce 1982: 99; Wanamaker 1990: 171–72).

This line of argumentation, however, reads far too much into the "we" of 1 Thess. 4:15. First, Paul's purpose in this verse is not to assert that he will be alive at Christ's return but that both groups of believers—the living as well as the deceased—will participate equally in the parousia. It is precarious to read anything beyond this into his words. Second, Paul does not use the personal pronoun "we" absolutely but qualifies it with two attributive participles ("those who are living, those who are left") so that the verse may be paraphrased "When I say 'we,' I mean those who are living, those who survive to that day" (Lightfoot 1904: 66). Third, given that Paul in this verse identifies only two groups (living believers and deceased believers), it is expected that he would locate himself in the group to which he and his readers currently belong (Ellicott 1864: 64). Fourth, Paul's later statement that "whether we wake or sleep" (5:10) suggests that he holds both states to be possible: "[Paul] did not know the date of the parousia but expected it soon and therefore had to reckon both with what would happen if he died prior to it and if he lived to it" (Best 1977: 195–96; see also Richard 1995: 241). This would explain how Paul in the same letter could envision both his restoration to life from death (1 Cor. 6:14) and his continued existence until Christ's return (15:51). Fifth, 1 Thessalonians was written over a decade and a half after Paul's conversion, during which time he experienced many life-threatening events (2 Cor. 11:23–28; see Acts 14:19–20) such that he could later say he was "often near death" (2 Cor. 11:23), so it strains credibility to believe that the apostle had never contemplated the possibility of his death before Christ's return (Stein 1988: 87–88). There are insufficient grounds, therefore, for concluding from the "we" in verse 15 that Paul expected to live until the parousia.

Paul further identifies the subject "we" as "those who are alive" (*hoi zōntes*) and "those who are left until the coming of the Lord" (*hoi perileipomenoi eis tēn parousian tou kyriou*). The first description serves as an expected counterpart to "those who have fallen asleep": Paul is contrasting the fate of living believers with deceased believers. The second description involves the use of *perileipomai* (remain, left behind), a term that occurs in the NT only here and in the identical expression in verse 17. Although Paul uses a cognate of this word to describe the "remnant" of Israel (Rom. 9:27), there is no evidence to suggest that this is the idea behind his reference here to "those who are left" (see V. Herntrich, *TDNT* 4:196–209). And even though the word does appear in nonbiblical texts to describe those who had survived a tragedy that left others dead, this does not necessarily imply that some of the deceased believers in Thessalonica had been martyred (*pace* Green 2002: 222). Instead, *perileipomenoi* is synonymous with *zōntes* and so simply refers to those who remain or live until the Lord's return.

This marks the third place in the letter (see also 2:19; 3:13) where Paul uses the term *parousia* to describe the "coming" of Christ, thereby evoking the image of a royal visit by a Roman emperor or official (see the fuller discussion of this key term in the comment on 2:19). This time, however, the image of a royal visit is more vividly evoked, as the apostle proceeds in the next verses to describe the pomp and circumstance connected with Christ's return, including his use of the technical term ἀπάντησις (*apantēsis*; see comment on v. 17).

Now that Paul has summarized in his own words the authoritative "word of the Lord" such that its significance for the specific situation at Thessalonica is highlighted (v. 15b), he proceeds to cite (though loosely) this authoritative Jesus logion: "because the Lord himself will descend from heaven, with a commanding shout, with a voice of an archangel, and with a trumpet call of God" (ὅτι αὐτὸς ὁ κύριος ἐν κελεύσματι, ἐν φωνῇ ἀρχαγγέλου καὶ ἐν σάλπιγγι θεοῦ, καταβήσεται ἀπ᾽ οὐρανοῦ, *hoti autos ho kyrios, en keleusmati, en phōnē archangelou kai en salpingi theou, katabēsetai ap᾽ ouranou*).

4:16

The material of verses 16–17 constitutes the most explicit description of the events surrounding Christ's return found anywhere in Paul's writings and probably in the whole NT as well. It is not surprising, therefore, that these verses have received a great deal of attention, particularly by those who use the Bible as a blueprint to predict the future. Yet, as Gaventa (1998: 66) observes, "This passage has more in common with poetry than with blueprints." The coming of the Lord is described in apocalyptic language that makes rich use of symbols and metaphors—language that ought to be read also literally rather than only literally. Marshall (1993: 128) comments: "A real event is being described, but it is one which cannot be described literally since the direct activity of God cannot be fully comprehended in human language. The biblical writers have therefore to resort to analogy and metaphor, the language of symbol, in order to convey their message." This was recognized long ago, for example, by Calvin, who, in explaining the "trumpet of God," refers readers to his comment about this instrument in 1 Cor. 15:52, where he states: "I prefer to regard it as a metaphor" (cited by Whiteley 1969: 72). It is important in any text, but especially in the apocalyptic language that marks these two verses, to distinguish between *meaning* and *referent*: the words found here clearly mean "trumpet," "shout," "snatched," "clouds," and so on, but may refer to other things as well. There is a danger, therefore, of reading this passage in a too-literal fashion, in which the main goal is to distinguish all the activities described here so that an exact timetable of future events emerges. This would involve a misuse of a text whose primary purpose is, as its concluding exhortation indicates (4:18), to provide pastoral comfort. Paul provides this comfort by clarifying for his readers the three stages of events that will take place at Christ's return, highlighting the fact that deceased believers will in no way be disadvantaged when compared with living believers.

First stage: The Lord descends from heaven. The conjunction *hoti* that opens the verse is causal, indicating that what follows supports Paul's summary in the preceding verse of the "word of the Lord," that living believers will certainly not precede deceased believers at Christ's parousia such that the latter group will miss that event or suffer some kind of disadvantage. The personal pronoun *autos* functions to add emphasis to the subject *ho kyrios*, stressing that it is "the Lord *himself*" who will come down from heaven. The image of an imperial visit that Paul evokes with his reference to the parousia in the previous verse does not necessarily involve the arrival of the emperor or king, since the term also referred to official visits of high-ranking officials. The authoritative saying of Jesus that Paul cites, however, highlights the fact that it is no mere angel or human representative but the Lord *himself* who will come from heaven (on Paul's use of the singular "heaven" instead of the plural "heavens," see comment on 1:10). This is especially important to the Thessalonians, who have just been assured by Paul in his first proof of 4:14 that God will bring their deceased fellow members "with him," that is, with Jesus when he returns. Therefore, if the parousia will involve the coming of the Lord *himself*, then the believers who have died will surely also be alive and present with him at his return.

The parousia or imperial visit of the Lord is described by three prepositional phrases, all of which begin with *en*, serving either as a marker of time ("in, while, when, at"; see BDAG 329.10; so the similar triple occurrence of *en* in 1 Cor. 15:52) or more likely as a marker of circumstance ("with"; see BDAG 329.7; Moule 1959: 78; so most commentators). The interrelationship of these three phrases has occasioned some disagreement. That (1) only the first phrase lacks a genitive modifier and that (2) only the second and third phrases are joined by the conjunction *kai* lead many to conclude that the final two phrases are intended to explain the opening one: "with a commanding shout, that is, with a call of an archangel and with a trumpet call of God" (so Findlay 1891: 100; Dobschütz 1909: 195; Frame 1912: 174; Howard 1988: 183; Richard 1995: 227; Malherbe 2000: 274; Nicholl 2004: 42; Fee 2009: 177; Luckensmeyer 2009: 242–43; Shogren 2012: 185).[10] Although this view is possible, these two grammatical points do not require that the relationship of the three phrases be read in this fashion since the three prepositional phrases can also be understood independently as three parallel events. Furthermore, if Paul did intend for the second and third prepositional phrases to explain the first, he could have made this clear by omitting the third preposition *en*, thereby linking more closely the second and third elements, just as he did earlier in the letter with the three prepositional phrases in 1:5 (see fuller explanation in the comment on that verse). Also, this alternative explanation of the relationship of the three phrases requires that an archangel (second phrase) issue the "commanding shout" (first phrase), whereas compelling evidence indicates that it is the descending Lord who gives this shout (see below). Finally, it is simpler and so preferable to read the three similar phrases as referring to three parallel events.

10. Hendriksen (1955: 115–16) argues that after "the commanding shout" in 4:16, "the voice of an archangel" ought to be identified with the sound of "the trumpet of God" (next phrase), as in Rev. 1:10 and 4:1, so that there are two events (shout, voice/trumpet) that accompany the Lord's return.

The first of the three circumstances or events that accompany the Lord's descent is "a commanding shout." The noun *keleusma* in Classical Greek functioned as a technical military term for the command of an officer to his soldiers but was also used to describe the cry or shout of a chariot rider to his horses, a hunter to his dogs, or a boat captain to his rowers (for texts, see L. Schmid, *TDNT* 3:656–59). The noun also became a technical term in political contexts to denote an official "order" or "decree" issued by government officials, ranging from the lowest of administrators to the emperor himself (L. Schmid, *TDNT* 3:657).[11] The presence of this term in verse 16—its only occurrence in the NT—thus likely refers to an authoritative cry given at a time of great importance and excitement: "a (cry of) command" (BDAG 538), "a shout of command" (L. Schmid, *TDNT* 3:657), or "a commanding shout" (NLT).[12]

The text does not state who issues this commanding shout: God, an archangel, or Christ? The first option (God) is perhaps supported by verse 14, where God is the one responsible for bringing the deceased believers with Jesus at his return, and by Philo's use of the same noun *keleusma* to claim that "God, by one single word of command [*keleusmati*], could easily collect together men living on the very confines of the earth, bringing them from the extremities of the world to any place which he may choose" (*Rewards* 117). The second option (archangel) would be supported by the interrelationship of the three prepositional phrases—if the final two phrases were actually intended to explain the first (a position rejected above). The third option (Christ) is the most natural reading, given that "the Lord" is not only the subject of the sentence but is also being emphasized ("the Lord *himself*"). Further support lies in John 5:25–29, which states: "The hour is coming, and now is, when the dead will hear the voice of the Son of God, and those who hear will live. . . . For the hour is coming when all who are in their graves will hear his voice and come out." This aforementioned text also answers another question that verse 16 does not explicitly address: to whom is the commanding shout directed? That it is aimed at deceased believers initiating their resurrection is suggested by Paul's immediately following statement that "the dead in Christ will rise" and supported by the words of John 5:25–29.

The second of the three circumstances that accompany the Lord's descent from heaven is "a voice of an archangel." The NT writers reveal very little interest in the higher rank of angels, with only one other reference, in Jude 9, to "the archangel Michael," the same figure described in Dan. 10:13 as "one of the rulers" (*heis tōn archontōn*) and Dan. 12:1 as the "great ruler" (*ho archōn ho megas*), who is also mentioned by name in Rev. 12:7. Jewish writers

---

11. The usage of *keleusma* in 4:16 leads Luckensmeyer (2009: 239–40) to consider it "possible that Paul intentionally uses the word to make a statement against the ideology of imperial eschatology by contrasting the κέλευσις of imperialism with the κέλευσμα associated with the coming of the Lord."

12. For an intriguing but ultimately unconvincing argument that the reference in 4:16 to Christ's descent from heaven with "a shout" echoes Ps. 47:5 (46:6 LXX), see C. Evans 1993; also Fee 2009: 176–77.

from the intertestamental period have much more to say about archangels, not only naming them (1 En. 20.1–7 identifies Suru'el [Uriel], Raphael, Raguel, Michael, Saraqa'el, Gabriel; a Greek fragment also adds the name Remiel) but also describing the various responsibilities they carry out on behalf of God (Tob. 12:15–22; 1 En. 9.1; 20.1–7; Sib. Or. 2.215; T. Isaac 2.1). Although the specific notion of a voice or something spoken by an archangel appears to be unparalleled in the literature of the day, the general presence and involvement of angels at events associated with the end of the present age is quite common both within the NT (Matt. 13:39, 41, 49; 16:27; 24:31; 25:31; Mark 8:38; 13:27; 1 Cor. 6:3; 2 Thess. 1:7; Jude 14; Revelation *passim*) and without (e.g., 1 En. 1.9; 2 Esd. [4 Ezra] 4:1–2; T. Levi 2.6–7; T. Isaac 2.1–2; Apoc. Zeph. 2.1–2). On the one hand, that the nouns "voice" and "archangel" are both indefinite suggests that these words do not have any specific figure in view. On the other hand, if these nouns, like the preceding "word of the Lord" (v. 15), ought to be understood as definite (NIV: "with *the* voice of *the* archangel"), then Paul may well be thinking of Michael (so BDAG 137; Fee 2009: 177; Shogren 2012: 186). This possibility becomes more convincing if the apostle's enigmatic reference to the restraining person and thing in 2 Thess. 2:6–7 refers, as seems plausible, to the activity and person of the archangel Michael (see the detailed discussion of "The Restrainer of 2 Thessalonians 2:6–7" in excursus 3).

The third circumstance to mark the parousia or imperial visit of the Lord is "a trumpet call of God." In antiquity the trumpet was infrequently used as a musical instrument and instead functioned primarily as a signal or sign (see G. Friedrich, *TDNT* 7:71–88; Bockmuehl 1991). The trumpet marked not only all types of military movement and activity but also signaled such diverse things as the beginning of athletic contests, the summoning of people to sacrifice, the call to silence by worshipers before prayer, and the mourning of loved ones in a funeral procession. In Judaism the trumpet similarly did not function first and foremost as a musical instrument but also as a signal, marking in particular the visible appearance of God not only in the past (Exod. 19:13, 16, 19; 20:18) but also at the future "day of the LORD" (Isa. 27:13; Joel 2:1; Zeph. 1:14–16; Zech. 9:14). The trumpet as an end-time sign becomes even more prominent in the intertestamental literature (2 Esd. [4 Ezra] 6:23; Pss. Sol. 11.1; Sib. Or. 4.173–74; 8.239; Apoc. Mos. 22.37–38; Apoc. Zeph. 9.1; 10.1; 11.1; 12.1; Apoc. Ab. 31.1–2; 1QM 7.13–9.6) and so not surprisingly is also found elsewhere in Paul (1 Cor. 15:52) and the NT (Matt. 24:31; Rev. 8:2, 6, 13; 9:14; 11:15). As with the apostle's other reference to a trumpet call, in 1 Cor. 15:52 ("the trumpet will sound, and the dead will be raised imperishable"), so also here in 1 Thess. 4:16 it is linked with the resurrection of the dead (note the immediately following clause "and the dead in Christ will rise first"). The sound of a trumpet, therefore, functions not only as a stereotyped sign of Jesus's return but, more important for the specific concern of the Thessalonians, also marks the moment when their deceased members will be brought to life such that they can participate equally in Christ's triumphal parousia.

Second stage: Deceased Christians will be resurrected. The first stage in the eschatological drama involving the Lord's descent from heaven with the three accompanying circumstances makes it possible for the second stage to occur (the initial *kai* is consecutive [BDF §442.2; BDAG 495.1.b.ζ] and so introduces the result of Christ's coming): "and the dead in Christ will rise first" (καὶ οἱ νεκροὶ ἐν Χριστῷ ἀναστήσονται πρῶτον, *kai hoi nekroi en Christō anastēsontai prōton*).

After referring to deceased believers three times in the passage so far with the euphemistic designation "those who are asleep / have fallen asleep" (vv. 13, 14, 15), Paul identifies them here for the first time as "the dead" (*hoi nekroi*), perhaps under the influence of the "word of the Lord" that he is loosely citing. The further designation that these dead believers are "in Christ" (*en Christō*) minimally means that these are those who belonged to Christ at the moment of their death: they died as Christians (see 1 Cor. 15:18, "those who have fallen asleep in Christ"; Rev. 14:13, "the dead who die in the Lord"). It is less clear whether it also "intimates, without defining precisely the condition of the believers in the intermediate state, that as in life and at death so from death to the *Parousia*, the believer is under the control of the indwelling Christ" (Frame 1912: 175; also Bruce 1982: 101; Williams 1992: 84; Weatherly 1996: 159). Some have objected on the ground that if this were Paul's intention, he would have written *hoi nekroi hoi en Christō*, that is, "the dead *the ones who are* in Christ" (Best 1977: 197; see also Malherbe 2000: 275; this reading actually occurs in F G*). But whether the phrase "the dead in Christ" presupposes the intermediate state, it is clear that the apostle believes that one's relationship with Christ does not come to an end even in death (Rom. 8:38–39). Nothing is said about the dead who are *not* "in Christ,"[13] just as there is no discussion about the nature of the resurrected body or the manner in which the living believers are transformed (such as in 1 Cor. 15:35–54; Phil. 3:21). Paul's concern is not to provide a comprehensive description of all that will happen at Christ's return but to comfort the Thessalonian believers, who were grieving over the death of their fellow believers.

The specific problem that Paul is trying to correct reveals itself in the assertion that the dead in Christ will not merely "rise" (note again [see comment on 4:14] the use of the rare—for Paul—verb *anistēmi* instead of his favored term *egeirō* [37x] for the resurrection) but that they will rise "first" (*prōton*). The unusual location of this adverb at the end of the clause instead of its expected opening position (Rom. 1:8; 3:2; 10:19; 15:24; 1 Cor. 11:18; 12:28; 15:46; 2 Cor. 8:5; 1 Tim. 2:1; 5:4) and the fact that it is immediately followed by another adverb "then" (*epeita*) lend an even greater emphasis to the temporal aspect than the term already has. This confirms my claim that the problem at

---

13. Contra Konstan and Ramelli (2007), who argue that the prepositional phrase "in Christ" likely goes not with the preceding noun "the dead" but with the following verb "will rise," with the result that Paul is referring not only to the resurrection of Christians ("the dead in Christ will rise") but also to the resurrection of all the dead ("the dead will rise in Christ").

Thessalonica is not whether the dead will be raised but how their resurrection coordinates with the triumphal return of Christ. Far from missing out on that glorious event or suffering some kind of disadvantage compared to those who are still alive on that day, the deceased believers will rise "first" and so be able to participate equally with living believers in the privilege of going up to meet the descending Lord and escorting him on the final leg of his return to earth. Some commentators conclude from this temporal reference that deceased believers will actually enjoy a privileged position over living believers, since they will rise first (so, e.g., Holmes 1998: 150; Green 2002: 227, 229). Yet the dead in Christ will rise not immediately into the presence of the returning Christ in the air, but to earth, from where they, along with living believers, will then be taken up to welcome the Lord in the air (v. 17, "then we who are alive, who are left, *together with them*, will be snatched . . .").

4:17 *Third stage: Both deceased (resurrected) and living (transformed)*[14] *believers will together be joined to the descending Lord.* After the Lord begins his descent from heaven with the three accompanying signs that mark his return and the dead in Christ are restored to live on earth, "then" (the temporal adverb *epeita*, coming right after another temporal adverb, *prōton*, emphasizes once again the sequence of events) the third stage of the eschatological drama occurs: "then we who are alive, who are left, will be snatched up together with them by means of clouds for a reception of the Lord in the air" (ἔπειτα ἡμεῖς οἱ ζῶντες οἱ περιλειπόμενοι ἅμα σὺν αὐτοῖς ἁρπαγησόμεθα ἐν νεφέλαις εἰς ἀπάντησιν τοῦ κυρίου εἰς ἀέρα, *epeita hēmeis hoi zōntes hoi perileipomenoi hama syn autois harpagēsometha en nephelais eis apantēsin tou kyriou eis aera*).

Modern readers typically focus on the second half of this sentence, with its description of believers being "snatched" (the so-called rapture, a term derived from the Vulgate's rendering of the Greek verb *harpazō* with the Latin *rapio*) and their "reception" of the descending Lord in the air. The Thessalonian readers, however, would have been struck by the first half, since it is here that Paul stresses the equal participation of the deceased believers with the living believers at Christ's parousia. The identical share that "the dead in Christ" will have in this event is expressed by the prepositional phrase *syn autois*, which is emphasized by virtue of its placement early in the sentence, before the main verb: "We who are alive, who are left *with them*, will be snatched." Further weight is given to this phrase by introducing it with *hama* (Rom. 3:12; Col. 4:3; 1 Thess. 4:17; 5:10; 1 Tim. 5:13; Philem. 22; see also Matt. 13:29; 20:1; Acts 24:26; 27:40), which may function as an adverb marking a simultaneous occurrence so that an idea separate from the prepositional phrase is being asserted: "*at the same time* with them" (so BDF §§194.3; 425:2; Moule 1959: 81–82; Ellicott 1880: 66–67; Rigaux 1956: 545; Best 1977: 198). This adverbial sense fits the context well: just as Paul earlier summarized the "word of the Lord" by asserting in the strongest language that living believers "will certainly

---

14. The transformation of living believers at Christ's return is not taught here in 1 Thess. 4:13–18 but is drawn from Paul's words in 1 Cor. 15:35–54 and Phil. 3:21.

not precede" deceased believers (v. 15b) such that the latter group will be at some kind of disadvantage at Christ's return, so here his loose citation of the Jesus logion similarly asserts that both the living and the dead will be taken up for the reception of the descending Lord "at the same time." What complicates this possible interpretation, however, is that *hama* also functions with the dative case as a preposition so that its pairing with *syn* might instead be a double preposition (Robertson 1934: 638) that emphasizes the locative sense: "*together* with them" (so BDAG 49.2; Lightfoot 1904: 68; Milligan 1908: 61; Malherbe 2000: 275). The choice between these two possible readings is difficult, but the latter sense is slightly stronger because of the parallel with 1 Thess. 5:10, the only other occurrence in the NT of the pair *hama syn*. What the two readings have in common, however, is that emphasis is placed on the equal participation of both living and deceased believers.

It is this reunited group of both living (transformed) and deceased (resurrected) believers that together "will be snatched up." The verb *harpazō* literally means "'snatch, seize,' i.e., take suddenly and vehemently" (BDAG 134; see also W. Foerster, *TDNT* 1:472–73) but was used by several NT authors with a wide range of meanings, mostly with a negative sense: "to steal" (Matt. 12:29); "to arrest someone by force" (John 6:15; Acts 23:10); "to tear out" seed that is sown (Matt. 13:19); "to be dragged away" by a wild animal (John 10:12); "to be taken" from God's hand (John 10:28, 29); "to seize" or claim for oneself the kingdom of heaven (Matt. 11:12). The verb can also be used with a positive sense: "to be snatched" from threatening danger (Jude 23); "to be taken away" by God and his Spirit to either an earthly (Acts 8:39) or heavenly (Rev. 12:5) location. Paul uses this verb elsewhere only in 2 Cor. 12:2, 4, where it has the positive sense of being "caught up" to the third heaven, that is, paradise, where he witnessed divine mysteries. This term also occurs in the apocalyptic writings of that day similarly to describe an ascent into the heavens, where the seer typically beholds events that will yet take place or learns other celestial secrets (e.g., 1 En. 39.3; 52.1; 2 En. 3.1; 7.1–2; 3 Bar. 2.1; Apoc. Zeph. 2.1). The use of *harpazō* here in 1 Thess. 4:17 clearly belongs to this latter category, where it positively describes the taking up of both living and deceased believers for a reception of the descending Lord.

Paul's choice of *harpazō* was intended not to teach "a secret rapture of the church"[15] but rather to make a possible wordplay, since this term was often used by non-Christian writers to speak of life or the living being "snatched away" by death (see esp. Malherbe 1983: 255n80; 2000: 275–76; also Holmes 1998: 151; Gaventa 1998: 66–67; Luckensmeyer 2009: 257). Plutarch, for example, a close contemporary of the apostle, used *harpazō* and its compounds

15. Fee (2009: 179–80) pointedly comments: "Paul himself could hardly have intended such a meaning [secret rapture] here. After all, for the Thessalonians themselves so to have understood it they would necessarily have needed *prior* instruction; but it is clear from this passage as a whole that Paul is informing them *for the first time* about the relationship of the 'living' and the 'dead' at the Parousia, so how could they have known about such an 'event' otherwise unknown in the church until the mid-nineteenth century?"

to refer to those who die an early death such that they are "snatched away" from "the advantages of life, such as marriage, education, manhood, citizenship, and public office" (*Con. Apoll.* 113C; see also 111D, 117B–D). Funerary inscriptions speak of how Fate has "snatched away" the living to the place of Hades (*IG* 2:1062a.3, 11477.9; 4:620.2; 5:733.12). Lucian uses a synonym of *harpazō* in the speech of a grieving father who cries out to his deceased son: "Dearest child, you are gone from me, dead, snatched away [*anērpasthēs*] before your time, leaving me behind alone and wretched" (*Funerals* 13). The Latin synonyms *rapio* and *eripio* are also frequently used in letters of consolation in the context of death. Seneca, for example, repeatedly refers to how Fortune has "snatched away" the deceased's wealth, friends, reputation, health, and breath (*Polyb.* 2.1–8; see also 11.1; 18.3; *Marc.* 6.1; Ovid, *Pontic Ep.* 4.11.5). Augustus, in his important funerary inscription, *Res gestae*, refers to the early death of his two adopted sons, Gaius and Lucius: "My sons, who as youths, were snatched from me by Fortune" (14.1). The colony of Pisae issued a commemorative decree at the death of Augustus's oldest adopted son that read in part: "When the news was brought to us that Gaius Caesar . . . was snatched by cruel fate from the Roman people, . . . this renewed and multiplied our grief" (*ILS* 140). A funerary monument from Moguntiacum (modern Mainz, Germany) dating to the first century AD states in part: "As you pass by, whoever reads this, stop, traveler, and look at how I lament in vain, unworthily snatched away [*raptus*]" (*CIL* 13.7070). Cicero quotes the *Iliad* in order to make the point that even the great god Jupiter "could not snatch his son Sarpedon from death" (*Div.* 2.25). Paul, therefore, may be cleverly inverting a common use of *harpazō* in referring to death: rather than the expected picture of death or fate "snatching away" to hades those who are living, the living "will be snatched up" so that they do not face the last enemy, death.[16] Though not stated explicitly, the living (but now transformed: 1 Cor. 15:51–54; Phil. 3:21) and deceased (but now resurrected) believers will be taken up by God, who is the implied agent of the passive form *harpagēsometha* (use of the so-called divine passive: see BDF §130.1; Wallace 1996: 437–38) and who earlier was said to bring those who had fallen asleep along with Jesus at his return (1 Thess. 4:14).

A brief prepositional phrase describes the instrument used by God to take believers up: "by means of clouds" (*en* does not likely convey location, which is expressed at the end of the sentence by *eis aera*, "in the air"—but signifies means or instrument). In the OT, clouds are so frequently associated with a theophany, that is, the appearance of God (e.g., Exod. 13:21–22; 14:19, 20, 24; 16:10; 19:16–17; Lev. 16:2; Num. 9:15–22; 10:11–12; 1 Kings 8:10–12;

---

16. Malherbe (1983: 255) concludes that Paul's deliberate choice of the verb ἁρπάζω in 4:17 involves a "neat twist": "Whereas the word usually denoted the separation from the living, Paul uses it to describe a snatching to association with the Lord and other Christians." In his later commentary, Malherbe (2000: 276) again refers to Paul's verb choice as a "neat twist" that also involves irony: "The dead in Christ will rise, and their separation from those who were left is overcome as, ironically, they are snatched up together with them."

2 Chron. 5:13–14; 6:1; Neh. 9:12, 19; Ps. 97:2; Isa. 19:1; Ezek. 1:4–28) that this meaning is naturally carried over to the NT (Matt. 17:5; Mark 9:7; Luke 9:34–35; 1 Cor. 10:1–2). Clouds as a sign of God's presence become connected not only with the ascension of Christ (Acts 1:9; see also the ascension of the two witnesses in Rev. 11:12) but also with his future return (Matt. 24:30; 26:64; Mark 13:26; 14:62; Luke 21:27; Rev. 1:7; 14:14–16), an image that can be traced back ultimately to Daniel's vision of "one like a son of man coming with the clouds of heaven" (7:13). The reference to believers being snatched up "by means of clouds," therefore, says less about the location of this gathering than it does about the presence of God and reassuring Paul's readers about the active part that the Divine will play in ensuring the equal presence and participation of both living and deceased believers in Christ's parousia.

The purpose (the preposition *eis* here denotes purpose: see BDAG 290.4.f) of believers being snatched up is "for a reception of the Lord" (*eis apantēsin tou kyriou*). The prepositional phrase *eis apantēsin* and the related verb *apantaō* occur frequently in the LXX in the ordinary sense of "to meet" someone, and this meaning also appears in the NT with the verbal form (Mark 14:13; Luke 17:12). The prepositional phrase, however, has a different connotation in the NT, because the noun *apantēsis* was a technical term referring to the well-known custom of a Hellenistic formal reception (E. Peterson 1930; see also his brief comments in *TDNT* 1:380–81).[17] This custom involved the sending of a delegation of leading citizens outside the city to welcome a visiting dignitary and escort that person on the final leg of the journey into their community.

Although there was no fixed form to what happened at these formal receptions, they frequently involved the following elements (see texts and discussion in E. Peterson 1930: 693–97; Cosby 1994). Once civic leaders became aware that a king or important official was coming to their city, they would adopt a formal resolution to pay tribute to that person by hosting a formal reception in his honor. Prominent citizens—including often priests and priestesses, officers and soldiers, leading teachers and their students, and victorious athletes—were then chosen to be part of the delegation that would meet the visiting dignitary outside the city walls, sometimes a great distance away. Those in the official reception party dressed in their finest clothes (frequently white) and wore laurel wreaths on their heads. Those who remained behind also often wore special clothes and garlands and decorated the city in festive

---

17. A few scholars have rejected this view, arguing either that Paul is instead influenced in his use of the phrase *eis apantēsin* (4:17) by the Sinai theophany (Exod. 19:10–18) and the LXX tradition (Dupont 1952: 64–73), or that the parallels with Hellenistic formal receptions are not as strong and clear as they are typically claimed to be (Cosby 1994). See the helpful survey of this debate in Luckensmeyer (2009: 260–65), who concludes: "It is apparent that the primary evidence does not support a technical meaning for ἀπάντησις and its cognates" (264), yet "the influence of Hellenistic formal receptions is significant," and so "an association of Paul's reference with Hellenistic formal receptions cannot be rejected" (265).

colors. The delegation would greet the coming dignitary with shouts of praise and song, and then escort him the rest of the way into their city, where the citizens would similarly welcome him with incessant shouts and applause. Once inside the city walls, the dignitary would offer sacrifices on the local altars and perhaps pronounce judgment on select prisoners, liberating some but sentencing others to execution.

Although not all of these elements of a Hellenistic formal reception parallel the events surrounding the return of Christ described in 1 Thess. 4:15–17 (see the six points raised by Cosby 1994: 28–31), the differences can be readily explained (see the response to Cosby by Gundry 1996); thus it is highly probable that Paul's use of *apantēsis* reflects this civic custom in antiquity (so most commentators). This conclusion is all the more convincing in light of the preceding reference to Christ's return with the term *parousia*. As Green (2002: 227–28) declares: "Since the context of this formal reception is the time of the royal *parousia* of the Lord (v. 15), there remains little doubt that this custom formed the background of this teaching." Indeed, this technical meaning of *apantēsis* was so common in that day that Cicero did not feel the need to translate it for his Latin readers when writing of Julius Caesar's triumphal return to Italy in 49 BC: "Just imagine what *apantēseis* he is receiving from the towns, what honors are paid to him!" (*Att.* 8.16.2); and mentioning the early success of Caesar's adoptive son, Octavian: "The municipalities are showing the boy remarkable favor. . . . Wonderful *apantēseis* and encouragement!" (*Att.* 16.11.6). The widespread understanding of *apantēsis* as referring to a formal reception is also seen in the rabbis' use of this term as a loanword (e.g., Midr. Tanḥ. 178a: "The great of the city moved out to meet [לאפנטי] the king"; cited by E. Peterson, *TDNT* 1:381).

The two other occurrences of *apantēsis* in the NT are also part of the identical prepositional phrase found in 1 Thess. 4:17 and similarly evoke the image of a Hellenistic formal reception. When the Christians in Rome learn that Paul the prisoner is approaching the imperial city, they send a delegation "for a reception" (*eis apantēsin*) of the apostle a good distance south of Rome and then escort him on the final leg of his journey (Acts 28:15). In the parable of the ten virgins, the women go out "for a reception" (*eis apantēsin*) of the bridegroom in which the five wise virgins use their lamps in an outdoor procession as they escort him to the wedding banquet (Matt. 25:6). There is compelling evidence, therefore, that the third remaining occurrence of *eis apantēsin* by Paul here in 1 Thess. 4:17 also intends to link the description of Christ's parousia with a Hellenistic formal reception—a connection that John Chrysostom highlighted long ago:

> For as when a king ceremoniously entered a city, certain dignitaries and city rulers, and many others who were confident toward the sovereign, would go out of the city to meet him; but the guilty and the condemned criminals would be guarded within, awaiting the sentence which the king would deliver. In the same way, when the Lord comes, those who are confident toward him will meet

him in the midst of the air, but the condemned, who are conscious of having committed many sins, will wait below for their judge.[18]

The location of this formal reception is "in the air" (the preposition *eis* here does not likely refer to direction but "a position within a certain area," since it is "frequently used where ἐν is expected": BDAG 289.1.a.δ). Since the Lord comes down "from heaven" and the believers are snatched up from earth, the "air" (*aēr*) can only be that space that lies between the heavenly and earthly realms. Since this region was widely believed to be the dwelling place of evil spirits and demons (see Eph. 2:2 as well as extrabiblical texts cited in BDAG 23.2.b; W. Foerster, *TDNT* 1:165n1 reports that "even today evil spirits are still called ἀερικά in Greece"), some find the location to be significant: "That the Lord chooses to meet his saints there, on the demons' home ground, so to speak, shows his complete mastery over them" (Morris 1991: 146; see also Otto 1997: 204–5; Holmes 1998: 151n17). But though Paul would surely affirm Christ's rule over the spiritual realm (see Eph. 1:20–22; Col. 1:16; 2:15), that is not his concern here. The apostle is similarly not emphasizing the final destination of believers, though his use of *apantēsis* to evoke the image of a Hellenistic formal reception strongly implies that, once all Christians are taken up to meet the returning Lord "in the air," they will escort him on the remainder of his victorious descent to earth (see further the comment on 4:14).

What Paul *does* stress in these verses is the consequence or result of the three stages of events described in 1 Thess. 4:16–17a for all the Thessalonian believers, both living and deceased—their eternal presence with the Lord: "and so we will always be with the Lord" (καὶ οὕτως πάντοτε σὺν κυρίῳ ἐσόμεθα, *kai houtōs pantote syn kyriō esometha*). This final clause of verse 17 is almost certainly not part of the "word of the Lord" that Paul has been loosely citing but his own summary (the adverb *houtōs* is "summarizing a thought expressed in what precedes": BDAG 742.1.b; see also Matt. 11:26; Acts 7:8; 1 Cor. 14:25) of the significance that this Jesus logion has for the problem faced at Thessalonica. Just as Paul concluded his first argument of verse 14 by reassuring the Thessalonian believers that God will bring the dead in their community "with him" (*syn autō*), that is, with Jesus at his return, so Paul similarly closes his second argument of verses 15–17 by asserting the eternal presence of believers "with the Lord" (*syn kyriō*). Paul's summary is so simple and brief that modern readers may well be disappointed that he does not spell out in more detail the nature of the eternal life that believers spend with the Lord. The apostle's concern, however, is to provide comfort to believers in Thessalonica who were grieving over the death of their fellow church members, and this concern has been fully met in his climaxing summary that all believers, both

---

18. John Chrysostom, *Ascens.* 50.450.57, as translated by Cosby 1994: 21. See also in his sermon on 1 Thess. 4:15–17: "For when a king drives into a city, those who are in honor go out to meet him; but the condemned await the judge within" (*Hom. 1 Thess.* 8).

living and deceased, will ultimately enjoy the blessing of being eternally present with the Lord.

4. Conclusion: Comfort One Another (4:18)

4:18   The eternal presence of believers with the returning, reigning Lord (v. 17b) serves as a natural culmination of not only the three-stage sequence of eschatological events described in verses 16–17a but also the argument of the passage as a whole, and so it is followed not surprisingly by a concluding statement: "Therefore comfort one another with these words" (ὥστε παρακαλεῖτε ἀλλήλους ἐν τοῖς λόγοις τούτοις, *hōste parakaleite allēlous en tois logois toutois*).

The particle *hōste*, when introducing an independent clause, means "for this reason, therefore" and serves to draw out an important conclusion from all that has been said in verses 13–17. Paul uses this particle in a similar fashion elsewhere to bring his discussion to a definitive close: thus 1 Cor. 7:38 concludes the discussion of virgins in 7:25–38; then 11:27, 33 conclude the discussion of division over the Lord's Supper celebration in 11:17–34; also 14:39 concludes the discussion of spiritual gifts in 12:1–14:40; and 15:58 concludes the discussion of resurrection in 15:1–58. Here the apostle concludes his discussion of the fate of deceased believers at Christ's return with an exhortation that confirms the paraenetic or pastoral concern that was suggested already in the purpose clause of the opening verse ("in order that you may not grieve like the rest who have no hope") and that has been at work in the whole passage: "Comfort one another." The verb *parakaleō* is a favorite Pauline term, occurring some fifty-four times in his letters as a whole and eight times in this letter (2:12; 3:2, 7; 4:1, 10, 18; 5:11, 14). Although the verb possesses a wide range of meanings (BDAG 764–65 lists five different senses), these possibilities can be grouped into two primary nuances: either command ("appeal, exhort, request, implore"), as in 2:12; 4:1, 10; 5:14; or comfort ("encourage, comfort, cheer up, console"), as in 3:2, 7; 5:11. That the latter nuance is intended here in 4:18 is clear from the context of grief over the death of fellow believers.

Paul's closing exhortation to "comfort one another" is nicely contrasted with a similar closing exhortation found in a second-century AD letter of consolation (P.Oxy. 115) already cited above (see comment on 4:13). In this letter addressed to a couple grieving over the death of their son, the author reasons to the parents that there was nothing that they or anyone else could have done to prevent this tragedy from happening ("One is able to do nothing against such things [i.e., death]")—a fact that leads immediately to the closing exhortation: "Therefore comfort yourselves." Paul, by contrast, grounds his exhortation to comfort not with the helplessness that humanity experiences in the face of death but "with these words" (the preposition *en* here functions as a marker introducing means or instrument: BDAG 328.5). "These words," of course, refer back to the two arguments that the apostle has presented in the preceding verses: first, the authoritative confession of the church concerning the resurrection of Jesus, which is a guarantee of the resurrection of deceased believers such that they will be alive and present at Christ's return (v. 14); and second, the authoritative "word of the Lord," which guarantees that deceased believers will in no way be at a disadvantage at Christ's return as compared with living believers but will be equally present with them at that eschatological event (vv. 15–17). These are the two reasons why the Thessalonians can now obey Paul's concluding call to "comfort one another." These are the two reasons why, in contrast to the hopelessness or despair that characterizes the way that those outside the church face the death of others, Christians grieve for deceased believers with hope.

Additional Notes

4:13. A few late minuscules and versions (104 614 630 1505 *pc* vg^mss sy; Aug^pt) replace the plural οὐ θέλομεν (we do not want) with the singular οὐ θέλω (I do not want), likely under the influence of other Pauline instances of the disclosure formula in the singular (Rom. 1:13; 1 Cor. 10:1; Phil. 1:12; Col. 2:1).

4:13. The present participle τῶν κοιμωμένων (those who are asleep: ℵ A B 0278 33 81 326 1175 1739 *pc*; Or) is preferred over the perfect participle τῶν κεκοιμημένων (those who have fallen asleep: D [F G, which have the corrupt form κεκοιμήνων] K L Ψ 88 104 257 𝔐) for two reasons: (1) it is supported by the older witnesses; (2) it is more likely to have been changed into the perfect participle in agreement with Matt. 27:52 and 1 Cor. 15:20, than (conversely) to have the perfect participle changed into present—a form found nowhere else in the NT (Lightfoot 1904: 63; B. Metzger 1994: 564–65).

4:15. Instead of KY = κυρίου (the coming of the *Lord*), Codex Vaticanus, "in one of its rare idiosyncratic moments" (Fee 2009: 164n3), reads IY = Ἰησοῦ (the coming of *Jesus*), likely under the influence of the preceding verse.

4:16. The adverb πρῶτον (first) is read as an adjective πρῶτοι in a few MSS (D* F G latt; Tert) in agreement with the subject οἱ νεκροί (the dead). Milligan (1908: 61) forwards the possibility that the alternate reading may be the result of an attempt to harmonize this passage with the wholly different "first resurrection" (πρώτη ἀνάστασις) of Rev. 20:5.

4:17. The attribute participle οἱ περιλειπόμενοι (the ones who are left) is omitted in some Western MSS (F G a b; Tert Ambst Spec), possibly because scribes felt that this rare expression (in the NT only here and in v. 15), which Paul repeats from 4:15 for emphasis, was unnecessarily redundant.

4:17. A few MSS replace ἀπάντησιν with the more common form ὑπάντησιν (so D* F G).

4:18. A few late MSS (1739^c *pc*) add τοῦ πνεύματος at the end of 4:18 so that the text reads: "with these words *of the Spirit*"—an obvious attempt by pious scribes to highlight the Spirit's role in inspiring Paul's words.

C. Comfort concerning Living Christians at Christ's Return (5:1–11)

Paul's stated desire for the Christians in Thessalonica is to "complete the things that are lacking in your faith" (3:10), and he has been preoccupied in the second, or exhortative, half of the letter body (4:1–5:22) with accomplishing this goal. All three of the topics foreshadowed in the transitional prayer of 3:12–13 have already been addressed: holiness in sexual conduct (4:3–8); the practice of *philadelphia*, or mutual love (4:9–12); and the return of Christ (4:13–18). That the apostle continues to discuss the return of Christ in 5:1–11 not only reveals the importance of this subject for the Thessalonian readers but also raises the question of the relationship between this and the preceding passage, which deals in a general way with the same subject. But while 4:13–18 concerns the fate of *deceased* believers at Jesus's return, 5:1–11 focuses on the fate of *living* Christians at the same eschatological event.[1] A variety of factors suggest that the believers in Thessalonica were not merely curious about the timing of the day of the Lord but also worried whether they would avoid the wrath connected with that future day, hoping instead to experience salvation and eternal life with Christ.

Paul responds to his readers' anxiety by asserting that, though the day of the Lord will involve a sudden destruction from which there will certainly be no escape, believers need not fear this eschatological event (vv. 1–3). The apostle then provides two supporting grounds for his assertion: first, their status as "sons of light" and "sons of day" (vv. 4–5); and second, their election by God to obtain salvation and eternal life with Christ (vv. 9–10). Sandwiched between these two grounds is an appeal to live vigilantly and sober-mindedly (i.e., to live ready and steady lives) in anticipation of Christ's return (vv. 6–8). Paul ends with a concluding exhortation based on the grounds given in the preceding verses, calling the Thessalonian Christians to comfort one another and build each other up (v. 11).

Literary Analysis

Character of the Passage

The material of 5:1–11, like the rest of the text belonging to the second half of the letter body (4:1–5:22), can best be identified as paraenesis or, as this term is best

---

1. Johanson (1987: 127): "The former passage [4:13–18] focuses on the recipients' anxiety more in relation to their grief and the question of the eschatological status of the deceased, while the latter passage [5:1–11] focuses on their anxiety more in relation to their own personal status in face of the imminent parousia."

translated, exhortation (for a general introduction to this formal category, see the introduction to 4:1–12). That this passage contains teaching about the day of the Lord and involves certain arguments or logical appeals, however, has led some to conclude that Paul's purpose is not paraenetic but primarily didactic or persuasive (Johanson 1987: 134–35: "5,1–11 is more adequately characterized as persuasion than parenesis"). Nevertheless, the intention of the apostle is not merely to inform or debate but also to change the conduct of the Thessalonians, so that the fear they now experience over their own fate on the day of the Lord would be replaced with the comfort that comes from knowing their privileged status of being "sons of light/day" and their election by God not to face his wrath but to obtain salvation and eternal life with Christ. The paraenetic character of the passage comes to the fore most clearly in the four hortatory subjunctives of verses 6–7 ("So then, let us not sleep like the rest, but let us stay awake and be sober; . . . let us be sober") and the two closing commands of verse 11 ("Therefore comfort one another and build each other up").

The traditional nature of paraenesis and its easy application to a variety of situations has caused some to argue that the exhortations of NT writers have little, if any, connection with the specific situation of their audience (Dibelius 1937). This presupposition about paraenesis might then lead to the conclusion that Paul's exhortations here in 5:1–11 are merely generic warnings about end-time concerns. But not only is this presupposition about paraenesis a faulty one; so also is its application to 5:1–11. Rather, there is compelling evidence that this passage, as with the paraenetical material in the other passages in 4:1–5:22, addresses an actual problem at work in the Thessalonian congregation.

Extent of the Passage

That 4:13–5:11 deals generally with the same subject matter, the return of Christ, might suggest that all of these verses form one lengthy literary unit within the letter. Indeed, such a conclusion seems to be further supported by the striking parallels in both content and form between the opening (4:13–18) and closing (5:1–11) sections of this unit (see the parallels cited in "Extent of the Passage" for 4:13–18; also see Plevnik 1979; Collins 1984: 154–72; Johanson 1987: 118–19; Howard 1988).

But while there clearly exists a close connection between the material of 4:13–18 and that of 5:1–11, there are compelling reasons for treating each of these passages as independent literary units, the second of which begins at 5:1. First, the subject matter shifts from the fate of deceased believers at Christ's return (4:13–18) to that of "the times and the seasons" concerning the day of the Lord, or more precisely, as the following verses suggest, the fate of living believers at this eschatological event. Second, 5:1 opens with two clear transitional markers: the "now about" (*peri de*) formula (see also 4:9, 13) and the vocative "brothers." Third, the use of the rhetorical device of paraleipsis ("you have no need to have anything written to you"; see BDF §495.1) in 5:1b and the particular form of the disclosure formula ("For you yourselves accurately know that . . .") in 5:2 both indicate that Paul has left the "new" teaching introduced in 4:13–18 and returned to previously shared material, teaching that the Thessalonians already know from his original ministry among them (so also the material in 4:1–12: see 4:1, 2, 6, 11). Fourth, after the concluding particle "therefore" (*hōste*) that opens 4:18 and the prepositional phrase "with these words" in this verse, which looks back to the preceding statements of 4:13–17, the reader expects a new topic to begin in the immediately following verse of 5:1.

The ending of the unit at 5:11 is likewise clearly marked by a variety of grammatical, epistolary, and other literary devices. First, the inferential conjunction "therefore" (dio) introduces a concluding statement that spells out the practical consequence of the argument presented in 5:1–10. Second, the fuller phrase in 5:11, "Therefore comfort one another" (dio parakaleite allēlous), appears to function as a stereotyped expression that concludes the preceding material of 5:1–10, just as the virtually identical phrase in 4:18, "Therefore comfort one another" (hōste parakaleite allēlous), concludes the preceding material of 4:13–17. Third, the ending at 5:11 is implied from the three transitional markers found in the immediately following verse, 5:12: the appeal formula ("We ask you . . .": the expected parakaloumen is replaced by the synonym erōtōmen: so also 2 Thess. 2:1; for an appeal formula where both verbs occur together, see 1 Thess. 4:1; also P.Oxy. 294.28; 744.6; P.Freib. 39; P.Col. 8.8–9, 21); the mildly adversative particle de (but); and the vocative "brothers." Finally, there is an obvious shift in subject matter from the eschatological concerns that predominate not only 5:1–11 but also 4:13–18 to a variety of ethical issues pertaining to community life in 5:12–22.

Structure of the Passage

The logical structure or rhetorical arrangement of Paul's discussion in 5:1–11 about the day of the Lord is less obvious than most of the other passages in 1 Thessalonians, and this difficulty accounts for the wide range of differing outlines that have been proposed. The confusion stems partly from many changes of person throughout the passage, a number of which occur *within* a literary unit (e.g., plural throughout, with a shift from second person in vv. 1–2 to third person in v. 3; from second person in vv. 4–5a to first person in vv. 5b–6; next to third person in v. 7 and then back to first person in v. 8). Nevertheless, there are enough grammatical, epistolary, and other more broadly literary clues to make a compelling case that 5:1–11 consists of five distinct units.

The first unit consists of verses 1–3, where the apostle employs a "now about" (peri de) formula to introduce the new topic of this passage. The transitional formula "Now about times and the seasons" by itself is elliptical and thus rather vague in identifying what this new topic entails. In the larger context, however, its meaning is clear, occurring as it does after the extended discussion of the second coming of the Lord in 4:13–18 and just before the reference to the "day of the Lord" in 5:2. The disclosure formula in verse 2 ("For you yourselves accurately know that . . .") is a second transitional device (see also 2:1; 4:2) by which the new topic of the day of the Lord is introduced. This first unit closes with a notable use of the emphatic future negation ("and they will certainly not escape"), which functions here as a sequence terminator. Semantic coherence in the opening unit can be found in the "coming" motif expressed through the verbs erchetai (v. 2) and ephistatai (v. 3).

The second unit comprises 5:4–5, whose opening is clearly marked by three elements: the personal pronoun "you" (hymeis), which is emphasized both by its mere presence (since the subject "you" is already expressed in the verb este) and its location at the head of the sentence; the mildly adversative de; and the vocative "brothers." The shift in subject from the third person "they" (two occurrences) and "them" of verse 3 to the second-person "you" that opens verse 4 creates a sharp contrast between the Thessalonian believers and those at the end of the preceding unit who embrace the Roman imperial propaganda "peace and security" and consequently will experience sudden destruction, from which "they will certainly not escape" (this contrast is further stressed by the emphatic position of the object "you" in the second half of v. 4, preceding the verb that controls it). The subject matter of the second unit involves the status of "all" (note the emphatic *pantes* that opens v. 5) the Christians in Thessalonica as demonstrated in the repeated use of the verb *eimi*. Paul's metaphorical use of "day/light" and "night/darkness" in this unit stems from his reference in the preceding unit to the "day" of the Lord coming like a thief "in the night" (5:2). The shift from the second-person "you" in verses 4–5a to the first-person "we" in verse 5b leads some commentators to begin the third unit already in this latter verse (Milligan 1908: 67; Holtz 1986: 209; Jurgensen 1994: 99n32; Holmstrand 1997: 65n80). That the second half of verse 5, however, still belongs to the second unit is clear from the *chiasm* it forms with the first half (light and day//night and darkness) and the presence again of the verb *eimi*. The shift here to the first person, therefore, more likely functions to foreshadow the cohortatives in the following unit as well as the inclusive "we/us" found in the rest of the passage, as Paul highlights his solidarity with the Thessalonian readers (Johanson 1987: 133).

The third unit includes verses 6–8 and is introduced by the particles *ara oun* (so then)—a combination found in the Bible only in Paul's Letters (Rom. 5:18; 7:3, 25; 8:12; 9:16, 18; 14:12, 19; Gal. 6:10; Eph. 2:19; 1 Thess. 5:6; 2 Thess. 2:15). These two particles normally function to signal a transition in the apostle's argument where he draws out the logical inference from what precedes (BDAG 127.2.b: "Here ἄρα expresses the inference and οὖν the transition"). This unit, therefore, sets forth the paraenetic, or exhortative, consequences of the assertions made about the Thessalonians' status in the preceding verses 4–5. The beginning of the third unit is further marked by the shift from the indicative to the hortatory subjunctive—a shift in keeping with the paraenetic function at work in these verses. The repetition of the verbal pairs *katheudō* (to sleep) and *grēgoreō* (to be awake) and also *nēphō* (to be sober) and *methyō* (to be drunk) give this unit lexical coherence.

The fourth unit involves verses 9–10, where the exhortations of the preceding unit are replaced with a causal statement (note the *hoti* that opens v. 9) about God's purpose for his people. The emphasis on divine purpose is expressed in the twofold repetition of the preposition *eis* in verse 9 ("not . . . for wrath, but for the obtaining of salvation") and the *hina* clause in verse 10 ("in order that, whether we are awake or asleep, together we may live with him"). The reference in the former purpose clause to "the obtaining of salvation" is anticipated by the final words of the preceding unit, which exhorts the readers to put on "the hope of salvation" as a helmet. The references in the latter purpose clause to being "asleep" and to living "with him" recall for the reader the primary issue addressed in the preceding passage of 4:13–18 (vv. 13, 14, 15, "those who are/have fallen asleep"; vv. 14, 17, "with him/the Lord") so that 5:10 functions as an appropriate summary of not just 5:1–9 but also the whole eschatological section of 4:13–5:11 and its treatment of the fate of both deceased and living believers at the parousia.

The fifth and final unit is 5:11, where the inferential conjunction *dio* (therefore) introduces a concluding statement that highlights the practical consequence of the argument presented in 5:1–10, just as the particle *hōste* (therefore) begins a similar summary sentence in 4:18. The break at 5:11 is also indicated by the shift from the indicative to the imperative mood. The closing character of verse 11 is further suggested by the exhortation "Comfort one another," since this repeats verbatim the closing command of 4:18. Here, however, Paul includes an additional exhortation, calling on his readers to "build each other up, one-on-one, just as you are indeed doing."

Now that the five units that make up 5:1–11 have been identified, we proceed to consider the relationship of these units to each other and what function they have within Paul's overall argument in this passage. The first unit of verses 1–3 introduces the new topic: "the times and the seasons" associated with Christ's coming, which is here referred to as "the day of the Lord." The way Paul addresses this topic in the remainder of the passage strongly implies that the Thessalonians are not merely curious about the timing of this eschatological day but rather question whether they are worthy enough to avoid the judgment associated with that end-time day and instead experience salvation and eternal life with Christ. Since the apostle (1) stresses the status of "all" (note the emphatic *pantes* that opens v. 5) his readers by three times describing them in terms of what they "are" and "are not," with the result that the day of the Lord will not surprise them like a thief (vv. 4–5); (2) in the armor metaphor emphasizes the third and final virtue, the "hope of salvation" (v. 8); (3) identifies God's purpose for them as being "not for wrath but for the obtaining of salvation" (v. 9); and (4) concludes with an exhortation that they "comfort each other and build each other up" (v. 11)—all this suggests a significant fear on the Thessalonians' part concerning their own position at the parousia. As Marshall (1990: 260) observes: "The members were worried not only about the fate of those who had already died at the imminent parousia but also about their own position; the character of the parousia as sudden, unexpected judgment upon unbelievers filled them with anxiety regarding themselves also" (so also Frame 1912: 178–79; Marshall 1983: 132; Johanson 1987: 127, 132; Holmes 1998: 165; Nicholl 2004: 49–79).

The first unit, verses 1–3, therefore functions not only to introduce the new topic of the day of the Lord but also to assert implicitly that the believers in Thessalonica need not fear its coming. For even though this day will bring about a sudden destruction upon the rest of humanity, from which there will certainly be no escape, the Thessalonians are sufficiently informed about its coming such that they have no need to receive any writing about this subject. The second unit, verses 4–5, provides an important reason *why* the Thessalonian Christians need not fear the day of the Lord: their status as "sons of the light/day" means that "the day will not overtake them like a thief." The third unit, verses 6–8, draws out the paraenetic, or exhortative, result of this status (note the opening *ara oun* of v. 6; also the logic of v. 8: "*Since* we are of the day, *let us be* sober"): this means living wakeful and sober-minded (ready and steady) lives by putting on the breastplate of faith and love, and as a helmet the hope of salvation. The fourth unit, verses 9–10, claims that God has destined the believers in Thessalonica for salvation and eternal life with Christ and thus provides another key reason why they need not fear the day of the Lord. The fifth unit, verse 11, concludes the discussion with an exhortation that they comfort one another and build each other up, based on the claims presented in the preceding verses.

The structure of 5:1–11, therefore, can be outlined as follows:

1. Opening assertion: Christians need not fear the day of the Lord (5:1–3)
2. Reason 1: You are "sons of light/day" (5:4–5)
3. Result: Live ready and steady lives (5:6–8)
4. Reason 2: God has destined us for salvation and life with Christ (5:9–10)
5. Conclusion: Comfort one another (5:11)

Exegesis and Exposition

[1]Now about the times and the seasons, brothers, you have no need to be written to;[2] [2]for you yourselves accurately know that the day of the Lord comes like a thief in the night. [3]Whenever ⌜ ⌝ people say: "Peace and security," then sudden destruction ⌜comes upon⌝ them, like birth pangs come upon a pregnant woman, and they will certainly not escape.

[4]But you, brothers, are not in darkness with the result that the day would surprise you like a ⌜thief⌝. [5]For you are all sons of light and sons of day; ⌜we are⌝ not of night or of darkness.

[6]So then, let us not sleep ⌜like the rest⌝, but let us stay awake and be sober. [7]For those who sleep, sleep at night, and those who get drunk, get drunk at night. [8]But as for us, since we are of the day, let us be sober, by putting on the breastplate of faith and love, and as a helmet the hope of salvation.

[9]For God did not destine us for wrath but for the obtaining of salvation through our Lord Jesus ⌜Christ⌝, [10]who died ⌜for⌝ us in order that, whether we are awake or asleep, together we may ⌜live⌝ with him.

[11]Therefore comfort one another and build each other up, one-on-one, just as you are indeed doing.

1. Opening Assertion: Christians Need Not Fear the Day of the Lord (5:1–3)

Paul opens the new topic concerning the day of the Lord by claiming the superfluous nature of his writing to the Thessalonians on this subject: "Now about the times and the seasons, brothers, you have no need to be written to" (περὶ δὲ τῶν χρόνων καὶ τῶν καιρῶν, ἀδελφοί, οὐ χρείαν ἔχετε ὑμῖν γράφεσθαι, *peri de tōn chronōn kai tōn kairōn, adelphoi, ou chreian echete hymin graphesthai*).

The "now about" (*peri de*) formula is an epistolary convention commonly employed in both secular (see White 1986 for examples from papyrus letters)

5:1

---

2. The Greek text includes the second-person plural pronoun ὑμῖν, so that the sentence literally reads: "you have no need to be written to *you*." Though the inclusion of the pronoun is redundant and awkward in English (hence its omission in our translation), it is not problematic in Greek, as evidenced by the fact that scribes made no attempt to "correct" the text as they did with the similar expression in 4:9 (on this, see additional notes).

and Pauline letters (1 Cor. 7:1, 25; 8:1, 4; 12:1; 16:1, 12; 1 Thess. 4:9, 13; 5:1) as a shorthand way of introducing a new topic that is readily known by both author and reader. The apostle has already used this formula to introduce the two preceding topics of "love for one another" (4:9) and the fate of "those who are asleep" (4:13), and now for the third time in the letter, he employs it to introduce the new topic that will preoccupy his attention in 5:1–11. Although several commentators conclude from the presence of this epistolary convention that the Thessalonians had written a letter to Paul with a series of questions to which he responds in 4:9, 13, and 5:1, it is more probable that the "now about" formula introduces a new subject that the apostle takes up in response to the oral report of Timothy (3:6; see further the comment on 4:9 and 4:13).

The new subject that Paul takes up deals with "the times and the seasons." The nouns *chronos* and *kairos* were sometimes distinguished in Classical Greek, and this has led several commentators, especially earlier ones, to differentiate between these terms here, claiming, for example, that the former term refers to the quantity of time (i.e., duration) and the latter term to the quality of time (see, e.g., Augustine, *Ep.* 197.2; Ellicott 1864: 67; Findlay 1891: 107; Lightfoot 1904: 70–71; Milligan 1908: 63; more recently Morris 1991: 148; Witherington 2006: 144). Yet the combination of these two nouns in both the LXX (Neh. 10:35 [10:34 Eng.]; 13:31; Dan. 2:21; 7:12; Wis. 8:8) and the NT (Acts 1:7; see 3:20–21) suggests that they are a conventional pair, thereby leading the majority of contemporary scholars to treat these words as a hendiadys, the two expressing the same idea.

In that period, the expression "the times and the seasons" is a fixed or stock phrase referring to the timing of eschatological events, as shown by several factors: (1) the use of this word pair in its only other NT occurrence as a shorthand reference to end-time events (Acts 1:7); (2) Paul's use of "the times and the seasons" as a topical heading for 5:1–11 without any accompanying explanation about the meaning of these terms; and (3) the widespread use of *kairos* in both biblical (e.g., in LXX: Jer. 6:15; 10:15; 18:23; 27:4, 31 [50:4, 31 Eng.]; Dan. 8:17; in NT: Matt. 8:29; Mark 13:33; Luke 21:8; Acts 3:20; 1 Cor. 4:5; Rev. 1:3) and nonbiblical (2 Bar. 14.1; 20.6; 2 Esd. [4 Ezra] 7:73–74) texts to refer to the judgment to take place at the end of time. The existence of a standard expression such as "the times and the seasons" is hardly surprising in light of the high level of interest that many in that day had with the timing of the day of the Lord (see Dan. 12:6–7; Matt. 24:3; Mark 13:32; Luke 17:20; Acts 1:6; 2 Esd. [4 Ezra] 4:33; 6:7; 2 Bar. 21.19; 25.1–4). It seems clear, therefore, that the Thessalonian Christians similarly have questions about the timing of this eschatological event. Yet, as noted above (see "Structure of the Passage"), the way Paul answers this question in the remainder of the passage indicates that the Thessalonians are not merely curious about the timing of the day of the Lord but also are experiencing a high level of anxiety as to whether that day will involve wrath or salvation for themselves.

Paul begins his treatment of the new subject concerning the day of the Lord and the Thessalonians' anxiety about the timing of this eschatological event by claiming that his readers "have no need to be written to" on this matter. For the third time in the letter, the apostle is employing the rhetorical device of paraleipsis: an expression that allows speakers or writers to address a subject that they outwardly claim does not need to be addressed (BDF §495.1). In 1:8 Paul refers to his readers' evangelistic activity while in the same breath he claims that he "has no need to say anything" about this very subject. In 4:9 the apostle asserts that he has no need to write to the Thessalonian believers "about love for one another" but then proceeds in the next verses to address this exact matter. Similarly, Paul here in 5:1 claims that he has no need to write to them "about the times and the seasons" but nevertheless takes up this same topic in the following verses. Such a claim functions to comfort the Christians in Thessalonica, for it implies that they already know all that is necessary pertaining to the timing of the day of the Lord. They are sufficiently informed about this eschatological event such that they need not fear its coming.

Although the Thessalonians' knowledge about the day of the Lord is implied in the paraleipsis expression of verse 1b, it is stated explicitly in the disclosure formula of verse 2: "for you yourselves accurately know that the day of the Lord comes like a thief in the night" (αὐτοὶ γὰρ ἀκριβῶς οἴδατε ὅτι ἡμέρα κυρίου ὡς κλέπτης ἐν νυκτὶ οὕτως ἔρχεται, *autoi gar akribōs oidate hoti hēmera kyriou hōs kleptēs en nykti houtōs erchetai*). **5:2**

The reason why (*gar* introduces a causal clause) Paul does not need to write to the Thessalonians "about the times and the seasons" connected with the day of the Lord is because they already possess the requisite knowledge about this subject. The apostle has used the verb *oidate* throughout 1 Thessalonians to appeal to the readers' personal knowledge about various matters (1:5; 2:1, 2, 5, 11; 3:3, 4; 4:2), and here he uses it yet again to refer to information that they already have about the day of the Lord's arrival. Paul stresses their possession of this knowledge through the addition of the pronoun *autoi* (yourselves; see also 2:1; 3:3; 2 Thess. 3:7) at the head of the sentence and the adverb *akribōs* (accurately). That the latter term is rare for Paul (elsewhere only in Eph. 5:15) leads some to conclude that the apostle is borrowing this word from the Thessalonians, who, either in a letter or report via Timothy, wanted to know "accurately" the timing of the parousia (so, e.g., Findlay 1891: 113; Best 1977: 204–5; Malherbe 2000: 289). The term, however, more likely is Paul's, since it forms an effective contrast between the accurate knowledge that the apostle claims the Thessalonians already have and the false knowledge of those who proclaim and embrace the Roman political propaganda "peace and security" (v. 3). Paul had apparently taught the believers in Thessalonica during his mission-founding visit about eschatological matters. That this instruction had been frequent is suggested not only by Paul's comment here that they know "accurately" about the day of the Lord but also his use of the imperfect tense in the second letter to stress the customary or repeated action of his teaching about events surrounding Christ's return (2 Thess. 2:5: "I was repeatedly saying [*elegon*] these things to you").

The content of what the Thessalonians accurately know is expressed by a *hoti* clause: "that the day of the Lord comes like a thief in the night." The expression "the day of the Lord" (*hēmera kyriou*) is a fixed phrase familiar to the Thessalonians, as indicated by the absence of the article with both terms (see BDF §259) and its use by Paul without any accompanying explanation. The day-of-the-Lord concept has its roots in the OT, where it refers to a future time when God would come both to punish the wicked and to vindicate his people, though the notion of judgment is more commonly stressed than that of deliverance (e.g., Isa. 2:1–4:6; Jer. 46:10; Ezek. 30:2–3; Obad. 15; Joel 1:15; 2:1, 11, 31–32; Amos 5:18–20; Zeph. 1:14–18; Zech. 14). The early Christians, for whom Jesus Christ was their "Lord," naturally applied the OT "day of the Lord" to the future time when Christ would come to punish the wicked and vindicate his followers.[3] The phrase is a favorite for Paul, occurring twice as frequently as "coming" (*parousia*) and in a variety of forms: "the day of the Lord" (1 Cor. 5:5; 1 Thess. 5:2; 2 Thess. 2:2); "the day of the Lord Jesus" (2 Cor. 1:14); "the day of our Lord Jesus Christ" (1 Cor. 1:8); "the day of Christ Jesus" (Phil. 1:6); "the day of Christ" (Phil. 1:10; 2:16); and simply "the day" (Rom. 2:5; 13:12; 1 Cor. 3:13; 1 Thess. 5:4; see Eph. 4:30) or "that day" (2 Thess. 1:10; 2 Tim. 1:12, 18). The apostle used the term "coming" (*parousia*) in his previous discussion about the fate of deceased believers at Christ's return (4:15) but switches here to the phrase "the day of the Lord," either because this expression was part of the Thessalonians' inquiry or, as is more likely, because it better conveys the notion of judgment associated with Christ's return, a point made in the following verse ("then sudden destruction comes upon them, . . . and they will certainly not escape").

With respect to the timing of the day of the Lord, Paul employs the first of multiple metaphors in this passage (v. 2b, thief in the night; v. 3b, birth pangs; vv. 4–5, darkness/light and its corresponding pair night/day; vv. 6–8a, to be asleep/awake and to be drunk/sober; v. 8b, military armor; v. 10b, "to be awake/asleep"). This one is intended to remind the Thessalonians of what they already accurately know, that this day "comes[4] like a thief in the night" (lit., "like a thief in the night, thus it comes," where the comparative particle *hōs* is correlative with *houtos*: BDAG 1104.2.a). This first metaphor is not a creation of the apostle but one that goes back to the teaching of Jesus (Matt.

---

3. Fee (2009: 188) highlights how this application of the OT phrase "day of the Lᴏʀᴅ" to Jesus's future coming reveals Paul's high Christology: "One should also note that 'the Lord' in this phrase is now Christ, rather than God the Father. The Christological significance of this transfer of language should not be missed. . . . As with prayer addressed to Christ in 3:11–12, this is another moment which demonstrates that a very high Christology was already in place for Paul by the time he wrote this his earliest letter." Similarly, Shogren (2012: 202) states: "What is remarkable from the standpoint of Paul's Christology is that the day of Yahweh predictions find their fulfillment in the coming of the Lord *Jesus*; all of the 'day' references are therefore indirect but unmistakable affirmations of Christ's deity."

4. In 5:2 the present tense of ἔρχεται instead of the expected future tense likely is intended to emphasize the certainty of the day of the Lord's coming (so, e.g., Eadie 1877: 176; Lünemann 1885: 545–46; Lightfoot 1904: 71; Morris 1991: 151; Malherbe 2000: 290). Note also the present tense of ἐφίσταται in 5:3.

24:43; Luke 12:39) and that was later used by other NT writers as well (2 Pet. 3:10: "But the day of the Lord will come like a thief"; Rev. 3:3; 16:15: "I will come/am coming like a thief"). The purpose of Jesus's teaching was to highlight the sudden and unpredictable nature of the Son of Man's arrival and the consequent need for believers to be always ready and prepared for his coming (Matt. 24:42, 44: "Watch, therefore, for you do not know on what day your Lord is coming. . . . Therefore you also must be ready, for the Son of Man is coming at an hour you do not expect"; see also Luke 12:40). Paul similarly uses the thief metaphor to stress the point that no one knows when the day of the Lord will come: it will arrive without warning, like the unpredictable arrival of a thief or burglar. But even though the precise timing of the day's arrival cannot be calculated, its coming is not unexpected for believers who are watchful and prepared (vv. 6–8) so that this day will not overtake them like a thief (v. 4). These words of reassurance and comfort, however, do not come until later in the passage. Here the metaphor functions to remind the Thessalonians not only of the impossibility of predicting when the day of the Lord will come, but also that this day will be one of judgment for those who are unprepared for its arrival—a point made more explicit in the following verse.

The prepositional phrase "in the night" (*en nykti*) is noteworthy, since it does not appear in any other text where the thief metaphor is used. There is a good possibility, therefore, that Paul has added it, not merely to add vividness to the threatening imagery of the thief (see Best 1977: 206; Gaventa 1998: 70) but also because it establishes a contrast between "day" and "night" and their related qualities of "light" and "darkness"—metaphors that the apostle will develop extensively in both the second (vv. 4–5) and third (vv. 6–8) units in the passage.

5:3

The rather negative picture in verse 2—with its note of judgment expressed through the coming "day of the Lord," and with the ominous character of the "thief in the night" metaphor—is intensified in verse 3, as Paul seeks to sharpen the contrast between the fate of the Thessalonian believers at Christ's return with that of the rest of humanity. Thus, before turning to the more positive and comforting picture that begins in verse 4, the apostle highlights the certain judgment that awaits those who do not have the accurate knowledge about the day of the Lord that the Christians in Thessalonica possess. Paul accomplishes this by first citing Roman political propaganda with which his readers would have been familiar and then following that quotation with another metaphor: "Whenever people say: 'Peace and security,' then sudden destruction comes upon them, like birth pangs come upon a pregnant woman, and they will certainly not escape" (ὅταν λέγωσιν· Εἰρήνη καὶ ἀσφάλεια, τότε αἰφνίδιος αὐτοῖς ἐφίσταται ὄλεθρος ὥσπερ ἡ ὠδὶν τῇ ἐν γαστρὶ ἐχούσῃ, καὶ οὐ μὴ ἐκφύγωσιν, *hotan legōsin: Eirēnē kai asphaleia, tote aiphnidios autois ephistatai olethros hōsper hē ōdin tē en gastri echousē, kai ou mē ekphygōsin*).

The absence of any connecting particle (asyndeton) makes the relationship of this verse to the preceding one uncertain—a grammatical ambiguity that some scribes tried to clarify (see additional notes). Nevertheless, the surrounding verses—both verse 2, which stresses what the readers accurately know about the day of the Lord coming like a thief, and verse 4, which emphasizes the current status of the readers with the result that the day of the Lord should not overtake them like a thief—indicate that Paul intends to contrast the fate of the Thessalonian believers at Christ's return with that of the rest of humanity who naively accept the Roman imperial propaganda "peace and security" and thus trust in the empire's political power instead of in God.

All translations place the brief phrase "peace and security" in quotation marks because it is clear from the introductory formula "whenever people say" that the apostle is not here creating the phrase but citing it. This is supported by several additional factors: the words *asphaleia* (security), *aiphnidios* (sudden), and *ephistatai* (it comes upon) occur only here in Paul; the impersonal use of *legōsin* (they say) is unusual for the apostle; and the word *eirēnē* (peace), which normally has a religious meaning in Paul, here has a secular sense such that it is paralleled with the word "security." These unique features already led Lightfoot (1904: 72) some time ago to observe: "The dissimilarity which this verse presents to the ordinary style of St. Paul is striking." Since the apostle, then, is not creating but citing these words, the question arises as to the source or identity of Paul's quotation.

The traditional answer is that the phrase "peace and security" echoes the OT prophetic warnings against false claims of peace uttered by wicked leaders or pseudo-prophets in Israel. In Jer. 6:14 God accuses the spiritual leaders in Jerusalem of treating "the wound of my people carelessly, saying 'Peace, peace,' where there is no peace" (so also 8:11, but not in the LXX). Similarly, in Ezek. 13:10 God claims that the prophets of Israel are false "because they have misled my people, saying, 'Peace, peace,' and there is no peace." And in Mic. 3:5 God complains about "prophets who lead my people astray: if you feed them, they proclaim 'Peace': if you do not, they prepare to wage war against you." Consequently, throughout the history of the church commentators have almost universally concluded that Paul in 5:3 is alluding to these OT warnings against false claims of peace (so, e.g., Marshall 1983: 134; Wanamaker 1990: 180; Williams 1992: 88; D. Martin 1995: 159; Malherbe 2000: 292, 303–5; Beale 2003: 142–43; Nicholl 2004: 54; Fee 2009: 189).[5] As further support that the apostle has these OT texts in view, some appeal to the birth-pangs metaphor found in the second half of the verse, a metaphor frequently employed by the prophets (for texts, see discussion below).

It is, of course, entirely feasible that Paul, who received extensive training in the OT and who in his other letters frequently quotes the Sacred Scriptures,

---

5. Malherbe (2000: 303–5) suggests that those advocating "peace and security" (5:3) are false prophets *within* the Thessalonian church and then connects their erroneous claim of "peace and security" with the problem of prophecy addressed in 5:19–20. Yet throughout the letter thus far, Paul's contrast has been between those *within* the church fellowship and "outsiders" (4:12), meaning their "fellow citizens" (2:14), "the rest" who have no hope (4:13) and are, spiritually speaking, "sleeping" (5:6). Here it is difficult to envision Paul as suddenly criticizing a group inside the church, such as false prophets.

is here echoing an OT prophetic warning. Nevertheless, there are at least five considerations that quickly place this conclusion in doubt. First, such a reference to the OT would be an anomaly in the Thessalonian correspondence, since nowhere else in 1 Thessalonians or 2 Thessalonians does Paul explicitly cite the Sacred Scriptures. Second, the Thessalonian congregation was a predominantly Gentile church, for whom the OT was a foreign and unknown text, and who thus would be less likely to hear a supposed reference to a prophetic warning. Third, Paul elsewhere never introduces an OT quotation or allusion with the ambiguous expression "whenever they say." Fourth, the use of the birth-pangs metaphor in the second half of the verse is not decisive since non-Christian writers in the ancient world also were familiar with this metaphor (Gempf 1994: 121). Fifth and most significant, the OT prophetic warnings deal only with the false claim of "peace" and say nothing about the false claim of "security," thereby differing in a significant way from Paul's joining of these two terms.

These problems with the traditional view, that Paul in 5:3 is echoing a prophetic warning, raise the possibility that the quoted phrase "peace and security" stems from a different source, quoting a popular theme or slogan of the imperial Roman propaganda machine (see esp. Weima 2012; also important are the earlier studies of Hendrix 1991: esp. 112–14; and vom Brocke 2001: 167–85; in recent times scholars have increasingly adopted this position: Donfried 1984; 1985: 344, 355n55; Koester 1997: 161–62; Holmes 1998: 167; Gaventa 1998: 70; Still 1999: 262–66; Green 2002: 233–34; Harrison 2002: 86–87; Oakes 2005: 317–18; Witherington 2006: 146–47; Furnish 2007: 108; S. Kim 2008: 43; Luckensmeyer 2009: 290–92). The Romans vigorously promoted themselves as those who secured not only "peace" but also, though to a lesser degree, "security" (either the Greek *asphaleia* or the Latin *securitas*). One of the various public media that Roman leaders used to promote themselves as providers of peace and security was the minting of coins, which would not only be disseminated throughout the empire but also, because of their value, endure over time; coins served as "portable billboards" by which Rome marketed itself. It is significant, then, that they widely issued coins bearing the image of the personified goddess "Peace" (*Pax*) or the word "peace" (*pax*) or the phrase "The peace of Augustus" (*pax Augusti*) on one side, with the image of various emperors on the other side; the same thing is true, though with less frequency, for the personified goddess "Security" (*Securitas*) and the word "security" (*securitas*), or the phrase "The Security of Augustis" (*Securitas Augusti*; for pictures and details, see Weima 2012: 333–41).

Monuments were another effective means by which the message of Roman peace and security was promulgated. For example, after his defeat of Marc Antony and Cleopatra, Octavian erected at the site of the battle a victory monument whose brief inscription, consisting of one-foot-high letters, highlighted his ability to provide universal peace: "after *peace* had been secured on land and sea" (restored translation proposed by Murray and Petsas 1989: 86). Another example is the *Ara Pacis* (Altar of Peace) built by the Roman Senate in 9 BC in honor of Augustus's successful military campaign to bring peace to the regions of Gaul and Spain. Although the altar itself as a whole conveys the message of peace and tranquility (Augustus in his *Res gestae* refers to it as "an altar of Augustan Peace"), this message is most clearly proclaimed in the eastern panel, which contains an image of the goddess *Pax*. The altar's image of peace and its propagandist message was spread well beyond Rome through the many travelers who visited the capital city, in the writings of ancient authors about this monument, and by the production of coins that display the Altar of Peace (*RIC* 1:461).

The most significant monuments for understanding the background of 5:3 are two memorials where the twin blessings of peace and security are found paired together, exactly as they are in Paul's First Letter to the Thessalonians. The first is a statue and accompanying description honoring the Roman military and political leader Pompey, discovered in Ilium, the ancient city of Troy. This monument was erected in the middle of the first century BC in gratitude to Pompey for preserving humankind from wars and pirates, thereby "restoring *peace and security* [*tēn eirēnēn kai tēn asphaleian*] on land and sea" (*SEG* 46:1562). The second monument to link the two blessings is the twin altars of *Pax Augusta* and *Securitas* discovered in Praeneste (Palestrina, Italy), whose citizens wanted to express their gratitude for the peace and security that they now enjoyed after years of civil war.

Roman peace and security was further promoted in official proclamations that were drafted, adopted, and inscribed for posterity. Key inscriptional evidence highlighting especially Roman peace can be seen, for example, in Augustus's funerary statement, the *Res gestae divi Augusti* (see esp. 12.2; 13.1–2; 25.1; 26.2–3); in a decree of the Asian League regarding changes to the provincial calendar (*OGIS* 458; copies of this decree have also been found around Asia Minor: *CIG* 3.3957; *CIL* 3.12240; 3.13651); and in a decree of Baetica (in Spain) celebrating the benefaction of Augustus (*ILS* 103). An important inscription where the twin benefits are again paired comes from Syria, where citizens thank the local Roman general in charge of the region, stating that he "has ruled over us in peace and given constant *peace and security* to travelers and to the people" (*OGIS* 613).

In addition to the numismatic, monumental, and inscriptional evidence cited above, the literary evidence is also compelling: many ancient authors, even those not particularly sympathetic to the empire, acknowledge the peace and security that Roman rule has provided. Literary sources where these two benefactions are linked include Josephus's recording of a decree from the citizens of Pergamum (*Ant.* 14.247–48), the first-century historian Velleius Paterculus's description of the Roman general Lucius Piso's battle against the Thracians (*History of Rome* 2.98.2) and of the start of Tiberius's reign (2.103.3–5), and the historian Tacitus (*Hist.* 2.12; 3.53; 4.74). The most striking parallel to Paul's phrase among the literary sources, however, is found in Plutarch's *Parallel Lives*, where he recounts Marc Antony's disastrous Persian campaign. Plutarch informs his readers that the Roman general was falsely promised safe passage by the enemy king Phraates, who "assured him of *peace and security*" (*eirēnēn kai asphaleian*; *Ant.* 40.4). This reference is remarkable because it not only exactly echoes the wording of Paul in 1 Thess. 5:3 but also possibly involves a deliberate use of irony by Plutarch: the very benefits that Roman rule was supposed to prove, peace and security, are instead offered to the Roman general Antony by his Parthian enemy. If so, this presupposes a widespread awareness of the phrase "peace and security" such that Plutarch, like the apostle Paul, could assume that his audience would pick up on such a satirical allusion.

Given the widespread nature of Roman imperial propaganda, the predominantly Gentile believers in Thessalonica would have immediately recognized in Paul's brief phrase, "peace and security," a clear allusion not to the warnings of the OT prophets, who spoke only about false claims of "peace," but the sloganeering of the Roman state and its claim of providing for its citizens the same two benefactions highlighted by the apostle. Paul's citation of such imperial propaganda is particularly appropriate for his Thessalonian readers in light of the close relationship between their city and Rome, as well as the financial and political benefits that this relationship offered (see further "A Favored Political Status" under "The City of Thessalonica" in the commentary introduction). It may well be that the "fellow citizens" (2:14) of the believers in Thessalonica responded to Christian claims about "the day of the Lord" (5:1) and the "coming wrath" (1:10; 5:9) by referring to Rome as the protector of their present peace and prosperity.

Paul, however, has a stern warning for all those who trust in the political power of Rome instead of in God: "then sudden destruction comes upon them." The noun *olethros* occurs only four times in the NT, always by Paul to refer to the eschatological destiny of the wicked (1 Cor. 5:5; 1 Thess. 5:3; 2 Thess. 1:9; 1 Tim. 6:9). That it is paired with ἀπώλεια (*apōleia*) in 1 Tim. 6:9 might suggest that the destruction that will fall upon the wicked is complete and results in their annihilation (see BDAG 127.2). In his Second Letter to the Thessalonians (1:9), however, Paul uses *olethros* to stress not the extermination of the wicked but their eternal separation from the presence of the Lord Jesus and his glory. Yet here in 5:3 the apostle does not spell out the precise sense of this term, and so one must be cautious about formulating an exact theological meaning for the word.

Paul continues to contrast the fate of the Thessalonian believers at Christ's return with that of their unbelieving neighbors by employing another metaphor. The day of the Lord will come not only like a thief in the night; the sudden destruction that will take place on that day will also fall upon the wicked "like birth pangs come upon [the verb *ephistatai* is implied from the preceding parallel clause] a pregnant woman." The symbolic or metaphorical use of labor pains is found with great frequency in the OT (Ps. 48:6; Isa. 13:8; 21:3; 26:17–18; 37:3; 42:13–14; 66:8; Jer. 4:31; 6:24; 8:21 [LXX only]; 22:23; 30:4–7; 48:41; 50:43 [27:43 LXX]; Hosea 13:13; Mic. 4:9; etc.) and the intertestamental literature (1 En. 62.4; 2 Esd. [4 Ezra] 4:40–43; 16:37–39; Sib. Or. 5.514; 1QH 11 [3].7–9; 13 [5].30–31; etc.). In these texts the images of labor pains function in differing, though related, ways (Gempf 1994): it can be an "intense" pain that makes clear the acuteness of suffering, a "productive" pain that leads to a positive outcome, a "helpless" pain that the sufferer cannot avoid, or a "cyclical" pain that once begun must run its course.

It is not clear, however, whether Paul's metaphorical use of labor pains fits any of these functions. On the one hand, the image comes after the adjective "sudden" (*aiphnidios* is emphasized by its location at the head of the sentence, separated from the main verb and subject) and also parallels the simile of a thief's surprise arrival at night found in the preceding verse, suggesting that Paul here in 5:3b is stressing the *unexpectedness* of the coming judgment—a use of this image that has no exact parallel in the OT. The objection against this view, "To what pregnant woman does labor come as a surprise?" (D. Martin 1995: 160), is not necessarily compelling, since Paul may be thinking about the unexpected timing of the onset of labor. On the other hand, the immediately following statement with its emphatic (note the double negative *ou mē*) claim that "they will certainly not escape" suggests that Paul may have in mind the *inevitableness* of the coming judgment—a use of this image that is paralleled in the OT. In light of the fluidity with which metaphors function, it is perhaps best to allow for both uses to be maintained.

The frightening picture of the day of the Lord, with its unexpected and inevitable destruction for all those who look to Rome instead of God for deliverance, reaches a climax with the emphatic statement: "and they will certainly not escape" (this emphasis is unfortunately missing in most translations). For the second time in this letter, Paul uses a grammatical construction found only two other times in his writings: the emphatic future negation (οὐ μή + aorist subjunctive), which is the strongest form of negation possible (see fuller discussion of this construction in comments on 4:15). In the preceding passage the apostle stresses that living believers would "certainly not precede" (4:15) deceased believers such that the latter group would be at a disadvantage at Christ's triumphal return; so also here, he underscores that those who buy into the Roman political propaganda "peace and security" will "certainly not escape" the destruction that accompanies the day of the Lord.

Before moving ahead to the new unit of verses 4–5, we need to clarify the role of verse 3 in Paul's overall argumentation in this passage, especially since there are two reasons why he could have simply omitted verse 3. First, the next verses (4–5) flesh out more fully the metaphor of darkness and light as well as the day-of-the-Lord theme—both first raised not in the immediately preceding verse (3) but in the earlier one (v. 2). Second, since the following verses (4–5) stress that the judgment described in verse 3 will *not* fall on the Thessalonian readers, why does Paul even raise this subject? As Nicholl (2004: 58) asks: "But why would Paul introduce the image [of sudden destruction from which there is certainly no escape] only to disavow [in vv. 4–5] its relevance to his readers?"[6]

6. Fee (2009: 190) similarly states: "One should note finally that the argument of this passage could have gotten by without the sentence that makes up our verse 3; . . . as Paul will go on to

The answer to this question must take seriously the primary function of the passage as a whole: to comfort the Thessalonian believers (v. 11). First and foremost, it is reassuring to an infant church overly anxious about their own status on the day of the Lord to be reminded that the judgment that is such a big part of that eschatological day will be experienced by others, not by them. Additionally, to readers who are encountering open hostility and opposition for their newfound faith (1 Thess. 2:2, 14–15; 3:1–5; 2 Thess. 1:4–7; see also 2 Cor. 8:1–2; Acts 17:5–7, 13), it also is comforting to be reminded of what they already accurately know, that the day of the Lord will be a time in which their opponents will be justly punished for their oppressive actions.[7]

2. Reason 1: You Are "Sons of Light/Day" (5:4–5)

In the opening unit of 5:1–3, Paul has not only introduced the new topic of the day of the Lord but also implicitly asserted that the believers in Thessalonica are sufficiently informed about this eschatological event that they need not fear its coming. Although the apostle opened this first unit by focusing on his Thessalonian readers ("*You* have no need for anything to be written to *you*. . . . For *you yourselves* accurately know that . . ."), he closed this unit by shifting attention to their unbelieving neighbors ("Whenever *they* say . . ."; "sudden destruction comes upon *them*, . . . and *they* will certainly not escape"). It is also in the latter part of the opening unit that the imagery and language about the day of the Lord becomes particularly threatening and ominous. All this serves to highlight the contrast formed with the second unit, verses 4–5, which provides the first reason why the Thessalonian Christians ought not to fear the coming day of the Lord: their status as "sons of light" and "sons of day."

The personal pronoun "you" (*hymeis*) in the opening and thus emphatic position, the contrastive particle *de* (but), and the vocative "brothers" all function to mark the transition to the second unit with its decidedly more positive and comforting message: "But you, brothers, are not in darkness with the result that the day would surprise you like a thief" (ὑμεῖς δέ, ἀδελφοί, οὐκ ἐστὲ ἐν σκότει ἵνα ἡ ἡμέρα ὑμᾶς ὡς κλέπτης καταλάβῃ, *hymeis de, adelphoi, ouk este en skotei hina hē hēmera hymas hōs kleptēs katalabē*).

5:4

The Christians in Thessalonica need not fear their fate on the day of the Lord because their status differs dramatically from that of their unbelieving neighbors. First, the Thessalonian believers are "brothers." The vocative *adelphoi* functions not only as a literary device marking the transition to the

---

say, believers are *not* going to be among those noted in this sentence. So the question remains, Why say it at all?"

7. A similar function appears in the thanksgiving of 2 Thessalonians, where in 1:5–10 Paul stresses the just character of God's judgments, thereby effectively comforting his persecuted readers with the reminder that they suffer not in vain but will ultimately be vindicated for their faith. This is to happen when God pays back their tormentors with the same torment that they have inflicted on the believers in Thessalonica and rewards these believers for their perseverance amid affliction (see further the comments on 2 Thess. 1:5–10).

second unit but also serves to remind the readers yet again (this marks the eleventh of fourteen occurrences of the vocative *adelphoi* in the letter: 1:4; 2:1, 9, 14, 17; 3:7; 4:1, 10b, 13; 5:1, 4, 12, 14, 25) of their status as members of a new social group—a family of "brothers" and "sisters" who will not experience judgment on the day of the Lord.

Second, the Thessalonian believers "are not in darkness." The use of the simple verb "to be" in the present tense here and twice more in the following verse suggests that Paul's concern in this second unit lies in reminding his readers of their current status. They have turned from idols to serve a living and true God (1:9) and thus enjoy the new and blessed status of being "brothers" who no longer are "in darkness." The earlier references in verse 2 to the "day" of the Lord and the thief's arrival "at night" lead Paul here and in the following verses to develop, in a metaphorical manner, the contrasts between not only "day" and "night" but also their corresponding qualities of "light" and "darkness." This metaphorical use of day/night and light/darkness to describe the human condition appears in many religious traditions, including the OT (e.g., Job 22:9–11; Pss. 27:1; 74:20; 82:5; 112:4; Prov. 4:18–19; Isa. 2:5; 5:20; 9:2; 60:19–20) and Jewish writings from the intertestamental period (e.g., 1 En. 41.8; 2 Esd. [4 Ezra] 14:20; T. Levi 19.1; T. Naph. 2.7–10; T. Benj. 5.3; 1QS 1.9–10; 3.13, 24–25; 1QM 1.1, 3). This usage undoubtedly influenced Paul's thinking, who elsewhere makes similar employment of this metaphor (Rom. 1:21; 2:19; 1 Cor. 4:5; 2 Cor. 4:6; 6:14; Eph. 4:18; 5:8–11; 6:12; Col. 1:13).

Some commentators wonder what specific aspect of the human condition this light/darkness and day/night metaphor has in view and consequently distinguish two possible meanings of the phrase "in darkness": (1) a moral state of sinfulness, or (2) a cognitive state of ignorance (see Wanamaker 1990: 181; Green 2002: 235). It is doubtful, however, that such a precise distinction is justified, given the fluid nature of a metaphor. Furthermore, there is an intimate link between morality and knowledge that also undermines such a distinction. Finally, both aspects fit well within the immediate context. On the one hand, the cognitive aspect is supported by the earlier statements of 5:1b–2 that Paul has no need to write to the Thessalonian believers about the day of the Lord, since they already "accurately know" about this subject. The cognitive aspect is also suggested by the following result clause of verse 4b, that this eschatological day will not "surprise" them, presumably because they are already well informed about its coming. On the other hand, the moral aspect is developed in the third unit of verses 6–8, with its exhortations to live vigilantly and sober-mindedly as sons of light/day. Therefore, both aspects are at work in Paul's use of this metaphor as he seeks to differentiate the current spiritual condition and future fate of the Thessalonian believers from that of their non-Christian neighbors. The "light" and "day" symbolize both the Thessalonians' state of righteousness and their knowledge about the imminent arrival of the day of the Lord, whereas "darkness" and "night" symbolize both the non-Christians' state of sinfulness and their ignorance about the impending judgment they will experience at Christ's return.

Paul spells out the comforting consequence of the readers' current status of not being "in darkness": "with the result [*hina* here does not have its more usual sense of purpose but instead expresses result: see BDAG 477.3; BDF §391.5] that the day would surprise you like a thief." The apostle is clearly looking back to his metaphor of verse 2, and thus "the day" is an abbreviated reference to "the day of the Lord," mentioned in that earlier verse. Similarly, his reference to "like a thief" (on the significance of the textual variant "thieves," see additional notes) also refers to that earlier metaphor, where he compared the coming of the day of the Lord to the unexpected arrival of a thief at night. Paul's point, therefore, is that his Thessalonian readers need not fear the day of the Lord, since their current status as "brothers" who are "not in darkness" means that this eschatological day of judgment would not "surprise" them (although the verb *katalambanō* often has the negative sense of "overtake" or "seize with hostile intent" [so BAGD 413], the metaphor of a thief's unexpected arrival more strongly suggests the sense of "surprise" [so BDAG 520]; see also texts cited by Malherbe 2000: 294). The Christians in Thessalonica may not know precisely when this event will take place, but they are adequately informed and prepared for this day of judgment.

Paul continues to stress the current status of the Thessalonians by extending the darkness metaphor introduced in the preceding verse: "For you are all sons of light and sons of day; we are not of night or of darkness" (πάντες γὰρ ὑμεῖς υἱοὶ φωτός ἐστε καὶ υἱοὶ ἡμέρας. Οὐκ ἐσμὲν νυκτὸς οὐδὲ σκότους, *pantes gar hymeis huioi phōtos este kai huioi hēmeras. Ouk esmen nyktos oude skotous*). **5:5**

The conjunction "for" (*gar*) links this verse with the preceding one, specifically with the earlier phrase "not in darkness." Whereas the previous verse stated the Thessalonians' condition in a negative fashion, here Paul makes clear (*gar* functions not as a marker of cause but of clarification: see BDAG 189.2) their current condition by positively claiming that "you are all sons of light and sons of day." Some commentators reject any significance in the adjective "all" (*pantes*), dismissing its presence as common within the apostle's letters (so, e.g., Best 1977: 210; Richard 1995: 253; Malherbe 2000: 294). The mere fact of its frequency, however, does not mean that "all" has no importance, particularly in this verse, where it is emphatically located at the head of the sentence. Its significance is suggested further by the eschatological fears facing the Thessalonian readers in this passage: will it be not just unbelievers but also Christians who are still alive on the day of the Lord and experience "destruction" (v. 3) and "wrath" (v. 9)? In such a context it would be comforting to hear that "you are *all* sons of light and sons of day" and that not one of them is excluded from this current status and the blessings that this status entails on the day of the Lord (see also the presence of "all" in 1:2; 4:10; 5:14, 26–27; 2 Thess. 1:3, 10; 3:18).[8]

---

8. Frame (1912: 184) goes too far in claiming that "πάντες [in 5:5] singles out the faint-hearted for special encouragement"—a specific group within the church who worry not only about their

The phrase "son/s of" (*huios/oi* with the genitive of a thing) is a Jewish expression[9] that denotes one or more persons who share in something or stand in a close relationship to something (in addition to its two occurrences here in 5:5 and once more in 2 Thess. 2:3, see Matt. 8:12; 9:15; 13:38; 23:15; Mark 2:19; 3:17; Luke 5:34; 10:6; 16:8; 20:34, 36; John 12:36; 17:12; Acts 3:25; 4:36; Eph. 2:2; 5:6; Col. 3:6). The specific phrase "sons of light" (in NT elsewhere only in Luke 16:8; John 12:36), therefore, identifies the Thessalonians as those who share in the quality of light—here a metaphorical reference to their moral status of righteousness and their knowledge about the imminent arrival of the day of the Lord (for a fuller explanation of this understanding, see discussion of "in darkness" in v. 4).

Paul does not stop, however, with the claim that the Thessalonians are "sons of light" but goes on to assert that they are also "sons of day." This latter phrase occurs nowhere else in the extant literature, so it may well be a creation of the apostle (see Focant 1990). Just as he uses "sons of light" to contrast the preceding reference to "darkness," so also he formulates the new phrase "sons of day" as a corollary to the just-mentioned "light" and as a contrast to the earlier reference to the thief coming "at night" (v. 2). A quick reading of this verse might suggest that these two parallel phrases stand in a synonymous relationship with each other and that no significant distinction exists between the readers' status as "sons of light" and "sons of day" (so Bruce 1982: 111; D. Martin 1995: 163). The second of these two phrases, however, has a "studied ambiguity" (Malherbe 2000: 294). On the one hand, "sons of day" is similar to "sons of light" in that it too refers metaphorically to the cognitive and consequent moral state of the Thessalonian believers. On the other hand, "sons of day" differs from the other phrase in that it also has an eschatological sense of referring to the coming day of the Lord. The eschatological sense of "sons of day" is strengthened by the close connection of this sentence to the previous verse (v. 4; the conjunction "for" opens v. 5), which mentions "the day"—an abbreviated but obvious reference to the "day of the Lord," discussed in verse 2. In the larger context, Paul's point is that the Thessalonians need not fear the day of the Lord with its accompanying "destruction" and "wrath" because they enjoy the status of being "sons of day"—that is, those who "belong to, are inheritors of, and are destined for the eschatological day to come" (Lövestam 1963: 53).

What has just been stated positively in the first half of verse 5 is now repeated negatively in the second half: "We are not of night or of darkness" (οὐκ ἐσμὲν νυκτὸς οὐδὲ σκότους, *ouk esmen nyktos oude skotous*). There is no need for any connecting particle to clarify the relationship of this second half

---

deceased fellow members (4:13–18) but also about their own salvation (5:1–11) and whom the apostle mentions in 5:14 ("Encourage the fainthearted").

9. Although Deissmann (1901: 161–66) cites several examples from Greek sources that have the phrase "sons of" (5:5) and appear to be free of Semitic influence, there is little doubt that Paul and the other NT writers are following Hebrew practice in their use of this expression (so BDAG 1025.2.β; BDF §162.6; MHT 3:207–8; Moule 1959: 174–75).

of the verse to the first half: connection is accomplished through the chiastic structure that Paul clearly intends to construct, in which the first and fourth elements (light/darkness) are contrasted with each other, as are the second and third (day/night):

A You are all sons of light
  B and sons of day.
  B′ We are not of night
A′ or of darkness.

Although this sentence adds nothing substantially new in terms of content but repeats in a negative fashion the point made already positively in the first half of the chiasm or verse, it has the rhetorical effect of emphasizing Paul's word of comfort to his Thessalonian readers: they ought not fear the day of the Lord, since they are "not of night or of darkness." The subtle but significant distinction observed above between "sons of light" and "sons of day" should also be followed for their corresponding negative counterparts "of night" and "of darkness." Another subtle but significant distinction is the change from the second-person "you" to the first-person "we," thereby signaling the upcoming shift to the third unit (vv. 6–8), where Paul tactfully includes himself and his cosenders in the subsequent exhortations (Frame 1912: 185; Johanson 1987: 133).

3. Result: Live Ready and Steady Lives (5:6–8)

In verses 4–5 Paul has emphasized the current status of the Thessalonian Christians as "sons of light/day," in sharp contrast to the status of their unbelieving neighbors, who are implicitly "of night/darkness" and will therefore certainly not escape destruction on the coming day of the Lord; now Paul proceeds in verses 6–8 to highlight the paraenetic, or exhortative, consequence of his readers' privileged status. That this third unit is intended to spell out the behavioral result of the status described in the second unit is clear from the particles *ara oun* (so then) that open verse 6 (see "Structure of the Passage" for a fuller discussion of these two particles), the logic of verse 8 ("*Since* we are of the day, *let us be* sober . . ."), and the typically Pauline shift from the indicative (who the readers *are*) to the imperative[10] (what the readers must now *do*).

Paul begins his exhortations of the third unit with an antithetical statement (not *x* but *y*) that develops further the cognitive and moral aspects implicit in the "light/darkness" and "day/night" metaphors of the previous verses: "So then, let us not sleep like the rest, but let us stay awake and be sober" (ἄρα οὖν μὴ καθεύδωμεν ὡς οἱ λοιποὶ ἀλλὰ γρηγορῶμεν καὶ νήφωμεν, *ara oun mē katheudōmen hōs hoi loipoi alla grēgorōmen kai nēphōmen*).

5:6

---

10. The hortatory subjunctive is used (three times in 5:6 and once in 5:8) instead of the imperative since there is no first-person imperative form in Greek.

The negative half of this antithetical statement employs a verb for sleeping (*katheudō*) that differs from the one (κοιμάω, *koimaō*) that Paul used three times in the preceding passage (4:13, 14, 15) and that he normally employs as a euphemism for death (see also 1 Cor. 7:39; 11:30; 15:6, 18, 20, 51). The apostle's choice of *katheudō* (rare for Paul: only in this passage and in a quote from an unknown hymn in Eph. 5:14) over *koimaō* likely stems from the fact that the former verb, although also used figuratively of death, has the additional metaphorical meaning of being spiritually apathetic—a meaning that Paul wants to invoke here in verse 6. The verb *katheudō*, therefore, has three possible connotations (BDAG 490), and all three occur in this passage: a literal reference to sleep (v. 7), a figurative reference to death (v. 10), and a second figurative reference to being spiritually indifferent (v. 6). The figurative use of this verb here in verse 6 follows quite naturally from the preceding material: it is not only a logical extension of the darkness/night metaphor of verses 4–5 (since sleep typically occurs in darkness and at night—a point that Paul will make explicitly in v. 7a) but is also implicit in the "thief" metaphor of verses 2 and 4 (since this metaphor brings to mind Jesus's words that, if the householder had known when the thief was coming, he would not have slept but would have stayed awake [Matt. 24:43]).

The comparative phrase "like the rest" (*hōs hoi loipoi*) recalls Paul's earlier exhortation that the Thessalonian believers should not grieve "like the rest who have no hope" (4:13). Just as the apostle used this phrase there to sharpen the distinction between the hopeful way the Thessalonian Christians ought to face death from the hopeless way of their unbelieving fellow citizens, so here he employs the identical phrase to contrast the conduct of these respective groups. The exhortation "Let us not sleep like the rest," therefore, is a continuing challenge[11] for the readers not to let their lives be characterized by the "sleep" of spiritual indifference like that of their unbelieving neighbors, whose ignorance about the coming day of the Lord and whose amoral conduct will ultimately result in a "sudden destruction," from which "they will certainly not escape."

The positive half of the antithetical statement consists of two verbs that also carry a metaphorical meaning. Paul's choice of the first verb, *grēgoreō*—a verb that occurs only four times in the apostle's letters (1 Cor. 16:13; Col. 4:2; 1 Thess. 5:6, 10)—is hardly surprising here since its literal meaning, "to stay awake," provides a perfect contrast with the literal meaning of *katheudō* (to sleep) used in the negative half of the verse. Like that verb, *grēgoreō* has two additional figurative meanings (BDAG 208): to be "in constant readiness, on the alert" and "to be alive." It is the former of these two metaphorical senses that Paul intends here, so that the command "Let us stay awake" refers to spiritual alertness and thus contrasts with the spiritual indifference countered by the command "Let us not sleep." The verb *grēgoreō* occurs elsewhere in

---

11. *Katheudōmen* (5:6), like the three other hortatory subjunctives in these verses, is in the present tense, thereby stressing the ongoing or continuous nature of this command.

the NT, frequently in connection with exhortations to be ready and prepared for Christ's return. It is found twice in Matt. 24:42–44, where Jesus exhorts his disciples to "stay awake, for you do not know on what day your Lord is coming." It occurs again in the parable of the wise and foolish virgins, which concludes with the command "Stay awake, therefore, for you know neither the day nor the hour" (25:13). It is used three times in a parable where the coming of the Son of Man is compared to a master who returns home unexpectedly and surprises his servants—a parable that ends with the one-word exhortation "Stay awake!" (Mark 13:32–37 par. Luke 12:37, 39 v.l.). The verb *grēgoreō* in an eschatological context also occurs a couple of times outside the Gospels (Rev. 3:2–3; 16:5).[12]

The second verb that Paul uses in the positive half of the antithetical statement is *nēphō*, which literally means "to be sober." In its six occurrences in the NT (1 Thess. 5:6, 8; 2 Tim. 4:5; 1 Pet. 1:13; 4:7; 5:8), however, *nēphō* never has this meaning but always possesses the metaphorical sense of being "well-balanced, self-controlled" (BDAG 672). The command "Let us be sober," therefore, is not concerned with prohibiting drunken behavior (though Paul did view literal sobriety as a required virtue of the Christian life: Rom. 13:13; 1 Cor. 5:11; 6:10; Eph. 5:18) but with the need for the Thessalonian believers to be "sober-minded." That *nēphō* occurs elsewhere in eschatological contexts (1 Pet. 4:7; probably also 2 Tim. 4:5 and 1 Pet. 5:8) and is paired with *grēgoreō*, which also typically occurs in eschatological contexts (see texts cited in the preceding paragraph) strongly suggests that the balance or self-control that Paul has in view here in the end-time context of 5:1–11 concerns not the Thessalonians' moral conduct in general but specifically their attitudes and practices connected with the coming day of the Lord. The first positive command to "stay awake" enjoins them to be alert and prepared for that day; the second positive command to "be sober" warns against any excessive concern or rash conduct in light of that eschatological event.[13] Put colloquially, the first command involves a call to be "ready" for the day of the Lord, while the second is to be "steady" in one's attitude and actions associated with that day. The latter exhortation would be particularly pertinent to the Thessalonian context argued for above—a significant fear on the Thessalonians' part

12. That *grēgoreō* (5:6) is not a common word in Paul's Letters but does occur frequently in many end-time sayings of Jesus is one of several indications (the "thief" metaphor in 5:2 and 5:4, the birth-pangs metaphor in 5:3, and some striking similarities between words and ideas found here and in Matt. 24) that has led some commentators to conclude that in this passage the apostle is borrowing from traditional eschatological material (see, e.g., Orchard 1938: 23–30; Best 1977: 211–12; Wanamaker 1990: 184; Wenham 1995: 303–14; Plevnik 1997: 117–19).

13. Contra the commentators who treat the two verbs *grēgoreō* and *nēphō* as synonyms, such as Hendriksen 1955: 125; Morris 1991: 157. The combination of these two verbs occurs elsewhere in the NT only in 1 Pet. 5:8. The motif of wakefulness is paired with sobriety by nonbiblical writers of that day (see texts cited by Lövestam 1963: 55; Malherbe 2000: 296), though a different verb for the concept of being awake is used (ἀγρυπνέω).

concerning not just deceased members (4:13–18) but also their own position at the parousia (5:1–11).[14]

5:7 Paul reminds the Thessalonian church of a "recognized fact" (Milligan 1908: 68) or "truism" (Wanamaker 1990: 184): "For those who sleep, sleep at night and those who get drunk,[15] get drunk at night" (οἳ γὰρ καθεύδοντες νυκτὸς καθεύδουσιν καὶ οἱ μεθυσκόμενοι νυκτὸς μεθύουσιν, *hoi gar katheudontes nyktos katheudousin kai hoi methyskomenoi nyktos methyousin*). This generalized observation about the typical timing of sleep and drunkenness functions to explain and thereby reinforce the exhortations of the previous verse, as is clear from the connecting particle "for" (*gar*). The apostle's readers lived in a culture that knew nothing about a "midnight" or "graveyard" shift and so would readily concur with his claim that those who sleep normally do so at night. They also lived in a culture that viewed drunkenness during the day as particularly contemptible conduct (Isa. 5:11; Eccles. 10:16; Acts 2:15; 2 Pet. 2:13; a similar attitude exists in nonbiblical sources: see Dobschütz 1909: 209n5) and so would also agree with his assertion that those who get drunk normally do so at night.

But while Paul is referring in a literal way to the human activities of "sleep" and "drunkenness" that typically take place "at night," his metaphorical uses of these words and their antonyms in the preceding verses show that the figurative sense is also very much in the apostle's mind.[16] The literal reference to "those who sleep" echoes the preceding exhortation "Let us not sleep," which metaphorically refers to the need to be alert and prepared, to be *ready* for the coming day of the Lord. Similarly, the literal reference to "those who get drunk" looks back to the previous command "Let us be sober," which metaphorically refers to the need to be well-balanced and self-controlled, to be *steady* in living while awaiting the eschatological day. So also the two literal references to "at night" (*nyktos* is a genitive of time, expressing the time within which something takes place; BDF §186.2) as the expected time for sleep and drunkenness recalls the metaphorical claim of verse 5 that the Thessalonians, along with the apostle and his fellow missionaries, are "not of night"; thus

---

14. A command to be steady is also particularly pertinent for the "idlers" in the Thessalonian church (5:14; see also 4:11; 2 Thess. 3:6–15), assuming that the cause of their slothful conduct is rooted in an excessive preoccupation with Christ's imminent return—a possible but by no means certain hypothesis.

15. The idea of drunkenness in 5:7 is expressed by two different but semantically linked verbs: the first participial form uses μεθύσκω (Eph. 5:18; Luke 12:45; John 2:10; Rev. 17:2), while the second indicative form has μεθύω (1 Cor. 11:21; Matt. 24:49). Although these verbs originally expressed a slight distinction from each other (the former to the act of becoming drunk, while the latter to the state of being drunk), no such nuance is likely intended here. Instead, like its preceding parallel clause οἱ καθεύδοντες καθεύδουσιν, so also οἱ μεθυσκόμενοι μεθύουσιν ought to be viewed simply as synonymous (note the alternate reading in Codex Vaticanus and Clement).

16. Best (1977: 212): "A metaphorical overtone clings to these facts of observation in Paul because he has been using 'night,' 'sleep,' and 'sobriety' metaphorically." Elias (1995: 198): "Evidently the thinking here flows back and forth between literal and metaphorical meanings, although the metaphorical level dominates."

the repeated phrase "at night" additionally sets the stage for the contrast that opens the following verse ("But since we are of the day . . ."). With his general observation about sleep and drunkenness in verse 7, therefore, Paul hardly "appears to interrupt the thought begun in v. 6" (Wanamaker 1990: 184, with a similar comment on 185) but instead in an effective manner recapitulates his exhortations given in the previous verse.

5:8

The close connection between the status of the Thessalonian Christians and the conduct that ought to result naturally from this status is once again highlighted by Paul: "But as for us, since we are of the day, let us be sober" (ἡμεῖς δὲ ἡμέρας ὄντες νήφωμεν, hēmeis de hēmeras ontes nēphōmen).

The placement of the personal pronoun hēmeis (we) in the emphatic opening position, along with the adversative particle de (but), functions to sharpen the contrast between the positive status of the apostle and his readers in comparison with the negative standing of their unbelieving neighbors, as described in the previous verse ("those who sleep" and "those who get drunk"). The distinction between these two groups is heightened further with the claim "We are of the day," since this contrasts with the double reference in the previous verse to "at night" (it also echoes Paul's claim in v. 5 that "we are all sons of light and sons of day"). The apostle, however, does not stop with stressing the distinctive status of believers but proceeds to link this status to their conduct: "*Since* we are of the day, *let us be sober*." Just as the particles *ara oun* (so then) in verse 6 connected the preceding description of believers' status as "sons of light and sons of day" with the following hortatory subjunctives, so here the causal participle *ontes* (since we are)[17] similarly ties the claim that "we are of the day" to the subsequent hortatory subjunctive "Let us be sober." As with its occurrence in verse 6, here too the verb *nēphō* does not literally refer to sobriety but has the metaphorical sense of being "well-balanced, self-controlled" (BDAG 672). The first half of verse 8, therefore, repeats and thus emphasizes the exhortation of verse 6: the Thessalonian readers ought not be excessively fearful about the day of the Lord or allow this eschatological event to cause them to act rashly, but they should instead be sober-minded in this matter, confident in their status as those who are "of the day."

Paul chooses not to repeat the other exhortation of verse 6: "Let us stay awake." This omission may be insignificant, especially if one treats the two commands "Let us stay awake" and "Let us be sober" as virtually synonymous. We have argued above, however, that the former exhortation enjoins believers to be alert and prepared for the day of the Lord (a call to be *ready*), while the latter exhortation warns against any excessive concern or rash conduct

---

17. Several translations treat the participle *ontes* as functioning adjectivally and thus render 5:8a as "We, who are of the day, should be sober" (so KJV, NKJV, GNT, NJB, NLT). However, the participle modifies the personal pronoun "we" and so, if it were functioning adjectivally, would normally have the definite article, which is missing here. It is better, therefore, to see the participle functioning adverbially with the following hortatory subjunctive and expressing cause: "*Since/because* we are of the day, let us be sober" (so NIV, ESV, HCSB, NASB, NRSV).

in light of that eschatological event (a call to be *steady*). If this distinction is justified, then the omission of the first command may be suggestive. For though there is a danger in reading too much from this nonoccurrence, it hints that the Thessalonians' problem (and thus Paul's concern) lies not with their indifference toward the day of the Lord, which needs to be corrected by a vigilant attitude of preparedness, but rather with their anxiety-filled fixation on this day, which needs to be corrected by a well-balanced attitude and self-controlled conduct.

Whereas the first half of verse 8 does not add anything new but repeats and so reinforces the exhortations of verse 6, the second half of this verse advances Paul's argument by presenting his readers with a new metaphor: "by putting on the breastplate of faith and love, and as a helmet the hope of salvation" (ἐνδυσάμενοι θώρακα πίστεως καὶ ἀγάπης καὶ περικεφαλαίαν ἐλπίδα σωτηρίας, *endysamenoi thōraka pisteōs kai agapēs kai perikephalaian elpida sōtērias*).

The precise function of verse 8b centers on whether the participle *endysamenoi* (putting on), which stands in an adverbial relationship with the hortatory subjunctive *nēphōmen* (let us be sober), expresses cause or means. The choice between these two options is partly determined by how one evaluates the aorist tense of the participle. One common view is that an aorist participle describes an action that *precedes* the main verb. Accordingly, the "putting on" of the armor precedes the action of being self-controlled and therefore provides the cause or reason for exercising self-control: "*Since* we put on, . . . let us be sober" (so, e.g., Wanamaker 1990: 185; Richard 1995: 254–55; Plevnik 1997: 112n52; Beale 2003: 150–51).[18] This understanding of the aorist participle, however, has long been questioned (BDF §339: "The notion of relative past time, however, is not at all necessarily inherent in the aorist participle"), and more recent studies have focused instead on word order: when the aorist participle occurs after the main verb, it describes an action *contemporary* with the main verb (Porter 1989: 381). Accordingly, the "putting on" of the armor occurs simultaneously with the action of being self-controlled and therefore provides the means by which believers exercise self-control: "Let us be sober *by* putting on . . ." (so, e.g., Findlay 1891: 114; Dobschütz 1909: 211; Frame 1912: 187; Malherbe 2000: 297; Green 2002: 240n193). The structure of this verse also works against a causal reading, since the grounds for the exhortation "let us be sober" have already been provided by the participial clause that precedes the main verb ("since we are of the day"). Therefore, although a causal reading remains possible, it is more probable that verse 8b is intended to provide the means by which believers can live sober-minded lives.

Another issue on which there exists some ambiguity is the logic of Paul's shift from the metaphor of day/night and light/darkness that has predominated

18. Gaventa (1998: 72) also argues for a causal reading, appealing not to grammar but to Paul's allusion in 5:8 to the OT, where the armor is worn by God. That Paul has significantly adapted his OT background (see discussion below), however, undermines the force of Gaventa's argument.

verses 4–8a to the new metaphor of military armor: why does the apostle suddenly introduce the martial metaphors of a breastplate and a helmet? Many commentators believe that the idea of vigilance expressed in the command of verse 6 ("let us stay awake") caused Paul to think of an armed sentry, who must stand ready and alert (so, e.g., Lightfoot 1904: 75; Frame 1912: 187; Best 1977: 215). But while this remains a plausible explanation, it would be more convincing if in verse 8 the apostle had repeated his use of the verb "let us stay awake," a command enjoining vigilance, rather than the verb "let us be sober," a command enjoining self-control and being well balanced. Perhaps the inherently fluid manner in which metaphors often function can account for the shift. Furthermore, elsewhere in Paul's writings is evidence that there existed in his mind at least a natural link between the metaphors of light/darkness and military armor (Rom. 13:12: "Let us put on the armor of light"; Eph. 6:11–12: "Put on the full armor of God, for our struggle is not against flesh and blood but against the powers of this dark world").

Happily, there is less uncertainty about the origin of this metaphor. The widespread presence of Roman soldiers meant that military armor could function quite easily as a metaphor for human ethical conduct, and certain philosophers and moralists of that day used it in exactly this way (see the texts cited by Malherbe 2000: 297–98). Paul's use of this metaphor, however, almost certainly stems from the OT, given the close verbal parallels between his words ("by putting on the breastplate of faith and love, and as a helmet the hope of salvation") and Isa. 59:17 ("He put on righteousness as a breastplate and placed a helmet of salvation on his head"; see also Wis. 5:17–18). The apostle's indebtedness to Isa. 59:17 explains why he doesn't add a third piece of armor to create a better parallel with the triad of faith, love, and hope. Nevertheless, Paul does adapt this OT text, such that it is no longer God who is the divine warrior but the human believer who wears the armor (a similar application to humans is found in a later rabbinic text: *b. B. Bat.* 9b).

Paul uses the image of armament several times in his letters (Rom. 13:12; 2 Cor. 6:7; 10:3–5; Eph. 6:11–17; Phil. 2:25; 2 Tim. 2:3–4), and these texts show how diverse he was in identifying the various virtues that the specific pieces of armor represented. That the apostle adapts this OT text so that it better suits the specific new context can be seen also here in verse 8b. Paul modifies the original text such that the breastplate no longer represents the single quality of "righteousness" but the two virtues of "faith and love." He also adds the third virtue of "hope" so that the original "helmet of salvation" now becomes "as a helmet the hope of salvation." The result of Paul's reapplication of this OT metaphor is that it now highlights the triad of faith, love, and hope, thereby echoing the same three virtues with which he opened the letter (1:3).

As with the earlier occurrence of this triad, there is less certainty on the meaning of the first two virtues than the third (see comment on 1:3). In light of what Paul has said thus far in the letter, however, "faith" almost certainly refers to their relationship with God (1:8, "your faith toward God")—a faith that Timothy was successfully sent to strengthen in the midst of trials (3:2,

5, 6, 7)—a faith that Paul nevertheless still seeks to complete (3:10). The "love" refers to the Thessalonians' relationship to their fellow Christians and all people (3:12; 4:9–10a) that manifests itself in a variety of particular ways (4:10b–12). The "hope" refers to the Thessalonians' confident expectation in Christ (1:3, "hope in our Lord Jesus Christ") and specifically in his second coming. That coming will mark the Thessalonians' rescue from the impending wrath (1:10), become an occasion for them to be Paul's crown of boasting before his Lord (2:19), put them in the presence of God the Father with hearts that are "blameless in holiness" (3:13), reunite them with their deceased loved ones and their Lord (4:13–18), and result in their "salvation" (5:8).

Although all three virtues of faith, love, and hope are important means for living sober-mindedly, several factors reveal that here the emphasis falls on the third and final element (Rigaux 1956: 569; Best 1977: 214; Malherbe 2000: 298; Furnish 2007: 110). First, faith and love are linked together with one part of armor (the breastplate), thereby leaving hope by itself to be connected with the remaining piece of armament (the helmet). Second, whereas faith and love are both expressed with a qualitative genitive ("breastplate *of* faith and *of* love"), hope is expressed with an accusative in apposition ("helmet, *that is,* hope"). Third, hope occurs in the final and climactic position (cf. 1 Cor. 13:13, where the order of the triad is changed but similarly places emphasis on the final element: "Now these three things remain: faith, hope, and love; but the greatest of these is love"). Fourth, hope is the only virtue that has an explicit object: "of salvation," meaning the salvation from wrath that Christ will bring about at his coming. Fifth, "the hope of *salvation*" is the only virtue among the three that Paul picks up in his subsequent grounding statement of verse 9 that "God did not destine us for wrath but for the obtaining of *salvation.*"[19] That Paul stresses hope is hardly surprising in light of the larger context of 5:1–11, where the concern of the Thessalonians lies in their own status at the judgment that will take place on the day of the Lord. The apostle asserts that they ought not to face this day with fear but with a sober-mindedness that is accomplished by clothing themselves with three virtues already in their possession, as they have amply demonstrated (1:3): their faith in God, their love for fellow believers as well as others, and especially their hope in the triumphant return of Christ, who will ensure that the day of the Lord is for them not a day of wrath but of salvation.

4. Reason 2: God Has Destined Us for Salvation and Life with Christ (5:9–10)

The beginning of a new paragraph here is somewhat artificial since the opening conjunction "for" (*hoti*) links verse 9 closely to what has just been written,

---

19. Nicholl (2004: 63): "The fact that Paul builds verses 9–10 upon this last piece of the armour . . . suggests that it has a special significance in this context. Paul apparently thinks that it is particularly urgent that the Thessalonians live with hope in their salvation at the parousia."

specifically the immediately preceding phrase "hope of salvation."[20] Nevertheless a discernible shift in Paul's argument takes place here as the apostle leaves behind his emphasis on the distinctive status of his Thessalonian readers (vv. 4–5) vis-à-vis unbelievers and the resulting conduct of that privileged status (vv. 6–8); here he proceeds to appeal to God's ultimate intention for them (the emphasis on divine purpose is expressed in the main verb *etheto*, the twofold repetition of the preposition *eis* in verse 9 ["destined not . . . for wrath, but for the obtaining of salvation"], and the *hina* clause in v. 10 ["in order that . . ."]). As such, verses 9–10 provide a second major reason in the overall argument of 5:1–11 as to *why* the Christians in Thessalonica ought not to fear the coming day of the Lord.

Paul makes his point by employing yet again an antithetical statement, thereby placing emphasis on the positive half, which is further stressed by the addition of a prepositional phrase: "For God did not destine us for wrath but for the obtaining of salvation through our Lord Jesus Christ" (ὅτι οὐκ ἔθετο ἡμᾶς ὁ θεὸς εἰς ὀργὴν ἀλλὰ εἰς περιποίησιν σωτηρίας διὰ τοῦ κυρίου ἡμῶν Ἰησοῦ Χριστοῦ, *hoti ouk etheto hēmas ho theos eis orgēn alla eis peripoiēsin sōtērias dia tou kyriou hēmōn Iēsou Christou*). **5:9**

The verb τίθημι (*tithēmi*) by itself simply means "he places," but the fuller construction *tithēmi tina eis ti* used here has the more specific sense of "consign someone to something" (BDAG 1004.5.β.b). That this fuller construction appears nowhere else in Paul's writings but does occur frequently in the LXX (e.g., Gen. 17:5; Ps. 65:9 [66:9 Eng.]; Jer. 25:12; Mic. 1:7; 4:7) and quotations of the OT in the NT (e.g., Acts 13:47; Rom. 4:17; 9:33) has led some to claim that this expression is a Hebraism (Ellicott 1880: 74; Rigaux 1956: 570; 1974–75: 333; Richard 1995: 255) and further that it is part of a preexisting formula that Paul here is borrowing (Harnisch 1973: 123–24; Rigaux 1974–75: 333; Havener 1981: 115–21). This overstates the evidence, however, since similar forms of this expression do occur elsewhere in the apostle's letters (Rom. 4:17; 1 Tim. 1:12; 2:7; 2 Tim. 1:11; note also how Paul utilizes κεῖμαι [*keimai*] as the passive of *tithēmi* in an identical construction in 1 Thess. 3:3 and Phil. 1:16).

Although the origin of the expression "God destined us to . . ." may be disputed, its function here in verse 9 is not: Paul uses this saying to highlight the notion of God's primary role in guaranteeing that on the day of the Lord the Thessalonian Christians will experience not wrath but salvation. This theme of the divine initiative has appeared several times throughout the letter thus far. The apostle opened the correspondence with this theme, grounding his thanksgiving on God's election of the believers in Thessalonica: "because we know, brothers loved by God, your election" (1:4). Paul's lengthy defense of his past conduct in their city includes the reminder that their holy lifestyle

---

20. Contra those who view 5:9 as providing another ground for the exhortation of 5:8 to be sober-minded (e.g., Wanamaker 1990: 186). That 5:9 instead has in view the closing words of the preceding verse is clear from the verbal link between "hope of *salvation*" and the purpose statement "not for wrath but for the obtaining of *salvation*."

is rooted ultimately not in anything that he did but in what God continues to do—"the one who is calling you into his own kingdom and glory" (2:12). God is in such control of the Thessalonians' lives that even the afflictions that they endure for their newfound faith are not the result of fate but part of his divine plan: "For you yourselves know that we are destined for this" (3:3). The challenge to live holy lives in sexual conduct is similarly rooted in God's election: "For God did not call us for impurity but in holiness" (4:7). The importance of this theme is also indicated in the letter closing, where Paul deviates from his normal pattern by adding to the peace benediction a word of assurance: "Faithful is the one calling you, who will indeed do it" (5:24). It is hardly surprising, therefore, that Paul seeks to allay his readers' concern about their own status on the coming day of the Lord by appealing yet again to their election. The doubt or fear that some believers had about the eschatological judgment ought to be replaced with the "hope of salvation," a hope that is rooted in the divine call of God, who "did not destine us for wrath but for the obtaining of salvation." Here, as in all the other occurrences of this theme in the letter, Paul merely asserts the divine call without offering any accompanying word of explanation. This suggests that such a topic must have been already well known to the apostle's readers from his original preaching ministry in their city.

In keeping with the antithetical structure of the verse, the result of God's choice for the lives of the Thessalonian Christians is stated first negatively and then positively: "not for wrath but for the obtaining of salvation." The reference to "wrath" looks back to this passage's earlier description of the judgment that awaits unbelievers, the "sudden destruction" from which "they will certainly not escape" (vv. 2–3). The mention of "wrath" also recalls the occurrence of this term in the opening section of the letter, where Paul gives thanks to God that his readers await Christ's glorious return from the heavens when he will rescue them "from the coming wrath" (1:10). The wrath to which the apostle is here referring, therefore, is not a divine judgment that has already been revealed and is now experienced in the present (see 2:16 and comments there) but the future punishment to be meted out at Christ's second coming. This notion of eschatological wrath originates from the OT, where "the day of the LORD" refers to a future time when God will come not only to vindicate the righteous but also, as the prophets emphasized even more, to punish the wicked (e.g., Isa. 2:1–4:6; Jer. 46:10; Ezek. 30:2–3; Obad. 15; Joel 1:15; 2:1, 11, 31–32; Amos 5:18–20; Zeph. 1:14–18; Zech. 14). Paul does not specify what this impending wrath entails (though see 2 Thess. 1:6–10 and 2:8–10), not because he is writing to believers for whom such a description would not apply (after all, a vivid description of God's wrath could function as a powerful warning for believers not to abandon their faith), but more likely because he does not want to exacerbate their already-existing fears about this eschatological day.

The apostle therefore quickly leaves behind the negative reference to wrath and moves on to the positive statement of God's activity in the Thessalonians' lives, the fact that he has destined them instead "for the obtaining of salvation." There is some uncertainty over the precise meaning of the verbal noun *peripoiēsis*, which occurs only five times in the NT but with three nuances (see BDAG 804): a passive sense in which the word refers to (1) "that which is acquired, *possessing*," or an active sense in which the term refers to either (2) the "experience of security, *preserving*" or (3) the "experience of an event of acquisition, *obtaining*." The second meaning can be quickly rejected, since it implies that the Thessalonians have already acquired salvation and that Paul comforts his readers by asserting that God has destined them to "preserve" what they currently possess (so, e.g., Rigaux 1956: 570–71; Holtz 1986: 228–29). That proposed meaning would contradict the overall context of the passage, which clearly has in view the future salvation that believers will experience on the day of the Lord. Furthermore, since the "wrath" is eschatological (1:10, "the coming wrath"), its counterpart, "salvation," must also refer to a future experience.

A choice between the first and third meanings is more difficult. This distinction between the passive sense of "possession" and the active sense of "obtaining" is not meaningless, since the latter rendering might imply that salvation involves human achievement rather than a divine gift. It is this concern that drives Lightfoot (1904: 76), for example, to adopt the passive sense of *peripoiēsin sōtērias*, taking the first term as signifying the act of God and the second term as being in apposition to the first, thereby spelling out what this act of God involves. Lightfoot defends his interpretation on the grounds that the noun *peripoiēsis* and its cognate verb function in the NT with the almost technical sense of referring to God's action of purchasing or setting apart for himself a chosen people, to the extent that this term is almost equivalent to the noun "election" (for a further defense of the passive sense, see also Rigaux 1956: 571; Holtz 1986: 571). The active sense of "obtaining," however, does not require an emphasis on human achievement to the exclusion of God's activity—a fact made clear in the following phrase, which states that salvation is "through our Lord Jesus Christ." And even though the passive sense of "possession" can be supported by the use of *peripoiēsis* in Eph. 1:14 and 1 Pet. 2:9 (see also certain LXX texts where this term similarly makes rare appearances: 2 Chron. 14:12; Hag. 2:9; Mal. 3:17), such a reading here in 5:9 must be rejected ultimately on grammatical grounds. For the genitive *sōtērias* that follows *peripoiēsis* is much more easily explained as functioning as the object of that preceding noun (so active sense) than as being in apposition to that term (so passive sense; see also the similar construction in 2 Thess. 2:14 and Heb. 10:39).

The positive half of the antithetical statement of 1 Thess. 5:9 is further emphasized with the addition of a prepositional phrase: "through our Lord Jesus Christ." This phrase modifies not the main verb, "he destined," but the immediately preceding expression, "for the obtaining of salvation." In this way Paul grounds the future salvation of his readers not in any human merit of his own or of theirs but in the work of Christ generally, and as the following words of verse 10a make clear, in his atoning death specifically. The mention of Christ's mediatory role (*dia*) in the same breath as the divine activity of God parallels the pattern found in the preceding passage, 4:13–18, where those believers who have already died will be brought back by God "through Jesus" (*dia tou Iēsou*, 4:14), that is, through the agency of Christ (see Malherbe 2000: 299). This also agrees with Paul's writing elsewhere, where the apostle employs the relatively fixed formula "through our Lord Jesus Christ" to highlight Christ's mediatory role in God's work of salvation (see Rom. 5:1, 11; 1 Cor. 15:57; Phil. 1:11; 1 Thess. 4:2; Titus 3:6).

5:10   The general reference to Christ's mediatory role ("through our Lord Jesus Christ") leads to a brief comment that states more precisely what that role entailed: "who died for us" (τοῦ ἀποθανόντος ὑπὲρ ἡμῶν, *tou apothanontos hyper hēmōn*).

In the context of discussing the future salvation of the Thessalonian Christians on the coming day of the Lord, it may seem surprising that Paul refers not to Christ's imminent return but to his past death. In the apostle's mind, however, their future obtaining of salvation instead of eschatological wrath is ultimately dependent on the previous work of Christ, "who died." Paul has referred to the death of Jesus two times in the letter thus far (2:15; 4:14; also implied in 1:10), but only here does he spell out its theological or soteriological significance: it is a death that is "for us" (*hyper hēmōn*).[21] As brief as the prepositional phrase "for us" may be, it clearly has in view the substitutionary character of Christ's death for believers' sins. This can be deduced from a number of instances elsewhere in Paul's Letters where he uses either exactly the same language ("to die for": Rom. 5:6; 14:15; 1 Cor. 15:3; 2 Cor. 5:15) or similar wording ("to give oneself for": Gal. 1:3–4; 2:20; Rom. 8:32; Eph. 5:25; 1 Tim. 2:6; Titus 2:14) and then often follows up these phrases with explicit statements about the atoning consequence of Christ's death. The absence of any such elaborating comments here in 1 Thess. 5:10 can be plausibly explained by the fact that the soteriological significance of Christ's death was part of Paul's mission-founding preaching in Thessalonica (see Acts 17:3) and was thus a topic with which the Thessalonian believers were already familiar such that it did not need to be stated overtly. That nothing is explicitly said about Christ's resurrection (but see 1:10 and 4:14) can be similarly explained and, in any case, is clearly inferred from the following claim that "together we may live with him."

In this section Paul's emphasis on God's ultimate intention for the Thessalonian believers, already expressed in the main verb *etheto* and the twofold repetition of the preposition *eis* in verse 9 ("destined not . . . *for* wrath, but *for* the obtaining of salvation"), is further stressed here in verse 10 with a *hina* clause, where the earlier reference to "salvation" is now defined as eternal life with Jesus: "in order that, whether we are awake or asleep, together we may

---

21. That some weighty MSS have περί in 5:10 instead of ὑπέρ has no impact on the interpretation of this phrase (see additional notes).

live with him" (ἵνα εἴτε γρηγορῶμεν εἴτε καθεύδωμεν ἅμα σὺν αὐτῷ ζήσωμεν, *hina eite grēgorōmen eite katheudōmen hama syn autō zēsōmen*).

The conjunction *hina* (in order that) leads the Thessalonian readers to expect a clause in the subjunctive mood that completes this purpose statement. But before Paul supplies such a statement, he inserts the correlative conditional clause "whether we are awake or asleep."[22] By means of this parenthetical addition, Paul skillfully reintroduces the concern of the preceding passage (4:13–18), the fate of *deceased* believers at Christ's return, and links it to the concern of the present passage (5:1–11), the fate of *living* believers at Christ's return. The apostle manages to bring these two concerns together by his careful choice of verbs in the correlative conditional clause: *grēgorōmen* and *katheudōmen*. Although literally meaning "to stay awake" and "to sleep," here these verbs have the figurative sense of "to be alive" (BDAG 208) and "to be dead" (BDAG 490; A. Oepke, *TDNT* 3:436). Consequently, the first half of the correlative conditional clause ("whether we are awake . . .") refers to believers who are still alive and so has in view the fate of living believers at Christ's return (5:1–11), while the second half of this clause (". . . or asleep") refers to believers who have already died and so has in view the fate of deceased believers at Christ's return (4:13–18). In this way Paul comforts his Thessalonian readers with the fact that *all* members of their church—both those who will still be alive on the day of the Lord and those who have already passed away—will not face "wrath" but "salvation": eternal life with the risen and returning Lord.

A few have challenged this interpretation (Kaye 1975: 51–52n27; Edgar 1979; Hodges 1982: 75–78; Lautenschlager 1990; D. Martin 1995: 168–69; Heil 2000; Luckensmeyer 2009: 306–13, 316–17) on the following grounds. First, these same two verbs occur earlier in the passage but with different meanings, and they ought to have the same meanings here: *grēgoreō* was used in verse 6 with the figurative sense of being "ready, alert," while *katheudō* was used in verse 6 with the figurative sense of being "spiritually indifferent." Second, if Paul had intended to refer to Christians who had died, he would not have used *katheudō*, which, it is claimed, never or at best rarely is used to refer to death, but *koimaō*, since this latter verb of "sleep" functions more commonly as a metaphor for death and was used three times as such in the preceding passage (4:13, 14, 15). Third, the other verb in the word pair, *grēgoreō* (to be awake), nowhere else has the metaphorical meaning of "to be alive." For these and other less weighty reasons it is then concluded that the two contrasting states referred to in the correlative conditional clause "whether we are awake

---

22. The *eite . . . eite* construction of 4:10 (see BDAG 279.6.o; BDF §§446; 454.3) occurs elsewhere in the apostle's letters, either in a verbal clause, as here (1 Cor. 12:26; 2 Cor. 1:6), or in a nonverbal clause (Rom. 12:6–8; 1 Cor. 3:22; 8:5; 2 Cor. 5:10; see also 1 Cor. 14:27). In a verbal clause, the indicative mood normally occurs (so 1 Cor. 12:26; 2 Cor. 1:6). The use of the subjunctive with this construction here in 1 Thess. 5:10 is usually explained as the result of attraction to the following subjunctive ζήσωμεν (e.g., Eadie 1877: 191; Ellicott 1880: 75; Lightfoot 1904: 77; Milligan 1908: 70).

or asleep" are not that of being "alive or dead" but that of being "vigilant or spiritually indifferent."

The obvious difficulty with this alternate interpretation, of course, is that it contradicts the sharp distinction that Paul has made earlier in the passage (vv. 4–5) between the status of believers as "sons of light/day" and that of non-Christians ("the rest") who are "of darkness/night." As Bruce (1982: 114) pointedly puts it: "It is ludicrous to suppose that the writers mean, 'Whether you live like sons of light or like sons of darkness, it will make little difference: you will be all right in the end.'" Similarly, it is difficult if not impossible to believe that the apostle would earlier exhort the Thessalonians to be ready and steady for the coming day of the Lord (v. 6) and then a few verses later undermine this command by stating that "whether we watch or fail to watch, we shall live together with him" (the translation proposed by Edgar 1979: 349).

In addition to the context, which ought to be decisive in determining the meaning of Paul's words here in verse 10b, there are also responses to the linguistic arguments forwarded by the minority challenging view. Although the use of *katheudō* as a metaphor for death is admittedly not common, there are parallels in the LXX (Ps. 87:6 [88:5 Eng.]; Dan. 12:2) and possibly other NT writers (Matt. 9:24; Mark 5:39; Luke 8:52) as well as extrabiblical literature (Aeschylus, *Cho.* 906; Plato, *Apol.* 40C–D).[23] Also, that Paul employs *katheudō* two times in verses 6–7 with two different senses (it has the metaphorical meaning of "spiritual indifference" in v. 6 but the literal meaning of "sleep" in v. 7) suggests that it would not be either unusual or impossible for the apostle to use this same verb with yet a third sense (i.e., to be dead) in verse 10 (so BDAG 490.3). As for the other verb in the word pair, there are a couple of examples where the root *grēgor-*, either in its verbal (Plato, *Symp.* 203A) or adverbial (Philo, *Dreams* 1.150, "sometimes alive and awake [ἐγρηγορώς, *egrēgorōs*], sometimes dead or asleep") form, does have the metaphorical meaning of "to be alive." Paul's use of *grēgoreō* and *katheudō* in 1 Thess. 5:10 involves a clever appropriation of vocabulary used in verses 6–7, but now with the new meaning of being alive or dead such that it recalls his earlier discussion in 4:13–18 on the fate of deceased believers at Christ's return. This varied use also seems clear from the reappearance of the marker of association *hama* (together; BDAG 49). As with its presence in 4:17, so here too in 5:10 the word "together" places emphasis on the equal participation of both living and deceased believers in the salvation to be received at Christ's return.[24]

Paul now completes the purpose statement that was introduced by the conjunction *hina* but then interrupted by the strategic insertion of the correlative

---

23. The concession on this point by Luckensmeyer (2009: 306), who ultimately adopts the alternative view that Paul with the verb "to be asleep" (5:10) is referring metaphorically not to death but to lack of vigilance, is significant: "First, the ridiculous claim that καθεύδειν is rarely or never used to refer to death, needs to be put away once and for all."

24. The marker of association *hama* (in 5:10) does not refer to the union of believers with Christ (which is expressed by the phrase "with him") but the union of believers with one another. For a fuller discussion of this marker, see comments on 4:17.

conditional clause. God has destined the Thessalonian Christians not to obtain wrath but salvation through the substitutionary death of Jesus—a death that paradoxically results in the life of the believer: "in order that . . . together we may live with him." As Best (1977: 219) states, it is difficult to understand this paradox of moving from the death of Jesus to the life of the believer without assuming the resurrection of Christ and the participation of believers in both his death and resurrection as the grounds of their new life in the Spirit—ideas clearly expounded at other places in his letters (see, e.g., Rom. 6:3–6; 8:9–11; 14:9; 1 Cor. 15:20–22; Gal. 2:20; Phil. 3:10–11; Col. 2:12–14; 1 Thess. 4:14). In this passage Paul's concern, however, is not with providing a theological explanation of how all this works. Instead, as the parallel with the preceding passage of 4:13–18 suggests, the apostle's concern is with providing comfort. He concluded the previous section by reassuring his readers that both deceased (4:13, 14, 15, "those who are/have fallen asleep"; 4:16, "the dead in Christ") and living (4:15, 17, "we who are alive, who are left") believers will participate evenly (4:17, "together with them") in the gift of eternal life with Christ at his return (4:17, "And so we will always be with the Lord"). Similarly he ends this section by comforting the Thessalonians that both living ("whether we are awake") and deceased ("or asleep") believers will share equally ("together") the blessing of eternal life with the returning Lord ("we may live with him").

Some have given the aorist *zēsōmen* the inceptive meaning of "begin to live" or "enter into life" (Best 1977: 219; Richard 1995: 256; Witherington 2006: 151n117) and so understand Paul to be describing the start of a new life with Christ experienced already in the present, as he does in 2 Cor. 5:14–15. This in turn might suggest that not just living ("whether we are awake") but also deceased ("or asleep") believers currently enjoy this life with Christ such that this verse becomes a proof text for the intermediate state: even though believers are dead, they nevertheless are presently alive with Jesus (see Green 2002: 244). But even though Paul elsewhere implies the continued existence of believers with Jesus after death and before their resurrection (Rom. 8:38–39; 2 Cor. 5:8; Phil. 1:21, 23), this idea is not in view here. Instead, in light of the heavy eschatological context, as well as the parallel with 4:17, the purpose clause "together we may live with him" clearly looks to the future: the resurrected (for those who have died) or transformed (for those who are still alive) life of believers with Jesus when he comes again.

5. Conclusion: Comfort One Another (5:11)

As the eternal presence of both deceased and living believers with the returning Lord (4:17) brought the preceding passage to an eschatological climax that led naturally to the concluding command "Therefore comfort one another with these words" (4:18), so also in the present passage the future resurrected or transformed life of believers with Christ leads to a closing exhortation that is similarly worded but also somewhat expanded: "Therefore comfort one another and build each other up, one-on-one, just as you are indeed doing"

5:11

(διὸ παρακαλεῖτε ἀλλήλους καὶ οἰκοδομεῖτε εἰς τὸν ἕνα καθὼς καὶ ποιεῖτε, *dio para-kaleite allēlous kai oikodomeite heis ton hena kathōs kai poeiete*).

The inferential conjunction *dio* (therefore), though different from the particle *hōste* used to introduce the closing command of 4:18, has the same function as that earlier term: it highlights the logical connection that exists between the preceding material and what follows. The two closing commands of 5:11 ("Comfort one another and build each other up"), therefore, look back to the claims made by Paul in 5:1–10. Although some downplay such a link (e.g., Wanamaker 1990: 189: "The conjunction διό is inferential, but v. 11 is certainly not a necessary or even obviously logical inference from what immediately precedes it"), this logical connection between 5:11 and the material of 5:1–10 is supported by the normal sense of the inferential conjunction *dio*, the parallel with 4:18, and the larger context. This means that the command "Comfort one another" looks back to Paul's two reasons for asserting that the Thessalonian believers who are still alive at Christ's return need not fear the day of the Lord: first, their status as "sons of light/day" (vv. 4–5) and, second, their election by God to obtain salvation and eternal life with Christ (vv. 9–10). Although the apostle does not here add to this command the prepositional phrase "with these words," there are no compelling grounds to assume that "Comfort one another" in 5:11 does not recall the specific reasons given in the preceding verses, just as "Comfort one another with these words" in 4:18 refers back to the arguments presented in the earlier verses of that passage.

Paul does, however, add something else to his stereotyped closing command "Comfort one another" (for a discussion of the verb *parakaleō*, see comments on 4:18), a second command: "and build each other up." The verb *oikodomeō* literally refers to the construction of a building, but in the apostle's writings this verb (Rom. 15:20; 1 Cor. 8:1; 10:23; 14:4, 17; Eph. 4:12, 16), along with its cognate noun (Rom. 14:19; 15:2; 1 Cor. 14:3, 5, 12, 26; 2 Cor. 12:19; 13:10; Eph. 4:12, 29), is always used figuratively of spiritual edification: "strengthen, build up, make more able" (BDAG 696.3). Although this figurative meaning of *oikodomeō* can be found in ancient Greek literature, Paul is more likely influenced by the OT, especially Jeremiah's repeated promise that God will "build up" Israel (Jer. 24:6; 38:4 [31:4 Eng.]; 40:7 [33:7 Eng.]; 49:10 [42:10 Eng.]; see also Ps. 27:5 [28:5 Eng.]) as well as its neighboring nations (Jer. 12:16). The term *oikodomeō* plays a particularly important role in Paul's Letters and his overall theology, describing not only his own apostolic responsibility to build up the church (2 Cor. 10:8; 12:19; 13:10) but also, as here in 1 Thess. 5:11, the responsibility of all members of the church to build each other up (see O. Michel, *TDNT* 5:140).

The point that all members share equally this responsibility for spiritual edification is stressed by the elliptical phrase "one-on-one" (*heis ton hena*). There is some disagreement about both the origin and meaning of this phrase. It is commonly claimed to be a Semitic expression that functions synonymously with "one another" (*allēlous*), a term that Paul has just used in the sentence and thus wishes to avoid using again (BDF §247.4; MHT 3:187; BDAG 293.5;

Moule 1959: 120; Fee 2009: 199n58: "an instance of 'elegant variation' [from the term *allēlous*], where there is no difference in meaning at all"). Both conclusions about its origin and meaning, however, may be challenged. That the same (T. Job 27.3) or similar (Theocritus, *Id.* 22, 65, *heis heni*; Plato, *Laws* 1.626C, *heis pros hena*; Herodotus 4.50, *hen pros hen*) forms of this expression appear elsewhere undermines its supposed Semitic origin. More important, that earlier in the letter the apostle stresses the individualistic nature of his dealing with the Thessalonian believers (2:11, "how we dealt with each one of you") suggests that a similar emphasis is also intended here (Richard 1995: 257; Malherbe 2000: 301; Witherington 2006: 153–54).

Paul does not explicitly state what teachings or truths the Thessalonian Christians are to use in mutually building each other up. The context suggests that the apostle primarily has in view the claims he presented in the previous verses, 5:1–10. Just as the first closing command calls on the Thessalonian believers to comfort one another with the message of their privileged status as "sons of light/day" (vv. 4–5) and their election by God to obtain salvation and eternal life with Christ (vv. 9–10), so also the second closing command demands that they build each other up with these same truths and that they do so in an intentionally personal ("one-on-one") manner. The second command, however, also looks ahead to the next section of the letter, where the general call to mutual edification is spelled out in terms of their conduct toward church leaders (5:12–13) and fellow church members (5:14–15). Although overstating the case, Malherbe (2000: 300) is ultimately correct in claiming that "this verse [5:11] could as well be treated with vv. 12–22, as the introduction to that section" (also Fee 2009: 184: this verse serves "as a kind of 'lead-in' to the series of exhortations with which the letter concludes"). The second command to "build each other up," therefore, has a transitional function: it first and foremost recalls the teaching of 5:1–10, yet it also sets the stage for the following exhortations of 5:12–22. This transitional function likely explains why Paul adds this command to the stereotyped expression "Comfort one another" (cf. 4:18; 5:11).

The section of 5:1–11 closes with a *kathōs* clause acknowledging that the Thessalonians are already engaged in mutual comfort and edification: "just as you are indeed doing" (*kathōs kai poeiete*). Paul has previously provided a similar affirmation in his introductory appeal that the readers conduct themselves in a manner that pleases God (4:1, "just as you are indeed walking") and in his discussion of love for one another (4:10, "For indeed you are doing it"). Just as these two earlier statements of affirmation do not mean that Paul has no concerns about the Thessalonian church or that he is not addressing concrete problems (see comments on 4:1 and 4:10), so also it would be wrong to conclude from this third statement of affirmation that the apostle is not dealing with an actual issue facing the congregation. Throughout the whole of 4:1–5:22, the apostle is fulfilling his stated desire to "complete the things that are lacking in your faith" (3:10), and this includes the Thessalonians' fear about the fate of living believers on the day of the Lord (5:1–11). But while there is a need for further comfort and building up within the body of believ-ers on this specific subject, such mutual edification was already taking place in the church, and Paul diplomatically acknowledges this fact.

Additional Notes

5:3. The absence of a transitional particle prompted a number of copyists to clarify the relationship of this verse to the preceding one: some (Ψ 0278 𝔐 a vg) viewed 5:3 as explanatory and so added γάρ (*gar*, for); others (ℵ² B D 0226 6 104 1505 1739 1881 2464 *pc* sy^h) saw 5:3 as contrastive and so added δέ (*de*, but). Although the context reveals the latter interpretation to be correct, the MS evidence supports the omission of any particle (so ℵ* A F G 33 it vg^ms sy^p Ir^lat Tert). Furthermore, the omission of any article best explains the arising of the two alternative readings, since, as Fee (2009: 185n8) rightly observes, "One would be hard pressed to account for either an omission or a change to the alternative conjunction."

5:3. Instead of the widely attested ἐφίσταται (comes upon), frequent in the LXX but found only here and in 2 Tim. 4:2, 6 in the NT, a few MSS have the alternate form ἐπίσταται (B 0226^vid lat; Ir^lat) or the different verb φανήσεται (will appear: F G b d; Aug^pt).

5:4. A couple of important uncials (A B), along with some Egyptian versions (bo^pt), replace the nominative singular κλέπτης (thief) with the accusative plural κλέπτας (thieves). This alternate reading slightly changes the sense of the verse. The nominative-singular "thief" modifies "the day" and so highlights the unexpected coming of the day of the Lord. The accusative plural "thieves," however, modifies the plural pronoun "you," with the result that the Thessalonian readers are likened to robbers who are unexpectedly caught by the morning light of a new day. Some commentators adopt the plural form on the grounds that it is (1) the more difficult reading and (2) more likely that a copyist changed the original plural to the singular (to agree with the form found in v. 2) than the converse (so Lightfoot 1904: 73–74; also Milligan 1908: 66; Frame 1912: 184; Förster 1916: 169–77; Neil 1950: 112). The textual support for the singular reading, however, is decidedly stronger with respect to number of witnesses, dates, and geographic distribution. It is also difficult to believe that Paul would use the thief metaphor differently here in 5:4 than what he had just used it for a mere two verses earlier in 5:2. Furthermore, the plural reading "appears to have arisen from scribal conformation to the preceding ὑμᾶς" (B. Metzger 1994: 565).

5:5. Some scribes found Paul's shift from the second-person ἐστε (you are) in the first half of the verse to the first-person ἐσμεν (we are) in the second half awkward and consequently tried to "correct" this reading (D* F G it vg^mss sy^p sa; Ambst). The reading "we are," however, is better attested, is the more difficult reading, and also functions well as a transition to Paul's inclusive use of the first-person plural in the following verses (vv. 5–10).

5:6. Although a number of MSS (ℵ² D F G [Ψ] 𝔐 it vg^cl sy^h co; Ambst) add the conjunction καί between ὡς and οἱ λοιποί, this reading ought to be rejected on both external and internal grounds. First, the older and more reliable witnesses support its omission (𝔓^46vid ℵ* A B 33 1739 1881 *pc* b f vg^st sy^p; Clement). Second, the conjunction was almost certainly added to assimilate this reading with that found in 4:13.

5:9. Instead of the fuller expression τοῦ κυρίου ἡμῶν Ἰησοῦ Χριστοῦ (our Lord Jesus Christ), a few MSS (𝔓^30vid B b m* sa vg^mss), two of them quite early, omit the last name, probably due to homoeoteleuton (similar ending).

5:10. That some weighty MSS (ℵ* B 33) have περί in 5:10 instead of the more widely attested ὑπέρ (so 𝔓³⁰ ℵ² A D F G Ψ 𝔐) has no impact on the interpretation of this phrase, since these two prepositions are likely synonymous. That both prepositions convey the same meaning is suggested by their presence together in Eph. 6:18–19 and Heb. 5:1, 3 (so Moule 1959: 63) as well as their frequent appearance as a textual variant for each other.

5:10. The presence of the present subjunctive ζῶμεν (D* E) and the future indicative ζήσομεν (A 2495* pc) in a few MSS may be due to the ambiguity of the widely attested aorist subjunctive ζήσωμεν as to whether this form refers to a present or future life with Christ. See further the comment on 5:10.

D. Exhortations on Congregational Life and Worship (5:12–22)

In the second half of the letter (4:1–5:22), Paul's overall concern is to "complete the things that are lacking in your faith" (3:10), that is, to address the issues facing the Thessalonian church that have been reported to him from the recently returned Timothy (3:6). These issues involve the congregation's ability to be holy in their sexual conduct; their practice of *philadelphia*, or mutual love; and their understanding and consequent comfort regarding the return of Christ—three subjects foreshadowed in the transitional prayer of 3:12–13 and subsequently taken up in detail in 4:3–8; 4:9–12; and 4:13–5:11, respectively. There still remain, however, additional matters where Paul finds the faith of the Thessalonians to be deficient and so, before bringing the body of the letter to a close, the apostle raises a variety of issues concerning their congregational life and worship. The commands in 5:12–22, therefore, despite their seemingly generic character, address specific issues at work in the Thessalonian church.

Although these final exhortations address a variety of topics related to congregational life and worship, they are not written in a haphazard manner but rather have been deliberately and skillfully arranged. The first section (vv. 12–13) exhorts the Thessalonian believers to respect their congregational leaders who work hard among them, rule over them, and admonish them. The second section (vv. 14–15) goes beyond the church's attitude and conduct toward its leaders to how it ought to minister to *all* congregational members, even though three specific groups of troubled believers are identified. The third section (vv. 16–18) commands the activities of rejoicing, praying, and giving thanks, which are an essential part of doing God's will in congregational worship. The fourth and final section (vv. 19–22) deals with another activity of communal worship that had become an issue within the Thessalonian congregation: prophecy. Here Paul strikes a careful balance between, on the one hand, strongly affirming the importance of prophecy, and on the other hand, commanding the church not naively to accept these Spirit-inspired utterances but to test them.

Literary Analysis

Character of the Passage

Although the entire second half of 1 Thessalonians (4:1–5:22) is best identified as paraenesis, or "exhortation" (for a general introduction to this formal category, see comments on 4:1–12), this literary category is most clearly illustrated in 5:12–22.

For here Paul issues no less than fifteen imperatives as well as an appeal formula (vv. 12–13a) whose two dependent infinitives also have an imperatival force. In fact, other than the explanatory comment of verse 18b ("For this is the will of God in Christ Jesus for you"), every one of the remaining clauses in the passage involves some kind of command.

But 5:12–22 differs from the rest of the letter not just because of its preponderance of imperatives and obvious exhortative character but also because of its other stylistic characteristics. This section is striking for the brevity of its many commands (twelve of the fifteen imperatival clauses consist of only two or three words each), not typical of the lengthy, dependent clauses found throughout the rest of the letter or of Paul's style in general. Another remarkable feature of this passage is the virtual absence of any connecting particles that indicate the syntactical relationship between all these tersely worded commands (the technical term for this is asyndeton). These unique characteristics of 5:12–22 have wrongly led some to conclude that this passage was not written with the kind of deliberate, logical argumentation found in the rest of the letter but instead consists of "a series of largely unrelated exhortations" (Best 1977: 223) presented in a loose and haphazard manner (for a refutation of this view, see "Structure of the Passage" below).

Another feature of 5:12–22, the seemingly generic character of Paul's commands in this passage, has similarly led to an unwarranted conclusion. Many commentators believe that the apostle here is borrowing from traditional paraenetic material and thus presume that the exhortations of 5:12–22 do not address specific issues at work in the Thessalonian congregation. Moore (1969: 79), for example, states: "There is no need to see behind each injunction a special situation supposedly requiring particular guidance; much of the advice and encouragement is of a general nature such as Paul would regard right and necessary for any church." Further support for this position is sometimes found in the similarities between Paul's commands here to the Thessalonian church and his commands to the congregations in Rome (see Selwyn 1947: 365–66; Best 1977: 223; Wanamaker 1990: 191):[1]

1 Thessalonians 5:12–22	Romans 12:9–18
Be at peace among yourselves. (13b)	*Be at peace* with all. (18)
Do not repay evil for evil. (15a)	*Do not repay evil for evil*. (17a)
Pursue the *good* . . . to all. (15b)	Consider the noble in sight of all. (17b)
Rejoice always. (16)	*Rejoice* in hope. (12a)
Pray continually. (17)	Persevere in *prayer*. (12c)
Don't quench the *Spirit*. (19)	Be fervent in the *Spirit*. (11b)
Hold fast to the *good*. (21b)	Cling to the *good*. (9c)
Abstain from every kind of *evil*. (22)	Hate what is *evil*. (9b)

The similarities between these two passages, however, are not as great as they may initially appear in this chart (see Marshall 1983: 146; Richard 1995: 273). The order of the commands is generally reversed and, though the same topics are addressed, the wording of these exhortations differs significantly. Even the verbal parallels are somewhat misleading since similar words take on particularized meanings in their

1. Comparative charts of the parallels between 1 Thess. 5 and Rom. 12 are given by Marshall 1983: 145–46; Wanamaker 1990: 191; and Richard 1995: 273. The chart of Richard, largely followed here, is the most helpful because it indicates not just parallels in content/subject matter but also the verbal parallels (italicized).

respective contexts. For instance, the commands to "hold fast to the good" and "hold yourselves away from every kind of evil" (1 Thess. 5:21b–22) in the Thessalonian context refer specifically to the testing of prophecy, whereas the commands to "hate what is evil" and "cling to the good" (Rom. 12:9b–c) in the Roman context refer to human conduct in general. Finally, the apparent similarities between the two passages should not overshadow the clear differences between them. In 1 Thess. 5 the subjects of respecting congregational leaders (vv. 12–13b); ministering to the rebellious idlers, the fainthearted, and the spiritually weak (v. 14); and testing prophecy (vv. 19–22)—these have no parallels in Rom. 12.

Therefore, even if some of the exhortations in 1 Thess. 5:12–22 are derived from traditional material of general applicability, Paul shapes this material to suit the specific needs of the Thessalonian congregation and supplements it with new material also aimed at their particular problems. This scenario is an entirely plausible one, as Marshall (1983: 146) points out: "The situation is the very natural one of a pastor who knows that a number of specific topics are usually important in exhortation and has a rough general pattern of teaching in his mind, but who presents it in such a way that he adapts it to the particular situation he has in mind." The final exhortations of 5:12–22, therefore, address specific issues at work in the Thessalonian congregation and so provide important clues in our reconstruction of the historical context of this early church.[2]

Extent of the Passage

The beginning of a new unit at 5:12 is suggested already in 5:11 by its two clues that it is bringing the preceding passage to a close: the inferential conjunction *dio* (therefore) and the summary command "Comfort one another" (as also in 4:18). That a major break does indeed occur at 5:12 is confirmed by the presence of several transitional markers: the mildly adversative particle *de* (but), the vocative *adelphoi* (brothers), and the appeal formula (though instead of the more common *parakaloumen* [We appeal . . .] there occurs the synonymous *erōtōmen* [We ask . . .]; so also 2 Thess. 2:1; Phil. 4:3; see 1 Thess. 4:1; P.Oxy. 294.28; 744.6; P.Freib. 39; P.Col. 8.8–9, 21 for an appeal formula where both verbs occur together). A fresh start at 5:12 is further signaled by a significant shift in content from the eschatological concerns that have preoccupied Paul's attention throughout the two preceding passages (4:13–18; 5:1–11) to a variety of ethical matters pertaining to relationships within the Thessalonian membership.

But although there is virtual unanimity over the beginning of this passage, there is some disagreement over its ending. The issue centers on the peace benediction of 5:23 and the immediately following word of encouragement in 5:24. A few commentators find an inclusio between the command of 5:13b, "Be at *peace* among yourselves," and the benediction of 5:23, "May the God of *peace* . . ." (so, e.g., Johanson 1987: 136–37; Lambrecht 2000b: 168; Beale 2003: 157) and consequently end the passage at 5:24. A greater number of scholars have been struck by the apparent parallel between the transitional prayers of 3:11–13 and the peace benediction of 5:23–24: just as the prayers of 3:11–13 close the first half of the letter (2:1–3:10), so the benediction of 5:23–24 ends the second half of the letter (4:1–5:22). Consequently

2. Contra Wanamaker (1990: 191): "On the whole the information in 5:12–22 has greater value for determining general characteristics of community life and personal relations within the Pauline mission than the specific situation prevailing at Thessalonica."

they similarly conclude that the peace benediction of 5:23–24 must go with the preceding material of 5:12–22 rather than with the subsequent material belonging to the letter closing (so, e.g., Rigaux 1956: 594–602; Bruce 1982: 128; Marshall 1983: 145; Gaventa 1998: 79, 85; Lambrecht 2000b: 165; Furnish 2007: 122).

There are, however, compelling reasons for limiting the present passage to 5:12–22 and locating the peace benediction of 5:23–24 in the letter closing. The claimed inclusio appears to be more of a coincidence than a deliberate creation by the apostle (note that the key word "peace" does not occur in the ideal position of vv. 12 and 24—the boundary verses of the passage—but in vv. 13 and 23). Also, the peace benediction of verses 23–24, like Paul's other peace benedictions (Rom. 15:33; 16:20a; 2 Cor. 13:11; Phil. 4:9b; 2 Thess. 3:16; see also Gal. 6:16), has a standard form that differs from that of 3:11; 3:12–13; and other prayers found in the bodies of the apostle's letters (2 Thess. 2:16–17; 3:5; Rom. 15:5–6; 15:13), thereby minimizing the significance of the claimed functional parallel between them (for a formal analysis of both types of prayers or benedictions, see Weima 1994a: 87–104). Whereas 1 Thess. 5:12–22 is addressed to "you," that is, the Thessalonians, and is predominated by the use of the imperative mood, verses 23–24 are directed to "the God of peace" and employ the rare optative mood. We also notice that the Pauline peace benediction is analogous to both the peace wish of Semitic letters and the health wish of Greco-Roman letters—epistolary conventions that are always located in the letter closing and not in the letter body. Finally, an analysis of Paul's other peace benedictions reveals that this epistolary convention typically serves as a literary heading that marks the beginning of the letter closing (Weima 1994a: 88–90). Therefore, despite some confusion over the proper location of the peace benediction of verses 23–24, these verses ought not to be included in the final exhortations, and the passage currently being examined must be limited to verses 12–22 (so the majority of commentators).

Structure of the Passage

An initial reading of the numerous commands of 5:12–22—commands that cover a variety of diverse topics and that typically have no syntactical connection between each other (asyndeton)—leads to the impression that this section was not written with the kind of tight, logical argumentation found in the rest of the letter. This impression is reinforced by the contemporary headings that are sometimes assigned to this passage: "General Exhortations" (Wanamaker 1990: 190; Weatherly 1996: 176); "Various Precepts" (Milligan 1908: 71; Moore 1969: 79); "Shotgun Paraenesis (Random Instructions)" (Roetzel 1975: 41; see also his 1972: 368, 375). To borrow an analogy from Gaventa (1998: 79), the exhortations in 5:12–22 at first glance appear to have all the coherence and logic of a grocery list in which the needed items have been haphazardly written down, without any careful thought as to the numbering and ranking of the listed goods. But as Gaventa goes on to note, a grocery list sometimes does have a deliberate structure, perhaps determined by the arrangement of aisles in the local supermarket. Similarly, Paul's final exhortations here in 5:12–22 do possess a conscious outline by which the apostle seeks to deal with a number of issues specifically connected to the situation in the Thessalonian church.[3]

---

3. Fee (2009: 201): "Although the imperatives in this series are for the most part very brief, so that they may be styled 'staccato,' they do not thereby lack order or substance in terms of the actual situation in Thessalonica."

The passage falls into four sections: verses 12–13, 14–15, 16–18, and 19–22. As noted above, the first unit, 5:12–13, is introduced by three transitional markers: the mildly adversative particle *de* (but), the vocative *adelphoi* (brothers), and the appeal formula ("We ask that . . ."). That this first unit ends with the exhortation to peace in verse 13b is implied by the presence of another appeal formula that immediately follows in verse 14, along with the adversative particle "but" and the vocative "brothers." The first unit is identified, however, not only by these formal features but also by its content: it deals with the church's attitude and conduct toward its leaders, then the second unit deals with the church's attitude and conduct toward all its members, especially those who are rebelliously idle, fainthearted, and spiritually weak.

In addition to this shift in content, the second unit, 5:14–15, is introduced with the same three transitional markers found in verse 12: the mildly adversative particle *de* (but), the vocative *adelphoi* (brothers), and the appeal formula, though this time with the expected verb *parakaloumen* (We appeal to you). Although the ending of this unit is less obvious, the material of verses 14e and 15 looks back to the three specific exhortations dealing with the rebellious idlers, the fainthearted, and the spiritually weak. These specific commands culminate in a general exhortation to "be patient to all" (v. 14e)—a topic that is developed in an antithetical manner first negatively (v. 15a: "Watch out that no one pays back evil for evil to anyone") and then positively (v. 15b: "But always pursue what is good for one another and for all"). The reference to "all" in verse 14e, referring internally to fellow believers, is expanded in verse 15b to include all people ("for one another and for all"), thereby creating a kind of concluding climax (Johanson 1987: 138).

The third unit, 5:16–18, contains no obvious transitional formula like those that introduce the first and second units. Nevertheless, the three very brief exhortations of verses 16–18a (only two-word or three-word clauses), after the long antithetical statement of verse 15, are suggestive of a new beginning. These three short commands are more clearly set apart from the preceding material by their common syntactical structure: an adverbial expression of time followed by an imperatival verb. This pattern is broken by the explanatory comment of verse 18b ("For this is the will of God in Christ Jesus for you"), which also sets off these three commands as a unit. That this explanatory comment of verse 18b belongs to and concludes the third unit is indicated by two facts: first, the demonstrative pronoun "this" (*touto*) does not look ahead to the subsequent exhortations but looks back (anaphoric function) to the preceding commands—not just to the immediately preceding command of verse 18a but to all three commands of the third unit; second, the statement "This is the will of God" involves an evaluation of what has just been said and so has a "rounding-off function" (Holmstrand 1997: 67).

The fourth unit, 5:19–22, also has no explicit transitional formula to indicate a shift from the preceding verses, and this has caused some commentators to lump all of verses 16–22 together. A few have found further support for the coherence of this larger section either in the alliteration of words beginning with the Greek letter *pi* (Johanson 1987: 142; Gaventa 1998: 84) or because all the commands in this larger section envision a common context of corporate worship (Elias 1995: 224). There are more compelling grounds, however, for distinguishing the material of verses 19–22 from that of verses 16–18. First, the presence of the explanatory clause of verse 18b ("For this is the will of God in Christ Jesus for you") divides the proposed larger section into two distinct parts. Second, verses 19–22, with its pattern of always listing first the direct object followed by the imperatival verb, is syntactically distinct from verses 16–18, with its pattern of always listing first an adverbial expression of time followed by the imperatival verb. Third and most significant, there is a striking shift in content in verses 19–22 to the new subject of testing prophecy. This new topic is taken up not only in the first two prohibitions that have explicit references to the Spirit and Spirit-inspired prophecy (vv. 19–20: "Do not quench the Spirit; do not despise prophecies") but, as is often overlooked, also in the following three commands (vv. 21–22: "But test all things: hold fast to the good; hold yourselves away from every kind of evil prophecy"). The adversative "but" (*de*) in verse 21 implies that the following three commands deal in a positive manner with the same subject addressed negatively in the two preceding prohibitions.

It is clear, therefore, that the exhortations of 5:12–22, despite covering a variety of topics, were not written in a haphazard manner but rather were deliberately and skillfully arranged according to the following structure:

1. Respecting congregational leaders (5:12–13)
2. Ministering to troubled congregational members (5:14–15)
   a. Ministering to rebellious idlers (5:14a)
   b. Ministering to the fainthearted (5:14b)
   c. Ministering to the weak (5:14c)
   d. Ministering to all members (5:14d–15)
3. Doing God's will in congregational worship (5:16–18)
4. Testing prophecy (5:19–22)

Exegesis and Exposition

[12]But we ask, brothers, that you respect those who work hard among you and ⌜rule over⌝ you in the Lord and admonish you, [13]and ⌜that you esteem⌝ them ⌜most highly⌝ in love because of their work. Be at peace among ⌜yourselves⌝.

[14]But we appeal to you, brothers: admonish the rebellious idlers; encourage the fainthearted; be devoted to the weak; be patient toward all. [15]Watch out that no one pays back evil for evil to anyone, but always pursue what is good for ⌜ ⌝ one another and for all.

[16]Rejoice always, [17]pray constantly, [18]give thanks in everything, for this is the will of God in Christ Jesus for you.

[19]Do not quench the Spirit; [20]do not despise prophecies, [21]⌜but⌝ test all things: hold fast to the good; [22]hold yourselves away from every kind of evil prophecy.

1. Respecting Congregational Leaders (5:12–13)

Paul brought the previous discussion to a close by exhorting the Thessalonian believers to "comfort one another and build each other up" (5:11)—two commands that first and foremost recall the teaching of the preceding

5:12

verses, 5:1–10. The second command to "build each other up," however, also looks ahead to the exhortations of 5:12–22, where this general call to mutual edification is spelled out in a variety of ways, beginning with their conduct toward congregational leaders: "But we ask, brothers, that you respect those who work hard among you and rule over you in the Lord and admonish you" (ἐρωτῶμεν δὲ ὑμᾶς, ἀδελφοί, εἰδέναι τοὺς κοπιῶντας ἐν ὑμῖν καὶ προϊσταμένους ὑμῶν ἐν κυρίῳ καὶ νουθετοῦντας ὑμᾶς, *erōtōmen de hymas, adelphoi, eidenai tous kopiōntas en hymin kai proistamenous hymōn en kyriō kai nouthetountas hymas*).

Instead of beginning this new section with a simple imperative—the form that he will employ throughout the rest of 5:12–22—Paul opens with an epistolary convention widely used in the ancient world: the appeal formula (for a fuller discussion of the form and function of the appeal formula, see comments on 4:1; see also Mullins 1962; Bjerkelund 1967). The apostle likely does so for two reasons. First, the appeal formula functions as a transitional device, marking the significant shift in subject matter from the day of the Lord (5:1–11) to issues pertaining to congregational life and worship (5:12–22). Second, the appeal formula gives, to this and the subsequent exhortations, a warmer or friendlier tone than a simple command (cf. Philem. 8–10, where Paul contrasts giving a command with issuing an appeal). This issuing of a softer "appeal" rather than a heavy-handed "command" fits well not only the overall tone of the letter, where Paul is generally pleased with the Thessalonians' spiritual condition, but also his just-mentioned concession that they are, in fact, comforting and building each other up as they ought to do (5:11, "just as you are indeed doing").

The appeal formula typically consists of four elements (Bjerkelund 1967: 43–50), the first of which involves the main verb of appeal from which this epistolary convention derives its name. Instead of the expected *parakaloumen* (Rom. 12:1; 15:30; 16:17; 1 Cor. 1:10; 4:16; 16:15; 2 Cor. 10:1–2; Phil. 4:2 [2x]; 1 Thess. 4:10b; 5:14; 1 Tim. 2:1; Philem. 9, 10), one finds here the rarer synonym *erōtōmen* (only three other times in Paul's writings: 4:1; 2 Thess. 2:1; Phil. 4:3). Since the apostle has just used *parakaleō* to express the idea of comfort or consolation (5:11), it would be awkward and potentially confusing to use the same verb in the immediately following verse with the different sense of appeal or exhortation, and so the apostle employs the synonym *erōtaō* instead.

The second element of the appeal formula consists of a reference to the recipients of the exhortation, here expressed simply by the second-person pronoun "you" (*hymas*). As often occurs in the Pauline version of this formula, the recipients are further specified by the vocative "brothers," another transitional device signaling the shift to a new subject. This twelfth occurrence of the vocative "brothers" in the letter thus far (1:4; 2:1, 9, 14, 17; 3:7; 4:1, 10b, 13; 5:1, 4, 12; also 5:14, 25) supplements the familial language and metaphors ("beloved," 1:4; "infants," 2:7b; "nursing mother," 2:7c; "father," 2:11; "orphaned," 2:17) found throughout 1 Thessalonians and is part of Paul's strategy to create community cohesion among the converts in Thessalonica, whose former relationships with family and friends would have been significantly impacted when they "turned to God from idols to serve the living and true God" (1:10). The close bonds they shared with their new spiritual "brothers and sisters" would be needed as they together faced opposition and hostility from their "fellow citizens" (2:14).

When the appeal formula occurs in official correspondence, a third element is frequently found: a prepositional phrase indicating the source of authority by which the letter sender issues his appeal. Although the Pauline version of the appeal formula often includes this third element (e.g., 4:1, "And so, brothers, we ask you and appeal *in the Lord Jesus* that . . ."), no such prepositional phrase is included here, perhaps because the apostle's authority to exhort them is not at all questioned by the Thessalonian church and because Paul does not want to appear heavy-handed in his request.

The fourth and final element involves the content of the appeal, typically introduced by either a ἵνα (*hina*) clause (4:1; 1 Cor. 1:10; see also Matt. 14:36; Mark 5:18; 6:56; 7:32; 8:22; Luke 8:32) or more commonly an infinitive clause (Rom. 12:1; 15:30; 16:17; 2 Cor. 10:1–2; Phil. 4:2; 1 Thess. 4:10b–11; 2 Thess. 2:1–2). Here Paul conveys the content of his appeal by means of not one but two infinitive clauses, which stand in a parallel relationship to each other: "that you respect . . . and esteem . . ." The first infinitive, *eidenai*, normally has the meaning "to know," and this is the sense it has elsewhere in the letter (1:4, 5; 2:1, 2, 5, 11; 3:3, 4; 4:2, 5; 5:2; in 4:4 with a following infinitive it has the specialized sense of "know *how to* . . ."). Since this meaning does not fit the context, it must here have the extended sense of knowing the worth of a person such that they are shown "respect, honor" (BDAG 694.6). This extended meaning is supported by the parallel with 1 Cor. 16:15, where an appeal formula is likewise followed by the same verb, with the sense that the Corinthians must not merely "know" but also "respect the household of Stephanus."[4] This reading seems confirmed a few verses later by Paul's command, though involving a different verb of "knowing" (*epiginōskete*), that the Corinthians treat Stephanus, along with Fortunatus and Achaicus, in a way that they "Honor such men" (1 Cor. 16:18). This use of *eidenai* with the extended sense of "respect, honor" also occurs in Ignatius of Antioch as a synonym for *timaō* (*Smyrn.* 9.1) and in Aelius Aristides (*Or.* 35.35).

A few commentators have objected to rendering the first infinitive in 5:12 as "to respect" on the grounds that such a reading would be tautological with the second infinitive in 5:13, which means "to esteem," and consequently they argue that the former term should instead be read as "to acknowledge" (Wanamaker 1990: 191–93; Richard 1995: 267–68; Holmes 1998: 178; Green 2002: 248). The grammatical structure of the appeal formula, however, presents the

---

4. Although the form οἴδατε in 1 Cor. 16:15 could be a simple indicative ("You know . . ."), its function in providing the content of the appeal formula suggests that it ought instead to be read as an imperative ("Know that . . .").

two infinitives as being in parallel with each other. Furthermore, the second clause is not completely identical with the first since it adds both the manner ("in love") and motivation ("because of their work") for bestowing respect. In any case, the distinction between acknowledging someone and respecting them is not great.

The group whom the Thessalonians must "respect" is described by three attributive participles: "those who work hard among you and rule over you in the Lord and admonish you." That only one definite article is used for all three attributives makes it clear that Paul has in view not three groups but one: congregational leaders whom he describes as having at least three distinct functions. Some commentators have tried to specify the relationship of these three functions, claiming that the first ("work hard") describes in a general way the task of congregational leaders, while the second ("rule over") and third ("admonish") are particular responsibilities that are subordinate to the first (Frame 1912: 192; Best 1977: 226; Holtz 1986: 242; Richard 1995: 268). Although such a shift from the general to the specific is natural, the three conjunctions that join the three attributive participles are all the simple *kai*, and so there is no grammatical reason not to treat the three functions of congregational leaders in a parallel or coordinate manner.

The first function that congregational leaders perform is that they "work hard among you" (*kopiōntas en hymin*). Paul elsewhere uses the verb *kopiaō* and its cognate noun *kopos* to refer both literally to his own demanding physical work with leather (1 Cor. 4:12; 2 Cor. 6:5; 11:23, 27; 1 Thess. 2:9; 2 Thess. 3:8; see also 1 Cor. 3:8; Eph. 4:28; 2 Tim. 2:6) and figuratively to the work of evangelism and related ministry tasks that he and others did (Rom. 16:6, 12b; 1 Cor. 15:10, 58; 16:16; 2 Cor. 10:15; Gal. 4:11; Phil. 2:16; Col. 1:29; 1 Thess. 1:3; 3:5; 1 Tim. 4:10; 5:17). The verb here in 5:12 clearly has the figurative meaning,[5] although it is not obvious what kind of specific church work Paul has in mind. The words of the apostle elsewhere, however, are suggestive. In addition to the subsequently mentioned activities of ruling and admonishing, such labor also involves preaching and teaching (1 Tim. 5:17, "those who work hard in the word and in teaching"), individual discipleship training (1 Thess. 2:11, "each one of you"), supporting the poor (2 Thess. 3:13; see Acts 20:35), and practicing pastoral care—the very thing that the whole church and not just the leaders are to do (1 Thess. 5:14–15).

The second function that congregational leaders perform is that they "rule over you in the Lord" (*proistamenous hymōn en kyriō*). The verb *proistēmi*, which occurs eight times in the NT and only in Paul, has two distinguishable meanings: either "to exercise a position of leadership, *rule,*

---

5. Note, however, McKinnish Bridges (2008: 150), who takes the verb literally and interprets it to refer not to spiritual leaders working in the church but "simply . . . people who produce goods for society," manual laborers (see also 157). Yet in 5:12–13 Paul has in view not manual laborers but spiritual leaders, as seems clear from the accompanying prepositional phrase that such folks are "in the Lord" and that the rest of the church should "esteem them most highly because of their work."

direct, *be at the head (of)*" (BDAG 870.1) or "to have an interest in, *show concern for, care for, give aid*" (BDAG 870.2). The issue, then, centers on whether the apostle in 5:12 is referring primarily to the notion of *authority* (first meaning) or *concern* (second meaning) that congregational leaders have over or for the members of the church. The notion of concern receives support from Rom. 12:8, where *proistēmi* occurs in a "gift" list between "the one who contributes" and "the one who does acts of mercy" and so in this context should be rendered "the one who gives aid." Further support for the notion of concern might be derived from the only occurrence of the cognate noun, in Rom. 16:2, used to describe Phoebe's relationship to the church of Cenchreae, though here it has the specialized meaning of "patron." Some commentators believe that *proistēmi* in 1 Thess. 5:12 refers to wealthy congregational members who act as "patrons" or "benefactors" to the church by providing it with aid (Meeks 1983: 134; Wanamaker 1990: 193; Richard 1995: 268, 275).

The notion of authority, however, is found in 1 Tim. 3:4–5, 12; and 5:17, where these four occurrences of *proistēmi* describe elders and deacons who "rule" their households well.[6] Some commentators dismiss this evidence from the Pastoral Letters, assuming these not to have been written by Paul. Yet even if one were to concede this questionable assumption, there are still numerous examples outside the NT where *proistēmi* is used to describe those who had a leadership or ruling capacity in ancient organizations (see texts cited by Milligan 1908: 72; MM 541; Rigaux 1956: 577–78). To give but one example, a second-century BC inscription (*OGIS* 728.4) from Thessalonica identifies a certain Marcus Annius as one who "ruled over" (*proistamenos*: the singular of the form found in 1 Thess. 5:12) the provincial council (*koinon*) in Macedonia (text cited by Milligan 1908: 72; and Green 2002: 249). Indeed, in the Greek literature of Paul's day, this ruling or authoritative sense of *proistēmi* can be said to be among its potential meanings "the most important of all" (B. Reicke, *TDNT* 6:700). That Paul has this meaning in view at least in 1 Thess. 5:12 seems clear from the addition of the phrase "in the Lord" (*en kyriō*), since this is a more fitting justification for those who exercise authority than care (see 4:1 and 2 Thess. 3:12, where Paul likewise grounds his authority to exhort the Thessalonians "in the Lord"). Similarly, the following participle (*nouthetountas*), whether it refers negatively to the act of admonishment or the more positive act of instruction, also better fits a context of those who wield authority than those who offer aid. Thus the tendency of several recent commentators (see esp. Malherbe 2000: 312–14) to exclude any notion of authority that these congregational members might have within the Thessalonian church and highlight instead only their care for others distorts the evidence.

---

6. The two remaining occurrences of *proistēmi*, in Titus 3:8, 14, are used with an impersonal object and are not relevant to its meaning in 1 Thess. 5:12.

Nevertheless, it would also be wrong to separate too sharply these two possible meanings of authority and concern, since those in leadership positions typically also provide support to those under their influence.[7] Paul expressly combines both senses in 1 Tim. 3:5, where he asks in a rhetorical fashion: "For if a man does not know how to rule over [*proistēmi*] his own household, how can he care for [*epimeleomai*] the church of God?" This linking of exercising authority and providing care, of course, is a characteristic feature of leadership in the NT, where the one who leads is to be like the one who serves (Luke 22:26).

The third function that congregational leaders perform is that they "admonish you" (*nouthetountas hymas*). The verb *noutheteō*, like the preceding *proistēmi*, is also a Pauline word, occurring seven times in the apostle's letters (Rom. 15:14; 1 Cor. 4:14; Col. 1:28; 3:16; 1 Thess. 5:12, 14; 2 Thess. 3:15; see also Titus 1:11 v.l.) and once in his farewell speech to the elders (Acts 20:31). A compound of *nous* (mind) and *tithēmi* (to put, place), the basic sense of the verb *noutheteō* is "to put something in someone's mind." As such, it might have the more positive sense of "to instruct" (it is paralleled with *didaskō* in Col. 1:28 and 3:16), and this is how some understand its meaning here in 1 Thess. 5:12 (Bruce 1982: 119). In its less ambiguous occurrences in Paul's Letters, however, *noutheteō* consistently has the negative sense of "admonish" (Milligan 1908: 72: "[It] has apparently always a sense of *blame* attached to it, hence = 'admonish,' 'warn'"). This sense is clearly seen, for example, in the apostle's rebuke to the Corinthians: "I am not writing this to shame you, but to admonish you as my dear children" (1 Cor. 4:14). Although the ambiguous context of 1 Thess. 5:12 would allow for either the positive or negative sense of *noutheteō*, the recurrence of this verb two verses later, involving a rebuke of a certain group within the church (5:14: "Admonish the rebellious idlers"), strongly suggests that the earlier occurrence similarly refers to the role that congregational leaders play in admonishing fellow believers.

Admonition, for Paul, never stems from a judgmental or vindictive spirit but rather is done out of genuine concern and love for others (J. Behm, *TDNT* 4:1021: "It denotes the word of admonition which is designed to correct while not provoking or embittering"). This can be seen in the example from 1 Cor. 4:14 cited above, where the apostle claims that he is writing "to admonish you *as my dear children*." Paul similarly commands the Thessalonians in their discipline of any member who is idle: "Do not look on him as an enemy, but admonish him as a brother" (2 Thess. 3:15).

Thus far I have been referring to "those who work hard among you and rule over you in the Lord and admonish you" as *congregational leaders*. A good

---

7. As Marshall (1983: 148) observes: "It seems likely that the two meanings can be combined. Paul is here thinking of those whose task it is to care for and supervise the church and who consequently have a certain measure of jurisdiction over its members and its activities." Green (2002: 249) similarly notes that "difficulties arise when we try to decide between the concepts of rendering aid on the one hand and leadership and authority on the other."

number of contemporary scholars insist that there is no justification here in 5:12 to believe that Paul is referring to "elders," since this and other church offices (deacons, bishops) supposedly did not exist until a later period, when the Christian movement had more time to develop such hierarchical structures. Among such scholars is what might be called an idealized or "romantic" view, counting the earliest churches as radically egalitarian groups without authoritative leaders, but with all members, equipped by the Spirit with particular gifts, participating equally in the various ministries of the church. It is clear, however, that Paul in 1 Thess. 5:12 is not referring to the whole church but to a specific group of people who perform the functions of working hard, ruling, and admonishing. Since the latter two functions in particular assume an authoritative position within the community, it is difficult not to think of individuals who possess a specific leadership position in the church like that of elder, even if that technical term was perhaps not yet used. The presence of elders at Thessalonica is further suggested by at least three other factors: (1) office bearers existed at nearby Philippi a short time later (Phil. 1:1b, "To all the saints in Christ Jesus who are at Philippi, with the bishops and deacons"); (2) the organization of the first churches was modeled to some degree on the synagogue, which had elders; and (3) well before his missionary work in Thessalonica, Paul's reported practice was to appoint elders for his newly founded churches (Acts 14:23).

Paul continues the content of his opening appeal by means of a second infinitive clause, which parallels the first: the Thessalonians are called on not only "to respect" their congregational leaders but also to "esteem them most highly in love because of their work" (καὶ ἡγεῖσθαι αὐτοὺς ὑπερεκπερισσοῦ ἐν ἀγάπῃ διὰ τὸ ἔργον αὐτῶν, kai hēgeisthai autous hyperekperissou en agapē dia to ergon autōn).

5:13

The verb hēgeomai normally for Paul (2 Cor. 9:5; Phil. 2:3, 6, 25; 3:7, 8a; 2 Thess. 3:15; 1 Tim. 1:12; 6:1) and other NT writers (Acts 26:2; Heb. 10:29; 11:11, 26; James 1:2; 2 Pet. 1:13; 2:13; 3:15) refers to an intellectual process and thus has the sense "think, consider, regard" (BDAG 434.2).[8] Although it could also have this sense here in 5:13, the parallel with the preceding infinitive ("to respect"), the following adverb ("most highly"), and possibly the following prepositional phrase ("in love") suggests that it instead has the stronger meaning "to esteem" (BDAG 434.2: "In 1 Th 5:13 there emerges for ἡγέομαι the sense esteem, respect"; see also F. Büchsel, TDNT 2:907, who cites a parallel meaning in Thucydides 2.89.9). That Paul intends for the Thessalonians not merely to acknowledge their congregational leaders but rather to esteem them is indicated by the hyperbolic adverb "most highly" (hyperekperissou), an uncommon form (elsewhere only in Eph. 3:20 and 1 Thess. 3:10; but see the related verbal form in Rom. 5:20 and 2 Cor. 7:4) whose double prefixes

---

8. The present participial form hēgoumenos occurs several times outside of Paul's Letters (Matt. 2:6; Luke 22:26; Acts 7:10; 14:12; 15:22; Heb. 13:7, 17, 24) with the specialized sense of one who performs a supervisory role: "leads, guides" (BDAG 434.1).

hyper and *ek* give the adjective *perissos* the superlative sense of the "highest form of comparison possible" (BDAG 1033). In other words, believers must treat their Christian leaders with a level of respect that is higher or greater than that shown any other person or official.

Two prepositional phrases provide both the *manner* and the *motivation* for bestowing such high respect. (1) The manner in which the Thessalonians ought to esteem their leaders is "in love" (*en agapē*; the preposition *en* likely functions adverbially: see BDAG 330.11). Since love ought to characterize the relationship between all believers (1 Cor. 13:1–3; Eph. 4:2, 15–16), it is hardly surprising that it also ought to characterize the way believers treat those who hold leadership positions in the church. Paul has demonstrated this love in his own relationship with the Thessalonians (see his loving-as-a-nursing-mother conduct in 2:7c–8) and now calls on his readers to act in a similar manner toward those in charge within the church. (2) The motivation for esteeming these congregational leaders is "because of their work" (*dia to ergon autōn*). The reference to "their work" recalls the three functions of "working hard," "ruling over," and "admonishing" just mentioned in the preceding verse. From this motivational phrase it is clear that respect and honor ought to be accorded congregational leaders not because of their position or office in and of itself, but because of the important pastoral work they perform. Although the church's leadership quite likely involved well-to-do members such as Jason (Acts 17:5–9)—whose education, financial freedom, and business experience in supervising others naturally allowed them to assume a leadership role in the congregation—such leaders are to be esteemed not for their high social status, family name, or position within the non-Christian community of Thessalonica, but rather for the crucial labor that they do within the congregation.

The opening paragraph of 5:12–13 dealing with congregational leaders comes to a close with a command whose wording is somewhat uncertain. Did Paul originally write "Be at peace among *them*," that is, the congregational leaders (so Witherington 2006: 161), or "Be at peace among *yourselves*"? The manuscript evidence is virtually equal (see additional notes), with many significant witnesses containing the simple pronoun "them" (*autois*) and many other significant witnesses containing the reflexive pronoun "yourselves" (*heautois*). But while the external evidence is evenly divided, the internal evidence suggests that the reflexive pronoun "yourselves" is original (so nearly all translations and commentators). The absence of any connective particle (asyndeton) likely caused scribes to clarify the connection that this command has with the preceding appeal by changing the reflexive pronoun "yourselves" to the simple pronoun "them." It is difficult to find any motivation for a scribe to make the reverse change. Furthermore, as the parallel with Rom. 12:18 suggests ("Be at peace *with* all people" [*meta* + genitive]), if Paul were actually thinking only of the peace that ought to exist between members of the church and its leaders, he would have likely used the prepositional phrase "with them" (*met' autōn*) rather than "among them" (*en autois*). Finally, even if the form *autois* were to be followed, it can also be read with a rough breathing as *hautois*—a contracted form of the reflexive pronoun *heautois* (MHT 3:41: "the simple personal pronoun often serves as a reflexive"; see also Moule 1959: 119)—such that the resulting translation is similarly "Be at peace among *yourselves*."

Although the original wording of the command has now been clarified, there still remains uncertainty about its relevancy to the church in Thessalonica. Since a call to peace is a very common part of Christian moral instruction (Rom. 12:18; 14:17, 19; 1 Cor. 14:33; 2 Cor. 13:11; Eph. 4:3; Col. 3:15; 2 Tim. 2:22; Heb. 12:14; James 3:18), echoing the command of Jesus (Mark 9:50), most commentators treat Paul's exhortation in 1 Thess. 5:13b as a traditional statement that does not reflect any specific problem at work in the Thessalonian congregation. This conclusion is strengthened by the fact that Paul's pattern here of moving from the specific commands dealing with congregational leaders (5:12–13a) to the general call to peace (5:13b) is seemingly followed in the subsequent paragraphs of this section as well (the three specific commands of 5:14 dealing with troubled congregational members conclude with the general call to be "patient to all," and the specific commands of 5:19–21 dealing with prophecy conclude with the general call to "hold yourselves away from every kind of evil"; so Lightfoot 1904: 80).

But while it would be wrong to read too much of the Thessalonian situation into the command to be at peace, it would be equally wrong to derive from this exhortation nothing at all. Paul would not have raised the topic of respecting congregational leaders if such a subject were not in some way directly relevant to the Thessalonian situation, and the same assumption should be true for the immediately following call to "be at peace among yourselves." Marshall (1983: 149) finds it noteworthy that Paul limits the command to peace within the church rather than with humanity in general, and that a similar exhortation occurs in letters where divisions were clearly present in the local congregation (Rom. 12:18; 2 Cor. 13:11). Although Paul does commend the Thessalonians for the loving way they treat each other (4:9–10a), he nevertheless appeals to them "to increase more and more" in such conduct (4:10b). The existence of some degree of tension in the Thessalonian congregation is also hinted at in the letter closing with the exhortation to greet each other with a holy kiss (5:26): this command occurs elsewhere in Paul's Letters always in contexts involving some degree of internal conflict (Rom. 16:16a; 1 Cor. 16:20b; 2 Cor. 13:12a; see Weima 1994a: 111–17, 184).

With regard to the relationship between church members and their congregational leaders, it is not difficult to envision how the latter group's work in "ruling over" and "admonishing" the former, even if carried out in the right spirit, could easily result in tension or feelings of bitterness. One situation that Paul may be thinking of in particular with his call to "be at peace among yourselves" is the problem posed by the *ataktoi*, the "rebellious idlers."[9] Although this possibility, first proposed by Frame (1911; 1912: 195; also adopted by Marxsen 1979: 62, 71–72; Marshall 1983: 149–50; Jewett 1986: 102–5; Green

---

9. For a justification of this translation of *ataktoi*, see comments on 5:14.

2002: 252; Beale 2003: 162), has been dismissed as "nothing more than a guess" (Wanamaker 1990: 196), it nevertheless is suggested by a couple of factors.[10] First, the call to peace is immediately followed with a command to admonish the *ataktoi* (5:14b), making a linkage between these two exhortations possible. Second, such a connection is further strengthened by the repetition of the verb "admonish" in 5:12b and 5:14b. Third, Paul concludes his extended treatment of the *ataktoi* in 2 Thess. 3:6–15 with a peace benediction (3:16) that has been deliberately altered to emphasize the theme of peace (see Weima 1994a: 188–90), providing yet another linkage between this particular group and the call to peace. Paul may well have had other specific situations in the Thessalonian congregation in mind with his command to "Be at peace among yourselves" (e.g., Green 2002: 252 claims that questions about the proper place of prophecy and the practice of sexual immorality were other issues that generated division in the Thessalonian church), but there is no evidence to substantiate any of these possibilities.

2. Ministering to Troubled Congregational Members (5:14–15)

The second unit broadens the focus from the church's attitude and conduct toward its leaders (5:12–13) to how it ought to minister to all congregational members (5:14–15), even though three specific groups of troubled believers are identified: "But we appeal to you, brothers: admonish the rebellious idlers; encourage the fainthearted; be devoted to the weak; be patient to all" (παρακαλοῦμεν δὲ ὑμᾶς, ἀδελφοί, νουθετεῖτε τοὺς ἀτάκτους, παραμυθεῖσθε τοὺς ὀλιγοψύχους, ἀντέχεσθε τῶν ἀσθενῶν, μακροθυμεῖτε πρὸς πάντας, *parakaloumen de hymas, noutheteite tous ataktous, paramytheisthe tous oligopsychous, antechesthe tōn asthenōn, makrothymeite pros pantas*).

As in 5:12, here too Paul employs the appeal formula in order both to mark the transition to a new subject matter and to continue the friendlier tone of his exhortations (for a fuller discussion of this epistolary formula, see comments on 4:1). The form of this appeal formula, however, differs slightly from its occurrence in the first unit. Instead of the rarer main verb *erōtōmen* (we ask: only four times in Paul: Phil. 4:3; 1 Thess. 4:1; 5:12; 2 Thess. 2:1), which was required in 5:12 (see comments above), here Paul can use the expected *parakaloumen* (we appeal: Rom. 12:1; 15:30; 16:17; 1 Cor. 1:10; 4:16; 16:15; 2 Cor. 10:1–2; Phil. 4:2 [2x]; 1 Thess. 4:10b; 1 Tim. 2:1; Philem. 9, 10).

The recipient of the exhortation is expressed in typical fashion with the second-person pronoun "you" (*hymas*) and the vocative "brothers," the latter functioning as yet another transitional device that signals the shift to a new subject. Some church fathers believed that with this reference to "you, brothers," Paul is addressing not the whole church but the congregational leaders

---

10. This is true only for the part of Frame's proposal where he links the problem of internal division to tensions between the congregational leaders and the rebellious idlers. Frame's further proposal that this conflict was due to the leaders' tactless treatment of the rebellious idlers is mere speculation and has no similar support.

mentioned in the preceding paragraph (John Chrysostom: "Here he addresses those who have rule," *Hom. 1 Thess.* 10 [PG 62:456]; see also Theodore of Mopsuestia, "On 1 Thessalonians" [Greer 2010: 490])—an interpretation that a few contemporary commentators have found convincing (e.g., Findlay 1891: 124; Masson 1957: 73; Schlier 1963: 97; Roetzel 1972: 368; Shogren 2012: 221). For a number of reasons, however, this view cannot be sustained (so most commentators; see esp. Best 1977: 229): (1) throughout this letter the vocative "brothers" refers to the whole church; (2) the expression "you, brothers," also as part of an appeal formula, occurs two verses earlier, where it clearly refers to the entire congregation, and there is no compelling reason to interpret it any different here; (3) the exhortations of the third unit (5:16–18), which have the whole church in view, are not introduced with any contrastive marker, thereby implying that the same audience is intended in the preceding unit; and (4) if Paul were referring only to leaders in 5:14–15, he could have easily indicated this by either changing the word order (so Dobschütz 1909: 220) or through some other means (Bruce 1982: 122). Therefore, although congregational leaders in Thessalonica no doubt played a key role in the practice of pastoral care, such ministry to others is the responsibility of all the church's members. This agrees with Paul's directions elsewhere to those in leadership positions that they are not to work alone but are "to equip the saints for the work of ministry" (Eph. 4:11–12).

The content of Paul's appeal to the whole church is expressed here not by means of a dependent clause, as is normally the case (either a *hina* clause [4:1; 1 Cor. 1:10] or more commonly an infinitive clause, as in 5:12 [see also texts cited there]), but an independent clause (see also 1 Cor. 4:16; 16:15). More precisely, Paul lists four tersely worded commands, each consisting of a present imperative (thereby highlighting the ongoing nature of the action enjoined) that is immediately followed by its direct object or a prepositional phrase.

a. Ministering to Rebellious Idlers (5:14a)

In the first command, the church is called on to "admonish the rebellious idlers." The importance of this command is suggested not only by its placement at the head of the list of imperatives but also because it is the only one of these four commands in which the main verb ("admonish") is repeated from the three activities of the congregational leaders mentioned above in 5:12. The context here in 5:14 demands that the verb *noutheteō* once again does not have the more positive meaning of "instruct" but the negative sense of "admonish," or "warn" (for fuller discussion of *noutheteō*, see comments on 5:12).

5:14a

There is some uncertainty about how to properly translate *tous ataktous*, the group whom Paul identifies and the Thessalonian congregation is to admonish. The Greek root *atakt-* occurs four times in the apostle's letters, all of them in his correspondence to the Thessalonians: the adjective *ataktoi* is found here in 5:14; the adverb *ataktōs* in 2 Thess. 3:6, 11; and the verb *ataktein* in 2 Thess.

3:7. This root originates from the prefix *a*- (the alpha privative, which expresses negation) and the verb *tassō* ("to give instructions as to what must be done, *order, fix, determine*": BDAG 991.2; see the related adjective *taktos* and noun *taxis*) and thus literally means "not in order, disorderly." The term refers in a general way to any kind of conduct that does not conform to established law or expected practice (for extended surveys of the use of this word in the ancient world, see Milligan 1908: 152–54; Rigaux 1956: 582–84; Spicq 1956; 1994: 1.223–26; G. Delling, *TDNT* 8:47–48). The root *atakt*- occurs most frequently in military parlance to describe insubordinate soldiers, negligent officers, or an army in disarray. But it also is used in a variety of other contexts as well, describing such diverse persons as those who do not follow the rules of conduct in the gymnasium at Berea (*NewDocs* 2:104.82), sons who fail to meet the financial needs of their parents (P.Eleph. 2.13), apprentices who miss work or fail to live up to the requirements of their contract (P.Oxy. 275.24; 725.39; P.Oslo 159.9; *SB* 10236.33; P.Cair.Zen. 59596; *BGU* 1125.8; P.Wisc. 4.22), or those who do not observe order and common law (Josephus, *Ag. Ap.* 2.151; Plutarch, *Cat. Maj.* 16.3). In light of this attested breadth of meaning, many translations and commentators understand Paul's use of *ataktoi* in 5:14 in a general way as referring to those who are "disorderly," "unruly," or "insubordinate."[11]

There are good reasons, however, for viewing the *ataktoi* in 5:14 more narrowly as those who act disorderly with respect to work, those who are "idle, lazy." First and foremost, the three other Pauline occurrences of the root *atakt*- (2 Thess. 3:6, 7, 11) occur in a context where some in the church are refusing to work, implying that the use of this term in 5:14 ought to be understood in the same way. Second, even if one dismisses these important parallels because of questions about the Pauline authorship of the second letter (so, e.g., Richard 1995: 270), the apostle's command in 4:11c ("to work with your hands") and the following purpose clause in 4:12 ("in order that you . . . may have need of no one") make clear that the problem of idleness is actually being faced by the Thessalonian congregation and is a problem whose roots go back to Paul's mission-founding visit to their city (4:11e, "just as we commanded you"; also 2 Thess. 3:6, 10). Third, the root *atakt*- occurs in a number of ancient texts with this narrow sense of being "idle" or "lazy" (see the texts examined by Milligan 1908: 153–54; Frame 1911: 194–96). In some of these texts, the verbal form *ataktein* is used interchangeably with *argeō* (to slack off, become idle).

In these non-Christian texts, however, the emphasis lies not on the slothful behavior alone but on the rebellious attitude toward the obligation of work (G. Delling, *TDNT* 8:48). This perhaps explains why Paul does not use more common words for laziness such as *argoi* or *apraktoi* but the rarer *ataktoi*

---

11. John Chrysostom, for example, understands the *ataktoi* in 5:14 in a general way as those who are guilty of revelry, drunkenness, and covetousness, thus as "all sinners, those who act against the will of God" (*Hom. 1 Thess.* 10 [PG 62:455]).

(Malherbe 2000: 317). On the one hand, this latter term's specific meaning of "idleness" captures the refusal of some in the Thessalonian church "to work with your hands" and so "have need of no one"; on the other hand, this latter term's general meaning of "disorderly" captures the resistance of such believers both to their congregational leaders (5:12–13) and to Paul, who earlier exhorted them to work during his original preaching ministry in their midst.[12] Therefore, Paul's reference to *tous ataktous* in 5:14 is best rendered as "the rebellious idlers"—those who are not merely lazy but who also compound their sin by rebelliously refusing to obey the command of both their congregational leaders and even Paul himself.[13]

b. Ministering to the Fainthearted (5:14b)

In the second of Paul's commands concerning how the Thessalonians ought to minister to troubled congregational members, he challenges the whole church to "encourage the fainthearted" (*paramytheisthe tous oligopsychous*). The verb *paramytheomai* is infrequent in Paul, appearing only here and earlier in the letter in 2:12. This term outside of Scripture "almost always has affective connotations, with the highly nuanced meanings of 'advise, encourage, console, comfort, speak calming words to, appease, soothe'" (Spicq 1994: 3.30–35; so also G. Stählin, *TDNT* 5:816–23). It frequently is used to describe the encouragement or consolation given to those who have suffered the death of a loved one or some other tragic event (BDAG 769; *NewDocs* 4:166), and this is the context in its only two other occurrences in the NT (John 11:19, 31).

5:14b

Those in the Thessalonian congregation who are to receive such encouragement are described as *tous oligopsychous*, literally, those with "little soul." The term occurs nowhere else in the NT and appears only rarely in nonbiblical Greek. Paul may thus know the term from the LXX, where it appears twenty times in a variety of forms (adjective, noun, verb) and most commonly describes an attitude of despondency or discouragement amid difficult circumstances (e.g., Exod. 6:9; Num. 21:4; Judg. 16:16; Isa. 25:5; 35:4; 54:6; 57:15; Jon. 4:8; Sir. 4:9; 7:10; Jdt. 7:19; 8:9; see G. Bertram, *TDNT* 9:666).

The question naturally arises as to the reason *why* some Thessalonian Christians were "fainthearted" or "discouraged" (BDAG 703): is Paul in a general way thinking about a variety of difficulties that these believers face, or does he have a specific concern in view? The brevity of Paul's directive, of

12. On the issue of *why* some members of the Thessalonian church were not willing to work, see comments on 4:11.

13. The NIV (2011) similarly renders *tous ataktous* in 5:14 not merely as "those who are idle" but with the fuller phrase "those who are idle *and disruptive*." My translation of "rebellious idlers" does not imply that it is permitted for believers to be idle as long as they are not idle in a rebellious way; as stated above, Paul rebukes both the sin of idleness *and* rebelliousness—two sins that happen to be combined in the lives of some members of the Thessalonian church. The weakness of the NIV's rendering is that it might mislead the modern reader into thinking that there are two groups of people in view (the idle and the disruptive) instead of one group—a point better captured with my translation "rebellious idlers."

course, demands that any answer to this question be tentative and that one guard against reading too much into this short command.[14] Nevertheless, that the previous charge concerning the "rebellious idlers" looks back to a specific problem taken up in 4:9–12 suggests that this command concerning the "fainthearted" similarly looks back to a particular issue addressed in the exhortative material of 4:1–5:11. The best candidate is the problem taken up immediately after 4:9–12, the discouragement ("to grieve like the rest who have no hope") that many in the church have concerning the fate of their fellow members who have died before Christ's return, as discussed in 4:13–18 (so, e.g., Ellicott 1880: 77; Frame 1912: 190; Hendriksen 1955: 136; Black 1982: 316; Marshall 1983: 151; Fee 1994a: 57n75; Richard 1995: 270, 277; Gaventa 1998: 82; Fee 2009: 210 [tentatively]). Strengthening this possibility is the point already noted above that the verb "encourage" frequently occurs in the context of death and that *paramytheomai* is often linked with *parakaleō* (Classen 1994–95: 327–28)—the verb that Paul uses in the concluding command of 4:18.

c. Ministering to the Weak (5:14c)

5:14c The third command challenges the whole church to "be devoted to the weak" (*antechesthe tōn asthenōn*). The verb *antechō*, though common in Hellenistic texts and the LXX, occurs infrequently in Paul (only here and Titus 1:9) and in the rest of the NT (Matt. 6:24; Luke 16:13). It expresses "a strong attachment to someone or something, *cling to, hold fast to, be devoted to*" (BDAG 87.1; see also H. Hanse, *TDNT* 2:827–28) and is even paralleled with the verb "to love" (Matt. 6:24; Luke 16:13). Paul enjoins his readers, therefore, not merely to "help" (so most translations) weak believers—perhaps allowing for a kind of assistance done in a detached, nonemotional manner—but to "be devoted to" such troubled members.

But who are "the weak" to whom the Thessalonian church must be devoted? The adjective *tōn asthenōn* might be referring to fellow believers who are *physically* weak, the "sick" and "ill" (Matt. 25:43–44; Luke 9:2; 10:9; Acts 5:15–16; 1 Cor. 11:30; the related noun *astheneia* and verb *astheneō* also frequently refer to physical ailments: see BDAG 142). But though this is possible (so Beale 2003: 166; Witherington 2006: 163), that the two previous groups whom Paul mentions were troubled in their moral conduct or religious character suggests that the third group similarly refers to those who are *spiritually* weak (so most commentators).[15] In two of his other letters, Paul uses the adjective "the weak" and its related forms (Rom. 14:1, 2; 15:1;

---

14. Holmes (1998: 180), however, is too cautious and overstates the case concerning "the fainthearted": "Nothing in the immediate context offers a clue to its precise nuance here or about its cause."

15. There is admittedly a danger in too sharply distinguishing between the physical and spiritual condition, since Paul links the two together in 1 Cor. 11:30 ("That [the abuse of poorer members in the celebration of the Lord's Supper] is why many of you are weak and ill and have died").

1 Cor. 8:7, 9, 10, 11, 12; 9:22) to refer to a specific group of Christians who stumbled over the eating of certain foods (either meat sacrificed to idols and eaten in a pagan temple [1 Cor. 8:1–11:1] or foods that were considered unclean [Rom. 14:1–23]) or the religious observance of special days (Rom. 14:5–6). The references to "the weak" in these letters, however, occur as part of lengthy discussions in contrast to its brief mention in 1 Thess. 5:14. Furthermore, there is nothing else in either of the Thessalonian Letters that even hints at the existence of a similar tension between "the weak" and "the strong" (contra Best 1977: 231).

More convincing than parallels in Paul's other letters are the theories that interpret "the weak" in its immediate context. Since the reference to "the rebellious idlers" almost certainly looks back to the exhortations of 4:9–12 and the "fainthearted" likely to the words of 4:13–18, it is plausible that "the weak" similarly has the exhortative material of 4:1–5:11 in view. Frame (1911: 198) proposes that Paul is referring to believers who struggle with living holy lives in their sexual conduct—the issue discussed in 4:3–8 (so also Hendriksen 1955: 136). But one might well expect that for those church members who conduct themselves sexually "in lustful passion, just as the Gentiles who do not know God" (4:5), who "take advantage" of other Christians in their sexual activity (4:6) and thereby "reject God" in this matter (4:8)—Paul would call on the rest of the church to rebuke or discipline such members rather than "be devoted to" them. Furthermore, the pattern in which the phrase "the rebellious idlers" looks back to 4:9–12 and "the fainthearted" to 4:13–18 suggests that "the weak" has in view not 4:3–8 but 5:1–11 (so Black 1982). In our analysis of this passage, we have already observed that some believers in Thessalonica were not merely curious about the timing of the day of the Lord but rather worried whether they would avoid the wrath connected with that future day and instead experience eternal life with Christ. This would mean that "the weak" refers to those in the Thessalonian church who are excessively anxious about their status at the eschatological judgment connected with Christ's return. Although the evidence is such that this identification of "the weak" can be only a hypothesis rather than a fact, it nevertheless is the interpretation that best fits the context.

d. Ministering to All Members (5:14d–15)

The final of the four three-word commands that are part of Paul's appeal to the whole church concerning ministering to troubled congregational members is that they "be patient to all" (*makrothymeite pros pantas*). Paul's use of *makrothymeō* and its cognates (verb: 2x; noun: 10x; for texts, see below) stems not from nonbiblical Greek writings, where the term occurs comparatively late and only infrequently, but rather from the LXX, where it takes on significant, theological importance in describing God's relationship to his covenant people (J. Horst, *TDNT* 4:374–87). This "patient" or, literally, "long-suffering" manner in which God deals with his people (the formula of Exod. 34:6, "The

5:14d

Lord God, the compassionate and merciful, *patient* and full of love" occurs repeatedly in biblical and later Jewish writings: Num. 14:18; Pss. 86:15; 103:8 [85:15; 102:8 LXX]; Joel 2:13; Jon. 4:2; 2 Esd. [4 Ezra] 7:33 NRSV; Neh. 9:17; Sir. 2:11; Pr. Man. 7; also Rom. 2:4; 9:22; 1 Tim. 1:16 [Christ]) is not only a characteristic feature of Paul's ministry (2 Cor. 6:6) but also the way in which the apostle calls upon his converts, including here the Thessalonians, to treat others (5:14; 1 Cor. 13:4; Gal. 5:2; Eph. 4:2; Col. 1:11; 3:12).

As with the three preceding commands, here too there is some debate about the identity of those who are the recipients of the Thessalonians' pastoral care. It is possible that the phrase "to all" refers more narrowly to the three groups of believers just mentioned: the rebellious idlers, the fainthearted, and the weak (note the NRSV: "Be patient with all *of them*"). But if Paul were thinking just of these three groups, he could have easily indicated so. Furthermore, elsewhere in the apostle's writings, it is clear that patience is a virtue that ought to be extended to all believers, not just certain kinds of troubled Christians. In contrast to this more narrow interpretation of "all," some wish to expand it to include not just believers but non-Christians as well (so, e.g., Wanamaker 1990: 198; Williams 1992: 98; Malherbe 2000: 320). But that those outside the church are not mentioned explicitly until 5:15 ("for one another *and for all*") suggests that they are not yet in view here in 5:14.

Many Christians find it hard to accept help, and especially discipline, from fellow believers; the difficulty of correcting one's vices and spiritual flaws means that relapses into old habits are to be expected. In such situations Paul exhorts the church not merely to admonish, encourage, and demonstrate devotion to troubled members, but also to do so in a patient, ongoing manner (note again the present tense of all the imperatives, highlighting the continuous nature of the action enjoined), thereby mirroring the long-suffering manner in which God continues to deal graciously with them.

5:15 Just as the general command to "be at peace among yourselves" in 5:13b concludes the specific commands of 5:12–13a, so the general command to "be patient to all" (5:14d) brings the three specific commands of 5:14a–c to a close. But before this second section dealing with the church's ministry to troubled congregational members comes to a definitive end, Paul expands this general call to patience in two ways: he restates the command in the form of an antithetical (not *x* but *y*) statement that highlights the principle of nonretaliation, and he enlarges the recipients of this nonretaliatory conduct to include not just fellow believers but also those outside the congregation as well: "Watch out that no one pay back evil for evil to anyone, but always pursue what is good for one another and for all" (ὁρᾶτε μή τις κακὸν ἀντὶ κακοῦ τινι ἀποδῷ, ἀλλὰ πάντοτε τὸ ἀγαθὸν διώκετε [καὶ][16] εἰς ἀλλήλους καὶ εἰς πάντας, *horate mē tis kakon anti kakou tini apodō, alla pantote to agathon diōkete [kai] eis allēlous kai eis pantas*).

16. See the additional notes for the possible addition of this conjunction in 5:15.

The positive half of the antithetical statement is introduced with the imperative *orate*, which functions here intransitively with the meaning "to be alert or on guard, *pay attention, see to it that*," or "*watch out!*" (BDAG 720.B.2). Although Paul elsewhere uses the synonym *blepete* (Gal. 5:15; 1 Cor. 8:9; 10:12; Col. 2:8) instead of *horate* (see also Matt. 8:4; 18:10; Mark 1:44), both words frequently introduce the construction *mē* plus the aorist subjunctive—a dependent clause whose construction expresses fear or apprehension (BDF §370; MHT 3:99).

What Paul is afraid of and thus warns the Thessalonian believers to "watch out" for is the temptation to "pay back evil for evil." The human desire for vengeance is so strong and destructive that it is not surprising that both biblical and nonbiblical sources speak against retaliatory behavior. Even the harsh-sounding OT principle of retribution—the lex talionis, "an eye for an eye and a tooth for a tooth" (see Exod. 31:23–25; Lev. 24:19–21; Deut. 19:21)—is actually intended to restrict vengeance to an exact equivalent of that which was wronged. Later OT and Jewish texts go further in their rejection of retaliation (Ps. 7:4–5; Prov. 20:22; 24:29; 25:21; Sir. 28:1–7; Jos. Asen. 23.9; 28.5; 29.3). Warnings against vengeance can also be found in the moral and philosophical writings of the Greco-Roman period (see texts cited by Malherbe 2000: 321; Green 2002: 255). In the NT, Jesus's explicit rejection of the lex talionis and his call to love one's enemies (Matt. 5:38–48; Luke 6:27–36) are echoed by other writers such as Peter ("Do not repay evil for evil or reviling for reviling": 1 Pet. 3:9) and Paul, both here and in his later letters ("Repay no one evil for evil. . . . Never avenge yourselves. . . . No, 'if your enemy is hungry, feed him; if he is thirsty, give him drink; for by so doing you will heap burning coals on his head'": Rom. 12:17–20; see also 1 Cor. 6:7).

The positive half of the antithetical statement shows that Paul does not command the Thessalonian believers to respond to those who treat them unkindly merely in a nonretaliatory manner but, more than that, also to seek the best interests of such individuals: "but always pursue what is good for one another and for all." The force of this command is strengthened in three ways. First, the adverb *pantote* (always) covers every type of imaginable situation; there is no context in which believers are not to seek the welfare of those around them. Second, the verb *diōkete* is a strong term that expresses not merely a willingness to "try" (NIV 1984) to do what is good but rather the great effort needed to "pursue" or "strive for" this goal. The term is so strong that it is often used to refer to those who persecute or oppress others (BDAG 254; see 2:15, where Paul uses a compound form to describe the Jews who drove him and his fellow missionaries out of Thessalonica). Third, the recipients of the good works that the Thessalonian church must pursue include not only their fellow Christians ("for one another") but also their non-Christian neighbors ("and for all").[17] The former group includes at least those church members

17. The prepositional phrase at the end of 5:15 refers to those *outside* the Christian community. As Fee correctly states (2009: 213n30), it would create an "awkward redundancy" if it had believers in view: "for one another and for all [of you]."

who are unfairly taking advantage of the generosity of other believers and who may well have reacted negatively to being "admonished" for their idle behavior (it is hard to envision Christians in Thessalonica responding negatively to the church's ministry of "encouraging" and "being devoted" to them). The latter group included those "fellow citizens" (2:14) who took an active part in the persecution that the church had to endure (1:6; 2:2, 14–15; 3:1–5; 2 Thess. 1:4–7; see also 2 Cor. 8:1–2; Acts 17:5–7, 13). The proper Christian response to harmful treatment from others, regardless of its source or its nature, is not merely that of patience and nonretaliation but additionally the aggressive pursuit of what is best for the offending person or party.

3. Doing God's Will in Congregational Worship (5:16–18)

The three commands that make up the third unit are so brief in length and so general in content that it is difficult to discern the specific situation in the Thessalonian church that they are intended to address. A few commentators have discerned a shift in content from the preceding two units, where the focus is on conduct toward *others*, to this third unit, which supposedly emphasizes conduct to *oneself*, with the result that verses 16–18 are viewed as a call to cultivate personal piety (e.g., Moore 1969: 83: "Verses 16–22 are injunctions concerning the individual Christian's right behavior"; Best 1977: 234: "vv. 16–18 take up the inner life of each believer"; Thomas 1978: 290, titling these verses "Responsibilities to oneself"). Yet a variety of subtle clues suggest that Paul's focus here is still very much communal and that his directives, although obviously relevant for individual devotional life, address first and foremost the congregational worship of the Thessalonian Christians. First, the imperatives continue to be plural and so, like the rest of 5:12–22, address the entire church. Second, the subsequent command not to despise prophecy in verse 20 clearly presupposes a worship context. Third, the following section of the letter (5:23–28) contains two exhortations that likewise suggest a context of congregational worship: one to greet fellow Christians with a holy kiss (5:26) and the other to ensure the public reading of the letter in the presence of all the believers (5:27).[18]

It is by no means obvious why Paul here includes three commands related to congregational worship or how this third unit of verses 16–18 fits within the rest of the passage. A plausible explanation is that in the apostle's mind the characteristics of joy, prayer, and thanksgiving are all intimately linked to the working of the Holy Spirit so that the three commands of the third unit function as a transition to the fourth unit, with its treatment of the Spirit and Spirit-inspired prophecy in the context of worship (see Fee 1994a: 53–55;

18. In his study of worship in the early church, R. Martin (1974: 135–36) claims that in 5:16–24 we find the "headings of a worship service," which includes a call to worship (vv. 16–18), guidelines for listening to the prophets (vv. 19–22), and a closing prayer (vv. 23–24). Although this conclusion goes beyond what the evidence allows, it does highlight the likely context of these verses: the communal worship of the Thessalonian congregation.

2009: 214). Paul connects joy with the Holy Spirit, for example, in the opening of this letter (1:6) and in his other letters as well (Gal. 5:22; Rom. 14:17). The apostle similarly links prayer to the Spirit (1 Cor. 14:15; Rom. 8:26–27; Eph. 6:18; Phil. 1:19) and Spirit-inspired prophecy (1 Cor. 11:4), as he also does with thanksgiving (1 Cor. 14:16). Thus, as Findlay (1891: 128) observed some time ago: "From *joy*, *prayer*, and *thanksgiving* it is a natural transition to *the Spirit* and *prophecy*" (cited by Fee 1994a: 54n66; 2009: 214n33).

The first of the three commands is "Rejoice always" (πάντοτε χαίρετε, *pantote chairete*). This is not the first time in the letter that Paul has sounded the note of "joy" or "rejoicing." The apostle opened his correspondence with the Thessalonians by giving thanks to God for how they received the gospel in much affliction yet "with joy that comes from the Holy Spirit" (1:6). Paul has also identified them twice as "my joy" on that future day when he will present them to the returning Lord as proof of his faithful missionary labors (2:19, 20). The twin facts that the Thessalonian church continues to love him despite his absence and that they remain steadfast in their faith despite enduring affliction have also caused Paul's fears about them to be replaced with "all the joy with which we rejoice because of you before our God" (3:9). Finally, the verbal form "rejoice" and noun form "joy" are important terms in Paul's Letters as a whole, occurring fifty times (see H. Conzelmann, *TDNT* 9:359–72; also W. G. Morrice, *DPL* 511–12, "Joy").

5:16

It is clear from these references that, despite the afflictions and hardships that characterized Paul's missionary endeavors, the Christian life was for him ultimately one of rejoicing and joy. The rest of the NT similarly portrays believers as joyful (see, e.g., Matt. 13:20; Luke 15:7, 32; 19:6; John 15:11; 16:24; 17:13; Acts 2:46; 8:8, 39; 13:48–52; 1 Pet. 1:8; 1 John 1:4; 2 John 12). Thus a good case can be made that joy is one of the distinguishing characteristics of Christianity, contrasting sharply with the hopelessness and pessimism of first-century paganism (so Spicq 1994: 3.498–99, noticing that a high percentage of uses of the noun *chara* in the papyri are of Christian origin, whereas pagan uses of the term are rare; see also comments on 4:13 about the pessimism that characterizes the pagan view of the afterlife). Paul calls on the Thessalonians, not only in their personal piety but, especially in their communal worship, to live this archetypal joyful life "always." In light of the preceding verse, this means that even when others—whether they be fellow believers or non-Christians—treat them unkindly or harshly, they must not hold on to grudges or in a vindictive way return evil for evil. In light of the larger context of the letter as a whole, this means that they must rejoice even when they suffer ridicule, abuse, and even worse at the hands of their unbelieving "fellow citizens" (2:14). Although the notion of joy in suffering seems paradoxical, it was the lifestyle exemplified by Paul, who rejoiced in harsh circumstances (Rom. 5:3; Col. 1:24; Acts 16:25; note also the emphasis of joy/rejoicing in Philippians—a letter written while the apostle was imprisoned) and who presented himself and his coworkers as "sorrowful, yet always rejoicing" (2 Cor. 6:10). Joy in suffering is also the lifestyle exhorted by Jesus and other NT writers (Matt. 5:10–12; Luke 6:22–23; John 16:20–22; 1 Pet. 4:13).

5:17   The second of the three commands is "Pray constantly" (ἀδιαλείπτως προσεύχεσθε, *adialeiptōs proseuchesthe*). Paul elsewhere also connects prayer with the activities of rejoicing and thanksgiving (1 Thess. 3:9–10; Phil. 1:3–4; 4:4–6). Yet the reference to prayer here, as noted above, may well be because in Paul's theology this, like rejoicing, is another activity linked to the Holy Spirit (Rom. 8:26–27; 1 Cor. 14:15; Eph. 6:18); thus the mention of prayer anticipates the treatment of the Spirit and Spirit-inspired prophecy in the worship context of the subsequent verses. This call to constant prayer is one that Paul frequently gives to his converts (Rom. 12:12; Phil. 4:6; Col. 4:2; Eph. 6:18; 1 Tim. 2:1, 8) and one that he exemplifies in his own prayer life, both in his unceasing prayer for others (Rom. 1:9; Phil. 1:4, 9–11; Col. 1:3, 9; 1 Thess. 1:2; 3:10; 2 Thess. 1:11–12; 2 Tim. 1:3; Philem. 4) and in his requests that they in return pray for him (Rom. 15:30; Eph. 6:19; Col. 4:3–4; 1 Thess. 5:25; 2 Thess. 3:1–2; see also 2 Cor. 1:8–11; Phil. 1:19; Philem. 22). Therefore, although the adverb "constantly" is formulaic and somewhat hyperbolic, it does stress the indispensable and frequent role that prayer ought to play in the life of the Christian community, particularly in its communal worship.[19]

If joy is one of the distinguishing characteristics of Christianity, the same thing cannot be said about prayer. Before the Thessalonians "had turned to God from idols to serve a living and true God" (1:9), they would have offered prayers to a variety of pagan deities as part of the cultic worship that was so much a part of their Greco-Roman world. Christian prayer, however, differed from pagan prayer in a fundamental way. Pagan prayer was typically done in a spirit of manipulation as worshipers sought to secure the favor of a particular deity (for texts illustrating this quid-pro-quo mentality in which worship was viewed as a transaction: "Do this for me, and I'll do that for you," see Green 2002: 33–34). Christian prayer, however, begins from the presupposition that God, our heavenly Father, already loves us and thus is eager to give good gifts to us as his children (Matt. 7:7–11; Luke 11:11–13).

5:18a   The third of the three commands is "Give thanks in everything" (ἐν παντὶ εὐχαριστεῖτε, *en panti eucharisteite*). This reference to giving thanks is not unexpected, given the close link elsewhere in Paul's Letters between the activities of rejoicing, prayer, and thanksgiving (1 Thess. 3:9–10; Phil. 1:3–4; 4:4–6) and even more so between the latter two (Rom. 1:9–10; 2 Cor. 1:11; Eph. 1:16; Phil. 1:3–4; 4:5; Col. 1:3; 4:2; 1 Thess. 1:2; 1 Tim. 2:1; 2 Tim. 1:3; Philem. 4). It also is hardly surprising in light of the apostle's theology, in which ingratitude to God is characteristic of pagan depravity (Rom. 1:21: "For although

---

19. Many commentators connect Paul's call to constant prayer in 5:17 with the parable of the persistent widow in Luke 18:2–8, which Jesus tells his disciples "in order that they should always pray and never lose heart" (18:1). Yet this parable, perhaps like the parable of the friend at midnight (11:5–8), teaches persistence in prayer, ongoing prayer for the same specific request, rather than constant or unceasing prayer.

they knew God they did not honor him as God or give thanks to him"), while thanksgiving to God is the natural and even obligatory response of believers for what he has done in their lives ("We *ought* to give thanks . . .": 2 Thess. 1:3; 2:13). Consequently, Paul frequently commands his readers, as he does here in 5:18, to give thanks to God (Eph. 5:4, 20; Phil. 4:6; Col. 1:12; 3:15, 17; 4:2; 1 Tim. 2:1), or he makes statements that presuppose their thanksgiving to God (Rom. 14:6; 1 Cor. 14:16; 2 Cor. 1:11; 4:15; 9:11–12; 1 Tim. 4:3–4). The apostle himself illustrates the importance of expressing gratitude to God in the way he structures his letters, typically including, between the letter opening and body, a thanksgiving section where he gives thanks to God for the believers to whom he is writing (see the extended discussion of this epistolary unit in the literary analysis of 1:2–10).

The command of 5:18, therefore, suggests that there ought to be a theocentric focus to the worship of the Thessalonian congregation: they gather not primarily to meet the needs of their members but more importantly to rejoice and pray and give God the thanksgiving that he is justly due for his gracious work in their lives and in their world. This theocentric focus can be seen even more clearly in Paul's concluding exhortation to the Colossians about the teaching, admonishing, and singing of psalms and hymns and spiritual songs that is part of their corporate worship: "Whatever you do, in word or deed, do everything in the name of the Lord Jesus, giving thanks to God the Father through him" (Col. 3:17 NRSV).

There is some debate among scholars about the exact meaning of the prepositional phrase that begins the command to give thanks: should *en panti* be understood temporally as "in every time," that is, "always," or does it have the sense of "in everything," that is, "in every circumstance or situation"? The first option is supported by (1) the parallelism with the temporal adverbs ("always," "constantly") that introduce the previous two commands and (2) the frequent presence of temporal adjectives with the verb "to give thanks" elsewhere in Paul's Letters, including 1 Thessalonians (1:2; 2:13; 2 Thess. 1:3; 2:13; 1 Cor. 1:4; Eph. 5:20; Phil. 1:3; Col. 1:3; Philem. 4). The second option is supported by the fact that (1) *en panti* is clearly distinguished from the temporal adverb *pantote* in 2 Cor. 9:8; (2) *en panti* elsewhere in Paul does not appear to have a temporal sense but rather means "in everything" or "in every circumstance" (1 Cor. 1:5; 2 Cor. 4:8; 6:4; 11:6, 9; Phil. 4:12); and (3) if Paul had intended a temporal sense, he could have easily done so with the same adjective *pas* (all) by either (a) using a different preposition (*dia pantos* = "forever"; so Rom. 11:10; 2 Thess. 3:16) or (b) adding a noun of time (*en panti kairō* = "in every time," as in Eph. 6:18; see Malherbe 2000: 330). Although the evidence is stronger for the second option, this is, as Marshall (1983: 155) declares, "surely a pointless controversy, since either translation is virtually equivalent to the other. Believers are to find reason to praise and thank God in whatever situation they may find themselves and thus at all times."

Concerning this prepositional phrase, it is more important to note that Christians are not to give thanks "*for* everything" but "*in* everything." Believers are never thankful *for* the specific trials and tribulations that they must endure either from living in a fallen, sinful world (general suffering endured by all people, Christian and non-Christian alike) or from their faith in Jesus Christ (specifically suffering as a Christian).[20] Nevertheless, even in these situations they are still able to express gratitude to God for a variety of spiritual truths, such as thanking God that they do not face these hardships alone but with the empowering and comforting presence of God's Spirit; that these burdens, no matter how great and painful, will not "be able to separate us from the love of God that is ours in Christ Jesus" (Rom. 8:38–39); that these troubles are "light and momentary" in comparison with eternity and are achieving for us "an eternal glory that far outweighs them all" (2 Cor. 4:17); that "in everything," even in these burdens, "God works for the good of those who love him, who are called according to his purpose" (Rom. 8:28).

5:18b   The third unit, with its three commands concerning congregational worship, closes with an explanatory statement: "for this is the will of God[21] in Christ Jesus[22] for you" (τοῦτο γὰρ θέλημα θεοῦ ἐν Χριστῷ Ἰησοῦ εἰς ὑμᾶς, *touto gar thelēma theou en Christō Iēsou eis hymas*). It is grammatically possible that the demonstrative pronoun "this" looks *ahead* to the subsequent exhortations about the Spirit and Spirit-filled prophecy in verses 19–22. In fact, in 4:3, the only other Pauline occurrence of the phrase "for this is the will of God," it refers to the following commands about holiness in sexual conduct. But whereas in that earlier passage the presence of a noun ("holiness") in apposition to "for this is the will of God" makes it clear that this phrase points forward, no similar construction is found here in 5:18b. As a result, the context suggests to virtually all commentators that the phrase "for this is the will of God" looks *backward*, though some see it referring only to the immediately preceding directive to give thanks (e.g., Ellicott 1864: 81; Eadie 1877: 208; Malherbe 2000: 330) while most believe that it has in view all three of the prior commands (e.g., Frame 1912: 203; Marshall 1983: 156; Wanamaker 1990: 200; Morris 1991: 174; Green 2002: 260). The latter position is to be preferred in light of the linking of rejoicing, prayer, and thanksgiving elsewhere in Paul's Letters (for texts, see above), as well as the parallel structure of all three commands. Although Paul considers all his instructions to be not merely "the word of human beings but, as it truly

---

20. Contra Beale (2003: 170): "Paul attaches *always, continually* and *in all circumstances* to the three precepts in 5:16–18 in order to highlight that his readers are not only to rejoice, pray and give thanks for the 'good things' but also for the 'bad things' that confront this church."

21. For an evaluation of the different explanations as to why the noun pair "will of God" in 5:18b lacks the definite article, see comment on 4:3a.

22. The exact meaning of the prepositional phrase "in Christ Jesus" is difficult to determine. The GNT connects it with the following prepositional phrase "for you" and so understands it to refer to the believer's union with Christ, which leads to the translation of 5:18b: "This is what God wants from you in your life in union with Christ Jesus." The word order, however, suggests that it ought to be linked with the preceding noun pair, "the will of God." Paul's point, therefore, is either that God's will is revealed "in Christ Jesus," that is, in his teaching and practice, or that it is only by being "in Christ Jesus" that we have power to do God's will (see Ellingworth and Nida 1975: 121–22; Morris 1991: 175).

is, the word of God" (2:13) and thus obligatory for his readers, by grounding these exhortations in the will of God, he infuses his words with the greatest authority. The gathering of the community to rejoice, pray, and give thanks is by no means optional but a requirement equal in importance with the call to live a holy or moral life.

4. Testing Prophecy (5:19–22)

The fourth unit continues to deal with congregational worship but involves a shift in subject matter from the general activities of rejoicing, praying, and giving thanks to the specific issue of testing prophecy. The five commands that make up this section can be easily misunderstood if one does not recognize the way in which Paul has carefully structured his presentation of these exhortations (see esp. Ellingworth and Nida 1975: 123; Fee 1994a: 57; 2009: 217). The section falls into two parts: first, two negative commands (vv. 19–20), which warn against an outright rejection of Spirit-inspired prophecy, and then three positive commands (vv. 21–22), which warn against an outright acceptance of prophecy by calling for it to be tested. The negative first part is further distinguished from the second positive part by the adversative particle "but" (δέ, *de*).[23] Within each of these two parts, there is a discernible shift from the general to the specific. In the negative commands that make up the first part, the meaning of the first imperative ("Do not quench the Spirit") is spelled out by the second ("Do not despise prophecies"). Similarly, in the three positive commands that make up the second part, the meaning of the opening general directive ("Test all things") is spelled out by the subsequent two commands ("Hold fast to the good; hold yourselves away from every kind of evil prophecy"). These final two commands form a couplet since it is clear that they make use of the contrasting word pair "good" and "evil" and employ the same root verb (ἔχω, *echō*) and differ only in their prefixes. The five commands of the fourth unit, therefore, ought to be outlined as follows:

Negative Commands (5:19–20)	
5:19: General:	Do not quench the Spirit;
5:20: Specific:	do not despise prophecies;
	but . . .
Positive Commands (5:21–22)	
5:21a: General:	test all things;
5:21b: Specific:	hold fast to the good;
5:22: Specific:	hold yourselves away from every kind of evil prophecy.

The outline or structure of this passage, however, is clearer than the historical situation that it seeks to address. If the emphasis is placed on the first half, with its negative commands, then the primary problem involves a rejection of prophecy by some in the Thessalonian congregation. Thus, for example,

23. On omission of *de* in some MSS of 5:21, see the additional notes.

Frame (1912: 204) conjectures that the idlers demanded via prophecies that they be supported financially, thereby causing the majority of the church in Thessalonica to doubt the validity of such spiritual utterances—a view that Paul seeks to correct with the negative commands of verses 19–20. Schmithals (1972: 172–75) similarly sees the apostle as defending the importance and value of prophecy but differently argues that the anticharismatic backlash was caused not by the idlers but by gnostic pneumatics similar to those who caused trouble in Corinth and elsewhere. Wanamaker (1990: 202–3) proposes that Paul is responding to leaders in the church (those referred to in 5:12–13) who disparaged the Spirit and the gift of prophecy because they felt threatened by the authority and prestige given to charismatic members of the church who could speak such spiritual utterances.

If, however, the emphasis is placed on the second half, with its positive commands, then the primary problem in the Thessalonian church involves its uncritical acceptance of prophecy, which leads to trouble. Thus, for example, Fee (1994a: 58; 1994b) argues that Paul may well be anticipating the kind of problem that he later had to address in his Second Letter to the Thessalonians (2:2): an untested prophecy that lies behind the false claim that "the day of the Lord has come." Malherbe (2000: 335) similarly puts the emphasis on the second half of the passage, claiming that "the problem was precisely that they were in thrall to the false prophets" and that in these verses the apostle is seeking to make the Thessalonian believers much more discerning in their acceptance of prophecies.

As the above discussion illustrates, it is sometimes difficult (and dangerous) to engage in mirror reading, that is, to discern the historical situation that lies behind a particular text. The specificity of the opening two negative commands (in contrast to the general nature of the following three positive commands) and the especially strong verb used in the second command (Paul prohibits not merely the neglect or rejection of prophecies but also holding them in disdain or contempt) are sufficient enough evidence to conclude that the apostle has in view not a generic but a particular situation. Nevertheless, there is not enough evidence to explain what is going on in the church that leads some to disparage prophecy. But whatever the problem may be, Paul clearly is concerned to *balance* his legitimization of Spirit-inspired utterances with the need for such prophecies to be tested according to the moral criteria of good and evil. As D. Martin (1995: 184) puts it: "Paul did not wish the church to become so cynical that they treated with contempt those who came with a word of prophecy. Neither was the church to be so gullible that they accepted whatever a so-called prophet said without carefully weighing it and determining that it was indeed a true word of God." This balanced approach of Paul toward Spirit-inspired utterances can also be seen in his First Letter to the Corinthians where, after a lengthy (chaps. 12–14) and at times sharply worded correction about their abuse of speaking in tongues and prophesying, he concludes with an affirmation of the very same spiritual gifts that have caused so much trouble in this church: "So then, my brothers, earnestly desire to prophesy, and do not forbid speaking in tongues" (14:39).

Paul opens the fourth unit with a general prohibition: "Do not quench the Spirit" (τὸ πνεῦμα μὴ σβέννυτε, *to pneuma mē sbennyte*). The apostle has mentioned the Holy Spirit explicitly only three other times in the letter thus far (1:5, 6; 4:8), and so here the reference to "the Spirit" may appear to come quite unexpectedly and abruptly. However, as noted above (see comment on 5:16), in Paul's mind the activities of rejoicing, praying, and thanksgiving are all intimately linked to the working of the Holy Spirit so that the three commands of the third unit function as a transition to this fourth unit, with its treatment of the Spirit and Spirit-inspired prophecy in the context of worship.

If the larger context is ignored, the mention of "the Spirit" could be interpreted in a general fashion to refer to ethical or moral conduct (see Gal. 5:18, 22–24). Thus, for example, John Chrysostom (*Hom. 1 Thess.* 11 [PG 62:461, 462]) reads into this verse a reference to the "fruit of the Spirit." However, in light of the immediately following reference to "prophecies," the mention of "the Spirit" must refer to the gifts or charismatic signs of the Spirit. A number of commentators argue that Paul has in view the gifts of the Spirit in general (e.g., see a list in 1 Cor. 12:7–11; also Rom. 12:6–8) and only in the next verse specifies the particular gift of prophecy (so, e.g., Ellicott 1880: 81; Frame 1912: 205; Best 1977: 238; Wanamaker 1990: 202). Others (Gunkel 1979: 30–31; Moore 1969: 84) think that the apostle already has a particular charismatic gift in mind, namely, speaking in tongues, since this gift proved to be a problem in the Corinthian church and Paul elsewhere pairs tongues speaking and prophesying in a manner that would parallel the references here to "the Spirit" and "prophecies" (1 Cor. 13:8: "as for prophecies, they will pass away; as for tongues, they will cease").[24] However, given (1) the pattern in this fourth unit of moving from the general to the particular (see comment above), (2) the content of the immediately following command, and (3) the use of the verb "to quench," it is more likely that the reference to "the Spirit" is, in the apostle's mind, already restricted to the particular gift of prophecy (so, e.g., Bruce 1982: 125; Holtz 1986: 259; Fee 1994a: 59; Malherbe 2000: 331; Fee 2009: 219). This understanding of "the Spirit" is supported by the occurrence of the same term (*pneuma*) in 2 Thess. 2:2, which in a context where it is set over against "a word" and "a letter," also has the sense of "prophecy" (so NIV) or "prophetic utterance" (Giblin 1967: 243; Fee 1994a: 74; 1994b: 207–8).

The word "S/spirit" (most often the Holy Spirit but sometimes the human spirit) is frequently linked with words meaning "fire" (see Rom. 12:11; 2 Tim. 1:6–7; elsewhere in the NT, see Matt. 3:11; Luke 3:16; Acts 2:3–4; 18:25).[25] This likely explains Paul's choice of, for him, the rare verb *sbennymi* (in Paul, only here and Eph. 6:16), which was used literally to refer to the extinguishing of

---

24. The appeal to 1 Cor. 13:8 is misleading, since tongues speaking and prophecy are not paired there but part of a list of three things (the third item is knowledge) that are temporary in contrast to the permanency of love.

25. This accounts for the NIV 1984 and TNIV translation of 5:19, "Do not put out the Spirit's fire," even though the word "fire" is not found in the Greek text. The NIV 2011 more accurately has "Do not quench the Spirit."

a fire and thus also possessed the figurative meaning of "to quench, stifle, suppress" (BDAG 917; for the widespread metaphorical use of this verb both in the LXX and secular literature, see F. Lang, *TDNT* 7:165–68; Spicq 1994: 3.242–43). The apostle, therefore, is forbidding the deliberate suppression of the person of the Holy Spirit or, more specifically, the manifestation of the Spirit's work in the form of spiritual utterances or prophecies given by believers in their communal worship. When those who are inspired by the Spirit to speak a divine word of prophecy are forbidden to practice this gift, or if what they say is rejected, then the body of believers is robbed of the opportunity to be built up, comforted, and encouraged (1 Cor. 14:3: "The one who prophesies speaks to people for their upbuilding and comfort and encouragement").

The grammatical construction of this prohibition—the negative *mē* with the present imperative instead of the aorist subjunctive—minimally stresses the ongoing or continuous nature of the command: "Do not *ever* quench the Spirit!" Many commentators (e.g., Milligan 1908: 76; Moore 1969: 83; Best 1977: 237; Marshall 1983: 157; Morris 1991: 176n65), however, believe that this construction expresses more than this: it has traditionally been understood to prohibit an action that is already taking place (Jackson 1904; MHT 1:122): "Do not *continue to* quench the Spirit!" If so, this would provide conclusive evidence that Paul's commands, both here and in the following verse, are not merely to prevent a potential issue but to correct an actual problem at work in the Thessalonian church. However, this traditional understanding of the distinction between prohibitions employing the present imperative versus those with the aorist subjunctive has been seriously called into question (McKay 1985; Boyer 1987; Fanning 1990: 325–88; Porter 1992: 220–29; see the brief but helpful survey of this debate in Wallace 1996: 714–17). Therefore, although Paul is likely responding to an actual problem, this conclusion must be based not on the grammatical construction of the prohibition but on other evidence such as the specificity and intensity of the next imperative (in 5:20).

5:20   The second prohibition clarifies the meaning of the first: "Do not despise prophecies" (προφητείας μὴ ἐξουθενεῖτε, *prophēteias mē exoutheneite*). The noun *prophēteia*, here in the plural (also in 1 Cor. 13:8 and 1 Tim. 1:18), occurs only a modest nine times in Paul's writings (Rom. 12:6; 1 Cor. 12:10; 13:2, 8; 14:6, 22; 1 Thess. 5:20; 1 Tim. 1:18; 4:14), and the majority of these occurrences are occasioned by the unique problem in Corinth. This might suggest that such Spirit-inspired activity did not play a large or important role in the early church. This figure, however, needs to be balanced by the following: (1) references to the noun "prophecy" are found in both the earliest (1 Thessalonians) and latest (1 Timothy) of the apostle's letters, (2) the verb "to prophesy" occurs eleven times (though all in 1 Corinthians), and (3) Paul mentions "prophecy" in Rom. 12:6 without any accompanying explanation. These facts "strongly suggest that this was a normal expression of the Spirit's activity in the early church" (Fee 1994a: 60). Paul's most detailed explanation of prophecy is found in 1 Cor. 14; from this and other references it can be defined as "a word or oracle given or revealed by God through the initiative and inspiration of the Holy Spirit and conveyed by a willing medium or participant sometimes designated as a 'prophet' or as 'one who prophesies.' A prophecy is given in order to meet one or more needs within the Christian community for guidance and direction, edification, encouragement, consolation or witness" (C. M. Robeck Jr., *DPL* 755). The high value that Paul accorded prophecy is clear from his exhortation, albeit in a polemical context, that the Corinthian Christians should "be zealous for spiritual gifts, especially that you prophesy" (1 Cor. 14:1; see also 14:39).

The esteem that Paul has for prophecy is also revealed in his command to the Thessalonians that they should not "despise" this spiritual gift. The verb *exoutheneō* is particularly strong, meaning "to show by one's attitude or manner of treatment that an entity has no merit or worth, *disdain*" (BDAG 352.1). For example, it is paired with the verb "to mock" in describing how Herod and his soldiers treated Jesus (Luke 23:11) and also is used in a parable to depict the attitude of the self-righteous Pharisee who contemptuously looks down on others, including a tax collector who has similarly gone to the temple to pray (Luke 18:9). Paul uses this verb elsewhere seven times to describe such things as God's choosing "what is low and despised in the world" (1 Cor. 1:28), congregational members in Corinth who take a legal matter before "those who are despised in/by the church" (1 Cor. 6:4), the Corinthian church's pejorative treatment of Timothy (1 Cor. 16:11: "Let no one disdain him!") and their critical evaluation of the apostle's preaching ability (2 Cor. 10:10: "His speech amounts to nothing"), the capacity of the Galatians to welcome the physically disabled Paul graciously rather than to "despise or scorn" him (Gal. 4:14), and those in Rome who look down on "the weak" because they abstain from eating meat (Rom. 14:3, 10). Here in 1 Thess. 5:20 the verb may refer not merely to the *attitude* of despising prophecy but the *action* of rejecting it in a contemptuous manner (so BDAG 352.2: "to have no use for something as being beneath one's consideration, *to reject disdainfully*"; see also Acts 4:11; Pss. Sol. 2.5; 1 En. 99.14).

The negative opening half of the fourth unit with its two prohibitions (5:19–20) is now balanced by the positive concluding half with its three commands, the first of which is general: "but test all things" (πάντα δὲ δοκιμάζετε, *panta de dokimazete*).[26] Paul does not want his strong affirmation of prophecy to be wrongly taken as a call to blindly accept any kind of purportedly Spirit-inspired

5:21a

---

26. Many early Christian writers (for a list of names and texts, see Lightfoot 1904: 85) believed that in this command to "test all things" (5:21a), Paul was borrowing from an *agraphon* of Jesus, a saying of Jesus not recorded in the Gospels: "Be tested/approved money-changers" (γίνεσθε δόκιμοι τραπεζῖται). In fact, they so closely connected the saying of Jesus with the command of Paul that they rarely quoted the one text without the other. This link was made easier by the fact that these early Christian writers frequently included in their version of Jesus's *agraphon* the words of Paul about "holding fast the good and abstaining from every evil" (5:21–22). The only possible connection between the two, however, is found in the root δοκιμ-, which is a too commonly used term to justify any claim of dependence by Paul on this Jesus saying (so Rigaux

utterance without discerning the truth of that particular utterance. The apostle knows how easily the gift of prophecy can be abused and cause harmful consequences that are at odds with its intended purpose of building up, comforting, and encouraging believers (1 Cor. 14:3). For example, it is likely a false prophecy claiming, "The day of the Lord has come!" that later triggers the Thessalonian church to be shaken out of their wits (2 Thess. 2:2). Counterfeit spiritual utterances sometimes involved obviously unchristian statements like "Jesus be cursed!" (1 Cor. 12:3). Fabricated prophecies were sometimes used to deny cardinal teachings of the Christian faith such as the full humanity of Christ (1 John 4:1–3; 2 John 7). Instead of serving the interests of others, prophecies could sadly serve the self-interests of the speaker, as demonstrated in this advice given in the Didache, a mid-to-late first-century Christian document: "Every prophet calling for a table of food in the Spirit will not eat of it; if he does, he is a false prophet. . . . If any prophet, speaking in the Spirit, says, 'Give me money' or anything else, do not listen to him" (11.9, 12). In light of this potential abuse of prophecy, therefore, Paul exhorts the Thessalonians not naively to believe all spiritual utterances but instead to put them to the test.

The need to test prophecy is also found in the apostle's extended discussion of spiritual gifts to the Corinthians (1 Cor. 12–14). Early in that discussion, Paul catalogs a variety of spiritual gifts and, immediately after referring to the gift of prophecy, lists the gift of "distinguishing [διάκρισις, *diakrisis*] between spirits" (1 Cor. 12:10)—a gift that presupposes the necessity for prophecy to be tested. Near the end of that same discussion, Paul commands: "Let two or three prophets speak, and let the others evaluate [διακρίνω, *diakrinō*] what is said" (1 Cor. 14:29). This notion of passing judgment on prophecy is here in 1 Thess. 5:21 expressed with the verb *dokimazō* (BDAG 255.1: "to make a critical examination of something to determine genuineness, *put to the test, examine*"). Earlier in 1 Thessalonians, Paul has used this verb twice to defend the integrity of his motives in preaching the gospel to them, claiming that he has been "tested" or "examined by God, . . . the one who examines our hearts" (2:4). Elsewhere he frequently uses this verb for testing or passing judgment about a person's moral character, either that of oneself (1 Cor. 11:28; 2 Cor. 13:5; Gal. 6:4; Eph. 5:10) or others (1 Cor. 16:3; 2 Cor. 8:22; 1 Tim. 3:10). Echoing the very point made by Paul here in 5:21 to the Thessalonians, the author of 1 John uses the same verb to challenge his readers similarly not to believe every spirit but to "test the spirits to see whether they are of God" (1 John 4:1).

The "all things" that are to be tested refer not to any aspect of the Christian life (contra Morris 1991: 178: "The words he uses are quite general, and they must be held to apply to all kinds of things and not simply to claimants to spiritual gifts"; so also Lightfoot 1904: 84) or even to all kinds of spiritual gifts (so Rigaux 1956: 592; Best 1977: 240; Wanamaker 1990: 203) but more narrowly to prophecy. Since the positive command to test all things stands

1956: 592; Jeremias 1958: 89–93; Fee 1994a: 60n92; Malherbe 2000: 333; Fee 2009: 221n63). Furthermore, Paul's saying lacks the key term "money-changers" (Best 1977: 241).

in an antithetical relationship to the two preceding negative commands, the adjective *panta* (all things), as Ellicott (1880: 82) notes, "must thus have a restricted sense, and be limited to the spiritual gifts previously alluded to" (so also, e.g., Eadie 1877: 211; Holtz 1986: 261; Malherbe 2000: 333; Green 2002: 264). The contemporary application of this command may justly be extended to other aspects of the Christian life, but its original intent is restricted to the testing of all prophecies.

Paul's clear call to test prophecy is unfortunately not accompanied by a clear statement of the criteria to be used in this discerning activity. Although the apostle spells out such criteria nowhere else either, a few of his statements are suggestive:

1. *Upbuilding.* Since prophecy is intended for the comforting, encouraging, and especially the upbuilding of the church (1 Cor. 14:3–5), as well as the "common good" (12:7), a general standard by which to evaluate prophecy is how well any given prophecy fulfills these purposes (Best 1977: 240; Fee 1994a: 61; Beale 2003: 175).

2. *Apostolic tradition.* A more specific standard for prophecy involves its agreement with apostolic teaching, which for contemporary believers has been recorded in the Bible. This criterion can be seen in Paul's treatment of the later crisis in Thessalonica over a false claim, almost certainly via a prophecy (2:2, "through a spirit"), that the day of the Lord has come (see esp. Fee 1994a: 61). The apostle responds to this crisis by appealing to the believers there to "stand fast and hold firm to the traditions that you were taught by us, either by word or letter" (2 Thess. 2:15). Paul therefore contrasts what was falsely taught them through a prophecy with what he truthfully taught them either through "word," meaning his original preaching ministry in their community, or through "letter," in his previous letter to them (1 Thessalonians). A similar appeal to the standard of agreement with apostolic teaching is found in 1 John 4:1–6, where the testimony of false prophets who deny that Jesus Christ has come in the flesh is contrasted with the testimony of the author, who presents himself as one who has apostolic authority to speak the truth.

3. *The prophet's character and conduct.* A third criterion from sources other than Paul, though not of prophesy per se but that of the person speaking a word of prophecy, involves the test of character or conduct (Stott 1991: 129; Green 2002: 264–65; Beale 2003: 174). Jesus warned his followers to "watch out for false prophets" whom "you will recognize by their fruits" (Matt. 7:15–20). The Didache similarly advises: "But not everyone who speaks in a spirit is a prophet, but only if he has the behavior of the Lord. . . . And every prophet who teaches the truth but does not do what he teaches is a false prophet" (11.8, 9–12).

Paul's general call to test all prophecies is now clarified with two further commands that form a couplet: "Hold fast to the good; hold yourselves away **5:21b–22** from every kind of evil prophecy" (τὸ καλὸν κατέχετε, ἀπὸ παντὸς εἴδους πονηροῦ ἀπέχεσθε, *to kalon katechete, apo pantos eidous ponērou apechesthe*). These two final exhortations can and have been taken out of their specific context and turned into universal maxims that are applicable to any and all situations, even by those who recognize that the preceding verses deal specifically with Spirit-inspired utterances (so, e.g., Eadie 1877: 212; Lünemann 1885: 556; Wanamaker 1990: 204; Holmes 1998: 185). But since this couplet is intended to specify the previous command to test all things (v. 21a), and this previous command is in turn intended to contrast with the preceding prohibitions about the Spirit and prophecies, there can be no doubt that in these closing verses Paul continues to be focused narrowly on the testing of these spiritual utterances. Thus, even though the word "prophecy" is not found in the Greek text, its addition to the translation of verse 22 accurately captures the intention of the apostle and thus is justified.

Paul's expected response to the Thessalonians' testing of prophecy is clear: if a given prophecy is tested and found to be "good," then they must "hold fast" to it; conversely, if a given prophecy is tested and found to be "evil," then they must "hold yourselves away" from it. The two verbs used here, both having the same root and differing only in a prefix, are strong and express wholehearted acceptance of prophecy that is judged good and absolute rejection of prophecy deemed evil. The first verb, *katechō*, functions almost as a technical term concerning the need for believers to embrace, keep, and defend key traditions or fundamental convictions of the Christian faith that have been passed on to them (1 Cor. 11:2; 15:2; Luke 8:15; Heb. 3:6, 14; 10:23; BDAG 533.2: "to adhere firmly to traditions, convictions, or beliefs, *hold to, hold fast*"). The second verb, *apechō*, when it occurs in the middle voice as it does here (also 1 Thess. 4:3; 1 Tim. 4:3; Acts 5:39 v.l.; 15:20, 29; 1 Pet. 2:11), means "to avoid contact with or use of something, *keep away, abstain, refrain from*" (BDAG 103.5). Paul has used this verb earlier in the letter while strongly exhorting the Thessalonians to have nothing to do with sexual immorality (4:3). The translation "hold yourselves away" is intended to highlight in English the contrast that is clearly seen in Greek with the preceding verb "hold fast."

The object of the second verb is unexpected and thus calls for some comment. For instead of balancing the positive command "Hold fast to *the good*"[27] with the negative command "Hold yourselves away from *the evil*," the apostle instead writes: "Hold yourselves away from *every kind of evil*." The noun *eidos* sometimes has the sense of "outward appearance" (Luke 3:22; 9:29; John 5:37), which here would mean that the Thessalonians must avoid not merely things that are actually evil but even things that appear to be evil. This understanding turns the command into a more general one and infuses it with an ethical understanding. We have seen from the context, however, that Paul's concern

---

27. Although Paul uses a different word for "good" in 5:21b (καλός) than a few verses earlier in 5:15 (ἀγαθός), there is no discernible difference in meaning between the two terms (see Rom. 7:18, where these two words appear to be used synonymously within the same verse).

still lies with the specific issue of prophecy. Furthermore, the contrast with the preceding command is not between what is actually good and what only appears to be evil but rather with what is actually evil. Thus a second meaning of *eidos* is preferred: "a variety of something, *kind*" (BDAG 280.2). It is less clear whether the adjective *ponēros* modifies this noun ("evil kind") or, as suggested by the parallel with "the good," it functions substantively ("kind of evil"). The fuller phrase "every kind of evil" may well be traditional, drawn from texts like Job 1:1, 8 and 2:3. Paul perhaps uses this fuller phrase instead of the shorter and expected "the evil" as the object of the second command because he views "the good" as a singular entity whereas evil comes in a variety of different forms (Lightfoot 1904: 86: "For 'the good' is one and the same essentially, while vice is manifold and variable"; so also Milligan 1908: 77; Best 1977: 240; Fee 1994a: 62; Weatherly 1996: 188).

Additional Notes

5:12. Instead of the expected form of the participle προϊσταμένους (B D F G Ψ 𝔐), a few weighty MSS have the Hellenistic form προϊστανομένους (𝔓30vid ℵ A). The meaning of the word is not affected.

5:13. A few MSS have replaced the infinitive ἡγεῖσθαι with the imperative ἡγεῖσθε (B Ψ 6 81 104 326 1739 *al* sy).

5:13. The adverb ὑπερεκπερισσοῦ (ℵ A D² Ψ 𝔐) is replaced with the simple form ἐκπερισσοῦ in perhaps one MS (𝔓30vid) and with the more traditional adverbial form ὑπερεκπερισσῶς in a few significant uncial MSS (B D* F G *pc*).

5:13. The manuscript evidence is virtually equal for the variants ἑαυτοῖς and αὐτοῖς, or even αὐτοῖς as a contracted form of the reflexive pronoun. Many significant witnesses contain the simple pronoun "them" (αὐτοῖς: 𝔓30 ℵ D* F G P Ψ 81 104 1881* 2464 2495* *pm* f vg; Cass); many other significant witnesses contain the reflexive pronoun "yourselves" (ἑαυτοῖς: A B D² K L 33 365 630 1175 1241 1739 1881ᶜ 2495ᶜ *pm*). Although the external evidence is evenly divided, the internal evidence suggests that the reflexive pronoun "yourselves" is original (so virtually all translations and commentators). The absence of any connective particle (asyndeton) likely caused scribes to clarify the connection that this command has with the preceding appeal by changing the reflexive pronoun "yourselves" to the simple pronoun "them." It is difficult to find any motivation for a scribe to make the reverse change.

5:15. The external evidence is evenly divided on whether the conjunction καί ought to be included (so 𝔓30 ℵ² B Ψ 𝔐 vgst syh) or omitted (so ℵ* A D F G 6 33 1739 1881 2464 *pc* it vgit syp; Ambst Spec) from the text after *diōkete*. The internal evidence, however, slightly favors its omission: (1) as the *lectio brevior* (shorter reading), it is more likely to be original; (2) the parallel phrase in 3:12 does not include the conjunction; and (3) the possibility that it was deliberately added by a later scribe to create a clearer and more polished reading: "but always pursue what is good *both* for one another *and* for all."

5:21. It is not clear whether the particle δέ was part of the original text. On the one hand, its omission has strong external support (ℵ* A 33 81 104 614 629 630 945 *pm* syp; Tert Did); its presence in other MSS may be explained as a later scribe's desire to make clear the contrast between the negative commands of 5:19–20 and the positive commands of 5:21–22. On the other hand, its presence also has strong external support (B D G K P Ψ 181 326 436 1241 1739 *pm* it vg co goth eth) and "is almost necessary for the sense" (Lightfoot 1904: 84). Some possible reasons for the omission of the particle include (1) the attempt to disconnect the command from the context and thus turn it into a maxim with wider application beyond prophecy (Eadie 1877: 211); (2) the result of the particle having "been absorbed by the first syllable of the following word" (B. Metzger 1971: 633, who follows Lightfoot 1904: 84; yet note that the following syllable is δοκ- and thus does not look or sound like the particle δέ); and (3) agreement with the whole series of commands in these verses, "all of which lack conjunctions" (Fee 1994a: 55n69; 2009: 216n39). In summary, the evidence for its inclusion is slightly stronger than for its omission, and this is the reading adopted in UBS[4] and NA[28].

V. Letter Closing (5:23–28)

Paul skillfully ends his letter by adapting the closing conventions so that this final epistolary unit not only better connects to the specific situation of the Thessalonian church but also echoes key themes taken up in the letter body. The peace benediction (v. 23) has been greatly expanded to recapitulate the two major themes of holy living and comfort concerning Christ's return. The word of encouragement (v. 24) recalls earlier statements about God's call and initiative in the Thessalonians' lives, thereby reassuring them that their ability to endure persecution and be preserved blameless at the coming of the Lord Jesus does not rest in their own talent or strength but in God's. Although the first hortatory section (v. 25) involves a general request for prayer, the subsequent kiss greeting (v. 26) and second hortatory section (v. 27) have also been adapted to address internal tensions at work in the Thessalonian congregation and to encourage reconciliation and concord among church members. The grace benediction (v. 28), along with the preceding peace benediction (5:23), forms an inverted or chiastic inclusio with the greeting of the letter opening (1:1, "Grace to you and peace"), thereby framing the letter and bringing Paul's correspondence to a definitive close.

Literary Analysis

Character of the Passage

First Thessalonians 5:23–28 consists of the fourth and final major section of Paul's correspondence: the letter closing. This final unit is the "Rodney Dangerfield" section of the apostle's letters: it does not get any respect. Whereas the first three major sections—the letter opening, thanksgiving, and letter body—have been subjected to a number of form-critical analyses, the letter closing has, by comparison, been largely neglected. Biblical commentaries generally treat the letter closing in a cursory manner and are typically at a loss to explain how a particular closing relates to its respective letter as a whole. The scholarly neglect of the Pauline letter closing and the failure to recognize the hermeneutical significance of this final section is due to one or more of the following three assumptions—all of them false (see Weima 1994a: 21–22; 2010b: 307–9).

First, it is believed that the closings (along with the openings) are primarily conventional in nature and serve merely to establish or maintain contact in contrast to the thanksgiving and body sections of the letter, which are judged to be more important, since here Paul takes up the specific issues that he wishes to address.[1] In

---

1. White (1981: 7), for example, states: "Whereas the body conveys the specific situational occasion of the letter, the opening and closing tend to convey the ongoing and general aspect of the correspondents' relationship."

colloquial terms, the opening and closing are viewed only as an appetizer and light dessert in contrast to the letter body, which provides the weightier main course. The closing (and opening) sections, however, are not without significance. As Jervis (1991: 42) recognizes: "The opening and closing sections are where Paul (re)establishes his relationship with his readers and where the function of each letter is most evident."[2] Furthermore, as Roetzel (1975: 30) observes: "Once the letter-writing conventions which Paul used are understood, the alert reader will also find clues to Paul's intent in his creative use of those conventions as well." This statement is just as true for the epistolary conventions found in the closing as it is in the other sections of Paul's Letters. Thus, rather than being insignificant, the letter closings serve an important function in the overall argument of the letter.

Second, there is a belief that the diverse formulas found within these final sections have been largely borrowed from the liturgical practices of the early church, and so any particular letter closing is assumed to be unrelated to the rest of the letter. For example, Champion (1934: 34), in his study of the benedictions and doxologies that frequently occur in the final sections of Paul's Letters, concludes that these two types of formulas "are not essential to the thought of the epistles and that they can be separated quite easily from their context." But even if one were to concede the debatable assertion that a liturgical origin exists for many (or all) of Paul's benedictions and doxologies, this does not preclude the possibility that these stereotyped formulas have been adapted by the apostle in such a way as to make them intimately connected to the concerns addressed in their respective letters.

A third possible explanation for the lack of attention typically given to Paul's letter closings involves a perceived parallel between the apostle's epistolary practices and those of other ancient letter writers. A survey of Hellenistic letters reveals that only a few epistolary conventions occur in the closings and that they do not always appear in the same order. These facts might suggest that ancient letter writers did not write the closing section with much care and that therefore Paul, following the epistolary practice of his day, did not do so either. A more careful analysis of Hellenistic letters, however, reveals the existence of a number of links between the closing sections and their respective body sections, thereby proving that ancient letter writers did not end their correspondence in a careless manner but instead tried to construct closings that were appropriate to each letter's contexts (Weima 1994a: 28–55, esp. the letters cited on 33–34, 53–55).

The neglect of the Pauline letter closing was ultimately corrected with a monograph-length study of this epistolary unit (Weima 1994a).[3] This detailed and comprehensive analysis demonstrates that the Pauline letter closings are carefully constructed units, shaped and adapted in such a way that they are related to, and sometimes even summarize, the major concerns and themes previously addressed in the body sections of their respective letters, and thus they are hermeneutically

---

2. Lyons (1985: 26–27) similarly observes that in a speech or written discourse the opening and closing are where the speaker makes his purpose explicit.

3. A few scattered articles on individual formulas or epistolary conventions found within letter closings appeared before this monograph: e.g., Bahr (1968) deals generally with subscriptions; Jewett (1969) and Mullins (1977) both cover benedictions; Mullins (1968) addresses closing greetings. But these, along with the more detailed studies of the Pauline letter closings by Gamble (1977: 65–83) and Schnider and Stenger (1987: 108–67), fail to demonstrate how these final epistolary sections relate in any significant way to the major concerns previously dealt with in the bodies of their respective letters.

significant. The letter closing, therefore, functions a lot like the thanksgiving, but in reverse. For as the thanksgiving foreshadows and points ahead to the major concerns to be addressed in the body of the letter (see esp. Schubert 1939 and O'Brien 1977), so the closing serves to highlight and encapsulate the main points previously taken up in the main section of the correspondence. This recapitulating function found generally in the Pauline letter closings is also evident in the closing of 1 Thessalonians, as will become clear in the comments on 5:23–28 given below (see also Weima 1994a: 174–86; 1995; 2010b: 313–17).

Extent of the Passage

There is some debate over the proper beginning of this letter closing. Since some commentators believe that the peace benediction (v. 23) and its accompanying word of encouragement (v. 24) conclude the preceding section concerning congregational life and worship (5:12–22), they begin the letter closing with Paul's request for prayer in 5:25. The vast majority of exegetes, however, view the peace benediction and word of encouragement as belonging to the letter closing and thus begin the final section of the letter at 5:23. The strengths and weaknesses of each of these positions have already been examined in the literary analysis of 5:12–22, and so there is no need to repeat those arguments here. Instead, I encourage the reader to review the extensive discussion found there; here I simply repeat my conclusion that several compelling reasons exist for including the peace benediction and word of encouragement in the letter closing and that this final epistolary unit is best seen as consisting of 5:23–28.

Structure of the Passage

The letter closing of 1 Thessalonians contains all five of the epistolary conventions typically found in the final sections of Paul's Letters.[4] It opens with the peace benediction (v. 23), whose form has been greatly expanded from the expected "May the God of peace be with you" (see Rom. 15:33; 2 Cor. 13:11; Phil. 4:9b; cf. Rom. 16:20a; 2 Thess. 3:16; Gal. 6:16) to a lengthy prayer that the God of peace will both "sanctify wholly" and "completely keep" the Thessalonians "blameless at the coming of our Lord Jesus Christ." This embellished peace benediction concludes with a word of encouragement (v. 24) in which Paul promises his readers that the God who calls them is faithful and so will ensure that the contents of the benediction are fulfilled in their lives. This is followed by a brief hortatory section (v. 25) that begins with the vocative "brothers," a standard introductory formula of this particular closing convention (Rom. 16:17–18; 1 Cor. 16:13–16; 2 Cor. 13:11a; Phil. 4:8–9a; Philem. 20–22). Paul exhorts the Thessalonians to pray for him and his coworkers. Next comes a greeting formula (v. 26) in which the apostle requests

---

4. The Pauline letter closings typically contain five epistolary conventions, usually given in the following order: (1) a "peace benediction" expresses Paul's prayer that the peace of God will be with his readers; (2) a "hortatory section" consists of some final commands or exhortations; (3) a "greeting section" conveys closing greetings from Paul and/or others with him to the readers, including an occasional command that they greet each other with a "holy kiss"; (4) an "autograph formula" indicates that Paul has taken over from his secretary and is now writing in his own hand; and (5) a "grace benediction" expresses Paul's prayer that the grace of the Lord Jesus Christ will be with his readers. See the extended discussion of these epistolary conventions in Weima 1994a: 77–155; 2010b: 310–45.

his readers to greet all the brothers with a holy kiss. In a second hortatory section (v. 27), probably written in his own hand (see comments below), Paul strongly adjures the Thessalonians to have his letter read to all the members of the church. The letter closing comes to a definitive end, in typical Pauline fashion, with a grace benediction (v. 28).

The letter closing of 5:23–28, therefore, ought to be outlined as follows:

A. Peace benediction (5:23)
B. Word of encouragement (5:24)
C. Hortatory section (5:25)
D. Kiss greeting (5:26)
E. Hortatory section (autograph) (5:27)
F. Grace benediction (5:28)

Exegesis and Exposition

[23]May the God of peace himself sanctify you completely, and may your whole spirit and soul and body be preserved blamelessly at the coming of our Lord Jesus Christ. [24]Faithful is the one who is calling you, who will indeed do this. [25]Brothers, pray ⌜also⌝ for us. [26]Greet all the brothers with a holy kiss. [27]I cause you to swear an oath in the name of the Lord that this letter be read to all ⌜the brothers⌝. [28]May the grace of our Lord Jesus Christ be with you.

A. Peace Benediction (5:23)

5:23   The letter closing begins with a peace benediction[5] that, along with the grace benediction of verse 28, forms an inverted, or chiastic, inclusio with the salutation "grace and peace" of the letter opening (1:1): "May the God of peace himself sanctify you completely, and may your whole spirit and soul and body be preserved blamelessly at the coming of our Lord Jesus Christ" (αὐτὸς δὲ ὁ θεὸς τῆς εἰρήνης ἁγιάσαι ὑμᾶς ὁλοτελεῖς, καὶ ὁλόκληρον ὑμῶν τὸ πνεῦμα καὶ ἡ ψυχὴ καὶ τὸ σῶμα ἀμέμπτως ἐν τῇ παρουσίᾳ τοῦ κυρίου ἡμῶν Ἰησοῦ Χριστοῦ τηρηθείη, *autos de ho theos tēs eirēnēs hagiasai hymas holoteleis, kai holoklēron hymōn to pneuma kai hē psychē kai to sōma amemptōs en tē parousia tou kyriou hēmōn Iēsou Christou tērētheiē*).

The peace benediction occurs seven times in Paul's various letter closings (Rom. 15:33; 16:20a; 2 Cor. 13:11; Gal. 6:16; Phil. 4:9b; 1 Thess. 5:23; 2 Thess. 3:16), and this epistolary convention exhibits a clear and consistent pattern involving four basic elements (see chart and discussion in Weima 1994a: 87–98; 2010b: 311–13).

First, there is the "introductory element," which consists of either the adversative particle *de* when the peace benediction occupies the first position in

---

5. This epistolary convention is referred to by a number of different titles: "prayer wish" (Wiles 1974: 63–68); "homiletic benediction" (Jewett 1969); "benedictory prayer" (Fee 1994a: 63; 2009: 225); "invocation" (Witherington 2006: 171).

a letter closing, as is the case here in 5:23 (so also Rom. 15:33; 2 Thess. 3:16; see Rom. 16:20a), or the conjunction *kai* when it is preceded in the closing by other epistolary conventions (2 Cor. 13:11b; Gal. 6:16; Phil. 4:9b).

Second, there is the "divine source" of the wish, which is normally "God" (only exception is 2 Thess. 3:16) in contrast to the grace benedictions, where the divine source is always "(our) Lord Jesus Christ." This pattern of aligning a peace benediction with God and a grace benediction with Christ follows naturally from the salutation in the letter opening, where the same two wishes are linked in chiastic fashion with the same two divine figures ("Grace and peace to you from God our Father and the Lord Jesus Christ"). Added consistently to the divine source is the qualifying genitive phrase "of peace," from which the peace benediction derives its name. The fuller expression "the God of peace," rare in the literature of Paul's day (only two other occurrences outside of Paul's closing peace benedictions: T. Dan 5.2; Heb. 13:20), describes God as the source and thus also the giver of peace. The meaning of this "peace" that God gives stems from the OT concept of *shalom* (*šālôm*; W. Foerster, *TDNT* 2:402–8) and thus does not refer merely to the resolution of conflict but has a much richer meaning, involving the restoration of the fallen created order to its former perfection and glory, thus as eschatological salvation (see Rom. 2:10; 8:6; 14:17; Eph. 6:15). Here in 1 Thess. 5:23 Paul adds to the divine source the intensive pronoun *autos* ("the God of peace *himself*"), thereby laying stress on God's role in the carrying out of the prayer rather than on the human ability of the Thessalonians themselves.

Third, the content or "wish" of the peace benediction is complicated by the fact that some of these closing benedictions use the copula (the verb "to be"), either given or implied, while others have a transitive verb. In the former type, the content of the wish is taken from the qualifying genitive phrase, so that Paul's statement "May the God of peace *be* with you" is tantamount to saying "May the God of peace *give* you peace." In fact, the peace benediction of 2 Thess. 3:16 states this wish explicitly: "May the Lord of peace himself give you peace." In the latter type, the content of the wish still includes peace (since the source is similarly "the God of peace") but also includes an additional wish expressed by the transitive verb.

The peace benediction here in 1 Thess. 5:23 belongs to this latter type as Paul uses not one but two transitive verbs: "to sanctify" and "to be preserved." These two optative verbs, along with two references to the Thessalonian recipients of the prayer ("you"; "your spirit and soul and body") and the two rare[6] and synonymous adjectives involving alliteration (*holoteleis*, completely; *holoklēron*, whole), are in a chiastic relationship to each other and form two distinct clauses:

---

6. The paired adjectives ὁλοτελής and ὁλόκληρος occur only here (5:23) in Paul's extant letters. In the rest of the NT, the first adjective occurs nowhere else, and the second adjective is found only once (James 1:4).

A verb: *hagiasai* (may he sanctify)
  B recipients: *hymas* (you)
    C adjective: *holoteleis* (completely)
      kai (and)
    C′ adjective: *holoklēron* (whole)
  B′ recipients: *hymōn to pneuma kai hē psychē kai to sōma* (your spirit and soul and body)
A′ verb: *tērētheiē* (may it be preserved)

These two distinct clauses in turn "form a kind of synonymous parallelism" (Fee 1994a: 65), which, when the remaining elements of the verse are added, can be rendered as follows:

first clause: "May the God of peace himself sanctify you completely"

second clause: "and may your whole spirit and soul and body be preserved blamelessly at the coming of our Lord Jesus Christ"

The fourth and final element in a Pauline peace benediction is the "recipient" of the wish. The recipient is frequently introduced with the preposition "with" (*meta*) and followed by the second-person-plural personal pronoun "you" (*hymōn*), a pattern identical to that used in the grace benediction. Although a few of the peace benedictions differ from this pattern slightly, the identity of the recipient is still indicated by the second-person-plural personal pronoun.

An understanding of the typical or expected form of the peace benediction reveals how unique and potentially significant is the form of this epistolary convention found here in 5:23. For instead of the simple and relatively fixed formula "May the God of peace be with you" (Rom. 15:33; 2 Cor. 13:11; Phil. 4:9b), Paul has greatly expanded the third element—the wish—to include two additional clauses that echo two major themes addressed earlier in the body of the letter: the call to holy or sanctified living and comfort concerning Christ's return (Weima 1994a: 174–86; 2010b: 313–17; see also Langevin 1989; 1990; Fee 2009: 225–26).

1. *Call to holy/sanctified living.* The first major theme of holiness, or sanctification, is expressed in the peace benediction by the two optative verbs that express the wish of the prayer: *hagiasai* (may he sanctify) and *amemptōs tērētheiē* (may it be preserved blamelessly). The chiasm formed by the two clauses that make up this peace benediction (see outline of the text given above) reveals that the second verb is intended to reiterate the meaning of the first, thereby adding emphasis to the theme of holiness. That holiness involves not just selected aspects or activities of a person's life but also their entire being and conduct is stressed by the two synonymous adjectives, *holoeteleis* and *holoklēron*, both of which refer "to being complete and meeting all expectations" or "a high standard" (BDAG 703, 704). The first adjective modifies "you" and thus describes Paul's prayer that the God of peace will sanctify

the Thessalonians "completely."[7] The second modifies "spirit and soul and body"[8] and thus describes Paul's prayer that God preserve blamelessly the Thessalonians' "whole" being. Thus the apostle petitions God (and so also implicitly exhorts his Thessalonian readers) for nothing less than their total and complete sanctification.

Although the call to holy or sanctified living comes distinctly to the fore in the second half of the letter (4:1–5:22) and most explicitly in 4:3–8, the same concern can also be found in the thanksgiving (1:2–10) and first half (2:1–3:13). Paul opens 1 Thessalonians by commending his readers for their "work of faith and labor of love," that is, for the outward and visible signs of a holy life that testify to how they have "turned to God from idols in order to serve a living and true God" (1:9). Indeed, their "faith toward God," manifested in their holy lives, has served as a powerful example to all the believers in Macedonia and Achaia (1:7–8). Paul then defends his mission-founding visit to Thessalonica by appealing to, among other things, "how holy and righteous and blameless [*amemptōs*] we were to you believers" (2:10). This holiness exemplified in the lives of Paul and his coworkers becomes in turn the ground on which the apostle challenges the Thessalonians "to lead a life worthy of God" (2:12). The concern for sanctified living also manifests itself in the purpose of the prayer that climaxes the first half of the letter: "in order to strengthen your hearts as blameless [*amemptous*] in holiness [*en hagiōsynē*] before our God and Father at the coming of our Lord Jesus with all his holy [*hagiōn*] ones" (3:13).

The second half of the letter, with its paraenetic (exhortative) focus, highlights to an even greater degree the theme of sanctification. God's will for the Thessalonians is explicitly identified as "your holiness [*hagiasmos*]" (4:3). Believers must abstain from sexual immorality and learn how to control their bodies "in holiness [*hagiasmos*] and honor" (4:4). The reason why they should live this way is because "God did not call us for impurity but in holiness [*hagiasmos*]" (4:7) and so he "gives his Spirit, who is holy [*hagion*], into you" (4:8b). Sanctified lives are further characterized by love for fellow Christians, which involves, among other things, working with one's own hands and thus being dependent on no one (4:9–12). The theme of holiness even occurs in the midst of a lengthy discussion about Christ's return (4:13–5:11), where Paul identifies his readers as "sons of light and sons of day" in contrast to those "of night or of darkness"

7. The form of the adjective ὁλοτελεῖς is masculine accusative plural and thus modifies ὑμᾶς: "May the God of peace himself sanctify you *as those who are in every way complete/quite perfect*." The sense of 5:23a is better captured in English, however, by rendering the predicate adjective as an adverb: "May the God of peace himself sanctify you *completely*" (so virtually all translations and commentaries; BDAG 704: "may God make you completely holy in every way").

8. Since the adjective ὁλόκληρον is neuter nominative singular, it technically modifies only the first noun with which it agrees: "spirit." Yet as Morris (1991: 182) states: "It is not uncommon for an adjective to agree in this way in number and gender with the nearest noun in a list, the whole of which it qualifies" (see also Green 2002: 267–68, citing BDF §135.3 in support). The adjective is in the predicate position and so could more literally be rendered "May your spirit and soul and body *as a whole* be preserved blamelessly."

(5:5; see also 5:4, 7, 8). These repeated metaphors of light and day versus darkness and night, common to the literature of the OT and Second Temple Judaism, are used here, as in Paul's other letters,[9] to refer to holy living, to the sanctified lives that the Thessalonians are leading. And though the term is not explicitly used, holiness continues to be a concern in the final exhortations about congregational life and worship (5:12–22). For if the Thessalonians want God to "sanctify" them "completely" and to preserve their "whole spirit and soul and body blamelessly," then they need to respect their congregational leaders (vv. 12–13a), be at peace among themselves (v. 13b), admonish the idlers (v. 14a), encourage the fainthearted (v. 14b), be devoted to the weak (v. 14c), deal patiently with all (v. 14d), pursue what is good (v. 15), and so on, to reiterate just a few of the listed activities that are characteristic of a holy life.

It is clear, therefore, that the emphasis on holiness expressed in the peace benediction of 5:23 echoes, both in content and in direct verbal links, the statements and exhortations given throughout the rest of 1 Thessalonians. Paul has carefully adapted and expanded this traditional epistolary convention belonging to the letter closing so that it recapitulates one of the key themes of his correspondence to the Thessalonians and thus functions to drive home to his readers one last time the importance of holy or sanctified living.

2. *Comfort concerning Christ's return.* A second major theme of the letter, comfort concerning Christ's return, is expressed in the peace benediction with the added prepositional phrase "at the coming of our Lord Jesus Christ." This reference to Christ's parousia is all the more striking because it does not occur in any other peace benediction.

Throughout the thanksgiving and body sections of the letter, the Thessalonian readers have been well prepared to be reminded about Christ's return in the closing. Paul opens his correspondence by giving thanks to God for the Thessalonians' "steadfastness of hope in our Lord Jesus Christ" (1:3), which, in the context of the letter as a whole, refers not merely to a general hope in the person and work of Christ, but more narrowly to their abiding confidence in his imminent return from heaven to bring about their deliverance. At the end of the thanksgiving section, this idea is confirmed with the climaxing statement that the Thessalonian readers have turned from idols not only to serve God but also "to wait for his Son from the heavens, . . . who rescues us from the coming wrath" (1:10). Paul therefore anticipates that the Thessalonian believers will be his "crown of boasting . . . before our Lord Jesus Christ at his coming" (2:19). To ensure that result, he closes the first half of the letter by praying that Christ will establish their hearts unblamable in holiness before God "at the coming of our Lord Jesus with all his holy ones" (3:13).

9. See Rom. 1:21; 2:19; 13:11–13; 1 Cor. 4:5; 2 Cor. 4:6; 6:14; Eph. 4:18; 5:8–11; 6:12; Col. 1:13. The metaphor of day/night and light/darkness as being connected with the concept of holiness or sanctified living is especially clear in Rom. 13:12–13: "The night is far gone, the day is at hand. Let us then cast off the works of darkness and put on the armor of light; let us conduct ourselves becomingly as in the day, not in reveling and drunkenness, not in debauchery and licentiousness, not in quarreling and jealousy."

The return of Christ is a theme developed much more explicitly in the second half of the letter, where Paul devotes two large sections (4:13–18; 5:1–11) to this very subject, highlighting in this material especially the pastoral concern of providing comfort (note the similar exhortation that concludes each section: "Therefore comfort one another" [4:18; 5:11]). The first passage (4:13–18) deals with the comforting message that deceased believers will neither miss nor be at a disadvantage at Christ's return, but that *all* Christians—those who have already "fallen asleep" as well as those who remain alive—will participate equally in the glory and splendor of his parousia. The second passage (5:1–11) comforts living believers with the truth that, though the day of the Lord will involve a sudden destruction from which there will certainly be no escape, believers need not fear this eschatological event: they not only enjoy the status of being "sons of light" and "sons of day"; they have also been elected by God not to suffer wrath but to obtain salvation and eternal life. Thus, the long section of 4:13–5:11 is permeated with references, both explicit and implicit, to the topic of Christ's return.

Such a preoccupation with the parousia of Christ, not only in 4:13–5:11 but also in the rest of the letter as well, makes it difficult to believe that the unparalleled reference to "the coming of our Lord Jesus Christ" in the peace benediction of 5:23 is fortuitous. Rather, as with the theme of being called to holy living, it seems apparent that Paul has deliberately adapted and expanded his typical closing peace benediction so that it echoes another main theme of this letter.

This recapitulating function of the peace benediction in 5:23 has potential significance for determining the correct meaning of the threefold reference to "spirit and soul and body." This is the only passage in the NT that speaks of a tripartite makeup of human nature. A number of diverse explanations have been forwarded, none of which has proved convincing to the majority of exegetes.[10] But understanding the peace benediction as echoing the major concerns of 1 Thessalonians as a whole suggests that the tripartite reference also harks back to some key issue previously addressed in the letter. The best

---

10. Various proposals for 5:23 may be briefly outlined as follows: (1) Dobschütz (1909), believing that Paul is describing the nature of a Christian as distinct from humankind in general, takes πνεῦμα to refer to the divine Spirit that enters into a believer alongside the human "soul" and "body." (2) Masson (1945) understands πνεῦμα to refer to the human being as a whole person (see Gal. 6:18; Phil. 4:23) and that "soul" and "body" then explicate this. (3) Stempvoort (1960–61) takes πνεῦμα as equivalent to the personal pronoun "you" and divides the verse so that ὁλόκληρον ὑμῶν τὸ πνεῦμα belongs to the first half of the sentence and is in parallel to ὑμᾶς ὁλοτελεῖς: "May the God of peace himself sanctify you wholly and your spirit completely. May both soul and body be kept blameless at the coming of our Lord Jesus." (4) Jewett (1971: 175–83) proposes that Paul is here taking over the language of enthusiasts in Thessalonica who adopted a gnostic type of understanding of humans in which the divinely given spirit was contrasted with the human body and soul. (5) Dibelius (1937: 229) believes that Paul has taken over a traditional formula (Ep. Apos. 24), and so any distinctions in it would not necessarily be his own. (6) Marshall (1983: 163) proposes reading the text as referring to three aspects, but not three parts, of a person's being.

candidate for this antecedent concern is one of the two themes that the rest of the peace benediction clearly intends to echo: either the call to holy/sanctified living or the comfort concerning Christ's return.

If the tripartite reference were intended by Paul to be connected with the latter theme of comfort concerning Christ's return, then it would be addressing yet again the Thessalonians' fear that their fellow believers who have already "fallen asleep" would not participate equally with living believers in the glorious events connected with the Lord's parousia, or triumphal coming (4:13–18). By closing the letter with a prayer that God may keep their spirit and soul and body "whole" (*holoklēron*) at the second coming of Christ, Paul responds one last time to such fears by assuring his readers that a believer's *whole* person will be involved in the day of Christ's return. Thus those who die before the parousia of Christ will neither miss that vindicating and magnificent eschatological event, nor will they be *in any way* at a disadvantage compared to believers who are still living.

But while this is a plausible explanation of the tripartite reference, there exists slightly stronger evidence that Paul intends to connect "spirit and soul and body" with the theme of sanctification. The apostle emphasizes this theme in the peace benediction even more than the theme of Christ's return, as shown by the presence of not one but two main verbs dealing with holiness. Paul further stresses the theme of holy living by using the two adjectives *holoeteleis* and *holoklēron* to emphasize the total and complete nature of the Thessalonians' sanctification. In a way similar to these adjectives, therefore, the reference to "spirit and soul and body" highlights that holiness pertains to their *whole* being and conduct. Just as Jesus's exhortation to love God with "all your heart, . . . soul, . . . mind, and . . . strength" (Mark 12:30 par.) is not intended to teach something about the makeup of humans but rather to stress the need for one's total and absolute devotion to God, so also Paul's prayer concerning "spirit and soul and body" says less about the apostle's view of anthropology than about his concern that sanctification be expressed in every aspect of the Thessalonians' being and conduct. As Bruce (1982: 130) observes: "The three [spirit, soul, body] together give further emphasis to the completeness of sanctification for which the writers pray." Williams (1992: 103) similarly observes: "The piling up of the nouns functions only to emphasize the completeness of the sanctification—it is to touch every aspect of their lives."[11]

B. Word of Encouragement (5:24)

5:24   The distinctiveness of the peace benediction in 5:23 is further heightened by the unusual addition of a word of encouragement that concludes the benediction

---

11. Fee (1994a: 66) also agrees that the tripartite reference has in view the completeness of sanctification but claims that the emphasis lies with the inclusion of the "body": "Paul is concerned that this early, almost totally Gentile (cf. 1:9–10), congregation understand that salvation in Christ includes the sanctification of the body: it is now to be holy, and wholly for God's own purposes" (so also 2009: 230).

(such added encouragement elsewhere only in 2 Thess. 3:16b): "Faithful is the one who is calling you, who will indeed do this" (πιστὸς ὁ καλῶν ὑμᾶς, ὃς καὶ ποιήσει, *pistos ho kalōn hymas, hos kai poiēsei*).

The preceding peace benediction already stressed the crucial role that God plays in the ability of the Thessalonians to live a holy life. As noted briefly above, this can be seen in the addition of the intensive pronoun *autos* (emphasized both by its placement at the head of the sentence and by its grammatical function), which underscores that it is God "himself" who will carry out the wish for sanctification expressed in the prayer. The Thessalonians' ability to endure persecution and be preserved blamelessly at the coming of the Lord Jesus does not rest in their own talent or strength but in God's.[12]

By means of this concluding word of encouragement, Paul continues to stress the divine role in the sanctifying process of the Thessalonians. As with the intensive pronoun *autos* in the preceding peace benediction, so also here the adjective *pistos* stands in the first position for emphasis: "Faithful" is the one to whom Paul prays to keep the Thessalonians completely holy at the return of Christ. The faithfulness of God, that is, his complete trustworthiness and reliability, is an important theme in Paul's theology: it stems from his Jewish heritage (Isa. 49:7: "Faithful is the holy one of Israel, who chose you"; see also Deut. 7:9; 32:4; Pss. Sol. 14.1), and he frequently appeals to it (1 Cor. 1:9, also in the context of God's "call"; 10:13, also in the context of God's ability "to do" something [the identical future form *poiēsei* is used]; 2 Cor. 1:18; 2 Thess. 3:3; 2 Tim. 2:13; see also Heb. 10:23; 11:11; 1 John 1:9). This faithful characteristic of God guarantees that he "will indeed do this": he will fulfill the wish of the peace benediction for the total sanctification of the Thessalonians at Christ's return.[13]

Paul's emphasis on the divine role in his readers' lives can also be seen in the description of God as "the one who is calling you" (*ho kalōn hymas*), where the present tense of the participle highlights the ongoing and continuous nature of the call. God has not called the Thessalonians once in the past and subsequently abandoned them to face their trials and tribulations on their own. Rather, as Paul puts it elsewhere, "he who began a good work in you will bring it to completion at the day of Jesus Christ" (Phil. 1:6).

This description of God as "the one who is calling you" encourages the Thessalonian believers in still another way: it recalls to their mind previous statements throughout the letter about God's role in their conversion (Weima 1994a: 181–83). The letter opens with the assertion that the ultimate reason why Paul and his coworkers give thanks to God about the converts in Thessalonica is because "we know . . . your election" (1:4). This divine initiative

---

12. Wiles (1974: 66) comments on 5:23a: "In the words αὐτὸς δέ he [Paul] seems to point away from the weakness of the converts' own unaided efforts and to place them under the supreme power of God."

13. The omission of an explicit direct object for ποιήσει in 5:24 has the effect of highlighting the verbal idea of God as "doing" or fulfilling the wish of the peace benediction (so Milligan 1908: 79; Morris 1991: 184; Malherbe 2000: 339).

is more clearly spelled out in 2:12, which identifies God as "the one who is calling [*tou kalountos*: the present tense of this participle is also significant] you into his own kingdom and glory." The suffering and persecution that the Thessalonians endure for their Christian faith is hardly a rare or unanticipated product of fate but an expected feature of the life that has been "destined" for them by God (3:3b). Similarly, Paul grounds his commands concerning sanctified living on the fact that "God did not call [*ekalesen*] us for impurity but in holiness" (4:7). And though the verb *kaleō* is not used in 5:9, God's involvement in the Thessalonians' deliverance is clearly central to Paul's reminder to them that "God has not destined us for wrath but for the obtaining of salvation through our Lord Jesus Christ." Thus, just as the peace benediction echoes the key themes of holiness and comfort concerning Christ's return, as developed previously in the letter, so also the word of encouragement in 5:24 recalls earlier statements about God's call and initiative in the Thessalonians' lives. This reminder in turn reassures them that their ability to be sanctified completely and to have their whole spirit, soul, and body be preserved blamelessly at the coming of Christ Jesus rests not in their own fallible abilities but in their faithful God, who continues to work out his call in their lives and thus "will indeed do this." As Morris (1991: 184) declares: "It is profoundly satisfying to the believer that in the last resort what matters is not his feeble hold on God, but God's strong grip on him."

C. Hortatory Section (5:25)

5:25   The second element in a typical Pauline letter closing[14] is a hortatory section, which is here very brief and general: "Brothers, pray also for us" (ἀδελφοί, προσεύχεσθε καὶ περὶ ἡμῶν, *adelphoi, proseuchesthe kai peri hēmōn*).

Hortatory material can be found in the closings of all the Pauline Letters, with the exception of 2 Thessalonians (see table 6 in Weima 1994a: 146; also table 2 in Weima 2010b: 321). It is clear that these final commands are far less tightly structured than the other epistolary conventions belonging to Paul's letter closings. They appear to be ad hoc creations of the apostle, and so it would be wrong to speak of their "form" in the same sense as that of the other stereotyped formulas also found in his letter closings. Nevertheless, there are a few features common to many of these hortatory sections. The most obvious is the use of the imperative mood, which naturally is to be expected in hortatory material. In those few instances where this mood does not occur, a verb of entreaty or adjuration expresses the imperative tone of Paul's words. Thus, for example, in a second hortatory section located a couple of verses later, in 5:27, the apostle writes: "I cause you to swear an oath by the Lord that this letter be read to all the brothers."

The closing exhortations are sometimes introduced with the adverbial use of the adjective "finally" (λοιπόν, *loipon*: 2 Cor. 13:11; Gal. 6:17; Phil. 4:8),

---

14. For a description of the five epistolary conventions typically found in Paul's letter closings, see note 4 above, under "Structure of the Passage."

though more frequently with the vocative "brothers," as is the case here (so also Rom. 16:17; 2 Cor. 13:11; Phil. 4:8; Philem. 20; see 1 Cor. 16:15). This marks the fourteenth time in the letter that Paul addresses his readers as "brothers" (1:4; 2:1, 9, 14, 17; 3:7; 4:1, 10b, 13; 5:1, 4, 12, 14, 25).[15] This repeated descriptor of his audience, along with the familial language and metaphors found throughout 1 Thessalonians (1:4, "beloved"; 2:7b, "infants"; 2:7c, "nursing mother"; 2:11, "father"; 2:17, "orphaned"), is part of Paul's strategy to create community cohesion among converts in Thessalonica, whose former relationships with family and friends would have been significantly impacted when they "turned to God from idols to serve the living and true God" (1:10). The close bonds they shared with their new spiritual "brothers and sisters" would be needed as they together faced opposition and hostility from their "fellow citizens" (2:14).

That Paul's letter closings frequently are related to—sometimes even summarize—subjects taken up in the body of the letter leads to the possibility that this recapitulating function also exists for the hortatory section. Some of the apostle's closing commands are related to concerns addressed previously in the body (2 Cor. 13:11; Rom. 16:17–20; see Weima 1994a: 147–48; 2010b: 322–24). Most hortatory sections, however, contain only general paraenetic, or exhortative, remarks that have no specific relation to the concrete epistolary situation. This is the case here in 5:25, where Paul's closing command that the Thessalonians "pray also for us" does not appear to be connected in any significant way to the material found in the letter body.[16] Instead, as the presence of the conjunction *kai* implies,[17] this command is connected to the preceding peace benediction: just as Paul has prayed for the Thessalonians, so they *also* ought to pray for him and his coworkers, Timothy and Silas (so most commentators: e.g., Milligan 1908: 79; Best 1977: 245; Wanamaker 1990: 207; Malherbe 2000: 340).

The presence of this command for prayer is hardly surprising, given the priority that this spiritual discipline plays in Paul's life and ministry. He opens most of his letters with a thanksgiving section that frequently refers to himself as remembering his readers in intercessory prayer (Rom. 1:9; Eph. 1:16; Phil. 1:4; Col. 1:3; 2 Tim. 1:3; Philem. 4). Some of these thanksgivings also conclude with a prayer report in which the apostle explicitly tells his readers the content of his prayers for them (Rom. 1:10; Phil. 1:9–11; Col. 1:9–14; 2 Thess. 1:11–12). Paul frequently asks his readers to reciprocate his intercessory prayers by requesting that they in turn pray for him (Rom. 15:30–33; 2 Cor. 1:11; Col. 4:3–4; 2 Thess. 3:1–2; see Eph. 6:18–19; Phil. 1:19; Philem. 22). Here in 5:25 the

---

15. This figure includes only the occurrences of the vocative form ἀδελφοί. The number is higher if one includes instances of this noun in other cases (see 3:2; 4:6, 10; 5:26, 27).

16. Contra Frame (1912: 215), who links this command in 5:25 with the exhortation of 5:17 that the Thessalonians should "pray constantly," not only for themselves and others in general but "also for us."

17. The textual evidence for including this conjunction in 5:25 is just slightly stronger than its exclusion. See discussion in additional notes.

apostle does not spell out what it is about which the Thessalonians ought to pray concerning him. Yet if one reads his request for prayer in 2 Thess. 3:1–2 ("As for other matters, brothers, pray for us that the word of God may run and be honored, just as it also is with you, and that we may be rescued from evil and wicked people, for not everyone has faith") in light of what Paul says about his present ministry in the rest of the Thessalonian correspondence, the apostle no doubt desires prayer for the success of his current mission work in Corinth and the surrounding area of Achaia, as well as for both physical and spiritual safety in the face of opposition and persecution (see 3:7, "in all *our* distress and affliction"; Acts 18:1–17).

D. Kiss Greeting (5:26)

5:26

Paul's closings normally include greetings, some of which bear the more specialized "kiss greeting" found here: "Greet all the brothers with a holy kiss" (ἀσπάσασθε τοὺς ἀδελφοὺς πάντας ἐν φιλήματι ἁγίῳ, *aspasasthe tous adelphous pantas en philēmati hagiō*).

The practice of giving a kiss as part of a greeting was widespread in the Orient (for a detailed study of the "holy kiss," as well as the kiss in general, see discussion and further sources in Weima 1994a: 112–14; 2010b: 330–32). Jewish examples of greeting others with a kiss, either when arriving or departing, can be found throughout the OT and intertestamental literature.[18] Greeting another person with a kiss continued to be a common practice in Jesus's day (Mark 14:45; Luke 7:45; 15:20; 22:47) and in Paul's (Acts 20:37). Thus the command in the apostle's letters to greet one another with a kiss reflects a widespread custom of that time, which explains why the command can be given in a rather simple and constant formulaic expression (Rom. 16:16a; 1 Cor. 16:20b; 2 Cor. 13:12a; 1 Thess. 5:26; see also 1 Pet. 5:14), without any accompanying word of explanation.

What is new in Paul's use of the practice, however, is that he explicitly refers to this kiss greeting as a "holy" kiss. Paul could be referring to the importance of maintaining proper and holy motives while practicing a kiss greeting.[19] But though this concern is surely part of Paul's thought in the exhortation, the

18. E.g., Gen. 29:11, 13; 31:28; 31:55 (32:1 LXX); 33:4; Exod. 4:27; 18:7; 2 Sam. 19:39 (19:40 LXX); 20:9; 1 Kings 19:20; Tob. 5:17; 10:12; 3 Macc. 5:49; Add. Esth. 15:8–12; 4 Bar. 6.3; T. Benj. 1.2; 3.7; T. Reu. 1.5; T. Sim. 1.2; T. Dan 7.1; T. Naph. 1.7; Jos. Asen. 4.1, 7; 18.3; 22.9.

19. The early church apparently experienced problems with the kiss greeting, with the exchange of the kiss between sexes becoming either for some believers an erotic experience or for nonbelievers an action that aroused suspicion. This explains Tertullian's comment that a pagan husband would not allow his wife "to meet any one of the brethren to exchange the kiss" (*Ux.* 2.4). Similarly, the apologist Athenagoras, a contemporary of Tertullian, states: "We feel it a matter of great importance that those, whom we thus think of as brother and sister and so on, should keep their bodies undefiled and uncorrupted. For our rule again tells us, 'If one kisses a second time, because he found it enjoyable, . . . [he sins]. Thus the kiss, or rather the religious salutation, should be very carefully guarded. If it is defiled by the slightest evil thought, it excludes us from eternal life'" (*Leg.* 32). Clement of Alexandria also warned against the improper practice of the kiss greeting, "which occasions foul suspicions and evil reports" (*Paed.* 3.11).

reference to a "holy" (*hagios*) kiss suggests that the apostle wants to distinguish the kiss greeting practiced between believers (*hagioi*: "holy" people, "saints") from that practiced between those outside the faith. For others, the kiss greeting "could be simply an expression of friendship and good will, but among Christians it assumed a deeper meaning; it symbolized the unity, the belonging together of Christians, in the church of Jesus Christ" (Benko 1984: 98). In other words, the kiss expressed not merely friendship and love but, more specifically, reconciliation and peace (see esp. Gen. 33:4; 45:15; 2 Sam. 14:33 LXX; Luke 15:20). This is what makes Judas's kiss of Jesus in the garden of Gethsemane so shocking and blasphemous: his action is motivated by an attitude that is completely opposite to its expected expression of unity and concord with the other person. The kiss exchanged between believers soon was referred to by early Christians as the *osculum pacis* (kiss of peace).[20] As a concrete expression of the oneness that exists between followers of Jesus, the exchange of the holy kiss naturally became an introductory step leading up to the celebration of the Eucharist—a further outward act that also powerfully symbolized the unity of believers as the body of Christ.

Paul's command to greet others "with a holy kiss," therefore, expresses more than an exhortation simply to greet each other. It serves, rather, as a challenge to his readers to remove any hostility that may exist among them and to exhibit the oneness that they share as fellow members of the body of Christ. It is analogous to our contemporary challenge that a married couple or close friends who are at odds with each other ought to "kiss and make up" (Witherington 2006: 176n6). This function of the kiss greeting explains why three of its four occurrences (Rom. 16:16a; 1 Cor. 16:20b; 2 Cor. 13:12a) are located in letters where some degree of conflict exists within the congregation and where Paul has addressed the issue of unity earlier in the body of the letter.

What, then, about the fourth occurrence of the kiss greeting, here in 5:26? The existence of a possible division within the Thessalonian congregation is at least suggested by the parallels with the other kiss greetings, which always occur in contexts involving some degree of internal conflict within the local church. This hint of internal tension is further suggested by the distinctive form of this kiss greeting in 5:26. For whereas all other occurrences of his command exhibit the fixed form "Greet *one another* with a holy kiss," Paul here has "Greet *all the brothers* with a holy kiss." The significance of this change from "one another" to "all the brothers" is further heightened by the fact that occurrences of the kiss greeting outside of Paul also uniformly use "one another" (1 Pet. 5:14; Justin, *1 Apol.* 61.65; Ap. Const. 8.9; Lit. James 2.20).

Many commentators are wary of reading too much into this change in the kiss greeting formula. Best (1977: 245), for example, claims that "*all* need not

---

20. Tertullian, *Or.* 18 (14). The kiss greeting became a test to ensure that peace and harmony existed among believers. In the East during the third century AD, it was explicitly asked, while the kiss was being exchanged, whether anyone harbored anger toward another, so that even at the last moment the bishop might make peace between them. See Dix 1945: 106–7.

be emphatic" and "it can hardly be taken as suggesting that some division within the church needs to be healed." Nevertheless, we have seen elsewhere in this letter closing that changes in Paul's expected form are not fortuitous but deliberate and related to the specific Thessalonian situation. Other commentators, therefore, have taken the shift from the expected "one another" to "all the brothers" to be significant, agreeing with Marshall (1983: 165): "In view of the fact that there was some tendency to division in the church, this stress on the fact that *all* belong to the one fellowship is probably intentional" (so also Frame 1912: 215–16; Hendriksen 1955: 142; Whiteley 1969: 86; Bruce 1982: 134). The evidence of an internal conflict is further suggested in the immediately following verse, where there is a similar stress that the letter be read to "*all* the brothers," implying that some in the church might not be so willing to hear and heed the apostle's words. This verse also marks the third time in three verses that Paul identifies his readers as "brothers," thereby stressing the familial relationship that ought to exist among members of the Thessalonian church.

Also relevant is the earlier command of 5:13b, "Be at peace among yourselves," which concludes an exhortation about respecting congregational leaders. Paul would not have raised the subject of esteeming leaders in the church (5:12–13a) if such a topic were not in some way directly relevant to the Thessalonian situation, and the same assumption should be true about the concluding call to "be at peace among yourselves" (5:13b). Although Paul commends the Thessalonians for the loving way that they treat each other (4:9–10a), he nevertheless exhorts them "to increase more and more" in such conduct (4:10b).

In light of the indirect and brief nature of the apostle's comments, the dissension within the congregation cannot have been widespread but limited in scope. It may have involved a general tension between church members and their congregational leaders, since it is not difficult to envision how the leaders' work in "ruling over" and "admonishing" the members (5:12), even if carried out in the right spirit, could easily result in feelings of resentment or bitterness. A more specific situation that Paul may be thinking of with the kiss greeting, however, is the problem with the "rebellious idlers," who were not only failing to heed Paul's instruction about the necessity of self-sufficient work but also refusing to obey the church's leaders on this matter (see comment on 5:13b for three factors that strengthen this possibility). The command "Greet all the brothers with a holy kiss," therefore, is not a perfunctory closing exhortation. Rather, just as the apostle has modified the peace benediction and word of encouragement to echo major themes presented in the letter body, so he here similarly adapts the kiss greeting to address the internal tensions at work in the Thessalonian congregation and to encourage reconciliation and concord among church members.

E. Hortatory Section (Autograph) (5:27)

5:27 The letter closing continues with a second hortatory section, where Paul has likely taken over from the secretary and now writes in his own hand: "I cause you to swear an oath in the name of the Lord that this letter be read to all the brothers" (ἐνορκίζω ὑμᾶς τὸν κύριον ἀναγνωσθῆναι τὴν ἐπιστολὴν πᾶσιν τοῖς ἀδελφοῖς, *enorkizō hymas ton kyrion anagnōsthēnai tēn epistolēn pasin tois adelphois*).

The Greek papyri demonstrate that ancient letters frequently ended with an autograph statement. Usually the letter body was dictated to a secretary, and then the letter closing—or at least part of the closing—was written by the sender in his own hand. It is hardly surprising, therefore, that the same phenomenon occurs in Paul's Letters. Greco-Roman letters rarely have an autograph formula in which it is explicitly stated that the sender has taken over the act of writing from the amanuensis, since a change in handwriting would have been visually obvious to the reader. Paul, however, knew that his letters would be read aloud in public gatherings where the size of the group prevented everyone from observing the change in handwriting. Consequently, he needed to make an explicit reference to closing material that he had written "in my own hand" (1 Cor. 16:21; Gal. 6:11; Col. 4:18a; 2 Thess. 3:17; Philem. 19).

Although Paul includes no such explicit statement here in 5:27, there are good reasons for viewing this second hortatory section and the subsequent grace benediction as an autograph. Since stereotyped formulas throughout this letter occur in the plural (e.g., thanksgiving formula: 1:2; 2:13; disclosure formula: 2:1; 4:9, 13; 5:1; appeal formula: 4:1, 10b; 5:12, 14), the petition given here in the singular has a particular significance. And in light of Paul's practice in his other letter closings, it seems natural to view this shift from the plural to the singular as evidence for an autograph. As Bruce (1982: 135) notes, "The most probable explanation is that Paul took over the pen at this point and added the adjuration and the concluding benediction with his own hand" (so also Best 1977: 246; Marshall 1983: 165; Wanamaker 1990: 208; Morris 1991: 186; Richards 1991: 179–80; D. Martin 1995: 191; Richard 1995: 292; Malherbe 2000: 342, 346; Witherington 2006: 176–77; Fee 2009: 232). Furthermore, Paul's remark in 2 Thess. 3:17 about his custom of closing all his letters in his own hand implies that *at least* his previous letter to the Thessalonians also contained a closing autograph, such as the material in 5:27–28.

Several features of this final hortatory section are striking. First, there is the shift from the plural "we" to the singular "I" (a similar shift is found earlier in the letter, at 2:18 and 3:5; see also 2 Thess. 2:5; 3:17). This shift supports my claim that, though the names of Silvanus and Timothy are included in the letter opening as cosenders, Paul is the real author of the letter and that the plurals used throughout the correspondence ought not to be taken literally but literarily (see comment on 1:1). Second, the verb *enorkizō* has a particularly strident tone since it involves causing someone to swear under oath to do something (BDAG 338: "to put someone under oath, *adjure*, cause someone to swear by something"; see also J. Schneider, *TDNT* 5:464). The root *orkizō*, which already is a strong term with the same meaning (see Mark 5:7; Acts 19:13; Matt. 26:63 v.l.), is here intensified by the addition of the preposition *en* (the resulting form *enorkizō* occurs only here in the extant writings of Paul and in the NT). This adjuration seems heavy-handed for a congregation with whom the apostle enjoys a good relationship and who would be expected to read eagerly a letter from the founder of their church. Third, the mere presence of this statement is notable because no other closing section of Paul's letter contains a similar adjuration.[21] Fourth, there is an obvious emphasis that this letter be read "to *all* the brothers."

What accounts for the presence of these unusual features? That no less than eight different answers to this question have been given (for a helpful listing of these answers, see Richard 1995: 291–92; Malherbe 2000: 334) suggests that one ought to be modest about any claims to having the definitive solution. Nevertheless, a plausible explanation in light of our observations about the preceding kiss greeting (5:26) and the earlier command to "be at peace among yourselves" (5:13b) is that Paul has in mind internal tensions in the church, particularly those involving the "rebellious idlers." As Green (2002: 271–72) observes: "The reason for such a strong exhortation is most likely found in the tension that existed between certain members of the congregation (4.6; 5.13–14, 20), especially between the majority of believers and the disorderly among them" (see also Frame 1912: 217; Bruce 1982: 135; Weatherly 1996: 194; Beale 2003: 177; Fee 2009: 233). These *ataktoi* (5:14) had already demonstrated an unwillingness to obey Paul's teaching to them during his mission-founding visit (4:11c, "to work with your own hands *just as we commanded you*"; see also 2 Thess. 3:6, 10), and the apostle understandably worries that they may continue to defy his teaching to them in this letter. Consequently, he places all his readers under oath that his correspondence be read to *all* the members of the Thessalonian church, including the "rebellious idlers."

Paul's fears about this group not complying with his letter proved true: the problem grew worse instead of better, thereby requiring the apostle to deal with it yet a third time and at great length in a later letter (2 Thess. 3:6–15). In this later discussion Paul again anticipates that these idlers will not all follow his directives, as evidenced in his closing statement: "If anyone does not obey our instruction in this letter, identify that person and have nothing to do with them." What is significant here is Paul's use of the first-class condition, which indicates that he assumes it to be true that some of the idlers will not heed his teaching on this matter.

F. Grace Benediction (5:28)

5:28 Secular letters of Paul's day typically ended with the "farewell wish," expressed either in the form of "Be strong!" (ἔρρωσο, *errōso*: Acts 15:29; 23:30 v.l.) or, less commonly, "Prosper!" (εὐτύχει, *eutychei*). This fixed formula served to signal the definitive end of a letter somewhat like the expression "sincerely" or

---

21. Paul's closing command in Col. 4:16 ("And when this letter has been read among you, have it read also in the church of the Laodiceans; and see that you read also the letter from Laodicea" [NRSV]) involves first and foremost not the *reading* of the letter but the *exchange* of that letter with another letter the apostle wrote to the Laodiceans.

"yours truly" is used to close our modern correspondence (for examples and discussion of the farewell formula, see Weima 1994a: 29–34). Paul, however, indicates the end of his letters by replacing this secular closing formula with a distinctively Christian one: "May the grace of our Lord Jesus Christ be with you" (ἡ χάρις τοῦ κυρίου ἡμῶν Ἰησοῦ Χριστοῦ μεθ' ὑμῶν, *hē charis tou kyriou hēmōn Iēsou Christou meth' hymōn*).

The grace benediction is the most common epistolary convention of Paul's letter closings: it ends every one of the apostle's letters. But not only is the grace benediction the most frequent of the closing conventions; it is also formally the most consistent. It exhibits a striking uniformity (see table 1 in Weima 1994a: 80; table 4 in Weima 2010b: 342), consisting of three basic elements: the wish, the divine source, and the recipient.

The wish or content of this benediction is "grace." Thus, in contrast to secular letters where the farewell wish expresses the desire that the recipients will have physical strength ("Be strong!") or prosperity ("Prosper!"), Paul calls on God to give his readers that which he believes to be a more valuable gift and one that is needed more: the gift of grace. This wish for grace, along with the preceding peace benediction (5:23), which is also typically found in the letter closing, forms an inverted, or chiastic, inclusio with the greeting of the letter opening: "Grace to you and peace" (1:1).

The divine source of this wish is expressed by means of the genitive phrase "of our Lord Jesus Christ." This genitive phrase is clearly used in a subjective sense, denoting source: the grace that Jesus Christ has and gives. Although Paul normally refers to God as the source of grace, he occasionally speaks of Christ in this fashion (2 Cor. 8:9; 12:9; Gal. 1:6; 5:4; 2 Thess. 1:12). On the whole, however, the depiction of Christ as the source of grace is a characteristic feature of the letter closings.[22]

The recipient of the wish or benediction normally consists of the prepositional phrase "with you" (*meth' hymōn*), as is the case here, though slight variations occur in other letter closings.

The omission of the main verb in the peace benediction calls for some comment. For though the copula "to be" is clearly implied, it is less obvious which mood of this verb Paul intends. If indicative, then the benediction would have the sense of a declarative statement: "The grace of our Lord Jesus Christ *is* with you." Another option is the imperative: "The grace of our Lord Jesus Christ *be* with you." A third possibility is the optative, in which the benediction expresses a holy or pious wish: "*May* the grace of our Lord Jesus Christ be with you." This last option is supported by peace benedictions and "other" benedictions in Paul's Letters, most of which use the optative (Rom. 15:5–6; 15:13; 1 Thess. 3:11, 12–13; 5:23; 2 Thess. 2:16–17; 3:5, 16).[23] By analogy, this

22. The letter openings also identify Christ as the source of grace, but there Christ possesses a secondary role to "God our Father": Rom. 1:7; 1 Cor. 1:3; 2 Cor. 1:2; Gal. 1:3; Phil. 1:2; 2 Thess. 1:2; Philem. 3.

23. Notice, however, the use of the indicative (future tense) in the peace benediction of Rom. 16:20; 2 Cor. 13:11; and Phil. 4:9.

practice suggests that the same mood is implied in the grace benedictions. Furthermore, although the opening benedictions or greetings of Paul's Letters also omit the verb, the opening benedictions of other NT letters have the optative (1 Pet. 1:2; 2 Pet. 1:2; Jude 2). Thus it seems best to view the grace benediction as a wish or prayer to Christ, to send his grace into the hearts and lives of the letter's recipients.[24]

Additional Notes

5:25. The external evidence for including the conjunction καί ($\mathfrak{P}^{30}$ B D* 0278 6 33 81 104 326 1505 1739 1881 2464 *pc* b sy^h sa; Ambst Epiph) is only slightly stronger than the evidence for omitting it (א A D² F G Ψ 𝔐 lat sy^p bo). With regard to the internal evidence, it might be argued that the conjunction is a later addition under the influence of Col. 4:3 (προσευχόμενοι ἅμα καὶ περὶ ἡμῶν). But if this were the case, one would expect that the particle ἅμα would also be added to 1 Thess. 5:25. The omission of the conjunction might instead be the result of scribes failing to connect this verse with the immediately preceding peace benediction, which functions as Paul's prayer for his readers. The editors of the standard Greek editions include καί in the main text, though they enclose it with square brackets, indicating some uncertainty about its presence (see B. Metzger 1994: 565).

5:27. A number of ancient MSS add the adjective "holy" before "brothers" ($\mathfrak{P}^{46vid}$ א² A K P Ψ 𝔐 33 81 614 1739 a vg sy bo). Most commentators reject this adjective as a later addition on the grounds that (1) the expression "holy brothers" occurs nowhere in Paul's Letters; (2) the external evidence is slightly stronger for its omission (א* B D F G 431 436 1311 1835 1907 2004 it sa; Ambst Ephraem Pel Cass); and (3) the possibility that ἁγίοις was accidentally omitted because of homoeoteleuton with ἀδελφοῖς appears less likely than the probability of its being added from ἁγίῳ in the previous verse (see B. Metzger 1994: 565–66). These grounds need to be balanced, however, by the fact that Paul earlier adapted the expected form of the peace benediction to highlight the theme of holiness or sanctification, and so a similar deliberate attempt to underscore this theme is possible here. Note also the use of the same adjective "holy ones" in 3:13, which likely refers not to angels but to believers (see comments on 3:13).

---

24. Van Elderen (1967: 48) recognizes that the optative in the NT often takes on a force similar to that of the imperative and speaks of an "imperatival optative"—an optative that expresses a stronger sense than mere volition: "The speaker intends more than a wish ('may it be so-and-so'); he expresses this with a strong confidence of fulfillment ('let it be so-and-so')."

2 Thessalonians

I. Letter Opening (1:1–2)

The letter opening of 2 Thessalonians is virtually identical with that of 1 Thessalonians except for two additions, both of which are noteworthy, even though these add-ons make explicit what was implicit in the previous letter. This letter opening, like that of 1 Thessalonians, has not been formally altered in any noteworthy way vis-à-vis some of Paul's other letters—a likely reflection of the good relationship that exists between the apostle and the Thessalonian church as well as his overall pleasure at their spiritual condition, despite his need to write to them only a short time later for a second time. Yet even this relatively simple letter opening serves the important function of laying down at least three significant points that have bearing on the rest of the letter. First, the inclusion of Silvanus and Timothy as cosenders gives further weight or authority to Paul's letter, for it not only shows the Thessalonians that the apostle is well informed about the current situation in their congregation but also that there is agreement between Paul and these other leaders about the required response expected from the recipients to their present circumstances. Second, the identification of the recipients with the term *ekklēsia* (church), a term used in the LXX to refer to Israel as God's covenant people, reflects Paul's understanding of the predominantly Gentile church of Thessalonica as the new people of God. This understanding manifests itself elsewhere in his Thessalonian correspondence as Paul similarly takes language formerly reserved for Israel and applies it to the congregation in Thessalonica. Finally, the prepositional phrase "in God our Father and the Lord Jesus Christ" (1:1b) and the greeting "Grace to you and peace," which is here expanded with the prepositional phrase "from God the Father and the Lord Jesus Christ" (1:2), both emphasize the primary and thus crucial role of the divine—both God and Christ—in the origin, ongoing life, and salvation of the readers. Such an emphasis would be comforting for the persecuted and frightened community of believers in Thessalonica.

Literary Analysis

For a literary analysis of the letter opening in Paul's Letters generally and a discussion of the degree to which the apostle both borrows from the letter-writing practices of his day but also adapts them to suit his particular audience and specific needs as seen, for example, in the way he "Christianizes" the greeting, see the comments on 1 Thess. 1:1. Compared to the expanded letter opening of Romans, 1 Corinthians, Galatians, or other Pauline Letters, the epistolary conventions that the apostle uses to open his Second Letter to the Thessalonians, like that of the first letter, are simple and unembellished. This is likely due to the good relationship that Paul enjoys with the Thessalonian congregation and the absence of any questions in this church about his apostolic status or authority.

Exegesis and Exposition

[1]Paul and Silvanus and Timothy. To the church of the Thessalonians in God our Father and the Lord Jesus Christ. [2]Grace to you and peace from God ⌜the⌝ Father and the Lord Jesus Christ.

Since the letter opening of 2 Thessalonians is, with two exceptions, identical to that of 1 Thessalonians, there is no need to repeat my observations about the first letter. Instead, the reader of this commentary ought to consult the detailed comments found there about that letter opening, which are equally true for understanding 2 Thess. 1:1–2. Here I limit my observations to the two additional elements found in the opening of the second letter, as well as a few other supplementary remarks.

A. Sender (1:1a)

1:1a   The mention of Silvanus and Timothy as cosenders indicates not only that they are still with Paul when he writes this letter (cf. 1 Thess. 1:1a) but also, along with the great similarities of this letter opening to that of the previous letter, strongly suggests that the second letter was written relatively briefly after the first. Some (Trilling 1972: 35) have viewed the inclusion of these two cosenders as problematic and as further evidence of the letter's pseudonymity on the grounds that these two individuals are never mentioned again in the rest of the document. This "problem," however, is only imaginary: in the undisputed Pauline Letters, there are at least three examples of cosenders who are never referred to again by name in the rest of the document: Silvanus (1 Thess. 1:1a), Sosthenes (1 Cor. 1:1), and Timothy (Philem. 1a).

The inclusion of the cosenders, along with the widespread use of the first-person plural "we" in the rest of the letter, raises the issue of whether Silvanus and Timothy had an active role in the composition of this Second Letter to the Thessalonians. When this question was raised in the first letter, it was observed that there are three instances where the text shifts significantly from the first-person plural, "we," to the first-person singular, "I" (2:18; 3:5; 5:27), suggesting that Paul is, in fact, the real author of the document. A similar shift to the first-person singular occurs two times in the second letter. In seeking to comfort the Thessalonian Christians, who are scared by the false claim concerning the supposed arrival of the day of the Lord, Paul rhetorically asks: "You remember, don't you, that, when I was still with you, I was repeatedly saying these things to you?" (2:5). More significant is the autograph greeting in the letter closing: "The greeting is in *my* own hand, that of *Paul*, which is the sign in every letter; thus *I* write" (3:17). These texts strongly imply that, though the names of Silvanus and Timothy are included as cosenders, Paul is the real author and that the plurals used throughout both letters ought to be taken literarily, not literally.[1]

B. Recipient (1:1b)

The second formal section of the Pauline letter opening—the recipient formula—contains the first of the two additions to the form found in the first letter: the addition of the possessive pronoun "our" to describe God:[2] "To the church of the Thessalonians in God *our* Father and the Lord Jesus Christ" (τῇ ἐκκλησίᾳ Θεσσαλονικέων ἐν θεῷ πατρὶ ἡμῶν καὶ κυρίῳ ᾽Ιησοῦ Χριστῷ, *tē ekklēsia Thessalonikeōn en theō patri hēmōn kai kyriō Iēsou Christō*).

This addition clarifies that the fatherhood of God to which Paul refers here is not God as Father of Christ (though this is a common Pauline idea: "the Father of our Lord Jesus Christ" occurs in Rom. 15:6; 2 Cor. 1:3; 11:31; Eph. 1:3; Col. 1:3) or as Father of all creation (Acts 17:28; also a Pauline idea) but as Father of believers—both the letter senders (Paul, Silvanus, and Timothy) and the letter recipients (the Thessalonian Christians). This concept of God as Father of believers is one of the distinctive teachings of the NT: "Whereas the contemporary pagan world held its gods in fear or uncertainty, the Christian view of God's parenthood brings an unparalleled element of intimacy into human relationships with God" ("God," in D. Guthrie and R. P. Martin, *DPL* 357–58). The expression "our Father" reflects Paul's basic assumption that the Thessalonians have "turned to God from idols to serve the living and true God" (1 Thess. 1:9) such that they have been adopted as "sons of God" and "children of God" (Rom. 8:14–17; Gal. 3:26; 4:4–7) and thus in a metaphorical sense now constitute his family.

That the fuller expression "our Father" occurs in virtually every one of Paul's letter openings (Rom. 1:7; 1 Cor. 1:3; 2 Cor. 1:2; Gal. 1:3, 4; Eph. 1:2; Phil. 1:2; Col. 1:2b; Philem. 3) might suggest that the addition of the possessive "our" here in 2 Thess. 1:1b does *not* mean that Paul is stressing to his Thessalonian readers their adoption by God, their spiritual Father. These references to "our Father," however, all occur in the opening greeting formula ("Grace to you and peace from God our Father and the Lord Jesus Christ") and not, as is the case here, in the recipient formula. Furthermore, the concept of God's fatherhood is raised again in the letter opening of 2 Thessalonians in

---

1. Contra several commentators, including Shogren (2012: 243), who goes further than most in attributing to Timothy a lesser role in the writing of the letter than that of Silas: "Also as in 1 Thessalonians, while Paul was the author, Silas and *to an extent* Timothy are involved in the production of the letter. That is, the plural verbs and pronouns ('we,' 'us') are not 'editorial' but truly reflect a plurality of people" (emphasis added). Unfortunately, Shogren never clarifies or justifies this active yet diminished role of Timothy.

2. That the possessive "our" occurs with both "Father" and "Lord" elsewhere in 1 Thessalonians (3:11, 13) and 2 Thessalonians (2:16, though the names occur in the reverse order) leads Fee (2007: 36–37) to conclude that the "our" here in 2 Thess. 1:1b (and in Paul's later letter openings, where the same prepositional phrase occurs) does double duty for both nouns: "Father" as well as "Lord."

the immediately following greeting formula of 1:2. Thus, without wanting to overstate the case, there is nevertheless a certain emphasis in Paul's addition of the possessive pronoun "our" in 1:1b. Its presence creates solidarity between the apostle and his readers, as well as infusing the letter opening with a greater degree of warmth and intimacy[3] (this fact is overlooked by many who claim that 2 Thessalonians has a decidedly cooler tone than 1 Thessalonians and go on to use this claimed difference as further grounds for accepting non-Pauline authorship of the second letter). In the letter it also serves Paul's overall goal of providing his persecuted and shaken readers with comfort, since the Thessalonians are hereby reminded, already at the very beginning of the letter, that they face their trials not alone as pagans but as a community, people who have been brought into the family of God, their spiritual Father.

C. Greeting (1:2)

1:2 The second way in which the letter opening of 2 Thessalonians differs from that of the previous letter is the addition to the greeting formula, a prepositional phrase indicating the source of this salutation: "Grace to you and peace[4] *from God the[5] Father and the Lord Jesus Christ*" (χάρις ὑμῖν καὶ εἰρήνη ἀπὸ θεοῦ πατρὸς καὶ κυρίου Ἰησοῦ Χριστοῦ, *charis hymin kai eirēnē apo theou patros kai kyriou Iēsou Christou*).

Whereas in the First Letter to the Thessalonians the source of grace and peace is merely implied (from the prepositional phrase in the preceding verse: "in God the Father and the Lord Jesus Christ"), here in the second letter it is made explicit. As a result, the two verses that make up the letter opening of 2 Thessalonians both end with the identical phrase: "in/from God our/the Father and the Lord Jesus Christ." This repeated reference to God and Christ has seemed to some not only awkward and overstated but also as further

---

3. So also Witherington (2006: 184): "This small but subtle difference from 1 Thess. 1.1 [of adding the possessive pronoun "our"] is perhaps deliberate, as Paul must exhort his audience more strongly here than in 1 Thessalonians and so must go the extra mile to stress the connection and rapport he has with them as members of the same family of God."

4. On the grounds that 2 Thessalonians both opens and closes with references to peace (1:2; 3:16), Bassler argues for an "inclusio of peace," which reveals that the theological goal of the letter is the restoration of peace: "References to peace form an *inclusio* about the body of the letter, and the arguments within each section of the letter body—though couched heavily in apocalyptic terms—have peace as their common goal" (1991: 79). Gaventa (1998: 98) finds Bassler's argument convincing and concludes that "framing the letter with talk of peace is no mere formality but provides a lens through which to read the letter." Although the letter closes with a peace benediction that has been slightly expanded (3:16), the opening greeting of peace (1:2) is identical in form to that found in all of Paul's other letter openings. More significantly, the word "peace" (εἰρήνη) occurs nowhere in the letter body, a fact that Bassler tries to mitigate by appealing to "outcome peace" (ἄνεσις) in 1:7 and "social peace" (ἡσυχία) in 3:12. The evidence, therefore, does not justify defining peace as the theological goal of the letter or using peace as the lens through which to read the whole letter.

5. In 1:2 some MSS give strong support for adding the possessive pronoun "our." But it is more convincing to assume the original omission of this word on both external and internal evidence (see additional note).

evidence of a pseudepigraphical hand (e.g., Richard [1995: 297] refers to it as "an anomalous, ponderous double reference to God the Father and the Lord Jesus Christ" resulting from the pseudepigraphic author's "strategy" involving "both the close imitation of Paul's letter to the Thessalonians and the use of other Pauline epistolary features"). Yet it is entirely in keeping with other back-to-back references to "God the Father and the Lord Jesus Christ" found in the undisputed letters of Paul (e.g., 2 Cor. 1:2–3; Gal. 1:1, 3; Col. 1:2–3; see also Eph. 1:2–3). Instead of viewing the double reference to God and Christ as problematic, it should instead be recognized that this repetition functions rhetorically to emphasize the primary and thus crucial role of the Divine—both God and Christ—in not only the origin of the Thessalonian church ("*in* God our Father and the Lord Jesus Christ") but also its ongoing life ("Grace to you and peace *from* God the Father and the Lord Jesus Christ"). Such an emphasis is comforting for the persecuted and frightened community of believers in Thessalonica.

The prepositional phrase added to the opening greeting, like the prepositional phrase of the preceding recipient formula, is also noteworthy for the way both divine persons function grammatically as the double object of a single preposition. Although a fuller discussion of this point has already been made in the comments on 1 Thess. 1:1b, we note again the implications that this juxtaposition of God and Christ has for Paul's Christology. That the apostle does not feel the need to explain or justify this juxtaposition suggests that he possesses a high Christology, which would have been an important part of his missionary preaching and which he can now safely assume to be accepted by his readers. As Wilson (1975) states: "That such a construction could be used without comment not only implies the writer's belief in the deity of Christ, but also takes the reader's acknowledgment of it for granted" (cited by Morris 1991: 192).[6] Speaking more broadly about the whole of 1 and 2 Thessalonians, Fee (2007: 33) concludes: "Paul's 'Christology' in these first two letters, therefore, is not a matter of christological assertions or explanations; rather, one is struck by the reality that this rigorous monotheist can speak about Christ in ways as remarkable as one finds here—statements that by their very nature would seem to put considerable pressure on that monotheism."

Additional Note

1:2. MSS give strong support for adding the possessive pronoun "our" (א A F G I 𝔐 lat sy sa bo^pt). If this reading is adopted, the omission of the possessive pronoun could have been done by later scribes for stylistic reasons, since the word already occurs in the immediately preceding verse (B. Metzger 1994: 567). This explanation, however, is less convincing than assuming the original omission of this word on both external evidence (there is strong textual support for its omission: B D P 0111^vid 33 1739 1881

6. On 2:2, Weatherly (1996: 212) similarly observes: "Paul, who was steeped in Jewish monotheism, attributes such gifts ['grace and peace'] to both God and Jesus with absolute ease and naturalness. Such is possible for him because he regards Jesus as fully divine."

pc m bo[pt]) and internal evidence (it is the shorter reading) and envisioning later scribes as adding the term to make this verse match virtually every other opening greeting of Paul: "*our* Father" (Rom. 1:7; 1 Cor. 1:3; 2 Cor. 1:2; Gal. 1:3, 4; Eph. 1:2; Phil. 1:2; Col. 1:2b; Philem. 3). If, as seems likely, the pronoun should be omitted, this weakens the claims of this letter's supposed pseudepigraphical character, since, as Fee (2007: 69n113) asks: "Would a pseudepigrapher have thus botched the borrowing of this phrase from the rest of the corpus?"

II. Thanksgiving (1:3–12)

Paul's epistolary pattern is not to move directly from the letter opening to the body of the letter but instead to include a "thanksgiving" section that serves at least three functions—all of which are at work here in 2 Thess. 1:3–12. First, it has a pastoral function: the thanksgiving reestablishes Paul's relationship with his Thessalonian readers by means of a positive expression of gratitude to God for the remarkable growth of their faith and love despite great opposition. Second, it has a paraenetic, or exhortative, function: the thanksgiving challenges—both implicitly in the thanksgiving of 1:3–10 and explicitly in the prayer report of verses 11–12—the believers in Thessalonica to live up to the praise and petitions that the apostle is giving them in his words of gratitude and prayer to God. Third, it has a foreshadowing function: the thanksgiving anticipates the eschatological issue that Paul takes up first and longest in the letter body: the false claim that the day of the Lord has already come (2:1–17). In the main passage of the letter body, however, the apostle's overriding concern is not so much to *correct* this false teaching as it is to *comfort* the shaken believers in Thessalonica. This concern of Paul with consoling his Thessalonian readers is well foreshadowed in the thanksgiving section.

The thanksgiving of 1:3–12 falls into three distinct sections. The first unit, verses 3–4, *commends* the Thessalonians for their remarkable spiritual growth in the face of persecution. To believers in Thessalonica who are suffering their fellow citizens' opposition to their faith, it will be greatly comforting to hear how Paul and his coworkers have found it not only "necessary" and "fitting" to give thanks to God because of their faith and love for one another but also to "boast" about them to other churches.

The second unit, verses 5–10, *comforts* the Thessalonians with the message of "the just judgment of God" (v. 5)—a judgment that will involve the punishment of those who are persecuting the believers in Thessalonica (vv. 6, 7b–9) and the reward of those being persecuted (vv. 7a, 10). For the majority of contemporary Christians who know embarrassingly little about suffering for their faith, it is difficult to hear the note of comfort in Paul's words about the just judgment of God. For the Thessalonian Christians, however, who are enduring persecution for no other reason than their faith in God and his Son, Jesus, it is comforting to hear about a final judgment that vindicates their faith, punishes their oppressors, and thus demonstrates that the God in whom they have placed their faith is indeed just.

The third unit, verses 11–12, *challenges* the Thessalonians to live up to the standard of conduct that Paul and his coworkers spell out in their prayer report. Yet even in this not-so-subtle exhortation for the Thessalonians to live up to the standard of conduct asked in prayer for them, Paul continues to console his readers not only by letting them know that he is praying for them but also by stressing, in the content of his prayer, the divine initiative in their salvation: *God* is the one who will make them worthy of their election and who will bring about their good desire and work, thereby ensuring that the name of the Lord Jesus Christ will be glorified in them and they in him.

Literary Analysis

Character of the Passage

Second Thessalonians 1:3–12 consists of a distinct epistolary unit typically found in Paul's Letters, located between the letter opening and the letter body, in which the apostle gives thanks to God for the believers to whom he is writing. This unit is normally labeled the "thanksgiving" section because of its key opening verb "to give thanks" (εὐχαριστεῖν, *eucharistein*) and the general content of this epistolary unit. For an extended discussion of the thanksgivings in the Pauline Letters as a whole, particularly their source, form, and function, see the comments on 1 Thess. 1:2–10 under the heading "Literary Analysis."

Extent of the Passage

The extent of this thanksgiving section is not in dispute; both its opening and conclusion are clearly marked. The beginning of this unit at verse 3 is indicated by three factors. First, it is strongly suggested by the greeting in 1:2, which normally signals the end of the letter opening and the start of the thanksgiving section. That verse 3 does indeed mark the beginning of the thanksgiving is, second, made clear by the presence of the key verb "to give thanks." And even though the fuller expression "We ought to give thanks" is used instead of the expected simple form "We give thanks," the key verb "to give thanks" is located, as it is in every other Pauline thanksgiving, at the head of the sentence, thus in the position of emphasis. Third, in verse 3 the presence of the vocative "brothers," a common transitional device in letters, confirms the beginning of a new unit here.

The closing of this unit after verse 12 is unmistakably indicated by a number of factors. First, verses 11–12 constitute a "prayer report," which, in Paul's other thanksgivings containing such a summary statement of the apostle's intercession for his letter recipients, always brings this epistolary unit to a close (Phil. 1:9–11; Col. 1:9–14; see also Rom. 1:10b). Second, in verse 12 the reference to the glorification of the name of the Lord Jesus has in view what will take place in the future at his parousia (note how the compound verb ἐνδοξασθῇ [*endoxasthē*] echoes the identical form found in verse 10, where the context is clearly eschatological: "whenever he comes to be glorified"). Thus in verse 12 the thanksgiving reaches an eschatological climax, just as Paul's other thanksgivings typically end on a futuristic note (1 Cor. 1:7–8; Phil. 1:10; 1 Thess. 1:10; on the eschatological climax as a transition from the thanksgiving to the letter body, see Schubert 1939: 4–5; O'Brien 1977: 170; Sanders 1962: 348–62; Roberts 1986: 29–35). Third, 2:1 opens with an appeal formula—an epistolary convention that in Paul's Letters typically signals a transition to a new topic or unit of thought. Finally, 2:1 also opens with the vocative "brothers," which is an even more common transitional device in letters, thereby confirming the end of the thanksgiving section and the beginning of the letter body.

Structure of the Passage

The thanksgiving of 1:3–12 consists of two sentences in Greek: verses 3–10 and 11–12. The first sentence is by far the longer of the two and has been variously described as "loosely connected" (Marshall 1983: 169), "complicated" (Morris 1991: 192), "poorly constructed" (Richard 1995: 312), "syntactically unclear" (Furnish 2007: 144), and having a "structure that leaves one gasping for grammatical oxygen" (Dunham 1981: 41). These descriptions need to be nuanced, however, since they are not true for verses 3–4, which match a typical Pauline style in which the apostle's argument is developed quite logically: a main clause (v. 3a) that is grounded with a causal *hoti* clause (v. 3b), which in turn leads naturally to a *hōste* result clause (v. 4). Furthermore, to a large extent verses 3–4 follow the form of Paul's other thanksgivings, which typically open with a main verb of thanksgiving, followed by the manner of thanksgiving (though here the expected participial construction is replaced with the parenthetical comment "as it is fitting") and the cause of thanksgiving (on the form of Paul's thanksgivings as a whole, see comments on 1 Thess. 1:2–10).

Verses 5–10, however, stand apart from the preceding material in terms of both its form and its style. Formally, this section does not match the "explanation" section that Paul normally has at this point in his thanksgiving—a section that usually modifies the preceding causal unit and so serves to elaborate on the cause for the apostle's thanksgiving to God. Stylistically, this section also differs from the preceding material in that the grammatical connection of its diverse parts is not made clear.

But despite the absence of connecting particles (asyndeton), these verses are linked in a variety of ways. In terms of its content, verses 5–10 are striking for the heavy concentration of eschatological references in contrast to verses 3–4, which deal with the present time. Also in terms of its content, verses 5–10 focus on divine action (God's just judgment accomplished at Christ's second coming) in contrast to verses 3–4, which highlight human action (the Thessalonians' remarkable spiritual growth in the face of persecution). In terms of its literary features, the key root δικ- (just, justice) occurs no less than four times (v. 5, δικαίας; v. 6, δίκαιον; v. 8, ἐκδίκησιν; v. 9, δίκην), thereby giving this section lexical coherence. This section is further joined together by the verb "to give (back)" ([ἀνταπο]δίδωμι, [*antapo*] *didōmi*), which is twice joined with the other key term of "justice": verse 6, "Since it is *just* before God to *give back* . . ."; and verse 8, "*giving justice* to those who do not know God." Finally, this section frequently employs parallelism, either contrastive (vv. 6b–7a, ". . . affliction to those who afflict you and rest to you who are being afflicted") or, more commonly, synonymous (v. 8, "to those who do not know God and to those who do not obey the gospel of our Lord Jesus Christ"; v. 9, "from the face of the Lord and from the glory of his might"; v. 10, "to be glorified in his holy ones and to be marveled at in all who believe").

The distinctive character of verses 5–10 has been variously explained. Way (1921: 41–42) finds in this passage, especially in verses 7–10, a "Hymn of the Second Coming," which is either Paul's own creation or an earlier work from which the apostle draws (see also Findlay 1891: lvii; Bornemann 1894; Wanamaker 1990: 234;

Williams 1992: 110). Other explanations stem from the observation that verses 5–10 contain a number of terms and theological themes from the OT. Particularly striking are the several parallels with Isa. 66—the final chapter of that important prophetic book, which describes what the Lord will do in the last days to prosper his chosen people and to punish the wicked. These parallels lead Aus (1971: 113–14; 1976: esp. 266–67) to propose that 1:5–10 is the result of a conscious reflection of Isa. 66, supplemented by a few other OT texts, in order to create an end-time scenario that will comfort the persecuted readers and counter the false claim concerning the day of the Lord (see also Richard 1995: 315–16). The several allusions to the OT in 1 Thess. 1:5–10 lead Bruce (1982: 148) to suggest that here Paul was borrowing from a "testimony collection"—a pre-Pauline compilation of OT passages that deal with the common subject of eschatological teaching. These two theories, however, have not found wide acceptance: most commentators view the OT parallels in 1:5–10 to be the result of unconscious allusions that come from the hand of the apostle himself rather than any preformed tradition. The situation is analogous to some Christians who are so familiar with the text of the Bible that their prayers unconsciously echo many biblical phrases or passages.

The second and shorter sentence in the thanksgiving, verses 11–12, is connected to the preceding unit by the opening prepositional phrase "to this end" (εἰς ὅ, *eis ho*), which looks back to the material of verses 5–10. Nevertheless, it constitutes a new, distinct unit in Paul's overall argument in 1:3–12. Formally, verses 11–12 make up the "prayer report" that the apostle sometimes uses to bring his thanksgiving to a close (Phil. 1:9–11; Col. 1:9–14; see also Rom. 1:10b). This final part of the Pauline thanksgiving typically involves the verb "to pray" (προσεύχεσθαι, *proseuchesai*) followed by a *hina* clause that gives in summary fashion the content of the prayer— exactly the form that is found here. That verses 11–12 make up a new section is further suggested by the parallel between the opening main clause of this third unit and that of the first unit: just as Paul and his coworkers "ought to give thanks *always concerning you*" (v. 3, πάντοτε περὶ ὑμῶν, *pantote peri hymōn*), so *also* (the conjunction καί [*kai*] in this main clause looks back to the only other main clause in the passage, found in v. 3) they "pray *always concerning you*" (v. 11, πάντοτε περὶ ὑμῶν, *pantote peri hymōn*).

The analysis given above makes clear that the thanksgiving of 2 Thess. 1:3–12 falls into three parts: verses 3–4, 5–10, 11–12.[1] This tripartite structure is adopted by most commentators, including a few who go further and see in the interrelationship of these three units a concentric arrangement (e.g., Rigaux 1956: 619, 628; Trilling 1980: 40, 61; Callow 1982: 28; Brunot 1985: 48; Menken 1990: 373–75). There is some correspondence between the outer units of verses 3–4 and verses 11–12: in addition to the parallel between the phrase "always concerning you" in each of these units that was already noted above, there is also a possible emphasis in both units on "faith" (vv. 3b, 4b, 11b). Nevertheless, these parallels are not strong enough to support the claim that Paul deliberately structured this thanksgiving in a concentric pattern.

---

1. If the thanksgiving is outlined on purely epistolary grounds, namely, on the basis of the form of Paul's other thanksgivings, a slightly different outline emerges: (1) Statement of thanksgiving (v. 3a); (2) Cause of thanksgiving (vv. 3b–4); (3) "Digression" on the just judgment of God (vv. 5–10); (4) Prayer report (vv. 11–12).

A discussion of the outline of this thanksgiving, its *form*, ought not to be completed without considering how this thanksgiving serves the larger purpose at work in 2 Thessalonians as a whole, its *function*. Paul's thanksgivings are not meaningless literary devices but rather integral parts of the apostle's letters, carefully crafted and adapted so as to support the key concern(s) developed in the body of the letter. The key concern of 2 Thessalonians is found in the issue that Paul takes up first and longest in the letter body: the false claim that the day of the Lord has come (2:1–17). As will become clear from the exposition of this main passage in the letter body, the apostle's overriding concern is not so much to *correct* this false teaching as it is to *comfort* the Thessalonian believers shaken by this false teaching. The thanksgiving of 1:3–12 anticipates this overriding concern of Paul to comfort his readers in Thessalonica. As Malherbe (2000: 381) observes: "A similar consolatory concern occupies Paul in this letter [2 Thessalonians], and it surfaces already in the first thanksgiving, in the beginning of the letter, which leads to encouragement of the discouraged readers."

The first unit, verses 3–4, *commends* the Thessalonians for their remarkable spiritual growth in the face of persecution. To believers in Thessalonica who have been suffering opposition to their faith from their fellow citizens, it would be greatly comforting to hear how Paul and his coworkers found it not only "necessary" and "fitting" to give thanks to God because of their faith and love for one another, but also to "boast" about them to other churches.

The second unit, verses 5–10, *comforts* the Thessalonians with the message of "the just judgment of God" (v. 5). For the majority of contemporary Christians who know embarrassingly little about suffering for their faith, it is difficult to hear the note of comfort in Paul's words about the just judgment of God. Yet for the Thessalonian Christians who are enduring persecution for no other reason than their faith in God and his Son, Jesus, it is comforting to hear about a final judgment that vindicates their faith, punishes their oppressors, and thus demonstrates that the God in whom they have placed their faith is indeed just.

The third unit, verses 11–12, *challenges* the Thessalonians to live up to the standard of conduct that Paul and his coworkers spell out in their prayer report (on the paraenetic, or exhortative, function of the thanksgiving section generally, see Schubert 1939: 26, 89; O'Brien 1977: 141–44, 165, 262–63). Yet even in this not-so-subtle exhortation for them to live up to the prayed-for standard of conduct, Paul continues to console his readers by not only letting them know that he is praying for them but also by stressing, in the content of his prayer, the divine initiative in their salvation: *God* is the one who will make them worthy of their election and who will bring about their good desire and work, thereby ensuring that the name of the Lord Jesus Christ will be glorified in them and they in him.

In light of the above discussion, the thanksgiving of 2 Thess. 1:3–12 can be best outlined as follows:

A. Commendation for spiritual growth in the face of persecution (1:3–4)
B. Comfort concerning the just judgment of God (1:5–10)
 1. The just judgment of God: Its assertion (1:5)
 2. The just judgment of God: Its evidence stated briefly (1:6–7a)

a. Negative judgment on the afflicters: Affliction (1:6)
b. Positive judgment on the afflicted: Rest (1:7a)
3. The just judgment of God: Its evidence restated more fully (1:7b–10)
a. Negative judgment on the afflicters: Eternal destruction (1:7b–9)
b. Positive judgment on the afflicted: Glorification (1:10)
C. Challenge: Prayer for God to work in the Thessalonians' lives (1:11–12)

Exegesis and Exposition

[3]We ought to give thanks to God always concerning you, brothers, as it is fitting, because your faith is growing abundantly, and the love of each one of you all for one another is increasing [4]so that we ourselves ⌜boast⌝ about you in the churches of God concerning your steadfastness and faith in all your persecutions and the afflictions that you are ⌜enduring⌝.

[5]Here is evidence of the just judgment of God so that you may be made worthy of the kingdom of God, on behalf of which you are also suffering, [6]since it is just in the sight of God to pay back affliction to the ones who are afflicting you [7]and [to pay back], to you who are being afflicted, rest with us, at the revelation of the Lord Jesus from heaven with the angels of his power [8]in ⌜a flame of fire⌝, ⌜inflicting⌝ punishment on those who do not know God and on those who do not obey the gospel of our Lord Jesus, [9]such people who will pay a penalty, eternal destruction from the presence of the Lord and from the glory of his might, [10]whenever he comes to be glorified in his holy ones and to be marveled at in all who believe (because our testimony to you was ⌜believed⌝) on that day.

[11]To this end we also are praying always concerning you, that our God may make you worthy of the calling and may ⌜complete⌝ every desire of goodness and work of faith in power, [12]so that the name of the ⌜Lord Jesus⌝ may be glorified in you and you in him according to the grace of our God and of our Lord Jesus Christ.

The discussion above concerning the structure of this thanksgiving (see "Structure of the Passage") highlighted the movement from Paul's *commendation* of the Thessalonian believers for their amazing spiritual growth in the face of persecution (vv. 3–4), to his *comfort* of them with the message of God's just judgment by which their persecutors would be punished and their own faith vindicated (vv. 5–10), and to his closing *challenge* via the prayer report (vv. 11–12). The following exegetical analysis unpacks this movement. Yet what ought not to be overlooked is the consolatory concern at work throughout the passage as a whole, which anticipates the apostle's ultimate purpose in the body of the letter. Paul aims to comfort the Christians in Thessalonica, who are enduring opposition to their faith and are badly shaken by a false claim concerning the day of the Lord (note the double reference to "comfort" in the prayer that closes 2:1–17: "But may our Lord Jesus Christ himself and God our Father, who . . . gave us eternal *comfort* and good hope by his grace, *comfort* your hearts"). To put it in colloquial terms, Paul's overriding concern in 2 Thessalonians is not to calculate the future but to comfort the church, and this consolatory purpose is at work already in the thanksgiving section.[2]

A. Commendation for Spiritual Growth in the Face of Persecution (1:3–4)

Paul opens this new section of the letter with words of thanksgiving that, though directed to God, involve a commendation of his Thessalonian readers: "We ought to give thanks to God always concerning you, brothers, as it is fitting, because your faith is growing abundantly, and the love of each one of you all for one another is increasing" (εὐχαριστεῖν ὀφείλομεν τῷ θεῷ πάντοτε περὶ ὑμῶν, ἀδελφοί, καθὼς ἄξιόν ἐστιν, ὅτι ὑπεραυξάνει ἡ πίστις ὑμῶν καὶ πλεονάζει ἡ ἀγάπη ἑνὸς ἑκάστου πάντων ὑμῶν εἰς ἀλλήλους, *eucharistein opheilomen tō theō pantote peri hymōn, adelphoi, kathōs axion estin, hoti hyperauxanei hē pistis hymōn kai pleonazei hē agapē henos hekastou pantōn hymōn eis allēlous*).

1:3

The opening part of Paul's thanksgivings typically consists of the following three elements: (1) a statement of thanksgiving involving the key verb "I/we give thanks" (*eucharistō/omen*); (2) a participial construction indicating the manner in which Paul gives thanks; and (3) a causal construction in the form of phrases using the conjunction *hoti* or participial clauses that give the reason(s) for the apostle's thanksgiving. The thanksgiving that opens 2 Thessalonians follows this form closely, except for two modest changes: the simple "I/we give thanks" is replaced by the fuller phrase "we ought to give thanks"; and the manner of thanksgiving has been replaced with the parenthetical clause "as it is fitting." Some commentators, however, find these two changes not at all modest but significant, and consequently they forward a variety of proposals to account for the unique formal features of this thanksgiving:

1. Frame (1912: 221) finds in the addition of "we ought" and "it is fitting" evidence that Paul is responding to a letter from the Thessalonian church "to the effect that they did not consider themselves worthy of the kingdom or entitled to the praise accorded them in the first epistle" (so also Bruce 1982: 144; Morris 1991: 193; Williams 1992: 110).
2. D. Martin (1995: 201) proposes that Paul is responding to the problem of 1 Thess. 2, where his opponents have accused him of being a flatterer, and so his language of obligation and fittingness here in verse 3 stems from his desire "to make it clear to the church that his praise for them was not flattery nor merely the biased appreciation of a loving father

2. Although the majority of exegetes either completely miss this consolatory purpose or fail to appreciate its importance both in the letter as a whole and in this introductory thanksgiving section, there are a few notable exceptions: Lünemann 1885: 557; Dobschütz 1909: 235; and esp. Malherbe 2000: 381, 388–89, who cites some patristic commentators.

for his children." Yet this interpretation, like the preceding one, is too speculative to be convincing and illustrates the danger of mirror reading: inferring from an ambiguous text too much about its specific historical context.

3. Aus (1973: 432–38) argues that statements about "the necessity and propriety of giving thanks" were common in Jewish and Christian liturgical settings and that Paul's statements here in verse 3 reflect this influence (so also Dobschütz 1909: 235; Richard 1995: 301; Gaventa 1998: 99). But as Wanamaker asks (1990: 216), even if such language does stem from a liturgical background, why is Paul influenced by this background only in this letter and in none of his other thanksgivings?

4. Several scholars view the language of "we ought" and "it is fitting" as decidedly distant and cool compared to the intimacy and warmth of his other thanksgivings and thus find in these two additions further evidence that 2 Thessalonians does not come from the hand of Paul (e.g., Dibelius 1937: 33; J. A. Bailey 1978–79: 137; Trilling 1980: 43–44; Furnish 2007: 132). However, this interpretation founders on the fact that the subsequent language of the thanksgiving is not only very warm and intimate (note the presence of the vocative "brothers") but even exuberant in its commendation (the Thessalonians' faith is not merely "growing" but "growing *abundantly*" [note the prefix *hyper* added to the verb *auxanō*] so that Paul boasts about them to other churches).

5. The best explanation is that the obligation of humans to give thanks to God is a common theme in both Jewish and Christian writings of Paul's day. The Mishnah, for example, in the context of reminding Jews during the Passover of how the Lord redeemed them from Egypt, states: "Therefore, we are obligated to thank him who wrought all these wonders for our fathers and us" (*m. Pesaḥ.* 10.5). The Christian letter known as 1 Clement exhorts its readers: "We ought in every respect to give thanks to him" (38.4). Similarly, the Epistle of Barnabas states: "The good Lord revealed everything to us beforehand, in order that we might know him to whom we ought to give thanks and praise for everything" (7.1; see also 5.3).

The fuller expression "We *ought to* give thanks to God," therefore, along with the parenthetical phrase "as it is fitting," does not mean that Paul views thanksgiving as a duty rather than a joy. Instead, the apostle is simply acknowledging, as do others of his day, the need for gratitude to be given to God since he is responsible for the growth of faith and love in the lives of the Thessalonian Christians. That this growth took place in the context of significant opposition and trial is, in Paul's mind, truly remarkable and thus precipitated his shift from the expected, simple "We give thanks" to the fuller and more powerful expression used here to open his thanksgiving. This shift also stems from the larger concern of Paul at work in the passage, to comfort his readers. To his recent converts in Thessalonica, who are suffering opposition to their faith from their fellow citizens (1 Thess. 2:14), it will be comforting to hear how Paul, their spiritual "father" (1 Thess. 2:11), has found it not only "fitting" but even obligatory to give thanks to God because of their remarkable spiritual growth.

In the discussion above, the emphasis on the commendation that the Thessalonians receive in this thanksgiving and its comforting function for these readers may lead one to miss the decidedly theocentric (God-centered) theology that underlies Paul's comments here. This theological perspective reveals itself in the simple but important fact that the apostle opens not with words of praise to his audience or words of congratulations to himself but words of thanksgiving "to God." The theocentric accent parallels the same theological perspective evident in the thanksgiving section of 1 Thessalonians: even though the Thessalonians are commended for their faith, love, and hope (1 Thess. 1:3), exemplary life in the midst of persecution (1:6–7), evangelistic activity (1:8), and conversion (1:9–10); and even though Paul and his fellow missionaries are to be recognized for the genuineness of their original ministry in Thessalonica (1:5)—all of these good things that have happened in that church are ultimately due to God's work of election (1:4); thus God is the one to whom thanksgiving must be given. Similarly in 2 Thessalonians, even though the church is commended for the abundant increase of their faith and love (2 Thess. 1:3b) such that Paul boasts about them to other churches (1:4), all this remarkable spiritual growth is ultimately due to God's activity in their lives, and so God is the one to whom thanksgiving must be given. The rest of the thanksgiving similarly highlights the primary role that God plays in the salvation of the Thessalonian Christians: verses 5–10 stress God's role in vindicating the believers in Thessalonica and punishing their enemies, and verses 11–12 give a report of prayer directed to "our God" to make the readers worthy of "his calling" by means of "[his] power." Also we notice the so-called second thanksgiving located in the body of the letter, with its double reference to God's election of the Thessalonian believers (2:13–14: "because God *chose* you . . . To this end he also *called* you").

Although Paul's thanksgiving is directed to God, it nevertheless has the Thessalonians as its subject matter: "always concerning you, brothers." The adverb "always" (*pantote*) and the prepositional phrase "concerning you" (*peri hymōn*) are both fairly regular features of the apostle's opening thanksgivings (1 Thess. 1:2; Rom. 1:8; 1 Cor. 1:4; Phil. 1:3–4; Philem. 4; Col. 1:3).[3] This might suggest that Paul's claim of "always" giving thanks to God for the Thessalonians is merely a rhetorical remark or epistolary nicety. But even though this claim is formulaic and somewhat hyperbolic, it gains more credibility in light of the addition of the vocative "brothers," which is not typically part

---

3. In 1:3 the adjective "all" found in the previous letter's thanksgiving—perhaps a deliberate addition by Paul so as to include all the believers in Thessalonica, including those who were rebelliously idle and would later come under rebuke for opposing the apostle and his appointed leaders in the church—is missing, in keeping with the form of his other thanksgivings. See further the comments on 1 Thess. 1:2a.

of the thanksgiving section (it occurs only in the thanksgivings of the Thessalonian correspondence). This vocative was used heavily in the first letter to characterize the relationship between Paul and his readers (1:4; 2:1, 9, 14, 17; 3:7; 4:1, 10b, 13; 5:1, 4, 12, 14, 25), as were intimate family metaphors such as "infants" (2:7b), "nursing mother" (2:7c), "father" (2:11), and orphans (2:17). The use of the vocative "brothers" here in a letter written to the same audience only a short time later, therefore, continues this use of kinship language and, along with the emphatic "we ourselves" in the following verse, stresses the affectionate nature of the relationship that exists between Paul and his readers (Malherbe 2000: 383). Given this intimate bond that the apostle has with the Thessalonians, it may well be true that Paul is "always" giving thanks to God concerning them.

The parenthetical phrase "as it is fitting" occurs only here in Paul's thanksgivings (but see Phil. 1:7, "as it is right"), replacing the expected participial construction indicating the manner in which the apostle gives thanks. The relationship between this phrase and the preceding main clause "We ought to give thanks" has engendered quite a bit of discussion, especially among older exegetes. A few propose a tautological relationship in which "as it is fitting" merely repeats the sense of "We ought to give thanks" for the sake of emphasis (e.g., Jowett 1894: 155). Most, however, distinguish between a "subjective" or "divine" obligation, expressed in the main clause, that stresses the thanks that is due to God for his role in the Thessalonians' lives and an "objective" or "human" obligation, expressed in the parenthetical clause, that stresses the thanks that is "fitting" because of the Thessalonians' praiseworthy conduct (e.g., Eadie 1877: 229; Ellicott 1880: 94; Lünemann 1885: 577; Milligan 1908: 86; Witherington 2006: 188). Lightfoot (1904: 97) paraphrases this distinction as follows: "It is not only a duty, which our conscience prescribes as owed to God; but it is also merited by your conduct." But while it is true that the phrase "as it is fitting" does not merely repeat the sense of "We ought to give thanks," the claimed distinction between the "subjective/divine" and the "objective/human" side of the obligation is too nuanced to be likely intended by Paul or picked up by his Thessalonian readers. It is more probable that the apostle first refers to the *necessity* of giving thanks to God and then the *propriety* of giving thanks to God, thereby adding emphasis to his overall commendation of the Christians in Thessalonica—an emphasis justified in light of their remarkable spiritual growth amid persecution and supporting Paul's larger goal, not just in the thanksgiving but also in the letter as a whole, of comforting his persecuted and shaken readers.

Here the conjunction *hoti* has a causal sense and so introduces two reasons why the giving of thanks to God concerning the Thessalonian believers is both necessary and fitting. The first reason involves the church's *faith*: "because your faith is growing abundantly." The term "faith" frequently occurs in Paul's writings as part of the triad "faith, love, and hope" (1 Thess. 1:3; 5:8; Rom. 5:1–5; 1 Cor. 13:13; Gal. 5:5–6; Eph. 4:2–5; Col. 1:4–5; see also Heb. 6:10–12; 10:22–24; 1 Pet. 1:3–8, 21–22; Barn. 1.4; 11.8; Polycarp, *Phil.* 3.2–3). Therefore the use of "faith" in this thanksgiving, along with the second member of the triad, "love," might lead to the conclusion that Paul's language here is formulaic and stereotypical, unconnected in any meaningful way to the specific situation of the Thessalonian church.

Against this conclusion, however, is the fact that the faith of the Thessalonians was of particular concern to Paul in his previous letter to them. Although their faith was sufficient to warrant thanksgiving to God (1 Thess. 1:3), it nevertheless was not great enough to overcome the apostle's anxiety about them, especially in light of the opposition to their faith that they were experiencing. Consequently, Paul sent Timothy "in order to strengthen you and comfort you concerning your faith" (3:2)—a purpose repeated virtually verbatim a few verses later (3:5: "I sent in order to learn about your faith"). Timothy's faith-strengthening ministry was successful enough to warrant a positive report when he returned to Paul: "But Timothy has now come to us from you and has brought good news about your faith" (3:6). Furthermore, the apostle was comforted in the afflictions that he himself was experiencing during his current ministry in Corinth "through this faith of yours" (3:7). Yet Timothy's report about the Thessalonians' faith was not completely free of concern, as evidenced by Paul's ongoing desire to visit them in person and so "complete the things that are lacking in your faith" (3:10)—something he attempts to accomplish in the remaining half of the letter (4:1–5:22). Faith is also an important piece of the spiritual armor (5:8) with which they need to clothe themselves in preparation for the coming day of the Lord.

In light of this background, that Paul opens his Second Letter to the Thessalonians by giving thanks for their abundantly growing faith is significant. Furthermore, in the thanksgiving of 1:3–12 a variety of features reveal a discernible emphasis on the readers' faith that continues in this letter. First, the verb *hyperauxanei*, occurring only here in the NT, is used to describe a faith that is not merely "growing" but "growing *abundantly*" (BDAG 1032), since the compound *hyper* is commonly used by Paul to express either emphasis or excess (MHT 2:326; of the twenty-five occurrences of *hyper-* compounds in the NT, all except three are in Paul's Letters). As O'Brien (1977: 172–73) notes, this form of the verb "points to the unusual, even unexpected, progress of the addressees' faith." Second, the present tense of *hyperauxanei* highlights the ongoing, continuous nature of this growing faith. Third, whereas both faith and love are mentioned here in verse 3, only faith is mentioned again in the immediately following verse as the thing that Paul boasts about to other churches. The second reference to faith in verse 4 is also significant for linking this word with the subject of persecution and affliction—the same link found in the previous letter to the Thessalonians (1 Thess. 3:1–5). Fourth, the term "faith" appears again (2 Thess. 1:11) in the prayer report that closes the thanksgiving section, perhaps forming an inclusio with the two earlier references to faith in verses 3 and 4. Finally, the verbal form of "faith" occurs twice in verse 10. This emphasis on faith throughout, not just in the thanksgiving section but also in the letter body, has not gone unnoticed by Giblin who, in his monograph treatment of the second chapter, considers the main theme of 1:3–12 to be "the fulfillment of faith" (1967: 8) and who titles his exposition of 2:1–17 as "The Threat to Faith."

The second reason why the giving of thanks to God concerning the Thessalonian believers is both necessary and fitting involves the church's *love*: "because . . . the love of each one of you all for one another is increasing." This love for other Christians, like their faith, was also of particular concern to Paul in his previous Letter to the Thessalonians. On the one hand, their mutual love was sufficient enough to warrant thanksgiving to God (1 Thess. 1:2–3). Nevertheless, Paul worried whether his ongoing inability to return in person to Thessalonica might be used by his opponents outside the church—the "fellow citizens" (2:14) who were oppressing the congregation and questioning the integrity of its founder—to raise further doubts about the genuineness of his love for the Thessalonian believers. In 2:17–3:10 the apostle responded to this concern by employing the apostolic parousia—an epistolary device that makes his presence more powerfully experienced among his Thessalonian readers such that they are reassured of his love for them. This explains why Paul is so pleased with the report of the just-returned Timothy, who brought double good news about not only the Thessalonians' faith but also their love: "But Timothy has now come to us from you and has brought good news about your faith and love and that you have a good remembrance of us always, longing to see us just as we also long to see you" (3:6). The second of the transitional prayers of 3:11–13 provides further evidence of Paul's concern with the subject of love among the Thessalonians: "But as for you, may the Lord cause you to increase and abound in love for one another and for all, just as we also increase and abound in love for you" (3:12). This prayer not only looks back to the concern about mutual love between the apostle and the church raised in 2:17–3:10, but also looks ahead specifically to the discussion of brotherly and sisterly love in 4:9–12 and more generally to the implications of loving one another taken up in 5:12–22. Love is also one piece of the spiritual armor (5:8) that the Thessalonians need to wear as they ready and steady themselves for the coming day of the Lord.

For the Thessalonian Christians who have recently heard Paul in his first letter to them raise so often the concern that love be evident in their congregation, it will be especially comforting to hear, at the opening of his second letter, that the increase of such love in their midst was one of the two reasons why the apostle was obligated to give thanks to God for them. The situation is similar to the encouragement a child feels when their parent, who has been exhorting them repeatedly in the past to develop a particular virtue, now praises them for the way they are demonstrating that very same virtue in their daily life. The manner in which Paul refers to this increased love reveals a degree of emphasis, though not nearly to the extent that "faith" was stressed. First, although the verb *pleonazei* is used rather than the compound form *hyperpleonazei* (which the apostle does use elsewhere in a thanksgiving section: 1 Tim. 1:14), the simpler form nevertheless gains emphasis from the preceding compound verb *hyperauxanei*, with which it shares a relationship of synonymous parallelism (Malherbe 2000: 385). Second, the verb *pleonazei*, like its preceding parallel form *hyperauxanei*, is in the present tense, thereby highlighting the ongoing, continuous nature of this increasing love. The third and most clear evidence of emphasis, however, is the fulsome phrase "the love of each one of you all for one another"—a phrase without parallel elsewhere in Paul or even in the rest of the NT. As Morris (1991: 194) states: "The expression is a strong one. Clearly Paul is making no exceptions. Love was a bond uniting the whole church."

The apostle's strong commendation of the Thessalonians for "the love of each one of you all for one another" is surprising in light of the problem taken up in 3:6–15: the rebellious idlers who are taking advantage of the love and generosity of their fellow congregational members. This leads Bruce (1982: 145) to assume that these idlers must constitute "an uncharacteristic minority, whose waywardness, though regrettable, did not detract from the satisfaction with which the community as a whole was viewed." It might additionally be observed that, though Paul exhorted the church to excommunicate those who rebelliously continued in their idle ways, he did not want such disciplinary action to come at the expense of the love for which he commends them in the opening thanksgiving. Paul thus concludes his lengthy treatment of the rebellious idlers by calling on the church to "not be discouraged in doing good" (3:13) and to "not consider . . . [an idler] as an enemy, but admonish him as a brother" (3:15).

The twin concerns of faith and love raised in the first letter and now mentioned again in the opening of the second letter as the reason for thanksgiving do not imply that the Thessalonians are living perfectly in these two areas and that Paul has no further worries about his readers. Thanksgivings in the apostle's letters have a paraenetic, or exhortative, function in which the readers are implicitly (or explicitly, in the closing prayer report) called on to live up to the praise that Paul gives them (Schubert 1939: 26, 89; O'Brien 1977: 141–44, 165, 262–63). Thus, as laudatory as Paul's words may be about "your faith" that "is growing abundantly" and "the love of each one of you all for one another" that "is increasing," the Thessalonians are nevertheless implicitly pressured to continue to grow in these two areas of their spiritual life.

1:4   Not only is Paul's commendation (and thus also his comfort) of the Thessalonian readers amplified by the fact that the apostle believes his thanksgiving to God for their remarkable spiritual growth is necessary and fitting (1:3), but it also causes him to brag about them to other congregations: "so that we ourselves boast about you in the churches of God concerning your steadfastness and faith in all your persecutions and the afflictions that you are enduring" (ὥστε αὐτοὺς ἡμᾶς ἐν ὑμῖν ἐγκαυχᾶσθαι ἐν ταῖς ἐκκλησίαις τοῦ θεοῦ ὑπὲρ τῆς ὑπομονῆς ὑμῶν καὶ πίστεως ἐν πᾶσιν τοῖς διωγμοῖς ὑμῶν καὶ ταῖς θλίψεσιν αἷς ἀνέχεσθε, *hōste autous hēmas en hymin enkauchasthai en tais ekklēsiais tou* *theou hyper tēs hypomonēs hymōn kai pisteōs en pasin tois diōgmois hymōn kai tais thlipsesin hais anechesthe).*

The emphasis expressed in the preceding verse (1:3) in a variety of ways (i.e., the statement about the obligation of giving thanks instead of the simpler and expected "we give thanks," the addition of the parenthetical comment about the propriety of giving thanks, the rare compound form of the verb "grow *abundantly*," and the fulsome and unparalleled phrase "the love of each one of you all for one another") continues in this subsequent result clause with the opening words "we ourselves," which is stressed both by its presence (the third-person personal pronoun, when modifying some other noun or pronoun in the predicate position, has an intensive function: BDF §288; Porter 1992: 130) and its location at the head of the sentence. Many exegetes have found these opening words so emphatic that they presume Paul to be contrasting the boasting that he and his coworkers make about the Thessalonian Christians with the boasting done by some other unidentified party. This assumption naturally leads to the attempt to identify who this unnamed group might be—an attempt that leads to a variety of proposals:

1. Paul has in view other Christians in general—not only "all the believers in Macedonia and Achaia" (1 Thess. 1:7–8) but in other places too (1:8), who not only report about the apostle's ministry in Thessalonica (1:9) but also boast about the Thessalonian believers. Here in 2 Thess. 1:4, then, Paul's point about boasting is that "If others had done so, why should not their own parents in the faith boast about them?" (Bruce 1982: 145; so also, e.g., Lünemann 1885: 578; Findlay 1891: 141).

2. Paul has in view himself and his general refusal to boast about anyone or anything except the Lord Jesus (1 Cor. 1:29–31) or the "cross of Christ" (Gal. 6:14). Whereas in his previous correspondence with the Thessalonians, the apostle follows this principle and "has no need to say anything" about spiritual gifts evident in this church (1:8), in this second letter "the qualities of which Paul speaks had been displayed in such outstanding measure that even those whose preaching had brought that church into being could not forebear to utter its praises" (Morris 1991: 194; so also Moore 1969: 91; O'Brien 1977: 175).

3. Paul has in view the Thessalonian believers whose faintheartedness (1 Thess. 5:14) or humility caused them to believe that they were not worthy of the apostle's praise of them in his first letter, let alone of his boasting about them. Paul, then, "contrasts his boasting to the Thessalonians' reluctance to speak about themselves" (Malherbe 2000: 386; so also Frame 1912: 223; Hendriksen 1955: 155; Marshall 1983: 171).

None of these proposals, however, have sufficient support to make them ultimately convincing. The first proposal suffers from the fact that there is nothing in the immediate context to suggest that Paul is thinking of other believers. The second proposal founders on the fact that elsewhere the apostle has already referred to the Thessalonians as his "crown of boasting" (1 Thess. 2:19) and also boasts about one of his other churches—the congregation in Corinth (2 Cor. 7:14; 8:1–5, 24; 9:3). The third proposal is mere conjecture: nothing is explicitly stated in either of the Thessalonian Letters about their supposed feelings of unworthiness. Nothing in the intensive use of the pronoun "we ourselves" demands a contrast with some other group. In fact, the intensive use of the third-person personal pronoun occurs frequently in the Thessalonian Letters and does not normally, if ever, imply a contrast with another person or party (see 1 Thess. 1:9; 2:1; 3:3, 11; 4:9, 16; 5:2, 23; 2 Thess. 2:16; 3:7, 16). It is more credible, therefore, to view its use here in the thanksgiving of the second letter as one further means by which Paul adds emphasis to his commendation of the Thessalonian readers. As Green (2002: 281) recognizes: "The most likely conclusion is that the emphatic 'we ourselves' was simply a way of underlining the author's strong sentiments about the church without putting them in contrast with anything or anyone."

Paul achieves still further emphasis in his commendation of the Thessalonian church through the particular form he uses to express the idea of "boasting." Whereas in his other letters the apostle commonly uses the simple form καυχάομαι (thirty-five occurrences), only here does he employ the compound form ἐγκαυχάομαι—the only occurrence of this form in the NT (this rare form does occur four times in the LXX: Pss. 51:3; 73:4; 96:7; 105:47 [Eng.: 52:1; 74:4; 97:7; 106:47]; also 1 Clem. 21.5). Although the significance of the compound form should not be overstated, it nevertheless expresses a slight emphasis that, in light of the other ways Paul adds weight to his commendation of the Thessalonians in these opening verses, is noteworthy. As Frame (1912: 224) observes, by choosing the compound form of the verb instead of his expected simple form, Paul "intensifies the point" (note the rendering of the JB: "we can take *special pride* in you"). In addition, the present tense is used, thereby highlighting the ongoing or continuous nature of the apostle's boasting, which serves to strengthen this emphasis even further.

The pride that the apostle has for the Thessalonian church is voiced publicly "in the churches of God."[4] It is not clear to what congregations Paul is referring since he does not include a specific geographic location. In his previous letter to them, Paul referred to "the churches of God" located "in Judea" (2:14); so it is possible that he similarly here has in view those same Jewish congregations who, like the Thessalonians, were enduring persecution for their faith. Given that Paul wrote the Thessalonian Letters from Corinth, another possibility is that he boasted about them to the churches in Corinth, Cenchreae (Rom. 16:1–2), and other Christian communities in the province

---

4. Several commentators claim that the expression "the churches of God" in 1:4 is unique in Paul: "In every other passage where Paul uses the plural 'communities' he delimits it with a geographical designation; where he means the whole Christian community he uses the singular" (Best 1977: 252; similar assertion by Wanamaker 1990: 218; Malherbe 2000: 387). This expression, however, is not so uncharacteristic of Paul since in other letters he employs the plural without designating a specific location: Rom. 16:4, 16; 1 Cor. 7:17; 11:16; 14:33, 34.

of Achaia (2 Cor. 1:1, "all the saints who are in the whole of Achaia"). The audience of the apostle's boasting, however, may well have been significantly larger than this in light of Paul's comment in his previous letter that believers not only in Achaia but also in Macedonia and "in every place" (1 Thess. 1:8) had learned of the Thessalonians' faith in God. Indeed, the phrase "the churches of God" with no geographic location specified is most naturally understood as a general reference to *all* those churches with which the apostle had contact. And though some commentators minimize Paul's statement of the previous letter concerning "in every place," claiming it to be mere hyperbole, there was much contact and exchange of information among the early Christian communities (see comments on 1 Thess. 1:8). Uncertainty about the exact location of these "churches of God," however, should not blind the contemporary reader to the powerful commendation of Paul's words: to the persecuted community of believers in Thessalonica, it will be comforting to hear that their founder, Paul, is so proud of their remarkable spiritual growth that he not only gives thanks to God for them but also boasts about them to other believers, both far and near.

Whereas the first prepositional phrase "in the churches of God" answers the question "*To whom* did Paul boast about the Thessalonian Christians?" the second prepositional phrase "concerning your steadfastness and faith" answers the question "*What* did Paul boast about these believers?" (the preposition *hyper* here is equivalent to περί [*peri*], with which it is frequently interchanged in the manuscripts; see BDAG 1031.3). That only one definite article is used for the two nouns of "steadfastness and faith" indicates that both these spiritual qualities are closely connected, though not so much so that we have here a hendiadys (contra, e.g., Moffatt 1897: 44, who refers to this construction as "a single conception = faith in its special aspect of patient endurance").

Paul has not chosen a couple of generic spiritual gifts that could be true of any first-century church but two that are specific to the Thessalonian congregation and their particular situation. The first characteristic of "steadfastness" (*hypomonē*) is a term widely used by the apostle and other NT writers in connection with the difficulties and persecution faced by believers for no other reason than their commitment to Christ (Rom. 5:3; 12:12; 2 Cor. 6:4; Luke 21:19; Heb. 10:32; 1 Pet. 2:20). The choice of this term, therefore, looks ahead to the third prepositional phrase ("in all your persecutions and afflictions"), which spells out that the Thessalonians' spiritual growth has taken place in the context of strong opposition from their fellow citizens. Indeed, there is clear evidence in the Thessalonian Letters and elsewhere that the church in Thessalonica experienced significant opposition and affliction because of their newfound beliefs (1 Thess. 1:6b; 2:2b, 14–15; 3:1–5; 2 Thess. 1:4–7; see also 2 Cor. 8:1–2; Acts 17:5–7, 13). The reference to "steadfastness," therefore, raises the historical context of persecution and so makes all the more remarkable the Thessalonians' spiritual growth in such a hostile environment, about which Paul boasts. The second characteristic of "faith" also fits the Thessalonian context well, since, as we have noted above (see comments on v. 3), this congregation's "faith toward God" (1 Thess. 1:8) was not only a concern that Paul frequently addressed in the previous letter but also one he stresses elsewhere in the thanksgiving of this second letter.

The third prepositional phrase provides the historical context in which the Thessalonians displayed their steadfastness and faith: "in all your persecutions and afflictions." This phrase makes explicit what was implied in the earlier term "steadfastness": the spiritual growth of the Thessalonian believers took place in a very difficult situation of open hostility from their fellow citizens. The first term, "persecution" (*diōgmos*), occurs relatively infrequently in Paul (Rom. 8:35; 2 Cor. 12:10; 2 Tim. 3:11 [2x]) and refers specifically to religious suffering. By contrast, the second term, "affliction" (*thlipsis*), occurs often in the apostle's letters (24x) and describes difficulties of all kinds, including but not restricted to religious persecution. It would be wrong here, however, to distinguish between these two terms since elsewhere they occur together as synonyms (Rom. 8:35; Matt. 13:21; Mark 4:17). The use of both terms together instead of one of them alone is nevertheless significant: Paul thereby stresses the context of religious persecution in which the Thessalonians' spiritual growth takes place. As Marshall (1983: 172) states: "They are used together for rhetorical effect."

This emphasis on the Thessalonians' difficult historical context is expressed still further by two other means. First, the adjective "all" is added before "persecutions," thereby implying that the opposition the believers in Thessalonica faced was not limited to a single event but involved numerous incidents. Second, the relative clause "which[5] you are enduring" also adds emphasis because it is another acknowledgment by Paul that his Thessalonian readers are suffering for their faith. The verb in this clause, *anechesthe*,[6] occurs in the present tense, indicating that "all your persecutions and afflictions" are not merely past events but also current realities. The believers in Thessalonica were persecuted from the very moment of their conversion (1 Thess. 1:6, "receiving the word in much affliction"; also Acts 17:5–9), and this opposition did not end when Paul and his fellow missionaries left town. Indeed, it was the ongoing nature of these persecutions that caused Paul to send Timothy in order to strengthen their faith in these afflictions (1 Thess. 3:1–5), and it seems clear that opposition from their fellow citizens was still an ongoing problem when the apostle wrote them his first letter (1 Thess. 3:3–4; contra Wanamaker 1990: 219, who, on the basis of the past tense in 1 Thess. 2:14, argues that persecution had stopped by the time of the first letter). Paul's words in the second letter, both here in 1:4 and elsewhere in the thanksgiving (vv. 5, 6), reveal that this opposition to the fledgling Christian movement in Thessalonica has still not stopped but is a present reality that actually seems to have become more intense (so almost

5. The relative pronoun (1:4b) is not in the expected genitive (ὧν) or accusative (ἅς) case (the verb ἀνέχω takes its object in either the genitive or accusative case; see BDAG 78) but in the dative (αἷς) case, due to its "attraction" (BDF §294) to its antecedent θλίψεσιν.

6. See the additional notes for text-critical analysis concerning this verb at the end of 1:4.

all commentators). It is important to assert once again (see discussion in the commentary introduction as well as comments on 1 Thess. 1:8 and 3:3) that this opposition likely did not involve physical death and martyrdom but brought severe social harassment and ostracism (Still 1999).

B. Comfort concerning the Just Judgment of God (1:5–10)

The second section of the thanksgiving (vv. 5–10), as noted in detail above (see "Structure of the Passage"), is distinct from the surrounding verses in terms of its form and stylistic features. This section also distinguishes itself by a marked shift in content from the preceding verses, which focus on the Thessalonians and their remarkable spiritual growth in the face of persecution, to these verses, which highlight God and his just judgment. Although the interrelationship of the various clauses in this second section is not clear due to the absence of any connecting particles (asyndeton), the subject matter nevertheless does follow a discernible pattern: (1) verse 5 opens with an assertion about the just judgment of God; (2) verses 6–7a spell out in brief the two sides of this just judgment: punishment for those persecuting the Thessalonian Christians and reward for the Thessalonian Christians who are being persecuted; and (3) in greater detail verses 7b–10 flesh out the two sides of this just judgment, beginning again with the punishment that awaits unbelievers (vv. 7b–9) and concluding again with the reward that will be received by the saints in Thessalonica (v. 10). This message continues the consolatory concern that is at work throughout the thanksgiving and also the rest of the letter: persecuted Christians find it comforting to hear about a divine judgment that vindicates their faith, punishes their oppressors, and thus demonstrates that the God in whom they have placed their faith is indeed just.

1. The Just Judgment of God: Its Assertion (1:5)

1:5 The second section of the thanksgiving opens with an assertion about the just judgment of God: "Here is evidence of the just judgment of God" (ἔνδειγμα τῆς δικαίας κρίσεως τοῦ θεοῦ, *endeigma tēs dikaias kriseōs tou theou*).

This transitional verse presents the exegete with two problems, both of which are difficult to solve with certainty. The first is grammatical and involves explaining how the opening word *endeigma* ("the proof of something, *evidence, plain indication*": BDAG 331), occurring only here in the NT, is connected to the preceding text. Only two solutions are typically viewed as possible (BDF §480.6): this neuter noun can be read as either (1) a nominative in an elliptical construction where the relative clause "which is" (ὅ ἐστιν, *ho estin*) is assumed, or (2) an accusative in apposition to the preceding clause. The first option is supported by a possible parallel in Phil. 1:28, where the related noun (ἔνδειξις, *endeixis*)[7] occurs (ἥτις ἐστὶν αὐτοῖς ἔνδειξις ἀπωλείας, ὑμῶν δὲ σωτηρίας, *hētis*

---

7. Both nouns are derived from the same verb, ἐνδείκνυμι: the noun *endeigma* in 1:5, with its -μα suffix, is a passive form, whereas the related noun, *endeixis*, with its -σις suffix, is an active form.

estin autois endeixis alpōleias, hymōn de sōtērias, which is a sign to them of [their] destruction, but of your salvation). The second option is supported by those few places elsewhere in Paul's writings where an accusative phrase is in apposition to a previous clause (e.g., Rom. 8:3; 12:1; 1 Tim. 2:6). This would not be the only time in the brief letter of 2 Thessalonians that Paul seemingly omits something (2:3 lacks a main clause, and something like "the day of the Lord will not come" is implied; 3:8b does not have a main verb but only a participle functioning independently), with the result that his grammar cannot be readily explained (anacoluthon).

The reason why there is no obvious and compelling explanation of how *endeigma* is grammatically linked to the preceding text, however, may not be due to Paul's confusing grammar but rather because of the seemingly overlooked third possibility, that the term is connected not to the *previous* text but rather to the *following* clause. The conditional conjunction εἴπερ (*eiper*, since) that opens verse 6 introduces a conditional clause whose protasis (the "if" clause) extends all the way to the end of verse 10. The apodosis (the "then" clause) of this conditional clause is not found anywhere in verses 6–10[8] but in the preceding words of verse 5 (although the protasis is normally given before the apodosis in conditional sentences, this order is frequently reversed for emphasis, as here). The whole conditional clause, therefore, runs as follows: "Since it is just in the sight of God to pay back affliction to the ones who are afflicting you and to pay back, to you who are being afflicted, rest with us . . . , [this is] evidence of the just judgment of God so that you may be made worthy of the kingdom of God, on behalf of which you are also suffering" (vv. 6–7, 5). Read this way, *endeigma* is a predicate nominative in the apodosis of a conditional clause in which the main verb "to be" is implied. Paul has reversed the normal order of the apodosis and protasis for emphasis: he wants to comfort his persecuted readers and does so by opening with an assertion about the just judgment of God.

The second significant problem in verse 5 involves the referent of the "evidence" to which Paul refers: what exactly constitutes the evidence that God's judgment is just? Here again exegetes typically consider two possibilities, though, as we will see, there is also a third option that, though largely overlooked, is attractive and preferred.

1. The older, traditional understanding takes "evidence" retrospectively as referring back to "your steadfastness and faith," so that it is the Thessalonian church's endurance of persecution that shows God's just judgment (so, e.g., Lightfoot 1904: 100; Frame 1912: 226; Best 1977: 254–55; Bruce 1982: 149; Morris 1991: 197–98; Richard 1995: 304, 316–18; Fee 2009: 253). Beale (2003: 184), for example, states: "Their enduring faith through suffering is

---

8. Richard's claim (1995: 305) that verses 9–10 function as the apodosis is grammatically impossible, since an apodosis, though semantically linked to the protasis, is grammatically independent, that is, it must be able to stand on its own as a complete sentence (Wallace 1996: 684). Neither 1:9, which opens with a relative clause, nor 1:10, which begins with an indefinite temporal clause, functions independently as a complete sentence.

the badge (the evidence or sign) by which they will be counted worthy of not being judged but of inheriting the kingdom of God at the end of history." In support of this position, proponents typically appeal to Phil. 1:28, where the Philippian church's boldness in the face of persecution ("not frightened in anything by your opponents") is said by Paul to be "evidence" (ἔνδειξις) to their enemies of their destruction, whereas to the believers it is "evidence" of their salvation. In both 2 Thess. 1:5 and Phil. 1:28, so the argument goes, the endurance of Christians amid persecution is evidence of how believers are rewarded with salvation while unbelievers are rewarded with destruction, thereby demonstrating the just judgment of God.

2. The more recent, challenging understanding of "evidence" also reads this term retrospectively but sees it as referring back to "all your persecutions and the afflictions that you are enduring" (v. 4), so that it is the persecutions themselves and not the Thessalonians' endurance of these persecutions that is evidence of God's just judgment (Bassler 1984; Wanamaker 1990: 220–23; Menken 1994: 85–86; Nicholl 2004: 149–50; Furnish 2007: 146–47). In support of this position, proponents cite at least four things. First, the closest antecedent to "evidence" is the prepositional clause that refers to the church's persecutions rather than their endurance of these persecutions. Second, verse 5 makes no mention of their steadfastness but does refer again to their persecutions (the verse closes with the prepositional phrase about God's kingdom: "on behalf of which you are also suffering"). Third, in the traditional view the appeal to Phil. 1:28 is ultimately unconvincing since the proposed parallel with 2 Thess. 1:5 is not exact: the "evidence" in Philippians is the destruction of the wicked and the salvation of the righteous, but in 2 Thessalonians it is the just judgment of God. Finally, in order to connect the Thessalonians' endurance amid persecutions with the righteous judgment of God, the traditional view requires that an unstated point be assumed, that God is the one who enables the Thessalonians to endure such suffering. As Wanamaker (1990: 221) observes: "It is difficult to conceive in what way the Thessalonians' perseverance presages the righteous judgment of God without introducing extraneous ideas into the text such as the notion that God has granted the Thessalonians the ability to persevere and remain faithful."

If, then, "evidence" in verse 5 refers to the persecutions themselves (option 2), how can one make sense of Paul's claim that this provides proof of God's just judgment? If anything, the suffering endured by the Thessalonian believers seems to prove the opposite, that God's judgment is unjust! The key to understanding Paul's logic, according to proponents of this challenging view, lies in a "theology of suffering" (*Leidenstheologie*) that can be found in Jewish literature of this time period (2 Macc. 6:12–16; Pss. Sol. 13.9–10; 2 Bar. 13.3–10; 48.48–50; 52.5–7; 78.5; Gen. Rab. 33.1).[9] In these writings,

---

9. Although the interpretation posing a "theology of suffering" had been advocated for some time already in a few German and French commentaries, it has only more recently appeared in English-language works: see, e.g., Dobschütz 1909: 242; Dibelius 1913: 26; Rigaux 1956: 620;

"suffering is no longer a sign of rejection by God" but "is viewed somewhat paradoxically as a sign of *acceptance* by God insofar as he offers through it an opportunity for his elect to receive in this age the punishment for their few sins, thus preserving the full measure of their reward in the age to come" (Bassler 1984: 502). Suffering in these Jewish texts, however, is not just a sign of God's acceptance but also of God's justice, since he insists on the punishment even of his elect. Paul, it is claimed, is using ideas from this theology of suffering to comfort his persecuted readers in Thessalonica with the assertion that the just judgment of God requires not only that their few sins be punished in the present time (hence their current experience of suffering) so that their full participation in the kingdom of God will be guaranteed in the end time, but also that their enemies who are responsible for their current suffering will be ultimately punished for their greater sins.

Although this "theology of suffering" provides a possible explanation of how Paul can logically refer to the present persecution endured by the Thessalonians as "evidence of the just judgment of God," it faces a number of objections. First, the Jewish texts cited in support do emphasize God's retributive justice, an idea clearly found in Paul's following words to the Thessalonians (1:6–10). Yet these Jewish texts do not in a very strong manner express the key idea required for Paul's statement of 1:5 to make logical sense, that the present suffering of the righteous is intended to pay for their relatively few sins now, thereby ensuring their full experience of salvation in the future. Second, Paul says nothing explicitly or even implicitly to suggest that the readers ought to view their present sufferings as payment for their few sins. As Gaventa (1998: 103) declares, "Our passage does not conform to this pattern [in the "theology of suffering"] entirely, since the writer says nothing about the few sins of the good that need to be expiated." Third, despite Paul's many statements about the persecution of believers, the specific idea about the just, temporary suffering endured by the elect is not an idea found elsewhere in Paul's writings (Morris 1991: 196n14). Finally, it may be questioned how familiar the predominantly Gentile readers of Thessalonica would have been with this Jewish theology of suffering and how likely they would pick up on the unstated principle that is claimed to underlie the apostle's statement in verse 5. These objections support the conclusion reached by Richard (1995: 317): "There is, in my reading, no evidence of a 'suffering theology' focusing on the just, temporary punishment of the elect. There is instead a stress on the just, final reward of the oppressor and oppressed (1:6–10)."

3. In light of the problems with the two preceding interpretations, both of which take "evidence" *retrospectively*, it may be best to follow a third position, which adopts a *prospective* reading of the term. Witherington (2006: 192) suggests that something like ὅδε ἐστιν (*hode estin*, here is) be supplied at the opening of verse 5 so that the sense of the verse is "Here is the evidence of the

---

Marxsen 1979: 68; Bassler 1984; Wanamaker 1990: 220–23; Menken 1994: 85–86; Gaventa 1998: 102–3; Green 2002: 284–85; Nicholl 2004: 149.

just judgment of God," with the actual evidence found not in the preceding verse (1:4) but in the following verses (1:6–10). That verse 5 does not look back but rather ahead to the subsequent material is suggested first by the grammar: as noted above, verse 5 functions as the apodosis of the conditional sentence that opens in verse 6. Second, the prospective reading of the term "evidence" is suggested by the fourfold repetition of the root δικ- (*dik-*), or "just/justice," throughout the unit of 1:5–10: "evidence of the *just* judgment of God" (v. 5) is linked lexically not to the preceding verse, where the term "just/justice" does not occur, but instead to the following verses, where this term reappears no less than three more times (v. 6, "since it is *just* to God"; v. 8, "giving *justice* to those who do not know God . . ."; and v. 9, "those who will receive *justice* [i.e., pay a penalty]"). Third, in addition to these lexical links, the internal structure of this section (1:5–10) also suggests that the "evidence" referred to in verse 5 finds its content not in the previous verses but rather in the following ones: evidence for the "just judgment of God" can be seen in the equitable way the divine judge will punish those afflicting the Thessalonian believers and reward the church members who are being afflicted—a truth that Paul presents first in brief (v. 6, punishment for those causing affliction; v. 7a, reward for those being afflicted) and then repeats in the same order at greater length (vv. 7b–9, punishment; v. 10, reward).

Complicating the already complex debate over the precise referent of "evidence" is a further question of whether the "just judgment of God" has in view only a future event, or whether Paul is thinking instead about a present experience, or perhaps a judgment that is both present and future. Although the majority of commentators understand the apostle to be referring to an end-time judgment, some argue for a present verdict, appealing to 1 Pet. 4:17–19, which refers to the suffering endured by Christians as a "judgment" that has already begun with the household of God (see, e.g., Olshausen 1851: 463; Marshall 1983: 173). Others claim that the options of a present or future judgment are not mutually exclusive: "as is the case with the kingdom of God, the day of the Lord, and other eschatological concepts, the judgment is in some way already present, preparing for the final judgment" (Malherbe 2000: 395; see also Beale 2003: 185). But though there does exist elsewhere in Paul's thinking a proleptic aspect to his eschatological framework, it does not logically follow that this aspect must also be found here in verse 5. Rather, there can be little doubt that the perspective of 1:6–10 is entirely focused on the future. If, as we have argued above, the "evidence" of verse 5 refers to the immediately following material of 1:6–10, then the "just judgment of God" must refer to an end-time event, when the Thessalonian believers will be rewarded for their suffering, and their tormenters will pay a terrible price for their opposition to God and his people. The future aspect of the judgment is an important corrective to the false claim taken up in the body of the letter that the day of the Lord has already come (2:2).

The consequence (although the construction *eis to* + infinitive can express either purpose or result [see BDF §402.2], the context here supports the latter function) of this just and future judgment is that the Christians in Thessalonica will be evaluated as commendable participants in the eschatological rule of God: "so that you may be made worthy[10] of the kingdom of God" (εἰς τὸ καταξιωθῆναι ὑμᾶς τῆς βασιλείας τοῦ θεοῦ, *eis to kataxiōthēnai hymas tēs basileias tou theou*). The use of the compound form *kataxiōthēnai* instead of the simple *axioun* (as in 1:11) gives a certain emphasis to the word and so strengthens its consolatory function: although the Thessalonian believers are suffering now, God's future judgment is just, and this means that he (the passive form of *kataxiōthēnai* implies that God is the unspoken agent: the so-called divine passive: BDF §130.1) will ensure that they are made worthy of full participation in the blessedness of his eschatological rule. Paul uses the term "kingdom" (*basileia*) only fourteen times in his writings, in sharp contrast to its many occurrences in the Gospels. Yet the apostle shares with the Gospels the view that the kingdom is both a present and a future reality. Sometimes Paul describes the kingdom as being inaugurated through the coming and ministry of Jesus Christ, so that it is something present and experienced now (Rom. 14:17; 1 Cor. 4:20). More often, as is the case here in verse 5, the kingdom is for the apostle both a time when God will vindicate his people and a place where God will fully establish his rule over all creation, as something future and experienced at Christ's glorious return (see also 1 Thess. 2:12; 1 Cor. 6:9, 10; 15:24, 50; Gal. 5:21).

Before Paul proceeds to present the evidence for the just judgment of God, he issues a relative clause that picks up the discussion of what God will yet do in the future and links it to what is happening to the Thessalonians right now: "on behalf of which you are also suffering" (ὑπὲρ ἧς καὶ πάσχετε, *hyper hēs kai paschete*). The inclusion of this brief relative clause contributes at least three things to Paul's overall argument in the thanksgiving section.

First, the use of the present tense ("you are suffering") allows the apostle to acknowledge yet again (see v. 4c: "in all your persecutions and the afflictions that you are enduring") their current state of suffering, thereby revealing his pastoral concern for their well-being. It is comforting for those enduring hardship to have the reality of their pain acknowledged by others.

Second, the addition of the conjunction *kai* (also) reminds the Christians in Thessalonica that they do not suffer alone but that their founder and spiritual leader also suffers along with them (Frame [1912: 227] renders the prepositional clause as "for which you too [as well as we, that is, the writers] are suffering"). It is possible that this conjunction has an emphatic meaning and that Paul is further acknowledging the reality of their suffering ("You are *indeed* suffering"). However, the following verse includes a reference to the apostle and his coworkers ("*and* . . . to pay back, to you who are being afflicted, rest *with us* [μεθ' ἡμῶν, *meth' hēmōn*]"), which suggests that the preceding *kai* (and) anticipates this communal aspect. Furthermore, when discussing his

10. On the distinction between being "made worthy" (1:5) and "considered worthy," see discussion of 1:11 below.

readers' suffering in the previous letter, Paul similarly mentions that he also was enduring persecution (1 Thess. 3:4, 7; see also 1:6; 2:2, 15–16; 2 Thess. 3:2). As Richard (1995: 305) states, "Focus on the common nature of these afflictions is part of the author's strategy."

Third, the preposition *hyper* clarifies the nature of the suffering being endured by both readers and apostle: the issue concerns not suffering in general but specifically Christian suffering, suffering "on behalf of the kingdom of God" (the antecedent of the feminine singular relative pronoun *hēs* is *basileia*). The preposition does not indicate motive or goal, as if suffering will achieve membership in the kingdom; rather, as in Phil. 1:29 (τὸ ὑπὲρ αὐτοῦ πάσχειν, *to hyper autou paschein*, to suffer for him [Christ]), the idea is one of suffering "for" or "on behalf of" the kingdom.

2. The Just Judgment of God: Its Evidence Stated Briefly (1:6–7a)

a. Negative Judgment on the Afflicters: Affliction (1:6)

1:6
After comforting his persecuted readers with the assertion that God's judgment is just (1:5), Paul now proceeds to present the evidence for this assertion, namely, the "eschatological reversal" (Shogren 2012: 239, 242): God at some point in the future will punish those who are currently persecuting the Thessalonian Christians and will reward these same believers for their endurance and faith in the midst of such persecution (1:6–10). The apostle begins with the negative side of this just judgment: "since it is just in the sight of God to pay back affliction to the ones who are afflicting you" (εἴπερ δίκαιον παρὰ θεῷ ἀνταποδοῦναι τοῖς θλίβουσιν ὑμᾶς θλῖψιν, *eiper dikaion para theō antapodounai tois thlibousin hymas thlipsin*).

The conditional particle *eiper* (only five other occurrences in the NT, all by Paul: Rom. 3:30; 8:9, 17; 1 Cor. 8:5; 15:15) introduces the protasis of a first-class condition, in which the speaker assumes the truth of what is being hypothesized—an idea that is best captured in English with the translation "since" (BDAG 279.6.1: "if indeed, if after all, since"; also BDF §454.2). As Marshall (1983: 174) observes, "Although the clause is conditional in form, the introductory conjunction (*eiper*) always indicates an assumed fact in Paul; hence the *RSV* translation *since* is justified." In this conditional clause, what is assumed is that "it is just in the sight of God to pay back affliction to the ones who are afflicting you." Paul does not feel the need to prove to the Thessalonians that God acts justly in punishing their persecutors (or in rewarding them with "rest"), since this justice of God is a fundamental teaching of both the OT (Gen. 18:25; 1 Kings 8:31–32; 2 Chron. 6:22–23; Job 8:3; 34:12; 37:23; Pss. 7:8–11; 9:4, 9, 16; 35:24; Isa. 5:16; Zeph. 3:5) and other Jewish writings (Tob. 3:2; 2 Macc. 12:6; Sir. 35:15–19), and thus not surprisingly appears elsewhere in the apostle's writings as well (see esp. Rom. 2:6–8; 12:19; 2 Cor. 5:10; Col. 3:25; 2 Tim. 4:8). But though not concerned with proving to his readers the just judgment of God, Paul is nevertheless emphasizing this truth to them. The stress on the "just" character of God's judgment, mentioned in the previous verse, is continued here by the location of the adjective "just" (*dikaion*), which, despite functioning as the predicate,[11] has been moved up to the head of the conditional clause, in a position of emphasis. This highlighting of the "just" character of God's judgment is continued in the rest of the section of 1:6–10 by means of two further (in addition to *dikaias* in v. 5 and *dikaion* here in v. 6) uses of this same root word (v. 8, *ekdikēsin*; v. 9, *dikēn*). By stressing the just character of God's judgment, Paul effectively comforts his persecuted readers with the reminder that they suffer not in vain but will ultimately be vindicated for their faith when God pays back their tormentors with the same torment that they have inflicted on the believers in Thessalonica and rewards these believers for their perseverance amid affliction. As Malherbe (2000: 397) correctly points out, "It is this practical, pastoral purpose that drives Paul's language, not an interest in divine retribution as part of theodicy."

The prepositional phrase *para theō* (in the sight of God: for *para* with the dative, see BDAG 757.2: "marker of one whose viewpoint is relevant, *in the sight or judgment of someone*") introduces the image of a heavenly courtroom scene where God is the judge, before whom all must appear in judgment. Thus, as the adjective "just" that emphatically opens verse 6 looks back to the same adjective in the key phrase "the just judgment of God" of verse 5, so the prepositional phrase "in the sight of God" similarly looks back to the expression "the judgment of God."

The infinitive *antapodounai* (BDAG 87.2: "to exact retribution, *repay, pay back*"), with its double prepositional form (*anti* + *apo*) giving the term a certain emphasis, also has here in this context a judicial sense (see Rom. 12:17; Heb. 10:30; both cite Deut. 32:35) and so continues the image of the divine tribunal before which the persecutors of the Thessalonian Christians will ultimately appear. This concern with reciprocity, expressed not only in the emphatic form of the infinitive "to pay back" but also in the fitting penalty and reward that each group—those persecuting and those being persecuted—receives, stems from the OT principle of the lex talionis, known from Exod. 21:23–25 and other passages ("an eye for an eye, a tooth for a tooth, a hand for a hand"). Scripture frequently affirms the theme of divine recompense, at times also using the identical verb "to pay back" (Deut. 32:35; Ps. 137:8; Obad. 15; see also Isa. 63:4). The allusions to Isa. 66 found in the following verses (vv. 8a, 8b, 12), however, strengthen the possibility that Paul has that same passage in view here. In fact, there are two verses from Isa. 66 that are relevant: verse 6, "The voice of the Lord paying back [*antapodidontos*] retribution to his enemies"; verse 15: "For the Lord will come like a fire, and his chariots like

11. The true subject of the protasis in the conditional clause of 1:6 is the infinitive ἀνταπο-δοῦναι (for the infinitive functioning as the subject of an impersonal construction, see BDF §393), which, as a verbal *noun*, is here a neuter singular nominative. The main verb of the protasis is the implied copula ("to be"), which in a first-class condition must be in the indicative mood. The adjective δίκαιον, therefore, is a neuter singular nominative that modifies the infinitive and functions as a predicate nominative.

the whirlwind to pay back [*apodounai*] his punishment with anger." The lex talionis is rejected as a principle of human conduct (Rom. 12:17; Matt. 5:38–48) since a person may easily act unjustly or out of vindictiveness. These dangers do not exist in divine conduct, however, since God's judgment is "just," and so this principle forms an essential aspect of any teaching about God's judgment (see Rom. 2:6–8; 12:19; 2 Cor. 5:10; Col. 3:25; 2 Tim. 4:8). Paul uses this OT principle to comfort his Thessalonian readers by pointing them to the future judgment as the time when the injustice of their present suffering will be redressed.

What God in his just judgment will pay back to those who are persecuting the Christians in Thessalonica is described briefly in just one word: "affliction" (*thlipsin*). This judgment is indeed just since it involves exact reciprocity: since they are "the ones who are afflicting" (*tois thlibousin*) the Thessalonian believers, it is just that God will pay "affliction" (*thlipsin*) back to them. Just what this affliction entails is spelled out later in the paragraph: those who are afflicting the recipients of this letter will not participate with the saints in the glory of Christ's return (v. 10); even worse, they "will pay a penalty, eternal destruction from the presence of the Lord and from the glory of his might" (v. 9).

This is perhaps the harshest language that Paul uses anywhere to describe God's just punishment of the wicked. Consequently, some have stumbled over the apostle's words here, finding such language of judgment to be at odds with the notion of a loving and merciful God. However, one cannot pit God's mercy against his love. The Heidelberg Catechism (1563), the most ecumenical and loved of the Reformed confessions, raises the following question as a potential objection to God's judgment of sinners: "But isn't God also merciful?" This historic confession then offers the following answer: "God is certainly merciful, but he is also just. His justice demands that sin, committed against his supreme majesty, be punished" (Question and Answer 11).[12] In a similar vein, Marshall (1983: 174–75) comments: "Nothing in the NT suggests that God's love is indifferent to justice, and that he bestows a free pardon on his enemies at the cost of failing to defend the persecuted against the persecutors. Indeed, it is difficult to see how the ultimate justice of God to those who suffer can be defended in a situation where the persecutor knows that in the end he will be freely forgiven."

b. Positive Judgment on the Afflicted: Rest (1:7a)

1:7a After offering as evidence for the just judgment of God the *negative* reward of "affliction" that the divine judge will pay back to those "fellow citizens" (1 Thess. 2:14) who are afflicting the believers in Thessalonica, Paul presents as further evidence for the just judgment of God the *positive* reward that awaits these persecuted believers: "and [to pay back], to you who are being afflicted, rest with us" (καὶ ὑμῖν τοῖς θλιβομένος ἄνεσιν μεθ' ἡμῶν, *kai hymin tois thlibomenos anesin meth' hēmōn*).

12. http://www.crcna.org/sites/default/files/Heidelberg%20Catechism_old.pdf.

The Greek word order, along with the threefold repetition of the root "afflict/affliction" (*thlib-*), suggests that Paul has deliberately created a contrasting parallel:

antapodounai	*tois thlibousin hymas*	*thipsin*	*kai*
[*antapodounai*]	*hymin tois thlibomenois*	*anesin*	*meth' hēmōn*
to pay back	to those who are afflicting you	affliction	and
[to pay back,]	to you who are being afflicted,	rest	with us

This contrasting parallel serves to sharpen the distinction between the two groups and especially the fittingness or justice of the judgment that each will receive: "affliction" or "rest." Here Paul's choice of the term *anesis* (BDAG 77.2: "relief from something onerous or troublesome, *rest, relaxation, relief*") is entirely expected, since it occurs elsewhere in his writings as the contrast to *thlipsis* (2 Cor. 7:5; 8:13; see also 2:13). But whereas its occurrence elsewhere has in view a *present* relief, here in this context it has the *future* sense of an eschatological blessing that believers will receive at the final judgment. The writer of Hebrews, though using a different term (κατάπαυσις, *katapausis*), takes the idea of "rest" as found in the OT and similarly develops it as a blessing to be received and enjoyed in the eschatological kingdom (Heb. 3:18–19; 4:1–11). Likewise 2 Esdras (4 Ezra) employs the notion of eschatological rest, contrasting it with the final dwelling place of the wicked: "Then the pit of torment shall appear and opposite it shall be the place of rest. . . . Look on this side and that: here are delight and rest, and there are fire and torments!" (7:36, 38; see also 7:75, 85, 95).

As the lone word "affliction" does not exhaust the full scope of God's negative and just judgment on the wicked but finds its fuller articulation later in the paragraph (vv. 7b–9), so also the meaning of the single term "rest" is explicated by the following words (v. 10). The positive and just judgment of rest on the persecuted Christians of Thessalonica, therefore, does not envision inactivity and a cessation to their physical labors. Rather, this eschatological rest consists of an end to their being persecuted for the Christian faith, "which in itself is a perfectly adequate fulfillment of the longings of those who suffer" (Marshall 1983: 175). It further involves their participation with all other saints in the glory and splendor of Christ's triumphal return (v. 10)—a sharp contrast to the fate of their oppressors, who will suffer "eternal destruction from the presence of the Lord and from the glory of his might" (v. 9). The Thessalonian readers would no doubt also connect this eschatological rest to the end-time blessings that the apostle highlighted in his previous letter to them: the resurrection of their deceased fellow believers, who would then join the living believers at Christ's return, and the full participation of both Christian groups in the magnificent events connected with the parousia—events that will culminate in their enjoyment of eternal presence with Christ (1 Thess. 4:13–18; 5:10–11).

The brief prepositional phrase "with us," foreshadowed by the "also" in verse 5 ("on behalf of which you are *also* suffering"), means that the Thessalonian readers will not only be reunited with their deceased fellow believers in this eschatological rest but also with Paul, their spiritual "mother" (1 Thess. 2:7) and "father" (2:11), along with his coworkers, Silas and Timothy (1 Thess. 1:1; 2 Thess. 1:1). Since these Christian leaders share in the Thessalonians' experience of "affliction," not only in the past at the founding of the church in Thessalonica (1 Thess. 1:6; 2:15–16) but also in the present as they currently serve the distant churches of Corinth and other communities in Achaia (1 Thess. 3:4, 7; 2 Thess. 3:2), they too—in keeping with the just judgment of God—will share with the readers in the eschatological blessing of "rest."

3. The Just Judgment of God: Its Evidence Restated More Fully (1:7b–10)

a. Negative Judgment on the Afflicters: Eternal Destruction (1:7b–9)

1:7b

It is a bit misleading to count 1:7b as beginning a new subsection, as in several commentaries (Frame 1912: 229; Moore 1969: 93; Best 1977: 257; Marshall 1983: 175; Menken 1994: 87; D. Martin 1995: 209; Nicholl 2004: 150), or as a new sentence, as in some translations (e.g., NIV: "This will happen when . . ."; GNT: "He will do this when . . ."). The Greek text contains no break with the preceding material but continues the protasis begun at 1:6. Nevertheless, there are compelling reasons for seeing a minor shift in Paul's argument at this point. First, whereas the primary actor in verses 6–7a is God and his just judgment (three references to "God"; none to "the Lord Jesus"), in verses 7b–10 this shifts to the Lord Jesus as the one who carries out this just judgment (eight references to "[our] Lord [Jesus]," six explicit and two implicit; only one reference to "God").[13] Second, another notable shift involves the change in persons being addressed: whereas verses 6–7a employ the second person as they address the specific situation of the Thessalonian readers, verses 7b–10 use the third person and so broaden the scope of those being addressed. Third, the content of Paul's argument supports a minor break here: the evidence presented briefly in verses 6–7a in support of the just judgment of God (v. 5) is now restated more fully in verses 7b–10, in both instances beginning with the fate of the persecutors and ending in climactic fashion with the reward of the Thessalonian believers who are enduring persecution.

Sandwiched between the evidence for the just judgment of God presented briefly in verses 6–7a and the more fully stated evidence given in verses 7b–10 is a prepositional phrase that indicates the timing of this divine judicial activity: "at the revelation of the Lord Jesus" (ἐν τῇ ἀποκαλύψει τοῦ κυρίου Ἰησοῦ,

---

13. Menken (1994: 87): "In comparison with what has preceded in 1.5–7a, there is a significant change: now 'the Lord Jesus' is the subject of the retribution. This shift is easily understood in a letter in which Jesus is preferably called 'the Lord': he bears God's own name and exercises God's functions, among them the office of eschatological judge." Note also the comment of Marshall (1983: 175): "While vv. 6–7a refer solely to the action of God, it is now [in vv. 7b–10] made clear that all along Paul has been thinking of his action through Christ."

en tē apokalypsei tou kyriou Iēsou). The preposition *en* can function as a "marker introducing means or instrument" (BDAG 328.5), and so a few have interpreted Paul's phrase to mean that God's judgment will take place "in and through" the revelation of Christ: "It is not simply that the retribution will take place 'at' the revelation; it will itself form part of the revelation" (Morris 1991: 201n25; so also Milligan 1908: 89). This, however, probably reads too much into the simple prepositional phrase. More likely *en* indicates a "point of time when something occurs" (BDAG 329.10.b lists 2 Thess. 1:7 under this heading). In fact, a temporal understanding of this prepositional phrase is supported by at least three things (Malherbe 2000: 398): the temporal clause of verse 10 ("when he comes . . ."); a similar expression in Rom. 2:5 ("on [*en*] the day of wrath and the revelation of God's just judgment"); and the occurrence of *en* with *parousia* in a temporal sense in 1 Thess. 2:19 and 1 Cor. 15:23.

The timing of God's just judgment, then, is at the return of the Lord Jesus. Paul's favorite word to refer to this future event is *parousia*, a preference witnessed in his previous letter to the Thessalonians (1 Thess. 2:19; 3:13; 4:15; 5:23; see also 2 Thess. 2:1, 8). Here, however, he employs a different term: *apokalypsis* (revelation). Although this word in both its noun and verbal forms occurs frequently enough in the apostle's letters (26 total: 13 occurrences for each form), it normally refers not to Jesus's return but to the revelation of certain transcendent secrets. Nevertheless, the apostle sometimes—as is the case here in 1:7b—uses this term to describe the revelation or manifestation of certain persons or circumstances in the end times (for the noun *apokalypsis*, see Rom. 2:5; 8:19; 1 Cor. 1:7; 2 Thess. 1:7; for the verb *apokalyptō*, see Rom. 8:18; 1 Cor. 3:13; Gal. 3:23; 2 Thess. 2:3, 6, 8). But though the word *apokalypsis* here shares with the word *parousia* an eschatological reference to, in this case, the future coming of the Lord, the two terms are not exactly identical in meaning. Whereas *parousia*, as a technical term in the Hellenistic world that referred to the coming of high-ranking officials or kings to a city for an official visit, highlights the power and presence of Christ when he comes (for a fuller explanation of this term, see comments on 1 Thess. 2:19), *apokalypsis* stresses the revelatory aspect of Christ's return. More specifically, the truth that Jesus the Judge will come to carry out the just judgment of God is a reality currently hidden from those persecuting the Thessalonian believers so that they are naively unaware of the "affliction" that will fall upon them. Conversely, since this truth is known to the Christians in Thessalonica, they are able to endure persecution until the "revelation of the Lord Jesus," when these hidden things will finally become manifest to all.

The prepositional phrase "at the revelation of the Lord Jesus" indicates the timing of God's just judgment and is itself modified by three additional prepositional phrases: "from heaven with the angels of his power in a flame of fire" (ἀπ' οὐρανοῦ μετ' ἀγγέλων δυνάμεως αὐτοῦ ἐν φλογὶ πυρός, [see my comments on 1:8 for a defense of this alternate reading] *ap' ouranou met' angelōn dynameōs autou en phlogi pyros*). These three prepositional phrases function to establish Christ's authority and power to come as the eschatological judge, who carries out the just judgment of God.

The first prepositional phrase, *ap' ouranou* (from heaven), is the least complicated of the three. That Jesus would return "from heaven" (so also 1 Thess. 1:10; 4:16; on the use of the singular "heaven" instead of the plural "heavens," see comment on 1 Thess. 1:10) is hardly surprising, given that, as the Son of God, this is his expected dwelling place. A return "from heaven" also fulfills the promise given to Christ's disciples at his ascension: "This same Jesus, who has been taken from you into heaven, will come back in the same way you have seen him go into heaven" (Acts 1:11). This phrase, however, indicates not merely the location from which Jesus comes but, more important, the divine authority with which he carries out the just judgment of God: "He comes from the dwelling place of God with the authority of God to execute judgment and recompense" (Marshall 1983: 176).

The second prepositional phrase, *met' angelōn dynameōs autou* (lit., "with the angels of the power of him"), is complicated by the different possible ways in which its three words can be connected to each other. The least likely option links the personal pronoun with the first noun, so that the resulting prepositional phrase refers to a distinct class of angels: "his angels of power" (so Frame 1912: 230). Not only is the evidence in Jewish writings for such distinct classes of angels weak (Frame cites only two texts in support; neither is compelling: 1 En. 61.10, "all the angels of governance"; T. Jud. 3.10, "a powerful angel"), the word order works against this possibility since the personal pronoun is much more likely to be modifying the immediately preceding noun "power" instead. A second option takes *dynameōs* as a qualitative genitive, thereby qualifying the kind of angels with which Christ will come: "his mighty angels" (RSV/NRSV) or "his powerful angels" (NIV). Although grammatically possible, there are easier and clearer ways to express this idea in Greek (e.g., instead of the noun form, Paul could have used the adjective *dynatos*—a form he frequently employs elsewhere), if this were actually the intention of the apostle. A third and preferred option takes *dynameōs* as an independent noun such that the phrase reads: "the angels of his power." This phrase would thus be expressing the idea that Christ's power to carry out the just judgment of God is mediated through his angels. Not only is this a more natural reading of the grammar, but it is also supported by the context, where the focus is less on the quality or nature of the angels who accompany Christ than on the coming of Christ and his authority and power to judge. But regardless of which option is adopted, the following point of Marshall (1983: 176) ought not to be overlooked: "The precise force of the words is not important; what matters is the impression of divine power and authority with which the Lord Jesus is invested."

1:8 The third and final prepositional phrase is complicated by a textual problem: did Paul write *en pyri phlogos* (in a fire of flame) or *en phlogi pyros* (in a flame of fire)? Most commentators, including the Nestle-Aland text, prefer the first reading on the grounds that it has slightly stronger textual support and is also the more difficult reading (see additional notes). The second reading is then explained as a copyist assimilation either to Isa. 66:15 or other less likely texts such as Isa. 29:6; Dan. 7:9; or Ps. 29:7 (so, e.g., Best 1977: 258; Malherbe 2000: 399–400). If this interpretation is correct, then the apostle may well have in view Exod. 3:2 ("And an angel of the Lord appeared to him in a fire of flame out of the bush"), where "flame" refers to a theophany. According to this understanding, the third prepositional phrase portrays Christ's return as the presence of the Divine, somewhat akin to God's appearance before Moses.

This hardly settles the matter, however, since at least one important manuscript of Exod. 3:2 has the alternate reading "a flame of fire" (the same variation occurs in Acts 7:30, which looks back to this OT text). Furthermore, the frequent allusions to Isa. 66 not only elsewhere in the thanksgiving of 1:3–12 (vv. 6, 12) but particularly in the latter half of this same verse (see comment on 1:8b) strongly suggest that here too Paul is drawing from Isa. 66:15 (so, e.g., Aus 1976: 266; Richard 1995: 307). This possibility gains further strength in that the apostle's reference to "fire" is intended to highlight not so much divine presence but rather the judgment that will take place—the point that is made not in Exod. 3:2 but in several other OT texts (Isa. 29:6; Dan. 7:9; Ps. 29:7; see also Sir. 21:9), including Isa. 66:15 ("For the Lord will come like a fire, and his chariots like the whirlwind to repay his punishment with anger, and his rebuke with a flame of fire"). It appears likely, therefore, that the alternative reading "in a flame of fire" is original and that this phrase involves an allusion to Isa. 66:15. Paul uses the imagery of a flaming fire to portray in a powerful manner the frightening judgment that awaits those who have been oppressing the Thessalonian believers.

Now that Paul has clarified the timing of the just judgment of God, namely, at the return of Jesus, who comes with divine authority ("from heaven") and power ("with the angels of his power") to execute the terrible judgment of God ("in a flame of fire"), he at greater length proceeds to restate the evidence for this just judgment. As in his earlier brief statement of the evidence (vv. 6–7a), the apostle here begins with the negative side of God's just judgment (vv. 7b–9) before moving on to the positive side (v. 10). This restatement of the evidence of God's just judgment (vv. 7b–10) differs, however, from the previous statement (vv. 6–7a), not only in length but also specificity, as this expanded section contains no explicit reference either to those persecuting the Christians in Thessalonica or to the Thessalonian believers themselves; instead Paul speaks more generically about "those who do not know God and who do not obey the gospel of our Lord Jesus" on the one hand, and "his holy ones" and "all those who believe" on the other hand.[14] This section

---

14. The only exception, which does give some specific reference, is the causal clause "because our testimony to you was believed" (v. 10b)—a clause that ought to be recognized as a parenthetical comment or an aside in the overall statement of 1:7b–10.

is also noteworthy for its high concentration of OT echoes or allusions (see Weima 2007: 883–86).

The emphasis on the *just* character of God's judgment introduced in the opening assertion of 1:5 ("Here is evidence of the just judgment of God") and the earlier statement of evidence in verses 6–7a ("Since it is just in the sight of God . . .") also manifests itself here as, for the third time, Paul employs the root *dik-*: Jesus comes "giving justice" (διδόντες ἐκδίκησιν, *didontes ekdikēsin*) or, as it can be translated in this context, "inflicting punishment" (BDAG 301.3: "penalty inflicted on wrongdoers, abs[olute] *punishment*"). With slight variations the phrase "inflicting punishment" occurs several times in the LXX (Deut. 32:35; Num. 31:3; 2 Sam. 4:8; 22:48; Ps. 17:48 [18:47 Eng.]; Ezek. 25:14, 17). It is striking, however, that this phrase also occurs in Isa. 66:15 (*apodounai . . . ekdikēsin*)—the same text alluded to in the immediately preceding phrase "a flame of fire." The action of "inflicting punishment" in Isa. 66:15, as in the other OT texts containing this phrase, is ascribed to God. In Paul's use of this phrase here, however, the divine work of meting out the just judgment of God is transferred to the returning Christ (the genitive participle *didontes* modifies the preceding *tou kyriou Iēsou*), as is also the case in his preceding letter to the Thessalonians (4:6: "Because the Lord is an avenger [*ekdikos*] concerning all these things"; see also 1 Thess. 1:10; 5:1–11; 2 Thess. 2:8–10; Rom. 12:19; Col. 3:23–25).

This punishment will be given not merely to the persecutors of the Thessalonian believers but also to a much larger group: "on those who do not know God and to those who do not obey the gospel of our Lord Jesus." Several commentators have concluded from this double clause that Paul has two distinct groups in mind: most likely Gentiles and Jews (so, e.g., Dobschütz 1909: 248; Frame 1912: 233; Marshall 1983: 177–78). This two-group interpretation appeals not only to the repetition of the definitive article *tois* in each clause but also to the description of the people in each clause. The first clause refers to "those who do not know God" (τοῖς μὴ εἰδόσιν θεόν, *tois mē eidosin theon*)— an OT expression that typically refers to Gentiles (Job 18:21; Ps. 78:6 [79:6 Eng.]; Jer. 10:25) and has this meaning elsewhere in Paul's Letters (Gal. 4:8–9; 1 Thess. 4:5; see also 1 Cor. 1:21). The second clause refers to "those who do not obey the gospel of our Lord Jesus" (τοῖς μὴ ὑπακούουσιν τῷ εὐαγγελίῳ τοῦ κυρίου ἡμῶν Ἰησοῦ, *tois mē hypakouousin tō euangeliō tou kyriou hēmōn Iēsou*)—an expression that may well allude to Isa. 66:4, where "they did not obey me [God]" (*ouch hypēkousan mou*) refers to the Jewish people.

Against the two-group interpretation, however, are at least three factors. First, these two OT expressions do not always refer exclusively to Gentiles and Jews: sometimes Jews are described in the OT as those who do not know God (Jer. 4:22; 9:6; Hosea 5:4) and sometimes Gentiles, along with Jews, are accused of not obeying the gospel (Rom. 10:16; 11:30). Second, it is doubtful whether the predominantly Gentile church at Thessalonica was knowledgeable enough of the OT to discern in Paul's allusions a reference to Gentiles and Jews as distinct groups (Wanamaker 1990: 227). Third and most important, the two clauses with their OT allusions are better read as being in synonymous parallelism, whereby the second clause restates or clarifies the first (so, e.g., Bruce 1982: 151; Wanamaker 1990: 227; Malherbe 2000: 401)—a reading that is supported by the parallelism found not only in the immediately following verse (v. 9b: "from the presence of the Lord and from the glory of his might") but also elsewhere in this opening section of the letter (vv. 6, 10). Therefore it is best to see Paul as describing a single group consisting of all those who will justly be punished for their failure to know God and obey the gospel.

Throughout verses 5–10 Paul's preoccupation with the *just* character of God's judgment, with the larger goal that this message of God's just judgment would function to comfort his persecuted readers, is evident yet again in verse 9 as now for the fourth time in this brief section (v. 5, *dikaias*; v. 6, *dikaion*; v. 8, *ekdikēsin*) he employs the key root δικ-: "such people who[15] will pay a penalty" (οἵτινες δίκην τίσουσιν, *hoitines dikēn tisousin*). The noun *dikēn*, rendered here as "penalty" (BDAG 250.1: "punishment meted out as legal penalty, *punishment, penalty*"), is further stressed by its location at the head of this lengthy relative clause and before the main verb with which it functions as the direct object. Paul's word choice and word location, therefore, emphasize "the idea of a just penalty, of a punishment meted out as the result of an evenhanded assessment of the rights of the case" so that "Paul leaves us in no doubt . . . of the justice of this proceeding" (Morris 1991: 204). The fuller phrase *dikēn tisousin* does not occur elsewhere in Scripture but is common enough in Classical Greek. A few commentators have found it "strange" (Best 1977: 261) or "noteworthy" (Malherbe 2000: 402) to find such a classical expression in a context saturated with apocalyptic and OT vocabulary (so also Masson 1957: 134). Since similar phrases can be found in the OT (see, e.g., Deut. 32:41, 43; Lev. 26:25; Ezek. 25:12; Prov. 20:22; 24:22, 44; 27:12), the apostle's word choice may not be so surprising after all, especially because it likely stems from "Paul's interest to stress the justice of God's judgment" (Malherbe 2000: 402).

Paul indeed has been so preoccupied with stressing the just character of God's judgment that he has not yet spelled out what the negative side of this just judgment means beyond three one-word descriptions: those who are afflicting the Thessalonian believers will be justly paid back with "affliction" (v. 6, *thlipsis*); those who do not know God or obey the gospel will be given "punishment" (v. 8, *ekdikēsin*) and will pay a "penalty" (v. 9, *dikēn*). Now the

1:9

15. Some grammarians claim that the distinction between the indefinite relative pronoun found in 1:9 (οἵτινες) and the definite relative pronoun no longer exists in NT writings (BDF §293; see BDAG 730.3). Others, however, disagree (MHT 1:91–92; Moule 1959: 123–25; see BDAG 729.2), arguing that "there are sufficiently large numbers of examples where the *generic* ('which, as other like things') and *essential* ('which by its very nature') senses of the indefinite relative pronoun are discernible to warrant distinction (see also Mt. 7.24; Acts 10.47; 17.11; Rom. 6.2; 9.4; 2 Cor. 8:10; Jas. 4.14)" (Porter 1992: 133). It is this latter distinction, namely, "to emphasize a characteristic quality" (BDAG 729.2.b), that is likely intended here, as Paul refers to a specific class of people ("such people") whom he has just characterized as "the ones who do not know God and who do not obey the gospel of our Lord Jesus."

apostle finally elaborates on what the just judgment of God for the unrighteous entails by describing it as "eternal destruction[16] from the presence of the Lord and from the glory of his might" (ὄλεθρον αἰώνιον ἀπὸ προσώπου τοῦ κυρίου καὶ ἀπὸ τῆς δόξης τῆς ἰσχύος αὐτοῦ, *olethron aiōnion apo prosōpou tou kyriou kai apo tēs doxēs tēs ischyos autou*). Even this more fulsome description, however, remains general and vague, especially when compared with the detailed and vivid descriptions found in Jewish apocalyptic writings. This is because that Paul's concern is not to construct a precise theology of divine retribution but to comfort his readers by providing them with "evidence of the just judgment of God" (v. 5).

The first part of this fuller explanation reveals the terrible price of the "penalty" that some will pay: "eternal destruction" (*olethron aiōnion* is in apposition to *dikēn*). The word *olethron* occurs three other times in Paul's Letters (1 Thess. 5:3; 1 Cor. 5:5; 1 Tim. 6:9), where it appears to have both the literal meaning of physical destruction and the metaphorical sense of disaster or ruin. Whereas in his previous letter to the Thessalonians Paul referred to this destruction as "sudden" (5:3), here the apostle calls it "eternal" (*aiōnion*), that is, "a period of unending duration, *without end*" (BDAG 33.3). That Paul does not have in view a destruction of a person that lasts forever (i.e., their annihilation) but rather their unending ruin (i.e., their continuing punishment) seems clear from three factors (Best 1977: 262; Marshall 1983: 179). First, this is the teaching of Jesus (e.g., Matt. 5:29–30; 12:32; 18:8–9; 25:41, 46; Luke 16:23–25), with which Paul would have been familiar. Second, the eternal punishment of the wicked was a common conviction in the apostle's Jewish heritage (e.g., 1QS 2.15; 5.13; Pss. Sol. 2.35; 15.11; 4 Macc. 10:15). Third, the following parallel phrases ("from the presence of the Lord and from the glory of his might") presuppose the ongoing existence of the wicked rather than their annihilation.

The second part of the fuller explanation of the just judgment of God for those who do not know God and do not obey the gospel shows more precisely what this "eternal destruction" entails: a separation "from the presence of the Lord and from the glory of his might." This description clearly echoes the triple refrain of Isa. 2:10, 19, 21, where the wicked on the day of the Lord are commanded to hide themselves behind rocks and in caves "from the presence of the fear of the Lord and from the glory of his might" (*apo prosōpou tou phobou kyriou kai apo tēs doxēs tēs ischyos autou*) "whenever he will rise to terrify the earth." Paul's omission of Isaiah's reference to "fear" has been interpreted by some (Best 1977: 264; Malherbe 2000: 403; Witherington 2006: 196–97) to reflect the apostle's reluctance to speak in active terms about the punishment of the wicked compared with other apocalyptic writers of his day (the term "fear" might suggest torture). This, however, is reading too much

---

16. In 1:9 the noun "destruction" (ὄλεθρον) is in apposition to the direct object "penalty" (δίκην) and so intends to explain that preceding term—an explanatory function that is captured in the following translation: "such people who will pay a penalty, eternal destruction."

into Paul's motives. More likely, the omission stems from a desire to express better the parallelism between "from the presence of the Lord" and "from the glory of his might" (the MT of Isa. 2:10, 19, 21 similarly omits the word "fear"). Since these two prepositional phrases are in synonymous parallelism with each other (see also vv. 8b and 10), it would be wrong to distinguish their meaning too sharply. Instead, in OT language the two phrases together express something of the glorious and powerful presence of Yahweh, which is here significantly applied to the Lord Jesus. Therefore the persecutors of the Christians in Thessalonica, along with all those who do not know God and do not obey the gospel, will be forever separated from this glorious and powerful presence of the Lord Jesus Christ—a sharp contrast to the fate of the Thessalonian believers, who will "always be with the Lord" (1 Thess. 4:17; see also 5:10) and who, as the following verse asserts, will witness and participate in the glory connected to Christ's return (see also v. 12).

The negative side of God's just judgment is described elsewhere in the NT in more graphic and fiery terms than those used here by Paul: "unquenchable fire" (Matt. 3:12); "fiery furnace" (Matt. 13:42, 50); "eternal fire" (Matt. 18:8; 25:41); "blackest darkness" (2 Pet. 2:17); "the punishment of eternal fire" (Jude 7); "the fiery lake of burning sulfur" (Rev. 21:8). Compared to these depictions, Paul's words about the separation "from the presence of the Lord and from the glory of his might" may appear tame. Nevertheless, two things ought to be remembered. First, the apostle's concern here is not to describe the fate of the wicked in such a hyperbolic manner that his readers will maliciously rejoice in the fate that awaits their oppressors.[17] Rather, his larger purpose in this section of the letter is to give evidence that God's judgment is just, or in colloquial terms, that "the punishment fits the crime": those who do not know God and who separate themselves from him in this life will justly be separated from God in the life to come. Conversely and comfortingly, "the reward fits the deed": those who have faithfully endured affliction will receive "rest" (v. 7) and glorification (v. 10). Second, in verse 9 Paul's description of what will happen to the wicked involves a most serious punishment, in his estimation. As Marshall (1983: 180) observes: "To be separated from God and his blessings—and to be forever in this situation—is for Paul the worst of prospects. This is the reality for which the other pictures are merely symbols."

b. Positive Judgment on the Afflicted: Glorification (1:10)

Having spelled out more fully in verses 7b–9 the negative judgment that will fall on those who are persecuting the Thessalonian believers, Paul shifts to the positive reward that awaits his Christian readers. This just judgment will take place "whenever he comes" (ὅταν ἔλθῃ, hotan elthē), both echoing the point

1:10

---

17. As Nicholl (2004: 152n27) explains: "If 'Paul' had wished to feed the hunger of 'the Thessalonians' for vengeance on *persecutors* in verses 8b–9, the offence of persecution would presumably have been explicitly stated (as in verse 6). As it stands, the reference is generic, simply differentiating 'the Thessalonians' from all unbelievers."

made in verse 7b that the punishment of the wicked and the vindication of the righteous occur "at the revelation of the Lord Jesus" and anticipating the same point made yet again at the end of verse 10 ("on that day"). This point is expressed here by means of an indefinite temporal clause ("when*ever*")—indefinite not because of any doubt about the reality of Christ's coming but only about the precise timing of that future event.

Paul's assertions in verse 10 about the positive fate of believers contrast well in both form and content with his just-stated claims in verse 9 about the negative fate of unbelievers. In terms of form, the apostle employs two infinitive clauses describing the positive judgment of God that are in synonymous parallelism ("to be glorified in his holy ones and to be marveled at in all who believe") to highlight the contrast with the two prepositional phrases describing the negative judgment of God, which are also in synonymous parallelism ("from the presence of the Lord and from the glory of his might"). In terms of content, Paul makes use of OT language to describe the reward of believers just as he did to describe the punishment of unbelievers. There is even a verbal link between the two contrasting consequences: whereas Christ's return results in unbelievers having no share in "the *glory* of his might" (v. 9), his coming for believers is the occasion when he will "be *glorified* in his holy ones" (ἐνδοξασθῆναι ἐν τοῖς ἁγίοις αὐτοῦ, *endoxasthēnai en tois hagiois autou*). The conclusion that this clause involves an allusion to Ps. 89:7 ("God is glorified in the assembly of the holy ones," *ho theos endoxazomenos en boulē hagiōn* [88:8 LXX]) is strengthened by the fact that the compound verb *endoxasthēnai* is relatively rare in the LXX and occurs in the NT only here and two verses later, in 2 Thess. 1:12. As in many of Paul's other OT allusions, once again we see how texts originally referring to God are now applied to Christ. Another significant change is that "the assembly of the holy ones" formerly refers to angels but here has in view believers, as the parallel phrase "all those who believe" clearly indicates (see also 1 Thess. 3:13).

It is less obvious, however, what specific point Paul intends with his claim that the Lord will "be glorified in his holy ones." The issue centers on the meaning of the preposition *en* (in), which could be instrumental (i.e., Christ is glorified by or through believers), causal (i.e., believers are the cause or reason for Christ to be glorified), or locative (i.e., Christ's glorification takes place in the presence of believers). Although a case can be made for each possibility, the third option is supported by a number of factors (see Marshall 1983: 180; Wanamaker 1990: 230–31). The locative meaning (1) agrees with the meaning of the preposition *en* in Ps. 88:8 LXX, which is being alluded to here; (2) matches the parallel clause "to be marveled at in all who believe"; and (3) contrasts well with the just-stated fate of unbelievers who will be excluded "from the presence of the Lord" (v. 9).

The positive side of God's just judgment is further explained by a second infinitival clause: "and to be marveled at in all who believe" (καὶ θαυμασθῆναι ἐν πᾶσιν τοῖς πιστεύσασιν, *kai thaumasthēnai en pasin tois pisteusasin*). As with the first infinitival clause with which it functions in synonymous parallelism, here too Paul's language echoes the OT, as in Ps. 68:35 (67:36 LXX): "God will be marveled at in the presence of his holy ones" (*thaumastos ho theos en tois hagiois autou*). Once again we see how Paul takes an OT text that originally refers to God and applies it to Christ. His pairing of "to be glorified" and "to be marveled at" (see also Exod. 34:10; Sir. 38:3, 6) suggests that the latter verb refers not so much to the notion of amazement or astonishment but to ascribing honor or glory (see Rev. 13:3, where *thaumazō* has the sense of worship). Christ's return will be the occasion when he is given the glory that he is justly due, and this glorification will take place in the presence of not just "his holy ones" but also, as the parallel clause clarifies, "*all* who believe."

Some have dismissed any idea that the adjective "all" is significant, claiming that Paul "constantly brings in 'all' and similar words, stressing universality without particular significance" (Best 1977: 266). But not only does the apostle have a strong track record of choosing his vocabulary with great care; the following parenthetical clause ("because our testimony to you was believed"), which explains the preceding "all who believe," also reveals that the "all" has in view specifically the Christians in Thessalonica. Other commentators, therefore, rightly recognize in the addition of the adjective "all" an emphasis aimed at reassuring the Thessalonian believers that they belong to that group of people who will experience the positive side of God's just judgment. Lightfoot (1904: 105), for example, states that "πᾶσιν points to the ellipsis, as if he had said: 'for all, you included.'" This implicit meaning in the word "all" explains why the translators of the NIV felt justified to add—even though it is not found in the Greek—the clause "This includes you" (see also the ISV; Ellingworth and Nida 1975: 151; Marshall 1983: 181; Richards 1995: 309). Such an understanding also lies behind the following paraphrase of this verse proposed by Hendriksen (1955: 162): "and to be marveled at in *all* who believed; and please notice that we said, 'In *all* who believed.' That includes you, Thessalonians."

That this sense is not reading too much into Paul's words but that he is indeed thinking about the situation of his Thessalonian readers is confirmed by the presence of a parenthetical statement: "because our testimony to you[18] was believed" (ὅτι ἐπιστεύθη τὸ μαρτύριον ἡμῶν ἐφ' ὑμᾶς, *hoti episteuthē to martyrion hēmōn eph' hymas*).[19] As Marshall (1990: 181) observes: "The statement is awkwardly placed and its inclusion must have had a special motive."

---

18. In 1:10 the precise meaning of the prepositional phrase ἐφ' ὑμᾶς is difficult to determine. It could function with the verb "was believed," with the sense "belief in our testimony *directed itself to reach you*" (Lightfoot 1904: 105). But not only is this rendering of the prepositional phrase awkward; it also goes against the word order, which more naturally links the prepositional phrase to the noun "testimony": "our testimony *to you*" (so virtually all commentators and translations). Yet its use here is unusual and without parallel (the only other NT occurrence where ἐπί with the accusative is paired with the noun "testimony" is in Luke 9:5, with the meaning "testimony *against them*").

19. Nicholl (2004: 153): "The ὅτι clause [in v. 10] reveals that the focus is squarely on 'the Thessalonians.'"

That motive lies in Paul's desire to clarify the preceding "all" and to reassure the believers in Thessalonica that, since they believed the "testimony" of himself and his fellow missionaries, they consequently belong to those for whom the just judgment of God will involve glorification rather than eternal destruction.[20] By choosing the verb "you believed," Paul links the Thessalonian Christians to "all who believe": those in whose presence Christ will be glorified and marveled (v. 10). By choosing the noun "testimony" as the object of what the Thessalonian Christians believed, Paul contrasts them with those who did not accept the "gospel" (in this context *to martyrion* is a synonym of *to euangelion* in v. 8b) and who will thus be eternally separated from the presence and glory of Christ (v. 9).

Here Paul does not merely provide to his persecuted readers further evidence of the just character of God's judgment such that he will punish their oppressors and reward them for their faith, but he additionally stresses that they do indeed belong to the group who will experience blessing at the return of Christ. This emphasis in turn suggests that some believers in Thessalonica worried about their own status on the day of the Lord. This anxiety of the Thessalonian believers surely lay behind Paul's extended discussion in the previous letter (5:1–11), where the apostle reassured them that "God did not destine us for wrath but for the obtaining of salvation through our Lord Jesus Christ" (5:9). This same unease is still held by Paul's readers in the second letter, where a false claim about the day of the Lord has caused some in the Thessalonian congregation to become so shaken in their faith that they again worried about their eternal destiny (2:1–17). It is this historical context that causes Hendriksen (1955: 162) to view verse 10 as a word of comfort: "This was a word of comfort for the congregation as a whole, but especially for those who wondered about the state of their salvation." Speaking more specifically about the addition of the adjective "all" in this verse, Malherbe (2000: 405) interprets this as done "for the sake of emphasis, emboldening those of his readers who may still have been uncertain about their salvation."

That Paul is already here thinking about the major concern of the letter taken up in 2:1–17 is suggested not only generally by the foreshadowing function of the thanksgiving section but specifically by the prepositional phrase with which the long, unwieldy sentence of verses 3–10 finally comes to an end: "on that day" (ἐν τῇ ἡμέρᾳ ἐκείνῃ, *en tē hēmera ekeinē*). Both by its position at the end of the lengthy sentence and its occurrence after the parenthesis (which cuts it off from the rest of the clause), this phrase is emphasized—an emphasis that most modern translations obscure by connecting it with the main verb at the head of the verse (e.g., ESV: "when he comes on that day") and that a few have tried to capture by rendering it as a separate sentence ("Yes; there will be justice when that day comes" [Knox Version]). "That day," of

---

20. Fee (2009: 262): "This [parenthetical remark in 1:10] is therefore not a sort of 'throwaway' clause, added at the end for their sakes; rather, it is quite the point toward which this entire recital has been heading right along."

course, is an abbreviated reference to the "day of the Lord" (1 Thess. 5:2, 4; 2 Thess. 2:2) and so refers to the future time when Christ returns ("whenever he comes") and the just judgment of God will be carried out. This brief phrase, perhaps prompted by its presence in Isa. 2:11, to which Paul has alluded in verse 9, anticipates the apostle's argument in 2:1–17. There is no need for the Thessalonian Christians to be disturbed by a claim that "the day of the Lord has come" (2:2), since that eschatological event cannot take place until the judgment of God has been carried out—a "just judgment" ensuring "on that day" that their persecutors are punished (vv. 6, 7b–9) and their faith is rewarded (vv. 7a, 10).

C. Challenge: Prayer for God to Work in the Thessalonians' Lives (1:11–12)

Formally, the third unit of verses 11–12 consists of the "prayer report"—not a direct prayer offered by Paul in the optative mood (as in 1 Thess. 3:11, 12–13; 5:23; 2 Thess. 2:16–17; 3:5) but a summarizing report of the content of his prayer—that the apostle sometimes uses to bring his thanksgiving to a close (Phil. 1:9–11; Col. 1:9–14; see also Rom. 1:10b). Functionally, this unit *challenges* the Thessalonians to live up to the standard of conduct that Paul and his coworkers spell out in their prayer report (on the paraenetic, or exhortative, function of the thanksgiving section generally, see Schubert 1939: 26, 89; O'Brien 1977: 141–44, 165, 262–63). Yet even in this not-so-subtle exhortation for them to live up to the standard of conduct for which the missionaries are praying, Paul continues to console his readers not only by letting them know that he is praying for them but also by letting the content of his prayer stress the divine initiative in their salvation (Malherbe 2000: 409): *God* is the one who will make them worthy of their election and who will complete their good desire and work, thereby ensuring that both the Lord Jesus Christ and they will be glorified. In a general way the prayer report also foreshadows the two concerns addressed in the rest of the letter: verse 11, dealing with the present conduct of the Thessalonians ("every desire of goodness and work of faith"), looks ahead to the exhortative material of 3:1–15, particularly the problem of rebellious idleness (3:6–15); verse 12, dealing with the end-time glorification of both the Lord Jesus and the Thessalonian believers, anticipates the eschatological matter taken up in 2:1–17.

1:11 The prayer report opens with a prepositional clause that is only loosely connected to the preceding sentence of 1:3–10: "To this end we also are praying always concerning you" (εἰς ὃ καὶ προσευχόμεθα πάντοτε περὶ ὑμῶν, *eis ho kai proseuchometha pantote peri hymōn*). The preposition *eis* often is used to express purpose (BDAG 290.4.f) and here conveys the goal of Paul's prayers: his intercessions before God on behalf of the Thessalonian Christians have a specific "end" in sight. Some (Lightfoot 1904: 105; Richard 1995: 310) have tried to narrow down exactly what this end is, arguing that the relative pronoun *ho* looks back to the Thessalonian believers "being made worthy of the kingdom of God" (v. 5) on the basis of the verbal link that exists between these two verses (v. 5, *kataxiōthēnai*; v. 11, *axiōsē*). Others (Frame 1912: 238; Menken 1994: 92; Beale 2003: 193) believe the antecedent of the relative pronoun lies more generally in the salvation described in the immediately preceding verse, 10b. The "end" that Paul's prayers have in sight, however, does not likely lie in any specific preceding word or words but rather in the whole of verses 5–10 and its comforting message of the just judgment of God, by which those persecuting the Thessalonian Christians will be punished and the believers in Thessalonica will be rewarded. The apostle lets his readers know he is praying that this just judgment of God will be a time not of punishment but of reward for them—something that, despite the divine initiative, will not happen automatically; it will require some action on their part, as the rest of the prayer report makes clear.

Paul's statement that he "also" (*kai*) is praying for his readers has been variously interpreted. Best (1977: 268) reads too little into the presence of this conjunction, arguing that "frequently in Paul καί after a relative pronoun may simply be omitted in translation (e.g. Rom. 5.2; 1 Cor. 1.8; 4.5)." Frame (1912: 238) reads too much into the presence of this conjunction, claiming that the apostle is responding to a letter from the fainthearted members of the Thessalonian church and reassuring them that he does indeed "also" pray for them. Also wrong are those who interpret the conjunction as referring to the reciprocal nature of Paul's intercessory prayer: he is "also" praying for his readers just as they are praying for him (even though this was the professed practice of the apostle [e.g., Rom. 1:10; Eph. 1:17; Phil. 1:4; Col. 1:3, 9; 1 Thess. 1:2; 2 Thess. 1:11; Philem. 4] and apparently also of his congregations [Rom. 15:30; Eph. 6:19–20; Col. 4:3; 1 Thess. 5:25; 2 Thess. 3:1–2]). Here the conjunction modifies not the pronominal subject "we" but the verb "are praying" so that the "also" looks back to the only other main clause in the thanksgiving, which is found in verse 3: just as Paul and his fellow missionaries "ought to give thanks always concerning you," so *also* they "are praying always concerning you" (so, e.g., Dobschütz 1909: 254; O'Brien 1977: 178; Marshall 1983: 182; Morris 1991: 208).

The force of the adverb "always" (*pantote*) is downplayed by some who view it as either hyperbole or a mere epistolary nicety. This interpretation is seemingly strengthened by the fact that Paul does frequently use this adverb in his opening thanksgivings (Rom. 1:10; 1 Cor. 1:4; Phil. 1:4; Col. 1:3; 1 Thess. 1:2; Philem. 4), as in 1:3 of this letter ("We ought to give thanks to God *always* concerning you"). But as noted in our comments on that earlier verse, Paul enjoyed an intimate bond with his Thessalonian converts that may well have led him to pray for them "always." Furthermore, such conduct would be appropriate and consistent for the apostle, who only a short time earlier had commanded his readers in his previous letter to "pray constantly" (1 Thess. 5:17). In colloquial terms, Paul practices what he preaches. The apostle, therefore, lets his readers know that his prayers to God on their behalf are not infrequent or irregular but constant and common (cf. Col. 1:9: "We have not stopped praying for you"). As such, this statement serves as a powerful expression of Paul's deep affection for the Christians in Thessalonica—a fact that no doubt will be both comforting and challenging for them.

It is difficult to determine whether the rest of verse 11 provides the purposes of Paul's intercessory prayers or the contents of these prayers, since the conjunction ἵνα (*hina*) can introduce clauses that express both ideas. On the one hand, the *hina* clause could continue the idea of purpose expressed already in the relative clause with which this sentence opens ("To this end . . ."). As Frame (1912: 239) explains: "Since the ἵνα resumes εἰς ὅ, it is to be taken not epexegetically as introducing the content of the prayer but finally," as expressing the purpose of the prayer. On the other hand, the idea of content is suggested by the presence of the ὅπως (*hopōs*) clause in the following verse. This is because in the alternating *hina-hopōs* pattern found elsewhere in the NT (Luke 16:27–28; John 11:57; 2 Cor. 8:14), the initial *hina* clause provides the content of a request while the subsequent *hopōs* clause provides the purpose of that request (so BDAG 718.2). The difficulty between choosing between these two options has led some exegetes to adopt both positions (e.g., Williams 1992: 118: "The conjunction *hina* introduces both the content and the purpose of the two-fold prayer"). Although a decision here can only be provisional, the latter option is made more likely by both the immediate context and other places in Paul's Letters where a verb of request or petition is followed by a *hina* that supplies the content of what is asked (e.g., 1 Cor. 1:10; 16:12; 2 Cor. 12:8; 1 Thess. 4:1; 2 Thess. 3:12).

The content of Paul's prayers for the Thessalonian Christians consists of two petitions: "that our God may make you[21] worthy of the calling and may complete every desire of goodness and work of faith in power" (ἵνα ὑμᾶς ἀξιώσῃ τῆς κλήσεως ὁ θεὸς ἡμῶν καὶ πληρώσῃ πᾶσαν εὐδοκίαν ἀγαθωσύνης καὶ ἔργον πίστεως ἐν δυνάμει, *hina hymas axiōsē tēs klēseōs ho theos hēmōn kai plērōsē pasan eudokian agathōsynēs kai ergon pisteōs en dynamei*). The first thing that the apostle petitions God to do deals with the moral status and ethical conduct of the believers in Thessalonica, specifically, their being "worthy of the calling." The use of the verb *axioō* recalls the occurrence of this same verb (though in the slightly emphatic compound form *kataxioō*) in verse 5. There Paul stressed the role of God by means of the divine passive. Here he again stresses the divine initiative by explicitly identifying the subject of the verb as "our God." This emphasis on God's role has an important implication on whether the verb should be translated as "*consider* worthy" or "*make* worthy." The first option agrees with the use of this verb elsewhere (1 Tim. 5:17; Heb. 3:3; 10:29; Luke 7:7; BDAG 523: "consider worthy"). The second option, however, fits better both the immediate context (which stresses the role of God) and Paul's theology. As Marshall (1983: 182) states: "God cannot deem worthy any whom he himself has not made worthy by his action rather than by their good works; hence the force of the verb is tantamount to 'make worthy.'"

---

21. The "you" is emphatic in 1:11b, placed before the verb, at the head of the ἵνα clause.

That which Paul asks God to make his readers worthy of is "the calling." The noun *klēsis* is used in the NT "almost exclusively . . . of the divine call" (BDAG 549), and so several translations add the personal pronoun "his" before the word "calling," even though it is not found in the Greek text (so ESV, HCSB, ISV, NET, NIV, NLT, NRSV). Paul's use of the noun "calling," therefore, is yet another way in which he stresses the divine initiative. Many exegetes—especially those who take the verb *axioō* as "consider worthy" and who are influenced by the concentration of eschatological references in the preceding verses—have located this divine call of God in the *future*: the eschatological prize that Paul anticipated receiving at the close of his life and ministry (Phil. 3:14) or the end-time call to attend the wedding or kingdom banquet (Matt. 22:3, 8). With one exception (Phil. 3:14), however, the divine call—whether expressed in the noun *klēsis*, the verb *kaleō,* or other terms—for Paul always refers to God's action in the *past*. For example, in his opening thanksgiving to the Corinthians, he reminds them: "Faithful is God, through whom you were called into fellowship with his Son, Jesus Christ, our Lord" (1 Cor. 1:9). He similarly opens the Letter to the Galatians by expressing his astonishment that "you are so quickly deserting him who called you in the grace of Christ" (Gal. 1:6). More important are the examples that come from his Thessalonian correspondence. Later in this letter, Paul will remind them that God "called you through our gospel . . . so that you may obtain the glory of our Lord Jesus Christ" (2 Thess. 2:14). In his previous letter to the Thessalonians, at strategic places the apostle makes repeated references to the theme of God's call or election (1 Thess. 1:4; 2:12; 3:3b; 4:7; 5:9, 24). All this suggests that the first petition of Paul's intercessory prayer, "that our God may make you worthy of the calling," refers to the apostle's desire that God will so work in the lives of the Thessalonian believers that their present conduct will demonstrate in clear and tangible ways that they have responded positively to the past call of God. By letting his readers hear this petition, Paul indirectly challenges them to live in such a way that is worthy of their divine calling.

The second petition, in keeping with the fact that it is grammatically parallel to the first petition, similarly deals with God's action in bringing about what the Thessalonians ought to do. Paul prays that God—the subject is still "our God," from the first purpose clause—"may complete" (*plēroō* here likely has the sense of "bring to completion that which was already begun, *complete, finish*": BDAG 828.3) two things connected with the Thessalonian believers: first, their inner desires ("every desire of goodness"); second, their outward actions ("[every][22] work of faith"). Since there is some confusion about the precise meaning of the first noun phrase, it is best to begin with the second noun phrase, which is clearer and also sheds light on the preceding phrase.

The second noun phrase, "work of faith" (*ergon pisteōs*), is identical to that found in the first letter (1 Thess. 1:3). There, as here, the genitive is subjective and so has the idea of "work produced by faith." Although Paul often places

22. In 1:11 the adjective πᾶσαν (every), though not repeated, goes with both noun phrases.

the plural "works" in an antithetical relationship with "faith," it would be wrong to conclude that he only views "works" in a negative manner. Indeed, he frequently uses the singular "work" in a positive sense (Rom. 2:7; 13:3; 14:20; 1 Cor. 3:13–15; 15:58; 1 Thess. 1:3; 5:13), and that is clearly its meaning here. Also, when the apostle is not addressing a historical context involving some kind of legalistic attitude or overemphasis of the Jewish law, he is not reticent about referring to the good works that characterize the life of faith. Here the phrase "work of faith," therefore, refers to Christian activity that results from faith—what Paul elsewhere refers to as "faith working itself out in acts of love" (Gal. 5:6). Paul does not clarify what kind of "work" he has in mind that God will complete in the lives of the Thessalonian believers. In light of both the first petition and the preceding noun phrase, the apostle no doubt has in view ethical works of faith that demonstrate the "calling" of God and an interest in the welfare of others (see below for the meaning of *agathōsynē*).

The first noun phrase is more difficult to interpret than the second, and its correct meaning depends on two issues. First, does the noun *eudokia* refer to the "desire, good will" of God or of the Thessalonian believers? Second, should the genitive *agathōsynēs* be read as objective or subjective? On the first issue, the noun *eudokia* refers primarily to the desire or will of God in the LXX (G. Schrenk, *TDNT* 2:743) and so, not surprisingly, also in half of the six occurrences of this term in Paul's Letters (Eph. 1:5, 9; Phil. 2:13). Two of the remaining three occurrences in the apostle's correspondence, however, refer to human desire or resolve (Rom. 10:1; Phil. 1:15), and so this sense is certainly possible here in 2 Thess. 1:11. This possibility moves to a probability (so most commentators; contra Calvin 1981: 320; Dobschütz 1909: 253–57; G. Schrenk, *TDNT* 2:746) because of three factors. First, the parallel noun phrase "work of faith" refers to the actions of the Thessalonians and consequently suggests that the same is true here. Second, the noun *agathōsynē*, to which *eudokia* is linked, always refers to human goodness (Rom. 15:14; Gal. 5:22; Eph. 5:9), never God's. Third, the adjective "every" fits better with the multiple desires that characterize humans than with the one or unified will of God (Wanamaker 1990: 234). On the second issue, if the genitive is taken objectively, then the phrase *eudokia agathōsynē* refers to the Thessalonians' "desire to do good." Although this fits the context well, a subjective reading of the genitive is supported by the parallelism with the second noun phrase: just as the Thessalonians' "work" originates from their "faith," so also their "desire" originates from their "goodness." As with "work," Paul does not clarify what the Thessalonians' "desire" entails, though the word "goodness" suggests a strong interest in the well-being of others (BDAG 4).

The two objects of the second petition of Paul's intercessory prayers may be parallel with each other, but they are not identical. Marshall (1983: 182) overstates the case, claiming that "the two phrases form a hendiadys in that it is difficult to detect any difference between resolves of goodness and works of faith." Instead, Frame (1912: 241) and others (e.g., O'Brien 1977: 181) are closer to the truth in observing "the progress from will (εὐδοκία) to deed (ἔργον)."

Paul prays that God may bring to completion not only the Thessalonians' "desire of goodness," that is, their good intentions, but also their "work of faith," that is, the turning of these good intentions into concrete acts. As the closing prepositional phrase "in power" (*en dynamei*) makes clear, neither this desire nor this work of the Thessalonian believers can be completed without God's assistance (see Rom. 1:4; 15:13; Col. 1:29). Even though Paul has been implicitly challenging his readers in the second petition concerning their responsibility to live morally upright lives, he leaves no doubt that this cannot happen through human merit: it requires the empowering work of God. As Malherbe (2000: 411) notes: "The second petition is bracketed by reference to God's activity, which rules out any possible claim to merit, yet it requires human action."

1:12   The purposes (plural: like the two petitions, there are also two purposes) of Paul's intercessory prayers shift the time frame from that of the present conduct of the Thessalonian believers made possible only through God's initiative (v. 11) to the future glorification of both the Lord Jesus and the Christians in Thessalonica: "so that the name of the Lord Jesus may be glorified in you and you in him" (ὅπως ἐνδοξασθῇ τὸ ὄνομα τοῦ κυρίου ἡμῶν Ἰησοῦ ἐν ὑμῖν, καὶ ὑμεῖς ἐν αὐτῷ, *hopōs endoxasthē to onoma tou kyriou hēmōn Iēsou en hymin, kai hymeis en autō*).

Paul's language is very similar to that found in Isa. 66:5 LXX: "so that the name of the Lord may be glorified" (*hina to onoma kyriou doxasthē*). Some (e.g., Best 1977: 270–71; Wanamaker 1990: 234–35) have questioned this OT allusion on the grounds that Paul employs *hopōs* instead of the original *hina* and the compound verb *endoxasthē* instead of the simple *doxasthē*. These two differences from the LXX, however, are easily explained. The use of *hopōs* likely stems not merely from stylistic variation after the preceding *hina* (so MHT 3:105 and most commentators) but also from Paul's desire to distinguish the petitions of the prayer from its ultimate purpose (BDAG 718.2: "the ἵνα-clause gives the content, the ὅπως-clause the purpose of the prayer"). The use of the compound *endoxasthē* instead of the simple form of this verb stems from the presence of the compound form two verses earlier, in v. 10, which in turn originates from its allusion to Ps. 89:7 (88:8 LXX). Furthermore, Paul has echoed Isa. 66 three times in the preceding verses (vv. 6, 8a, 8b), thereby strengthening the likelihood that he is doing so once again here in verse 12. Finally, even though "the name of the Lord" is a common phrase for Paul (Rom. 10:13; 1 Cor. 1:2, 10; 5:4; 6:11; Col. 3:17; 2 Thess. 3:6), "of the six occurrences of *onoma* with *doxazein* in the LXX, only Isa. 66:5 uses *to onoma kyriou*," thereby making "the identification of the allusion certain (Aus 1976: 267). The words of Isa. 66:5 were originally addressed to those in Israel who were being despised and mocked for their faith in God: "Speak, our brothers, to those who hate you and detest you, so that the name of the Lord may be glorified, and may be seen in gladness; but they shall be put to shame" (LXX). Hence these OT words are fitting for the Thessalonian believers, who are similarly suffering opposition and ridicule for their newfound faith. In such a context, Paul prays that God will work in their lives (v. 11) for the twofold purpose that "the name of the Lord may be glorified in you and you in him."

When does this double glorification take place? Several commentators argue that, since the petitions of the prayer deal with the present conduct of the Thessalonian Christians, the glorification of Christ and believers also takes place in the current time period (so, e.g., Dobschütz 1909: 257; Trilling 1980: 64; Wanamaker 1990: 235; D. Martin 1995: 219; Richard 1995: 311; Nicholl 2004: 155). This view typically takes the following prepositional phrase "in you" (*en hymin*) as instrumental, so that Christ is glorified through the actions of his followers. There are stronger reasons, however, to view Christ's glorification and that of believers as a future event that will occur at his second coming. First and foremost is the parallel between this verse and verse 10, which clearly deals with the eschatological glorification of Christ. Although those advocating a present-time understanding of verse 12 question this parallel, it is made obvious by the common use of the compound form *endoxazō* (a rare form in the NT, found only here in 1:10, 12) and also to a lesser degree by the subsequent prepositional phrase ("in you" of v. 12 parallels "in his holy ones" of v. 10). Second, though the glorification of believers can have for Paul a present aspect (2 Cor. 3:18), it much more commonly refers to the future—either a general end-time sharing in the glory of God and/or Christ (e.g., Rom. 5:2; Col. 3:4; 2 Thess. 2:14) or a more specific transformation of believers' bodies at the parousia (Rom. 8:18–19; 1 Cor. 15:42–44; Phil. 3:20–21). Third, although Paul elsewhere speaks of believers glorifying *God* through their present conduct (Rom. 15:6; 1 Cor. 6:20; 10:31; 2 Cor. 9:13; Gal. 1:24), he nowhere refers to *Christ* as being glorified in this manner. Fourth, Paul's thanksgivings typically end on a futuristic note (1 Cor. 1:7–8; Phil. 1:10; 1 Thess. 1:10; on the eschatological climax as a transition from the thanksgiving to the letter body, see Schubert 1939: 4–5; O'Brien 1977: 170; Sanders 1962: 348–62; Roberts 1986: 29–35). Finally, as Best (1977: 271) puts it: "Above all the whole tenor of 2 Th. 1.3ff is eschatological and it would take strong arguments to force us to see in v. 12 a movement from this, and an alteration in meaning in a word unique to Paul in v. 10 and v. 12 to make it refer to the present existence of believers. God is changing believers now (v. 11) so that glorification can take place at the End."

That this eschatological glorification involves not "our Lord Jesus" but "*the name* of our Lord Jesus" has been claimed to be significant. O'Brien (1977: 182–83) is illustrative of many commentators (e.g., Eadie 1877: 252; Ellicott 1880: 105; Milligan 1908: 94; Best 1977: 271; Morris 1991: 210; Green 2002: 299) when he states: "In the Old Testament, far from being a mere label, a person's name was of profound significance, disclosing the essential character of the person. . . . Here the glorification of the name means the showing forth of the Lord Jesus as He really is." Wanamaker (1990: 235) also sees significance, but of a different sort: "Paul is forced to make the name of the Lord his point of reference in v. 12, not the person of the Lord as in v. 10, because he is writing about the present glorification of the Lord who remains in heaven, not his future glorification, when he will be physically present with his people." These interpretations, however, are guilty of reading too much into the text. The simpler and more convincing reason why Paul refers to "the name" of the Lord is that this expression is found in Isa. 66:5, to which (as we have already concluded) the apostle alludes. "We should not, therefore, attach too much significance to the use of the word, for example, by asking which particular name or title of Jesus was in Paul's mind. The thought is simply that the Lord Jesus is glorified" (Marshall 1983: 183).

This end-time glorification will happen "in you" (*en hymin*)—a likely parallel to "in his holy ones," which follows the same verb in verse 10. If so, then the preposition *en* (in) should not be taken as instrumental or causal but as locative, for the three reasons cited above (see comments on v. 10). Thus a clear and comforting contrast is formed between the fate of the Thessalonian believers and that of their tormentors: whereas the Christians in Thessalonica will witness firsthand and participate fully in the glorification of the Lord Jesus, their persecuting fellow citizens "will pay a penalty, eternal destruction from the presence of the Lord and from the *glory* of his might" (v. 9).

We have argued that the glorification of Christ referred to in verse 12 is the same as that in verse 10: both are eschatological and both take place in the presence of believers. Yet there is an important difference between these two verses: verse 10 refers to the glorification only of the Lord Jesus; verse 12 adds the glorification also of believers: "and you in him" (*kai hymeis en autō*). This brief elliptical clause presents a second purpose of Paul's intercessory prayers, whose comforting promise should not be missed: the Thessalonian Christians will not only have their faith vindicated when they are personally present and participate in the eschatological glorification of Christ but will also themselves be glorified. There is a rich OT and Jewish background to the apostle's understanding of "glory" that cannot be fully explained here (see G. Kittel, *TDNT* 2:233–55; Spicq 1994: 1.353–61; R. B. Gaffin Jr., *DPL* 348–50). Basically, glory refers to the visible radiance of God's being or character that is revealed in heaven and given by him to his human creatures (Rom. 5:2; 8:18; Col. 1:27). Although humanity has lost its original share in God's glory (Rom. 3:23), believers will recover this divine glory on the eschatological day when Christ returns—a day when the Lord Jesus will be glorified in the presence of his believers, and they will be glorified in the presence of him (so also Col. 3:4: "When Christ, who is your life, appears, then you also will appear with him in glory"). Among other things, for believers this glorification will specifically involve the transformation of their current "lowly" or "physical" bodies into "glorified" or "spiritual" bodies that resemble that of Christ's resurrected body (1 Cor. 15:42–44; Phil. 3:20–21). This glorification involves not just believing people, however, but also "creation itself will be liberated from bondage to decay and brought into the freedom and glory of the children of God" (Rom. 8:21).

The apostle's prayer report concludes with another reminder (see also "our God" and "in power" in v. 11) that both the contents and the purposes of his intercessory prayers can happen not through the human effort of the Thessalonians alone, as important as their effort may be, but through the gracious work of God and Christ: "according to the grace of our God and of our Lord Jesus Christ" (κατὰ τὴν χάριν τοῦ θεοῦ ἡμῶν καὶ κυρίου Ἰησοῦ Χριστοῦ, *kata tēn charin tou theou hēmōn kai kyriou Iēsou Christou*). The presence of only one definite article for the two nouns, "our God" and "Lord Jesus Christ," has raised questions about Paul's intent here. Some (see esp. Turner 1965: 13–17; also Green 2002: 300n21) argue on the basis of the Granville Sharp Rule that this grammatical construction joins together "our God" and "Lord" as a double description of the one person, "Jesus Christ" (cf. Titus 2:13; also John 20:28; 2 Pet. 1:11), so that this verse should be translated and punctuated as "the grace of our God and Lord, Jesus Christ" (so NLT, ISV; also marginal reading in GNT, RSV, NIV)—a rendering that provides support for the deity of Christ.[23] The Sharp rule, however, excludes personal names, and this would apply to the word "Lord," which was for the apostle virtually a personal name. Furthermore, elsewhere in the Thessalonian correspondence, Paul frequently refers to "Lord" without the article (1 Thess. 3:8; 4:1, 6, 17; 5:2; 2 Thess. 1:1, 2; 2:13; 3:4, 12), so that its absence here may not be significant. It is more likely that Paul has two distinct figures in view in describing the work of grace. He mentions "our God," not only because he has opened the letter by referring to the grace that comes from "God the Father" (1:2), but also because throughout the prayer report he has been stressing the divine initiative of "our God" (v. 11). He adds a reference to "[the] Lord Jesus Christ" not only because in Paul's theology more generally the grace that comes from God is mediated to believers through their relationship to Christ, but also because in the thanksgiving the apostle has been highlighting the return of Christ as the historical moment when the Thessalonian readers will be rewarded for their faith and their persecutors will be punished.

Additional Notes

1:4. Instead of the compound ἐγκαυχᾶσθαι, a number of MSS have the simple form καυχᾶσθαι (D F G Ψ 𝔐). Not only is there overwhelming MS support for the compound form (ℵ A B P 0111 33 81 2464 *pc*), but the simple form also clearly originates as a perceived correction by scribes to that form commonly used (thirty-five times) by Paul.

1:4. The important uncial Vaticanus (B) has a different compound verb: ἐνέχεσθε (you are loaded down). This variant, however, not only lacks other MS support; it may also have been occasioned by the preceding relative pronoun, which, due to attraction to the case of *thlipsesin*, is in the unexpected dative case—the case that the verb ἐνέχω normally takes (BDAG 336). Thus the copyist of Vaticanus

---

23. Dobschütz (1909: 258) interpreted the grammatical construction in this way and concluded that such a claim to deity (in 1:12b) could not be genuinely Pauline but rather must have been a later interpolation. Aside from the fact that an ascription of the title "God" to Jesus was done enough times by other authors of Scripture (e.g., John 1:1, 18; 20:28; Heb. 1:8–9; 1 John 5:20) that Paul could have made a similar claim (see Rom. 9:5), the biggest weakness to Dobschütz's hypothesis of interpolation is that it has absolutely no textual support.

may have thought that he was "correcting" an apparent grammatical problem by changing the prefix of the verb so that it agrees with its dative object.

1:8. Some MSS have (as accepted above) ἐν φλογὶ πυρός instead of ἐν πυρὶ φλογός (NA[28], UBS[4]). See my comments on 1:8 for discussion of this choice.

1:8. In place of the genitive διδόντος, the nominative διδούς is read by D* F G Ψ *pc* b vg[ms]. This change likely stemmed from the attempt of scribes to clarify the flow of Paul's sentence, since the participle is separated by some distance from the words that it modifies (τοῦ κυρίου Ἰησοῦ).

1:10. Although the variant ἐπιστώθη (was confirmed) is favored by Hort (see W-H) and Moffatt (1897: 46), it has far too little textual support (107 *pc*) to warrant replacing the reading ἐπιστεύθη (was believed). Furthermore, Paul's choice of ἐπιστεύθη was undoubtedly prompted by his use of πιστεύσασιν two words earlier.

1:11. In place of the aorist subjunctive πληρώσῃ, expected after the preceding ἵνα, the future indicative πληρώσει is found in several MSS (A K P Ψ 6 326 1241 2464 *al*). This shift from the aorist subjunctive to the future indicative occurs frequently in the ancient MSS, likely due to their similar-sounding endings.

1:12. Many MSS add Χριστοῦ (so A F G P 33 81 104 365 1739 1881 2495 *pm* lat sy bo[pt]; Ambst) to the noun phrase "the name of our Lord Jesus," likely under the influence of its presence at the end of this verse. The shorter and preferred reading has stronger textual support (ℵ B D K L Ψ 0111 6 323 630 1175 1241 2464 *pm* b sa bo[pt]).

III. Comfort concerning the Day of the Lord (2:1–17)

My alternate title for this section is "The Slaying of Satan's Superman and the Sure Salvation of the Saints: Paul's Word of Comfort" (Weima 2006). Second Thessalonians 2:1–17 is a difficult passage, likely the most exegetically challenging text in all of Paul's Letters. But even though much in this passage is debatable and open to various interpretations, the apostle's overall goal or larger purpose remains quite clear: not to *predict* the future (contrary to the claims of so-called prophecy experts who approach this passage as a blueprint for spelling out what yet must take place) but to *pastor* the Thessalonian church. The consolatory theme already present and foreshadowed in the preceding thanksgiving section (1:3–12) comes to fuller expression here in the body of the letter. To a young congregation that is persecuted by their unbelieving fellow citizens and frightened by a false claim that the day of the Lord has already come, Paul speaks a word of comfort.

This message of comfort is presented in five distinct sections. The first unit, verses 1–2, introduces the *crisis* that the rest of the passage seeks to address. Someone has claimed, likely by means of a prophetic utterance asserting the authority of Paul, that the day of the Lord has come. Even though this claim may have seemed obviously false, it nevertheless has caused the young church of Thessalonica, already apprehensive about their eschatological fate (1 Thess. 5:1–11), to be scared out of their wits, fearful of whether they would avoid the wrath of God connected with the day of judgment and instead experience salvation.

The second unit, verses 3–12, consists of Paul's *correction* of this false claim, which is the source of the Thessalonians' fear. The apostle reassures the shaken church members that the day of the Lord cannot have come because this future event will not take place until certain clearly defined events take place first, foremost of which involves the appearance and destruction of the man of lawlessness, who for the present time is being restrained. Paul's description of the coming destruction that will fall upon not only this "superman of Satan," but also his followers, who are persecuting the believers in Thessalonica, is ultimately a message of comfort to the apostle's readers, because this future judgment will vindicate their faith, punish their enemies, and demonstrate that God's judgment is just (cf. 1:5–10).

The third unit, verses 13–14, involves *comfort*: Paul reassures the Thessalonian Christians with the message that God's election of them guarantees that they will not receive judgment on the day of the Lord but salvation. The apostle thanks God that, in sharp contrast to the unbelievers who are perishing, the Christians in Thessalonica are sure to receive "salvation"—a salvation that is sure due to God's prior work of choosing (v. 13) and calling (v. 14) them.

The fourth unit, verse 15, involves the *command* that corrects the crisis introduced at the beginning of the passage: if the problem is mental instability ("too easily shaken from your mind or alarmed") due to a *new* assertion about the day of the Lord originating from a prophetic utterance that claims the authority of Paul, the solution is to "stand firm and hold fast" to the traditions that the apostle has *previously* taught them, either in a spoken word or written letter.

The fifth and final unit, verses 16–17, consists of the *closing*, as Paul ends his lengthy word of comfort with a double-petition prayer. The prayer's first and longer half (vv. 16–17a) *looks back* and summarizes the apostle's concern in the preceding verses, his aim to comfort the Thessalonian church. To a congregation frightened by a new claim that the day of the Lord has come, Paul offers a prayer that the Lord Jesus Christ and the God who gives "eternal comfort" may "comfort" their shaken hearts. This double reference to "comfort" reveals Paul's pastoral purpose at work throughout the passage. The second and shorter half of the prayer (v. 17b) *looks ahead* and anticipates the apostle's concern in the remaining verses of the letter body (3:1–15), to "strengthen" the church "in every good work and word" in sharp contrast to the rebellious idlers in their midst.

Literary Analysis

Character of the Passage

Even though 2 Thess. 2:1–17 obviously belongs to the genre of a letter and constitutes the body section of Paul's second correspondence to the Thessalonians, in this passage the apostle at times employs a different style of writing: apocalyptic.[1] Already a century ago, Milligan (1908: 95) noted about these verses that "instead of conveying his warning in a clear and definitive form, the Apostle prefers to embody it in a mysterious apocalyptic picture, which has not only no parallel in his own writings, but is unlike anything else in the N.T., unless it be certain passages in the Revelation of St John." Ellingworth and Nida (1975: 157), in their treatment of this passage, refer to "this kind of writing, technically known as 'apocalyptic.'" More recently Dunn (1998: 304) has stated about this passage: "Nothing in the Pauline letters is closer to the genre of apocalypse." Nevertheless, it is one thing to see Paul in 2 Thess. 2:1–17 making use of apocalyptic images and themes; it is another to claim that this section constitutes full-blown apocalyptic or is very close to the writing style used in the last book of the canon. The apostle does employ images and themes that are similarly found in apocalyptic writings of his day, but he does so only in one section of this passage (vv. 3–12) and not to the same degree as is found in true apocalyptic texts. Thus some restraint should be exercised in the use of the term "apocalyptic" to describe the literary character of 2:1–17.

---

1. Much of the material in the following three sections is adapted from Weima 2006: esp. 68–75.

The apocalyptic images and themes in this passage have caused great difficulties for interpretation. Gaventa (1998: 107) admits: "Readers of the New Testament stumbling for the first time into the middle of 2 Thessalonians may be forgiven if they feel like Alice tumbling down a dark hole in Wonderland. The residents of this Wonderland are new and mysterious, their relationship to one another unclear, and the stranger responds with a sense of disorientation." The residents of this Wonderland to which Gaventa refers involve such intriguing figures or events as the man of lawlessness, who is also called the son of destruction, the apostasy, the restraining person and the restraining force, the day of the Lord, and two parousias, or "comings": one by the man of lawlessness, and one by the Lord Jesus Christ. Not only is the precise meaning of these apocalyptic events and persons difficult to ascertain, but also the Greek text of this passage contains several grammatical irregularities, incomplete sentences, and textual variants. Neil (1950: 155) some years ago made the claim that 2 Thess. 2:1–17 is "probably the most obscure and difficult passage in the whole of the Pauline correspondence." Those who have wrestled with this passage might justly criticize Neil's claim, not because he is guilty of overstatement but quite the opposite—because he understated the problem by including the adverb "probably." Holmes (1998: 228) declares that this passage is "by common consent one of the most obscure in the Pauline corpus." Commentators typically appreciate the honesty of the great church leader Augustine, who, after wrestling with this passage, stated: "I frankly confess that the meaning of this completely escapes me" (*City* 20.19).

The difficulty of this passage drives home the important principle of "shouting" where Scripture demands that one should shout but "whispering" where Scripture demands that one should whisper. In other words, there are many subjects that the Bible addresses frequently and with great clarity, and these are the things that the exegete ought to shout. But there are some subjects that the Bible addresses infrequently and with less clarity, and these are the things that the exegete ought to whisper. Thus it may well be that the reader ends up whispering about the meaning of the diverse characters and events described in 2 Thess. 2:1–17. In this situation whispering is not a sign of treating God's Word in a wimpy or wishy-washy manner; rather, it is evidence of having such a high respect for the biblical text that one dares not speak more definitively than the text allows.

But even though much in this passage is debatable and open to various interpretations, Paul's overall goal or larger purpose in describing these things to the Thessalonians remains quite clear: to comfort his readers (see esp. the discussion below under "Extent of the Passage" and the comments on the concluding prayer of 2:16–17, with its double reference to "comfort" [v. 16, *paraklēsin*; v. 17, *parakalesai*]). The consolatory theme already present and foreshadowed in the preceding thanksgiving section comes to fuller expression here in the body of the letter. It is this message of comfort that any faithful explanation of 2:1–17 must clearly convey or "shout."

Extent of the Passage

The first mistake that one can easily make in the interpretation of 2:1–17 is potentially major: failing to recognize the proper boundaries of the passage and ending the reading too soon. The *beginning* of the passage at 2:1 is quite clear from a variety of epistolary clues:

a. The appeal formula "Now we ask you . . ." (ἐρωτῶμεν, *erōtōmen*, is a synonym for the more common παρακαλοῦμεν, *parakaloumen*: see 1 Thess. 4:1; 5:12, 14; Phil. 4:2–3; P.Oxy. 294.28; 744.6; P.Freib. 39; P.Col. 8.8–9, 21) primarily functions in Paul's Letters to signal a major transition, either from the end of the thanksgiving to the beginning of the letter body, as is the case here (also 1 Cor. 1:10; Philem. 8–9), or as more typically happens, a transition within the letter body (Rom. 12:1; 15:30; 16:17; 1 Cor. 16:15; 2 Cor. 10:1; Phil. 4:2; 1 Thess. 4:1; Eph. 4:1).

b. The vocative ἀδελφοί, *adelphoi* (brothers) is an epistolary device in Paul's Letters commonly used to introduce a new unit or subunit (e.g., 1 Thess. 2:1, 17; 3:7; 4:1, 13; 5:1, 12; 2 Thess. 1:3; 2:1, 13, 15; 3:1, 6).

c. The prayer report of 1:11–12, as in Paul's other thanksgivings (Phil. 1:9–11; Col. 1:9–14; see also Rom. 1:10b), formally concludes the thanksgiving section of 1:3–12 and so leads the reader to expect the beginning of the letter body in the immediately following verse, 2:1.

d. The phrase "but concerning" (ὑπὲρ δέ, *hyper de*) in 2:1 may well be a synonym for the epistolary formula περὶ δέ, *peri de*, frequently used by Paul to introduce a new topic (1 Thess. 4:9, 13; 5:1; 1 Cor. 7:1, 25; 8:1; 12:1; 16:1, 12).

But while the beginning of the passage is clear, the *ending* of the passage is less obvious, with the result that many exegetes stop reading after verse 12. This is understandable, given that the editors of the Greek text (NA[28], UBS[4]) and modern translations (e.g., KJV, NIV, RSV, NRSV, JB, NLT, ESV) always begin a new paragraph at verse 13 and frequently also add a heading at this point, suggesting that a new section of the letter begins here. The vast majority of commentators treat verses 1–12 as a complete unit, dealing with the topic of the man of lawlessness and thus distinct from the following material, verses 13–17, which deals with the different topic of thanksgiving for the Thessalonian readers; thereby they downplay or even exclude any connection between these two sections. Best (1977: 311), for example, states of 2:13: "Paul is apparently returning deliberately to the theme of thanksgiving and *making a new beginning*" (emphasis added). Marshall (1983: 184) likewise asserts: "But it is doubtful whether the whole chapter [2:1–17] should be regarded as one section. It seems best, however, to regard vv. 1–12 as forming a section of teaching, since v. 13 starts afresh in the form of a thanksgiving." On the basis of a rhetorical reading of the letter, Witherington (2006: 206) similarly concludes: "While the argument proper begins at v. 3, the argument does not extend beyond v. 12. In vv. 13–17 we have a separate section on thanksgiving followed by another wish prayer which should not be seen as part of the refutation itself" (see also, e.g., Frame 1912; Bruce 1982; Morris 1991; Richard 1995; Malherbe 2000; Beale 2003; Furnish 2007; Shogren 2012).

But although ending the section at verse 12 may be understandable in light of the thanksgiving that opens verse 13 and the seemingly abrupt shift in subject matter here from that of the preceding verses, it is clearly wrong. There are a number of indisputable links between verses 1–12 and verses 13–17—links that demonstrate Paul's intention that the whole of chapter 2 be read together as a literary unit. What is at stake here is not merely a technical point or scholarly debate as to where the passage ends but, as I will spell out shortly, the key to discovering Paul's overall and thus primary purpose in this discussion: to comfort his Thessalonian readers.

The compelling reasons for extending the reading to the end of the chapter at verse 17 are as follows:

a. There is a verbal inclusio between verse 2 ("either by a spiritual utterance or by a word or by a letter supposedly from us") and verse 15 ("either by a word or by a letter from us"). The connection between these two verses is strengthened by not just the repetition of the two prepositional phrases (the omission of the first prepositional phrase in v. 15 is significant) but also the same order of these prepositional phrases.

b. There is a thematic inclusio between the problem of mental *instability* articulated in verse 2 ("that you not be too easily shaken from your mind or alarmed") and the solution of mental *stability* in both the command of verse 15 ("Stand firm and hold fast!") and the prayer of verse 17 (May Jesus and God "strengthen" you). That the command to mental stability in verse 15 does indeed look back to the problem of mental instability in verse 2 is supported by the two particles ἄρα οὖν (*ara oun*, so then) that introduce this command (in v. 15)—particles that elsewhere draw a conclusion based on what has been said beforehand (see also Rom. 8:12; 14:12, 19; Gal. 6:10; 1 Thess. 5:6). That the prayer for mental stability in verse 17 also does look back to the earlier problem of mental instability is supported by a striking parallel with the first letter: just as Paul's prayer in 1 Thess. 3:13 that the Lord "strengthen your hearts" (στηρίξαι ὑμῶν τὰς καρδίας, *stērixai hymōn tas kardias*) looks back to the earlier problem in 1 Thess. 3:3 that "no one be shaken in these trials," so also Paul's prayer in 2 Thess. 2:17 that the Lord "strengthen your hearts" (ὑμῶν τὰς καρδίας . . . στηρίξαι, *hymōn tas kardias . . . stērixai*) looks back to the earlier problem identified in 2 Thess. 2:2, that the Thessalonians are "shaken from your mind or alarmed."

c. There are a couple of significant contrasts between the description of *unbelievers* in verses 3–12 and that of the Thessalonian *believers* in verses 13–17 (so also Giblin 1967: 46–48; D. Martin 1995: 221–22). A sharp contrast is created between the two groups through the use of the word pair "truth" and "lie." On the one hand, unbelievers are said to "not accept the love of the truth" (v. 10b, τὴν ἀγάπην τῆς ἀληθείας οὐκ ἐδέξαντο, *tēn agapēn tēs alētheias ouk edexanto*), "to believe the lie" (v. 11a, εἰς τὸ πιστεῦσαι . . . τῷ ψεύδει, *eis to pisteusai . . . tō pseudei*), and are "those who have not believed the truth" (v. 12, οἱ μὴ πιστεύσαντες τῇ ἀληθείᾳ, *hoi mē pisteusantes tē alētheia*); on the other hand, the Thessalonian Christians have been chosen by God through their "belief in the truth" (v. 13b, ἐν . . . πίστει ἀληθείας, *en . . . pistei alētheias*). This contrast between the two groups is further heightened with another word pair: "to be destroyed" and "to be saved/salvation." On the one hand, unbelievers are "those who are being destroyed" (v. 10a, τοῖς ἀπολλυμένοις, *tois apollymenois*) and who do not accept the truth "so that they may be saved" (v. 10b, εἰς τὸ σωθῆναι αὐτούς, *eis to sōthēnai autous*); on the other hand, the Thessalonian Christians are elected by God as firstfruits "for salvation" (v. 13b, εἰς σωτηρίαν, *eis sōterian*).

d. There is a parallel between the structure of Paul's argument in the first letter and that found here in 2:1–17. Just as the two interconnected problems of Paul's absence and the Thessalonians' persecution in 1 Thess. 2:17–3:10 are concluded with two transitional prayers in 3:11–13 (optative mood) and followed by the phrase "Finally, brothers" in 4:1, which introduces the next topic, so also the problem of the false claim about the day of the Lord in 2 Thess. 2:1–15 is concluded with a transitional prayer in 2:16–17 (optative mood) and followed by the phrase "Finally, brothers" in 3:1, which introduces the next topic:

1 Thessalonians		2 Thessalonians	
2:17–3:10	Main paragraph	2:1–15	Main paragraph
3:11–13	Transitional prayers (optative)	2:16–17	Transitional prayer (optative)
4:1	"Finally, brothers, . . ."	3:1	"Finally, brothers, . . ."

e. If one assumes that the new passage begun in 2:1 extends only to 2:12 and that a major break therefore occurs at the immediately following verse of 2:13, then this results in separating the material of 2:13–17, with no compelling explanation of how this isolated section is integrated into the surrounding material or the logic of the letter body as a whole (D. Martin 1995: 221).

Determining the proper ending of Paul's argument in 2 Thess. 2 is of crucial importance for properly discerning his primary purpose in this discussion. If one reads only up to verse 12, the passage closes with *a note of judgment for unbelievers*. In fact, the final three verses speak in a very sobering way about those who "are on the way to destruction because they did not accept the love of the truth so that they might be saved" and how "because of this God sends them a powerful delusion in order that they believe the lie so that all who have not believed the truth but delighted in wickedness will be condemned" (vv. 10b–12). If, however, one reads all the way to verse 17, the passage closes with *a note of comfort for the Thessalonian Christians*. In sharp contrast to the doom facing their unbelieving fellow citizens, they are comforted by the knowledge that God has elected them to receive not judgment but salvation. That Paul's overall purpose in this passage truly is to comfort his Thessalonian readers can be seen in his closing prayer in verses 16–17, which contains a double reference to comfort: "But may our Lord Jesus Christ himself and God our Father, the one who loved us and gave us eternal *comfort* [the noun παράκλησιν, *paraklēsin*] and good hope by his grace, *comfort* [the cognate verb in the optative παρακαλέσαι, *parakalesai*] your hearts and strengthen them in every good work and word" (vv. 16–17).

A proper understanding of where the passage ends, therefore, is an important corrective to so-called prophecy experts, who approach this passage as a blueprint for spelling out what will happen in the future. An exegete who concentrates only on the words of verses 1–12 and mines them merely for clues about what yet must still take place, such a reader misses and, even worse, violates Paul's primary purpose in this passage, a purpose that becomes clear from verses 13–17. The apostle's first and foremost intention is not to *predict* but to *pastor*.[2] To a young congregation that is persecuted by their unbelieving fellow citizens and frightened by a false claim that

---

2. Giblin (1967: 41) perceptively observes: "What seems to have been neglected in studying this passage is attention to the repeated subordination of apocalyptic flights to a point of pastoral concern or pastoral reaction. Paul seems to be more concerned with the pastoral problem of

the day of the Lord has come, Paul speaks words of comfort. As Gaventa (1998: 123) declares about the closing prayer of verses 16–17: "Throughout this chapter [2 Thess. 2], the writer has attempted to strengthen and *comfort* Christians who have been frightened out of their wits by false announcements of the day of the Lord. Finally, however, the acknowledgment comes that God is the one who grants *comfort* and hope and strength" (emphasis added).

Structure of the Passage

The many difficult interpretive issues faced in this passage lead potentially to a second danger for the exegete, namely, "missing the forest for the trees." In other words, one must guard against spending so much time and energy in explaining the specific details about the man of lawlessness, the apostasy, the restraining person and restraining force, and the other apocalyptic events and characters found in this chapter that the overarching pastoral concern of the passage is either downplayed or even missed completely. Thus special care must be given to understanding the overall structure of the passage and how its respective units support the consolatory function at work in the passage as a whole.

Paul presents his word of comfort in five discernible units. The first unit consists of verses 1–2, which introduce the *crisis* that the rest of the passage seeks to address. The beginning of this unit is clearly marked by several epistolary conventions (see "Extent of the Passage" above, which identifies four of these transitional markers) and is held together grammatically by the fact that it consists of one lengthy sentence. Here we discover that the Thessalonian Christians are frightened out of their wits over a false claim that the day of the Lord has come.

The second and longest unit involves verses 3–12 and presents Paul's *correction* of this false claim, which is the source of the Thessalonians' fear. The day of the Lord cannot have come "because" (note the causal ὅτι [*hoti*] that opens this unit in v. 3b) this future event will not take place until certain clearly defined events take place first, foremost of which involves the appearance and destruction of the man of lawlessness, who for the present time is being restrained. It is this second unit that is referred to in the first part of my alternate longer heading for this passage: "The Slaying of Satan's Superman."

The third unit, verses 13–14, involves the *comfort* and is set apart from the preceding material in three ways: (1) the personal pronoun "We," emphasized both by its mere presence (since the subject is already expressed in the verb "we ought") and its location at the head of the sentence, thereby signaling the shift from the fate of the man of lawlessness and his deceived followers to that of the Thessalonian Christians; (2) the soft adversative particle δέ (but); and (3) the vocative phrase "brothers loved by the Lord." Here Paul gives thanks to God that, in sharp contrast to the unbelievers, who are perishing, the Christians in Thessalonica are sure to receive "salvation"—a salvation that is guaranteed by God's prior work of choosing (v. 13) and calling (v. 14) them. This third unit accounts for the second part of my alternate heading: "The Sure Salvation of the Saints."

The fourth unit, verse 15, consists of the *command*. That this verse marks another shift in the argument is witnessed by three clues: (1) another occurrence of the

---

correcting the Thessalonians' outlook than he is with describing the coming of the Antichrist or even the coming of the Lord."

transitional marker, the vocative "brothers" (ἀδελφοί, *adelphoi*); (2) the use of the double particles ἄρα οὖν (*ara oun*, so then) in which "ἄρα expresses the inference and οὖν the transition" (BDAG 127.2b; see also Rom. 5:18; 7:3, 25; 8:12; 9:16, 18; 14:12, 19; Gal. 6:10; Eph. 2:19; 1 Thess. 5:6; 2 Clem. 8.6; 14.3); and (3) the shift from the indicative mood that predominates the preceding verses to the double imperative in this verse. Paul here begins to bring his discussion to a close with two concluding commands, which offer the solution to the crisis introduced in verses 1–2. If the problem is mental instability ("too easily shaken from your mind or alarmed") due to a *new* claim about the day of the Lord, likely through a spiritual utterance that claims the authority of Paul, the solution is to "stand firm and hold fast" to the traditions that the apostle has *previously* taught them in a spoken word or written letter.

The fifth and final unit involves verses 16–17, which function as the *closing* of Paul's argument. These verses are formally distinct from the rest of the material in the passage in that they make use of the optative mood and constitute a prayer or "benediction," which the apostle always uses elsewhere to bring a discussion to a definitive close (Rom. 15:5–6; 15:13; 1 Thess. 3:11, 12–13; 2 Thess. 3:5; see Weima 1994a: 101–4). Like the immediately preceding command of verse 15, the prayer of verses 16–17 also looks back to the problem of mental instability introduced at the beginning of the chapter. To a congregation frightened by a new claim that the day of the Lord has come, Paul offers a prayer that the Lord Jesus Christ and the God who gives "eternal comfort" may "comfort" their hearts. It is this closing prayer that most clearly reveals Paul's overall purpose in the passage and explains the third part of my alternate heading: "Paul's Word of Comfort."

The structure of 2:1–17, therefore, is as follows:

A. Crisis: Fear over the claim that "the day of the Lord has come" (2:1–2)
   1. The nature of the false claim (2:1)
   2. The meaning of the false claim (2:2a)
   3. The source of the false claim (2:2b)
   4. The connection of the false claim to Paul (2:2c)
B. Correction: Events that must precede the day of the Lord (2:3–12)
   1. Future: The apostasy and the man of lawlessness (2:3–5)
      a. The apostasy (2:3a)
      b. The man of lawlessness (2:3b–4)
      c. A mild rebuke (2:5)
   2. Present: The restraining thing/person and the mystery of lawlessness (2:6–7)
   3. Future: The coming of the man of lawlessness and his deceived followers (2:8–10)
   4. Present: The judgment of unbelievers (2:11–12)
C. Comfort: God ensures the salvation of the Thessalonians (2:13–14)
D. Command: Stand firm by holding fast to Paul's teachings (2:15)
E. Closing prayer that God will comfort the Thessalonians (2:16–17)

Exegesis and Exposition

[1]Now we ask you, brothers, concerning the coming of ⌜our⌝ Lord Jesus Christ and our gathering to him, [2]that you not be too easily shaken from your mind or alarmed, whether through a prophetic utterance or through a spoken word or through a written letter, supposedly through us, claiming that the day of the ⌜Lord⌝ has come.

[3]Do not let anyone deceive you in any way, because that day will not come unless the apostasy comes first and the man of ⌜lawlessness⌝ is revealed, the son of destruction, [4]the one who opposes and exalts himself over every being called god or every object of worship, so that he ⌜   ⌝ takes his seat in the temple of God, proclaiming that he himself is God. [5]You remember, don't you, that when ⌜I was⌝ still with you, I was repeatedly saying these things to you? [6]And you know the thing that is now restraining in order that he might be revealed at ⌜his own⌝ fixed time. [7]For the mystery of lawlessness is already at work only until the one who is now restraining is out of the way. [8]And then the lawless one will be revealed, whom the Lord ⌜Jesus⌝ ⌜will slay⌝ with the breath of his mouth and will destroy by the sudden appearance of his coming. [9]The coming of the lawless one will be in conformity with the work of Satan in all power—both deceptive signs and wonders—[10]and in all deception of ⌜   ⌝ wickedness ⌜   ⌝ to those on the way to destruction because they did not accept the love of the truth so that they might be saved. [11]And because of this God ⌜sends⌝ them a powerful delusion in order that they believe the lie, [12]so that all who have not believed the truth but delighted in wickedness will be condemned.

[13]But as for us, we ought to give thanks to God always concerning you, brothers loved by ⌜the Lord⌝, because God chose you ⌜as firstfruits⌝ for salvation by means of the sanctifying work of the Spirit and your belief in the truth. [14]To this end he ⌜also⌝ called you through our gospel for the obtaining of the glory of our Lord Jesus Christ.

[15]So then, brothers, stand firm and hold fast to the traditions that you were taught either by our word or by our letter. [16]But may our Lord Jesus Christ himself and ⌜God our Father⌝, the one who loved us and gave us eternal comfort and good hope by his grace, [17]comfort your hearts and strengthen them in every good ⌜work and word⌝.

A. Crisis: Fear over the Claim That "the Day of the Lord Has Come" (2:1–2)

It is no exaggeration to say that the Thessalonian church was facing a crisis.[3] In other words, Paul in 2:1–17 is not merely satisfying their curiosity about eschatological matters but rather is providing desperately needed pastoral comfort to believers who were frightened about end-time events and unsure about their salvation on that eschatological day. The seriousness of the situation is suggested by two facts: (1) this subject matter is the first thing the apostle discusses in the letter body; (2) he goes to great lengths to treat this

---

3. Contra Moore (1969: 98): "We must not exaggerate the dimensions of this problem for there is no evidence that it had reached anything like a crisis." Shogren (2012: 273) also downplays the seriousness of the problem, suggesting that "Paul was simply guarding against a potential danger."

matter. Actually, the other subjects taken up in the letter—their unjust suffering described in the opening thanksgiving of 1:3–12 and their ongoing problem with rebelliously idle members described in 3:1–15—almost certainly are connected with the problem taken up here in 2:1–17.[4]

1. The Nature of the False Claim (2:1)

2:1   Paul introduces the first and biggest concern of the letter body with an epistolary convention widely used in the ancient world: the appeal formula (for a fuller discussion of the form and function of the appeal formula, see comments on 1 Thess. 4:1; see also Mullins 1962; Bjerkelund 1967). This formula typically consists of four elements (Bjerkelund 1967: 43–50), the first of which involves the main verb of appeal from which this epistolary convention derives its name. However, instead of the expected "we appeal" (παρακαλοῦμεν, *parakaloumen*: Rom. 12:1; 15:30; 16:17; 1 Cor. 1:10; 4:16; 16:15; 2 Cor. 10:1–2; Phil. 4:2 [2x]; 1 Thess. 4:10b; 5:14; Philem. 9, 10), here occurs the rarer synonym "we ask" (ἐρωτῶμεν, *erōtōmen*: only three other times in Paul: 1 Thess. 4:1; 5:12; Phil. 4:3). Paul's use of the appeal formula, especially with the verb "we ask," gives the following section of 2:1–17 a warmer and friendlier tone. Instead of being heavy-handed and commanding the Thessalonians, the apostle deliberately employs the softer and more user-friendly appeal formula. That Paul is aware of the difference between "commanding" and "appealing" is clear from his comment to Philemon that "although I have much boldness in Christ to *command* you to the necessary thing, more because of love I *appeal*" (vv. 8–9). The use here of the softer "we ask" fits well with the overall tone of not only the preceding thanksgiving section of 1:3–12, where Paul expresses his deep thanksgiving for the church's impressive endurance of significant persecution, but also the tone of the following material of 2:1–17, where, as I have argued above, his overriding concern is pastoral, to comfort his Thessalonian readers. Here the appeal formula also possesses its expected transitional function, indicating a major shift either within the letter body (Rom. 12:1; 15:30; 16:17; 1 Cor. 16:15; 2 Cor. 10:1; Phil. 4:2; 1 Thess. 4:1; Eph. 4:1), or as here, the shift from the thanksgiving to the letter body (also 1 Cor. 1:10; Philem. 8–9).

4. Fee (1994a: 71; 2009: 268) argues that 2 Thess. 2 is the most crucial chapter in the letter because "it serves as the primary occasion for the letter. Indeed, the other concerns—their unjust suffering (ch. 1) and the continuing difficulty with the 'unruly idle' (ch. 3)—are best understood as related to this one. Whatever some of them had come to believe about 'the day of the Lord' (see 1 Thes 5:1–11), it had resulted in their being shaken with regard to their present sufferings and had caused others to take a dim view toward 'working with their own hands.'" Although not all commentators connect the topics of suffering (2 Thess. 1) and idleness (chap. 3) with the false claim concerning the day of the Lord (chap. 2), there is a consensus that chap. 2 constitutes the primary reason why 2 Thessalonians was written: e.g., Olshausen 1851: 470; Dobschütz 1909: 261; Staab 1965: 50; Bruce 1982: 162; Holmes 1998: 227–28; Malherbe 2000: 427.

The second element of the appeal formula consists of a reference to the recipients of the appeal, here expressed simply by the second-person pronoun "you" (ὑμᾶς, *hymas*). As he often does with this formula, however, Paul further specifies the recipients with the vocative "brothers" (ἀδελφοί, *adelphoi*). In addition to functioning as yet another transitional device that signals the major shift from the thanksgiving to the letter body, this marks the second of seven occurrences of the vocative "brothers" in this brief letter (1:3; 2:1, 13, 15; 3:1, 6, 13; see also 3:15). This vocative term was used heavily in the first letter to characterize the relationship between Paul and his readers (1:4; 2:1, 9, 14, 17; 3:7; 4:1, 10b, 13; 5:1, 4, 12, 14, 25), as were intimate family metaphors such as "infants" (2:7b), "nursing mother" (2:7c), "father" (2:11), and "orphans" (2:17). The frequent use of the vocative "brothers" here in a letter written to the same audience only a short time later, therefore, continues this use of kinship language and stresses the affectionate nature of the relationship that exists between Paul and his readers.

When the appeal formula occurs in official correspondence of the Greco-Roman world, it frequently has a third formal element: a prepositional phrase that indicates the source of authority by which the letter writer issues his appeal. Paul's employment of the appeal formula sometimes parallels this pattern and also contains this same third element (e.g., 1 Thess. 4:1: "And so, brothers, we ask you and appeal *in the Lord Jesus* that . . ."). At other times, however, as here in 2:1, the apostle does not include such a prepositional phrase, partly because his authority to exhort them is not at all questioned by the Thessalonian church (note in this regard the absence of the expected title "apostle" in the opening of both letters; see comments on 1 Thess. 1:1a and 2 Thess. 1:1a), but more because an appeal to his authority does not fit well with his pastoral purpose of comforting his readers.

But while there is no prepositional phrase indicating the source of authority by which Paul issues his appeal to the Thessalonians, there is a prepositional phrase indicating something else: "concerning the coming of our Lord Jesus Christ and our gathering to him" (ὑπὲρ τῆς παρουσίας τοῦ κυρίου ἡμῶν Ἰησοῦ Χριστοῦ καὶ ἡμῶν ἐπισυναγωγῆς ἐπ' αὐτόν, *hyper tēs parousias tou kyriou hēmōn Iēsou Christou kai hēmōn episynagōgēs ep' auton*). This prepositional phrase does not indicate the content of Paul's appeal. That typically is expressed in the appeal formula by means of an infinitive clause (Rom. 12:1; 15:30; 16:17; 2 Cor. 10:1–2; Phil. 4:2; 1 Thess. 4:10b–11), and thus the content of the appeal is instead found in the subsequent double infinitive of verse 2. Here the preposition *hyper* is equivalent to the preposition περί (*peri*: so BDAG 1031.3; Moule 1959: 64–65), with which it is frequently interchanged in the manuscripts (see, e.g., 1 Thess. 3:2). Thus the preposition *hyper*, combined with the particle *de* (the two have been separated because *hyper* has been pushed forward in the sentence due to the presence of the appeal formula, while the particle has to remain in the postpositive position), is a synonym for the epistolary formula περὶ δέ (*peri de*) frequently used by Paul to introduce a new topic (1 Thess. 4:9, 13; 5:1; 1 Cor. 7:1, 25; 8:1; 12:1; 16:1, 12). Along with the appeal formula and the vocative, this is the third epistolary convention that signals the major transition at 2:1 from the thanksgiving to the body of the letter.

The new topic that the prepositional phrase introduces concerns "the coming of our Lord Jesus Christ and our gathering to him." The close connection between the two key nouns, "coming" (*parousia*: for a full discussion of the meaning and significance of this key term, see comments on 1 Thess. 2:19) and "gathering" (*episynagōgē*), is suggested by the two parts of the prepositional clause that are in synonymous parallelism with each other and confirmed by the use of one definite article for both nouns. It would be wrong, therefore, to distinguish too sharply between the words "coming" and "gathering." Although the former term refers to Christ's action while the latter term to the activity of the Thessalonian believers, both words have in view the same eschatological event. The immediate reference of both terms is to the comforting picture given in the previous letter of how all believers, both those who have already died and those who are still alive, will be gathered together to Jesus at his return (1 Thess. 4:16–17; 5:10). The motif, however, goes back beyond this to the widespread OT hope in the gathering together of the scattered exiles to their own land on the day of the Lord (Ps. 106:47 [105:47 LXX]; Isa. 27:13; 43:4–7; 52:12; 56:8; Jer. 31:8; Ezek. 28:25; Joel 3:1–2; Zech. 2:6–7; 2 Macc. 1:27; 2:7, 18; Tob. 14:7; T. Asher 7.6–7; T. Naph. 8.3). The noun "gathering" (*episynagōgē*) in particular, found only here in Paul's writings,[5] along with the cognate verb, was a technical term that referred to the hope in an end-time reunion of God's dispersed people (Isa. 27:13; 2 Macc. 2:7, 18; Pss. Sol. 17.50). This hope was taken over by Jesus and his followers to refer to the final gathering of God's people with the Messiah (Matt. 24:31; Mark 13:27; Luke 13:34). Just as in 1 Thessalonians, Paul stresses the ultimate presence of believers with Christ (in both texts the Greek word order indicates emphasis: 4:17, "and thus always *with the Lord* we will be"; 5:10, "*with him* we will live"), so also here in 2 Thessalonians the eschatological gathering or reunion of all believers is explicitly stated to be "to him" (*ep' auton*).[6] In the first letter there was grief among the Thessalonian believers concerning the full participation of deceased believers at this eschatological reunion (4:13–18) and fear whether even the living members of the church would experience salvation on that day—a grief and fear that Paul sought to correct with a message

---

5. The only other occurrence of ἐπισυναγωγή in the NT is in Heb. 10:25, to refer to the regular gathering of Christians for worship—a gathering that anticipates and symbolically rehearses the great assembling of Christ's followers at his return (so Frame 1912: 245; Ward 1973: 153; Green 2002: 302).

6. Gaventa (1998: 109) argues that this prepositional phrase (2:1b) could also be translated as "before him" in the sense that "believers gather to witness and receive justice." She prefers this rendering on the grounds that it is supported by the stress on God's retributive justice in the preceding thanksgiving section. Her argument would be stronger if the preposition were used with the genitive, since this is the construction typically found in juridical contexts (BDAG 363.3). The precise meaning of ἐπί is often difficult to determine, given its wide range of meanings (BDAG 363–67 lists eighteen different possibilities), something witnessed even in this brief letter (see 1:10; 2:4; 3:4).

of comfort (4:18 and 5:11: "Therefore comfort one another"). Likewise here in the second letter (2:1–17) there once again is a fear in the church over their participation in the end-time gathering of believers—a fear that the apostle similarly seeks to correct with a message of comfort (2:16–17, "May the God . . . who gives eternal comfort . . . comfort you").

2. The Meaning of the False Claim (2:2a)

The fourth and final element of the appeal formula involves the content of the appeal. This is typically introduced by either a ἵνα (*hina*) clause (1 Thess. 4:1; 1 Cor. 1:10) or, more commonly, an infinitive clause (Rom. 12:1; 15:30; 16:17; 2 Cor. 10:1–2; Phil. 4:2; 1 Thess. 4:10b–11). Here the content of the appeal is expressed by not one but two infinitive clauses, which are in synonymous parallelism: "that you not be too easily[7] shaken from your mind or alarmed, whether through a prophetic utterance or through a spoken word or through a written letter, supposedly through us, claiming that the day of the Lord has come" (εἰς τὸ μὴ ταχέως σαλευθῆναι ὑμᾶς ἀπὸ τοῦ νοὸς μηδὲ θροεῖσθαι, μήτε διὰ πνεύματος μήτε διὰ λόγου μήτε δι᾽ ἐπιστολῆς ὡς δι᾽ ἡμῶν, ὡς ὅτι ἐνέστηκεν ἡ ἡμέρα τοῦ κυρίου, *eis to mē tacheōs saleuthēnai hymas apo tou noos mēde throeisthai, mēte dia pneumatos mēte dia logou mēte di᾽ epistolēs hōs di᾽ hēmōn, hōs hoti enestēken hē hēmera tou kyriou*). Not until the very end of this verse does Paul spell out the cause of the crisis experienced in the Thessalonian church: the deceptively simple but false claim that "the day of the Lord has come." This claim raises three questions, all of which are difficult to answer: First, what is the precise meaning of the assertion: "The day of the Lord has come"? Second, what is the means by which this false claim has been communicated? Third, how is this false claim connected to Paul?

On the first question, the issue centers on whether the verb *enestēken*, which is in the perfect tense, conveys the *presence* of the day of the Lord (the day of the Lord has already happened) or its *imminence* (the day of the Lord is about to happen). Some have found the first notion of presence impossible on the grounds that the events surrounding the parousia, or second coming, of Christ are far too dramatic and public to be missed by the Thessalonian believers and thus argue for the translation "The day of the Lord *is at hand*" (KJV), or even better, "*is just at hand*" (ASV).[8]

The second notion of imminence, however, suffers from even more weighty objections. First, the perfect tense in general highlights a past action having significance that is present, not just imminent. Second, the exact same verb

2:2a

---

7. BDAG (992.1.β) classifies the adverb ταχέως in 2 Thess. 2:2 as having "a remonstrative sense . . . *too easily*" and cite Gal. 1:6 and 1 Tim. 5:22 as two further Pauline examples of this use. The adverb here has less the sense of "haste" than the idea of too quickly or "easily" being influenced by the false claim.

8. See esp. Stephenson 1968; also Warfield 1886: 37; Lightfoot 1904: 110; Dobschütz 1909: 267–68; Dibelius 1937: 29; A. Oepke, *TDNT* 2:544: "in process of coming"; Peerbolte 1996: 73–74; Green 2002: 305; Shogren 2012: 275–77.

ἐνίστημι (*enistēmi*) occurs five additional times in Paul's Letters, four of which are also, as here in 2 Thess. 2:2, in the perfect tense. In two of these additional occurrences the apostle uses the perfect to distinguish carefully between "things present" and "things to come" (Rom. 8:38; 1 Cor. 3:22), and the two remaining occurrences similarly refer to a present reality, not merely an imminent one (1 Cor. 7:26, "present crisis"; Gal. 1:4, "present evil age"). Third, the perfect form of *enistēmi* describes a present reality in other documents of that day, including the Letter to the Hebrews (9:9), the writings of Philo and Josephus, and the Epistle of Barnabas, as well as in the Septuagint, classical literature, and the papyri (for specific texts, see Nicholl 2004: 116nn4–7, 9). Fourth, if Paul had intended to describe the imminence of the day of the Lord and not its presence, it may be asked why he did not employ the verb ἐγγίζω (*engizō*, to draw near), with which he is clearly familiar, using it elsewhere to say about the day of the Lord: "The day is near" (Rom. 13:12; see also Phil. 2:30). This last text raises a fifth and final point: Paul *agrees* with the claim that the day of the Lord is "imminent" or "near" (Rom. 13:12; also 1 Thess. 5:2; 2 Thess. 1:5–10; 2:1) and thus would not warn the Thessalonians against anyone deceiving them with such an assertion (2 Thess. 2:3). By contrast, a claim that the day of the Lord has already come is a position that the apostle rejects and seeks to correct in the second major section of this passage, verses 3–12. These are the key reasons why the vast majority of Bible translations and commentators render the false claim that was frightening the Thessalonians as "the day of the Lord *has come*."

This conclusion, however, raises the problem of how the Thessalonians could be disturbed by a claim that was so clearly false. After all, it would have been obvious to them that none of their fellow believers who had "fallen asleep" had been resurrected (1 Thess. 4:14, 16), that "sudden destruction" had not yet fallen on their unbelieving neighbors (5:3), and that there had been no cry of command, voice of an archangel, or "trumpet call of God" to signal the glorious parousia of Christ (4:16). Why, then, would the Thessalonian church be so severely shaken about a bizarre claim that "the day of the Lord has come"?

Most commentators conclude that the Christians in Thessalonica likely did not understand the day of the Lord to be a single and instantaneous happening but rather to be a complex number of events, of which Christ's parousia was just one part (so, e.g., Frame 1912: 248; Best 1977: 279; Marshall 1983: 186; Morris 1991: 217; Wanamaker 1990: 240; Dunn 1998: 301n37; for objections, see Nicholl 2004: 117). The claim that "the day of the Lord has come," therefore, would be interpreted by the Thessalonians to mean that the series of events connected with that eschatological day have begun to unfold and that "the coming [parousia] of our Lord Jesus Christ and our gathering to him" (2 Thess. 2:1) are about to take place.

But whereas in the first letter this hope in Christ's imminent return and in believers' reunion with him was a message that comforted the Thessalonians (1 Thess. 4:18; 5:11), here in the second letter it is a message that causes them to be "too easily shaken[9] from [their] mind or alarmed"[10] (2:2a), or in idiomatic terms, to be scared out of their wits.[11] The false claim, however, did not concern the parousia, which the Thessalonians eagerly anticipated, but the day of the Lord, which the Thessalonians apparently viewed with some nervousness and apprehension. A variety of factors in 1 Thess. 5:1–11 suggest that the believers in Thessalonica were not merely curious about the timing of the day of the Lord (as the opening phrase "about times and seasons [dates]" might imply) but instead worried whether they would avoid the wrath connected with that future day and instead experience salvation. This fear stemmed from the day-of-the-Lord concept in the OT, where, though it refers to a future time when God will come both to punish the wicked and to vindicate his people, the notion of judgment is more commonly stressed than that of deliverance (e.g., Isa. 2:1–4:6; Jer. 46:10; Ezek. 30:2–3; Obad. 15; Joel 1:15; 2:1, 11, 31–32; Amos 5:18–20; Zeph. 1:14–18; Zech. 14). In 1 Thess. 5:1–11, then, Paul responds to his readers' anxiety by asserting that, though the day of the Lord will indeed involve a sudden destruction from which there will certainly be no escape (v. 3), they as believers need not fear this eschatological event because they have been elected by God "not for wrath but for the obtaining of salvation" (v. 9). Here in 2 Thess. 2:1–17, Paul comforts his readers with exactly the same line of reasoning: God has elected and called them as "firstfruits for salvation" (vv. 13–14).

Given this already existing apprehension about their fate on the day of the Lord, it is perhaps not surprising that the Thessalonian church is reacting with fear to the claim that this eschatological day of judgment has already come. Furthermore, as revealed in the classic fable of "Chicken Little"—in which an acorn falls on Henny-Penny's head, and she runs around, yelling, "The sky is falling! The sky is falling!" (cited in this context by Gaventa 1998: 123)—fear is often as irrational as it is contagious. Thus, even though the claim "the day of the Lord has come" may have seemed obviously false, it nevertheless has caused the young church of Thessalonica to be greatly alarmed, fearful of

---

9. In 2:2a the verb σαλεύω, which occurs fifteen times in the NT (Matt. 11:7; 24:29; Mark 13:25; Luke 6:38, 48; 7:24; 21:26; Acts 2:25; 4:31; 16:26; 17:13; Heb. 12:26, 27 [2x]) but only here in Paul's Letters, can have the figurative meaning of "to disturb inwardly, *disturb, shake*" (BDAG 911.2).

10. The verb θροέω, like that of the preceding infinitive in 2:2a, to which it is closely joined by one article controlling both infinitives, also occurs only here in Paul's Letters. The verb appears infrequently in the rest of the NT (Matt. 24:6; Mark 13:7; Luke 24:37 v.l.), where it also is used in an eschatological context. The change from the aorist σαλευθῆναι to the present θροεῖσθαι may reflect a slight shift in emphasis on the ongoing or continuous nature of the readers' fear or alarm.

11. Bruce (1982: 161, 163) renders the Greek (2:2a) to be "shaken out of your wits"; Hendriksen (1955: 168) and Giblin (1967: 244) use the colloquial expression "lost their head." See also Nicholl (2004: 126–32), whose careful study of the meaning of the two infinitives leads to the following conclusion: "We conclude that θροέομαι and σαλεύω ἀπὸ τοῦ νοός should be interpreted as indicating that the false claim was frightening and violently shook those who accepted it. Rather than being enthused and positively excited, they were disorientated and terrified, needing stabilizing and reassurance" (131).

whether they will avoid the wrath connected with that day of judgment and instead experience salvation.

3. The Source of the False Claim (2:2b)

2:2b   The second difficult question of verse 2 involves the source of the false claim about the day of the Lord (see esp. the detailed analysis of Fee 1994b). In other words, what is the precise meaning of the three prepositional phrases "through the Spirit, through a word, through a letter"? That the apostle lists three options suggests that he does not know for certain the source of the false claim. Nevertheless, there is some evidence that he suspects the guilty member of the triad to be the first one mentioned: the Spirit, or, as *pneuma* is better rendered here, "spiritual/prophetic utterance" (so most commentators: e.g., Frame 1912: 246; Best 1977: 279; Bruce 1982: 163; Wanamaker 1990: 239; Richard 1995: 325; Witherington 2006: 213) or simply "prophecy" (so NCV, NIV). Since Paul is familiar with the noun "prophecy" (προφητεία, *prophēteia*; the noun occurs nine times in his writings), one may wonder why he here employs the noun "Spirit" (*pneuma*) instead. Yet in the previous letter to the Thessalonians, the apostle places the word "Spirit" (*pneuma*) in a parallel relationship with "prophecy" (*prophēteia*; 1 Thess. 5:20–21). Furthermore, elsewhere Paul uses "Spirit" (*pneuma*) as a "shorthand" (Green 2002: 303) to refer to prophetic utterances given through the work of the Holy Spirit (1 Cor. 2:10, 13; 12:10; see also 1 John 4:1–3).

In the rest of the passage, the apostle suspects a spirit-inspired prophecy to be the likely source of the false claim about the day of the Lord, as suggested by his affirmation of the remaining two members of the triad—"a word" and "a letter"—and his notable nonmention of the first member, "a prophecy." In order to correct the false claim that the day of the Lord has come, Paul twice affirms "a word," that is, the oral message (nonecstatic speech in distinction from Spirit-inspired prophecy and the written letter) that made up his former teaching to the Thessalonians. First, in verse 5 he asks rhetorically about the things he is mentioning in the surrounding verses: "You remember, don't you, that, when I was still with you, I was repeatedly saying these things to you?" Second, in verse 15 he again affirms his former "word" to them—a word that proves the falsehood of the claim that the day of the Lord has come—by commanding the Thessalonians to hold fast to the traditions they were taught "through a word [*dia logou*]." This prepositional phrase in verse 15 clearly looks back to the identical prepositional phrase in verse 2. The third member of the triad is also affirmed in verse 15 with the additional prepositional phrase "through a letter [*di' epistolēs*]"—also a clear allusion back to the identical prepositional phrase in verse 2. In verse 15 the omission of the first member of the triad, "through a prophecy," is significant. As Fee (1994a: 75) observes: "What is conspicuously missing in this instance, of course, is the first member of the former triad, 'through the Spirit'—because in this view that is what Paul himself most likely believed to be the ultimate source of his difficulty." This conclusion is further supported by the apostle's command in the previous letter, where Paul already seems aware of the danger of the Thessalonian church being misled by a false prophecy and so exhorts them not naively to accept every spiritual utterance but instead to "test all things," then "hold fast to the good," and "hold yourselves away from every kind of evil prophecy" (1 Thess. 5:21–22).

4. The Connection of the False Claim to Paul (2:2c)

The third difficult question of verse 2 is how the false claim about the day of the Lord is connected to Paul. The answer depends on the precise meaning of yet another brief prepositional phrase: "supposedly[12] through us" (hōs di' hēmōn). Several commentators connect this phrase only with the immediately preceding member of the triad, with the result that Paul is referring to a forged letter claiming the apostle as its sender or writer (so, e.g., BDF §425.4; BDAG 1105.3.c; Bruce 1982: 164; Richard 1995: 325; Green 2002: 304; Witherington 2006: 214; Furnish 2007: 154). Advocates of this position typically appeal for support to 3:17, where Paul's reference to writing the closing greeting in his own hand as a distinguishing sign of all his letters is interpreted as a response to a forged letter supposedly from Paul, just like the situation claimed to be in view here in 2:2. But this interpretation fails in three ways. First, the appeal to 3:17 for support is unconvincing since the function of this autograph lies not with authenticating 2 Thessalonians as genuinely Pauline in contrast to a pseudonymous letter, but rather with underscoring Paul's authority in this letter and the resulting need for the "rebellious idlers" (3:6–15) to obey its injunctions (see Weima 1994a: 126–27, 189; also the comments on 3:17). Second, this interpretation suffers from the fact that later in this passage Paul commands the Thessalonian church to hold fast to what he has previously taught them "through our letter" (2:15), an unlikely exhortation if Paul fears that their eschatological error was communicated by means of a letter forged in his name. Third, Paul's choice of the preposition *dia*, which expresses instrumentality ("by, through"), rather than *apo*, which expresses source ("from")—two prepositions that he elsewhere carefully distinguishes (see Gal. 1:1)—strongly suggests that the apostle is not referring to a counterfeit letter claiming to come "from us" but rather to a genuine Pauline letter that has been misinterpreted in such a way that a false claim about the day of the Lord has been mediated "through us," as though with the support of Paul and his cosenders (see Dobschütz 1909: 266; Giblin 1967: 149n3; esp. Fee 1994a: 73; 1994b: 205–6).

In light of these observations, the prepositional phrase "supposedly through us" more likely refers to all three members of the preceding triad,

2:2c

---

12. The adverb ὡς can function as a "marker introducing the perspective from which a person, thing or activity is viewed" (BDAG 1104.3). Here in 2:2 it occurs before the prepositional phrase to express "what is objectively false or erroneous" (BDAG 1105.3.b): "supposedly, allegedly, purporting to be."

a position that the majority of commentators adopt. The use of the preposition *dia* in these three elements is also significant. Paul's concern is not that the false claim about the day of the Lord by means of a prophetic utterance or a spoken word or a written letter has originated with him (*"from* us"), but rather that one of these three means—he does not know for certain which one but suspects it is a prophetic utterance—has been attributed to him (*"through* us"). To cite Fee (1994b: 206) once again: "[Paul] is not so much concerned with the form in which the error came to them, but with the fact that the content of the error itself has been attributed to him in some way." Whether someone claimed, "The *Spirit* has revealed to me that what Paul really meant in his preaching or his letter is this," or "Paul must mean this about the day of the Lord because I heard the *word* from his own lips during his ministry in our city," or "Paul's *letter* may not say this explicitly but it clearly implies that this is the truth about the day of the Lord"—all three possible scenarios are ultimately less important to the apostle than the fact that the false claim that the day of the Lord has come is being attributed to him and his authority. This is why he will begin the next unit (vv. 3–12) with the exhortation "Let no one deceive you *in any way.*" It is crucial that the Thessalonian believers do not allow anyone, regardless of the means (whether "through a prophetic utterance or through a spoken word or through a written letter" or through anything else), to appeal to Paul's authority ("supposedly through us") such that they are deceived into thinking that the day of the Lord has come.

B. Correction: Events That Must Precede the Day of the Lord (2:3–12)

Paul corrects the false claim by reminding them of what he previously taught them (v. 5; see also v. 15) and what they therefore already know (v. 6): the day of the Lord cannot come until certain clearly defined events occur. That the apostle in his correction of the false claim is not really saying anything new to the Thessalonians is also indicated by his comment in the first letter that he has no real need to write to them about the day of the Lord, since they already "accurately know" about this eschatological day (1 Thess. 5:1–2) and this knowledge will result in that day not surprising them like a thief (5:4). This knowledge that the Thessalonians already have about the coming apostasy and man of lawlessness is also revealed in the imperfect tense of the verb ἔλεγον (*elegon*) in verse 5 of our passage, which highlights the customary or repeated nature of the action: "I was *repeatedly* saying these things to you." Paul obviously had devoted more than one sermon to this eschatological subject during his mission-founding ministry in Thessalonica. Furthermore, the apostle introduces the question of verse 5 with the negative οὐ (*ou*), which changes it from an ambiguous question into a rhetorical one that expects a positive answer (BDF §427.2): "You remember, don't you, that when I was with you, I was telling you these things?"

The modern reader of 2 Thess. 2, therefore, is walking into the middle of a conversation between Paul and the Thessalonian believers, a dialogue with a rather extensive history. If we, then, struggle at times to understand what the apostle is talking about, we ought not to conclude that Paul is engaged in poor reasoning or that our exegetical abilities are embarrassingly weak. The difficulties in interpretation stem from the simple but important fact that the Thessalonian believers' already existing knowledge about the eschatological events leading up to the day of the Lord allow Paul to speak about these things in an elliptical manner (Shogren 2012: 274: "Paul is speaking in a kind of shorthand") that they could easily understand but we cannot.

A further reason why Paul's correction in verses 3–12 is difficult for contemporary readers to grasp stems from the fact that he does not present events in chronological order but alternates a future-present pattern (so Marshall 1983: 185; see also Malherbe 2000: 414). The apostle begins in verses 3–4 with the future, describing what has to happen "first" (v. 3), before the day of the Lord comes: the apostasy and the man of lawlessness. Paul interrupts his description of these future events with a parenthetical question in verse 5 by which he reminds the Thessalonians that they know these things from his previous preaching ministry among them. Then in verses 6–7 the apostle proceeds to talk about the present time (note the temporal adverbs "now" [vv. 6, 7] and "already" [v. 7]), in which lawlessness is already at work, but there is both a restraining thing and a restraining person who prevents the human embodiment and climax of that lawlessness, the man of lawlessness, from coming on the scene. Verses 8–10 move ahead again in time to the future (note the opening adverb "then" [v. 8]) when there will occur two parousias: first, the coming of the man of lawlessness; second, the coming of the Lord Jesus Christ. Finally, in verses 11–12 Paul moves back to the present, describing the judgment of unbelievers. This alternating temporal shift between the future and the present suggests that Paul is not interested in spelling out a detailed "timetable of apocalyptic events" (so wrongly Hughes 1989: 58)—something that many modern "prophecy experts" are very much interested in discovering in this text—but rather in proving to the Thessalonians that the claim about the day of the Lord being present cannot be true.[13]

1. Future: The Apostasy and the Man of Lawlessness (2:3–5)

Paul transitions to the second unit, which seeks to correct the false claim about the day of the Lord by issuing a command that not only summarizes the point of the preceding verse but also broadens that point: "Do not let

13. McKinnish Bridges (2008: 235) rightly notes: "The lack of attention to chronological presentation and the more emotional presentation of material, without the sustained linguistic attention to Greek syntax, create the impression that the events described in vv. 3–12 are universal descriptions of the atmosphere and quality of life that occurs before the final day of the Lord. In other words, I cannot see how anyone could develop a graph or timetable for the Lord's return from these words. They do not appear to ask for such an interpretation."

anyone deceive you in any way" (μή τις ὑμᾶς ἐξαπατήσῃ κατὰ μηδένα τρόπον, *mē tis hymas exapatēsē kata mēdena tropon*). This exhortation both recapitulates the preceding reference to the three means by which the false claim has been communicated ("through a prophetic utterance or through a spoken word or through a written letter") but also expands it to include any other possible means ("in any way") and an appeal to any other possible authority beyond that of just Paul ("anyone"). This broadening of the scope of the command puts greater pressure on the Thessalonian church to comply with the apostle's exhortation, for they will not be able to excuse their deception about the day of the Lord by appealing to *any* kind of means of communication or *any* source of authority.

This transitional command that opens the second unit is not only broadened but also intensified in a couple of ways. First, it is the only direct command in 2:1–17 other than the concluding double imperatives of verse 15. Although here Paul employs the rarer third-person subjunctive (elsewhere in his letters only 1 Cor. 16:11; 2 Cor. 11:16), which is less direct than the second-person imperative, the command is nevertheless strong, especially given the overall consolatory function at work in the passage. The apostle's use of a strong prohibition is certainly justified in light of the significantly harmful effect that the false claim was having on the church. There may also be present here, however, a hint of rebuke that stems from Paul's disappointment with the Thessalonian believers, given his previous teaching to them about these eschatological matters and their expected knowledge of such things (v. 5). Second, the choice of the word "deceive," here the compound verb *exapataō* (used in NT writings only by Paul: Rom. 7:11; 16:18; 1 Cor. 3:18; 2 Cor. 11:3; 1 Tim. 2:14), giving it slightly greater emphasis than the simple form *apataō* (Eph. 5:6; 1 Tim. 2:14; James 1:26), adds an aspect that may go beyond what was mentioned in the preceding verse. Whereas verse 2 indicates that the false claim about the day of the Lord might be due to a naive or genuine misunderstanding about a communication attributed to Paul, here the apostle's verb selection raises the possibility of a conscious or deliberate deception. The lack of reference to any specific person or group, however, makes it unlikely that Paul has in view individuals outside the church who are falsifying the apostle's teaching and deliberately deceiving the Thessalonian church. The advocates of the false claim about the day of the Lord may have been well-meaning but misguided members of the congregation (D. Martin 1995: 231).

The pointed command against deception is followed by the conjunction ὅτι (*hoti*), which here functions as a "marker of causality, *because, since*" (BDAG 732.4). This marker plays an important role in showing that the remainder of not just the sentence in verses 3b–4 but also the rest of the second unit (vv. 3–12) is intended to give the reason *why* the claim of verse 2 is false. The day of the Lord cannot have come "because" certain specific events must take place "first." Two of these prerequisite events—the coming of "the apostasy" and the appearance of "the man of lawlessness"—are described in the remainder of the sentence by way of a conditional clause that is grammatically incomplete:

the protasis ("if") half is present, but the apodosis (concluding, "then") half is missing.[14] It appears as if Paul's mention of the man of lawlessness (v. 3b) has prompted him to launch into an extended description of this figure (v. 4) that goes on for so long that either (1) the apostle loses track of the structure of the sentence (something that happens with some frequency to Paul, especially when he is animated or emotional about something: see, e.g., 1 Thess. 2:11–12, 19; 2 Thess. 2:7; Rom. 4:16; 5:12; 1 Cor. 1:31; 2 Cor. 8:13; Gal. 1:20; 2:4) or, more likely, (2) he interrupts the structure of the conditional clause with a parenthetical question (v. 5) to remind the readers that he has already spoken to them about the apostasy and this rebellious figure on several occasions, so they should be well informed about these end-time events.

Whatever the reason for its absence, however, the grammatical problem of the missing or implied apodosis is only minor since the omitted words are easily reconstructed from the context, from the false claim given at the end of the immediately preceding verse.[15] In fact, virtually all translations insert the words "it will not be/happen" or, more commonly, "that day will not come." Paul likely intended this implied apodosis to come at the *end* of the lengthy protasis: "Unless [lit., "if not"; see BDAG 267.c.β] the apostasy comes first and the man of lawlessness is revealed, the son of destruction, the one who . . . , *that day will not come.*" Modern translations, however, place the implied apodosis *before* the lengthy protasis so that the sentence reads smoother and the contemporary reader does not lose track of the logical link between the two halves of this conditional clause: "*that day will not come*, unless the apostasy comes first and the man of lawlessness is revealed. . . ."

14. Many commentators refer to this incomplete conditional clause as an "anacoluthon," a grammatical construction that does not logically follow (from the Greek verb ἀκολουθέω with an alpha privative prefix). The construction here in 2:3, however, is not so much *illogical* (the sense of the sentence is logical and clear enough, as evidenced by the fact that Greek scribes did not feel the need to add something here and so "correct" the text) as it is *incomplete*, and so it would be better to refer to this as an "ellipsis" (Lightfoot 1893: 110). The presence of this ellipsis makes the claim about 2 Thessalonians' pseudonymous character highly unlikely. As Wanamaker (1990: 244) observes: "A self-conscious literary forger would almost certainly have made his point with great care rather than allowing an anacoluthon with its inherent ambiguity to occur precisely at a key point in his argument."

15. Giblin (1967: 115–39) proposes that the missing apodosis (in v. 3) be supplied not from the preceding context but from the following one such that the omitted clause should be something like "the judgment of God will not have been executed against the powers of deception, removing them once and for all" or "the Lord will not have come in judgment to end definitively the deception that is the work of Satan" (135). The point that Giblin wants to make is that Paul is not discussing primarily the temporal aspects of the parousia but rather its qualitative aspects. In other words, the apostle's concern lies not with the chronological sequence of events but the conditions necessary for the manifestation of God's just judgment and vindication. Two things, however, make Giblin's proposal, as suggestive as it may be, unlikely. First, the context created by the false claim of 2:2 requires an answer that includes a strong temporal element, a point strengthened by the occurrence of several temporal adverbs in the following verses. Second, and more important, Giblin's interpretation requires the reader to supply the missing apodosis with something that Paul has not yet written rather than with something that has just been stated in the preceding verse (Marshall 1983: 188).

Paul's correction of the crisis that has emerged in the Thessalonian church from the false claim that the day of the Lord has come is both simple and clear: this claim is obviously wrong because that day cannot take place until two related events occur: "the apostasy comes first and the man of lawlessness is revealed" (ἔλθῃ ἡ ἀποστασία πρῶτον καὶ ἀποκαλυφθῇ ὁ ἄνθρωπος τῆς ἀνομίας, *elthē hē apostasia prōton kai apokalyphthē ho anthrōpos tēs anomias*). There is some confusion about the precise relationship of these two events: are they sequential or simultaneous? Placing the adverb "first" after the noun "apostasy" and before the reference to the man of lawlessness, and presenting two parallel clauses with a separate verb for each event—these features have convinced some of the former option: the apostasy comes first, and then after this, the man of lawlessness is revealed (so Ellicott 1864: 109; Findlay 1891: 167; Milligan 1908: 98; Witherington 2006: 216). However, Paul does not include the expected "then" (ἔπειτα, *epeita*: so 1 Cor. 15:46; 1 Thess. 4:16) or "second" (δεύτερον, *deuteron*: so 1 Cor. 12:28) before the second event, and the character and actions of "the man of lawlessness" described later in the sentence are in keeping with the idea of apostasy. These features have led the vast majority of commentators to adopt the latter option: the coming of the apostasy and the appearance of the man of lawlessness are two simultaneous events that ought not to be distinguished sharply from each other. These grounds for the latter option, though suggestive, are nevertheless not weighty, since it is always dangerous to draw too much from an "argument from silence" (what Paul did not say) as well as the fact that the apostle occasionally begins with a reference to the adverb "first" without continuing the series with a "next" or "second" (see Rom. 1:8; 3:2; 1 Cor. 11:18). The reality that Paul is not clear about the precise relationship of the two events (the grammar is ultimately ambiguous: Lightfoot 1904: 111; Frame 1912: 252; Neil 1950: 160) confirms the point made above: the apostle is less concerned in verses 3–12 with laying out a specific timetable for these eschatological happenings than with correcting the false claim about the day of the Lord and thereby comforting his Thessalonian readers. Whatever the precise relationship between the coming of the apostasy and the manifestation of the man of lawlessness, the church in Thessalonica knows that these two events must clearly occur "first," that is, before the day of the Lord can come.

a. The Apostasy (2:3a)

2:3a One of the future events that must precede the coming of the day of the Lord is the "apostasy" (*apostasia*).[16] Three facts indicate that the Thessalonian

16. A few exegetes (English 1954: 67–71; Wuest 1957: 63–67; House 1995), appealing to the use of the cognate verb ἀφίστημι in Classical Greek, where it has the meaning "stand away from, depart," take the noun ἀποστασία (in 2:3) to mean "departure" and thus see here a reference to the sudden departure or "rapture" of believers immediately prior to the seven-year period of tribulation. There are strong reasons, however, why this interpretation is implausible (see Gundry 1973: 113–18; Beale 2003: 204–5). First, it is generally a mistake to have a cognate verb determine the meaning of a given noun, since a noun often acquires a special meaning distinct from the

readers are familiar with this future event: (1) Paul can simply refer to the apostasy without providing any explanatory comments about what this event involves. (2) Paul uses the definite article to describe this event: "*the* apostasy," a specific and defined event about which the readers know (BDAG 686.2.a: the "individualizing use" of the article in which "it focuses attention on a single thing or single concept, as already known"). (3) Paul explicitly states in 2:5 that he has discussed this and other end-time events with them. But while those in Thessalonica know well of what the apostle is speaking, the modern reader does not and so faces difficult questions about the character of this apostasy (is it political or religious?) and its participants (does it involve Jews, Christians, or non-Christians?). Answers to these questions are not made easier by the fact that the noun occurs nowhere else in Paul's writings (the verbal form, *aphistēmi*, meaning "to distance oneself from some person or thing," occurs three times: 2 Cor. 12:8; 1 Tim. 4:1; 2 Tim. 2:19) and is rare elsewhere in the NT (only Acts 21:21, where Jewish Christian leaders report to Paul that he has been accused of being responsible for Jews' "abandonment" of Moses).

A political or religious apostasy? The noun *apostasia* in secular Greek writings refers to political or military "rebellion" (see H. Schlier, *TDNT* 1:513), and it also has this meaning in at least one LXX text (1 Esd. 2:21 [2:27 NRSV]). In the Greek version of the OT, however, the noun occurs more often with a religious sense of "apostasy" from God (Josh. 22:22; 2 Chron. 29:19; 33:19; Jer. 2:19). The same term is used to describe the forsaking of the law by certain Jews at the time of the Maccabean revolt (1 Macc. 2:15). A much greater number of Jewish writings from the Second Temple period also speak of people as abandoning God and his law, but that apostasy is dated in the future, shortly before the appearance of the Messiah (Jub. 23.14–21; 2 Esd. [4 Ezra] 5:1–12; 14:16–18; 1 En. 91.3–10; 93.8–10; 2 Bar. 41.3; 42.4; 1QpHab 1.5, 12–13; 2.1–8; see also Str-B 3:637). Writings from the rest of the NT similarly express a general belief that the end times will be marked by opposition to God, an increase of immorality and wickedness, and the activity of false prophets and religious leaders who seek to direct the elect away from God (1 Tim. 4:1; 2 Tim. 3:1–9; Matt. 24:11–24; Mark 13:3–23; 2 Pet. 3:3–4; Jude 17–18).

In light of this background, "the apostasy" mentioned by Paul here in 2:3 likely refers to a rebellion against God, which is primarily religious in nature. It is the failure to receive the gospel of truth, which leads to salvation (v. 10), instead accepting a false gospel (v. 11), which leads to the worship of a pseudo-god (v. 4) and results in condemnation (v. 12). But while the apostasy will be primarily religious in nature, one should not too quickly rule out the possibility that it also has a political aspect involving civil rebellion. Any disobedience against God and his commands would naturally spill over to include a revolt

---

verbal root from which it is derived. Second, the noun ἀποστασία in the LXX, intertestamental literature, and NT has the special sense of religious "apostasy" or political and military "rebellion" and never the nuance of "departure." Third, it is highly unlikely that ἀποστασία could have the positive sense of referring to the "departure" of Christians from earth to heaven prior to the tribulation since in 2:3 this noun is paired with the revelation of the man of lawlessness.

against the general laws and morals of society as a whole. Furthermore, since public order is maintained by governing agencies whose authority has been established by God (Rom. 13:1–2), any rebellion against these institutions and their laws would involve a rebellion against God (Bruce 1982: 167). Finally, in analyzing the ancient world, there is a danger in distinguishing too sharply between the religious and political realms.

An apostasy by Jews, Christians, or non-Christians? Closely connected with the issue over the apostasy's character is the issue of its participants. A few have seen here a future and decisive rejection of the gospel by Jews (Best 1977: 282–84; see also Kennedy 1904: 218; Davies 1977–78: 8). This view is highly unlikely given that such a significant rejection had already happened in the past, in the Jewish rejection of Christ and involvement in his death—an event that Paul mentions in his previous letter (1 Thess. 2:15–16). In addition to this, the apostle elsewhere describes the Jewish rejection of the gospel not in terms of "apostasy" but of misplaced "zeal" (Rom. 10:2). Another possibility is that the apostasy involves Christians and the community of faith. Support for this interpretation lies in the following three observations: First, apostasy by definition seems to presuppose an original relationship to God. Second, the immediate context of the false claim about the day of the Lord involves deception *within* the Thessalonian church. Third, Paul elsewhere uses the verbal form of the noun "apostasy" to refer to the sobering reality that "in later times some will depart from the faith" (1 Tim. 4:1; see also 2 Tim. 3:1–9).

Nevertheless, there is nothing here or in the apostle's other letters suggesting that he expected a large-scale Christian defection. Quite the opposite: throughout both his letters to the Thessalonian church, Paul expresses the great confidence he has in their ability to endure persecution and persevere in the faith to the end (1 Thess. 1:2–3, 6; 2:14; 3:6–8, 13; 5:4, 9; 2 Thess. 1:3–4, 10, 11–12; 2:13–14). Also, the references in the subsequent verses to "those on the way to destruction because they did not accept the love of the truth so that they might be saved" (v. 10) and "all who have not believed the truth but delighted in wickedness" (v. 12) surely do not refer to the Christians in Thessalonica, but to those outside the community of faith. Finally, if we are correct above in identifying the apostasy as involving a rebellion against God that involves not just the religious realm but the political and moral spheres as well, then this too suggests the participation of non-Christians. To the objection that such people do not have an original relationship to God such that they can be guilty of rebelling against him, Paul might well respond by asserting that such an original relationship to God does actually exist via God's revelation of himself in creation such that all humanity is now without excuse (Rom. 1:18–32). It may be best, therefore, to see in the term *apostasia* more generally "the rebellion of the creature against the Creator" (Morris 1991: 219n18) and recognize the word as referring to the apostasy of humankind as a whole, including those in the church who are outwardly associated with the people of God but who have not inwardly committed themselves to the

Christian faith such that they can withstand the "deceptive signs and wonders" (v. 9) of the man of lawlessness.

b. The Man of Lawlessness (2:3b–4)

The second of the future events that must precede the coming of the day of the Lord is the manifestation of one who apparently emerges out of the apostasy to become its leader, the one in whom the rebellion against God reaches its climax, "the man of lawlessness" (*ho anthrōpos tēs anomias*). This figure is not Satan himself, as verse 9 makes clear, but is the servant of Satan, or in colloquial terms, "Satan's superman." He is typically identified with the figure whom John calls "the antichrist" (1 John 2:18, 22; 4:3; 2 John 7) as well as the unnamed individuals ("many") and "false christs" referred to by Jesus, who will appear at the end of time (Matt. 24:5, 23–24; Mark 13:21–22; Luke 21:8). Yet whereas John is referring to individuals within the church of his day who are denying that Christ has come in the flesh, Paul has in view an eschatological individual who will appear at the end of time yet prior to the day of the Lord. There is, however, no fundamental conflict between these two biblical writers, since John leaves room for the coming of a future, personal antichrist (1 John 2:18), and Paul recognizes that the power of lawlessness is already at work in the present time (2 Thess. 2:7).

2:3b

The phrase "man of lawlessness" involves a Semitic idiom in which a generic personal noun ("son," "man," "master," et al.) followed by an adjectival genitive designates the person's essential condition or quality (BDF §162). Paul therefore depicts this person as one who is the very personification of lawlessness. This is why the apostle later in the passage identifies this person with the abbreviated phrase "the lawless one" (v. 8). The key word in the first title, *anomia*, consists of the alpha privative and the noun "law" so that it literally means "without the law," that is, someone who acts as if there is no law of God. Paul elsewhere uses this term as a synonym for "sin" (ἁμαρτία, *harmatia*: Rom. 4:7; so also 1 John 3:4 and Heb. 10:17; this pairing of "lawlessness" and "sin" stems from the LXX: Pss. 30:19; 50:4; 58:3; 102:10 [Eng.: 31:18; 51:2; 59:2; 103:10]) and "immorality" (ἀκαθαρσία, *akatharsia*: Rom. 6:19), as a parallel with spiritual "darkness" (σκότος, *skotos*: 2 Cor. 6:14), and as something from which humans need to be "redeemed" (λυτρόομαι, *lytroomai*: Titus 2:14). The lawlessness referred to here is not so much the rejection of the Mosaic law—an antinomianism or libertine lifestyle of the type that Paul dealt with in Corinth—but, in light of the apostle's use of this term elsewhere (see texts cited above), involves more broadly rebellion against God and his will (Marshall 1983: 189; Malherbe 2000: 419). The title "man of lawlessness," therefore, reveals this superman of Satan to be the archopponent of God, who actively rebels against his divine will.

Although Paul's description of the man of lawlessness has similarities with a number of OT texts, the closest parallels are found in the part of Daniel's prophecy that finds its initial fulfillment in the desecration of the Jerusalem temple by Antiochus IV, who set up an altar to the pagan god Zeus in the holy of holies (Vos [1930: 111] comments: "That Paul in 2 Thess. ii is dependent on Daniel hardly requires pointing out"; see also Ridderbos 1975: 512; Beale 2003: 206–7). This desecration of the temple as prophesied in Daniel was an event kept alive in Jewish and early Christian thinking through various rulers who also were guilty of violating the sanctity of the Jerusalem sanctuary: in addition to the initial defilement by Antiochus IV, there was also the Roman general Pompey, who entered the holy of holies in 63 BC (Josephus, *Ant.* 14.69–76), and the emperor Caligula, who considered himself to be a god and in AD 40 tried to have his statue erected in the Jerusalem temple (Philo, *Embassy* 203–346; Josephus, *Ant.* 18.261–309). Paul therefore is employing a familiar theme to portray the supremely evil character of the coming lawless one and his usurpation of God's place in the world.

The title "man of lawlessness" (for the alternate reading "man of sin," see additional notes) may be influenced by Dan. 12:10, which describes the apostasy at the end of time when "the lawless ones will do lawlessness, and all the lawless ones will not understand."[17] The designation "the lawless one"—not the exact title "man of lawlessness" but the abbreviated form used later, in verse 8—occurs in Pss. Sol. 17.11, where it describes how the "lawless one laid waste our land, . . . massacred young and old and children, . . . expelled them [Jewish leading citizens] to the west, . . . and he did in Jerusalem all the things that Gentiles do for their gods in their cities." These words may well refer to the infamous act of 63 BC, when the Roman general Pompey conquered the region of Palestine and entered the holy of holies in the Jerusalem temple. Since Paul will go on in the subsequent verse to describe how the man of lawlessness will take his seat in the temple and show himself to be god, "it is quite possible that Paul has in view some future pagan ruler who will recapitulate the sins of Antiochus Epiphanes, Pompey, and Caligula" (Witherington 2006: 218; see also Wanamaker 1990: 245; Malherbe 2000: 419).

The phrase "the son of destruction" (ὁ υἱὸς τῆς ἀπωλείας, *ho huios tēs apōleias*), like the preceding phrase "the man of lawlessness" with which it is in a parallel or appositional relationship, also involves a Semitic idiom where a generic personal noun (here "son") followed by an adjectival genitive (here "of destruction") designates the person's essential condition or quality (BDF §162). The key word in this second title, *apōleia*, can have either a transitive sense ("the destruction that one causes": Matt. 26:8; Mark 14:4) or an intransitive sense ("the destruction that one experiences": Rom. 9:22; Phil. 1:28; 3:19; 1 Tim. 6:9; Matt. 7:13; John 17:12; Acts 8:20; 25:16 v.l.; Heb. 10:39; 2 Pet. 2:1; 3:7, 16; Rev. 17:8, 11; BDAG 127). Evidence for the first option lies in the two clauses that surround this one, which both have a transitive sense: the man of

---

17. Other less likely OT parallels to 2:2 include Ps. 89:22 (88:23 LXX) ("The enemy shall have no advantage against him, and the son of lawlessness shall not hurt him") and Isa. 57:3–4 ("But as for you, come here, you sons of lawlessness. . . . Are you not children of destruction, a lawless seed?").

lawlessness is one who aggressively rebels against God and his will and who also actively "opposes and exalts himself above every being called god or every object of worship." Thus it is possible that the second title refers to the destruction that this eschatological figure will cause (Wanamaker 1990: 245: "The term 'son of destruction' probably denotes his role as an agent of destruction for Satan"). Paul's use of the term *apōleia* elsewhere, however, always has the intransitive sense, and this is also by far its more common sense in other NT writings (see the texts cited above). Furthermore, Paul and other NT writers regularly use this term in eschatological contexts, like the one here in verse 3, to refer to the eternal destruction that the wicked will receive as punishment.

These observations provide compelling reasons for concluding that the second title refers to the lawless one's ultimate destiny: he is the one "doomed to destruction" (NIV; also the GNT: "destined to hell"). As such, this title foreshadows the future destruction not just of this end-time enemy described in verse 8 ("whom the Lord Jesus will slay with the breath of his mouth and will destroy by the sudden appearance of his coming") but also of his deceived followers mentioned in verse 10 ("those on the way to destruction" employs the verbal root [ἀπόλλυμι, *apollymi*] from which the noun "destruction" is derived). The second title, therefore, also supports the consolatory function at work in the passage as a whole: the Thessalonian believers are comforted in the assurance that this eschatological enemy of God, however powerful and deceptive he may be (v. 9), will be ultimately destroyed.

The rebellious nature of the man of lawlessness is further highlighted by means of a lengthy participial clause that is in apposition to the two previous brief noun clauses: in addition to being "the man of lawlessness, the son of destruction," this eschatological enemy is also "the one who opposes and exalts himself over every being called god or every object of worship" (ὁ ἀντικείμενος καὶ ὑπεραιρόμενος ἐπὶ πάντα λεγόμενον θεὸν ἢ σέβασμα, *ho antikeimenos kai hyperairomenos epi panta legomeonon theon ē sebasma*). In addition to the content of Paul's words here, the mere presence of this verse is significant, since as of this point the apostle has said enough already to prove that the claim "The day of the Lord has come" is false. But instead of ending here after reminding his readers of the two events that must precede that day, Paul goes on to spell out at greater length the God-opposing and God-supplanting character of the man of lawlessness. As Vos (1930: 95) proposed:

2:4

> But for correcting that [the false claim of v. 2] the simplest reference to a well-established eschatological program would have been sufficient. When instead of this the Apostle launches out into a somewhat detailed exposition of the entire subject, it becomes difficult to escape from the impression that Paul took a certain personal delight in drawing the figure at full length.

The word "delight" may not be entirely justified in light of the serious crisis that has fallen on the Thessalonian church concerning the false claim about the day of the Lord. Nevertheless, Paul was certainly animated about this matter, so much so that he never completes the conditional clause that he has begun but instead goes on at some length to spell out the rebellious character of this eschatological enemy doomed to destruction.

The two participles in this clause are linked together by one article, and both govern the same prepositional phrase ("every being called god or every object of worship"). Consequently, rather than viewing the participles as substantives which provide two more titles of the end-time adversary ("the Opposer" and "the Self-Exalter": so Lightfoot 1904: 112; Hamann 1953: 422), it is better to treat them together as providing further clarification about the character of the lawless one. The first participle, *antikeimenos*, involves a verbal root used elsewhere by Paul to describe enemies "opposed" to his ministry (1 Cor. 16:9); the desires of the flesh, which are "opposed" to the desires of the Spirit (Gal. 5:17); the "opponents" who are intimidating the Philippian believers (Phil. 1:28); "lawless" (*anomoi*) and other ungodly sinners who are "opposed" to sound doctrine (1 Tim. 1:9–10); and also "*the* opposer," that is, Satan (1 Tim. 5:14; also 1 Clem. 15.1; Mart. Pol. 17.1). Its use here, therefore, reinforces the aspect of rebelliousness expressed in the first title: the man of lawlessness is one who opposes not just God but, as the following prepositional phrase indicates, every god or object of human worship. That this participle (and the second one too) occurs in the present tense highlights the ongoing nature of his opposing or rebellious activity: "It is no passing phase" (Morris 1991: 222).

The second participle, *hyperairomenos*, advances the picture of arrogance and impiety that is emerging for the man of lawlessness. Not content with opposing God, he goes even further and "exalts himself" in an attempt to replace God as the object of human devotion. This compound word, consisting of the preposition *hyper* (above) and the verb *airō* (to raise), thus means "to have an undue sense of one's self-importance, *rise up, exalt oneself, be elated*" (BDAG 1031). It occurs only one other place in the NT: Paul states that God sent him his "thorn in the flesh" to prevent the apostle from becoming too elated or proud of himself (2 Cor. 12:7 [2x]). The selfish ambitions of the man of lawlessness, however, are not hindered in any way as he instead seeks to build himself up to such a high level that he supplants even God himself.

This opposing and self-exalting activity will be directed against "every being called god or every object of worship." The prepositional phrase *epi panta legomeonon theon* can be taken in two slightly different ways: it refers either to beings that are believed to be gods but in reality are not—a skepticism captured nicely by the English expression "*so-called* gods" (so most translations)—or more comprehensively to both false gods and the real God alike. The former, restricted meaning gains support from Paul's use of the same present-passive participle *legomenos* in 1 Cor. 8:5–6 ("although there may be so-called gods in heaven or on earth, . . . yet for us there is one God, the Father"), where he does not intend to concede the actual existence of various claimed gods (see also Gal. 4:8). The immediate context, however, should be given greater consideration, and it supports the latter, more comprehensive meaning. First, the rest of the verse ("so that he takes his seat in the temple of God, proclaiming that he himself is God") makes it clear that the ultimate goal of the man of lawlessness is not merely to be acknowledged as one of the gods that people may worship but as the ultimate, supreme God. Second, the blasphemous aspect of the lawless one's actions require that he challenge not just claimed false gods—after all, Paul challenges their status too—but the one and only true God. The man of lawlessness, therefore, will oppose and exalt himself "over every being called god," that is, whatever people may worship as god, including the one true God. It makes sense, then, that this superman of Satan additionally opposes and exalts himself over "every [the adjective *panta* governs both *theon* and *sebasma*] object of worship." The noun *sebasma*, as in its only other NT occurrence in Acts 17:23, where Paul draws attention to the multiplicity of gods and altars viewed as sacred by the Athenians, refers to anything that is worshiped, whether it be deities, images, shrines, altars, or other venerated objects. The arrogance and audaciousness of the man of lawlessness is so great that he will not tolerate any rival of any kind.

We have observed above (see comments on v. 3) that Paul's description of the man of lawlessness finds its closest parallels in Daniel's prophecy about end-time challenges faced by the people of God. The parallel between the title "man of lawlessness" and Dan. 12:10, with its description of the lawless conduct characteristic of individuals living in the last days, has already been noted. Now, however, we see another, even closer parallel between Paul's description of the man of lawlessness here in 2 Thess. 2:4 and Daniel's prophecy about a future king of the north who "will exalt and magnify himself above every god" (Dan. 11:36)—a prophecy that most exegetes believe finds its initial fulfillment in the Hellenistic king Antiochus IV Epiphanes, who desecrated the Jerusalem temple during the time of the Maccabees by setting up an altar to the pagan god Zeus. Nevertheless, it is not necessary to conclude that Paul himself is drawing on the Daniel material. The striking parallels between 2 Thess. 2 and the eschatological teachings of Jesus as recorded in the Synoptic Gospels (see Orchard 1938; Ford 1979: 198; Beasley-Murray 1954: 233; Hartman 1966: 194; Wenham 1984: 179) suggest that the apostle is more likely drawing from traditional material of early Christian eschatology, which was based on the teaching of Jesus, who in turn incorporated the prophecy of Daniel in expounding his views of the end times.

The God-opposing and self-exalting conduct of the man of lawlessness reaches its climax in a result clause,[18] which reveals the depth of this eschatological enemy's defiance against the divine God: "so that he takes his seat in

---

18. A few commentators claim that the Greek construction in 2:4 expresses not *actual* result but *intended* result, so that one should not necessarily conclude that the man of lawlessness actually does take his seat in the temple of God but rather desires to do so (Frame 1912: 256–57; Menken 1994: 107). The distinction between actual result (ὥστε + indicative) and intended result (ὥστε + infinitive), however, is true only of Classical Greek and not of the later Koine Greek of the NT (BDF §391.3; Wallace 1996: 593n14). Furthermore, Paul's concern is to convey the height of the lawless one's rebellion against God—a point that is expressed equally well regardless of whether the result clause is intended or actual.

the temple of God, proclaiming[19] that he himself is God" (ὥστε αὐτὸν εἰς τὸν ναὸν τοῦ θεοῦ καθίσαι ἀποδεικνύντα ἑαυτὸν ὅτι ἔστιν θεός, *hōste auton eis ton naon tou theou kathisai apodeiknynta heaton hoti estin theos*). Several details of the text, though in themselves not so seemingly significant, work together to intensify the blasphemous nature of this rebellious act. First, the personal pronoun "he" (*auton*) is emphatic: it is "placed prominently forward to mark the individualizing arrogance of this impious intruder" (Ellicott 1880: 111; see also Malherbe 2000: 420). The man of lawlessness takes his seat (the infinitive *kathisai* is intransitive: BDAG 492.3) in the temple. This is not a position that has been given to him or that he has earned; rather, he aggressively and brazenly takes a position that belongs to none but God alone. Second, the word used for "temple" is not *hieron*, which refers to the entire temple complex, but *naos*, which has in view the inner court of the temple. The man of lawlessness, therefore, does not merely take his seat in the outer courtyard or some other less important location in the temple complex but in the most holy inner court, reserved for only God. Third, the compound verb *apodeiknymi* was becoming a technical term for the appointing of a person to a particular office (BDAG 108.1: "to show forth for public recognition"). This makes the ongoing and persistent (note the present tense) proclamation of the lawless one concerning his own divinity more of a formal and public act, which heightens its offensiveness. Fourth, the final participial clause ("proclaiming that he himself is God") is to some degree redundant since it repeats in the form of an indirect statement what the action of taking a seat in the temple has already symbolically expressed. Yet by spelling out that this action involves a public proclamation "that he himself is God," the sacrilegious character of such conduct is heightened even further. Fifth, the reflexive pronoun *heauton*, both by its presence and its placement before the ὅτι clause, adds emphasis: "proclaiming *himself*, that he is God."

But while this verse clearly conveys the blasphemous nature of the lawless one's usurpation of God's position and power, it remains somewhat ambiguous as to what Paul intends in his reference to "the temple of God." The most obvious meaning is the Jerusalem temple, an interpretation seemingly confirmed by the double occurrence of the article before the nouns *naos* and *theos*: "*the* temple of *the* God." Nevertheless, claimed problems with this interpretation have led to two alternate proposals. The least likely option is that Paul is referring to a heavenly temple. Neil (1950: 164), for example, states that it is "not likely that the actual Temple at Jerusalem is in Paul's mind at all, but that he is thinking rather in the sense of Ps. 11:4, of the Temple of God in heaven" (so also Frame 1912: 257; Gaventa 1998:

---

19. The exact force of this adverbial participle is difficult to determine, though it may well be expressing purpose: the man of lawlessness takes his seat in the temple of God *in order to* show that he is God (so Frame 1912: 257). In Classical Greek this purpose, or telic, function was expressed by the future participle, but in Koine Greek this function is increasingly taken over by the present participle and typically follows the controlling verb (Wallace 1996: 636); both these characteristics are true of the participle found here in 2:4.

112). The notion of a heavenly temple does occur in the writings of the OT (Pss. 11:4; 18:6; Isa. 66:1; Mic. 1:2; Hab. 2:20), in the intertestamental period (e.g., 1 En. 14.17–22; 2 Bar. 4.2–6; T. Levi 5.1–2; b. Ḥag. 12b), and in the book of Revelation (11:19; 14:15, 17; 15:5–6, 8; 16:1, 17). Yet there is nothing in the context to support this view: the man of lawlessness's manifestation, deceptive works, and ultimate defeat at Christ's return all take place on earth. Additionally, the idea of a heavenly temple occurs nowhere else in Paul's writings. Finally, that the God-opposing and self-exalting activity takes place on earth (where every god is "named" and every object of worship is located) suggests that the resulting action of taking the seat in the temple occurs in the same locale.

A second and more persuasive alternative is that "the temple of God" refers to the church. This view was adopted first by some church fathers (John Chrysostom, *Hom. 2 Thess.* 3; and the Antiochian school), then later by the Reformers in their struggle against the papacy, and it remains a commonly held view today (its strongest proponents include Giblin 1967: 76–80; and more recently Beale 2003: 207–11). The weightiest evidence in support of this interpretation is Paul's figurative usage of the noun "temple" elsewhere: it occurs seven times outside 2 Thess. 2:4 and never refers to a literal temple, whether in Jerusalem or elsewhere, but instead to believers: individually (1 Cor. 6:19), congregationally (1 Cor. 3:16–17 [3x]; 2 Cor. 6:16 [2x]), or universally (Eph. 2:21). Further evidence for the ecclesiastical view, it is claimed, lies in the previous reference to "the apostasy," which supposedly presupposes a religious falling away by those who originally had a relationship to God, that is, members of the church. Additionally, that the "church as temple" idea was part of Paul's teaching to other churches suggests that he would have also taught this concept to the Thessalonian church such that they would understand the reference to the temple in 2:4 in this way (note especially 1 Cor. 3:16 and 6:19, which expect the answer "Yes" to Paul's rhetorical question of whether his Corinthian readers know that they are a temple of God: Giblin 1967: 76n4). It is therefore concluded that "to 'sit in the temple of God' is likely not a reference to the antichrist's literal positioning of himself in the center of a physical temple but to a figurative sitting, a ruling. . . . 2:3–4 teaches that the latter-day assailant will come into the midst of the church and cause it to become predominantly apostate and unbelieving" (Beale 2003: 210).

As weighty as such arguments seem to be, most exegetes have rightly not found the ecclesiastical interpretation convincing. The reasons include the following:

1. The appeal to the apostle's figurative use of *naos* elsewhere is weakened by the fact that this noun does not always refer to the church: in 1 Cor. 6:19 it refers to the physical body of a Christian. This appeal to Paul's usage elsewhere is further undermined because in these texts he never uses the exact articular phrase "the temple of the God": the closest is the anarthrous expression "a temple of God" (1 Cor. 3:16; 2 Cor. 6:16),

and other texts exhibit an even greater difference: "a temple of the Holy Spirit" (1 Cor. 6:19) and "a holy temple in the Lord" (Eph. 2:21).

2. As a general hermeneutical rule, "Context is king," that is, the meaning of a particular word or phrase should be determined first and foremost by the context in which it occurs. The eschatological context of 2 Thess. 2 and especially its employment of apocalyptic imagery is quite different from that found in occurrences of the noun *naos* in Paul's other letters.

3. At this stage in its history, the church was still in its infancy, and there was no united ecclesiastical organization or even one leading congregation that could justly represent the whole of the Christian community and so provide the kind of power base where the man of lawlessness might take his seat and operate (Bruce 1982: 169).

4. It was observed above (see comments on v. 3) that the term "the apostasy" likely referred not in a limited way only to those associated with the church but more generally to the rebellion of the creature against the Creator, in which humankind as a whole would participate. The ecclesiastical interpretation of "temple" is thus too narrow, since the goal of the man of lawlessness is to be worshiped as god not merely by those in the church, but also by all of humanity.

5. The "temple = church" view does not fit well with the historical context of the Thessalonian congregation and especially Paul's concern throughout the passage to comfort this church. As Witherington (2006: 220n68) observes: "We might add pastorally that for a group of Christians under persecution and experiencing anxiety it would hardly be encouraging to regale them with a description of how their congregation and others would fall apart at the seams, suffer major defections, and worse, suffer the horrible influence of a lawless teacher who saw himself as a deity!"

6. The double presence of the article means that the phrase "*the* temple of *the* God" most naturally is understood as a reference to the Jerusalem temple. The congregation at Thessalonica, even though it was predominantly made up of Gentile believers, would have been well familiar with the sanctuary in Jerusalem from Paul's previous teaching, as the apostle clearly asserts in the following verse.

7. Perhaps the strongest evidence that Paul has in view the Jerusalem temple is that the desecration of this sanctuary and the action of taking a seat there and claiming to be God are ideas that are part of a well-known theme from Jewish history that, in light of Jesus's teaching, became part of the early church's eschatology.

   a. This theme has its roots already in the OT, where certain foreign kings made claims to divinity. In Ezek. 28:2 the king of Tyre is condemned for saying in the pride of his heart: "I am a god; I sit on the throne of a god in the heart of the seas." Isaiah 14:13–14 reveals that the king of Babylon has similar blasphemous thoughts of grandeur: "I will ascend to heaven; I will raise my throne above the stars of God; I will sit enthroned on the mounts of the assembly, on the utmost heights of

Mount Zaphon [the place the Canaanites believed to be the dwelling place of the gods, much like Mount Olympus for the Greeks]. I will ascend above the tops of the clouds; I will make myself like the Most High."

b. Paul's language here of taking a seat in the temple and claiming to be God, as was noted already above, finds its closest parallel in Daniel's prophecy about a coming ruler: "The king will do as he pleases. He will exalt and magnify himself above every god and will say unheard-of things against the God of gods. . . . He will show no regard for the gods of his ancestors, . . . nor . . . regard any god, but will exalt himself above them all" (11:36–37). Daniel also prophesies that this future ruler "will put an end to sacrifice and offering. And at the temple he will set up an abomination that causes desolation" (9:26–27). These prophecies find their initial fulfillment in King Antiochus IV, both in his claims to divinity (he demanded to be called Epiphanes, that is, "[God] manifest"), and his actions in 168 BC of plundering the Jerusalem temple, abolishing all sacrifice to the God of Israel and in the sanctuary offering a pig on an altar dedicated to Zeus (Josephus, *J.W.* 1.31–35; *Ant.* 12.248–56; 1 Macc. 1:20–23, 41–57; 2 Macc. 6:2). Daniel's prophecy concerning the temple's defilement entered into the end-time expectation of Christians because of Jesus's explicit reference to this prophecy (Matt. 24:15; Mark 13:14).

c. This theme of the desecration of the Jerusalem sanctuary and usurpation of God's place there by an archenemy was kept alive by subsequent infamous events in Jewish history. One of these involved the Roman general Pompey, who, after capturing the city of Jerusalem in 63 BC, entered the holy of holies in the temple (Josephus, *Ant.* 14.69–76). His defilement of the temple is likely referred to in Pss. Sol. 17, where he is described as "the lawless one" (17.11)—the same abbreviated title that Paul gives to the man of lawlessness in 2 Thess. 2:8.

d. Another well-known desecration—or more accurately, potential desecration—of the Jerusalem temple occurred just over a decade before the writing of Paul's Second Letter to the Thessalonians. In AD 40 the emperor Caligula (Gaius) had plans to turn the Jerusalem sanctuary into a place of worship dedicated to himself as a god and so gave instruction for his statue to be set up in that sacred site. As Josephus reports: "The insolence with which the emperor Gaius (Caligula) defied fortune surpassed all bounds: he wished to be considered a god and to be hailed as such; . . . his impiety extended even to Judea. In fact, he sent Petronius with an army to Jerusalem to install in the sanctuary statues of himself" (*J.W.* 2.184–85; see also *Ant.* 18.261–309; Philo, *Embassy* 203–346). The Syrian legate, Petronius, wisely delayed in carrying out Caligula's orders, during which time the emperor was assassinated, so his violation of the temple ultimately never took place. Nevertheless, Caligula's intentions were well known among Jews—so much so that it almost caused a revolt in Judea. This "close call" may well have helped keep alive the end-time expectation for the desecration of the temple.

It is sometimes objected that none of these events from Jewish history involved the exact action of someone who sits himself in the temple of God and then proclaims that he himself is God (Frame 1912: 257; Weatherly 1996: 258). However, the desecration of the temple by Antiochus IV does match Paul's description here of the lawless one's actions better than is typically recognized. Antiochus, in his religious zeal for Zeus, of whom he believed himself to be a "manifestation" (hence his additional name "Epiphanes"), set up in the Jerusalem temple an image of Zeus in his own (Antiochus's) likeness, such that the king can be justly said to have taken his seat or presence in the temple of God. But even if this violation of the temple by Antiochus or different desecrations by others in Jewish history do not exactly match that described by the apostle, it is, as Menken (1994: 106) recognizes, "only a small step from their actions to the action of the lawless one in 2 Thess. 2.4, a step that is easily taken by someone who is reflecting on these past models of human arrogance in light of expected eschatological evil."

Some have understood Paul's reference here to the Jerusalem temple as grounds for believing that, in light of this temple's destruction in AD 70, it must be rebuilt at some time in the future so that it will be possible for the apostle's prediction about the man of lawlessness's blasphemous actions to take place. Thomas (1978: 322), for example, states: "This ['the temple of God'] is evidently a Jewish temple to be rebuilt in Jerusalem in the future" (this interpretation goes back all the way to Hippolytus, *Antichr.* 25, 63; and Cyril of Jerusalem, *Cat. Lect.* 15.15).

But while Paul is here referring to the historic temple of Jerusalem, he is more likely using this sanctuary metaphorically by picking up the well-known theme of its desecration as a graphic description of the lawless one's usurpation of God and his divine authority. If so, this means that *the verse says more about the character of the man of lawlessness than the location where he will make his appearance.* As Bruce (1982: 169) puts it: "It may be best to conclude that the Jerusalem sanctuary is meant here by Paul and his companions, but meant in a metaphorical sense. Had they said, 'so that he takes his seat on the throne of God,' few would have thought it necessary to think of a literal throne; it would simply have been regarded as a graphic way of saying that he plans to usurp the authority of God." Marshall (1983: 191–92) similarly states: "Paul was using a well-known motif metaphorically and typologically. Taking up a motif derived from Ezekiel and Daniel and given concrete illustration in previous desecrations of the Jewish temple, both actual and attempted, he has used this language to portray the *character* of the culminating manifestation of evil as an anti-theistic power which usurps the place of God in the world" (emphasis added; so also, e.g., Fee 2009: 284; Shogren 2012: 284–85). It is also worth citing, given the intense debate about the meaning of the phrase "the temple of God," the conclusion of Ridderbos (1975: 520–21):

> With the temple certainly the temple at Jerusalem is in the first instance to be thought of. One must not, however, fail to appreciate the apocalyptic character of the delineation. That which is still hidden, which as future event is still incapable of description, is denoted with the help of available notions borrowed from the present. To sit in the temple is a divine attribute, the arrogating to oneself of divine honor. No conclusions are to be drawn from that for the time and place in which the man of sin will make his appearance.

c. A Mild Rebuke (2:5)

The conditional clause begun in 2:3, whose protasis or "if" part deals with the two events—the apostasy and the man of lawlessness—that must precede the day of the Lord, is never brought to completion by its expected apodosis, or "then" part. Instead, Paul interrupts his vivid description of the coming eschatological enemy with a parenthetical question: "You remember, don't you, that, when I was still with you, I was repeatedly saying these things to you?" (οὐ μνημονεύετε ὅτι ἔτι ὢν πρὸς ὑμᾶς ταῦτα ἔλεγον ὑμῖν; *ou mnēmoneuete hoti eti ōn pros hymas tauta elegon hymin?*).

2:5

Two grammatical features suggest that Paul's words here involve a mild rebuke of his readers in Thessalonica (so most commentators, but see Morris 1991: 224; Richard 1995: 329). First, the question is introduced with the negative *ou*, which clearly expects a "Yes" answer (BDF §427.2). Paul, therefore, is not asking a genuine question that seeks an answer, but a rhetorical question that makes an assertion: the Thessalonian believers do actually remember "these things," that is, the details concerning the coming of the apostasy and the revelation of the man of lawlessness (the demonstrative pronoun *tauta* does not look ahead to the content of the following verses but backward to the two preceding ones). The apostle's wording here does not involve as strong a reprimand as is expressed in his ten-times repeated question, "You know, don't you, that . . . ?" (1 Cor. 3:16; 5:6; 6:2, 3, 9, 15, 16, 19; 9:13, 24), to the Corinthians—a church in which his relationship with them was strained. This stronger reprimand would be inappropriate not only in light of the much better relationship Paul enjoys with the Thessalonian congregation, but also in light of the significant spiritual crisis that this church is facing. Nevertheless, there is in this question the not very subtle point that Paul expects the Thessalonian Christians to remember his teaching about these preliminary eschatological events, which prove the claim concerning the day of the Lord's arrival to be bogus. The unspoken and logical follow-up question is "Since you do remember these things, why are you shaken by an obviously false claim that the day of the Lord has come?"

Second, a mild rebuke is additionally indicated by the use of the rarer imperfect tense, *elegon*, which conveys the notion of ongoing or recurring action: "I was *repeatedly* saying these things to you." Paul's teaching and preaching to them during his mission-founding ministry in Thessalonica did not consist merely of one or two brief discussions concerning the end-time events such that they could be justly excused for not remembering these things. Instead, eschatological matters were of such importance to the apostle that they were at the core of his gospel presentation (note in 1 Thess. 1:9–10 how the conversion of the Thessalonians is immediately followed with a reference to how they also "wait for his Son from heaven, . . . Jesus, . . . who rescues us from the coming wrath") and also, in light of the weightiness of this subject, were frequently the subject matter of Paul's preaching.[20] That the apostle had spoken often to the Thessalonian church about the day of the Lord is further suggested by the fact that in the first letter he can tell them on this subject, "You yourselves accurately know" (1 Thess. 5:2), with the result that the day would not surprise them like a thief (5:4). It is the repeated nature of this previous instruction that explains why Paul here does not spell out in detail all the events connected with the coming apostasy and the revelation of the lawless one: the apostle can justly assume that his readers remember his teaching about these things. Of course, the modern reader has not enjoyed the benefit of Paul's recurring preaching on such end-time matters and so understandably finds many of the apostle's references in 2 Thess. 2:3–12 ambiguous and difficult to comprehend.

The rhetorical question of verse 5 is made more personal and thus more pointed by the move from the plural (2:1, "*We* ask you . . ."; 2:2, "as from *us*") to the singular (". . . when *I* was still with you, *I* was repeatedly saying these things to you"). Although this shift is not as emphatic as it could have been if he had also used, as in 1 Thess. 2:18 and 3:5, the personal pronoun "I," Paul is nevertheless stressing the role that he personally played in teaching his Thessalonian readers about the eschatological events such that he knows them now to be well informed about these matters. This shift from the plural to the singular is hardly surprising, given that the same phenomenon occurs in the first letter (1 Thess. 2:18; 3:5; 5:27; see also 2 Thess. 3:17), especially at moments when the apostle is very emotionally involved and animated in his response to a particular problem in the church. This shift to the singular also confirms that the plural "we" used so frequently throughout both letters ought not to be read *literally* but *literarily*: Paul is the real author of the two letters but includes Silvanus (Silas) and Timothy, who have played a key role in the Thessalonian church—the former in the establishing of the church (Acts 17:1–10) and the latter in the subsequent strengthening of the church (1 Thess. 3:1–5)—to give his letter further weight or authority (see comments on 1 Thess. 1:1a and 2 Thess. 1:1a).[21]

20. The repeated instruction on eschatological matters implied by the imperfect tense of ἔλεγον in 2:5 is further evidence that Paul's mission-founding ministry in Thessalonica lasted longer than three Sabbaths (see the introduction for further discussion).

21. Witherington (2006: 220): "This [v. 5] surely makes clear that Paul is the primary author of this material (cf. 2 Thess. 3:17), while Silas and Timothy are presumably simply offering the 'amen' to Paul's teaching." Spitta (1896: 111–25) proposes the interesting but implausible theory that the "I" here is not Paul but Timothy and that this letter, other than the closing autograph (3:17–18), was written by the apostle's helper. Spitta argues that this explains the more Jewish

A few have found it puzzling or even problematic that Paul takes his readers back to his oral teaching given during his mission-founding visit rather than to his more recently written letter, which in 4:13–5:11 similarly deals with eschatological matters. Trilling (1980: 88n333) uses this observation to support his claim that 2 Thessalonians is pseudepigraphical, while Wanamaker (1990: 249) sees in this same observation further evidence for his claim that 2 Thessalonians was written before 1 Thessalonians. Both conclusions, however, are unwarranted. Paul does not refer back to his previous letter because it does not deal with exactly the same problem here in 2 Thess. 2:1–17 (Marshall 1983: 192–93). There 1 Thess. 4:13–18 deals specifically with the fate of deceased believers at Christ's parousia or return, and so differs significantly from the topic taken up in the second letter. Then 1 Thess. 5:1–11 deals with the fate of living believers on the day of the Lord and so does come closer to addressing the issue treated in his later correspondence, though again the specific concern in each passage is different. Yet the apostle's argumentation in both letters is the same: he contrasts the knowledge that his readers already have from his earlier oral teaching (1 Thess. 5:2, 4: "You yourselves accurately know. . . . But you, brothers, are not in darkness with the result that the day would surprise you like a thief"; 2 Thess. 2:5: "You remember, don't you, that, when I was still with you, I was repeatedly saying these things to you?") with the ignorance that unbelievers have about these end-time things such that they face future judgment (1 Thess. 5:3: non-Christians do not know what will happen, and so the day of the Lord will overtake them like a thief in the night; 2 Thess. 2:9–12: non-Christians do not know about the coming apostasy and the man of lawlessness and so will be misled by his false signs and wonders).

2. Present: The Restraining Thing/Person and the Mystery of Lawlessness (2:6–7)

The second section of Paul's correction in 2:3–12 shifts the temporal perspective from what must take place "first" (v. 3) in the future, before the day of the Lord comes, to what is currently taking place "now" (vv. 6, 7) and "already" (v. 7). In terms of the function that verses 6–7 play in the overall argument of 2:3–12, the two verses are readily understood: the two *future* events—the coming of the apostasy and the revelation of the man of lawlessness—that must precede the day of the Lord (vv. 3–5) are contrasted with two *present* events or realities (vv. 6–7): the rebellion against God that the lawless one will embody is already at work in the world, and the future appearance of that eschatological enemy is currently being restrained by a thing (the neuter τὸ

---

character of the second letter compared to the first, and also better accounts for the adverb ἔτι, since Timothy was with the Thessalonian church more recently than Paul. But not only are both these claims vulnerable to criticism; the assertion of Timothy's authorship additionally suffers from the fact that the shift from the plural to the singular elsewhere in the Thessalonian correspondence clearly refers to Paul (1 Thess. 2:18; 3:5; 5:27; 2 Thess. 3:17). Therefore, if Timothy were the author of 2 Thessalonians, he would have felt the need to add here in 2:5 the words "I, Timothy" or a similar expression to clarify the situation (Milligan 1908: xc).

κατέχον, *to katechon*) and a person (the masculine ὁ κατέχων, *ho katechōn*). These verses, therefore, function to correct or clarify further why the crisis-creating claim that "the day of the Lord has come" cannot be true. In terms of identifying the specific referent of the restraining thing and the restraining person, however, these verses are anything but clear. In fact, "these two verses are among the most problematic texts in the whole of the Pauline corpus" (Wanamaker 1990: 249). In order to take into account the immediate context, I will hold off discussing the "riddle of the restrainer" (Farrow 1989) until after explaining the remaining elements found in both these verses.

2:6   Paul continues to appeal to the knowledge that his readers have from his mission-founding preaching but changes the time frame from future events to present-day happenings: "And you know the thing that is now restraining in order that he might be revealed at his own fixed time" (καὶ νῦν τὸ κατέχον οἴδατε εἰς τὸ ἀποκαλυφθῆναι αὐτὸν ἐν τῷ ἑαυτοῦ καιρῷ, *kai nyn to katechon oidate eis to apokalyphthēnai auton en tō heautou kairō*).

The adverb "now" (*nyn*) could modify the main verb "you know" so that it functions to connect logically this new sentence with the preceding one in verse 5: "And now, *in light of your remembering my previous oral teaching given during my mission-found ministry*, you know . . ." Another possibility, however, is that the adverb modifies the substantive participle so that it functions temporally: "what is now restraining." Although the first option is followed in several translations (e.g., KJV, ASV, NIV), the second possibility is supported by five factors. First and foremost, the heavy concentration of temporal markers in the surrounding verses (v. 3, "first"; v. 6, "at his own fixed time"; v. 7, "already," "now," "until"; v. 8, "then") suggests that here also the adverb functions temporally. Second, there is the parallel between verses 6 and 7: just as the adverb ἄρτι (*arti*) modifies the masculine form of the key participle, "the one who is restraining *now*" (v. 7), so the adverb *nyn* modifies the neuter form of the same participle, "the thing that is restraining *now*" (v. 6). Third, throughout this correction section (vv. 3–12), Paul presents a chronological framework that seeks to prove false the claim concerning the day of the Lord's arrival, and a temporal understanding of the adverb "now" agrees with that framework. Fourth, the adverb is separated from the main verb "you know" and placed immediately in front of its likely modifier: the substantive participle "the thing that is restraining." Fifth, the logical connection to the previous verse is likely expressed not by the adverb "now" but by the conjunction "and," which Paul rarely uses to begin a new sentence, except when he intentionally links sentences that are coordinate (the technical term is *parataxis*: BDAG 494.1.b.β; BDF §458). But even if "now" were not taken temporally, it would still remain clear from the adverbs "already" (*ēdē*) and "now" (*arti*) in verse 7 that in these two verses Paul has shifted his perspective from future events to present-day happenings.

The temporal shift in Paul's argument is further marked by the verb "you know" (*oidate*), since a verb of "knowing" typically occurs in a disclosure formula (Mullins 1964)—an epistolary convention that elsewhere in the Thessalonian letters (1 Thess. 2:1; 4:2, 13; 5:2; 2 Thess. 3:7) and in the apostle's other correspondence (e.g., Rom. 1:13; 1 Cor. 12:1; 15:1; 2 Cor. 1:8; Gal. 1:11; Phil. 1:12) marks transition. Giblin (1967: 159–66) proposes that the verb "you know" has in view a special kind of knowledge: it does not refer to speculative or conceptual knowledge but to "some form of experiential knowledge or knowledge in which some form of immediate personal awareness, realization, recognition and the like is stressed" (160). This in turn means, so Giblin claims, that here Paul is not referring, as he did in the preceding verse ("You remember, don't you, that . . ."), to the catechetical teaching he gave the Thessalonian believers during his mission-founding visit but instead to the knowledge his readers have subsequently acquired through their own personal experience of the restraining force. But if Paul were actually contrasting the knowledge about the restraining thing/person that his readers originally received from him (v. 5) with that knowledge about the restraining thing/person from their own personal experience (v. 6), he would likely have introduced this verse not with "and now"—a grammatical construction that, as we have noted above, strengthens the logical link to the previous verse—but instead with the contrastive "but now" (Best 1977: 290). Furthermore, their experiential knowledge of the restraining force does not preclude the likelihood that this subject was included in "these things" (tauta) about which Paul had previously instructed them and which, especially in light of their subsequent awareness of this restraining force due to that previous instruction, they thus "remember" (v. 5) and "know" (v. 6).

The purpose (eis to + infinitive typically expresses purpose or result: BDF §402.2)[22] of the restraining force is to ensure that the revelation of the man of lawlessness happens at his fixed time. The text does not clearly specify either *who* will be revealed or in *whose* time this appearance will take place, stating instead somewhat ambiguously "in order that he [auton] may be revealed in his/its own [heautou] time." Theoretically, there are three possible antecedents for the personal pronoun "he" (auton): "the thing that is now restraining," described earlier in the verse; "the man of lawlessness," mentioned in verse 3; or "our Lord Jesus Christ," referred to in verse 1. In reality, however, there is little doubt about whom Paul has in view. The restraining force, despite being the nearest possible antecedent, is neuter and so does not agree in gender with the masculine personal pronoun auton. And though this problem

22. Giblin (1967: 204–10) goes on at some length to show that the connection between this infinitive phrase (in 2:6) and the first half of the sentence is not one of purpose but rather "is little more than an expression of temporal consequence between the present experience of a force analogous to the ἄνθρωπος τῆς ἀνομίας [of 2:3] and the future manifestation of this latter figure at a determined moment" (210). Elsewhere in the letter, however, the construction εἰς τό with the infinitive expresses purpose or result (1:5; 2:10, 11; 3:9; but see 2:2, where this construction expresses the content of the appeal), and this is by far its most common function in the rest of Paul's Letters (BDF §402.2). Since its widely attested function of expressing purpose or result makes good sense in this context, there is little justification for adopting a different meaning here.

may be mitigated somewhat by the fact that the immediately following verse refers to the restraining force in the masculine, the problem of the mismatched genders severely undermines this candidate as the likely antecedent of "him." The possibility that Paul is referring to the revelation of the Lord Jesus Christ suffers from the great distance that would exist between the pronoun and its supposed antecedent. The one remaining option is the man of lawlessness, and that he is in view here is made virtually certain by the strong parallelism between this verse and two surrounding verses: "and the man of lawlessness is revealed . . ." (v. 3); "and then the lawless one will be revealed" (v. 8). Since both of these surrounding verses involve the verb "to reveal" in the passive voice, there can be little doubt that the "he" who functions as the subject of the passive infinitive "to reveal" in the current verse also refers to the man of lawlessness.

The same ambiguity exists over *whose* time it is when the revelation of the man of lawlessness takes place, since there are again three options as to whom or what the reflexive pronoun "his own" (*heautou*; on the textual variant, see additional notes) refers: (1) the restraining force, (2) the man of lawlessness, or (3) the Lord Jesus Christ. This time the first option does not suffer from the problem of mismatched genders, since the reflexive pronoun is in the genitive case, so the form for masculine and neuter is identical. Nevertheless, the second option is clearly preferred, since the closest possible antecedent, the personal pronoun "he" (*auton*), refers to the man of lawlessness.

The connection between the possessive pronoun and this antecedent is stressed both through its mere presence ("his own" instead of the simple pronoun "his") and the word order (it comes before rather than, as expected, after the noun): the man of lawlessness will be revealed in *his own*—that is, the lawless one's—fixed time. The emphasis, however, lies on who will be revealed at this time, not who will control the timing of this future event. In other words, even though the one to be revealed is the man of lawlessness, it is not he but God who determines when this superman of Satan will make his appearance (contra Wanamaker 1990: 254: "This may indicate that the 'appointed time' of the person of rebellion is under the dominion of Satan rather than God because the person of rebellion is Satan's agent"; see also Best 1977: 292). The notion of God's sovereignty is indicated first by the purpose clause that introduces the second half of this verse. As Bruce (1982: 170) states about the construction *eis to apokalyphthēnai*: "If purpose is indicated, the purpose is God's, to which both the man of lawlessness and the restraining power are perforce subservient" (so also Lightfoot 1904: 114; Morris 1991: 228n47). The idea of God's control over these future events is suggested, second, by the choice of the word for "time": *kairos* does not refer generally to time and its passing but more narrowly to "a defined period for an event, *definite, fixed time*" (BDAG 498.2). Although not always spelled out, the unspoken agent who sets or establishes such a fixed time is God. Paul, therefore, "is not describing some great series of events that take place in violation of the will of God, while God, so to speak, has to work out some plan as a counter. Paul thinks of God as being in control of the whole process" (Morris 1991: 228). This stress on God's sovereign control over these future events will undoubtedly comfort the Thessalonian church in their crisis of confusion about the claim of verse 2 and, as such, it strengthens the consolatory purpose at work in the passage of 2:1–17 as a whole.

Verse 7 is closely linked to the preceding verse not only by its shared present-time perspective (note the two adverbs "already" and "now") but also by the connecting particle γάρ (*gar*), which functions to express neither cause nor inference (so wrongly Richard 1995: 330) but clarification (BDAG 189.2): "For the mystery of lawlessness is already at work only until the one who is now restraining is out of the way" (τὸ γὰρ μυστήριον ἤδη ἐνεργεῖται τῆς ἀνομίας· μόνον ὁ κατέχων ἄρτι ἕως ἐκ μέσου γένηται, *to gar mystērion ēdē energeitai tēs anomias monon ho katechōn arti heōs ek mesou genētai*). The clarification concerns not the identity of the restraining force (the readers apparently already know what this is) but how the future revelation of the man of lawlessness relates chronologically to the lawlessness that is presently at work in the world. By explaining the sequence of these current and future events, Paul further proves the claim about the day of the Lord's present arrival (v. 2) to be false and thus comforts his shaken readers.

2:7

The phrase "mystery of lawlessness" is a unique expression that has no exact parallel in the NT or other literature of that day. The closest equivalents are found in Josephus, who describes the life of Antipater the son of Herod the Great as "a mystery of evil" (*J.W.* 1.470), and in several Qumran documents that have the plural "myster*ies* of sin" (1QH 13 [5].36; 1QM 14.9; 1Q27 1, 2, 7). The phrase "mystery of lawlessness," therefore, appears to be a creation of the apostle. The main stress in this ad hoc formulation of Paul rests on the first term "mystery," which is located not only in the opening and emphatic position in the sentence, but also separated sharply from the genitive "of lawlessness," which comes after the main verb. In the secular writings of the Greco-Roman world, the word "mystery" (*mystērion*), especially when occurring in the plural, functions as a technical term for the secret teachings and ceremonies connected with the increasingly popular mystery religions and cults (see BDAG 661; G. Bornkamm, *TDNT* 4:802–28). Consequently, some believe that Paul has such mystery cults in view (Green 2002: 317: "The term 'mystery' was also commonly employed to speak of the secret and sacred rites of various religions of that era, and it is likely that Paul has some such cult in mind"; see also Donfried 1985: 353; Holland 1988: 114).

The apostle's use of this term elsewhere, however, makes a reference to any pagan group highly unlikely. The word "mystery" occurs twenty-eight times in the NT, all but seven coming from the hand of Paul, where "the usual sense—indeed, almost the only sense—is a 'divine truth, once kept secret by God, but now revealed to His faithful'" (Furfey 1946: 186).[23] Such truths are

23. Beale (2003: 218) argues that elsewhere in the NT the word "mystery," when linked closely to OT allusions, is used to indicate that prophecy is being fulfilled but in a manner unexpected

appropriately identified as a "mystery" because it is impossible for unbelievers to comprehend them apart from their being revealed by God. And since such revealed truths cannot be fully grasped by the human mind or reason, to some degree they also remain a mystery even to those believers to whom God has revealed them. The emphasis in the term "mystery," however, lies less on the notion of incomprehensibility than of hiddenness unless revealed by God. As Witherington (2006: 222) declares: "*Mystērion* here surely has the sense not of something incomprehensible but rather of something hidden from plain view but nevertheless extant and at work."

The hidden but divinely revealed mystery in this verse is identified as "lawlessness" (*anomia*). The genitive *tēs anomias* likely functions as an appositive or epexegetical so that the fuller phrase "the mystery of lawlessness" means "the mystery which is lawlessness." As noted above (see comments on v. 3), Paul elsewhere uses the term "lawlessness" as a synonym for "sin" (Rom. 6:19) and a parallel with spiritual "darkness" (2 Cor. 6:14). Therefore this word, despite its etymology (lit., "without the law"), has in view not narrowly a rejection of the Mosaic law but more broadly rebellion against God and his will. It is this rebellion against God—a "mysterious" rebellion in that it is hidden and unobservable to unbelievers but revealed by God to believers and so readily known to them—that "is already at work" (*ēdē energeitai*).[24] Paul thus clarifies (the particle *gar* opens this verse) the chronological relationship that exists between the "man of lawlessness" and the "mystery of lawlessness." Although both involve opposition and rebellion against God, they operate in different time periods: the mystery of lawlessness is "already" operative in this world, albeit in a limited fashion due to the influence of the restraining force/person; once this restraining force/person is removed, "then" (v. 8) the man of lawlessness will be revealed "at his own fixed time" (v. 6).

The remainder of verse 7 is grammatically awkward and literally reads: "only the one who is now restraining until he is out of the way." Most commentators see here an ellipsis (so, e.g., Ellicott 1880: 114; Lightfoot 1904: 114; Frame 1912: 264; Morris 1991: 229n49; D. Martin 1995: 241; Malherbe 2000:

---

by its OT readers. This leads him to assert further: "Paul uses the word *mystery* in 2:7 because he understands the antichrist prophecy from Daniel [referred to in 2:4] as beginning to be fulfilled in the Thessalonian church in an enigmatic manner not clearly foreseen by Daniel." If, as is argued below, the references to "the restraining thing" (2:6) and "the restraining person" (2:7) have in view the angel Michael and his restraining work as described in Dan. 10–12, this would strengthen Beale's assertion. Nevertheless, his claim about the term "mystery" appears to be more true of its sparse occurrences in Revelation than in its high frequency in Paul's Letters, where the word consistently refers to a divine truth hidden from general humanity but revealed by God and thus known to his believers.

24. In 2:7 the present tense ἐνεργεῖται can be either middle ("is at work": so BDAG 335.b), which simply describes the lawless force at work in the world, or passive ("is made [by God] to work": so Best 1977: 293; Wanamaker 1990: 253), which highlights God's role in these events. The issue of what voice is intended in this verb, however, is ultimately not significant: "in either case, the context shows that the activity takes place within and is circumscribed by God's eschatological plan" (Malherbe 2000: 423).

423) in which a verb needs to be supplied with *monon ho katechōn*—either *energeitai* (is at work) from the preceding main clause, or the verb *genētai* (is) from the following temporal clause. A better explanation, however, is that there is no ellipsis at all but a change in word order for emphasis (Milligan 1908: 102; Richard 1995: 331; Wanamaker 1990: 257): just as in the previous verse the neuter reference to "the thing that is now restraining" was moved forward in the sentence, so also here the masculine reference to "the one who is now restraining" has been placed before the beginning of the temporal clause (introduced with the conjunction *heōs*). This explanation of the grammar of verse 7 is not only supported by a similar construction in Gal. 2:10 (the adverb "only" and the noun "the poor" are moved up before the beginning of the purpose clause) but also enjoys two other advantages: it avoids the need to supply a missing verb and, more important, it makes clear who is the subject of the temporal clause.[25] In both verses 6 and 7, therefore, Paul has changed the expected word order so that he can place emphasis on the thing and person that are restraining lawlessness in the present time period (note in each verse the temporal adverb "now") in contrast to the revelation of Satan's superman, which will take place in the future.

The verse closes with the clause "is out of the way" (*ek mesou genētai*). Although this expression does not occur in the same form anywhere else in the NT, close parallels in two of Paul's other letters (1 Cor. 5:2; Col. 2:14) refer to the act of removing something and thus lead to the translation given above. The subject of the verb almost certainly is "the one who is restraining now," and so the temporal clause refers to a future time when this figure will be removed and his present-day work of restraint will come to an end, thereby allowing the man of lawlessness to make his grand appearance. In order to gain additional insight into the identity and role of the restraining force/person (is it/he viewed positively or negatively?), some have tried to find in the phrase "is out of the way" an indication of whether the restraining one's removal will take place through violent or voluntary means. Fulford (1911: 41–42), for example, finds close parallels to Paul's statement here in some secular Greek writers who also combine the prepositional phrase *ek mesou* with the verb *ginomai*; from these similar constructions, he concludes that "St. Paul contemplates the Restrainer rather as retiring voluntarily from the scene of action than as forcibly removed or overthrown" (see also Bruce 1982: 170; Green 2002: 318). Dobschütz (1909: 282), by contrast, finds in the clause "is out of the way" a negative connotation that in turn implies a violent removal of the one who

---

25. Even if the second half of 2:7 did involve an ellipsis and a missing verb had to be supplied, the most natural reading of the verse would be to see the subject of the clause, "only the one who is now restraining [is at work]," as also being the subject of the temporal clause: "until he—the one who is now restraining—is out of the way." But although this is the most natural reading, the grammatical construction allows the possibility of a different subject in the temporal clause. This is the claim of Barnouin (1977: 489) and Aus (1977: 551), who hold that the subject of γένηται is "the mystery of lawlessness," while Farrow (1989) argues that the subject is the man of lawlessness.

is now restraining. These contradictory conclusions illustrate the danger of reading too much into Paul's words. As Frame (1912: 265) succinctly states: "The fact, not the manner, of removal is indicated" (so also Milligan 1908: 102; Best 1977: 295).

Thus far my discussion has avoided any explanatory comments about the restraining thing (*to katechon*) and the restraining person (*ho katechōn*) referred to in verses 6 and 7 respectively. Now that the remaining elements in these two verses have been examined, the pressing challenge is to resolve the riddle of the restrainer. This is no small challenge, given the failure of NT scholarship to reach any kind of consensus other than the all-too-common admissions of ignorance by those commentators who tackle the issue. Nevertheless, the detailed evidence presented in excursus 3 ("The Restrainer of 2 Thessalonians 2:6–7") suggests that this vexing exegetical issue may well be solved. The key to resolving the riddle of the restrainer lies in recognizing yet another allusion by Paul in this passage to the vision of Dan. 10–12: just as (1) Paul's use of the title "the man of lawlessness" in 2:3b is likely influenced by Dan. 12:10, with its description of the lawless conduct characteristic of individuals living in the last days, and (2) Paul's description of the eschatological enemy in 2:4 parallels even more closely Daniel's prophecy about a future king of the north who "will exalt and magnify himself above every god" (11:36) and desecrate the temple (11:31), so also (3) Paul's description of the restraining entity here in 2:6–7 is similarly influenced by the role that Michael, the patron angel of the Jews, plays in the vision of Dan. 10–12. The apostle's argument follows exactly the chronological schema found in Dan. 10–12: eschatological tribulation will come upon God's people only when Michael, the guardian of God's people, ends his protecting or restraining work (see excursus 3 for a fuller explanation of how the chronological schema in Dan. 10–12 parallels perfectly the order of events presented by Paul in 2 Thess. 2:3–12).

The two references to the restraining entity in verses 6–7, therefore, can be understood as follows: the neuter attributive participle in verse 6 focuses on the restraining activity of the archangel Michael, and the masculine attributive participle in verse 7 has in view the archangel Michael as a person. If it is wondered why Paul does not simply use the word "angel" or the name "Michael,"[26] the likely answer is that the apostle wants to emphasize for his readers not the identity of the *katechon/katechōn* figure but his restraining function.[27] The readers, of course, already know both of these things, but it is the function of restraint that addresses head-on their specific fear over the claim that the day of the Lord has come. Such a claim is obviously false since

---

26. Note the objection raised by Krodel 1990: 442: "All of these hypotheses have at least one fatal flaw. They are unable to explain why the author of this short letter used the word *katechon* (-*ōn*) instead of emperor, or governor, or apostle, or angel, or God."

27. Hannah (1999: 134, also 122–23; 2000: 44) offers a different explanation, appealing to a Pauline tendency to avoid explicit references to angels in favor of terms like ἀρχαί, ἐξουσίαι, and δυνάμεις, out of a concern that his Hellenistic audience would find references to angels or archangels as uncultured. Hannah observes a similar apprehension in Philo.

there is a clear sequence of events that must take place before that eschatological day will arrive: (1) The archangel Michael is restraining "now" (mentioned twice [v. 6, *nyn*; v. 7, *arti*] and thus emphasized) while the mystery of lawlessness is already at work in the world. (2) Hence the apostasy and the man of lawlessness are still in the future. (3) Thus the day of the Lord, the sequel to these two events, is even further in the future.

3. Future: The Coming of the Man of Lawlessness and His Deceived Followers (2:8–10)

The third section (vv. 8–10) of Paul's correction (vv. 3–12) shifts the time frame from present happenings to future events (note the adverb "then" in v. 8, opening this section). Once the current restraining activity of the archangel Michael is removed, "then" will occur the future event described already at some length in verses 3b–4 and referred to briefly in verse 6b ("in order that he might be revealed at his own fixed time"): the coming of the man of lawlessness. Although this superman of Satan will later be destroyed by the Lord Jesus, he will nevertheless have a parousia or coming that will deceive many and cause their destruction. The consoling purpose at work in 2:1–17 as a whole also ought to be recognized in this third subsection of the correction: Paul is reassuring his readers not just that the day of the Lord has not yet come, but also that they will ultimately be vindicated for their current affliction. As Fee (2009: 290) rightly observes about these verses: "Everything about the passage suggests that Paul is here offering a word of encouragement to these persecuted believers, since the emphasis is now altogether on God's ultimate, righteous judgment of their persecutors."

Although Paul rarely begins a new sentence with the conjunction "and" (the technical term is *parataxis*: BDAG 494.1.b.β; BDF §458), he does so three times in close proximity (vv. 6, 8, 11) in the correction of verses 3–12, each *kai* marking the shift to a new temporal perspective. Just as this conjunction opened the previous subunit (vv. 6–7) dealing with present happenings, so also here in verse 8 it marks, along with the temporal adverb "then," the transition to the next subunit (vv. 8–10) dealing with what will take place in the future: "And then the lawless one will be revealed" (καὶ τότε ἀποκαλυφθήσεται ὁ ἄνομος, *kai tote apokalyphthēsetai ho anomos*).

2:8

This numbers the third time (see also vv. 3b, 6b) that Paul refers to the future coming of the eschatological enemy, albeit in both differing and similar ways. Whereas the apostle earlier described this figure with the Semitic idiom "the man of lawlessness" (v. 3b), here he employs the typically Greek formulation "the lawless one." The change in title likely stems merely from stylistic variation and does not involve any significant shift in meaning: both expressions capture well the essential condition or quality of this individual as one who rebels against God and his will. But though the titles of this end-time enemy change slightly, the verb used to describe his future coming does not: for the third time not only is the same verb "reveal" (ἀποκαλύπτω, *apokalyptō*) used but also, as in its previous occurrences (vv. 3, 6), it is found in the passive voice. Both of these grammatical observations are significant. First, the thrice-repeated use of the verb "reveal" emphasizes the contrast between lawlessness in its present *hidden* state and its future *revealed* state: the rebellion against God is currently being restrained and thus is hidden from humanity's full view (thus it is "the mystery of lawlessness," that is, something known only to believers, to whom such knowledge has been revealed); in the future it will be fully exposed in the person of the lawless one, with his God-usurping and blasphemous, self-exalting conduct (v. 4) plainly visible to all. Second, the thrice-repeated use of the passive voice emphasizes that God, as the unspoken agent, controls the revelation or appearance of the lawless one. Since God is the one who, through the angelic agency of Michael, is currently restraining lawlessness, it logically follows that he also is the one who determines when that restraint will end and when the man of lawlessness will be revealed. As Beale (2003: 221) states: "God (or Christ) is always the subject of the verb 're-veal' throughout the New Testament, and 2:8 is no exception. God causes the revelation of the lawless one." Morris (1991: 230) similarly observes: "[Paul] puts his emphasis on the overriding sovereignty of God." The Thessalonian believers are comforted, therefore, by the consistent message that not only their current circumstances but also the events they will endure in the future are fully under God's control.

The main clause of verse 8a is followed by two relative clauses: the first deals with the parousia, or coming, of Christ, which results in the destruction of the lawless one (v. 8b); the second treats the parousia, or coming, of the lawless one, which results in the destruction of those whom he deceives (vv. 9–10). The order of these two relative clauses is clearly illogical and temporally out of sequence, since Paul describes the end of the lawless one *before* he describes his coming. This sequencing, however, reflects the apostle's pastoral priority of providing his readers with a word of comfort: although the Thessalonian believers are justly sobered by the future revelation of the lawless one, they nevertheless are comforted in the knowledge that this upcoming event not only remains within God's providential control (the passive voice of the verb "reveal") but also that this superman of Satan and his destructive work will be brought to a quick and certain end at Christ's return.[28] The pastoral priority that explains this illogical sequencing was foreshadowed in verse 3b: after mentioning the man of lawlessness for the first time, Paul immediately refers to this character's end by describing him as "the son of destruction," the one doomed to destruction (see comments on v. 3b).[29]

28. Menken (1994: 113): "An effect of this illogical sequence is, that the reader or hearer of the letter is fortified in his trust in the final victory of the Lord Jesus, and that beforehand the sting is taken out of the actions of the lawless one as depicted in the following verses."

29. Holmes 1998: 244–45: "The pattern Paul models here—he keeps his primary focus on Jesus and speaks of Antichrist no more than he has to—is a pattern we would do well to follow. When novels about Antichrist [e.g., the Left Behind series] outsell books about Jesus, it seems to me that there is something seriously out of balance. Christ our Savior, not Antichrist, his

The antecedent of the first relative clause is "the lawless one," mentioned at the end of the main clause, and his destruction at the coming of Christ is described by means of synonymous parallelism: "whom the Lord Jesus will slay with the breath of his mouth and will destroy by the sudden appearance of his coming" (ὃν ὁ κύριος Ἰησοῦς ἀνελεῖ τῷ πνεύματι τοῦ στόματος αὐτοῦ καὶ καταργήσει τῇ ἐπιφανείᾳ τῆς παρουσίας αὐτοῦ, *hon ho kyrios anelei tō pneumati tou stomatos autou kai katargēsei tē epiphaneia tēs parousias autou*).

In the first half of the parallel clauses, Paul employs language reminiscent of Isa. 11:4 LXX, where the prince from David's house "will strike the earth with the word of his mouth, and with the breath of his lips he will slay the ungodly." The allusion to this OT text is strengthened by adopting the more strongly attested future indicative *anelei* (he will slay)—the same form found in Isa. 11:4—rather than the aorist optative ἀνέλοι (*aneloi*, may he slay!), the different verb ἀναλοῖ (*analoi*, he consumes), or ἀναλώσει (*analōsei*, he will consume; for more on this textual variant, see additional notes). Paul has combined the two phrases from the Isaiah text ("with the word of his mouth and with the breath of his lips") into one ("with the breath of his mouth"). Although some (Frame 1912: 265; see also Best 1977: 303; Malherbe 2000: 424) have attributed this compression to "an unconscious reminiscence" of Ps. 33:6 (32:6 LXX; "By the word of the Lord the heavens were established; all the hosts of them by the breath of his mouth"), a number of biblical and intertestamental passages similarly refer to the destruction of the wicked by means of breath or the force of the mouth (Job 4:9; Isa. 30:27–28; 1 En. 14.2; 62.2; 84.1; 2 Esd. [4 Ezra] 13:10–11; Pss. Sol. 17.24, 25; Rev. 19:15).

The larger context of Isa. 11:4 was interpreted in the early church as a prophecy about the Messiah, and so Paul not surprisingly applies this OT text to the coming of "the Lord Jesus" (even if "Jesus" is a later scribal addition [see additional notes], "the Lord" for Paul is Jesus). The "breath" of God is always depicted as something powerful and mighty (see the texts cited at the end of the preceding paragraph). The image that Paul presents here with this OT allusion, therefore, is not one whereby the man of lawlessness will be easily blown over by the mere breath of the Lord Jesus (contra many; e.g., Hendriksen 1955: 183; Morris 1991: 231; Menken 1994: 114; Gaventa 1998: 115; also the line from Martin Luther's famous hymn, "A Mighty Fortress Is Our God": "One little word shall fell him"). Rather, this breath is a potent and fearful weapon of war used by the returning Christ to destroy this eschatological enemy.[30] This image of the Lord Jesus's power expressed in the metaphor of breath is

---

antagonist, deserves our attention." Best (1977: 302) expresses the same sentiment more succinctly: "There is a minimum which the Thessalonians must know about the Rebel but their gaze is not to be on him but on the Lord." Even briefer is the comment of Fee (2009: 290): "Paul is simply incapable of giving him [the man of lawlessness] top billing."

30. Giblin (1967: 91–95) proposes that the word for "breath," which in Greek is πνεῦμα, refers to the (Holy) Spirit emanating from the mouth of the Lord Jesus. This understanding, however, goes against the imagery at work in this verse (both in its original Isa. 11:4 context and here) and the clearly metaphorical meaning intended with the word πνεῦμα (Fee 1994a: 75–76).

intensified by the verb *anelei*, which, though chosen by Paul because of the allusion to Isa. 11:4 (the apostle uses this verb nowhere else), conveys Christ's ability not merely to "overthrow" the lawless one (so NIV), but violently to slay him (BDAG 64.2: "*do away with, destroy*, mostly of killing by violence").

In the second half of the parallel clauses that make up verse 8, Paul employs the verb *katargēsei*, which is rare in the rest of the NT, yet a favorite term of the apostle, whose writings account for all but two of its twenty-five occurrences. The issue arises whether the verb here has its more literal[31] sense of "make ineffective" (BDAG 525.2: "to cause something to lose its power or effectiveness, *invalidate, make powerless*") or the stronger sense of "destroy" (BDAG 525.3: "to cause something to come to an end or to be no longer in existence, *abolish, wipe out, set aside*"). The former sense conveys a different nuance than that expressed in the first half of the parallel clauses: the Lord Jesus will not only "slay" the lawless one but also "render [him] useless": the lawless one will be robbed of all significance (so Morris 1991: 231n53; Richard 1995: 333). The latter sense conveys a similar or perhaps intensified nuance than that expressed in the first half: the Lord Jesus will "slay" the lawless one, and he will also similarly "destroy" or, even more strongly, "annihilate" him (Menken 1994: 114; G. Delling [*TDNT* 1:454] renders the verb here as "complete destruction"; NRSV: "annihilating him"). Three observations provide slightly stronger support for the latter sense of "destroy." First, this understanding avoids the chronological or anticlimactic problem of the lawless one's death preceding his inactivation. Second, the striking parallelism in grammatical form found in the two halves of the relative clause (they are perfectly identical: future indicative verb, article plus instrumental dative noun, article plus defining genitive noun, and possessive third-person personal pronoun)[32] strengthen the case that the second half is intended to express the identical point made in the first half. Third, the use of the verb "slay" in the first half, to refer not merely to the overthrow of the lawless one but also his violent death, suggests that the verb *katargēsei* in the second half also has in view not merely the lawless one being rendered powerless but also his destruction (see also 1 Cor. 15:24, 26).

The instrument or means[33] by which the Lord Jesus will destroy the lawless one is "by the appearance of his coming" (*tē epiphaneia tēs parousias autou*). Here Paul combines two nouns that appear at first glance to be synonymous, since he uses them both elsewhere to describe the coming or return of Christ: "appearance" occurs in the so-called Pastoral Letters (1 Tim. 6:14; 2 Tim. 4:1, 8; Titus 2:13; see also 2 Tim. 1:10, where it refers to Christ's first appearance

---

31. This compound verb is made up of a preposition, the alpha privative, and the verb "to work": κατά + α + ἐργέω.

32. The relative clause of 2:8 charted:

first half of relative clause:	ἀνελεῖ	τῷ πνεύματι τοῦ στόματος	αὐτοῦ
second half of relative clause:	καταργήσει	τῇ ἐπιφανείᾳ τῆς παρουσίας	αὐτοῦ

33. Although the dative phrase (in 2:8c) could express time ("*at* the appearance of his coming"), the strong parallelism with the dative phrase in the preceding clause (which clearly indicates instrumentality) indicates that it instead expresses means ("*by* the appearance of his coming").

on earth), while "coming" is found in the remaining letters (1 Cor. 15:23; 16:17; 2 Cor. 7:6, 7; 10:10; Phil. 1:26; 2:12; 1 Thess. 2:19; 3:13; 4:15; 5:23; 2 Thess. 2:1, 8; see also 2 Thess. 2:9, where it refers to the lawless one's coming). On the assumption that these two terms are identical, some view their combination here either negatively as being "clumsy" (Menken 1994: 114), or positively as emphasizing the splendor and glory of Christ's return (Morris 1991: 231; D. Martin 1995: 243; see also Ellingworth and Nida 1975: "his dazzling presence"; NIV: "the splendor of his coming"). Others, however, argue for a distinction between the two words. One proposal is that *epiphaneia* has a more hostile sense than *parousia* (see LXX: 2 Sam. 7:23; Joel 2:11; Mal. 3:22 [4:5 Eng.]; 2 Macc. 2:21; 3:24; 12:22; 14:15; 3 Macc. 5:8) and that this distinction fits well in this context of the lawless one's destruction (Best 1977: 304; Marshall 1983: 200). The passages cited in support of this hostile sense, however, are not so convincing since they describe how the divine manifestation helped God's people to defeat their enemy (Malherbe 2000: 424). It is also questionable whether the nuance of *epiphaneia* ought to be located in Jewish sources rather than in Greek literature, where the word was a technical term referring to "a visible and frequently *sudden* manifestation of a hidden deity, either in the form of a personal appearance, or through some deed of power or oracular communication by which its presence is made known" (BDAG 385, emphasis added). If, as is more likely with such a widespread technical term, Paul is influenced by its Hellenistic background, then *epiphaneia* stresses the sudden or unexpected aspect of Christ's appearance: just when all may appear lost due to the revelation of the lawless one, this eschatological enemy will be destroyed by the abrupt manifestation of Christ at his coming (see Wanamaker 1990: 258; Menken 1994: 114; Witherington 2006: 223; cf. Giblin 1967: 179).

2:9 Paul began the third unit by referring to the future revelation of the lawless one (v. 8a) but then immediately digressed with a relative clause that stressed the certain and sudden destruction of this eschatological enemy at the parousia, or "coming," of Christ (v. 8b). Here in verse 9 the apostle once again returns to the future revelation of the lawless one, using a second relative clause that describes how this superman of Satan has, just like the Lord Jesus, his own parousia, or "coming": literally, "whose coming is in conformity with the work of Satan" (οὗ ἐστιν ἡ παρουσία κατ' ἐνέργειαν τοῦ σατανᾶ, *hou estin hē parousia kat' energeian tou satana*).

Most translations make two changes to the original Greek text. First, since the nearest antecedent of the relative pronoun "whose" (*hou*) is "the Lord Jesus" (v. 8b), even though the context shows that it refers to "the lawless one" (v. 8a), there is the danger of confusing exactly whose coming is being described. Translations, therefore, typically begin a new sentence at verse 9 and add a clarifying reference: "The coming *of the lawless one* . . ." Second, the time reference for the lawless one's coming is future, as indicated by the adverb "then" and the future tense of "he will be revealed" found in the opening of verse 8. Translations, therefore, further clarify the situation by turning Paul's present tense "is" (*estin*) into the future: "The coming of the lawless one *will be* . . ." The present tense lends a certain vividness to this future event and so stresses its certainty (see similarly 1 Thess. 5:2: The day of the Lord "comes" [*erchetai*] like a thief in the night; 5:3: Sudden destruction "comes upon" [*ephistatai*] nonbelievers).

The predicate of this future coming is likely[34] the prepositional phrase "in conformity with the work of Satan" (*kata* functions as a "marker of norm of similarity or homogeneity, *according to, in conformity with*": BDAG 512.5). In other words, the features connected with the lawless one's coming will be in fundamental agreement with the "work of Satan" (*energeia tou satana*). The choice of this term for "work" is significant, since in Paul's writings it always refers to the working or operation not of humans but of transcendent beings (BDAG 335)—usually God (Phil. 3:21; Eph. 1:19; 3:7; 4:16; Col. 1:29; 2:12; 2 Thess. 2:11; 1 Cor. 12:10 v.l.), or in this lone case, Satan (for more on this name or title, see comments on 1 Thess. 2:18). Thus, just as Satan is the supernatural power lying behind the mystery of lawlessness that is secretly "at work" in the present (v. 7: note the use of the verb *energeō*, from which the noun *energeia* is derived), so also Satan (genitive of source or origin) empowers his servant, the man of lawlessness, in his deceptive and destructive work, which will be publicly on display at his future coming (cf. Rev. 13:2).

What this "work of Satan" manifested in the coming of the lawless one consists of is spelled out in two clauses (vv. 9b–10a), whose parallelism is signaled by their common use of the preposition "in," along with the adjective "all" to open the clause, and a concluding genitive:

> in all power and signs and wonders of falsehood and
> in all deception of wickedness

> ἐν πάσῃ δυνάμει καὶ σημείοις καὶ τέρασιν ψεύδους καὶ
> ἐν πάσῃ ἀπάτῃ ἀδικίας

> *en pasē dynamei kai sēmeiois kai terasin pseudous kai*
> *en pasē apatē adikias*

The exact grammatical interrelationship of all the words found in the first half of these two parallel prepositional clauses is not clear as three questions emerge: First, does the opening adjective "all" modify only the first noun ("all power") or all three ("*all kinds of* power and signs and wonders")? Second, should the three nouns "power and signs and wonders" be viewed as a triad of equal members or grouped differently? Third, does the closing genitive "of falsehood" govern only the last noun, the final two, or all three? Although these questions are closely connected, it is the second that most determines the answers to the other two. The three nouns do occur elsewhere as a triad

---

34. The object of "whose coming is" (2:9a) could be either (1) the prepositional phrase "in conformity with the work of Satan," (2) the parallel prepositional phrases "in all power . . . and in all deceit," or (3) the attributive participle "to those who are perishing." The word order slightly favors the first option, but the overall meaning is not greatly affected regardless of which option is chosen.

(2 Cor. 12:12; Acts 2:22; Heb. 2:4), but significantly in a different word order and with the noun "power" always in the plural, in contrast to Paul's use of the singular here in 2 Thess. 2:9. Much more often do the last two nouns "signs and wonders" occur as a word pair denoting supernatural and miraculous happenings (Exod. 7:3; Deut. 4:34; 6:22; Isa. 8:18; 20:3; Jer. 32:21 [39:21 LXX]; Rom. 15:19; Matt. 24:24; Mark 13:22; John 4:48; Acts 2:19, 43; 4:30; 5:12; 6:8; 7:36; 14:3; 15:12). The fixed nature of the word pair "signs and wonders," along with the fact that the first noun, "power," occurs in the singular in contrast to the next two in the plural, suggest that these three nouns should not be viewed together as a triad. Rather, the first noun "power" is the key word, paralleled in the following prepositional phrase by the singular noun "deception" (*apatē*, in v. 10); what "power" means is then spelled out by the following word pair in verse 9: "in power—both signs and wonders" (see also Richard 1995: 334; Fee 1994a: 76; 2009: 293).

The adjective "all" (*pasē*) is feminine singular dative and thus is best seen as modifying the first noun only—the only one of the three with which it matches in gender, number, and case: "in *all* power." The closing genitive "of falsehood" (*pseudous*) governs not just the last noun "wonders," which it follows, but the word pair "signs and wonders," which clearly belong together and refer to a single reality. The genitive is qualitative (reflecting Hebrew usage: see BDF §165), and as such might be highlighting the fake or *unreal* character of the signs and wonders (RSV: "with pretended signs and wonders"; NIV 1984: "counterfeit miracles, signs and wonders"). But Paul does not question the reality of miracles and so is unlikely to be claiming that the lawless one's coming will be accompanied by "false" or "spurious" supernatural actions. Rather, precisely because his signs and wonders are real, they are so dangerous. The qualitative genitive is expressing the *deceptive* character of the miraculous signs and wonders (BDAG 1097: "deceptive wonders"; TNIV and NIV 2011: "signs and wonders that serve the lie"). The misleading aspect of the lawless one's coming is supported by the reference to "deception" in the parallel prepositional clause of verse 10a and the reference in verse 11 to the "powerful delusion" (lit., "work of deception") that causes some to believe "the lie." This understanding is supported more generally by Jesus's warning that "false Christs and false prophets will appear and perform great signs and wonders to deceive even the elect—if that were possible" (Mark 13:22; Matt. 24:24). The book of Revelation also speaks of the great beast that will arise and do great signs in order to "deceive those who dwell on earth" (Rev. 13:13–14).

2:10 The description of the deceptive nature of the lawless one's coming, which will be in keeping with "the work of Satan," is continued by a second parallel prepositional phrase: "and in all deception of wickedness" (καὶ ἐν πάσῃ ἀπάτῃ ἀδικίας, *kai en pasē apatē adikias*). The noun "deception" (*apatē*), not common for Paul (elsewhere only Eph. 4:22; Col. 2:8), parallels "power" in the previous phrase and thus confirms that the purpose of the "signs and wonders" that will accompany the lawless one's coming is to mislead or deceive. The genitive "of wickedness" parallels "of falsehood" and thus is also likely qualitative: it highlights the evil or malicious character of the deception (BDAG 99: "wicked deception"). However, since deception by its very nature is wicked, this interpretation might result in making the expression "wicked deception" redundant. Another understanding is suggested by the parallel to the preceding prepositional phrase. Just as the qualitative genitive "of falsehood" highlights the intention of the signs and wonders to mislead, so also the qualitative genitive "of wickedness" expresses the purpose of the deception: to bring about wickedness. This leads a couple of commentators to render the phrase "deception of wickedness" as "enticement to wickedness" (Richard 1995: 334) or "deception leading to unrighteousness" (Beale 2003: 222). In other words, the lawless one's coming will not only involve miraculous signs that will deceive people but also deceptive signs that will induce them to engage in wicked or unrighteous acts. This understanding gains support from Paul's comment in verse 12 about those who "delighted in wickedness."

At this point in Paul's correction, an important shift takes place even though this shift is not signaled grammatically but instead indicated by the content. The apostle shifts his readers' attention away from the deceptive and wickedness-inducing coming of the lawless one to those who are negatively impacted by his coming. Indeed, the remainder not just of verse 10 but also all of verses 11–12 deals not with the coming of Satan's superman, but with those whom he deceives and their ultimate destruction. The likely reason for this shift from the lawless one's coming to his deceived followers is that these people are the ones who are persecuting the Thessalonian church.[35] Though the problem of persecution is not explicitly identified in 2:1–17, it is a major theme in the immediately preceding chapter and thus very much still in the mind of the apostle and his readers. As will be made clear below, Paul's description of the coming destruction that will fall upon not only the man of lawlessness but also his followers who are persecuting the believers in Thessalonica is ultimately a message of comfort to the apostle's readers, because this future judgment will vindicate their faith, punish their enemies, and demonstrate that God is just.

The lawless one's coming is directed "to[36] those on the way to destruction" (τοῖς ἀπολλυμένοις, tois apollymenois) and not, by way of contrast, to the believers in Thessalonica. Although Christians will certainly experience the revelation of the lawless one as severe persecution, his misleading "signs and wonders" and wickedness-inducing deception will have an effect only on those outside the community of faith. They are the ones who are presently blind to the "mystery of lawlessness" already at work in the world (2:7) and who have refused to accept the truth of the gospel, thereby leaving themselves vulnerable

---

35. Gaventa (1998: 115–16) observes that Paul has two distinct but related targets in view: not only the anxiety of the Thessalonian Christians over the false claim that the day of the Lord has come but also the problem of persecution: "Although the second target is not explicitly identified, there does seem to be one, namely, those who are afflicting the church."

36. The dative here in 2:10 likely functions to express not disadvantage (so Marshall 1983: 202; Malherbe 2000: 426) but the indirect object of "coming" (*parousia*).

to the destructive work of Satan's superman. The expression "the ones being destroyed" (*tois apollymenois*) is a typical expression of Paul (1 Cor. 1:18; 2 Cor. 2:15; 4:3), which he elsewhere contrasts with "the ones being saved" (1 Cor. 1:18; 2 Cor. 2:15; see also Luke 13:23; Acts 2:47). The present tense of the substantive participle represents the action as a process: "those on the way to destruction" (Fanning 1990: 103). In other words, Paul views the destruction of the wicked not merely as a simple event that will take place in the future but also as a process already begun, which will reach its logical conclusion after the lawless one makes his grand appearance. The verb *apollymi*, used to describe the deceived followers, is the same root already employed in 2:3 to label further the man of lawlessness: "the son of destruction," meaning "the one doomed to destruction." Thus this eschatological enemy fittingly leads his deceived followers to the very fate for which he himself is destined (Best 1977: 307).

Paul puts the blame for their destructive end not at the feet of God's reprobation nor even the deceptive handiwork of the lawless one, but squarely on the shoulders of their own misconduct: "because they did not accept the love of the truth so that they might be saved" (ἀνθ᾽ ὧν τὴν ἀγάπην τῆς ἀληθείας οὐκ ἐδέξαντο εἰς τὸ σωθῆναι αὐτούς, *anth' hōn tēn agapēn tēs alētheias ouk edexanto eis to sōthēnai autous*). The classical construction *anth' hōn*, which occurs only here in Paul's Letters but often in Luke's writings (Luke 1:20; 12:3; 19:44; Acts 12:23) and even more frequently in the LXX, literally means "in return for which" and thus "because" (BDAG 88.5; BDF §201.1). The words following this construction, therefore, are intended to spell out the reason why some are on the way to destruction: "because they did not accept the love of the truth." That this reference to "the truth" refers not to some philosophical truth or truth in a wider sense (such as the truth of God's existence revealed in creation: so Trilling 1980: 110; Marshall 1983: 203) but narrowly to the gospel message is clear from three factors. First, Paul elsewhere uses the word "truth" as a synonym for the gospel (e.g., 2 Cor. 4:2; 13:8; Gal. 2:5, 14; 5:7; Eph. 1:13; Col. 1:5, 6; see BDAG 42.2.b: "the content of Christianity as the ultimate truth"). Second, the same verb "receive" was used twice in the previous letter to refer to the Thessalonian church's acceptance of "the word," that is, the gospel (1 Thess. 1:6; 2:13; so also 2 Cor. 11:4). Third, in Paul's theology it is only the truth of the gospel that can bring about salvation ("so that they might be saved"). Therefore, the followers of the lawless one are on their way to destruction not because of forces outside their control but because of their own deliberate rejection of the truth of the gospel.

Paul, however, grounds their destruction not merely in their rejection of "the truth" but more fully and thus precisely in their rejection of "the love of the truth." Although the apostle combines the noun "love" with a genitive elsewhere in letters (e.g., "the love of God" in Rom. 5:5; 2 Thess. 3:5; "the love of Christ" in Rom. 8:35; 2 Cor. 5:14), this is the only time he joins it with "truth" (this combination occurs nowhere else in the NT either). The fuller expression "love of the truth" (the genitive is objective) goes beyond the idea of accepting the gospel on an intellectual level as something that is factually true or accurate, moving deeply to a passionate, emotional attachment to the gospel: one is personally and fully devoted to this truth. Several translations try to capture this greater involvement of the heart and will by rendering the literal expression "they did not accept the love of the truth" as "they refused to love the truth" (RSV, NRSV, NIV, NLT, NCV).

The past tense of "they did not accept" (*ouk edexanto*) is puzzling, since the time perspective in this section (vv. 8–10) involves future events. Some take the past tense to mean Paul is viewing events from the future point of view of the lawless one's coming (Best 1977: 307; Malherbe 2000: 426). It is more plausible, however, that Paul views events from his current point of view such that the past tense refers to the apostle's preaching of the gospel during his mission-founding ministry in Thessalonica: this was the time when the Thessalonian believers "accepted the word" (1 Thess. 1:6; 2:13) and when by contrast their persecutors "did not accept the love of the truth." As Wanamaker (1990: 261) observes about the past tense *edexanto*: "It is probable that Paul is alluding broadly to those who refused to accept the gospel at the time it was preached at Thessalonica and became the persecutors of the Christians" (see also Menken 1994: 117). This past rejection of the gospel by the believers' "fellow citizens" (1 Thess. 2:14) explains why they can justly be identified as "those [already] on the way to destruction" and also why the future comings of the lawless one and then of the Lord Jesus will not result (the construction *eis to* + infinitive can express either purpose or result: here result better fits this negative context) in their salvation ("so that they might be saved").

4. Present: The Judgment of Unbelievers (2:11–12)

The fourth section (vv. 11–12) of Paul's correction (2 Thess. 2:3–12) shifts the time perspective from future events back to present happenings. As with the previous temporal shifts begun at verse 6 (present time) and verse 8 (future time), here too the transition back to present happenings is marked with the conjunction "and." Paul rarely begins a new sentence with this conjunction (the technical term is *parataxis*: BDAG 494.1.b.β; BDF §458), but does so three times in such close proximity, suggesting that its presence here again at verse 11 can hardly be accidental but rather is due to Paul's careful composition of the larger unit of verses 3–12. The contrast here in verses 11–12 with the preceding subunit of verses 8–10, however, has less to do with *time*—a shift from future events to present happenings—than with *persons*—a shift from the lawless one and his coming to those whom he deceives and their ultimate destruction. This shift is understandable since it is these deceived and doomed unbelievers who are persecuting the Thessalonian congregation. Paul's goal in verses 8–10, therefore, is not merely to continue to correct the false claim about the day of the Lord but also, as I have argued throughout the exegesis of this complex passage, to comfort his oppressed readers. [37]

37. Wanamaker (1990: 264): "Naturally, this rhetoric [in vv. 11–12] provided considerable encouragement for Paul's converts to persevere, in spite of their experience of oppression, by

The Thessalonian citizens' rejection of the gospel preached by Paul during his past mission-founding visit then causes God to act: "And because of this God sends them a powerful delusion in order that they believe the lie" (καὶ διὰ τοῦτο πέμπει αὐτοῖς ὁ θεὸς ἐνέργειαν πλάνης εἰς τὸ πιστεῦσαι αὐτοὺς τῷ ψεύδει, *kai dia touto pempei autois ho theos energeian planēs eis to pisteusai autous tō pseudei*).

The conjunction "and" (*kai*), omitted in some translations (e.g., NLT, NIV, NRSV, ESV), is important since it functions as a coordinating conjunction that strengthens the connection between Paul's words in this verse with the immediately preceding one. The apostle emphasizes this connection further by means of the prepositional phrase "because of this" (*dia touto*), which also looks back (anaphoric function) to his just-mentioned statement that "they did not accept the love of the truth" (v. 10b). Since this preceding verse with its past tense refers to Paul's mission-founding ministry in Thessalonica as the time when many in the city "did not accept the love of the truth," it is a logical outcome that God in the present time, as a direct consequence of that past rejection of the gospel, "sends them a powerful delusion." There is no need, therefore, to view the present-tense verb *pempei* (for the variant future reading πέμψει, *pempsei*, see additional notes) as a "prophetic present" (Lightfoot 1904: 118), referring to a future event that will occur when the apostasy comes and the man of lawlessness is revealed (so, e.g., Frame 1912: 217; Marshall 1983: 204). Rather, "it is a true present, describing what is happening now" (Malherbe 2000: 427).

What God sends to those who reject the gospel is a "powerful delusion" or, literally, "a working of deception" (*energeian planēs*). In Paul's writings the noun *energeia* always refers to the working or operation not of humans but of transcendent beings—typically, as is the case here, God (Eph. 1:19; 3:7; 4:16; Phil. 3:21; Col. 1:29; 2:12; 1 Cor. 12:10 v.l.), or with one exception found two verses earlier, Satan (2 Thess. 2:9, "in conformity with the *work* of Satan"). The divine source of this working means that it is no weak or impotent force but a "strong" (KJV, ESV) or "powerful" (NIV, NRSV) one.

The goal of God sending this strong or powerful working to unbelievers is their "delusion" or "deception" (Frame 1912: 272: "πλάνης is a genitive of the object, and denotes the goal of the active inward energy, namely, 'delusion,' the state of being deceived"). This is confirmed in the subsequent purpose clause, "in order that they believe the lie." The use of the singular *pseudos* along with the article ("*the* lie") suggests that Paul is not referring to error or falsehood in general but to something specific. Many commentators believe the apostle is referring back either to the false claim by the man of lawlessness to be God (v. 4) or to the "false" wonders that will accompany his coming (v. 9). Both of these possible antecedents for "the lie," however, suffer from the defect that they deal with a *future* falsehood, whereas verse 11 speaks of

---

ultimately promising their vindication." Also Fee (2009: 295): "All of this [vv. 11–12] is intended not as a threat to the Thessalonians, but as comfort for them in the midst of present persecution."

a *present* delusion. It is more likely that "the lie" refers to the rejection of the gospel: since "the truth" refers to the gospel that Paul preached to the citizens of Thessalonica and that they did not accept (v. 10b), "the lie" plausibly refers to the rejection of this gospel truth (Best 1977: 309; Bruce 1982: 174; Fee 2009: 295). Further support lies in Rom. 1:25, where "the lie" is used to describe those who "exchanged the truth about God for the lie and worshiped and served the creature rather than the Creator."

2:12   The result[38] of people's rejection of the gospel and of God's subsequent sending of a powerful delusion is hardly surprising: "so that all who have not believed the truth but delighted in wickedness will be condemned" (ἵνα κριθῶσιν πάντες οἱ μὴ πιστεύσαντες τῇ ἀληθείᾳ ἀλλὰ εὐδοκήσαντες τῇ ἀδικίᾳ, *hina krithōsin pantes hoi mē pisteusantes tē alētheia alla eudokēsantes tē adikia*).

The verb *krinō* by itself is a neutral term, implying neither acquittal nor condemnation. Yet in this context of "not accepting the love of the truth" but instead "believing the lie," the notion of condemnation is clearly in view (BDAG 568.5: "to engage in a judicial process, *judge, condemn*") and so refers to the final judgment. The past rejection of the gospel by unbelievers, which leads to the present delusion sent to them by God, will result in their future judgment. Paul does not spell out who executes this future judgment or what this upcoming condemnation involves, but both of these are easily discerned. The use of the passive voice (the so-called divine passive), the explicit reference to "God" in the main clause of verse 11, and the larger context portraying all these activities as occurring under God's sovereign control—these features reveal God to be the judge who executes his just judgment against those who have rejected his gospel. As to what such just judgment or condemnation entails for unbelievers, this was already described by Paul in the opening thanksgiving section: since they have "afflicted" the Thessalonian Christians, it is just that God will pay them back with "affliction" (1:6); they will also receive "a penalty, eternal destruction from the presence of the Lord and from the glory of his might" (1:9).

Paul does not identify either the agent or the nature of the condemnation that unbelievers will receive. The apostle, does, however, mention and emphasize these unbelievers as the recipients of that condemnation—an emphasis that is accomplished in three ways. First, since the subject of the verb "they will be condemned" is clear from the preceding context, the explicit mention of "those who have not believed the truth but delighted in wickedness" is emphatic and functions "to bring home the gravity of the action and of God's judgment" (Best 1977: 309; also Wanamaker 1990: 263). Second, Paul further highlights the oppressors of the Thessalonian church as recipients of the future

---

38. Although ἵνα followed by the subjunctive typically expresses purpose, it can also express result (BDAG 477.3). This latter sense of result is more likely here in 2:12, given that the notion of purpose is already expressed in the preceding articular infinitive (εἰς τὸ πιστεῦσαι). Some commentators refer to this verse as indicating the "ultimate" purpose in contrast to the "initial" purpose expressed in the preceding verse (Frame 1912: 272; Marshall 1983: 204).

condemnation by describing them not in a short and formally simple phrase, but in a longer, antithetical clause (not *x* but *y*) that justifies their punishment both negatively ("who have not believed the truth") and positively ("but delighted in wickedness"). Third, the addition of the adjective "all" broadens the condemnation to include not just those unbelievers in Thessalonica but also all those in other places who similarly reject the gospel and so deserve God's just judgment. The nouns "truth" and "wickedness" occur as a word pair elsewhere in Paul's Letters (Rom. 2:8; 1 Cor. 13:6) and show that in the apostle's thinking (as in the rest of the canon), morality is always closely linked to truth: right conduct naturally emerges from right belief; conversely, wrong or evil conduct naturally emerges from wrong belief.

At first glance, the words of these two past verses (vv. 11–12) are puzzling and problematic. Christians do not easily accept the idea that God sends a powerful work of delusion that leads people to believe the lie and ultimately results in their condemnation. However, at least three important points need to be remembered when hearing these words. First, the significance of the opening prepositional phrase in verse 11 ("because of this") should not be overlooked: God acts not as a cause but as a consequence of people's previous rejection of the truth of the gospel. Second, God's action is similar not only to Paul's statements elsewhere that God gives sinners over to their own sin (Rom. 1:24, 26, 28; 11:8; 2 Tim. 4:4), but also to certain OT texts where God employs evil spirits to inspire false prophets and so carry out his just judgment against the wicked (2 Sam. 24:1; 1 Kings 22:23; Ezek. 14:9). Third, Paul's purpose here is not to give a theological exposition of God's role in the judgment of sinners, but to comfort the persecuted Christians in Thessalonica. As Witherington (2006: 226) observes: "There is meant to be some comfort here for believers under pressure and persecution that God is still in charge and that they are not among those who are perishing but rather among those who love the truth."

C. Comfort: God Ensures the Salvation of the Thessalonians (2:13–14)

The importance of including this paragraph with the preceding verses of this chapter cannot be overstated. If one reads only up to verse 12, as most commentators unfortunately do, then this passage closes with a note of judgment for unbelievers. If, however, one reads all the way up to verse 17, then this passage closes with a note of comfort for the Thessalonian believers.[39] This message of comfort is found not only in the twofold occurrence of "comfort" in the closing prayer of verses 16–17 (v. 16, the noun παράκλησιν, *paraklēsin*; v. 17, the verb παρακαλέσαι, *parakalesai*), but earlier here in the paragraph of verses 13–14. Whereas the immediately preceding verses stress the just judgment of God on the unbelievers in Thessalonica who are persecuting the

39. For a justification that 2:13–17 belongs to 2:1–12, as well as an explanation of the significance of this fact, see the extensive discussion above, under "Extent of the Passage."

church, the present paragraph (vv. 13–14) emphasizes God's election of the Thessalonian believers such that they are guaranteed to receive not judgment but salvation. In the words of my alternative heading for 2:1–17, the present paragraph highlights "the sure salvation of the saints."

2:13 After the gloom and doom in the preceding verses, which characterized the fate of those persecuting the Thessalonian church, here Paul in sharp contrast gushes with gratitude about the different fate that awaits his beloved converts in Thessalonica: "But as for us, we ought to give thanks to God always concerning you, brothers loved by the Lord, because God chose you as firstfruits for salvation by means of the sanctifying work of the Spirit and your belief in the truth" (ἡμεῖς δὲ ὀφείλομεν εὐχαριστεῖν τῷ θεῷ πάντοτε περὶ ὑμῶν, ἀδελφοὶ ἠγαπημένοι ὑπὸ κυρίου, ὅτι εἵλατο ὑμᾶς ὁ θεὸς ἀπαρχὴν εἰς σωτηρίαν ἐν ἁγιασμῷ πνεύματος καὶ πίστει ἀληθείας, *hēmeis de opheilomen eucharistein tō theō pantote peri hymōn, adelphoi ēgapēmenoi hypo kyriou, hoti heilato hymas ho theos aparchēn eis sōtērian en hagiasmō pneumatos kai pistei alētheias.*

Paul's words repeat virtually verbatim those used in 1:3 to open this letter. The similarities with 1:3 are so strong that the apostle must be intending to remind the readers of his earlier words of thanksgiving, thereby adding emphasis to what he had said about them there and now repeats about them here. This stress on Paul's overwhelming thanksgiving or gratitude about the Thessalonian believers is further heightened by four subtle but significant changes from the statement of 1:3.

First, there is the addition of the personal pronoun "we," which is emphatic not only by its mere presence (since "we" is already expressed in the verbal form *opheilomen* and thus not needed to be stated explicitly) but also by its location at the head of the sentence. Milligan (1908: 106) refers to "the emphatic 'we' in the present passage lending additional stress to the writer's keen sense of indebtedness to God for the good estate of the Thessalonian church." In light of the sharp contrast that Paul forms between the fate of unbelievers in the previous verses and that of the Thessalonian Christians in this paragraph, one might have expected the apostle to use the second-person pronoun "you" instead of the first person "we." Paul's word choice, however, allows him to convey the strong emotional attachment he has to the believers in Thessalonica: he, along with Silas and Timothy, is personally invested in their welfare, and his concern for their well-being is inseparably linked with that of their own (O'Brien 1977: 185n114).

Second, there is the addition of the particle *de* (but). It occurs in none of the other thanksgiving formulas of Paul (Rom. 1:8; 1 Cor. 1:4; 2 Cor. 1:11; Eph. 1:15; Phil. 1:3; Col. 1:3; 1 Thess. 1:2; 2:13; 2 Thess. 1:3; Philem. 4), and thus its presence cannot be explained as belonging to the form of this epistolary convention. Instead, the particle functions to enhance the contrast that Paul creates between the just judgment of God against the church's oppressors (vv. 11–12) and the sure salvation of the Thessalonian believers (vv. 13–14).

Third, the word order of the key verbs is changed: whereas in 1:3 the main verb "we ought" occurs after the infinitive "to give thanks," here it comes before the infinitive. Although one should not read too much into this minor modification, the change in the word order does emphasize Paul's sense and feeling of obligation to give thanks to God concerning his readers. A few scholars view the apostle's language of "We ought to give thanks" as distant and cool compared to the intimacy and warmth of his other thanksgivings, where he simply says, "We give thanks," and see in the expression of obligation further evidence that 2 Thessalonians does not come from the hand of Paul (e.g., J. A. Bailey 1978–79: 137; Trilling 1980: 119; Furnish 2007: 132). This interpretation, however, fails to see the obvious affection that the apostle has for his readers, evident not only in the use of the first-person pronoun "we," as noted above, but also in the expanded vocative phrase "brothers loved by the Lord." The obligation to give thanks of which Paul speaks here, therefore, refers not to a reluctant or forced expression of gratitude but instead to a great compulsion that naturally arises out of the apostle's great joy for them. Paul is acknowledging, as others of his day do, the need for gratitude to be given to God, since he is responsible for the readers' election and ultimate salvation, in sharp contrast to the judgment facing their oppressors (for further discussion, see comments on 2 Thess. 1:3).

Fourth, whereas Paul in 1:3 identifies his readers with the vocative "brothers," he here expands that identification with the remarkable phrase "brothers loved by the Lord" (*adelphoi ēgapēmenoi hypo kyriou*). This phrase is striking for two reasons. First, Paul has replaced the expected reference to *God* ("loved by God": so 1 Thess. 1:4; see also Col. 3:12) with a reference to *the Lord*.[40] Some have downplayed this replacement, understanding the Greek *kyrios* here as a reference to God rather than to Jesus (so Rigaux 1956: 371; Ellingworth and Nida 1975: 182; Malherbe 2000: 436; Beale 2003: 225). In support of reading *kyrios* this way, proponents appeal to the following factors, all of them based on the context: (1) God is the primary actor in both verses 11–12 and verses 13–14; (2) there is an explicit reference to "God" both immediately before and after the reference to "the Lord"; and (3) the subsequent prayer of verses 16–17 identifies God as "the one who loves us." Nevertheless, there remain compelling reasons why *kyrios* here refers not to God but to Jesus. This is supported more generally by Paul's use of this term elsewhere in his writings, including both Thessalonian Letters. More specific and ultimately decisive support lies in the grammar of verse 13. For if Paul had actually intended to refer to God's love rather than Jesus's love, this would have resulted in two changes to what he actually wrote. Since Paul has already referred to God ("We ought to give thanks to God"), he could have more simply stated: "loved by *him*, because *he* chose you." However, since Paul intended to refer to the love of Christ, this necessitated his writing "loved by *the Lord*" and adding another explicit reference to "God" as the subject of the verb "he chose" in order to mark

---

40. In 2:13 some copyists "corrected" the text to "God" (see additional notes below).

the shift in person (so already Eadie 1877: 291; also Best 1977: 311; Fee 2009: 300n98). There can be little doubt, therefore, that the apostle is saying that the Thessalonian believers are "loved by the Lord," that is, by Jesus Christ. Since the other instances where Paul speaks about Christ's love have in view specifically his saving work on the cross (Rom. 8:35, 37, 39; 2 Cor. 5:14; Gal. 2:20; Eph. 3:19; 5:2, 25; 1 Tim. 1:14; 2 Tim. 1:13), that is its likely meaning here as well (Fee 2009: 301).

Why did Paul replace the expected reference to "God" with "the Lord"? A few scholars do not bother answering this question on the conviction that this change has little or no significance (Best 1977: 312: "We ought not then to make too much of this variation"; Morris 1991: 238: "There is probably no significance in the change from 'loved by God' to 'loved by the Lord'"). Others, however, see such a replacement as especially appropriate for this context, where the antichrist's followers are being contrasted with Christ's beloved ones: "In the present context it [the shift from God to Christ] may be deliberate in order to reassure the readers that the Lord Jesus, who is coming for his own people and who will destroy the wicked, loves them in particular and will keep them in safety for final salvation" (Marshall 1983: 206; so also Moore 1969; O'Brien 1977: 186; Weatherly 1996: 273). Although this is surely part of the answer for the change, an additional reason is also probable. The exact expression "loved by the Lord" in Greek occurs elsewhere only in Deut. 33:12 LXX, where it is used in Moses's blessing to the tribe of Benjamin.[41] Since Paul was a Benjamite—the tribe to which his namesake, King Saul, also belonged, and the tribe with which he explicitly identified himself with a certain degree of pride (Phil. 3:5; Rom. 11:1), he obviously would be very familiar with this OT expression. It appears, therefore, that Paul has taken his ancestral blessing and applied it to his converts in Thessalonica: they, like him, are "loved by the Lord" (so O'Brien 1977: 186; D. Martin 1995: 251; Fee 2009: 299).

The second reason why the phrase "loved by the Lord" is so striking is that it provides another example of how Paul takes language originally applied to Israel (in addition to the full phrase, found in this exact form only in Deut. 33:12, see also the identification of Israel as "loved" in Deut. 32:15 LXX; Pss. 60:5; 108:6; Isa. 44:2 LXX; Jer. 11:15; 12:7; Sir. 45:1; Bar. 3:36 [3:37 LXX]; etc.) and reapplies it to the Christian church. Especially in this context, where Paul grounds his obligation to thank God in God's election of the Thessalonian believers ("because God chose you"), there can be little doubt that Paul's taking terms originally reserved for Israel (or more specifically, for Benjamin, a particular tribe of Israel) and applying them to the predominantly Gentile

41. The similar expression "loved by his Lord" occurs in Sir. 46:13 LXX, which differs slightly from Paul's wording with the addition of the personal pronoun "his." The absence of the article before "Lord" in Paul's wording (ἠγαπημένοι ὑπὸ κυρίου) is notable, since the parallel expression "loved by God" in the previous letter (1 Thess. 1:4; see also Col. 3:12) does have the article. This leads Fee (2009: 299n94) to state, "That Paul is borrowing [from Deut. 33:12 LXX] his ancestral language seems certain in this case because of the anarthrous κυρίου."

congregation of Thessalonica cannot be coincidental but stems from his conviction that the church—made up of both Jewish and Gentile Christians—now constitutes the renewed Israel of God (see comments on 1 Thess. 1:1, 4; 4:8; also Thielman 1994: 73–74; Weima 1996: esp. 101–3). What Marshall (1990: 262) states about the similar phrase in 1 Thess. 1:4 is equally true of Paul's words here: "It is clear that by this early stage in his thinking Paul has already developed the concept of the church as the Israel of God. The conviction that God's love is now extended to the church composed of Jews and Gentiles is already present, and it does not need to be defended in any way. The church has inherited the position of Israel."

After the opening main clause that expresses strongly the missionaries' obligation to give thanks to God for the Thessalonian converts comes a subordinate clause, introduced with the conjunction *hoti*. The conjunction here is causal and so introduces the first of two explicit[42] and parallel reasons *why* there is the obligation to give thanks to God (the second explicit reason is given in the relative clause that immediately follows in 2:14): "because God chose you" (*hoti heilato hymas ho theos*). Paul's reason for thanksgiving differs from that given in the opening of this letter: whereas in 1:3–4 the apostle highlights what his readers have done (their remarkable spiritual growth in the face of heavy persecution), here he focuses on what God has done (his election of the Thessalonian Christians), the very thing also cited in the first letter as the reason for giving thanks (1 Thess. 1:2–4: "We give thanks to God . . . because we know, brothers loved by God, your election"). The apostle is seeking to comfort his readers, and so he grounds his thanksgiving not in their own praiseworthy yet ultimately fickle conduct, but instead in the eternal and unchanging choice of God. The idea of God's election or primary role in the Thessalonians' salvation appears throughout 1 Thessalonians, where, as is the case also here, it is never explained but assumed to be known (1 Thess. 1:4; 2:12; 3:3b; 4:7; 5:9, 24). Furthermore, although the idea of God's election is constant in Paul's writings, the words he uses to express this concept are not, as the apostle employs some six or seven different terms (see list in Frame 1912: 280; Morris 1991: 238n67; Malherbe 2000: 436). Here he uses the verb *haireō*, which in the middle voice has the sense of "choose" (BDAG 28.2). Since the only other two occurrences of this term in the NT refer to human choice (Phil. 1:22; Heb. 11:25), Paul's word selection for the idea of God's election may seem "odd" (Witherington 2006: 232). The explanation may be that the apostle is influenced by Deut. 26:18 LXX, where exactly the same verbal form is used to describe God's choosing of Israel in an important text known to Paul because it involves the renewal of the Sinai covenant. But regardless of the origin of Paul's word selection, it will be comforting for the Thessalonian believers to hear that their salvation depends not on their own human effort but on God's divine choice.

---

42. In 2:13 an implicit reason for giving thanks appears in the striking vocative address of the readers as "loved by the Lord."

Next one faces a tough textual problem that involves the difference of only a single Greek letter, yet it results in a considerable difference in meaning: did Paul write after the clause "God chose you" either (1) a prepositional phrase "from the beginning" (ΑΠΑΡΧΗΣ = ἀπ᾽ ἀρχῆς), or (2) a second object "as firstfruits" (ΑΠΑΡΧΗΝ = ἀπαρχήν)? The external evidence—the number, date, location of the manuscripts—is almost evenly split: both readings enjoy strong manuscript support from both the East and West.[43] Nevertheless, the internal evidence—what Paul likely wrote and what the copyists likely did—in at least five ways favors the reading "firstfruits" as original (see esp. B. Metzger 1994: 568; Fee 1992: 179–80; 2009: 298n92, 301–2). First, Paul nowhere else uses the exact phrase "from the beginning" and so is unlikely to be doing so here. Second, when the apostle wants to express the idea of something going back to the very beginning of time, he uses different prepositional phrases than "from the beginning" (1 Cor. 2:7, "before the ages"; Col. 1:26, "from the ages"; Eph. 1:4, "before the foundation of the earth"; 2 Tim. 1:9, "before the times of the ages"). Third, Paul normally uses the noun *archē* with the meaning "ruler, authority" (Rom. 8:38; 1 Cor. 15:24; Eph. 1:21; 3:10; 6:12; Col. 1:16; 2:10, 15; Titus 3:1) and only rarely with the temporal sense of "beginning" (Col. 1:18, which may be part of a hymn; Phil. 4:15). Fourth, the term "firstfruits" is a Pauline word that occurs in his other writings six times (Rom. 8:23; 11:16; 16:5; 1 Cor. 15:20, 23; 16:15), two of which occur without a qualifying genitive, as is the case here in 2:13. Fifth, there are two instances where copyists apparently took offense at the original reading "firstfruits" and substituted it with "from the beginning," even though this latter "corrected" reading did not fit the context (Rom. 16:5, in 𝔓[46] D* g m; Rev. 14:4, in 𝔓[47] ℵ 336 1918).

Counterarguments, of course, can be made against these points. A few claim that the original and rare phrase "from the beginning" was replaced with the more common "firstfruits" (Richard 1995: 356). But while this is a possibility, it is not a weighty enough argument to override the five factors cited above. Some object that the Thessalonian believers were not technically "firstfruits" since others in Macedonia had become believers before them, such as the Christians in Philippi. But this argument assumes that Paul intended something that he does not say: "firstfruits *of Macedonia*." It is more likely the case, however, that, "since Paul does not qualify 'first fruits' in any way, he almost certainly intended these believers to see themselves more narrowly as God's 'first fruits' *in Thessalonica*" (Fee 2009: 302), that is, the first of many others from their city who would yet become believers. But even if Paul were thinking more broadly of the Thessalonian believers as the firstfruits of Macedonia, such a metaphor could justly be made in light of both the brief time that had elapsed between Paul's ministry in Philippi and that in Thessalonica, and also the striking success of his Thessalonian ministry (Milligan 1908: 106–7). Furthermore, the word "firstfruits" in the LXX refers not just chronologically to the first produce of the land or firstborn of domestic animals

---

43. See MS support for each option in the additional notes below.

but also qualitatively to the best produce or best animal that one offers to God (Spicq 1994: 1.145–52; BDAG 98: "such sacrifices would begin with 'firstlings' or 'first fruits,' frequently distinguished for quality"). Paul's reference to the Thessalonian church as "firstfruits," therefore, may well have in view not just their priority in sequence but also their quality (Malherbe 2000: 437).

Perhaps the strongest objection to the reading "firstfruits" is the charge that it does not fit Paul's purpose of comforting his readers. Frame (1912: 281), for example, states that "in a section written for the encouragement of those who were losing the assurance of their salvation, ἀπ' ἀρχῆς [from the beginning] is more appropriate than ἀπαρχήν [firstfruits]." Marshall (1983: 207) similarly asserts: "The decisive argument against the variant [firstfruits] is that it does not make sense in the context." But this objection fails to recognize how comforting the metaphor of firstfruits would have been to the Thessalonian believers. To a community of believers scared out of their wits (2:2a) over claims that the day of the Lord has come (2:2b) and therefore afraid that they might not be part of the assembly gathered to Christ at his parousia (2:1), it would be greatly reassuring to hear that their eternal destiny will not be the destruction that awaits the man of lawlessness (2:8–10) and his deceived followers (2:11–12), but rather that they have been chosen by God as firstfruits—first and perhaps also choice fruit at the great eschatological harvest. In this metaphor the Thessalonian believers would have been comforted, however, not only by hearing again about their own presence at the eschatological harvest, but also how they are the vanguard of many others from their community whom God has likewise chosen for salvation. Although the Christians in Thessalonica may look at themselves as a small and persecuted community, they should instead see themselves from God's perspective, as firstfruits—forerunners of many others from their own families and home city who will join them in the abundant end-time harvest.

The causal clause "because God chose you as firstfruits" is qualified by two prepositional phrases, the first of which is introduced with *eis* and so expresses the *purpose* (BDAG 290.4.f) of the Thessalonian believers being elected by God: "for salvation" (*eis sōtērian*). The word "salvation" is one that Paul has used elsewhere in the two Thessalonian Letters, both in its noun (1 Thess. 5:8, 9) and verbal (1 Thess. 2:16; 2 Thess. 2:10) forms. Some assert, "The word [salvation] must be given here its widest possible meaning embracing both the present life and the life of the End" (Best 1977: 314). However, the use of the word elsewhere in the two letters, as well as the present context with its heavy eschatological focus, indicates that Paul is thinking primarily about the salvation that the Thessalonian believers will enjoy on the day of the Lord. The apostle's word choice is controlled by the comforting contrast he wants to create between his readers and those who are persecuting them: while their fellow citizens in Thessalonica who are opposing them are "those on the way to destruction" because they refused to love the truth with the result "that they might be saved" (v. 10b), the Thessalonian Christians have been chosen by God "for salvation."

The second prepositional phrase that qualifies the causal clause "because God chose you as firstfruits" is introduced with *en* and so expresses the *means or instrumentality* (BDAG 328.5.b) by which the divine choice takes place: "through the sanctifying work of the Spirit and your belief in the truth" (*en hagiasmō pneumatos kai pistei alētheias*). The Greek text is more ambiguous than this English translation suggests. The issue centers on whether the genitive *pneumatos* is subjective and thus refers to the holiness that the Spirit (that is, the Holy Spirit)[44] has and causes to exist within a believer, or whether it instead is objective and thus refers to the holiness that the spirit (that is, the human spirit [1 Thess. 5:23]) receives. Those who advocate the latter position (e.g., Findlay 1891: 189–90; Moffatt 1897: 50; Witherington 2006: 232–33) do so for at least two reasons, neither of which are ultimately convincing. First, that *pneumatos* lacks both the definite article and the adjective "holy" is not decisive, since there are other instances of this phenomenon where the Holy Spirit is clearly intended (e.g., Rom. 8:4, 13; see esp. 1 Pet. 1:2, where the Third Person of the Trinity is obviously in view). Second, that the parallel genitive *alētheias* in this same prepositional phrase is objective ("your belief in the truth") is suggestive but not weighty enough to override other compelling evidence. The immediate context stresses God's role in the salvation of the readers ("God chose you"), which suggests that the same thing is intended in the prepositional phrase "through the holiness of the Spirit." The larger context of the Thessalonian Letters states this idea exactly, similarly connecting the sanctifying work of the Spirit with God's election: "your election . . . in the Holy Spirit" (1 Thess. 1:4–5); "God call[ed] us . . . in holiness. . . . God . . . gives his Spirit, who is holy, into you" (4:7–8). Furthermore, Paul's other letters link the Spirit of God with the sanctification of believers (Rom. 15:16; 1 Cor. 6:11–12; 1 Thess. 4:7–8). Finally, the sequence of the elements in the prepositional phrase supports reading *pneumatos* as a subjective genitive that refers to the Spirit of God, since Paul normally places the divine means ("the sanctifying work of the Spirit") before the human ("your belief in the truth"; Fee 2009: 303). To take *pneumatos* as an objective genitive that refers to the human spirit would result in an illogical sequence, where sanctification occurs after belief (Menken 1994: 121).

The divine initiative of the Spirit as the means by which God works out his choice of the Thessalonian believers is balanced by their human response:

44. This means that there is a reference to all three divine persons within the same verse (2:13): "But as for us we ought to give thanks to God always concerning you, brothers loved by the **Lord** [Jesus Christ], because **God** chose you as firstfruits for salvation by means of the sanctifying work of the **Spirit** and your belief in the truth." Although Paul does not stress these references, it is another striking instance of how the apostle, "rigorous monotheist though he was, joins Father, Son and Spirit in ways that indicate the full identity of the Son and Spirit with the Father, while not losing that monotheism" (Fee 2009: 300n96). For a list of over thirty other such proto-Trinitarian passages in Paul's Letters, see Fee 1994a: 48n39.

"through[45] . . . belief in the truth" (*en . . . pistei alētheias*). Again there is the ambiguity of whether the genitive *alētheias* is subjective and thus refers to the "truth" that creates "faith," or is instead objective and thus refers to the "faith *in* or directed to the truth," that is, belief in the truth of the gospel. Since the subjective reading is awkward and does not balance well the other half of this prepositional phrase, the objective reading is strongly preferred. Paul, then, is referring to the "faith," meaning his readers' belief in the "truth." The apostle's word choice here of "faith" (in the sense of belief) and "truth" is again determined by the comforting contrast that he continues to create between his readers and those who are persecuting them: whereas their fellow citizens in Thessalonica "believed [*pisteusai*, the same root as the noun "faith"] the lie" (v. 11b) and are identified as "those who did not believe [*pisteusantes*, the same root as the noun "faith"] the truth" (v. 12), the Thessalonian Christians are saved by "your belief in the truth." Since "truth" in verse 13 looks back to the same word in verse 12, where that term refers to the gospel (see comments on these verses), that is also its meaning here: the church in Thessalonica is saved by their belief in the truth, that is, the gospel. This meaning is confirmed by the parallel prepositional phrase in the immediately following verse, where God called the Thessalonian believers "through our gospel."

Paul parallels the *hoti* clause of verse 13b, which gives the first reason why he and his cosenders must give thanks to God for the Thessalonian believers, with a relative clause that gives a second yet similar reason why such thanksgiving is necessary: "To this end he also[46] called you through our gospel for the obtaining of the glory of our Lord Jesus Christ" (εἰς ὃ καὶ ἐκάλεσεν ὑμᾶς διὰ τοῦ εὐαγγελίου ἡμῶν εἰς περιποίησιν δόξης τοῦ κυρίου ἡμῶν Ἰησοῦ Χριστοῦ, *eis ho kai ekalesen hymas dia tou euaggeliou hēmōn eis peripoiēsin doxēs tou kyriou hēmōn Iēsou Christou*).

2:14

The parallels in both content and grammar between this second reason and the first are so striking that they can hardly be accidental: both open with a main verb (indicative mood, aorist tense) that stresses God's past initiative in the salvation of the readers (v. 13b, "God chose you"; v. 14, "he called you"), which is then followed with two prepositional phrases, one spelling out the *goal* (*eis* plus the accusative) of God's action (v. 13b, "for salvation"; v. 14, "for the obtaining of the glory of our Lord Jesus Christ"), the other spelling out the *means* of God's action (v. 13b, "through the sanctifying work of the Spirit and your belief in the truth"; v. 14, "through our gospel"). Although each of the parallel elements in the second reason clarifies to a slightly further degree the elements in the first reason, the content remains fundamentally the same. In other words, Paul provides no new information in verse 14 that he has not

45. In 2:13c the close link between the sanctifying work of the Spirit and the Thessalonian belief in the truth of the gospel is indicated by the single preposition ἐν used to introduce both the divine initiative and the human response.
46. On the textual question of whether this conjunction in 2:14 belongs to Paul's original letter or is a later addition, see the additional notes below.

already stated more generally in verse 13b. Nevertheless, the repetition provided in verse 14 serves an important rhetorical purpose: providing emphasis. By repeating and clarifying that God not only "chose" the Thessalonian readers but also "elected" them, that God's purpose was not only their "salvation" but also their "obtaining of the glory of our Lord Jesus Christ," and that this happened not only "through the sanctifying work of the Spirit and your belief in the truth" but also "through our gospel," Paul strengthens the comforting function that this unit (vv. 13–14) has within 2:1–17. His readers are further reassured that God has acted in such a way so as to guarantee their future salvation and glory.

Paul introduces the second reason why he, along with Silas and Timothy, ought to give thanks to God for the Thessalonian readers, using a prepositional clause ("to this end") that looks back not to any specific noun in the preceding causal clause (the nouns "salvation," "holiness," "belief," and "truth" are all masculine or feminine and so do not agree with the neuter relative pronoun) but more generally to the whole clause made up of these nouns. Just as the identical expression "to this end" in 1:11 (introducing the prayer report) refers back generally to the whole of 1:5–10, so here (introducing the second parallel reason for giving thanks) it refers back to the whole of 2:13b. The preceding main clause, "God chose you," is clarified by the statement that "he also elected you" (*kai ekalesen hymas*). By far the verb *kaleō* is Paul's favorite term among the five or six different terms he uses to describe God's initiative in human salvation, occurring thirty-three times in his various letters. Such a high frequency suggests that the concept of God's election must be an important and recurring one in the apostle's preaching ministry. This fact also explains why he can again use either the specific term (1 Thess. 2:12; 4:7; 5:7, 24) or the broad concept (1 Thess. 1:4; 3:3b; 5:9; 2 Thess. 2:13) without feeling any need to explain or illustrate it for his readers in Thessalonica. Paul's concern here is not didactic but pastoral: God has elected the Thessalonian believers, and so the salvation of these saints is sure.

Paul proceeds to clarify the *means* of God's elective work: whereas the previous clause described this abstractly as happening "through the sanctifying work of the Spirit and your belief in the truth," here the apostle states more specifically that this happened "through our gospel" (*dia tou euaggeliou hēmōn*), that is, through the good news that he and his coworkers preached during their mission-founding visit to Thessalonica. As Best (1977: 316) puts it: "The pre-historical or meta-historical choice by God became actual in the historical event of Paul's visit to Thessalonica and his preaching of the gospel." The word "gospel" (*euaggelion*) occurs some sixty times in the apostle's letters, very often accompanied by the genitive descriptors "of God" (stressing the origin of the gospel—from God: so 1 Thess. 2:2, 4, 8, 9) or "of Christ" (stressing the content of the gospel—about Christ: so 1 Thess. 3:2; 2 Thess. 1:8). Here Paul deviates from his typical manner of referring to the gospel and employs the personal pronoun "our" (*hēmōn*), which stresses the crucial role that he and his fellow missionaries played in the Thessalonians' conversion and their experience of election (so also 1 Thess. 1:5).[47] Paul's reference to "*our gospel*," therefore, does not appear to be merely a "personal touch" intended to "stress his care for his converts" (so Morris 1991: 240). Rather, it more likely has a polemical thrust, as Paul is already anticipating the command that he is about to give in the following verse to hold fast to the traditions that *he and his coworkers* taught them "either by our word [our original preaching the gospel to them] or by our letter" as opposed to a "prophetic utterance" (2:2b) by *others*—the likely source of the false claim that the day of the Lord has come.[48]

Paul also clarifies the *purpose* of God's elective work: whereas the previous clause stated in a generic way that God chose the Thessalonian believers "for salvation," here the apostle spells out that God elected them "for the obtaining of the glory of our Lord Jesus Christ" (*eis peripoiēsin doxēs tou kyriou hēmōn Iēsou Christou*). There is some uncertainty over the precise meaning of the verbal noun *peripoiēsis* and whether it has the passive meaning of "possession" or the active sense of "obtaining" (see BDAG 804)—not a meaningless distinction, since the latter rendering might imply that eschatological glory involves human achievement rather than a divine gift (see comments on 1 Thess. 5:9 for extended discussion of the similar phrase "the obtaining of salvation").

The nuances of this debate, however, should not distract us from the more important phrase with which Paul chooses to parallel "salvation": "the glory of our Lord Jesus Christ" (the genitive *doxēs* functions as the object of the verbal noun *peripoiēsin*). Here the Greek word *doxa* does not have the secular meaning of "fame, recognition, renown, honor, prestige" (BDAG 257.3) but the religious and OT sense of "divine glory," the visible radiance and majesty of God (BDAG 257.1). Paul elsewhere reflects this OT idea by normally connecting glory to God (e.g., 1 Thess. 2:12: "God, the one who is calling you into his own kingdom and glory"). Here, however, Paul strikingly ascribes to "our Lord Jesus Christ" the attribute of glory that in the OT is reserved for God. Paul's immediate purpose, though, is not to teach his readers about the divine attribute of glory that Christ shares with God but to comfort them about their ultimate destiny: God elected them for the purpose of their future obtaining of the glory of Christ. This agrees with many later statements by the apostle that believers will share in Christ's glory "if indeed we share in his sufferings in order that we may also share in his *glory*. I consider that our present sufferings are not worth comparing with the *glory* that will be revealed in us"

---

47. The personal pronoun "our" or "my" with "gospel" occurs elsewhere only four times: Rom. 2:16; 16:25; 2 Cor. 4:3; 2 Tim. 2:8.

48. Gaventa (1998: 124) has an important insight concerning the application of the brief phrase "through our gospel" for modern-day preachers: "That little phrase in verse 14, 'through our proclamation of the good news,' stands as an important reminder for preachers themselves. God calls people to faith by a variety of means, and one of those means is preaching. Too often preachers persuade themselves that the task is outmoded, that no one listens, that preparation can be shortened and sloppy. Here we are faced with the claim that God works through that preaching to bring salvation into the lives of women and men. It cannot be neglected."

(Rom. 8:17–18); "who will transform our lowly body to be like his *glorious* body" (Phil. 3:21); "the elect, that they too may obtain the salvation that is in Christ Jesus, with eternal *glory*" (2 Tim. 2:10; see also Rom. 8:21; 1 Cor. 2:7; 15:43; 2 Cor. 4:17). This blessed end-time fate of the Thessalonian converts differs diametrically from that of their persecutors, "who will pay a penalty, eternal destruction from the presence of the Lord and from the *glory* of his might, whenever he comes to be *glorified*" (1:9–10a).

D. Command: Stand Firm by Holding Fast to Paul's Teachings (2:15)

The double particles ἄρα οὖν (*ara oun*, so then) that open verse 15 not only mark the beginning of a new unit (along with the transitional marker, the vocative "brothers") but also emphasize the strong connection between the commands given in this verse and the material of the preceding verses (Thrall [1962: 10] refers to the combination *ara oun* as "an emphatically inferential connective"). The two commands of verse 15, however, do not look back merely to the immediately preceding paragraph but also to everything Paul has said thus far in this chapter, especially his opening words in verse 2. The link to verse 2 is particularly clear from the apostle's intentional echo of it in the phrase "either by a word or by a letter," thereby forming an inclusio between the opening and closing sections of this chapter. This connection is further evident thematically, as the commands of verse 15 are intended to correct the crisis introduced in verses 1–2: if the problem is mental instability ("easily shaken in mind or alarmed") due to a *new* assertion about the day of the Lord originating from a spiritual utterance that claims the authority of Paul, the solution is to "stand firm and hold fast" to the traditions that he has *previously* taught them in a spoken word or written letter. The importance of verse 15 is additionally indicated by the shift from the indicative mood, which predominates in the preceding verses, to the imperative—the only occurrence of this mood in the whole of 2:1–17.[49] Here the apostle finally gives the Thessalonian congregation their marching orders, telling them what specifically they must now do.

2:15 Paul begins to bring his lengthy eschatological discussion to a close with two closely connected commands, both in the present tense, thereby stressing the ongoing nature of the exhorted action: "So then, brothers, stand firm and hold fast to the traditions that you were taught either by our word or by our letter" (ἄρα οὖν, ἀδελφοί, στήκετε καὶ κρατεῖτε τὰς παραδόσεις ἃς ἐδιδάχθητε εἴτε διὰ λόγου εἴτε δι' ἐπιστολῆς ἡμῶν, *ara oun, adelphoi, stēkete kai krateite tas paradoseis has edidachthēte eite dia logou eite di' epistolēs hēmōn*).

The first command, "stand firm" (*stēkete*), involves a verb used in the NT primarily by Paul (seven of its approximately twelve occurrences). Whereas other biblical writers use this verb with its literal sense of being in a standing

---

49. Note, however, the use of a prohibition—the negative μή with the aorist subjunctive—in 2:3a: "Let no one deceive you in any way."

position (Mark 3:31; 11:25; see also John 1:26 v.l.; Rev. 12:4 v.l.), Paul always has the figurative sense of "to be firmly committed in conviction or belief, *stand firm, be steadfast*" (BDAG 944.2; see Rom. 14:4; 1 Cor. 16:13; Gal. 5:1; Phil. 1:27; 4:1; 1 Thess. 3:8). The apostle employed this same verb in his First Letter to the Thessalonians (3:8), where it looks back to his previously stated concern that none of his readers "may be shaken by these afflictions" (3:3a), and so the command "stand firm" serves as a fitting antidote to that fear. Here in the second letter, Paul employs this same verb in a parallel manner; it looks back to his previously stated concern that his readers "not be easily shaken from your mind or alarmed" (2:2a) about a false claim concerning the arrival of the day of the Lord, and so the command to "stand firm" again serves as a fitting antidote to that fear.

Paul often follows the verb "stand firm" with a clarifying prepositional phrase such as "in the Lord" (1 Thess. 3:8; Phil. 4:1), "in the faith" (1 Cor. 16:13), or "in one spirit" (Phil. 1:27). Here, however, as in Gal. 5:1, he follows the verb with a second verb that clarifies the means by which his readers are to stand firm. The conjunction "and" (*kai*) that joins these two verbs is explicative: it introduces another verb, which explains what goes before it (BDAG 495.1.c; Malherbe 2000: 440). The second command, "hold fast" (*krateite*), therefore, does not refer to an action that is independent from the first command but rather one that is closely connected to it: "stand firm *by holding fast*" (so Best 1977: 317; Fee 2009: 305). The verb *krateō* has a variety of nuances, but in its two occurrences in Paul (elsewhere only in Col. 2:19), it is an aggressive term with the sense of "to adhere strongly to, *hold fast*" (BDAG 565.6). In the face of false eschatological claims that have caused the believers in Thessalonica to be scared out of their wits, Paul exhorts the church not merely to know or remember but, in a more forceful and proactive manner, to "hold fast" to something: "the traditions that you were taught" (*tas paradoseis has edidachthēte*).

The noun "traditions," derived from the compound verb παραδίδωμι (*paradidōmi*), meaning "hand down/over," refers to the content of instruction that was originally received and then passed down to others. Although Paul here and elsewhere uses semitechnical terminology from Judaism for the receiving and handing down of traditional material (see, e.g., F. Büchsel, *TDNT* 2:171–73; M. B. Thompson, *DPL* 944–45), the idea of divine revelation that was received by one generation and passed on to the next was well known in the Hellenistic world as well.[50] The apostle uses the noun "traditions" or its associated verbal forms mostly in a positive way[51] to refer to important

---

50. Green (2002: 329n102) helpfully cites Plato, *Phileb.* 16C: "The ancients, who were better than we and lived nearer the gods, handed down [*paredosan*] the tradition [*tautēn phēmēn*] that all the things which are ever said to exist are sprung from one and many and have inherent in them the finite and the infinite."

51. Paul uses the word *paradosis* negatively twice: once to refer to the Jewish "traditions" for which he was extremely zealous in his pre-Christian life (Gal. 1:14); the other to refer to human "tradition" that underlies hollow and deceptive philosophy (Col. 2:8).

teachings that do not originate with him but that he first received and subsequently handed down to his converts. These teachings deal with diverse subjects such as the sayings of Jesus at the institution of the Lord's Supper (1 Cor. 11:23), the resurrection of Christ (1 Cor. 15:3), the importance of self-sufficient labor (2 Thess. 3:6), and more generally the Christian life (Rom. 6:17) and gospel message (1 Thess. 2:13). Here the term "traditions" refers to teachings about Jesus's glorious return that Paul has given the Thessalonian converts both during his mission-founding visit and in his previous letter. That the apostle uses the term "traditions" rather than "teaching" (either διδαχή, *didachē*, or διδασκαλία, *didaskalia*—terms he employs elsewhere frequently: nineteen times for the latter term and six times for the former) suggests that he wants to highlight the extensive approval of his eschatological teachings: his instructions are not unique to himself but enjoy widespread acceptance among the larger Christian community. In this way the apostle adds weight not only to his previous teachings but also to his current command that the Thessalonian church ought to hold fast to these teachings.

But even as Paul connects his eschatological teaching with the "traditions" of the larger Christian community, he at the same time stresses the key role that he played in teaching them these traditions. This emphasis, foreshadowed in the prepositional phrase "through *our* gospel" in the preceding verse, is expressed by the double prepositional phrase "either through our word or through our letter" (*eite dia logou eite di' epistolēs hēmōn*). The first phrase "through our[52] word" refers to the eschatological instruction that Paul and his coworkers gave the Thessalonian church during their mission-founding visit (perhaps also the oral teaching that Timothy gave during his follow-up visit), while the second phrase "through our letter" refers to the eschatological instruction that Paul and his cosenders gave in 1 Thessalonians.[53] The deliberate echo of the earlier words of 2:2b ("whether through a prophetic utterance or through a word [i.e., oral message] or through a [written] letter") is clear both from the similarities in vocabulary and also the order of these prepositional phrases. What is strikingly absent in 2:15 from that earlier verse is the prepositional phrase "through a prophetic utterance." The reason for this notable omission stems from Paul's suspicion that the source of the false claim about the day of the Lord is a spirit-inspired prophecy (see further the comments on 2:2b). The apostle thus corrects the mental instability ("too easily shaken from your mind or alarmed") that such a prophetic utterance was causing among members of the Thessalonian church by commanding them to stand

52. At the end of 2:15, the personal pronoun ἡμῶν (our) does double duty in that it refers to both preceding nouns.

53. Some have disagreed with this interpretation, arguing instead that in 2:15 Paul is referring to the present letter—our 2 Thessalonians (so esp. Wanamaker [1990: 269] as part of his argument that the order of the two Thessalonian Letters ought to be reversed). But if Paul had wanted to refer to the present letter, he would have used the definite article (*the* letter = this letter) as he does in the following chapter (3:14), his previous letter (1 Thess. 5:27), and elsewhere (Rom. 16:22; Col. 4:16).

firm and hold fast to the eschatological teachings that *he* previously taught them, as part of the broader church's "traditions," either in a spoken word or written letter. Paul's commands here are in agreement with his exhortations in the previous letter (5:19–22) not to accept naively all prophetic utterances but instead to test them—a test that is spelled out here in the second letter and consists of determining whether such prophecies agree with what he taught them in either spoken word or written letter.

E. Closing Prayer That God Will Comfort the Thessalonians (2:16–17)

Paul brings his lengthy eschatological discussion to a close by means of a double-petition prayer that in its first and longer half (vv. 16–17a) *looks back* and summarizes the apostle's concern in the preceding verses, namely, to comfort the Thessalonian church. To a congregation frightened by a new claim that the day of the Lord has come, Paul offers a prayer that the Lord Jesus Christ and the God who gives "eternal comfort" may "comfort" their shaken hearts. This double reference to "comfort" reveals Paul's pastoral purpose at work throughout the passage and justifies my main heading for 2:1–17 ("Comfort concerning the Day of the Lord") as well as the subtitle of my alternative longer heading: "Paul's Word of Comfort." The second and shorter half of the prayer (v. 17b) *looks ahead* and anticipates the apostle's concern in the remaining verses of the letter body (3:1–15), his concern to "strengthen" the church "in every good work and word" in sharp contrast to the rebellious idlers in their midst. The prayer of verses 16–17, therefore, like the prayers of 1 Thess. 3:11–13, does not have merely a summarizing function (though this function predominates here) but also a transitional one (so recognized by only a few commentators: Elias 1995: 303; Witherington 2006: 239; Fee 2009: 309).

The first and longer half of the double-petition prayer calls on both Christ and God to comfort the shaken congregation in Thessalonica: "But may our Lord Jesus Christ himself and God our Father, the one who loved us and gave us eternal comfort and good hope by his grace, comfort your hearts" (αὐτὸς δὲ ὁ κύριος ἡμῶν Ἰησοῦς Χριστὸς καὶ ὁ θεὸς ὁ πατὴρ ἡμῶν ὁ ἀγαπήσας ἡμᾶς καὶ δοὺς παράκλησιν αἰωνίαν καὶ ἐλπίδα ἀγαθὴν ἐν χάριτι παρακαλέσαι ὑμῶν τὰς καρδίας, *autos de ho kyrios hēmōn Iēsous Christos kai ho theos ho patēr hēmōn ho agapēsas hēmas kai dous paraklēsin aiōnian kai elpida agathēn en chariti parakalesai hymōn tas kardias*).

The form of this prayer fits with the petitions or benedictions that are located in the letter body (Rom. 15:5–6; 15:13; 1 Thess. 3:11, 12–13; 2 Thess. 3:5; see also Heb. 13:20–21) and are formally distinct from the grace benedictions and peace benedictions located in the letter closing. These "body" benedictions or prayers, though possessing a less consistent form than the two closing benedictions, nevertheless have a common structure, consisting of five basic elements (Weima 1994a: 101–4): (1) the introductory element, always the adversative particle δέ (*de*) in its expected postpositive position; (2) the

2:16–17a

divine source of the prayer, given in the nominative and usually elaborated on by means of a genitive phrase or participial clause; (3) the content of the prayer, normally expressed by the verb in the optative mood; (4) the object of the prayer, involving some form of the personal pronoun "you"; and (5) the purpose of the prayer, expressed by either a ἵνα (*hina*) or εἰς (*eis*) clause.

Here the prayer opens with its expected introductory element—the adversative particle *de*. Since this particle introduces all the other "body" benedictions or prayers, most commentators and translations downplay any adversative force in *de* by either omitting the term or rendering it as "now" rather than "but" (BDAG 213.2). It is true that the contrastive sense of the particle should not be overstated (it is much more moderate than ἀλλά, *alla*). Yet Paul could have more closely linked the prayer with the immediately preceding material by shifting from the particle *de* to the simple conjunction καί (*kai*, and), as he does in some closing prayers or benedictions for peace (cf. *kai* in 2 Cor. 13:11b; Gal. 6:16; Phil. 4:9b; with *de* in Rom. 15:33; 16:20a; 1 Thess. 5:23; 2 Thess. 3:16). Furthermore, the presence of the intensive pronoun "himself" (*autos*) at the head of the prayer suggests that the particle *de* does have a slight adversative sense: in contrast to the immediately preceding command, which spells out what the Thessalonians must now do, the prayer highlights what Christ *himself* and God will do. The comfort available to the shaken believers in Thessalonica rests ultimately not on their human ability to obey the command to stand firm by holding fast to the traditions that they have received through Paul's oral and written teaching, but on the divine activity of both Christ and God, which makes their obedience to such a command possible (so also Frame 1912: 285).

The second part of the prayer, the divine source, is striking for at least three reasons. First, there is the use of two subjects ("our Lord Jesus Christ himself and God our Father") with a singular verb ("may *he* comfort," *parakalesai*; note also the singular verb used in the second prayer, "may *he* strengthen," *stērixai*). This grammatical oddity cannot be accounted for by claiming that Paul "forgot" he had used a plural subject (so Wanamaker 1990: 271) since the apostle did exactly the same thing in the body prayer of the earlier Thessalonian Letter (1 Thess. 3:11). Also unconvincing is the claim that with two subjects the verb often agrees with the nearer of the two (Bruce 1982: 71), since the examples cited in support involve conventional word pairs (1 Cor. 15:50, "flesh and blood"; Matt. 5:18, "heaven and earth"; Mark 4:41, "wind and sea"; James 5:3, "gold and silver") so that the parallel with the two persons mentioned here is not exact. Instead, this grammatical construction does, in fact, have implications for the deity of Jesus, even though one must not overstate these implications. On the one hand, the repetition of the definite article for both persons[54] suggests that Paul views "our Lord Jesus Christ

---

54. On the textual question of whether the article should be read before "God" in 2:16, see the additional notes below. Even if this article is not viewed as original, there is the presence of two additional articles before both "Father" and the participle "who loved."

himself" and "God our Father" as two individual entities and so avoids the danger of a *complete merging* of the two figures to whom he prays. On the other hand, that these two individual figures are closely linked together with a singular verb suggests that Paul views Jesus as sharing the deity of God and so avoids the danger of a *complete separation* of these two figures to whom he prays (Hewett 1975–76: 54). As Milligan (1908: 108) observes: "We have another striking example of the equal honour ascribed to the Son with the Father throughout these epistles."[55]

The second notable feature about the divine source of the prayer is the order of the two subjects: "our Lord Jesus Christ himself" comes before "God, our Father." When mentioning both divine persons, Paul's normal pattern is to list God first and Jesus second, yet this ordering is not rigid but can be reversed (as in 2 Cor. 13:13; Gal. 1:1). Here the mention of Jesus first may be due to the christological emphasis found throughout this passage (2:1, 2, 8, 13, 14) as well as throughout the letter (so Rigaux 1956: 690; Menken 1994: 123; Malherbe 2000: 441–42). This emphasis on Christ is also seemingly reflected in the addition of the intensive pronoun to the first of the two listed sources: "our Lord Jesus Christ *himself*."

Yet this christological emphasis is offset by a third remarkable aspect about the divine source of the prayer, namely, the extended description of the second listed source, "God our Father," as "the one who loved us and gave us eternal comfort and good hope by his grace." The two attributive participles used to describe God as "the one who loved" (*ho agapēsas*) and "gave" (*dous*) are introduced with only one article, thereby joining these two divine actions closely together. Paul, therefore, has in view not two distinct activities of God, each of which has some specific past referent (i.e., "loved" refers to God's election of the Thessalonians [2 Thess. 2:13–14] or his sending of Christ [John 3:16] to die for sinners [Rom. 5:8; Gal. 2:20], whereas "gave" refers to the gift of the Spirit [1 Thess. 4:8; Rom. 5:5; Gal. 4:6] or something else: so most commentators). Rather, the first activity of God is clarified by the second: God loved *by* giving (Best 1977: 320 states: "'given' really explains 'loved'").

What God has given the Thessalonian believers out of his love for them is "eternal comfort and good hope" (*paraklēsin aiōnian kai elpida agathēn*). Paul's choice of the noun "comfort" reveals his pastoral concern that has been at work throughout the whole passage. The apostle does not describe God as the one who gave "knowledge" or "truth" or some other gift appropriate for correcting false teachings about eschatological events. Instead, he describes God as the one who gave "comfort" (*paraklēsis*)—the only fitting antidote for the anxiety and fear gripping the Thessalonian church due to the false claim about the day of the Lord. Paul further consoles his readers by describing

---

55. On 2:16, note also the comment of Fee (2009: 306): "Paul's very high Christology is especially noticeable, not as something (ever) argued for, but as something simply assumed to be the common stock of early Christian belief." Similarly, Shogren (2012: 307) sees in the unique grammar and content of this prayer "a subtle but undeniable attestation of the divinity of Christ."

this comfort as "eternal" (*aiōnia*). The eschatological context has led a few commentators to take this adjective as describing the object of comfort: a comfort concerning eternity or end-time matters (Best 1977: 320; Ellingworth and Nida 1975: 186; D. Martin 1995: 258–59). But this interpretation would require that the adjective "eternal" be in the genitive case and function objectively. Since the adjective "eternal" is instead in the accusative case, agreeing with the direct object "comfort," it functions to describe the character of that comfort: it is a comfort that exists not only for the present crisis but also is "eternal," an unending or inexhaustible comfort that will sustain the Thessalonian readers until the end of time (BDAG 33.3: "pertaining to a period of unending duration, *without end*").

In addition to this never-ending comfort, God has also given the converts in Thessalonica "good hope" (*elpida agathēn*). Although similar expressions are used by Paul ("firm hope," 2 Cor. 1:7; "blessed hope," Titus 2:13) and other NT writers ("living hope," 1 Pet. 1:3; "better hope," Heb. 7:19), the exact phrase occurs nowhere else in the Bible. The rarity of this phrase contrasts sharply with secular sources of that day, where the same two words occur together frequently. Some of these nonbiblical references to "good hope" describe a general optimism that certain individuals have despite their discouraging circumstances (e.g., Xenophon, *Cyr.* 1.6.19; Josephus, *Ant.* 1.325; 5.222; 8.214; 13.201; 14.96). Other references to "good hope," however, describe a specific hope for life after death that existed in the mystery religions and certain pagan cults (e.g., Julian, *Ep.* 20.452c: "You will give me still greater good hope for the future life"; see also texts cited in Cumont 1949; Otzen 1958). It may well be, therefore, that Paul's reference to "good hope" stems from his borrowing "a contemporary secular idiom" (Holmes 1998: 255; so also, e.g., Best 1977: 321; Marshall 1982: 211; Wanamaker 1990: 271; Witherington 2006: 239). If so, the phrase "good hope" does not describe a second gift in addition to "eternal comfort" but rather restates the first gift. Paul's intended meaning can be colloquially rendered: "God has given us eternal comfort, or, as some people would commonly put it, good hope."

The extended description of "God our Father" as the second source of the prayer closes with the brief prepositional phrase "by [his] grace" (*en chariti*). Grace, like election, is a fundamental concept in Paul's theology that he never explains anywhere in his Thessalonian Letters (1 Thess. 1:1; 5:28; 2 Thess. 1:2, 12; 2:16; 3:18) but simply assumes to be known by his readers from his mission-founding ministry in their midst (1 Thess. 2:8: "We . . . were pleased to share with you not only the gospel of God but also our own selves"). Here in 2 Thess. 2:16 the brief reference to grace further reminds the readers that God's love for them, displayed concretely in his giving them eternal comfort, does not originate from any accomplishment on their part but from his unmerited favor.

The third part of the prayer, the content, is expressed by two optative verbs, the first of which asks that Jesus and God "may comfort your hearts" (*parakalesai hymōn tas kardias*). The optative mood in the NT often takes on a force similar to that of the imperative so that it is legitimate to speak of an "imperatival optative"—an optative that expresses a stronger sense than mere volition: "The speaker intends more than a wish ('may it be so-and-so'); he expresses this with a strong sense of fulfillment ('let it be so-and-so') (van Elderen 1967: 48; BDF §384: "The optative proper used to denote an attainable wish"). The optative *parakalesai*, therefore, conveys not merely Paul's faint hope but also his confident prayer that Jesus and God will comfort the shaken minds and fearful hearts of the believers in Thessalonica. Paul's verb selection of "comfort," coming so quickly after his choice of the noun "comfort" as the object of what God gave, lends emphasis to the term and reflects the apostle's pastoral concern at work throughout this lengthy eschatological passage. This pastoral concern likely accounts for the object "your hearts," which expresses a warmer and more affectionate tone than the simple pronoun "you."

Paul has another major concern, however, that he still wants to address in the letter and so transitions in the closing prayer from the end-time discussion of 2:1–17 to the problem of the rebellious idlers, which ultimately lies behind his subsequent discussion of 3:1–15. This transition occurs in the second and shorter half of the double-petition prayer and is also expressed with an optative verb: "and strengthen them[56] in every good[57] work and word" (καὶ στηρίξαι ἐν παντὶ ἔργῳ καὶ λόγῳ ἀγαθῷ, *kai stērixai en panti ergō kai logō agathō*).

2:17b

The pairing of the verbs "comfort" and "strengthen" is not unexpected since Paul used both of these terms together (though in reverse order) in the previous letter (1 Thess. 3:2) when describing the purpose of Timothy's return visit to the Thessalonian church (they are also joined as a word pair in Acts 14:22 and 15:32). There the two verbs, given in the form of articular infinitives, were closely linked by means of one article, which did double duty for both. Here, however, the two verbs are less directly connected together and have in view different concerns: whereas the first petition in the prayer to "comfort" looks *back* to the anxiety over a false eschatological claim, the second petition to "strengthen" looks *ahead* to the remaining material of the letter body.

Three factors suggest that the second petition anticipates the upcoming discussion of 3:1–15. First, there is the striking parallel between the double-petition prayer of 2 Thess. 2:16–17 and the two prayers of 1 Thess. 3:11–13. Since the second prayer in the previous letter clearly foreshadows the key concerns taken up in the rest of the letter body, a strong possibility exists that the second petition here in 2:17b does the same thing. Second, Paul chooses the identical verb in the introductory unit of 3:1–5 to reassure his readers that the Lord "will strengthen" (στηρίξαι, *stērixai*) them (3:3)—the only two

---

56. The object of the second verb "strengthen" is not stated in 2:17 but implied from the object of the first verb "comfort," namely, "your hearts."

57. The adjectives "every" and "good" are located in the first and last positions, respectively, in the prepositional phrase ἐν παντὶ ἔργῳ καὶ λόγῳ ἀγαθῷ. This "typical inclusio" (Fee 2009: 309n124) means that both adjectives are intended to go with both nouns. The same phenomenon occurs earlier in the passage (2:9) where the prepositional phrase has one adjective in the opening position and another in the last, yet both adjectives describe all three intervening nouns.

occurrences of this verb in the letter. Third, the prepositional phrase "in every good work and word" (*en panti ergō kai logō agathō*) that clarifies the second petition almost certainly has in view Paul's extended exhortations concerning the "rebellious idlers" and the requirement for self-sufficient work in the major unit of 3:6–15. As Elias (1995: 303) notices: "In desiring a community witness which reflects an authentic integration of *good work and word*, the writers clearly anticipate the issue of *the unruly*, addressed in 3:6–15." Witherington (2006: 239) likewise states: "This ['in every good work and word'] foreshadows the subject matter of the argument coming in ch. 3 about work." Paul uses the word pair "work and word" elsewhere in his letters (Rom. 15:18; Col. 3:17; see also Luke 24:19; Acts 7:22), though the typical order of each term here is reversed,[58] likely in order to emphasize the importance of the first element, "every good work." Whereas in 2:1–17 the apostle has been preoccupied with right thinking, his emphasis in 3:1–15 shifts slightly to right conduct. He desires that the "good hope" they have about the future will also manifest itself in every "good work" in the present. Such "good work" is the antithesis of the conduct adopted by the rebellious idlers, whom the church ought to avoid (3:6, 14–15). Instead, "good work" involves self-sufficient labor, following both Paul's example (3:7–9) and his teachings about work (3:10–13).

Additional Notes

2:1. The personal pronoun ἡμῶν that identifies the "coming" as that of "*our* Lord Jesus Christ" is omitted in some MSS, including a few important ones: B Ψ 33 *pc* vg^{ms} sy^h. The text-critical rule of following the shorter reading supports the omission of this pronoun. Nevertheless, the testimony of the greater number of major MSS argues for its inclusion, as do the facts that (1) Vaticanus (B) has a scribal tendency to omit seemingly unimportant details in the text (Richard 1995: 323), and (2) its omission can be explained for stylistic reasons, namely, the second occurrence of the pronoun "our" only four words later (Fee 1994b: 198n8; 2009: 271n5).

2:2. Despite the overwhelming support for the reading κυρίου ("the day of the *Lord*": so ℵ A B D* F G L P Ψ 6 33 81 104 365 1241 1739 1881 2464 *al* latt sy co; Or Epiph), 𝔐 has Χριστοῦ ("the day of Christ": so also D^2). This substitution likely stems from the desire to clarify that "Lord" refers not to God but to Christ.

2:3. There is significant external evidence—both in the number of MSS and in the representation from each of the three text types—for the reading "man *of sin*" (ἁμαρτίας: A D F G L P Ψ 𝔐 lat sy; Ir^{lat} Eus). Nevertheless, the alternate reading "man *of lawlessness*" is preferred. Not only does it too have strong textual support (ℵ B 6 81 88^{mg} 104 326 365 1739 1881 2464 *pc* m co; Marcion Tertullian), but more significantly, the presence of ἀνομία in verse 7 and ἄνομος in verse 8 presupposes the occurrence of the same word in verse 3. The presence of the reading "man of sin" likely stems from copyists who replaced the rare ἀνομία (15x in the NT) with the far more common ἁμαρτία (173x; see B. Metzger 1994: 567).

2:4. The phrase "as God" (ὡς θεόν) is added before the infinitive "to take his seat" in some MSS (D^2 G^2 K L sy$^{p, h**}$) including 𝔐 so that the KJV reads: "so that he *as God* sitteth in the temple of God."

58. Some copyists "corrected" the text to the usual order (see additional notes).

That this phrase is a later addition is initially suggested by the text-critical principle of *lectio brevior* (favoring the shorter reading) and then confirmed by the facts that (1) there is overwhelming textual support for its omission (א A B D* P Ψ 6 33 81 104 323 330 365 629 1739 1881 2464 *pc* lat co; Ir^lat Or Epiph), and (2) it likely originated as an explanatory gloss that spells out the implicit claim in the lawless one's action of taking his seat in the temple of God, which is then stated explicitly in the subsequent ὅτι clause ("that he himself is God").

2:5. Instead of the nominative participle ὤν, a few Western texts (D* b; Ambst) have the genitive absolute ἐμοῦ ὄντος. The former reading is surely the original because of its support by all the major MSS and because Paul, when referring to himself, regularly employs the nominative participle rather than the genitive absolute (e.g., 1 Cor. 9:19–21; 2 Cor. 10:1; 13:2; 1 Thess. 5:8; Philem. 9; etc.). The latter reading likely arose from those few Western MSS that replaced the active ταῦτα ἔλεγον (I was saying these things) with the passive ταῦτα ἐλέγετο (These things were being said)—a change that then required the nominative participle to be "corrected" with the genitive absolute (Bruce 1982: 162).

2:6. The external evidence—the number, age, text type, and geographic distribution of the MSS—is almost evenly divided between the possessive pronoun "his/its own" (ἑαυτοῦ: א^2 B D F G Ψ 𝔐) and the personal pronoun "his/its" (αὐτοῦ: א* A I K P 33 81 323 326 365 630 2464 *al*; Origen). The third-person personal pronoun in Koine Greek often has a reflexive sense (BDF §283; MHT 3:41: "the simple personal pronoun often serves as a reflexive") so that the meaning is not altered greatly regardless of which reading is adopted as original.

2:8. Although the name "Jesus" (Ἰησοῦς) is omitted in some texts (D^2 K 88 614 1739 1881 𝔐 bo^ms), including one important uncial (B), it does enjoy a wide range of Greek and versional support (א A D* F G L^c P Ψ 0278 33 81 104 365 1241 1271 2464 *pc* latt sy cop; Ir Or Did). The internal evidence is inconclusive. On the one hand, the name may have been intentionally added, either for pious reasons (note how some Latin MSS add the word "Christ" here) or for clarifying that the Lord refers not to God but to Jesus. On the other hand, the name may have been intentionally deleted in order to have Paul's allusion conform more accurately to Isa. 11:4. The editors of the Greek text (NA^28, UBS^4) include the name (although in square brackets), as do virtually all translations.

2:8. No less than four different readings for the first verb in the relative clause appear in the MSS: (1) the future indicative ἀνελεῖ (he will slay: A B P 81 88 104 365 451 2464 *pc* latt; Hippolytus); (2) the aorist optative ἀνελοῖ (may he slay!: F G 37 424^c 1739 *pc* Did); (3) the present indicative of a different verb, ἀναλοῖ (from ἀναλόω, he consumes: א*); and (4) the future indicative of the same different verb, ἀναλώσει (from ἀναλόω, he will consume: D^2 Ψ 𝔐 co). It is difficult to reconstruct the history of how these different readings arose (see Frame 1912: 266), but the most likely scenario is as follows. Although the first reading ἀνελεῖ (he will slay) might have resulted from an assimilation to Isa. 11:4, it has by far the strongest external evidence and thus is likely to be original (B. Metzger 1994: 636). The third reading ἀναλοῖ (he consumes) can be explained as a gloss that clarifies the metaphor of "the breath of his mouth" (consuming goes more naturally with a reference to the mouth than slaying, especially to a scribe who failed to recognize the allusion to Isa. 11:4). The fourth reading ἀναλώσει (he will consume) involves a correction of the third reading in order to bring the present tense into agreement with the future tense used in the second half of the clause (καταργήσει, he will destroy). The second reading ἀνελοῖ (may he slay!), which is grammatically impossible (a relative clause does not allow the use of the optative mood), would then be a compromise between the first and third readings (Milligan 1908: 103; Giblin 1967: 53). A few commentators have argued that the third reading is original (Findlay 1891: 149; Zimmer 1893: 79; Lightfoot 1904: 115), but its textual support is far too weak, especially compared to the first reading.

2:10. Some later MSS ($\aleph^2$ D Ψ 𝕸) add the article τῆς before the adjective ἀδικίας so that the text reads "of the wicked one" and refers to Satan himself as the source of the deceptive coming of the lawless one. The exclusion of the article, however, is supported by both external evidence ($\aleph$*A B D F G P 6 33 81 104 1739 1881 2464 *pc*; Or) and internal evidence (it is the shorter reading, and it parallels the genitive ψεύδους in the preceding prepositional phrase, which is also anarthrous).

2:10. Confusion about the precise function of the dative τοῖς ἀπολλυμένοις led some copyists ($\aleph^2$ D^1 Ψ 𝕸 sy) to add the preposition ἐν, thereby locating the deceptive signs and wonders of the lawless one "in" or "among" his doomed followers ("the ones on the way to destruction"). Older and more reliable MSS support the omission of this preposition ($\aleph$* A B D* F G 33 81 1739 2474 *pc* latt).

2:11. Instead of the present "he sends" (πέμπει: $\aleph$* A B D* F G 6 33 1739 1881 *pc* b vgst sa^{ms}; Tert), some MSS have the future "he will send" (πέμψει: $\aleph^2$ D^2 Ψ 𝕸 it vg^{cl} sa^{mss} bo; Ambst). The MSS that support the future tense, however, are all either secondhand or decidedly late, and also likely due to scribes who changed the text to match the preceding references to the two eschatological comings—one by the lawless one and the other by the Lord Jesus Christ (2:8–9).

2:13. Some copyists were so struck by the substitution of "the Lord" for "God" that they viewed it as a scribal error and thus "corrected" the reading to the expected "God": so D* b m vg.

2:13. (1) ἀπ᾽ ἀρχῆς (from the beginning): $\aleph$ D K L Ψ 104 181 330 436 451 614 629 630 1241 1962 1984 1985 2127 2492 2495 *Byz Lect* it$^{ar, d, e, g, mon}$ syr^p cop^{sa} arm eth Ambst Chr Pel Theodore^{lat} Theodoret Vigilius John-Damascus^{txt}. (2) ἀπαρχήν (firstfruits): B F G^{gr} P 33 81 326 1739 1877 it$^{c, dem, div, f, x, z}$ vg syr^h cop^{bo} Didymus Ambr Cyril Euthalius John-Damascus^{comm}.

2:14. It is difficult to be certain whether the prepositional phrase that opens 2:14 (εἰς ὅ [To this end]) includes the conjunction καί. The external evidence favors its omission (A^{vid} B D Ψ 33 1739 1881 𝕸 a b m* vg^{mss} sy^p Ambst), though only barely so, since strong support remains for its inclusion ($\aleph$ F G P 0278 81 365 2464 *al* vg sy^h). The internal evidence slightly favors its inclusion since it fits Paul's practice earlier in the letter, in 1:11. Fee (2009: 298n91) claims that this is also the harder reading since "it is difficult to imagine the circumstances in which scribes would have *added* a καί here when it seems so unnecessary to the overall sense." Yet a scribe might have wanted to make Paul's practice here conform to his earlier expression in 1:11 or wanted to highlight the way in which 2:14 adds a second reason for which Paul must "also" give thanks to God for his Thessalonian converts (2:13a). The difficulty in deciding between the two readings is reflected in both the NA^{28} and UBS^4 Greek texts, which include the conjunction in the main text but place it within square brackets.

2:16. The exact expression ὁ θεὸς ὁ πατὴρ ἡμῶν is unique among Paul's writings, and this fact led copyists to alter the reading so that it better agreed with the apostle's practice elsewhere. Some replaced the article before πατήρ with the conjunction καί (A D^2 I Ψ 𝕸 b d m vg sy^h), resulting in a reading frequently found in Paul's writings (e.g., 2 Cor. 1:3; 11:31; Gal. 1:4; Eph. 1:3; Phil. 4:20; 1 Thess. 1:3; 3:11, 13). The external evidence supporting the article as original, however, is quite strong ($\aleph$ B D* F G 33 1739 1881 *pc* a vg^{mss} sy^p co; Ambst). Others instead deleted the article before θεός (B D* K L 33 1175 1739 1881 *al*), though here too the external evidence for its presence is weighty, albeit slightly less so ($\aleph$ A D^2 F G I Ψ 𝕸), thereby causing the editors of the Greek text to place it within square brackets.

2:17. Some copyists "corrected" the text by putting the two nouns "work and word" in their usual order, "word and work": F G K 6 323 630 1175 *al* b m (sy^p).

Excursus 3
The Restrainer of 2 Thessalonians 2:6–7

The Riddle of the Restrainer

The difficulty of resolving the riddle of the restrainer is attested, first, by the abundance of academic articles dealing with this specific subject (see sources listed in Weima and Porter 1998: 246–72 and more recently in P. Metzger 2005: 313–43). Giblin (1967: 14) does not exaggerate when he states of the restrainer: "This figure's notoriety now surpasses that of [the] Antichrist." The difficulty is evident, second, in the all-too-common admission of ignorance by commentators who wrestle with these verses. For example, it is worth citing again the candid confession of Augustine, who stated about the restraining force and the restraining person: "I frankly confess that the meaning of this completely escapes me" (*City* 20.19). Frame (1912: 258) expresses similar pessimism: "Unfortunately, the allusions are so fragmentary and cryptic that it is at present impossible to determine precisely what Paul means." Equally gloomy is the opinion of Koester (1990: 457): "The question of the identity of the retarding element and/or person will probably never be solved." Gaventa (1998: 114) likewise states in a frank and terse manner: "The identity of the restrainer is utterly hidden from us." But though the possibility of identifying the restrainer may be difficult, it is not as hopeless as these quotes suggest. Nevertheless, any conclusions reached about this matter are not so settled and sure that they justify being shouted rather than whispered.

Grammatical Issues

Before taking up the difficult task of identifying the restrainer, we begin with two grammatical issues closely connected to this identification. First, there is the obvious observation that the restraining activity is described both impersonally with the neuter *to katechon* (v. 6, "the *thing* that is restraining") and personally with the masculine *ho katechōn* (v. 7, "the *person* who is restraining"). Any proposed identification of the restraining power, therefore, must involve an entity that can be regarded both as an impersonal force and as a person. A parallel exists between lawlessness and restraint: just as rebellion against God manifests itself in both impersonal (v. 7, "the mystery of *lawlessness*") and personal (v. 3, "the *man* of lawlessness"; v. 6, "in order that *he* may be revealed at *his* own fixed time"; v. 8, "the lawless *one*") ways, so also the restraint of this rebellion against God appears as both a power and a person. Yet whereas lawlessness takes place in different temporal schemes (the mystery of lawlessness is already at work in the present time, while the figure who embodies this lawlessness will be revealed at his fixed time in the future), the restraining thing and the restraining person are both active as present-day realities.

The second and more difficult grammatical issue involves the precise meaning of the compound verb *katechō* (the preposition *kata* + the common verb *echō*, to have), used in both the neuter and masculine participles. The difficulty lies in that this verb, occurring ten times in Paul and eight times in the rest of the NT, has a variety of nuances, depending on the context (BDAG 532–33 and Spicq 1994: 285–91 both list no less than eight different translations for its eighteen occurrences). If its two occurrences here in 2:6–7 are included, the most common meaning of *katechō* is "to prevent the doing of something or cause to be ineffective, *prevent, hinder, restrain*" (BDAG 523.1): Paul desired to prevent or restrain Onesimus from returning to his master so that the slave could help the apostle in his imprisonment (Philem. 13); unregenerate humanity suppresses or restrains truth by their wickedness (Rom. 1:18); believers have died to the law, which once bound or restrained them (Rom. 7:6); the crowd prevented or restrained Jesus from leaving (Luke 4:42); individuals are confined or restrained from movement by disease (Luke 4:38 v.l.; John 5:4 v.l.). The second most common meaning of *katechō* is "to adhere firmly to traditions, conviction, or beliefs, *hold to, hold fast*" (BDAG 533.2): Paul commands his readers to hold fast to such things as spiritual prophecies that are judged to be "good" (1 Thess. 5:21), the "teachings" that he has passed on to them (1 Cor. 11:2), and his "preaching" concerning the resurrection (1 Cor. 15:2; see also Luke 8:15; Heb. 3:6, 14). The verb less frequently refers to possessing material things (1 Cor. 7:30; 2 Cor. 6:10; Matt. 21:38 v.l.) and occupying a place (Luke 14:9); it also functions as a technical legal (Rom. 1:18) or nautical (Acts 27:40) term (BDAG 533.2–7).

In light of its wide diversity of meanings, the intended sense of *katechō* here in 2:6 and 2:7 must be determined less by its use elsewhere (though this will still play an important role) than by its context. Paul stresses that the mystery of lawlessness is operative in the present (note the twofold occurrence of "now": v. 6, *nyn*; v. 7, *arti*) but "only" (v. 7, *monon*) until the time when the *katechōn* figure leaves the scene: "then" (v. 8, *tote*) and only then will the man of lawlessness be revealed at his fixed time. The most natural way to read this emphasized sequence of events, especially the presence of the adverb "only," is that the *katechōn* figure currently *prevents* the lawless one from making his appearance. When it is additionally observed that the idea of restraint is the most common meaning of the verb *katechō* elsewhere in Paul and in the NT, and that the idea of restraint also is frequently found with this verb's occurrences in the secular literature of that day (LSJ 926; see also the extensive list of sources cited by Nicholl 2004: 227n10), then the most plausible conclusion is that its two occurrences here convey the notion of holding back or hindering. As Nicholl (2004: 227) observes: "In this context, where the operation of the κατέχον causes rebellion to stay in its unrevealed state until the point when the κατέχων is removed from the scene, it is little wonder that most scholars have interpreted κατέχω in its common (especially in classical literature) sense of 'hold back' or 'restrain.'" It is also significant that the meaning of restraint was adopted by the early church fathers (see Tertullian, *Res.* 24; John Chrysostom, *Hom. 2 Thess.* 4). Finally, although the specific term *katechon/katechōn* is not found elsewhere in the Jewish literature of this period, in discussing the end times these writings do contain the general idea of a "delaying" or "restraining" factor that is under the direct control of God (see texts and discussion in Menken 1994: 109, 111–12; Hannah 1999: 55–56; Malherbe 2000: 433).

The strength of translating *katechō* as "restraint" to some degree increases with the objections that can be raised against the two alternative meanings that have been proposed. Since neither the neuter nor the masculine participle (both used substantively here) have a direct object, a few (Robinson 1964: 635–38; Frame 1912: 258; Vos 1930: 133n20; Best 1977: 299; Weatherly 1996: 260) have argued that they should be taken intransitively to mean something like "to hold sway, rule." The significant feature of this view is that the *katechon* thing and the *katechōn* person thus function as being supportive of the man of lawlessness rather than opposed to him: they are an evil power and person who serve as agents of Satan rather than of God. Although some examples of the sense "to hold sway, rule" occur in the LXX and Classical Greek, there is not one example elsewhere in Paul or in the rest of the NT where the verb has this meaning. Furthermore, all the remaining NT occurrences of *katechō* are transitive (except for its use as a technical term in Acts 27:40; so BDAG 532–33), as are all its fifty occurrences in the LXX (H. Hanse, *TDNT* 2:829), suggesting that this is also the case here in 2:6 and 2:7. If, then, the implied and expected object of both participles is the man of lawlessness—a likely assumption given that he is the key figure in view immediately before (vv. 3b–4), after (vv. 8–10), and even during the two references to the *katechon* and the *katechōn* in 2:6–7 (he is the likely antecedent in the purpose clause "in order that *he* might be revealed in *his* fixed own time")[1]—then the alternative meaning of "hold sway, rule" becomes even more improbable.

Yet another connotation has been proposed by Giblin (1967: 167–204, 234–42; 1990) who takes *katechō* in the active sense of "seize, possess," in which an evil, pseudo-prophetic force "seizes" or "possesses" certain individuals in the Thessalonian congregation and especially one particular "prophet" who was misleading the church about the day of the Lord's arrival (so also Green 2002: 316, who states of the *to katechon*: "This is a power that 'seizes' or 'possesses' and may imply some form of demonic possession such as that which was found in the cults of Dionysus and Serapis"). But while there is

---

1. On 2:6, Malherbe (2000: 422) observes: "Grammatically, matters are complicated by the fact that *to katechon* ('what restrains') has no object, although there can be little doubt that the *auton* ('he') in the second part of the sentence is already in mind."

some evidence in the LXX and secular Greek writings that the passive voice of *katechō* denotes the possession of a person by an evil spirit, this meaning occurs, as Giblin himself admits, only "rarely" (1967: 197; on 240 he similarly states: "It is true that the active form of the verb is quite rare in this connection"). And though Green (2002: 316n52) cites two examples of this meaning in the active voice (P.Lond.Lit. 52.12; Justin, *2 Apol.* 6.6), still *katechō* in the sense of possession by a spirit occurs nowhere else in Paul's writings or other NT documents. Furthermore, Giblin's interpretation makes the cosmic, end-time events connected with the day of the Lord dependent on the removal of one false prophet in the small, localized church of Thessalonica (Best 1977: 299; Marshall 1983: 199; Menken 1994: 111). As Wanamaker (1990: 252) states: "That Paul believed the coming of Christ would or could be held up until some local false prophet was out of the way seems highly unlikely."

The examination undertaken above concerning the precise meaning of *katechō* is of great significance for determining the identity of this power and person. Although this compound verb possesses a wide variety of meanings and nuances, (1) the immediate context of 2:3–12, (2) the most common meaning this verb has elsewhere in Paul's writings and in the NT, (3) its use in extrabiblical documents, (4) its understanding by the early church fathers, and (5) the weaknesses of all proposed alternative meanings all form persuasive evidence that *katechō* here in 2:6 and 2:7 expresses the idea of restraint. It is hardly surprising, therefore, that every major translation renders the two attributive participles as "holds back" or "restrains" and that a wide consensus exists among commentators in understanding this restraining influence to be positive and beneficial.

The Identity of the Restrainer: Proposed Solutions

We now turn to the task of resolving the riddle of the restrainer, identifying the restraining thing and the restraining person. Some have questioned the legitimacy of this task. Ridderbos (1975: 525), for example, states: "There is no basis for wishing to be specific here, nor is it in harmony with the apocalyptic character of the text to do so. Paul does not allude here—so we think—to specific historic phenomena or events, but speaks in apocalyptic language of the supernatural factors that determine the restraining of the last things." But though the apostle does employ apocalyptic language, he does not refer to the restraining thing and the restraining person as if they are abstract concepts without any defined or concrete identity. Quite the opposite: he explicitly states that he has talked to the Thessalonians about this subject with sufficient frequency and clarity during his mission-founding visit (v. 5) that they "know" (v. 6) this restraining entity. Furthermore, an appeal to the apocalyptic language employed here ought not to be used to justify abandoning any attempt to determine the identity of the restraining power and person. As Witherington (2006: 208) observes: "Apocalyptic symbols and terminology are often deliberately vague so they may be multivalent, but they are seldom nonreferential."

At least seven[2] different proposals have been presented to identify the restraining thing and the restraining person to which Paul refers:

1. The Roman Empire and the Roman emperor
2. The principle of law and order and the political leaders in general
3. The proclamation of the gospel and Paul
4. The presence of the church and the Holy Spirit
5. The power of evil and Satan
6. The false prophecy and the false prophet
7. The activity and the person of the archangel Michael

We will review and briefly evaluate these proposals[3] before explaining and defending in greater detail the last option: the restraining force involves the activity and the person of the archangel Michael.

1. *The Roman Empire and the Roman emperor.* A view that dates back to Tertullian (*Res.* 24) and Hippolytus of Rome (*Comm. Dan.* 4.21), about AD 200, and until recent times was popular (Milligan 1908: 101: this interpretation has "won the support of the great majority of ancient and modern scholars") is that the neuter participle refers to the Roman Empire, and the masculine participle to the Roman emperor. This proposal is based primarily on the belief that Paul had a positive attitude toward the established government (Rom. 13:1–7), which he viewed as holding evil in check, and also that the apostle frequently made use of his Roman citizenship, which provided him protection from various opponents who were seeking to stop his missionary activities.

Several objections against this view, however, can be raised. First, although Paul at times benefited from the Roman Empire and its implementation of law and order, his ministry has also suffered from it in several ways, thus far already including beating, imprisonment (1 Thess. 2:2; Acts 16:19–24), and the prevention of his repeated attempts to return to his beloved converts in Thessalonica (1 Thess. 2:17–18; 3:10). Second, Paul's Letters, including his correspondence with the Thessalonians, contain a greater anti-imperial message than has often been recognized in the past (see esp. 1 Thess. 5:3). Third, both Jewish (Sib. Or. 7.108–13; 8.37–193) and Christian (Rev. 17–18) eschatological

---

2. The number of different proposals for 2:6–7 runs higher than this; in our survey we have omitted views that have not garnered at least a degree of widespread support (e.g., Warfield [1886] argues that the restraining power is the Jewish state and the restraining person is James of Jerusalem). Further complicating the situation are explanations that combine one or more of the different proposals: e.g., Hendriksen (1955: 182) combines views 2 and 7; Ford (1979: 219), 2, 3, and 4; Beale (2003: 215–17), 3 and 7.

3. See also the following works, which offer a detailed explanation and evaluation of most of these proposals: Frame 1912: 259–62; Marshall 1983: 196–99; Wanamaker 1990: 250–52; Richard 1995: 337–40; L. Morris, *DPL* 592–94; Hannah 2000: 31–37; Beale 2003: 214–16; Nicholl 2004: 228–30; P. Metzger 2005: 15–47.

writings tend to portray Rome not in a positive manner but as a force opposed to God's people (Peerbolte 1996: 142). Fourth, the emperor Caligula's recent attempt (just eleven or twelve years earlier, in AD 40) to have his image set up in the Jerusalem temple and turn that sanctuary into a place of worship dedicated to himself as a god involves activity that resembles rather than restrains the kind of blasphemous desecration to be carried out by the man of lawlessness. Fifth, since lawlessness (*anomia*) primarily involves a rebellion against God and his will, the restraint of such lawlessness would logically involve a religious rather than a political entity (though it is dangerous to distinguish these realms too sharply in the ancient world). Finally, this view would mean that Paul was wrong since in our own time the Roman Empire is "out of the way," but obviously neither the apostasy nor the man of lawlessness has appeared, nor have any of the other expected end-time events.

A few commentators (Robinson 1964: 635–38; Wanamaker 1990: 256–57; Elias 1995: 283; P. Metzger 2005: 271–95) similarly argue that Paul is referring to the Roman Empire and emperor, but instead of seeing the empire as a beneficial force that "restrains" the coming of the lawless one, they view it as an evil power that foreshadows or prepares the way for the coming of that eschatological enemy. This understanding is based on taking the key verb *katechō* intransitively as "hold sway, rule." Yet, not only are there grammatical considerations that undermine this rendering of the verb (see discussion above), but the context also strongly suggests that the *katechon* and the *katechōn*, whatever or whoever they may be, are positive and good, and thus opposed to the man of lawlessness.

2. *The principle of law and order and the political leaders in general.* This interpretation is virtually identical to the preceding one except that it takes the specific references to the Roman Empire and emperor and broadens them to refer to the principle of law and order and a political ruler in general (so, e.g., Ellicott 1880: 112; Lightfoot 1904: 114; Milligan 1908: 101; Morris 1991: 227; Richard 1995: 338–40). Although this view avoids the problem of Paul being mistaken in his prophecy about future events, it suffers from most of the remaining criticisms raised against the previous view. Additionally there is the problem that the masculine singular *ho ketechōn* more naturally refers to one specific individual, about whom Paul preached and the Thessalonians know, rather than being used in a collective sense of all persons throughout human history who embody the principle of law and order.

3. *The proclamation of the gospel and Paul.* A view found already in the church fathers (Justin, *1 Apol.* 45; Theodore of Mopsuestia [Swete 1880: 50–54]; Theodoret of Cyrrhus [R. Hill 2001: 129]) and later also in Calvin (1981: 332–33) but revived in more recent times (Cullmann 1936; Munck 1959: 36–42; see also Beale 2003: 215–16) proposes that the restraining thing is the preaching of the gospel, and the restraining person is Paul in his role as a preacher to the Gentiles. This interpretation is based primarily on the idea expressed in Mark 13:10 (cf. Matt. 24:14) that the gospel must be preached "first" to all the nations before end-time tribulations, which include seeing

"the abomination that causes desolation standing where it does not belong [in the temple]" (Mark 13:14), after which time Christ, "the Son of Man," will return (13:26)—a chronology that in broad strokes follows that expressed by Paul here in 2:3b–10.

The biggest or "fatal" (Marshall 1983: 198) flaw with this proposal is that at the time of his writing the Thessalonian Letters, the apostle clearly anticipated remaining alive until the return of Christ (1 Thess. 4:15, 17). It may also be legitimately questioned whether Paul viewed his individual preaching ministry as playing such a decisive role in ushering in end-time events such as the revelation of the lawless one, which would have cosmic consequences. Furthermore, the expression "until he is out of the way" is a highly unusual and cryptic way of referring to his own death, especially when there is no obvious reason for the apostle to speak about it in such a circumspect manner. Finally, this view also would mean that Paul was mistaken in his description of future events, since his death has not resulted in the appearance of the man of lawlessness. This last concern has caused some to modify the interpretation slightly so that the neuter participle still refers to the preaching of the gospel, but the masculine participle refers not to Paul but to "the preacher," that is, anyone who proclaims the gospel (Cerfaux 1959: 47; Moore 1966: 112–14; 1969: 103; Berkhof 1966: 130–35). This modification, however, is weakened by the masculine singular *ho katechōn*, which more likely has in view a particular individual rather than an indefinite group of persons throughout all of history who preach the gospel.

4. *The presence of the church and the Holy Spirit.* Exegetes from a dispensationalist theological perspective argue that the restraining entity of 2:6 and 2:7 is the Holy Spirit, who is currently holding back evil but who will be taken out of this world when the church is removed or raptured (so, e.g., English 1954: 72–80; Scofield 1967: 1294–95n1; Walvoord 1976: 77–78; Thomas 1978: 324–25; Powell 1997: 328–32; see also MacDougall 1993: chap. 5). In these two verses Paul's shift from the neuter to the masculine either parallels the manner in which the Holy Spirit is spoken of elsewhere in Scripture (the upper-room discourse in John's Gospel refers to the Spirit in both the neuter, agreeing with the gender of the noun πνεῦμα, *pneuma*; and the masculine, agreeing with the person of the Spirit: see esp. John 14:26; 15:26; 16:13–14), or the neuter has in view the restraining work of the Spirit in the church while the masculine refers to the person of the Spirit.

The key concept on which this view is predicated (i.e., the rapture of the church along with the Spirit from earth to heaven), however, is difficult to defend exegetically (see comments on 1 Thess. 4:17). There is also the problem of why Paul would refer to the Spirit in such an enigmatic way when only a few verses later within the same passage he refers explicitly to "the Holy Spirit" (2 Thess. 2:13). Finally, nothing in Paul's writings or in the rest of Scripture allows for the idea that the Spirit will ever be "out of the way"; the Holy Spirit is God, and it would be impossible for God ever to be not present in the world.

5. *The power of evil and Satan.* Whereas the previous proposals take the verb *katechō* transitively and see the two participles as referring to a positive force that "restrains" the coming of the man of lawlessness, this view takes the verb intransitively and sees the two participles as referring to an evil force that "rules" or "holds sway" until the coming of the lawless one: the neuter describes either the power of evil (Frame 1912: 261–62) or the mystery of lawlessness (Dixon 1990), while the masculine describes Satan himself (see also Best 1977: 299–301). As we have demonstrated above, however, there are significant problems with taking the verb intransitively and viewing the *katechon/katechōn* entity as being morally evil or bad. The chronological sequence of one evil character (Satan) disappearing to make room for another evil character (the man of lawlessness) has also seemed to most interpreters highly improbable. Furthermore, since the lawless one's parousia will be "in conformity with the work of Satan" (2:9), we may wonder how this would be possible now that Satan is supposedly "out of the way."

6. *The false prophecy and the false prophet.* Giblin (1967: 167–204, 234–42; also 1990: 459–69) takes the verb *katechō* in the active sense of "seize," understands the neuter participle as referring to a pseudo-prophetic force captivating ("seizing, possessing") certain believers in Thessalonica, and counts the masculine participle as referring to one particular individual or false prophet, who must be removed before the man of lawlessness can be revealed (see also Green 2002: 316). The significant objections that can be raised against this interpretation have already been reviewed above.

7. *The activity and the person of the archangel Michael.* The possibility that the restrainer is an angel has been suggested by several commentators (Dibelius 1937: 46–51; Ridderbos 1975: 525; Marshall 1983: 199–200; Holland 1988: 110–13; Müller 1988: 50–51; Menken 1994: 113; Beale 2003: 216–17) on the conviction that only a supernatural being is powerful enough to restrain the mystery of lawlessness that is already at work in the world. Although one might naturally think of God as playing the role of the restrainer, this possibility has to be rejected on the grounds that it is impossible for God to disappear from the scene ("until he is out of the way"). The next logical candidate would be a supernatural being such as an angel, through whom God's power is currently at work in restraining lawlessness and preventing Satan's superman from making his grand appearance. An angelic identification of the restrainer is supported by several apocalyptic texts in the NT and Jewish writings where angels have a binding or restraining function. For example, an unnamed angel in Rev. 20:1–3 binds Satan, thereby restraining his work of deception.[4] Also, four angels in Rev. 7:1 seize the four winds of the earth, holding them back for a temporary period from bringing calamity to the

---

4. This binding of Satan and resulting restraint of his deceptive work last for "a thousand years" (Rev. 20:2). Although many locate the millennial reign of Christ to a future period begun after his second coming, there are good reasons for viewing this as the present reality ushered in during Christ's first coming and ministry so that the restraint of Satan's deceptive work spoken of here ought to be dated to the current age—exactly the point asserted by Paul in 2 Thess. 2:7.

land and sea. Or again, the angels Raphael and Michael in 1 En. 10.4 and 10.11–12 bind two leaders of the watchers, Azaz'el and Semyaza, for seventy generations underground until the day of judgment. The possibility that the restrainer is an angel gains further credence from the fact that Paul believed such supernatural creatures to have an important role in carrying out the will of God, especially in connection with end-time events, as evidenced in his statement to the Thessalonians in the previous chapter that Christ's return would be accompanied by "the angels of his power" (1:7b) and his statement in the previous letter that Christ's return would be signaled by "a voice of an archangel" (1 Thess. 4:16). The most likely angel candidate by far, given his preeminent position in both Jewish and Christian writings, is the archangel Michael (see Hannah 1999 and esp. Nicholl 2004: 231–32 for a lengthy list of texts that highlight Michael's role as the most important of the archangels, protector and interceder of God's people, military leader of the heavenly hosts, and primary opponent of and even victor over Satan).

The strongest evidence that the restrainer is not just an angel but more specifically the archangel Michael, however, lies in the likely allusions in our passage to the vision of Dan. 10–12, where Michael, the patron angel of the Jews, is said to withstand (restrain?) the evil patron angels of Israel's enemies, Persia and Greece. Since (1) Paul's use of the title "the man of lawlessness" in 2 Thess. 2:3b is likely influenced by Dan. 12:10, with its description of the lawless conduct characteristic of individuals living in the last days; and (2) Paul's description of this eschatological enemy in 2 Thess. 2:4 parallels even more closely Daniel's prophecy about a future king of the north who "will exalt and magnify himself above every god" (11:36) and desecrate the temple (11:31)—these facts enhance the possibility that the apostle's description of the restraining entity in 2 Thess. 2:6–7 is similarly influenced by material from the same vision of Dan. 10–12. Hannah (2000) and Nicholl (2004: 225–49) examine this possibility in greater detail and demonstrate not only that the identity of the archangel Michael as restrainer stems from Dan. 10:13, 20–21 but also, in Nicholl's case, that Paul's reference to the removal of Michael's restraining work ("until he is out of the way") originates from Dan. 12:1a (see also Witherington 2006: 211–12, 221; Shogren 2012: 287–88b).

The context of Dan. 10–12 involves a vision of a heavenly figure who has been sent to tell the prophet about a "war" (10:1) that is apparently taking place in two dimensions: a heavenly dimension, where Michael, the "chief prince" or patron angel of Israel, fights against the "princes" or patron angels of Persia and Greece (10:20–21; see also 10:13); and an earthly dimension, where kings of the south and kings of the north do battle against each other (11:2–45). The pattern then repeats itself with a brief description of an incident that takes place in the heavenly realm: "at that time Michael, the great prince who protects your people, will arise" (12:1a). This is followed by earthly events involving first a time of unparalleled distress for God's people (12:1b) and then their blessed deliverance (12:1c–3). What happens in the heavenly realm impacts what happens in the earthly realm. The evil, patron angels of Persia and Greece work through the earthly kings of both the south and the north in ways that negatively impact the people of God. Yet Michael, the patron archangel of Israel, who "protects" God's people (12:1a), fights against these evil angels (10:20–21; see also 10:13), thereby restraining their destructive impact in the earthly realm as each human king rises only briefly before finally falling in the quest for ultimate power. Michael's role in the vision of Dan. 10–12, then, is that of one who restrains the forces of evil, similar to Paul's depiction of the *katechon/katechōn* figure in 2:6–7 as one who restrains "the mystery of lawlessness" already at work in the world.

The apostle's sequencing of events—the restraining thing/person will one day become absent, and this departure paves the way for lawlessness to reach its climax in the coming of the apostasy and the appearance of the lawless one (2 Thess. 2:3–8)—also parallels the chronology found in the vision of Dan. 10–12. The key verse is 12:1a, where Michael is said to "stand" (MT) or, as rendered in the LXX, "stand aside, pass by" (παρέρχομαι, *parerchomai*). Although the specific nature or purpose of Michael's action is not stated, the context suggests that his conduct is conditional for the next event to occur: it is only after Michael "stands" or "stands aside" (12:1a) that the unparalleled distress of God's people takes place (12:1b). As Nicholl (2004: 44) puts it: "The logic seems to be that the eschatological tribulation could only come upon God's people if Michael, the guardian of God's people, ceases from protecting them." The chronological schema in Dan. 10–12, therefore, parallels exactly that followed by Paul in 2 Thess. 2:3–12:

a. The archangel Michael currently restrains evil (Dan. 10:20–11:45; 2 Thess. 2:6a, 7a: "And you know the thing that is now restraining"; "the one who is now restraining").

b. Michael, the restrainer, will be removed from the scene (Dan. 12:1a: "At that time Michael, the great prince who protects your people, will arise/stand aside"; 2 Thess. 2:7b: "only until he is out of the way").

c. God's people endure a time of unequaled tribulation (Dan. 12:1b: "There will be a time of distress such as has not happened from the beginning of the nations until then"; 2 Thess. 2:3–4, 8–10: the coming of the apostasy and the revelation of the man of lawlessness).

d. The final judgment takes place when God's people are delivered and their enemies are punished (Dan. 12:1c–3: "But at that time your people—everyone whose name is found written in the book—will be delivered. Multitudes who sleep in the dust of the earth will awake: some to everlasting life, others to shame and everlasting contempt. Those who are wise will shine like the brightness of the heavens, and those who lead many to righteousness like stars for ever and ever"; 2 Thess. 2:3–14: the arrival of the day of the Lord [v. 3] will involve not only the destruction of the man of lawlessness [v. 8b] and his deceived followers [vv. 10b–12], but also the salvation and glorification of the Thessalonian believers [vv. 13–14]).

Finally, a text, though dating to a time well after the writing of 2 Thessalonians, indicates that others within Judaism, like Paul, not only understood the archangel Michael as a restrainer but also used the same verb as the apostle to describe his restraining function. An incantation from a magical papyrus dating to the third or fourth century refers to "Michael, . . . who restrains [κατέχων, *katechōn*] him whom they call the great dragon" (*PGM* 4.2770). As Hannah (1999: 134; also 2000: 44) observes: "This text demonstrates that Michael was known to some individuals in antiquity, who were at least acquainted with Jewish or Christian angelology, as (ὁ) κατέχων" (see also Nicholl 2004: 38–41).

IV. Exhortations about the Rebellious Idlers (3:1–15)

The second and final major topic of the letter deals with the problem of the "rebellious idlers" (ἄτακτοι, *ataktoi*; 1 Thess. 5:14a)—those in the Thessalonian church who rebelliously refuse to obey Paul's repeated instructions about the need for self-sufficient work and who instead continue to live a lazy lifestyle in which they take advantage of the charity of fellow congregational members and use their resulting free time to engage in meddlesome behavior. The apostle first addressed this problem during his initial visit to Thessalonica (1 Thess. 4:11b; 2 Thess. 3:6, 10) and dealt with it again, albeit briefly, in his first letter (1 Thess. 4:11b–12; 5:14a). Instead of getting better, however, the problem apparently grew worse. Thus, for yet a third time and at much greater length, Paul takes up the issue here in 2 Thess. 3:1–15.

Paul's exhortations fall into two major units: verses 1–5 and 6–15. The first unit can be labeled "General" since it deals in a wide-ranging way with various subjects: exhortation to pray for Paul and his fellow missionaries (vv. 1–2a), reason why such intercessory prayer is needed (v. 2b), word of encouragement about the Lord's work of strengthening and guarding the Thessalonians (v. 3), Paul's confidence in his Thessalonian readers (v. 4), and a prayer for what the Lord will do for them (v. 5). These disparate topics are joined together by a common function: to prepare the original readers to hear and heed the exhortations that come in the immediately following unit of verses 6–15.

The second unit can be labeled "Specific" since it contains Paul's particular commands on how the church ought to deal with the rebelliously idle behavior of some of their fellow members. The apostle frames this discussion with opening (v. 6) and closing (vv. 13–15) commands to keep away from those who persist in their lazy and meddlesome ways. The significant negative impact that these commands "to avoid" (v. 6) and "not to associate with" (v. 14) would have on such wayward members can be easily missed by those today who live in a Western society that is highly individualistic and largely shameless. For the believers in Thessalonica, however, who by contrast lived in a heavily communal culture, where honor and shame were among the most powerful forces controlling social behavior, such disciplinary action would have a devastating impact ("in order that he may be put to shame") that Paul hopes in turn will ultimately lead to their repentance and restoration.

Sandwiched between the opening and closing commands to practice church discipline are three subunits (vv. 7–9, 10, 11–12). The first two are intended to provide the grounds or basis for the framing commands: the example of Paul (vv. 7–9) and the teaching of Paul (v. 10). In the first subunit (vv. 7–9), Paul reminds his readers of his example of self-sufficient work—how, despite his "right" as an apostle to receive support from the church, he worked both hard ("in labor and toil") and long ("night and day") to provide for them a model to be imitated. In the second subunit (v. 10), Paul additionally reminds his readers of his repeated teaching about self-sufficient work summarized in the command, "If someone is not willing to work, let him not eat!" In the third subunit (vv. 11–12), Paul takes the general principle of self-sufficient work recalled in both his past example and former teaching and applies it specifically to the rebellious idlers in Thessalonica, who are commanded to "eat their own bread," that is, they must provide for their own basic daily needs rather than live from the benevolence of fellow church members. Paul's primary purpose is not punitive but redemptive, as evidenced by the "brotherly" or loving way in which the rebellious idlers ought to be treated throughout the disciplinary process (vv. 6, 15).

Literary Analysis

Character of the Passage

The material of 3:1–15 is best identified in terms of its genre as exhortation or, by its more technical term, *paraenesis* (for an extended discussion of this formal category, see comments on 1 Thess. 4:1–12). Paul's pattern here parallels exactly that adopted in his previous letter: the main topic(s) taken up in the body of the letter (1 Thess. 2:1–3:10; 2 Thess. 2:1–15) is brought to a close by transitional prayers (1 Thess. 3:11, 12–13; 2 Thess. 2:16–17a, 17b); then, after two transitional markers (the adverbial use of λοιπόν [*loipon*] and the vocative ἀδελφοί [*adelphoi*]; 1 Thess. 4:1; 2 Thess. 3:1), this is followed by various exhortations (1 Thess. 4:1–5:22; 2 Thess. 3:1–15) until the peace benediction (1 Thess. 5:23; 2 Thess. 3:16) signals the start of the letter closing. The exhortative character of 3:1–15 is evident not just *explicitly* in the use of the imperative mood (vv. 1, 10, 13, 14, 15 [2x]), the verb "to command" (vv. 4, 6, 10, 12) and indirect commands (vv. 6, 14), but also *implicitly* in such things as the confidence formula (v. 4). On this epistolary convention, Malherbe (2000: 446) states: "Paul on occasion expresses confidence about his readers as a hortatory or paraenetic device, urging upon them precisely what he says he is confident about." The prayer in verse 5 also involves implicit paraenesis, since Paul's sharing of the content of his prayer to God for the Thessalonians not so subtly also lets his readers know what the apostle hopes will happen in their lives. The exhortative character of 3:1–15 sets this passage formally apart from the preceding passage, whose only imperatives are found in the double closing commands in 2:15. This stronger hortatory quality of 3:1–15 reflects a shift in Paul's overall purpose in the two passages: whereas the apostle in 2:1–17 is primarily *comforting* the Thessalonian congregation, here in 3:1–15 he is *challenging* and even *commanding* them to deal appropriately with a select group within the congregation: the ἄτακτοι (*ataktoi*), or "rebellious idlers."

Extent of the Passage

Several literary features clearly identify the beginning of a new unit at 3:1. The first petition of the transitional prayer in 2:16–17a brings the preceding discussion to a close and so leads the reader to expect in the subsequent verse the beginning of the next major issue to be addressed in the letter body. This expectation is confirmed by the second petition of the prayer in verse 17b, which in a subtle yet clear way anticipates matters taken up in 3:1–15 (the verb "to strengthen" is picked up in 3:3, and the noun phrase "every good work" looks ahead to the exhortations about the "rebellious idlers" and the requirements for self-sufficient work in 3:6–15; for a fuller explanation, see the comments on 2:17b). Two epistolary devices further corroborate the start of a new unit at 3:1: the presence of *to loipon*, which often introduces the last item or subject matter to be treated in the letter body (in addition to 1 Thess. 4:1, see also 2 Cor. 13:11; Gal. 6:17; Phil. 4:8), and the vocative *adelphoi*, commonly used by Paul and other NT writers to signal the beginning of a new section. Finally, there is also a shift in topic as Paul moves away from end-time matters and the Thessalonians' unjustified fears about this subject in 2:1–17 and takes up issues of conduct and how the church ought to discipline certain wayward members within their fellowship.

But where does this new passage end? A good number of commentators see a major break occurring at 3:6, such that there are two distinct units (3:1–5 and 3:6–15), not in any significant way connected to each other (so, e.g., Best 1977; Bruce 1982; Marshall 1983; Morris 1991; Williams 1992; D. Martin 1995; Beale 2003; see also the commentators who begin the first unit not at 3:1 but earlier, at 2:13: e.g., Holmes 1998; Malherbe 2000). This failure to see how the two resulting paragraphs of 3:1–5 and 3:6–15 might be interrelated leads such commentators in turn to make negative judgments about the logic of Paul's argument, especially in the first paragraph. Wanamaker (1990: 273), for example, claims that 3:1–5 is "roughly composed" and "disjointed" and goes on to postulate that "perhaps he [Paul] was interrupted in his composition of the letter after 2:17, and in returning to the letter did not give enough care to continuing his train of thought smoothly." Some years earlier, Rigaux (1956: 693) commented negatively about the coherence of Paul's argument here by stating: "Every speaker has his good and bad days." Even the conservative Marshall (1983: 212) declares: "The structure of the epistle at this point is not altogether clear."

It is true that a significant transition takes place at 3:6 such that there are two distinct paragraphs: 3:1–5 and 3:6–15. This is clear from the prayer, or "body-benediction," of 3:5, which in Paul's Letters always functions to bring a discussion to a close (Rom. 15:5–6; 15:13; 1 Thess. 3:11, 12–13; 2 Thess. 2:16–17; Weima 1994a: 101–4). The break at 3:6 is further indicated by two epistolary conventions that in the apostle's letters typically mark the beginning of a new paragraph: the vocative "brothers" and the "command" formula—an epistolary convention that follows the form of the more common "appeal" formula (Bjerkelund 1967), with the important difference that it employs the harsher verb "command" (παραγγέλλω, *parangellō*) instead of the softer, more user-friendly "appeal" (παρακαλέω, *parakaleō*).

It is not true, however, that the two resulting paragraphs of 3:1–5 and 3:6–15 are unconnected to each other. An important lexical link between the two paragraphs lies in the verb "command" (*parangellō*: vv. 4, 6, 10, 12). Furthermore, this key lexical link is stressed in both paragraphs: in 3:1–5 it is emphasized by word order as the relative clause where the verb occurs is moved from its expected position at the end of the main clause to the beginning: "*what things we are commanding*, you are indeed doing and will continue to do" (v. 4b); in 3:6–15 the verb "command" is emphasized by both its selection to open the new paragraph (v. 6, "Now we command you . . .") and its twofold repetition within the paragraph (v. 10, "For when we were with you, we also were repeatedly commanding to you this . . ."; v. 12, "To such people we command . . .").

Since Paul has consciously connected these two paragraphs together, what function does he intend 3:1–5 to have in relation to 3:6–15? Why does the apostle not jump immediately to the exhortations of the latter paragraph, dealing with the rebellious idlers, but instead first spend five verses on what appears to be unrelated matters? The answer is that the first paragraph, 3:1–5, prepares the readers to hear and heed the strong commands given in the second paragraph, 3:6–15. Frame (1912: 288–89) rightly states of the function of 3:1–5: "Wishing to get their willing obedience to the command of vv. 6–15, he seeks their sympathy in requesting their prayer for him and his cause, and delicately commends their faith. . . . Still wishing to get their willing obedience, Paul . . . avows tactfully his faith in them that they will be glad to do what he commands, as indeed they are even now doing." Menken (1994: 125) likewise notes how Paul in 3:1–5 "makes them receptive to his specific injunctions that will follow in 3.6–12." Fee (2009: 310–11) adopts a largely similar position in his proposal that Paul in 3:1–5 borrows "a common feature from ancient rhetoric, . . . a *captatio benevolentiae* (vv. 1–5), an introductory word of praise intended to gain a good hearing from them before addressing this difficult issue [those in the church who are rebelliously idle] once more."

It would be wrong, therefore, to end the new unit introduced in 3:1 already at 3:5 since that would cut off this paragraph from the following larger paragraph of 3:6–15, to which it is lexically linked. Even worse, this arrangement would prevent one from seeing the important role that 3:1–5 plays in relation to 3:6–15, namely, to prepare the original readers to hear and heed the later commands connected with the rebellious idlers in the Thessalonian congregation. Instead, the passage must be extended all the way to 3:15.[1]

Structure of the Passage

The exhortative material of 3:1–15 falls into two major units: verses 1–5 and 6–15 (for a justification of these two units, see discussion above on "Extent of the Passage"). The first unit can be labeled "General" since it does not deal with

---

1. The weakness in extending the passage all the way to 3:16 (so, e.g., Findlay 1891; Milligan 1908; Marshall 1983; Menken 1994) is that verse 16 consists of a peace benediction—an epistolary convention that not only belongs to the letter closing but also typically functions as a literary heading that marks the beginning of the letter closing (Weima 1994a: 88–90). Ending the passage earlier, at 3:12 (so, e.g., Trilling 1980: 154–55; Müller 1988: 166; Holland 1988: 52; Menken 1994: 141–42; Furnish 2007: 179), makes it difficult to provide a compelling explanation for how the resulting small section of 3:13–15 functions in the overall structure of the letter. As Nicholl (2004: 170) states: "Verses 14–15 clearly belong with verses 6–12, for there is no other issue in 2 Thessalonians which merits discipline." Furthermore, 3:14–15 is best understood as a closing command to "not associate with" idle members—a command that forms a thematic inclusio with the opening command of 3:6 to "keep away" from such members. Finally, there is also a lexical inclusio between the singular, nonvocative "brother" in 3:6 and 3:15.

any specific or clearly defined problem but instead in a wide-ranging way refers to various subjects: exhortation to pray for Paul and his fellow missionaries (vv. 1–2a), reason why such intercessory prayer is needed (v. 2b), word of encouragement about the Lord's work of strengthening and guarding the Thessalonians (v. 3), Paul's confidence in his Thessalonian readers (v. 4), and a prayer for what the Lord will do for them (v. 5). Many commentators struggle to make sense of the logic of Paul's argumentation, agreeing with the assessment of Richard (1995: 373) about this section's "lack of unity and focus." Yet, as was explained above, these disparate topics are joined together by a common function: to prepare the original readers to hear and heed the exhortations that come in the immediately following unit of verses 6–15.

The second unit can be labeled "Specific" since it contains Paul's commands related to a particular difficulty facing the church: how they ought to deal with the rebelliously idle behavior of some of their fellow members. The apostle frames this discussion with opening (v. 6) and closing (vv. 13–15) commands to avoid those who are idle (Gaventa 1998: 127). These commands are similar in content (v. 6, "that you keep away from . . ."; v. 14, "that you not associate with . . .") and thus form a thematic inclusio that marks the boundaries of the second unit (vv. 6–15). The boundaries are further supported by a lexical inclusio between the singular, nonvocative "brother" in verse 6 and verse 15—a term that not only identifies the recipient of the church's discipline as a fellow congregational member but also highlights the "brotherly" or loving way in which this discipline is to be practiced.

Sandwiched between these opening and closing commands are three subunits (vv. 7–9, 10, 11–12), each one introduced with the conjunction "for" (γάρ, *gar*). The first two are intended to provide the grounds or basis for the framing commands: Paul's example (vv. 7–9) and teaching (v. 10). The first subunit (vv. 7–9), involving the example of Paul, is introduced with a disclosure formula ("For you yourselves know . . ."), which typically functions as a transitional device in the apostle's letters. The boundaries of this first subunit are demarked not only thematically by its similar content—the example of Paul—but also literarily by the lexical inclusio that is formed between the key infinitive "to imitate" (μιμεῖσθαι, *mimeisthai*), found in verse 7 and repeated in verse 9. The second subunit (v. 10), involving the teaching of Paul, is introduced not merely with the conjunction "for" that opens the first subunit but with the fuller construction "for also" (καὶ γάρ, *kai gar*), indicating that this clause presents an additional second ground for the framing commands to discipline the rebellious idlers. The third subunit (vv. 11–12) also opens with the conjunction "for," though this time it introduces not a third ground but instead an explanatory comment on how the first two grounds dealing with the past example and past teaching of Paul about work ought to be applied to the contemporary problem facing the Thessalonian congregation. This third subunit of application is linked lexically to the two preceding subunits by the key imperative phrase "let them *eat* their own *bread*" (v. 12, τὸν ἑαυτῶν ἄρτον ἐσθίωσιν, *ton heautōn arton esthiōsin*), which looks back to the phrase "*eat bread*" (v. 8, ἄρτον ἐφάγομεν, *arton ephagomen*) in the first subunit dealing with the example of Paul and the imperative "Let him not *eat!*" (v. 10, μηδὲ ἐσθιέτω, *mēde esthietō*) in the second subunit dealing with the teaching of Paul.

The closing commands of verses 13–15 are set apart literarily by the transitional marker, the vocative "brothers," and the emphatic personal pronoun "you" in verse 13. After a general exhortation to continue doing good (v. 13), there follows a specific command "that you not associate with this one" (v. 14), which echoes the opening command "that you keep away from every brother . . ." (v. 6).

The following thus shows the structure of 3:1–15:

A. General exhortations: The Lord's work in Paul's ministry and the Thessalonian church (3:1–5)
   1. Command for intercessory prayer (3:1–2a)
   2. Reason for the command (3:2b)
   3. Word of encouragement (3:3)
   4. Confidence formula (3:4)
   5. Concluding prayer (3:5)
B. Specific exhortations: Discipline the rebellious idlers (3:6–15)
   1. Opening command (3:6)
   2. The example of Paul (3:7–9)
   3. The teaching of Paul (3:10)
   4. Applying Paul's example and teaching (3:11–12)
   5. Closing commands (3:13–15)

Exegesis and Exposition

¹As for other matters, brothers, pray for us that the word of ⌜the Lord⌝ may run and be honored, just as it also is with you, ²and that we may be rescued from evil and wicked people. For not everyone has faith. ³But faithful is the ⌜Lord⌝, who will ⌜strengthen⌝ and guard you from the evil one. ⁴Furthermore, we have confidence in the Lord about you, that what things we are commanding, ⌜you are indeed doing and will continue to do⌝. ⁵Now may the Lord direct your hearts to God's love and to Christ's endurance.

⁶Now we command you, brothers, in the name of ⌜our⌝ Lord Jesus Christ, that you keep away from every brother who continues to walk in a rebelliously idle manner and not according to the tradition that ⌜they received⌝ from us. ⁷For you yourselves know how it is necessary to imitate us: we were not idle among you, ⁸and we did not eat bread from anyone without paying for it, but we were working in labor and toil ⌜night and day⌝ in order not to burden any of you— ⁹not that we do not have the right, but in order that we might give ourselves to you as an example so that you might imitate us. ¹⁰For when we were with you, we also were repeatedly commanding this to you: "If anyone is not willing to work, let him not eat." ¹¹We say this because we hear that some are continuing to walk among you in a rebelliously idle manner by not being busy but by being busybodies. ¹²To such people we command and appeal ⌜in the Lord Jesus Christ⌝ that they eat their own bread by working with quietness. ¹³But as for you, brothers, do not ⌜be discouraged⌝ in doing good. ¹⁴But if anyone does not obey our command in this letter, take special notice of that person ⌜so as to not associate⌝ with him in order that he might be put to shame. ¹⁵And do not consider him as an enemy but admonish him as a brother.

A. General Exhortations: The Lord's Work in Paul's Ministry and the Thessalonian Church (3:1–5)

1. Command for Intercessory Prayer (3:1–2a)

3:1 Paul begins the second and final major topic of the letter body with a command for intercessory prayer, which initially suggests that the concern of this new unit will be on him and his missionary activity. The parenthetical clause at the end of the opening verse, however, hints that already here the apostle's primary concern is more focused on the situation of his Thessalonian readers, and that the general exhortations of verses 1–5 are intended to secure his readers' obedience to the specific exhortations coming in verses 6–15: "As for other matters, brothers, pray for us that the word of the Lord may run and be honored, just as it also is with you" (τὸ λοιπὸν προσεύχεσθε, ἀδελφοί, περὶ ἡμῶν ἵνα ὁ λόγος τοῦ κυρίου τρέχῃ καὶ δοξάζηται καθὼς καὶ πρὸς ὑμᾶς, *to loipon proseuchesthe, adelphoi, peri hēmōn hina ho logos tou kyriou trechē kai doxazētai kathōs kai pros hymas*).

The general exhortations of verses 1–5 as a new section in the letter are signaled first by the adjective *to loipon*, which, when used adverbially as here, functions "as a transition to something new, especially when it comes near the end of a literary work" (BDAG 603.3.b; see 2 Cor. 13:11; Phil. 3:1; 4:8; 1 Thess. 4:1). It need not necessarily introduce the very last topic of a letter or indicate that the letter will soon come to an end, and so the translation "finally" (so virtually all English versions) in many cases is misleading. In this context it is better rendered "as far as the rest is concerned" or "as for other matters" (NIV). Nor does *to loipon* necessarily introduce a topic of lesser importance than matters previously taken up in the letter body. For example, *loipon* was used in 1 Thess. 4:1 to introduce the important exhortations raised in 4:3–5:22 and similarly in Phil. 3:1 for the weighty matters that follow in Philippians. Here in 2 Thess. 3:1 it introduces the topic of idle and meddlesome members in the church—a topic whose importance is suggested both by the great length (vv. 1–15) with which Paul treats this subject as well as by the strong language of "command" that he repeatedly employs in addressing this problem (vv. 4, 6, 10, 12).[2]

The beginning of the new section of verses 1–5 is signaled, second, by the vocative "brothers." This marks the sixth of seven occurrences of the term in this brief letter (1:3; 2:1, 13, 15; 3:1, 6, 13; see also the singular in 3:6, 15) and continues Paul's heavy use of this vocative in his previous correspondence with the Thessalonian church to characterize his relationship with them (14x: 1:4; 2:1, 9, 14, 17; 3:7; 4:1, 10b, 13; 5:1, 4, 12, 14, 25), a much higher frequency

---

2. Fee (2009: 313) overstates the importance of 3:1–15, claiming that "as a point of emphasis, he [Paul] has saved the final word for a matter that concerns him greatly" (cf. also 333). It is unlikely that Paul "saved" the problem of the idlers for last because it was so important; rather, he treats it here in chap. 3 because he had finished dealing with the primary problem facing the Thessalonian congregation, which is addressed in 2:1–17—a problem foreshadowed in the thanksgiving section and then taken up first and treated the longest in the letter body.

than in any of his other letters. The presence of the vocative "brothers" yet again here in 2 Thess. 3:1 functions not merely as a transitional marker but also stresses the intimate bond that Paul enjoys with his Thessalonian readers and so makes them more disposed to obey the exhortations—both general (vv. 1–5) and specific (vv. 6–15)—that he is about to give.

Paul opens the general exhortations with the only explicit command found in this paragraph: "Pray for us" (*proseuchesthe peri hēmōn*). The presence of this command for intercessory (not for oneself but for others) prayer follows quite naturally from the prayer that concludes the previous eschatological discussion: just as Paul prays for his Thessalonian readers (2:16–17), so he asks that they reciprocate by praying for him and his fellow missionaries.[3] The apostle's command for intercessory prayer also agrees well with the priority and practice that this spiritual discipline has in his own life. Paul opens most of his letters with a thanksgiving section that typically refers to him remembering his readers in such intercessory prayer (Rom. 1:9; Eph. 1:16; Phil. 1:4; Col. 1:3; 1 Thess. 1:2–3; 2 Tim. 1:3; Philem. 4). Some of these thanksgivings, including the one in this letter, also conclude with a prayer report in which the apostle shares with his readers the content of his prayers for them (2 Thess. 1:11–12; also Rom. 1:10; Phil. 1:9–11; Col. 1:9–14). Paul frequently calls on his readers to reciprocate his intercessory prayers by requesting that they in turn pray for him (Rom. 15:30–33; 2 Cor. 11:1; Col. 4:3–4; see Eph. 6:18–19; Phil. 1:19; Philem. 22).

Here Paul's command "Pray for us" repeats exactly his words in the closing of the first letter (5:25). In both places he uses the present-tense imperative, thereby stressing the ongoing or continuous nature of their prayers on his behalf. The apostle expects the Thessalonians not merely to utter a quick prayer for him that will make them briefly feel good about themselves before they return to the concerns that preoccupy their own lives. Instead, Paul challenges, even commands, the converts in Thessalonica to regularly and repeatedly bring the issues of his life and his ministry to the throne of God in prayer.

But whereas the apostle's command in the first letter did not specify *what* the Thessalonian Christians ought to include in their intercessory prayers, here in the second letter he adds two *hina* clauses (vv. 1b, 2a) that spell out the content (BDAG 476.2; Moule 1959: 145–46)[4] of these expected prayers. The first of these *hina* clauses reveals that the apostle desires prayers not so much for himself personally as for his ministry: "that the word of the Lord may run and be honored" (*hina ho logos tou kyriou trechē kai doxazētai*). The phrase "the word of the Lord" is an unusual way for Paul to refer to the gospel message, as it occurs only one other time in his letters (1 Thess. 1:8). The expected way for the apostle to refer to the gospel is to use either the noun

---

3. Yet in 3:1 Paul does not stress this reciprocity by including in the exhortation to pray the adverb "also" (καί, *kai*) as he did in his previous letter (1 Thess. 5:25: "Pray *also* for us").

4. Contra those (e.g., Wanamaker 1990: 274; Richard 1995: 369; Shogren 2012: 316) who take the ἵνα clauses (3:1b–2a) as giving the *purpose* of the prayers.

"word" absolutely (e.g., 1 Thess. 1:5, 6) or the expression "the word of *God*" (Rom. 9:6; 1 Cor. 14:36; Eph. 6:17; Phil. 1:14 v.l.; Col. 1:25; 1 Thess. 2:13; 1 Tim. 4:5; 2 Tim. 2:9; Titus 2:5).[5] Consequently, it is difficult to determine whether the rare phrase "the word of the Lord" ought to be taken objectively ("the word about the Lord") or subjectively ("the word that comes from the Lord"). Here Paul may be influenced by the OT, where the phrase "the word of the LORD" occurs over 250 times, always with the sense of a message originating from God. If so, the apostle's rare wording would refer to the fact that the gospel message he proclaims originates not from him or any other human source but from a divine source. Paul differs from the OT usage, however, since the divine source is identified no longer as God (so, e.g., Williams 1992: 31; Witherington 2006: 241) but as "the Lord," that is, Jesus Christ, following the apostle's consistent use of this term throughout his letters (so most commentators; see esp. Fee 2009: 31–34).

The only other time Paul uses the phrase "the word of the Lord," he pairs it with the unique verb "to echo forth," thereby creating a powerful image of a sound—the gospel message—that emanates from the Thessalonian Christians and reverberates on and on throughout the hills and valleys of Macedonia, Achaia, and beyond (1 Thess. 1:8). Here in 2 Thess. 3:1 Paul combines the phrase with the verb "to run" (τρέχω, *trechō*), thereby creating yet another potent image, though there is debate about its source. Many commentators believe that Paul is alluding to Ps. 147:4 LXX (147:15 Eng.), whose second strophe in the LXX reads: "his word runs swiftly" (ἕως τάχους δραμεῖται ὁ λόγος αὐτοῦ, *heōs tachous drameitai ho logos autou*). In the context of the psalm, God sends his word to the earth and, just as God is in control of the seasons such that he sends snow, hail, and wind and nothing can stop him, so he is in control of his word such that nothing can hinder it from "running" or spreading swiftly. The image Paul is evoking here in 3:1, therefore, is one where the gospel message "runs": it "proceeds quickly and without restraint" (BDAG 1015.3).

This claimed allusion to Ps. 147:4 LXX suffers, however, from the fact that Paul's words differ from their supposed OT source in two key ways. First, the verbal forms are not identical since Paul writes *trechē*, whereas Ps. 147:4 has *drameitai*.[6] Second, the apostle does not include the prepositional phrase *heōs tachous* (swiftly), stressed by virtue of word order in Ps. 147:4 and crucial to making the point that God's word does not merely "run" but that it "runs swiftly." It seems more likely, then, that the apostle is not alluding to this OT text but instead is evoking the image of an athletic race.[7] The metaphor of running a race was common in Paul's day, and he used it often in his letters

---

5. A few copyists changed the text of 3:1 to "the word of God" (see additional notes).

6. Fee (2009: 313n13) tries to minimize this problem by claiming that a native Greek speaker would not have stumbled over the different verbal forms, just as a native English speaker has no problem in moving from "go" to "went."

7. Marshall (1983: 213) argues: "It is not necessary to choose between these two sources, since the metaphor of a race was also Jewish (Ps. 19:5); Paul is able to make use of an OT picture which would be meaningful to Greek readers."

(Rom. 9:16 KJV; 1 Cor. 9:24–27; Gal. 2:2; 5:7; Phil. 2:16; 2 Tim. 4:7). Indeed, although lacking the key verb "run," his previous letter to the Thessalonians makes a clear allusion to such athletic contests, where the victor receives a wreath (2:19: "For who is our . . . crown of boasting—Is it not, in fact, you?").

This picture of the victory wreath likely lies behind the second verb in the clause, which continues the athletic metaphor: the Thessalonian believers are commanded to pray for Paul that the gospel message he proclaims may not only "run" but also "be honored" (*doxazētai*). As Green (2002: 335) observes: "The combination of 'run' and 'be honored' suggests that the apostles visualize the word as a runner who competes in the games and wins the prize, and so receives the honor that is due." The gospel must not only run or compete in the public arena with other religions or worldviews; it must also win the competition and "be honored," that is, be accepted "not as the word of human beings but, as it truly is, the word of God" (1 Thess. 2:13). Just as a winning athlete is openly honored in the bestowing of the victory wreath, so the gospel message is to be publicly praised in the words and obedient conduct of its adherents. This is what happened in response to Paul and Barnabas's ministry in Antioch Pisidia, where its citizens "honored the word of the Lord" (Acts 13:48).

Before proceeding to the second *hina* clause, which spells out what else ought to be included in the content of the Thessalonians' intercessory prayers on his behalf, Paul adds a parenthetical statement that is more important than commonly recognized: "just as it also is with you" (*kathōs kai pros hymas*). The implied subject of this clause, "it," refers back to "the word of the Lord," the gospel message. The absence of any verb in the Greek text has resulted in confusion over whether the apostle is commenting about the *past* acceptance of the gospel message in Thessalonica or its *present* success in that city (the translations and commentaries are virtually equally divided in their conclusion; a few believe that both past and present are intended: e.g., Best 1977: 325; Menken 1994: 126; Beale 2003: 238). But if Paul wanted to stress the timing of this victory of the gospel, he would have been sure to include a verb (as he does in 3:4, for example, to stress both the readers' present and future obedience: "you are indeed doing and will continue to do"). Its absence, therefore, suggests that "what Paul is after here is the *reality* of the success of the gospel among them, not *when* this success occurred" (Fee 2009: 314).

The importance of this parenthetical statement lies in its strong commendation of the Thessalonian readers and how this commendation sets them up to obey the commands that are coming in verses 6–15. The phrase "just as it also is with you," as brief and innocuous as it may seem to be, functions to identify the Thessalonian believers as those among whom the gospel has "run" and been "honored." Such an affirmation from one who is spiritually both their "nursing mother" and "father" (1 Thess. 2:7c, 11) would no doubt endear the apostle that much more to his readers and induce them to be favorably disposed to the commands that he will soon share with them. As Frame (1912: 291–92) observes about this parenthetical comment: "The praise implied in the prayer that the gospel may succeed with all as it succeeds with the readers is designed probably as an incentive not to their prayers for him but to their obedience to the command in mind (v. 6). Sympathy for Paul is to create a willing compliance; if they love him, they will keep his commands." Furthermore, this brief aside shifts the focus away for a moment from the situation of Paul and his coworkers ("Pray for *us*") to that of the Thessalonian believers ("just as it also is with *you*"). This shift anticipates verses 3–5, showing the apostle's preoccupation with the circumstances of his readers (v. 3: "who will strengthen *you* . . ."; v. 4: "We have confidence in the Lord about *you*. . . . You are indeed doing and will continue to do"; v. 5: "Now may the Lord direct *your* hearts . . .") and suggests that their situation—not his—is his primary concern already here in the opening verses of 3:1–5 (see further comments below on v. 3).

3:2a   A second *hina* clause, parallel to the first (v. 1b), provides an additional item to be included in the Thessalonians' intercessory prayers for Paul and his fellow missionaries, Silas and Timothy: "and that we may be rescued from evil and wicked people" (καὶ ἵνα ῥυσθῶμεν ἀπὸ τῶν ἀτόπων καὶ πονηρῶν ἀνθρώπων, *kai hina rhysthōmen apo tōn atopōn kai ponērōn anthrōpōn*).

This second prayer request is logically connected to the first: if the word of the Lord is to run and be honored, then the proclaimers of that word, Paul and his coworkers, must be rescued from certain evil individuals who are thwarting them from carrying out their evangelistic activity. The verb "rescue" (ῥύομαι, *rhyomai*), though not as frequent as "save" (σῴζω, *sōzō*), is by no means rare in the apostle's writings (Rom. 7:24; 11:26; 15:31; 2 Cor. 1:10 [3x]; Col. 1:13; 1 Thess. 1:10; 2 Tim. 3:11; 4:17, 18) and typically conveys the idea of being delivered "out of" (ἐκ, *ek*) or, as here, "from" (ἀπό, *apo*) something negative or harmful. Paul used this verb in his previous letter to refer to the *future* rescue from the impending wrath of God, on the final day of judgment (1:10). Here, however, it refers to the *present* rescue from human opponents who are currently obstructing the preaching and acceptance of the gospel. The apostle's prayer request is very similar to that which he would give later in his life to other churches: "[Pray] that I may be rescued [*rhyomai*] from the unbelievers in Judea" (Rom. 15:31); "On him we have set our hope that he will continue to rescue [*rhyomai*] us, as you help us by your prayers . . ." (2 Cor. 1:10–11). In still another letter, Paul also uses the verb "rescue" to describe God's work of delivering him from enemies and situations of persecution (2 Tim. 3:11; 4:17, 18), which has led a few commentators to read this prayer request in 2 Thess. 3:2a as generic and to conclude that "no specific threat is in view here" (Furnish 2007: 171; also Best 1977: 325: "The reference then may be quite general since Paul was constantly hindered in his preaching"). Two things, however, argue for a different conclusion. First and foremost, the presence of the definite article to describe those from whom he prays to be rescued—from "*the* evil and wicked people" (*tōn atopōn kai ponērōn anthrōpōn*)—strongly suggests that the apostle has particular people and a specific situation in mind. Second, the aorist tense of "rescue" (in contrast to the present tense used in both verbs in the immediately preceding prayer request) suggests a single and specific event rather than a repeated and generic one. Consequently, the apostle more likely is referring to a particular challenge to his evangelistic ministry from which he needs to be rescued (so the majority of commentators).

Paul does not provide any details about this danger, apparently because his readers already know about his situation. Instead, he broadly identifies those undermining his outreach activity as "evil and wicked people" (*tōn atopōn kai ponērōn anthrōpōn*). The first term, *atopos*, a rare one occurring only four times in the NT and only here in Paul, consists of the alpha privative (no, not) plus the noun *topos* (place) and so literally refers to something "out of place." When used metaphorically, it can have the neutral sense of "being out of the ordinary, *unusual, surprising*" (BDAG 149.1; so Acts 28:6), or more commonly, the negative sense of "being behaviorally out of place, *evil, wrong, improper*" (BDAG 149.2; so Luke 23:41; Acts 25:5). That this latter and negative sense is intended here is obvious both from the context and the second term with which it is paired. The second term, *ponēros*, is common in the NT (78x in NT; 13x in Paul) and refers to "being morally or socially worthless, *wicked, evil, bad, base, worthless, vicious, degenerate*" (BDAG 851.1). In Paul's description of his opponents, many hear an echo from the OT, either Isa. 25:4 LXX ("From wicked people you will rescue them") or Ps. 139:2 LXX (140:1 Eng.: "Deliver me, O Lord, from the evil person; from the unjust person rescue me"). Against this possibility, however, is the fact that the combination of terms *atopos* and *ponēros* used by Paul here occurs nowhere in the Septuagint (Frame 1912: 293). Beyond the apostle's description of his opponents as "evil and wicked persons," it is difficult to know anything with certainty about the situation to which he refers. Since Paul was ministering in Corinth at the time of writing this letter, it is plausible to envision opposition in that city and surrounding region from nonbelievers[8]—not only Jews but Gentiles too—who sought to undermine the gospel ministry in ways similar to those alluded to in his letters (e.g., questioning the integrity and motives of Paul, as in 1 Thess. 2:1–12) and described more specifically in Acts (e.g., slandering Paul: 13:45; 14:2, 19; 19:9; plotting to end his life: 14:5; bringing formal charges against Paul before local and regional officials: 16:19–21; 17:5–7; 18:12–13).

It is important to recognize the rhetorical or persuasive function that this second prayer request has in Paul's overall argument in verses 1–5. By asking his readers to pray for his deliverance from "evil and wicked persons," the apostle creates their empathy for his situation and so enhances their compliance to his request for prayer: as they persevere despite significant suffering for their faith (2 Thess. 1:3–12), so also Paul must endure such strong opposition that he needs their prayer for divine deliverance. At the same time the second request also comforts the Thessalonian believers through the implicit reminder

---

8. On 3:2, there is no justification for Beale's (2003: 239) claim that Paul's opponents are false believers "who profess belief and are part of the church community but are 'out of place' there because they are not genuine saints."

that God is one who can not only rescue Paul from his enemies but also rescue them from their own enemies.

2. Reason for the Command (3:2b)

3:2b After his command that the Thessalonian believers pray for him, Paul continues with a brief statement that, though seemingly trite and insignificant, has the important function of justifying not only his two preceding prayer requests but also his following word of encouragement: "For not everyone has faith" (οὐ γὰρ πάντων ἡ πίστις, *ou gar pantōn hē pistis*).

The Greek text is elliptical and thus difficult to render precisely in English, as it literally reads "For not of all [is] the faith." This way of speaking is technically a litotes (so already Lightfoot 1904: 125; also Hendriksen 1955: 195; Furnish 2007: 171; Fee 2009: 317n29)—a deliberate understating of a situation, often expressed negatively, for effect. Instead of saying positively "a few have faith," Paul makes the same point more powerfully by stating in a negative manner "not all have faith" (for another Pauline litotes, see Rom. 10:16: "Not all [the Israelites] accepted the gospel"). The noun "faith," especially when it has the definite article as it does here, could refer to the content of the gospel: a system of belief, the body of Christian teaching, "the Faith." In this context, however, the noun "faith" refers to the human response of belief in the gospel: the faith that the gospel requires from people, their trust and commitment to "the word of the Lord" (v. 1b). What Paul is saying here, in an understated yet emphatic way, is that "not everyone has faith," that is, the vast majority of people have not responded to his preaching ministry with trust and commitment to the gospel.

Although this point is "a truism that at first sight hardly seems necessary" (Fee 2009: 316–17), in a weighty way such a statement justifies (note how it is introduced with the conjunction *gar* [for], which has its common meaning as "a marker of cause or reason": BDAG 189.1) both Paul's preceding and following statements. It substantiates his two just-mentioned prayer requests: since there are many who do not have faith, such people (1) need to hear and heed the gospel proclaimed by Paul (first prayer request: "that the word of the Lord may run and be honored") yet also (2) pose a serious threat to those like Paul who proclaim that good news (second prayer request: "and that we may be rescued from evil and wicked people"). It substantiates also the following word of encouragement in verse 3: since there are many who do not have faith, such "evil and wicked people" (and "the evil one" who is working through these individuals) pose a threat not just to Paul but also to his converts in Thessalonica, who need to be encouraged with the message "Faithful is the Lord, who will strengthen and guard you from the evil one." Therefore, the brief statement "For not everyone has faith," far from being "banal and unnecessary" (Marshall 1983: 214),[9] functions

---

9. Marshall (1983: 214) actually disagrees with this quote, going on to argue that the statement of 3:2b "acquires greater significance if it is seen not so much as a conclusion to what

as an important hinge verse, justifying not only the previous verse but the following verse as well.

3. Word of Encouragement (3:3)

Since "not everyone has faith," these faithless folks predictably threaten not only Paul's current ministry in Corinth but also the Thessalonian church such that the believers in this city need a word of encouragement from their founder: "But faithful is the Lord, who will strengthen and guard you from the evil one" (πιστὸς δέ ἐστιν ὁ κύριος, ὃς στηρίξει ὑμᾶς καὶ φυλάξει ἀπὸ τοῦ πονηροῦ, *pistos de estin ho kyrios, hos stērixei hymas kai phylaxei apo tou ponērou*).

Here Paul's shift from speaking about his own situation in the previous verses ("Pray for *us*," vv. 1–2) to that of his readers ("strengthen and guard *you*," vv. 3–5) has appeared to many to be "surprising" (Marshall 1983: 215), "abrupt" (Wanamaker 1990: 276; Furnish 2007: 171), and "awkward" (Gaventa 1998: 125). Yet the apostle accomplishes this transition quite skillfully by means of a double wordplay: the previous verse involves a prayer for rescue from "evil" (the adjective *ponēros*) people because not everyone has "faith" (the noun *pistis*); the current verse involves a word of encouragement that the Lord is "faithful" (the adjective *pistos*) and so will strengthen and guard believers from the "evil" (the adjective *ponēros*) one. The second wordplay is especially stressed by means of word order: the final word in verse 2 is the noun "faith," and the first word in verse 3 is the related adjective "faithful." The presence of two nouns in the Greek language that are spelled virtually the same (they differ in only one letter) and placed immediately beside each other without any punctuation or break would be impossible for the original readers to miss (so also Fee 2009: 317). The technical term for this construction is paronomasia—"the recurrence of the same word or stem in close proximity" (BDF §488.1)—and it is an especially effective way of speaking to highlight a contrast, as is the case here. The addition of the particle *de*, which has here an adversative sense, completes this clever transition and contrast: although unbelievers or "*evil*" people lack *faith*, *faithful* is the Lord, who protects his followers from the "*evil*" one.

Here at verse 3 the shift from "us" to "you" is made more natural not just by the double wordplay but also by the parenthetical clause at the end of verse 1, which anticipates this transition. It was noted above that the brief aside "just as it also is with you" foreshadows the apostle's preoccupation with the circumstances of his readers (in vv. 3–5) and suggests that their situation—not his—is his primary concern already in his request for prayer in verses 1–2. As Fee (2009: 317) states about the change of object at verse 3 from "us" to "you": "This appears to be primary evidence that the preceding request for

---

has just been said but rather as an introduction to the next verse." His conclusion is only half correct, however, since it downplays the significant way that 3:2b justifies both of the two preceding prayer requests.

prayer is as much about the Thessalonians themselves as it is for the apostolic trio from whom this letter has come to them."

Paul's word of encouragement for his Thessalonian readers involves a formulaic statement found five times in the apostle's writings: "Faithful is the Lord" (1 Cor. 1:9; 10:13; 2 Cor. 1:18; 1 Thess. 5:24; 2 Thess. 3:3). There are, however, two differences here from its other occurrences—one minor, the other major. The minor change involves the addition of the verb "is" (*estin*): elsewhere its presence is assumed, as is typical in such predicate-nominative constructions, but here it is explicitly stated, thereby lending a degree of emphasis to the statement (Frame 1912: 204: "emphasizes the reality of the faithfulness of Christ"; so also Malherbe 2000: 445). The major change involves the subject: elsewhere the faithful one is identified as "God," but here he is "the Lord" (*ho kyrios*). To many ancient copyists, this second change seemed to be a mistake, so they "corrected" it to "God," in keeping with Paul's other uses of this formulaic expression (for details, see additional notes below). A few contemporary scholars also stumble over this change, claiming that the apostle really is referring to God even though he uses "the Lord" (so Williams 1992: 141; Malherbe 2000: 445; Green 2002: 337). Yet in Paul's writings the designation "the Lord" consistently refers to Jesus Christ, as it does explicitly, for example, just a few verses earlier, in the prayer that closes the preceding discussion (2:16–17). The designation "the Lord" occurs additionally in the sentences that both precede and follow its occurrence here (v. 1: "the word of the Lord"; v. 4: "We have confidence in the Lord"), where it also has in view Jesus Christ. Furthermore, since Paul in this formulaic expression normally identifies the faithful one as "God," it is difficult to explain why he would change it here to "the Lord" unless he deliberately wanted to refer to a different subject (Fee 2009: 318–19). Finally, this change agrees with the emphasis throughout this letter on "the Lord," that is, the Lord Jesus Christ. This emphasis is most noticeable in 2:13 ("loved by the Lord") and 3:16 ("the Lord of peace"), where expected references to "God" have been replaced with "the Lord," just as is the case here in 3:3. Paul therefore is stressing to his Thessalonian readers that "the Lord" (= Jesus Christ) is "faithful." The attribute of faithfulness that is part of this formulaic saying almost certainly stems from OT descriptions of God (Deut. 7:9; 32:4; Ps. 145:13b [144:13a LXX]; Isa. 49:7) as the one in whom humans can have full confidence. Paul again demonstrates how natural it is for him to take attributes of God and apply them directly to the Lord Jesus Christ.

The specific ways in which the Lord Jesus Christ demonstrates his faithfulness to the Thessalonian believers is identified in the following relative clause: "who will strengthen and guard you from the evil one." The first verb, "will strengthen" (*stērixei*),[10] was foreshadowed in the transitional prayer of 2:16–17, where Paul petitions both "our Lord Jesus Christ himself and God our Father" (v. 16) to "strengthen" the Christians in Thessalonica in all their good deeds and words (v. 17b). That earlier prayer about what Paul hopes Christ (and

---

10. See the additional notes regarding the textual variants στηρίσει and τηρήσει in 3:3.

God) will do in the lives of his readers is here restated as a confident assertion, intended to encourage them in their struggle to live the Christian life. What is the problem facing the Thessalonian church for which it needs to be strengthened? The most obvious candidate is opposition from the unbelieving "fellow citizens" (1 Thess. 2:14) who, like the "wicked" and "faithless" people oppressing Paul in Corinth, are also harassing believers in Thessalonica. That this is the historical context the apostle has in mind is supported by the fact that the same verb "strengthen" was used in the previous letter to describe the goal of Timothy's past mission in strengthening the Thessalonian church in the face of persecutions that they continued to endure (1 Thess. 3:2; see also 3:13). But Paul's word of encouragement about the Lord's work of strengthening may also have in view the upcoming problem of the idlers, especially since the transitional prayer of 2:17b, which employs the same verb "strengthen," foreshadows that concern with its reference to "every good work." In other words, the Lord Jesus will strengthen the Thessalonian believers in their ability to obey the exhortations given in 3:6–15.

The second verb, "will guard" (*phylaxei*), is nowhere else in Paul or in any other biblical text paired with the first verb "will strengthen." The former term, which occurs eight times in the apostle's writings, does not here have the sense of "observing, keeping" the OT law or certain instructions (Rom. 2:26; Gal. 6:13; 1 Tim. 5:21) but rather "guarding, protecting" someone or something from that which is dangerous or harmful (so also 1 Tim. 6:20; 2 Tim. 1:12, 14; 4:15). Paul's thought and verb choice may well be influenced by the Psalms, where God is frequently claimed or petitioned to "guard" his people from their enemies (Pss. 12:7; 16:1; 41:2; 121:7; 141:9 [LXX: 11:8; 15:1; 40:3; 120:7; 140:9]). Paul identifies the danger facing the Thessalonian believers, from which the Lord will guard them, as "the evil one" (*tou ponērou*). Although the adjective "evil" could be neuter and so refer abstractly to the power of evil at work in the world (KJV: "keep you from evil"),[11] several factors strongly support reading it as masculine such that it has in view a personal being: "the evil one," that is, Satan. The four most compelling reasons include the following (for the full list of arguments supporting each position, see Best 1977: 327–28): First, in the immediate context, the use of the adjective "evil" to describe persons (v. 2a, "evil and wicked people") from whom Paul needs to be rescued is more naturally paralleled by a personal being from whom the Thessalonian church needs to be guarded. Second, "the evil one" functions as a more suitable antithesis to "the Lord" mentioned earlier in verse 3. Third, in the larger context of both Thessalonian Letters, Satan and his evil activity play a prominent role (1 Thess. 2:18; 3:5; 2 Thess. 2:9). Finally, the title "the

---

11. Fee (2009: 319) observes how reading τοῦ πονηροῦ as the neuter "evil," especially in the KJV rendering "keep you from evil," has led to a significant misunderstanding of this verse as meaning "keep you from doing anything that is evil." The context, however, clearly shows that the intent of this verse is not to keep believers from doing evil but rather that believers are protected from evil, or as has been argued above, "from the evil one." Fee rightly concludes: "Thus this is not a subtle exhortation but a word of encouragement."

evil one" occurs elsewhere in Paul's writings (Eph. 6:16) and was current in the early church (Matt. 13:19, 38; 1 John 2:13–14; 5:18–19).

Paul's word of encouragement does not involve a health-and-wealth gospel, in which believers are promised to enjoy a life free from hardship and opposition. The apostle has been consistent on this: already during his mission-founding visit, he told the believers in Thessalonica that they would suffer for their faith (1 Thess. 3:4); so there is nothing surprising about "your persecutions and the afflictions that you are enduring" (2 Thess. 1:4). But in the midst of this sober reality is the comforting message that the Lord Jesus Christ is "faithful": he will not let them down but "will strengthen and guard" them from whatever trials and tribulations "the evil one" may send their way.

4. Confidence Formula (3:4)

3:4
The word of encouragement in 3:3 seeks not only to comfort the Thessalonian believers but also to spur on their obedience to the faithful Lord, who is at work in their lives. That this too was in the mind of Paul becomes clear from his subsequent expression of confidence in their present and ongoing ability to obey apostolic commands: "Furthermore,[12] we have confidence in the Lord about you, that what things we are commanding, you are indeed doing and will continue to do" (πεποίθαμεν δὲ ἐν κυρίῳ ἐφ' ὑμᾶς, ὅτι ἃ παραγγέλλομεν καὶ ποιεῖτε καὶ ποιήσετε, *pepoithamen de en kyriō eph' hymas, hoti ha parangellomen kai poieite kai poiēsete*).

In verse 3 Paul encouraged obedience with a formulaic statement, and he does the same thing here with what has been called a "confidence formula" (White 1972: 104–6) or "expression of confidence" (Olson 1985; also 1984). In the apostle's writings are several instances where he expresses confidence by means of the verb πείθω (*peithō*) in the perfect tense and first person, which is the form found here (see also Rom. 14:14; 2 Cor. 2:3; Gal. 5:10; Phil. 2:24; Philem. 21). This verbal form is followed frequently by two elements also present here: a prepositional phrase giving the ground of Paul's confidence and a *hoti* clause giving the content of what he is confident about. The existence of similar expressions of confidence in the secular letters of the apostle's day (see the letters cited by Olson 1984; also Spicq 1994: 3.71) suggest that such statements are not a Pauline invention but an epistolary convention of that time. Rhetorically, the confidence formula functions to exert pressure on letter recipients to live up to the confidence that the writer has in them. As Olson (1985: 289) observes: "The evidence of a variety of parallels suggest that such expressions [of confidence] are usually included to serve the persuasive purpose. Whatever the emotion behind the expression, the function is to undergird the letter's requests or admonitions by creating a sense of obligation through praise."

Here in 3:4 Paul's statement of confidence is clarified by two prepositional phrases: "in the Lord" (*en kyriō*) and "about you" (*eph' hymas*). The first

12. As 3:4 begins, the particle δέ introduces an additional yet distinct point to Paul's argument in this paragraph.

phrase, similar to the more common "in Christ," refers to the relationship believers have with the Lord Jesus Christ. The second phrase identifies the recipients toward whom Paul's confidence is directed (the preposition *epi* in this context is a "marker of feelings directed toward someone, *in, on, for, toward*, w[ith] acc[usative] after words that express belief, trust, hope": BDAG 366.15; see also 2 Cor. 2:3; Matt. 27:43). The apostle's confidence, therefore, is ultimately grounded not in the Thessalonian Christians themselves but rather "in the Lord," that is, in the Lord Jesus Christ and what he is doing in and through these believers. The confidence formula is a logical consequence of Paul's just-stated assertion that the Lord is faithful and will strengthen the Christians in Thessalonica and guard them from the evil one. This also explains why, in the immediately following verse, Paul's intercessory prayer for the Thessalonian church is directed to "the Lord," since he is the ultimate power behind the changed lives of these believers.

The content of what Paul is confident about concerning Christ's work in the Thessalonian congregation is given, as it is in most other confidence formulas (Rom. 14:14; 2 Cor. 2:3; Gal. 5:10; Phil. 2:24), in a *hoti* clause that introduces indirect discourse: "that what things we are commanding, you are indeed doing and will continue to do." The apostle draws attention to the relative clause "what things we are commanding" (*ha parangellomen*) by moving it from its expected position at the end of the main *hoti* clause to its beginning. This highlighting of Paul's action of "commanding" the Thessalonians foreshadows the key role that the same verb plays in the upcoming paragraph of verses 6–15, where the verb "command" is emphasized both by its selection to open the new paragraph (v. 6: "But we command you") and also by its twofold repetition within the paragraph (v. 10: "For when we were with you, we also were repeatedly commanding this to you"; v. 12: "To such people we command"). There can be little doubt, therefore, that the referent of the action "we are commanding" is found not by looking *back* to the call for the Thessalonians to remember Paul in prayer in verse 1 (so wrongly Lightfoot 1904: 127; Marshall 1983: 217) but by looking *ahead* to the commands in verses 6–15 concerning self-sufficient work and how to deal with church members who are rebelliously idle. The present tense of *parangellomen* does not create a problem for this interpretation, as if Paul should have instead used the future "what things we *will* command you [in the upcoming verses of 3:6–15]." During his mission-founding visit, the apostle gave the church instructions regarding self-sufficient work (1 Thess. 4:11; 2 Thess. 3:6, 10) and again in his previous letter (1 Thess. 4:11; 5:14) so that the commands he is about to give in 2 Thess. 3:6–15 are not new but repeat his earlier injunctions.

Since Paul has in view commands concerning work given in the past (and about to be repeated in the present discussion), he is in a position to render a judgment about the way the majority of the Thessalonian church has thus far responded to these commands: "you are indeed doing and will continue to do" (*kai poieite kai poiēsete*).[13] In his previous letter the apostle three times, in the middle of paraenetic material, acknowledged the good progress that his Thessalonian converts were making (4:1, "just as you are indeed walking"; 4:10, "For you are indeed doing it"; 5:11, "just as you are indeed doing"). Here he adopts the same strategy of affirming that most members of the church have actually obeyed his commands with regard to the necessity of self-sufficient work. This too is an effective rhetorical tactic: on the one hand, those who are acting properly in this area of their life feel pressure to maintain their obedient conduct in order to live up to the praise that they are receiving from the apostle; on the other hand, those who are adopting an idle lifestyle do experience pressure to live the same praiseworthy life that the majority of their fellow church members do. Additionally, such affirmation from the apostle softens the harsher language of "command," which Paul feels compelled to use in addressing this ongoing and persistent problem, instead of his preferred softer language of "appeal" or its synonym "ask" (1 Thess. 4:1, 10b; 5:12, 14; 2 Thess. 2:1).

5. Concluding Prayer (3:5)

3:5 Paul brings the general exhortations of verses 1–5 to a close with a prayer that, like the similar prayers in 1 Thess. 3:11, 12–13 and 2 Thess. 2:16–17, anticipates the immediately following material and so also has a transitional function: "Now may the Lord direct your hearts to God's love and to Christ's endurance" (ὁ δὲ κύριος κατευθύναι ὑμῶν τὰς καρδίας εἰς τὴν ἀγάπην τοῦ θεοῦ καὶ εἰς τὴν ὑπομονὴν τοῦ Χριστοῦ, *ho de kyrios kateuthynai hymōn tas kardias eis tēn agapēn tou theou kai eis tēn hypomonēn tou Christou*).

The previous two verses both consisted of formulaic statements—a word of encouragement in verse 3 and a confidence formula in verse 4—and the same thing is true here in verse 5, which contains a prayer, or "body-benediction." Benedictions located in the letter body (Rom. 15:5–6, 13; 1 Thess. 3:11, 12–13; 2 Thess. 2:16–17; see also Heb. 13:20–21) are formally distinct from the grace and peace benedictions located in the letter closings. Although possessing a less consistent form than the closing grace and peace benedictions, the body benedictions, or prayers, have a common structure, consisting of the following basic elements (Weima 1994a: 101–4).

First, there is the introductory element, which is always the adversative particle *de* in its expected postpositive position. Here the particle has a slightly adversative function: whereas the previous verse focused on *the Thessalonian believers* and Paul's confidence in what *they* are doing and will continue to do (albeit "in the Lord," that is, through Christ's empowering presence), the prayer in this verse places the emphasis once again (see v. 3) on *the Lord* and what *he* will do for the converts in Thessalonica.

Second, there is the divine source of the prayer, which is here simply expressed as "the Lord" (*ho kyrios*). Although a few understand this as a reference to God the Father (e.g., Malherbe 2000: 447; Beale 2003: 243–47; Witherington

13. On the textual questions surrounding this clause, see the additional notes below.

2006: 243), there is no reason to understand "the Lord" in a way different than Paul himself defines the term in the preceding body benediction of 2:16–17, namely, "our Lord Jesus Christ himself."[14] This marks the fourth time in this brief, five-verse introductory paragraph that Paul uses the designation, thereby throughout verses 1–5 stressing the Lord's crucial role in the ministry of Paul and the Thessalonian congregation.

Third, there is the content of the prayer, expressed as it typically is in the optative mood, which asks that the Lord "may direct your hearts" (*kateuthynai hymōn tas kardias*). The optative mood in the NT often takes on a force similar to that of the imperative so that it is legitimate to speak of an "imperatival optative"—an optative expressing a stronger sense than mere volition: "The speaker intends more than a wish ('may it be so-and-so'); he expresses this with a strong sense of fulfillment ('let it be so-and-so')" (van Elderen 1967: 48; BDF §384: "The optative proper used to denote an attainable wish"). The optative *kateuthynai*, therefore, conveys not merely Paul's faint hope but indeed his confident expectation that the Lord Jesus will indeed "direct" the hearts of his Thessalonian readers. The verb *kateuthynai* is not common in Paul's writings, occurring elsewhere only in the prayer, or body benediction, of 1 Thess. 3:11, where it retains its literal meaning of "make straight": Satan had "blocked" Paul's path to the Thessalonian church (2:18), and so the apostle prays that God and the Lord Jesus will "make straight" that path, allowing him to be reunited with his converts in that city. Here, however, the verb *kateuthynai* has a metaphorical or ethical meaning—a meaning it frequently has in the Septuagint: to make straight or "correct" a person's steps in the moral way that they should go (Pss. 37:23; 40:2 [36:23; 39:3 LXX]; Prov. 4:26) or, in a closer parallel to Paul's words here, to make straight or "direct" people's "hearts" to God (1 Chron. 29:18; 2 Chron. 12:14; 19:3; 20:33; 30:19; Prov. 21:2; 23:19; Sir. 49:3; 51:20).[15] The apostle, therefore, employs a common Septuagint expression to petition the Lord Jesus to take the "hearts"—the deepest emotions and desires—of his Thessalonian readers, which apart from Christ's influence wander in diverse directions after things that are not always healthy and holy, and instead "make them straight" such that they are directed in a single-minded, focused way toward a specific goal or purpose.

This purpose—the final element of these body benedictions, or prayers—is expressed here by a double εἰς (*eis*) clause. Paul prays that the Lord will direct

14. That Paul in 3:5 prays for "the Lord" to direct the hearts of the Thessalonians "to *God's* love and *Christ's* endurance" (rather than "*his* endurance") led many patristic commentators (e.g., Theodoret, "Interpretation of 2 Thessalonians 3"; Basil of Caesarea, *On the Holy Spirit*) to the position that "the Lord" refers to the Holy Spirit.

15. Fee (2009: 322n42), following several other commentators (e.g., Richard 1995: 372), claims that Paul is deliberately citing 1 Chron. 29:18 LXX because this verse, along with 1 Thess. 3:5, "are the only two places [in the Bible] where 'the Lord' is the subject of this Greek verb and 'the heart' is the object." His claim, however, is not accurate: the same subject, verb, and object also occur in an even closer parallel form in Prov. 21:2 LXX: "But the Lord directs the hearts" (κατευθύνει δὲ καρδίας κύριος). It is more likely, therefore, that Paul is not echoing a particular verse (1 Chron. 29:18) but more generally a common Septuagint expression.

the readers' hearts in an attentive and undistracted way to two things: "to God's love and to Christ's endurance" (*eis tēn agapēn tou theou kai eis tēn hypomonēn tou Christou*). In both purpose clauses the issue is whether the genitive nouns ("the love *of God* and the endurance *of Christ*") ought to be read subjectively or objectively. In other words, does the first purpose clause refer to God's love for the Thessalonian Christians (subjective genitive) or their love for God (objective genitive)? Although both interpretations are grammatically possible, there is compelling evidence that Paul intended the first option. The phrase "the love of God" occurs three other times in the apostle's writings (Rom. 5:5; 8:39; 2 Cor. 13:13; see also Eph. 2:4, "the love of him") where the context clearly has in view God's love for believers. The subjective genitive is also supported by the immediate context, where just a few verses earlier in another body benediction, or prayer, Paul identifies God as "the one who loved us" (2:16). Finally, this interpretation fits better the persuasive force of Paul's overall argument in 3:1–15, where this prayer in verse 5 (along with the rest of vv. 1–5) prepares the Thessalonian readers to hear and heed the specific instructions about to come in verses 6–15. As Best (1977: 330) declares: "If the Thessalonians continually remember how God loves them, their hearts will be steeled to keep the instruction he has given and is about to give through Paul."

It is more difficult, however, to decide between the two grammatical options in the second purpose clause ("to the endurance *of Christ*"), which occurs nowhere else in Paul's writings.

1. The *objective* genitive would refer to an action that the Thessalonian Christians carry out in relation to Christ. The situation is further complicated in that there are two possibilities under the objective genitive option, depending on how one understands the initial, or "head," noun *hypomonē*.

   a. If it describes "the act or state of patient waiting for someone, *expectation*" (BDAG 1040.2), then the fuller phrase "the expectation of Christ" (objective genitive) refers to how the Christians in Thessalonica ought to steadfastly wait for the return of Jesus: "the patient waiting for Christ" (so KJV; also Calvin 1981: 351; Dobschütz 1909: 309; Menken 1994: 129; Lambrecht 2000a). This interpretation fits the larger context of 2 Thessalonians, which deals extensively with issues surrounding Christ's return (2:1–17; also 1:5–12). Nevertheless, this topic is not addressed anywhere in the immediate context of 3:1–15. More problematic is the fact that understanding *hypomonē* as "expectation" is a connotation that it never has in Paul's fourteen other uses of this noun.

   b. If, however, the noun *hypomonē* describes "the capacity to hold out or bear up in the face of difficulty, *patience, endurance, fortitude, steadfastness, perseverance*" (BDAG 1039.1), then the fuller phrase "the steadfastness of Christ" (objective genitive) refers to how the Christians in Thessalonica ought to remain firm in their commitment to Christ despite strong opposition and even persecution: "your steadfastness to Christ" (so Trilling 1980: 330–31; see also MHT 3:212). This interpretation is supported by the use of the noun *hypomonē* elsewhere in the Thessalonian Letters (1 Thess. 1:3; 2 Thess. 1:4), where it refers to the endurance of the Thessalonian congregation in the face of strong opposition, and also the larger context of 2 Thessalonians, which commends them for such endurance (1:3–4). Yet once again this topic is not directly[16] addressed anywhere in the immediate context of 3:1–15.

2. The *subjective* genitive would refer to an action that Christ carries out in relation to the Thessalonian Christians. If the head noun *hypomonē* has its normal meaning of "endurance," then the fuller phrase "the endurance of Christ" (subjective genitive) refers to "Christ's endurance," that is, the fortitude that Christ has demonstrated, especially during his passion (so, e.g., Ellicott 1880: 127; Marshall 1983: 218; Wanamaker 1990: 278–79; Richard 1995: 372; Holmes 1998: 258; Fee 2009: 322–23). This interpretation is supported by the obvious parallelism between the two purpose clauses: if the first *eis* clause clearly has in view a subjective genitive, then it is most likely (though not certain)[17] that the second *eis* clause was intended to be read this way too. The same grammatical construction with the idea of endurance (*hypomonē*) as an example to be followed occurs also in James (5:11, "the steadfastness of Job") and Polycarp (*Phil.* 8.2, "the steadfastness of him [Christ]"). Finally, as with the phrase "God's love," so also the phrase "Christ's endurance" as a subjective genitive makes better sense as a ground for promoting the readers' obedience to the upcoming commands of verses 6–15. Paul prays that the Lord Jesus will direct the hearts of the Thessalonian believers in a single-minded way both to God's love for them and to Christ's exemplary endurance so that they will respond with compliance to the specific injunctions he is about to give concerning work and their treatment of those in their midst who are rebelliously idle. As Wanamaker (1990: 279) concludes: "Thus Paul's wish-prayer is for the Lord to direct the reader's heart to God's love for them and to the perseverance which Christ demonstrated *as a basis* for encouraging what Paul considers proper Christian behavior" (emphasis added).

B. Specific Exhortations: Discipline the Rebellious Idlers (3:6–15)

The preceding unit of verses 1–5 can be justly labeled "General Exhortations," since it does not deal with any clearly defined problem but instead in

---

16. Yet it may be conceded that the theme of persecution/opposition is indirectly addressed in 3:2, which describes the situation not of the Thessalonians but of Paul, who needs to be "rescued" from "evil and wicked people" because "not everyone has faith."

17. It must be conceded that it is possible to have a mixed parallelism where the use of the genitive in the first half of a noun clause does not parallel the genitive in the second half, as is the case earlier in the letter in 2:13c.

a wide-ranging way addresses a variety of different subjects joined together by a common function, namely, to prepare the original readers to hear and heed the exhortations that come in the immediately following unit of verses 6–15. That subsequent unit, by contrast, can be rightly labeled "Specific Exhortations," since it contains Paul's commands related to a particular difficulty facing the church: how they ought to deal with the rebelliously idle behavior of some of their fellow members.

Before turning to Paul's treatment of this specific problem, there are three questions that need to be answered in order to place the apostle's exhortations in their proper context. Since all three have been dealt with in detail elsewhere in this commentary, I will only summarize the previous examinations of these questions and refer the reader to these earlier discussions for both further elaboration of the issue and justification for the conclusion reached.

First, what is the proper meaning of the Greek root ἀτακτ- (atakt-), used three times in this passage to describe the improper behavior of some believers in Thessalonica (vv. 6, 7, 11; also see 1 Thess. 5:14)? In other words, what specific problem is being addressed in this passage? On the one hand, in a general way this Greek root refers to any kind of conduct that does not conform to established law or expected practice and so refers to those who are "disorderly," "unruly," or "insubordinate" (BDAG 148). This sense captures the resistance of some Christians in Thessalonica both to their congregational leaders (1 Thess. 5:12–13) and to Paul, who has first exhorted them to work already during his mission-founding visit (1 Thess. 4:11b; 2 Thess. 3:6b, 10) and then a second time in his previous letter (1 Thess. 4:11b; 5:14). On the other hand, in this context the Greek root refers in a specific way to those who refuse to work, in other words, those who are "idle, lazy," as is clear from Paul's appeal here to both his example of self-sufficient work (vv. 7–9) and his explicit teaching (v. 10). These two aspects are captured well in the description of such erring believers as "rebellious idlers"—those who were not merely lazy but who compounded their sin by rebelliously refusing to obey the command of both their congregational leaders and even Paul himself. As Frame (1912: 299) observes: "The fault is not idleness but deliberate, disobedient idleness" (for an expanded discussion of this issue, see comments on 1 Thess. 5:14).

Second, why were some in the Thessalonian congregation rebelliously idle? The traditional explanation involves the church's eschatological excitement over the imminent return of Christ. The belief that Jesus would return soon caused some believers to abandon ordinary earthly pursuits, such as working for a living, so that they could give full attention to spiritual preparation, eschatological discussion, and perhaps evangelism. This group likely reasoned to themselves, "Since the end is near, work is a waste of time." An alternative explanation, however, proposes a sociological cause for the idle behavior. A few commentators appeal to the general disdain toward physical labor prevalent in the Greco-Roman world. More turn to the patron-client relationship that was popular in that day. In this relationship, members of the lower class attached themselves to benefactors from among the upper class, from whom they then received sustenance and help in various matters in exchange for the obligation to reciprocate with expressions of gratitude and support. It is argued that Paul's converts included those of the urban poor who had formed client relationships with wealthy members in the Thessalonian church, but who exploited the generosity of their new Christian patrons. Within this debate, there is both "bad news" and "good news." The "bad news" is that, though the evidence tilts more strongly to the eschatological explanation, both reasons are not free from criticism, and there does not appear to be sufficient information available to reach a definitive conclusion. The "good news" is that our understanding of both the past meaning and present application of this passage is not hindered in any meaningful way by this fact. Fee (2009: 325) is correct to concede in this debate over why some were rebelliously idle that "we simply do not know; and in fact getting an answer to this question would hardly affect our understanding of the text at all" (for an expanded discussion of this issue, see comments on 1 Thess. 4:11b).

Third, how does Paul treat the problem of the rebellious idlers in this passage? Whereas in the previous letter he settled for a brief exhortation that each member should work with their hands (1 Thess. 4:11c) and that the church should admonish those who refused to do so (5:14), here the apostle feels the need to address the issue in a much longer and more direct fashion, almost certainly because the problem has grown worse instead of better. Paul frames his comments with opening (v. 6) and closing (vv. 13–15) commands to avoid those who are idle. These commands, which begin and end the passage, are similar in content (v. 6: "that you keep away from . . ."; v. 14: "that you not associate with . . .") and thus form a thematic inclusio that marks the boundaries of the overall unit of verses 6–15. The apostle grounds these framing commands with an appeal to two differing arguments (each introduced by the conjunction "for" [γάρ, *gar*]): the first based on the example of self-sufficient work that he provided during his past ministry in their midst (vv. 7–9); the second based on his repeated teaching on this very subject (v. 10). Paul then applies his former example and former teaching to the contemporary problem in the church posed by the rebellious idlers (vv. 11–12). Throughout the passage his primary purpose is not punitive (the section closes with the command in verse 15: "And do not consider him as an enemy but admonish him as a brother") but redemptive: although exclusion from the community will cause the rebellious idlers initially to "feel ashamed" (v. 14), they will hopefully respond with repentance and restoration within the fellowship of believers.

1. Opening Command (3:6)

Paul opens his treatment of the persistent problem of the rebellious idlers with a specific command that was anticipated already in the general exhortations of verses 1–5, especially in the confidence formula of verse 4: "Now we command you, brothers, in the name of our Lord Jesus Christ, that you keep

3:6

away from every brother who continues to walk in a rebelliously idle manner and not according to the tradition that they received from us" (παραγγέλλομεν δὲ ὑμῖν, ἀδελφοί, ἐν ὀνόματι τοῦ κυρίου ἡμῶν Ἰησοῦ Χριστοῦ στέλλεσθαι ὑμᾶς ἀπὸ παντὸς ἀδελφοῦ ἀτάκτως περιπατοῦντος καὶ μὴ κατὰ τὴν παράδοσιν ἣν παρελάβοσαν παρ' ἡμῶν, *parangellomen de hymin, adelphoi, en onomati tou kyriou hēmōn Iēsou Xristou stellesthai hymas apo pantos adelphou ataktōs peripatountos kai mē kata tēn paradosin hēn parelabosan par' hēmōn*).

It is worth highlighting once again (see also "Literary Analysis" above) how the new unit of verses 6–15 is connected to the preceding unit of verses 1–5, particularly in light of claims to the contrary (e.g., Marshall [1983: 218] opens his treatment of vv. 6–15 by stating: "Without any apparent link to what has preceded, there now comes a section . . ."). Not only have the general exhortations of verses 1–5 in a broad way prepared the readers to hear and heed the specific exhortations of verses 6–15, but an important lexical link between the two paragraphs lies in the verb "command" (*parangellō*): the confidence that Paul has in his Thessalonian readers that "what things we are commanding, you are indeed doing and will continue to do" (v. 4) anticipates the commands that the apostle gives in the immediately following unit (vv. 6, 10, 12). The conclusion that this lexical link is not accidental but deliberate is strengthened by the fact that Paul has stressed this verb in both sections: in verse 4 he emphasized it through word order by moving the verb "command" from its expected position at the end of the main clause ("you are doing and will do what things we are commanding") to the beginning ("what things we are commanding, you are doing and will do"); in verses 6–15 he emphasizes the verb "command" both by selecting it as the main verb to open the new paragraph (v. 6: "Now we command you . . ."), and then also by repeating the verb two more times within the paragraph (v. 10: "For when we were with you, we also were repeatedly commanding this to you . . ."; v. 12: "To such people we command . . .").

What makes this lexical link even more striking is that Paul employs the verb "command" only infrequently (other than the four occurrences here in 2 Thess. 3:1–15, it is used eight times: 1 Cor. 7:10; 11:17; 1 Thess. 4:11; 1 Tim. 1:3; 4:11; 5:7; 6:13, 17). Paul's preference by far is to issue his exhortations by "appealing" (παρακαλέω, *parakaleō*: 54 occurrences) to his readers, often in the form of an epistolary convention widely used in the ancient world: the appeal formula (see esp. Mullins 1962; Bjerkelund 1967). This formula typically consists of four elements (Bjerkelund 1967: 43–50): (1) the verb of appeal from which this epistolary convention derives its name in the first person; (2) a reference to the recipients of the appeal; (3) a prepositional phrase indicating the source of authority by which the letter sender issues the appeal (this element normally occurs only in official correspondence and not in private letters); and (4) the content of the appeal, typically introduced by either an infinitive or a ἵνα (*hina*) clause.

All four of these formal elements are found in verse 6. However, the first element—the verb of petition—has been altered as the expected "we appeal" has been replaced with the harsher "we command." On the one hand, this change is surprising, given Paul's clear preference for the softer, more user-friendly verb "appeal." Fee (2009: 327) therefore notes that "the command itself is especially unusual for Paul and thus quite unexpected." On the other hand, this change is entirely understandable in light of two considerations. First, the apostle's foreshadowing comments in verse 4 ("what things we are commanding, you are indeed doing and will continue to do") prepare the reader for Paul's "command" here. Second, this is now the third time that the apostle has needed to address the problem of idleness (first time, in Paul's mission-founding visit: 1 Thess. 4:11c; 2 Thess. 3:6b, 10; second time, in Paul's previous letter: 1 Thess. 4:11c; 5:14), and that the problem has grown worse instead of better justifiably requires Paul to shift from the softer "appeal" in his earlier letter (1 Thess. 5:14) to the stronger "command" here.

The second element, the recipients of the specific exhortation, is expressed simply with the second-person pronoun "you" (*hymin*). But this element, though brief and simple, is important, for it shows that Paul expects not just the leaders to deal with the problematic behavior of the rebellious idlers, but the congregation as a whole. Even though the apostle will have a command later in the passage that is directed more narrowly to the guilty members themselves (v. 12), he chooses not only here in the opening command but also throughout this passage to address his commands and supporting arguments to all the church's members, thereby reminding the congregation of their corporate responsibility to discipline their errant members. As is often the case with the appeal formula (or more precisely here, command formula), Paul further specifies the recipients with the vocative "brothers" (*adelphoi*). In addition to functioning as a literary device signaling the transition to the specific exhortations that begin at verse 6, this sixth (of seven) direct address to "brothers" in this brief letter (1:3; 2:1, 13, 15; 3:1, 6, 13) also serves to soften the harsher tone conveyed in the verb choice "we command." Furthermore, since Paul includes the rebellious idlers in his reference to the "brothers," he exemplifies the very thing that he later commands the church to do in the treatment of their wayward members: "Do not consider him as an enemy but admonish him as a brother" (v. 15).

The third element of the appeal or command formula consists of a prepositional phrase indicating the source of authority by which Paul issues his exhortation: "in the name of our Lord Jesus Christ" (*en onomati tou kyriou hēmōn Iēsou Christou*). The rhetorical force of this prepositional phrase becomes clearer in light of the apostle's use of this same expression earlier in the letter. Paul brought his opening thanksgiving to a close with a prayer for the future glorification of both the Lord Jesus and the Christians in Thessalonica: "so that the name of our Lord Jesus may be glorified in you and you in him" (1:12). As Gaventa (1998: 128) states: "If the goal of the Christian is to live so that the name of Jesus is glorified, then appeal to the name at the beginning of an ethical admonition indicates the high seriousness of the instruction that follows." The command to discipline the rebellious idlers may ostensibly come from Paul, but the addition of the prepositional phrase makes clear that it ultimately comes from the Lord Jesus Christ himself and thus is a command that the Thessalonian church must obey.[18] If, as seems likely, the pronoun "our" is original ("in the name of *our* Lord Jesus Christ"),[19] then the sense of obligation to obey the command is heightened even further as Paul draws his readers' attention to the fact that Jesus Christ is not just his Lord alone but "our" common Lord.

The fourth element is the content of the appeal or command, introduced here, as it most commonly is, by an infinitive clause (see Rom. 12:1; 15:30; 16:17; 2 Cor. 10:1–2; Phil. 4:2; 1 Thess. 4:10b–11; 2 Thess. 2:2): "that you keep away from every brother who continues to walk in a rebelliously idle manner and not according to the tradition that they received from us" (*stellesthai hymas apo pantos adelphou ataktōs peripatountos kai mē kata tēn paradosin hēn parelabosan par' hēmōn*). The verb *stellō* is rare not just in Paul's writings but in the rest of Greek literature as well, thereby making it difficult to determine its precise meaning here in verse 6. Its only other occurrence in the apostle's letters is in 2 Cor. 8:20, but this potential parallel suffers because its meaning too is unclear. The verb literally means "to send," and so the middle form (which often has a reflexive sense) followed by the preposition *apo* (from) has the sense of "to send oneself away from" something or someone. This meaning gains further support from the context,[20] where the corresponding command in verse 14 is used to frame the whole unit of verses 6–15: "Do not mingle/associate with him" (μὴ συναναμίγνυσθαι αὐτῷ, *mē synanamignysthai autō*). Additional support lies in the compound form ὑποστέλλω (*hypostellō*) in Gal. 2:12, where Paul describes how Peter, out of fear of reprisal from James's representatives, "drew back and separated himself" from Gentile believers. Paul's intent in his opening command, therefore, is quite clear: he is commanding the church as a whole "to keep their distance, *keep away, stand aloof*" (BDAG 942.1) from fellow congregational members who are rebelling against both Paul and congregational leaders by continuing in their idle ways.

The effectiveness of Paul's strategy of calling on the Thessalonian church to practice mutual discipline can be easily missed by those today who live in a Western society that is highly individualistic and largely shameless. By contrast, the believers in Thessalonica lived in a strongly communal culture, where honor and shame were powerful forces controlling social behavior. When they "turned to God from idols in order to serve a living and true God" (1 Thess. 1:9), they were cut off from the familial and social networks that were such

18. Wanamaker (1990: 281): "At a theological level the addition of 'in the name of the Lord Jesus Christ' to a command implies that the command is not simply Paul's but that it has the sanction of the Lord Jesus Christ himself. At a functional level the formula makes failure to keep the command a matter of disobedience not merely to Paul but to the Lord himself. In other words it is one of the most powerful forms of theological coercion available to Paul."

19. On the inclusion of the possessive "our" in 3:6 despite its absence in some MSS, see the additional notes.

20. K. H. Rengstorf (*TDNT* 7:589) claims that Paul's use of *stellesthai* (in 3:6c) "is without exact parallel linguistically and is thus to be expounded directly from the context."

an important part of their daily life and so needed to establish a new network made up of fellow "brothers" and "sisters" in Christ—a social network called "the church." The identity of these new converts, in keeping with the communal nature of their culture, was strongly connected to the larger group of believers to whom they belonged. In such a context, the effectiveness of Paul's call to practice church discipline becomes clear. As Green (2002: 345) observes, "The separation of the disorderly believer from the new family would have been devastating. It is hard to imagine a more forceful way of bringing these people into harmony with the apostolic teaching."

Paul strikingly refers to such wayward church members as "every brother" (*pantos adelphou*). As inappropriate as their rebelliously idle behavior may be, it does not yet exclude them from membership in the church or place them in the category of "evil and wicked people" who do not have "faith" (v. 2). Nor does their improper conduct justify the church's treatment of them in a harsh and cruel manner; rather, following the example of the apostle who here identifies such an individual as a "brother," the church is to "consider such a person not as an enemy but admonish him as a brother" (v. 15).

Paul further identifies these errant church members as anyone who "continues to walk"[21] in two ways: "in a rebelliously idle manner" and "not according to the tradition that they received from us." The first description, here rendered in English with a prepositional phrase consisting of five words, is in the original Greek text only a single term: the adverb *ataktōs*. We have already explained above how the key root *atakt-* (see also vv. 7, 11) expresses both the general sense of insubordination to both Paul and his appointed leaders in the congregation and the specific sense of laziness. The second description of the wayward members needing to be disciplined identifies these individuals as walking "not according to the tradition that they received from us" (*mē kata tēn paradosin hēn parelabosan par' hēmōn*). In the previous chapter (2:15), Paul has already used the noun "traditions" in the plural to refer to teachings about Jesus's glorious return that he has given the Thessalonian converts, both orally during his mission-founding visit and in writing via his previous letter. He calls them "traditions" because these important teachings did not originate with him: first he received them and then subsequently handed them down to his converts. Here he uses the singular "tradition" to refer to material that, though dealing with different subject matter, he similarly received and then passed on to the believers in Thessalonica. Later in this passage Paul will explicitly cite such traditional material, reminding them of his previous teaching about the need for self-sufficient work: "If anyone is not willing to work, let him not eat" (v. 10). Manuscripts disagree on whether this tradition is something that "*you* received" (so NIV, RSV, ESV), "*he* received" (KJV),

---

21. The present tense participle *peripatountos* in 3:6d highlights the ongoing nature of the action—a fact confirmed by the apostle's need repeatedly to address the problem of idleness. For the metaphorical use of "walking" as Paul's favorite term to describe moral conduct, see comments on 1 Thess. 2:12.

or as the evidence strongly supports (see discussion below, in the additional notes), "*they* received" (ASV, NRSV, NLT). This textual problem is important (contra Morris 1991: 253n12, who states, "Not much hangs on the decision") since the third-person plural "they" indicates that the erring church members have truly been taught to live differently and thus have no excuse for their rebelliously idle behavior. As Witherington (2006: 249n13) observes: "Paul is claiming that those who are idle have personally received the tradition about working and so know better."

2. The Example of Paul (3:7–9)

3:7 To ground his opening command to the whole church that they keep away from fellow members who persist in living in a rebelliously idle manner, Paul presents two arguments: the first appeals to his *example* of self-sufficient work (vv. 7–9), and the second to his *teaching* on this very subject (v. 10). The apostle introduces his first argument with the disclosure formula (Mullins 1964), an epistolary convention that he frequently employs to begin a new section: "For you yourselves know how it is necessary to imitate us" (αὐτοὶ γὰρ οἴδατε πῶς δεῖ μιμεῖσθαι ἡμᾶς, *autoi gar oidate pōs dei mimeisthai hēmas*).

The conjunction "for" (*gar*) looks back not to the preceding relative clause ("the tradition which they received from us": contra Fee 2009: 329) but to the main clause containing the opening command to keep away from erring members of the congregation. Thus the reference in verses 7–9 to the exemplary work of Paul, which the Thessalonian church must imitate, is not part of the "tradition" that the congregation received (contra the claim of many commentators: e.g., Marshall 1983: 221: "Thus the tradition which the Thessalonians received [v. 6] was given in both the instruction and the example of the apostles") but rather serves as one of the grounds supporting the opening command. In other words, the first reason why the church should distance itself from the rebellious idlers is that such behavior contradicts the example of self-sufficient work provided by the apostle during his mission-founding visit in Thessalonica.

Paul emphatically (note the addition of the third-person pronoun: "you *yourselves* know," *autoi oidate*) asserts that his readers already know about the need to imitate his working lifestyle. The apostle is thus following a strategy often employed in both of his Thessalonian Letters: appealing to the firsthand knowledge they have about something (1 Thess. 1:5; 2:1, 2, 5, 9, 10, 11; 3:3; 4:2; 5:2; 2 Thess. 2:5, 6). This is an effective rhetorical tactic since it removes any possible excuse for idle behavior: all the church members, including the rebelliously idle, have not only received the "tradition," that is, the apostolic teaching about self-sufficient work that was passed on to them by Paul and his fellow missionaries (v. 6b), but they also know of the apostolic example (v. 7). The members of the Thessalonian church need only go back in time and recall in their minds how the apostle, along with Silas and Timothy, worked hard and long to provide for their own daily needs. Paul has already reminded the believers in Thessalonica of his self-sufficient work in his earlier letter (1 Thess. 2:9) as one of the several arguments he forwards to defend the integrity of his motives during his original visit to their city. Now he reminds them yet again of his past labor in their midst but this time with a different goal: to provide the first reason why the idle conduct of certain believers is inappropriate and why such members should thus be shunned by the larger congregation.

Although the *vocabulary* of imitation is not so common in Paul's Letters (1 Thess. 1:6; 2:14; 2 Thess. 3:7, 9; 1 Cor. 4:16; 11:1; Phil. 3:17; see Eph. 5:1), the *idea* of imitation does occur quite frequently. As examples to be emulated, the apostle holds up not only himself (in addition to the aforementioned texts, see 1 Cor. 7:7–16; Gal. 4:12–20; Phil. 1:30; 4:9a) but also God (Eph. 5:1), Christ (1 Thess. 1:6; 1 Cor. 11:1; Phil. 2:5–11), the churches of Judea (1 Thess. 2:14), and his coworkers: Timothy (Phil. 2:19–24; 1 Tim. 4:12), Epaphroditus (Phil. 2:25–30), and Titus (Titus 2:7). The theme of imitation, therefore, plays an important, though sometimes misunderstood, role in Paul's theology (on the wrong reading of the imitation theme, see comments on 1 Thess. 1:6). At the end of verse 9, the apostle stresses this theme in our passage by repeating the same infinitive form *mimeisthai* (v. 9: "so that you might imitate us"), so that the key verb "to imitate" forms an inclusio marking the boundaries of this unit (vv. 7–9) dealing with the example of Paul.

Three considerations ought to be kept in mind in understanding Paul's double reference here to the Thessalonians' imitation of himself and his coworkers. First, the notion of imitating some sort of moral exemplar was widespread in the ancient world. Seneca, for example, states that a model of conduct "will help you more than the written word. You must go to the scene of action, first, because men put more faith in their eyes than in their ears; and second, because the way is long if one follows precepts but short and helpful if one follows examples" (*Ep.* 6.5–6; see also 7.6–9; 11.9; Isocrates, *Demon.* 4.11; Quintilian, *Inst.* 2.28; Plutarch, *Demetr.* 1.6; Philostratus, *Vit. Apoll.* 1.19; 4 Macc. 9:23; 2 Macc. 6:27–28; see further Malherbe 1986). Paul, therefore, is not only following a widespread practice of his day; his failure to employ the imitation theme might also have opened himself up to accusations that he did not consider himself a teacher worthy of emulation.

Second, Paul's call for believers to imitate himself is grounded not in his own authority but in his own imitation of Christ (see 1 Cor. 11:1, likely a fuller expression of 1 Thess. 1:6). Paul's status, therefore, is exactly the same as that of his Thessalonian readers: one who along with them is called to be an imitator of Christ.

Third, it is an axiom in education that verbal instruction must be supplemented, if not preceded, with a model of the desired behavior or skill. By presenting himself as a model to be imitated, therefore, Paul is enacting an effective teaching strategy. And though the apostle sometimes uses others as a model, the example of himself and his coworkers is best known to his Thessalonian readers and thus more effective. There is a superficial difference between the imitation theme in the two letters of Paul to the Thessalonians:

in the first letter the apostle acknowledges that his readers have been engaged in the activity of imitation (1:6: "You on your part became imitators of us and of the Lord"; 2:14: "You yourselves, brothers, became imitators of the churches of God in Christ Jesus which are in Judea"), whereas here in the second letter he presents imitation as an obligatory action (3:7: "It is necessary to imitate us").[22] There is no actual divergence, however, since the obligation to engage in imitation is presupposed in the laudatory statements of 1 Thess. 1:6 and 2:14, and is also confirmed by Paul's other letters, where he explicitly commands the readers to imitate either himself or others (1 Cor. 4:16; 11:1; Phil. 3:17; Eph. 5:1).

The main clause of verse 7a ("For you yourselves know how it is necessary to imitate us") is followed by a lengthy dependent clause, which extends to the end of verse 8 and is introduced by the conjunction *hoti*. It is possible that this conjunction functions as a marker of causality ("because") in which the lengthy dependent clause of verses 7b–8 answers the question *why* the Thessalonians know how they must imitate Paul and his coworkers.[23] In this context, however, it is better to view the conjunction as serving to mark an explanatory clause (= "namely" or a colon; see BDAG 732.2) in which the lengthy dependent clause of verses 7b–8 answers the question *what* it is about the life of Paul and his coworkers that must be imitated. The apostle uses the explanatory clause of verses 7b–8 to highlight a specific aspect of his life that needs to be imitated—his self-sufficient work—which is most relevant for the problem of those living in a rebelliously idle manner. This lengthy explanation is given in the form of an antithetical statement (not *x* but *y*) that contains two clauses in the opening negative half and one in the closing positive half. The structure of verses 7–8, therefore, should be outlined as follows:

Main clause:	[7]For you yourselves know how it is necessary to imitate us,
Explanatory conjunction:	namely,
Negative statement 1:	we were *not* idle among you,
Negative statement 2:	[8]and we did *not* eat bread from anyone without paying for it,
Positive statement:	*but* we were working in labor and toil night and day in order not to burden any of you.

The rhetorical effect of such an antithetical statement is to create emphasis: not only does this structure allow the speaker to use more words to make the same basic point (this is especially true of vv. 7b–8, which contain not one but two negative statements in the opening half of the antithetical construction), but it also stresses the positive statement that comes in the concluding, climactic position.

22. In 3:7a the impersonal verb δεῖ (*dei*) means "to be under necessity of happening, *it is necessary, one must, one has to*, denoting compulsion of any kind" (BDAG 214.1).

23. If this were the intended meaning of the ὅτι (*hoti*) clause in 3:7b–8, we would more naturally expect a different statement than what Paul actually gives, something like "because we commanded you to do so" or "because we taught this to you."

The first negative statement in the opening half of the antithetical clause states in a brief and broad manner that Paul did not live among the Thessalonians with the same rebelliously idle conduct exhibited by some of the church's members: "We were not idle among you" (οὐκ ἠτακτήσαμεν ἐν ὑμῖν, *ouk ētaktēsamen en hymin*). For the second time in this passage, here we meet the root *atakt-* (see v. 6; also v. 11) and the debate over its precise meaning. A few translations and even more commentators highlight the term's general meaning of "insubordination" and thus render this verse "We were not *disorderly* among you" (KJV; Hendriksen 1955; Menken 1994: 134; Richard 1995: 380; Malherbe 2000: 450; Green 2002: 346) or "We did not act in an *undisciplined* manner among you" (NASB; Holmes 1998: 273). In the following clauses, however, Paul draws attention to his self-sufficient work, which indicates that here he is using the root *atakt-* with its more specific meaning of being "idle" or "lazy."

The second negative statement in the opening half of the antithetical clause spells out in more specific detail what was involved in the apostle's not living an idle life: "and we did not eat bread[24] from anyone without paying for it" (οὐδὲ δωρεὰν ἄρτον ἐφάγομεν παρά τινος, *oude dōrean arton ephagomen para tinos*). The phrase "eat bread" (*argon ephagomen*) is likely a Semitic expression referring not merely to the act of eating bread or even other types of food but more broadly to the act of receiving basic daily needs. For example, the same verb and noun combination "eat bread" occurs in Gen. 3:19 LXX, where the statement "By the sweat of your face you will *eat* your *bread*" (φάγῃ τὸν ἄρτον σου, *phagē ton arton sou*) refers to the need for Adam (and the rest of humanity) after the fall to work hard to supply his own daily needs. Similarly, David's statement to Mephibosheth, son of Jonathan, that "you shall *eat bread* [φαγῇ ἄρτον, *phagē arton*] at my table continually" (2 Sam. 9:7 LXX) refers not merely to the provision of bread or other food but more broadly to all his daily needs (see also Ps. 41:9 [40:10 LXX]; Ezek. 12:18–19; Amos 7:12). Paul's claim, therefore, is that during his mission-founding visit in Thessalonica he did not accept any provision of food, housing, or other daily needs "as a gift" (the accusative *dōrean* functions as an adverb: BDAG 266.1; see also BDF §160), that is, without paying for it (for a similar adverbial use of *dōrean* in the accusative, see Rom. 3:24; 2 Cor. 11:7; Matt. 10:8; Rev. 21:6; 22:17; Gen. 29:15; Exod. 21:11; P. Tebt. 5.187, 250; PSI 400.16; 543.19). By placing the adverbial accusative *dōrean* at the head of the clause, Paul emphasizes that he did not accept any help from believers in Thessalonica "as a gift."

The apostle's refusal to accept support for his daily needs was part of a deliberate missionary strategy that he followed not only in his Thessalonian ministry but elsewhere as well (see 1 Cor. 9:1–18; 2 Cor. 11:7). Although Paul

3:8

---

24. We retain the literal meaning "eat bread" in the translation of 3:8 so that the connection of this verse with verses 10 and 12, which also employ this phrase, can be heard and appreciated. The lexical link between these verses is hidden in most translations, which render the phrase "eat bread" here more broadly as "take food" or more broadly yet as "accept support."

vigorously defended his right as an apostle to receive financial support (see the immediately following verse of 2 Thess. 3:9; also 1 Cor. 9:3–7), he chose not to make use of this right during his *initial* ministry in a particular city. The apostle's expressed reason for doing so was "in order not to burden any of you" (v. 8b; similarly 1 Thess. 2:9), but a deeper motivation was to not "put an obstacle in the way of the gospel of Christ" (1 Cor. 9:12). The obstacle to which Paul is alluding, of course, is that his hearers may view him (or his opponents may portray him) as just another itinerant teacher whose coming was selfishly rooted in financial gain, personal glory, or both. The reality of this potential danger is all too clearly demonstrated in the apostle's lengthy defense of his integrity in 1 Thess. 2:1–16. Paul's *later* ministry in a particular church, however, followed a different strategy. Once a church had been established and the apostle left that congregation, he expected them to contribute to the cause of the gospel (J. M. Everts, *DPL* 297). This explains why Paul accepts monetary support from the Philippian church (Phil. 4:15–16) at the very same time he is ministering in Thessalonica, where he "did not eat bread from anyone without paying for it."

The two negative clauses that open the antithetical clause of verses 7b–8 are now concluded in a climactic fashion with the balancing positive clause: "but we were working in labor and toil night and day in order not to burden any of you" (ἀλλ' ἐν κόπῳ καὶ μόχθῳ νυκτὸς καὶ ἡμέρας ἐργαζόμενοι πρὸς τὸ μὴ ἐπιβαρῆσαί τινα ὑμῶν, *all' en kopō kai mochthō nyktos kai hēmeras ergazomenoi pros to mē epibarēsai tina hymōn*).

Paul skillfully stresses his self-sufficient work as a powerful counterexample to the rebelliously idle conduct of certain church members in five ways. First, as noted above, he employs an antithetical statement placing the emphasis on his claim here in the second positive half that instead of being idle and accepting support without paying for it, "we were working" (*ergazomenoi*).[25] There is no need for the apostle to state what kind of work he did since his readers would have known this well from the time he spent laboring in their midst (for a discussion of Paul's profession, see comments on 1 Thess. 2:9). Second, he uses the present-tense participle, which, though creating a grammatical problem,[26] highlights the ongoing or continuous nature of his labor (hence the emphatic translation "we were working" rather than the unstressed "we worked"). Third, he stresses the difficulty of his self-sufficient work through the addition of the word pair "in labor and toil" (*en kopō kai mochthō*). These two nouns constitute a fixed unit (the same word pair occurs also in 2 Cor. 11:27 and 1 Thess. 2:9) that Paul uses to describe in a more emphatic way the

---

25. There is a grammatical problem here: the positive clause of 3:8b lacks a main verb in the indicative mood to balance the indicative verbs used in the two corresponding negative clauses of 3:7b (ἠτακτήσαμεν) and 3:8a (ἐφάγομεν). If the presence of the participle *ergazomenoi* in 3:8 is not an accidental error stemming from the haste with which the letter was written (so Wanamaker 1990: 284), then one might explain it as either an independent or periphrastic participle construction in which the main verb ἦμεν (we were) is implied.

26. See the preceding footnote.

physical exertion connected with the work he endured during his original ministry in Thessalonica. Fourth, he underscores the length of his self-sufficient work through the addition of another word pair: "night and day" (*nyktos kai hēmeras*). These two nouns also occur as a fixed unit in Paul's Letters (1 Thess. 2:9; 3:10; 1 Tim. 5:5; 2 Tim. 1:4) and are used here to stress the great amount of time that the apostle spent in his work: he labored not merely for a brief moment but actually for great lengths of time, during both the night and the day.[27] Fifth and finally, both word pairs emphasizing the difficulty of the work ("in labor and toil") and the length of the work ("night and day") are further underscored by their location at the front of the sentence. The cumulative effect of all these emphases is that Paul presents a powerful example of himself that functions as not only an explicit challenge for the Thessalonian believers to imitate (v. 7: "You yourselves know how it is necessary to imitate us") but also an implicit rebuke for the idle members of the church, whose conduct is strikingly at odds with that of their spiritual father.

Paul's stated purpose (the preposition *pros* plus the articular infinitive expresses purpose: BDAG 875.3.e.ε) for working hard and long is "in order not to burden any of you" (πρὸς τὸ μὴ ἐπιβαρῆσαί τινα ὑμῶν, *pros to mē epibarēsai tina hymōn*). The rare verb *epibarēsai* (elsewhere in the NT, only 2 Cor. 2:5; 1 Thess. 2:9), which means *weigh down, burden*," denotes material support such as the provision of food, lodging, and financial remuneration. The larger purpose clause is word for word the same as an identical claim in the earlier letter to the Thessalonians (1 Thess. 2:9). But whereas in that letter this assertion was part of a series of proofs intended to defend Paul's integrity, here it is presented as part of the example that the Thessalonian church is called on to imitate (see both v. 7a and v. 9). As Green (2002: 348) recognizes: "More than one factor motivated Paul and company to refrain from seeking to support themselves through the preaching of the gospel." This purpose clause also involves yet another implicit rebuke of the rebellious idlers: it is clear that their conduct, contrary to that of the apostle, is putting a burden on their fellow church members.

The first argument based on the example of his self-sufficient work (vv. 7–9)   **3:9** that Paul uses to undergird his opening command for the church to keep away from their rebelliously idle fellow members (v. 6) comes to a close with an elliptical statement that intensifies even further the significance of his paradigmatic practice: "not that we do not have the right, but in order that we might give ourselves to you as an example so that you might imitate us" (οὐχ ὅτι οὐκ ἔχομεν ἐξουσίαν, ἀλλ' ἵνα ἑαυτοὺς τύπον δῶμεν ὑμῖν εἰς τὸ μιμεῖσθαι ἡμᾶς,

---

27. The genitive expresses "time within which" (BDF §186.2), "during" the night and "during" the day, in distinction from the accusative, which conveys "extent of time" (BDF §161.2), and thus the idea that Paul is claiming in hyperbolic style that he worked for the whole day and the whole night. Lightfoot (1904: 130) follows the accusative form found in the later MSS (see additional notes below) as original and concludes that this reading "implies the uninterruptedness of the labour."

ouch hoti ouk echomen exousian, all' hina heautous typon dōmen hymin eis to mimeisthai hēmas).

Several commentators identify this verse as a "parenthetical remark" (Wanamaker 1990: 285; also Best 1977: 337; Green 2002: 348) and thus imply that it is merely an explanatory comment that digresses from the preceding main point of Paul's argument. Still others argue that the apostle's concern here is that his example of working to provide for himself might be "misapprehended and misapplied" (Ellicott 1880: 130) and that he "does not want anyone to think that his refusal to accept support in any way undermines his authority" (Holmes 1998: 273n15). These observations, however, fail to recognize how verse 9 advances Paul's first argument by making his example of self-sufficient work an even more powerful model to be imitated. The logic of this verse is clear: if Paul, who had a right not to engage in physical labor but instead receive support from the church, nevertheless voluntarily worked hard and long to provide for his own basic daily needs, how much more should the rebelliously idle members who do not have this right[28] follow the example of Paul and earn their own living (see Best 1977: 337; Bruce 1982: 206)! Paul could have made his point in the first argument of vv. 7–9 by simply appealing to his self-sufficient work, but he cleverly increases the persuasive force of his argument by stressing how hard ("in labor and toil") and long ("night and day") he was working. Here in verse 9 he skillfully increases the persuasive force of his argument even further by reminding the readers that he was working even when he had a right as an apostle and preacher not to engage in physical labor but to receive support from the church.

Paul makes this point in a highly elliptical fashion, letting the reader fill in the implied missing words at three places. The opening expression "not that" (*ouch hoti*) is an abbreviated formula of the fuller clause "We are not saying that . . ." (οὐκ λέγομεν ὅτι, *ouch legomen hoti* . . . ; BDF §480.5) and one that the apostle employs at times to introduce a new point or clarifying comment (2 Cor. 1:24, 3:5; Phil. 3:12; 4:11, 17; also John 6:46; 7:22). The new point that follows, like the one made just before it (vv. 7b–8), is given in the form of an antithetical statement (not *x* but *y*). The negative half of this construction, which, as the opening expression "not that" indicates, Paul rejects, is that "we do not have the right" (*ouk echomen exousian*). Here we meet the second elliptical clause in this verse, since the object of "the right" is implied: "to eat bread as a gift" (v. 8a), "to eat and drink" (food provided by the church; 1 Cor. 9:4), or "not to work" (1 Cor. 9:6). The meaning of the key word "right" (*exousia*) becomes clear from Paul's extended discussion in 1 Cor. 9:1–18, where the term occurs six times (vv. 4, 5, 6, 12 [2x], 18) and refers to the expectation that those engaged in full-time ministry justly have, for the

---

28. Nicholl (2004: 169n59) comments: "This [that the rebellious idlers did not have the right to support like Paul did] suggests that the ἄτακτοι were not preachers," so they were not using their free time to engage in preaching, as is sometimes asserted (so Lightfoot 1904: 60; Jewett 1986: 177; Menken 1994: 140; Richard 1995: 384, 394).

larger church community to provide for their food, housing, and other basic needs. This same "right" or expectation lies behind Paul's later quotation to Timothy of the OT mandate that "the worker ["those who labor in preaching and teaching," v. 17] deserves his wages" (1 Tim. 5:18).

The positive and concluding half of the antithetical construction contains the third ellipsis, as Paul follows the strong adversative "but" (*all'*) not with a main clause as expected and implied (something like "we waived this right" or "we were working"), but with a purpose clause that spells out an additional motivation for his self-sufficient labor: "in order that we might give ourselves to you as an example" (*hina heautous typon dōmen hymin*).[29] In the previous verse the apostle has already claimed that his reason for working was to guard against creating a financial burden for any church member in Thessalonica. Here he cites the further reason that his working lifestyle serves as an "example" (*typos*) for the Thessalonian believers to imitate (on the meaning of the noun *typos*, see comments on 1 Thess. 1:7). It is impossible to determine with certainty the relationship of these two stated reasons, such as whether the first (not to become a financial burden to the church) was Paul's original motivation for working with his hands (cf. 1 Thess. 4:11), and the second (to provide the church with a model to be imitated) was a later purpose stemming from the need to correct the idle behavior of certain congregational members.[30] What is clear, however, is that the paradigmatic purpose predominates since it addresses head-on the key problem that is being addressed in this passage. Additional evidence lies in the concluding clause of verse 9, which gives the ultimate purpose or result[31] of providing the Thessalonian believers with an example of self-sufficient work: "so that you might imitate us" (*eis to mimeisthai hēmas*). Richard (1995: 381) implies that this concluding clause is redundant since it "restates what the term *typos* ('example') already expresses."

29. A comparison of this clause with the same idea as it is expressed in Phil. 3:17 ("You have us as an example") has led some commentators to find Paul's wording here in 3:9 emphatic. Whereas the Philippian text employs the verb "you have" (ἔχετε), 3:9 has the stronger verb "we give" (δῶμεν), leading Best (1977: 339) to state: "The Thessalonians do not just 'have' this example; it has been deliberately set before them." While the Philippians text contains the simple pronoun "us" (ἡμᾶς), 3:9 uses the reflexive pronoun "ourselves" (ἑαυτούς), leading Frame (1912: 304) to claim: "The ἑαυτούς here is likewise more emphatic than the ἡμᾶς just cited from Phil. 3:17; Paul gives not simply the command to work (v. 10), but also himself as an example of industry." Morris (1991: 225) agrees: "'Ourselves' is emphatic. They gave not only a message, but [also] themselves."

30. That the problem of idleness by some in the church goes back already to the mission-founding visit of Paul to Thessalonica suggests that the paradigmatic purpose of his self-sufficient work must have come into play very early in his ministry there. Fee (2009: 332) states: "Most likely he [Paul] understood the two reasons to be two sides of the same coin. On the practical side of things, he worked 'night and day' so as not to burden them; at the same time what was born of necessity came to be understood as offering them a model to imitate."

31. The construction εἰς τό + infinitive typically expresses purpose (BDF §402.2). Since in 3:9 it immediately follows a construction that also expresses purpose (ἵνα + subjunctive), it is best to view this concluding clause as giving either the "ultimate" purpose or result of the preceding purpose clause.

The addition of this concluding clause is important, however, since it forms an inclusio with the opening words of verse 7a, thereby marking the boundaries of the unit (vv. 7–9) that makes up Paul's first argument. The repetition of the key verb "to imitate" (*mimeisthai*: vv. 7a, 9c) also adds emphasis to the theme of imitation that is at work throughout this unit.

3. The Teaching of Paul (3:10)

3:10

While the first argument Paul uses to ground the opening command to keep away from any rebelliously idle member (v. 6) appeals to his *example* (vv. 7–9), the second argument appeals to his *teaching* (v. 10). Since the time frame of his paradigmatic practice in the first argument looks back to Paul's mission-founding work in Thessalonica, the second argument involving his teaching understandably begins by also taking the readers back to that past visit: "For when we were with you, we also were repeatedly commanding to you this: 'If anyone is not willing to work, let him not eat'" (καὶ γὰρ ὅτε ἦμεν πρὸς ὑμᾶς, τοῦτο παρηγγέλλομεν ὑμῖν ὅτι εἴ τις οὐ θέλει ἐργάζεσθαι μηδὲ ἐσθιέτω, *kai gar hote ēmen pros hymas, touto parēngellomen hymin hoti ei tis ou thelei ergazesthai mēde esthietō*).

The verse opens with the conjunction *kai*, which, despite its innocuous appearance, has the important function of bringing together the first argument introduced by the causative marker *gar* (for) in verse 7 with the second argument introduced here in verse 10 also with the causative marker *gar* (for). This *coordinating* function of *kai* is unfortunately hidden in virtually every English translation, which renders the conjunction *intensively* as "even": "For *even* when we were with you . . ." This translation emphasizes the presence of Paul and his coworkers in Thessalonica, which is unlikely to be the apostle's intention since the preceding verses (vv. 7–9) already refer to this fact (so Dobschütz 1909: 312; Marshall 1983: 223). The *kai* instead emphasizes the additional reason (Paul's teaching about work in distinction from his example) that the apostle is about to present for obeying the opening command to keep away from rebelliously idle members: "For when we were with you, we *also* were repeatedly commanding this to you."[32]

In his correspondence with the Thessalonians, this is not the first time that Paul reminds his readers of what he has formerly taught them during his original visit to their city: he did so in the first letter on the topic of persecution (1 Thess. 3:4); he did so previously in this second letter on the topic of the end times (2 Thess. 2:5); and he does so here for the third time on the topic of work. All three instances follow the same pattern: Paul begins with a

---

32. Frame (1912: 304) comments on 3:10: "The γάρ is parallel to γάρ in v. 7, and the καί coordinates the first reason for the command of v. 6, that is, the example of industry (vv. 7–9), with the second reason, namely, the oral precept repeatedly given when he was with them (v. 10)." The coordinating, rather than intensive, function of καί is also recognized by Lightfoot (1904: 131), who translates the καὶ γάρ that opens 3:10 as "'*for also*'; i.e. 'not only did we set before you our own example, but we gave you a positive precept to this effect, when at Thessalonica.'"

temporal clause ("when we were with you," *hote ēmen pros hymas*) that takes the readers back in time to his mission-founding visit and follows that with a verb in the imperfect tense that highlights the repeated nature of his original teaching. Here in 3:10 the temporal clause confirms that some believers' idleness was not a recent issue but one whose roots trace to the earliest days of the Thessalonian church (suggested also by the past tense in 1 Thess. 4:11c, "to work with your hands, just as we *commanded* you"; and in 2 Thess. 3:6, "the tradition that they *received* from us"). This was the last time when Paul was with them in person and was "repeatedly commanding" (the imperfect *parēngellomen* looks back to the opening command of 3:6, which in turn looks back to the confidence formula of 3:4) them about the necessity of work. The apostle's teaching on this subject matter was not something mentioned only briefly in passing; instead, Paul frequently commanded them about their need to work and so provide for their own basic needs. No one in the church can plead ignorance about the necessity of self-sufficient work.

Paul proceeds to quote (the *hoti* introduces direct speech) to his readers one of these commands making up the "tradition" that the whole Thessalonian church, including the rebellious idlers, "received" (v. 6) and that he had originally shared with them in a repeated manner: "If anyone is not willing to work, let him not eat" (*ei tis ou thelei ergazesthai mēde esthietō*). Although numerous parallels to this quotation have been forwarded, they differ from Paul's statement in two ways. First, whereas the apostle's words constitute a moral command that explicitly obligates its hearers to conduct themselves in a particular way (note the use of the third-person imperative "let him not eat" [*mēde esthietō*]), other claimed parallels are truisms that articulate an obvious fact and only implicitly call the hearer to action. For example, we read in the Proverbs: "Lazy hands make for poverty, but diligent hands bring wealth" (10:4) or "The one who works his land will have abundant food" (12:11) or "Laziness leads to sleep and negligence to starvation" (19:15). This is also true of what is the closest parallel found thus far—a fifth-century rabbinic commentary on Gen. 3:19: "If I do not work, I have nothing to eat" (Gen. Rab. 2.2; see Str-B 3:641–42). The same basic point appears also in Greek sources: in Phaedrus's *Fables*, written in the early first century AD, the ant says to the fly: "You don't work? That's why you don't have anything when you need it" (4.25.17). Thus, as Malherbe (2000: 452) concludes, "Paul may reflect a popular sentiment, but it is not at all clear that he is quoting something."

The second and more significant way in which the apostle differs from these parallels is that he speaks not broadly of those who do not work but narrowly of those who refuse to work: "If anyone is *not willing* [*ou thelei*] to work." The fundamental problem of the rebellious idlers is not their lack of employment but their deliberate refusal to work.[33] Paul does not have in view church

---

33. This fact undermines the proposal of Russell (1988: 112) that the problem in the Thessalonian church stemmed from the urban poor, for whom "even [in] the port trading center of Thessalonica, the opportunities for employment were limited."

members who cannot find work or are not able to work due to illness, injury, or old age. To believers who are genuinely in need, Paul expects the broader church community to "not be discouraged in doing good" (v. 13), that is, to minister to them in a compassionate way (Gal. 6:10; Eph. 4:28; 1 Tim. 5:3–8; Titus 3:14; note also Paul's involvement in the "collection" for needy Christians in Judea: Gal. 2:10; 1 Cor. 16:1–4; 2 Cor. 8–9; Rom. 15:25–27). Regarding believers who obstinately refuse to work even when they have the opportunity and means to do so, however, Paul commands the church membership as a whole not to provide them with food and other basic daily needs ("Let him not eat!") as part of the broader disciplinary process (v. 6, "keep away from"; v. 14, "not associate with").

4. Applying Paul's Example and Teaching (3:11–12)

3:11   As Paul leaves behind the two reasons why his readers should distance themselves from their fellow rebelliously idle members, his argument shifts slightly in both temporal perspective and purpose. Because such conduct contradicts the principle of self-sufficient work both exemplified and taught by Paul in the past, he applies this principle directly to the current situation facing the Thessalonian church: "We say this because we hear that some are continuing to walk among you in a rebelliously idle manner by not being busy but by being busybodies" (ἀκούομεν γάρ τινας περιπατοῦντας ἐν ὑμῖν ἀτάκτως μηδὲν ἐργαζομένους ἀλλὰ περιεργαζομένους, *akouomen gar tinas peripatountas en hymin ataktōs mēden ergazomenous alla periergazomenous*).

The presence yet again of the conjunction "for" (*gar*) to open this verse (see also v. 7 and v. 10) naturally suggests that Paul might be presenting a third reason why erring church members ought to be disciplined. But if this were what the apostle intended, we would expect to find again the fuller construction "for also" (*kai gar*), as in verse 10. Furthermore, the content of the next two verses reveals that Paul is not forwarding an additional reason to supplement the two already given in verses 7–9 and verse 10 but rather is explaining or, more precisely, applying those previous points. As Best (1977: 339) comments elliptically about the function of verses 11–12: "Paul has completed the 'tradition' (v. 6); now its application." Fee (2009: 33) makes the same point but states it more fully: "Thus, in two (Greek) sentences (vv. 11 and 12), Paul gathers together what has been said to this point and aims [applies] it directly at those needing correction."[34] This explanatory function of *gar* (BDAG 189.2) is brought out well by rendering it as "We say this because . . ." (so GNT; Ellingworth and Nida 1975: 205).

The reason why Paul has raised the principle of self-sufficient work in his past conduct and former teaching is because "we hear that some are continuing

---

34. Though not explicitly using the vocabulary of "application," the concept is implied in Morris (1991: 257), who introduces 3:11 as follows: "Paul comes out into the open. He has not been speaking simply in general terms, laying down precepts against some possible future need. He has in mind a definitive situation."

to walk among you in a rebelliously idle manner." The present tense "we hear" (*akouomen*) should not be overinterpreted to mean that the problematic behavior of some church members "has only recently come to light" (Furnish 2007: 178), since there is compelling evidence that the issue of idleness goes back not just to the preceding letter (1 Thess. 4:10b–12; 5:14) but also to the founding of the Thessalonian church (1 Thess. 4:11c; 2 Thess. 3:6, 10). Nor does the present tense require that Paul was hearing "ongoing reports" about such inappropriate conduct (D. Martin 1995: 283; see also Morris 1991: 257); yet the apostle must have received at least one earlier report from the recently returned Timothy (1 Thess. 3:6) before writing the first letter, in addition to the report to which he refers here. The present tense, rather, marks the shift in Paul's argument away from his past example and former teaching to the current situation in the church. The apostle has received a report, likely in oral form rather than via a letter (this is the most natural way to interpret "we hear"), from either the returning carrier of the first letter (Timothy?) or someone else with a connection to the Thessalonian congregation (Aristarchus or Secundus are less likely candidates since they do not seemingly connect with Paul until after the writing of both Thessalonian Letters: Acts 19:29; 20:4; 27:2; Col. 4:10; Philem. 24).

But while the form and source of the report ultimately remain uncertain, its content is not: "some are continuing to walk among you in a rebelliously idle manner." This clause repeats virtually verbatim a key phrase from the opening command of verse 6. There the identity of the wayward members was identified with the collective singular "every brother"; here the indefinite plural "some" (*tinas*) is used. Although it is impossible to know how many in the church belong to this category, "some" strongly suggests more than just one or two members, a fact supported further by the great length that Paul devotes in the letter to addressing this problem (contra Witherington 2006: 254, who interprets Paul in 3:14 to be speaking of "an isolated offender, of one person" and so claims that this is an "isolated problem"). The present tense participle *peripatountas* stresses again the ongoing nature of the improper conduct: some in the church are "continuing to walk." The adverb *ataktōs* marks the third occurrence of this key root in the passage (see also vv. 6, 7). As noted in our previous discussion of this term, it would be wrong to limit, as almost all translations do, the problematic behavior to either the general sense of insubordination alone or the specific sense of laziness alone, since the context of 3:6–15 reveals that *both* aspects are in view: thus "in rebellious idleness" or "in a rebelliously idle manner" (see also the NIV 2011: "We hear that some among you are idle *and* disruptive").

Not everything in verse 11, however, merely repeats the wording of the opening command of verse 6. Paul adds two adverbial participles in the form of yet another (see also vv. 7b–8, 9) antithetical (not *x* but *y*) statement that by means of a clever wordplay gives the manner by which some were living in rebellious idleness: "by not being busy, but by being busybodies" (*mēden ergazomenous alla periergazomenous*). The technical term for this kind of skillful pun is paronomasia: "the recurrence of the same word or word stem in close proximity. . . . In contrasts, so that a certain subtlety and occasionally a sort of humor is present" (BDF §488.1b). Paul contrasts the verb *ergazomai* with the compound form of the same verb *periergazomai*, thereby creating a striking and witty pun that, though difficult to capture in translation, nevertheless in the rendering given above can still be readily appreciated by the modern reader.[35] This should not be thought of negatively as a "rhetorical trick" (so Best 1977: 340) but instead positively as yet another persuasive means by which Paul catches the attention of his audience and makes his point, not only in a more memorable fashion but also in a more gentle manner, since the criticism involved in describing some readers as "busybodies" is softened by the humor contained in the wordplay. Paul is a gifted communicator who engages such wordplays throughout his letters (e.g., Rom. 12:3; 1 Cor. 7:31; 2 Cor. 1:13; 3:2; 4:8; 6:9; 10:12; Phil. 3:3), and so the presence of this rhetorical device here is not surprising. That the exact same pun had been made over three centuries earlier by the Athenian statesman and orator Demosthenes (4 *Philip.* 72 [150]: ἐργάζῃ καὶ περιεργάζῃ) has led a few to conclude that the apostle is borrowing "a saying familiar to the Thessalonians, making it all that much more rhetorically effective here as advice not just from Paul but also from previous sages" (Witherington 2006: 252; also see Rigaux 1956: 711). No other parallels to this wordplay, however, have been found, suggesting that it was not widely known in the ancient world and thus more likely originates with the apostle himself, who, as his other letters testify, is easily capable of creating such a statement (see texts cited above).

The negative half of the antithetical statement, "by not being busy," literally means "by not working" (*mēden ergazomenous*) and shows once again that it would be wrong to exclude the idea of idleness or laziness from the problem being addressed. Some members of the Thessalonian church are not working, or more precisely, as the former teaching of Paul clarifies (v. 10), are not willing to work. What they are doing instead is indicated by the positive half of the antithetical statement: they spend their free time "by being busybodies" (*periergazomenous*). The compound verb *periergazomai* occurs only here in the NT but is frequently used in secular writings of that day such that its meaning is clear: "to be intrusively busy, *be a busybody, meddler*" (BDAG 800). The term has a strongly negative connotation and was often employed to accuse philosophers of interfering in other people's business (Plutarch, *Busybody* 516A; Lucian, *Icar.* 20), a charge common and weighty enough to require sustained rebuttal (e.g., Epictetus, *Disc.* 3.22.97; Dio Chrysostom, *Or.* 21.2–3; see fuller discussion in Malherbe 2000: 453). Paul claims, therefore, that some in the Thessalonian congregation are refusing to work and using their resulting

---

35. Another translation of 3:11 that captures well the wordplay is "not by working hard but by hardly working" (Holmes 1998: 273). The weakness of this rendering, however, is that it fails to capture the aspect of meddlesome behavior expressed in the second verb περιεργάζομαι (BDAG 800).

free time to meddle into the affairs of others. The situation is likely similar to that addressed in 1 Tim. 5:13, where the cognate noun describes young widows who "get into the habit of being idle and going from house to house, not only being idlers but also gossips and busybodies [περίεργοι, *periergoi*], saying things that they should not say." Still highly questionable are attempts to specify further the historical setting by locating the meddlesome activity either to an inner-community context (an in-house situation involving only church members) or a public setting (a situation involving contact between the Thessalonian believers and their non-Christian fellow citizens)—or to identify the action implied in such "busybody" behavior. There is not enough information available, even with the help of insights based on 1 Thess. 4:10b–12, to decide these issues with a high degree of confidence.[36]

The reference in verse 11 to the problematic behavior of the rebellious idlers prepares the way in verse 12 for a command aimed at this specific group—a command that applies the principle of self-sufficient work recalled in the double appeal to Paul's past example (vv. 7–9) and his former teaching (v. 10): "To such people we command and appeal in the Lord Jesus Christ that they eat their own bread by working with quietness" (τοῖς δὲ τοιούτοις παραγγέλλομεν καὶ παρακαλοῦμεν ἐν κυρίῳ Ἰησοῦ Χριστῷ, ἵνα μετὰ ἡσυχίας ἐργαζόμενοι τὸν ἑαυτῶν ἄρτον ἐσθίωσιν, *tois de toioutois parangellomen kai parakaloumen en kyriō Iēsou Christō, hina meta hēsychias ergazomenoi ton heautōn arton esthiōsin*).

3:12

This is the only place in the whole discussion where Paul addresses the problematic church members directly, and even here he does so in a muted manner by using not the second-person pronoun "you" but the third-person correlative adjective "such people" (*toioutois*). The discipline of wayward members is not merely a private concern limited to either the individuals involved in inappropriate behavior or the congregational leaders alone; rather, it constitutes a shared problem that needs to be addressed by the entire community of faith, and so throughout verses 6–15 the apostle directs his comments to the church as a whole. Here, however, he deviates from that practice out of his desire to spell out—for the rebellious idlers described in verse 11, who are the antecedent of "such people"—how they ought to live. This shift in focus from the broader congregation to the much smaller group of problematic members is signaled also by the placement of "such people" in a position of emphasis at the head of the sentence.

Paul gives further emphasis to his words by using not one but two main verbs: "we command and appeal" (*parangellomen kai parakaloumen*). This combination is unique in the apostle's writings; he typically employs just one of these verbs as part of the appeal or command formula (for more on this epistolary convention, see comments on 3:6). His use of the first verb "we

---

36. Contra, e.g., Green (2002: 351), who with unjustified certainty asserts: "The problem is rather the involvement of the clients in the public assembly where they supported the causes of their patrons, entangling themselves in issues that were properly none of their concern. At issue is their political participation in favor of their patron."

command," though infrequent elsewhere (eight occurrences outside this chapter), is not surprising here in light of the key role that it plays in this passage (vv. 4, 6, 10). His use of the second verb, "we appeal," however, despite being common elsewhere (54x for Paul), is surprising, since Paul does not use this word as a synonym of "command" but rather as a contrast (Philem. 8–10: "Although having boldness in Christ to *command* you to do what is necessary, I prefer to *appeal* to more because of love. . . . I *appeal* to you for my child, Onesimus"). This suggests that its addition here is intended to emphasize not so much Paul's authority (contra Wanamaker 1990: 287: "The combination of the two [verbs] underscores the authority behind the exhortation and the necessity of obedience. . . . Paul constructed the exhortation to the disorderly in the strongest terms possible"; so also, e.g., D. Martin 1995: 283; Green 2002: 352) as his empathy for these wayward church members (so, e.g., Menken 1994: 136: "The severity of the command is immediately mitigated to the gentleness of the exhortation"; also Frame 1912: 306; Best 1977: 340; Morris 1991: 257–58; Malherbe 2000: 454). This is not to deny any notion of authority, which clearly is present in the opening verb "we command" and also even in the softer, more user-friendly "we appeal": Paul is issuing no mere advice but a strong word of exhortation that the rebellious idlers are obligated to obey. Yet it would be wrong not to hear and appreciate how the addition of the second verb "we appeal" "injects a note of passionate pastoral pleading into the instruction" (Nicholl 2004: 170).

The same juxtaposition of authority and compassion is likely expressed in the prepositional phrase "in the Lord Jesus Christ" (*en kyriō Iēsou Christō*). This phrase acknowledges not only the authoritative ground by which Paul issues his command but also the relationship that both Paul and his readers, including the rebellious idlers, have with Christ, a relationship that underlies their obedience to this command. As Marshall (1983: 225) notes: "The point may be underlined: this was the third occasion at least on which Paul had had to raise the matter, and yet he still does so in a brotherly fashion on the basis of their standing in Christ" (see also Morris 1991: 258). This "brotherly fashion" in which the apostle deals with troublesome church members fits the larger context of verses 6–15, where Paul opens by referring to these individuals as "every brother" (v. 6) and closes by exhorting the congregation not to consider such a person "as an enemy" but "as a brother" (v. 15).

The content of the command/appeal is introduced by the conjunction ἵνα (*hina*, that)[37] and uses vocabulary that is clearly intended to echo wording found in the preceding verses: "that they eat their own bread" (*ton heautōn arton esthiōsin*). The exhortation to "eat their own bread" is linked lexically to the earlier appeal both to Paul's example in verses 7–9 ("We did not *eat bread* from anyone") and to his teaching in verse 10 ("If anyone is not willing to work, let

---

37. In 3:12 the conjunction ἵνα does not have its common function as a marker denoting purpose, aim, or goal but as a marker denoting the content of the preceding main verbs (BDAG 476.2; Moule 1959: 145–46): see 1 Thess. 4:1; Rom. 15:30–31; 1 Cor. 1:10.

him not *eat*"). Thus there is a close relationship between the current verse and those earlier ones: Paul takes the general principle of self-sufficient work recalled in his past example and former teaching and now applies it specifically to the rebellious idlers in Thessalonica, who must "eat their own bread," that is, they must provide for "their own" (*heautōn* is emphatic) basic daily needs rather than live from the generosity of fellow church members (on the phrase "eat bread" as a Semitic expression referring not merely to the act of eating bread or even other types of food but more broadly the act of receiving basic daily needs, see comments on 3:8).

Paul specifies not only what the rebellious idlers must do (become self-sufficient) but stresses (note the word order) also the manner by which they must do it: "by working with quietness" (*meta hēsychias ergazomenoi*). That the conduct described in this clause is intended to function as a direct contrast to that of the previous verse ("by not being busy but by being busybodies") is clear (contra Frame 1912: 307) from two factors: lexically, both clauses make use of the same verb "to work" (*ergazomai* and its compound form *periergazomai*); syntactically, both clauses are adverbial participles expressing manner. Thus, if "by not being busy but by being busybodies" is the clever description of the meddlesome virus afflicting certain members of the Thessalonian church, then "by working with quietness" is the much-needed antidote. The noun "quietness" (*hēsychia*) does not mean saying very little or nothing ("silence": 1 Tim. 2:11; Acts 21:14; 22:2) but acting in a manner that does not cause unrest or disturbance to others (BDAG 440.1: "state of quietness without disturbance, *quietness, rest*"; see also Spicq 1994: 2.178–83). Paul's point is identical to that made in his previous letter, where he used the verbal form of this noun to command his Thessalonian readers "to make it your ambition to live a quiet life" (4:11, φιλοτιμεῖσθαι ἡσυχάζειν, *philotimeisthai hēsychazein*). Elsewhere the apostle exhorts believers to pray for governing authorities "so that we may lead a peaceful and quiet [*hēsychios*] life" (1 Tim. 2:2), that is, to conduct themselves in a calm and "well-ordered" manner (BDAG 440). Perhaps the best parallel to illustrate the apostle's meaning of working "with quietness" is Philo's contrast of the "quiet" man with the

> vulgar man, who spends his days meddling, running around in public, in theaters, tribunals, councils, and assemblies, meetings and consultations of all sorts; he prattles on without moderation, fruitless, to no end; he confuses and stirs up everything, mingling truth with falsehood, the spoken with the unspoken, the private with the public, the sacred with the profane, the serious with the ridiculous, not having learned to remain quiet [*hēsychian*], which is the ideal when the situation calls for it; and he pricks up his ears in an excess of bustling busyness. (*Abraham* 20)

Paul therefore is calling on the rebellious idlers to engage in self-sufficient work and to do so in a deliberate manner whereby they live a quiet life free from the kind of busybody or meddlesome behavior that disturbs others.

5. Closing Commands (3:13–15)

A shift in Paul's argument takes place at verse 13—not a shift in topic, as he continues to deal with the problem posed by the rebellious idlers, but a shift in focus. He leaves behind his words of application directed narrowly to the troublesome members within the Thessalonian congregation and issues closing commands that are more broadly aimed at the church as a whole. The apostle issues four commands: the first (v. 13) is short and general, functioning to introduce the exhortations that follow (Fee [2009: 336] speaks of this command "as the 'heading' of the conclusion found in verses 14–15"); the second (v. 14) is long and specific, functioning as the key exhortation in this closing section (note how this command "that you not associate with him" echoes and thus forms a thematic inclusio with the opening command "that you keep away from every brother" [v. 6]); and the final two (v. 15) are combined in an antithetical statement intended to clarify the disciplinary action called upon in the preceding specific command.

3:13 Paul signals the shift in his argument literarily with the emphatic personal pronoun "you" (in contrast to the correlative adjective "to such people" used to open the previous verse) and the vocative "brothers," a common transitional marker: "But as for you, brothers, do not be discouraged in doing good" (ὑμεῖς δέ, ἀδελφοί, μὴ ἐγκακήσητε καλοποιοῦντες, *hymeis de, adelphoi, mē enkakēsēte kalopoiountes*).

The compound verb ἐγκακέω (= ἐν + κακέω), which appears only rarely outside the NT, literally means "to do evil in, behave badly in regard to," but its precise nuance varies according to the context. The word occurs four other times in Paul's Letters, always (as here) with the negative particle, where it has the sense "to lose one's motivation in continuing a desirable pattern of conduct or activity, *lose enthusiasm, be discouraged*" (BDAG 272). For example, the term occurs twice in 2 Cor. 4, where Paul affirms that, in spite of the trials and tribulations that are constantly a part of his ministry, "we do not lose heart" (vv. 1, 16). In Gal. 6:9 the apostle promises his readers that there will be a spiritual harvest, if they do not give up the work of the gospel, and uses this promise of positive results to ground his command to "not become weary in doing good." Writing to the Ephesians, who know about their apostle's imprisonment and seeming abandonment by God, Paul asks them "not to be discouraged because of my sufferings for you" (Eph. 3:13). The only other occurrence of this verb in the NT is in Luke 18:1, where it introduces and spells out the meaning of the parable of the persistent widow: "They should always pray and not give up." Thus both Paul and Luke have made this verb "a Christian technical term to express the unflagging pursuit of the goal of service to neighbor or of apostolic ministry as well as the 'tautness' of the determined heart that does not let up, does not lose courage" (Spicq 1994: 1.399). Here the apostle's prohibition is in the form of the aorist subjunctive (instead of its alternate form with the present imperative), which supposedly forbids an action not yet begun; this fact has led some to conclude that the

Thessalonians were not already waning in their acts of benevolence: "Do not *begin now* to be discouraged in doing good" (so Best 1977: 342; Morris 1991: 258n28; Malherbe 2000: 458; see also MHT 3:76–78). However, the traditional understanding of the distinction between prohibitions employing the aorist subjunctive versus those with the present imperative has been seriously called into question (McKay 1985; Boyer 1987; Fanning 1990: 325–88; Porter 1992: 220–28; see the brief but helpful survey of this debate in Wallace 1996: 714–17). It remains an open question whether the Thessalonians were already discouraged by the support that they were extending to their fellow members or if Paul is issuing a preemptive command against this danger.

The content of the activity about which the Thessalonians are not to be discouraged is identified with a supplementary participle: "in doing good" (*kalopoiountes*). The present tense in this verbal form is significant: it stresses the ongoing or continuous nature of doing good. The good envisioned by Paul involves not general acts of proper conduct but specific acts of Christian charity to those in need (contra Hendriksen 1955: 204, who asserts that "the meaning is general; that is, it is not specifically 'giving to the poor' that is meant, but performing what accords with God's will in every walk of life"; so also Müller 1988: 166). In the previous letter, Paul exhorts the Thessalonians to "hold fast to the good" (5:21), which in that context is not a universal maxim applicable to any and all situations but a specific reference to Spirit-inspired utterances. Similarly, the command "Do not be discouraged in doing good" in this context refers narrowly to the kind of benevolent acts extended to the rebellious idlers and others in need. Although Paul does not want the Thessalonian church to enable their idle members to continue to take advantage of the congregation's generosity, he also does not want it to overreact and give up all acts of charity completely. As Malherbe (2000: 458) observes: "The context here suggests that the reference is to the material support the church had given to their fellow members in need rather than in doing good in general or to doing what is right. Paul is rather warning against overinterpretation of his directions."

Paul does not explicitly identify who are the intended recipients of these ongoing acts of charity. Some claim that the apostle has in view anyone in need, including the rebellious idlers: "This would be entirely in accord with the early Christian spirit of showing love to those who do not deserve it and do not return it" (Marshall 1983: 226). Others go further and assert that Paul actually is thinking primarily of the good that ought to be shown to the rebellious idlers: "Paul feared the church would react with a harsh and unchristian manner toward the idle. . . . The church should react with Christian love even toward those believers who would abuse their generosity" (D. Martin 1995: 284–85). This interpretation, however, contradicts what the apostle says in verse 10 about repeatedly having taught the church to not offer food and other kinds of aid to any church member who refuses to work. Such an understanding also seriously undercuts Paul's opening and closing commands to "keep away from" (v. 6) and "not associate with" (v. 14) erring members. Although the apostle does not want the Thessalonian church to treat the rebellious idlers in a harsh and unloving manner (see his clarifying commands in v. 15), that is not his concern here. Paul has in view those believers who, unlike the rebellious idlers, are genuinely in need, and he does not want the Thessalonian church to become discouraged from extending specific acts of benevolence to these legitimately disadvantaged members.

3:14   Paul anticipates the sobering reality that, despite all his careful argumentation in the preceding verses, some of the rebellious idlers will still not change their lazy and meddlesome ways, thereby requiring the church to discipline these members: "But if anyone does not obey our command in this letter, take special notice of that person so as to not associate with him in order that he might be put to shame" (εἰ δέ τις οὐχ ὑπακούει τῷ λόγῳ ἡμῶν διὰ τῆς ἐπιστολῆς, τοῦτον σημειοῦσθε μὴ συναναμίγνυσθαι αὐτῷ, ἵνα ἐντραπῇ, *ei de tis ouch hypakouei tō logō hēmōn dia tēs epistolēs, touton sēmeiousthe mē synanamignysthai autō, hina entrapē*).

The second and most important imperative in the closing commands is given in the form of a first-class conditional (if *x* then *y*) clause. The pairing of the particle *ei* with the indicative typically assumes the truth of the protasis, or "if" statement (BDF §372.1), suggesting that Paul does, in fact, expect one or more among the rebellious idlers to "not obey our command in this letter." This discouraging likelihood is supported not only by the grammar but also by Paul's history with the Thessalonian church: several members have rebelliously refused to change their idle conduct despite admonitions from the apostle both during his mission-founding visit and in his previous letter, and so it would be not at all surprising if they do not now obey "our command in[38] this[39] letter." The Greek actually says "our word" (*tō logō hēmōn*); hence a few commentators, based on their belief that verses 13–15 are not connected with the prior material of verses 3–12 but stand as an independent unit, view this term as referring to the whole letter of 2 Thessalonians (Trilling 1980: 154–55; Müller 1988: 166; Holland 1988: 52; Menken 1994: 141–42). Most, however,

---

38. The preposition used here is διά (*dia*), which, when followed by a genitive object (as here), expresses agency: "through, by means of." Some kind of verbal action must be supplied for the preposition's literal meaning to make sense in English: "But if anyone does not obey our command [given/communicated/expressed] through this letter, take special notice of that person."

39. The Greek of 3:14 does not contain the demonstrative pronoun "this" but refers more generally to "the" letter, thereby raising the question as to what letter Paul has in view. It is possible to take the prepositional phrase διὰ τῆς ἐπιστολῆς as belonging not to the protasis, but to the apodosis so that it modifies the imperative σημειοῦσθε: "by a letter take special notice of that person." The idea would be that Paul commands the church to send him a letter containing the names of members whom they have identified as not obeying his command (so Calvin: "[Paul] desires that they be reported to him"; also see some nineteenth- and early twentieth-century commentators). But while possible, this interpretation is improbable due to two factors: first, the word order suggests that the prepositional phrase goes with the preceding protasis; second and more significant, the presence of the definitive article ("through *the* letter" rather than the indefinite "through *a* letter") is inappropriate for a future letter sent by the Thessalonians to Paul but is a natural way to refer to the current letter at hand (see 1 Thess. 5:27; also Rom. 16:22; Col. 4:16).

rightly view "our word" to be looking back to the immediately preceding material of verses 6–13, especially the command given directly to the rebellious idlers in verse 12 that "they eat their own bread by working with quietness."

If, as Paul expects, someone disobeys this command, then the Thessalonian church is exhorted to discipline such a member: "take special notice of that person so as to not associate with him." The verb *sēmeiousthe*, occurring only here in the NT, can be used either positively, as in Josephus, who describes how the Persian king Artaxerxes commanded his historians "to note" the name of Mordecai as worthy of honor (*Ant.* 11.208), or negatively, as Paul does here "to take special notice of" someone (BDAG 921) for blame or censure (see also K. H. Rengstorf, *TDNT* 7:265–66). The meaning of this imperative is illuminated by Paul's similar appeal to the Romans that they "look out for/ take note of [σκοπεῖν, *skopein*] those who create dissensions and difficulties, in opposition to the doctrine that you have learned, and keep away from them" (Rom. 16:17). In both his Letter to the Romans and 2 Thessalonians, the apostle directs his call for disciplinary action to not merely the church leaders but the entire congregation. The church as a whole has a corporate responsibility to discipline their fellow wayward members. Indeed, discipline will never accomplish its restorative goal unless the entire congregation is involved in the process.

Like many details of this disciplinary process, Paul does not spell out how the church is to "take special notice" of anyone who disobeys the command to self-sufficient work.[40] He does, however, give the purpose[41] of this initial step of identification: "so as to not associate with him" (BDAG 965; H. Greeven, *TDNT* 7:853–55). The double compound *synanamignysthai*—which occurs elsewhere in the apostle's writings twice in his dealing with another discipline case, in Corinth (1 Cor. 5:9, 11)—echoes the opening call to discipline of verse 6: he began the passage by commanding the Thessalonians to "keep away" (στέλλεσθαι, *stellesthai*) from church members who rebelliously continue their idle ways. Now he brings his lengthy treatment of these troublesome church members to a close with a synonymous command to "not associate" with such people. This nonassociation does not involve cutting off all forms of contact with the person (excommunication), since the corrective commands in the following verse presuppose some degree of ongoing interaction. It minimally involves not admitting the person to the church's worship gatherings, including the communal meal, which is part of their Lord's Supper celebrations (1 Cor.

---

40. Malherbe (2000: 460) postulates that Paul "expected the person who carried this letter to its recipients to supply the details or that he left matters of procedure to the church, so long as his commands were carried out."

41. The infinitive συναναμίγνυσθαι in 3:14 ought to be read as having its common "final" or purpose function (BDF §390) rather than its much rarer imperatival function (contra Frame 1912: 308; Hendriksen 1955: 206n134). Later scribes tried to smooth the awkwardness of this grammatical construction (asyndeton) by adding the conjunction καί and changing the infinitive form to another imperative so that the text now read: "Take special notice of that person and do not associate with him." See the additional notes for a more detailed discussion of these textual changes.

11:20–22; also 5:11). Since the church met not in a public building but in the private home of a wealthy member like Jason, it would have been easy to carry out Paul's command at this communal level. Nonassociation must have also excluded hosting a private meal for such a person, since this would violate the clear command of verse 10 as well as the application of that command in verse 12. This leaves only informal personal contact, during which they are to treat the disciplined member not as an "enemy" but as a "brother" (v. 15).

The initial purpose of not associating with any disobedient member has a secondary or further goal: "in order that he might be put to shame." The compound verb *entrepō* literally means "to turn about," but in Paul (1 Cor. 4:14; Titus 2:8) it always has the metaphorical meaning of "to reprove, shame," or in the passive, as we have here, "to be put to shame, be ashamed" (BDAG 341.1). Paul is not at all speaking about a malicious intent to embarrass or ridicule someone in public; rather, he issues this statement from a Greco-Roman perspective in which "shame" and its corresponding value of "honor" were among the most powerful factors impacting social behavior. As Green (2002: 355) observes: "In a society oriented primarily toward the group rather than the individual and in which honor and shame were fundamental motivations for human action, the prescribed social separation that provoked shame would have been a powerful discipline." Fee (2009: 338) similarly recognizes that "all of what is said here makes sense only in such a culture where 'honor' and 'shame' stand at the highest level of values." Any member of the Thessalonian church who ends up being identified by the larger fellowship as someone who has disobeyed Paul's command and consequently someone with whom they ought not associate is thus in a highly precarious position. This person has already been rejected and shamed by their pagan fellow citizens (1 Thess. 2:14) following conversion, and so they likely cannot find fellowship and support from that community. Now they also face rejection and shame from their new social network, the church. As a result they will experience huge pressure to change their idle and meddlesome ways and return to their newfound family of brothers and sisters in Christ. Although Paul does not explicitly state that this restoration is his ultimate purpose in commanding the Thessalonian church to discipline wayward members, it is suggested both by the corrective commands in the following verse as well as his statements in other situations that called for the discipline of a church member (1 Cor. 5:5: "so that his spirit may be saved on the day of the Lord"; Gal. 6:1: "Brothers, if someone is caught in sin, you who are spiritual should restore him").

3:15   The third and fourth imperatives that make up the closing commands are combined in an antithetical statement intended to clarify the discipline enjoined in the preceding command: "And do not consider him as an enemy but admonish him as a brother" (καὶ μὴ ὡς ἐχθρὸν ἡγεῖσθε, ἀλλὰ νουθετεῖτε ὡς ἀδελφόν, *kai mē hōs echthron hēgeisthe, alla noutheteite hōs adelphon*).

The enforcement of discipline is always difficult—not only for those on the receiving end, who naturally get defensive and upset at others who highlight their sin(s), but also for those on the giving end, who can easily become contemptuous and unduly harsh. Paul anticipated the problems connected with discipline already in the preceding letter, where he concluded the section on respecting congregational leaders in their task of working, ruling, and admonishing (5:12–13a) with the command: "Be at peace among yourselves" (5:13b). Here too the apostle understands the potential danger and so adds two clarifying commands that address the attitude of the Thessalonian church as it engages in the difficult task of discipline. Paul emphasizes the proper attitude in which discipline must be carried out by placing the two clarifying commands within an antithetical construction—the fourth one in this passage (see also vv. 7b–8, 9, 11b). Rhetorically, this construction stresses the apostle's point by allowing him to say it both negatively ("not as an enemy") and positively ("but as a brother") and also by putting emphasis on the second command, which comes in the concluding, climactic position.

The conjunction "and" (*kai*) that opens this verse catches many commentators off guard, since they are expecting instead the strong adversative particle "but" (ἀλλά, *alla*). Fee (2009: 338), for example, states: "In one of the more surprising moments in this letter, Paul begins this qualifying sentence not with an expected 'but,' but with an 'and.'" Translations either omit this opening conjunction (RSV, NLT, NAB, ESV) or give it a contrasting meaning by rendering it as "yet" (KJV, NASB, NIV) or more strongly as "but" (NCV). Nevertheless, the presence of "and" here is important in showing continuity rather than contrast between the clarifying commands of verse 15 and the preceding command of verse 14. As Morris (1991: 261) observes: "The point is that Paul is not contrasting the behavior outlined in this verse with that in the previous one, but carrying on a consistent line of thought. Throughout this whole section he aims at having the dissident reclaimed in a spirit of love. The actions enjoined in verse 14 are just as kindly intentioned as those in this verse" (so earlier Ellicott 1880: 134).

The initial negative half of the antithetical construction contains the prohibition "Do not consider him as an enemy" (*mē hōs echthron hēgeisthe*). That this prohibition employs the present imperative instead of the aorist subjunctive is significant, not to indicate an action that is already happening ("Do not *continue to* consider him as an enemy") but one that is ongoing and continuous ("Do not *ever* consider him as an enemy"). The emperor Marcus Aurelius (AD 121–180) gives a similar instruction on how to deal with someone who behaves rudely in the gymnasium: "We keep an eye on him, not though as an enemy [οὐ μέντοι ὡς ἐχθρόν, *ou mentoi hōs echthron*] nor from suspicion of him but with good-humored avoidance" (*Med.* 6.20). Unlike Paul, however, Aurelius demonstrates no interest in the reform of this offensive person and "recognizes no duty of remonstrance towards the offender ὡς ἀδελφόν" (Moffatt 1910).

Paul's concern for the rehabilitation and return of the wayward church member comes out especially in the concluding and climactic half of the antithetical construction: "but admonish him as a brother" (*alla noutheteite hōs adelphon*). Although the verb *noutheteō* (Rom. 15:14; 1 Cor. 4:14; Col. 1:28; 3:16; 1 Thess. 5:12, 14; 2 Thess. 3:15; see also Titus 1:11 v.l.) is sometimes claimed to have the positive sense of "to instruct," in its less ambiguous occurrences, such as here, it consistently has the negative sense of "admonish" (Milligan 1908: 72: "[It] has apparently always a sense of *blame* attached to it, hence = 'admonish,' 'warn'"). This is clearly the meaning of the term in Paul's exhortation in the previous letter to "admonish the rebellious idlers" (1 Thess. 5:14) and also in the preceding description of the role that congregational leaders play in "admonishing" fellow believers (5:12). For the apostle, however, admonition never stems from a judgmental or vindictive spirit but rather is done out of genuine concern and love for others. Such concern can be seen in 1 Cor. 4:14, where Paul asserts that he is writing "to admonish you *as my dear children.*" This concern also manifests itself here as Paul commands the Thessalonians to discipline any rebellious idler in a way that does not treat that person "as an enemy" but "as a brother." Marshall (1983: 229) spells this out: "*As a brother* . . . means that the discipline must be exercised in love." That the only occurrences of the singular, nonvocative "brother" in the letter are both here in the closing (v. 15) and opening (v. 6) verses of this passage is unlikely to be coincidental. This intended inclusio functions not only literarily to mark the boundaries of this passage (vv. 6–15) but also thematically to highlight the "brotherly" or loving way that discipline ought to be carried out in the church.

Additional Notes

3:1. Since using either "word" or "the word of God" is the expected way for the apostle to refer to the gospel, a few copyists changed the rarer "the word of the Lord" (κυρίου) to the common and expected "the word of God" (θεοῦ: so G P 33 489 927 vg^(mss)).

3:3. Several MSS have replaced κύριος ("But faithful is the *Lord*") with θεός ("But faithful is *God*"): A D* F G 2464 *pc* it vg^(cl) bo^(ms); Ambst. Such a change is clearly an attempt by copyists to bring this verse into alignment with Paul's other uses of this formulaic statement (1 Cor. 1:9; 10:13; 2 Cor. 1:18; 1 Thess. 5:24). But not only is κύριος the more difficult reading and thus more likely to be original; it also enjoys strong MS support: ℵ B D¹ Ψ 𝔐 vg^(st) sy cop.

3:3. The form στηρίσει, found in B, involves an alternate future (and aorist) ending often found in verb stems ending in a consonantal stop (BDF §71; MHT 2:259). The verb τηρήσει (he will keep), found only in F and G, likely originates from treating the two verbs in this relative clause as synonyms, along with the fact that τηρέω is sometimes paired with φυλάσσω (John 17:12).

3:4. The clause καὶ ποιεῖτε καὶ ποιήσετε (you are indeed doing and will continue to do) exhibits some variation in the MSS. A few important uncials (ℵ* A D*), along with later texts and versions (6 629 1739 *pc* lat), omit the conjunction καί (which functions here adverbially to express emphasis), and it is hard to discern whether it was deleted as either redundant or awkward, or if it was added to agree with similar Pauline expressions of affirmation (1 Thess. 4:1, 10; 5:11). The difficulty in determining the original reading has led the editors of NA²⁸ to include the word but place it in square brackets. The present and future verbs in the clause (so ℵ² D² Ψ 𝔐 f vg sy^(h); Ambst) are different in some MSS: a couple of uncials have the aorist and present tense (ἐποιήσατε καὶ ποιεῖτε: F G) while the weighty Vaticanus (B) has all three tenses (ἐποιήσατε καὶ ποιεῖτε καὶ ποιήσετε).

3:6. The pronoun ἡμῶν (our) in the prepositional phrase "in the name of [our] Lord Jesus Christ" is omitted in two important MSS: B and D*. It may be, then, that the pronoun is a later addition, under the influence of the similar phrase earlier in the letter in 1:12 (so Ellicott 1880: 127; Frame 1912: 299). However, the omission of the word is "considerably weakened when one considers Vaticanus' tendency to omit seemingly unimportant terms during the copying process" (Richard 1995: 378). Furthermore, the inclusion of the word enjoys widespread support (ℵ A D¹ F G Ψ 𝔐 lat sy co).

3:6. The extant MSS have four different readings of the main verb in the relative clause that ends this verse: (1) παρελάβοσαν (*they* received: ℵ* A [D* ἐλάβοσαν] 33 88 1827 1845 2005 Basil); (2) παρέλαβον (*they* received: ℵ^c D^c K L P 𝔐 81 614 1739); (3) παρελάβετε (*you* received: B F^gk G 104 327 436 442 1611 2005 2495 syr^h cop goth arm); and (4) παρέλαβε (*he* received: 5 76 218 234 1962 Basil Ps-Oecumenius). The most strongly attested reading, the most difficult reading (which is most likely to be the original reading), and the reading that best explains the origin of the remaining three is the first one (see B. Metzger 1994: 569). The third-person plural form παρελάβοσαν is awkward and surprising in a context where the second-person plural form "you" is smoother and expected in light of the following verses, which address not just the rebellious idlers but also the whole community and so make use of the second-person plural form (note οἴδατε [*you* know] that opens the immediately following verse). This caused several later scribes to make the original wording more natural to read by changing it to the second-person plural form παρελάβετε. The original third-person plural form παρελάβοσαν, however, had a further difficulty: it contained the irregular ending -οσαν (a first-aorist ending on a second-aorist verb—a phenomenon that occurs with some frequency in the LXX), which led other scribes to "correct" it to the expected regular ending -ον. The third-person singular, which has only minimal external support, is also a likely "correction" intended to make the original plural form match the singular παντὸς ἀδελφοῦ (every brother) used in the earlier part of the verse. A few (e.g., Frame 1912: 300; Morris 1991: 253n12) have argued that the second-person plural form is original on the grounds that it would more naturally lead to the second-person plural form in the following verse. They then account for the third-person plural form by appealing to an "ocular confusion" (MHT 2:209) with the similar ending of the preceding noun παράδοσιν. This explanation, however, is highly implausible, given not only the unlikelihood of confusing two words separated at some distance from each other but also that the ending of the noun is not identical with the ending of the verb.

3:8. There is some disagreement among the MSS over whether the word pair "night and day" was originally written in the accusative (A D I Ψ 𝔐) or genitive case (ℵ B F G 33 81 104 365 2464 *pc*). The genitive reading is supported by both the older MSS and Pauline practice, which elsewhere always gives this word pair in the genitive (1 Thess. 2:9; 3:10; 1 Tim. 5:5; 2 Tim. 1:3). The accusative reading likely came about under the influence of its occurrence in the Gospels and Acts (Mark 4:27; Luke 2:37; Acts 26:7). This textual issue has exegetical significance since the genitive expresses the actual situation of Paul as working periodically during the night and during the day (the genitive expresses "time within which": BDF §186.2), whereas the accusative in a hyperbolical manner expresses the impossible situation of Paul as working for the whole day and the whole night (the accusative expresses "extent of time": BDF §161.2).

3:12. The prepositional phrase connected with the two main verbs "we command and appeal" differs among the MSS: the oldest and most reliable texts have ἐν with the dative (ἐν κυρίῳ Ἰησοῦ Χριστῷ: ℵ* A B D* F G 0278 33 81 104 365 1739 1881 2464 *pc* lat [sy^p co]), while less ancient texts have διά with the genitive (διὰ τοῦ κυρίου ἡμῶν Ἰησοῦ Χριστοῦ: ℵ² D² Ψ 𝔐 sy^h). It is not clear why Fee (2009: 332n71) identifies the first of these two readings as the more difficult "by far," since the construction ἐν with the dative object(s) "the Lord (Jesus Christ)" occurs elsewhere in Thessalonian correspondence in similar constructions (3:4, 6; 1 Thess. 4:1; see also 1 Thess. 2:14; 3:8; 5:18) and is readily understandable in this context.

3:13. The compound form ἐκκακήσητε, which combines the verb κακέω with the preposition ἐκ, occurs in some MSS: D² F G Ψ 𝔐. The older and more reliable texts, however, support the form ἐγκακήσητε, which uses the preposition ἐν: ℵ A B D* (but with the present tense imperative ἐγκακεῖτε) 323 326 *pc* co.

3:14. Uncertainty about the grammatical function of the infinitive συναναμίγνυσθαι and the slightly awkward construction of this clause (asyndeton) caused later scribes to add the conjunction καί (D*·² F G 𝔐 vg sy; Ambst Spec) and change the ending of the infinitive to an imperative (συναναμίγνυσθε: D² 𝔐 sy; Ambst) so that the text read more clearly and smoothly as two imperatives: τοῦτον σημειοῦσθε καὶ μὴ συναναμίγνσθε αὐτῷ (Take special notice of this one and do not associate with him). The infinitive form, however, is not only the more difficult reading and thus original, but it also has overwhelming textual support: ℵ A B D¹ (D* F G) Ψ 33 (1739 2464) *pc* (it) bo.

V. Letter Closing (3:16–18)

The letter closing of 2 Thessalonians, despite its brevity, has several formally distinctive features compared with other letters in the Pauline corpus. In fact, every one of the epistolary conventions found in this particular final section is, in one or more ways, formally unique. (1) Whereas all other peace benedictions identify the divine source of the wish as "God," here the apostle refers to the giver of the wish as "the Lord." (2) Paul stresses the role that the Lord plays in the carrying out of the prayer for peace by adding the intensive pronoun "the Lord *himself*." (3) The apostle repeats the noun "peace" so that the resulting double reference to this term emphasizes the content of the wish. (4) The application of the prayer for peace is expanded by means of the double prepositional phrase "at all times in all ways." (5) Paul adds a word of encouragement ("May the Lord be with you all") borrowed from his Jewish background but changes it in two ways: (a) he transforms the meaning of the term "the Lord" so that it no longer refers to God but to Christ, and (b) he expands the recipients of this wish by adding the adjective "all." (6) The autograph greeting is distinctive because of its unparalleled explanatory clause that follows this epistolary convention: "which is a sign in every letter; this is the way I write." (7) Finally, even the grace benediction, which throughout Paul's Letters exhibits a striking consistency in form, has been expanded by adding the adjective "all" to the recipients of the wish. These unique features are not fortuitous but stem from the apostle's deliberate and skillful adaptation of the closing conventions so that this final epistolary unit better connects to the specific issues raised previously in the letter body.

Literary Analysis

Character of the Passage

Second Thessalonians 3:16–18 consists of the fourth and final major section of Paul's correspondence: the letter closing. A detailed and comprehensive analysis of the Pauline letter closings in general reveals that they are carefully constructed units, shaped and adapted in such a way that they are related to—sometimes even summarize—the major concerns and themes addressed in the body sections of their respective letters, and so these closings are hermeneutically significant (Weima 1993; 1994a; 1995; 2010b). The letter closing, therefore, functions much like the thanksgiving but in reverse. For as the thanksgiving foreshadows and points ahead to the major concerns to be addressed in the body of the letter, so the closing serves to highlight and encapsulate the main points previously taken up in the main section of the correspondence. This recapitulating function was seen in the closing of

1 Thessalonians (see comments on 1 Thess. 5:23–28), and so there is good reason to expect it to be present in the closing of 2 Thessalonians as well.

Extent of the Passage

Several scholars do not include the peace benediction of verse 16 as the first element of the letter closing but as the final element of the letter body, believing that its function parallels that of the earlier prayers in the letter: just as the prayer of 2:16–17 concludes 2:1–15 and the prayer of 3:5 concludes 3:1–4, so the prayer for peace in 3:16 concludes the immediately preceding material of 3:6–15 (so, e.g., NA[28]; Milligan 1908: 117–18; Whiteley 1969: 111–12; Trilling 1980: 156–60; Bruce 1982: 211–13; Marshall 1983: 230–31; Menken 1994: 143; Richard 1995: 384–85, 392). This reasoning is not completely wrong, as 3:16 does indeed look back to the previous section. Yet there are additional considerations to take into account. First and foremost is the fact that the peace benediction in Paul's Letters typically serves as a literary heading that marks the beginning of a letter closing (Weima 1994a: 88–90). Second, the peace benediction of 3:16 is, as I will demonstrate, linked to issues taken up in other parts of the letter and not just in the immediately preceding section (the double prepositional phrase "at all times in all ways" is too broad to refer only to the problem of disciplining the rebellious idlers). Third, the peace benediction of 3:16, like Paul's other peace benedictions (Rom. 15:33; 16:20a; 2 Cor. 13:11; Phil. 4:9b; 1 Thess. 5:23; see also Gal. 6:16), has a standard form that differs from the prayers (more accurately, the "body benedictions") of 2 Thess. 2:16–17 and 3:5 and those found elsewhere in the apostle's letters (Rom. 15:5–6, 13), thereby minimizing the significance of the claimed functional parallel between them (for a formal analysis of both types of prayers or benedictions, see Weima 1994a: 87–104). Finally, the Pauline peace benediction is analogous to both the peace wish of Semitic letters and the health wish of Greco-Roman letters—epistolary conventions that are always located in the letter closing and not in the letter body. These considerations provide compelling grounds for beginning the letter closing of 2 Thessalonians with the peace benediction of 3:16.

Structure of the Passage

Second Thessalonians, despite its brief letter closing, contains three of the four epistolary conventions typically found in the final section of Paul's correspondence. The closing begins with a slightly altered and expanded peace benediction in which the apostle prays that "the Lord of peace himself" will give believers at Thessalonica peace "at all times and in all ways" (3:16a). This wish for peace concludes with a word of encouragement: "May the Lord be with you all" (v. 16b). Then Paul briefly greets them in his own hand and explains that a closing autograph section is a characteristic sign of all his letters (v. 17). Finally, the letter comes to a definitive close with an expected second wish, the "grace benediction," which always concludes the apostle's correspondence: "May the grace of the Lord Jesus Christ be with you all" (v. 18).

The letter closing of 2 Thessalonians, therefore, ought to be outlined as follows:

A. Peace benediction (3:16a)
B. Word of encouragement (3:16b)
C. Autograph greeting and explanatory comment (3:17)
D. Grace benediction (3:18)

Exegesis and Exposition

[16]May the Lord of peace himself give you peace at all times in every ⌜way⌝. May the Lord be with you all. [17]The greeting is in my own hand, that of Paul, which is a sign in every letter; this is the way I write. [18]May the grace of our Lord Jesus Christ be with you all.

A. Peace Benediction (3:16a)

The letter closing begins with a peace benediction,[1] which, along with the grace benediction of verse 18, forms an inverted or chiastic inclusio with the salutation "grace and peace" of the letter opening (1:2), thereby framing the boundaries of the letter: "May the Lord of peace himself give you peace at all times in every way" (αὐτὸς δὲ ὁ κύριος τῆς εἰρήνης δῴη ὑμῖν τὴν εἰρήνην διὰ παντὸς ἐν παντὶ τρόπῳ, *autos de ho kyrios tēs eirēnēs dōē hymin tēn eirēnēn dia pantos en panti tropō*).

3:16a

The unique and potentially significant features of this epistolary convention in verse 16 become clear when it is compared with the typical form of the peace benediction elsewhere in Paul's letter closings. The peace benediction occurs seven times in the final section of the apostle's correspondence (Rom. 15:33; 16:20a; 2 Cor. 13:11; Gal. 6:16; Phil. 4:9b; 1 Thess. 5:23; 2 Thess. 3:16), where it displays a clear and consistent pattern involving four basic elements (see chart and discussion in Weima 1994a: 87–98; for a fuller explanation of these four basic elements, see comments on 1 Thess. 5:23). Here Paul deviates from his expected form in three ways, all of which to varying degrees draw the reader's attention to major issues and key themes taken up earlier in the letter. As Richard (1995: 392) observes, the peace benediction is "a prayer which brings together some of the letter's principal concerns."

First, whereas all other peace benedictions identify the divine source of the wish as "God" (*theos*), here the apostle refers to the giver of the wish as "the Lord" (*ho kyrios*). Paul stresses the role that the Lord plays in carrying out the prayer for peace by adding the intensive pronoun *autos*: "the Lord *himself*" (not found in any other peace benediction except for 1 Thess. 5:23). In a general way this change in the identity of the divine source recalls the emphasis throughout the letter on Christ: a similar substitution happens in the phrase "loved by the Lord" (2:13); the prayers of 3:5 and 3:16 are likewise directed to "the Lord"; Paul's confidence in the Thessalonians is grounded

---

1. This epistolary convention is referred to by a number of different titles: "prayer wish" (Wiles 1974: 63–68); "homiletic benediction" (Jewett 1969); "benedictory prayer" (Fee 1994a: 63; 2009: 225).

"in the Lord" (3:4); his commands to them are based on the authority of "the Lord" (3:6, 12); and the concluding word of encouragement in 3:16b does not involve "God" (as in 1 Thess. 5:24; see also 1 Cor. 1:9) but "the Lord." In a more specific way this change also recalls the major concern of the letter, the confusion over the claim that "the day of the Lord has come" (2:2). Nicholl (2004: 175) observes: "The unique formulation here ["the Lord of peace" instead of the expected "God of peace"] is probably inspired by the fact that the main issue troubling 'the Thessalonians' relates to ἡ ἡμέρα τοῦ κυρίου (2:2; cf. 2:8b; 3:3–5), as is perhaps reinforced by the addition of αὐτός."

Second, whereas the wish or prayer for peace in other peace benedictions is typically taken from the qualifying genitive phrase "the God *of peace*" along with the copula (the verb "to be"), either given or implied, so that this epistolary convention typically reads "May the God of peace *be* with you," here Paul employs the transitive verb "give" (*dōē*) and repeats the noun "peace" (*tēn eirēnēn*) so that the prayer now reads "May the Lord of *peace* himself give you *peace*." The double reference to "peace" clearly emphasizes the content of the wish—an emphasis on peace that is understandable in light of the major issues addressed in the letter. This wish looks back minimally to the immediately preceding section, dealing with the lazy and meddlesome members of the church and the internal tensions that have resulted from their ongoing rebellious behavior and need to be disciplined. Just as Paul in his first letter anticipated strained relations from the admonishment of the rebellious idlers (1 Thess. 5:12, 14) and consequently commanded the church to "Be at peace among yourselves" (5:13b), so here he similarly expects that his commands to discipline wayward members will cause internal tensions and thus prays in an emphatic manner that "the Lord of peace" will "give peace" to the Thessalonian congregation.

The third unique feature of this peace benediction, however, suggests that the emphasis on peace also looks back to other issues in the letter. The addition of the double prepositional phrase "at all times in all ways" (*dia pantos en panti tropō*) indicates that it would be wrong to limit the prayer for peace only to the problem of disciplining the rebellious idlers. These two prepositional phrases show that Paul expects his prayer for peace to be applied to the Thessalonian church in a very broad manner, both temporally ("at all times") and experientially ("in all ways"). This prayer for peace, therefore, also looks back to the readers' fear connected with the increased opposition that they endure from their fellow citizens (1:3–12) as well as the anxiety connected with the false claim about the day of Christ (2:1–17). As D. Martin (1995: 291) observes: "The phrase ["at all times in all ways"] implies a multitude of troubles, and the letter has revealed a persecuted, doctrinally confused, and socially troubled church. Thus the plea for peace should be understood as broadly as this phrase and the larger context demand."[2]

---

2. On 3:16, note also the comment of Fee (2009: 340): "In light of the preceding content (God's coming judgment on their enemies; the timing of the day of the Lord; and unrest caused by the disruptive-idle), this prayer is precisely what is needed."

B. Word of Encouragement (3:16b)

The distinctive features of the peace benediction in verse 16a are further heightened by the unusual addition of a word of encouragement that concludes this prayer for peace (elsewhere only in 1 Thess. 5:24): "May the Lord be with you all" (ὁ κύριος μετὰ πάντων ὑμῶν, *ho kyrios meta pantōn hymōn*).

The crucial role that Christ plays in providing the peace which the congregation requires in the face of outside opposition (2 Thess. 1), eschatological confusion (chap. 2), and internal conflict (chap. 3) was stressed in the preceding peace benediction by the addition of the intensive pronoun *autos*: it is "the Lord of peace *himself*" who will carry out the prayer to give them this much-needed peace. Paul now further stresses Christ's role by means of a word of encouragement that he borrows from his Jewish heritage but also adapts in light of the specific situation at Thessalonica. The statement "May the Lord be with you" is an opening greeting that Jews often used to encourage the ones being addressed that they were not alone but that "the Lord" (= God) was with them: this is the greeting used by Boaz to his field workers (Ruth 2:4), the angel to Gideon (Judg. 6:12), the prophet Azariah to king Asa of Judah (2 Chron. 15:2), and the angel to Mary (Luke 1:28).[3]

Paul, however, does not simply repeat this common Jewish greeting but adapts it in two significant ways that are both relevant to the Thessalonian context. First, he transforms the meaning of the term "the Lord" so that it no longer refers to God but to Christ. As Fee (2009: 341) correctly observes: "Paul has appropriated what strictly belonged to Yahweh in an Old Testament passage and applied it directly to Christ." This second reference to Christ in the letter closing looks back, as already noted above in the striking substitution of "the Lord of peace" for the expected "God of peace," not only in a general way to the emphasis on Christ's role throughout the letter but also in a specific way to the letter's central concern about "the day of the Lord." Second, within the Jewish word of encouragement, Paul inserts the adjective "all": "May the Lord be with you *all*." With this addition the apostle stresses that his prayer for the Lord's presence among them includes all the members of the Thessalonian church, not just those who are discouraged and fearful of outside opposition and of end-time confusion, but also those who are the cause of internal tension and the object of his disciplinary commands.

3. In all these examples, the sentence lacks a main verb and so implies the presence of the copula ("to be"), exactly the form found in Paul's statement. This implicit presence of the verb leaves ambiguous what mood is intended: an indicative, which would give the expression the sense of a declarative statement ("The Lord *is* with you all"); an imperative, which would turn it into a command ("*Let* the Lord be with you all!"); or, as is most likely, the optative, which would render it a holy or pious wish ("*May* the Lord be with you all"). For a defense of the last option, see comments on 1 Thess. 5:28.

C. Autograph Greeting and Explanatory Comment (3:17)

3:17   The third epistolary convention found in this letter closing is the greeting, which unlike everything in the letter thus far is written not by Paul's secretary but by the apostle himself: "The greeting is in my own hand, that of Paul" (ὁ ἀσπασμὸς τῇ ἐμῇ χειρὶ Παύλου, *ho aspasmos tē emē cheiri Paulou*).

The greeting is a common element of Paul's letter closings, found in the endings of all his letters except for Galatians (likely reflecting Paul's strained relations with these churches), Ephesians (perhaps because it was a circular letter), and 1 Timothy. The apostle typically expresses greetings by using the verb form ἀσπάζομαι (*aspazomai*, I greet; for the classification of first-person, second-person, and third-person greetings using the verbal form, see table 4 in Weima 1994a: 106–7), though the noun form *aspasmos* found here occurs in two other letter closings as well (1 Cor. 16:21; Col. 4:18). Best (1977: 346–47) argues that the noun *aspasmos* refers back to the content of the previous verse so that the actual greeting itself consists of the wish for peace (v. 16a) and for the Lord's presence (v. 16b). Against this, however, is the fact that Paul's other two occurrences of the noun "greeting" do not include a preceding wish for peace (1 Cor. 16:21; Col. 4:18). Also, it is simpler and thus preferred to understand the noun "greeting" as conveying the actual greeting of the apostle to his readers.

Within the closing Paul follows his typical practice of including not only a greeting but also an autograph—writing the greeting "in my[4] own hand, that of Paul" (*tē emē cheiri Paulou*). In that day the sender would commonly construct a letter with the help of a secretary (the technical term is *amanuensis*) but then oneself write the letter closing, or at least part of the closing. The phrase "in my own hand" occurs five times in the apostle's letters (1 Cor. 16:21; Gal. 6:11; Col. 4:18a; 2 Thess. 3:17; Philem. 19) and implies that to this point Paul has been using a secretary (note also Rom. 16:22, where the secretary, Tertius, greets the recipients) but now takes up the pen himself to write personally to his readers. A few parallels to Paul's expression "in my own hand" can be found in the correspondence of his day. Ziemann (1912: 365) cites a Greek letter that closes: "I have written these things to you in my own hand" (ταῦτά σοι γέγραφα τῇ ἐμῇ χειρί, *tauta soi gegrapha tē emē cheiri*). The sender of P.Grenf.II 89 states: "I wrote all in my own hand" (ὁλόγραφον χειρὶ ἐμῇ, *holographon cheiri emē*). The letters of Cicero contain a number of references to "in my own hand" (*mea manu*), apparently a preferred formula signaling the shift from the secretary to his own hand (e.g., *Att.* 8.1; 13.28; see Richards 1991: 173). Despite these examples, Greco-Roman letters rarely

---

4. Note the shift in 3:17 from the first-person plural used throughout the letter to the first-person singular: "my," "Paul," and "this is how I write." This, along with a similar shift at 2:5 ("You remember, don't you, that when I was still with you, I was repeatedly saying these things to you?"), reveals that, though the names of Silvanus and Timothy are included as cosenders (1:1a), Paul is the real author, and thus the plurals used throughout the letter ought to be taken literarily, not literally. A similar shift happens in the first letter (2:18; 3:5; 5:27).

speak of a change of hand since such a shift is obvious to the reader. Paul, however, knows that his letters will be read in public worship, where the size of the group prevents everyone from seeing the change in handwriting styles, and so he frequently makes an explicit reference to the closing material that he has written "in my own hand."

But while the autograph greeting in the first half of verse 17 follows expected Pauline practice, the addition of an explanatory comment in the second half is unique and striking: "which is a sign in every letter; this is the way I write" (ὅ ἐστιν σημεῖον ἐν πάσῃ ἐπιστολῇ οὕτως γράφω, *ho estin sēmeion en pasē epistolē; houtōs graphō*). Two questions need to be answered: To what does the "sign" refer? What is Paul trying to signal to the Thessalonian readers by this sign?

On the first question, the sign could refer either to the greeting itself or to the fact that the greeting is written in Paul's own hand. The former option must be rejected on grammatical grounds, given that the relative pronoun *ho* that introduces this clause is neuter and so refers not to the masculine noun "greeting" but to the whole clause. Additionally, the greeting formula, whether in its verbal or noun form, is *not* found in every letter of the apostle. The "sign," therefore, has in view the handwritten script of Paul. The phrase that concludes this explanatory comment supports this interpretation, since "this is the way I write" (*houtōs graphō*) refers to the *manner* in which Paul closes his letters (i.e., with an autograph) and not to the *content* of his closing (i.e., with a greeting). The prepositional phrase "in every letter" suggests, therefore, that Paul always ends his letters with an autograph statement and that this fact should be assumed to be true even in those letters that make no such explicit reference to the apostle's own handwriting.[5] Thus, for example, it is most probable that in the closing of his previous letter to the Thessalonians, Paul also takes over from the secretary, likely at 5:27, where he pens in his own hand a command written no longer with the literary plural but the singular ("I cause you to swear an oath"). This is certainly true of the closing of Galatians—another Pauline letter likely already written by this time—where Paul opens the final section of this correspondence by stating, "See with what large letters I write to you in my own hand" (Gal. 6:11).

On the second question, the vast majority of commentators believe that with his handwritten "sign" Paul intends to signal the authenticity of this letter. The possible existence of a forged correspondence claiming to be from Paul and his fellow workers (2:2) has caused the apostle to write part of the closing in his own hand, thereby establishing the letter's genuineness. This interpretation leads F. W. Danker, for example, to render the explanatory clause as "this is the mark *of genuineness* in every letter" (BDAG 920.1, emphasis added).

---

5. This conclusion receives further support from the secular papyrus letters of that day, the vast majority of which indicate that the sender closed the correspondence in his own hand without expressly saying so (see the examples and discussion in Weima 1994a: 45–50). Recognizing the weight of these parallels, Deissmann (1910: 158–59) concluded that it would be begging the question to assume that Paul "only finished off with his own hand those letters in which he expressly says that he did."

A couple of factors, however, suggest a different or at least additional purpose. First, a closing autograph in letters of that day functioned not just to authenticate a letter but also to accomplish a variety of different purposes, such as to make a letter legally binding, to give a letter a more personal touch, to ensure confidentiality (Weima 1994a: 48–50). Paul's autographs, therefore, should not be limited to only one possible function (to establish a letter's authenticity) but rather can serve various purposes, depending on the specific context and concern at work in any given letter. Second, there is strong evidence that Paul suspects the source of the false teaching about the day of the Lord to be not from a letter supposedly from him but from a prophecy claiming his authority (see comments on 2 Thess. 2:2, 15). This in turn suggests that the apostle in this letter closing is not concerned primarily with establishing the authenticity of the current letter. Another possibility is that the autograph makes Paul's presence more powerfully experienced by the Thessalonian readers and thus enhances the letter's *authority*. The mention of his handwritten greeting as a distinguishing sign in all his letters not only evokes more vividly in the readers' mind the image of the apostle writing to them but also makes his words harder to ignore. As Menken (1994: 144) notes, the autograph "serves to suggest the personal, authoritative presence of the apostle in the letter." Witherington (2006: 263) similarly observes that "the final words in one's own hand is an indirect means of asserting that what is in this letter has the authority of Paul himself and must be taken seriously."[6] The apostle may have in view especially the rebellious idlers and anticipate that not all of them will obey his command to be engaged in self-sufficient work (recall the first-class condition of 3:14).

D. Grace Benediction (3:18)

3:18 The letter closing comes to a definitive end with a grace benediction that, along with the peace benediction of verse 16, forms an inverted, or chiastic, inclusio; thereby the salutation "grace and peace" of the letter opening (1:2) paired with "peace" (3:16) and "grace" (v. 18) frames the boundaries of the letter: "May the grace of our Lord Jesus Christ be with you all" (ἡ χάρις τοῦ κυρίου ἡμῶν Ἰησοῦ Χριστοῦ μετὰ πάντων ὑμῶν, *hē charis tou kyriou hēmōn Iēsou Christou meta pantōn hymōn*).

The grace benediction is not only the most common epistolary convention of Paul's letter closings (it ends every one of the apostle's letters) but also the most formally consistent. It exhibits a striking uniformity (see table 1 in Weima 1994a: 80), consisting of three basic elements: the wish, the divine source, and

6. An authoritative function for the autograph greeting is also acknowledged by others: Marshall (1983: 232): "It seems more probable that Paul's purpose is to emphasize the authority and authenticity of this letter rather than to deny the authenticity of other alleged letters of his"; Holmes (1998: 277): "The apostolic signature also lends a note of authority, reinforcing the tone of 3:6–15"; and Wanamaker (1990: 292): "Paul wrote v. 17 to underscore the authority of the letter for its recipients."

the recipient (for a fuller description of each of these elements, see comments on 1 Thess. 5:28). The formal consistency of this epistolary convention accentuates the one way in which the grace benediction of 2 Thess. 3:18 is unique: the addition of the adjective "all" to the recipients of the wish. Further evidence that this addition is not fortuitous but deliberate and thus significant (contra Best 1977: 348, who states: "little emphasis should be laid on the addition"; also Malherbe 2000: 463; Furnish 2007: 183) lies in the fact that a similar addition takes place in the word of encouragement in verse 16b: Paul takes the common Jewish greeting "May the Lord be with you" and expands it to read "May the Lord be with you *all*." With this same addition the apostle stresses that his prayer for the Lord's grace to be with them includes all the members of the Thessalonian church, both the majority who are fearful in the face of outside opposition (1:3–12) and of end-time confusion (2:1–17), as well as the minority whose rebelliously idle behavior requires disciplinary action (3:1–15). As Fee (2009: 342–43) states, "This [the addition of "all"] seems to be yet another way (subtle perhaps, but real nonetheless) of embracing the entire community in the concluding grace. Looked at in this way, it is perhaps his own offering of the right hand of fellowship to some who otherwise need correction in order to be part of the 'all.'"

Additional Note

3:16. Although the reading "in every *way*" (τρόπῳ) enjoys strong support (ℵ Aᶜ B Dᶜ K P Ψ 𝔐 81 614 1739 sy co), several MSS, including the important Alexandrinus, have the reading "in every *place*" (τόπῳ: A* D* F G 33 76 itᵈ·ᵍ·⁶¹·⁸⁶ vg goth Ambst Chr). This variation involves only one letter in Greek and so likely was an accidental change from the rarer "way" (13x in the NT; no other use of the precise prepositional phrase "in every way" [but see Rom. 3:2 and Phil. 1:18]) to the more common "place" (94x in the NT; 4 occurrences of the fuller prepositional phrase "in every place": 1 Cor. 1:2; 2 Cor. 2:14; 1 Thess. 1:8; 1 Tim. 2:8). The context also supports the reading "in every way" (contra Lightfoot 1904: 135).

Works Cited

BD The Anchor Bible Dictionary. Edited by D. N. Freedman et al. 6 vols. New York: Doubleday, 1992.

hn, J. Y.-S.
1989 "The Parousia in Paul's Letters to the Thessalonians, the Corinthians, and the Romans, in Relation to Its Old Testament Judaic Background." PhD diss., Fuller Theological Seminary.

ford, H.
1865 "The First Epistle to the Thessalonians." Vol. 3 / pp. 248–83 of The Greek New Testament. 4th ed. London: Rivingtons.

nphoux, C. B.
2003 "1 Th 2,14–16: Quel Juifs sont-ils mis en cause par Paul?" Filología neotestamentaria 16:85–101.

NRW Aufstieg und Niedergang der römischen Welt. Edited by H. Temporini and W. Haase. Part 2: Principat. Berlin: de Gruyter, 1972–.

th. Pal. Epigrammatum anthologia Palatina. Edited by F. Dübner, P. Waltz, et al. Paris: Firmin-Didot; et al., 1864–.

cough, R.
2003 Paul's Macedonian Associations: The Social Context of Philippians and 1 Thessalonians. Tübingen: Mohr Siebeck.

ne, D. E.
1987 The New Testament in Its Literary Environment. Library of Early Christianity 8. Philadelphia: Westminster.
1989 "Trouble in Thessalonica: An Exegetical Study of I Thess 4:9–12, 5:12–14 and II Thess 3:6–15 in Light of First-Century Social Conditions." Master's thesis, Regent College.

s, R. D.
1971 "Comfort in Judgment: The Use of the Day of the Lord and Theophany Traditions in Second Thessalonians 1." PhD diss., Yale University.

1973 "The Liturgical Background of the Necessity and Propriety of Giving Thanks according to 2 Thessalonians 1:3." Journal of Biblical Literature 92:432–38.
1976 "Relevance of Isaiah 66:7 to Revelation 12 and 2 Thessalonians 1." Zeitschrift für die neutestamentliche Wissenschaft 67:252–68.
1977 "God's Plan and God's Power: Isaiah 66 and the Restraining Factors of 2 Thess. 2:6–7." Journal of Biblical Literature 96:537–53.

Baarda, T.
1984 "'Maar de torn is over hen gekomen' (1 Thess. 2:16c)." Pp. 15–74 in Paulus en de andere Joden: exegetische bijdragen en discussie. Edited by H. Jansen, S. J. Noorda, and J. S. Vos. Delft: Meinema.
1985 "1 Thess 2:14–16: Rodrigues in 'Nestle-Aland.'" Nederlands theologisch tijdschrift 39/3:186–93.

Bacon, B. W.
1922 "Wrath 'unto the Uttermost.'" The Expositor, 8th series, 24:356–76.

Bahr, G. J.
1968 "Subscriptions in the Pauline Letters." Journal of Biblical Literature 87/1:27–41.

Bailey, J. A.
1978–79 "Who Wrote II Thessalonians?" New Testament Studies 25:131–45.

Bailey, J. W., and J. W. Clarke
1955 "The First and Second Epistles to the Thessalonians." Vol. 11 / pp. 243–339 in The Interpreter's Bible. Edited by G. A. Buttrick. 12 vols. Nashville: Abingdon.

Baltensweiler, H.
1963 "Erwägungen zu I Thess 4:3–8." Theologische Zeitschrift 19/1:1–13.
1967 Die Ehe im Neuen Testament: Exegetische Untersuchungen über Ehe, Ehelosigkeit und Ehescheidung. Abhandlungen zur Theologie des Alten und Neuen Testaments 52. Zurich: Zwingli Verlag.

Bammel, E.
1959   "Judenverfolgung und Naherwartung: Zur Eschatologie des ersten Thessalonicherbriefs." *Zeitschrift für Theologie und Kirche* 56/3:294–315.

Barclay, J. M. G.
1987   "Mirror-Reading a Polemical Letter: Galatians as a Test Case." *Journal for the Study of the New Testament* 31:73–93.

1993   "Conflict in Thessalonica." *Catholic Biblical Quarterly* 55:512–30.

Barnouin, M.
1977   "Les problems de traduction concernant II Thess. II.6–7." *New Testament Studies* 23:482–98.

Barrett, C. K.
1998   *A Critical and Exegetical Commentary on the Acts of the Apostles.* 2 vols. International Critical Commentary. Edinburgh: T&T Clark.

Bassler, J. M.
1984   "The Enigmatic Sign: 2 Thessalonians 1:5." *Catholic Biblical Quarterly* 46/3:496–510.

1991   "Peace in All Ways: Theology in the Thessalonian Letters; A Response to R. Jewett, E. Krentz, and E. Richard." Vol. 1 / pp. 71–85 in *Pauline Theology.* Edited by J. M. Bassler, D. M. Hay, and E. E. Johnson. Minneapolis: Fortress.

Baumert, N.
1987   "*Homeiromenoi* in 1 Thess 2:8." *Biblica* 68/4:552–63.

1992   "'Wir lassen uns nicht beirren.' Semantische Fragen in 1 Thess 3,2f." *Filología Neotestamentaria* 5:45–60.

Baur, F. C.
1845   *Paulus: Der Apostel Jesu Christi.* Stuttgart: Becher & Müller.

1855   "Die beiden Briefe an die Thessalonicher, Ihre Echtheit und Bedeutung für die Lehre de Parusi Christie." *Theologische Jahrbücher* 14:141–68.

1875   *Paul, the Apostle of Jesus Christ: His Life and Work, His Epistles and His Doctrine,* vol. 2. Translated by E. Zeller. Edited by A. Menzies. 2nd ed. London: Williams & Norgate.

BDAG   *A Greek-English Lexicon of the New Testament and Other Early Christian Literature.* By W. Bauer, F. W. Danker, W. F. Arndt, and F. W. Gingrich. 3rd ed. Chicago: University of Chicago Press, 2000.

BDF   *A Greek Grammar of the New Testament and Other Early Christian Literature.* By F. Blass and A. Debrunner. Translated and revised by R. W. Funk. Chicago: University of Chicago Press, 1961.

Beale, G. K.
2003   *1–2 Thessalonians.* IVP New Testament Commentary Series. Downers Grove, IL: InterVarsity.

Beasley-Murray, G. R.
1954   *Jesus and the Future: An Examination of the Criticism of the Eschatological Discourse, Mark 13, with Special Reference to the Little Apocalypse Theory.* London: Macmillan.

Beauvery, R.
1955   "ΠΛΕΟΝΕΚΤΕΙΝ in 1 Thess 4,6a." *Verbum domini* 33:78–85.

Beck, N. A.
1985   *Mature Christianity: The Recognition and Repudiation of the Anti-Jewish Polemic of the New Testament.* Selinsgrove, PA: Susquehanna University Press.

Becker, J.
1976   *Auferstehung der Toten im Urchristentum.* Stuttgart: KBW Verlag.

Beker, J. C.
1980   *Paul the Apostle: The Triumph of God in Life and Thought.* Philadelphia: Fortress.

Benko, S.
1984   "The Kiss." Pp. 79–102 in *Pagan Rome and the Early Christians.* By S. Benko. Bloomington: Indiana University Press.

Benson, G. P.
1996   "Note on 1 Thessalonians 1.6." *Expository Times* 107:143–44.

Berger, K.
1974   "Apostelbrief und apostolische Rede: Zum Formular frühchristlicher Briefe." *Zeitschrift für die neutestamentliche Wissenschaft* 65:190–231.

Berkhof, H.
1966   *Christ the Meaning of History.* Translated by L. Buurman. Richmond, VA: John Knox.

Best, E.
1977   *A Commentary on the First and Second Epistles to the Thessalonians.* Reprinted with additional bibliography. Black's New Testament Commentaries. London: Black.

Bienert, W.
1954　　*Die Arbeit nach der Lehre der Bibel: Eine Grundlegung evangelischer Sozialethik.* Stuttgart: Evangelisches Verlagswerk.

Bjerkelund, C. J.
1967　　*Parakalô: Form, Funktion und Sinn der parakalô-Sätze in den paulinischen Briefen.* Oslo: Universitetsforlaget.

Black, D. A.
1982　　"The Weak in Thessalonica: A Study in Pauline Lexicography." *Journal of the Evangelical Theological Society* 25/3:307–21.

Bock, D. L.
2007　　*Acts.* Baker Exegetical Commentary on the New Testament. Grand Rapids: Baker Academic.

Bockmuehl, M. N. A.
1991　　"'The Trumpet Shall Sound': *Shofar* Symbolism and Its Reception in Early Christianity." Pp. 199–225 in *Templum Amicitiae: Essays on the Second Temple Presented to Ernst Bammel.* Edited by W. Horbury. Journal for the Study of the New Testament: Supplement Series 48. Sheffield: JSOT Press.

Boer, W. P. de
1962　　*The Imitation of Paul: An Exegetical Study.* Kampen: Kok.

Boers, H.
1975–76　"The Form Critical Study of Paul's Letters: I Thessalonians as a Case Study." *New Testament Studies* 22/2:140–58.

Bornemann, W.
1894　　*Die Thessalonicherbriefe.* Göttingen: Vandenhoeck & Ruprecht.

Bornkamm, G.
1971　　*Paul.* New York: Harper & Row.

Boyer, J. L.
1987　　"The Classification of Imperatives: A Statistical Study." *Grace Theological Journal* 8:35–54.

Bradley, D. G.
1953　　"The 'Topos' as a Form in the Pauline Paraenesis." *Journal of Biblical Literature* 72:238–46.

Bradley, K. R.
1986　　"Wet-Nursing at Rome: A Study in Social Relations." Pp. 201–29 in *The Family in Ancient Rome: New Perspectives.* Edited by B. Rawson. Ithaca, NY: Cornell University Press.

Bristol, L. O.
1943–44　"Paul's Thessalonian Correspondence." *Expository Times* 55:223.

Brocke, C. vom
2001　　*Thessaloniki—Stadt des Kassander und Gemeinde des Paulus: Eine frühe christliche Gemeinde in ihrer heidnischen Umwelt.* Wissenschaftliche Untersuchungen zum Neuen Testament 2/125. Tübingen: Mohr Siebeck.

Broer, I.
1983　　"'Antisemitismus' und Judenpolemik im Neuen Testament: Ein Beitrag zum besseren Verständnis von 1 Thess 2:14–16." *Biblische Notizen: Beiträge zur exegetischen Diskussion* 20:59–91.

Bruce, F. F.
1977　　*Paul: Apostle of the Heart Set Free.* Grand Rapids: Eerdmans.
1979　　"St. Paul in Macedonia." *Bulletin of the John Rylands University Library* 61/2:337–54.
1982　　*1 & 2 Thessalonians.* Word Biblical Commentary. Waco: Word Books.

Brunot, A.
1985　　*Le génie littéraire de saint Paul.* Lectio divina 15. Paris: Cerf.

Buck, C., and G. Taylor
1969　　*Saint Paul: A Study in the Development of His Thought.* New York: Scribners.

Burke, T. J.
2000　　"Pauline Paternity in 1 Thessalonians." *Tyndale Bulletin* 51/1:59–80.
2003　　*Family Matters: A Socio-Historical Study of Kinship Metaphors in I Thessalonians.* Journal for the Study of the New Testament: Supplement Series 247. London: T&T Clark.

Burton, E. D.
1898　　"The Politarchs." *American Journal of Theology* 2:598–632.

Bussman, C.
1971　　*Themen der paulinischen Missionspredigt auf dem Hintergrund des spätjüdisch-hellenistischen Missionsliteratur.* Bern: Herbert Lang.

Callow, J.
1982　　*A Semantic Structure Analysis of Second Thessalonians.* Dallas: Summer Institute of Linguistics.

Calvin, J.
1981　　*The Philippians, Colossians, and Thessalonians.* Grand Rapids: Baker.

Caragounis, C.
2002 "Parainesis on ΑΓΙΑΣΜΟΣ (1 Th 4:3–8)." *Filología neotestamentaria* 15:133–51.

Carras, G. P.
1990 "Jewish Ethics and Gentile Converts: Remarks on 1 Thes 4,3–8." Pp. 306–15 in *The Thessalonian Correspondence.* Edited by R. F. Collins. Bibliotheca ephemeridum theologicarum lovaniensium 87. Louvain: Leuven University Press.

Carson, D. A., and D. J. Moo
2005 *An Introduction to the New Testament.* 2nd ed. Grand Rapids: Zondervan.

Castelli, E. A.
1991 *Imitating Paul: A Discourse of Power.* Literary Currents in Biblical Interpretation. Louisville: Westminster/John Knox.

Cerfaux, L.
1925 "'Les Saints' de Jérusalem." *Ephemerides theologicae lovanienses* 2:510–29.
1959 *Christ in the Theology of St. Paul.* New York: Herder & Herder.

Chadwick, H.
1950 "1 Thess. 3:3: σαίνεσθαι." *Journal of Theological Studies* 1:156–58.

Champion, L. G.
1934 *Benedictions and Doxologies in the Epistles of Paul.* Oxford: Kemp Hall.

Chapa, J.
1994 "Is First Thessalonians a Letter of Consolation?" *New Testament Studies* 40/1:150–60.

CIG *Corpus inscriptionum graecarum.* Edited by A. Boeckh et al. 4 vols. Hildesheim: G. Olms Verlag, 1977.

CIJ *Corpus inscriptionum judaicarum.* Compiled by J.-B. Frey. Rome: Pontificio Institutu di Archeologia Christiana, 1936–. Reprinted as *Corpus of Jewish Inscriptions: Jewish Inscriptions from the Third Century B.C. to the Seventh Century A.D.* New York: Ktav, 1975.

CIL *Corpus inscriptionum latinarum.* Berlin: Reimer, 1862–.

Clark, K. W.
1940 "Realized Eschatology." *Journal of Biblical Literature* 59/3:367–83.

Clarke, A. D.
1998 "'Be Imitators of Me': Paul's Model of Leadership." *Tyndale Bulletin* 492.2:329–60.

Classen, C. J.
1994–95 "Philologische Bemerkungen zur Sprache des Apostles Paulus." *Wiener Studien* 107/8:321–35.
2000 *Rhetorical Criticism of the New Testament.* Tübingen: Mohr Siebeck.

Clemen, C. C.
1894 *Die Einheitlichkeit der paulinischen Briefe: An der Hand der bisher mit Bezug auf sie aufgestellten Interpolations- und Compilationshypothesen geprüft.* Göttingen: Vandenhoeck & Ruprecht.

Collins, R. F.
1983 "'This Is the Will of God: Your Sanctification' (1 Thess 4:3)." *Laval théologique et philosophique* 39:27–53.
1984 *Studies on the First Letter to the Thessalonians.* Bibliotheca ephemeridum theologicarum lovaniensium 66. Louvain: Leuven University Press.
1988 *Letters That Paul Did Not Write: The Epistle to the Hebrews and the Pauline Pseudepigrapha.* Good News Studies 28. Wilmington, DE: Glazier.
1993 *The Birth of the New Testament: The Origin and Development of the First Christian Generation.* New York: Crossroad.
1998 "The Function of Paraenesis in 1 Thess 4,1–12; 5,12–22." *Ephemerides theologicae lovanienses* 74/4:398–414.

Cosby, M. R.
1994 "Hellenistic Formal Receptions and Paul's Use of ΑΠΑΝΤΗΣΙΣ in 1 Thessalonians 4:17." *Bulletin for Biblical Research* 4:15–34.

Cranfield, C. E. B.
1979 "A Study of 1 Thessalonians 2." *Irish Biblical Studies* 1:215–26.

Crawford, C.
1973 "The 'Tiny' Problem of 1 Thessalonians 2:7: The Case of the Curious Vocative." *Biblica* 54/1:69–72.

Crüsemann, M.
2010 *Die pseudepigraphen Briefe an die Gemeinde in Thessaloniki: Studien zu ihrer Abfassung und zur jüdisch-christlichen Sozialgeschichte.* Beiträge zur Wissenschaft vom Alten und Neuen Testament 191. Stuttgart: Kohlhammer.

Cullmann, O.
1936 "Le caractère eschatologique du devoir missionaire et de la conscience apostolique de saint Paul: Étude sur le κατέχον (-ων) de 2. Thess.

2:6–7." *Revue de l'histoire des religions* 16:210–45.

Cumont, F.
1949   *Lux perpetua*. Paris: Geuthner.

Davies, W. D.
1948   *Paul and Rabbinic Judaism*. London: SPCK.
1977–78   "Paul and the People of Israel." *New Testament Studies* 24 (1977–78): 4–39.

Deidun, T. J.
1981   *New Covenant Morality in Paul*. Analecta biblica 89. Rome: Biblical Institute Press.

Deissmann, A.
1901   *Bible Studies: Contributions, Chiefly from Papyri and Inscriptions, to the History of the Language, the Literature, and the Religion of Hellenistic Judaism and Primitive Christianity*. Edinburgh: T&T Clark. 2nd ed., 1903.
1910   *Light from the Ancient East*. Translated by L. R. M. Strachan. London: Hodder & Stoughton.

Delobel, J.
1995   "One Letter Too Many in Paul's First Letter? A Study of (ν)ηπιοι in 1 Thess 2.7." *Louvain Studies* 20:126–33.

Denis, A.-M.
1957   "L'Apôtre Paul, prophète, 'messianique' des Gentils: Étude thématique de I Thess., II.1–6." *Ephemerides theologicae lovanienses* 33:245–318.

De Vos, C. S.
1999   *Church and Community Conflicts: The Relationships of the Thessalonian, Corinthian, and Philippian Churches with Their Wider Civic Communities*. Atlanta: Scholars Press.

Dibelius, M.
1913   *Die Briefe des Apostels Paulus: Die neun kleinen Briefe*. Handbuch zum Neuen Testament 3.2. Tübingen: Mohr Siebeck.
1937   *An die Thessalonicher I, II*. Handbuch zum Neuen Testament 11. Tübingen: Mohr.

Dix, G.
1945   *The Shape of the Liturgy*. Glasgow: Glasgow University Press.

Dixon, P. S.
1990   "The Evil Restraint in 2 Thess 2:6." *Journal of the Evangelical Theological Society* 33:445–49.

Dobschütz, E. von
1909   *Die Thessalonicherbriefe*. Kritisch-Exegetischer Kommentar über das Neue Testament 10. Göttingen: Vandenhoeck & Ruprecht.

Dodd, C. H.
1932   *The Epistle of Paul to the Romans*. Moffatt New Testament Commentary. New York: Harper & Row.

Donfried, K. P.
1984   "Paul and Judaism: 1 Thessalonians 2:13–16 as a Test Case." *Interpretation* 38:242–53.
1985   "The Cults of Thessalonica and the Thessalonian Correspondence." *New Testament Studies* 31/3:336–56.
1987   "The Kingdom of God in Paul." Pp. 175–90 in *The Kingdom of God in 20th-Century Interpretation*. Edited by W. L. Willis. Peabody, MA: Hendrickson.
1991   "War Timotheus in Athen? Exegetische Überlegungen zu 1 Thess 3,1–3." Pp. 189–96 in *Die Freude an Gott—unsere Kraft: Festschrift für Otto Bernhard Knoch zum 65. Geburtstag*. Edited by J. J. Degenhardt. Stuttgart: Katholisches Bibelwerk.
1993a   "The Theology of 1 and 2 Thessalonians." Pp. 1–113 in *The Theology of the Shorter Pauline Letters*. Edited by J. D. G. Dunn. New Testament Theology. Cambridge: Cambridge University Press.
1993b   "2 Thessalonians and the Church of Thessalonica." Pp. 128–44 in *Origins and Method: Towards a New Understanding of Judaism and Christianity; Essays in Honour of John C. Hurd*. Edited by B. H. McLean. Journal for the Study of the New Testament: Supplement Series 86. Sheffield: JSOT Press.
1997   "The Imperial Cults of Thessalonica and Political Conflict in 1 Thessalonians." Pp. 215–23 in *Paul and Empire: Religion and Power in Roman Imperial Society*. Edited by R. A. Horsley. Harrisburg, PA: Trinity.
2002   *Paul, Thessalonica, and Early Christianity*. Grand Rapids: Eerdmans.

Doty, W. G.
1973   *Letters in Primitive Christianity*. Philadelphia: Fortress.

DPL   *Dictionary of Paul and His Letters*. Edited by G. F. Hawthorne and R. P.

Martin. Downers Grove, IL: InterVarsity, 1993.

Dunham, D. A.
1981   "2 Thessalonians 1:3–10: A Study in Sentence Structure." *Journal of the Evangelical Theological Society* 24:39–46.

Dunn, J. D. G.
1988   *Romans.* 2 vols. Word Biblical Commentary. Dallas: Word.
1998   *The Theology of Paul the Apostle.* Grand Rapids: Eerdmans.

Dupont, J.
1952   "'Avec le Seigneur' a la Parousie." Pp. 39–79 in ΣΥΝ ΧΡΙΣΤΩΙ: *L'union avec le Christ suivant Saint Paul.* Paris: Desclée de Brouwer.

Eadie, J.
1877   *A Commentary on the Greek Text of the Epistles of Paul to the Thessalonians.* Edited by W. Young. London: Macmillan.

Eckart, K.-G.
1961   "Der zweite echte Brief des Apostels Paulus an die Thessalonicher: Ernst Fuchs, dem Scheidenden, zum 'Andenken.'" *Zeitschrift für Theologie und Kirche* 58/1:30–44.

Edgar, T. R.
1979   "The Meaning of 'Sleep' in 1 Thessalonians 5:10." *Journal of the Evangelical Theological Society* 22:345–49.

Edson, C.
1940   "Macedonia." *Harvard Studies in Classical Philology* 51:125–36.
1948   "Cults of Thessalonica (Macedonia III)." *Harvard Theological Review* 41/3:153–204.

Elderen, B. van
1961   "The Pauline Use of the Participle." PhD diss., Pacific School of Religion.
1967   "The Verb in the Epistolary Invocation." *Calvin Theological Journal* 2:46–48.

Elgvin, T.
1997   "'To Master His Own Vessel': 1 Thess 4:4 in Light of New Qumran Evidence." *New Testament Studies* 43/4:604–19.

Elias, J. W.
1995   *First and Second Thessalonians.* Believers Church Bible Commentary. Scottdale, PA: Herald.

Ellicott, C. J.
1864   *A Critical and Grammatical Commentary on St. Paul's Epistles to the Thessalonians: With a Revised Translation.* 2nd ed. Andover, MA: Draper.
1880   *St. Paul's Epistles to the Thessalonians: With a Critical and Grammatical Commentary, and a Revised Translation.* 4th ed. London: Longman.

Ellingworth, P.
1974   "Which Way Are We Going? A Verb of Movement, Especially in 1 Thess 4:14b." *Bible Translator* 25/4:426–31.

Ellingworth, P., and E. A. Nida
1975   *A Translator's Handbook on Paul's Letters to the Thessalonians.* Helps for Translators 17. Stuttgart: United Bible Societies.

Ellis, E. E.
1978   *Prophecy and Hermeneutic in Early Christianity.* Grand Rapids: Eerdmans.

English, E. S.
1954   *Re-thinking the Rapture.* Travelers Rest, SC: Southern Bible Book House.

Erhardt, A.
1969   *The Acts of the Apostles.* Manchester: Manchester University Press.

Esler, P.
2000   "2 Thessalonians." Pp. 1213–20 in *The Oxford Bible Commentary.* Edited by J. Barton and J. Muddiman. Oxford: Oxford University Press.

Evans, C. A.
1993   "Ascending and Descending with a Shout: Psalm 47.6 [47.5 ET = 46.6 LXX] and 1 Thessalonians 4.16." Pp. 238–53 in *Paul and the Scriptures of Israel.* Edited by C. A. Evans and J. A. Sanders. Journal for the Study of the New Testament: Supplement Series 83. Studies in Early Judaism and Christianity 1. Sheffield: JSOT Press.

Evans, R. M.
1968   *Eschatology and Ethics: A Study of Thessalonica and Paul's Letters to the Thessalonians.* Princeton, NJ: McMahon.

Exler, F. X. J.
1923   "The Form of the Ancient Greek Letter: A Study in Greek Epistolography." PhD diss., Catholic University of America.

Fanning, B. M.
1990   *Verbal Aspect in New Testament Greek.* Oxford: Clarendon.

Farrow, D.
1989   "Showdown: The Message of Second Thessalonians 2:1–12 and the Riddle of the 'Restrainer.'" *Crux* 25/1:23–26.

Faulkenberry Miller, J. B.
1999   "Infants and Orphans in 1 Thessalonians: A Discussion of ἀπορφανίζω and the Text-Critical Problem in 1 Thess. 2:7." Paper presented at the annual meeting of the Society of Biblical Literature, Boston.

Faw, C. E.
1952   "On the Writing of First Thessalonians." *Journal of Biblical Literature* 71:217–25.

Fee, G. D.
1992   "On Text and Commentary on 1 and 2 Thessalonians." Pp. 165–83 in *SBL 1992 Seminar Papers*. Edited by E. H. Lovering Jr. Atlanta: Scholars Press.
1994a   *God's Empowering Presence: The Holy Spirit in the Letters of Paul.* Peabody, MA: Hendrickson.
1994b   "Pneuma and Eschatology in 2 Thessalonians 2.1–2: A Proposal about 'Testing the Prophets' and the Purpose of 2 Thessalonians." Pp. 196–215 in *To Tell the Mystery: Essays on New Testament Eschatology in Honor of Robert H. Gundry.* Edited by T. E. Schmidt and M. Silva. Journal for the Study of the New Testament: Supplement Series 100. Sheffield: JSOT Press.
2007   *Pauline Christology: An Exegetical-Theological Study.* Peabody, MA: Hendrickson.
2009   *The First and Second Letters to the Thessalonians.* New International Commentary on the New Testament. Grand Rapids: Eerdmans.

Ferguson, E.
1982   "Canon Muratori: Date and Provenance." *Studia Patristica* 18:677–83.
1993   *Backgrounds of Early Christianity.* 2nd ed. Grand Rapids: Eerdmans.
2009   *Backgrounds of Early Christianity.* 3rd ed. Grand Rapids: Eerdmans.

Findlay, G. G.
1891   *The Epistles to the Thessalonians.* Cambridge Bible for Schools and Colleges. Cambridge: Cambridge University Press.

Fiore, B.
1986   *The Function of Personal Example in the Socratic and Pastoral Epistles.*

Analecta Biblica. Rome: Biblical Institute Press.

Fitzmyer, J. A.
1968   "New Testament Epistles." Vol. 2 / pp. 223–26 in *The Jerome Biblical Commentary.* Edited by R. E. Brown et al. Englewood Cliffs, NJ: Prentice-Hall.
1998   *The Acts of the Apostles: A New Translation with Introduction and Commentary.* Anchor Bible 31. New York: Doubleday.

Focant, C.
1990   "Les fils du Jour (1 Thes 5,5)." Pp. 348–55 in *The Thessalonian Correspondence.* Edited by R. F. Collins. Bibliotheca ephemeridum theologicarum lovaniensium 87. Louvain: Leuven University Press.

Ford, D.
1979   *The Abomination of Desolation in Biblical Eschatology.* Washington, DC: University Press of America.

Förster, G.
1916   "1 Thessalonicher 5,1–10." *Zeitschrift für die neutestamentliche Wissenschaft* 17:169–77.

Foster, P.
2012   "Who Wrote 2 Thessalonians? A Fresh Look at an Old Problem." *Journal for the Study of the New Testament* 35:150–75.

Fowl, S. E.
1990   *The Story of Christ in the Ethics of Paul: An Analysis of the Function of the Hymnic Material in the Pauline Corpus.* Journal for the Study of the New Testament: Supplement Series 36. Sheffield: JSOT Press.

Fraikin, D.
1974   "Note on the Sanctuary of the Egyptian Gods in Thessaloniki." *Numina Aegaea* 1:1–6.

Frame, J. E.
1911   "Οἱ Ἄτακτοι (1 Thes. 5.14). Pp. 191–206 in *Essays in Modern Theology and Related Subjects: Gathered and Published as a Testimonial to Charles A. Briggs.* New York: Scribners.
1912   *A Critical and Exegetical Commentary on the Epistles of St. Paul to the Thessalonians.* International Critical Commentary. Edinburgh: T&T Clark.

Fredriksen, P.
1991   "Judaism, the Circumcision of Gentiles, and Apocalyptic Hope: Another Look

at Galatians 1 and 2." *Journal of Theological Studies* 42:532–64.

Friedrich, G.
1965 "Ein Tauflied hellenistischer Judenchristen: 1 Thess 1:9f." *Theologische Zeitschrift* 21/6:502–16.
1973 "1 Thessalonicher 5:1–11: Der apologetische Einschub eines Späteren." *Zeitschrift für Theologie und Kirche* 70/3:288–315.
1976 "Der Erste Brief an die Thessalonicher und der Zweite Brief an die Thessalonicher." Pp. 203–76 in *Die Briefe an die Galater, Epheser, Philipper, Kolosser, Thessalonicher, und Philemon.* By J. Becker, H. Conzelmann, and G. Friedrich. Das Neue Testament Deutsch 8. Göttingen: Vandenhoeck & Ruprecht.

Fulford, H. W. (ed.)
1911 *The Epistles of Paul the Apostle to the Thessalonians, 1, 2 Timothy, Titus: Revised Version Edited for the Use of Schools.* Cambridge: Cambridge University Press.

Funk, R. W.
1967 "The Apostolic Parousia: Form and Significance." Pp. 249–68 in *Christian History and Interpretation: Studies Presented to John Knox.* Edited by W. R. Farmer, J. Knox, C. F. D. Moule, et al. Cambridge: Cambridge University Press.

Furfey, P. H.
1946 "The Mystery of Lawlessness." *Catholic Biblical Quarterly* 8:179–91.

Furnish, V. P.
2007 *1 Thessalonians, 2 Thessalonians.* Abingdon New Testament Commentaries. Nashville: Abingdon.

Gaebler, H.
1935 *Die antiken Münzen Nord-Griechenlands,* vol. 3: *Makedonia und Paionia.* Berlin: G. Reimer.

Gager, J. G.
1983 *The Origins of Anti-Semitism: Attitudes toward Judaism in Pagan and Christian Antiquity.* Oxford: Oxford University Press.

Gamble, H., Jr.
1977 *The Textual History of the Letter to the Romans.* Grand Rapids: Eerdmans.

Gardner, R.
1958 *Cicero,* vol. 13: *Orations: Pro Caelio; De provinciis consularibus; Pro Balbo.*

Loeb Classical Library 447. Cambridge, MA: Harvard University Press.

Gauthier, P., and M. B. Hatzopoulos
1993 *La loi gymnasiarchique de Béroia.* Μελετήματα 16. Athens: de Boccard.

Gaventa, B. R.
1986 "Galatians 1 and 2: Autobiography as Paradigm." *Novum Testamentum* 28/4:309–26.
1991 "Apostles as Babes and Nurses in 1 Thessalonians 2:7." Pp. 193–207 in *Faith and History: Essays in Honor of Paul W. Meyer.* Edited by J. T. Carroll, C. H. Cosgrove, and E. E. Johnson. Atlanta: Scholars Press.
1998 *First and Second Thessalonians.* Interpretation. Louisville: John Knox.

Gempf, C.
1994 "The Imagery of Labor Pangs in the New Testament." *Tyndale Bulletin* 45:119–35.

Gerhardsson, B.
1961 *Memory and Manuscript: Oral and Written Transmission in Rabbinic Judaism and Early Christianity.* Translated by E. J. Sharpe. Acta seminarii neotestamentici upsaliensis 22. Uppsala: Gleerup.

Getty, M. A.
1990 "The Imitation of Paul in the Letters to the Thessalonians." Pp. 277–83 in *The Thessalonian Correspondence.* Edited by R. F. Collins. Bibliotheca ephemeridum theologicarum lovaniensium 87. Louvain: Leuven University Press.

Giblin, C. H.
1967 *The Threat to Faith: An Exegetical and Theological Reexamination of 2 Thessalonians 2.* Analecta biblica 31. Rome: Pontifical Biblical Institute.
1990 "2 Thessalonians 2 Re-read as Pseudepigraphical: A Revised Reaffirmation of *The Threat to Faith.*" Pp. 459–69 in *The Thessalonian Correspondence.* Edited by R. F. Collins. Bibliotheca ephemeridum theologicarum lovaniensium 87. Louvain: Leuven University Press.

Gilliard, F. D.
1989 "The Problem of the Antisemitic Comma between 1 Thessalonians 2:14 and 15." *New Testament Studies* 35/4:481–502.
1994 "Paul and the Killing of the Prophets in 1 Thess. 2:15." *Novum Testamentum* 36/3:259–70.

Gillman, J.

1985   "Signals of Transformation in 1 Thessalonians 4:13–18." *Catholic Biblical Quarterly* 47/2:263–81.

1990   "Paul's *Eisodos*: The Proclaimed and the Proclaimer (1 Thes 2,8)." Pp. 62–70 in *The Thessalonian Correspondence.* Edited by R. F. Collins. Bibliotheca ephemeridum theologicarum lovaniensium 87. Louvain: Leuven University Press.

Glasson, T. F.

1988   "Theophany and Parousia." *New Testament Studies* 34:259–70.

Goulder, M. D.

1992   "Silas in Thessalonica." *Journal for the Study of the New Testament* 48:87–106.

Green, G. L.

2002   *The Letters to the Thessalonians.* Pillar New Testament Commentary. Grand Rapids: Eerdmans.

Greer, R. A.

2010   *Theodore of Mopsuestia: The Commentaries on the Minor Epistles of Paul; Translated with an Introduction and Notes.* Atlanta: Society of Biblical Literature.

Gregson, R.

1966   "Solution to the Problems of the Thessalonian Epistles." *Evangelical Quarterly* 38/2:76–80.

Gribomont, J.

1979   "*Facti sumus parvuli*: La charge apostolique (1 Th 2,1–12)." Pp. 311–38 in *Paul de Tarse: Apôtre de notre temps.* Edited by A.-L. Descamps, L. de Lorenzi, and G. Benelli. Série monographique de "Benedictina": Section paulinienne 1. Rome: Abbaye de S. Paolo.

Grimm, C. L. W.

1850   "Die Echtheit der Briefe an die Thessalonicher, gegen D. Baur's Angriff vertheidigt." *Theologische Studien und Kritiken* 23:753–816.

Grimm-Thayer

    A Greek-English Lexicon of the New Testament: Being Grimm's Wilke's "Clavis Novi Testamenti." Translated, revised, and enlarged by J. H. Thayer. New York: American Book, 1889.

Grotius, H.

1640   *Commentatio ad loca quaedam N. Testamenti quae de Antichristo agunt, aut agere putantur, expendenda eruditis.* Amsterdam: Cornelium Blaeu.

Gschnitzer, F.

1973   "*Politarchēs.*" Pp. 483–500 in *Paulys Realencyclopädie der classischen Altertumswissenschaft.* Edited by G. Wissowa. Supplement 13. Munich: Druckenmüller.

Gundry, R. H.

1973   *The Church and the Tribulation.* Grand Rapids: Zondervan.

1987   "The Hellenization of Dominical Tradition and the Christianization of Jewish Tradition in the Eschatology of 1–2 Thessalonians." *New Testament Studies* 33:161–78.

1996   "A Brief Note on 'Hellenistic Formal Receptions and Paul's Use of ΑΠΑΝΤΗΣΙΣ in 1 Thessalonians 4:17.'" *Bulletin for Biblical Research* 6:39–41.

Gundry Volf, J. M.

1990   *Paul and Perseverance: Staying in and Falling Away.* Louisville: Westminster/John Knox.

Gunkel, H.

1979   *The Influence of the Holy Spirit.* Philadelphia: Fortress. Original German ed., 1888.

Hahneman, G. M.

1992   *The Muratorian Fragment and the Development of the Canon.* Oxford: Clarendon.

Hamann, H. P.

1953   "A Brief Exegesis of 2 Thess. 2:1–12 with Guidelines for the Application of the Prophecy Contained Therein." *Concordia Theological Monthly* 24:418–33.

Hannah, D. D.

1999   *Michael and Christ: Michael Traditions and Angel Christology in Early Christianity.* Tübingen: Mohr Siebeck.

2000   "The Angelic Restrainer of 2 Thessalonians 2.6–7." Pp. 28–45 in *Calling Time: Religion and Change at the Turn of the Millennium.* Edited by M. Percy. Sheffield: Sheffield Academic Press.

Harnack, A. von

1924   *Die Mission und Ausbreitung des Christentums in den ersten drei Jahrhunderten.* Leipzig: Hinrichs.

1962   *The Mission and Expansion of Christianity in the First Three Centuries.* Translated and edited by J. Moffatt. 2 vols. Harper Torch Books. New York: Harper.

Harnisch, W.
1973   *Eschatologische Existenz*. Göttingen: Vandenhoeck & Ruprecht.

Harrer, G. A.
1940   "Saul Who Also Is Called Paul." *Harvard Theological Review* 33:19–33.

Harris, J. R.
1898   "A Study in Letter-Writing." *The Expositor*, 5th series, 4:185–204.

Harrison, J. R.
2002   "Paul and the Imperial Gospel at Thessaloniki." *Journal for the Study of the New Testament* 25:71–96.

Hartman, L.
1966   *Prophecy Interpreted: The Formation of Some Jewish Apocalyptic Texts and of the Eschatological Discourse Mark 13 Par.* Coniectanea biblica: New Testament Series 1. Lund: Gleerup.

Haufe, G.
1985   "Reich Gottes bei Paulus und in der Jesustradition." *New Testament Studies* 31:467–72.

Havener, I.
1981   "The Pre-Pauline Christological Credal Formulae of 1 Thessalonians." Pp. 105–28 in *SBL Seminar Papers*. Society of Biblical Literature Seminar Papers 20. Chico, CA: Scholars Press.

Heikel, J. A.
1935   "1. Thess. 3,2." *Theologischen Studien und Kritiken* 106:316.

Heil, J. H.
2000   "Those Now 'Asleep' (Not Dead) Must Be 'Awakened' for the Day of the Lord in 1 Thess 5.9–10." *New Testament Studies* 46:464–71.

Helly, B.
1977   "Politarques, poliarques et politophylaques." Pp. 531–44 in *Ancient Macedonia II: Papers Read at the Second International Symposium Held at Thessaloniki, 19–24 August 1973.* Edited by M. Andronikou et al. Thessaloniki: Institute for Balkan Studies.

Hemberg, B.
1950   *Die Kabiren*. Uppsala: Almquist & Wiksells.

Hemer, C. J.
1985   "The Name of Paul." *Tyndale Bulletin* 36:179–83.
1989   *The Book of Acts in the Setting of Hellenistic History.* Edited by C. H. Gempf. Wissenschaftliche Untersuchungen zum Neuen Testament 49. Tübingen: Mohr.

Reprinted Winona Lake, IN: Eisenbrauns, 1990.

Hendriksen, W.
1955   *Exposition of I and II Thessalonians.* New Testament Commentary. Grand Rapids: Baker.

Hendrix, H. L.
1984   "Thessalonicans Honor Romans." ThD diss., Harvard University.
1986   "Beyond 'Imperial Cult' and 'Cults of Magistrates.'" Pp. 301–8 in *SBL Seminar Papers*. Edited by K. H. Richards. Atlanta: Scholars Press.
1987   "Thessalonica." Vol. 1 / pp. 1–49 in *Archaeological Resources for New Testament Studies: A Collection of Slides on Culture and Religion in Antiquity.* Edited by H. Koester and H. L. Hendrix. Philadelphia: Fortress.
1991   "Archaeology and Eschatology at Thessalonica." Pp. 107–18 in *The Future of Early Christians: Essays in Honor of Helmut Koester.* Edited by B. A. Pearson. Minneapolis: Fortress.

Hengel, M.
1966   "Die Synagogeninschrift von Stobi." *Zeitschrift für die neutestamentliche Wissenschaft* 57:145–83.

Henneken, B.
1969   *Verkündigung und Prophetie im Ersten Thessalonicherbrief: Ein Beitrag zur Theologie des Wortes Gottes.* Stuttgarter Bibelstudien 29. Stuttgart: Verlag Katholisches Bibelwerk.

Hewett, J. A.
1975–76   "1 Thessalonians 3.13." *Expository Times* 87:54–55.

Hilgenfeld, A. H.
1862   "Die beiden Briefe an die Thessalonicher, nach Inhalt und Ursprung." *Zeitschrift für wissenschaftliche Theologie* 5:225–64.

Hill, C. E.
1995   "The Debate over the Muratorian Fragment and the Development of the Canon." *Westminster Theological Journal* 57:437–52.

Hill, J. L.
1990   "Establishing the Church in Thessalonica." PhD diss., Duke University.

Hill, R. C. (trans.)
2001   "I and II Thessalonians." Vol. 2 / pp. 107–35 in *Commentary on the Letters of St. Paul.* By Theodoret, Bishop of

Cyrrhus. Brookline, MA: Holy Cross Orthodox Press.

Hobbs, H. H.
1971   "1–2 Thessalonians." Vol. 11 / pp. 257–98 in *The Broadman Bible Commentary*. Edited by C. J. Allen. Nashville: Broadman.

Hock, R. F.
1978   "Paul's Tentmaking and the Problem of His Social Class." *Journal of Biblical Literature* 97:555–64.
1979   "The Workshop as a Social Context for Paul's Missionary Preaching." *Catholic Biblical Quarterly* 41:438–50.
1980   *The Social Context of Paul's Ministry: Tentmaking and Apostleship*. Philadelphia: Fortress.

Hodges, Z. C.
1982   "The Rapture in 1 Thessalonians 5:1–11." Pp. 67–79 in *Walvoord: A Tribute*. Edited by D. K. Campbell. Chicago: Moody.

Hodgson, R., Jr.
1982   "1 Thess 4:1–12 and the Holiness Tradition (HT)." Pp. 199–215 in *SBL 1982 Seminar Papers*. Edited by K. H. Richards. SBL Seminar Papers 21. Chico, CA: Scholars Press.

Hofmann, J. C. K. von
1869   *Die heilige Schrift neuen Testaments*, vol. 1: *Der erste und zweite Brief Pauli an die Thessalonicher*. Nördlingen: C. H. Beck.

Holland, G. S.
1988   *The Tradition That You Received from Us: 2 Thessalonians in the Pauline Tradition*. Hermeneutische Untersuchungen zur Theologie 24. Tübingen: Mohr Siebeck.
1990   "'A Letter Supposedly from Us': A Contribution to the Discussion about the Authorship of 2 Thessalonians." Pp. 394–402 in *The Thessalonian Correspondence*. Edited by R. F. Collins. Bibliotheca ephemeridum theologicarum lovaniensium 87. Louvain: Leuven University Press.

Hollmann, G.
1904   "Die Unechtheit des zweiten Thessalonichrbriefs." *Zeitschrift für die neutestamentliche Wissenschaft* 5:28–38.

Holloway, J. O.
1992   *Peripateō as a Thematic Marker for Pauline Ethics*. San Francisco: Mellen Research University Press.

Holmes, M. W.
1998   *1 & 2 Thessalonians*. NIV Application Commentary. Grand Rapids: Zondervan.

Holmstrand, J.
1997   *Markers and Meaning in Paul: An Analysis of 1 Thessalonians, Philippians and Galatians*. Coniectanea biblica: New Testament Series 28. Stockholm: Almqvist & Wiksell International.

Holsten, C.
1877   "Zur Unechtheit des Ersten Briefes an die Thessalonicher und zur Abfassungszeit der Apokalypse." *Jahrbucher für Protestantische Theologie* 36:731–32.

Holtz, T.
1986   *Der erste Brief an die Thessalonicher*. Evangelisch-katholischer Kommentar zum Neuen Testament. Zurich: Benziger.
1991   "Paul and the Oral Gospel Tradition." Pp. 380–93 in *Jesus and the Oral Gospel Tradition*. Edited by H. Wansbrough. Sheffield: JSOT Press.
2000   "On the Background of 1 Thessalonians 2:1–12." Pp. 69–80 in *The Thessalonians Debate: Methodological Discord or Methodological Synthesis?* Edited by K. P. Donfried and J. Beutler. Grand Rapids: Eerdmans.

Hooker, M. D.
1996   "1 Thessalonians 1:9–10: A Nutshell—but What Kind of Nut?" Pp. 435–48 in *Geschichte—Tradition—Reflexion: Festschriften für Martin Hengel zum 70. Geburtstag*, vol. 3: *Frühes Christentum*. Edited by H. Cancik, H. Lichtenberger, and P. Schäfer. Tübingen: Mohr Siebeck.

Hopkins, K.
1983   *Death and Renewal*. Sociological Studies in Roman History 2. Cambridge: Cambridge University Press.

Horbury, W.
1982   "1 Thessalonians 2:3 as Rebutting the Charge of False Prophecy." *Journal of Theological Studies* 33/2:492–508.

Horsley, G. H. R.
1982   "Politarchs." Pp. 34–35 in *New Documents Illustrating Christianity*, vol. 2: *A Review of the Greek Inscriptions and Papyri published in 1977*. Liverpool: Liverpool University Press.
1994   "The Politarchs." Pp. 419–31 in *The Book of Acts in Its First Century Setting*, vol. 2: *The Book of Acts in Its*

Graeco-Roman Setting. Edited by D. W. J. Gill and C. Gempf. Grand Rapids: Eerdmans.

House, H. W.
1995   "Apostasia in 2 Thessalonians 2:3: Apostasy or Rapture?" Pp. 261–95 in *When the Trumpet Sounds.* Edited by T. Ice and T. J. Demy. Eugene, OR: Harvest House.

Howard, T. L.
1988   "The Literary Unity of 1 Thessalonians 4:13–5:11." *Grace Theological Journal* 9:163–90.

Hughes, F. W.
1989   *Early Christian Rhetoric and 2 Thessalonians.* Journal for the Study of the New Testament: Supplement Series 30. Sheffield: JSOT Press.
1990   "The Rhetoric of 1 Thessalonians." Pp. 94–116 in *The Thessalonian Correspondence.* Edited by R. F. Collins. Bibliotheca ephemeridum theologicarum lovaniensium 87. Louvain: Leuven University Press.

Hunter, A. M.
1961   *Paul and His Predecessors.* Philadelphia: Westminster.

Hurd, J. C.
1967   "Pauline Chronology and Pauline Theology." Pp. 225–48 in *Christian History and Interpretation: Studies Presented to John Knox.* Edited by W. R. Farmer, C. F. D. Moule, and R. R. Niebuhr. Cambridge: Cambridge University Press.
1968   "The Sequence of Paul's Letters." *Canadian Journal of Theology* 14:189–200.
1972   "Concerning the Structure of 1 Thessalonians." Paper presented at the Annual Meeting of the Society of Biblical Literature, Los Angeles, November.
1983   "Concerning the Authenticity of 2 Thessalonians." Paper presented at the Annual Meeting of the Society of Biblical Literature, Dallas, November.
1984   "The Jesus Whom Paul Preaches (Acts 19:10)." Pp. 73–89 in *From Jesus to Paul: Studies in Honour of Francis Wright Beare.* Edited by P. Richardson and J. C. Hurd. Waterloo, ON: Wilfrid Laurier University Press.

Hyldahl, N.
1972–73   "Jesus og joderne ifolge 1 Tess 2,14–16." *Svensk Exegetisk Arsbok* 37/38:238–54.

1980   "Auferstehung Christi—Auferstehung der Toten (1 Thess 4,13–18)." Pp. 119–35 in *Die Paulinische Literatur und Theologie: Anlässlich der 50. jährigen Gründungs-Feier der Universität von Aarhus.* Edited by S. Pedersen. Teologiske Studien 7. Århus: Forlaget Aros.

IG   *Inscriptiones graecae.* Editio minor. Berlin: de Gruyter, 1924–.

ILS   *Inscriptiones latinae selectee.* Edited by H. Dessau, 3 vols. Berlin: Weidmann, 1882–1916; plus various reprints.

ISBE   *International Standard Bible Encyclopedia.* Edited by G. W. Bromiley. Fully revised. 4 vols. Grand Rapids: Eerdmans, 1979–88.

IT   *Inscriptiones graecae,* vol. 10: *Inscriptiones Thessalonicae et viciniae.* Edited by C. Edson. Berlin: de Gruyter, 1972.

Jackson, H.
1904   "Prohibitions in Greek." *Classical Review* 18:262–63.

Jensen, J.
1978   "Does *Porneia* Mean Fornication? A Critique of Bruce Malina." *Novum Testamentum* 20/3:161–84.

Jeremias, J.
1958   *Unknown Sayings of Jesus.* London: SPCK.
1964   *Unknown Sayings of Jesus.* 2nd ed. London: SPCK.

Jervis, L. A.
1991   *The Purpose of Romans: A Comparative Letter Structure Investigation.* Library of New Testament Studies. Sheffield: JSOT Press.

Jewett, R.
1969   "Form and Function of the Homiletic Benediction." *Anglican Theological Review* 51/1:18–34.
1970–71   "The Agitators and the Galatian Congregation." *New Testament Studies* 17:198–212.
1971   *Paul's Anthropological Terms.* Leiden: Brill.
1972   "Enthusiastic Radicalism and the Thessalonian Correspondence." 1972 *Proceedings of the Society of Biblical Literature* 1:181–232.
1979   *A Chronology of Paul's Life.* Philadelphia: Fortress.
1986   *The Thessalonian Correspondence: Pauline Rhetoric and Millenarian Piety.*

Foundations and Facets. Philadelphia: Fortress.

Johanson, B. C.

1987   *To All the Brethren: A Text-Linguistic and Rhetorical Approach to 1 Thessalonians.* Coniectanea biblica: New Testament Series 16. Stockholm: Almqvist & Wiksell.

Johnson, L. T.

1992   *The Acts of the Apostles.* Collegeville, MN: Liturgical Press.

Johnson, S. E.

1941   "Notes and Comments (I Thess 2:16)." *Anglican Theological Review* 23:173–76.

Jowett, B.

1894   *The Epistles of St. Paul to the Thessalonians, Galatians and Romans.* Edited and condensed by L. Campbell. 3rd ed. London: Murray.

Judge, E. A.

1971   "The Decrees of Caesar at Thessalonica." *Reformed Theological Review* 30:1–7.

Jurgensen, H.

1994   "Awaiting the Return of Christ: A Re-examination of 1 Thessalonians 4.13–5.11 from a Pentecostal Perspective." *Journal of Pentecostal Theology* 4:81–113.

Kaye, B. N.

1975   "Eschatology and Ethics in 1 and 2 Thessalonians." *Novum Testamentum* 17/1:47–57.

Keener, C. S.

2012   *Acts: An Exegetical Commentary*, vol. 1: *Introduction and 1:1–2:47.* Grand Rapids: Baker Academic.

2014   *Acts: An Exegetical Commentary*, vol 3: *15:1–23:35.* Grand Rapids: Baker Academic.

Kelcy, R. C.

1963   "A Grammatical and Syntactical Analysis of 1 Thessalonians." PhD diss., Southwestern Baptist Theological Seminary.

Kemmler, D. W.

1975   *Faith and Human Reason: A Study of Paul's Method of Preaching as Illustrated by 1–2 Thessalonians and Acts 17,2–4.* Supplements to Novum Testamentum 50. Leiden: Brill.

Kennedy, H. A. A.

1904   *St. Paul's Conceptions of the Last Things.* London: Hodder & Stoughton.

Kim, C.-H.

1972   *Form and Structure of the Familiar Greek Letter of Recommendation.* Society of Biblical Literature Dissertation Series 4. Missoula, MT: Scholars Press.

Kim, S.

2002   "The Jesus Tradition in 1 Thess 4.13–5.11." *New Testament Studies* 48:225–42.

2005   "Paul's Entry (εἴσοδος) and the Thessalonians' Faith (1 Thessalonians 1–3)." *New Testament Studies* 51:37–47.

2008   *Christ and Caesar: The Gospel and the Roman Empire in the Writings of Paul and Luke.* Grand Rapids: Eerdmans.

Klassen, W.

1978   "Foundations for Pauline Sexual Ethics as Seen in I Thess. 4:1–8." Pp. 159–81 in *SBL 1978 Seminar Papers.* Edited by P. J. Achtemeier. Atlanta: Scholars Press.

Kloppenborg, J. S.

1993   "Philadelphia, Theodidaktos and the Dioscuri: Rhetorical Engagement in 1 Thessalonians 4:9–12." *New Testament Studies* 39/2:265–89.

Knox, A. D.

1924   "Τὸ μηδένα σαίνεσθαι ἐν ταῖς θλίψεσιν ταύταις (1 Thess. iii 3)." *Journal of Theological Studies* 25:290–91.

Knox, J.

1950   *Chapters in a Life of Paul.* Nashville: Abingdon.

Koester, H.

1979   "I Thessalonians—Experiment in Christian Writing." Pp. 33–44 in *Continuity and Discontinuity in Church History: Essays Presented to George Huston Williams on the Occasion of His 65th Birthday.* Edited by F. F. Church and T. George. Studies in the History of Christian Thought 19. Leiden: Brill.

1982   *Introduction to the New Testament,* vol. 2: *History and Literature of Early Christianity.* Philadelphia: Fortress.

1985   "The Text of 1 Thessalonians." Pp. 219–27 in *The Living Text: Essays in Honor of Ernest W. Saunders.* Edited by D. E. Groh and R. Jewett. Lanham, MD: University Press of America.

1990   "From Paul's Eschatology to the Apocalyptic Schemata of 2 Thessalonians." Pp. 441–58 in *The Thessalonian Correspondence.* Edited by R. F. Collins. Bibliotheca ephemeridum theologicarum lovaniensium 87. Louvain: Leuven University Press.

1997 "Imperial Ideology and Paul's Eschatology in 1 Thessalonians." Pp. 158–66 in *Paul and Empire*. Edited by R. A. Horsley. Harrisburg, PA: Trinity.

2007 *Paul and His World: Interpreting the New Testament in Its Context*. Minneapolis: Fortress.

Konstan, D., and I. Ramelli
2007 "The Syntax of ἐν Χριστῷ in 1 Thessalonians 4:16." *Journal of Biblical Literature* 126:579–93.

Koskenniemi, H.
1956 *Studien zur Idee und Phraseologie des griechischen Briefes bis 400 n. Chr.* Suomalaisen Tiedeakatemian toimituksia: Series B, 102/2. Helsinki: Akateeminen Kirjakauppa.

Koukouli-Chrysanthaki, C.
1981 "Politarchs in a New Inscription from Amphipolis." Pp. 229–41 in *Ancient Macedonian Studies in Honor of Charles F. Edson*. Edited by H. Dell. Thessaloniki: Institute for Balkan Studies.

Kramer, W. R.
1966 *Christ, Lord, Son of God*. Translated by B. Hardy. Studies in Biblical Theology 50. London: SCM.

Kreitzer, L. J.
1987 "The Parousia and the Final Judgment in Paul." Pp. 93–129 in *Jesus and God in Paul's Eschatology*. Journal for the Study of the New Testament: Supplement Series 19. Sheffield: JSOT Press.

Krodel, G. A.
1978 "2 Thessalonians." Pp. 73–96 in *Ephesians, Colossians, 2 Thessalonians, the Pastoral Epistles*. By J. P. Sampley et al. Philadelphia: Fortress.

1990 "The 'Religious Power of Lawlessness' (*Katechon*) as Precursor of the 'Lawless One' (*Anomos*): 2 Thess 2:6–7." *Currents in Theology and Mission* 17:440–46.

Kümmel, W. G.
1973 *Einleitung in das Neue Testament*. 17th rev. ed. Heidelberg: Quelle & Meyer.

1977 *Introduction to the New Testament*. Rev. and enlarged English ed. Translated by Howard Clark Kee from the 16th rev. German ed. Nashville: Abingdon.

Lake, K.
1911 "The Epistles to the Thessalonians." Pp. 61–101 in *The Earlier Epistles of St.*

Paul: Their Motive and Origin. By K. Lake. London: Rivingtons.

Lambrecht, J.
1990 "Thanksgivings in 1 Thessalonians 1–3." Pp. 183–205 in *The Thessalonian Correspondence*. Edited by R. F. Collins. Bibliotheca ephemeridum theologicarum lovaniensium 87. Louvain: Leuven University Press–Peeters.

2000a "Loving God and Steadfastly Awaiting Christ (2 Thessalonians 3,5)." *Ephemerides theologicae lovanienses* 76:435–41.

2000b "A Structure Analysis of 1 Thessalonians 4–5." Pp. 163–78 in *The Thessalonian Debate: Methodological Discord or Methodological Synthesis?* Edited by K. P. Donfried and J. Beutler. Grand Rapids: Eerdmans.

Langevin, P.-É.
1965 "Le Seigneur Jésus selon un texte prépaulinien, 1 Th 1:9–10." *Sciences ecclésiastiques* 17/2:263–82; 17/3:473–512.

1989 "L'intervention de Dieu, selon 1 Thess 5,23–24: Deja le salut par grace." *Science et esprit* 41/1:71–92.

1990 "L'intervention de Dieu, selon 1 Thess 5,23–24." Pp. 236–56 in *The Thessalonian Correspondence*. Edited by R. F. Collins. Bibliotheca ephemeridum theologicarum lovaniensium 87. Louvain: Leuven University Press.

Lattimore, R.
1942 *Themes in Greek and Latin Epitaphs*. Urbana: University of Illinois Press.

Laub, F.
1973 *Eschatologische Verkündigung und Lebensgestaltung nach Paulus: Eine Untersuchung zum Wirken des Apostels beim Aufbau der Gemeinde in Thessalonike*. Biblische Untersuchungen 10. Regensburg: Pustet.

1985 *1. und 2. Thessalonicherbrief*. Würzberg: Echter.

1990 "Paulinische Autorität in nachpaulinischer Zeit (2 Thes)." Pp. 403–17 in *The Thessalonian Correspondence*. Edited by R. F. Collins. Bibliotheca ephemeridum theologicarum lovaniensium 87. Louvain: Leuven University Press.

Lautenschlager, M.
1990 "Εἴτε γρηγορῶμεν εἴτε καθεύδωμεν: Zum Verhältnis von Heiligung und Heil in 1 Thess 5,10." *Zeitschrift für*

Lee, R., and C. Lee
1975   "An Analysis of the Larger Semantic Units of 1 Thessalonians." *Notes on Translation* 56:28–42.

Légasse, S.
1997   "Vas suum possidere (1 Th 4,4)." *Filología neotestamentaria* 10:105–15.
1999   *Les Épîtres de Paul aux Thessaloniciens.* Paris: Cerf.

Lenski, R. C. H.
1937   *The Interpretation of St. Paul's Epistles to the Colossians, to the Thessalonians, to Timothy, to Titus and to Philemon.* Columbus, OH: Lutheran Book Concern.

Levine, L. I.
2000   *The Ancient Synagogue: The First Thousand Years.* 2nd ed. New Haven: Yale University Press.

Levinskaya, I.
1996   *The Book of Acts in Its First Century Setting,* vol. 5: *Diaspora Setting.* Grand Rapids: Eerdmans.

Lightfoot, J. B.
1893   *Biblical Essays.* London: Macmillan.
1904   *Notes on the Epistles of St. Paul from Unpublished Commentaries.* 2nd ed. London: Macmillan.

Linder, J. R.
1867   "1 Thess. 4,3–5." *Theologische Studien und Kritiken* 40:516–21.

Lipsius, R. A.
1854   "Über Zweck und Veranlassung des ersten Thessalonicher-briefs." *Theologische Studien und Kritiken* 27:907–34.

Lohfink, G.
1971   *Die Himmelfahrt Jesu: Untersuchungen zu den Himmelfahrts- und Erhöhungstexten bei Lukas.* Studien zum Alten und Neuen Testaments 26. Munich: Kösel.

Lövestam, E.
1963   *Spiritual Wakefulness in the New Testament.* Translated by W. F. Salisbury. Lunds Universitets Årsskrift 1/55.3. Lund: Gleerup.

LSJ   *A Greek-English Lexicon.* By H. G. Liddell, R. Scott, and H. S. Jones. 9th ed. with rev. supplement. Oxford: Clarendon, 1996.

Luckensmeyer, D.
2009   *The Eschatology of First Thessalonians.* Novum Testamentum et Orbis Antiquus; Studien zur Umwelt des Neuen Testaments 71. Göttingen: Vandenhoeck & Ruprecht.

Lüdemann, G.
1984   *Paul, Apostle to the Gentiles: Studies in Chronology.* Translated by F. Stanley Jones. Philadelphia: Fortress.

Lünemann, G.
1885   *Critical and Exegetical Hand-Book to the Epistles to the Thessalonians.* Translated by P. J. Gloag. Meyer's Commentary on the New Testament. New York: Funk & Wagnalls.

Lütgert, E. W.
1909   "Die Volkommenen im Philipperbrief und die Enthusiasten in Thessalonich." *Beiträge zur Förderung christlicher Theologie* 13/6:547–654.

Luz, U.
1968   *Das Geschichtsverständnis des Paulus.* Beiträge zur evangelischen Theologie 49. Munich: Evangelischer Verlag.

Lyons, G.
1985   *Pauline Autobiography: Toward a New Understanding.* Society of Biblical Literature Dissertation Series 73. Atlanta: Scholars Press.

MacDougall, D.
1993   "The Authenticity of II Thessalonians with Special Reference to Its Use of Traditional Material." PhD diss., University of Aberdeen.

MacMullen, R.
1981   *Paganism in the Roman Empire.* New Haven: Yale University Press.

Makaronas, C. I.
1951   "Via Egnatia and Thessalonike." Pp. 380–88 in *Studies Presented to David Moore Robinson on His Seventieth Birthday,* vol. 1. Edited by G. E. Mylonas. St. Louis: Washington University Press.

Malherbe, A. J.
1970   "'Gentle as a Nurse': The Cynic Background to I Thess ii." *Novum Testamentum* 12:203–17.
1983   "Exhortation in First Thessalonians." *Novum Testamentum* 25:238–56.
1986   *Moral Exhortation: A Greco-Roman Sourcebook.* Philadelphia: Westminster.

1987   *Paul and the Thessalonians: The Philosophic Tradition of Pastoral Care.* Philadelphia: Fortress.

1988   *Ancient Epistolary Theorists.* Society of Biblical Literature Sources for Biblical Study 12. Atlanta: Scholars Press.

1989   *Paul and the Popular Philosophers.* Philadelphia: Fortress.

1990   "Did the Thesssalonians Write to Paul?" Pp. 246–57 in *The Conversation Continues: Studies in Paul and John.* Edited by R. Fortna and B. Gaventa. Nashville: Abingdon.

1995   "God's Family in Thessalonica." Pp. 117–28 in *The First Christians and Their Social World.* Edited by L. M. White and O. L. Yarbrough. Minneapolis: Fortress.

2000   *The Letters to the Thessalonians: A New Translation with Introduction and Commentary.* Anchor Bible 32B. New York: Doubleday.

Malina, B.
1972   "Does *Porneia* Mean Fornication?" *Novum Testamentum* 14:10–17.

Manson, T. W.
1953   "St. Paul in Greece: The Letters to the Thessalonians." *Bulletin of the John Rylands University Library of Manchester* 35/2:428–47.

Manus, C. U.
1990   "Luke's Account of Paul in Thessalonica (Acts 17,1–9)." Pp. 27–38 in *The Thessalonian Correspondence.* Edited by R. F. Collins. Bibliotheca ephemeridum theologicarum lovaniensium 87. Louvain: Leuven University Press.

Marshall, I. H.
1982   "Pauline Theology in the Thessalonian Correspondence." Pp. 173–83 in *Paul and Paulinism: Festschrift for C. K. Barrett.* Edited by M. D. Hooker and S. G. Wilson. London: SPCK.

1983   *1 and 2 Thessalonians: Based on the Revised Standard Version.* New Century Bible Commentary. Grand Rapids: Eerdmans.

1990   "Election and Calling to Salvation in 1 and 2 Thessalonians." Pp. 259–76 in *The Thessalonian Correspondence.* Edited by R. F. Collins. Bibliotheca ephemeridum theologicarum lovaniensium 87. Louvain: Leuven University Press.

Martin, D. M.
1995   *1, 2 Thessalonians.* New American Commentary 33. Nashville: Broadman & Holman.

Martin, M.
1999   "'Example' and 'Imitation' in the Thessalonian Correspondence." *Southwestern Journal of Theology* 42:39–49.

Martin, R. P.
1974   *Worship in the Early Church.* Rev. ed. London: Marshall, Morgan & Scott.

Marxsen, W.
1969   "Auslegung von 1 Thess 4,13–18." *Zeitschrift für Theologie und Kirche* 66:22–37.

1979   *Der erste Brief an die Thessalonicher.* Zürcher Bibelkommentare. Zurich: Theologischer Verlag.

1982   *Der zweite Thessalonicherbrief.* Zürcher Bibelkommentare. Zurich: Theologischer Verlag.

Masson, C.
1945   "Sur I Thessaloniciens V, 23: Notes d'anthropologie paulinienne." *Revue de théologie et de philosophie* 33:97–102.

1957   *Les deux Épîtres de Saint Paul aux Thessaloniciens.* Commentaire du Nouveau Testament. Neuchâtel: Delachaux & Niestlé.

McGehee, M.
1989   "A Rejoinder to Two Recent Studies Dealing with 1 Thess 4:4." *Catholic Biblical Quarterly* 51/1:82–89.

McKay, K. L.
1985   "Aspect in Imperatival Constructions in New Testament Greek." *Novum Testamentum* 27:201–26.

McKinnish Bridges, L.
2008   *1 & 2 Thessalonians.* Smyth & Helwys Bible Commentary. Macon, GA: Smyth & Helwys.

Mearns, C. L.
1980–81   "Early Eschatological Development in Paul: The Evidence of I and II Thessalonians." *New Testament Studies* 27/2:137–57.

Meeks, W. A.
1983   *The First Urban Christians: The Social World of the Apostle Paul.* New Haven: Yale University Press.

1986   *The Moral World of the First Christians.* Library of Early Christianity 6. Philadelphia: Westminster.

Mellor, R.

1975   Θεὰ Ῥώμη: *The Worship of the Goddess Roma in the Greek World.* Hypomnemata: Untersuchungen zur Antike und zu ihrer Nachleben 42. Göttingen: Vandenhoeck & Ruprecht.

Menken, M. J. J.

1990   "The Structure of 2 Thessalonians." Pp. 373–382 in *The Thessalonian Correspondence.* Edited by R. F. Collins. Bibliotheca ephemeridum theologicarum lovaniensium 87. Louvain: Leuven University Press.

1994   *2 Thessalonians.* New Testament Readings. London: Routledge.

Merk, O.

1968   *Handeln aus Glauben: Die Motivierungen der paulinischen Ethik.* Marburger theologische Studien 5. Marburg: Elwert.

Merklein, H.

1992   "Der Theologe als Prophet: Zur Funktion prophetischen Redens im theologischen Diskurs des Paulus." *New Testament Studies* 38/3:402–29.

Metzger, B. M.

1971   *A Textual Commentary on the Greek New Testament.* Stuttgart: United Bible Societies.

1992   *The Text of the New Testament: Its Transmission, Corruption, and Restoration.* 3rd ed. Oxford: Oxford University Press.

1994   *A Textual Commentary on the Greek New Testament.* 2nd ed. Stuttgart: Deutsche Bibelgesellschaft / United Bible Societies.

Metzger, P.

2005   *Katechon: II Thess 2,1–12 im Horizont apokalyptischen Denkens.* Beihefte zur Zeitschrift für die neutestamentliche Wissenschaft und die Kunde der älteren Kirche 135. Berlin: de Gruyter.

MHT   *A Grammar of New Testament Greek.* By J. H. Moulton, W. F. Howard, and N. Turner. 4 vols. Edinburgh: T&T Clark, 1908–76.

Michel, O.

1967   "Fragen zu 1 Thessalonicher 2,14–16: Antijüdische Polemik bei Paulus." Pp. 50–59 in *Antijudäismus im Neuen Testament? Exegetische und systematische Beiträge.* Edited by W. P. Eckert, N. P. Levison, and M. Stohr. Abhandlung zum christlich-jüdischen Dialog 2. Munich: Kaiser.

Milligan, G.

1908   *St. Paul's Epistles to the Thessalonians: The Greek Text with Introduction and Notes.* London: Macmillan.

Mitchell, M. M.

1989   "Concerning ΠΕΡΙ ΔΕ in 1 Corinthians." *Novum Testamentum* 31/3:229–56.

1992   "New Testament Envoys in the Context of Greco-Roman Diplomatic and Epistolary Conventions: The Example of Timothy and Titus." *Journal of Biblical Literature* 111/4:641–62.

MM   *The Vocabulary of the Greek New Testament Illustrated from the Papyri and Other Non-literary Sources.* By J. H. Moulton and G. Milligan. London: Hodder & Stoughton, 1930. Reprinted Peabody, MA: Hendrickson, 1997.

Moffatt, J.

1897   "The First and Second Epistles of Paul the Apostle to the Thessalonians." Vol. 4 / pp. 1–54 in *The Expositor's Greek New Testament.* Edited by W. R. Nicholl. London: Hodder & Stoughton.

1910   "2 Thessalonians iii.14, 15." *Expository Times* 21/7:328.

Moore, A. L.

1966   *The Parousia in the New Testament.* Leiden: Brill.

1969   *1 and 2 Thessalonians: Based on the Revised Standard Version.* Century Bible: New Series. London: Nelson.

Morgan-Gillman, F.

1990   "Jason of Thessalonica (Acts 17,5–9)." Pp. 39–49 in *The Thessalonian Correspondence.* Edited by R. F. Collins. Bibliotheca ephemeridum theologicarum lovaniensium 87. Louvain: Leuven University Press.

Morris, L.

1956   "ΚΑΙ ἍΠΑΞ ΚΑΙ ΔΙΣ." *Novum Testamentum* 1/3:205–8.

1959   *The First and Second Epistles to the Thessalonians: The English Text with Introduction.* New International Commentary on the New Testament. Grand Rapids: Eerdmans.

1960   *The Biblical Doctrine of Judgment.* Grand Rapids: Eerdmans.

1991   *First and Second Epistles to the Thessalonians.* Rev. ed. New International Commentary on the New Testament. Grand Rapids: Eerdmans.

Moule, C. F. D.
1959   *An Idiom Book of New Testament Greek.* Cambridge: Cambridge University Press.

Müller, P.
1988   *Anfänge der Paulusschule: Dargestellt am zweiten Thessalonicherbrief und am Kolosserbrief.* Abhandlungen zur Theologie des Alten und Neuen Testaments 74. Zurich: Theologischer Verlag.

Mullins, T. Y.
1962   "Petition as a Literary Form." *Novum Testamentum* 5/1:46–54.
1964   "Disclosure: A Literary Form in the New Testament." *Novum Testamentum* 7/1:44–50.
1968   "Greeting as a New Testament Form." *Journal of Biblical Literature* 87/4:418–26.
1973   "Visit Talk in New Testament Letters." *Catholic Biblical Quarterly* 35:350–58.
1977   "Benediction as a New Testament Form." *Andrews University Seminary Studies* 15/1:59–64.

Munck, J.
1959   *Paul and the Salvation of Mankind.* London: SCM.
1967   *Christ and Israel: An Interpretation of Romans 9–11.* Philadelphia: Fortress.

Murphy-O'Connor, J.
1996   *Paul: A Critical Life.* Oxford: Oxford University Press.

Murray, W. M., and P. M. Petsas
1989   *Octavian's Campsite Memorial for the Actian War.* Transactions of the American Philosophical Society 79, part 4. Philadelphia: American Philosophical Society.

NA²⁷   *Novum Testamentum Graece.* Edited by Eberhard Nestle, Erwin Nestle, B. Aland, K. Aland, J. Karavidopoulos, C. M. Martini, and B. M. Metzger. 27th ed. Stuttgart: Deutsche Bibelgesellschaft, 1993.

NA²⁸   *Novum Testamentum Graece.* Edited by Eberhard Nestle, Erwin Nestle, B. Aland, K. Aland, J. Karavidopoulos, C. M. Martini, and B. M. Metzger. 28th ed. Stuttgart: Deutsche Bibelgesellschaft, 2012.

Neil, W.
1950   *The Epistle of Paul to the Thessalonians.* Moffat New Testament Commentary. London: Hodder & Stoughton.

1957   *St. Paul's Epistles to the Thessalonians: Introduction and Commentary.* Torch Bible Commentaries. London: SCM.

Nestle, E.
1906   "Ein neues Wort für das Wörterbuch des Neuen Testaments." *Zeitschrift für die neutestamentliche Wissenschaft* 7:361–62. ET: "1 Thess. iii.3." *Expository Times* 18/10 (1907): 479.

NewDocs   *New Documents Illustrating Early Christianity.* Edited by G. H. R. Horsley and S. R. Llewelyn. 8 vols. Grand Rapids: Eerdmans, 1981–98.

Neyrey, J. H.
1980   "Eschatology in 1 Thessalonians: The Theological Factor in 1:9–10; 2:4–5; 3:11–13; 4:6 and 4:13–18." Pp. 219–31 in *SBL Seminar Papers.* Edited by P. J. Achtemeier. Society of Biblical Literature Seminar Papers 19. Chico, CA: Scholars Press.

Nicholl, C. R.
2004   *From Hope to Despair in Thessalonica: Situating 1 and 2 Thessalonians.* Society for New Testament Studies Monograph Series 126. Cambridge: Cambridge University Press.

NIDNTT   *New International Dictionary of New Testament Theology.* Edited by C. Brown. 4 vols. Grand Rapids: Zondervan, 1975–85.

Nigdelis, P. M.
2010   "Voluntary Associations in Roman Thessalonikē: In Search of Identity and Support in a Cosmopolitan Society." Pp. 13–46 in *From Roman to Early Christian* Thessalonikē: *Studies in Religion and Archaeology.* Edited by L. S. Nasrallah, C. Bakirtzis, and S. J. Friesen. Harvard Theological Studies 64. Cambridge, MA: Harvard University Press.

Oakes, P.
2005   "Re-mapping the Universe: Paul and the Emperor in 1 Thessalonians and Philippians." *Journal for the Study of the New Testament* 27:301–22.

O'Brien, P. T.
1977   *Introductory Thanksgivings in the Letters of Paul.* Leiden: Brill.

Oepke, A.
1933   *Die Briefe an die Thessalonicher.* Neue Testament Deutsch 8. Göttingen: Vandenhoeck & Ruprecht.

1963   "Die Briefe an die Thessalonicher." Pp. 157–87 in *Die kleineren Briefe des Apostels Paulus*. By H. W. Beyer, P. Althaus, H. Conzelmann, G. Friedrich, A. Oepke, et al. Neue Testament Deutsch 8. Göttingen: Vandenhoeck & Ruprecht.

Ogara, F.
1938   "'Haec est . . . voluntas Dei, sanctificatio vestra.'" *Verbum domini* 18:65–72.

OGIS   *Orientis graeci inscriptiones selectae.* Edited by W. Dittenberger. 2 vols. Leipzig: S. Hirzel, 1903–5.

Olshausen, H.
1851   *Biblical Commentary on St. Paul's Epistles to the Galatians, Ephesians, Colossians, and Thessalonians.* Edinburgh: T&T Clark.

Olson, S. N.
1984   "Epistolary Uses of Expressions of Self-Confidence." *Journal of Biblical Literature* 103:585–97.
1985   "Pauline Expressions of Confidence in His Addressees." *Catholic Biblical Quarterly* 47:282–95.

Orchard, B.
1938   "Thessalonians and the Synoptic Gospels." *Biblica* 19/1:19–42.

Osiek, C., and D. L. Balch
1997   *Families in the New Testament World: Households and House Churches.* Louisville: Westminster/John Knox.

Otto, R. E.
1997   "The Meeting in the Air (1 Thess 4:17)." *Horizons in Biblical Theology* 19:192–212.

Otzen, P.
1958   "Gute Hoffnung bei Paulus." *Zeitschrift für die neutestamentliche Wissenschaft und die Kunde der älteren Kirche* 49:283–85.

Papagiannopoulos, A.
1982   *History of Thessaloniki.* Thessalonikē: Rekos.

Parry, R. St. J.
1923–24   "Σαίνεσθαι, I Thess. iii 3." *Journal of Theological Studies* 25:405.

Pearson, B. A.
1971   "1 Thessalonians 2:13–16: A Deutero-Pauline Interpolation." *Harvard Theological Review* 64/1:79–94.

Peerbolte, L. J. L.
1996   *The Antecedents of Antichrist: A Traditio-Historical Study of the Earliest Christian Views on Eschatological Opponents.* Leiden: Brill.

Perdelwitz, R.
1913   "Zu σαίνεσθαι ἐν ταῖς θλίψεσιν ταύταις, 1 Thess. 3,3." *Theologische Studien und Kritiken* 86:613–15.

Perdrizet, P. M.
1894   "Voyage dans la Macédoine première." *Bulletin de correspondence hellenique* 18:416–45.

Peterson, D. G.
2009   *The Acts of the Apostles.* Pillar New Testament Commentary. Grand Rapids: Eerdmans.

Peterson, E.
1930   "Die Einholung des Kyrios." *Zeitschrift für systematische Theologie* 1:682–702.

Pfitzner, V. C.
1962   *Paul and the Agon Motif.* Supplements to Novum Testamentum 16. Leiden: Brill.

PG   Patrologia graeca. Edited by J.-P. Migne. 162 vols. Paris, 1857–86.

Plevnik, J.
1979   "1 Thess 5:1–11: Its Authenticity, Intention and Message." *Biblica* 60/1:71–90.
1984   "The Taking Up of the Faithful and the Resurrection of the Dead in 1 Thessalonians 4:13–18." *Catholic Biblical Quarterly* 46:274–83.
1997   *Paul and the Parousia: An Exegetical and Theological Investigation.* Peabody, MA: Hendrickson.
2000   "The Destination of the Apostle and of the Faithful: Second Corinthians 4:13b–14 and First Thessalonians 4:14." *Catholic Biblical Quarterly* 62:83–95.

Plummer, A.
1918   *A Commentary on St. Paul's First Epistle to the Thessalonians.* London: Robert Scott.

Pobee, J. S.
1985   *Persecution and Martyrdom in the Theology of Paul.* Journal for the Study of the New Testament: Supplement Series 6. Sheffield: JSOT Press.

Popkes, W.
1996   *Paranese und Neues Testament.* Stuttgarter Bibelstudien 168. Stuttgart: Verlag Katholisches Bibelwerk.

Porter, S. E.
1989   *Verbal Aspect in the Greek of the New Testament, with Reference to Tense and Mood.* New York: Peter Lang.

1992   *Idioms of the Greek New Testament.* Sheffield: JSOT Press.

1993   "The Theoretical Justification for Application of Rhetorical Categories to Pauline Epistolary Literature." Pp. 100–122 in *Rhetoric and the New Testament: Essays from the 1992 Heidelberg Conference.* Edited by S. E. Porter and T. H. Olbricht. Sheffield: JSOT Press.

Porter, S. E., and B. Dyer
2012   "Oral Texts? A Reassessment of the Oral and Rhetorical Nature of Paul's Letters in Light of Recent Studies." *Journal of the Evangelical Theological Society* 55/2:323–41.

Powell, C. E.
1997   "The Identity of the 'Restrainer' in 2 Thessalonians 2:6–7." *Bibliotheca sacra* 154:320–32.

Radl, W.
1981   *Ankunft des Herrn: Zur Bedeutung und Funktion der Parusieaussagen bei Paulus.* Beiträge zur biblischen Exegese und Theologie 15. Frankfurt am Main: Peter Lang.

Ramsay, W. M.
1920   *St. Paul the Traveller and the Roman Citizen.* London: Hodder & Stoughton.

Reese, J. M.
1979   *1 and 2 Thessalonians.* New Testament Message. Wilmington, DE: Michael Glazier.

Reicke, B.
1984   "Judaeo-Christianity and the Jewish Establishment, A.D. 33–66." Pp. 145–52 in *Jesus and the Politics of His Day.* Edited by E. Bammel and C. F. D. Moule. Cambridge: Cambridge University Press.

Reinhartz, A.
1987   "On the Meaning of the Pauline Exhortation 'μιμηταί μου γίνεσθε—Become Imitators of Me.'" *Studies in Religion / Sciences religieuses* 16/4:393–403.

Reinmuth, E.
1998   "Die erste Brief an die Thessalonicher" and "Die zweite Brief an die Thessalonicher." Pp. 105–204 in *Die Briefe an die Philipper, Thessalonicher und an Philemon.* By N. Walter, E. Reinmuth, and P. Lampe. Das Neue Testament Deutsch 8.2. Göttingen: Vandenhoeck & Ruprecht.

Richard, E. J.
1995   *First and Second Thessalonians.* Sacra pagina. Collegeville, MN: Liturgical Press.

Richards, E. R.
1991   *The Secretary in the Letters of Paul.* Tübingen: Mohr Siebeck.

Ridderbos, H. N.
1975   *Paul: An Outline of His Theology.* Grand Rapids: Eerdmans.

Riddle, D. W.
1940   *Paul, Man of Conflict: A Modern Biographical Sketch.* Nashville: Cokesbury.

Riesner, R.
1998   *Paul's Early Period: Chronology, Mission Strategy, Theology.* Translated by D. Stott. Grand Rapids: Eerdmans.

Rigaux, B.
1956   *Les épîtres aux Thessaloniciens.* Études bibliques. Paris: Gabalda.

1968   *The Letters of St. Paul: Modern Studies.* Chicago: Franciscan Herald.

1974–75 "Tradition et rédaction dans 1 Th. V.1–10." *New Testament Studies* 21:318–40.

Roberts, J. H.
1986   "The Eschatological Transitions to the Pauline Letter Body." *Neotestamentica* 20:29–35.

Robertson, A. T.
1934   *A Grammar of the Greek New Testament in the Light of Historical Research.* Nashville: Broadman.

Robinson, D. W. B.
1964   "II Thess. 2,6: 'That Which Restrains' or 'That Which Holds Sway'?" Pp. 635–38 in *Studia Evangelica,* vol. 2: *Papers Presented to the Second International Congress on New Testament Studies Held at Christ Church, Oxford, 1961,* part 1: *The New Testament Scriptures.* Edited by F. L. Cross. Texte und Untersuchungen zur Geschichte der altchristlichen Literatur 87. Berlin: Akademie Verlag.

Roetzel, C. J.
1972   "1 Thess 5:12–28: A Case Study." Pp. 367–83 in *SBL 1972 Proceedings,* vol. 2. Edited by L. C. McGaughy. Chico, CA: Society of Biblical Literature.

1975   *The Letters of Paul: Conversations in Context.* Atlanta: John Knox.

1982   *The Letters of Paul: Conversations in Context.* 2nd ed. Louisville: Westminster/John Knox.

1986   "Theodidaktoi and Handwork in Philo and I Thessalonians." Pp. 324–31 in *L'Apôtre Paul: Personalité, style, et conception du mnistère*. Edited by A. Vanhoye. Bibliotheca ephemeridum theologicarum lovaniensium 73. Louvain: Leuven University Press.

Roller, O.
1933   *Das Formular der paulinischen Briefe: Ein Beitrag zur Lehre vom antiken Briefe*. Stuttgart: Kohlhammer.

Rongy, H.
1909   "De Adjunctis et Scopo Scriptionis 2ae Ep. ad Thessalonicenses." *Revue ecclésiastique de Liège* 5:97–100.

Rosner, B. S.
1995   "Seven Questions for Paul's Ethics: 1 Thessalonians 4:1–12 as a Case Study." Pp. 351–60 in *Understanding Paul's Ethics: Twentieth-Century Approaches*. Edited by B. S. Rosner. Grand Rapids: Eerdmans.

Ross, J. M.
1975   "1 Thessalonians 3.13." *Bible Translator* 26/4:444.

Russell, R.
1988   "The Idle in 2 Thess 3:6–12: An Eschatological or a Social Problem?" *New Testament Studies* 34/1:105–19.

Ryken, L.
1993   "The Literature of the New Testament." Pp. 361–75 in *A Complete Literary Guide to the Bible*. Edited by L. Ryken and T. Longman. Grand Rapids: Zondervan.

Sabbe, M.
1961   "De Paulinische beschrijving van de parousie." *Collationes Brugenses et Gandavenses* 7/1:86–114.

Sailors, T. B.
2000   "Wedding Textual and Rhetorical Criticism to Understand the Text of 1 Thessalonians 2.7." *Journal for the Study of the New Testament* 80:81–98.

Sanders, J. T.
1962   "The Transition from Opening Epistolary Thanksgiving to Body in the Letters of the Pauline Corpus." *Journal of Biblical Literature* 81:348–62.

SB   *Sammelbuch griechischer Urkunden aus Ägypten*. Edited by F. Preisigke et al. Vols. 1–. Strassburg: Trübner; et al., 1915–.

Schippers, R.
1966   "Pre-Synoptic Tradition in 1 Thessalonians 2:13–16." *Novum Testamentum* 8:223–34.

Schlier, H.
1963   "Auslegung des 1. Thessalonicherbriefes (4,13–5,11)." *Bibel und Leben* 4:19–30.

Schlueter, C. J.
1994   *Filling Up the Measure: Polemical Hyperbole in 1 Thessalonians 2:14–16*. Journal for the Study of the New Testament: Supplement Series 98. Sheffield: JSOT Press.

Schmidt, D. D.
1983   "1 Thess 2:13–16: Linguistic Evidence for an Interpolation." *Journal of Biblical Literature* 102/2:269–79.
1990   "The Syntactical Style of 2 Thessalonians: How Pauline Is It?" Pp. 383–93 in *The Thessalonian Correspondence*. Edited by R. F. Collins. Bibliotheca ephemeridum theologicarum lovaniensium 87. Louvain: Leuven University Press.

Schmidt, J. E. C.
1801   *Vermutungen über die beiden Briefe an die Thessalonicher*. Bibliothek für Kritik und Exegese des Neuen Testaments und ältesten Christengeschichte 2/3. Hadamar: Gelehrtenbuchhandlung.

Schmithals, W.
1964   "Die Thessalonicherbriefe als Briefkompositionen." Pp. 295–315 in *Zeit und Geschichte: Dankesgabe an Rudolf Bultmann zum 80. Geburtstag*. Edited by E. Dinkler. Tübingen: Mohr Siebeck.
1971   *The Office of Apostle in the Early Church*. London: SPCK.
1972   *Paul and the Gnostics*. Translated by J. E. Steely. Nashville: Abingdon.

Schnabel, E.
2012   *Acts*. Zondervan Exegetical Commentary on the New Testament. Grand Rapids: Zondervan.

Schnelle, U.
1990   "Die Ethik des 1. Thessalonicherbriefes." Pp. 295–305 in *The Thessalonian Correspondence*. Edited by R. F. Collins. Bibliotheca ephemeridum theologicarum lovaniensium 87. Louvain: Leuven University Press.

Schnider, F., and W. Stenger
1987   *Studien zum neutestamentlichen Briefformular*. New Testament Tools and Studies 11. Leiden: Brill.

Schoon-Janssen, J.
1991   *Umstrittene Apologien in den Paulus-briefen: Studien zur rhetorischen Situation des 1. Thessalonicherbriefes, des Galaterbriefes und des Philipperbriefes.* Göttinger theologische Arbeiten 45. Göttingen: Vandenhoeck & Ruprecht.

Schrader, K.
1836   *Der Apostel Paulus*, vol. 5. Leipzig: C. E. Kollmann.

Schubert, P.
1939   *Form and Function of the Pauline Thanksgivings.* Berlin: Töpelmann.

Schuler, C.
1960   "The Macedonian Politarchs." *Classical Philology* 55:90–100.

Schürer, E.
1973–87   *The History of the Jewish People in the Age of Jesus Christ (175 B.C.–A.D. 135).* Edited by G. Vermès, F. Millar, and M. Black. Rev. ed. 3 vols. Edinburgh: T&T Clark.

Scofield, C. I.
1967   *The New Scofield Reference Bible: Holy Bible, Authorized King James Version, with Introductions, Annotations, Subject Chain References, and Such Word Changes in the Text as Will Help the Reader.* Edited by E. S. English et al. New York: Oxford University Press.

SEG   *Supplementum epigraphicum graecum.* Leiden: Brill; et al., 1923–.

Selwyn, E. G.
1947   *The First Epistle of Peter: The Greek Text with Introduction, Notes and Essays.* London: Macmillan.

Senior, D. P. (ed.)
1990   *The Catholic Study Bible.* New York: Oxford University Press.

Seventer, J.
1961   *Paul and Seneca.* Leiden: Brill.

Sherwin-White, A. N.
1963   *Roman Society and Roman Law in the New Testament.* Oxford: Clarendon.

Shogren, G. S.
2012   *1 & 2 Thessalonians.* Zondervan Exegetical Commentary on the New Testament. Grand Rapids: Zondervan.

Siber, P.
1971   *Mit Christus leben: Eine Studie zur paulinischen Auferstehungshoffnung.* Abhandlungen zur Theologie des Alten und Neuen Testaments 61. Zurich: Theologischer Verlag.

Silva, M.
1996   *Explorations in Exegetical Method: Galatians as a Test Case.* Grand Rapids: Baker.

Smith, A.
1990   "The Social and Ethical Implications of the Pauline Rhetoric in I Thessalonians." PhD diss., Vanderbilt University.

Smith, J. E.
2001a   "Another Look at 4Q416 2 ii.21, a Critical Parallel to First Thessalonians 4:4." *Catholic Biblical Quarterly* 63/3:499–504.

2001b   "1 Thessalonians 4:4: Breaking the Impasse." *Bulletin for Biblical Research* 11/1:65–105.

Snaith, N. H.
1944   *The Distinctive Ideas of the Old Testament.* New York: Schocken.

Soden, H. F. von
1885   "Der erste Thessalonicherbrief." *Theologische Studien und Kritiken* 58:263–310.

Söding, T.
1992   *Die Trias Glaube, Hoffnung, Liebe bei Paulus: Eine exegetische Studie.* Stuttgarter Bibelstudien 150. Stuttgart: Katholisches Bibelwerk.

Spicq, C.
1956   "Les Thessaloniciens 'inquiets' étaient-ils des paresseux." *Studia theologica* 10/1:1–13.

1994   *Theological Lexicon of the New Testament.* Translated and edited by J. D. Ernest. 3 vols. Peabody, MA: Hendrickson.

Spitta, F.
1896   *Zur Geschichte und Litteratur des Urchristentums*, vol. 1. Göttingen: Vandenhoeck & Ruprecht.

Staab, K.
1965   *Die Thessalonicherbriefe, die Gefangenschaftsbriefe* [by K. Staab] *und die Pastoralbriefe* [by J. Freundorfer]. Regensburger Neues Testament 7. 4th ed. Regensburg: Pustet.

Stamps, D. L.
1995   "Rhetorical Criticism of the New Testament: Ancient and Modern Evaluations of Argumentation." Pp. 77–128 in *Approaches to New Testament Studies.* Edited by S. E. Porter and D. Tombs. Sheffield: Sheffield Academic Press.

Steck, O. H.
1967   *Israel und das gewaltsame Geschick der Propheten.* Wissenschaftliche Monographien zum Alten und Neuen Testament 23. Neukirchen-Vluyn: Neukirchener Verlag.

Stegemann, W.
1985   "Anlass und Hintergrund der Abfassung von 1 Th 2,1–12." Pp. 397–416 in *Theologische Brosamen für Lothar Steiger.* Edited by G. Freund and E. Stegemann. Diehlheimer Blätter zum Alten Testament und seiner Rezeption in der Alten Kirche 5. Heidelberg: Esprint.

Steimle, C.
2008   *Religion im römischen Thessaloniki: Sakraltopographie, Kult und Gesellschaft 168 v. Chr.–324 n. Chr.* Tübingen: Mohr Siebeck.

Stein, R. H.
1988   *Difficult Passages in the Epistles.* Grand Rapids: Baker.

Stempvoort, P. A. van
1960–61   "Eine stilistische Losung einer alten Schwierigkeit in 1. Thess. v.23." *New Testament Studies* 7/3:262–65.

Stephenson, A. M. G.
1968   "On the Meaning of ἐνέστηκεν ἡ ἡμέρα τοῦ κυρίου in 2 Thessalonians 2,2." Pp. 442–51 in *Studia evangelica,* vol. 4: *Papers Presented to the Third International Congress on New Testament Studies Held at Christ Church, Oxford, 1965.* Edited by F. L. Cross. Texte und Untersuchungen zur Geschichte der altchristlichen Literatur 102. Berlin: Akademie-Verlag.

Still, T. D.
1999   *Conflict at Thessalonica: A Pauline Church and Its Neighbours.* Journal for the Study of the New Testament: Supplement Series 183. Sheffield: Sheffield Academic Press.

Stott, J. R. W.
1991   *The Gospel and the End of Time: The Message of 1 & 2 Thessalonians.* Downers Grove, IL: InterVarsity.

Stowers, S. K.
1986   *Letter Writing in Greco-Roman Antiquity.* Philadelphia: Westminster.

Str-B   *Kommentar zum Neuen Testament aus Talmud und Midrasch.* By H. L. Strack and P. Billerbeck. 6 vols. Munich: Beck, 1922–61.

Strelan, J. G.
1975   "Burden-Bearing and the Law of Christ: A Re-examination of Galatians 6:2." *Journal of Biblical Literature* 94:266–76.

Sumney, J. L.
1990   *Identifying Paul's Opponents: The Question of Method in 2 Corinthians.* Sheffield: JSOT Press.

Sundberg, A. C., Jr.
1973   "Canon Muratori: A Fourth Century List." *Harvard Theological Review* 66:1–41.

Swete, H. B. (ed.)
1880   *In Epistolam B. Pauli ad Thessalonicenses I, II.* Vol. 2 / pp. 1–66 in *In Epistolas B. Pauli Commentarii.* By Theodore of Mopsuestia. Cambridge: Cambridge University Press.

Taatz, I.
1991   *Frühjüdische Briefe: Die paulinischen Briefe im Rahmen der offiziellen religiösen Briefe des Frühjudentums.* Novum Testamentum et Orbis Antiquus 16. Freiburg: Universitätsverlag; Göttingen: Vandenhoeck & Ruprecht.

TDNT   *Theological Dictionary of the New Testament.* Edited by G. Kittel and G. Friedrich. Translated and edited by G. W. Bromiley. 10 vols. Grand Rapids: Eerdmans, 1964–76.

Thielman, F.
1994   *Paul and the Law: A Contextual Approach.* Downers Grove, IL: InterVarsity.

Thomas, R. L.
1978   "1–2 Thessalonians." Vol. 11 / pp. 227–337 in *The Expositor's Bible Commentary.* Edited by F. E. Gaebelein. Grand Rapids: Zondervan.

Thompson, E.
1944–45   "The Sequence of the Two Epistles to the Thessalonians." *Expository Times* 56:306–7.

Thrall, M. E.
1962   *Greek Particles in the New Testament.* Grand Rapids: Eerdmans.

Thurston, B.
1995   *Reading Colossians, Ephesians, and 2 Thessalonians: A Literary and Theological Commentary.* Macon, GA: Smyth & Helwys.

Thurston, R. W.
1973   "Relationship between the Thessalonian Epistles." *Expository Times* 85/2:52–56.

TLG   Thesaurus Linguae Graecae: A Digital Library of Greek Literature. Irvine: University of California, 2001–. http://www.tlg.uci.edu/.

Tomson, P. J.
1990   *Paul and the Jewish Law: Halakha in the Letters of the Apostle to the Gentiles.* Compendia rerum iudaicarum ad Novum Testamentum 3.1. Minneapolis: Fortress.

Touratsoglou, I.
1988   *Die Münzstätte von Thessalonike in der römischen Kaiserzeit.* Berlin: de Gruyter.

Travis, S. H.
1986   *Christ and the Judgment of God.* Basingstoke: Marshall Pickering.

Trilling, W.
1972   *Untersuchungen zum zweiten Thessalonicherbrief.* Erfurter theologische Studien 27. Leipzig: St.-Benno-Verlag.
1980   *Der zweite Brief an die Thessalonicher.* Evangelisch-katholischer Kommentar zum Neuen Testament. Neukirchen-Vluyn: Neukirchener Verlag.

Trudinger, P.
1995   "The Priority of 2 Thessalonians Revisited: Some Fresh Evidence." *Downside Review* 113:31–35.

Turner, N.
1965   *Grammatical Insights into the New Testament.* Edinburgh: T&T Clark.

Tzanavari, K.
2003   "The Worship of Gods and Heroes in Thessaloniki." Pp. 177–262 in *Roman Thessaloniki.* Edited by D. V. Grammenos. Thessaloniki: Archaeological Museum Publications.

UBS⁴   *The Greek New Testament.* Edited by B. Aland et al. 4th rev. ed. Stuttgart: Deutsche Bibelgesellschaft/United Bible Societies, 1994.

Unger, M. F.
1962   "Historical Research and the Church at Thessalonica." *Bibliotheca sacra* 119:38–44.

Unnik, W. C. van
1964   "Die Rücksicht auf die Reaktion der Nicht-Christen als Motiv in der altchristlichen Paränese." Pp. 221–34 in *Judentum, Urchristentum, Kirche:*

Festschrift für Joachim Jeremias. Edited by W. Eltester. 2nd ed. Beihefte zur Zeitschrift für die neutestamentliche Wissenschaft 26. Berlin: Töpelmann.

Vacalopoulos, A. E.
1972   *A History of Thessalonica.* Thessaloniki: Institute for Balkan Studies. Reprinted 1984.

Verhoef, E.
1995   "Die Bedeutung des Artikels τῶν in 1 Thess 2.15." *Biblische Notizen* 80:41–46.
1997   "The Relation between 1 Thessalonians and 2 Thessalonians and the Inauthenticity of 2 Thessalonians." *Hervormde teologiese studies* 53:163–71.
1998   *De Brieven aan de Tessalonicenzen.* Kampen: Uitgeverij Kok.

Vickers, M. J.
1972   "Hellenistic Thessaloniki." *Journal of Hellenic Studies* 92:156–70.

Vidal Garcia, S.
1979   "La formula de resurreccion 'cristologica simple.'" *Salmanticensis* 27:385–417.

Vogel, W.
1934   "Εἰδέναι τὸ ἑαυτοῦ σκεῦος κτᾶσθαι. Zur Deutung von I Thess 4,3ff. im Zusammenhang der paulinischen Eheauffassung." *Theologische Blätter* 13:83–85.

Vokotopoulou, J.
1996   *Guide to the Archaeological Museum of Thessaloniki.* Athens: Kapon.

Vos, G.
1930   *The Pauline Eschatology.* Grand Rapids: Eerdmans.

Wainwright, A.
1980   "Where Did Silas Go? (And What Was His Connection with *Galatians?*)." *Journal for the Study of the New Testament* 8:66–70.

Wallace, D. B.
1990   "A Textual Problem in 1 Thessalonians 1:10: Ἐκ τῆς Ὀργῆς vs. Ἀπὸ τῆς Ὀργῆς." *Bibliotheca sacra* 147:470–79.
1996   *Greek Grammar beyond the Basics.* Grand Rapids: Zondervan.

Walton, S.
1995   "What Has Aristotle to Do with Paul? Rhetorical Criticism and 1 Thessalonians." *Tyndale Bulletin* 46/2:229–50.

Walvoord, J. F.
1976   *The Thessalonian Epistles.* Grand Rapids: Zondervan.

Wanamaker, C. A.

1990   *The Epistles to the Thessalonians: A Commentary on the Greek Text.* New International Greek Testament Commentary. Grand Rapids: Eerdmans.

Ward, R. A.

1973   *Commentary on 1 & 2 Thessalonians.* Waco: Word Books.

Ware, J. P.

1992   "The Thessalonians as a Missionary Congregation: 1 Thessalonians 1,5–8." *Zeitschrift für die neutestamentliche Wissenschaft* 83:126–31.

Warfield, B. B.

1886   "The Prophecies of St. Paul, I: 1 and 2 Thessalonians." *The Expositor*, 3rd series, 4:30–44.

Way, A. S.

1921   *The Letters of St. Paul to Seven Churches and Three Friends.* London: Macmillan.

Weatherly, J. A.

1991   "The Authenticity of 1 Thessalonians 2.13–16: Additional Evidence." *Journal for the Study of the New Testament* 42:79–98.

1994   "Responsibility for the Death of Jesus in Paul: 1 Thessalonians 2:14–16." Pp. 176–94 in *Jewish Responsibility for the Death of Jesus in Luke-Acts.* Journal for the Study of the New Testament: Supplement Series 106. Sheffield: Sheffield Academic Press.

1996   *1 & 2 Thessalonians.* College Press NIV Commentary. Joplin, MO: College Press.

Weima, J. A. D.

1993   "Gal. 6:11–18: A Hermeneutical Key to the Galatian Letter." *Calvin Theological Journal* 28:90–107.

1994a   *Neglected Endings: The Significance of the Pauline Letter Closings.* Journal for the Study of the New Testament: Supplement Series 101. Sheffield: JSOT Press.

1994b   "Preaching the Gospel in Rome: A Study of the Epistolary Framework of Romans." Pp. 337–66 in *Gospel in Paul: Studies in Corinthians, Galatians and Romans for Richard N. Longenecker.* Edited by L. A. Jervis and P. Richardson. Journal for the Study of the New Testament: Supplement Series 108. Sheffield: JSOT Press.

1995   "The Pauline Letter Closing: Analysis and Hermeneutical Significance." *Bulletin for Biblical Research* 5:177–98.

1996   "'How You Must Walk to Please God': Holiness and Discipleship in 1 Thessalonians." Pp. 98–119 in *Patterns of Discipleship in the New Testament.* Edited by R. N. Longenecker. Grand Rapids: Eerdmans.

1997a   "An Apology for the Apologetic Function of 1 Thessalonians 2.1–12." *Journal for the Study of the New Testament* 68:73–99.

1997b   "What Does Aristotle Have to Do with Paul? An Evaluation of Rhetorical Criticism." *Calvin Theological Journal* 32/2:458–68.

2000a   "'But We Became Infants among You': The Case for ΝΗΠΙΟΙ in 1 Thess 2.7." *New Testament Studies* 46:547–64.

2000b   "The Function of 1 Thessalonians 2:1–12 and the Use of Rhetorical Criticism: A Response to Otto Merk." Pp. 114–31 in *The Thessalonians Debate: Methodological Discord or Methodological Synthesis?* Edited by K. P. Donfried and J. Beutler. Grand Rapids: Eerdmans.

2001   "Literary Criticism." Pp. 150–69 in *New Testament Criticism and Interpretation.* Edited by D. A. Black and D. S. Dockery. Nashville: Broadman & Holman.

2002   "Infants, Nursing Mother and Father: Paul's Portrayal of a Pastor." *Calvin Theological Journal* 37/2:209–29.

2006   "The Slaying of Satan's Superman and the Sure Salvation of the Saints: Paul's Apocalyptic Word of Comfort (2 Thessalonians 2:1–17)." *Calvin Theological Journal* 41:67–88.

2007   "1–2 Thessalonians." Pp. 871–89 in *Commentary on the New Testament Use of the Old Testament.* Edited by G. K. Beale and D. A. Carson. Grand Rapids: Baker Academic.

2010a   "Paul's Persuasive Prose: An Epistolary Analysis of the Letter to Philemon." Pp. 29–60 in *Philemon in Perspective: Interpreting a Pauline Letter.* Edited by D. F. Tolmie. Berlin: de Gruyter.

2010b   "Sincerely, Paul: The Significance of the Pauline Letter Closings." Pp. 307–45 in *Paul and the Ancient Letter Form.* Edited by S. E. Porter and S. A. Adams. Leiden: Brill.

2012   "'Peace and Security' (1 Thess 5.3): Prophetic Warning or Political

Propaganda?" *New Testament Studies* 58:331–59.

Weima, J. A. D., and S. E. Porter
1998   *An Annotated Bibliography of 1 & 2 Thessalonians.* New Testament Tools and Studies 26. Leiden: Brill.

Weiss, J.
1937   *The History of Primitive Christianity.* New York: Harper & Row.

Weiss, W.
1993   "Glaube—Liebe—Hoffnung: Zu der Trias bei Paulus." *Zeitschrift für die neutestamentliche Wissenschaft* 84:196–217.

Wengst, K.
1972   "Der Apostel und die Tradition: Zur theologischen Bedeutung urchristlicher Formeln bei Paulus." *Zeitschrift für Theologie und Kirche* 69/2:145–62.

Wenham, D.
1984   *The Rediscovery of Jesus' Eschatological Discourse.* Gospel Perspectives 4. Sheffield: JSOT Press.
1985   "Paul's Use of the Jesus Tradition: Three Samples." Pp. 7–37 in *Gospel Perspectives 5: The Jesus Tradition outside the Gospels.* Edited by D. Wenham. Sheffield: JSOT Press.
1995   *Paul: Follower of Jesus or Founder of Christianity?* Grand Rapids: Eerdmans.

West, J. C.
1914   "The Order of 1 and 2 Thessalonians." *Journal of Theological Studies* 15:66–74.

W-H
        The New Testament in the Original Greek. The text revised by B. F. Westcott and F. J. A. Hort. Cambridge: Macmillan, 1881. 2nd ed., 1896.

Whitaker, G. H.
1921   "Love Springs No Leak." *The Expositor*, 8th series, 21:126–29.

White, J. L.
1971   "The Structural Analysis of Philemon: A Point of Departure in the Formal Analysis of the Pauline Letter." Vol. 1 / pp. 1–47 in *One Hundred Seventh Annual Meeting Seminar Papers—28–31 October 1971, Regency Hyatt House, Atlanta, Ga.* Missoula, MT: Scholars Press.
1972   *The Body of the Greek Letter.* Society of Biblical Literature Dissertation Series 2. Missoula, MT: Scholars Press.
1981   "The Ancient Epistolography Group in Retrospect." *Semeia* 22:1–14.

1986   *Light from Ancient Letters.* Philadelphia: Fortress.

Whiteley, D. E. H.
1969   *Thessalonians in the Revised Standard Version: With Introduction and Commentary.* New Clarendon Bible 7. London: Oxford University Press.

Whitton, J.
1982   "A Neglected Meaning for *Skeuos* in 1 Thessalonians 4.4." *New Testament Studies* 28/1:142–43.

Wilckens, U.
1963   *Die Missionsreden der Apostelgeschichte.* 2nd ed. Wissenschaftliche Monographien zum Alten und Neuen Testament 5. Neukirchen-Vluyn: Neukirchener Verlag.

Wilder, T. L.
2004   *Pseudonymity, the New Testament, and Deception: An Inquiry into Intention and Reception.* Lanham, MD: University Press of America.

Wiles, G. P.
1974   *Paul's Intercessory Prayers: The Significance of the Intercessory Prayer Passages in the Letters of St. Paul.* Cambridge: Cambridge University Press.

Williams, D. J.
1992   *1 and 2 Thessalonians.* New International Biblical Commentary. Peabody, MA: Hendrickson.

Wilson, G. B.
1975   *I & II Thessalonians: A Digest of Reformed Comment.* Edinburgh: Banner of Truth Trust.

Winter, B. W.
1989   "'If a Man Does Not Wish to Work . . .': A Cultural and Historical Setting for 2 Thessalonians 3:6–16." *Tyndale Bulletin* 40/2:303–15.
1993   "The Entries and Ethics of Orators and Paul (1 Thessalonians 2:1–12)." *Tyndale Bulletin* 44/1:55–74.
1994   *Seek the Welfare of the City: Christians as Benefactors and Citizens.* First-Century Christians in the Graeco-Roman World. Grand Rapids: Eerdmans.

Witherington, B., III
1990   *Women and the Genesis of Christianity.* Cambridge: Cambridge University Press.
1998   *The Acts of the Apostles: A Socio-Rhetorical Commentary.* Grand Rapids: Eerdmans.

2006   *1 and 2 Thessalonians: A Socio-Rhetorical Commentary*. Grand Rapids: Eerdmans.

Witmer, S. E.
2006   "Θεοδίδακτοι in 1 Thessalonians 4.9: A Pauline Neologism." *New Testament Studies* 52/2:239–50.

2008   *Divine Instruction in Early Christianity*. Wissenschaftliche Untersuchungen zum Neuen Testament 2/246. Tübingen: Mohr Siebeck.

Witt, R. E.
1977   "The *Kabeiroi* in Ancient Macedonia." Vol. 2 / pp. 67–80 in *Ancient Macedonia II: Papers Read at the Second International Symposium Held in Thessaloniki, 19–24 August 1973*. Edited by B. Laourdas and C. I. Makaronas. 2 vols. Thessaloniki: Institute for Balkan Studies.

Wohlenberg, G.
1909   *Die erste und zweite Thessalonicherbrief*. 2nd ed. Kommentar zum Neuen Testament 12. Leipzig: Deichert.

Wrede, W.
1903   *Die Echtheit des zweiten Thessalonicherbriefs*. Texte und Untersuchungen zur Geschichte der altchristlichen Literatur 2/24. Leipzig: Hinrichs.

Wuest, K. S.
1957   "The Rapture—Precisely When?" *Bibliotheca sacra* 114:60–69.

Yarbrough, O. L.
1986   *Not Like the Gentiles: Marriage Rules in the Letters of Paul*. Society of Biblical Literature Dissertation Series 80. Atlanta: Scholars Press.

Yarbrough, R. Y.
1999   "Sexual Gratification in 1 Thess 4:1–8." *Trinity Journal* 20:215–32.

Ziemann, F.
1912   *De epistularum Graecarum formulis sollemnibus quaestiones selectae*. Berlin: Haas.

Zimmer, F.
1893   *Der Text der Thessalonicherbriefe: Samt textkritischem Apparat und Kommentar*. Güdlimburg: C. F. Viewegs.

Index of Subjects

Index of Authors

Index of Greek Words

Index of Scripture and Other Ancient Writings

Old Testament *685*
New Testament *688*
Old Testament Apocrypha *705*
Old Testament Pseudepigrapha *706*
Rabbinic Writings *707*
Qumran/Dead Sea Scrolls *707*

Papyri, Inscriptions, and Coins *707*
Josephus *708*
Philo *708*
Classical Writers *709*
Church Fathers *710*

Old Testament

Genesis

1 320
3:19 615
3:19 LXX 609
8:21–22 320
9:11 320
12:1–3 91
15:16 LXX 175
17:5 365
18:25 464
29:11 426n18
29:13 426n18
29:15 609
31:28 426n18
31:55 426n18
32:1 LXX 426n18
33:4 426n18, 427
45:15 427
47:30 309

Exodus

2:11 89
3:2 471
4:27 426n18
6:9 393
7:3 539
7:4 277
12:12 277
13:21–22 332
14:19 332

14:20 332
14:24 332
16:8 281
16:10 332
18:7 426n18
19:5–6 91
19:5–6 LXX 265
19:6 241
19:10–18 333n17
19:13 328
19:16 328
19:16–17 332
19:19 328
20:18 328
21:11 609
21:23–25 465
31:23–25 397
32:12 249
32:25 249
34:6 109, 395
34:10 477

Leviticus

11:44 241
11:44 LXX 265
11:45 157, 241, 265
16:2 332
17–26 265
18:6–23 266
19:2 241, 265

19:18 289
20:7 241, 265
20:23–26 LXX 265
20:26 265
22:32 241, 265
24:19–21 397
26:12 109
26:25 473

Numbers

6:22–27 22
9:15–22 332
10:11–12 332
14:14–16 249
14:18 396
14:21 109
14:28 109
21:4 393
23:27 137, 249, 258
31:3 472

Deuteronomy

4:34 539
4:37 91
6:22 539
7:9 423, 592
9:10 68
9:13 199
9:25–29 249
15:3 89

15:12 89
18:6 68
19:21 397
23:2–4 68
25:3 26
26:18 LXX 549
26:18–19 LXX 265
26:19 241
31:16 309
31:30 68
32:4 423, 592
32:15 90
32:15 LXX 548
32:35 277, 465, 472
32:40 109
32:41 473
32:43 473
33:12 90
33:12 LXX 548, 548n41

Joshua

22:22 511

Judges

6:12 635
16:16 393
19:5 240
19:8 240
20:2 68

New Testament

Colossians

1 Thessalonians

Revelation

1:3 344
1:7 333
1:10 326n10
2:2 290
2:10 203, 213
2:14 262
2:20 262
3:2–3 359
3:3 347
4:1 326n10
6:9–11 309
7:1 574
8:2 328

8:6 328
8:13 328
9:14 328
9:20–22 262
11:12 333
11:15 328
11:19 519
12:4 225, 557
12:5 331
12:7 327
13:2 538
13:3 477
13:13–14 539
14:4 550

14:6 219
14:13 329
14:14–16 333
14:15 519
14:17 519
14:19 179
15:1 179
15:5–6 519
15:7 179
15:8 519
16:1 519
16:5 359
16:15 347
16:17 519

17–18 571
17:2 360n15
17:8 514
17:11 514
18:14 273
19:15 179, 535
20:1–3 574
20:2 574n4
20:5 337
21:1–2 320
21:6 609
21:8 475
21:10 320
22:17 609

Old Testament Apocrypha

Additions to Esther

15:8–12 426n18

Baruch

3:36 90, 548
3:37 LXX 548

2 Esdras

4:1–2 328
4:33 344
4:34–37 175
4:40–43 351
5:1–12 511
6:7 344
6:23 328
6:25 313
7:26–44 313
7:32 309
7:33 396
7:36 467
7:38 467
7:73–74 344
7:74 175
7:75 467
7:85 467
7:95 467
13:10–11 535

13:24 313
14:16–18 511
14:20 354
16:37–39 351

Judith

7:19 393
8:9 393

1 Maccabees

1:20–23 521
1:41–57 521
2:15 511
3:30 199

2 Maccabees

1:1 71
1:1–10 71
1:27 500
2:7 500
2:18 500
2:21 537
3:24 537
6:2 521
6:12–16 460
6:14 175

6:27–28 98, 607
9:23 607
12:6 464
12:22 537
12:44–45 309
12:45 309
14:15 537

3 Maccabees

5:8 537
5:49 426n18

4 Maccabees

9:23 98
10:15 474

Prayer of Manasseh

7 396

Sirach

2:11 396
4:9 393
7:10 393
21:9 471
28:1–7 397

35:15–19 464
38:3 477
38:6 477
45:1 90, 548
46:13 LXX 548n41
49:3 237, 597
51:20 237, 597

Tobit

3:2 464
5:17 426n18
7:12 71
10:12 426n18
11:14 242
12:15 242
12:15–22 328
14:7 500

Wisdom of Solomon

1:6 140
5:17–18 363
8:8 344
10:21 145
14:12 274
14:22–26 274
19:4 175

Old Testament Pseudepigrapha

Rabbinic Writings

Qumran/Dead Sea Scrolls

Papyri, Inscriptions, and Coins

Josephus

Philo

Classical Writers

Church Fathers